SOCIAL PROBLEMS
AS SOCIAL MOVEMENTS

Contributors*

Stan L. Albrecht
Richard R. Bennett
Reginald W. Bibby
Lee H. Bowker
Robert Davis
Stuart C Hadden
Clay W. Hardin
Jill Gilbert McKelvy
Michael J. Ohr
Lorne A. Phillips
Vicki L. Rose
John M. Taves
Julie Camille Wolfe

*See page 659.

SOCIAL PROBLEMS AS SOCIAL MOVEMENTS

Armand L. Mauss
Washington State University

J. B. LIPPINCOTT COMPANY
Philadelphia   New York   Toronto

Table 5-1 is taken from Hugo A. Bedau, *The Death Penalty in America,* published by Doubleday & Co., Inc. © 1964 and 1967 by Hugo A. Bedau. Reprinted with permission of the publisher.

Tables 6-1 and 6-2 are taken from Irving Louis Horowitz, *The Struggle Is the Message.* © 1970 by Irving Louis Horowitz and Glendessary Press. Reprinted with permission of the author and publisher.

Figure 7-3 is taken from Alfred E. Lindesmith, *The Addict and the Law.* © 1965 by Indiana University Press, and reprinted with their permission.

Table 12-2 is taken from *Population, Resources, Environment,* by Paul R. Ehrlich and Anne H. Ehrlich. © 1970 by W. H. Freeman & Co.

Figure 15-1 is taken from "Energy and Power," by Chauncey Starr. © 1971 by Scientific American, Inc. All rights reserved.

Figure 15-2 is taken from "The Flow of Energy in an Industrial Society," by Earl Cook. © 1971 by Scientific American, Inc. All rights reserved.

Figure 15-3 is taken from "Human Materials Production as a Process in the Biosphere," by Harrison Brown, in *Man in the Ecosphere,* by Paul Ehrlich, *et al.,* eds. © 1971 by W. H. Freeman & Co.

Table 15-8 is taken from John C. Maloney and Lynn Slovansky, "The Pollution Issue: A Survey of Editorial Judgments," in Leslie L. Rose, Jr., ed., *The Politics of Ecosuicide.* © 1971 by Holt, Rinehart & Winston.

Table 16-1 is taken from *Population Dynamics,* by Ralph Thomlinson. © 1965 by Random House, Inc.

Copyright © 1975 by J. B. Lippincott Company

All rights reserved.

With the exception of brief excerpts for review, no part of this book may be reproduced in any form or by any means without written permission from the publisher.

ISBN 0-397-47325-7

Library of Congress Catalog Card Number 75-1229

Printed in the United States of America

135798642

Library of Congress Cataloging in Publication Data

Mauss, Armand L.
Social problems as social movements.

Bibliography: p.
Includes index.
1. Social movements. 2. Social problems.
I. Title.
HN13.M38   309.1'73   75-1229
ISBN 0-397-47325-7

To Ruth the Refuge, and the Incredulous Eight.

Contents

Preface ix
Prologue xv

PART ONE/ THE THEORETICAL FRAMEWORK 1
1 Social Problems and Their Champions 3
2 Social Problems as Social Movements 38

PART TWO/ LAW AND ORDER 73
3 Crime and Law 75
4 Juvenile Delinquency 115
5 Corrections and Punishment 148
6 Radical Protest 201

PART THREE/ PERSONAL DEVIATION 235
7 Drug Use 237
8 Alcohol Use 281
9 Mental Illness 319
10 Sexual Behavior: Prostitution, Pornography, and Homosexuality 357

PART FOUR/ THE CHANGING STATUS OF WOMEN 403
11 Feminist Movements as Social Problems 405
12 Abortion 442
13 Emerging Modes of Marriage 475

PART FIVE/ GENERAL SOCIETAL ISSUES 509
14 Race and Ethnic Relations 511
15 The Environment 556
16 Population 606

About the Contributors 659
Bibliography 661
Index 705

Preface

This book is offered as a creative effort that is at once synthetic and original. It is synthetic because it integrates in somewhat new ways a diversity of materials and ideas from the literature of social problems, deviant behavior, symbolic interaction, collective behavior, social movements, and even social epistemology. It is, on the other hand, original because it is the first book, as far as we know, to (1) pose a comprehensive theoretical framework explaining social problems *totally* from an interactionist/collective behavior perspective (whether they involve deviance or not); to (2) apply that framework consistently to that analysis of a long *series* of social problems, historical and contemporary; and to (3) carry that theoretical framework to its logical conclusion by *identifying* social problems with social movements, i.e., to treat social problems simply as a sub-type of social movement.

We are trying to reach audiences at both extremes of sociological sophistication. On the one hand, the book is deliberately designed as a text for the standard college courses in social problems. It provides systematic treatments and explanations for the major problems of contemporary American society, as will be clear from a glance at the table of contents. Its reading level may be a bit more demanding than that of some competing books, but it certainly is not as demanding as that of others, including a widely adopted reader in social problems co-edited by two respected colleagues. It is almost as well suited as a text in a course on social movements as it is for one on social problems, since it offers a comprehensive and consistent theoretical approach to problems that have been associated with some of the most important social movements of our time. It would even be a very useful secondary text in the sociology of law, since it reviews the sociological and historical origins of much of the important legislation that has emerged over the years in the effort to "solve" our social problems.

On the other hand, we feel that our efforts here deserve the attention of our professional colleagues, as well as of beginning students, for the book is intended as a serious contribution to social problems theory and not merely as the usual superficial undergraduate review of the nation's ills. To be sure, even our fairly long chapters on each of the various social problems are of necessity more superficial than we would prefer, given our space limitations. However, the theoretical chapters at the beginning are developed in some depth, and we trust that the relative parsimony of the subsequent topical chapters will still provide our professional colleagues with enough data to validate our major theoretical contentions, while, at the same time, providing undergraduate students the necessary overview of each social problem.

As we look back over the work we have done here, and compare it with our original vision of two years ago, we recognize that some parts of it are stronger than other parts. There are some gaps which, for one reason or another, we were not able to fill. There are doubtless others that we have not noticed, and which will, we trust, be called to our attention by critical colleagues. We have, of course, tried hard for accuracy in details, both large and small. We have tried to be theoretically consistent, as well as empirically sound and thorough, insofar as the materials available to us would permit. We have tried to avoid moralizing, whether from the point of view of "the establishment" or that of "the radicals." We have tried as dispassionately as we could to apply the same basic theoretical perspective to the "favorite" social problems of both these "camps." We do not delude ourselves that we have succeeded fully in all these attempts, and we are counting on our colleagues and students (from whatever "camp") to call to our attention our gaps, lapses, inaccuracies, and biases, so that we may subsequently refine and strengthen the present effort.

Even after allowing for any and all shortcomings of our work, however, we feel that it has been basically quite successful. We have taken a new theoretical approach in social problems textbooks and applied it to a variety of data. In doing this, of course, we have ourselves done what we have so often attributed in this book to others: We have constructed our own definitions of reality, and, in testing those definitions, we have used data selectively as well as systematically. We trust, however, that our selectivity has not made for serious distortions. Whether our readers will agree or not with our conclusions in every detail, we feel that we have at least made a convincing general case for several of the most important postulates in our theoretical framework: (1) that social problems are, after all, only a type of social movement; (2) that social problems, like other social movements, have a "natural history" characterized by a "*rise-and-fall*" pattern; and (3) that this natural history has an existence of its own that is independent of the so-called "objective conditions" in the society which were addressed by the movement in the beginning. In addition, we would suggest that we have demonstrated the enormous importance of the study of *history* if we are to understand the origins of social problems, by which we mean here not merely the well-springs of this or that problematic social *condition* (e.g. the industrial revolution, urbanization), but, even more importantly, the cultural, social, and intellectual sources of the *movements* which define some conditions as problematic.

The ebbing and flowing around us of social problem-movements led to some ambivalence about the contents of this book, even as it was being written. What new social problems were emerging that should be covered in this book? Which other problems were clearly past their peak and disappearing? As the book began to grow large, and deadlines began to close in, some editorial judgments had to be made, and these resulted in the eventual elimination of chapters on topics that might have added even more interest to our endeavor, and which may well appear in subsequent editions of the book. Of at least historical interest, for example, are the "social problems" of poverty and of mass society, both of which were once standard fare in textbooks. One scarcely hears of them any more, however, not necessarily because the underlying social conditions to which they referred have disappeared, but only because the collective interest in them has waned. On the other hand, considerable collective interest and activity seem to be building up for the "problems" of welfare (rather than poverty *per se*), old age, euthanasia, suicide, and political corruption. We maintain that it is one of the attributes of a society characterized by relatively high levels of education, leisure, and civil liberties to generate a variety of social problems continuously. If this is true, our history suggests that we are a fortunate people indeed.

Armand L. Mauss
Pullman, Washington
January, 1975

Preface

Acknowledgments

This enterprise, like any comparable one, has been made possible through the good will and hard work of many different persons, some of whom (like the kind professional colleagues who reviewed early portions of the manuscript for our publisher) remain unknown to us. Our gratitude to them, and to our many other unknown assistants, is no less for their anonymity. Chief among those whom we do know, however, are the marvellous people on the editorial staff of the Higher Education Division at J. B. Lippincott Company. A. Richard Heffron, Senior Editor, backed our project when it was just an idea and continued with patient persistence to push it along even in the face of our frequently missed deadlines. The editorial staff showed an extraordinary degree of professional competence and conscientiousness in dealing with the manuscript. Deserving of special mention in this regard are Gale Schricker and Val Rementer.

Among my colleagues and students at Washington State University there were also many who invested heavily of themselves in this project, and without whom it would not have been possible for a much longer time. Prominent mention has been made elsewhere of my collaborators, and their contributions to these pages will speak for themselves. There were several others, however, who are entitled to be considered "early stage collaborators," since they contributed some excellent material to the first draft of the manuscript. Concerns over total length of the work, together with certain other editorial imperatives, however, resulted in the eventual trimming out of their portions, but much credit and gratitude are due them for enormous contributions to the initial success of the project as a whole. We are referring here to the work of Dr. James H. Frey, Robert B. Heffernan, Eric L. Jensen, Joyce Kemp Jones, Charles C. Maynard, and Roy L. Schmidt, all currently or formerly of Washington State University. Special thanks must go to Julie C. Wolfe, who was not only one of the author-collaborators, but also prepared the thorough test manual to accompany the book and attended to a constant stream of editorial and clerical details for us throughout the life of the project. Also rendering valuable editorial and clerical services was Pamela Petelchuk.

Many of the tables, charts, and graphs for this book were taken from other publications, and we would like to acknowledge our enormous debt to their authors and publishers for the important contribution which these materials have made to our work. Some of these were government documents, at least in their original form, and thus in the public domain, but we wish to express our appreciation for them nevertheless: to the U.S. Department of Justice we are grateful for making available the Uniform Crime Reports of the F.B.I., which we used in Tables 3-1 through 3-5, 3-7, 3-8, 4-1, and 5-8, and in Figures 3-1, 3-2, and 3-3, and the U.S. Bureau of Prisons reports, which we used in Tables 5-2, 5-3, 5-4, and 5-6, and in Figures 5-1, 5-2, and 5-3. We appreciated having a number of Bureau of Census reports (e.g. Statistical Abstracts and Current Population Reports for 1972), from which we took Tables 16-2 through 16-5 and Figures 16-3, 16-4, 16-5; and Bureau of Labor Statistics reports, from which we took Tables 11-1 and 11-2; as well as Bureau of Narcotics data (for Figure 7-2), Department of Health, Education, and Welfare special reports for 1971 (for Figures 8-1 through 8-6), and HEW's National Institutes of Health 1971 and 1972 NIMH/HSM reports (for Table 9-3). During the late 1960's and early 1970's, a number of important reports were produced by a variety of special federal or presidential commissions, from which we also benefitted greatly: Table 3-6 came from the 1966 report of the Commission on Law Enforcement and the Administration of Justice; Table 6-3 from the 1969 report of the Commission on the Causes and Prevention of Violence; Table 6-4 from the 1968 report of the Commission on Civil Disorders; Figure 16-2 from the 1971 report of the Commission on Population Growth and the American Future; and Figure 7-4 and Tables 7-1, 7-2, 7-3, and 7-5 from the 1973 report of the Commission on Marijuana and Drug Use. A generous grant from the National Science Foundation, together with one from the Russell Sage Foundation, has made possible also the rich body of data in the annual General Social Surveys conducted by the National Opinion Research Center (NORC) and the Roper Public Opinion Research Center, from the 1972 codebook of which we took the data for Tables 5-7, 11-4, and 12-3 through 12-8. Mr. Jerry M. Wood, of the Tarrant County, Texas, Juvenile Probation Department was kind enough to provide us the data for Tables 4-2 and 4-3 and for Figure 4-1.

In addition to all of the above valuable materials from public sources, we have drawn much also from private and commercial sources, which are indicated below. We express our deepest gratitude for the permissions which we received from the respective publishers, and, where required, from the authors as well, for the use and reproduction of these materials:

The Gallup public opinion data in Tables 5-7, 11-3, 11-5 through 11-10, 12-1, 15-9, 15-10, and 16-6 through 16-9. Copyright 1966, 1969, 1972, and 1973, by the American Institute of Public Opinion, Princeton, N.J.

The Harris public opinion data in Tables 15-4, 15-5, and 15-6. Copyright 1972 by Louis Harris and Associates, New York, N.Y.

The NORC public opinion data in Table 15-3. Copyright 1972 by the National Opinion Research Corporation, Chicago, Ill.

Some of the poll data cited just above was obtained via regular reviews in *Public Opinion Quarterly* (Columbia University, New York, N.Y.), including the data for Tables 16-8 and 16-9 (Copyright 1967 by POQ) and for Tables 15-3 through 15-6 (Copyright 1972 by POQ). Author in all cases Hazel Erskine.

The New York Times of April 14, 1974, was our original source for Table 3-9; of September 26, 1971, for Table 5-5; and of February 16, 1969, for Table 5-7. Copyright by *New York Times* for those dates.

Table 3-10 came from "Public Reaction to Crime in the Streets," *The American Scholar* 40 (Autumn, 1971). Author Frank F. Furstenberg. Copyright 1971 by United Chapters of Phi Beta Kappa, Washington, D.C.

Table 15-11 came from "Politics and Ecology: A Profile of Student Eco-Activists," *Youth and Society* 3 (1972). Authors Riley E. Dunlap and Richard P. Gale. Copyright 1972 by Sage Publications, Inc., Beverly Hills, Calif.

Table 16-8 originally appeared in *Look Magazine* for June 29, 1965 (Vol. 24) in an article entitled, "America's Mood Today." Author: Leonard Gross. Copyright 1965 by Cowles Magazine and Broadcasting Company, Inc., Des Moines, Iowa.

Table 16-10 came from two sources: "Zero Population Growth, Inc.," *BioScience* 21 (July, 1971), copyright 1971 by the American Institute of Biological Sciences, Washington, D.C.; and "Zero Population Growth, Inc.; A Second Study," appearing in the *Journal of Biosocial Science* 6 (January, 1974), published in Cambridge, England. Author in both cases Larry D. Barnett.

Table 15-8 came from "The Pollution Issue: A Survey of Editorial Judgments," by J. C. Maloney and L. Slovansky, in *The Politics of Ecosuicide,* edited by Leslie L. Roos, Jr. Copyright 1971 by Holt, Rinehart, and Winston, New York, N.Y.

Figure 7-3 came from *The Addict and the Law* by Alfred R. Lindesmith. Copyright 1965 by Indiana University Press, Bloomington, Indiana.

Table 5-1 came from *The Death Penalty in America* by Hugo A. Bedau. Copyright 1964 and 1967 by Hugo A. Bedau and Doubleday & Co., Garden City, N.Y.

Table 16-1 came from *Population Dynamics* by Ralph Thomlinson. Copyright 1965 by Random House, Inc., New York, N.Y.

Tables 9-1 and 9-2, though originally compiled from NIMH data, came via the *1973 World Almanac and Book of Facts.* Copyright 1974 by the Newspaper Enterprise Association, New York, N.Y.

Figure 7-1 came from "Psychotherapeutic Drugs: Prescriptions Filled in U.S. Drug Stores, 1964-1970," by M. B. Balter and J. Levine, which appeared in *Licit and Illicit Drugs,* by E. M. Brecher and the Editors of *Consumer Reports.* Copyright 1972 by the Consumers' Union, Mt. Vernon, N.Y.

Table 7-4 came from the 4th edition of the *Conscientious Guide to Drug Abuse,* by Vic Pawlak. Copyright 1973 by Vic Pawlak and the Do-It-Now Foundation of Phoenix, Arizona.

Tables 6-1 and 6-2 were condensed and compiled from Tables 1 and 2 in the Appendix of *The Struggle is the Message,* by I. L. Horowitz. Copyright 1970 by Glendessary Press, Berkeley, Calif.

Tables 12-2 and 15-2 both came from *Population, Resources, Environment,* by Paul and Anne Ehrlich. Copyright 1970 and 1972 by W. H. Freeman and Co., San Francisco, Calif.

Figures 15-1 and 15-2 came, respectively, from "Energy and Power," by Chauncey Starr, and from "The Flow of Energy in an Industrial Society," by Earl Cook, both appearing in *Energy and Power: A Scientific American Book.* Copyright 1971 by W. H. Freeman and Co., San Francisco, Calif.

Figure 15-3 came from "Human Materials Production as a Process in the Biosphere," by Harrison Brown, appearing in *Man in the Ecosphere,* edited by Paul R. Ehrlich, et al. Copyright 1971 by W. H. Freeman and Co., San Francisco.

Tables 15-7, 15-9, 15-10, and Figure 15-4, though originating in other places, came to us via "American Public Opinion and Environmental Pollution," by Donald Munton and Linda Brady, a mimeographed research report of the Ohio State University Behavioral Science Laboratory, 1970, and published here by permission of Donald Munton.

Figure 15-5, deriving originally from U.S. Forest Service data, came to us via "Neospartan Hedonist Adult Toy Afficionados and the Development of Bureaucratic Purgatory," a 1973 unpublished paper by John Baden, and published here with his permission.

Finally, the material on prostitution in Chapter 10 came in large part from unpublished work by Professor Charles E. Reasons, of the University of Calgary, and was published here with his permission.

Prologue

> (W)e must not say that an action shocks the common conscience because it is criminal, but rather that it is criminal because it shocks the common conscience. We do not reprove it because it is a crime, but it is a crime because we reprove it.
> (Emile Durkheim, 1933:81)

As this quotation shows, sociologists have known at least since the time of Durkheim that social problems originate in public opinion rather than in objective reality. They have been applying this insight fruitfully in recent years to the study of crime and deviance (e.g., Becker, 1963; and Schur, 1965), but only rarely and by allusion have they applied it to the study of *social problems* more generally. Indeed, Herbert Blumer (1971) is one of the very few social scientists to have clearly called for this approach to social problems (see also Kitsuse and Spector, 1973; and Spector and Kitsuse, 1973), but so far his call has not been taken very seriously in the textbooks on social problems. The standard textbooks reflect only an occasional recognition of the Durkheim-Blumer insight, and none of them attempts a systematic theory of social problems on this basis.

With but few exceptions, most textbook authors seem to hold that social problems derive from the nature of reality itself—that is, that certain social conditions are inherently problematic. While some authors recognize that public opinion or collective definitions may play a part, they still seem generally to regard public opinion as a mere catalyst that draws the attention of the masses to social conditions already, by their nature, undesirable and in need of change. One of the best-established standard textbooks in the field, for example, defines a "social problem" as follows:

> ... a condition affecting a significant number of people in ways considered undesirable, about which it is felt something can be done through collective action. (Horton and Leslie, 1974:4)

This definition raises many questions which, to some extent, the authors attempt to answer: What is a "significant number" of people? Considered "undesirable" by whom? Whose "collective action"? In spite of the enormous relativity in answers to such questions, however, the authors seem to have little doubt that at least some social conditions are "undesirable" by *anyone's* definition and are therefore social problems in an obvious and objective sense. They tell us, for example, that a "population explosion is a serious problem" these days (Horton and Leslie, 1974:9), but they do not say *to whom* it is a problem. They remark elsewhere (p. 10) that "social problems are the logical, normal, and inevitable products of present social values and practices," which seems to mean that social problems are objective realities created by *social institutions* rather than by public opinion. While recognizing that the mass media and other vehicles of public opinion may play a part in generating social problems, these authors claim (p. 11) that "unless real grievances exist, no amount of publicity will create a problem." Presumably, then, some grievances are objectively "real." In short, while according some importance to public opinion and collective definition, these authors seem to regard many social problems as ultimately real and objective phenomena in society.

Basically, the same view on social problems is taken by a second prominent textbook in the field: "The first and basic ingredient of a social problem consists of a substantial discrepancy between widely shared social standards and actual conditions of social life" (Merton and Nisbet, 1971:799). It is clear from the author's development of this point that he regards the "discrepancy" in question as an objective reality, not depending on any collective recognition or public opinion. He claims, in fact, that social scientists can sometimes recognize the discrepancy before the rest of society (Merton and Nisbet, 1971:806-810). To him, public opinion functions primarily to bring about the *recognition* of problems already there, rather than to generate the problems themselves.

A third established textbook on social problems is highly critical of both texts just described (and of most others in the field) for being "overly relativistic and lacking in intellectual direction" (Skolnick and Currie, 1970:2). The authors of this third book take a forthrightly moralistic stance, arguing that the study of social problems should begin with the study of such basic processes as "institutional decay," which they (and presumably any alert social critic) should be able to see. To them, there are certain "problematic aspects of American society" which, while often neglected in textbooks, are objectively real and are properly "open . . . to public scrutiny." There is little recognition in this text of moral relativity or of collective definitions as the genesis of social problems (Skolnick and Currie, 1970:14-16).

There are two textbooks which give a much greater recognition to the importance of public opinion processes in the production of social problems, and further reference will be made to them later on (Davis, 1970; and Becker, 1966). Most of the books on social problems, however, fail to utilize Durkheim's insight. For if it is true, as Durkheim says, that "we do not reprove [an action] because it is a crime, but it is a crime because we reprove it," then it is equally true that we do not deplore a social condition because it is a problem; rather, it is a problem because we deplore it. Such, then, is the first premise guiding the treatment of social problems in this textbook: *No social condition, however deplorable or intolerable it may seem to social scientists or social critics, is inherently problematic*. It is made a problem by the entrepreneurship of various interest groups, which succeed in winning over important segments of public opinion to the support of a social movement aimed at changing that condition. Since, therefore, a social problem is dependent on a social movement for its very existence and is, practically speaking, coterminous with it, we might say that a *social problem is simply a kind of social movement*. This position carries to a logical conclusion the ideas of such theorists as Durkheim, Blumer, and Becker, as well as the perspectives of certain earlier (but generally forgotten) social problems writers like Waller (1936), Fuller and Myers (1937 and 1941), and Cuber, Harper, and Kenkel (1956). Their ideas will be discussed somewhat more fully later on. For now, it is enough to note that the treatment of social problems in this book *reverses* the causal connection they are usually believed to have with social movements. Whereas most authors assert or imply that

Prologue

social problems generate (ameliorative) social movements, the present author takes the position that *social movements generate social problems*.

The essential similarity between social problems and social movements can be seen in the definitions developed for each in sociological literature. Most definitions of social *movements* emphasize the element of collective behavior, which is relatively spontaneous, unstructured, and unorganized (as distinguished from behavior in established groups and institutions, which is structured by the role that members are expected to play). In its most unstructured form, collective behavior includes panics, mobs, crowds, fads, and so on, but it occurs also in the partially organized publics and interest groups which make up social movements.

Among the definitions which point to the collective element in social movements is Blumer's (1971): "Social movements can be viewed as collective enterprises to establish a new order of life. They have their inception in a condition of unrest, and derive their motive power . . . from dissatisfaction . . . and . . . from . . . hopes for a new scheme . . . of living." Gusfield (1968:445) defines movements as "socially shared demands for change in some aspect of the social order." Turner and Killian (1957) recognize that movements can also arise to *resist* change, when they define a social movement as "a collectivity [which acts] with some continuity to promote or resist a change in the society or group of which it is a part." In all these definitions, particular attention is given to the elements of collective behavior, dissatisfaction, unrest, and shared demands for change or against change.

When we look at the definitions of social *problems* offered by current textbooks, we find a great deal of overlap with these definitions of movements. Recall the definition of Horton and Leslie (1974:4) given at the beginning of this prologue, which stresses a social condition deemed "undesirable" by a significant number of people and their desire to do something about it through "collective action." Most other textbook definitions of social problems also point to collective decisions to "do something" about unsatisfactory conditions in a society. Because of the similarity in their established definitions, then, and especially because of the collective behavior which characterizes both, we shall hereafter be considering social problems as a type of social movement.

Chapter 1 attempts to locate the origins of social problems. It combines the insights of Blumer and Becker with those of Berger and Luckmann by examining in some detail the importance of a variety of *interests* in society and the *social constructions of reality* associated with those interests. Interest groups and their publics are the creators or "discoverers" of social problems and their valiant champions. Sociological theories about deviant behavior and about other social problems are presented here as simply constructions of reality offered by social scientists as interest groups.

Chapter 2 is concerned mainly with the social movements which the various interest groups generate and which become part and parcel of the social problems themselves. Various social movement theories are considered, and, in large part, adopted, as the framework for understanding "what happens" to social problems. In particular, this chapter applies a "career" concept, or "natural history model," to an examination of what happens to social problems as movements over time. As an addition to other frameworks that have used this model, Chapter 2 develops in particular the *decline and demise* portion of the natural history of social problems. Social problems are rarely "solved" in the sense that a substantial change is made in the "parameters of reality" which the interest groups and their champions have addressed, but the movements do come to an end in a variety of ways, independently of their impact on reality. They also frequently leave behind a "legacy" in the form of normative and legal changes. That legacy, in turn, may have many unintended consequences that become problematic for other interest groups in other generations.

The first two chapters, then, expound a general theory for analyzing the social problems discussed in succeeding chapters. Each chapter in Parts II through V begins the study of a particular "social problem" by illustrating briefly the relativity that has surrounded the problematic social condition in various times or places. Then the chapter goes on to review the "parameters of reality"—that is, those official indicators which most people in the society would regard as reflecting the scope and nature of the social condition the interest groups are addressing. Each chapter next devotes some considerable space to a description of the various kinds of interests and constructions of reality (ideologies, theories, propaganda) that have resulted in defining those parameters of reality as problematic. This description is followed by an analysis of the social movements involved in generating and promoting the problems, with particular focus on the natural histories of those movements. Finally, each chapter closes with a brief review of the legacy of these movements and the implications of that legacy for the future.

A genuinely different approach has been taken to social problems from that found in other textbooks, though this approach has benefitted greatly from ideas presented by others in the literature for some time. We hope that the synthesis and application of these ideas to an undergraduate textbook will be as much appreciated by the scholars to whom we are indebted as by the students who are the ultimate beneficiaries.

PART ONE

THE THEORETICAL FRAMEWORK

Chapter 1

Social Problems and Their Champions

THE SOCIAL CONSTRUCTION OF REALITY
The Relativity of Truth

Considering that cultural and moral relativity is one of the most important principles in the social sciences, it is curious that social problems analysts have not applied this principle more thoroughly and systematically than they have. Every beginning student in sociology learns that behavior which is considered immoral and outrageous in one culture or subculture might be acceptable or even encouraged in another culture. Thus, cannibalism might be abhorrent to Americans, but it is still practiced in other parts of the world. Relativity applies across time, too, even within the same culture. Women who smoked in 19th-century America were regarded as immoral, but such is certainly not the case today. It is therefore not at all difficult to understand that any kind of behavior is neither moral nor immoral in itself; it is *made* moral or immoral (as Durkheim pointed out) *only* by the collective decision and definition of a group or society. The same relativity of time and place applies to social conditions: they are never problems in and of themselves; they are always *made* problems by the collective decision and definition of a group or society. For example, Americans tend to feel that India has an enormous population problem; indeed, many feel that our own country is overpopulated, even though it has only a fraction of the growth rate and density of India. The ordinary Indian villager, though, is likely to see the problem more as a shortage of food than as a surplus of population. (See Chapter 16.)

This principle of cultural relativity derives from an even more fundamental epistemological concept in sociology—the social construction of reality itself. While this concept has been understood in the social sciences for some time, one of the more recent and thorough treatises on the subject is that of Berger and Luckmann (1967). When we speak of the "social construction of reality," we are referring to the theory that there is no such thing as a single "objective" definition of reality; there are only various (and sometimes competing) realities, each of which is defined by a different group, public, or culture. We are dealing here with various definitions not only of social reality, but even of physical reality. The same empirical data, whether about society or about the universe, can be used to support a variety of conceptions of reality; indeed, we might say that a certain socially defined design, organization, or meaning is simply *imposed* on data or "facts" which otherwise have no meaning in and of themselves. Take, for example, our solar system: for many centuries people have been watching the sun rise in the east and set in the west, but the meaning of this fact, prior to Galileo, was that the sun revolved around the earth; even the scientists and the Church in Europe taught this theory. In more recent years, however, our scientists (and most people) believe that the earth revolves around the sun, and that the rising and setting of the sun is due to the rotation of the earth on its own axis. Which theory is really "true"? Indeed, how do we even know that there is any such thing as a "solar system," with a sun in the center and a number of planets revolving around it? Is that design objectively present in space, or is it in the minds of the people who study it, as is the "Big Dipper" or "Orion the Hunter"? Just as certain "primitive peoples" looked upon the chaos of stars in the skies and imposed on it designs in the form of hunters and animals, perhaps we (on the advice of our astronomers, instead of our "medicine men") are simply imposing the design called "solar system" on the chaos of outer space. We continue to believe that our solar system is objectively real, because (1) most people we know so believe—that is, we have a cultural "consensus" about it; and (2) whether we have merely imposed the design or not, *it works*—that is, it enables us to land men on the moon and to put satellites in orbit around our own planet and others. As long as this theory, or definition of reality, seems to work and to be supported by a consensus, we will doubtless continue to regard it as "true." However, it is entirely possible that future generations of scientists will persuade us that the present theory is partially or totally wrong, just as we are convinced that the medieval astronomers were wrong, and then there will be a new theory, a new truth, a new definition of reality; and perhaps we will adopt this new truth from a totally different culture, such as China, just as we are starting to learn from the Chinese a new theory about anaesthesiology (acupuncture). So it is that even physical or "scientific" reality can be socially constructed and thus relative to a particular people and a particular time.

What has just been discussed with respect to physical reality is at least as true also of social reality. The same data of facts may have different meanings to different groups or peoples at different times, and thus will constitute *different realities*. These different realities, furthermore, are usually expressed in different words and symbols, which come to have a reality of their own; or, as Berger and

Luckmann (1967) say, language "objectivates" the common experiences and perceptions of a people. Language actually structures our thinking in the ways that we look at "facts," so that we tend to forget the difference between those facts themselves and the meanings that we give them, as though the facts and the words or symbols about them are all part of the same reality. For example, given the fact that black children in our northern cities tend to go to different schools from those attended by white children in the suburbs, what is the meaning that we should attach to that fact? To some, this state of affairs constitutes "racial segregation and discrimination," while to others it constitutes "preserving our neighborhood schools." These two different meanings involve different words and symbols, and they evoke different emotions. Indeed, to the segments of the population who hold the two different perspectives, there are two different realities.

Facts and Interpretations

Examples can be multiplied almost endlessly of cases where the same basic data or "facts" yield different meanings or realities to different groups or segments in the society. If there is a steady increase in the divorce rate during a period of twenty years, that fact or data has no meaning in and of itself, until it is given a meaning by a certain interest group or public in the society. To a religious denomination or interest group, it might mean that there has been a "moral decline" in the society, since people no longer "take seriously their marriage covenants." To a women's liberation chapter, however, the same divorce rate might mean that millions of unhappily married women have found the courage and the opportunity to assert themselves against the "stultifying situation of traditional family life" and become "self-actualizing individuals." Or, if there is a sudden increase in the rate of arrests for public drunkenness, what does that mean? Again, to religious and moral interest groups, it might mean that there is a widespread "character breakdown" in our society and that alcoholic beverages should be banned or made harder to get for people with "weak characters." Medical, psychiatric, and social work experts, however, might conclude that we have a new "public health" problem, since they tend to define alcoholism (and frequent drunkenness) as a "disease," rather than as a character disorder. (See Chapter 8.) Still another possible meaning (from among many) of an increase in drunkenness arrests might well be that an increasing number of our cities have passed new laws against public drunkenness; or else police departments in those cities have increased the number of patrolmen working in skid row neighborhoods, where much of the drunkenness occurs.

Similarly, a startling statistical increase in the rate of juvenile delinquency in a given period might mean that parents are "not doing their job" and that there is a "breakdown of the American home and family." It might also mean that a numerous and powerful group of well-meaning citizens has launched a campaign to identify children with "problems," remove them from their "unwholesome environments," and extend to them the "protection of the juvenile courts." (See Chapter 4.) Of course, an increase in delinquency might also mean that many school districts or state legislatures have increased the mandatory age for public school attendance, thereby automatically increasing the number of children who will be listed as "truant" and therefore delinquent. One can see a great variety also in the public and official definitions surrounding "crime," as well as "delinquency." When the FBI's Uniform Crime Report shows an increase in murders, rapes, and robberies, many people, and many government officials, will express concern about a "crime wave" and about the "breakdown of law and order" in our society. However, when there are public disclosures indicating widespread illegal activities during election campaigns on the part of government officials and their aides in both parties, extending back perhaps to the last several elections, many people are inclined to dismiss these disclosures as mere "politics." Indeed, the Governor of California was reported as feeling that leniency was in order for those government officials involved in the Watergate scandal, on the ground that they were not really criminals "at heart." Thus, even when we talk about crime as a great "social problem," we tend to have in mind somewhat different definitions of "crime," depending upon our political, economic, and moral interests. (See Chapter 3.)

We will return later to the question of how people's interests influence their definitions of reality. At this point, it needs to be asked how people can live together in the same society when they cannot agree even on such a fundamental matter as the definition of reality. The answer, in part, is that much of the turmoil and conflict in history has been precisely over different definitions of truth or reality. Such differences have also provided the basis for the great variety of religious, political, economic, and other institutions that we see around the world. However, beneath all these differences, there does tend to be basic agreement among the members of a society, at least about what constitutes data or evidence. That is, people may disagree about the meaning of government statistics on population growth, but there is probably widespread agreement that the statistics themselves are "true." Such generalized agreement about what is true or factual we will call "consensual reality"—that is, reality which has its basis in public opinion.

Reality by Consensus

Whether or not consensual reality is true in some objective sense does not really matter; for, as W. I. Thomas, an early American sociologist pointed out, whatever people *believe* to be real will be real in its consequences. Consensual reality is therefore extremely important, both socially and psychologically, for it is the only operative reality that most people have. That is, most of us believe and act upon whatever we have learned to be true from our family, our friends, and our society in general. That is what is meant by a "social definition of reality." Like any social definition, consensual reality varies greatly, of course, from one culture to another and even from one time to another in the same culture. Some important social problems, indeed, have had their origins in factual data that we would not consider "real" today. For example, one of the great "crime waves" that colonial Massachusetts had to cope with was an outbreak of witchcraft (Erikson, 1966). No matter how ridiculous it may seem to us three centuries later, witchcraft was a great social problem in its time. Though there may have been some differences of opinion about which women were witches, few in Salem doubted that there really were such things as witches or that certain data indicated the presence of witches. Much more recently, but of less importance, were the "mad gasser" and "windshield pitting" epidemics (Medalia and Larsen, 1958; and Johnson, 1945). In the first of these, a widespread collective belief developed that a mysterious person was sneaking about and spraying some kind of toxic gas in unexpected places. As this report spread through the news media, many people began calling the police with claims that they had been victimized by the "mad gasser" and had experienced mild nausea and temporary unconsciousness. No gasser was ever sighted, nor was there ever any real evidence of the presence of an unusual gas in any of the places from which complaints originated. To all appearances, and after careful investigation, there never was any "mad gasser." The "evidence" was imaginary, but it still produced a temporary and small-scale social problem. The "windshield pitting epidemic" was also the result of apparently imaginary evidence. Once again responding to news reports, people began checking their windshields for the appearance of small pits or chips that had been reported by other townspeople. Suddenly, all over the city, people were reporting strange and unexplained pits in their car windshields, which they had never seen before. Speculation about the cause included the fallout of atomic particles from nuclear weapons tests. After a thorough investigation, it was concluded that the "mysterious" windshield pits had in every case developed from normal vehicle use and had simply never been noticed before by the drivers, until they had been sensitized by the rumors.

Now, probably all of us hope and assume that consensual reality in the form of government statistics is more substantial and reliable than the widely accepted reality of pitted windshields and mad gassers. The point, however, is that both these kinds of reality are socially constructed and created and can become the basis for collective interpretations, which, in turn, can lead to social movements to solve the problem supposedly reflected in that evidence. The kind of consensual reality illustrated here reminds us once again of the observations of Berger and Luckmann (1967), who emphasized the importance of understanding reality as it is constructed by ordinary people (as opposed to intellectuals and tastemakers). This kind of "common sense" reality, or "everyday life" reality, is the "common social stock of knowledge," as Berger and Luckmann put it; it is what "everybody knows." As long as it works, or continues to provide satisfactory explanations for the surrounding world, almost everyone in a society will take it for granted and will have very little interest in pressing beyond it to anything deeper or more complicated. When, however, this consensual reality, or common stock of knowledge, fails to "deliver the goods," or to make possible the solution of everyday practical problems, then people will begin to question it and will be open to new constructions of reality being offered by special interest groups.

Parameters of Consensual Reality

Generally speaking, it is possible to divide consensual reality into two main types: formal and informal. This distinction may have little significance to "the man on the street," but it does refer to two different qualities or levels of reality that can be observed in societies like our own. *Formal* consensual reality is that which originates from persons or institutions generally regarded as authorities. Examples of this kind of reality are government reports and statistics, pronouncements by religious leaders (in religiously homogeneous societies), scientific articles and books, and various sorts of "expert" testimony. Social commentators, as well as ordinary people, are likely to be impressed by "facts" cited from such sources in conversations with friends and in newspaper and magazine articles. Even the experts themselves, for that matter, such as scientists and educators, are likely to regard data from such sources as the ultimate or most reliable level of "truth." Most scientists, however, are well aware of the flaws, gaps, and misinterpretations which so often characterize even this formal and official kind of truth, especially with regard to social problems. A few examples will perhaps suffice. Suppose that in a population of stable size the incidence of a certain crime is 100 in 1971, 150 in 1972, and 175 in 1975. Now, there are at least two different ways to look at those same figures. We can emphasize the continuing increase in the incidence of the crime by pointing out that it has increased 75 percent in a period of only two years; or, we can emphasize the decrease in the rate of growth (only 16.67 percent from 1972 to 1973, compared with 50 percent from 1971 to 1972). In addition to such variations in interpretation, statistics, however "official" they may be, are subject to many contingencies in their very origin. A city can experience a simultaneous increase in homicide and decrease in suicide in a given year simply by a change in coroners, if the new coroner is more competent or alert than his predecessor and recognizes that some apparent suicides are actually very clever homicides. Police can increase the incidence or outbreak of certain kinds of crimes or misdemeanors simply by putting on an enforcement campaign as they often do when prostitution, for example, becomes too open and offensive. Darrell Huff, in his excellent little book, *How to Lie with Statistics* (1954), offers numerous examples, in ten different chapters, of all the various kinds of flaws, misinterpretations, selective interpretations, and misleading presentations that are often found in formal and "official" reports or articles. The point is *not* that these formal constructions of reality are useless or mostly unreliable; rather, the point is that they need to be examined and considered with great care, which most people in a society fail to do in their ready acceptance of "truth" from these formal sources.

In using the term *informal consensual reality,* we are referring to such "truth" as is found in folklore, myth, anecdotes, and certain episodes. These are distinguished from the more formal parameters of reality primarily by ther unsystematic character. Formal scientific studies and reports usually try, at least, to base themselves upon some kind of adequate sample or cross-section of whatever they are investigating and to offer empirical evidence (or experiences) from a number of different tests, experiments, or observations. Informal consensual reality, by contrast, comes from accumulated traditions (that may or may not have originated from systematic experience) or widely told stories that are taken to be typical of some fact. To many people, the number 13 is unlucky, especially if it falls on a Friday, and they behave accordingly. More importantly, there are widespread cultural myths in our society about Indians or blacks and "what they are like." These myths are widely enough believed among Caucasians to affect their attitudes and behavior toward these ethnic minorities, and thus must be considered part of the "common stock" of consensual reality. In addition to such traditional folk beliefs, informal consensual reality includes anecdotes and episodes from news reports, from friends, and from associates of various kinds. An example from recent years would be the celebrated case of Kitty Genovese in New York City, who was tracked down over a space of several blocks and stabbed repeatedly while many residents of the area watched without interfering or even calling the police. This incident was widely reported in the news media and has been offered as an example in articles and books of the "loss of civic conscience" among our citizens, the "breakdown of community life" in our big cities, and so on. In a similar way, episodes of youthful extravagance or violence will frequently be cited as examples of a growing "loss of respect" by our youth. While such episodes or anecdotes really cannot properly be offered as evidence of anything in a systematic or reliable sense, they nevertheless tend to become part of the popular "stock" of truth or reality. They will be cited also by moral crusaders as "proof" of the need for a "crackdown" or a campaign to eliminate this or that social evil or social problem, which is why they become important in any discussion of the genesis of social problems.

In previous examples, frequent mention has been made of the mass media and the part which they have played in spreading the "consensus" or "common stock" of reality. The nature and variety of media effects on public opinion are not fully understood. In a recent study, Hubbard (1973) reviewed a number of investigations which social scientists have made into media effects, with particular attention to "creative effects"—i.e., those additions or "distortions" which the media contribute to "objective reality" as it actually exists. It is clear from Hubbard's work, and from the work of others that he reviews, that the media do certainly generate such "creative effects." What is questionable, however, is whether public opinion is as much molded or affected by media interpretations as is often claimed. People may be influenced more by friends and family than by the media in their constructions of reality. On the other hand, some studies have emphasized the importance of the news media, and of the interest groups with greatest access to the media, in the construction of reality surrounding social problems (Molotch and Lester, 1974). Whatever may be the impact of the media in the actual *construction* of reality, however, there is no doubt about the importance of the media in the *dissemination* of information and ideas, and therefore in the spreading of consensual reality of all kinds.

However much consensual reality may be informed by the mass media, one of the most interesting things about it is the potential for discrepancy between the formal and informal levels. What we generally call "public opinion" is apt to rest more upon informal than formal parameters of reality, because so many people, while accepting the authority of the formal sources, are ignorant of what these sources actually report. For example, the Bill of Rights in the United States Constitution is certainly one of the more widely accepted repositories of "truth" in our society. Yet, in a widely publicized national survey, majorities of our citizens (sometimes large majorities) expressed such beliefs as that it was all right to search radicals without a warrant, that radicals might appropriately be arrested and held without bail, and similar propositions equally in violation of the Bill of Rights (Horton and Leslie, 1974: Chapter 18). Chapter 3 of this book presents evidence from formal sources of consensual reality (i.e., FBI reports) that crimes against persons and property are much more likely to occur in downtown city neighborhoods than in the suburbs. Nevertheless, surveys of public opinion show that residents of the suburbs fear that *they* are the most likely victims of such crimes, on the basis, probably, of a selective reading of the newspapers, dramatic but unrepresentative episodes, and other varieties of informal reality. As subsequent chapters in this book will show, many "social problems" have been generated by the informal reality held by public opinion, with very little regard for the actual contents or evidence available to the public from authoritative parameters of reality.

To summarize the Preface and this chapter so far, we started by pointing out the need for a new approach to the study of social problems, one which would give more attention than do most textbooks to the importance of public opinion in the genesis of social problems. We stated the guiding premise of this book, that social problems are actually produced by social movements (indeed, in a sense, they *are* a kind of social movement) and that these social movements are largely based in public opinion. We then discussed the relativity of the truth or reality of public opinion, observing that all reality, whether about society or about the physical universe itself, is a *social product;* it is constructed by groups and societies in accordance with their own traditions and their own interests. At the basis of public opinion are two levels of consensual reality: formal and informal. The first of these is of an official, authoritative, and usually systematic nature. People tend to regard it as "true" even without knowing much about its actual contents. Data or evidence from formal parameters of reality are often selectively presented in an effort to provide authoritative "proof" for a point of view. Informal consensual reality, on the other hand, is unsystematic. It is made up of traditional myths, dramatic episodes, and widely believed anecdotes. Public opinion may be informed more by informal than by formal types of consensual reality, though it can be changed or persuaded by the introduction of weighty evidence from official or scientific reports and the like. Public opinion or consensual reality is extremely important in the study of social problems. It constitutes the only truth that people have, in the operational sense, for it is the basis for people's attitudes and behavior toward society and toward each other. Public opinion, as derived from consensual reality, also provides the raw material for social problem-movements and the context within which these movements are acted out.

It is time now to turn to a discussion of those individuals and groups who, in their own interests, attempt to influence public opinion and the collective definitions of reality, and who thereby *generate* social problems via social movements. We are calling them the "champions" of social problems.

CHAMPIONS AND THEIR INTERESTS
Publics and Pressure Groups

That people are largely motivated by their own interests has been observed by many philosophers, including those as ideologically different as Thomas Hobbes, Adam Smith, Karl Marx, and Sigmund Freud. Indeed, at the collective level, the "interest group" has long been recognized as a very important part of our political system and process. The larger collective context, of which the interest group is a part, is called a "public." We are not referring here, as we have above, to the *general* public, but rather to a particular *issue-specific public,* made up of all the people who care about a certain issue, no matter what side of the issue they may be on. From within that public emerges *interest groups,* usually at least one group for each position or point of view on the issue, made up of those individuals who have the most to gain or lose by the outcome of the issue. Or sometimes, as is often the case with social problems, the interest groups may form first and then generate a surrounding public by their publicity and activity. In any case, the interest groups tend to recruit people who have a lot at stake, and these people increasingly cooperate in communicating their point of view, in raising funds to further their cause, and in organizing themselves for the activities they deem necessary. If the interest group reaches an advanced stage of organization and activity, and if it begins to engage in lobbying and other political activities aimed directly at government, then it is called a *pressure group*.

Making up the arena of the general public, then, and trying to exert influence on general public opinion, are often certain special publics. A public in the sense is still an amorphous and unorganized collectivity of people, but they have in common a concern over a current issue.

Some concrete examples might serve to make clearer the relationships among publics, interest groups, and pressure groups. For the past decade or so, there has been an "abortion public," made up of all those who have listened to, watched, or participated in discussions concerning laws to regulate abortion. (See Chapter 12.) The question has been not so much whether women should have abortions at all as whether there should be laws to prevent abortions in the early stages of pregnancy. Until a 1973 Supreme Court decision, most states had rather restrictive laws regulating abortions, while at the same time there have been many abortions performed each year illegally. In the early 1960's, it was discovered that the use of thalidomide, a tranquilizer widely used among pregnant women, was implicated in the birth of many deformed infants. As publicity about this risk of deformity began to spread, the desirability of abortion came to be seriously considered by many expectant mothers who had been using thalidomide. One of these, Mrs. Sherri Finkbine, in a celebrated and highly publicized case, went to Sweden for an abortion. While public response to the "thalidomide scare" never produced a major new issue, there has continued to be a growing chorus of discussion about the desirability, and even the constitutionality, of laws which, in effect, require women to have children they do not want or else to travel abroad for their abortions. Religious spokesmen have been widely heard on both sides of the issue. Political and legal exponents have argued the constitutional questions. Social scientists and social workers have expressed their opinions. Millions of ordinary people, especially women, have listened and have formed opinions of their own. All such people, whether they have directly communicated with each other or not, have comprised what we are here calling the "abortion public."

In more recent years, however, it has become possible to identify certain conspicuous *interest groups* which have organized to take a more active part in the controversy. Some of these, like the Roman Catholic Church, had, of course, existed for a long time, but they began to focus more effort and concern upon the issue. Joining the Catholic Church in arguing against more liberal abortion laws have been other conservative religious groups and political leaders, including an incumbent president. The Voice of the Unborn in Michigan and elsewhere is a philosophical and political organization, in part overlapping with religious elements, which has been active on the same side. On the other side, in favor of abolishing or greatly relaxing the laws on abortion, has been a great variety of interest groups, many of whom have derived their positions on abortion from other interests. Some of the more liberal religious groups, most notably the American Friends, have been on this side. So have many of the orginizations associated with the Women's Liberation Movement, such as NOW (National Organization for Women). Birth control forces have also been represented on the side opposing abortion legislation, including Zero Population Growth and Planned Parenthood. An important political interest group on the same side has been the American Civil Liberties Union. On both sides of the abortion question, then, interest groups have developed to promote interests which they regard as critical on moral, religious, legal, political, or other grounds.

In order to promote their interests more effectively and with greater political impact, both sides of this issue have increasingly worked toward coordination and cooperation among their respective groups and organizations. This process has led to the emergence of large "umbrella" organizations, such as the National Right-to-Life Committee on the side of restrictive abortion legislation and the National Association for Repeal of Abortion Laws (NARAL) on the side of relaxed (or nil) abortion legislation. These nationwide organizations, backed by most of their constituent pressure groups, have functioned as very active and effective *pressure groups* for their causes. While the existence of nationwide organizations has in no way precluded pressure tactics by their member organizations (many of which have been politically active in their own right), these "umbrella" organizations comprise particularly good examples of how pressure groups develop from interest groups, for their activities have been typical (including lobbying, picketing, and propagandizing) and have been more effective than those of most of the member groups, which have had smaller resources and other campaigns to expend them on besides abortion. In any case, the abortion issue, widely regarded as an important emerging "social problem" in America, illustrates how publics can generate (and be acted upon by) interest groups, many of which then generate (or themselves become) pressure groups. It is the position of this book that all social problems are produced by the behavior of publics, interest groups, and/or pressure groups and that these are therefore very important social phenomena to understand. The actual social movements that result from their activity will be the main subject of the next chapter.

Varieties of Interests and Their Champions

The abortion issue also serves to illustrate the great range of possible interests that can be represented in the genesis and development of a social problem. When we use terms like "interest group," many of us tend to think first of *economic* or business interests. To be sure, this kind of interest is among the most important in generating movements of all sorts, including those called "social problems." It is easy to see the operation of economic interests in some social problems, but in other cases such interests are more subtle, or can only be inferred or suspected. A number of social scientists recently have demonstrated the class basis for many laws and punishments; that is, certain crimes, such as prostitution, are created by laws which originate mainly in the middle class but which hit hardest against the lower class (Quinney, 1970a and 1970b). More obvious (and perhaps more justifiable to most of us) is the whole category of laws against property crimes, such as shoplifting, theft, and vandalism. Many social critics are fond of pointing out, however, that such crimes receive a disproportionate amount of attention and enforcement, compared to certain favorite "white-collar" crimes, such as embezzlement, price-fixing, and income tax evasion. (See Chapter 3.) Quite aside from issues of crime, it is easy to see the economic interests involved on both sides of many racial confrontations in our society. Minority groups have understandable economic motives (among other kinds) for wanting legislation guaranteeing their right to buy homes in neighborhoods of their own choosing; and real estate interests worried about the consequent risk of "declining property values" are certainly expressing an economic motivation. The chapters in this book will offer many other examples of economic interests as these are involved in the creation of social problems. Sometimes such interests remain rather vaguely defined as the property of an amorphous public, but more often they are given concrete expression by interest groups and pressure groups specifically organized for that purpose, such as the National Association of Manufacturers, the Committee on Political Education (COPE) or organized labor, the National Welfare Rights Organization, and innumerable others.

Frequently overlapping with other kinds of interests are the *political* ones. Political interest groups are those which seek to acquire, exercise, and/or influence the exercise of *power* in the social or political sense. The best known among these, of course, are the multitudes of pressure groups representing a variety of other kinds of interests, such as those in the women's movement, the various ethnic movements, and the like. Political parties themselves, indeed, are a kind of ultimate expression of political interests, though each party is likely to have many specific interests within it. Not all political interest groups become pressure groups in the active sense, however; some, like the conservative Intercollegiate Studies Institute (ISI), limit their activities to publication, education, and communication. In the purest sense of the term, political interest groups are those apparently motivated by political ideals not directly linked to economic or other kinds of interests, such as perhaps the American Civil Liberties Union. Often, however, the quest for power by a political group is clearly a means to serving interests of a different kind.

Political and economic interests sometimes overlap with (but can be distinguished from) *occupational* interests. These arise from a desire to maintain or expand the status, importance, or prerogatives of an occupational or professional community. As is the case with other kinds of interests, there may be only a kind of unorganized public involved, such as "teachers" or "construction workers," but interest groups and pressure groups formed within these occupational publics are among the most important kinds in our society. The American Medical Association, for example, not only exercises considerable control over the practice of medicine in this country, but it actively takes stands, raises money, and lobbies in favor of specific positions on such modern social issues as abortion, euthanasia, drugs, and alcohol. The same can be said for the American Association of University Professors (though not necessarily on the same issues). In addition to physicians and professors, occupations having organizations which represent them on various social and political issues include social workers, policemen, juvenile authorities, and many other groups with a direct interest in the outcome of certain current social problems. One of the best known of these is the National Council on Crime and Delinquency (NCCD), an inter-occupational organization made up of scholars, judges, lawyers, and various kinds of enforcement people. It is important to note, however, that the putative interests of an occupational group or public are not always the same over time or under all circumstances. It may be in the interests of the police, for example, when they are trying to improve their chances for bigger budgets and more personnel, to publicize statistics indicating the existence of a great "crime wave" (indeed, police even have the power to "create" such statistics by changing their patterns of enforcement). On the other hand, at times when political or public relations considerations call for an image of great police effectiveness, it may serve police interests instead to focus on evidence of a "declining crime rate." (See Chapter 3.)

A fourth category of interests that becomes particularly important in the genesis of social problems is that of *moral* interests, which may be ultimately *religiously* motivated, but not necessarily. Moral interests are very diverse and frequently evoke great fervor in those who hold them. In a sense, of course, many political ideals are moral in nature, but we are attributing these to political interest groups. Moral interests that have been important in producing social problems have included temperance (anti-alcohol), anti-drug concerns, "child-saving" (i.e., control of delinquency), sexual virtue and purity, and the "work ethic." All such interests are based upon ideals that are seen as having ultimate, or even eternal, importance, either because they were handed down by God or because they are critical to the survival of society or even mankind. Infraction of such moral ideals carries with it the connotation of sin, of fundamental wrong-doing, even of horror for those whose moral interests have been offended, and they usually strive to transform such sins into crimes—that is, to get laws passed that will enforce their moral ideals upon everyone. Howard S. Becker (1963) has coined the term "moral entrepreneurs" to refer to such crusaders, and he shows clearly how moral "enterprise" was mainly responsible for our anti-marijuana legislation. The same case could be made, of course, for the origin of alcohol regulations (especially during the Prohibition era), obscenity and pornography legislation, and a host of other types of legislation. Kai Erikson's study of colonial American Puritans (1966) is one among many studies that have traced the moralistic tendencies in American culture back to early Puritan times. Nor has moral entrepreneurship in our society been limited to "crimes without victims," as Schur (1965) calls infractions of *personal* piety and morality. Indeed, moral entrepreneurs have been active on all sides of such issues and "social problems" as abortion, race relations and civil rights, war, and poverty. As with political interests, moral interests may attract a great variety of publics. Some of these publics could be more or less accurately characterized as "liberals" or "conservatives" in a political, social, or religious sense, and some of them could be strictly religious publics, depending on the issue, such as "American Catholics" or "middle-America Protestants." Frequently, of course, interest groups and pressure groups emerge from these various publics. Examples of groups representing primarily moral interests, drawn from a range of recent issues, would be The Women's Christian Temperance Union, the Sierra Club (environmental issues), Citizens for Decency, and the Euthanasia Society of America.

A kind of public somewhat more vague and difficult to distinguish than others we have discussed might be called a *psychological public*. This kind of public is not likely to produce its own interest and pressure groups; rather it feeds other interest groups. A psychological public, as the term is used here, is a collection of individuals having certain psychological or emotional needs and dispositions that make them ready recruits for interest groups and movements. Such individuals are exemplified by the literature on the "Authoritarian Personality." (Adorno, et al., 1950.) According to this literature, an authoritarian personality is characterized by intolerance for diversity, by a narrow and dogmatic view of right and wrong, by discomfort with ambiguity, frequently by a hyper-patriotic or nationalistic approach to world problems, by a need to see social groups in a hierarchical arrangement, and other traits. The authoritarian personality is theoretically determined by its style, rather than by its specific content; that is, authoritarians may be liberal or conservative, middle class or working class, Catholic or Protestant. We would expect the "authoritarian psychological public" to appear on both sides of some issues, perhaps, but on many issues (such as obscenity and pornography) it is more likely to be found on the conservative side.

Other possible examples of psychological publics are the "true believers," so well described by Eric Hoffer (1951) in a book by that name, and those who are experiencing the various kinds of "deprivation" outlined by Charles Y. Glock (1973). In some ways, the "true believer" is like the "authoritarian personality," but Hoffer attributes the immense fanaticism of true believers explicitly to their personal weaknesses. Their inability to relate to an existing social order leads them to seek change of almost any kind at almost any cost. In outlining what he calls "the role of undesirables" in history, Hoffer gives particular attention to different types of poor people and "misfits." He illustrates their involvement in a great variety of causes and social movements, particularly of a left-wing kind. Glock's formulation of the role of *deprivation* has been especially well tested and illustrated with data from religious movements, but he is explicit on the point that secular movements can often be explained by the same factor, and, indeed, many social movements and interest groups having no religious significance whatever will frequently take on a zeal characteristic of new religious sects. In using the concept "deprivation," Glock is going beyond the economic use of that term (which was the most significant to Marx), and he is going beyond the notion of "the poor" or the "misfit" in Hoffer's sense. Glock distinguishes five different types of deprivation: economic, social, psychological, ethical, and organismic (physical). Any or all of these can provide a basis for the recruitment of a person so deprived to a new movement or interest group, and for the zeal of such a person after recruitment. As in the case of "authoritarians" and "true believers," it is not always predictable just what kind of cause or movement a "deprived" person will support; furthermore, it is important to remember that his "deprivation" in any case is defined by his own perceptions and is likely to be relative to time, place, and situation. Nevertheless, as Glock has shown, it is possible, with empirical support, to make inferences about a person's predispositions for active membership in certain organizations from certain putative kinds of deprivation.

So far we have discussed five kinds of publics and interest groups that may be involved in the genesis of social problems: economic, political, occupational, moral, and psychological. There is still a sixth kind, which we will call the *scientific* public and interest group and which includes social scientists like the present author. Before moving on to the more lengthy treatment in store for the reader on the scientific public, however, a few other observations seem to be in order here.

First while our discussion of interests and their exponents has been in collective terms (i.e., publics, interest groups, etc.) primarily, it should be noted that individuals can also be important in generating social problems. This is true not only in the obvious sense that publics and groups are ultimately composed of individuals, but also in the sense that individuals can frequently generate and motivate publics and interest groups by means of their charisma, their eloquence, or simply their ability to personify and represent the feelings of others (Hoffer, 1951; Weber, 1964). Some personalities have been so important that their names are attached to the movements which they founded (for example, see the reference to Comstock in Chapter 10). Others, while not founders, have made themselves at least prominent spokesmen for certain movements or interests; for example, we think of Jane Addams in connection with pioneer efforts to define and control juvenile delinquency, and we recognize Roy Wilkins as an important contributor to the civil rights movement. Still other individuals, like Ralph Nader, are important as figures whose work has resulted in much publicity and legislation even without the pressure of a major movement (though, to be sure, he represents a definite public). Zealous individuals, whatever their motives, are likely to be especially important in the early stages of a movement, when amorphous publics are in the process of being galvanized into effective interest groups and pressure groups. (See next chapter.)

The question of motives relates to another observation that needs to be made before moving on to the perspectives of the scientific public. It is perhaps an easy and natural thing to assume that the various kinds of interests we have discussed will lead to ulterior motives, that interest groups are made up of people who are simply "grinding their own axes" or working off their own "hang-ups." *We make no such judgment,* and it is irrelevant to the main point to think of interest-oriented behavior in terms of ulterior motives or fanatical conspiracies. It is simply a matter of the social constructions of reality, an idea which was introduced earlier in this chapter. As Berger and Luckmann (1967:120) explain, "there will always be a social-structural base for competition between rival definitions of reality," and furthermore:

Rival definitions of reality are thus decided upon in the sphere of rival social interests whose rivalry is in turn "translated" into theoretical terms. Whether the rival experts and their respective supporters are "sincere" in their subjective relationship to the theories in question is of only secondary interest for a sociological understanding of these processes. (Berger and Luckmann, 1967:120)

Since, as Berger and Luckmann (1967:120-124) point out, theories and ideologies are validated more by social support than by empirical evidence, the important thing sociologically is the breadth and strength of that support, which will determine the ultimate success of interest groups in their efforts to promote a cause social problem. An interest group may use moral rhetoric and appeals whate its interests may be, but in the final analysis it is likely to have adopted its the or ideology "because of specific theoretical elements that are conducive to interests" (124). In the ongoing struggle among interest groups for social chang however, there is always a dialectical relationship between ideas and social pro cesses; that is, theories or reality constructions will often be used to legitimate o to delegitimate institutions, but institutions might also be changed sometimes so that they will better conform to generally accepted ideas (128).

The different definitions of reality held with equal sincerity by different interest groups and publics are explained in large part by what Berger and Luckmann call "the social distribution of knowledge"; definitions of truth or "knowledge" may be distributed by social class, age, sex, religion, occupation, and so on. This kind of segmentation produces publics and interest groups having their own "socially segregated subuniverses of meaning." Deviant and marginal groups, acting out their own interests, will frequently produce "counter-definitions" or "counter-realities" as a way of resisting established societal definitions and "treatments." Whether a deviant group or not, however, the subuniverse of meaning promoted by a group or public will be related to its concrete social interests; that is, groups and individuals can be quite sincere and still be promoting their own interests of an economic, moral, or other kind, for these interests have come to be (for them) an inherent part of the definition of reality (Berger and Luckmann, 1967:II).

Scientists as Publics and Interest Groups

The various *scientific* publics and interest groups, including sociologists, are no more exempt from this principle of reality than are the other kinds of interest groups we have discussed. Indeed, "scientific theory" in any field of science is a kind of social construction of reality, a point that we illustrated earlier in this chapter with the different theories about the solar system. This textbook itself presents one among competing definitions of the "reality" or "truth" about social problems, based upon many assumptions and premises accumulated from the culture and the discipline of which the authors are a part. Like all other theories in all other fields of science, our theory about social problems can be expected to gain currency and become part of the consensus of our public only to the extent that it works, that is, to the extent that it seems to explain satisfactorily and consistently the phenomena (social problems) that it is addressing. The fact that we even have scientific groups and their theories is itself a kind of cultural contingency; for, as Berger and Luckmann (1967:46) point out, not all societies can afford to include scientific publics and theories in their "social distribution of knowledge." It is really only in societies with an economic surplus and a considerable division of labor that it is "possible for certain individuals or groups to engage in specialized activities not directly concerned with subsistence." This condition leads to "specialization and segmentation in the common stock of knowledge . . . (and) . . . Thus we have the 'theoretical life,' with its luxurious proliferation of specialized bodies of knowledge, administered by specialists whose social prestige may actually depend upon their inability to do anything but theorize. . . ." (1967:81) This quest for social prestige by our scientists, a concomitant of their quest for "truth," has produced quite a body of literature in social science about the causes and consequences of various social problems. Let us review briefly the main theories about social problems, particularly from sociology, that have developed over the years. Since there will be many references to these theories in subsequent chapters, it will perhaps serve the reader well if we outline them here.

SOCIOLOGICAL THEORIES ON SOCIAL PROBLEMS
Constructions of Reality by Social Scientists

Certain introductory comments might first be in order about some of the assumptions which sociologists generally make in their theorizing. First, as sociologists we do not usually give much attention to theories of other disciplines, even related ones like psychology and physiology. Explanations for certain kinds of problematic behavior have been derived from physiology by Lombroso, Sheldon, and others. Criminal and other anti-social behavior, for example, have been attributed in large part to head shape, body type, a double-y male chromosome, and other physical characteristics (Clinard, 1974: Chapter 5). Psychologists and psychiatrists too have offered us theories from the field of abnormal psychology, beginning with the classical Freudian work on psychosexual development, neurotic conflicts, and so on (Clinard, 1974: Chapter 6). The reasons that sociologists do not utilize such theories more often are probably threefold: (1) such theories may help us to understand individual cases, but they do not go very far in explaining the variation between deviants and nondeviants in a population; (2) such theories do not address social problems which do not involve deviant behavior (such as population and environment issues, old age, etc.); (3) psychological problems, at least, are generally believed by sociologists to have their origins in social relationships anyway.

The Normative System

An important set of assumptions lying behind much sociological theory on social problems has to do with what we call a *normative system*. This is an abstract construction of reality, diagrammed in Figure 1-1, which refers to the various

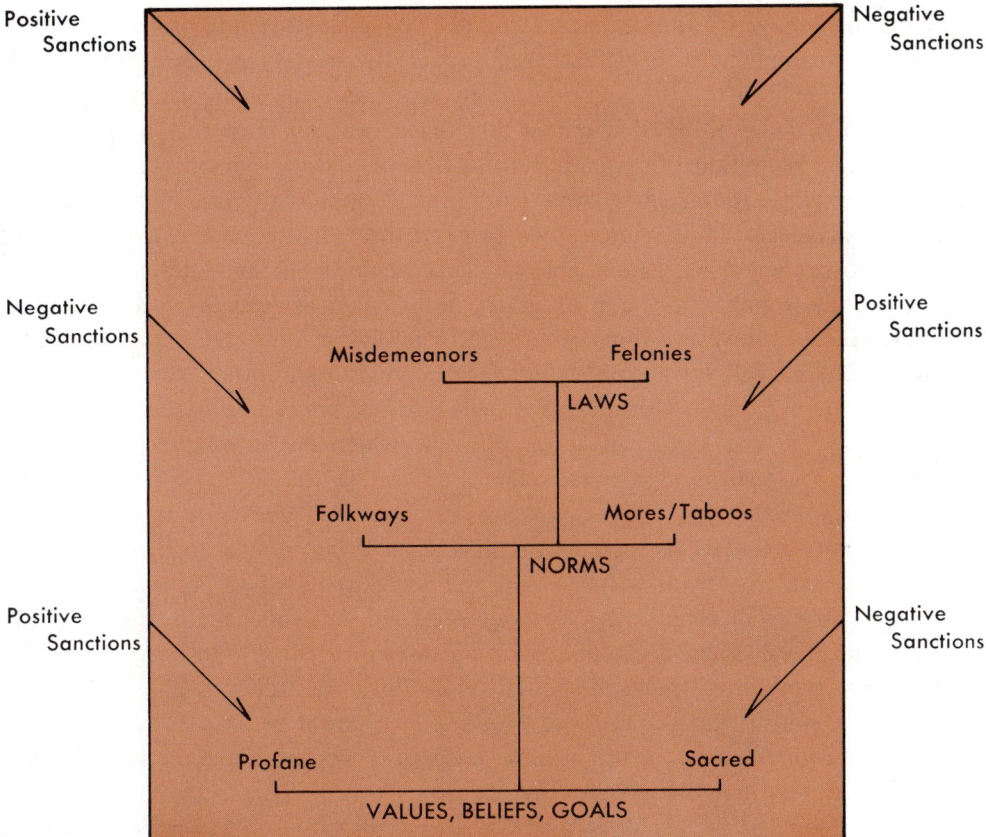

Figure 1-1   Diagram of a Normative System

ideals, standards of behavior, and laws which govern the social life of a society or small group, such as a family, church, or ethnic subculture. As the diagram indicates, a normative system might be seen as having two dimensions—vertical and horizontal. Let us look at the vertical dimension first: At the bottom is a level of the normative system representing *values*. The values of a society or group are those ideals or principles that people hold dear, such as "equality," "patriotism," or "love," in our own society. Particular forms of behavior are not specified by values, for they are of a very abstract nature; the ideal of equality, for example, has been espoused during our history by people whose actual behavior has ranged from slave-holding to civil rights demonstrations. Nevertheless, values are supposed to provide rough abstract guides to behavior at the level of principle.

To get a more accurate and predictive guide to actual behavior, we have to move up a level to the *norms* of a society or group. Norms are actual concrete standards of behavior required of individuals. Norms are supposed to derive from values and to implement them, and they provide the observer with a fairly good operational definition of the values held by a group. For example, if a person crowds into a line waiting at a movie box office, we can infer that he probably has a different definition of "equality" from that of another person who waits his turn, for the prescription "first come first served" implies that no one is entitled to special privileges in the quest for scarce items. The person who crowds in will also be subjected to considerable abuse, perhaps including forcible removal, though he will probably not be arrested, for he has not (in most instances) broken any law. He has, however, violated a norm, which is an *informal prescription for behavior,* and he will be the object of various kinds of informal social pressure to get him to conform. ("Norms," used in this sense, are not to be confused with "norms" used in the statistical sense for that which is "normal" or regularly recurring; as the term is used here, rather, it refers to that which is "normative" or socially required.)

Some norms come to be regarded as having such importance to a people that they do not want to rely merely on informal social pressure to enforce them; or sometimes norms will come to be so widely violated that some more weighty kind of enforcement will seem necessary. Such norms will then be translated into *laws* (in societies that have legal and legislative institutions). Laws might be defined as formalized norms that are enforced by the police power of the state. Most of us have seen volumes, such as the vehicle code of a certain state, in which laws pertaining to the use of vehicles are clearly set down, with the terminology carefully defined and the penalties spelled out explicitly. The civil rights acts passed by Congress during the 1960's reflected a widespread belief that the *value* of equality was not sufficiently well implemented by the informal *norm* "first come first served" when, for example, some of our minority citizens attempted to buy homes in better neighborhoods. Some of the civil rights legislation, accordingly, raised this norm to the level of *law.* Just as norms, then, are more concrete and explicit than values, laws are more specific, explicit, and formal than norms. Thus, the vertical dimension of a normative system goes from abstract to concrete.

The horizontal dimension (*cf.* Figure 1-1) refers to the scaled property of a normative system, its tendency at all three levels to range *from the less to the more important.* Laws, norms, and values each comprise a scale or continuum of seriousness or importance. In societies like our own, at least, not all laws carry equally severe penalties. These range from minor *misdemeanors,* which usually carry fines or short jail sentences, to *felonies,* which carry much heavier fines, long jail sentences, and, in some cases, even a death penalty, perhaps.

Norms too can usually be understood as comprising a continuum from "folkways" (less important norms) to "mores" (more important norms), to use the terminology of Sumner (1960). Mores that are phrased negatively (e.g., "thou shalt not . . .") are sometimes called "taboos" (tabus). Folkways might be exemplified by the clothing and hair customs among us. Though quite a range is permitted, people who wear clothes that are too "grubby" or too outlandish are likely to receive stares and comments. Men whose hair is very long, or who wear beards, are likely to get a certain amount of light hazing, and may even be the objects of insult from our more conservative citizens, but since their behavior violates only some rather vague folkways, they are not likely to endure much heavy social pressure. Mores, on the other hand, govern behavior regarded as somewhat more crucial to the successful maintenance of social life and social peace. In our society, and in most others, norms regulating relations between the sexes are often toward the *mores* end of the scale. Indeed, our English word "moral" is derived from the Latin *mores,* and when we say an act is "immoral," we are usually referring to a violation of norms at the right-hand extremity of the diagram, whether there is a law against that behavior or not.

The level of *values* at the bottom of our diagram also has a scaled property, which we might describe, at least approximately, by the distinction which Durkheim (1961) made between "sacred" values and "profane" values. The latter term refers to values of a common, ordinary, and changeable nature, in contrast to sacred values, which are more essential, enduring, and unquestionable. Most of our profane values sit so lightly upon us, and have so few conspicuous behavioral outcomes, that we are not even aware of them; an example might be the emphasis which many students and other young people place upon being fashionable and popular. Most professors probably wish that the value of scholarship would take precedence over the values of popularity and fashionability among students, for these latter values are probably even more profane to professors than they are to students. They are profane in a sociological sense, though, because they deal with everyday things and because they are subject to fairly rapid shifts in definition and importance. Every society (and many groups and subcultures) has *sacred* values, on the other hand, which have become part of its traditions and cannot seriously be questioned by people in the society without their running a severe risk of being branded as troublemakers or traitors, even if their actual behavior is acceptable. Political extremists, for example, even in the United States, often find it difficult to speak to large audiences. They might be denied permission by the authorities (perhaps on the grounds that their speech can cause a breach of the peace), or they might be booed and hooted down by the audiences themselves. People on the "wrong side" of a social issue or social problem might suffer the same treatment, such as those who advocate too "permissive" a corrections program in this time of "law and order" or those women who are considered "traitors" to the women's movement because they prefer male dominance. Certain sacred principles or values are challenged and threatened by such dissenters from the "established truth" of the contemporary political or social scene. Symbols like the flag, which represent sacred values, are also supposed to be treated reverently by all members of the society, and those who refuse to salute the flag on appropriate occasions are likely to suffer some abuse, even though they are not breaking any law or otherwise behaving in dangerous or anti-social ways.

The horizontal dimension of a normative system, then, refers to the range of lesser-to-greater importance found at each of the three levels, and the vertical dimension refers to the increasing specificity and concreteness of the normative system as we go from values (at the bottom) to norms and to laws (at the top). Theoretically, a sociologist or anthropologist making a thorough study of a society or group should find it possible to catalogue various ideals and behavioral standards into one of these vertical categories and to rank all values, norms, and laws in order from weak to strong. How can one tell which values and norms are weak and which are strong? We can tell by the *sanctions,* that is, by the rewards and punishments used by the society or group to get individuals to conform. *Rewards* (sometimes called "positive sanctions") can come in subtle forms, such as smiles and kind words, or in more obvious forms, such as money and public acclaim. Punishments or *penalties* (sometimes called "negative sanctions") can range from raised eyebrows to executions, depending on the severity of the violation. In a sense, sanctions almost constitute a third dimension of the normative system, running back and forth across all three levels to *enforce* the various values, norms, and laws involved. Since this is difficult to show on two-dimensional paper, however, sanctions are presented in Figure 1-1 simply as pressures coming from both left and right (negative and positive) to keep the thoughts, expressions, and behavior of people where they "belong" on each level.

Normative Systems and Relativity

Earlier in this chapter we discussed the importance of relativity in defining "reality" or "truth," and the same principle must be kept in mind in discussing normative systems: they are, of course, relative to *time,* to *place* (or culture), and to *situation.* When we say that they are relative to time, we mean that in the same society or culture there might be quite a difference in normative systems from one generation to another. Our grandmothers can probably recall when it was considered "immoral" for women to smoke or wear lipstick, and we all know it was once illegal for women to vote or to own property in their own names. In these and in many other respects, we could say that, in effect, we have a different normative system in our society now from the one we had fifty years ago. Normative systems are relative to place also, in the sense that the norms and values of one society or group are different from those of another society or group. We all realize that headhunting tribes in South

America hold quite different values and norms from our own with respect to killing (and probably in many other respects as well); but we don't have to look to such exotic places to see this kind of relativity illustrated. In our own rather heterogeneous society, we see many normative differences among our religious subcultures, our social classes, our ethnic groups, and, of course, our deviant subcultures. The family values and norms of the Mafia do not fully coincide with those of the society in general, although they are not completely different either. In addition to the relativity of time and place, normative systems are affected also by the relativity of situation, which determines in large part the priorities by which we rank our values and norms. (This idea is close to what some theologians call "situational ethics.") For example, even though we may esteem both honesty and loyalty as values (with their derivative norms), we may feel obliged to put honesty above loyalty if we witness a serious crime committed by a friend; on the other hand, we may wish to reverse the priorities if we are prisoners of war under interrogation (or if we are members of a deviant subculture being interrogated by the police).

These three kinds of relativity greatly complicate the process of law enforcement in complex societies like our own, particularly the relativity of time and place. Sometimes, for example, values and norms change and become obsolete before the laws based upon them have been changed. This is true of many of the "Blue Laws" inherited from our Puritan past. Laws against profanity, obscenity, prostitution, and adultery no longer have the support that they once had in our underlying norms and values, and consequently we do not really expect the police to enforce them very conscientiously. If such laws are rigorously enforced, we are likely to become hostile or to demand that they be abolished. Indeed, laws that do not have widespread support in the underlying norms and values, for whatever reason, will create enormous enforcement problems and will probably result in the outbreak of various kinds of "secondary crime" (i.e., crimes committed in the process of trying to evade the principal or primary laws). We have all heard, for example, of the difficulties of enforcing alcohol abstinence during the Prohibition Era, because a large minority (if not a majority) did not really believe in the law (that is, their values and norms did not support it). As Chapter 7 shows, a similar problem now exists with respect to the use of marijuana. Bootlegging, black markets, underworld control and other kinds of "secondary crime" have resulted from efforts to prohibit alcohol, marijuana, and other substances or behavior not in violation of important norms or values in the normative system. Recent literature in criminology has demonstrated that many of our laws are class-based or otherwise represent interests or normative systems different from those of the people most likely to break these laws, and, in that sense, such laws are seen as "culture-bound," biased, illegitimate, and oppressive according to the definitions of reality in some of our subcultures (Quinney, 1970a and 1970b). Gaps of these kinds in the public consensus about normative systems, then, derive from the relativity we have discussed above, and they create serious problems of law enforcement. Most police programs and procedures are based upon the assumption that laws will be obeyed voluntarily almost all of the time by almost all of the people, because of the influence or pressure from the popular norms and values upon which the laws are supposed to be based. When that assumption can no longer be made, much more money and effort must be put into law enforcement, and much more conflict erupts between the police and the populace.

The normative system is believed by sociologists to be "operating" in any culture or subculture. It is an abstraction offered by sociologists as a working "definition of reality," and much of the sociological theory about social problems deals with elements of that abstraction. As a scientific interest group, sociologists have advocated or promoted a variety of theories, some of them complementary. Since many of our social problems are defined by sociologists as involving *deviant behavior,* we will look first at some of the sociological theories on that subject. Though there are many ways that deviance theory can be classified, we will review four perspectives which, taken together, comprise the most influential and widely utilized theories about deviance from the discipline of sociology.

Theories About Deviant Behavior

Functionalism

The first of these we might call the *functionalist perspective,* which dates back at least to the work of Durkheim (1933 and 1964) around the turn of the present century. This perspective begins with the assumption that the various elements and institutions of society are tied together into a structure of interdependent parts, somewhat like an organism or an ecosystem, so that what happens in one part affects other parts. Deviant behavior has been defined by some theorists from this point of view as being *functional*—that is, as contributing to the operation of the existing structure; on the other hand, some theorists have treated deviance as *dysfunctional,* or disruptive of the social structure.

Several functional aspects of deviance have been proposed. Deviance helps define the normative boundaries of a society, for the punishment meted out to deviants helps to clarify the limits of public tolerance. Deviance helps promote social change needed for the overall health of the society, for innovative or law-evading behavior often results in a relaxation of norms or a change in the laws that are obsolete or dysfunctional. It also helps provide outlets for the occasional release of pressure that would otherwise destroy institutions that are normatively demanding; and it helps increase the solidarity of a group or society when its members cooperate to fight deviance in their midst and punish the offenders. One or more of these functions of deviance have been illustrated by Durkheim's (1964) treatment of crime, by Davis's (1937) analysis of prostitution, by Erikson's (1966) historical work on sin and crime in Puritan New England, and by other works.

Deviance is also seen sometimes as *dys*functional: it weakens public commitment to the normative structure if it is very widespread; it taxes the resources of the society to hunt down and punish deviants; and it disrupts the public peace. The notion of dysfunction is very close to the conception that most ordinary people have about the nature of crime and deviance in society.

Another aspect of functionalist theory that has been usefully applied to deviance is the distinction between *manifest functions* and *latent functions,* first propounded in a different context by Robert Merton (1957). In reference to deviance, manifest functions (or dysfunctions) are those which a form of deviance is intended to serve, such as public sexual gratification in the case of prostitution, or, in the case of income-tax cheating, the protection of private profits even at the cost of undermining the revenue system. Latent functions of these same forms of deviance, on the other hand, might be to make more tolerable (and therefore endurable) the monogamous form of marriage for males, in the case of prostitution, and to generate a whole new professional category of tax lawyers, to handle litigation in cases of tax cheating.

In any event, the scientists using a functionalist perspective asks how a given form of deviance serves or disrupts an existing social order, whether or not intentionally, how deviance is tied in with other customs and institutions in the society, and how it contributes to change from one structural arrangement to others.

Strain and Control

The second theoretical perspective on deviance often advanced by the sociological scientific interest group might be called *strain theory*. This theory is advanced on two levels, the societal level and the individual level. On the societal level, variations of strain theory can be seen in concepts like *anomie, social disorganization,* and *value conflict*. All of these concepts refer to some kind of breakdown in the traditional social order, caused sometimes by external events (such as wars, invasions, natural disasters, or migrations) and sometimes by internal changes (such as population shifts and swells, economic crises, and the like). Especially in the case of internal developments, it is often hard to tell which ones are causes of the breakdown and which ones are symptoms. Nevertheless, the general idea is that some kind of unexpected or large-scale phenomenon has spread confusion or chaos, where before there was order and peace. Many such theories have attributed the breakdown in recent generations to the industrial revolution (e.g., Dynes, et al., 1964). *Anomie,* a term used by the French sociologist Durkheim (1933 and

1951), connotes a breakdown of the *normative system,* in which norms and values have become vague, confused, or contradictory. Large numbers of people have become unsure of the culturally prescribed goals in life and the means by which they are expected to obtain them. As a result, old definitions of right and wrong lose their power, and people no longer feel constrained by them. Deviance of various kinds becomes more common, partly because of this generalized loss of commitment to traditional norms and partly just as a form of boundary-testing in a time when normative boundaries are not clear. For some of the same reasons, deviance increases also during times of *social disorganization,* which refers to a breakdown in the *social structure* more than in the normative system. (Of course, in large part the two kinds of breakdown would go together). Social disorganization (which is what functionalists often mean when they speak of "dysfunctions") implies that social roles are not as well defined as they once were, so that people do not behave in the ways that their positions once required them to behave; that traditional social institutions (like family, church, etc.) do not work as well as they once did, or do not carry out the same functions that they used to; and that, consequently, behavior has become more unpredictable and social interaction of all kinds more risky and problematic. *Value conflict,* the third of these concepts used to imply a societal breakdown of some kind, deals with the normative system and the social structure simultaneously. Conflicts occur in the *norms and values held from one segment of the society to another.* For example, different ethnic and religious subcultures will inculcate different values and norms in their members to some degree, and this difference will set the stage for conflicts (political, economic, moral, or even physical) among competing groups or subcultures, particularly in a society as varied and heterogeneous as the American society. Of course, value conflicts can occur also between social classes, regions, occupational interest groups, and a host of other kinds of groups. Many social theorists indeed, beginning with Karl Marx, have regarded the normative system of any society as simply the norms and values *of the groups in power,* which they have imposed upon all other segments of the society who are weaker in numbers or resources. Laws, from this point of view, are always class-based and will be resisted by those classes or subcultures in the society who do not share the norms and values upon which the laws are based. Deviance is thus seen simply as the rejection of (or resistance to) the laws of the "establishment" by the "oppressed peoples" of that society. But whether the issue is class-based law or not, the general idea is that the different subcultures and interest groups in the society disagree in certain important respects over values, goals, or norms, either because of differential socialization or because of changes over time in the normative system that have affected the different groups unevenly (Horton and Leslie, 1974, Chapter 2; Quinney, 1970a, 1970b).

The variations of strain theory discussed so far have dealt with the society-wide kinds of strain. The same theoretical perspective can be applied at the individual level, and it is here that sociological and psychological theories are most likely to be parallel and similar. Individual or psychological strain can lead to deviance in a variety of ways. For example, people can try to "retreat" or "escape" from their internal conflicts or their interpersonal conflicts through suicide, alcoholism, drugs, or withdrawal into some psychotic state. The term "anomie" itself, which we used earlier to refer to a condition in society, can also be used to refer to a condition within the individual (whether or not it exists objectively in his society). If the individual *perceives* normative ambiguity or irregularity, then he is subjectively "anomic," and he runs a higher risk than most people of turning to suicide, alcohol, etc. (The terms "anomie" and "anomic," in fact, were first used by Durkheim [1951] in his study of suicide.) Merton (1957), followed by Cloward and Ohlin (1960), have elaborated the concept of anomie to explain how it may take different forms and have different deviant outcomes, according to the particular kinds of discrepancies that exist in a society among its *goals,* its acceptable *means,* and differential *opportunities* for people to achieve the goals by the means available to them. Psychological strain theories trace certain kinds of deviant behavior to the difficulties that individuals have in coping with frustration (often leading to severely aggressive behavior), thwarted ego needs, repressed libidinous drives, and many other personal problems, most of which sociologists would be inclined to attribute to social experiences in the family or elsewhere (Clinard, 1974: Chapter 6). If sociologists and psychologists frequently look to individual psychological conditions for the causes of deviant behavior, they do not have very clear explanations as to *what causes these conditions,* and certainly there has not been much success in making *predictions* about deviance from various kinds of psychological strain.

Whether dealing at the individual (psychological) level or at the societal level, then, many sociological theories attribute deviant behavior (and the consequent social problems) to some kind of *strain.*

Somewhat related to strain theory is a line of reasoning that might be called *control theory,* recently revised, elaborated, and tested in an important book by Travis Hirschi (1969). While Hirschi clearly distinguishes between strain and control theory, it might be more useful here to consider what they have in common. They both look at the *ties or bonds* that people have to other people and to the society, classified by Hirschi as attachment, commitment, involvement, and belief. With some oversimplification, we could say that strain theories tend to explain *deviance* by the *absence* of such bonds, whereas control theories tend to explain *conformity* by the *presence* of these bonds. The *strain theorists* ask why people commit crimes or deviant acts, and they answer the question by focusing on those conditions (societal or psychological) that weaken the bonds holding the social structure together and holding individuals to the structure: anomie, social disorganization, value conflicts, and so forth. The *control theorists,* on the other hand, ask the opposite question: Why do people conform? Why do they *not* deviate and commit crimes? While not necessarily using concepts like anomie or social disorganization, the control theorists still focus on the individual's ties to traditional social institutions, such as home, school, peers, occupations, and recreation, and upon the degree to which the individual holds clear and strong beliefs in traditional *values*. In these respects, then, strain and control theories might be considered different sides of the same theoretical coin.

Social Learning

A third and very different kind of deviance theory we shall call *social learning or transmission* theory. This general line of theorizing posits that people *learn* to be deviant just as they learn anything else; that no more complicated theory is needed to explain why people become deviant or criminal than is needed to explain why they become Catholic. In the words of the song, "You've got to be taught to hate" (or to steal, etc.). When a gang of juvenile delinquents fights, steals, or vandalizes, for example, they may be deviant or criminal according to the society at large, but not to themselves; they are only acting out the "code of the gang" (that is, the normative system of the gang). In fact, if they do not act out that code, they will be subjected to severe sanctions by the other gang members. In this conceptualization, then, a gang is seen as a kind of subculture in about the same sense as an ethnic or religious group would be considered a subculture. Many sociological treatises on juvenile delinquency have been written from this theoretical perspective, as have studies on drug use, violence, prostitution, and other forms of deviance (e.g., Cohen, 1955 and 1959; Akers, 1973). A classical criminology textbook by Sutherland and Cressey has expressed the same basic idea with the term "differential association"; that is, people tend to take on the values and norms of those with whom they principally associate. The psychological mechanism involved in this socialization process, according to Sutherland, is simply that a person becomes a criminal or deviant "because of an excess of definitions favorable to violation of law over definitions unfavorable to violation of law" (Akers, 1973: Chapter 3). Such a statement comes close to the behavioral psychological theories of psychologists like B. F. Skinner (Akers, 1973: Chapter 4). This perspective, however, is not limited to deviant gangs or peer groups; it attributes deviance also to the socialization a person might receive in other cultural settings, especially while growing up. The culture of the lower class, in particular, has been blamed by many scholars for teaching its members values and norms that are deviant from the middle-class point of view (Cohen, 1955 and 1959; Miller, 1958). In one way or another, then, social or cultural learning theories explain deviant behavior (and the social problems resulting from it) as something that is learned in subcultures, peer groups, or class settings that have deviant normative systems.

Social Interactionism

The fourth of the theoretical perspectives on deviance that we are considering here has gained special currency in recent years. It is often called the *interactionist* perspective, or the social interaction perspective. Derived largely from the symbolic interaction theoretical tradition of G. H. Mead and other early American sociologists of the Chicago School, this perspective has been given cogent contemporary application to the study of deviance by Becker (1963), Erikson (1966), Goffman (1961 and 1963), Lemert (1972), Rubington and Weinberg (1973), Schur (1965 and 1971), and several others. It is fundamentally different in its approach from the other theoretical perspectives we have been looking at, for they have mainly attempted to explain deviant acts by looking at the deviant and asking why he does what he does. These other theories are interested in the deviance or conformity of the *members* of a social system, with little or no attention to that social system itself and why it has the kind of normative system that it has. While agreeing that it is important to ask why some people deviate from the norms and laws while others do not deviate, interaction theorists say that it is equally important to ask why a given society regards certain kinds of behavior as deviant, sinful, or criminal and how it came to have laws against such behavior. Instead of taking the normative system of a society as "given" and defining deviance by reference to that system, Becker (1963) suggests that deviance should be defined as a "transaction" (or interaction) "that takes place between some social group and one who is viewed by that group as a rule-breaker." From this perspective, an understanding of deviant behavior must focus upon the processes by which rules are made, broken, and enforced, rather than simply upon the "strange" behavior of a class of people called "deviants" or "criminals." One of the key concepts of the interactionist perspective is that of *labelling,* the attaching of a negative status to a person as a result of an adverse collective definition of his behavior. Once a person has been so labelled, he is treated accordingly; he is expected to behave as a "delinquent" or as a "homosexual," etc., and others will even make selective perceptions of his subsequent behavior that reinforce their definition of him. Behavior that they would not necessarily see as delinquent or homosexual in others now comes to be so defined in the labelled person. With a variety of verbal and nonverbal clues in their responses to him, the "straight" people will communicate to the labelled one that they expect him to deviate, and, partly as a consequence of their expectations, he will continue to do so. This sets up the "self-fulfilling prophecy" by which the labelled person ends up "as everyone knew he would," at odds with society. Becker (1963) has described in some detail what might be called a "dialectic of mutual ostracism," through which the labelled and the labellers, interacting through the definitions implied in the label, grow further and further apart, until finally the deviant joins an organized deviant group, takes on a new, deviant worldview or ideology and a new self-concept as "junkie," "gay," "crook," etc. The development of deviance, then, is seen from this perspective as a *bilateral process,* involving not only a certain kind of behavior on the part of the one labelled deviant, but also the making and enforcing of a set of rules or laws, in the first place, followed by a continuing general response to the deviant that helps to "lock him into" his new status and role.

It is, of course, true that without the misbehavior of the deviant, there would be no deviance; but it is equally true that without the presence of rules (laws) against that behavior there would be no deviance. In this sense, the chief cause of crime is law. One holding a less relativistic view of the causes of deviance might object that every society has to have laws or norms, a truism that is inherent in the very definition of society. But there is no reason in the nature of things that a society has to have any particular laws or norms, for, as we have abundantly illustrated earlier in this chapter, there is an immense variety from time to time and place to place in normative systems, in what is considered criminal or sinful.

There is a great variety, too, in what is considered a "social problem" in different times and places, since social problems are created by the same process of collective definition that creates laws and labels law-breakers. As will doubtless be clear to the reader by now, this process is the main subject of the present textbook, which means that we are deriving the theoretical framework of the book largely from the *social interactionist* perspective briefly outlined above. We are, however, applying this theoretical perspective, not only to the kinds of "social problems" involving deviant behavior, but to *all* kinds of social problems.

General Social Problems Theories

Objectivist Theories

There are, of course, other theories about social problems among sociologists as a scientific interest group, and we alluded briefly to some of these theories in the Preface. Whether or not drawing upon the deviance theories just outlined, many sociologists have looked for the causes of modern social problems *in rapid social change,* particularly the far-reaching changes derived from industrialization, mechanization, cybernation, and other fundamental developments of social life in the present century (e.g., Clinard, 1974; Dynes et al., 1964; Horton and Leslie, 1974; and Weinberg, 1970). This tendency has led to the use of concepts from the functional (dysfunctional) and disorganization or "strain" schools of thought primarily, even in explaining social problems that do not involve deviance. The explanation has been that, because of important economic and technological changes in the past century and a half, social systems do not work as well as they used to. Values and norms, roles and role expectations, have changed to meet the times. However, these social and cultural changes have taken place unevenly across the society, creating problems for those individuals and segments of the society not able to adjust readily to the new situations. For example, family life has been disrupted by the new opportunities and evolving roles of the wife and mother; ethnic minorities, too, have had new roles opened up to them by industrial development and migration. Some, unable to realize legitimate goals in these new times, have turned to one or another kind of crime to "make it." Others have retreated or escaped from the stress of these new times into alcohol, drugs, suicide, or mental illness. While the ideas in this paragraph oversimplify the explanation for social problems offered by most sociologists, they form their general line of reasoning. Almost all these sociologists see social problems as caused mainly by *objective changes in the social structure* rather than by the actions of individuals and groups, even if the problem in question involves deviant behavior. Accordingly, we might call this theoretical orientation toward social problems an "objectivist" one, as opposed to a more subjectivist theory (like the one employed by this book), which looks for the definition (or even the cause) of social problems in the subjective perceptions and interests of individuals and groups.

There is, however, another kind of "objectivist" sociological theory on social problems, one which still sees the origin of problems in the objective facts of the social structure. Rather than looking for the explanation of social problems in social change, however, this other objectivist orientation blames the *lack* of needed change in the existing social structure. Usually the capitalist system itself is either implicitly or explicitly indicted for such characteristics as materialism, exploitation, imperialism, racism, and the like, which characteristics are seen as generating the pressing social problems of our time. Racial conflict, for example, is explained as arising naturally from the racism and exploitation inherent in our economic system. Poverty is similarly explained and considered inevitable under capitalism, even the modified capitalism in our society. War, too, arises from the natural imperialist impulses of capitalism. Oppressed people will often turn to crime, or to alcohol and drugs, as a means of coping with their oppression. This general line of theorizing, which owes much to Marxist social thought, has constituted the main thrust of a few social problems textbooks appearing in more recent years (e.g., Skolnick and Currie, 1970 and 1973; Chambliss, 1973; Lindenfeld, 1973; and Carnoy and Weiss, 1973). It might be called "left-wing objectivism" in contrast to the "right-wing objectivism" described above. Both regard social problems as objectively real in the sense that they are *objectively generated from the social structure itself,* rather than arising from the various social constructions of reality found in the minds of men and women.

It would be incorrect and unfair, however, to characterize all other social problems theories and textbooks as totally lacking in a recognition of the part played by social constructions of reality, interest groups, public opinion, and other processes of collective definition. Even those of an objectivist theoretical orientation (both left and right) differ considerably among themselves in the amount of attention and importance they accord to subjective factors and collective definitions. Many of them recognize that collective behavior and interest group activities help to raise public consciousness and concern about modern social problems, but only with the understanding that those problems are inherently and objectively present in the first place, independent of public recognition. This approach is very different from saying, as the present book says, that certain individuals and interest groups in the society, for their own reasons, *choose to make problems* out of social conditions that other groups, societies, and generations would not notice. Nevertheless, even within an objectivist theoretical framework, most theorists recognize that public opinion plays an important part in the rise of social problems. One of the more sophisticated and widely adopted formulations of the tie between social problems and objective reality was first put forth by Merton (1971), who distinguished between "manifest" and "latent" social problems, as he had earlier done between manifest and latent functions. Manifest problems are those which everyone in a society can see, those which have been publicly recognized as needing attention. Latent problems, in contrast, are those which have not yet been recognized by the public, but which can be pointed out by experts, such as social scientists. This position is still objectivist, since both kinds of social problems are objectively present. They are both the result of *discrepancies in the social system* between "widely shared social standards and actual conditions of social life" (Merton, 1971:799). It is just that the latent problems have not yet received general recognition through the processes of interest group activity and public opinion formation. This distinction between manifest and latent social problems, while explicitly recognized in one way or another by several of the "right-wing" objective textbooks, is often implicit in the presentations of the "left-wing" objectivists as well. They, too, say that the social problems are *objectively there,* usually in the capitalist system, whether everyone recognizes them or not. These theorists see themselves as merely sounding the alarm and calling our attention, usually in very moralistic terms, to serious problems, injustices, and hypocrisies in our system that anyone ought to be able to see as objectively present (Skolnick & Currie, 1973; Chambliss, 1973; and Lindenfeld, 1973).

Subjectivist Theories

In addition to the two kinds of objectivist theories about social problems, which we have briefly discussed above, there are a few theorists who use a more *subjectivist* perspective, built around such concepts as interest groups, collective definitions, public opinion, and the like. Probably the chief proponent of this perspective at the present time is Howard S. Becker (1963 and 1966), whose work has served as a mainspring and point of departure for the present book. Becker, in turn, has drawn upon the ideas of earlier sociologists like Blumer (1951 and 1971), Mills (1943 and 1959), and Fuller and Myers (1941a and b). The major difference between Becker's perspective and those of the two kinds of objectivists discussed above is his contention, which we share, that *objective conditions have very little directly to do* with the cause or origin of social problems. Objective reality (or, as we have called it, "consensual reality") may provide to interested people in the society certain data or "facts," which they, in turn, may interpret according to their own social and psychological constructions. Whatever these "objective facts" may be, however, they are *neither necessary nor sufficient* to produce social problems. People can create social problems with *no* basis in reality, as the Puritans of New England created witchcraft; or, people can fail to see problems in conditions which they later consider outrageous, such as the conditions of reservation and urban Indians in the United States. Individuals and interest groups will simply generate social problems out of their own interests, with or without the data from objective reality. This is the theoretical point of view of what we might call "subjectivists" (to distinguish them from the "objectivists").

A treatise on social problems that largely shares the subjectivist view of Becker (but not fully) is that of F. James Davis (1970), who provides a rather thorough account of the parts played by collective behavior, value conflict, and public opinion formation in generating social problems. Since Davis, however, sees social change, together with "marked social unrest," as necessary conditions in the society for the rise of social problems, he still retains a measure of the objectivist viewpoint. Also, Davis stops short of tying social problems to social movements, as the perspective of Blumer and Becker would do, though he recognizes that movements are sometimes involved. Except for the work of Becker, Davis, and the present text, then, sociological theories about social problems tend to be objectivist in their perspective and to draw upon a variety of deviance theories in explaining the causes of problems. The four kinds of deviance theories we have reviewed, and the two or three kinds of social problems theories themselves, have all been widely analyzed and criticized, often by each other. Our interest here has been more in describing these various theoretical perspectives as "constructions of reality" offered by social scientists, rather than in critiquing them. In any case, it is not so much a question of whether these various theories are ultimately "true" or "false"; it is more a matter of *which kinds of social problems* are more usefully explained by which kinds of theories and (we would here insist) to what extent these theories recognize the process of collective definition and behavior in generating social problems.

SUMMARY*

After trying, in the Preface, to distinguish our approach to the study of social problems, we began the present chapter with a discussion of the relative nature of truth and reality. We gave particular emphasis to the socially constructed character of reality, whether scientific theory or "common sense." The only reality there is in a society is that which people agree to believe. In all societies, most people will share a consensus about the kinds of formal and informal reality they will accept, and in our society much credence is given to official statistics, scientific reports, and the like, as sources providing the "parameters of reality." However, the interpretations and selective perceptions of that reality are derived from the reality constructions of various subgroups and segments within the society. Their reality constructions, in turn, are closely related to their *interests,* which tend to be of one or more of six types: economic, political, moral, occupational, psychological, and scientific. *Publics* form around these interests, and these publics frequently give rise to *interest groups,* which are somewhat organized, and *pressure groups,* which are interest groups that focus mainly on the political process to pursue their interests. It is these interest (pressure) groups, together with certain influential individuals within or outside them, that we call "the champions" of social problems, for they are the ones who fight to establish certain conditions as "problems" in the public eye, and then work for the solution of these problems.

Most interest groups have definitions of reality that are specific to the problems which they promote, and these definitions are examined in some detail later in this book. The *scientific* interest groups, however, or at least the social scientists, have certain more general constructions of reality about social problems. Called socio-

---

* After the text for this book was already in press, I discovered an excellent treatise on the sociology of social problems theory: Ritchie P. Lowry, *Social Problems: A Critical Analysis of Theories and Public Policy* (Lexington, Mass.: D. C. Heath, 1974). While Lowry's treatment differs conceptually in certain particulars from what I have presented here, there are also some important parallels. *Social Problems* serves to amplify and illustrate well much that I have been able only to touch upon with regard to the fads and fashions in social science theory, the intellectual interests of various "scientific interest groups" (as I have called them), and the social and intellectual wellsprings of these interests. I strongly recommend the book to all who have an interest in the sociology of sociology.

logical theories, these reality constructions are of various kinds. We first reviewed an abstract construction called a *normative system,* which lies at the root of many of the theories. Then we presented briefly four different perspectives on *deviant behavior,* which is behavior that violates the normative system and thus often becomes problematic for some segments of the society. These four different theoretical perspectives we called functionalism, strain and control, social learning or transmission, and social interactionism. As for more *general* theories about social problems (those which do not necessarily involve deviance), we distinguished between those of an "objectivist" kind, which see social problems as objectively present in the social system, and those of a "subjectivist" kind, which find the origin of social problems in the various subjective constructions of reality among interest groups and individuals. The present textbook draws upon the subjectivist definition of social problems and upon the social interactionist perspective on deviance. Having thus located the source of social problems in the differential reality constructions of interest groups, we will go on in Chapter 2 to outline the typical "careers" of the social movements generated by these interest groups.

Chapter 2

Social Problems as Social Movements

THE GENESIS OF SOCIAL PROBLEM-MOVEMENTS

We have presented the case for considering social *problems* as simply a special kind of social *movement*. This case rests in large part upon the proposition that the characteristics of social problems are typically also those of social movements. These characteristics have been discussed in preceding sections and include subjective definitions of reality, the formation of interest groups with their respective constructions of reality, the efforts of such groups to mobilize public opinion, and various other processes typical of collective behavior and social movements. In the present chapter, we shall see further how well social movement theory fits the case of social problems. Accordingly, we shall hereafter use the two terms more or less interchangeably. When we speak of social problems, it will be with the understanding that we are thinking of them as movements; and when we speak of movements, we shall be referring to social problem-movements, unless we specify some other kind.

In the previous chapter, we emphasized the importance of subjective constructions of reality over objective social conditions in generating social problem-movements. Among the reasons for this choice of emphasis were: (1) the cultural and temporal *relativity* surrounding the issue of what is a problem—that is, the same social conditions may or may not be defined as problematic, depending on time and place; (2) the *insufficiency* of "objective" social conditions to produce social problems in and of themselves; and (3) the *unpredictability* of social problems, especially of any particular social problem, from given social conditions. Our de-emphasis of objective social conditions, however, should not be construed to mean that such conditions have *no* importance—only that the part which they play is much more dependent upon collective definition than the latter is upon them. Nevertheless, historical studies have indicated that social unrest, social problems, social movements, and the like are more likely to occur under some social conditions than under others. One important and rather obvious example of such a contingency is whether the political system *permits* the collective expression of new constructions of reality by interest groups. Totalitarian states do not, usually, and that restriction is probably why social movements of any kind are rare in such states, except, perhaps, those movements that result in a political coup. But this example is only a superficial instance of the susceptibility of social structures to the generation of social movements.

Structural Conduciveness and Strain

Neil Smelser (1962), among other sociologists, has pointed out that certain conditions can make societies susceptible to outbreaks of collective behavior, including social movements; and his book on the subject spells out what those conditions are: structural conduciveness, structural strain, the growth and spread of generalized belief, special precipitating factors, the mobilization of participants, and certain facilitating processes in the social control system. Of special interest to us here are the first two of these factors, conduciveness and strain, since these in particular exist before the movement begins and provide the setting in which it must arise. "Conduciveness" refers to the arrangements in a society that may either facilitate or restrain the rise of a particular kind of movement. For example, a society which already encourages individual autonomy in its political system and depends upon a market arrangement for its economic system, is probably more likely to get a women's liberation movement than is a society based on a traditional caste system. (See Chapter 11.) The other concept, "strain," refers to the inadequate functioning of society, particularly ambiguities and discrepancies in the normative system and inconsistencies between ideals and realities. Smelser explains the rise of social movements and other forms of collective behavior by means of a "value-added" model: no one of the factors listed above will produce collective behavior by itself, but each of the factors adds to the likelihood through its own additional weight and through its interaction with all the other factors. With all six of the factors present in certain ways, the likelihood of a movement's arising approaches certainty. However, it is very difficult, if not impossible, to predict just what kind of movement (Smelser, 1962: Chapter V).

The difficulties in prediction are increased to the extent that we try to rely on only one or two of the factors in the value-added model. Smelser's caution about relying upon "strain" could apply as well to "conduciveness" or to any of the other factors: structural strain, he reminds us (p. 66), is a necessary but not sufficient condition for the rise of movements, and any type of strain may give rise to any kind of collective behavior (including expressions other than movements). He qualifies considerably the "objectiveness" of strain, furthermore, in a way that illustrates the *subjective nature* of the "underlying social conditions" for a movement:

> Before we can classify any event or situation as a source of strain, we must assess (it) with reference to *cultural standards and personal expectations.* . . . One worker, for instance, may face unemployment as a temporary hardship to be endured calmly until business improves. Another may see unemployment as a threat to his whole personal identity. Strain, then, always expresses a *relation between an event or situation and certain cultural and individual standards.* (Smelser, 1962:51; italics added.)

No doubt "cultural standards" here could refer just as well to "subcultural" or "interest group" standards, and thus, even where "objective" strains in the social structure are thought of as prerequisites to the rise of social movements, we are still confronted with *subjective* definitions of reality.

In addition to his recognition of the importance of subjective ideas in the definition of "structural strain," Smelser (1962) has as one of the major components in his value-added model "the growth and spread of generalized belief," which corresponds to what we have been calling "public opinion." The types of generalized belief of greatest importance for the present study are probably those which Smelser (1962: IX and X) calls "norm-oriented" and "value-oriented" beliefs, but his "hostile" beliefs and "wish-fulfillment" beliefs also appear to get involved in many social problem-movements. Even though Smelser, then, is dealing with what many people would assume are objective factors in the underlying social setting, he makes very clear the dependence of these factors, and the movements they generate, upon the social constructions of reality held by the participants and the public at large. This approach would seem to undermine much of the explanation on which objectivists rely when they trace the rise of social problems to discrepancies between shared social standards and actual social conditions, to social disorganization, to social dysfunctions, to hypocrisies in the system, to rapid social change, and to other characteristics of the system "external" to the movement.

Even if one could confidently regard systemic factors as totally external to social constructions of reality, they still give us very limited explanation of the causes of social problems or other movements. Wilbert Moore (1963) has convincingly characterized societies of all kinds as "tension-management systems," and he has shown that all societies at all times undergo changes even without dramatic historical developments like revolutions or technological breakthroughs. Societies are constantly generating their own changes from such natural occurrences as gradual changes in population size and density or from the imperfections inevitable in any socialization process across generations. If all societies are constantly changing, if they are constantly in a state of "tension-management," and if, as Moore points out, there are always discrepancies between the ideals and the realities, then we can expect only a rather superficial explanation and understanding of the causes of social problems (or other movements) if we look primarily to such phenomena as rapid social change, social disorganization, normative inconsistencies, and the like. Lewis Killian (1964), who has made major contributions to the study of collective behavior, suggests, in a vein similar to Moore's, that we need no special theory to explain the rise of social movements from a particular social system. We must look for social movements, they suggest, in the very nature of the social order itself and in the natural gaps in the process of socialization. Since no social order can be expected to function equally well for everyone all the time, we can expect a certain amount of dissatisfaction or unrest in any society at any time.

Let us posit, then, that (1) societies can be considered "tension-management systems," in which there are always, to some degree, normative discrepancies, dysfunctions, and other strains brought about by continuous large- and small-scale changes in the society; (2) some societies (especially large and heterogeneous ones like our own) have to contend with (or "manage") more change and strain than do other societies; (3) such societies will generate more social problems (and other movements) than will the less dynamic and mobile ones; *but* (4) it is very difficult (if not impossible) to predict which social problem-movements will arise or when, from knowing the susceptibility factors in the social structure itself; *because* (5) the critical and ultimate determinants of social problems will be the perceptions and definitions held by publics and interest groups about the changes and strains in their social setting.

Stability and Change in the Incidence of Social Problems

A historical observation that further complicates the prediction of social problems on the basis of structural factors alone is the ebb and flow in their incidence over time in the same society, which does not always seem closely related to structural complexity or rates of change. In recent American history, for example, the periods which spawned the largest number of social problems and reform movements were the so-called Progressive Era (late 19th century up through World War I) and the Kennedy-Johnson years (the late 1950's and the 1960's). It would be difficult to make the case that these periods were very different in structural characteristics from the decades on either side of them, but they were periods when many people were concerned with a variety of social problems and concomitant reform movements. This observation raises the question of what causes fluctuation in the incidence of social problems.

The very fact that there are periods or eras which stand out as times of "social reform" would suggest that most of the time the incidence of social problems is fairly stable. Kai Erikson (1966) has an insight that may be applicable here. As a part of his analysis of "crime rates" in 16th-century Massachusetts, he argues that rates of crime and, indeed, rates of deviance in general tend to remain constant over long periods of time. Although there may be shifts in the particular *kinds* of deviance that receive attention every few years, the amount of deviance, including crime, *taken as a whole* does not fluctuate much. There seems to be a "quota" of deviance that any society can afford, because its social control apparatus is necessarily finite. This apparatus simply cannot be "spread thin" enough to handle heavy and unpredictable demands on its financial and logistical system. As a result, if the social control agencies (including police, courts, perhaps clergy and kinship authorities, too, in traditional societies) are called upon to cope with sudden "waves" of one or two kinds of deviance, they must pay less attention to other kinds—a process which Erikson calls "displacement" of social control efforts. This theoretical position is derived ultimately from the functional model put forth by Durkheim (1964:67), who viewed deviance as "an integral part of all healthy societies" (though "regrettably" so). Hence, deviance (or crime) fulfills certain important functions in society, such as boundary-maintenance for the normative system (when culprits are punished as an example to others) and the reinforcement of group solidarity when members band together to punish or expel the culprit. Severe deviance, furthermore, serves the function of maintaining a fair amount of leeway for individual and group diversity, or even eccentricity, by keeping the social contol agencies so busy with *serious* crimes that they cannot be used to crack down on lesser forms of deviance. Even in a society in which crimes in the usual sense were no longer committed, Durkheim explains (1964:67-69), "crime would not thereby disappear; it would only change its form, for the very cause which would thus dry up the sources of criminality would immediately open up new ones.... Imagine a society of saints, a perfect cloister of exemplary individuals. Crimes, properly so called, will thereby be unknown; but faults which appear venial to the layman will create there the same scandal that the ordinary offense does in ordinary (societies). This (hypothetical, perfect) society ... will define these acts as criminal and treat them as such." It is in this sense, says Durkheim (67), that "crime is normal, because a society exempt from it is utterly impossible." So, putting the ideas of Durkheim and Erikson together, the argument is that every society generates or defines its own normal level of deviant behavior, and this level is likely to remain stable over time, although the particular offenses defined as deviant (or enforced as such) may vary from time to time.

We propose here that this Durkheim-Erikson argument be broadened beyond deviance to include all social problems. We therefore maintain that every society in a given span of time has its own normal quota of social problems. Although the specific social conditions which interest groups may pick out to define as problems will vary from time to time, the incidence of problems will remain stable. Not only is there a limit on the resources available for the sponsorship of causes, but there is also a limit on the challenges to the status quo which can be managed by social control agencies. As we shall see later, these agencies will attempt, with a combination of co-optation and repression, to keep the outbreak of social problems within manageable limits.

For those who would question this extension of Erikson's theory about deviance to the whole arena of social problems, several arguments can be offered. (1) Many of the social problems in our society center on deviant behavior anyway: crime, delinquency, sexual deviations, radical protest, mental illness, alcoholism, drug "abuse," and so on. (2) Even those social problems that do not address deviant behavior seem to develop through the same processes of definition and mobilization that define deviance, or they undertake to create and define new kinds of deviance. While we may not think of social problems like population, conservation, or poverty as involving deviance, the interest groups promoting such problems will always point the finger at certain "offenders" and question their morality. Thus, producing large families is considered immoral for those who have the means and the know-how to limit their offspring to two. Litterbugs are definitely "bad guys" for the environmentalist. Stingy, insensitive politicians stand in the way of programs for the poor. The male chauvinist is the "criminal" for the women's liberation movement. Though social problems of these kinds do not involve "deviant behavior" as we normally define it, they certainly do involve labelling certain recalcitrant types as though they were deviant (and, indeed, an effort to get them collectively defined as deviant). (3) All social problem-movements, whether they involve deviance or not, are, in Smelser's terminology, norm-oriented or value-oriented movements. They all attempt either to reaffirm or to redefine some aspects of the normative system. Thus, they are all "boundary-oriented" in the normative sense. Furthermore, even the social problem-movements not involving deviance share the same quality and style of those which do: campaigns and crusades which build and enhance the solidarity of the participants, the rallying slogans, and, as we observed above, the identification and definition of enemies or opponents.

We would therefore explain the stability in the incidence of social problems, not so much by reference to any lack of change or disorganization in the social structure as by postulating, with Durkheim and Erikson, a "normal quota" of social problems logistically possible for a society. Why, then, do we sometimes see periods in the history of a society which seem to produce outbreaks or fluctuations in the incidence of social problems? We would suggest at least three answers to that question. (1) The fluctuations may be only apparent, when a more thorough accounting for a period of history would show considerable stability. It is important to keep in mind that the incidence of social problems must be judged by their severity as well as by their sheer number. Thus, for example, we usually find very few social problems during times of world war or national disaster, probably because total wars constitute such a drain on the resources, energy, and emotions of a people that it is difficult for many of them to get aroused over other problems. The war becomes the one all-consuming problem. Also, those are typically times when special interests and their campaigns receive very little tolerance from the government or from the public at large, for no distractions must be permitted from the objectives of the war effort (or whatever the all-consuming problem is). In such periods, then, it is not that the total "quota" of social problems has changed, but rather that most of it is being "allocated" to one great problem. (2) There may actually be an increase or decrease in "the size and complexity of its social control apparatus," as Erikson would put it. Such a change in the "control apparatus," or the coping mechanisms of the society, could be expected to increase its quota of social problems. The quota might also be increased by a rapidly expanding economy, which would make available to interest groups more resources and leisure for campaigns. It may be noteworthy in this regard that the Progressive Era and the 1960's were both periods of great economic growth and prosperity, and they were also periods remarkable for the number and severity of social problems which they produced. (3) In times of a rapidly increasing division of labor and a growing economic surplus, it becomes more and more possible "for certain individuals and groups to engage in specialized activities not directly concerned with subsistence. These specialized activities . . . lead to specialization and segmentation in the common stock of knowledge. . . . This means that certain individuals are . . . freed from [subsistence activities] to fabricate myths . . ." and to generate theories (Berger and Luckmann, 1967:81). In other words, the rise and fall of social problems *is* related to changes in the social structure and to changes in the economic and technological realms, but not in the way that objectivist theories maintain. Our argument is that social problems arise during these times of social change, not so much because of concomitant conditions like strain, disorganization, anomie, and the like, but *simply because more people have more time, more resources, and more energy* to address social conditions, to define some of them as problematic and to engage in the processes of collective behavior which will produce social problem-movements.

Types of Social Movements

Having discussed the part played by objective social conditions *vs.* that played by subjective definitions in the generation of social problems, let us take a closer look at social problem-movements. More than two decades ago, Herbert Blumer (1951) set forth a typology of social movements which still seems relevant. His main distinction is between *general* and *specific* social movements, which differ according to the degree of their focus and organization. He describes also some kinds of movements which are distinguished mainly by their *quality* or *style: expressive movements* (including some religious movements and fashion movements), which seek to cope with personal and social dissatisfactions without aiming to change external social conditions; and *nationalistic* or *revival* movements, which seek to impose on present-day society certain idealized values or arrangements from the past. While the reform movements around social problems frequently partake of expressive or revivalist qualities, we are most concerned here with the more "quantitative" distinction Blumer makes between general and specific social movements.

General social movements consist mostly of "groping and unco-ordinated efforts" toward vague goals or objectives. They lack organization, leadership, and structure. They grow gradually out of what Blumer calls "cultural drifts," which are "gradual and pervasive changes in the values of a people." As a general movement begins to form from a cultural drift, it gradually acquires spokesmen who are more like "voices in the wilderness" than real leaders. A literature of protest and advocacy begins to develop, and the "media of interaction" among the people interested in the issues are in the form mainly of discussions, reading, and the selective perception and exchange of examples from social life to support their uneasiness. There is little or no concerted action by groups; most of the activity is on an individual basis. A general movement is carried by a vague collectivity of individuals—a "mass," as Blumer calls it, or perhaps a "public," as we have called it in the previous chapter.

A *specific* social movement usually grows out of a general movement as the latter grows out of a cultural drift. Instead of being carried by a mass or a public, the specific movement is an expression of the activities of interest groups and pressure groups, which have fairly well-defined goals. Blumer offers the example of the anti-slavery movement of the 19th century, which grew out of a more general humanitarian movement beginning somewhat earlier. Specific movements are apt to be of either a reform or revolutionary nature. They have certain generally acknowledged leaders, an overall organization broken down into a division of labor and roles, a guiding philosophy and set of rules, a body of traditions and expectations, and a kind of "we-consciousness." In short, a specific social movement is a kind of social organization, though not always as organized as established groups and institutions. Its organization and other characteristics are not, of course, present from the beginning, but they develop with the passage of time, largely out of the interaction of the movement with the rest of the society. For this reason, Blumer stresses the importance of the time dimension in the "career" of a specific social movement, a point to which we shall return later in this chapter. Most social problems are characterized by the traits of a *specific* social movement, though they often begin, and remain for a fairly long time, in the *general* movement stage.

As part of his comprehensive treatment on collective behavior, Smelser (1962:IX and X) deals with two kinds of specific movements: norm-oriented and value-oriented movements. The first of these seeks to "restore, protect, modify, or create norms in the name of a generalized belief." It addresses existing norms and laws and concrete ways of doing things in a society, sometimes out of conservative tendencies, but usually out of a desire for some kind of change. In terms of the outline of a normative system, discussed in Chapter 1, we would say that norm-oriented movements deal with the two top levels of the diagram (i.e., norms and laws). Those movements which deal with the bottom level of the diagram, however, Smelser calls *value-oriented movements:* collective attempts to "restore, protect, modify, or create values in the name of a generalized belief." Because value-oriented movements deal with the most fundamental and all-inclusive aspects of a culture, they might be described as trying, in effect, to create a new culture. They include many of the movements called by Blumer "expressive" and "nationalist," many of the religious movements of history, especially those that have swept whole societies and continents, and probably all of the movements based on the great "isms," such as Communism, Fascism, millenarianism, and the like, which attempt to reorder entire ways of life. By contrast, *norm-oriented* movements are content to leave the underlying culture and organization of a society pretty much intact, striving only for changes in (or preservation of) some of the social arrangements, rules, norms, laws, and other less fundamental aspects. Most social problems are of the norm-oriented type and only very rarely value-oriented, for they do not typically address the basis of the culture itself. The population problem-movement, for example, does not call for a basic change in the economy, in family life, or in any other institution; it advocates only that we establish as a norm the two-child family and encourage that norm through a variety of social and legal sanctions. To the extent, however, that a social problem-movement defines the source or cause of a problem as lying within the basic nature of the society (as, for example, when "radical" social theories claim that certain problems can be solved only by the abolition of capitalism), they take on some characteristics of a value-oriented movement; but the typical social problem is norm-oriented. Most of the movements dealt with in this textbook will be of the specific, norm-oriented kind, with all of the characteristics that Blumer, Smelser, and others have attributed to them.

ORGANIZATION AND MOBILIZATION OF SOCIAL MOVEMENTS

Thus far, this chapter has dealt with how social problems or movements get started, and in this connection, we have considered both the underlying social conditions and the importance of collective definitions in identifying these conditions as problematic. In this section, we shall be concerned with the next logical question:

Once social movements get going, by whatever means or causes, what are they like and what do they do? There is quite a voluminous literature on this question, some of which is represented in the bibliography at the end of the book. Here we shall be able to draw on such literature only in a general and summary way, with special focus, of course, on those ideas that are of special relevance to the theoretical stance of this book. Let us look first at the kind of structure or organization a social movement is likely to have.

Structural Characteristics of Social Movements

The usual pattern for a social movement resembles a series of three concentric rings or circles. The outermost ring represents a kind of public, or portion of the public, of the type that usually carries a general movement, except that in the case of a specific movement this public is made up of those whose sympathies definitely lean in the direction of the particular movement's program or ideology. These are not, however, the enthusiasts of a movement, for their interests are not yet critically involved. Their support for the movement waxes and wanes with the movement's own success and with the amount of pressure applied to the movement from the outside. They are often considered "fair weather friends" by the more deeply committed movement members. Nevertheless, they can be very important in (1) providing a good deal of the financial support and other resources that the movement needs; and (2) in using their votes and sheer numbers to add political strength (or at least the semblance of it) to the movement.

Within this ring comprising the sympathetic public, there is a much smaller one containing the active membership. This consists of individuals and organizations who have definite interests in the success of the movement, but these interests are not necessarily exclusively focused on the movement. They may have equally strong interests in quite other causes, and/or they may be more willing than some of the more zealous members to compromise with the existing situation and accept some reform and amelioration. Nevertheless, these are very important members of the movement. They are frequently well educated and skilled in committee work and other kinds of organizational behavior. They are often influential people whose public support for a movement will help to give it legitimacy and acceptance, especially if it begins as an unpopular movement suffering from repressive efforts by the government or by other traditional institutions.

The innermost ring of a social movement is its *heart* or *core*. It contains the principal leaders and the organizations having their goals exclusively in the success of the movement. The most zealous and committed members are also found in this core. If there is a central coordinating organization, committee, or other steering body for the movement, it is also located here, but there might be two or three separate major organizations committed to the movement who share this center space with a greater or lesser degree of cooperation and harmony. The attitudes of people at the core of the movement are likely to be rather uncompromising, sometimes a little paranoid, and in many ways rather like those of religious enthusiasts in a new sect. If the movement fulfills its goals, or for some other reason becomes obsolescent, the members and organizations at this inner core will frequently try to keep the movement going in new directions with new goals and causes, rather than permit it to die out (Gusfield, 1955; and Messinger, 1955). The success of any social movement depends upon the *quality* of the membership distributed among the three rings, as well as upon their sheer numbers. Mere size in the outermost circle will be very important, of course, but it is no substitute for commitment and skill in the two inner circles, especially in the core itself. A fairly small public can give the appearance of a powerful mass movement, if it has a committed leadership, skilled in propaganda. Such appears to have been the case in many movements, ranging from totalitarian party coups, as in Russia in 1917, to the mental health movement in the United States (*cf.* Chapter 9). The optimum circumstances for a successful movement, of course, would be a large outer circle of sympathizers, mobilized by an able and committed inner circle, which is surrounded by an aroused and influential middle circle. This is probably a fairly accurate description of the ecology and conservation movement discussed in Chapter 15.

Perhaps we can use the abortion issue again to illustrate the three-circled distribution of membership in a social movement. If we look just at the movement to promote easy abortions, we see that it has a sizeable public made up of the 40 percent (approximately) of the nation who reported in a survey that they would advocate abortions under nearly any circumstances for nearly any woman who wanted one. (See Chapter 12.) This public, perhaps along with women who themselves have wanted abortions but have been unable to get them, and other directly interested people, would comprise the outermost ring of the movement. In the middle ring, we would have organizations like the National Organization for Women, Planned Parenthood, the American Civil Liberties Union, and the American Friends Service Committee, which have a variety of other causes and interests as well, but which give a portion of their time, energy, and resources to the promotion of more liberal abortion laws. Individual leaders and spokesmen in these movements, along with individuals from certain professions or walks of life who just happen to feel strongly about this issue, will also be part of the middle circle. Finally, in the core of the movement, are organizations formed specifically and exclusively to pursue its goals, such as the National Association for Repeal of Abortion Laws, the Association for the Study of Abortion, and the Women's National Abortion Action Coalition, which attempts, among other things, to coordinate the efforts of the other organizations and to spearhead the whole movement. In many cases, of course, individuals may belong to more than one of these organizations at the same time, even without being leaders in any of them. Such individuals also belong in the core.

Recruitment and Retention of Members

In this section, we will explore why people join and support a movement, particularly those people in the inner core, who give heavily of their time and resources. A "common sense" answer to the question is *altruism;* that is, some people have a strong desire to "do good" and therefore join movements that share this objective. While altruism should not be cynically dismissed as a motivation, the concept has no generally accepted operational definition. Defining altruism or "doing good" is like trying to define the "true religion": many people think they have it, but they cannot agree among themselves. People on all sides of nearly any social issue will claim that they are doing good, even though they are working for quite different and often opposite goals. Even if altruism were an objective, value-free term, it would be necessary to ask, as social scientists, why some people are more altruistic than others or have no altruism at all. In this text, we will not be questioning the altruism or sincerity of anyone, but we will be seeking more objective explanations for why people join and work for movements.

There is much literature on the personal and psychological reasons behind decisions to affiliate with movements, but there is little consensus among behavioral scientists about these motivations (see, e.g., Cantril, 1941; Heberle, 1951; Lang and Lang, 1961; and Toch, 1965). We alluded to this issue in the last chapter when we discussed the psychological publics from which interest groups might be recruited. There is indeed some reason to believe that people who join movements might be giving expression to a need for affiliation, a sense of dissatisfaction, or some other special psychic or emotional need. Glock's (1973) typology of "deprivation," to which we referred in the last chapter, is an attempt to specify the various kinds of deprivation which people might be seeking to assuage when they join movements, and others have pointed out the importance of economic needs and deprivations, as well as social lacks like status, affective ties, and the like. Two important theories of revolution, moreover, point out the tremendous importance in those extreme kinds of movements of personal dissatisfactions and frustrated rising expectations (Brinton, 1952; and Hopper, 1950). Some theorists have gone so far as to posit that joiners have psychological traits that are not altogether healthy and desirable. They point to a kind of fanaticism found in the "authoritarian personality" or in the "true believer" (Adorno, et al., 1950; and Hoffer, 1951).

There may well be some psychologically pained or disturbed people at the center of social movements, but such people are also found in the classroom and in the office. Since these characteristics are not likely to apply to many of the active participants in a movement, they are probably not helpful in shedding light on the motivation of joiners. Furthermore, if people do feel needs for affiliation, status, affection, identity, and the like, then it is probable that there is a distinctly social origin for these needs; hence we would do better to look to less esoteric and more plausibly demonstrable motivations. Some of these might even be in accidental situations, such as a certain crisis or turning point in one's life, of the kind Lofland and Stark (1965) have posited.

All in all, it is probably not necessary to look to theories about personal problems and inadequacies to understand why people join movements, or why they stay in them once they have joined. In the last chapter, we reviewed different kinds of interests that lead people to form interest groups and derivative pressure groups. Since these interest groups, whether or not formally organized, comprise in large part the middle and inner circles of a movement, then a sufficient explanation of people's joining and participating in a movement can be found in an investigation of the number and intensity of their interests. If a person's economic, occupational, political, moral, or other interests are threatened, or, rather, if he perceives that they are, then no other special theory is needed. Of course, a person is likely to have more than one kind of interest in his lifetime, and he must be expected to weigh *all* his interests and to arrange them in some kind of hierarchy before deciding how much support and time to give to a movement. In short, social movement joiners and activists are just like anybody else in these respects. Oberschall puts the matter rather succinctly:

No one is in a position to disregard where his next meal is coming from and whether he is going to have a roof over his head. Leaders and active participants in social movements are no different from other people: they fear punishment; they are vulnerable to social and economic pressures; they seek support and economic security; some can be co-opted, others corrupted. (Oberschall, 1973:159-60)

Oberschall, in fact, casts our contention about interests into a kind of "calculus" framework: whatever people's interests may be, they are likely to calculate the *risks vs. the rewards* of acting on those interests before they join a movement (Oberschall, 1973:162). People can be expected to be as much concerned with what they will be *losing* in those aspects of their lives *outside* the movement as they are with what they might gain by participating *inside* the movement. These gains and losses, of course, can be derived from any kind of interest. A person who stands to lose his job, his best friends, or his status in the community by joining a movement will have to be able to look forward to many compensations from life within the movement. Of course, a person who has few or no such involvements in life will have nothing to lose, and perhaps much to gain, by joining. Oberschall

(1973:168-70) explains much of the participation that took place in the student movement of the 1960's as coming from the relatively young and uninvolved, who stood to lose little in "outside" society by joining the movement. We regard it as a sufficiently complex and helpful theory to say simply that as long as a person's "calculus" of interest risks and rewards balances in favor of participation, he will participate, and the more so the heavier that balance. When the calculus balances in the other direction, he will withdraw from the movement or become less active. We must always keep in mind, though, that a person's interests are varied. They are by no means necessarily economic and may indeed be psychological. The interests of people are more likely than not to be derived from *their positions in the social structure*. Social class, ethnicity, age, sex, religion, occupation, and many other elements in the social structure can provide the social base from which a movement draws its members. We expect, for example, that almost all the participants in the women's liberation movement are women (*cf*. Chapter 11). The civil rights movement of the 1950's and 1960's was carried mainly by a membership drawn from the most unassimilated ethnic groups, aided to some extent by many others. Participants on all sides of the abortion issue, the obscenity issue, and other social problems come from certain religious groups disproportionately (Chapters 10 and 12). The older people will be more involved than the younger in the problem-movement dealing with old age and death. Other examples abound. In summary, then, we are saying that: (1) a person becomes, and continues to be, an active member of a social movement out of certain interests that are usually quite plausibly inferred and easily understood from (a) his or her position in the social structure, and/or (b) his or her special interests of an economic, social, political, occupational, moral, or psychological kind; (2) a person's participation in and enthusiasm for a social movement can be expected to rise or fall in accordance with his own calculus of the risks vs. the rewards he is likely to encounter inside and outside the movement, taking into account the variety and hierarchy of his interests.

Leadership

Many of the observations made above will apply also to the leaders of a movement, who, after all, are among its most active and committed participants. Leaders emerge from a certain social base, have certain interests, and may possess certain personality traits that render them especially susceptible to service in the leadership of a movement. Perhaps even more than their followers, they must contend with the risk-reward calculus, and they are more vulnerable to a variety of *risks within the movement*. Leadership in movements is much more risky than leadership in regularly organized institutions or bureaucracies, because the leaders of movements usually serve without regularly designated authority and without salaries. When they do draw salaries, as in certain long-standing voluntary organizations, these are subject to the continuing acceptance and goodwill of their followers. They must rely for their effectiveness among their followers on delicate techniques of persuasion, motivation, and reinforcement. Considering that such skills are required, it is unlikely that many leaders of social movements are marginal people, wild-eyed fanatics, or otherwise psychologically disturbed, as some social theorists have suggested (Oberschall, 1973:146-56). Of course, such a personality type may well appear in the leadership of a movement now and then, just as it does in regular social institutions, and such types may even make unique contributions to the success of a movement. It may also be true that certain kinds of movements, especially those defined by the public as "bizarre," may have, in both their leadership and their membership, a relatively large number of people regarded by the general public as "nuts" or "kooks." Nevertheless, it is important to keep in mind that characterizations of this kind are likely to develop about leaders *after* they have become prominent in a movement, partly as a result of the collective definition of "deviants" by the public at large and partly because the strains, frustrations, and other pressures upon leaders in a "cause" are liable to generate abnormal behavior in even the most stable and happy people (Oberschall, 1973:148-49).

Many of the studies of social movements indicate that their leaders come from a cross-section of mankind or are a cut above average in social background, intelligence, and skill. After reviewing some of these studies, Oberschall concludes that such is the case, at least, for political opposition movements, and we would suggest that it is even more likely in reform movements of a less militant and more problem-oriented kind:

> It is difficult to escape the conclusion that the upper and middle strata in society supply the substantial bulk of opposition leaders to all manners of social movements in proportions far above that of their percentage in the population at large. But this is equally true for political leaders in . . . parties and in other institutionalized groups . . . (Oberschall, 1973:155)

In other words, the same qualities that make for successful leadership in more conventional social settings will be needed in successful social movements. A number of scholars have noted that the Progressive Movement, a general social movement which spawned and included a number of more specific ones like the anti-trust movement, feminism, and prohibition, was led by people from the upper strata of society. As we look around today at most of the social problem-movements in present society, we see the same phenomenon. Those who are leaders and spokesmen of the movements for "law and order," for population control, for ecology and the environment, for and against more liberal abortion laws, and on various sides of most of our other social problems or issues, are predominantly from the middle- and upper-middle classes. Even those problem-movements having specifically ethnic or lower-class memberships are often led in large part by people from the more privileged sectors of the society (e.g., civil rights or the war on poverty). Oberschall (1973:154-56) makes the interesting observation that leaders and spokesmen in movements are especially likely to come from the "free professions," to be lawyers, teachers, writers, and other intellectuals, who are freer, both socially and temporally, to conceive and advocate new ideas and policies. This observation recalls that of Berger and Luckmann (1967:81) about the "theoretical life" that is possible for intellectual "specialists" and theorists in societies like ours, with relative abundance and an extended division of labor.

Leaders can be classified according to *style* and *function*. For style, we shall draw upon the classical formulation of Max Weber (1957), which has been somewhat developed and elaborated by others. Weber pointed to three different types of *authority* upon which leaders can draw in order to gain the compliance of their followers (authority might be defined as "legitimate power"): charismatic, rational-legal, and traditional. The first type is especially common among leaders of new movements. It is derived from the personal charisma of the leader. *Charisma,* a Greek word, is a kind of extraordinary power or influence, sometimes appearing mystical or supernatural. To what extent charisma comes from a leader's own personality traits, and to what extent it is projected by a membership or by a certain crisis situation, is not clear. But he who has it is followed because the membership believes that he has truth and justice on his side and that he has the right to lead them. As used in social science, charisma is a value-neutral term, which can be applied to historical figures as diverse as Moses, Jesus, Napoleon, and Hitler. Not all social movements, of course, have charismatic leaders, but many do. One thinks of Martin Luther King as having this quality in the civil rights movement, but so, probably, did Joseph McCarthy in the anti-communist movement of the 1950's. Among contemporary social problem-movements, charismatic leaders might include Ralph Nader (environment and consumer protection), Gloria Steinem and Bella Abzug (Women's Liberation), and Thomas Hayden or Abbie Hoffman (New Left).

A kind of leadership and authority more familiar to us, probably, is the *rational-legal* type, characteristic of modern corporations, bureaucracies, and other formal organizations. If there is any charisma in this kind of leadership, it will inhere in the office rather than in the leader who holds it (e.g., President of the United States), though one sometimes finds a charismatic personality in a charismatic office. Usually, however, one's legitimacy or right to lead in this situation is based upon his having been elected or appointed to the position according to a pre-existing set of rules and procedures. As a social movement grows and develops, it is increasingly likely to generate voluntary but formal organizations (e.g., Common

Cause), sometimes even with salaried staffs, to carry on its work full time. Those social problem-movements which involve such formal organizations as part of their strength and support will include leadership of the rational-legal type, frequently along with individual charismatic leaders.

The third kind of leadership, *traditional,* is rarely found as part of any social movement, because by definition it takes time to develop, and most social movements are short-lived. Traditional leadership is the kind represented by kings, patriarchs, and similar leaders, who get their authority by means of a system of succession, usually, in which individual training, competence, and skill play little or no part, as they do in the rational-legal setting. An element of traditional leadership might be seen in the case of the "elder statesman" who occasionally associates with a movement for most of his life and continues to lead, just because he always has, perhaps long after his usefulness has disappeared. This phenomenon has occurred now and then in the radical movements and labor movements of the past, but it rarely if ever has occurred in the movements dealing wtih social problems.

While these three styles of leadership can be distinguished and discussed as ideal types, they are frequently mixed in actual practice. All three types can be useful in the same movement: the "old man" to give the movement a continuity and venerability; the efficient bureaucrat to keep it organized and supported; and the charismatic "firebrand" to capture the public imagination. Also, movements frequently evolve over time, so that a predominantly charismatic leadership gives way to a more rational-legal one as the movement outgrows its early struggling days and becomes more stable. Weber called this the "routinization" of charisma. Some movements, especially very unpopular ones, die out while still in the charismatic stage of leadership. Others evolve into either rational-legal or traditional forms. Still others may evolve into rational-legal and then traditional, or vice-versa. The changing patterns of leadership will depend largely on the needs of the movement in its interaction with the rest of its "host society."

The same observation can be made as we examine leadership of a movement according to its *functions*. Leaders, charismatic or not, are needed for different purposes at different stages of a movement's history. While some scholars have elaborated rather complex typologies of movement leaders (e.g., Hoffer, 1951 and Heberle, 1951), Smelser suggests that there are usually two basic types of leadership needed, according to function: "leadership in formulating the beliefs and leadership in mobilizing the participants for action. Sometimes the same person performs both these functions; in other cases, a division of leadership roles appears within a movement" (Smelser, 1962:297-98 and 355-56). And, one might add, there may be more than one person involved in providing each kind of leadership. One of the most interesting and troubling aspects of a movement's history, indeed, is the changing behavior of its leaders. Some no longer seem needed and drop out.

Others engage in a power struggle to see whose program will prevail. Leadership in a movement is especially vulnerable to problems of this kind because it usually comes into existence without the regular legitimizing procedures characteristic of more settled organizations. Either the leadership begins as charismatic and experiences a "succession crisis" when the founding leaders disappear, or else regularly installed leaders in a variety of related but rival voluntary organizations compete for overall leadership. In any case, sudden and drastic transformation in the leadership of a movement may be wrought by the risk-reward calculating of the leaders, by the changing needs of the movement, and by the changing perceptions and definitions of the membership, to say nothing of the occasional fanatic or defector among the leaders. In some ways, it is surprising that social movements maintain any effective leadership over time at all!

Mobilization

Oberschall (1973:158) has characterized the central problem of mobilization for a social movement as one of "resource management"—the acquisition and use of money, time, talent, energy, and commitment, frequently in the face of opposition and repression from a hostile "host society" trying to deny the movement such resources. Two of the most important resources, of course, are the membership and the leadership. Given fair success in recruiting and arousing these, the rest of the needed resources may not be difficult to raise and manage. The relationship between leaders and members will also be very important, especially in the *voluntary* organizational frameworks characteristic of most social movements. Some of the organizations within the movement will be of an *informal* kind; people will get together in small community meetings under temporary or rotating chairmen, or they will communicate occasionally with likeminded friends and with emerging spokesmen of the movement. In these respects, they will be acting simply as "concerned citizens." However, when a group of such citizens assembles under a name like the "Society Against Problems" (SAP), draws up a charter or set by bylaws, raises money, divides into committees with specific functions, etc., then there is a *formal* organization. Whether formal or informal, these organizations will have to grapple with problems like coordinating efforts with those of related organizations, motivating members to work, finding some feasible system of sanctions (rewards and punishments) for members who do not work, or who seem otherwise "undesirable" in the organization, and so on. Such organizational problems greatly complicate the marshalling of resources in social movements, especially since almost all movements are based upon voluntary participation and leadership.

Once a movement has a viable organizational structure, formal or informal, with committed members and able leaders, then we can point to other critical elements in a successful mobilization. One of these is an appealing *ideology* or set of beliefs.

These beliefs must be capable of providing a satisfactory explanation to members and prospective members concerning the causes of the problem and the steps that must be taken to solve it. One of the most important functions of an ideology is the legitimation of a movement, the explanation of the need for the movement and why it "belongs." Frequently the important elements of an ideology will be expressed in the form of slogans and symbols, which succinctly sum up the legitimacy of a movement and what it stands for, though usually in oversimplified terms. Most of us became acquainted with the peace symbol during the 1960's, which showed a stylized bomber, lest we forgot the damage it could do. The clenched fist atop the female cross symbolizes the women's liberation movement. Right-wing patriotic organizations distributed bumper stickers saying, "America: Love it or Leave it!" to which the liberal reformist organizations responded, "America: Change it or Lose it!" During the War on Poverty and the Civil Rights Movement in the 1960's, many reform-oriented groups, and sometimes even the federal government, used the slogan, "If you're not part of the solution, you're part of the problem." All such symbols and slogans are intended to give brief and impressive expression to the basic ideals of an ideology, and, to the extent that they "catch on" and become popular and faddish, they provide important support to a movement even though their full meanings may not be understood by those who sport them. Ideologies, symbols, and slogans also, it must be remembered, have important personal functions for the members, quite aside from the help they give to the mobilization process. They help the members feel a part of something important, and they provide a sense of certainty and meaning where before there may have been confusion or alarm. In many respects, the symbols and ideologies characteristic of social movements (especially social problems) resemble those of religious sects; indeed, conversion to a movement has many of the same functions for recruits as religious conversion has.

Beyond ideology and slogans, mobilization involves a repertory of successful strategies and tactics, which will help to build membership, influence politicians, or raise money. By "strategy" we mean a long-range plan or policy, while "tactic" refers to a specific means or technique for carrying out the plan. Sometimes violence is involved as a strategy, a tactic, or both, or it develops accidentally. It is rarely a deliberate technique of the movement, however, and is more often perpetrated by hostile elements in the society in opposition to the movement. Especially in the case of social problem-movements in our society, violence is usually detrimental to the cause. Strategies and tactics in movements are generally those which we associate with any political action in our system: the seeking and forming of alliances, lobbying, picketing, fund-raising, speech-making, pamphleteering, broadcasting in the media, and so on. Sometimes a successful tactic can consist of no more than a skillful reaction to an unplanned *precipitating incident*. Smelser points to the boost which many movements have received from such incidents and their successful exploitation: spectacular crimes play into the hands of "law and order" movements; the arrest of a charismatic leader can produce solidarity in a movement that has been waning and breaking up (Smelser, 1962:292-96). Or, it can work the other way: a gasoline shortage, even if a product of collective definitions, can blunt the efforts of conservationists to "protect the environment" against petroleum exploitation. In any case, whether in response to unforeseen incidents or in the day-to-day struggle toward a movement's goals, the nature and timing of strategies and tactics are critical to successful mobilization. Frequently, a movement will change tactics or strategies in response to failures and successes. Smelser calls our attention to the Prohibition Movement, for example, which at first worked only through Protestant churches and then switched to special temperance organizations at the local level. Later on, mobilization focused mainly on the state level and the organization of Prohibition Parties to pressure the state legislatures, but then, around the turn of the present century, it reverted to work at the local level. Finally, it turned again to the state level and galvanized its various state organizations into a national movement that brought the passage of the 18th Amendment (Smelser, 1962:282-83). These shifts were not the result merely of the whims of the leadership, but, as is the case with any movement, they were responses to the interaction going on with the host society. It is to this interaction, and its consequences for a movement more generally, that we now turn.

THE NATURAL HISTORY OF SOCIAL MOVEMENTS

By the "natural history" of a social movement, we mean the process of evolution through which a movement typically passes as a result primarily of its interaction with its social environment. While no two movements are exactly alike, of course, in the details of their history, there are still certain recurring patterns and regularities. Since we are conceiving of social problems here as a kind of social movement, we are positing that they, too, have a natural history. Quite a number of social scientists have used the natural history model in their treatment of social movements. One of the best known and most successful of these treatments has been that of Crane Brinton (1952), who applied the model to the development of revolutions, which represent an extreme kind of social movement. A German scholar, Ernst Troeltsch (1931), drawing somewhat upon the work of his colleague Max Weber, applied the same general notion to the development of new religious sects and their gradual transformation into regular churches. Herbert Blumer (1951), taking an idea from Dawson and Gettys in the 1920's traced five stages through which social movements typically pass. Since then, the scholars whose treatment of social movements has involved the idea of stages, implicitly or explicitly, have included Hopper (1950), Heberle (1951), Hoffer (1951), King (1956), Lang and Lang (1961), and Killian (1964).

It is interesting that other scholars, while not recognizing social problems as social movements *per se,* have nevertheless recognized that social problems also have a natural history and pass through stages. We would, of course, point out that the reason for this parallel is that problems are movements themselves. The natural history model for social problems was postulated as early as 1940 by Fuller and Myers (1941b), though it was criticized a decade later by Lemert (1951), not so much for its use as a general model as for the particular application of it that Fuller and Myers had made. In more recent years, Howard Becker (1966) has recommended the work of Fuller and Myers for further consideration, but he has not yet elaborated upon their work. Herbert Blumer, himself one of the originators of the natural history model for social movements (1951), suggested the model again more recently (1971) for application to social *problems,* without, apparently, seeing these as identical with social movements. Again he posits five stages, but not the same five as he had used for social movements a generation earlier. Even more recently, the idea of stages for the analysis of social problems was put forth by Leonard Reissman (1972), who conceives of social problems as having a "solution cycle" of three stages: identification, shaping, and disappearance. Reissman emphasizes the part played by collective definition and redefinition in the passage of a social problem through these stages. As we review the varied literature on both social movements and social problems, with particular reference to the use of a natural history model, we find two deficiencies which we feel can be remedied by our presentation in this book. (1) No one, as far as we know, has yet *identified* social problems with social movements, recognizing that, in fact, they are the same thing. Some have come close, especially Blumer, and we fully acknowledge our debt to their thinking, but they do not seem to have taken the last logical step of recognizing problems as movements. The importance of this last step is implied in Blumer's own recent article (1971), where he stresses the importance of an adequate theory of social problems as collective behavior, especially with regard to what happens at each stage of a problem's development. We would suggest that recognizing problems as movements makes it possible to apply to the analysis of problems *all of the work that has already been done on movements,* to which we propose to add our own modest contribution here. (2) Few, if any, of the existing formulations of natural history models, especially where social problems are concerned, have paid sufficient attention to the *end of the life-cycle,* to what might be called the "decline" or disappearance of social problems and/or movements. Most formulations, except possibly Reissman's, take the natural history model up through the "full blown" stage (e.g., "institutionalization," "development of tactics," "implementation," "reform," and the like), without much attention to what happens to a problem-movement after that. The same is true of the more recent formulation of Spector and Kitsuse (1973), although they apply different names to their stages. Our work will present some discussion of decline and demise, as well as of the earlier stages of the movement.

The Interaction of the Movement with the Host Society

It is perhaps obvious that the natural history of a social movement, whether of a problem kind or not, is dependent primarily upon the nature of its interaction with its "host society" (i.e., the society which produces it). Both the society and the movement are changed by this interaction, as Killian (1964:454) has so well pointed out. Later in this chapter, we shall discuss briefly some of the changes which the society experiences as the result of a social problem-movement, but here we are concerned mainly with the effect of the interaction upon the movement itself. Again, as Killian (1964:445) observed, a movement is always of an emergent nature, and what happens to it and its members "as a consequence of their interaction within the movement is vastly more important than the reasons why they first came into the movement," a commentary on personal interaction within the movement as well as on interaction between the movement and the milieu.

The crucial underlying fact in the relationship of a movement to its social environment is that each must contend with its own dilemma. For the movement, the dilemma consists of trying to maintain an identity, an integrity, and a continuing commitment to principles, while still trying to broaden its membership base. In terms of the concentric circle model used earlier, the movement must try to get as many members as possible into the outer and middle circles, without sacrificing the commitment and zeal of the membership in the core circle. The most zealous members are likely to take a rather uncompromising and purist stance toward the movement's goals; whereas a movement, to be effective, usually has to make certain pragmatic compromises in order to attract as much support as possible. For the host society, on the other hand, the dilemma consists of trying to accommodate the movement while still containing or controlling it, so that it does not go "too far" and create a general problem of social control. (This response assumes a society which recognizes reform movements as legitimate in the first place, of course.) These reciprocal dilemmas provide the context within which the movement and the society enter into an almost dialectical relationship, each making a series of responses and counter-responses to the moves of the other.

The host society makes its moves through traditional institutions, not just the government and, indeed, sometimes not involving the government at all. These institutions—government, business, churches, families—are not necessarily coordinated in their responses, except through the common commitment of their membership to certain traditional values and norms. Of course, representatives from these institutions might form a conservative opposition movement to the emerging social problem, but normally the traditional institutions of society can be expected to resist the reforms called for by the social problem-movement simply by a generalized inertia, apathy, or hostility. As traditional definitions and constructions of reality become less useful and satisfactory, defectors from traditional institutions may begin to support the movement in one or more of its three "rings," and it is the object of the movement's mobilization precisely to encourage such defection. Generally, however, the "burden of proof" stays with the movement, and the process of changing collective definitions of the situation is usually a laborious one. Sometimes the movement receives unintended help from the government or some other agency in the form of an incident or provocation which has the effect of galvanizing sentiment within the movement and increasing its circle of sympathizers. These incidents become episodal or anecdotal data of the kind mentioned in Chapter 1, which help to reshape "consensual reality." Thus, word of the murder of civil rights workers in the South increases public sentiment or sympathy for their movement, even among many Southerners. Or a series of prison riots may increase public interest in, and desire for, some kind of reform in our corrections system. The same episodes, however, might strengthen the call for "law and order."

It is rare for a movement to outlast its host society, except in those extreme cases where the movement is a successful revolution, and, even then, as Brinton (1952) has shown, a society has a way of "absorbing" a revolution, as the leaders of it turn to the hard realities of trying to govern in an established social or cultural setting. Especially in relatively permissive and assimilationist societies like our own, reformist movements tend to be tamed or absorbed through an accommodation in which both sides make compromises and come to terms with the other's position. The only alternatives to accommodation for the movement are revolution *or* elimination, the latter coming either from complete repression by the society or through the movement's own secession. While the movement is struggling to expand its own resource and membership base, without unduly compromising its critical goals, the host society is responding with a "double death-squeeze," made up of the twin pressures of co-optation and repression (Mauss, 1971c). by "co-optation," we mean ameliorative gestures in the direction of meeting and neutralizing the movement's criticisms, combined with a propaganda effort emphasizing those interests and values which the society shares with the reform movement. By "repression," we refer to social control techniques ranging from police action to ridicule, which can and do occur across all the institutions of the society. Smelser is among those who have pointed out that repression cannot be so severe that all avenues for dissent and agitation are closed, for that may crystallize the emerging movement and aid its mobilization. At the same time, co-optation cannot be so cordial as to raise unduly the aspirations of the movement's members, for then they may escalate their demands for reform. For the society, the problem is to maintain a "precarious balance" between repression and co-optation, appropriate to the movement's own "precarious balance" (Smelser's term), at a given stage of development, between power and oblivion (Smelser, 1962:282-86). The fortunes of a movement are thus determined in large part by the particular *mixture* of co-optation and repression applied by the society, and by its own manipulation of, and responses to, that mixture.

Stages in the Natural History of a Social Movement

It is neither novel nor profound to postulate, as we have done, that something as dynamic as a social movement has a career or natural history as it interacts with the rest of society. To go a step further and specify *stages* in that natural history, however, carries risks of oversimplification and distortion. Let us make clear, therefore, that we are offering the following formulation, not as an accurate and specific outline of every social movement, but as an ideal type of reality, to make possible empirical observations on the extent to which various movements correspond to this typification. While this formulation was developed mainly with radical protest movements in mind (Mauss, 1971c), any kind of movement fits it reasonably well, and the social problems discussed in this book are better understood in the light of this model. The five stages we call: (1) incipiency, (2) coalescence, (3) institutionalization, (4) fragmentation, and (5) demise. Some of these, especially the first three, are similar to what has been proposed by others; the last two have few, if any, parallels in the literature. A growth curve representing this five-stage life-cycle would have a shape approximating the normal curve, with the third stage at the apex. For some movements, however, the hypothetical curve would be sharper or flatter than normal. The chief impetus or force which projects a movement through these stages is the interaction between the movement and the society, with particular reference to the changing mix of co-optation and repression applied by the society and the movement's responses to that "mix."

Incipiency

The inception of a movement or social problem occurs while it is still in what Blumer calls the *general* stage, characterized by "groping, uncoordinated efforts . . . unorganized, with neither established leadership nor recognized membership, and little guidance or control" (Blumer, 1951:200-01). Such following as it has is in the form primarily of a *concerned public* of the kind which we represented above as the "outer ring" of the movement—people who have begun to feel a mild threat to the preservation or realization of certain vital interests. They begin to read and write articles in the media, hold occasional *ad hoc* meetings, write letters to congressmen, and the like. The initial response of the society is likely to be indulgent with a "mix" containing very little repression and a lot of co-optation (unless the movement is perceived as a highly subversive or abhorrent value-oriented one, in which case repression is likely to be immediate, formal, and thorough). Rather than generate conflict, most of the institutions and agencies of the society will attempt a restoration of the consensus through conciliation, compromise, and absorption. This response, in turn, requires the members having serious concerns to seek for an "identity," for a definition of their concerns, and thus for clear boundaries separating their definitions from those of the public at large. This boundary-testing will begin to arouse some hostility in the society, for it will involve some rejection of the compromise and co-optation being offered by the society. Unless the movement is already very large, and much more focused than is likely at this stage, the co-optive efforts of the society may keep the movement in this incipient stage for quite a long time. An example is the "death with dignity" movement associated with the "old age problem" in our society, in which there is a growing sentiment, centered in the medical professions, that "something should be done" and even a small organization in favor of euthanasia. In the society at large, probably everybody agrees that artificially keeping sick old people alive indefinitely is an undesirable practice. In some hospitals a compromise has been made in the form of withholding "artificial props" to life and letting the incurably ill die as quickly as nature takes its course. There is still considerable general sentiment, however, that more might be done to hasten the passing of one who is suffering severely, and, if that sentiment begins to crystallize into demands for euthanasia legislation, a repressive response is likely from most of the society, followed by further organization and mobilization by the euthanasists. This development will bring the next stage in the life of the movement.

Coalescence

The next stage is *coalescence,* which is marked by the gradual formation of the two inner rings of the movement. Formal and informal organizations begin to develop out of segments of the sympathetic public that have become the most aroused by perceived threats to the preservation or realization of their interests. In the words of Turner and Killian, such people will begin to "supplement their informal discussion with some organization to promote their convictions effectively and insure more sustained activity" (Turner and Killian, 1957:307). This development will be in response to repressive and provocative acts on the parts of the government or of other institutions of the "establishment"; it may also occur as the result of disappointment from perceived failures of the government or society to take ameliorative action after raising general hopes and expectations that such would be forthcoming. There may not yet be much (if any) society-wide coordination at this stage, but there will be alliances formed, ad hoc committees and caucuses springing up here and there, and some more formal associations organized at local and regional levels. In short, a change in the "mix" toward a larger proportion of repression will usually bring coalescence of the movement. The movement cannot usually be stopped at this point without massive repression, or else massive co-optation approaching capitulation on the part of the society. The current ecology movement reached this stage after a series of provocations like off-shore oil spills and the Alaska pipeline plan. Prior to those provocations, it was largely co-opted, for who could be opposed to clean air, clean land, and clean water? However, this movement has now begun to coalesce and is moving steadily toward the next stage. (See Chapter 15.) Another movement that passed through the stage of coalescence in recent years is the anti-obscenity/pornography campaign. (See Chapter 10.) Starting in the 1950's as a generalized sentiment for "decency" and against "smut," it gradually coalesced in response to increasingly liberal decisions by state and federal courts. It finally came sufficiently to the attention of the government to require the appointment of a Presidential Commission to survey the problem. This was a sign that it had reached the next stage.

Institutionalization

When the government and other traditional institutions take official notice of a problem or movement and work out a series of standard coping mechanisms to manage it, the movement is *institutionalized*. A distinction must be made here, however, between the institutionalization of a *movement,* to which we are referring, and the institutionalization of its *program*. The latter use of the term implies a widespread and/or official adoption of many of the movement's goals or objectives, which is frequently accompanied by the rapid decline of the movement itself. We are here referring instead to the institutionalization of the movement, which implies that it is still mobilizing toward getting its program adopted. Institutionalization in this sense is accompanied by all the characteristics of a "full blown" movement: society-wide organization and coordination (unless the movement happens to deal with strictly local issues); a large base of members and resources; an extended division of labor; regular thrusts into the political processes of the society (e.g., lobbying, campaigning in elections); and growing respectability.* It is during this stage that the movement enjoys its greatest success: the mass media begin to take it seriously, politicians begin to vie for its favor, and some of its spokesmen become fashionable and perhaps well-paid speakers at rallies, meetings, and other public events. Legislation begins to be passed in an effort to "solve the problem" which the movement has defined. Thus, institutionalization means, for the movement, its

---

* As used here, "institutionalization" thus encompasses Stages Two, Three and Four of the model proposed by Spector and Kitsuse (1973), while their first stage and mine are very similar.

period of greatest power, support, and fashionability; for the society, it means taking account of the movement with a repertory of routines which have the effect of greatly increasing the co-optation element in the mix. Repression is now reserved only for the fanatics and extremists, usually very few, who refuse to be "bought off" by the co-optation and begin to try other strategies and tactics to justify their *raison d'etre*. Most of the social problems that come to mind today have reached the institutionalization stage or have even begun to pass out of it and go into decline. Still enjoying the hey-day of institutionalization are the law and order movement (including crime and delinquency definitions); drug and alcohol problems; the movement against obscenity and pornography; women's liberation; the ecology and environment movement; and the population problem. The chapters in this book devoted to these topics will describe those characteristics which seem to warrant placing such problems in the institutionalization stage. Other problems, which seem to have passed the peak of institutionalization, will be mentioned in the discussion of the fourth stage.

Fragmentation

An irony in the natural history of social movements is that their very success leads to *fragmentation*. Of course, fragmentation can occur through conflicts and pressures at any stage of a social movement's life (Smelser, 1962:304-05; Oberschall, 1973:143), but here we are referring to "normal fragmentation," which occurs typically *after* a movement has enjoyed a period of success and respectability, and is caused more by co-optation than by repression; that is the irony. Smelser seems to be referring to this phenomenon when he speaks of the "divisive effects of institutional accommodation" (1962:363). There are several reasons for the process of fragmentation. (1) In terms of the concentric circle structure, accommodations and co-optations have stripped away the outer ring and much of the middle ring; that is, many of the sympathetic public and active supporters have come to feel that "things have really improved" and that the threat to their vital interests has greatly subsided. This redefinition of the situation will cause them to turn to other (perhaps related) causes or to drop out altogether. At the same time, they will join with the rest of the society in labelling the uncompromising purists in the center circle as "fanatics," "far-out extremists," etc., thereby actually participating in the growing repression which now becomes the fate of the movement's survivors. (2) Those who remain in the movement will fall to fighting among themselves over strategy and tactics for the future: some will call for continuing the original struggle until total success has been achieved; others will call for a modification of program; still others will advocate displacement of original goals altogether and a turning toward new objectives. In large part, these controversies will have a basis in the differential interests of the participants, deriving from their respective locations in the social structure, as well as from their personal commitments. The radical or New Left movement of the 1960's, for example, began to break up in the middle and latter half of that decade over differential interests of the blacks and whites in the movement and, among the blacks, the differing interests of the middle and lower classes (Mauss, 1971c:198-99). (3) Not the least of the reasons for fragmentation will be the changing requirements of leadership as the movement's earlier charisma is routinized and the rational organizer becomes more important than the charismatic ideologue. Leaders may begin contending with each other for supremacy and each may attempt to collect his own following or fragment from the movement. Not only will the different styles and functions of leadership be at stake in this process, but also the various personal interests of the leaders themselves (Smelser, 1962:359-63). Some will be "bought off" by the co-optive efforts of the society, but others' interests will be better served by trying to lead segments of the movement into new paths. Besides the radical protest movement and the civil rights movement, the war on poverty began to show signs of fragmentation in the late 1960's. In all three movements, institutionalization was enjoyed in the earlier part of that decade, but since that time different spokesmen and different segments of the movements have gone in different directions. (See Chapters 6 and 14.)

Demise

The final stage of a movement is its *demise*. Within the movement, the demise is seldom recognized. Instead, this stage might be defined by the movement as "success," since most of its goals may have been accomplished through co-optation, or it might be defined as a temporary setback for an otherwise still vital movement. However the demise is defined by the movement, it is simply a "mopping up" phase for the establishment or the society. The co-optation process has appropriated the most critical elements of the movement's program, has "bought off" many of its leaders and most effective members, and has choked off most of its outside support. This leaves only small bands of "true believers" who appear increasingly ridiculous and who, in desperation, may even resort to violence or terrorism to keep the movement alive (as, for example, the Weathermen did at the end of the New Left movement). Their behavior alienates them still further from the rest of the society and from their erstwhile reformist colleagues, and they are either driven to complete secession from the society or left to face the onslaught of total repression from a now unrestrained public consensus. The mix of co-optation and repression with which the interaction began has now been transformed from almost total co-optation, in the incipiency stage, to almost total repression, in the final stage. While the society at large is also surely affected in many ways by this process, it seems inescapable that a social problem-movement will ultimately experience fragmentation and demise.

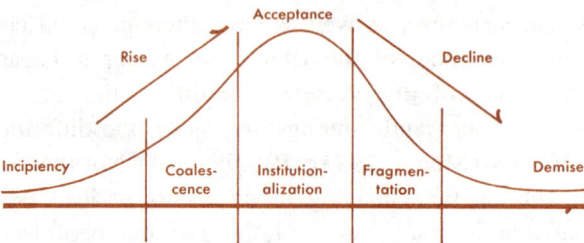

Figure 2-1 Normal Pattern for the Natural History of a Social Movement

Let us here re-emphasize that the process just described is an *ideal type* of historical reality, one only approximated by the actual histories of social problems. It will not always be possible, without considerably more historical research, to specify the "cutting points" between the five stages of a problem or movement. There is still much room, therefore, among scholars and students, for controversy over the number of stages, their demarcations, and their appropriate designations. It is less debatable, however, that, whatever the specifics, social problems and other movements have a life-cycle involving a rise, a thriving, and a decline, though little attention in the scientific literature has been paid to the process of decline. (Figure 2-1 offers a simple graphic outline of the life-cycle.)

We have argued also that this *life-cycle occurs independently of objective reality* for the most part. It has its inception in the collective definitions of its members and sympathizers of the nature of reality, and it is moved through its various stages by its interaction with the host society, an interaction that involves a process of mutual definitions and selective perceptions. While the objective reality of those who are co-opted or repressed may change, no objective change is needed in the putatively problematic social conditions in order for the movement's life-cycle to run its course. The cycle begins and ends with individuals and groups on all sides of an issue acting out their own perceived interests in response to each other. When the interaction we have described brings the movement to an end, *then* the social problem disappears, whatever may be the case with the social conditions which had once be defined as problematic.

THE DECLINE AND LEGACY OF A SOCIAL PROBLEM

Social problems are rarely "solved" in anything near the sense originally expected and demanded by the interest groups that identify them. Their disappearance may take several forms and may seem, in fact, rather mysterious. Blumer (1971) himself recently observed the proclivity of some social problems to "languish, perish, or just fade away." Edward Banfield, after reviewing the great problems of our cities and noting the important part played by collective and interest-group definitions in the rise of these problems, observes, "Hard as it may be for a nation of inveterate problem-solvers to believe, social problems sometimes disappear in the normal course of events," and he devotes some attention to those events (Banfield, 1970:257). Smelser, too, observes the "inherent tendency for even successful movements to leave a residue of disappointment," because the expectations and hopes of the proponents are always unrealistically high (1962:305).

Patterns and Varieties of Demise

Much of this chapter has been devoted to a discussion of the ideal-typical pattern which is normally followed in the development of a social problem through the various stages in its natural history (Figure 2-1). Certain important variations of that pattern might be noted at this time. The first of these is the *abortive* pattern represented by Figure 2-2. Applicable here is the observation by Smelser that a movement "under conditions of continuous repression tends to become moribund." (1962:366) In terms of our model, a society (usually through the government) almost always has the power to bring to bear overpowering repression in either of the first two stages of growth, thereby unbalancing the risk/reward ratio too much for it to be in anyone's interest to continue in the movement. This is the usual response to movements (even benign, mildly reformist ones) in totalitarian societies, and it is at least theoretically possible even in our own society. Indeed, this seems to be the appropriate characterization for the abortive end to certain American

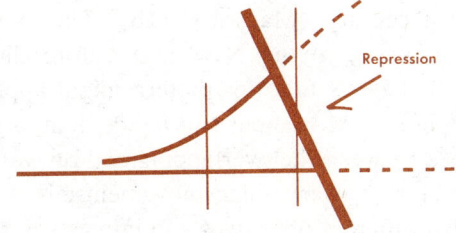

Figure 2-2

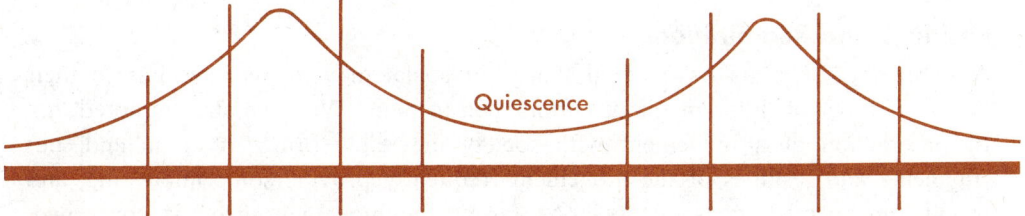

Figure 2-3

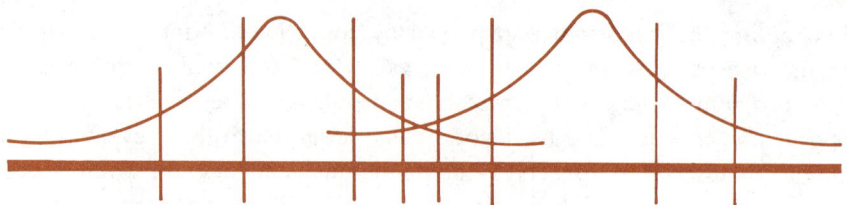

Figure 2-4 Overlapping Pattern

Indian religious movements that got started late in the last century (LaBarre, 1970). A second variation of our model, one which permits the movement to go almost to complete demise, is the *revival* pattern (Figure 2-3). In this case, a movement retains a flicker of life even after severe decline and flares up again later, sometimes a generation or two later, in response to new definitions by the appropriate interest groups. An example of this pattern is the Feminist Movement, which became moribund after its co-optation with the passage of the 19th Amendment and a variety of protectionist measures on behalf of women. It seems to have remained quiescent for almost fifty years, with only an occasional public notice, until it was revived in the form of the contemporary Women's Liberation Movement. (See Chapter 11.) The current ecology and environment movement has revived concerns similar to those of early conservationists. Still a third variation of our model is represented in Figure 2-4—the *overlapping* pattern. In this pattern, a sequel to an earlier movement gets going before the latter has completely died out. We have suggested elsewhere that this variation might fit the left-wing radical movements of the present century (Mauss, 1971b). The Old Left seems to have "passed the torch," as it were, to the New Left before disappearing from the national scene. Chapter 8 suggests that this pattern might apply to the relationship between the earlier Temperance Movement and the contemporary campaign against alcoholism. The difference between the overlapping and revival patterns, besides the coincidence in time peculiar to overlapping movements, is that revivals are more likely to involve somewhat different objectives and interests in the sequel movement. Apart from all these variations, it might be observed again that the basic "normal" pattern is itself subject to considerable variation in "flatness" and "steepness."

Residues and Redefinitions

A number of scholars have noted that after social movements have passed their peak a number of different things can happen to them. We have already noted that the interaction of a movement with society inevitably brings it to an end, but fragments and residues of the movement frequently provide some interesting, and usually unexpected, consequences. As far as the movement itself is concerned, though its original form will die out, it may, as Messinger (1955) shows, survive as quite a different entity, perhaps even a recreational one! Also, its various fragments may join with other emerging movements to provide new causes. If a movement has had any degree of success, however, that success is most likely to take the form of at least partial adoption or institutionalization of its program by the society. This is especially true in the case of social problems movements. Even less successful movements will usually leave behind some residues, if only in the form of new fads.

In general, one can find the residues of social movements at three different levels of the society. At the most general level, that of *popular culture,* a movement may at least bring changes in argot, jokes, leisure-time activities, styles, and the like. The New Left and related hippie movements of the 1960's, while achieving few of their formal objectives, left a residue of long hair styles for men and new word usages ("freak out," "right on"). As a result of the civil rights movement of the same period, Negroes are now called "Blacks," a term which was insulting a generation earlier. Of even more importance are the new definitions of social phenomena that come into currency in the wake of a problem-movement. As a result of the "child-savers" movement, non-conforming adolescents were defined as troubled children needing "protection" from a bad social environment, instead of merely "juvenile delinquents" or "young thugs." As a result of the mental hygiene movement, certain forms of deviant behavior are now defined as "mental illness" and treated as such by a class of physicians called psychiatrists. The campaign against alcoholism has likewise succeeded in getting that condition defined as a "disease" and a public health problem, rather than a character disorder or crime. Certain literary products are variously defined as "art" or as "smut," depending on the fortunes of the anti-pornography interest groups in our society.

At a somewhat more critical level, that of *norms* (and sometimes values), a social movement may also leave a telling residue. Some such changes involve only folkways. One can no longer tell "nigger" jokes in polite society without scorn. Indeed, such long-standing American entertainment institutions as minstrel shows and "Amos 'n' Andy" programs are clearly casualties of the civil rights movement and of the concomitant emergence of black consciousness and pride. More important normative boundaries are also changed by movements. Certainly more freedom and opportunity are accorded to women in our society as a result of "women's lib"; quite aside from actual changes in the law, the very role definitions of the "place of the woman" have been drastically altered. The population movement seems to have contributed to a new definition of large families as unfashionable, if not downright immoral. A great many of the problem-movements examined in this book have already made important normative changes in our culture, or are clearly in the process of doing so, whether they have been "successful" movements or not.

The most conspicuous level at which social problems leave their residues and redefinitions is the level of *laws and law enforcement*. One could almost say that the volume and depth of change at this level is the most important indicator of the "success" of a social problem-movement, or at least of its historical importance. It is at this level, too, that there so often appears the discrepancy between the "manifest" and the "latent" functions of new laws, or between what the new laws are intended to do and what they actually end up doing unexpectedly. One of the most celebrated examples of this discrepancy is to be seen in the Prohibition amendment, which spawned an enormous amount of "secondary" crime in the process of making alcoholic beverages illegal. Almost all problem-oriented laws which create contraband products have the same impact: the creation of new crimes and a new class of criminals. In a recent posthumous essay, Arnold Rose has considerably elaborated on this principle. As he states his theme: "Laws are attempts to deal with social problems; they usually transform the social problems in some unanticipated way; in so doing, they often create new social problems" (Rose, 1968). He then goes on to point out the part played by law in generating juvenile delinquency, race conflict, drug problems, and a great many other social problems through the unexpected consequences of new laws. The entire legal structure of our nation's welfare system has produced a new social problem, that of welfare itself. Whereas before we had only the one problem of indigence and poverty, we now have that problem *plus* a second one, welfare, created to "solve" the first one.

There are several reasons for this kind of outcome or "legacy" from social problems. (1) In our zeal to solve problems through laws, we often pass laws that do not have sufficient support in the traditional norms of the society, so that enforcement is an awesome burden. (2) As Blumer (1971) has pointed out, the laws actually designed by reformers are often watered down in the legislative or enforcement process, with the result that they fail to fulfill their intended or manifest functions, while still fulfilling a host of undesirable latent functions. (3) As a related point, Ross and Staines, as well as Leonard Reissman, have pointed to the essentially political nature of both the definition and the solution of social problems (Ross and Staines, 1972; and Reissman, 1972); that is, the laws that are passed and enforced around a given social problem are likely to be a reflection more of the interests of politicians and enforcement officials than of the imperatives of the "problem situation." Becker (1963) has made a similar point.

SUMMARY

After establishing in Chapter 1 the importance of interest groups and their constructions of reality in the genesis of social problems, we began Chapter 2 with a consideration of the part played by conditions in the social structure itself in the genesis of social problems. We applied the theoretical notions of Durkheim and Erikson in arguing that the incidence and severity of social problems in a society depend, not so much upon objectively "problematic" conditions, as upon the "quota" which is logistically possible for a society to manage.

We then moved on to describe the nature and structure of social problem-movements, distinguishing between general and specific ones and, among specific ones, between value- and norm-oriented movements, noting that almost all social problems are movements of the specific, norm-oriented kind. We described movements as having a structure resembling three concentric circles or rings, with the more active and zealous segments found in the inner two rings. Next we considered some characteristics of members and leaders in social movements, using a risk/reward calculus to account for the ability of a movement to mobilize them.

The natural history of a social movement occupied a major portion of the chapter, in which passage of a movement through the five stages of its life-cycle or natural history was explained as a function of the twin pressures of co-optation and repression, which are applied in various mixtures by the host society. Particular attention was given to the part played by those pressures in the fragmentation and demise of a movement.

In the final section of the chapter, we considered what happens to the movement and to the society after the movement has declined and disappeared. We stressed that the putatively "problematic" conditions around which the movement was started play little or no part in what happens to it and that it, in turn, often leaves those conditions unchanged, if not worse. The "legacy" of a movement, as we conceived of it, consists of residues and redefinitions at the levels of popular culture, norms, and laws. The laws are probably the most important legacy of the movement, and they are frequently responsible for generating new problems unforeseen when they were so eagerly legislated.

In the chapters that follow, we will apply the theoretical model, developed in these first two chapters, to a variety of actual social problems.

PART TWO
LAW AND ORDER

Chapter 3
Crime and Law

> Loose talk about war against crime too easily infuses the administration of justice with the psychology and morals of war.
>
> —Justice Felix Frankfurter

THE SOCIAL CONSTRUCTION OF REALITY

The most simple definition of crime is that it is a violation of the law. Reality, however, is far more complicated than that, for there is enormous variation from age to age and from place to place, not only in the laws that are passed, but also in the rigor of their enforcement and in the penalties exacted for their violation. During the present century, there has been some international tendency, especially in the industrial countries, for laws and penalties to become more similar from one nation to another, particularly with respect to acts that are clearly *predatory,* i.e., where there are obvious losses of life, health, or property suffered by specific *victims.* In general, however, cultural variety is more the rule than universal uniformity.

Crime and Relativity

A study of history and anthropology would show the full range of the cultural relativity which has prevailed in attitudes toward law and crime. A young man who drags a struggling girl into the bushes in order to have sexual relations with her is likely to be charged with rape in our society, even if she is his girl friend; but in parts of Polynesia, this is considered standard courting behavior for a man with serious matrimonial intentions. Or, if we were to look at the survivals of the old Puritan "Blue Laws" that are still on the books in some of our states, we would get a glimpse into a time not so long ago when it was a misdemeanor to kiss a woman in public. Further, in the Soviet Union today, acts that our legal system would probably regard as serious predatory violations, such as murder, rape, and assault, normally carry a maximum penalty of 15 years imprisonment, whereas "crimes against the state" (including political offenses) carry much heavier penalties, including long-term exile or even execution. In the United States, by contrast, "political crimes" are generally more difficult to define, are extremely controversial, convictions for them are hard to get (except for a few celebrated cases through history), and penalties are relatively light, unless some sense of "national emergency" or wartime treason prevails. On the other hand, convictions for predatory crimes against the person (e.g., murder, rape, kidnapping) may carry life sentences (or, until recently, the death penalty) in the United States, and convictions for property crimes such as burglary carry a maximum penalty of 30 years imprisonment (Knudten, 1970).

For the so-called "victimless crimes," the United States has some of the strictest laws and harshest punishments in the world. For homosexual relations, for example, some states prescribe a penalty of 15 years in the penitentiary, and such relations are against the law everywhere in the United States, even between consenting adults. In England, by contrast, homosexual behavior with mutual consent is no longer regulated or penalized at all. Similarly, England applies no criminal sanctions against narcotics users, but refers them to medical treatment, whereas in the United States, the Boggs Amendment of 1965 provides for a 40-year prison sentence on the third conviction for illegal possession of narcotics, and a maximum penalty of death for the sale of narcotics to minors. Some 1973 legislation in the state of New York is even more severe in its narcotics penalties (cf. Chapter 7).

Thus it is apparent that the same acts evoke different meanings and definitions in different cultures, leading to different laws and different penalties. From the sociologist's point of view, it is irrelevant to ask which culture is "right" and which is "wrong" about these matters; sociology is likely to be more interested in what laws reveal about a *culture,* than in what they reveal about *criminals.*

Variation and relativity in crime and its laws can be seen not only in comparisons among different societies. Even within our own society there are many differences among states and regions of the country, not only in the laws themselves, but in the penalties for the same violations, and in enforcement practices. In sex offenses, particularly, penalties may range from a mild rebuff by the judge in one state to a heavy prison sentence in another. Even definitions of crimes vary. In most states, prostitution is defined as the marketing of sexual services for payment, while in one state, Tennessee, compensation need not be involved. Standards by which severity of penalties is established for different crimes are sometimes difficult to understand: in Pennsylvania, statutory rape (i.e., with a willing but "underage" female) carries a maximum prison sentence of 15 years, five times the length of the sentence for assault with intent to do bodily harm!

The rigor and extent of the enforcement of a law is also important, because that defines the real or operational limits to citizen behavior, rather than merely what is "on the books." Most of us who have perpetrated such "folk crimes" as exceeding the speed limit are well aware that we are influenced much less by the posted speed limit than by our estimates of actual police enforcement practices. Similarly, the principal author of this chapter knows from first-hand experience as a former police officer that "moonshining" (illegal production of liquor) in the Appalachian Region of the United States is widely tolerated by local enforcement officers, in spite of explicit state and local laws against it, because public opinion in that region does not support strict enforcement. Many other so-called "vices," such as prostitution and gambling, are permitted by slack enforcement to thrive in many American cities, as long as it is in no one's interest to "crack down" on them.

Time itself brings considerable change, not only in enforcement practices, but in the very definition of the nature or seriousness of an act. Acts or practices that have been illegal for a long time are sometimes later legalized, such as abortion and Sunday business. Misdemeanors (crimes carrying penalties of up to a year in jail) may be made felonies (which carry sentences of one year or more): in the 1930's marijuana use (in some states) was changed by federal legislation from a misdemeanor to a felony. Legal behavior (e.g., alcohol consumption) may suddenly be made illegal (the 18th Amendment), and then later legalized again (the 21st Amendment). Considering all the elements and contingencies that go into the operational definition of "crime" at a particular time and place, it is apparent that the definition is considerably more complicated than the one given at the beginning of this chapter. Even after an agreement has been reached on the definition of crime, however, we face still more complexity in attempting to measure the amount and seriousness of crime.

Parameters of Consensual Reality

Considering the complications involved in defining crime, the unevenness in the enforcement of laws, and the amount of lawbreaking that is likely to go unreported or undetected for various reasons, it is probably impossible ever for us to know how much crime there *really* is in any complete or objective sense. By consensus or general agreement, however, most of us are willing to rely on certain official records and statistics for at least a rough measure of how many and what kinds of crimes are being committed, what kinds of people are mainly involved as criminals and victims, and a great many other details about the incidence of crime. The most important and widely used source of official data about crime is probably the

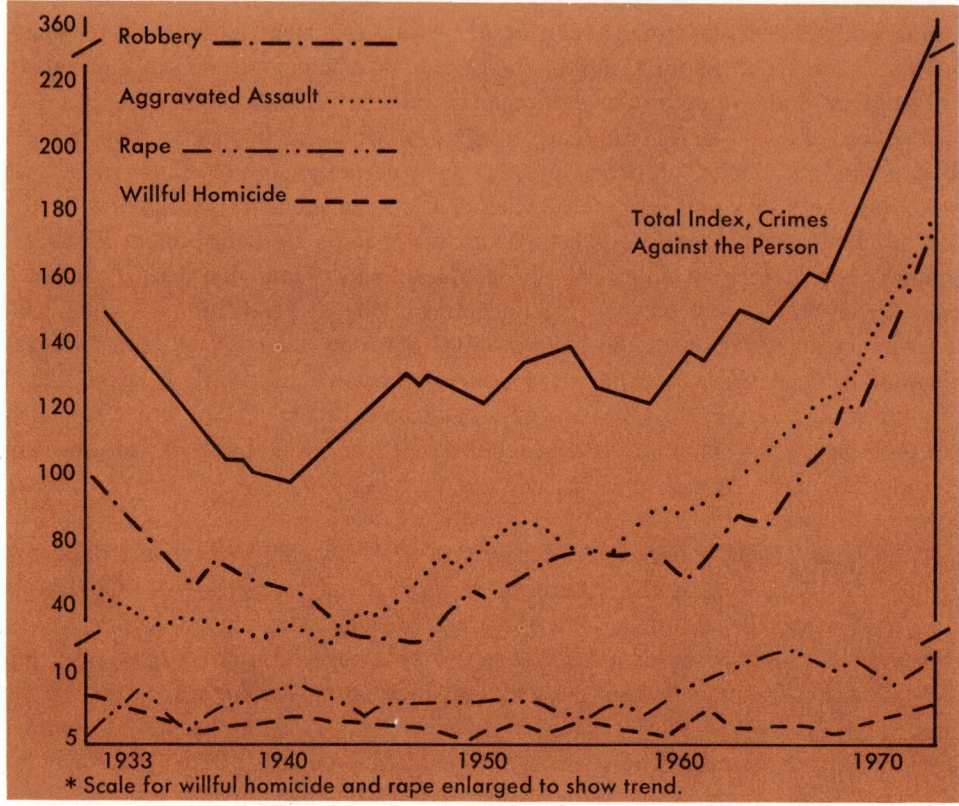

Figure 3-1   Index Crimes, 1933-1970: Reported Crimes Against the Person
SOURCE: FBI Uniform Crime Reports Section: unpublished data

Uniform Crime Reports (UCR) gathered by the FBI and issued periodically. Other relevant reports on crime are issued by the Federal Bureau of Prisons, the National Office of Vital Statistics, and the Children's Bureau of the Department of Health, Education, and Welfare (HEW), the latter dealing mainly with statistics on delinquency.

Street or Index Crimes

The UCR distinguishes between Index Crimes and Non-Index Crimes. The Index Crimes, which are the ones mainly used as the basis for estimating the general incidence, growth, and distribution of "the crime problem" in the United States, are crimes against persons or property, the kinds citizens are most likely to worry about. Let us look briefly at some of the available data (mostly from the 1970 UCR) about crime in America, starting with what might be called "street crimes" (more or less the same as Index Crimes). We will look later at Non-Index Crime, such as white-collar crime and organized crime.

Figure 3-1 shows us the incidence of (Index) crimes against persons for the period from 1933 to 1970. The increase in the "rate" of crime from 154 to 360 during this period means that there were 154 victims per 100,000 people at the beginning of the period, and that, after some fluctuation, the number of victims more than doubled to 360 per 100,000 at the end of the period. (Note that these figures reflect *not* arrests but citizen reports.) As Figure 3-1 indicates, not all crimes against the person follow the composite trend. Some kinds of crimes fluctuated more than others. Overall, however, a sharp rise in the rate began about 1960 and accelerated after 1965.

Figure 3-2 is a similar graph showing Index Crimes against property, rather than

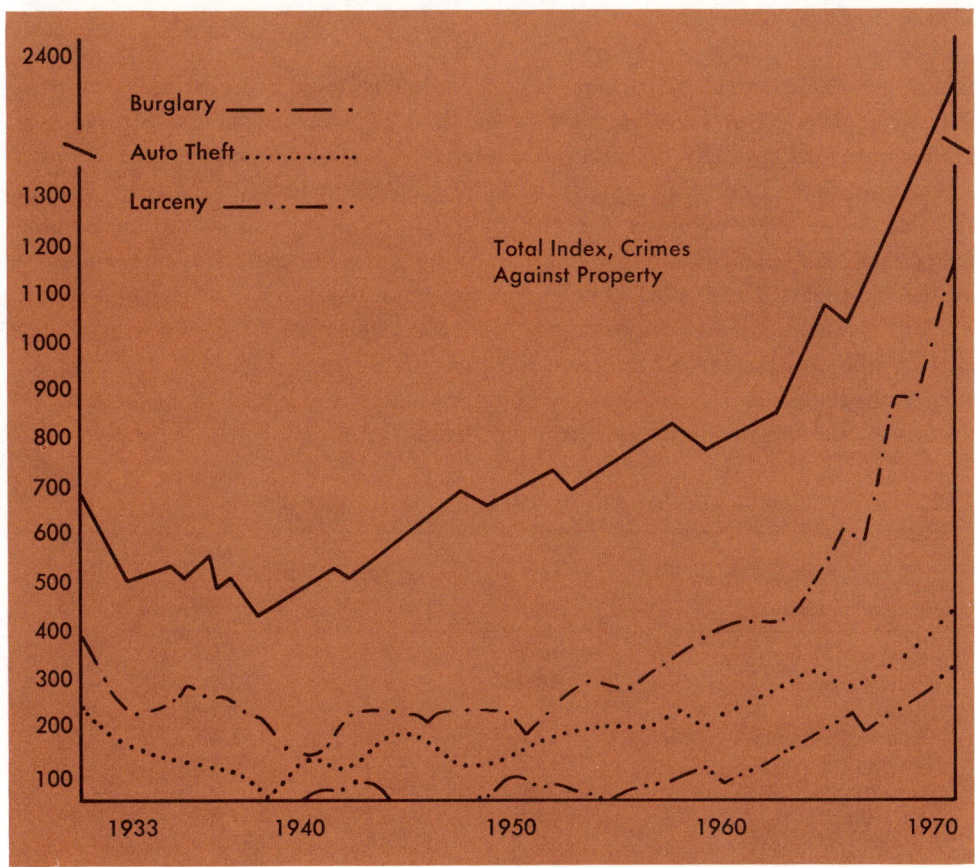

Figure 3-2 Index Crimes, 1933-1970: Reported Crimes Against Property
SOURCE: FBI Uniform Crime Reports Section: unpublished data

TABLE 3-1 CRIME RATE BY REGION, 1970 (RATE PER 100,000 INHABITANTS)

Crime Index Offense	North-eastern States	North Central States	Southern States	Western States
Murder	5.8	6.5	11.2	6.4
Forcible rape	12.7	17.0	18.0	28.9
Robbery	232.8	172.7	130.2	157.5
Aggravated assault	134.0	127.0	202.7	187.3
Burglary	1065.5	896.6	960.7	1541.8
Larceny	823.2	759.7	750.2	1269.3
Auto theft	571.9	419.3	372.1	570.2
Total	2845.9	2398.7	2400.2	3761.4
Violent	385.5	323.2	362.2	380.0
Property	2460.6	2075.5	2038.0	3381.3

Source: Uniform Crime Reports, 1970, p. 6

against persons. Here, also, there has been a gradual increase in recent years, particularly since 1965. Burglary, auto theft, and larceny have accounted for most of the increase. Interestingly enough, while the *incidence* of property crimes is much higher than that of personal crimes, the latter has had the greater increase in *rates*.

Table 3-1 enables us to see the distribution of crime in various regions around the country. It is clear that the western states have the highest crime rate, followed by the Northeast. Further breakdowns of the figures indicate that personal crime is more frequent in the northeastern states, whereas property crimes account for most of the western states' dubious first-place distinction. Murder rates vary the most from region to region, with the southern states way ahead of the rest of the country, while the western states lead the nation in rapes.

TABLE 3-2 CRIME RATE BY AREA, 1970

Crime Index Offense	Total U.S.	Cities over 250,000	Suburban	Rural
Murder	7.8	17.5	3.8	6.4
Forcible rape	18.3	39.7	13.0	9.9
Robbery	171.5	589.4	58.3	14.1
Aggravated assault	162.4	333.9	101.6	89.6
Burglary	1067.7	1947.9	871.7	434.1
Larceny	859.4	1290.1	800.8	302.7
Auto theft	453.5	1116.7	287.8	70.7
Total	2740.5	5335.1	2137.0	927.4
Violent	360.0	980.4	176.7	120.0
Property	2380.5	4354.7	1960.3	807.4

Source: Uniform Crime Reports, 1970, p. 6

Chapter 3 / Crime and Law

TABLE 3-3 TOTAL ARRESTS, DISTRIBUTION BY SEX, 1970

Offense Charged	Persons Arrested		
	Total	Male	Female
Murder	12,836	10,857	1,979
Manslaughter	3,020	2,697	323
Forcible rape	15,411	15,411	—
Robbery	87,687	82,340	5,347
Aggravated assault	125,971	110,057	15,914
Burglary	285,418	272,047	13,371
Larceny	616,099	443,902	172,197
Auto theft	127,341	120,858	6,483

Source: Uniform Crime Reports, 1970, p. 129

The differences in crime rates between urban and rural areas are shown in Table 3-2. At present, as historically, urban areas account for most of the crime in the United States, and by a considerable margin. Suburban areas have rates that are generally between those of urban and rural areas, except for the murder rate, which is lower in suburbia than in either the country or the big city.

Factors other than region and population density affect the distribution of crime rates. Table 3-3 shows the differences by sex. It is clear from the figures that males are much more likely than females to be arrested for most kinds of crimes, particularly for burglary and auto theft, where they outnumber females by 20 to 1. While the female proportions in the crime statistics have increased in recent years, they are still far below those for the males. The most common Index Crimes for women are larceny (28 percent of the cases), aggravated assault (13 percent) and murder (15 percent). Among the Non-Index Crimes, women account for

TABLE 3-4 TOTAL ARRESTS BY AGE, 1970

Offense Charged	Total	Ages under 18	Ages over 18
Murder	12,836	1,346	11,490
Manslaughter	3,020	243	2,777
Forcible rape	15,411	3,205	12,206
Robbery	87,687	29,289	58,398
Aggravated assault	125,971	20,756	105,215
Burglary	285,418	148,296	137,122
Larceny	616,099	312,066	304,033
Auto theft	127,341	71,456	55,885
Percent	100.0	25.3	74.7

Source: Uniform Crime Reports, 1970, p. 126

TABLE 3-5 TOTAL ARRESTS BY RACE, 1970

Offense Charged	Total	White	Black	Other
Murder	11,874	4,503	7,097	247
Manslaughter	2,930	2,238	613	79
Forcible rape	14,419	7,260	6,900	259
Robbery	74,484	24,770	48,282	1,432
Aggravated assault	114,153	59,567	52,323	2,263
Burglary	270,498	174,512	91,305	4,681
Larceny	590,660	392,769	186,720	11,171
Auto theft	120,082	73,687	43,341	3,054
Total	6,257,104	4,377,157	1,688,389	195,588

Source: Uniform Crime Reports, 1970, p. 141

79 percent of commercialized vice arrests (mostly prostitution), 52 percent of the (juvenile) runaways, and 27 percent of the forgeries.

The distribution of crime is greatly affected also by age, as we can see in Table 3-4. Minors below the age of 18 account for 25 percent of the entire Index population and for 52 percent of all property crimes (e.g., burglary, auto theft, larceny). Crimes against the person are more frequently committed by young adults in their 20's than by minors, but after the age of 30, involvement in all crimes drops off sharply to less than 2 percent for people of retirement age (65 or older).

One of the most significant and controversial factors in the distribution of the crime statistics is race. On the one hand, it is clear from Table 3-5 that whites outnumber blacks in all crime categories except robbery and murder; on the other hand, blacks account for more than 25 percent of the total arrest statistics, whereas they comprise only about 11 percent of the total population of the country. Sociologists do not, however, attribute the black over-representation in crime statistics to the factor of race. It is more likely a result of social class differences between the races. American blacks are disproportionately found in the lower classes, which have historically dominated our crime statistics, partly, perhaps, because of their greater motivation, provocation, or opportunity for crime, and partly, to be sure, because of differential and often prejudicial labeling and enforcement practices on the part of officials. Early in the present century, the contribution to the crime statistics of the Italian immigrants to this country was totally out of proportion to their numerical representation in the population, as is now the case with the black population. Before the Italians it was the Irish who occupied that position. More recently, Spanish-speaking immigrants from Mexico and Puerto Rico have joined the blacks in over-representation among arrestees

Chapter 3 / Crime and Law

TABLE 3-6 VICTIM-OFFENDER RELATIONSHIPS BY RACE AND SEX IN ASSAULTIVE CRIMES AGAINST THE PERSON (EXCEPT HOMICIDE)

Victim by Race and Sex	Offenses Attributed to—			
	White Offenders		Black Offenders	
	Male	Female	Male	Female
White males	201	9	129	4
White females	108	14	46	6
Black males	58	3	1,636	256
Black females	21	3	1,202	157
Total population[a]	130	10	350	535

[a] The rates are based only upon 14 years of age or older in each category. The "total population" category in addition excludes persons from racial groups other than black or white.

Source: President's Commission on Law Enforcement and Administration of Justice, The Challenge of Crime in a Free Society, p. 40

(Block and Geis, 1970). This general point was noted in the 1967 report of the President's Commission on Law Enforcement and Administration of Justice:

The Commission is of the view that if the conditions of equal opportunity prevailed, the large difference now found between the Negro and white arrest rates would disappear (p. 45).

Index Crimes, Victims, and Reporting

Reports of victims offer another source (along with arrest statistics) for finding out about the incidence and distribution of crime. Unfortunately, however, victims may themselves be disinclined to report their difficulties to the police for a variety of reasons, including fear of embarrassment, especially in the case of rape victims, or on the part of victims whose own gullibility or misbehavior may have contributed to the crime. Other reasons for reticence to report crimes include lack of faith or confidence in the integrity or efficiency of the police, the complications which victims see in the reporting process, and victims' fear of retaliation by the offender (*The Bulletin,* Philadelphia, April 16, 1974). Nevertheless, victims do report crimes, and so do witnesses, and sometimes interesting discrepancies can be seen between police reports and victim reports. This is especially true when the reports of victims are made to non-official parties, such as poll interviewers.

Table 3-6, which originates from police records, shows how victims are distributed according to the race and sex of their assailants. Contrary to what many people seem to think, victims are far more likely to be men than women, and to be black than white. The victims of black offenders, in other words, are themselves much more likely to be black than white. Less than 7 percent of the murders, and 20 percent of the rapes, are cross-racial (a category which includes white against

TABLE 3-7 MURDER BY CIRCUMSTANCE, 1970

Circumstance	Percentage
Spouse killing spouse	12.1
Parent killing child	3.1
Other family killings	8.1
Romantic triangle and lovers' quarrels	7.1
Other arguments	40.8
Known felony type	20.4
Suspected felony type	8.4
Total	100.0

Source: Uniform Crime Reports, 1970, p. 9

TABLE 3-8 CRIMES CLEARED BY ARREST, 1970

	Against the Person			Against Property	
	Cleared	Not Cleared		Cleared	Not Cleared
Murder	86%	14%	Robbery	29%	71%
Manslaughter	81%	19%	Burglary	19%	81%
Forcible rape	56%	44%	Larceny	18%	82%
Aggravated assault	65%	35%	Auto theft	17%	83%

Source: Uniform Crime Reports, 1970, p. 32

black, as well as the other way around). Robbery is an exception; it is disproportionately committed by blacks against whites (Knudten, 1970).

Murder in particular, besides being mostly a crime between people of the same race, is also usually a crime between relatives, friends, or acquaintances. As Table 3-7 shows, nearly 75 percent of all murders are in that category, frequently occurring after arguments between friends or family members, rather than being coolly premeditated first-degree slayings. Motives (e.g., jealously, fear, etc.) are also fairly easy to identify in assaultive crimes where the victim knows the assailant, and witnesses are often present as well. This is why police depend so heavily upon victims and/or witnesses to help in the solution of crimes against the person; the victim is almost always able to identify the assailant (except, of course, in the case of murder) but will not always do so for some of the reasons mentioned above. This is also why these crimes are more easily solved (see Table 3-8). With other kinds of crimes, however, such as those involving property but not assault, solution is much harder. Only 29 percent of our robberies, 19 percent of our burglaries,

18 percent of our larcenies, and 17 percent of our auto thefts reported are ever solved. Figure 3-3 indicates that while our crime rates have been rising, our clearance rates have been dropping, and that, in fact, the gap between them has been widening. (A crime is considered "cleared" if an arrest is made.)

A 1972 national interview survey conducted by the U. S. Census Bureau and the Law Enforcement Assistance Administration (LEAA), and reported in *The Bulletin* (April 16, 1974) in Philadelphia, found some interesting similarities and differences in the statistics that we have just reviewed. This survey is particularly revealing because it is based on self-reports of victims to anonymous interviewers, rather than upon official reports to police. It is probably thus not surprising that the study found that 80 percent of all serious crimes in Philadelphia over the period were not reported to the police! Aside from this large discrepancy between police statistics and those of the survey, however, the two were in agreement that men were much more likely to be victims than were women, and that blacks were much more likely to be victims than were whites. All in all, the survey found that 63 of every 1,000 Philadelphians had been victims of violent crimes in 1972, and that 95 of every 1,000 had been robbed. Since Philadelphia ranks high among U. S. cities with the highest crime rates, the situation there may be worse than in other parts of the country. Table 3-9 presents more extensive results of the same national survey which was carried out in 13 cities, and we can see that Philadelphia is unusually high in its ratio of unreported to reported crime. In other respects, it is higher than some cities and lower than others; overall, it isn't too much different. By way of comparison, Gallup poll for the same year (1972) revealed that "one person in every three living in densely populated center-city areas of the nation

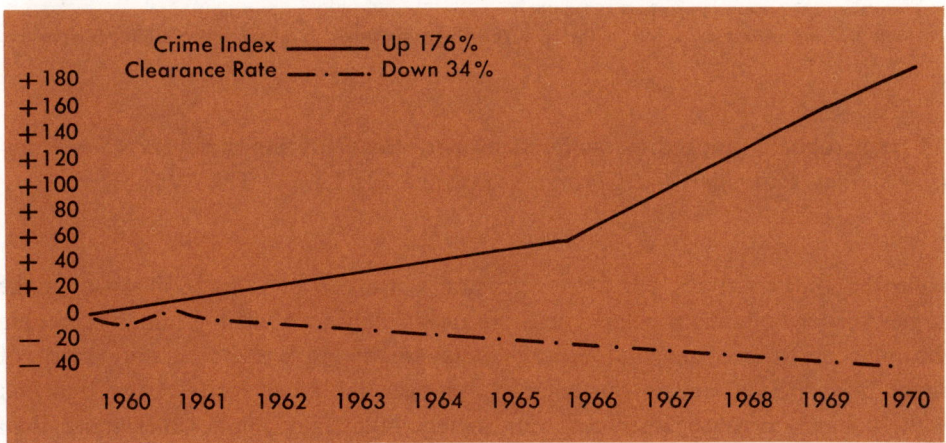

Figure 3-3 Crime and Crimes Cleared, 1960-1970: Percent Change over 1960
SOURCE: FBI, *Uniform Crime Report, 1970*, p. 34

TABLE 3-9 CRIME VICTIMIZATION IN 13 SELECTED CITIES

	Crime Victimization Rate per 1,000 Residents 12 and Over				Household Victimization per 1,000 Households			Commercial Victimization per 1,000 Business Establishments		
	(Crimes of Violence)	Rape and Attempted Rape	Robbery	Assault	Burglary	Household Larceny	Auto Theft	Burglary	Robbery	Ratio of Unreported Crime to Reported Crime
a Detroit	(68)	3	32	33	174	106	49	615	179	2.7 to 1
Denver	(67)	3	17	46	158	168	44	443	54	2.9 to 1
a Philadelphia	(63)	1	28	34	109	87	42	390	116	5.1 to 1
Portland, Ore.	(59)	3	17	40	151	149	34	355	39	2.6 to 1
Baltimore	(56)	1	26	28	116	100	35	578	135	2.2 to 1
a Chicago	(56)	3	26	27	118	77	36	317	77	2.8 to 1
Cleveland	(54)	2	24	28	124	80	76	367	77	2.4 to 1
a Los Angeles	(53)	2	16	35	148	131	42	311	47	2.9 to 1
Atlanta	(48)	2	16	30	161	102	29	741	157	2.3 to 1
Dallas	(43)	2	10	31	147	147	24	355	48	2.6 to 1
Newark	(42)	1	29	12	123	44	37	631	98	1.4 to 1
St. Louis	(42)	1	16	25	125	81	47	531	94	1.5 to 1
a New York	(36)	1	24	11	68	33	26	328	103	2.1 to 1

Source: National Crime Panel Surveys, Law Enforcement Assistance Administration, Justice Department
a Information for five largest cities covers 1972. Information for eight others is based on surveys carried out in July-October 1972 covering previous 12 months
(This table was taken from an article in *The New York Times* by David Burnham, which originally appeared on April 14, 1974)

had been robbed, mugged, or suffered property loss" during that year (*San Francisco Sunday Examiner and Chronicle,* January 21, 1973, "This World," p. 10).

Organized Crime

While the Index Crimes (or "street crimes") are the ones most likely to make the newspaper columns regularly, and are most likely to be in the minds of people who advocate more "law and order," these are by no means the only kinds of crimes being perpetrated in our society, nor even the most costly. Organized and "white-collar" crime together cost our society financially many times more than street crime, perhaps even a hundred times more. The President's Commission (1967) estimated that seven billion dollars a year passes into the hands of organized crime from their control over gambling, loan-sharking, narcotics, prostitution, and so on. Thus, the income of organized crime, on which it pays no taxes, is as great as the combined income of our ten largest industrial corporations (Clark, 1971).

As one authoritative criminologist has pointed out, however (Cressey, 1969) the greatest cost of organized crime may be from the civic damage done by using that money to neutralize and corrupt both our criminal justice system and our political processes. Organized crime could not operate successfully without large-scale bribery and/or intimidation of powerful people. Some of its success, however, must be attributed to a public which, to some degree, is in awe of, and occasionally even glorifies in the mass media the courage and cunning of, the "successful" mobster, and creates a continuing demand for the "vices" which are the lucrative marketable products of organized crime. Also contributing to the incidence of organized crime are a variety of "vice laws" which are often not widely supported in cultural norms or public opinion, because they create "victimless" crimes. For a variety of reasons, statistics on the actual incidence of organized crime are very hard to come by and only fragmentary when they exist.

White-Collar Crime

Another kind of crime that seldom arouses the same degree of public concern and outrage as "street crime" is "white-collar crime," that is committed by people in the white-collar occupations, usually by the relatively powerful or well-to-do, and usually as a more or less natural (but not legal) extension of normal occupational or professional activities. This category includes embezzlement, political corruption, check forgery, pilfering, "con games," and many other activities that usually involve middle-class criminals and the use of fraud in preference to force. The Watergate scandal of the Nixon Administration was probably the most notorious and extensive example of white-collar crime in this generation. Lower down in the ranks of traditional American organizations, as if nothing were sacred any longer, even the Boy Scouts of America had its own "Watergate" (in the words of its chief executive) in mid-1974, when it was discovered that members of the professional BSA staff in Chicago had been padding the scout membership rolls in order to get federal funds. Less than 50 percent of the scouts listed on the rolls actually existed (*San Francisco Sunday Examiner and Chronicle,* June 16, 1974, "This World").

Even before Watergate, the 1967 report of the President's Commission on Law Enforcement and Administration of Justice pointed out that

... information as is available, though not systematically compiled, indicates that white-collar crime is pervasive in our society and causes enormous economic and social harm. (p. 103)

The report estimated that income-tax evasion costs the government from 25 to 40 billion dollars annually, and that security frauds cost the public from one-half to one billion dollars each year. Ordinary citizens lose a total of one to two billion dollars a year in auto-repair swindles alone, to say nothing of the costs of other swindles, misrepresentations, and deceptive practices in the business world. As in the case of organized crime, however, the civic costs of white-collar crime may be more important than the financial ones, and even harder to measure. Widespread public demoralization about the values of our economic system or our political institutions may be generated by a Watergate type of scandal, with incalculable consequences. On the other hand, Americans seem to have been less concerned about, and quicker to forgive, white-collar crimes than street crimes. It is open to question whether without the persistent interest-group activity, fact-finding, and reporting on the part of the press, the opposition party, and others, the Nixon Administration would have suffered any more from the Watergate scandal than Lyndon Johnson did from the Bobby Baker episode. We are not quick to think ill of our substantial citizens. This brings us to the question of public opinion as a "construction of reality" about crime, and of the differences between public opinion and "objective" reality.

Public Opinion

While the public has been expressing itself in various collective ways about crime and the law for some years, it seems to have become particularly sensitive to these issues beginning with the racial disturbances, student protests, and other disorders in our larger cities in the mid-1960's. For at least a decade thereafter, and continuing into the present, the "law and order" issue, in one form or another, has remained near the top of public concerns expressed both to political leaders and to opinion pollsters. In early 1968, a Gallup poll asked people what they thought was "the most important problem" facing their country and their community. The answer, "crime and lawlessness," ranked second only to the Viet-Nam War as the most important problem in the country, and absolutely first (on a list of 13) as the most important problem facing their community (Gallup, 1968). In 1967, 31 percent of Gallup's respondents reported that there were areas near their homes where they would feel unsafe walking alone at night; in early 1972, that figure had increased to 41 percent (Gallup, 1967 and 1972). According to the report of the President's Commission (1967), however, survey respondents tend to feel that neighborhoods other than their own have higher crime rates, whether this is true or not. A 1969 Harris poll asked many questions similar to those raised by Gallup, and got very similar results. A 1972 Gallup survey showed, furthermore, that more than half of the nation believed that there was more crime in their area than there had been a year earlier (*San Francisco Sunday Examiner and Chronicle,*

TABLE 3-10 RELATIONSHIP BETWEEN CONCERN ABOUT CRIME AND THE RISK OF VICTIMIZATION

Concern about Crime	High Crime Area	Medium Crime Area	Low Crime Area
Crime not "most serious" problem	74%	71%	66%
Crime "most serious" problem	26%	29%	34%

Source: Frank F. Furstenberg, 1971

Jan. 21, 1973, "This World," p. 10). This alarming perception of increased crime rates, however, is not shared universally, even though it may well be true (judging from Figures 3-1, 3-2, and 3-3). A more detailed comparison of the 1967 and 1972 Gallup polls shows that perceptions of increased violent crime were related to the age of the sample: older respondents (50-70) felt that violent crimes had increased, while the youngest groups (18-30) tended to feel that violent crime was on the decrease!

Often there is a considerable gap between public opinion and objective reality, insofar as the latter can be measured. New York City, for example, has the reputation at home and abroad of being a crime-ridden city, very unsafe for the unwary visitor, much to the dismay of its Convention and Visitors Bureau (*San Francisco Sunday Examiner and Chronicle,* Jan. 28, 1973, "This World," p. 25). This is in spite of the fact, as we can see from Table 3-9, that New York was the safest of the 13 large cities sampled in the crime victimization survey; that is, it had the lowest overall crime rate, and one of the most accurately reported. Its crime rate was far below such "safe" western cities as Denver and Portland. Table 3-10 shows, furthermore, that public opinion is equally far removed from reality at a neighborhood level. The lower the crime rate in an area, the greater the likelihood that its residents will regard crime as their "most serious" problem when interviewed by pollsters. People with the least likelihood of becoming victims apparently feel they have the most to fear. The 1967 report of the President's Commission on Law Enforcement came to a similar conclusion:

> ... The available data indicate that for most people, attitudes about serious crimes and crime trends come largely from vicarious sources. ... The Commission found little statistical relationship between having been directly victimized by crime, and attitudes toward most aspects of the crime problem. (1967, 6:86)

The irony in all this, and one of potentially great importance for crime-related social movements, is that not only are the citizens who are the least likely to be victimized the most likely to be concerned about crime as a "serious problem," they are also the ones most likely to favor a harsh "law-and-order" approach to dealing with street crime. This attitude prevails despite the fact that in 1970 the violent Index Crimes accounted for only 15 percent of all Index Crimes, and for only 3½ percent of all reported crimes (Furstenberg, 1971). Ramsey Clark (1971) has estimated that the "average American" has only one chance in 400 years of being a victim of a violent personal crime, although a black or Spanish-speaking American has one chance in eight years. As we have observed, furthermore, the assailant is not likely to be some mysterious stranger, but rather a person of the victim's own race and social circle.

Such discrepancies as sometimes exist between "reality" and public opinion are not entirely the consequence of exaggerated definitions by an anxious citizenry. Law enforcement agencies themselves have been known to manipulate the official statistics. Sometimes the statistics are magnified in importance simply as a result of the reporting format used. Thus, when the late J. Edgar Hoover was director of the FBI, a stolen-vehicle case, when solved, would be reported first in the UCR in a section listing all the related arrests and convictions, then again in a section dealing with "automobiles recovered," and finally in a section on the value of recovered stolen property. One incident could thus produce a number of entries in official reports, and easily lead to a misinterpretation of statistics (Turner, 1970). Another kind of format manipulation of statistics can be seen in the case of robbery reports. In most police-based reports (including the UCR), robberies are listed under crimes against the person (e.g., Figure 3-1), since, by definition, they involve personal threats by the robber. Like most crimes against the person, as we noted above, robbery has a relatively high clearance rate (compared to property crimes). Thus when the UCR clearance reports (e.g., Table 3-8) show robbery under property crimes, the overall effect is to enhance the generally low clearance rates for property crimes.

Still another form of statistical manipulation can be seen in the manner of presentation of a given statistical fact. If a community of 100,000 people has one rape incident in a year, and two in the next year, we can either say that there was a 100 percent increase in rapes, or we can say that there was only one more rape this year than last. Both statements are true, but the choice of emphasis is important in influencing public opinion. In the 1970 UCR, for example, it was reported that the homicide rate had increased 56 percent since 1960, a statement that was technically true but based upon an increase of only 2.1 homicides per 100,000 people. "Official statistics," then, are affected both by choice of presentation or emphasis, and by choice of (or changes in) the reporting category.

Other instances of statistical manipulation are even more obviously self-serving. In one case personally known to one of the authors, a county sheriff, running for re-election, in order to stack the figures in his favor, reported in his speeches a "crime rate" (rate of arrests) based on figures not only for his own rural area, but for a small urban area within his county, which had its own police department and therefore little or no operational relation to the sheriff. Furthermore, the town had a better conviction rate than did the surrounding county. Thus, by first lumping together all the figures for the entire county and then selectively isolating them to serve his purposes, the sheriff could stand on a record that was artificially high (for him) both in arrests (or "crime rate") and in convictions. In another incident known to the author, a police commissioner in a Tennessee city began to insist that the officers and dispatchers record all illegal incidents, major or minor, that came to their attention, which had not been their policy formerly. The result, as the commissioner had hoped, was a greatly increased operating budget for the police department based on a rise in the crime statistics; another result was an unnecessary increase in the collective anxiety of the public. For a great variety of reasons, then, the public is more likely to be aware of (and concerned about) Index Crimes than either organized or white-collar crime.

Now that we have seen some of the factors that lie behind the official facts or "parameters of reality," and some of the public responses to the published "facts" about crime, let us turn to a consideration of the various publics and interest groups which are concerned with the alleviation of problems in the incidence and distribution of crime and its victims.

CHAMPIONS AND THEIR INTERESTS

In the abstract, behavior defined as "crime" is likely to be considered a "social problem" anywhere. We have seen, however, that as far as the public is concerned, there is "crime," and then there is "crime" (of quite a different kind). Of considerable importance in understanding crime as a "social problem" is to understand what kinds of crime are generally defined as part of the problem and why. Various publics and interest groups play a crucial part in this definition.

Psychological Interests and Publics

There is some reason to believe that we have in America what might be called a "law and order" mentality among some segments of the population. People with such an outlook are not characterized by any special or coherent ideological stance, but they tend to be among the "respectable middle class," generally hard-working citizens and very concerned about protecting the property and goods that their efforts have accumulated. Whether or not they live in unsafe neighborhoods (and they rarely do), they are the ones most likely to report in public opinion polls that "law and order" is a serious problem (cf. the above discussion on public opinion and reality). This does not necessarily mean that they are hyperscrupulous in their own observances of the law; they may occasionally violate traffic laws or commit other "folk crimes" that they feel don't "really matter." They nevertheless see themselves as good citizens, who ought to be protected from "criminal elements." Such a mentality is easily recruited to support "law and order" campaigns and, in its more extreme forms, participate in vigilante movements.

In part, a person's outlook toward crime, and his definition of "criminals," are counterparts of his outlook on the police; and attitudes toward both the police and criminals are largely learned through interaction with police and criminals, respectively. Differential interaction with or exposure to these elements, in turn, is related largely to one's social-class background. One interesting study shows that fear of crime and criminals (particularly of the "street" variety) is inversely related to fear of the police. That is, those who worry most about crime are the ones who do not worry about the police, and vice versa (Block, 1971). People who have learned, as have many of our citizens from ghettos and "crime-ridden" neighborhoods, to associate harassment, brutality, or other negative and threatening behavior with the police, will be inclined to fear the police as much as (or more than) they fear the criminal, and are not likely to be found in the ranks of "law-and-order" supporters, even though their neighborhoods may be relatively unsafe. The very fact, ironically, that the police select such neighborhoods for more heavy patrolling and surveillance may make the residents more wary of police (and, indeed, may itself generate disproportionately high "crime statistics" from those neighborhoods) (Chevigny, 1969; Hudson, 1970; and Cray, 1972). In the same vein, interestingly enough, a U.S. Civil Rights Commission report (1965) showed that southern blacks, even in rural areas, had had such unpleasant encounters with police when reporting crimes that they were more wary of the police than of potential assailants.

In middle-class neighborhoods, however, where police are seen more infrequently, they may be more appreciated and regarded as friendly symbols of safety and help. Middle-class interactions with the police are more likely to be courteous and unstrained and to involve relatively minor issues, such as traffic violations or neighborhood matters. When police appear in "nice" neighborhoods for more than perfunctory patrols, it is usually because they have been called by a middle-class victim who needs their help. Such contacts generate a much more favorable image of the police, and a much greater public tendency to "support your local police" in the struggle for "law and order."

Selective middle-class indignation about "street crime" (as opposed to organized or white-collar crime) is probably also a consequence of the greater threat which these crimes represent to middle-class goals and values. While by no means necessarily condoning organized or white-collar crime, middle-class "law-and-order" people can understand those crimes better and sympathize somewhat with their perpetrators, who, in some ways, are exhibiting such praiseworthy middle-class values as hard work, monetary acquisitiveness, cleverness, and courage. (Or, as a former Governor of California once expressed it, the Watergate offenders were not "criminals at heart.") Organized and white-collar crimes, furthermore, often do not make the newspapers. By contrast, crimes of violence, destruction, or theft are constantly being brought to the public attention in the mass media. These crimes are incomprehensible from the viewpoint of middle-class values. They show no respect for property or property rights, usually result in little or no financial gain for the criminal, and seem to destroy life and goods uselessly.

There is also an element of fear of the unknown and the unpredictable in the way that many people react to stories of "street crimes." The criminologist Sutherland makes this point especially well in his discussion of the development of "sexual psychopath" laws in our history: "Fear [of sexual attacks] is greater because the behavior is so incomprehensible" (1969:75). Sutherland goes on to explain that many of our laws intended to control "sexual psychopaths" are irrational, are based on faulty and unscientific beliefs, and often result in the unjust and unnecessary harassment of some essentially harmless people.

A search for identity in a time of rapid social and cultural change is believed by some social scientists to account for some of the strong "law-and-order" motivations of "respectable" citizens. When the traditional normative boundaries are no longer too clear, and some people seem to be getting away with behavior that might have been sternly punished in an earlier time, other people seem to need reassurance that they are really "good guys," in contrast to the "bad guys" who are out there picking on innocent citizens. Such a feeling often lies behind the complaint sometimes heard from an otherwise law-abiding citizen who, when stopped by a patrolman for speeding, will angrily demand, "Why aren't you out catching the *real* criminals instead of harassing us good citizens?!" By *real* criminals, of course, is meant the murderers, rapists, thieves, and vandals. It thus becomes important to some citizens' own egos to be able to think of "them" as the real criminals. From doubtless similar motivations, according to an extensive study of shoplifters, the hardest problem faced by the otherwise "decent," naive, amateur shoplifter (as often as not a middle-class housewife!) is the inability to face the definition of oneself as a "criminal" (Cameron, 1964).

Moral Interest Groups

There is a great variety of moral interest groups involved in trying to define certain kinds of behavior as criminal, and, accordingly, to restrict such behavior. For the most part, the efforts of these groups are specifically directed at one or another kind of behavior which they consider objectionable, such as drinking, drugs, sex, and so on, and therefore they will be considered separately in the various chapters of this book which deal with the individual "problem" behaviors. We might point out here only that churches have been influential many times in anti-crime movements, but not often with the best of understanding (Hissong, 1968). In large part also, some of the groups considered below as essentially "civic" or "political" in nature represent moral interests as well.

Political and Civic Interest Groups

The crime issue seems to attract quite a variety of groups which attempt to exert political pressure on police, on lawmakers, or on public opinion to get "solutions" to the crime "problems" that they have defined. Perhaps the most blatantly political type of interest group is the political campaign organization or party, which will sometimes use the crime issue to embarrass the opposition and/or to convince the voters that a certain candidate is critically needed to "fight crime." Reference was made above to the example of the county sheriff who used such a ploy, and it is well-known as a resort of ambitious prosecutors seeking to promote their own careers (Blumberg, 1970; Cipes, 1968; and Knudten, 1970). As we will point out under the heading of political and civic enterprise later on, a number of presidential and congressional campaigns have also stressed crime as an issue, most recently during the campaigns of the 1960's. Occasionally a candidate will use the "law-and-order" issue as the main plank in his political platform.

On a more local level, we sometimes find citizens' groups seeking to support and cooperate with the police in fighting crime, such as "block committees" that have been formed in some of our larger cities to assist the police in surveillance, and to offer help and refuge to potential victims (especially children). Groups of this kind are clearly pledged to work "within the system." Other citizen groups have more of a "vigilante" mentality, finding the police inadequate, corrupt, or otherwise "falling down on the job." They create a continuing pressure and anxiety for the police by threatening or attempting to take the law into their own hands, thereby becoming a police problem themselves.

Civic and political pressure groups are not always on the side of stricter enforcement, however. Some of them are more concerned with protecting those whom they feel are being unjustly treated by the police. On the local level, the Black Panthers in Oakland, California, and the Baton Rouge (Louisiana) Deacons have had some serious and violent confrontations with the police, partly over their self-ascribed protective functions of standing between "the people" and "the pigs" (Marx and Archer, 1973). Less pugnacious, and probably more effective, were the "truth squads" that circulated in cities like Berkeley, California, during the late 1960's; they would follow the police around "to keep them honest," or to serve as willing and uninvolved witnesses to any instances of police "brutality" or "harassment." At the national level, one of the most important functions of the American Civil Liberties Union (ACLU) historically has been to provide political pressure and legal support on behalf of individuals (especially relatively powerless ones) who seem to have been abused by the police or deprived of "due process" or other civil liberties.

One could add here a variety of *ad hoc* congressional committees and local citizens' groups formed to "clean up" this or that "crime problem," such as in the case of prostitution in New York's "Hell's Kitchen" during the late 1960's and early 1970's (Sheehy, 1972; Cipes, 1968). It is clear from the record in this case that the actual *incidence* of prostitution did not decrease appreciably after the citizen agitation, but for a time it was defined as "out of control," so citizens' groups put pressure on the police to "clean it up." Most such citizen crusades are moralistic in their motivation, and can thus be considered as much moral as political interest groups.

In discussing some of the dynamics of the most recent anti-crime movement later on, civic and political groups, as well as economic groups, formed to deal with various aspects of the "crime problem," will be described in greater detail.

Economic Interest Groups

Aside from organized crime itself, and the perpetrators of smaller-scale property crimes, who obviously have vested economic interests in crime, there are at least three kinds of legitimate economic interest groups related to the crime issue. The first of these is the victims of the criminals, who often join defensive or protective organizations such as Chambers of Commerce, retailers, associations of various kinds, insurance companies, and so on. All of these groups can be expected to bring a lot of property crime to their members' attention and to demand more effective protection and enforcement. A second economic interest group manufactures and supplies police equipment. It is not necessary to assign ulterior motives to such industries to see that they profit from "crime waves" and from the appropriations of funds to fight crime. Companies such as Smith and Wesson and Federal Laboratories, Inc., have enjoyed good profits in recent years. Finally, a third kind of economic interest group manufactures and sells a variety of security devices to anxious citizens: gadgetry to protect homes from criminals can range from 300 to several thousand dollars per home. Expensive guard dogs are also included in this category (Alpren, 1972). Security device industries have also enjoyed high profits in this age of "law and order," as have private protection and security agencies.

Occupational Interest Groups

While social workers, parole officers, prison-keepers, criminologists, and a variety of other related workers have some real occupational interests in crime, the occupation with the greatest and most direct interest is, of course, the police, since they face the issue on a daily basis and at the "grass-roots" level. The police interests are of both an organizational and a personal nature; that is, police organizations depend for their existence and support upon a public perception that they are really needed, and policemen as individuals have the same needs as others to feel that they are important.

The organizational interests on which the police act involve maintaining a delicate balance between two kinds of public perceptions: on the one hand, the public must be persuaded that there really is a crime problem; but, on the other hand, the public must not blame the police for the problem. They must feel that the police are doing their best and need only more financial and moral support to deal more effectively with crime. Therefore, it is sometimes in the interests of the police to emphasize how much crime there is; at other times, it is more in their interests to emphasize what a good job they've been doing to control it, and thus to minimize somewhat the extent of criminal activities. As an example of the latter, as late as 1962 J. Edgar Hoover, the Director of the FBI (1924-1972), apparently did not regard, or did not act as though he regarded, organized crime as a major destructive force in America (Turner, 1971). He tended to disregard both the evidence from the well-known "Appalachian Conference" (Nov., 1957) of important Mafia figures (Tyler, 1971) and the incriminating testimony of Joseph Valachi before a Senate investigating committee (Turner, 1970). A former U. S. Attorney General, Ramsey Clark, has claimed that a frontal assault on organized crime would have made the FBI look bad at that time, because it was not prepared or equipped to win such a battle (Clark, 1971). Valachi himself had testified that the Mafia or Cosa Nostra did not fear the FBI, for it considered it too reticent to attack for fear of losing too many court cases (Mass, 1969).* To the extent that these allegations about the FBI are true, they would constitute an extreme example of the more unusual police tendency to minimize criminal behavior.

More common is the police practice of emphasizing and manipulating crime statistics to help establish the urgent public need for police work, and thus to

---

* The precise reasons for such apparent FBI hesitancy to engage organized crime are not clear. It may have been simply a matter of official staffing priorities, for Valachi claimed that in 1959, only four FBI agents in New York City were assigned to work on organized crime, compared to more than 400 assigned to deal with domestic Communists (Mass, 1969:28). In 1967, then Attorney General Ramsey Clark was quoted as saying, "Vast segments of our (FBI) agent personnel must be switched from non-essential counting of meaningless statistics to matters involving top Mafia, so that their power can be broken" (Turner, 1970:169).

enhance public support for police organizations. We have seen some examples of this tactic above under the discussion of public opinion. A recent study of the Soviet NKVD (The People's Commissariat of Internal Affairs) during the 1930's makes some interesting points about the organizational pressures brought to bear on police units to make enough arrests to demonstrate that there really is a "problem," and that they are serving the public well (Conner, 1972). (We are not comparing American and Soviet police in any other respect.) Whatever tactics the police may use to garner community support, they are seen as essential to their occupational interests.

Public esteem for individual police officers is also an important occupational interest, as it is for any people of any occupation (Glasser, 1965). In order to enjoy a strong self-concept, an officer needs to feel that his community regards his work as vital. This is an especially critical issue for police officers, since, on the average, they are recruited from lower- and lower-middle-class backgrounds and are very interested in upward social mobility. The opinions of articulate middle-class citizens are therefore very important to them (McNamara, 1967). In dealing with public opinion, the police sometimes see themselves as suffering from the same problems experienced by members of minority groups in our society. They are often referred to as the "they" in citizen "we"/"they" characterizations; they are subject to a certain amount of public stereotyping, in which unpleasant citizen encounters with one or a few policemen are generalized to *all* police, with consequent feelings of "depersonalization" or hostility toward the officers; and they feel discriminated against in matters of social and economic rewards and benefits from society (Bennett, 1971). For all these reasons, the police sometimes feel quite justified in using certain exaggerations or deceptions when describing the crime problem, in order to gain support from what they see as a basically unappreciative public.

In order to promote favorable public interest and to gain some political influence at the same time, the police have organized themselves into a number of professional (occupational) associations and societies. These include the Fraternal Order of Police, the Benevolent Police Association, or the Patrolmen's Benevolent Association, which are national organizations, as well as a number of state and regional counterparts of these, such as the Washington Association of Sheriffs and Police Chiefs, the Tennessee Law Enforcement Officers' Association, and countless others. For more specialized interests within the occupation, there are the International Association of Chiefs of Police, the National Academy Alumni Association, and others. For police officers of black minority groups, the Afro-American Police League and the Black Guardians have been organized in some cities, to protect their members against professional discrimination, and, in part, to protect citizens of the same race from undue harassment by white officers (Jones, 1969).

All these organizations engage in various kinds of publicity and promotion, lobbying, fund-raising, and so on, in the interests of members. An example from the 1960's of particularly effective work by the Patrolmen's Benevolent Association in New York City was its successful campaign against the establishment of Civilian Review Boards, which will be discussed further on.

Scientific Interest Groups

For many decades now, crime as a social and behavioral phenomenon has been investigated scientifically by a number of different kinds of scientists. While some of the resulting theory and research has come from physiologists, their work on the subject has gained little acceptance, and even the most acceptable work has not offered much promise of accounting for a very large proportion of criminal behavior. The most widely studied scientific work, therefore, but not necessarily the most revealing, has come from psychologists or psychiatrists, sociologists, and criminologists. (See also the review of scientific interest groups in Chapter 5.)

The psychological or psychiatric perspective has focused mainly on the individual himself and his personality traits. A number of psychological theories have been advanced to explain criminal behavior. Generally, the individual is seen to acquire both criminal and non-criminal tendencies from a variety of sources. Criminal tendencies might result from a defective ego, defective superego, or both (Abrahamsen, 1960). Or, criminal behavior might result from mistreatment or oppression, leading to feelings of helplessness or despair, which, in turn, produce criminal behavior (Halleck, 1967). The main significance of such theories is that they call for "treatment" or correction that is directed at changing the personality rather than at punishment *per se.*

Sociologists, on the other hand, tend to assume that the genesis of crime lies with the social influences on the individual, or with the nature of society and its rules, or both. For the most part, we have already covered the main sociological theories about crime or deviance in Chapter 1. We might recall, however, that the structural-functional perspective sees crime as arising naturally in a society and having certain contributions to make to the maintenance of that society's structure and smooth functioning. Durkheim, Erikson, Merton, Davis, and Bell are included among the theorists here. A somewhat related outlook is the *strain* perspective, which has many variations. One version is that there are gaps and lags in the organization of a society, which produce inconsistencies and unpredictabilities that are hard for an individual to cope with. Various kinds of *anomie,* for example, might result from an individual's inability to achieve the valued *goals* of a particular society or culture with the limited *means* available to him because of his lack of opportunity (Merton, Cloward and Ohlin, Shaw and McKay, and others). This will lead him to choose illegitimate means with which to meet his goals or to retreat altogether into some kind of "personal pathology," such as alcoholism. Another variation of strain theory might be called "conflict" theory, which holds that crime is the result of one or another kind of social conflict, usually between those who make the laws and those against whom the laws are usually directed and enforced. Thus, the middle-class establishment may be seen as imposing a variety of moral prescriptions and values upon a subculture (or set of subcultures) which considers them invalid or irrelevant and therefore resists obeying them. A recent version of this conflict view has been called "the new criminology" (Ian Taylor, et al., 1973); it takes the somewhat Marxist stand that laws constitute an oppression of the "have-nots" by the "haves" in capitalist societies, and that crime is therefore the inevitable product of a capitalist system.

Another kind of focus on deviant subcultures can be seen in what we sometimes call "social learning" or "cultural transmission" theories about crime. From this perspective, criminal behavior is seen as simply *learned,* like any other kind of behavior, in the setting of delinquent peer groups or other deviant cultural settings. Albert Cohen (1955) is well-known for having applied this idea (as well as an anomie perspective) to delinquent boys, and Edwin Sutherland (1947) offered one of the classical formulations of this perspective in his discussion of "differential association." Walter Miller (1958) and Wolfgang and Ferracuti (1967) have also made contributions in this theoretical tradition.

Perhaps the most recent theoretical perspective on criminal behavior to receive special attention in sociology is the social interactionist one (including the so-called "labeling" perspective). Well-known exponents of this perspective include Matza, Tannenbaum, Becker, Lemert, Glaser, and Schur. On the one hand, this view stresses a kind of "sociology-of-law" outlook, i.e., a study of why certain kinds of behavior are against the law in certain cultural settings, but not others, and how certain class and other biases enter into law-making and law enforcement. On the other hand, the interactionists observe the impact of the process of social labeling on the individual and his or her behavior, with particular reference to how one's self-concept is affected. The self-concept is seen as the chief determinant of behavior, i.e., people behave like criminals when they think of themselves as criminals; and the self-concept, in turn, is created in social interaction.

Criminologists tend to draw on psychological theories, sociological theories, or both, and they most often perform their work in academic departments of universities, in research institutes, and in government agencies (Mannheim, 1967). All of these scientific interest groups, but particularly criminologists, benefit professionally from public definitions of crime as a major and growing "social problem" (Manning, 1972). This does not mean, of course, that they consciously try to manipulate public opinion, but they obviously do have a professional stake in "generating knowledge" about crime and criminals, which, in turn, helps to formulate collective definitions in textbooks and other scientific writings.

CRIME AND ITS SOCIAL MOVEMENTS

Social movements surrounding the crime issue can take a number of forms and can be generated at national, regional, or local levels. Some movements are national in scope and involve a number of interest groups in a variety of places, all focusing on a common national concern. A good example here would be the social movement generated by the marijuana issue, which produced the legislation and restrictions of the 1930's (Becker, 1963). Local and regional chapters of the International Association of Chiefs of Police, combining forces with congressional elements and spokesmen from the Bureau of Narcotics, succeeded in gathering enough public and legislative support to carry the day. Other movements are addressed to local crime issues, often types of "vice" like prostitution (Sheehy, 1972), and they may or may not have counterparts in other communities at the same time. When a number of local communities focus attention on the same crime issue at the same time, however, we have the basis for a nationwide "sweep" by a new movement. The national mass media play an important part in the process of "nationalizing" a social movement.

Historic Crime Movements

Leaving aside purely local movements and those limited to a specific form of "vice" or crime, we can identify two major, national movements aimed at "cracking down" on "general lawlessness" in the past half-century. The first of these occurred in the 1920's (related in part to the "crime wave" accompanying Prohibition) and culminated in the election of a conservative Republican, Herbert Hoover, in 1928 (Cipes, 1968). The second occurred in the 1960's, and was generated largely by public reactions to the student and racial unrest of that period. It, too, culminated in the election of a "law-and-order" president, Richard Nixon in 1968, and was probably involved again, though to a lesser extent, in his re-election in 1972.

A principal indicator of the rise and development of these crime movements is the waxing and waning of the incidence of crime-related publications listed in the *Reader's Guide to Periodical Literature*. In the years 1922-1924, some 60 articles were published on crime and criminals and listed in *Reader's Guide*. In the next three years, some 284 such articles appeared, as politicians and journalists of various persuasions debated the crime issue. Immediately after Hoover's election, however, with no decrease in the actual incidence of crime, the relevant articles listed in *Reader's Guide* dropped to 257, then to 211 in the next three-year period, and finally, from 1935-1937, to no more than 127. No doubt the diminished public interest in the issue reflected a general belief that something "had been done" about the "crime problem." The "something" was in part the election of Hoover himself, but perhaps even more significant was his appointment of a special commission on "law observance and enforcement," better known as the Wickersham Commission. This body surveyed the crime situation in 1929 and made its recommendations to the President. It is not clear to what extent, if any, the Commission's work actually affected the control of crime, but it apparently had some effect on calming public opinion (Leonard and More, 1967).

The publication pattern in *Reader's Guide* for the more recent anti-crime movement is similar, though the actual numbers of articles are quite different because of a change in the cataloging policies of this reference work. From 1963 to 1965 there were 99 articles listed on the crime issue, a number which increased to 176 in the next three years. In the election year of 1968 alone, there were some 222 crime-related articles, reflecting the heavy emphasis which this issue was receiving at its height of popularity (Block, 1971). In the two succeeding years, 1969-1971, the number of articles dropped to some 150. Because this movement is so close to us in time and so relevant to our present concerns about crime, it might be interesting to consider in more detail how it came about.

The Recent Crime Movement: Strategies and Tactics of Interest Groups

A number of different interest and pressure groups have been responsible for generating the most recent anti-crime movement, which has continued, although somewhat attenuated, into the 1970's. Focusing originally upon the campus and racial disturbances of the mid-1960's, the movement expanded its focus to a more general one of "law and order" after those initial disturbances began to diminish (Furstenberg, 1971; Cipes, 1968). Political campaigns of various kinds and citizens' groups at various levels made their contributions to the collective definition that there was a "crime problem."

Political and Civic Enterprises

It is understandable that political parties and candidates want to appeal to the principal concerns of voters and to represent themselves as effective champions of those concerns. The effect of such legitimate political activity, however, in the case of crime, is sometimes to magnify public concern. Where there are relatively few issues in a campaign, the one or two most volatile ones are especially likely to be emphasized and to be uppermost in the minds of the voters (Block, 1971). These observations seem especially applicable to the issue of crime in the political campaigns of 1968. Even though a presidential Commission on Law Enforcement and Administration of Justice, just the year before, had reported that there was no real "crime wave" in the 1960's (Cipes, 1968), the crime issue became one of the major concerns of the campaign.

The more conservative (but not necessarily Republican) candidates in 1968 were the more likely to fasten onto the "crime issue." George Wallace received his loudest applause whenever he discussed the "law-and-order" theme (Cipes, 1968). Gerald Ford, then a congressman campaigning for the Republican Party, was quoted by *U.S. News & World Report* (1967:48) as criticizing the courts for leniency: ". . . [the courts] should uphold the rights of law-abiding citizens with the same fervor as they uphold the rights of the accused." After the withdrawal of Lyndon Johnson from the 1968 campaign, and the optimistic promises of the Republicans about ending the Viet-Nam War, the only other issue left was the "crime" war, which quickly became the main target of the Republican campaign (Cipes, 1968). Richard Nixon, in a *Reader's Digest* article near the time of the presidential election, made the following statement, now so ironic in retrospect:

. . . America has become among the most lawless and violent in the history of free peoples . . . [with a] decline in respect for public authority and the rule of law . . . [Criminals have been turned loose] to prey on an innocent society . . . [and] immediate and decisive force must be the first response. (Nixon, 1967:49)

Such statements by public figures who "ought to know" contributed to the collective public perceptions that there was a "crime problem," and, in turn, contributed to the election of those who were making the statements. Governor Nelson Rockefeller, in his campaign for re-election in New York State during the same period, portrayed the "drug problem" as the major cause of violence in his state: "Tens of thousands of innocent victims are robbed, mugged, and murdered by those addicted" (Leary, 1973); and he promised to defend the public against such violence if re-elected. Even Mayor John Lindsay of New York, generally considered a liberal, associated himself with a "drive against prostitution" pushed by the Times Square Development Council and certain women's organizations in 1972. After much publicity and agitation, and a few "dragnet" arrests, the mayor and the Council simply defined the problem as "cleaned up" and went back to their business, while prostitution continued unabated, though more discreetly. This outcome seemed to justify the prediction of an unruffled brothel operator during the campaign that the "church will go before we go!" (Sheehy, 1972b).

Aside from campaigns for political office, there are many other political enterprises to combat crime by civic groups, which are sometimes morally motivated, and usually local or regional in scope. Frequently such civic groups are of long standing, such as Parent-Teacher Associations or churches, and are periodically aroused to action by specific moral or criminal issues, such as a rash of sexual attacks (Sutherland, 1969). Other groups are more *ad hoc* in nature, originating in a response to a specific and temporary "problem." After the problem is defined as solved, the group usually disbands, as was the case with the anti-prostitution crusade mentioned above (Sheehy, 1972; Cipes, 1968). Sometimes, however, an *ad hoc* group remains alive and refocuses its concerns. An example here would be the Indianapolis Women's Anti-Crime Crusade formed in the late 1960's by concerned middle-class women in the wake of the purse-snatching and savage beating of an elderly psychologist (Remsberg, 1968). When police surveillance of the streets seemed to bring an end to the original "problem" of street crime, the Crusade branched out into such activities as youth drop-out counseling, community surveillance of public parks, self-help programs for the city's disadvantaged, and other services.

The recruits and activists of these organizations differ somewhat according to the nature of the civic group in question. As in the above Indianapolis and New York City cases, *ad hoc* groups addressed to ephemeral and/or "victimless" crimes tend to recruit solid middle- and upper-middle-class people. On the other hand, citizen bands aimed at preventing recurrent predatory crimes will be more likely to recruit from lower-income neighborhoods which are subject to an especially large amount of such crime. An example here would be the so-called vigilante groups (citizen patrols or self-defense bands), about whom the following observation has been made:

For many young, lower-status males, a group's symbols of authority—badges, uniforms, and such—provide a sense of respect and responsibility ordinarily unavailable to them. . . . The desire for novelty and the opportunity to act out *machismo* fantasies also prompt persons to join. . . . (Marx and Archer, 1973:47)

Joiners of the highest status are likely to be associated with the civic and church groups that have long standing. This has been found to be true on a relative basis even in ghetto areas (Remsberg, 1968). Such persons usually have more leisure time to give to the organizations and perhaps stronger vested interests in "solving the problem." Leaders of these various kinds of civic and religious groups tend to be representative of the joiners, with perhaps even stronger commitments.

The success of such civic and political groups depends largely on getting their "problems" legitimized, i.e., generally accepted as problems by public opinion; and the legitimization of a problem largely depends, in turn, on the legitimacy which the public accords to the organization(s) promoting it. Well-established civic groups and churches, of course, enjoy a certain "built-in" and long-standing legitimacy, which lends greater credibility to their definitions of "problems." *Ad hoc* civic groups, especially if they are of only marginal status such as vigilante groups, have a much harder time getting legitimized. Of course, the legitimacy and credibility of any interest group gets a boost if it focuses on a condition which has already received a great deal of public support and concern. Thus, a public already disposed to believe that there has been a "wave of street crime" will accord greater legitimacy to a civic group formed to fight crime of that kind. It usually takes a scandal of the magnitude of a "Watergate," however, to arouse much public interest in an organization or movement aimed at reducing white-collar crime.

Public acceptance of a civic-interest group and its "problem" also is greatly enhanced by the effectiveness of a group in (1) forming strategic coalitions; and (2) disseminating persuasive material through the media. In the Indianapolis Crusade, for example, the women formed coalitions with merchants by distributing literature for them on the shoplifting problem; with the police, by supporting their efforts for increased salaries; and with local neighborhood improvement units, by helping with clean-up campaigns. Churches, likewise, have been urged to enlist support for their public positions by placing competent church members on the boards and councils of secular agencies; pressuring political leaders to improve services to youth; and inviting judges, probation officers, police, and social workers to participate in church study groups (Hissong, 1968).

As for a group's dissemination of persuasive information to publicize its cause, Sutherland has observed, in connection with the campaign for sexual psychopath laws mentioned above, that:

. . . The diffusion of sexual psychopathic laws consequently has occurred under the following conditions: a state of fear developed, to some extent, by the general, nationwide, popular literature and made explicit by a few spectacular sex crimes. . . . (Sutherland, 1969:79)

Following this example, the Indianapolis Women's Anti-Crime Crusade held a series of discussion groups, in which women brought scrapbooks depicting common and spectacular crimes against women, in order to "show" the seriousness of the crime problem (Remsberg, 1968).

Economic Enterprises

Two kinds of economic interests converge to promote anti-crime crusades in the public mind. The first of these might be called the "loser interests," referring to industries and organizations which stand to incur losses from criminal behavior on the part of employees or outside predators. The second might be considered the "gainer" interests, by which we mean those organizations or enterprises that stand to gain in moral or economic support through their efforts to reduce crime or to supply crime fighters. An example of "loser" activity would be the collaboration that developed in Dallas among a group of store owners after a rash of armed robberies occurred (*U.S. News & World Report,* 1970). Their efforts involved not only mutual exchange of information and protection, but also combined support for publicity about their plight, in an effort to get greater community (and police) assistance. The by-product of such activity, of course, was increased public perception that there was a local crime problem.

Chicago has had an Association of Commerce and Industry organized since 1919, which has been particularly active in defining the crime problems in that city, one of its successful efforts having been the funding and organizing of the Chicago Crime Commission. In 1967, more than half-a-million pieces of literature were disseminated there to business employees in order to educate them on the crime problems of the business community. The merchants of Chicago have also promoted a "Crime-Stop" campaign, in which, among other things, they distributed 800,000 wallet reference cards describing the individual citizen's responsibilities in the "crime problem" (*Nation's Business,* 1967).

Sometimes the "loser" interests will finance special efforts by other bodies to promote the "truth" about the crime problem. Thus Indianapolis businessmen during the 1960's raised and contributed $12,000 a year to finance a Law Enforcement Committee to search out the causes and cures for the local "crime problem." Without making it public, businessmen will sometimes also contribute money to law enforcement agencies for "special" police activities (*Nation's Business,* 1967). In Washington, D.C., the Board of Trade, in alliance with a bankers' association, has been actively lobbying with government agencies and Congress to promote their definition of the "crime problem." Letters to congressmen and public officials, speeches to community groups, and full-page ads in local newspapers are among the tactics being used here (Cipes, 1968).

A clear example of "gainers'" activities can be seen in the case of an Atlanta firm that specializes in the sale of burglar alarms. It also runs full-page ads which appeal strongly to public fears about burglars, and it maintains a list of individuals and companies recently burglarized to which its salesmen are regularly referred for good sales leads—rather the equivalent of "ambulance chasing" by unscrupulous lawyers (Alpren, 1972). Police-equipment manufacturers use similar practices for the promotion of their products.

Some "gainers" are found in academic life, rather than in the business world. In order to promote the continuation of funds from the Law Enforcement Assistance Administration in 1972, the Southern Association of Criminal Justice Educators lobbied in Congress and disseminated information to the public on the seriousness of the "crime problem," and the need for continued public funding of enterprises like their own.

For somewhat different reasons, then, both those enterprises which stand to lose from crime, and those which gain from public concern about the existence of crime, can promote public perceptions that crime is a "serious social problem."

Police Enterprise

As we have indicated briefly in the section of this chapter on occupational interest groups, the police face a continuing need to have their activities looked upon by the public as vitally important. In an effort to maintain this image, the police frequently use both a "positive" and a "negative" approach in their community relations efforts. The positive approach consists of a variety of strategies to gain public esteem and appreciation, while the negative approach plays upon public fears of crime and criminals. From the latter point of view, of course, a "crime wave" is advantageous to the police, for it causes an anxious public to look to the police as its chief protection from criminals. Kamisar (1969) has observed that the police strategy with regard to crime waves must be a delicate one; it requires that the public believe that there really is a crime wave, but not blame the police for it. A common police device is to lay the blame on the courts for "letting criminals go" and claim that they (the police) must be given greater authority and prerogatives (Levine, 1970; Kamisar, 1969). The public must also be made to see that the police are simply responding faithfully to citizen needs and demands for more protection, rather than fostering a "scare campaign" (Bayley and Mendelsohn, 1969). One way to convince the public is by the selective presentation of crime statistics, as we have observed earlier (Black, 1970; Conner, 1972). A classic example of the negative or fear-generating approach is considered in greater detail in the chapter on drugs: the energetic entrepreneurship of H. J. Anslinger and the Bureau of Narcotics in the 1930's to outlaw marijuana (Becker, 1963). The Bureau began by "alerting" local law enforcement agencies across the country to the new evil of marijuana-smoking. Then came an extensive "educational campaign" to inform the public of the evil effects of this weed. Horrid episodes were recounted in the mass media of crimes by dope-crazed marijuana users, as, for example, one in which a young marijuana "addict (sic) with an ax had killed his father, mother, two brothers and a sister . . ." (Becker, 1963:142). At local levels, as we have already seen, the selective presentation of statistics about police activities can arouse a fearful public, which the police can then mollify with new statistics about their intensified clean-up activities. When "crackdowns" occur, they are often directed against various kinds of powerless "undesirables," such as drunks, drifters, and vagrants, who make easy additions to arrest statistics after having been labeled by police as "potential" troublemakers (Cipes, 1968; Quinney, 1970b; Wilson, 1968).

New York City in the late 1960's witnessed a good example of effective local police public relations in the case of the Civilian Review Board issue. The mayor and city government had instituted the Civilian Review Board to exercise some surveillance over police activity in 1966, in response to complaints, especially from minority groups, about police harassment and brutality. Subsequently, however, the Patrolmen's Benevolent Association in the city succeeded in gathering more than the required 45,000 petition signatures to place the issue of the Review Board on a referendum ballot. Then began the campaign to win over the public:

> The major thrust of the PBA's campaign was the growing menace of crime in the streets, and what the PBA saw as the Civilian Review Board threat to deprive the police of the support and confidence they needed if they were to be effective. (Bellush and David, 1971:78)

The PBA campaign was very effective: civilian review boards were voted down by 60 percent to 36 percent. Police political activities, based upon such public appeals, are used in many other ways, such as pressuring legislatures for heavier penalties for assaulting an officer, or for other special penalties, and for increased police benefits (More, 1967).

Styles and Problems of Law Enforcement as an Occupation

It would be a great mistake, and a disservice to the police, however, to create the impression that the principal approach of the police to community relations is the negative one of juggling statistics and engendering fear. Indeed, such police behavior is not often relied upon, and can be quite counterproductive. If police constantly point to the rising crime statistics, they must run the risk that at least some of the public will blame them for what has happened, which would undermine the whole function of such police publicity (Skolnick, 1967; Hudson, 1970; Black and Riess, 1967). Actually, it is more common for the police to try quite hard to assess community expectations realistically and to work accordingly. Variations in community needs and expectations result in one of three general models or "styles" of police operation, though sometimes they may be mixed (Banton, 1964; Wilson, 1968).

First is the "watchman" style of enforcement, which is most appropriate for the smaller and more homogeneous rural communities, where conformity primarily occurs in response to informal social pressures, rather than to fear of formal sanctions. In such places, the police can simply stand by to serve in unusually severe cases or emergencies and keep a generally "low profile." Second is the "legalistic" style, which is common in the larger and more complex urban communities. This style is characterized by an impersonal, bureaucratic kind of police behavior, the effectiveness of which is judged not so much by the maintenance of order as by the number of arrests. In case of difficulty, police are likely to fall back on acting "by the book," rather than according to personal judgments. Finally, the third style is the "service" style, common to quiet, homogeneous middle-class suburban areas, where criminal activity seems relatively sparse. Here the police attempt to function as real "professionals" and to render a variety of social services having little or nothing to do with actual law enforcement. This "service" style of police work has lately become more common also in many urban areas, as part of an effort to enhance the image of the police there (Wilson, 1968). Such differential police behavior must be understood not only as trying to adapt to specific community needs, but also as trying to elicit maximum support from community opinion for the appropriateness of their behavior in that community (President's Commission on the Causes and Prevention of Violence, 1969).

In their attempts to serve their communities in such a way as to maximize public support, however, the police face a number of difficulties and complications inherent in their roles and in their organizational structure. One problem is that the successful accomplishment of a certain goal may produce undesirable but unavoidable side effects. For instance, the need to produce a fast, mobile "strike force" for ghettos and other high-crime areas has come from a combination of a shortage of staff and an acuteness of certain manifestations of crime. The "strike-force" concept, then, is an alternative to the saturation of certain areas with large numbers of "stand-by" police. However, when strike forces encounter residents, they tend to do so under conditions of stress and emotion, with the result that the community sees the police mainly at their meanest, while the police see the residents at their most volatile and suspicious, and mutual stereotyping is the inevitable outcome (Kuykendall, 1970). This is only one example of the more general problem of "cross-rippling," in which undesirable side effects, usually harmful to police relations with the community, come from legitimate police efforts to do their job (Wilson, 1972; Gourley, 1970). The stereotyping is especially unfortunate, since it tends to predispose mutual expectations and influence the definitions of other encounter situations (Garmire, 1970).

Public stereotyping complicates another "occupational hazard" of the police, namely the loose and undefined nature of many police encounters. Most police work does not occur in situations that are strictly defined by the law, and provide no room for flexibility in the officers' responses (Wilson, 1968; LaFave, 1965; Black, 1970). Officers must usually, then, rely on their own assessments of a situation and of a citizen under scrutiny, and they must mediate between a citizen's right to civil liberties and their own responsibilities as guardians of the public order. Under such pressures, many officers simply fall back on their role of formal authority, thereby increasing tension and the likelihood of an altercation (Hudson, 1970; Goffman, 1959). If an altercation occurs, the officer may then feel compelled to arrest the person on some "catch-all" law such as disturbing the peace (Hudson, 1970; Chevigny, 1969; Black and Riess, 1965). This contributes negatively to police efforts to maintain community support. Instead of relying mainly on such support for their sense of mission, importance, and self-esteem,

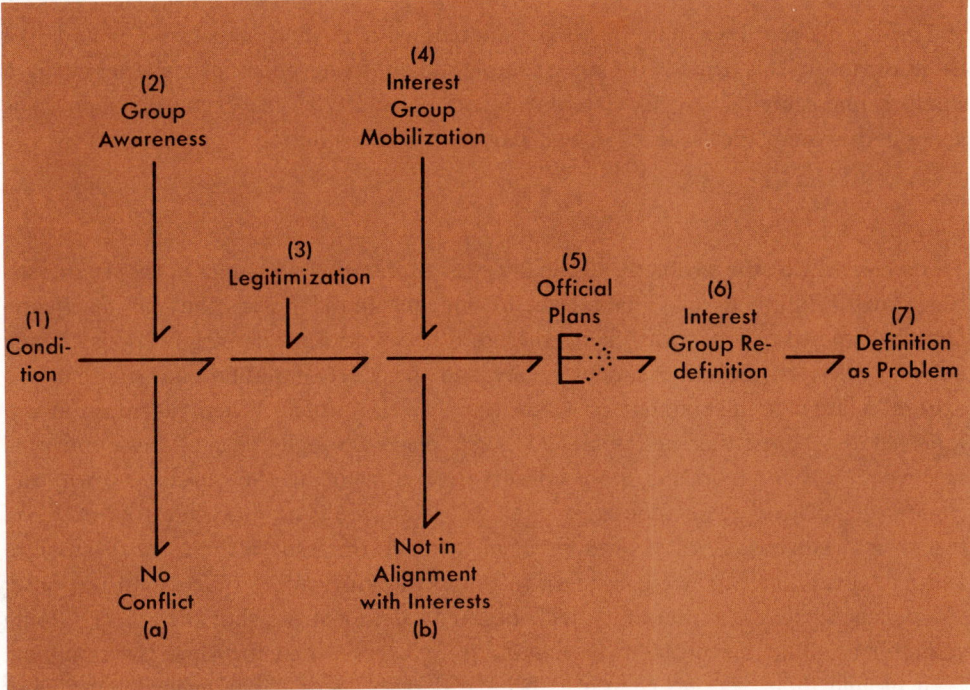

Figure 3-4 Composite Rendering of Two Models of the Development of a Crime Problem
SOURCE: Sutherland (1969) and Blumer (1971)

therefore, there is a tendency on the part of police officers to look instead to their own organization for such rewards; this, in turn, increases their isolation from the community, and leads to attempts to try to manipulate the community through some of the means we have discussed above (Skolnick, 1967; Hudson, 1970).

The Natural History of Crime Movements

Edwin Sutherland (1969) and Herbert Blumer (1971) have both offered kinds of "life-cycle" models of the process by which a crime *condition* comes to be defined as a crime *problem*. Sutherland uses the sexual-psychopath problem as his illustration. These models resemble the natural-history model being employed in this book. A composite of the Sutherland and Blumer models is summarized in Figure 3-4, which shows, first, the recognition of the condition by one or more interest groups, and then public spread of such recognition and concern. The original interest group(s), if they are not to remain a "dissident few," must arouse and mobilize other interest groups, in coalition with whom they pressure public opinion and the establishment for action, usually in the form of new laws or restrictions. This model is intended to apply either to national or local levels.

Turning to our own natural-history model, with its five stages, we would like to illustrate it this time with an example taken from personal experience in a small Tennessee city. In this city, during the early 1970's, a "crime problem" was generated around the issue of drugs, particularly marijuana.

Incipiency

The *incipiency* of the problem, ironically, was marked by a change in the Tennessee state laws relating to marijuana use, in which "simple possession" of marijuana (one-half ounce or less) was changed from a felony to a misdemeanor. This change actually reflected the enforcement policy and the level of public concern that had existed relative to marijuana for some time, i.e., minimal. When the mass media reported the "loosening up" that had taken place through the new law, murmurs began to be heard from the more conservative citizenry in the observed town, and rumors began to spread about the "addicts" who would now be free to "prey" on the upright citizens. Church groups began to make the issue a topic for discussion, and to express their growing concern to the local enforcement officers. In response, the police, sensing a community will, began to demonstrate that they were "doing something" about the problem by making more arrests than they had been making, even though there was no reason to believe that the actual incidence of marijuana use had changed. The arrests, significantly, were almost entirely of students at the local college, whom "everybody knew" to be the chief marijuana users. Children of local citizens were very rarely arrested.

Coalescence

In order for a few church groups and prominent citizens to become an actual movement, however, it was necessary for them to form some alliances with other legitimized groups in the community, such as the PTA, additional church groups, and some women's organizations. This was the beginning of *coalescence,* and delegates from the town coalition began to consult with both the town's police chief and the county sheriff about a "crash program" of education and tightened enforcement. The coalescence was gradually broadened at the same time by the addition of new kinds of interests, such as prominent local merchants concerned about the theft which was sure to occur as the "addicts" looked for ways to support their habit. (Actually, it later came out that users of marijuana and other drugs there were supported almost entirely by "pushing.") The police, meanwhile, intensified their arrest efforts even more, thus producing horrifying statistics on the growing "problem."

Institutionalization

The growing coalition was eventually given official recognition by the mayor's office and by other local politicians, who joined in sponsoring and planning "crackdowns" and "roundups" with such catchy slogans as "Operation Impel" and "Operation Search." It may or may not have been coincidental that the two operations were launched a month before the political incumbents involved were up for re-election. Such official sponsorship was indicative of the *institutionalization* of the movement. This institutionalization was developed (and the "problem" partly co-opted) by the preparation and implementation of three new programs which were a result of the combined efforts of city government and civic groups: (1) an expanded educational program in the schools to warn the children of the evils of drug use; (2) the elevation of drug investigations to first priority by the police; and (3) the petitioning of the courts to levy the heaviest permissible penalties on those convicted of drug offenses.

Fragmentation and Demise

Fragmentation of the movement began soon, however. The three new programs had to compete with each other for public funds and other resources, and the police won out when they succeeded in persuading the city government to eliminate the other programs and assign all available resources to them, so that they could do "the kind of job" which the community required. Groups with vested interests in the abandoned programs were angered by these developments and began to lose their zeal. Some of the most zealous were further disenchanted with the movement when the police, with their renewed support and official vote of confidence, began arresting the high-school children of prominent citizens, as well as college students. The withdrawal of support from these formerly interested groups eventually brought about the complete *demise* of the movement.

Thus, in accordance with the postulate of Blumer (1971) and of this book, that "problems" exist as a matter of collective definition, rather than as "objective" realities, the arrests for marijuana use and sale dropped from 47 during the first half of 1972 to only 4 during the second half of the same year. By every other available indication, the incidence of marijuana possession and related offenses had remained quite stable during the entire "crisis." The mass media and the citizenry took the changes in arrest figures to mean that the problem had been "solved," as indeed it had been by process of collective definition. The police, however, knew of certain other explanations for the change, including their own desire to escape the criticism of former allies and prominent citizens for some of the arrests they had been making.

THE LEGACY OF THE CRIME MOVEMENTS

Much of the legacy of the history of crime in our society takes the form of an accumulation of folklore and general attitudes about criminals and their activities. This process has been going on for a long time, of course, and did not start just with the "law-and-order" period of the 1960's and 1970's. Our culture has always had a certain ambivalence about some crimes and a certain selective moral outrage about criminals, for as far back as there are records. For the most part, we have thought of our "crime problem" in terms of the vicious and wanton predatory attacks against persons or property by criminals who are pathological in some sense: "drug-crazed" or drunk, sexually perverted, desperately deprived, and so on. We have tended to look upon organized crime and white-collar crime as somehow more understandable in motivation than these "pathological" crimes, and therefore not quite so reprehensible. The "Robin Hood" legend, after all, is nearly a thousand years old, and many more recent criminal characters, like Jesse James, have taken on some of the Robin Hood traits, i.e., basically good-hearted people who have tried to avoid killing except when forced to do so, and have dealt kindly with the poor. It would be greatly overstating the point to say that we have actually condoned organized and white-collar crime, but we have tended to see a certain heroism in some of these criminals, and we have not generally considered them a significant part of our "crime problem." One has only to recall the recent portrayals of criminal figures in films and books, such as *The Godfather,* to see the mixture of fascination, sympathy and horror which has been typical of our outlook on organized crime; or the generally sympathetic handling of the "criminal" characters in the *Flim-Flam Man* or *Paper Moon* which reflects our outlook on white-collar crime.

At the same time, we have glorified the police in our numerous books, movies, and television programs about them. The enormous popularity of police programs, from the early age of radio to the present age of television, testifies to the fascination with which we view their work and the support which most Americans are ready to offer their "local police" and FBI heroes, and the like. While we are glad to see them win their "fight against crime" in most of these portrayals, we are happiest when their victory is against the "vicious" street criminals. When they are struggling against organized and white-collar crime, the issues are often not as clear-cut.

In more recent years, this mentality, which shows a certain ambivalence and indulgence for some kinds of crime, and certainly for "folk crimes" like traffic offenses, but which demands that you "support your local police" against street crime, has come to be included in the term "silent majority." This term emerged in the vocabulary of establishment politicians during the "crime problem" of the

1960's, and it refers to that great mass of "middle America" which has been keeping quiet and working hard all these years, only to be assaulted by hippies, racial extremists, and political radicals full of envy for and unjustified hostility toward the American way of life. While these "noisy minorities" have been making "non-negotiable demands" and tearing up society, the "silent majority" has been plugging along and trying to keep the peace. They have finally gotten "fed up" and have risen up to elect public officials who will crack down on all this mayhem and restore "law and order" to our society. This mentality, which has been identified and measured repeatedly in public-opinion polls in recent years, is one of the most important cultural and social legacies of the "crime problem" of the 1960's. It has had an enormous impact not only on our political life, but also on our media and other institutions.

The "silent majority," however, has not been without opposition. Civil libertarians, led especially by the ACLU, have consistently invoked the tradition of "due process" and equal application of the law, both in their publicity and in court defenses of certain defendants who seemed to be victimized by the "silent majority's" zeal for law and order. At the same time, organizations devoted to the support and protection of dissenters and racial minorities, who have been victims of police misbehavior or judicial miscarriage, have also come out of the tumultuous sixties. Some of these have been of an *ad hoc* nature, as in the case of support for the "Chicago Seven," while others, such as the Black Panthers, are of a more enduring variety.

In more formal ways, the "crime problem" of the 1960's and 1970's has left us a legacy of considerable political and judicial importance. Since the election of 1968, there has been a considerable shift in emphasis toward a harder line in the government's approach to crime. There has been a phasing out of the functions (and even existence) of the Office of Economic Opportunity, once conceived of as a great help in the prevention of crime through the alleviation of misery and the creation of jobs, while more funding and official support have been given to drug prevention and enforcement programs and to programs such as the Law Enforcement Assistance Administration, which strengthen the training and effectiveness of enforcement personnel around the country. In the same vein, the Warren Burger-led Supreme Court, largely appointed by President Nixon, has handed down some significant decisions reversing much of the impact of the earlier Warren Court, regarded by the "silent majority" as too soft and permissive. For example, by a vote of 8 to 1, the Supreme Court in mid-1974 reversed some of the impact of the 1966 *Miranda* decision, by ruling that in certain situations, prosecutors could use evidence indirectly obtained from defendants who had not been fully informed of their rights (the *Miranda* decision had established a virtually absolute privilege against self-incrimination for persons in custody, even prior to court proceedings). The courts also have allowed the reinstatement of police practices formerly considered an infringement of privacy, such as "preventive detention" and the "no-knock entry" (*Newsweek,* 1973).

Other important outcomes of the "silent majority's" reaction to the 1960's have been (1) the "overcriminalization" of certain life-styles or forms of behavior which are largely "victimless" or have little social impact. The condemnation of drug use, particularly marijuana, is one example of this; the continued harassment of homosexuals in many of our cities is another. (2) An increase in the support for police establishments: larger salaries, better and more equipment, higher educational standards for police officers, and so on. These have not, of course, occurred universally or been equally distributed, but they have characterized most of our larger cities. (3) A tendency on the parts of legislative bodies, both federal and state, to increase penalties for certain kinds of crimes, rather than to continue an earlier trend (from the 1950's and early 1960's) relying more on "preventive measures" to reduce crime.

As of the mid-1970's, the "crime situation" is still very much in flux. There are survivals of earlier, more "liberal" and libertarian traditions in our courts and legislatures, but at the same time the impact of the "silent majority" is still being felt, and will doubtless continue to be for some time. In the future, collective definition of "the crime problem" probably will undergo some change, and will give heavier emphasis to white-collar crime as a result of the Watergate revelations, the impact of which is only starting to be felt.

Chapter 4
Juvenile Delinquency

THE SOCIAL CONSTRUCTION OF REALITY
Delinquency and Relativity

> At present, it is predicted that one out of every six boys will end up in court for other than traffic offenses sometime before his 18th birthday.... (HEW, 1969:2)

He is 16, of Spanish descent with long, slicked-back hair and the look of poverty in his dress. The room had cost him nearly a day's wages, so he was making it look as presentable as possible. He did not want her to be turned off by the somewhat dank smell of the cheap motel room. After a while she showed, looking quite striking in her short miniskirt, long black hair, and flashing dark eyes.

This scene, which could be an instance of juvenile delinquency in this country, is a typical method by which youth in parts of Mexico begin their "free union." After spending the night together, they will go to his parents' home and begin living together under their supervision. If the arrangement proves satisfactory, they will eventually be married. (See Cavan and Cavan, 1968.) In the United States, a country whose mores and laws evolved out of English common law, this episode would exemplify for many the "decadence" of today's youth. Adult complaints about youthful "decadence" arise in part, some would say, from a modern "generation gap," which goes beyond mere misunderstanding between the age groups to refer to gross differences in values and behavior. An extreme form of such a gap is noted by Yablonsky (1970:12):

> The distrust of adults by young rebels in the hip drop-out movement is clearly declared in the phrase that has become a facetious American platitude: "Never trust anyone over 30."

The seriousness of the official view on juvenile misbehavior was echoed by the special President's Commission (1967:37): "America's best hope for reducing crime is to reduce juvenile delinquency and youth crime...." In many other societies as well as our own, juvenile delinquency is a "social problem." Cavan and Cavan (1968) point out that, although the definitions of juvenile delinquency vary, nearly all cultures have a long tradition of the problem. One might well ask how delinquency is defined in our society, and how widespread it is. The relativity in the answers to such questions can be seen in the following list (compiled by Sussman, 1959) of behaviors that are included in the definition of delinquency from state to state, though no one state uses all of the items on the list:

1/ (A juvenile delinquent is one who) violates any law or ordinance;
2/ (Who is) habitually truant;
3/ (Knowingly) associates with thieves, vicious or immoral persons;
4/ Incorrigible;
5/ Beyond control of parent or guardian;
6/ Growing up in idleness or crime;
7/ So deports self as to injure self or others;
8/ Absents self from home (without just cause) without consent;
9/ Immoral or indecent conduct;
10/ (Habitually) uses vile, obscene, or vulgar language (in public places);
11/ (Knowingly) enters, visits house of ill repute;
12/ Patronizes, visits policy shop or gaming place;
13/ (Habitually) wanders about railroad yards or tracks;
14/ Jumps train or enters car or engine without authority;
15/ Patronizes saloon or dram house where intoxicating liquor is sold;
16/ Wanders streets at night, not on lawful business;
17/ Patronizes public poolroom or bucket shop;
18/ Immoral conduct around school (or in public place);
19/ Engages in illegal occupation;
20/ In occupation or situation dangerous or injurious to self or others;
21/ Smokes cigarettes (or uses tobacco in any form);
22/ Frequents place the existence of which violates the law;
23/ Is found (in place for permitting of which) adult may be punished;
24/ Addicted to drugs;
25/ Disorderly;
26/ Begging;
27/ Uses intoxicating liquor;
28/ Makes indecent proposal;
29/ Loiters, sleeps in alleys, vagrant;
30/ Runs away from state or charity institution;
31/ Found on premises occupied or used for illegal purposes;
32/ Operates motor vehicle dangerously while under the influence of liquor;

33/ Attempts to marry without consent, in violation of law;
34/ Given to sexual irregularities.
(As quoted by Kittrie, 1971:119)

Parameters of Reality

The conception of juvenile delinquency in the United States was developed from English common law, in which juveniles were not legally responsible for their actions until the age of seven. From seven to fourteen, youths were capable of intention to commit antisocial behavior, unless evidence demonstrated that a youth was immature (Cohen and Short, 1971). The main point of the English conception was that youth should not be subject to the same laws as adults; they should receive separate treatment, "rehabilitation" instead of "punishment." The main focus of juvenile law in Britain and the United States has been on what is best for the youngster, rather than on the protection of society. Implied is the belief that young people are not truly capable of "hard core" criminality as adults are. One may expect a youth to deviate a bit ("boys will be boys"); but the strongest sanctions of the state are to be used sparingly and only in cases of extreme youthful deviance.

Foremost in the definition of juvenile delinquency, then, is that it is deviant behavior by *juveniles*. In most parts of the United States, a "juvenile" is younger than 16 or 18. "Delinquent" behavior may be classified into three broad categories. The first includes those behaviors which are "mal in se," or bad by their very nature, and which would be criminal even if committed by adults. Examples are murder, rape, robbery, and larceny. A second category includes behaviors which are permitted adults, but are defined as delinquent for youth, such as curfew violation, drinking, truancy, and some types of sexual license, which are considered harmful or undesirable for the youths themselves rather than for society. A third category includes a very broad and vague set of behaviors, also delinquent for youth only, but regarded as a threat to established authority, such as general incorrigibility, "negativeness," and disrespect for authority. In this last category are often youths for whom the state feels it must take some preventive action, including sometimes total custody, because of "undesirable" conditions at home.

Sometimes, indeed, a youth having "unfit parents" will be made a "ward of the state" even if he has never committed any of the offenses mentioned in any of these three categories, and he will likely be handled by the same authorities, and have many of the same restrictions placed upon him, as regular "delinquents." After the youth reaches adult age, he or she is no longer held responsible, in most states, for offenses committed as a juvenile. The record is usually retired to a "dead file" and not consulted again.

Though the behavior of delinquents often has a prankster-like quality, they are certainly capable of serious offenses. Winslow (1969) presents 1965 data from

TABLE 4-1 PERCENT OF CRIME BY TYPE OF CRIME, 11 TO 17 YEARS OF AGE

Type of Crime	
Willful homicide	8.4
Forcible rape	19.8
Robbery	28.0
Aggravated assault	14.2
Burglary	47.7
Larceny	49.2
Motor vehicle theft	61.4

Source: Uniform Crime Report, FBI, Department of Justice, Washington, D.C., 1965 (unpublished)

the Uniform Crime Report (unpublished) which indicate that 18.3 percent of all willful homicide, forcible rape, robbery, and aggravated assault is committed by offenders under the age of 18. What is perhaps more surprising is that over half of all burglary, larceny, and motor vehicle theft is committed by juveniles. About 1 percent of violent acts like murder, rape, and assault are committed by persons under ten! When the data are taken from self-reports of delinquent behavior, instead of from official records, we find that nearly 90 percent of all youths report offenses for which they could have been brought to court (Winslow, 1969). Thus, the actual incidence of juvenile delinquency may far exceed official figures. (See Table 4-1. See also Gould, 1969, and Short and Nye, 1957.)

There is reason also, from official records, to believe that delinquency is on the increase. In the Uniform Crime Reports (UCR), the percentage of homicide, rape, robbery, and aggravated assault committed by juveniles rose from 18 percent to 23 percent from 1965 to 1970. The percentage of burglary, larceny, and motor vehicle theft committed by juveniles in that period stayed at around 51 percent. Spielberger (1971), in looking at an earlier period, found a 103 percent increase from 1958 to 1967 in the number of youths referred to Florida juvenile courts and a 23 percent increase in their commitment rate. Such increases may not, however, be as serious as they appear. As Spielberger himself points out, though the referrals in Florida (1958 to 1967) did increase 103 percent, at least an 85 percent increase could have been predicted based entirely upon the changing age structure of the state; that is, the cohort of "high risk" aged youngsters increased relative to the other ages. Thus, while there has been some increase in juvenile delinquency, the extent of that increase is open to question.

The literature on juvenile delinquency indicates that a number of social background factors are related to it, including sex, socio-economic status, broken homes, number of siblings, school failure, poverty, race, and age (Ohr, 1972). Psychological characteristics like self-concept and the perceived expectations of others have also been implicated in delinquency.

Chapter 4 / Juvenile Delinquency

TABLE 4-2 DELINQUENT REFERRALS BY AGE, RACE, AND SEX

Age	Race and Sex						Total
	White Male-Female		Negro Male-Female		Chicano Male-Female		
11 year old	3	0	2	0	1	0	6
12 year old	6	0	5	0	5	1	17
13 year old	12	6	2	1	3	0	24
14 year old	22	12	4	4	8	2	52
15 year old	21	14	5	5	6	2	53
16 year old	39	13	8	5	5	3	73
Total	103	45	26	15	28	8	225

Source: Unpublished Report, Tarrant County Juvenile Probation Department, Fort Worth, Texas, November, 1972

With respect to sex, for example, Winslow (1969) in reviewing the UCR reports for 1965, found that boys were five times as likely to be arrested as girls. Other data (e.g., Table 4-2) usually indicate similar disproportions between boys and girls. Also, while half of the girls are arrested for juvenile-only offenses, fully four-fifths of the boys arrested have committed an act that would be criminal for adults.

McKay and Kobrin (1966) found that the incidence of delinquency and crime increased the closer one approached to the center of a city. Thus, the number of delinquents toward the center of Chicago approach ten per hundred, while at the outer ring (ten miles from the center), only two of one hundred boys had been arrested.

The Gluecks found that 60 percent of 500 delinquents they studied came from broken homes, compared to only 34 percent of 500 nondelinquents (Glueck, 1963). Bowlby (1952) found that mother separation was related both to mental illness and to juvenile delinquency. Baker and Adams (1963) demonstrated in a study of glue-sniffers that 50 percent of them came from families with eight or more children, while only 18 percent of non-glue-sniffers had that many siblings. Glueck (1934) also demonstrated that sibling size was positively related to incidence of juvenile delinquency.

A variety of statistical reports like the one in Table 4-3 indicate that black children are more likely than white ones to become delinquent. There is much evidence, however, to indicate that race is not the decisive factor in black-white differences. When blacks and whites are compared within social class categories, the differences between them nearly disappear, indicating that class, rather than race, is what makes the difference. Many black children at present have lower-class origins. Earlier ethnic groups to occupy the lower class (e.g., Italians) have also

TABLE 4-3 DELINQUENT REFERRALS BY TYPE OF REFERRAL, RACE, AND SEX

Reason for Referral	White Male	White Female	Negro Male	Negro Female	Chicano Male	Chicano Female	Total
Murder	0	0	0	0	1	0	1
Robbery: Purse-Snatching	0	0	1	0	0	0	1
Aggravated Assault	1	0	2	3	1	0	7
Assault Exc. Aggravated	0	1	0	0	0	0	1
Burglary: Breaking or Entering	14	1	6	0	17	0	38
Auto Theft: Unauthorized Use	1	1	0	0	0	0	2
Auto Theft: Exc. Unauthorized Use	2	1	0	0	0	0	3
Larceny: Shoplifting	11	4	3	7	1	3	29
Larceny Exc. Shoplifting	6	1	4	0	0	0	11
Narcotics	1	2	0	0	0	0	3
Marijuana	19	3	1	0	0	0	23
Glue Sniffing	2	0	0	0	0	0	2
Drugs: Exc. Narcotic	2	0	0	0	0	0	2
Drunkenness	0	0	0	0	1	0	1
Disorderly Conduct	7	1	4	3	0	0	15
Vandalism	7	0	1	0	0	0	8
Runaway	15	25	3	1	0	3	47
Truancy	4	0	0	0	0	0	4
Curfew Violation	3	3	0	0	0	0	6
Paint Sniffing	4	0	0	0	4	2	10
Prowling	0	0	1	0	0	0	1
Witness to Murder	0	0	0	1	0	0	1
Illegal Entry	0	0	0	0	3	0	3
Courtesy Supervision	2	0	0	0	0	0	2
Arson	1	0	0	0	0	0	1
Fraud	0	1	0	0	0	0	1
Killing Domestic Animal	1	0	0	0	0	0	1
Forgery	0	1	0	0	0	0	1
Total	103	45	26	15	28	8	225

Source: Unpublished Report, Tarrant County Juvenile Probation Department, Fort Worth, Texas, November, 1972

had disproportionately high rates of crime and delinquency, no doubt for the same reason. Middle-class youngsters of all ethnic groups tend to have lower rates of delinquency than do lower-class youngsters.

Other factors, equally unrelated to race, have also contributed to the black tendency for high delinquency rates. Schwartz and Stryker (1970) have shown that white, middle-class teachers have tended to respond to black, lower-class children through stereotypes that have adversely affected their estimate of their ability to compete with middle-class peers in school. The teacher's evaluation of a youngster as a potential delinquent, as Reckless had also found, was not only a good predictor, but a self-fulfilling prophecy. Biases against nonwhite races in official statistics may also help to explain the relatively high rate of delinquency for blacks. Gould (1969) compared officially reported delinquency rates with self-reported rates, finding quite a discrepancy between the two. However, in the case of self-reported delinquent behavior, he found no differences among white, black, or Oriental boys.

Public Opinion and Juvenile Delinquency

The general public's concern about juvenile delinquency is demonstrated by the answer to a Gallup poll (April, 1972) question: "What should be done to reduce crime?" The second most frequent response was "More parental control." Another question asked of the public (Gallup, September, 1972) was "Which . . . would you like your elementary schools (grades 1-6) to give more attention to?" Third on the list was "Teaching students to respect law and authority." When the same question was asked for high schools, respect for law and authority was rated first, above learning. When Gallup (April, 1972) asked what the causes of crime were, third on the list of responses was "lack of supervision of parents." Other responses included "lack of responsibility among younger people" (eighth on the list). When Gallup asked what the major problem in education was today, the most common answer (18 percent) was "discipline." The same response was first on the list to the same question in December, 1970.

It appears, therefore, that the U.S. public not only believes that juvenile delinquency is a major problem, but also that the chief cause for this problem lies in a lack of discipline in the home and in the school. Unlike some of the other social problems discussed in this book, public opinion about the causes of delinquency receives considerable support from social scientists. A number of studies have found that discipline of a *fair and consistent kind* in the socialization or rearing process is very likely to produce a nondelinquent child (Nye, 1958; Slocum and Stone, 1963; and Lees and Newsome, 1954).

Having reviewed the nature and extent of juvenile delinquency as defined by official interest groups and public opinion, let us turn to an examination of the kinds of interest groups that have concerned themselves with this problem and what they have done about it.

CHAMPIONS AND THEIR INTERESTS

Warden Martin . . . placed two bricks at each end of the prison yard and giving the black baby two more, ordered him to carry them to one of the piles, lay them down, pick up the other two, which he in turn carried to the further end . . . and so on . . . all day long. . . . He served in all seventeen years and some months. (Powell, 1891:16)

It is only in relatively recent times that the kind of treatment described above for youthful offenders has been generally considered extreme or inappropriate. Though occasionally more "enlightened" voices were raised in protest from the earliest times, it was only toward the end of the last century that interest groups, especially moral interest groups, began to concern themselves extensively with juvenile delinquency and its cures. Since then, the approaches advocated for the solution of this social problem have tended to take either of two philosophical forms. The first of these might be called the "child-saver" approach; and more recently we have seen the rise of a "children's rights" orientation. A number of interest groups have espoused both philosophies.

Moral Interest Groups

The concern of the moral interest groups has been chiefly with the type of treatment which the juvenile offender has received. The central philosophy has been that the child is unable to comprehend the wrongness of his acts and needs to be treated as though he were ill, instead of being punished like a criminal. Anthony Platt's book, *The Child Savers* (1969), points out that moral indignation over the treatment of juveniles has been expressed by numerous groups in different ways. Homer Folks, for example, in an address to the National Conference of Charities and Corrections in 1891, pointed out that an "inherent evil of the reformatory system was its tendency to fasten an 'enduring stigma' on its inmates" (Platt, p. 62).

As early as 1787, the Philadelphia Society for Alleviating the Miseries of Public Prisons was advocating the removal of chlidren from the jails, a demand repeated a generation later (1819) by the Society for the Prevention of Pauperism, as well as other such groups. John Augustus, a Boston shoemaker, sought in the early 19th century to protect the child (as well as some adults) from being thrown into institutions with hardened criminals:

We desire something different from a House of Correction or Alms-house, in order to save an honest man (or child) from being thrust into a den of thieves and robbers. (Teeters and Reinemann, 1950:386)

The emphasis of the moral interest groups is thus on removing the child from the miseries of prisons, on rehabilitation and treatment rather than on punishment, and on insuring the welfare of the child.

In 1853, Charles Loring Brace founded the Children's Aid Society of New York, which was to be the first of a series of societies for the aid of children. Brace's main claim was that the children of New York were being uncared for by their parents and left to roam the streets; it was the bad influence of the city environment which was seen to be the cause of delinquency among the children of New York. The Children's Aid Society took children from the streets and out of the almshouses and sent them to farms and homes in the country, where they could be taught the values of hard work and have secure homes. Altogether this society sent 48,000 such children out to farms. The Society for the Protection of Destitute Roman Catholic Children (1863) was opposed to Brace's technique, considering it to be an indentured servant system. Instead, they sent out children as "apprentices" to various businesses and factories.

Other such moral interest groups included the Salem Fraternity (1887), Playground Association of America (1909), the Chicago Woman's Club, Hull House Group, Child Study Association (1890), Catholic Home Bureau (1899), and the Child Welfare League of America (1915). The Society for the Prevention of Cruelty to Children (1875) was formed one year *after* the Society for the Prevention of Cruelty to Animals; it is perhaps ironic that the latter organization continues today while the former faded out from lack of continued interest. Several prominent judges gave support to these moral interest groups, including especially Julian Mack of Chicago, Harvey Baker of Boston, and Timothy Hurley of Chicago.

To these moral interest groups, delinquency is created by environmental factors. There is nothing inherently evil about the child; he has either had a poor upbringing, or he has been "forced" into his behavior by a bad environment. To prevent delinquency, then, one needs to change the child's environment. This is done either by changing his actual residence (as attempted by Charles Brace, for example) or by altering the socialization process.

A more complete discussion of the activities and philosophy of these moral interest groups, as well as other interest groups, will be presented later in this chapter.

Professional and Occupational Interest Groups

Those who have been charged with the professional responsibility for "handling" the juvenile problems in our society have developed special interests in addition to moral ones. As Lemert (1970) has observed:

While nineteenth century legal reform movements appear to have sprung from humanitarian motives . . . those of the twentieth century have been fathered by administrative concerns, technological and organizational complexities, and sheer population growth.

The concerns of these groups have been of four kinds: First, there are the ethical issues: What is the proper way to treat juvenile offenders? Should they or should they not be treated as adults, with the same rights and privileges? It is to such concerns as these that the groups in the children's rights movements have addressed themselves. Second has been the concern with the professional level of the handling and treatment facilities and personnel, expressed by such groups as the National Probation and Parole Association, the various police associations (e.g., the International Association of Chiefs of Police), the Council on Social Work Education, the Children's Bureau of the Health, Education, and Welfare Department, and the National Committee on Employment of Youth. All of these are opposed, for example, to having untrained personnel handling juvenile offenders.

A third issue has concerned the process of handling juvenile offenders, particularly the establishment of a standardized treatment system *vs.* the more informal, and sometimes arbitrary, procedures found in many juvenile corrections and treatment centers. The primary groups which have addressed this issue are the National Council on Crime and Delinquency and the Children's Bureau of the Department of Health, Education, and Welfare.

Finally, there is the concern on behalf of "society"—i.e., that the juvenile offender is "getting away with murder." Judge Lester Loble of Montana, for example, believes that youthful offenders are conscious of their special status as children and use this status to commit their crimes without fear of punishment. He feels that the "soft" approach to juveniles teaches them a disrespect for the law that carries on into their adult lives and leads them into a life of permanent crime. He feels that only by showing them the strong arm of the law and publicizing their names and offenses may the wayward youth be taught to refrain from delinquent activities. His chief concern, therefore, has been with the restrictions placed upon the juvenile court—that the very "softness" of the courts has given the juvenile delinquent the freedom to perpetuate his delinquency. If granted a freer hand for "tougher" administration, Judge Lobel believes that the juvenile court could be a place where youngsters are taught to respect the law (Loble and Wylie, 1967).

The National Council on Crime and Delinquency, mentioned above, is a current interest group that shows increasing influence in promoting its ideologies and procedures for the "correction" of juvenile offenders. Established in 1907, the Council consists of over 60,000 citizens and crime-control officials working to improve the criminal justice system and to maximize the effectiveness of law enforcement. In their "Crime and Delinquency Literature" publication (Vol. 4, No. 3, September, 1972), NCCD states that it "carries out programs designed to help protect the public against organized crime." But its main strength seems to lie in its ability to protect the citizen from the increasing bureaucratic control of the various law enforcement agencies. It is a citizen's pressure group which designs professional standards and guidelines for police, judges, correctional workers, and laymen. It drafts model legislation and provides legal advisory service to legislatures, criminal justice agencies, and citizens' groups; and it publishes literature for interested people, both professional and lay.

Scientific Interest Groups

As indicated in the previous chapter, some physiological scientists, beginning with Lombroso, have argued that a person is born with either "delinquent" or "normal" tendencies. Psychologists (and psychoanalysts), however, have de-emphasized physiological factors, focusing instead on failures in the socialization process. An example of such an approach is the Freudian theory that sometimes a "fixation" occurs at an early stage in the psycho-sexual development which permanently damages the person's ability to ward off "id" impulses.

In the 19th century, Durkheim (1951) began to neutralize the heavy influence which the fields of psychology and physiology had had in the prevalent theories about human behavior, particularly deviant behavior. Prior to Durkheim, it was generally believed that certain external and internal conditions worked upon the psyche of man to lead him into deviance. Whether climatic or biological, however, these conditions lacked explanatory power. Durkheim saw that such causal theories did not explain, for example, the massive variations among societies in suicide rates (Durkheim, 1951). He proposed the theory of *anomie,* or normlessness, to explain these rate disparities in societies. The key concept of his theory was that of "social integration." When the individual is sufficiently "integrated" into his society, he adheres to its norms and mores so that integrated societies will have relatively little deviant behavior, compared to societies that are "anomic," or lacking in integration.

At the same time, however, Durkheim argued that a certain amount of deviant behavior helps to identify and maintain the "normative boundaries" of a society by evoking public scorn and punishment (Durkheim, 1938). Such "boundary-testing" is particularly common when the norms break down due to large-scale and rapid changes in the economic order of a society. Durkheim, as well as Kai Erikson (1966) and others, has developed the theoretical basis for what may be called a "structural-functional" approach to delinquency. That is, the structure of the society itself is seen as generating a certain amount of delinquency by the kinds of laws it passes and the kinds of boundary-testing they call forth. (See Chapter 2.)

A second approach to the sociological study of delinquency (also derived from Durkheim) is sometimes called the "disorganization" approach. Merton (1957), for example, has extended Durkheim's theory of specifying that anomie arises mainly from the inability of a delinquent (or other deviant) to reach the generally valued goals of our culture (e.g., wealth) by culturally approved or legitimate means. Thus, the structure frustrates certain members of society and leads them into acceptance of illegitimate means to obtain their goals. This general idea has been refined by Cloward and Ohlin (1960), as well as by others, to emphasize the part played by "differential opportunity" in generating delinquency, in particular the location of adolescents in the age structure of the society, as well as in its social-class structure. More recently, Hirschi (1969) has identified as a cause of delinquency the breakdown of certain social and emotional bonds between the youth and the social structure.

The perspective of a third scientific interest group in sociology is sometimes called "social learning theory" and includes the ideas of Sutherland, Cohen, Short, and others. Shaw and McKay (1942) observed a generation ago that crime and delinquency persist in certain city neighborhoods despite the population changes occurring within them. They explain this phenomenon by reference to the transmission of a criminal tradition or "culture" within these areas: new residents, either by birth or by in-migration are indoctrinated into the culture of crime through group memberships. LaMar Empey (1967) has argued that 60 to 90 percent of all delinquency by young offenders occurs in such groups, most of them quite small (e.g., two to four members). Yablonsky (1962) characterized these groups as having diffuse role definitions, limited cohesion, impermanence, shifting membership, disturbed leadership, and limited definition of membership expectations. This is quite different from the earlier picture of delinquent gangs that Cohen (1955) offered. For him, the delinquent subculture was characterized as nonutilitarian, malicious, and negative. The delinquency-oriented individual, one who has been unable to "make it" in legitimate society, creates or joins a delinquent subculture as a vehicle for "revenge" and compensation, totally denying the legitimacy of the larger society's norms and laws. That is, "the delinquent's conduct is right, by the standards of his subculture, precisely because it is wrong by the norms of the larger culture" (Cohen, 1955:26).

Sutherland (1966), in his argument against any physiological, deterministic view of delinquency, proposes the theory of "differential association." This theory views delinquency as simply being learned in the same manner as any human behavior—that is, through interaction with other persons, mainly within small primary groups. This theory has been further developed by Akers (1973). The individual is confronted with definitions of expected behavior, some of which favor delinquency. If he is confronted with an excess of delinquent definitions over nondelinquent ones, and his interaction with the definers is intense enough, he is likely to accept their delinquent definitions. In the delinquent friendship group, the individual learns both the operations of delinquent behavior and the rationalizations for partaking of it. This would help to explain even the rather extreme case in which one member of a family becomes a priest and another a criminal: the latter has probably belonged to a delinquent group outside the family.

A fourth sociological perspective may be termed "interactionist." Tannenbaum has argued that the response of the society figures prominently in a youth's acceptance of a delinquent role. The society, represented by parents, teachers, and police, will often define the more or less normal activities of youth as delinquent. Occasional "rough-housing" or mischief may be strongly disapproved of by such persons, who impose sanctions that help to define some youth as delinquent. Once this label has been applied, all of the institutions join in this redefinition of the youth and respond to him in a manner reserved for the delinquent. He is thereby drawn into a self-fulfilling prophecy, which leads him to the internalization of a permanently delinquent self-image.

The emphasis on self-concept is one of the most important aspects of interactionist theory. Young people are likely to be especially sensitive about falling short of a goal so highly valued in our society as wealth. Other societies have established nondelinquent ways for the poor to maintain their self-esteem. The status of the traditional peasant, with his fierce pride in a subcultural, nondelinquent value system, serves to ward off the type of degradation inherent in being poor in our society. The reference groups for the poor in other societies are other poor people; but, constantly exposed to the middle-class orientation of our mass media, poor youth in the United States are unable to compare themselves favorably with others. A second source of status degradation are upwardly mobile peers, who may cause the individual to feel left behind. Thus, working-class boys, worried about low status in middle-class terms, are likely to have serious problems of adjustment. These problems may be resolved in a variety of ways, one of which is the creation and maintenance of a delinquent subculture. As long as a working-class boy clings to a version of middle-class values, he is forced to give himself a low evaluation. The delinquent subculture helps to free him from this burden of low self-esteem (Cohen, 1955).

As a society becames more concerned about juvenile delinquency, however, the tendency to use the label may increase, causing a greater number of persons to be so labeled, even without any change in their actual behavior. As Deutscher once put it:

The only reasonable conclusion that can be drawn, from the sometimes invalid and frequently unreliable data on delinquency trends, is that there is no consistent evidence of any general increase in the rates of misbehavior among children and adolescents. (Deutscher, 1960:469)

Thus, independent of the actual rate of juvenile delinquent acts, there may be an increase in the number of youngsters that the society is willing to *label* as delinquent. Deutscher's formula for the extent of the social problem of juvenile delinquency is that it is equal to the amount of *deviant behavior,* which is relatively constant, divided by the amount of community *tolerance,* which lately has been decreasing. Thus, the problem has been increasing without any increase in the actual incidence of delinquent acts. Aware of the critical impact of such a process on the individual, Deutscher calls for three questions to be answered through future research: What is the effect on the child's definition of himself and of his expected role in society, when he is labeled "delinquent"? What is the effect on others who know such a label has been applied? How is the interaction process, and eventually the socialization process, affected by such labeling?

The self-concept is seen by the interactionists as the key to understanding the process of becoming delinquent. Thomas *et al.* (1964:1) demonstrate that the "functional limits of one's ability to learn are determined by his self-conception of his ability as acquired in the interaction with significant others." This is in line with the general theory of G. H. Mead (1934), which explains an individual's adherence to any mode of behavior, deviant or nondeviant, in terms of the subjective understanding of his expectations in the situation. If the individual perceives that he is "expected" to perform delinquent acts by the society, by his "generalized other" (the social system of which he feels a part), by his peers, and by his parents, then, to him, *not* being deviant would be the violation of expectation.

Reckless (1956) showed in his research that the perceived conception of others is highly correlated with one's own self-concept and that it is the self-concept, favorable or unfavorable, which accounts for behavioral patterns. Boys in his study were selected by their teachers as potentially either nondelinquent or likely to be in future contact with the juvenile courts. The "good" boys had higher self-concepts, lower scores on a delinquency proneness test, and higher scores on a social responsibility test. Tangri and Schwartz (1967) have argued that the teachers in Reckless's study used middle-class standards by which to judge their lower-class students; and it is, of course, middle-class standards by which boys are designated delinquent or nondelinquent in the courts. (See also Schwartz and Stryker, 1970.)

Having reviewed the constructions of reality about delinquency by the moral, professional, and scientific publics and interest groups, let us now turn to a discussion of some of their efforts to promote their points of view.

THE DELINQUENCY PROBLEM AND SOCIAL MOVEMENTS

Two major social movements in our history have addressed the issue of juvenile delinquency, and we shall call these the "child savers" and the "children's rights" movements. The first of these, because it is the oldest, the most enduring, and the one with greater impact on our juvenile justice system, will receive much greater attention here. More recent, however, is the "children's rights" movement, which has been challenging some aspects of the traditional juvenile justice process. Since the courts have figured especially prominently in this recent challenge, we will give them more attention in that part of our discussion, although, of course, the courts have been important in the "child-savers" approach also.

The Child Savers

The child savers were persons deeply concerned about the welfare of children in the society. They believed in the basic goodness of the child and believed that children became delinquent due to a "bad environment." The way to curb delinquency, therefore, was simply to remove wayward children from the environment to which they had been subjected. Although these child savers were characterized, in large part, by a sincere desire to protect children, they were motivated also by other interests. At least three elements in 19th century society combined with the interest in children to motivate the child savers.

First, in the 19th century, the United States was in the throes of perhaps the fastest change that any society had ever undergone. The Industrial Revolution, the tremendous immigration of European peasantry, the rapidity of urban expansion, and the tremendous growth of the economy all created a situation in which many of the traditional ways of life were eroded. With the "decline of traditional religion, increased leisure and boredom, the rise of public education, and the breakdown of communal life in the impersonal, crowded cities," philanthropic work filled the void (Platt, 1969:77). Women who had less to do in the home with increasing mechanization and who found the traditional avenues for outside activity (e.g., the church) either no longer functioning or no longer interesting turned to child-saving organizations and activity.

Second, as will be discussed in a later chapter, women's rights were becoming a topic of great importance in the late 19th century. Among the demands of the feminists was the "right to work." Opposing the feminists were those who believed in the basic "purity" and "femininity" of women, i.e., that women were far more moral than men, and, as such, must be the rearers of the children to assure them the proper moral guidance. The child-saving movement provided a vehicle which offered militant feminists an opportunity to work at something that was not objectionable to antifeminists, since all agreed that women should work for the moral improvement of the youth:

Middle-class women were now better educated and had more leisure time, but their choice of careers was limited. Child saving, however, was a reputable task for any woman who wanted to extend her housekeeping functions into the community without denying antifeminist stereotypes of woman's nature and place. (Platt, 1969:76)

Third, there had been for some time a "child-saving" attitude in our cultural heritage in the form of the *parens patriae* doctrine which had originated much earlier in England. This was the general notion that the state was ultimately the "parent" of everyone and ought to function directly as such for any children with "inadequate" parents. Of course, many elements of our social milieu have served to keep the "child-saving" outlook alive, not the least of which has been the growth of the psychoanalytic conceptions of child-rearing. From Freud to Spock, there has been a continuing demand to consider the child's welfare as paramount in matters of socialization, punishment, and day-to-day relationships.

If certain elements in the social structure and cultural heritage helped to create a favorable environment for the child savers, they seemed also to have certain motivations of their own, making them "moral entrepreneurs" or perhaps the kind of psychological interest group mentioned in Chapter 1. Platt (1969:3) has characterized the child savers thus:

The term "child savers" is used to characterize a group of "disinterested" reformers who regarded their cause a matter of conscience and morality, serving no particular class or political interests.

What type of background did the person have who led or joined the child-saving movement? The three main characteristics of these people, whether men or women, were (1) rural background, (2) upper-middle-class or upper-class membership and (3) higher education.

Enoch C. Wines, described as the "foremost American authority on reformatories and institutions for children prior to the twentieth century" (Platt, 1969:48), was one of the leading child savers. He spent his childhood working on a farm, earned his Ph.D. from Middlebury College, and was the organizer of the National Prison Association (1872). Like most of his contemporaries, he believed that "the normal place of education for . . . children is in the fields" (Wines, 1888:608).

Although "child saving was essentially a middle-class movement, launched by the 'leisure class' on behalf of those less fortunately placed in the social order," it was especially middle- and upper-class women who concerned themselves with child saving (Platt, 1969:72). Men were more interested in the juvenile courts, and more recently in children's rights. The reasons for greater female involvement in the movement have been, in part, suggested above. Women were concerned with the "morality" of the children, having been defined by their society as more "moral" than men. They also had little difficulty in seeing child saving as an extension of their homemaker role. Quoting Bowen, Humphrey states:

If, on our charity boards, we had more women who were conversant with the daily lives of the poor, they would be a great asset in the work of relief and construction. If a woman is a good housekeeper in her own home, she will be able to do well at larger housekeeping. (Humphrey, 1939:633)

That these women were well-educated, widely traveled, and had access to political and financial resources is clearly pointed out by Platt's description of many of the leaders of the movement:

Louise Bowen and Helen Henrotin were both married to bankers; Mrs. Potter Ralmer's husband was an influential broker and hotel owner; Mrs. Perry Smith's husband was Vice President of the Chicago and Northwestern Railroad; and the fathers of Jane Addams and Julia Lathrop were both Republican senators in the Illinois legislature. (77)

One of her [Jane Addams] colleagues founded a school in Japan, another became a missionary in Korea, and another taught in a school for blind children. (94)

Dorothy Powers (1939) described the members of her club as being middle-class housewives with families of two or fewer children living in residential areas. Because of their background, these women were particularly concerned with the traditional (rural) family and sought to give wayward children such an environment:

Although the child savers were bored at home and unhappy with their lack of participation in the "real world," they vigorously defended the virtue of traditional family life . . . (Platt, 77)

Men concurred with the definition of the woman in the child-saving movement. G. E. Howe, for example, advocated giving the wayward boy a mother, a home, a woman's ear to tell his trouble to, and, most of all, a woman's love. George Hoover, Superintendent of the American Home-Finding Association (1898), remarked:

No institution is so well adapted to develop the better elements of human character as is God's institution, namely the family home. (Platt, 79-80)

And C. D. Randall (1884) believed that the woman has a "unique capacity for understanding human problems." We see, therefore, a picture of the "typical" child saver as a middle-class, well-educated woman of rural background. Child saving was for them the "truest and noblest scope for the public activities of women in the time which they can spare from their primary domestic duties" (Lynde, 1879). And child saving, as we noted earlier, was one occupation which satisfied both the feminists and antifeminists:

The only claim to rights here made is the equal right with men to minister to and labor for the sick, the suffering, the helpless, the depraved. . . . Because of fitness for the positions referred to should both men and women, one just as much as the other, be appointed, not at all as a question of sex. . . . It is not intended to advocate the appointment of women on boards with a view to their advancement as women, but as a means of bringing into useful activity all feminine qualities which shall supplement those of men and round out to harmonious proportions organizations formed for facilitating charity work. (Richardson, 1892:216-222)

Of all the many child savers, there were two who perhaps did most to instigate and maintain the movement: Platt (83-96) presents us with sketches of these, Louise De Koven Bowen and Jane Addams.

Louise Bowen exemplifies the child saver described above. She was the child of a rural Protestant family, attended private school and college, was widely traveled, was associated with the Republican party, and lived in suburban, upper-class Chicago. She attended the Dearborn Seminary, where she learned grace and self-sacrifice, which were to serve her well in her charity work. The Hull's Woman's Club gave her the opportunity to do "something worthwhile for the poor, a means of establishing a sympathetic relationship between the 'well-to-do and those less well off'" (87).

Jane Addams, also country-born, was educated at Rockford Seminary, was well-traveled, and demonstrated "a preoccupation with making amends for her own good fortune for being born into wealth and luxury" (94). Both Louise Bowen and Jane Addams showed the characteristics which typify what we called psychological interest groups in Chapter 1:

> Jane Addams recognized that her generation, especially the women, lacked a "heritage of noble obligation" and were driven by a "desire for action" and "the wish to right wrong and alleviate suffering." The new religion of social service—"this renaissance of the early Christian humanitarianism"—was designed to provide an outlet for the "active faculties" of a "fast growing number of cultivated young people" whose lives lacked vitality and purpose. (Platt, 95)

Louise Bowen was President of the Hull House, Chairman of the Lower North-Side District United Charities, President of the Juvenile Protective Association, and Auditor of the National Woman's Suffrage Association, as well as a member or leader in numerous other political and charitable organizations. In addition, she contributed huge sums of money, donating a new wing for the Maurice Porter Hospital and building an auditorium for the Hull House.

Jane Addams devoted her life to numerous organizations, including Hull House itself, which she helped to establish. Her main interest was the use of recreation to replace delinquency. This idea was adopted by the Salem Fraternity, which was founded in 1887 to provide recreational facilities for youth and which was important in creating other clubs for children, such as the New York City Neighborhood Guild (1889), the Playground Association (1909), the Boy Scouts (1912), and the Girl Scouts (1912).

Connections may easily be made between the social and cultural motivations for child saving and the organizational forms which reflected them. Two of these, the reformatory system and the cottage plan, will be discussed here at some length. Both of them seemed to offer help for coping with more social problems of those times than merely the control of obstreperous children:

It seems that the child saving movement went beyond mere instrumental reforms in the social control of youth. It was also a symbolic movement which seemed to be defending the sanctity of fundamental institutions—the nuclear family, the agricultural community, Protestant nativism, woman's domesticity, parental discipline, and the assimilation of immigrants. (Platt, 1969:73-74)

The Reformatory System

As early as 1787, the Philadelphia Society for Alleviating the Miseries of the Public Prison made the claim that was to become the basis of the reformatory system:

Children both in the gaol and workhouses are frequently suffered to remain with their parents whereby they are initiated in early life to scenes of debauchery, dishonesty, and wickedness of every kind . . . [and] are gradually seduced from their original innocence (Teeters and Reinemann, 1950:70)

In other words, new surroundings were needed to protect the "inherently good" children from the ill effects of a poor environment. As the cities grew and the child savers became increasingly concerned with the "moral climate" of the impersonal city environment, with its threat to cherished traditions, the city itself increasingly came to be seen as the cause of youthful delinquency. Thus, "reformatories for children should develop as far as possible the conditions of home life, and they should be built in the country, for the normal place of education for such children is in the fields" (Platt, 1969:49). These reformatories should be managed by women, should give children moral and religious training, and, above all, should instill in them good work habits. There should be a personal interest in each child to counter the demoralizing effect of impersonal city life. An emphasis should also be placed on simplicity in dress, diet, and surroundings (Platt, 1969:50). Instead of treating just the "symptom" of delinquency, an effort must be made to reach the "whole child."

To make a good boy out of this bundle of perversities, his entire being must be revolutionized. He must be taught self control, industry, respect for himself and the rights of others. (Caldwell, 1886:71)

Platt has comprehensively delineated the purposes of the reformatory system:

(1) Young offenders must be segregated from the corrupting influences of adult criminals. (2) "Delinquents" need to be removed from their environment and imprisoned for their own good and protection. Reformatories should be guarded sanctuaries, combining love

and guidance with firmness and restraint. (3) "Delinquents" should be assigned to reformatories without trial and with minimal legal requirements. Due process is not required because reformatories are intended to reform and not to punish. (4) Sentences should be indeterminate, so that inmates are encouraged to cooperate in their own reform and recalcitrant "delinquents" are not allowed to resume their criminal careers. (5) Reformation should not be confused with sentimentality. Punishment is required only insofar as it is good for the punished person and only when other methods have been exhausted. (6) Inmates must be protected from idleness, indulgence, and luxuries through military drill, physical exercise, and constant supervision. (7) Reformatories should be built in the countryside and designed according to the "cottage plan." (8) Labor, education, and religion constitute the essential program of reform. Inmates should not be given more than an elementary education. Industrial and agricultural training should predominate. (9) The value of sobriety, thrift, industry, prudence, "realistic" ambition, and adjustment must be taught. (Platt, 1969:54-55)

The Cottage Plan

From the reformatory system evolved the cottage plan, which had as its main goal the complete removal of the child from the city and surrounding him with a "home in the country."

Children should deal with elemental things of the world—earth, stones, trees, animals, running water, fire, open spaces—instead of pavements, signboards, subdivided lots, apartment houses, and electric percolators. Civilization has been hardest on children. (Addams, 1925:221)

Education which was learned out of books was deemed all but useless: true education came from *doing*. Of particular importance was learning to perform a task or a series of tasks, such as cooking, housework, or chopping wood. Indoctrination emphasized the Puritan work ethic and the acceptance of one's lot in life.

It must be emphasized at this point that, although the late 19th and early 20th centuries were times of rapid change, many of the ideals of the agricultural society were very much in effect. The child savers themselves had been reared in an agricultural setting and believed in its inherent value. As Durkheim (1933) has indicated, in times of changing social structure, a sense of anomie may develop from trying to adhere to traditional norms in the face of such change. Thus, anomie or alienation may have been a motivating factor in the child-saving movement. As the President of the Illinois Conference of Charities remarked:

Salvation for the "city waif" and "gamin of the alley" was only possible if they were returned to a "simpler and saner life," "the normalities of the country," and "the simplicities of the farm." In order to truly help delinquents, they must be given simplicity, protection, and seclusion." (Jones, 1898, in Platt, 1969:61)

There was some resistance to such new institutional arrangements as cottages. Homer Folks, for example, spoke of the "enduring stigma" given the child who was sent to reformatories or cottages (Folks, 1891:137). However, the desire to save these children and give them a sense of individuality, an awareness of family responsibility, and a good home, outweighed any opposition. As Brace expressed it:

> Under a new atmosphere of kindness, sympathy, comfort and self-respect, many of their vices drop from them like the old and verminous clothing they left behind. . . . They are not so liable to fall in with bad company. (Brace, 1876:137)

Institutional Transformation of the Child-Saver Ideals

As often happens even with the best intentions, the child-saving movement produced institutional forms which seemed to violate the original ideals. For example, even before the cottage plan, Charles Loring Brace's organization, The Children's Aid Society (founded 1853), had had as its goal the removal of children from the evils of the almshouses and general environment of New York City. Their plan was to place these "unwanted" children in good foster homes in the countryside to teach them the value of hard work and love of nature. What gradually developed, however, was a profit-making indentured servant organization that saw 48,000 New York City youth drafted into agricultural work until the age of 18. Similarly, the Society for the Prevention of Cruelty to Children, founded by E. Fellow Jenkins, and a number of other such organizations, sent children out to the country to be worked until their 18th birthdays. The Society for the Prevention of Destitute Roman Catholic Children, founded in 1863, for the express purpose of countering the indentured servant system, ended up with only a less visible and threatening kind of indenturing under the guise of "apprenticeship."

> The transfer of the reformatory from city to country also meant that delinquents became invisible and removed from civilized society. (Platt, 1969:66)

In the meantime, the city reformatories continued to operate and were changing toward greater regimentation. Less concerned with returning the child to nature, and more interested in forcing the child to adapt to the city's environment in a law-abiding manner, the reformatory became increasingly military in style. About the Elmira Reform School, Brockway wrote:

> Reformation is socialization of the anti-social by scientific training while under the completest government control. . . . The reformatory became like a garrison of a thousand prison soldiers. . . . By means, mainly of military organization . . . the general tone had gradually changed from that of a convict prison to the tone of a conscript fortress. (Brockway, 1878:310-311)

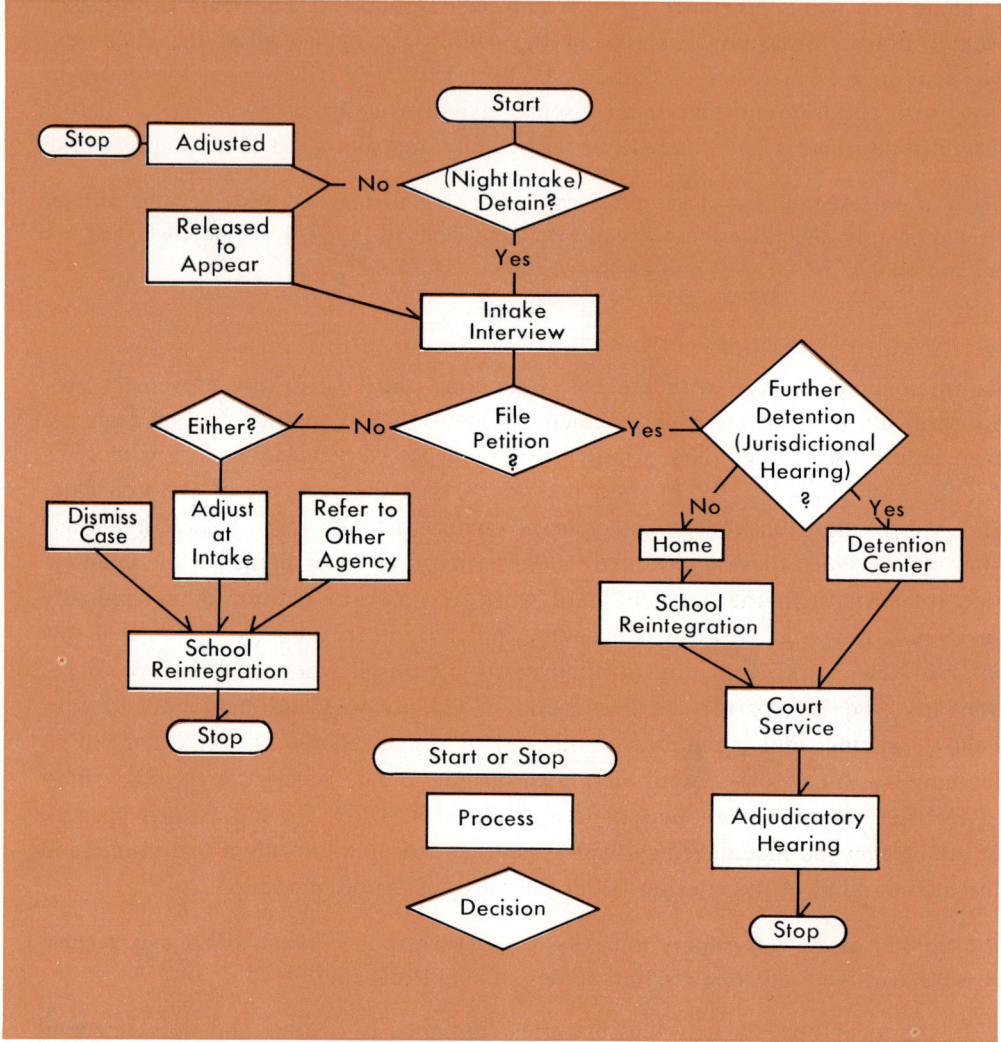

Figure 4-1 Flow Chart of Intake Process
SOURCE: Tarrant County Juvenile Department, Ft. Worth, Texas, 1972

In each of the two major types of institution, the cottage plan and the city reformatory, the child savers tried to avoid stigmatization of the child through bypassing regular court procedures, but stigmatization was inevitable. For all practical purposes, our juvenile corrections system even today is based upon these same institutions, which deny to juveniles the due process of regular courts in an effort to save them from unwholesome influences and from stigmatization.

The Juvenile Court System

No institutional expression of the child-savers movement has been more typical or more influential than the Juvenile Court System that has existed in our society throughout the present century.

The first juvenile court was established by the Illinois legislature in 1899, in which:

> The fundamental idea of the [juvenile court] law is that the state must step in and exercise guardianship over a child found under such adverse social or individual conditions as to develop crime. . . . It proposes a plan whereby he may be treated, not as a criminal . . . but as a ward of the state. (Pound, 1944:13-14)

Shortly after Illinois, California and other states created their own systems.*

> Women and women's organizations more or less spearheaded the drive in California, as they had in Illinois. . . . The California Club of San Francisco, which took the lead in getting the bill introduced, was directly patterned after a comparable women's organization in Chicago. (Lemert, 1970:37)

As the juvenile court first emerged out of the child-saving movement, it adopted the English formulation of *parens patriae*. That is, the juvenile court, as a representative of the state, was to be as a "father" to a wayward child. The young person was seen to be inherently good, and delinquent only because of unwholesome environmental factors. Thus, it was the duty of the court to treat the wayward child, not as a criminal, but as a son. The child was not to be punished, in the legalistic sense, but guided firmly to a realization of the wrongness of his actions. The proceedings in a juvenile case "must carry out consistently the purely educational principles of the court, and any suggestion of an old fashioned criminal trial should be avoided" (Henderson, 1905:340-341). Of course, some children continued to be treated like adult criminals and placed in jails (Platt:146), but the *parens patriae* idea came to be the dominant philosophy. See Figure 4-1 for an example of the complicated process which, for juveniles, normally takes the place of the usual due process and trial.

The "Natural History" of the Child Savers Movement

The incipiency of the child savers movement can be seen both in the cultural heritage from England of the *parens patriae* doctrine and in the early stirrings of humanitarian penological concerns through such organizations as the Philadelphia Society in 1787. With a couple of exceptions in the mid-19th century, it would be

---

* For a thorough analysis of the history of the juvenile court, see "Task Force Report: Juvenile Delinquency and Youth Crime," President's Commission on Law Enforcement and Administration of Justice, Washington, D.C., U.S. Government Printing Office, 1967:1-40.

fair to say that the movement remained incipient until after the Civil War; such was the fate, in fact, of many potential reform movements at a time when the nation's energies were consumed with the Abolition issue. Once that war was over, a number of new movements got started, including the feminist or female suffrage movement, on which the child savers were able to "ride," in a sense, as we observed earlier. The organizational and lobbying successes of important women, such as Addams and Bowen, signaled the coalescence of the child savers' movement by the end of the 19th century.

The institutionalization of a movement (including a social problem), it will be recalled, occurs when the establishment has come to take it seriously and to respond in patterned ways to its challenge. An indication of institutionalization early in the 20th century was the establishment of the special "juvenile court," at first state by state but eventually nationwide. This was the official judicial implementation of the child savers' definition of reality about the nature of delinquency. The development of reformatories and of cottage systems, some of them even before the juvenile court idea had spread, represented a growing institutionalization of the child-savers' philosophy in the penological area as well. Still another important symptom of institutionalization was the organization, in 1907, of the National Council on Crime and Delinquency (NCCD), embracing, as it does, professional practitioners, scholars, lawyers, and lay people with an interest in crime and delinquency. The mere fact that this organization in its name has given "delinquency" equal official status with crime is a sign that the social problem-movement of delinquency has been "institutionalized."

It is too early to speak of fragmentation or demise in the child-savers' movement but its response to the challenge of the newer children's rights movement has been somewhat fragmentary and piecemeal, and it seems definitely to be giving ground, especially in the higher courts. Still, its legacy, which we will discuss later, is likely to be with us for some time.

The Children's Rights Movement

The second major social movement to address the problem of juvenile delinquency has been the children's rights movement, whose primary position is that the juvenile offender, though in need of separate and special care, is still to be considered a citizen of the country and to be afforded the same constitutional rights as an adult. These rights must be observed in all phases of incrimination, from arrest to verdict.

Many recent developments in juvenile justice in certain states, as well as nationwide, have been the result of this growing movement, which has expressed itself mainly in the juvenile courts. Perhaps ironically, the juvenile court system was first instigated by the child-saving movement. Though originally the juvenile court was certainly not intended by the child savers to safeguard the child's constitutional rights, it has been the main vehicle through which the newer children's rights movement has operated.

Even at an early time, however, when the child savers' philosophy was coming into its own, the competing philosophy of children's rights was emphatically expressed by Mr. Justice Thornton of the Supreme Court of Cook County, Illinois (1870):

Can the State, as parens patriae, exceed the power of the natural parent, except in punishing crime? These laws provide for the "safe keeping" of the child; they direct his "commitment" and only a "ticket of leave" or the uncontrolled discretion of a board of guardians, will permit the imprisoned boy to breathe the pure air of heaven outside his prison walls, and to feel the instincts of manhood by contact with the busy world. . . . The confinement may be from one to fifteen years, according to the age of the child. Executive clemency cannot open the prison doors, for no offense has been committed. The writ of habeas corpus, a writ for the security of liberty, can afford no relief, for the sovereign power of the State as parens patriae has determined the imprisonment beyond recall. Such a restraint upon natural liberty is tyranny and oppression. If, without crime, without the conviction of an offense, the children of the state are thus to be confined for the "good of Society," then Society had better be reduced to its original elements and free government acknowledged a failure. . . . The welfare and rights of the child are also to be considered. . . . Even criminals cannot be convicted and imprisoned without due process of law. (People v. Turner, 55 Ill. 280 [1870] as quoted by Platt, 103-104)

In the case just cited, the child savers succeeded in discrediting Justice Thornton's position, and they gained general acceptance for their own position until very recent times. Eventually, however, the juvenile courts were to begin giving much more credence to the children's rights view expressed by Thornton.

It was not until the 1940's that murmurings of the child's rights philosophy began to be heard in official settings, however. Lemert (62-63) discusses some of the changes in the social structure which helped to give rise to growing doubts about the conception of the juvenile court as *parens patriae*. He points out that this concept has been developed in small communities in which there was a direct, continuous, and informal interaction. As California, for example, saw more in-migration and urbanization, a more impersonal and formal outlook developed. The growth and specialization of police departments—as well as an increase in the number of automobiles and thus in juvenile contact with police for traffic offenses—accelerated the formalization and impersonalization of the juvenile courts. What had once been a friendly, fatherly judge became a brisk arbiter, rushing the juvenile to a quick verdict and then turning him over to a variety of specialists whose efforts were often poorly coordinated:

Without comprehensive provisions for coordination, the result has been fragmented juvenile programs in which little case accountability and follow through is possible. (Kittrie, 1971:113)

Since juvenile staffs have come to be greatly overworked, with little accountability and tremendous power, juveniles have often been locked up without the benefit either of a truly rehabilitative program or constitutional rights. Examples are given by Kittrie (1971):

A youth of fourteen found access to an unoccupied house and with two friends of the same age proceeded to build a "clubhouse." Their offense was in entering the garage attached to the house and removing a flashlight and three fuses. They were detected when the clubhouse caught fire. The parents made immediate restitution, amounting to $14. The juvenile court had found the youths delinquent even in the face of their clean records, regular attendance at school and Sunday school, and favorable recommendations by a minister and deputy sheriff.

Mills, a fourteen-year-old boy with no previous record of any misconduct, phoned the local school and falsely reported the presence of a bomb. Under the state statute, a person molesting or disturbing any free school is guilty of a misdemeanor and can be jailed up to thirty days. But the jurisdiction of the juvenile court determined Mills a delinquent and accordingly committed him to the state training school until he attained the age of twenty-one. On review, the West Virginia Supreme Court of Appeals affirmed the youth's seven-year commitment for an act which, if committed by an adult, would carry a maximum jail sentence of thirty days. (W. Va. Code 6040[14] [1961] as quoted in Kittrie, 1971:121-122)

As professional and public dissatisfaction has grown, both with the *parens patriae* doctrine itself and with the abuses of the juvenile justice system supposedly derived from it, two major publics have emerged to promote the children's rights movement: (1) those who demand that the youthful offender hold on to some of the benefits of the juvenile court, while at the same time being guaranteed his constitutional rights as a citizen; and (2) those whom Platt (156-158) calls the "legal moralists." We will discuss each in turn.

Due-Process Constitutionalists

The constitutionalists see the traditional juvenile court as "arbitrary, unconstitutional," and contrary to "the principles of fair trial" (Platt, 152-153). They are concerned particularly about the "invasion of personal rights under the pretext of 'welfare' and 'rehabilitation'" (Platt, 158). And, as has been observed by social scientists like Platt (159) and Garfinkel (1956), the current *parens patriae* courts have served to degrade rather than to rehabilitate the youth without granting them their constitutional safeguards. Although it is difficult to identify all the groups comprising constitutionalists, the NCCD and the American Bar Association have been especially prominent in the fight to guarantee children's rights. In the NCCD's "Crime and Delinquency Literature" (V.3, No. 3, September, 1972), the policy of NCCD toward children's rights is outlined:

The juvenile's ability to exercise his right to take voluntary, informed action for his own benefit is enhanced by the development of hot-lines, free clinics, legal aid drop-in centers, information and referral services, and voluntary facilities for temporary stays. The National Center for Child Advocacy was recently established at the federal level to deal primarily with the welfare-type needs of children. It could also serve as a vehicle for achieving significant legislative change in much the same way as the state-level Children's Lobby is already working in California.

Meanwhile, however, thousands of children remain incarcerated in custodial institutions throughout the country, many of them "for their own protection," all of them allegedly for rehabilitative purposes. Non-criminal minors are still placed in detention "to teach them a lesson"; young people are still harassed for unconventional dress or appearance and denied the means of self-help because of their age; parents still take their children to court to enforce demands for obedience; and young people still have little recourse to the law in defense of their interests as they perceive them.

In California, the Governor's Special Study Commission on Juvenile Justice, directed by John A. Pettis, an Oakland attorney, made a list of recommendations which were bitterly debated. These included:

the right to counsel, separate jurisdictional categories of dependent, neglected, and delinquent children, restrictions on dispositions derived from these categories, bifurcated hearings to establish jurisdiction of the court before it considered dispositions, procedures for juvenile traffic hearings, recordings of hearings, special rules of evidence, elimination of "double jeopardy," requirement that "findings" be made by judges, standards for the appointment of referees, provision for detention hearings, clarification of juvenile arrest procedures, establishment of probation departments as agencies of county government, and the organization of annual conferences of juvenile court judges. (Lemert, 1971:119)

Opposition to these recommendations came from three main groups: parole officers, judges, and police. The California Probation Parole and Corrections Officers Association, speaking for parole officers, stated in 1960: ". . . the California Probation Parole and Correctional Officers Association opposed repeal of the present Juvenile Court Law . . ." (Resolution No. 5, CPPCA, Long Beach, June 10, 1960, as quoted by Lemert: 129). It appears, however, that the main cause of their opposition was their feared loss of power, since they had not been consulted in the drafting of the proposal.

There is no quarrel with the expressed principles of the Juvenile Justice Commission, but its proposals underwrite the principles only vaguely where they do at all. . . . [W]hat the Commission says it wants . . . can be provided by changing the law in specific details, and should be done by a cooperative effort of the judges, probation officers and law enforcement officials who have the job to do after the changes are made, as well as before. (Robert Mowrers to Senate Judiciary Committee, n.d., as quoted by Lemert: 132)

Judges, on the other hand, were opposed on a stronger philosophical basis:

The Commission seems to have fixed the idea of protecting juveniles from cruel, inhuman, irresponsible, and sometimes incompetent judges (Ross Carkett, a judge, November, 1960).

I think that somewhere along the line the people who make the law are going to have to repose some trust in the juvenile judges. I don't think the juvenile court law should be rewritten just because it was fifty years old, because it worked well for fifty years and it's done a very fine job. Just because we had some rotten areas, some judges abusing rights—that situation should have been cleaned up; the judges are the ones that should have been taken to task, not the law. (Lemert: quoting an unnamed judge, 135)

Their influence as a professional interest group in opposition to the proposed changes in the status quo was diminished by the fact that the judges were not organized in their opposition, while the forces for change had organized solidly and worked hard.

The police opposition is summarized by Collins, as quoted by Lemert (139):

In retrospect, I suppose it was inevitable that the brand of legal fetishism, which in recent years has made our adult courts a mockery, would attempt invasion of our Juvenile Courts. The steady parade of decisions by Appellate Courts, which have given protection to the criminal at the expense of the community, stands as a contributor to the appalling and increasing crime rate.

This [recommendations of the Juvenile Justice Commission] appears to be an extension of the obvious trend in legislative and judicial decrees in recent years. The police are charged with the responsibility of protecting the community, and no group does more to protect the rights of individuals who compose the community than the police. However, there are those who have developed and continue to foster the theory that on one hand is the community and on the other is the law violator, and somewhere out in space is the enemy of both.

That the police opposition was somewhat successful is indicated from a statement made by Harold Stallings, Los Angeles County Sheriff's Department, to a legislative group after approval of Recommendation 24, which permitted juveniles to be placed into custody without warrant by the police (Lemert, 141): ". . . this is a high honor and a sacred trust given to law enforcement. We want to say that we will not take it lightly, that we will increase our efforts to screen and we do appreciate this trust that has been placed."

Legal Moralists

The second (and more "hard-nosed") kind of children's rights opponents to the *parens patriae* court is what Platt has termed the "legal moralists." Their philosophy is summarized thus by Platt:

> The juvenile court is a politically ineffective and morally improper means of controlling juvenile crime. . . . Judicial punishment can never be imposed merely for the purpose of securing some extrinsic good, either for the criminal himself or for civil society; it must in all cases be imposed (and can only be imposed) because the individual upon whom it is inflicted has committed an offense. . . . The right of retaliation . . . is the only principle which . . . can definitely guide a public tribunal as to both the quality and quantity of a just punishment. (153)

The primary concern of the moralists is the protection of the community from youthful law-breakers, while giving the latter "realistic, adult" treatment in the courts, rather than "coddling" them. Perhaps the most prominent spokesman for the moralists has been Judge Lester H. Loble of Montana. After becoming a judge, Loble grew increasingly restless with the juvenile system, which seemed to require him "to join the conspiracy to hide these [juvenile delinquency] horrors from the same public that was every night their victim" (Loble and Wylie, 1967:8).

> The case workers and psychologists seemed to know everything but the main subject, the juvenile offender. They kept ducking him. They backgrounded all their cases until mountains of massive minutiae piled up. There finally became so much minutiae that there ceased to be a case. This led to an extraordinary concept, not only alive today but spreading. Here it is: No youth should be held accountable for any action; no youth should be punished for any crime, no matter how vicious; no youth is responsible; and, finally, if we had a proper society, we would have no misbehavior problem in our young people. Therefore, let us eliminate the problem by correcting the society that created it. (12)

> But I believe that I am rehabilitating them and that the theorists are ruining them; that the theorists are not only returning them, time after time, to the opportunity for their second or third or fourth (or fortieth) offense, but are supplying the young with invitations to commit them. (13)

To Loble, there are two major enemies in society: (1) the juvenile delinquent, "no-goods—the black-jacketed night-riding Hell's Angel with a knife in his boot and a stone in his heart" (15); and (2) "all those who are preventing the public from knowing the names and histories of our young felons" (15). This includes social workers, sociologists, and judges. Outside of Montana, public support for

Loble has not been very large, but it is interesting that the "moralists" like Loble come to many of the same conclusions as those in the mainstream of the children's rights movement, but out of quite different motives.

With an incipiency going back to Justice Thornton in 1870, and a coalescence extending from the 1940's to the 1960's, the children's rights movement seems to be approaching institutionalization through a series of responses by the courts, especially the Supreme Court. With the Gault decision of 1967, the Kent Decision of 1966, and other such major Supreme Court decisions granting the juvenile the basic constitutional rights of a citizen, this movement is offering a critical challenge to the waning child-saver's movement. Jerry M. Wood, Supervisor of Intake of the Tarrant County Juvenile Probation Department, Fort Worth, Texas, has observed that "Beginning with this [Gault] decision, [our] courts have begun to appoint lawyers for those children who cannot retain them and the 'guardian ad litem' concept has come about in the juvenile court" (personal communication, December 18, 1972).

THE LEGACY OF THE CHILDREN'S MOVEMENTS

Since the child-savers movement still holds considerable sway in our juvenile courts and correctional institutions, and since the children's rights movement has only just begun to take hold, it may be premature to speak of the "legacies" of these movements. However, certain observations can be made about their impact so far. Both movements have contributed to the collective definition of certain juvenile behaviors as problematic. One result is that today one of every six males in the U.S. will be confronting the juvenile court before his 18th birthday. But what about other effects of these movements? Is today's society different because the child savers have had their day? Have the legal moralists or children's rights advocates in any significant manner affected the experiences of youth in trouble? Or have these movements done nothing more than change the level of public consciousness about juvenile delinquency?

The child-saving movement has fed (and itself been fed by) the psychoanalytic (or "soft") way of thinking about youthful misbehavior. Replacing the previously popular explanations that some juveniles are biologically or physiologically predetermined to be delinquent, the child-saving movement has succeeded in establishing the official view that delinquency is the result of factors beyond the child's control, such as the urban environment or simply poor socialization. The prevalence of this definition of delinquency has greatly altered the ways in which children are treated in the home, at school, and in the courts. A general societal effort has been made to improve the social environments of children during the present century, from the establishment of parks and playgrounds to the rise of the Boy Scouts. Out of the child-saving movement have also come certain new conventions in child discipline. It is no longer fashionable to hit one's misbehaving child in public, and schools have long been under pressure to eliminate all corporal punishment. Fairly or not, the "permissive" Dr. Benjamin Spock has been widely implicated as both a prophet and a symptom of this "new look" in child-rearing. The movie coding system is another outgrowth of the child-saving mentality: parents are warned not to send their children to an "R" movie, as it may prove damaging to them, and children are legally barred from X-rated films.

The children's rights legalists have not yet had such a general cultural impact, although their influence has certainly been felt in the courts. It shows also in such newly established institutions as student grievance committees in high schools, in legal resistance by some students and parents to school dress and hair codes, and perhaps even in the recent reduction of legal voting age.

A kind of ideological conflict thus continues. On the one hand, the child-saver movement has been having its greatest influence within the political and legislative processes. The social programs created in the 1960's under the Kennedy and Johnson administrations were strongly influenced by the philosophy that it is the social environment which generates juvenile delinquency and other social problems. As reported by Short (1973), there is a drive to create for the juvenile delinquent, especially the black gang member, an environment in which the youth are encouraged actively to participate in the improvement of their own communities.

It is important to note that a program to prevent and control delinquency—Mobilization for Youth—became the first "Great Society" agency and the spearhead for the National Welfare Rights Organization. . . . (Short, 1973:13)

The youth gangs were encouraged to "go conservative," that is, participate in legitimate enterprises. The Youth Organization United (YOU), for example, was reported by Blackman (1971) as being active in four areas:

The conservative Vice Lords have converted some old rundown buildings into youth centers.

In New Orleans, Thugs United, Inc., operates a record shop, paperback bookstore, an Afro-American clothing store and variety shop, and a recreation program for youngsters.

In Philadelphia, the Young Great Society runs a half-way house for boys from problem homes, a tutoring program, a day-care center and, in cooperation with hospitals, a narcotics and alcoholic-rehabilitation center.

In San Francisco's Chinatown, LeWays (legitimate ways) operates a recreation center and tutoring service to help Chinese-American youths with school problems. (as quoted in Short, 1973:18-19)

The child-saver philosophy seems to be expressed in these federally funded programs in the streets. The youth are still seen as at least potentially delinquent unless the environment is altered and the traditional values of self-help and hard work are made to replace the subculture of the lower-class youth gang.

The children's rights movement, on the other hand, has gained its greatest momentum within the judicial process. The Supreme Court, operating both in response to, and in leadership of, the children's rights movement, has made four especially important rulings since the mid-1960's. In *Kent* v. *U.S.* (1966), three major issues were decided: the child is entitled to a hearing before his case is waived to criminal court; his attorney is entitled to access to probation records used by the court in making its decision; and the court must make clear the reasons for its decision if it waives jurisdiction to the criminal court.

Shortly afterwards, the Court ruled in *In Re: Gault* (1967) that the child has the right to official notice of the charges against him; the right to counsel; the right to confrontation and cross-examination; and the privilege against self-incrimination. In *In Re: Winship* (1970), the Court extended these trends by ruling that the child must be proven guilty beyond reasonable doubt, instead of only by the preponderance of evidence, as had been the case.

At the same time, however, the child-saver philosophy has continud to have some influence and has partly mitigated the recent court victories of the children's rights movement. The Supreme Court ruled in *McKiver* v. *Pennsylvania* (1971), for example, that a child could be denied the right to a trial by jury. While this ruling by no means reversed the provisions in the Kent, Gault, and Winship cases, it did indicate that the effort to grant children the total legal rights of the adult citizen still faces considerable opposition from the child savers. The latter continue also to have great influence in the actual operation of the local juvenile court. Lefstein, Stapleton, and Teitelbaum (1969) have shown, for example, that the local courts are not yet following the Supreme Court decisions in at least three respects: the right to counsel; the privilege against self-incrimination; and the right of confrontation and cross-examination.

Concerning the right to counsel, they found in two courts that the judge made no attempt to advise the child of his right to counsel in 85 percent and 32 percent of the cases respectively and that he gave "prejudicial" advice to 15 percent and 65 percent of the cases respectively. As an example of "prejudicial" advice, they quote a judge in an actual court hearing:

At this time, I'd like to inform you that you have a right to have an attorney. If you cannot afford an attorney, I'll appoint an attorney for you. Or, on the other hand, if you'd like, *we can have the case heard today.*

Also, a case has been made by Carver and While (1968) that none of the Supreme Court decisions have actually granted the juvenile his constitutional rights. They have merely been gradually extending the due process clause to one such right after another. This means that juveniles will require separate rulings on every issue which has not been specifically ruled upon. Thus, the children's rights advocates apparently have a long road to travel in order to bring about full implementation of constitutional rights within the juvenile court system.

Chapter 5

Corrections and Punishment

THE SOCIAL CONSTRUCTION OF REALITY

No single penological doctrine can be identified as ever having guided the evolution of the prison. Today's prison administrator is the unhappy inheritor of a penological crazy-quilt whose pieces originated in religious beliefs, popular dogmas, humanitarian sentiments, military traditions, "scientific" theories, and administrative expediency. Now one, now the other of these sources achieved pre-eminence in the past as particular groups won the ear of legislators and policy-makers. (Taft and England, 1971:394)

Historical Relativity and Corrections

An important point that has recurred frequently in the preceding chapters is that the passage of laws is an outgrowth of collective definitions about the nature of reality, and that these definitions are, in turn, subject to much social, cultural, and situational relativity. We can learn much about the value system and normative priorities of a society by studying its laws and the stringency with which they are enforced. By investigating a society's arrangements for dealing with violators of the laws, we can also learn much about its definitions of the causes of and cures for deviance, and, indeed, its definitions of human nature itself. Erikson (1966) has identified two main competing philosophies which inform the American penal system and go all the way back to colonial times. The Quakers, who developed the Philadelphia system (or Pennsylvania system), were concerned mainly with changing the inner spiritual condition of the criminal, in the belief that a natural consequence would be a change in his behavior. The Puritans, on the other hand, were advocates of the so-called Auburn system, which was based on the belief that any hope of basic change in the character or spiritual condition of a criminal was futile, since he was probably only acting out his "predestined" nature.

TABLE 5-1 CAPITAL CRIMES IN THE UNITED STATES BY TYPE OF OFFENSE, JURISDICTIONS, AND EXECUTIONS (1967)

Type of Offense	Number of Capital Jurisdictions[a]	Number of Mandatory Jurisdictions	Number of Executing Jurisdictions[b]
Capitally punishable homicide	44	9	44
Murder	40	0	—[d]
Other homicide[c]	20	8	—[d]
Kidnapping[e]	34	1	6
Treason	21	11	0
Rape[f]	19	0	18
Carnal knowledge[g]	15	0	—[d]
Robbery[h]	10	0	7
Perjury in a capital case[i]	10	6	0
Bombing[j]	7	0	0
Assault by life term prisoner[k]	5	3	1
Burglary[l]	4	0	2
Arson	4	0	0
Train wrecking	2	0	0
Train robbery	2	0	0
Espionage[m]	2	0	1
Other[n]	17	5	0
Total[o]	44	22	45

[a] Fifty-five jurisdictions: Fifty states, District of Columbia, Puerto Rico, Virgin Islands, Federal civil and military.
[b] From National Prisoner Statistics, "Executions 1961." Alaska and Hawaii excluded. Executions in years prior to 1930 excluded.
[c] Includes sixteen special capital homicide statutes.
[d] Information not available; see note b.
[e] Included kidnapping for ransom, kidnapping with bodily harm, kidnapping for ransom and with bodily harm, taking a hostage.
[f] Includes rape, attempted rape, assault with intent to rape, drugging with intent to rape.
[g] Includes carnal knowledge of a minor and of a mentally deficient or mentally ill person.
[h] Includes robbery, aggravated robbery, armed robbery, bank robbery.
[i] Includes perjury and subornation leading to the death of a guilty person or to the death of an innocent person.
[j] Includes bombing, dynamiting, and bomb throwing.
[k] Includes assault and assault with a deadly weapon.
[l] Includes burglary and armed burglary.
[m] Includes gathering or giving information to an enemy or foreign power during wartime.
[n] Includes twenty-one special capital statutes.
[o] Because of duplications, the totals are less than the sum of the numbers in each column.
Source: H. A. Bedau, The Dealth Penalty in America, p. 46

Accordingly, the emphasis of the Auburn system was on changing the outward behavior only, by disciplining an offender into submission.

The relativity of our definitions of crime and the criminal can also be seen in the fact that even the severity of punishment for different offenses has constantly changed over time. Only a century or so ago in England, literally hundreds of crimes were punishable by the death penalty, whereas today in the United States it is doubtful whether many people believe any longer that the death penalty should be applied for any offenses at all. In recent years, our society has defined relatively few offenses as capital crimes, as Table 5-1 indicates. Homicide, rape, kidnapping, and treason have most often been punishable by the death penalty (Bedau, 1967a:46). From the 1930's through the 1960's, 86 percent of all executions were for murder, about 12 percent for rape, and about 2 percent for all other capital crimes (U.S. Bureau of Prisons, *National Prisoner Statistics,* August, 1969). It is interesting to consider the different labels that have been used over the years to define what we do to convicted criminals. We once spoke openly of punishment, and described our treatment program as a penal system. Now, increasingly, we are starting to use the euphemism "corrections" to describe our handling of the criminal. To get a deeper historical perspective on the evolution of our present penal or corrections system, however, and the enormous historical relativity which has molded that system, let us review some background information.

In general, four primary modes of dealing with offenders have been employed in the United States. During the colonial period, corporal punishment (e.g., flogging) was used almost exclusively to discipline those who violated the law. Capital punishment (death) was often used in dealing with what were considered more serious offenders in early America, and has persisted, but with decreasing frequency, up to modern times. The third method is imprisonment. The practice of depriving offenders of their freedom, as a means of punishing or treating them, first gained serious acceptance with the establishment of a small penitentiary, the Walnut Street Penitentiary, in Philadelphia in 1790.* Taft and England (1971: 403) point out that William Penn, Quaker founder of Pennsylvania, in his charter of 1682 for the colony, provided for imprisonment rather than corporal punishment for all offenses but murder (a capital offense), and that this charter was in effect until Penn's death in 1718, when it was revoked and the severe practices of corporal and capital punishments of the preceding period were revived. It was not until 1790, then, that imprisonment became an established form of penology in this country. The fourth, and most recently developed, means of dealing with criminals is the supervision and partial restriction of their activities by means of either probation or parole, which will be discussed further on.

The heaviest use of corporal punishment in America occurred among the colonial Puritans. Branding, flogging, and ear-clipping (severing the offender's ear from his head) were among the most frequently used penalties. Tongue-boring, accomplished with the aid of a hot iron, was practiced less frequently. According to Merrill (1945:769), breaking on the wheel also was employed in both New

---

* For a comprehensive account of the development of the Walnut Street Penitentiary see Negley K. Teeters, 1955.

York and Virginia during the colonial era. The stocks, the pillory, and the ducking stool were used for minor offenses. In some cases, the criminal's ear was nailed to the pillory and was torn or cut off upon his release. In the case of branding, most marks were in the form of letters indicating the type of offense committed ("B" for blasphemy, "A" for adultery, etc.), which were placed either on the thumb or forehead. Sentences were carried out publicly and, as indicated by Merrill (1945: 770), apparently without regard for sex differences.

Although the incidence of corporal punishment declined considerably following the Revolutionary War, it did not become extinct, and even after its use by the courts was generally abandoned, it was still employed by prison authorities in dealing with troublesome convicts. Until after the Civil War, the legal punishment in North Carolina for perjury in a capital case was cutting off the offender's right ear (Steiner and Brown, 1927:11-12). Court-ordered floggings, though rare by the 20th century, were administered as recently as 1948, in Maryland, and June, 1952, in Delaware. The pillory was also used in Delaware until 1905 (Barnes and Teeters, 1959:290-292). Sterilization was used as a punishment to some extent during the early part of the 20th century, especially for sex offenders. Whenever tested in the courts during the 20th century, however, sterilization for *punitive* reasons (as opposed to eugenic) has been held unconstitutional (Morris, 1934: 332-333). (See also George T. Felkenes, "Sterilization and the Law," in Harold K. Becker, et al. (eds.), *New Dimensions in Criminal Justice,* Metuchen, N.J.: Scarecrow Press, Inc., 1968.)

During the 20th century, the use of corporal punishment has been restricted mainly to prison inmates. Prior to the administration of Warden Thomas Mott Osborne (1914), the guards at Sing Sing Prison in New York were infamous for their frequent and merciless use of the whip in enforcing complete silence among the prisoners. Robert Burns, a prisoner, in a fascinating account of his experiences as part of a Georgia chain gang during the 1920's, relates how it was not uncommon for a convict to be placed in tight-fitting stocks if it was felt that he had not exhibited sufficient industry during a 14-hour day in the fields. After such placement, the bench upon which he was supported was removed, and he would be left to hang there in agony for an hour (Burns, 1932:171). MacCormick (1954:23) has stated that at Kilby Prison in Alabama in 1949 "flogging with a heavy leather strap was the routine punishment. . . ." A survey (Teeters, 1952) of 58 state and federal prisons indicated that by the early 1950's, the use of corporal punishment within these institutions had been virtually abandoned. It must be noted, however, that these findings were based on the replies of prison administrators, and may not have been strictly congruent with actual practice. For example, as recently as June 30, 1965, seven prisoners received ten lashes each for leading a sitdown strike at the Tennessee State Prison. As reported by *The New York Times* (July 1, 1965:14), it was the "first time . . . in more than a year" that such measures had been taken, thus indicating that the event was hardly considered an isolated occurrence. On September 5, 1966 (*The New York Times,* September 6, 1966:52), a strike at the Cummins Prison Farm in Arkansas (later to become the subject of a widely publicized scandal involving murder of, and extreme cruelty toward, inmates) led to the whipping of ten black inmates with a five-foot-long leather strap. As recently as October, 1971, abuse of prisoners in Virginia, including the use of corporal punishment, prompted a United States federal district judge (case of *Landman* v. *Royster*) to declare the treatment of prisoners by the Virginia state prison system unconstitutional on the grounds that it was a violation of the 8th Amendment prohibiting cruel and unusual punishment (*The New York Times,* November 1, 1971:1).

In colonial America, the legal system and, consequently, the administration of justice, largely conformed to that existing at the time in England. The frequent use of both corporal and capital punishment by the colonists was a natural outgrowth of their cultural heritage. Such crimes as idolatry, witchcraft, blasphemy, sodomy, and adultery were all punishable by death in 17th-century Puritan Massachusetts (Bedau, 1967a:5). Executions were carried out by hanging, burning, and, in at least one case, crushing (Bedau, 1967a:15). Occasionally, the corpse was cut into sections (quartered), and displayed publicly at various locations for a deterrent effect.

In early America, executions were almost always conducted in public, often in the town square. Gradually, a tendency developed for executions to take place within the privacy of prison walls, with an ever-decreasing number of witnesses, although executions were conducted in public as late as the middle 1930's. All executions within the last 35 years have been conducted privately, usually in the presence of ten or twenty official witnesses. The trend toward more humane methods of execution in America began with the 8th Amendment to the Constitution, which stipulated that punishments were to be neither cruel nor unusual. Since 1789, with very few exceptions, only four types of executions have been utilized in the United States: hanging, shooting, electrocution, and lethal gas. In 1825, a Negro was burned to death in an unusual legal execution in South Carolina, according to Teeters (1967:109-110). This was accomplished, judging from the constable's bill, with wood and "two bottles of Spirits Turpentine." In 1790, Congress made first-degree murder and rape capital offenses, with a mandatory sentence of hanging. Legal provision for a jury to specify life imprisonment instead of hanging was approved in 1875 (Kirchway, 1927). The electric chair was first used to execute William Kemmler on August 6, 1890, in the state of New York (Bedau, 1967a:17). On February 8, 1924, Gee Jon became the first person to be

Chapter 5 / Corrections and Punishment

TABLE 5-2 UNITED STATES PENITENTIARIES FOR ADULT MALE FELONS

Facility	Date Opened	Date Closed
McNeil Island, Washington	1-22-1865	—
Leavenworth, Kansas	7-1-1895	—
Atlanta, Georgia	1-31-1902	—
Lewisburg, Pennsylvania	11-15-1932	—
Alcatraz, California	9-1-1934	3-20-1963
Terre Haute, Indiana	10-18-1940	—
Marion, Illinois	6-3-1963	2-5-1965

Source: U.S. Bureau of Prisons, Statistical Report: Fiscal Years 1971 and 1972, Washington, D.C.: U.S. Department of Justice, Bureau of Prisons

put to death by the use of lethal gas. The execution took place in Nevada (Bedau, 1967a:18). In June, 1972, the United States Supreme Court ruled that the death penalty was unconstitutional, not in principle, but as it had historically been applied in practice; that is, capital punishment had been disproportionately meted out to those who were black, poor, and male.

The various forms of corporal and capital punishment, however, have increasingly given way to sentences of imprisonment. Strange as it may seem to us today, prisons for long-term incarceration are a fairly recent development in the long history of penology. The first such prison seems to have been the small Walnut Street Penitentiary established in Philadelphia in 1790 (Teeters, 1955). Until 1800, prisoners in this facility were treated quite humanely. With the exception of the most serious offenders (who were kept in solitary confinement), the inmates were provided with work, which they performed in congregate work areas. At night they slept in dormitory-type facilities. Food, clothing, and sanitary facilities were all adequate. By 1800, however, overcrowding and a fire which destroyed the prison's industrial facilities resulted in a deterioration of conditions. Virginia and Massachusetts followed the lead of Pennsylvania by building their first prisons in 1800 and 1805, respectively. New York's Auburn Prison was completed in 1819. In 1829, Pennsylvania's Eastern State Penitentiary was opened (Barnes and Teeters, 1959).

A large percentage of the structures in use as prisons today exhibit many of the same undesirable features present in these earliest penitentiaries (see Table 5-2). In a number of cases, structures which have extremely outdated facilities are still maintained. Taft and England (1971:417) suggest that one reason for the continued use of these archaic structures may be the expense involved in building new prison institutions. Pennsylvania's Eastern State Penitentiary had been in use for more than 140 years when it was closed in April, 1970. Of the five federal penitentiaries presently in use, three have been operating for over 70 years; construction on all three was begun prior to the turn of the century. The penitentiary at McNeil Island, Washington, is the oldest in the federal system, having opened on January 22, 1865.

Although a lack of constructive activities has been a serious problem in the history of penology in this country, early prisons, such as Auburn and Sing Sing, were quite successful in providing their inmates with work. At first such tasks were largely for the benefit of prison administrators, but in recent years efforts have been directed toward providing work which is primarily in the interests of the convict. Several methods have been used to employ prisoners over the years (Taft and England, 1971). One has been contract labor, in which prisoners have been gainfully employed by private industry, either under the direct supervision of guards within the prison walls, or (in the case of less dangerous convicts) in the temporary custody of industrial entrepreneurs. In either case, the convict's wages, which were very small, went to the state. Later on, the state began to employ convicts directly, either marketing the goods they manufactured, or using them to make products which the state supplied to the public (e.g., license plates). State and public use of convict labor on roads, in forests and parks, and so on, has also been common. However, this use of cheap prison labor in competition with free-market labor has drawn much criticism from both organized labor and private industry, as we will see in the sections on prisoner utilization and the reformatory movement.

One of the most infamous methods of employing prisoners has been the chain gang, which is a row of prisoners connected to each other by chains, usually at the ankles. Both private and public use has been made of these gangs, and it is difficult to say where the worst abuses have occurred. The first chain gangs were formed in post-revolutionary Pennsylvania in an attempt to remove prisoners from deteriorating prison conditions (Taft and England, 1971:404). The abuses which subsequently developed from the new practice, however, soon brought an end to the use of chain gangs in Pennsylvania. Although chain gangs were used to varying degrees in all parts of the country, they reached their peak in the Reconstruction period in the South. Steiner and Brown (1927:16-17) report that in North Carolina during the period from June 30, 1922 to June 30, 1925, 48 percent of those convicted of serious crimes were sentenced to chain gangs, while only 8 percent were sent to the state prison. While serving in chain gangs, prisoners lived in small, mobile, steel cages measuring 18 feet by 7 feet, and holding 18 men apiece. These were intended mainly as sleeping quarters, but on Sundays and during bad weather, the men had to remain in these cramped conditions for long periods of time (Steiner and Brown, 1927:55-56). An alternative scarcely preferable to the chain gang was that of languishing day after day in a prison cell. Albert Morris (1934: 442) has noted that in 1928, approximately 16 percent of the nation's prisoners

TABLE 5-3 PRISONERS EMPLOYED AT PRODUCTIVE (NOT INSTITUTIONAL MAINTENANCE) TASKS

Year	Percent Employed Productively		Percent Employed at Institutional Maintenance Tasks
	State and Federal	Federal Only	State and Federal
1885	75	—	—
1895	72	—	—
1905	65	—	—
1923	61	—	30
1928	58	26	29
1966-1970	(California only) 11–11.5	—	—
1970	—	32	—
1971	—	30	—

Sources: Figures up to and including 1928 are taken from L. N. Robinson, Should Prisoners Work?, 1931, pp. 6-11. Figures for California are from the report of the California Auditor General and Legislative Analyst, 1971, p. 2. The federal figures for 1970 and 1971 were computed from figures for those in the Federal Prison Industries or Federal work-release programs provided in the Federal Prison Industries, Inc., Annual Report, 1971, p. 2, and the total number of prisoners in the Federal system as given in the U.S. Bureau of Prisons, Statistical Report: Fiscal Years 1971 and 1972, p. 23.

was not provided with work of any kind (this figure may have included some who were physically or psychologically unemployable). During the present century, however, most prisoners have been kept gainfully employed. Between 50 percent and 75 percent of all state and federal prisoners have been employed in productive tasks other than institutional maintenance, and most of the rest are employed in prison maintenance tasks (Robinson, 1931:6-11), as Table 5-3 indicates.

Parameters of Consensual Reality

Valid statistical data on the various types of punishment and their supposedly ameliorative effects are hard to obtain. This has always been true. In Puritan times, when the codes of justice frequently called for different kinds of corporal punishment, no systematic data were kept on rates of recidivism, but the record does indicate that many persons were repeatedly punished for the same offense, so a recidivism problem doubtless existed. Data on capital punishment and its consequences are unavailable until recent times. In 1930, the U.S. Bureau of Prisons began compiling such statistics, and these indicate that capital punishment was regularly employed up through 1967. During this period it can be seen that there was a general trend toward making the administration of capital punishment less painful, as well as toward decreasing the number of crimes calling for its use. In very recent years, capital punishment has been retained only for the most serious

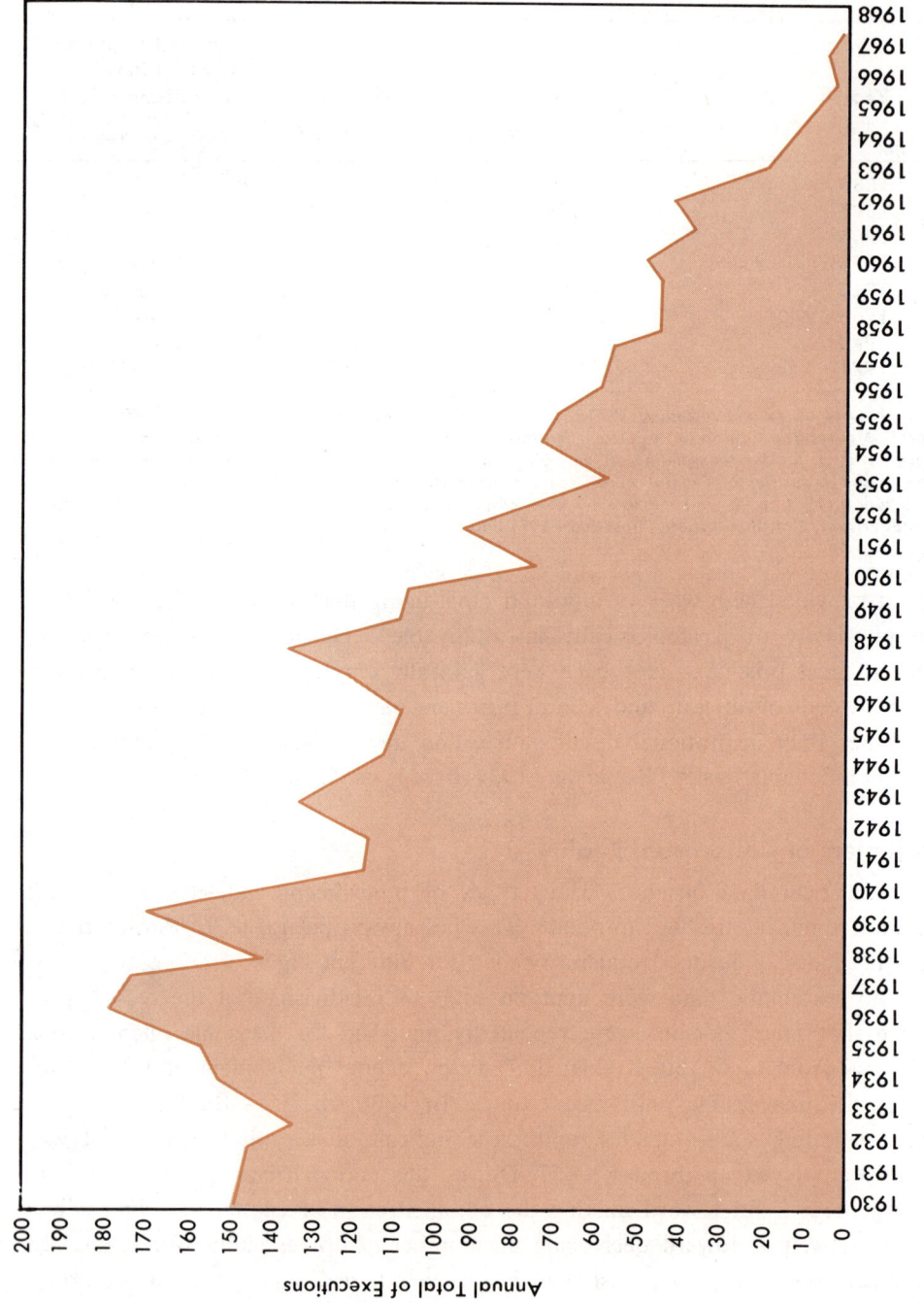

Figure 5-2 Frequency of Use of Capital Punishment, 1930 to 1968
SOURCE: U.S. Bureau of Prisons, *National Prisoner Statistics Bulletin*, 46, August 1971

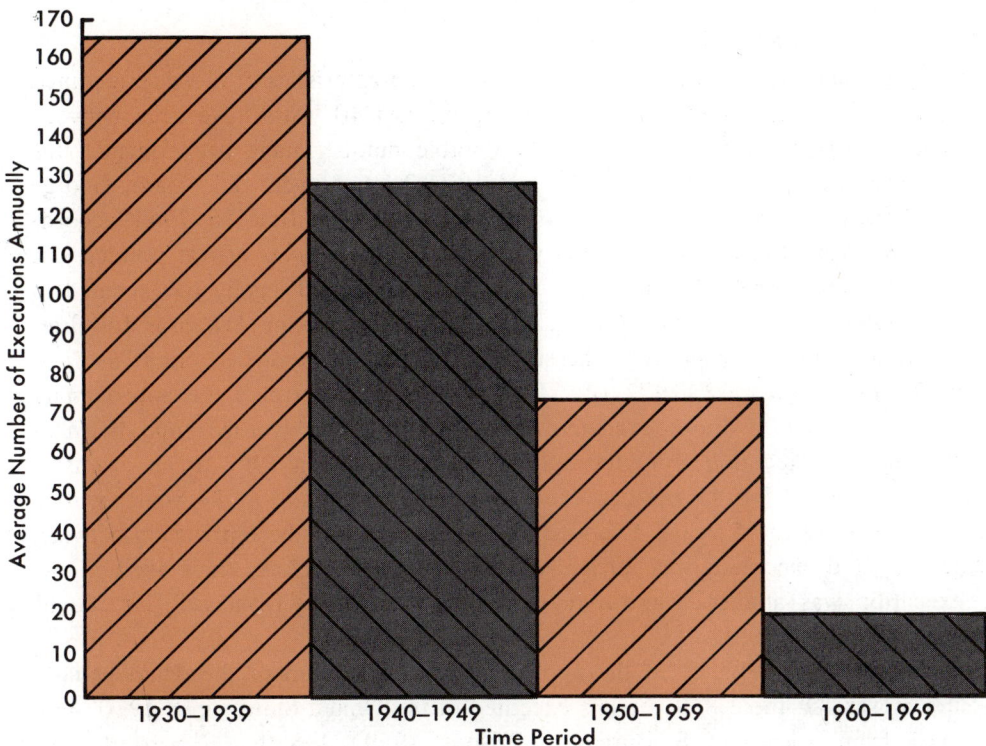

Figure 5-1 Decline in the Use of Capital Punishment
SOURCE: U.S. Bureau of Prisons, *National Prisoner Statistics Bulletin*, 46, August 1971

crimes, and its incidence has been steadily declining (see Figures 5-1 and 5-2). During the years 1930-1939, between 140 and 199 executions occurred annually. For the years 1940-1949, those figures dropped to between 153 and 117. From 1950 to 1959, the highest annual figure was 105, and the lowest was 49. Figures for subsequent years have been as follows:

1960	56	1964	15
1961	42	1965	7
1962	47	1966	1
1963	21	1967	2

There have been no executions in the United States since 1967.*

---

* All the data reported in this paragraph come from U.S. Bureau of Prisons, 1969. (See Bibliography.)

Characteristics of the Condemned

Some systematic data have been collected on the characteristics of those condemned and executed. Most persons executed during the last 40 years have been between the ages of 20 and 35, although a considerable number have been outside this range (U.S. Bureau of Prisons, 1963 and 1971a). A 14-year-old Negro, George Stinney, Jr., was executed for murder in South Carolina on June 16, 1944, according to *The New York Times* (January 7, 1962). The *Times* article pointed out that as of January, 1962, children as young as seven could legally be executed in several states. A 15-year-old boy was sentenced to death in Arkansas for first-degree murder in 1971, although the sentence has not been carried out (*The New York Times,* January 22, 1972:14). It is possible to determine the approximate age at sentencing of those executed by subtracting the average time between sentencing and execution from the age at execution. Using 1962 as an example, the median age of the 47 persons executed during the year was 28 years, with a range of from 19 to 45 years. The median elapsed time for these prisoners between sentencing and execution was 20 and-a-half months. Therefore, their average age at execution was about 26 and-a-quarter years (computed from U.S. Bureau of Prisons, 1971a).

The greatest discrepancy in the application and execution of the death penalty occurs by sex. Of the 3,859 persons executed in the United States since 1930, only 32 have been women (U.S. Bureau of Prisons, 1969), less than 1 percent. This is undoubtedly influenced to some extent by the fact that women are less likely to be involved in capital offenses than men. Of the 648 persons under sentence of death in the United States on May 14, 1971, only seven were women (*U.S. News & World Report,* May 31, 1971:37-38).

With reference to race, 53.5 percent of all persons executed since 1930 have been black, 45.4 percent have been white, and 1.1 percent have been members of other races (U.S. Bureau of Prisons, 1969, No. 45). In relation to their numbers in the population in general, blacks have been conspicuously overpresented in the ranks of those executed. Furthermore, blacks have received the death penalty for rape far more frequently than have whites. According to Silver (1972:138), ". . . 405 of 455 executions for rape between 1930 and 1971 were carried out on blacks; 58 of 61 such executions in Georgia were of blacks. . . ." She also points out that 190,971 persons were arrested for rape in the United States during 1969 and 1970 (see Figure 5-3).

Prisoner Living Conditions

American penal institutions have grown increasingly overcrowded through the years. In 1930, the normal capacity of institutions in the federal system was 7,434. The number of prisoners accommodated by these institutions exceeded 20,000,

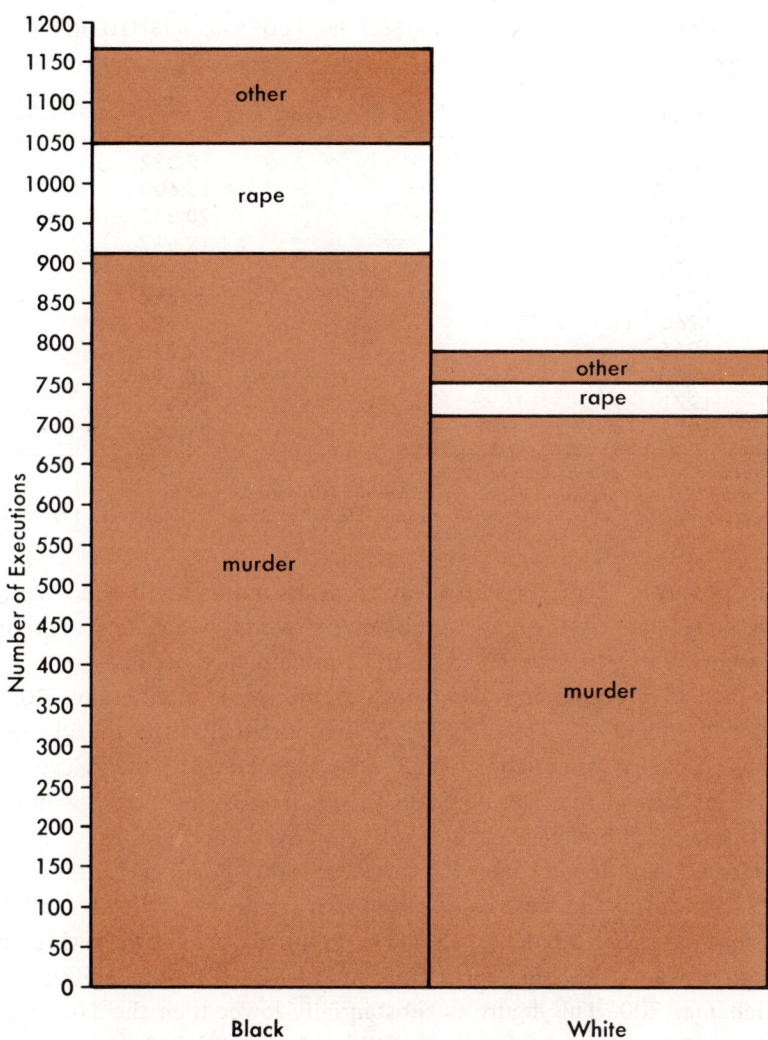

Figure 5-3 Executions by Crime and Race of Offenders, 1937 through 1950
SOURCE: U.S. Bureau of Prisons, *National Prisoner Statistics Bulletin*, 5, April 1952

and in 1960 the number reached almost 24,000. In 1972, there were 21,280 inmates in federal facilities alone (see Table 5-4).

The problem of overcrowding has been even more acute in many state systems. Federal prisoners, after all, represent only between 10 and 15 percent of those persons in prison facilities (not counting those housed in county or municipal jails and workhouses). Although some states, such as California and Massachusetts, have closed down several of their correctional facilities (especially those serving

TABLE 5-4 SENTENCED PRISONERS HOUSED IN FEDERAL INSTITUTIONS, 1930-1972

Year	Number of Sentenced Prisoners
1930[a]	12,332
1935[b]	15,600
1940[c]	20,345
1945	19,987
1950	17,930
1955	21,606
1960	23,974
1965	22,346
1970	20,686
1971	20,820
1972	21,280

[a] Source: U.S. Bureau of Prisons, Annual Report, 1930, p. 3
[b] Source: U.S. Bureau of Prisons, Statistical Report: Fiscal Years 1969 and 1970, p. 21
[c] Source for the years 1940-1972: U.S. Bureau of Prisons, Statistical Report: Fiscal Years 1971 and 1972, p. 23

juveniles), as a result of a recent shift away from institutionally based correctional programs, in most state systems the problem of overcrowding has continued to worsen in recent years. In several cases the problem has become so acute that officials have had to prohibit or restrict new commitments. In January 20, 1972, for example, *The New York Times* (1972:57) reported that the Florida Director of Corrections, Louis Wainwright, issued an order banning the acceptance of any additional inmates at the Florida State Prison because of overcrowding there.

Road-work gangs, although they are still employed, are not as common, no longer use chains, and have somewhat better conditions than formerly. As of October, 1971, however, their use in five southern states was still substantial (*The New York Times,* October 23, 1971:35): The number of convicts serving on road gangs in Virginia was 2,000; in North Carolina, 1,800; Florida, 1,500; Georgia, 800; and Alabama, 700. This figure is substantially lower than the 100,000 road-gang prisoners employed in the South in 1935. Mississippi ended the practice of chain gangs before World War II, and Louisiana followed suit shortly thereafter. A steady decline in the use of all kinds of road-gang convicts has taken place since that time. In 1960, there were 16,000 prisoners employed in such gangs; in 1965, 11,000; and in 1970, only 7,000. The use of road gangs in North Carolina was ended by legislative decree in July, 1973.

Prisoner Utilization

After the Hawes-Cooper Act of 1934, which severely limited the marketing of prison-made goods, the level of "unemployment" in prisons rose sharply, converting them into what Taft and England (1971:407) have described as "houses of idleness." Most prison-labor programs were forced to convert to the state-use, i.e., to produce goods or services for use or sale by federal or state governments. State use meant a highly restricted and limited market for products. Even the most successful state-use systems, such as the one developed in California, have not been able to provide employment for more than a small minority of their inmates. The federal government has developed one of the more successful state-use programs: Federal Prison Industries, Inc. was established in 1934, and sales for its first year totaled about $3 million. By 1970, this figure had reached over $58 million (Federal Prison Industries, Inc., *Annual Report,* 1971:3). Despite its financial success, less than 25 percent of federal prisoners are able to participate in the program.

It is not often that a man in free society is asked to do something for nothing, but this has frequently been the case in prison society. Even up to the present, prisoners receive ridiculously low pay for their labors if, indeed, they receive any pay at all. *The New York Times* reported on September 12, 1972 (p. 1) that most inmates in the New York State prison system make 35 cents per day or less. Wages paid in California's highly praised inmate employment system reportedly ranged from 2 cents to 16 cents per hour in 1970 (*Report* of the Georgia Legislature Penal Affairs Study Committee, 1971:3). In the federal program, average monthly wages for inmates were $38 in 1965, $40 in 1966, $41 in 1967, and $58 in 1970 (see Federal Prison Industries, Inc., *Annual Report,* 1966, 1967, and 1971). The special problems encountered by prison-labor systems make their production much less efficient than labor in private industry.

Various work-release programs have recently begun to provide the inmate with a higher level of compensation for his labors. In this type of program the inmate is released from prison during working hours in order to pursue a job in private industry, where he receives the same pay as free men working in the same position. (See below.)

Prison Staff Personnel

Until recently, prison administration was a political rather than a professional occupation. In a number of states, prison administrators are still political appointees. MacCormick (1954:26) has pointed out that the practice of making high administrative positions in corrections subject to political appointment has had several deleterious effects. Those who are appointed often gain their positions as a result of political expertise rather than through their skills in the area of corrections. Furthermore, such appointees are sensitive to political pressures, which often discourage the development of innovative programs. The extreme degree of job insecurity generated by such a system also makes it difficult to attract highly qualified individuals.

TABLE 5-5   EDUCATION AND INCOME OF PRISON GUARDS IN 1971

Education		Income	
Masters Degree	1%	Over $14,000	1%
Some Graduate Study	3%	$12,000–$14,000	2%
Bachelors Degree	3%	$10,000–$12,000	2%
1–3 Years of College	25%	$8,000–$10,000	16%
High School Graduate	52%	$6,000–$8,000	43%
Did Not Complete High School	16%	Under $6,000	36%

Source: The New York Times, September 26, 1971, 1:3

At the level of guards or custodians, low pay and undesirable working conditions are factors which operate against obtaining high-quality personnel. In many institutions, there is little difference between the guards and the convicts. One might even conclude that the convicts have the edge. In 1964, Bennett stated (1954:13) that the pay of a prison officer was ". . . usually less than that of a semiskilled industrial worker." In 1971, a nationwide survey (*The New York Times,* September 26, 1971:1) indicated that most prison guards received annual salaries of less than $8,000. Furthermore, fewer than half had any education beyond high school, and 16 percent had not even graduated from high school (see Table 5-5).

Alternatives to Imprisonment

The development of various methods of supervised release undoubtedly grew out of the realization that prisons were ineffective in accomplishing the goals of rehabilitation, and the reduction of recidivism. Probation (supervised release *in place of* prison) and parole (supervised release *after* a period in prison) have been the most commonly utilized means. Both were the outcome of the efforts of well-intentioned private citizens, and both finally gained legal sanction at the same time as the establishment of the Elmira Reformatory in 1876 (Chute and Bell, 1956:211). A Boston shoemaker, John Augustus, is considered to have been the first person to assume (unofficially) the duties of a probation officer. His voluntary work was performed in the period between 1849 and 1864. Although the first few probation laws were directed at offenders of all ages, initially, probation gained widespread use for juveniles. The practice of parole was officially accepted for adults even more quickly than the practice of probation. The federal government adopted the practice of parole in 1910, and by 1934, it was legal in all but two states, Virginia and Mississippi (Morris, 1934:475). It was not until March 4, 1925, however, that President Calvin Coolidge signed the Federal Probation Law (Chute and Bell, 1956:111). A full-time three-member Federal Board of Parole was established in 1930, and 48 percent of the prisoners released from state and

Chapter 5 / Corrections and Punishment

TABLE 5-6 FEDERAL ADULT PRISONERS RELEASED ON PAROLE OR AT EXPIRATION OF SENTENCE

Year	Paroled (a)	Mandatory Release (b)	Percent of (a) + (b) Paroled
1963	3,155	3,740	46
1964	2,992	3,788	44
1965	2,984	3,652	45
1966	3,396	3,388	50
1967	4,225	3,080	58
1968	3,418	2,739	56
1969	3,160	2,398	57
1970	2,673	2,625	50
1971	3,016	2,649	53
1972	3,257	2,562	56

Source: U.S. Bureau of Prisons, Statistical Report: Fiscal Years 1971 and 1972, pp. 190-191. Figures in final column were computed based on data presented in the above source.

federal prisons that year were released on parole. (The remainder had finished their sentences.)

Both parole and probation have continued to gain in popularity as methods of supervised release among those in charge of administering justice. Of those federal prisoners who were released in 1963, 46 percent were paroled. By 1966, this figure had risen to 50 percent, and the comparable figure for 1972 was 56 percent (see Table 5-6). Probation has enjoyed a similar level of acceptance during the last several years. By 1956, probation was legally sanctioned in every state (Taft and England, 1971:376). In Minnesota, probation is now used quite extensively; only about 19 percent of convicted felons are sent to prison (*The New York Times*, December 12, 1971:69), and the rest are placed on probation. In many states more than 50 percent of those convicted of crimes are placed on probation. This is especially true for first offenders.

Public Opinion and Punishment

The general public is scarcely aware of "facts and figures" of the kind we have been presenting here concerning the treatment of convicts, but this does not, of course, prevent people from forming definite opinions on the subject. The attitudes of the public toward corrections and punishment, and toward criminals themselves, are informed largely by the kind of law-and-order mentality that we discussed in the previous chapters; that is, most people seem inclined to favor a "hard line" toward those convicted of crimes, and to be more interested in their punishment than in their rehabilitation. We might note in passing that Americans have not been known to be too concerned with upholding the constitutional rights of those who

TABLE 5-7 THE OPINION OF THE GENERAL PUBLIC

Year	Favor Capital Punishment	Oppose Capital Punishment	No Opinion
1936[a]	62%	—	—
1953[b]	68%	25%	7%
1960[b]	51%	36%	13%
1965[b]	45%	43%	12%
1966[b]	42%	47%	11%
1969[b]	51%	40%	9%
1972[c]	53%	39%	8%

[a] G. S. McClellan, Capital Punishment, p. 93
[b] "Gallup Poll Sees Concern on Crime," The New York Times, February 16, 1969, 47:1
[c] National Opinion Research Center, Roper Poll, Spring, 1972

have unpopular ideas, to say nothing of those who have been convicted of deviant behavior. For example, in its 1972 Spring Social Survey, the National Opinion Research Corporation (NORC) found that 55 percent of the people in its national sample felt that they would like to prevent those "who are against all churches and religion" from teaching in a college or university; 32 percent would like to prevent those with such beliefs even from making a public speech; and 35 percent would like to remove any books written by them from public libraries.

Against such a low threshold of tolerance, it is not surprising to find in the same survey that 63 percent of the sample population felt that the courts were not dealing harshly enough with criminals, and that 53 percent favored the death penalty "for persons convicted of murder" (not necessarily even first-degree murder). Such opinions were expressed at almost exactly the same time (Spring, 1972) that the Supreme Court ruled against the current practice of capital punishment, indicating a considerable disparity between public and judicial opinion. Of the same sample, incidentally, 70 percent also favored requiring a firearm permit to purchase a gun.

The distribution of attitudes about capital punishment among various segments of the population in the 1972 NORC survey is also interesting (Petersen, 1974). Women were more likely than men to oppose capital punishment; Democrats more likely than Republicans; and blacks were twice as likely as whites to oppose it (perhaps because they have been affected by it in greater numbers). Opposition to capital punishment was stronger among those in the lower social classes than among those in the upper classes; stronger among the young than among the middle-aged and elderly; and strongest of all in the southern states. A Gallup poll taken several months after this NORC survey showed similar results, with a slight increase in the proportion favoring capital punishment (Berck, 1973).

Table 5-7 shows the changes in public opinion toward capital punishment over the past generation. For a long time, the proportion of our citizens favoring capital punishment remained at about two-thirds (62 percent to 68 percent), but then, in the 1960's, approval for this kind of punishment began to drop rapidly, reaching a low of 42 percent in the mid-1960's, and probably reflecting the national mood of social reform characteristic of the Kennedy-Johnson years. However, the rising crime rate of this same period (cf. Chapter 3) gave rise to a renewed law-and-order mentality, which is reflected in the continued upswing of sentiment favoring capital punishment since that time.

CHAMPIONS AND THEIR INTERESTS

The general public, although it does not usually take an active part in the process of correctional reform, does play an indirect role through its acceptance (or at least tolerance) of the reforms advocated by activist groups. The public probably played a more significant part in influencing correctional standards prior to the development of the complex, bureaucratic, impersonal structure surrounding the penal system which exists today. Crime and the criminal were perceived more personally when the victims often knew those who had victimized them, or those who were being publicly punished for victimizing others, and when the losses suffered could not be recovered through insurance companies. Modern methods of justice tend to isolate the criminal from his actual and potential victims, which may reduce the victims' desire for personal revenge, thus depersonalizing the whole process. This generalization would probably not apply in the case of violent crimes, where the public concern tends to be high, although more of our citizens are beginning to place the blame for some lawlessness on social conditions, rather than on the individual criminal.

The movements for correctional reform have not been homogeneous, closely integrated, or highly coordinated. They might better be conceptualized in terms of a *series* of movements, sometimes overlapping. Within each movement, different interest groups, although seeking similar ends, were often motivated by somewhat different needs, perceptions, and beliefs. Let us review the variety of interests, interest-groups, and publics that have been involved in the various reform movements.

Religious Interests

As we indicated previously, corporal and capital punishment flourished under the Puritan culture of early New England. The Puritans held strictly to rigid moral and religious doctrines, and attempted to suppress the slightest deviation from their standards. Kindness and affection were clearly subordinated to moral righteousness. Erikson (1966:189) has provided a clear picture of the consequences of such an orientation for the Puritan concept of justice: ". . . justice was governed by a relentless kind of certainty. Little attention was paid to the motives of the offender, the grief of the victim, the anger of the community, or any other human emotion: the whole process had a flat, mechanical tone because it dealt with the laws of nature rather than with the decisions of men. [Deviance was seen as an offense against] . . . the symmetry and orderliness of nature itself" (Erikson, 1966:187). Although they believed in the doctrine of predestination, which placed the ultimate destiny of a person beyond his own control, the Puritans (somewhat paradoxically) still felt that a man was responsible for his actions (Erikson, 1966:191). They believed that the wicked could be coerced and terrorized into conformity, but that true inner reformation was impossible.

The influence of Puritan ideology has not been completely eradicated from the attitudes of many present-day Americans. As pointed out by Erikson (1966:198),

The theological views which sustained this development pattern have largely disappeared from the religious life of the society, but the attitudes toward deviation which were implied in the pattern are still retained in many of the institutions we have built to process and confine deviant offenders. We are still apt to visualize deviant behavior as the product of a deep-seated characterological strain in the person who enacts it, rather than as the product of the situation in which it took place, and we are still apt to treat that person as if his whole being was somehow implicated in what is often no more than a passing deviant episode.

This puritanical approach to corrections has guided a number of interest groups involved in correctional reform. The concept of retribution—the feeling that the offender must "pay his debt to society" by forfeiting either his life or his freedom—has occupied a prominent position in the minds of many reformers.

The Quakers, unlike the Puritans, believed it was possible to improve the inner moral quality of a person. They did not consider the fate of an individual to be predestined or beyond his control. Rather than attempting merely to repress undesirable behavior, they sought to bring about moral reformation in the wayward (Erikson, 1966:199-205). Furthermore, the means which they pursued to achieve such transformation did not involve the bloody penalties often exacted by the Puritans. The Quaker religious orientation was one of love, brotherhood, and gentleness. They disliked physical violence, and in almost all cases opposed taking a human life on moral grounds. It is not surprising, therefore, that they have played a leading role in developing penological alternatives to corporal and capital punishment. The Quakers' emphasis on reformation has received strong support from many contemporary correctional reform groups. In the opinion of one writer (Leary, 1972), the major sustaining factor in the movement against capital punishment has been the theological position of the Quakers that taking a human life is never justified.

The establishment of centers of imprisonment tended to remove the correctional process from public scrutiny. People no longer crowded expectantly around the whipping post, or subjected those in the stocks or pillory to jeers and insults. The treatment of the offender grew less personal and more professional. Initially, those persons who were working for changes in the goals and methods employed in prisons were religiously committed professionals motivated by a humanitarian concern for the welfare of human beings subjected to intolerable conditions. They were often judges, lawyers, and prison administrators who were directly exposed to the plight of prisoners and more sensitive to penal abuses. In many cases, by virtue of the background required for their occupational positions, they were well-educated, socially aware people. Doctors, lawyers, teachers, and members of the clergy were prominent among those working for prison reforms. The prospects for "moral reclamation" of prisoners often appealed to churchmen, while those in the field of education were eager to demonstrate the value of their services in preparing the inmate for successful participation in society.

In recent times, religious representatives can be found on both sides of penological controversies, particularly those surrounding the capital punishment issue. The more liberal religionists tend to favor abolition of capital punishment and of other punitive approaches to corrections. In 1955, three chaplains at the Massachusetts State Prison sponsored a bill in the state legislature to outlaw capital punishment (*The New York Times,* December 7, 1955). During the 1960's, various well-organized religious groups took an influential stand against capital punishment. In January, 1960, the New York State Council of Churches offered its support to five bills coming before the state legislature aimed at limiting capital punishment, and shortly thereafter the Union of American Hebrew Congregations criticized important politicians who had not yet taken a public stand against capital punishment (*The New York Times,* January 14, and February 28, 1960). By early 1961, the National Council of the Protestant Episcopal Church was urging its members to support efforts to end the use of the death penalty on the grounds that it ". . . violates Christian teaching, brutalizes society, and fails to deter crime" (*Christian Century* 78, 1961:382). Mather (1965:382) suggests that the repeal of capital punishment in Iowa on February 18, 1965, may well have been partially due to the influence of a legislative seminar conducted by the Iowa Council of Churches and attended by a number of legislators. The successful repeal vote occurred the day after the seminar, at which church representatives spoke against the death penalty. Shortly thereafter *Time* (85, 1965:62-63) summarized the situation as follows: "The drive against the death penalty is gathering new momentum, gaining support from such religious groups as the Methodist Church, the Protestant Episcopal Church, the American Baptist Convention, and the Presbyterian Church in the U.S.A." The following year the Lutheran Church in America (an organization claiming 3.3 million members) went on record opposing the use of the death sentence (*The New York Times,* June 30, 1966). In 1968, the National Council of Churches publicly stated its opposition to capital punishment, and requested that member denominations take active steps to support legislation to end its use (*The New York Times,* September 14, 1968:37). A brief opposing capital punishment, on the grounds that it was "cruel and unusual," was filed with the United States Supreme Court in October, 1971, by 14 religious organizations and individuals, including the National Coalition of American Nuns (2,000 members) and the 42-million member National Council of Churches of Christ in the U.S.A. (*Nation,* 213, 1971:228). That same year the World Council of Churches also voiced its support for abolition of capital punishment.

A religious organization which is still very prominent in corrections reform is the Society of Friends (Quakers), working largely through its social-service arm, the American Friends Service Committee (AFSC). Active in most American cities, the AFSC works to abolish the use of prisons and to improve conditions within existing prisons. In 1972, the Center for Peace and Social Justice was established by a group of Franciscan priests in San Francisco. Its aim is to coordinate the efforts of all reform-oriented religious groups in working for greater justice in the prisons (Daniels, 1974). There are many such local religious-interest groups concerned with prisoner conditions in cities across the country.

Moral Interest Groups

Moral interest groups and individuals outside of organized religion have also been very important in agitating for penological changes over the years. In 1787, Benjamin Franklin and Benjamin Rush, both prominent early reformers, were influential in the establishment of the Philadelphia Society for Alleviating the Miseries of Public Prisoners. This was the organization mainly responsible for the institution of the "new penitentiary" at the Walnut Street Jail in Philadelphia three years later (Teeters, 1955:29-32). Now known as the Pennsylvania Prison Society, this organization is still active in correctional reform.

The state of New York has also produced many active correctional reformers. In 1846, the New York Prison Association was organized, with the stated goals of ". . . amelioration of the condition of prisoners, . . . improvement of prison discipline and . . . government . . . , [and the] support and encouragement of reformed convicts after their discharge . . ." (New York Prison Association, *Annual Report,* 1910:4). Although the reformatory concept, emphasizing training rather than punishment, had been applied to juveniles at the New York House of Refuge as early as 1825 (Taft and England, 1971:443), the New York reformers of the

1860's, joined by the enthusiastic support of Franklin Sanborn from Boston and Zebulon Brockway of Detroit, urged the application of the reformatory concept to the treatment of adult offenders as well. Brockway, especially, was strongly impressed by the mark system then in use in Ireland whereby indeterminate sentences were given to offenders, with the individual earning his freedom in degrees by exhibiting evidence of his "reformation" (Conrad, 1967:89-90). (Cf. the section later in this chapter on The Reformatory Movement.)

Thomas Mott Osborne was one of the most progressive penologists of the reformatory movement. First, as head of the prison at Auburn, New York, and later as warden at Sing Sing Prison, Osborne transformed "disgraceful, inhumane institutions" into promising correctional facilities. Various individuals and interests opposed to Osborne kept his programs from receiving very extensive testing or support, and he retired rather early in life. Osborne always treated his inmates as normal human beings, and he attempted to make conditions within the prison resemble those of free society as much as possible. Rather than repressing and coercing those under his command, he attempted to encourage them to make their own decisions, and to accept responsibility for conducting their own society. Osborne assisted the inmates in establishing their own government, consisting of elected representatives and appointed committees. He guided them in setting up their own judicial system to deal with disciplinary problems within the prison. The inmates even had their own parole board, which was empowered to decide if the sanctions imposed on those violating prison rules could be lifted early (this did not apply to release from the institution). A system by which inmates were compensated for their work was also developed, and a bank was opened in which inmates could accumulate savings. Morris (1934:505) reports that seven months after its founding, prisoner accounts in the bank totaled $31,424.41, an average of slightly over $30 per inmate depositor.

More recently, many moral interest groups have sprung up in various states to work for certain reforms in the corrections system. California has a particularly large number of active interest and pressure groups, moral and political, as well as religious (see above). For example, the Committee for Prisoner Humanity and Justice, based in San Francisco, was started in 1971 as a private, non-profit organization working on the legal, medical, and educational problems of prisoners. The Medical Committee for Human Rights is a national organization dating back to the early 1960's, with interests in prison-health care and maintenance. Formed to help with the problems of prisoners' families is the Friends Outside, another San Francisco organization that offers free food and clothing to families of prisoners, and child care for mothers visiting prisons (Daniels, 1974). Among those moral-interest groups working specifically against capital punishment have been Citizens

Against Legalized Murder (1966) and the American League to Abolish Capital Punishment (1925), which will be discussed at length in the section on The Movement to Abolish Capital Punishment.

Economic and Political Interest Groups

Economic and political interests have also appeared on both sides of the corrections-reform issue. Industrial interests at first exploited prisoners on many occasions, and opposed the development of prison-labor programs which were operated on a more equitable basis by the state. The American Federation of Labor has often joined forces with organized groups in management to resist the expansion of prison industries, and to avoid the competition which might develop between prisoners and free-market laborers. On the other hand, political leaders, desiring to keep taxes for prison maintenance and administration to a minimum, have often tried to develop profitable prison industries, but with only secondary concern for the rehabilitative influences on the inmates. Both labor and management, then, tend to see prisoners as possible competitors, while politicians tend to view them as a source of public income. More recently, inmates have been able to exert some economic and political influences for themselves.

Political interest groups concerned with civil rights and liberties have recently taken very active positions in the movement for correctional reform. As criminals have come to be viewed more as unfortunate victims of deviant societal influences than as inhuman monsters, guarantees of their rights have been added to the objectives of civil rights organizations. These groups see the prison inmate as a part of our disadvantaged minorities, and as subject to discrimination and prejudice by the larger society. They also consider the disproportionately high number of blacks in prison as symptomatic of repression by white society, from which convicts need special protection. The American Civil Liberties Union and the National Association for the Advancement of Colored People have become increasingly effective and influential in their defense of minority prisoners' rights. Although the ACLU did not officially join the movement to abolish capital punishment until 1965, and the NAACP until two years later, their influence in this area was felt somewhat earlier. Prior to the execution of Carryl Chessman in 1960, more than 200 persons from various abolition organizations mobilized to protest the execution and marched down New York's Fifth Avenue, while another large group held a protest vigil around San Quentin Prison in California, where the execution was to take place (*Life* 48, May 9, 1960:45).

Although prisoners themselves have had little influence over trends in correctional policy in the past, lately they have begun to gain more influence. Although they are most directly affected by correctional policy, throughout the entire history of penology they have had almost no influence on such policies and practices. Under the influence and guidance of various reformist groups, prisoners are attempting to redefine themselves and their situation. Instead of viewing their criminal actions as sinful, and their punishment as just, they have begun to view their conduct as a justifiable reaction to the injustices of a corrupt social organization and an inequitable opportunity structure; and they see the retribution demanded of them by society as a confirmation of its unjust and repressive nature. Supported by such a construction of reality, prisoners are becoming increasingly militant in demanding their rights as human beings. Particular expressions of this view will be discussed below.

The issues on which political interest groups tend to focus are the low wages (usually only pennies per hour) paid for prisoners' labor, and the lack of due process and other ordinary civil rights in life within the prison. In some states, there are special grievances besides, which are an outgrowth of a particular system. In California, for example, which many experts have regarded as having an especially "progressive" and "enlightened" corrections system, political-interest groups (including prisoners' groups) have been very critical of the indeterminate sentence (discussed further at the end of this chapter), and of the California Adult Authority. The latter acts as a parole board which passes judgment on when and whether prisoners are ready for release on parole. Prisoners feel that the police-related backgrounds of most of the nine CAA members make them unsympathetic and arbitrary in their judgments. The indeterminate sentence, though originally intended to allow for shortened prison terms after sufficient "rehabilitation" of prisoners had occurred, has apparently been used by the CAA instead for justifying additional time of incarceration before parole. California now has the highest average period in the nation of first-sentence time served before parole (two to three-and-half years) (Daniels, 1974; Mitford, 1971).

Among the economically and politically oriented organizations fighting against current conditions of prison life are the Prison Law Collective, a private non-profit organization founded in San Francisco in 1970, which helps prisoners with legal problems in a variety of ways; the Prisoners' Union, a national outfit in existence since 1971, which focuses on prisoners' civil rights and wages; and the United Prisoners' Union, similar in orientation to the Prisoners' Union, but more self-consciously radical (Daniels, 1974). Politically oriented pressure groups working against capital punishment, in particular, are the special units (or projects) which have been organized within both the ACLU and the NAACP, both of which have also traditionally worked in the more general area of prisoner rights and treatment (Schardt, 1973, and Berck, 1973).

Scientific Interest Groups

In the distant past, when crime was believed to be caused by evil spirits which possessed humans, corrective action was taken mainly to propitiate the deities offended by these spirits. It was merely incidental that such action might involve a particular person. As the individual came to be seen as responsible for his own actions, however, punishment came to be applied for purposes of both revenge and deterrence. Most recently, with the development of the biological sciences, the idea that a person is totally responsible for his own actions has been partly replaced by the idea that his actions constitute an illness or abnormality, and the emphasis on punishment has given way to pathology and the need for rehabilitation. Further, the rise of the social sciences has resulted in a search for the societal genesis of both law and crime. Crime is coming to be seen more as an indicator of social, rather than of individual, "problems." Such a perspective seems to dictate treatment and change of the society rather than of the individual. Exponents of this view have comprised some of the most influential professional interest groups yet to become involved in correctional reform movements. Psychologists, psychiatrists, and sociologists have been eager to justify their theories. Scientific theories require empirical tests, and the prisons have provided an ample supply of subjects for their study. Today, criminology is definitely an important field in sociology, with many academicians devoting their careers to the study of corrections and correctional reform. Whereas psychologists have focused on changing the individual, sociology has emphasized the need for broader changes in society's criminal-justice system. In the words of McAnany,

> While humanitarian-minded men have always been associated with the penal systems in the past, their position was, at best, personal and uncertain. With the advent of social science to the arena of punishment, however, a now clearly defined school of thought has arisen whose insistence on the reform of the convict as the central theme of criminal sanctions excludes or subordinates all other ends of punishment. . . . Science became the means, replacing religion and moral exhortations, whereby bad men were turned into good. (1971:128)

Whereas McAnany goes on to stress changing the individual, others have more strongly advocated a change in the opportunity structure offered by society (e.g., Ohlin, 1971:36).

The various scientific definitions of the criminal have been somewhat at odds with the definitions of the various reformers.

The disciplines of both psychology and sociology have greatly influenced prison policies. Psychology began gaining recognition as a genuine scientific discipline in early 20th-century America, and this was reflected in some of the new methods of treatment applied to criminals at that time. The Boston Municipal Court became the first to use clinical evaluation in dealing with adult offenders in 1914, and in 1921, the Detroit Recorder's Court was the first to set up a completely equipped clinic for treatment of adult offenders (Morris, 1934:305). Psychologists were accustomed to looking at individuals and individual pathology, and they naturally looked for the causes of criminal behavior within the individual. Somewhat later, in the 1940's and 1950's, sociologists, having gained a degree of stature in the scientific community, began to exert some influence over the directions taken in correctional reform, and a new conception of the prisoner began to develop in the minds of both prison administrators and the general public, as Conrad has pointed out:

Our perception of the criminal has changed. We no longer view him as one who has wilfully chosen to do evil in preference to good. We now see him as one who has been caused by unfavorable circumstances to offend against society. The circumstances which led him to crime might be found within him by the psychologist or around him by the sociologist. Whatever their origin, the belief prevails that both circumstances and their effects can and should be changed. The thrust of this belief has had a profound effect on prison management and reform. (1967:90-91)

Obviously, the way in which a criminal is defined will determine society's response to him. The major contribution of psychology and sociology in creating a new definition of the criminal was to emphasize that those factors responsible for his criminological behavior might well be beyond his control, or inherent in certain social situations, and that they should be dealt with in a rational, scentific manner. The most important theories about crime from this perspective have already been reviewed in Chapters 1 and 3.

Social scientists, in alliance with cooperative prison administrators, have assumed considerable leadership in the contemporary correctional reform movement. Service on federal and state advisory or planning commissions has been a frequent means by which psychologists and sociologists have been able to put their ideas into practice. Recommendations and reports presented to political and administrative officials by such groups as the American Correctional Association and the National Council on Crime and Delinquency have also had an impact on penological practices.

The application of scientific research procedures to the problems of corrections has probably been responsible for the increasing emphasis on parole and probation during the 20th century. The few existing analyses of data on prisoners and on recidivism rates reveal that imprisonment often has done more harm than good in attempting to "reform" offenders. A result of such research has been an increasing tendency in contemporary corrections theory and policy to place offenders in non-institutional programs, but so far the results have been no better than those

TABLE 5-8   RECIDIVISM BY TYPE OF CRIME, 1970-1972

Robbery	77%	Gambling	65%
Forgery	74%	Weapons (illegal poss.)	62%
Auto theft	73%	Larceny	61%
Burglary	71%	Narcotics	60%
Fraud	69%	Embezzlement	34%
Assault	68%	All others	66%

Average for all—65%

The above figures refer to the percents of repeaters found among 228,032 adults arrested in the United States for federal violations during 1970, 1971, and 1972. Their average age was 29 at last arrest, and 24 at first arrest, for an average criminal career length of 5 years. Among these arrestees, 25% had one prior conviction, 9% had two, 5% had three, and 8% had four or more.

Source: Federal Bureau of Investigation, Uniform Crime Report, 1972, pp. 37 and 38

produced by conventional methods of incarceration (see Table 5-8). It will probably be some time, actually, before we will know much about the effects of new corrections theories and policies, since the FBI began only in 1970 to do systematic research on criminal biographies (FBI, Uniform Crime Report, 1972:35-39).

James Q. Wilson, an eminent contemporary criminologist, has explained very perceptively why social science theories have not been very helpful in rehabilitating criminals, or even in reducing their rates of recidivism. In the first place, the interest of social scientists in penology itself (as opposed to criminology) is comparatively recent:

It was not until 1966, fifty years after criminology began as a discipline in this country, and after seven editions of the leading text on crime had appeared, that there began to be a serious and sustained inquiry into the consequences for crime rates of differences in the certainty and severity of penalties. (Wilson, 1974:52)

Furthermore, as Wilson points out, scientific theories which look for the causes of criminal behavior in forces outside the individual, over which he has little or no control, are probably incapable by definition of helping to further the processes of reform and rehabilitation, because they are deterministic. That is, they "explain" not only why persons commit crimes, but also why they *must* do so. Such "explanations" do not help in the development of rehabilitative methods. Wilson goes on to show, from the 1966-1967 report of the Federal Crime Commission, that social-science theories and recommendations about crime and rehabilitation had little basis in actual scientific research, reflecting instead the personal and ideological biases of individual social scientists (Wilson, 1974). Thus, at present, there are no truly scientific grounds for believing that any methods of correction work better than any others, either in deterrence or in rehabilitation (Wilson, 1974; Wilkins, 1969; and Martinson, 1974).

SOCIAL MOVEMENTS IN CORRECTIONS AND PUNISHMENT

As we have already indicated, the earliest penological methods employed in this country consisted almost exclusively of various forms of physical punishment. Such methods were expedient for the time and place: a developing frontier society struggling for survival in an unknown land could hardly be expected to support a nonproductive prisoner population for long. The whipping post, the stocks, and the branding iron were very economical penological techniques. Furthermore, the Puritans, whose influence was far wider than the Quakers', were not really concerned with reformation as such. Their goal was simply deterrence: to make punishment so unpleasant that criminals would not dare to repeat their offenses. When offenses were repeated, the same punishments were simply applied with increasing severity. The Puritan character was well-suited to severe corporal punishments. Their religious doctrines, perhaps the most basic aspect of their culture, emphasized the physical horrors which awaited the sinful after death. The severe abuses inflicted on criminals could easily be seen as an extension of divine wrath to life on earth (Erikson, 1966:188-190).

Penological Social Movements and Their Natural Histories

As we look back over the variety of movements, reformers, crusaders, and interest groups that have defined the "social problem" of punishment and corrections in our history, we can see certain patterns that are consistent with the theoretical perspective of this book. The nature and definition of this social problem have shifted from one generation to the next, and public or interest-group concern for the treatment of convicts has waxed and waned with little regard for the realities of changing prisoner conditions. More important in determining the "career patterns" of reform movements have been general societal events and conditions such as wars, depressions, and the rise and fall of other social movements, which have sometimes helped and sometimes displaced the corrections reform movements. Throughout the history of the social movements in the area of corrections, it is possible to see a continuing (and still unresolved) tension between the two opposing philosophies present from the beginning: the Puritan, with its emphasis on punishment, control, and retribution, and the Quaker, with its belief in regeneration or rehabilitation. This tension has expressed itself in all of the penology reform movements that we have had, while in general these movements have each followed the natural history pattern suggested in Chapter 2 (either Figure 2-1 or Figure 2-4).

Aside from the movement to abolish capital punishment, which we will consider separately, the three major reform movements in penology have been: (1) the prison or penitentiary movement, (2) the reformatory movement, and (3) the prisoners'-rights movement. For each of these, we can see a period of incipiency, characterized by murmurs and criticisms of existing arrangements on the part of occasional social commentators, perhaps inspired by Quaker traditions. Then gradually there follows a period of coalescence, when the dissenters form new organizations to promote their criticisms and to define for the public the nature of the "social problem" found in the correctional institutions. In response to these organizations, but without making drastic or widespread changes in the existing arrangements, the establishment, in the form of legislators and prison administrators, initiates new and usually "experimental" programs in corrections reform, thus taking account of the reform movements or institutionalizing them. Encouraged by such developments, the reformist interest groups and individuals then tend to turn their attention to other pursuits, and at length the corrections programs and institutions revert to the same "deplorable" conditions as existed before, with the establishment pleading financial problems, citizen pressures, and the like. These are the symptoms of the fragmentation and demise stages of the reform movements, and the end (at least temporarily) to the "social problems" originally defined by them.

The Prison or Penitentiary Movement

Starting about the same time as the nation itself, and lasting well into the 19th century, this movement had its incipiency in Pennsylvania, where Quaker influence was relatively strong. Benjamin Rush and Benjamin Franklin were two of its earliest and most eminent spokesmen. The main objective of this movement was to persuade society to depart from the traditional Puritan-based system of stocks, pillory, and physical mutilation, and instead put convicted offenders in solitary confinement; here a program of isolated but humane treatment would help them to meditate upon their errors and their circumstances and thus to develop a "penitent" attitude. Places for such confinement were called new prisons or penitentiaries (as distinguished from jails, which had long been in use for short-term confinement). The coalescence of this movement was evidenced by the organization of the Philadelphia Society for Alleviating the Miseries of Public Prisoners (a descendant of which has continued down to the present, with somewhat different objectives, as the Pennsylvania Prison Society). This organization was influential in the establishment of the Walnut Street Penitentiary in Philadelphia just before the turn of the 19th century, as we have mentioned earlier; this was the first of a few new prisons which represented the institutionalization of the movement.

Other new prisons established as part of this movement about the same time included one in New Jersey (1798), in Virginia (1800), in Massachusetts (1805), in Vermont (1808), in Maryland and New Hampshire (1812), Ohio (1816), and the Western State Penitentiary at Allegheny, Pennsylvania (1828). Of all of these, New York's Auburn Prison (1819) and Pennsylvania's Eastern State Prison (1829) came to be perhaps the best known nationally and internationally as prototypes or models of the Auburn System and the Pennsylvania System, respectively (Sutherland and Cressey, 1966:505-508). The chief difference between the two was that Auburn modified the strict practice of solitary confinement common to Pennsylvania (intended to keep the prisoners from having unwholesome influences on each other and to encourage their meditation), applying it only at night. During the day, Auburn prisoners worked together in productive labor, but under a rule of silence. Some rivalry developed between the two models, each claiming the greater effectiveness. Many Europeans seemed impressed by the Pennsylvania model, but the Auburn approach gained greater currency in the United States, partly, no doubt, because of the greater expense of maintaining a totally solitary arrangement (Sutherland and Cressey, 1966:508-509). In any case, these two approaches dominated American penological thought and practice until Brockway and the Reformatory Movement (see below).

Many other innovations in the treatment of prisoners occurred beginning in 1790, including paying them for their labor at free-market rates; classification of prisoners on the basis of their rehabilitative potential; providing them with books and basic schooling; and giving them some degree of medical attention (Teeters, 1955:127). Visiting privileges were also in effect at least as early as 1808 (Teeters, 1955:57), depending on the behavior of the inmate. Furthermore, a pardoning procedure gradually became more common until 1820, when Pennsylvania Governor William Findlay refused to approve pardons simply on the basis of recommendations by the prison's board of inspectors. Instead, the Governor suggested the use of the limited indeterminate sentence, but this was not officially introduced until much later.* (The prison board recommended for pardon those whom they felt had undergone appropriate reformation [Teeters, 1955:82].)

The new penitentiaries and other innovations were considered progressive models for the world in the early 19th century, and were visited by a number of European reformers. Ironically, however, the very fact that these penitentiaries removed prisoners from the public exposure they had had previously made the "social problem" of treatment of prisoners more remote from the public consciousness. At the same time, the country was beginning to be caught up in other, more immediate and pressing social movements, such as the rise of Jacksonian democracy, and the movement to abolish slavery, which seemed to use up the society's

---

* The indeterminate sentence had been employed in this country since the beginning (and still is) in a variety of penological programs. The first truly legal and widespread use of it, however, was at the Elmira Reformatory, with adult offenders, in New York in 1889 (Sutherland and Cressey, 1966:627-628).

"quota" of social problems, and left little public attention for the prisoner issue. After an initial period of some improvements the prisons of the country, including the new kinds resulting from this early movement, reverted to conditions of overcrowding, poor treatment of prisoners, etc., in which they pretty much remained until after the Civil War. This "relapse" signaled the decline and demise of this first reform movement in penology.

The Reformatory Movement

After the Civil War, a new penological movement began to take shape, whose origins have been described by Grünhut:

> The tasks of Reconstruction aroused and deepened the sense of social responsibility. Enthusiastic interest in an active and conscious penal policy spread over the United States. . . . Enoch Cobb Wines, secretary of the New York Prison Association, and Theodore W. Dwight, the first head of Columbia Law School, were the "heralds" of the new movement. All seemed to agree upon the ultimate aim, i.e., to make the utmost efforts, by appealing to the positive side of the prisoner's character, to reclaim the criminal for useful membership in society. (1948:89)

STRATEGIES OF THE MOVEMENT AND SOCIETAL RESPONSES In 1867, the efforts of the New York Prison Association began to bear fruit when it succeeded in persuading the Legislature to provide funds for the establishment of the Elmira Reformatory, the first institution of its kind in the United States for adult offenders (Morris, 1934:373-4). The facility was not ready for use until 1876, and while awaiting its completion, the reformers organized the first National Prison Congress in Cincinnati, Ohio in 1870. Grünhut (1948:90) has termed this event ". . . the peak of the [reformatory] movement. . . ." According to Alper and Boren (1972: 17-23), the ideas of reformation, moral direction, and personalized justice were advocated in an almost religious atmosphere. Those attending the conference voted to establish the American Prison Association (now the American Correctional Association), and elected Enoch Wines as its first secretary. Wines, an ardent proselytizer for the reformatory cause, went on to become the primary force behind the organization of the International Prison Congress of 1872 held in London.

The ideals of the leaders of the reformatory movement were quite radical for their time. Public acceptance for the institution was won from Elmira residents largely through the persuasive efforts of the Reverend Thomas K. Beecher, an influential Elmira minister who approved of the new correctional approach. Several political and judicial ties of the reformers also helped to insure the success of the project (Brockway, 1912:161-2).

When the Elmira Reformatory opened in 1876, Zebulon Brockway was its first superintendent. This gave Brockway a perfect opportunity to put his ideas into practice. Work, education, and religion were seen as the means for reforming the individual, while the motivation for reform was supplied by the flexibility of the indeterminate sentence. Brockway's reforms included

> ... uniform but not degrading clothing; a liberal dietary; gymnasium and appliances for physical culture and athletics; instruction in trades; military band; school of letters with classes from kindergarten through high school; library; weekly institutional paper; entertainments in the auditorium; optional religious attendance. (Taft and England, 1971:413)

Brockway was a very dedicated reformer, who spent almost his entire life in the movement. His commitment to the use of the indeterminate sentence as a tool of reform was especially strong, and he gave speeches and wrote papers advocating it at every opportunity.

The New York Prison Association has continued to be a staunch supporter of the reformatory movement well into the present century. The report of the Association for the year 1910 clearly indicates its commitment:

> Recognizing ... that legitimate publicity is of importance in gaining and holding friends, the Association has during the year frequently availed itself of the columns of the New York daily press. We have published a number of leaflets depicting in a simple and graphic manner our various activities, illustrated when possible by photographs. During the year the Association has maintained a press service, sending specially prepared articles to about 200 newspapers in New York State; these articles had educational value and were widely printed. The general secretary of the Association, acting as the chairman of the publicity committee of the International Prison Congress, carried on during the earlier months of 1910 a national press service with gratifying results. During the year several members of the staff of the Association have been active on the lecture platform, especially in churches in New York city and vicinity. (1910:20)

Obviously this was a well-organized and highly energetic pressure group.

In addition to the above activities, the Association sponsored a "prison-day" campaign for which special coverage by the newspapers was obtained. This campaign consisted also of circulating to churches "... material containing adequate information in printed form for use in sermons and addresses," and introduced several new prison reform bills in the legislature (New York Prison Association, *Annual Report,* 1910:24). It was also during this period that the principle of supervised release, now embodied in probation and parole, began to gain widespread official sanction.* The professionals working in these areas established

---

* Probation as a form of supervised release was first instituted as state policy in Massachusetts in 1880. Parole, while it had been used in a limited way in New York as part of the Elmira Reformatory program as early as 1869, was first officially adopted by a state in Ohio in 1884 (Sutherland and Cressey, 1966:627-628).

national professional organizations to further the development of supervised release procedures.

However auspicious the reformatory movement may have been for a while, it was gradually undermined by overcrowded facilities and by the opposition of unions and industry to the use of prison labor. Vocational training and productive employment had been important elements in the basic philosophy of the reformatory movement, but, as Robinson explained it:

> Throughout the entire nineteenth century and down to the present time the steady pressure of union labor has been applied to restrict the sale of prison-made goods and the use of prison labor on building construction; occasionally road work by prisoners has been protested against. (1931:61)

The American Federation of Labor, established in 1881, had become a powerful political influence by the early part of the 20th century. In the face of opposition from such a strong union, politicians were unlikely to support the interests of convicts, who were not even allowed to vote. Later on, the depression of the 1930's probably served to step up the efforts of both labor and industry in opposing prison production. Pushed by the lobbying and pressure group of the AFL, the Hawes-Cooper Act was approved on January 19, 1929. Designed to take effect five years after its passage, it gave states the right to ban the importation of prison goods if they so chose. During the five-year interim period between the passage and the implementation of the Act, the AFL managed to gain the support of several state legislatures, assuring that the provisions of the Act would be applied to the advantage of organized labor in those states. Further, the Ashhurst-Summers Act of 1935, as well as additional federal legislation, amounted to a virtual ban on the shipment of prison goods in interstate commerce by 1941.* Predictably enough, however, World War II brought prison labor into new action. There was little objection to employment of inmates both inside and outside the prison during the wartime economic boom, but after the war the opposition from free labor and industry was renewed (Taft and England, 1971: chap. 25, and Robinson, 1931).

The movement against prison labor demonstrates the extent to which the definition of a social problem can be selectively manipulated and controlled by the actions of certain interest groups. Each time an economic crisis developed, organized labor would accelerate its assault on prison industries, but during times of economic

---

* "The Ashhurst-Summers Act of 1935 prohibited (by federal law) transportation of goods into states forbidding their entry, and required the labelling of prison-made goods shipped in interstate commerce. In the face of mass unemployment during the depression, every state had passed legislation by 1940 to take advantage of this opportunity to ban prison-made goods of other states" (Johnson, 1968:562). See also Frank T. Flynn, "The Federal Government and the Prison—Labor in the States, I: the Aftermath of Federal Restrictions," *Social Services Review* 24 (March, 1950), 20-21.

prosperity these protests would die down. The objections had little to do with the realities of the situation. Prison industry, after all, was conducted in areas where private industry had little interest. Furthermore, even in the 1920's when prisons were relatively productive, their products in most areas comprised only a fraction of a percent of the free-labor output (Robinson, 1931:55-57). Nevertheless, the young organized labor movement saw convicts as a useful issue in gaining recognition for free labor. At the same time, however, as Taft and England have pointed out (1971:455), the employment of convicts on state farms did not meet with any opposition to speak of, probably because of the lack of organization among farmers and farm workers in those days.

The political tactics of the "free-market" interests eventually forced the reformatory system to seek new means of providing labor for convicts. Past experience had made correctional administrators reluctant to allow private interests to control prison labor. State industries had become increasingly difficult and impractical to maintain, because this meant that the state had to confine consumption of products made by prisoners to its own agencies. Many difficulties have arisen in this effort, including low production efficiency and high costs. Therefore the idea of making prisons self-supporting has by now pretty well been abandoned.

Federal law has not placed as many restrictions upon federal prison labor as upon state prison labor, however, so convict labor continues to be fairly productive in the federal prisons.* According to the *Annual Report* of the Federal Prison Industries, Inc., for 1972 (pp. 2 and 3), the sales volume for goods made in federal prisons reached an all-time high of more than $52 million in 1970, followed by $44.5 million in 1971 and $51.3 million in 1972, with the profit margins running at around 12 percent of those figures. In 1971, 4,621 federal prisoners were paid wages totalling $3,224,602, and in 1972, 5,005 were paid a total of $3,654,713, for an average annual income per prisoner of between $700 and $800 during those years. It is apparent that even in the relatively well-off federal prisons, the industrial output comes nowhere near supporting either the prisoners or the institutions.

THE REFORMATORY MOVEMENT AND THE NATURAL HISTORY PERSPECTIVE Even while the earlier prison-penitentiary movement was in progress, and several of these new "model" institutions had been established, there were those who were questioning the value of prisons which, however much they might be working on the "inner man" to elicit penitence, were doing little or nothing to "retrain" him to rejoin society. What was needed, it was argued, was reform and rehabilitation;

---

* The work done today by the inmates in the Federal Prison Industries Program includes printing, electronic cable repair and manufacture, furniture construction and refinishing, brush-making, data processing, textile manufacturing, and shoe manufacturing (Federal Prison Industries, Inc., *Annual Report,* 1972, p. 4).

that is, a program within the prison system not only to change the attitude of the prisoner, but also to reform his behavior. This could be done, it was suggested, by giving him meaningful and productive tasks to perform while in prison, which would pay him legitimate wages during his sentence and train him in skills that he could use in the world of work after his release. This general concept took a number of specific forms, as we have observed earlier, some of which ran afoul of the interests of business and labor organizations. The earliest and most sustained voices to arise in favor of the reformatory approach during its period of incipiency were those of Franklin Sanborn, Zebulon Brockway, Thomas Mott Osborne, Enoch Wines, and the Reverend Thomas Beecher, all of whom were critical of the "deterioration" of conditions in American prisons, even in those which had been established under the earlier penitentiary concept. While the New York Prison Association was established around mid-century to promote some of these ideas, the new movement did not really enjoy coalescence until after the Civil War, when the diminution of the anti-slavery movement liberated some reformist energy to nourish another corrections-reform campaign. In the years just after the Civil War, the institutionalization of this new reformatory movement was reflected in: (1) the establishment of national (instead of just regional or statewide) organizations such as the National Prison Congress and the American Prison Association (later named the American Correctional Association) (cf. pp. 245-246); (2) the wide breadth of support given to the movement through these organizations by a variety of occupational groups, including social scientists; (3) the establishment of new prisons (or the reorganization of existing ones) in line with the "reformatory" concept, including the Elmira Reformatory and Sing Sing Prison in the state of New York; and (4) the attention (and sometimes opposition) which the movement received from political and economic interests in society. The opposition of organized labor and of certain business interests to any kind of productive (and thus competitive) labor in the reformatories was, indeed, an important factor in the eventual decline and demise of the reformatory movement, which gradually reverted, as had the earlier penitentiary movement, to a situation of mere incarceration under increasingly unpleasant circumstances.

The conditions at Elmira began to deteriorate as a result of overcrowding and legislation limiting the utilization of prison labor, and ". . . what had begun as a bold experiment lost the inspiring impulse of its first promoters, and became routine work and mass treatment. The spirit of Cincinnati died with the first generation of humanitarian reformers" (Grünhut, 1948:92). By the early 1930's Albert Morris was prompted to state: ". . . the high ideals of its founders have not been realized. The modern reformatory has, with a few progressive exceptions, become essentially a prison" (1934:376).

It is ironic that by the 1930's, Sing Sing Prison, which had once been the "hope of the future," had come to symbolize the worst in prison life and experience. With the attention of reformers and the "energy quota" for social problems both pre-empted by World War I, the "gangster problems" of the 1920's, and Prohibition, the prisons were overcrowded with new kinds of criminals convicted by sedition and prohibition laws. The reformatory movement was dead, and further developments in this direction were effectively prevented by the onset of the Great Depression and World War II. During the 1930's, 1940's, and much of the 1950's, therefore, though prison conditions and convict recidivism rates were as "bad" as ever, no more "social problems" relating to corrections were generated until the 1960's.

The Prisoners'-Rights Movement

STRATEGIES OF THE MOVEMENT AND SOCIETAL RESPONSES As part of the increased interest and awareness in crime and criminals during the era of social reform of the 1960's, legislators, journalists, and reformers have begun to take an increased interest in prison conditions, and to insist upon greater accessibility of the prisons to outsiders. An example of this development was the October, 1966, special CBS television report, "Men in Cages," which was nationally broadcast. This program pointed out the problems of overcrowding in our prisons, confinement of first offenders with hardened criminals, and the difficulties faced by released inmates in gaining employment. Such media coverage has served to make the public more accepting of programs designed to overcome these problems, and to reinforce the idea that prisoners are human beings with feelings, needs, and rights. The result has been a new climate of acceptance and understanding conducive to the recent rise of the prisoners'-rights movement.

The ACLU and the NAACP are often remembered for their successful battles against capital punishment, but both of these groups also have taken an active role in securing prisoners' rights in several areas. In these efforts, they have been assisted by other groups with related interests. In April, 1971, the American Bar Association's Commission on Correctional Facilities and Services announced plans to mount a campaign against state and federal laws restricting employment opportunities for released inmates, as well as against those prohibiting the use of convict labor (*The New York Times,* April 14, 1971:25).

The ACLU has been especially effective in the prisoners'-rights movement. In 1971, for example, a representative of that organization was able to gain the cooperation of the warden of the New York State Prison at Comstock, without going to court, in negotiating several requests by prisoners (*The New York Times,* December 19, 1971). The ACLU now hopes to extend this practice to other institutions, in an effort to increase communication between prisoners and prison administrators. The organization has also served to bring undesirable conditions in correctional facilities to public attention. Early in 1973 *The New York Times* (January 13, 1973:68) reported a request from ten inmates of New Jersey's Leesburg State Prison to establish an ACLU chapter in the prison. With the cooperation of prison officials, the ACLU is now opening such a branch, the first in a United States prison. Its activities will include distributing civil rights literature, providing legal counsel, conducting programs with ACLU speakers, and gathering information on prison conditions and inmates' rights.

Pressure groups for prisoners' rights have also met with considerable success in the courts. Racial segregation in prisons was brought to an end through suits initiated by civil rights groups. The use of corporal punishment and mail censorship in prisons has been successfully opposed in the courts. Recently, pressure by civil liberties groups prompted the Washington State Department of Social and Health Services to declare unconstitutional the denial of a prisoner's right to see visitors, including family, friends, representatives of the mass media, attorneys, and other professionals; prisoners were also given the right to refuse to see visitors (*Spokane Daily Chronicle,* June 21, 1973). The courts furthermore have recently supported claims that prisoners are entitled to hearings with "due-process" rights, prior to the employment of disciplinary action or the revocation of parole.

One example of the many cases on behalf of prisoners' rights that have increasingly hit the courts beginning in the early 1970's was the 1971 case of *Landman* v. *Royster* in the state of Virginia. In this case, a permanent injunction was obtained by an ACLU lawyer, on behalf of a number of inmates, which prevented the state prison system from using a bread and water diet, chains, corporal punishment, nudity, or mail censorship for disciplinary purposes. The court ruled these cruel and unusual punishments in violation of the 8th Amendment, and it ruled also that an inmate must be granted a hearing, where the rules of due process are observed, prior to the imposition of any disciplinary measures in a prison. The attorney hailed this development as a "Bill of Rights for inmates" (B. A. Franklin, *The New York Times,* Nov. 1, 1971, Section I, p. 3).

The adoption of some such Bill of Rights in all federal and state prisons was called for in 1972 by a joint statement of 450 religious, racial, business, labor, and civic groups, represented by the National Council of Churches, the United States Catholic Conference, the American Jewish Committee, the National Urban League, the NAACP, the National Council on Crime and Delinquency, the International League for the Rights of Man, and the International Union of Electrical, Radio, and Machine Workers. In a statement sent simultaneously to the U.S. Attorney General, the Judiciary Committees of Congress, and the Governors and legislative leaders of the various states, the religious and civic spokesmen pointed to the "tragedy of Attica" and asserted that "prisons must no longer create embittered, hopeless people, but (must) be a real force in the process of rehabilitation." Pennsylvania was the only state that had adopted a prisoners' Bill of Rights (*The New York Times,* Feb. 16, 1972, 23:4).

The highly publicized bloody 1971 uprising at the Attica, New York, prison, to which the civic leaders' statement referred, was itself instrumental in bringing some improvements in the lot of prisoners there and elsewhere in the state. Of the thirty original demands of the rebelling Attica prisoners, only four were *not* at least partially met by the state or by the prison administration within a year of the uprising: (1) payment of a minimum wage to prisoners; (2) grand jury investigation of the use of prison industry profits; (3) an end to administrative resentencing of parole violators; and (4) an end to solitary confinement as a form of discipline. Among the more numerous demands that *were* at least partially met were: greater professionalization and increased training of staff; inclusion of representatives for minority groups on prison staffs; increases in the number of correctional officers; higher educational requirements for superintendents; more showers; reduced mail censorship; more library books (especially those dealing with minority groups); removal of wire mesh from visiting rooms; and the creation of inmate liaison committees (Paul L. Montgomery, *The New York Times,* Sept. 12, 1972, I:1).

Lately, prisoners themselves have not been content simply to sit back and let others fight for their rights; they have been active participants in the struggle. Since the early 1950's, prison riots have frequently centered around demands for improved living conditions and educational and vocational training programs. In many cases, these riots were not consciously planned, but were later taken over by prisoners who saw the utility of converting them into formal protests. In some cases, prisoners' protests have taken on rather dramatic proportions. At the Kansas State Penitentiary, 300 prisoners severed their Achilles tendons or mutilated themselves in various other ways between July 1, 1969 and December 3, 1969 in an effort to get satisfaction for their demands for a new warden and a federal investigation of conditions at the prison (*The New York Times,* December 4, 1969:37). Although self-mutilation was not previously unknown, in the past convicts had usually mutilated themselves only to avoid work or to gain admission to hospital facilities.

Black Muslim groups began promoting the use of the courts for the benefit of prisoners in the early 1960's. Most suits which they initiated were based on the contention that prison practices were in violation of the prisoners' legal rights. In the year 1969, a total of 2,500 convicts filed suit in the federal courts (*The New York Times,* January 4, 1970, 4:6). Similar efforts by older religious movements (mentioned earlier), such as the AFSC (i.e., the Quakers), go back even before those of the Muslims.

Beginning in the early 1970's, there has been a proliferation of new prison-reform and prisoners'-rights organizations, many of which were mentioned earlier in this chapter. Especially important have been the efforts of the Prison Law Collective, based in San Francisco, which publishes and distributes *The Jailhouse Lawyers' Manual* and helps prisoners with legal problems; and the Prisoners' Union, which also started in California in 1970, and now publishes *The Outlaw*, a journal with a circulation of about 20,000, mostly inside the prisons (Daniels, 1974). The Union has organized several prisoner strikes, with solitary confinement resulting for some of its strike leaders. Within a year after its emergence, it had become a national organization, its stated goals including the unionization of prisons, the protection of prisoners' rights, payment of the prevailing wage rates to prisoners for their labor, observance of minimum-wage laws, full civil-service job rights, and the right to hold elective office upon release. The Union has embraced the traditional tactics of strikes and other work stoppages in order to achieve its goals.

A somewhat more militant outgrowth of the Prisoners' Union is the United Prisoners' Union (UPU), which is composed of both inmates and former inmates. This organization has been seeking the advice and backing of the United Auto Workers, the United Farm Workers, and the ACLU in developing its strategy. It was reported by *The New York Times* on May 16, 1972 (p. 86) that another group, the National Prisoners Alliance, composed of prisoners, former inmates, and those sympathetic to the plight of inmates, was planning a nationwide prisoner sitdown strike to protest low wages and visiting restrictions. Still another group, the National Prisoners Reform Association, recently filed a class-action suit in Massachusetts to force that state to give inmates the right to vote (*The New York Times,* October 9, 1972:28).

The black liberation movement and elements of the New Left may also have been moving forces behind some of the recent prisoner uprisings (Morris, 1971). These groups tend to view prisons simply as vehicles of repression by the larger white society. In spite of some evidence for such radical influences in the Attica Prison riot, however, the New York State Investigating Commission concluded that the Attica uprising was not planned in advance by militant, politically oriented activists, but was, rather, a spontaneous reaction to the tensions and hatred generated by the harassment and racism existing within the institution. Only after the initial takeover did inmate leaders begin to emerge and make demands (New York State Special Commission on Attica, 1972).

THE PRISONERS'-RIGHTS MOVEMENT AND THE NATURAL HISTORY PERSPECTIVE

The latest reform movement to arise and define the nature of the "penology problem" in our society is the prisoners'-rights movement. This movement had its incipiency in the late 1950's and early 1960's with the efforts of the black liberation movement, the Black Muslims, and of certain elements of the emerging New Left to (1) call the attention of the public once again to the "deplorable" conditions in our overcrowded prisons, and (2) to organize the prisoners for collective action which involved the development of new and better self-concepts. Organizations have been more noteworthy than individuals in the creation of this new movement; indeed, one of the major differences between this movement and its predecessors has been its ability to attract organizations which are not limited in their interests to prison reform but which have a broad base of concerns and support, e.g., the ACLU, the NAACP, the National Council on Crime and Delinquency, and the American Bar Association. As long as the movement was supported by relatively "radical" groups on the fringes of society, such as the Muslims and the New Left, it could only remain in an incipient stage. With the establishment of the National Prisoner Association and the United Prisoners' Union, in the late 1960's and early 1970's, and the organization of both incarcerated and released prisoners, the movement can be said to have coalesced into the first movement in history in which prisoners began promoting their own interests, instead of relying on outside "reformers." As they were joined by the broader-based organizations mentioned above, especially the ACLU, the NCCD, and the ABA, they gained the attention of the establishment. Occasional prison riots and bloody shoot-outs in the late 1960's and early 1970's punctuated and emphasized the need for the establishment to begin to cope with the newly aroused prisoner movement. The new court decisions on prisoners' rights, and the new developments in the field of civil rights and penological reform since the late 1960's, some of which are noted in the legacy section of this chapter, make it clear that this movement is now in the stage of institutionalization. The relatively broad base of support which this movement has acquired is likely to give it greater longevity and impact than its predecessors have had, but its eventual fate and accomplishments are yet to be assessed. Because of the far-reaching influence of this movement thus far, however, it is clear that at the very least we are in the midst of another "social problem" in the area of penology reform.

The Movement to Abolish Capital Punishment

We will consider the movement against capital punishment apart from the other, more general penological movements, since it has existed as an independent movement almost from the very beginning of the nation, thus antedating most of the other movements.

MOVEMENT STRATEGIES AND SOCIETAL RESPONSES The movement to abolish capital punishment was born among the Quakers of colonial Pennsylvania. The Quakers were a persecuted people who came to America hoping to find a chance to practice their beliefs in peace. When they arrived in this country, however, they were met by the harsh and uncompromising Puritans. The Quakers often suffered severe treatment at the hands of the Puritans for their failure to conform to Puritan ideals, and this forced them to establish their own settlements where they could be free from Puritan domination. Once they were able to live by the precepts prescribed by their religion, they were quick to apply their concepts of love and mercy even to those who broke the law. Capital punishment was reserved only for those who had committed homicide.

When the colonies grew into a young nation, the atmosphere of freedom and independence, including the somewhat greater religious freedom, enabled the Quakers to expand their activities throughout the new country. Even in Puritan Massachusetts we find that "The Society of Friends (i.e., Quakers) within the state were ever urging in their petitions to the legislature for the abolition of the death penalty" ("The Death Penalty as a Preventive of Crime": 368). Evidently the Quakers did not have a great deal of influence over the legislators, for capital punishment persisted. The Quakers did serve to create a general awareness of what they saw as a social problem, however, and as a result of their efforts, the American Society for the Abolition of Capital Punishment was organized in 1845 (Bedau, 1967a:9).

While the movement for abolition of the death penalty did not gain strong support until the early part of the 20th century, there were other indications of doubt about capital punishment. Juries, for example, began to show reluctance to convict persons accused of capital crimes. In 1920, ". . . only 15 percent of the people tried for murder were convicted in Maine prior to the abolition of the death penalty, and such convictions rose to 64 percent after its abolition. It is well-known that juries are less inclined to find men guilty when guilt means death than when it means a milder punishment ("The Death Penalty": 620). Beginning in 1915, bills calling for the abolition of the death penalty were presented before the New York State legislature every year until 1965, when the death penalty was abolished in that state (*The New York Times,* March 20, 1965:1). According to Playfair (1957:32), the strength of the movement reached a peak in 1917, at which time a nationwide repeal of capital punishment seemed likely. He considers the "atmosphere of insecurity" created by World War I as the reason for the failure of the movement to achieve its goals at that time.

Although the abolition movement may have been set back by the war, it was revived in 1925 with the founding of the American League to Abolish Capital Punishment in New York, an organization with strong leadership and coordination. Many of its members were prominent in the field of corrections. Lewis E. Lawes, a well-known New York prison administrator, was the first president of the League. Its main function was explained by its first secretary, Vivian Pierce:

[Previous] campaigns have been brief and discouraging. Often they were inadequately financed and organized. We believe that with a national organization always on the watch to lend aid, these costly defeats will be unnecessary. ("Abolishing the Death Penalty," 29)

Members of the League spoke at theaters and various public gatherings, often collecting donations from sympathetic listeners. Following speeches by several members of the League at Broadway's Hampden Theatre in 1929, a solicitation for funds resulted in pledges of approximately $600 from the audience (*The New York Times,* February 18, 1929:9).

According to Bedau (1967a:10), the lawlessness of the Prohibition era dealt another setback to the movement for abolition of the death penalty. Nevertheless, by 1930 the League was still mounting campaigns in New York, New Jersey, Colorado, California, and Vermont (*The New York Times,* February 4, 1930:27), if less successful ones. During the next 25 years, support for abolition dropped considerably in both public opinion and in the legislatures (see Table 5-7). Writing in 1957, Playfair (p. 32) described the nationwide abolitionist cause as "almost dead." Bedau (1967a:14-15) has suggested several factors which may have hampered the success of the abolition movement: (1) elimination of the most violent and repulsive methods of execution; (2) making executions private; (3) limiting the use of the death penalty to such crimes as first-degree murder; and (4) allowing the jury the power to grant mercy. It is somewhat ironic that the matter of jury discretion eventually influenced the Supreme Court to declare capital punishment, as it had been practiced, unconstitutional.

In the late 1950's, and throughout the 1960's, two new forces joined the abolitionist cause: religious organizations and groups concerned with the protection of human rights. The Protestant and Jewish denominations showed an increased concern for social problems, beginning with civil rights and extending later to the abolitionist cause. The efforts of the churches included not only public resolutions and legislative lobbying, but also the promotion of collective protest activities, such as the prison vigil at the execution of Carryl Chessman. Perhaps the largest collective effort supported by churches and other abolitionist groups was the mass protest which occurred at the execution of Aaron Mitchell, the last person to be executed in California (April, 1967). Almost 500 persons picketed outside of San Quentin Prison, and others picketed both the home and the office of Governor Ronald Reagan, who was a death-penalty advocate (*Time* 89:25, April 21, 1967). Protestors wearing black armbands staged protests at the Colorado State Prison and Statehouse in response to the execution of Jose Monge, the last person to be executed in the United States, on June 9, 1967 (*Time* 89:33, June 9, 1967).

TABLE 5-9 APPROXIMATE TIME OF ENTRANCE OF VARIOUS GROUPS INTO THE ABOLITION MOVEMENT

17th Cent.	Quakers
1845	American Society for the Abolition of Capital Punishment
1925	League to Abolish Capital Punishment National Save-a-Life League
1931	First Humanist Society (New York)
1959	Union of American Hebrew Congregations New York Committee to Abolish Capital Punishment
1960	General Conference of the Methodist Church (10,000,000 members) United Lutheran Church (2,500,000 members) New York State Council of Churches
1961	Protestant Episcopal Church
1965	New York State Association of Trial Lawyers American Correctional Association American Civil Liberties Union New York State Temporary Commission on Revision of the Penal Law and Code of Criminal Procedure National Council on Crime and Delinquency New Mexico Council of Churches Iowa Council of Churches
1967	National Association for the Advancement of Colored People (California and Florida executions blocked)
1968	National Council of Churches (Witherspoon decision)
1969	National Urban League
1970	American Psychiatric Association
1971	National Commission on Reform of Federal Criminal Laws World Council of Churches National Coalition of American Nuns (2,000 members) Citizens Against Legalized Murder (Governor Winthrop Rockefeller of Arkansas commutes 15 death sentences)
1972	California Supreme Court United States Supreme Court

Individual prisoners had occasionally attempted to avoid executions through legal maneuvering for a number of years, but it was not until the ACLU and the NAACP entered the abolitionist movement in the 1960's that these methods began to be fully exploited. Both organizations had won major successes in court battles in the civil-rights movement, and were fully cognizant of the effectivenesss of court processes in furthering their goals. Furthermore, they had access to experienced legal staffs. It was only natural, then, that their chief strategy in attacking capital punishment should focus on the courts, adding a new and potent dimension to the abolitionist effort. In April, 1967 (*The New York Times,* April 5, 1967:35) the ACLU and the NAACP Legal Defense Fund brought suit in a Florida federal district court to block the use of the death penalty in that state. The suit was based on the claim that the state's capital punishment laws were unconstitutional. A similar suit was filed in a San Francisco federal district court on June 27, 1967 (*The New York Times,* June 28, 1967:41). In May, 1971, the NAACP organized a conference for lawyers involved in fighting the death penalty in order to develop comprehensive and coordinated legal strategies for opposing capital punishment, including legislative and judicial appeals, as well as attempts to obtain commutations from governors (*U.S. News & World Report,* May 1, 1971). Appeals against the death penalty eventually resulted in the ruling by the California Supreme Court in February, 1972, that it was unconstitutional, and a similar ruling by the United States Supreme Court brought a nationwide end to executions on June 29, 1972. Table 5-9 outlines the historical development of the movement to abolish capital punishment.

Since the 1972 Supreme Court decision, a vigorous countermovement has begun to grow in an effort to restore the death penalty. The proponents of capital punishment, though disappointed at the Court's decision, were somewhat encouraged by the fact that (1) the decision had been very close (5 to 4), and (2) it had been directed against the *usual practice* of capital punishment, rather than against the principle. Accordingly, many legislators and citizens have been hard at work trying to draft proposals for "air-tight" state and federal death-penalty laws that will satisfy the Supreme Court's objections to the "wanton" and "freakish" manner in which the penalty has been imposed.* Meanwhile, almost 100 condemned men (and one woman) across the nation (most of them in the South)

---

* This crucial Supreme Court decision was the outcome of its simultaneous consideration of three cases: (1) that of William Henry Furman of Savannah, Georgia, charged with murder, after being surprised in the process of a burglary and shooting the victim through a door (#69-5003); (2) that of Lucius Jackson, Jr., also of Savannah, Georgia, charged with rape (#69-5030); and (3) that of Elmer Branch of Vernon, Texas, charged also with rape (#69-5031). All three men were black, and the two rape victims were white but not seriously injured.

The Supreme Court decision was 5 to 4 in favor of overturning the death sentences (not the verdicts). In general, the majority based its conclusion on the argument that application of the death penalty had become capricious and unusual, thereby violating the 8th Amendment of the Bill of Rights. Each of the nine justices wrote a separate opinion on the cases. The four dissenting justices argued that the court would be exceeding its constitutional authority and usurping legislative duties if it were to prevent the use of a legally sanctioned form of punishment. Two of the 5-man majority argued that the use of capital punishment was cruel and unusual per se and therefore unconstitutional (White and Marshall). The other three (Douglas, Brennan and Stewart) focused mainly on the arbitary and uneven results which had occurred from allowing judge and jury discretion in the application of the death penalty. These three left open the possibility that a mandatory death penalty for some crimes, or some other arrangement eliminating the discretionary element, might pass a constitutional test. It is this latter "loophole" on which some states are now basing their hopes for the constitutionality of new capital punishment laws which they have passed (or are in the process of passing). (The above is taken mainly from *United States Reports* 408 [1972]:238-470.)

have been awaiting the final outcome. By 1975, nearly half of the states in the union had passed new death-penalty laws which attempted to satisfy the Supreme Court requirements, mainly by specifying certain offenses for which conviction would bring a mandatory death penalty (e.g., hired assassinations, killing policemen, mass murders, murders by convicts already under life sentences, and several other offenses). Supporters of such new laws hope that by defining capital offenses clearly, and by removing any possibility of unequal mercy granted by impressionable juries, the new laws will pass a Supreme Court test in the future.

In many other states, new death-penalty laws have been voted down or vetoed by the governors. At the federal level also, bills both for and against capital punishment have been introduced in Congress. Both public and official opinion are thus very much divided on this issue, and we can expect movements on both sides, with strongly contrasting definitions of "the problem," to thrive for some time (Schardt, 1973; Marshall, 1974; Stewart, 1974; and Berck, 1973).

THE MOVEMENT TO ABOLISH CAPITAL PUNISHMENT AND THE NATURAL HISTORY PERSPECTIVE Although it has overlapped in some ways with the various corrections-reform movements we have discussed, the movement to abolish capital punishment has had a separate development of its own. This movement seems to have followed the "revival" pattern of social movements which we have outlined (see Figure 2-3); it originated as early as the 17th century with the Quakers, and then submerged for almost two centuries, surfacing briefly and occasionally during this period. Only in very recent years has the issue of the abolition of capital punishment gained enough support to challenge seriously the practice of execution. A glance at Table 5-9 shows that except for the Quakers only one organization to abolish capital punishment existed until the 20th century, and it produced only a "mini-movement." From 1920 to 1960, a somewhat more important (but still incipient) movement was carried by three abolitionist organizations. Since 1960, however, a great many organizations have gotten into the act, most of them influential multi-purpose organizations such as the mainstream Protestant churches. As the coalescing movement was forged out of the "questionable" political executions in this country in the 1940's and 1950's, it rapidly developed under the leadership and support of the respectable organizations listed in Table 5-9; these were in sharp contrast to the more isolated and marginal groups which had led the incipient phase of the movement.

The initial response of the establishment to the abolition movement was to reduce greatly the number of actual executions in the 1950's and 1960's (see Figure 5-2), while keeping capital punishment "on the books." Probably in response to the growing influence of an increasingly institutionalized movement, juries became more and more reluctant to find defendants guilty of capital offenses, and judges became more and more reluctant to give out sentences of execution.

It appeared for a while that this *de facto* response of the justice system might co-opt the abolitionist movement and put an end to capital punishment as a "social problem." However, the interest groups involved carried the issue all the way to the Supreme Court, which, in 1972, declared capital punishment to be unconstitutional in practice. In spite of this favorable decision, however, the movement has been kept alive by the increased efforts of a countermovement attempting to pass capital punishment laws in the various states which will be constitutionally acceptable to the Supreme Court. As matters stand in the mid-1970's, therefore, we have a very much institutionalized movement to abolish capital punishment, as can be seen by the accommodations that have been made for it by both political institutions and counter-interest groups. Whether the abolition movement dies out, however, and with it the "social problem" it has addressed, depends upon the success of the countermovement now in progress.

THE LEGACY OF PENOLOGY REFORM MOVEMENTS

The penological and correctional practices in our society are a strange and often illogical mixture of many legacies accumulated over the past three centuries. To the Puritans, the deviant represented a problem of social control, but to the Quakers, he constituted a moral obligation. The proponents of reformatory and rehabilitation movements felt he needed to be changed in some way, and particularly that he ought to be equipped to respond more effectively to his environment. Organized labor sought to keep him unemployed, and the civil rights movement attempted to protect him. Lately, the prisoner himself is attempting to defend his interests and determine his own destiny. Meanwhile the ultimate penalty, capital punishment, continues to be promoted by those who regard it as a necessary deterrent, and opposed by those who consider it cruel and unusual punishment. Elements of all of these traditions (and others) make up the penological patchwork quilt in contemporary society. On the whole, the current legacy of the various penological movements and theories is not a very promising one, but there are some interesting intimations of possible future directions in some of the newer "experimental" developments around the country.

De-emphasis of Imprisonment

One of the most important modern trends in correctional reform is toward disposing of conventional imprisonment as it has been used in the past. Confinement of the offender has increasingly been called into question as an effective means of dealing with the large majority of criminals. Conrad (1971:90), for example, has stated,

Modern penologists now agree that one of the special disadvantages of confinement is the separation of the offender from the community, resulting in the dislocation of his ties to family, to the economic system, and to the ordinary course of life as a citizen at large.

Morris (1965:276) has noted that,

. . . only a very few prisoners require the cells and walls to keep them in, and the cells and walls grossly increase the social isolation of the prison, impede re-education, and inhibit the preservation of those ties which are so often determinative of social conformity. The open institution is a most promising diversification of prison.

The Model Penal Code of the American Law Institute (1962) recommends imprisonment only when clearly necessary for the protection of society, and the report of the National Advisory Commission on Criminal Justice Standards and Goals (1973) recommended abandonment of the prison concept for juveniles and the strict limitation of its use for adults. In May, 1972, the Wisconsin Task Force on Offender Rehabilitation, appointed by the Governor following the Attica, New York, prison riot, recommended that the state end its use of prisons by 1975. As a replacement for these institutions, the committee recommended the development of community-based treatment centers in which convicted persons could receive special supervision and guidance. These centers would be small and would accommodate only three or four persons at a time. The community would be responsible for setting up programs for the educational and vocational training of these offenders, and would maintain various crisis-intervention and psychological treatment programs (*The New York Times,* May 28, 1972:26). Several other states, including Massachusetts, California, Minnesota, and Washington, are planning to end their use of prisons. It is probably not widely realized, in fact, that prison populations have actually declined in recent years (Gibbons, 1974).

As of mid-1972, 80 percent of California offenders were in community-based noninstitutional programs, with a similar percentage in such programs in Wisconsin. Rhode Island has, for the past decade, successfully employed a "deferred-conviction" program, whereby accused felons can be placed in community-probation programs, rather than face court conviction and imprisonment (*The New York Times,* July 27, 1972:31). In mid-1972, the General Assembly of the United Presbyterian Church also announced its decision to work toward ending the use of prisons as a part of the correctional apparatus (*The New York Times,* May 24, 1972:16). The public, however, has often been reluctant to go along with such radical reforms. Both fear and indignation were expressed by residents of Kingston, Rhode Island, at the prospect of having a noninstitutional home for ten delinquent youths established in their community, and Kingston was not the first town to have opposed the project (*The New York Times,* July 10, 1966:58).

Prisoner Education

Another area in which the recognition of inmate potential has occurred is in the educational field. San Quentin Prison in California, assisted by the Extension Division of the University of Southern California, and the Wisconsin State Prison, aided by the University of Wisconsin, were pioneers in developing serious educational programs for inmates as early as the 1930's (Morris, 1934:430). In 1966, a Ford Foundation grant of nearly $100,000 was provided to the University of Southern California for the purpose of developing a four-year college for San Quentin inmates. Other states, including Washington and North Carolina, have developed experimental study-release programs in which inmates are permitted to attend classes at public educational institutions. A law which went into effect October 1, 1972, allows inmates in Connecticut prisons to remain in prison up to 90 days past their release date if they choose to do so, in order to complete educational or drug rehabilitation programs.

Furloughs and Visits

From the realization that isolation of the prisoner may have deleterious effects on his rehabilitation has come a tendency toward allowing him greater contact with family and friends through a variety of visiting and furlough programs. According to Hopper (1970), a liberal visitation and leave program began at the Parchman, Mississippi, prison in 1944. As the program developed it included ten-day furloughs and conjugal visits. These were at first unofficial, but their success soon resulted in official acceptance. Such visits have been credited with improving prisoner morale, preserving family relationships, and reducing homosexuality among the prisoners. In mid-1972 the conjugal visit program at Parchman, Mississippi, was extended to females, with the requirement that oral contraceptives and other birth-control devices be employed.

In April, 1971, a Family Visit Plan was initiated at California's Soledad, San Quentin, and Corona facilities (*Life* 71, August 13, 1971:24-29), the first time such a program has been provided for maximum-security inmates. Inmates are permitted one three-day visit with their families each month. The prisoner and his family are provided with a furnished apartment near the prison, but beyond its walls. The only restrictions are that no alcohol is allowed, and the inmate must show himself before a tower prison guard three times a day. In addition to this outside visit, convicts are allowed unrestricted visits in a special visitors' room within the institution. The inmate is not separated from the visitor by the glass or wire barriers common in other prisons.

In New Jersey, facilities were recently completed which allow inmates contact visits with friends and family in small, but colorfully decorated cubicles. Other

New Jersey prisons have had such programs in operation for some time. Convicts are allowed two contact visits per month and one non-contact visit (*The New York Times,* December 7, 1972:110). Legislation was recently introduced in New Jersey proposing the development of a conjugal-visit program for that state (*The New York Times,* April 9, 1972:110).

A number of states have developed furlough programs on an experimental basis. The purpose of these programs is to allow the inmate to seek employment, attend to family affairs, obtain medical treatment, and join his family on holidays such as Christmas and Thanksgiving. On approval by the New York State Legislature, a program of furloughs was begun in that state in July, 1972. Over 1,200 furloughs were granted in the first six months of the program, and of 680 inmates given furloughs over the 1972 Christmas holidays, only seven failed to return on schedule. The furloughs ranged from two to seven days in length (*The New York Times,* January 9, 1973:43). In Connecticut, where 3,016 furloughs were granted during 1972, only 14 prisoners violated the conditions of their furlough (*The New York Times,* December 29, 1972:20). By late 1972, Massachusetts was also developing a furlough program for its inmates, and the state of Washington had a 30-day furlough program in operation. Plans for a "prerelease" center at Boston State Hospital in Mattapan, Massachusetts, call for inmates to be allowed to have free access to the community during the day within 90 days of their parole, as long as they check into the center by 11 p.m. (*The New York Times,* October 22, 1972, 4:6). This arrangement provides "graduating" prisoners with an opportunity to seek employment and housing, and to attend to personal affairs in advance of their full release.

Prison Accommodations

A number of changes have been brought about in both the design and administration of prisons as a result of changing views of the convict and methods of responding to him. Walled, fortress-like institutions are being replaced by less distinctive, more attractive structures. Security is being made less conspicuous. Taft and England (1971:419) point out that the first U.S. penitentiary to be built without a wall was the facility at Terre Haute, Indiana (completed in 1940). More recently, however, a rooftop swimming pool has been planned for the Jefferson County Jail in Louisville, Kentucky, in hopes that it will create a less strained atmosphere at the institution (*The New York Times,* July 18, 1971:34).

Various administrative changes have recently been aimed at creating a more "normal" atmosphere within correctional institutions, in which the convict will no longer be degraded and humiliated, but encouraged and aided in reclaiming his self-respect. One indication of this orientation is the practice of referring to prisoners as residents, and to guards as correctional officers. Recently, the newspaper at the Stillwater, Minnesota, prison announced that it would refer to all male citizens and inmates alike as "Mr." (*The New York Times,* February 5, 1966:11). Such approaches are not present in all institutions, of course, but they are gradually gaining some acceptance. At the Washington State Prison, officials have allowed inmates to form their own Resident Government Council, which cooperates with correctional authorities in planning and developing a number of rehabilitative programs. The inmates, referred to as residents, are free to dress as they please. Hairstyles, including mustaches and beards, are at the discretion of the individual. Prisoners are also allowed to attend and participate in disciplinary hearings. At the Federal Correctional Institution at Fort Worth, Texas, a similar set-up is developing. Again, inmates are referred to as residents and the institution is called a campus (*The New York Times,* July 8, 1972:27), and family picnics are permitted in an area outside the facility. Another distinctive feature of this institution is that it is the nation's first adult "co-educational" prison; 20 percent of its residents are female.

Additional changes in prison practices have made prison staff more responsive to inmates' needs. In Minnesota, an ombudsman, who is completely independent of the correctional department, receives inmate complaints and has the authority to confer directly with the governor in resolving them (*The New York Times,* August 14, 1972:25). Another promising program being developed in Minnesota is the "contract" system, under which an inmate can choose to fulfill the obligations of a contract, working toward his release rather than merely waiting for his sentence to expire (*The New York Times,* December 12, 1971:69). The conditions of the contract may require the completion of a business-training program, other educational courses, a marriage-relations course offered by the prison, the demonstration of good behavior over a period of time, or other things. This program is designed to improve the motivation of convicts in rehabilitative programs, and allows correctional authorities to induce each inmate to do those things which they feel will be most effective in helping him to succeed in society.

Work Release

Work-release programs represent an important part of the new techniques being developed to assist prisoners in regaining their status as productive citizens. These programs allow the offender to maintain his role as family provider, as well as requiring him to accept regular responsibilities in the performance of his work. A strong trend toward the integration of the inmate into the free economy has received considerable support from a number of states.

According to England (1961:24), work-release was first used in Massachusetts at the Massachusetts Reformatory for Women in 1910. Other reports (*The New York Times,* November 18, 1972:21) suggest it may have been used as early as

1879 at the Framingham House of Corrections (for women) in Massachusetts. It was not until 1972, however, that the program was extended to males in that state. Wisconsin's Huber Law, enacted in 1913, provided that misdemeanants could be released during the day to pursue jobs in the community. In 1956, five states were experimenting with work-release programs, and by 1965 this number had risen to 24. The federal government, under authorization from the Law Enforcement Assistance Act,* also began developing a work-release program in 1965 (Zalba, 1970). Several other states have initiated work-release programs since 1965, and a number (including Washington, North Carolina, and Illinois) have also begun day-release of prisoners for educational or vocational-training programs. In almost all cases, work-release programs have met with encouraging success, though to some extent limited job openings are hampering them. Inmates have enthusiastically approved such programs, and escape rates have been low, usually less than 1 percent.

"Open Institutions" and Halfway Houses

The open institution is no longer merely a dream of correctional reformers. Several open correctional facilities are now in existence, such as the Bucks County Jail in Pennsylvania. Although the escape rate there has been relatively high (about 4 percent), officials at the jail feel that the program is successful. Of the offenders sentenced in the county, 56 percent were on work-release programs in June, 1970, and a halfway house is aiding the reintegration of released offenders into the community (*The New York Times,* July 2, 1970:37). A number of public and private organizations have developed such halfway houses; although only a few were in existence prior to 1965, almost 500 of them opened between 1967 and 1972. This rapid development was made possible through funds provided by the federal Law Enforcement Assistance Act (*The New York Times,* November 26, 1971:32). Though frequently opposed by people residing near them (on the grounds that they do not enhance the character and safety of a neighborhood) halfway houses

---

* "The Law Enforcement Assistance Act of 1965 was a facet of President Johnson's 'war on crime'; the Act was to implement a three-year experimental program of providing federal funds to encourage innovation in State and local criminal justice systems. The language in the 1965 Act, which gave the granting authority to the Attorney General, authorized, under Sections 2 and 3 of the Act, (the providing of) grants for 'the purpose of improving the quality of State and local law enforcement and correctional personnel,' and for 'the purpose of improving the capabilities, techniques, and practices of State and local agencies engaged in law enforcement, (and) the administration of criminal laws.' In practice, however, expenditures . . . for the fiscal years 1966 and 1967 were negligible." (Law Enforcement Assistance Administration, "The Dollars and Sense of Justice: A Study of the Law Enforcement Assistance Administration as it Relates to the Defense Function of the Criminal Justice System," *Hearings before the Subcommittee No. 5 of the Committee on the Judiciary, House of Representatives,* 93rd Congress, First Session on the Law Enforcement Assistance Administration, pp. 536-578.)

seem to be providing an effective method for reintegrating the convict into society.

It is quite obvious from all of the above innovations that modern society has started to redefine correctional policy, and has developed somewhat different perceptions of the criminal from those held by previous generations. Increasing emphasis is being placed on helping the convict to adapt more effectively to society, and to make society more flexible and tolerant in dealing with those who fail to conform to its laws. Much remains to be done, of course, and it is clear that elements of both our punitive Puritan and our reformist Quaker legacies are still very much with us.

Survivals of the Past

The review that we have just offered of some of the newer developments in the corrections field, however promising they may seem, must be viewed in the light of at least three important considerations: (1) They do not yet represent the typical approaches to punishment and corrections in our society, which are still overwhelmingly custodial and punitive, with little regard for the prisoner's real rehabilitation and successful re-entry into society, his civil rights, or his creature comforts (Menninger, 1968; Irwin, 1970; Mitford, 1971 and 1973; and Wilkins, 1969). (2) Even if the new directions which we have described were to replace totally the existing and traditional modes of punishment and correction, there is as yet no scientific basis for expecting any reduction in either crime or recidivism rates, or any improvement in "rehabilitation." The fact is that we still don't know what "works" with people who are convicted of crimes (Gibbons, 1974; Wilson, 1974; and Wilkins, 1969). (3) Finally, even the most promising innovation in corrections practices may produce the opposite of the expected and desired effect or outcome, either as a result of unanticipated loopholes and side effects, or of subversion by staff, or both.

Perhaps the best recent example of this third caveat is the use of the indeterminate sentence, which has been tried off and on in many places during penal history, and is currently a prominent feature of the California corrections system, widely regarded as one of the most "progressive" and "successful" in the nation (Mitford, 1971 and 1973). The original intention behind the indeterminate sentence was to reward prisoners who showed rapid progress in rehabilitation and good conduct while in prison. Instead of requiring them to serve out a standard fixed sentence of, say, ten years, convicts could be sentenced to a modest minimum of a year or two, with the maximum left open, so that the sooner a prisoner showed that he was "rehabilitated," the sooner he could be released, rather than having to serve the whole ten years.

However enlightened and humane this idea might have been at its inception, parole boards such as the California Adult Authority have been using it, according to some investigators, as a kind of "club" over the heads of helpless convicts to keep them from protesting about anything, or making any kind of "fuss," for fear that such "misbehavior" will be taken as evidence that they need another few years of incarceration. Also, it has been charged that the changing composition and criteria of boards from one meeting to the next result in arbitrary and unpredictable requirements from aspiring parolees, who are left in constant fear and doubt as to exactly what they must do or not do in order to be deemed worthy of parole. Whatever the intentions may be of "the system," and particularly of the parole board, the prisoners generally seem to despise and fear the indeterminate sentence and to prefer by far the "flat-time" kind of penalty. Evidence that their fears are well-grounded can be seen in the fact that California leads the nation in the average number of months served by its first-term convicts before parole (Mitford, 1971 and 1973; Gibbons, 1974; and Daniels, 1974).

We can expect corrections and punishment to continue to be a "social problem" in our society, if only because we have never achieved a consensus among our legislators or in our public opinion as to the main objectives of a corrections system. Our Puritan legacy teaches us to despair of any true rehabilitation of the "criminal nature" and to simply keep lawbreakers locked up until they conform. Our Quaker legacy teaches us, on the other hand, that we must strive for a true change of heart in the criminal, whereupon his behavior will follow suit. Our social scientists tell us that manipulating a convict's social and physical environment will change both his attitudes and his behavior, but there is little scientific agreement about which elements in the environment should be manipulated. The "ordinary citizen" is not nearly so concerned with theories of rehabilitation as he is with protecting his own life and property, and he has little patience for any program that does not have that objective as its highest priority. Indeed, there are few "social problems" in which there is greater competition among definitions of "reality" than in the area of punishment and corrections.

Chapter 6
Radical Protest

THE SOCIAL CONSTRUCTION OF REALITY

> There was indiscipline and rebellion everywhere . . . the boys occupied the school for two days and hoisted the red flag . . . two companies of troops with fixed bayonets had to be called in to suppress a rising of the pupils . . . the pupils set fire to their books and desks and withdrew to an island which had to be taken by assault by the army. (Aries, 1965:317-318)

This vivid description could well be a wire service report in recent years from an American city with a college or university campus, but it is nothing of the sort; it is a description of student protest at an English Jesuit college (La Flèche) in 1646. Collective disorderly protest has occurred throughout history. In ancient days, protesting crowds gathered at the marketplace or in front of the palace to express their grievances. In 18th-century Western Europe, the forcible occupation of fields and forests by the landless, revolts against tax collectors, anti-conscription rebellions, food riots, and attacks on machines were the most frequent forms of collective protest (National Violence Commission Report, 1969:16).

The right to protest is an essential part of the American system of government. The leaders of the revolutionary movements of the 1770's and 1780's, and the framers of the Constitution and the Bill of Rights, seemed to be well aware of the importance of this right. Hence, the right of peaceful protest was enshrined in the First Amendment. But because people with strong grievances are often impatient and because peace-keepers often overreact, protest in the United States has not always remained peaceful.

Protest has been defined as "an expression or declaration of objection, disapproval, or dissent, often in opposition to something a person is powerless to prevent or avoid" (*Random House Dictionary,* 1967). Professor Ralph H. Turner adds that an act of protest includes the following:

The action expresses a grievance, a conviction of wrong or injustice; the protestors are unable to correct the condition by their own efforts; the action is intended to draw attention to the grievances; the action is further meant to provoke ameliorative steps by some target group; and the protestors depend upon some combination of sympathy and fear to move the target group in their behalf. (Turner, 1969:861)

Protest sometimes emphasizes persuasion, sometimes concern, but always involves both elements (Bayley, 1962:663-672). Many forms of protest involve no violence or disruption, but these will not concern us in this chapter.

Historical Relativity

Some commentators continue to write as if radical protest were a creation of the 1960's, as if the past had nothing to say to the present. On the contrary, there is nothing new about radical protest in America. Protest over social, political, and economic grievances has a long history in the United States. Since the War of Independence, there have been major eras of protest comparable to the 1960's: the 1830's and 1840's, the 1880's and 1890's, and the 1930's, to name the most significant. Especially well known in our history have been disorders relating to economic issues, ethnic and religious minorities, the draft (even during the Civil War!), labor organization, and female suffrage (Skolnick, 1969:12).

Following the quiescence of the Eisenhower years, American society began to be aroused by the social and political actions of dissenting individuals and groups. From the relatively peaceful days of sit-ins and freedom rides, protest spread and became more militant to the point where university buildings were occupied, sections of major cities were burned to the ground, and a national political convention had to be held behind barbed wire. Recent radical protest of this nature has been identified primarily with students and blacks, but actually various middle-class groups and "respectable" professionals have been involved in protest that has been at least militant and not always legal. Teachers have picketed schools in New York City. Doctors, nurses, researchers, and others from the medical profession have demonstrated against the war in Viet-Nam. Clergymen have also protested. On several Sundays in September and October, 1968, parishioners demonstrated near Catholic churches in Washington, D.C., to protest sanctions against priests who did not support the Pope's edict against artificial birth control. Even the staffs of law enforcement agencies have not refrained from demonstrating. On October 1, 1968, one-hundred "welfare patrolmen" picketed New York City's Social Services Department (Etzioni, 1970:5).

Despite its historical roots, radical protest in the 1960's and 1970's has a number of characteristics which set it apart from that of earlier eras, according to Boskin and Rosenstone:

Chapter 6 / Radical Protest

(1) The current protest has occurred in a period of prolonged prosperity.
(2) It has reflected the increasing pluralistic nature of society, including not only ethnic groups, but also emerging subcultures centering around school, youth, and dropouts from society.
(3) It has been essentially activist rather than ideological in orientation.
(4) It has seen the emergence of nationwide black organizations which have excluded white membership.
(5) It has been led by the younger generation, which has set the tone and direction of the movements. (Boskin and Rosenstone, 1969:1)

The term *protest* is sometimes applied to trivial and chronic challenges that express a general tradition of dissent, rather than to deep grievances. But the subject matter of this discussion is *radical protest,* by which we mean protest that stems from a deep feeling of grievance, that attempts to provoke ameliorative action (Turner, 1969:861), and that at least occasionally violates some laws of the society as a calculated tactic. Infraction of the law is a universal and necessary feature of the kind of protest that concerns us here. The term *radical* is not used here to characterize the political orientation of individuals, but rather to describe the *nature or form of the protest itself;* that is, protest becomes *radical when it is viewed by the body politic* as breaking the law and therefore as illegitimate. This chapter will focus primarily upon three recent types of radical protest: that of blacks, of students, and of the anti-war movement. These overlapping forms of radical protest occurred with increasing frequency in the 1960's and early 1970's. Some have claimed that America has had more protest during this period than at any other time in the nation's history. Our historical statistics are probably not complete enough to be sure about such a claim, but we do have some figures on the protests of more recent years.

Parameters of Reality

According to *The Report to the National Commission on the Causes and Prevention of Violence,* more than two million Americans resorted to demonstrations, riots, or terrorism to express their political demands and private antagonisms during the five-year period between June, 1963, and May, 1968. No more than a fifth of them took part in activities proscribed by law, but their actions reportedly resulted in more than 9,000 casualties, including some 200 deaths, and more than 70,000 arrests (Violence Commission, 575).

Civil Rights demonstrations mobilized about 1.1 million Americans, anti-war demonstrations about 680,000, and urban ghetto riots an estimated 200,000 (Violence Commission, 575). According to a study conducted by the National Student Association, students staged at least 221 demonstrations in 101 colleges between January 1 and June 15, 1968, involving 38,911 participants (Skolnick, 1969:22).

In America, from 1963 to 1968, about 11 out of every 1,000 persons took part in some form of protest (Violence Commission, 575).

Student Protest

American student activism has a long history, although it was only in the 1960's that it received national attention and serious analysis. In 1823, half the Harvard senior class was expelled shortly before graduation for participating in disruptive activity, and students were involved in anti-conscription campaigns during the Civil War (Lipset, 1971:128).

The Berkeley student protest of 1964 began the current era. According to the National Student Association, during the first half of the 1967-1968 academic year there were 71 separate demonstrations on 62 campuses, counting only those demonstrations involving 35 or more students (Peterson, 1968:79). During one academic year (1968-1969), the American Council on Education counted over 9,400 campus incidents (American Council on Education, 1971). More than a million and a half students were involved in radical protest after the Cambodia, Kent State, and Jackson State incidents in 1970 (Peterson, 1970). From a 1964-1965 analysis of 849 colleges, it was estimated that there were about 370 campus protests per 100 colleges. A roughly comparable study conducted in 1969-1970 showed a small rise to 386 protests per 100 colleges (American Council on Education, 1971).

By the middle of the 1960's, approximately 20 percent of all accredited colleges had experienced some campus disorder. During the 1967-1968 academic year, one out of every four colleges had an organized protest against military recruiting on campus, and one out of five had a protest against Dow Chemical, the CIA, or other agencies involved in the war. The 1968-1969 academic year saw a slight increase in campus disorders, with contemporary estimates indicating occurrences at 29 percent of all institutions of higher education (Ehrlich, 1971). The academic years of 1970-1971 and 1971-1972 witnessed declines in campus disorders, the Jackson-Kent State confrontations being the major disorders.

One measure of student protest can be seen in the increase of disciplinary action against students on campuses. One study of 28 colleges and universities showed that campus protests resulted in 950 suspensions or expulsions of students, with another 800 reprimands during one year (Scranton Commission, 1971). Another study found that radical protests were followed by campus or civil court penalties in over 75 percent of the colleges where they occurred (Bayer and Austin, 1969, Table 6). The percentage of campuses reporting student arrests increased from under 5 percent in 1968-1969 to almost 12 percent in 1969-1970 (Bayer and Austin, 1969, Table 6). If we study in detail some of the most publicized campus disorders, like Berkeley in 1964, the University of Chicago in 1969, Columbia in

Chapter 6 / Radical Protest

1968, or Harvard in 1969, we see that many students were in each case either convicted by the courts (almost 800 at Berkeley) or suspended and expelled by the university (123 at the University of Chicago) (Keniston and Lerner, 1971).

Anti-War Protest

By 1970, protest against American military involvement and conduct in Viet-Nam became so familiar to our national life that it almost acquired the status of an institution. The first pebbles of protest against American involvement were thrown in the late 1950's, but by March 31, 1968, when President Johnson announced his decision not to seek re-election, the protest had become a landslide. From the spring of 1965 to the spring of 1968, anti-war demonstrations are estimated to have grown from approximately 100,000 participants a year to about 280,000 (Horowitz, 1969). Many, but not all, of the participants were students.

On February 16 and 17, 1962, more than 4,000 student demonstrators came to Washington, D.C., to protest the war (Solomon and Fishman, 1963). In April, 1967, 200,000 New Yorkers marched in a mobilization against the Viet-Nam war (Etzioni, 1970:25). During the period from 1965 to 1968, it is estimated that there was an average of 3 to 4 anti-war protests per month (Violence Commission, 563). The average number of people protesting the war increased from

TABLE 6-1 ANTI-WAR DEMONSTRATIONS BY 1,000 PERSONS OR MORE, 1965-1968

Period (Season)	By Time of Occurrence				
	1965	1966	1967	1968	Total
January-March	1	8	3	1	13
April-June	2	3	2	4	11
July-September	1	3	0	0	4
October-December	9	1	10	1	21
Totals	13	15	15	6	49

Number	By Number of Participants				
	1965	1966	1967	1968	Total
1,000-4,999	6	9	8	2	25
5,000-9,999	1	2	3	0	6
10,000-14,999	2	2	0	2	6
15,000-19,999	2	0	0	0	2
20,000 or more	2	2	4	2	10
Totals	13	15	15	6	49

Source: Irving Louis Horowitz, The Struggle Is the Message: The Organization and Ideology of the Anti-War Movement, Berkeley, Calif.: Glendessary Press, 1970, Appendix, Table I

TABLE 6-2 ANTI-WAR DEMONSTRATIONS BY FEWER THAN 1,000 PERSONS, 1965-1968

	By Time of Occurrence				
Period (Season)	1965	1966	1967	1968	Total
January-March	3	15	6	6	30
April-June	6	14	5	4	29
July-September	5	7	1	1	14
October-December	29	2	30	0	61
Totals	43	38	42	11	134
	By Number of Participants				
Number	1965	1966	1967	1968	Total
fewer than 100	16	9	12	3	40
100-299	9	12	15	2	38
300-499	12	6	5	3	26
500-699	2	0	4	1	7
700-899	2	5	4	0	11
900-999	0	0	0	0	0
not known	2	6	2	2	12
Totals	43	38	42	11	134

Source: Irving Louis Horowitz, The Struggle Is the Message: The Organization and Ideology of the Anti-War Movement, Berkeley, Calif.: Glendessary Press, 1970, Appendix, Table II

approximately 14,400 to 38,700 per month during this same time period. (See also Tables 6-1 and 6-2.)

One study has listed the following as some of the major characteristics of anti-war demonstrators:

They were, by and large, a group in their early college years. They had come to Washington, D.C. . . . from 57 different colleges and universities. . . . The mean age of the demonstrators was 18½ . . . The sex distribution of the sample was 3:2, male:female. Approximately three-fourths of the sample had their homes in urban areas. Demonstrators came from middle class families with four or more children. Forty-five percent of all demonstrators were the oldest in their families. (Solomon and Fishman, 1963:57)

The number of anti-war rallies, protests, and demonstrations increased steadily from 1965 through 1967, while in 1968 it tapered off as anti-war protest became enmeshed in the presidential campaign. The demonstrations held in 1968, however, were almost always large, and they engendered the sharpest confrontations between demonstrators and law enforcement officials (Cox Commission, 1968:113).

Black Protest

Alternating extremes of elation and despair have characterized black protest in the 1960's and early 1970's. During a three-year period in the mid-sixties, there were more than a hundred major revolts in as many American cities. This suggested to many blacks, especially those who had been used to the more passive protest tactics of the 1950's and early 1960's, that the new course of protest could be expected to be violent and disruptive (Boskin and Rosenstone, 1969:2).

In 1966, approximately 40 cities experienced civil disorders. By 1967, civil disorders occurred in approximately 168 cities. The most reliable estimate for 1969 is that there were approximately 688 disorders (Ehrlich, 1971:297). During the first nine months of 1967, 164 disorders occurred in 128 cities. Twenty-five (20 percent) of these cities had two or more disturbances. New York had five separate disorders, Chicago had four, six cities had three, and seventeen cities had two (Cox Commission, 1968:113).

In the violent summer of 1967, Detroit became the scene of the bloodiest racial disturbance in half a century and the costliest, in terms of property damage, in U. S. history. At week's end, there were 41 known dead, 347 injured, and 3,800 arrested. Some 5,000 people were homeless (the vast majority black), while 1,300 buildings had been reduced to mounds of ashes and bricks and 2,700 businesses pillaged (*Time,* 1967: 13-15).

Between 1964 and 1967, approximately 130 civilians, mainly blacks, and 12 enforcement personnel, mainly Caucasian, were killed. Approximately 4,700 blacks and enforcement personnel were injured. Over 20,000 persons were arrested during the melees; property damage mounted into the hundreds of millions of dollars; and many urban areas resembled the hollowed remnants of war-torn cities (Boskin and Rosenstone, 1969:8).

After Martin Luther King, Jr., was killed on April 4, 1968, civil disorders occurred throughout the country. The month of April alone (1968) saw nearly as many disorders as in the entire year of 1967. More National Guard troops were called up than in all of 1967 (34,900 to 27,700), and more federal troops as well (23,700 to 4,800) (Lemberg Center, 1968:60). Major riots took place in several cities during this time period. In Chicago, 9 were killed and 500 injured; in Washington, D.C., 11 died and 1,113 were injured. There were 6 deaths and 900 injuries in Baltimore, and 6 deaths in Kansas City, Missouri. Racial protest of some degree occurred in 36 states and at least 138 cities (Lemberg Center, 1968:60).

High school protest by black students escalated in 1968. In Cincinnati, sit-ins and demonstrations in six of the city's eight high schools resulted in the suspension of 1,300 and arrest of 100 students. In South Bend, Indiana, 72 adults and 59 juveniles were arrested after a sit-in at the school system's administration building

TABLE 6-3 CHARACTERISTICS OF MAJOR TYPES OF CIVIL STRIFE IN THE UNITED STATES, JUNE 1963 - MAY 1968[a]

Type of Event	Number of Events Identified[b]	Estimated Number of Participants[c]	Reported Number of Casualties[d]	Reported Arrests[e]	Total Magnitude of Events[f]
Civil rights demonstrations[g]	369	1,117,600	389	15,379	7.53
Antiwar demonstrations[h]	104	680,000	400	3,258	5.62
Student protests on campus issues[i]	91	102,035	122	1,914	4.02
Antischool integration demonstrations[j]	24	34,720	0	164	1.66
Segregationist clashes and counter-demonstrations[k]	54	31,200	163	643	3.24
Negro riots and disturbances[l]	239	(200,000)	8,133	49,607	8.30
White terrorism against Negroes and rights workers[m]	213	(2,000)	112	97	2.48
All turmoil[a]	—	2,174,655	9,285	—	13.40
All conspiracy[a]	—	2,040	122	—	3.00
All strife[a]	—	2,176,695	9,407	—	13.64

[a] The data in this table include many estimates; all are imprecise. A number of less extensive forms of strife are not specifically shown, among them interracial clashes not involving civil-rights activities; terrorism within the Black Muslim movement; organized black terrorism against whites (negligible in this period); the local rebellion of Mexican-Americans in New Mexico in June 1967; and labor violence. Data on these events are included in the summary measures of magnitudes of strife.
[b] As reported in news sources, with the inclusions and exclusions listed in footnotes (g) to (m). Demonstrations and riots that last for more than 1 day are counted as one. Simultaneous demonstrations in several neighborhoods or cities are counted separately.
[c] Despite the apparent precision of some of the figures, the component figures for many events are rough estimates and in some instances "guess-estimates" assigned by coders. Figures in parentheses are especially tentative.
[d] Including deaths and injuries. Riots reportedly resulted in the death of 191 persons; white terrorism in the deaths of 23. Injury reports are of questionable reliability, since there are no standard reporting practices for them. Minor injuries usually are unreported.
[e] People reported in news sources to have been detained. No totals are shown because of incomplete data on arrests for types of strife not separately listed.
[f] The magnitude scores are not additive. Scores should be expanded to their fifth power to determine the actual average of their component Pervasiveness, Intensity, and Duration scores.
[g] As reported in the New York Times Index, including civil rights and school integration demonstrations. Excluded are events involving less than 100 people, boycotts, and demonstrations that become riots or clashes with segregationists. Also see (i), below.
[h] Based on data reported by Irving Louis Horowitz, "The Struggle Is the Message," paper prepared for the Task Force on Group Protest and Violence, National Commission on the Causes and Prevention of Violence, Sept. 1968, Tables 1, 2, and 3. The Horowitz data were revised to maintain comparability with other data by elimination of events involving less than 100 people and by exclusion of indoor rallies and protest meetings. Also see (i), below.
[i] Student demonstrations on issues other than civil rights and peace, as reported in the New York Times Index. Student civil-rights protests are included under civil-rights demonstrations; student antiwar protests are included under antiwar demonstrations.
[j] Demonstrations opposing busing, integration, and local control of schools by Negroes, as reported in the New York Times Index. Excluded are demonstrations involving less than 100 people; and boycotts, strikes, and walkouts.
[k] Demonstrations by white segregationists opposing civil-rights demonstrations and collective public attacks by segregationists on rights demonstrators, as reported in the New York Times Index. Excluded are events in which less than 100 white demonstrators or attackers were involved.
[l] "Hostile outbursts" initiated by blacks, as reported by Bryan T. Downes with Stephen W. Burke, "The Black Protest Movement and Urban Violence," paper read at the annual meeting of the American Political Science Association, Washington, D.C., Sept. 1968, pp. 12-15.
[m] Small-scale, clandestine acts of terror and violence, including bombings, arson, shooting, beatings, and major cross-burning incidents, as reported in the New York Times Index. Ordinarily no estimates of the number of participants are available.

Source: Hugh Davis Graham and Ted Robert Gurr, Violence in America: Historical and Comparative Perspectives, a staff report to the National Commission on the Causes and Prevention of Violence, Vol. 2, Washington, D.C.: Government Printing Office, June, 1969, pp. 446-447.

Chapter 6 / Radical Protest

TABLE 6-4 DISTRIBUTION OF 1967 CIVIL DISORDERS BY LEVEL, MONTH, REGION, AND CITY POPULATION

	Disorders by Month and Level			
Month (1967)	Number of Major Disorders	Number of Serious Disorders	Number of Minor Disorders	Totals
January	—	—	1	1
February	—	—	—	—
March	—	1	—	1
April	—	1	3	4
May	—	3	8	11
June	3	3	10	16
July	5	22	76	103
August	—	3	14	17
September	—	—	11	11
Total	8	33	123	164

	Disorders by Region and Level			
Region	Number of Major Disorders	Number of Serious Disorders	Number of Minor Disorders	Total (percent)
East	3	10	44	35
Midwest	4	11	44	36
South and border	1	7	19	16
West	—	5	16	13
Total	8	33	123	100

	Disorders by Level and City Population			
City Population (in thousands)	Number of Major Disorders	Number of Serious Disorders	Number of Minor Disorders	Totals
0-50	1	5	31	37
50-100	0	3	27	30
100-250	0	8	23	31
250-500	5	10	15	30
500-1,000	1	4	10	15
Over 1,000	1	3	13	17
Totals	8	33	119	160

Source: Report of the National Advisory Commission on Civil Disorders ("Kerner Commission"), March 1, 1968, Government Printing Office, p. 66

(*U. S. News,* 1968:37). The teaching of black history was a central issue in many protests, as in the boycott of three high schools in Waterbury, Connecticut (*The New York Times,* 1968a:22). (See Chapter 14 for more on black protest.)

Public Opinion

Thus far, data have been presented on the incidence of radical protest in the 1960's and 1970's. What has been the public's definition of student, black, and anti-war protest? James Reston observed in the fall of 1968 that "the prevailing mood of the country is against demonstrators in the black ghetto and the universities" (*The New York Times,* 1968b). In a Harris survey released in December, 1965, one-third of the American public thought that people had no right "to conduct peaceful demonstrations against the war." By 1967, four out of ten Americans doubted the right of persons to protest peacefully, and seven out of ten construed demonstrations as "acts of disloyalty" and as hurting the cause of peace (Harris, December, 1967). As campus-based protest expanded, public rejection even of the *right* of students to protest passed the half-way mark. In March, 1969, when Harris pollsters asked, "Do you feel that students have the right to make their protest or not?" 52 percent of the American public replied that they had no right.

Rather than focusing on the needs communicated by the protestors, the majority on the sidelines concentrated their attention on the communicative acts themselves, condemning both them and those who participated in them. For instance, 74 percent of the adult public in a California poll expressed disapproval of the student demonstrations at Berkeley in 1964 (Miller, 1965:347). A Harris poll (September 27, 1965) reported that 68 percent of Americans found anti-Viet-Nam pickets "more harmful than helpful" (5 percent "more helpful than harmful"). Two-thirds versus 16 percent felt the same way about civil rights demonstrations and about student demonstrations at colleges. A later poll (Harris, June 5, 1967) showed that the public had grown even more critical of black "demonstration tactics"; those disapproving of them had grown to 82 percent.

CHAMPIONS AND THEIR INTERESTS

The three concurrent streams of the protest movement, while focusing largely on their own respective interests in the campus, the war, and race relations, nevertheless shared certain beliefs and definitions about the nature of social and political reality in the United States. All three groups opposed the Viet-Nam War, either for the "imperialism" which it represented, or for its perceived racial overtones, or for its wastefulness, or for all these (and other) reasons. All three groups advocated a fundamental redistribution not only of wealth, but of power in favor of the poor, the minorities, and the students. "Participatory democracy," a major plank in the protest platform, meant greater day-to-day participation by the "powerless" in those political and legal decisions which most affected their lives, and "liberation" meant not only such political participation, but also the freedom for individuals to adopt unusual life-styles as they chose. Critics of the protestors frequently pointed to the anomaly in their using aggressive (and occasionally violent) tactics in support of "peace," and when protestors demanded "power to the people," their critics would sometimes counter with "which people?" Nevertheless, to the protest groups themselves, their stance on foreign and domestic policies of the "establishment" seemed clear, consistent, and comprehensive (Mauss, 1971a).

In Chapter 2, it was pointed out that social movements tend to have a three-ringed structure, in which the "hard core" of the movement is surrounded by two rings of progressively less militant supporters. Some movements generate countermovements having a similar structure, or perhaps the two opposing movements will arise concomitantly in response to each other. The radical student, anti-war, and black liberation movements of the 1960's actually had their origins somewhat earlier in the mid-1950's, and their rise was paralleled by that of a powerful countermovement which defined the radical agitation as part of a subversive, foreign-led, anti-American conspiracy and as a threat to the law and order of the land. The radical movements comprised the inner core of a much larger (but less militant) liberal public, sympathetic to the universal extension of civil rights, to an increase in student autonomy on the college campuses, and to a conciliatory diplomatic stance for the United States in foreign policy. At the same time, the countermovement to radicalism was expressed most conspicuously by a militantly conservative hard core surrounded by a very large public, holding the kinds of views about radical protest which were described above in the section on public opinion polls. While the general public was perhaps not willing to go to the ideological extremes of the conservative hard core, it clearly tended to accept the latter's definition of radical movements as "law-and-order" problems.

We will look first at the general structure and ideas of the radical movements and then at those of the conservative countermovement.

The Radical Interest Groups

It is sometimes difficult to distinguish clearly between *moral* publics or interest groups and *political* ones, since both espouse moral principles and act upon them. We will here consider as moral interest groups those whose efforts are more propagandistic than political, while those which engage primarily in the time-honored political pressure tactics we will consider political groups.

Moral Interest Groups

The anti-war moral interest groups were particularly offended by increasing U. S. involvement in Viet-Nam. Most of these groups have an ideological concern for peace and nonviolence going back beyond Viet-Nam to the issue of militarism and the testing of nuclear arms. The more prominent of these groups have been Women Strike for Peace, SANE, War Resister's League, Committee for Nonviolent Action, the Fellowship of Reconciliation, Student Peace Union, Veterans for Peace, and Veterans and Reservists to End the War in Viet-Nam. At the beginning (in the late 50's), the most influential of these organizations were SANE and the Student Peace Union. The Student Affiliate of the National Committee for a Sane Nuclear Policy (SANE) was founded in 1958 and, although it included many left-wing students, generally followed SANE's liberal policies (Altbach and Peterson, 1971:12). Its major interests were ending nuclear testing and the Viet-Nam War. Dr. Benjamin Spock, one of SANE's members, was eventually put on trial by the U. S. government for his anti-war activities. The other major moral interest group, the Student Peace Union (SPU), was founded in 1959 by a combination of pacifists and moderate radicals. The SPU was for a period the largest student peace group in the United States, with a membership of about 5,000 on some 100 campuses (Altbach and Peterson, 1971:12). By 1964, Students for a Democratic Society had taken over most of its activities within the context of a broader program and absorbed most of the SPU's former membership in the process. SPU's major interests were the same as SANE's, i.e., ending nuclear testing and the Viet-Nam War. The strictly *moral* interest groups tended to focus mainly on the war and peace issue. Black and campus protest emerging in this period was almost by definition carried on by *political* interest groups.

Political Interest Groups

In addition to moral interest groups, political interest groups have also been active in radical causes. The major concern of these organizations has not been merely with protest but with the organization of youth and blacks for social change. Most of the student-oriented groups are now defunct.

STUDENTS FOR A DEMOCRATIC SOCIETY (SDS) Founded on the campus of the University of Michigan in 1960, and until 1962 identified as the Student League for Industrial Democracy, the Students for a Democratic Society (SDS) conceived of themselves as a new radical movement to change the American political process fundamentally and to reinvigorate it. Such would be the result, they believed, if universities could become centers of controversy and arenas for active discussion of alternatives to present policies, if the civil rights and anti-war movements could succeed in mobilizing large numbers of people at the grass-roots level; and if established reform groups, such as the labor movement, liberal organizations, and religious bodies, would join forces with the civil rights, peace, and student movements to offer new alternatives to the electorate at the local and national levels (Skolnick, 1969:89). SDS was the most influential of the student political groups formed in the early 1960's. At its height, it claimed about 7,000 "national" (i.e., dues-paying) members and another 35,000 members in its several hundred local chapters (*Life,* 1968). Two of SDS's major personalities were Jerry Rubin and Tom Hayden.

THE PROGRESSIVE LABOR PARTY (PLP) Originating in Brooklyn in 1961, PLP originally designated itself the Progressive Labor Movement. Its pro-Peking, Marxist orientation makes it one of the more radical of the far-left organizations. In 1966, its membership was estimated at about 700, with a very high turnover (McReynolds, 1966:530). The Progressive Labor Party has published a monthly organ, *Progressive Labor;* a New York bi-weekly, *Challenge;* and an occasional paper in San Francisco, *Spark*. The PLP's program is designed to exploit issues on campuses and elsewhere in order to turn conflicts between young people and the power structure into large-scale social change (Luce, 1965:33).

THE W.E.B. DUBOIS CLUB Though in existence locally on the West Coast for some time, Dubois Clubs became a national organization in 1964 and had a membership of close to 4,000 in 1966 (Monat, 1966:3). Essentially Marxist-Leninist and pro-Soviet in orientation, the Dubois Club had as its eventual goal the formation of a third political party, which was never really accomplished.

THE MAY SECOND MOVEMENT (M2M) Organized by members of Progressive Labor, M2M was a student group that derived its name from the first rally it sponsored (May 2, 1964) to oppose the war in Viet-Nam. M2M had its own publication, the *Free Student*. Its membership was probably not more than 500 at its peak. Although it was initially established as a "radical peace organization," and maintained its concern with urging American withdrawal from Southeast Asia, M2M organizers in the late sixties engaged in stirring up student grievances on college campuses (Mead, 1971:201).

THE NATIONAL ASSOCIATION FOR THE ADVANCEMENT OF COLORED PEOPLE (NAACP) Founded in 1909, the NAACP led a direct frontal attack on the system of racial segregation and discrimination by lobbying for civil rights legislation and, more important, by fighting in the courts for the enforcement of the Reconstruction Amendments. It also sponsored and coordinated mass marches, boycotts, and picketing. It is the largest black liberation organization in the nation, with some 400,000 dues-paying members and probably millions of supporters, black and white (Meier and Rudwick, 1970:42).

THE CONGRESS OF RACIAL EQUALITY (CORE) Founded in 1942 by James Farmer, CORE is generally regarded as one of the more militant of the black protest organizations. CORE was originally an integrationist organization but eventually changed its program to a basis of Black Power and Black Nationalism.* Over the past several years, CORE has suffered a decline in activity, membership, and financial support. Its present leader is Roy Innis.

THE SOUTHERN CHRISTIAN LEADERSHIP CONFERENCE (SCLC) Established by Dr. Martin Luther King, Jr., in Atlanta, Georgia, in 1957, SCLC coordinates nonviolent direct action in Southern cities. After Dr. King's assassination in 1968, the Reverend Ralph David Abernathy became the leader. Through the zeal of its collective leadership, variable support from Southern black churches, and financial help from a wide variety of private donors, SCLC has achieved some remarkable victories in its nonviolent action program. For example, it was SCLC that was mainly instrumental, particularly in the earlier days, in integrating public accommodations, greatly increasing voter registration, and in organizing self-help programs for the poor, such as "Operation Breadbasket." SCLC, incidentally, was also the organization that gave "birth" and early sustenance to SNCC.

THE STUDENT NONVIOLENT COORDINATING COMMITTEE (SNCC) A "nonmembership" organization with a staff that varied in size from 150 to 250, SNCC was formed in April, 1960, in Raleigh, North Carolina (Mead, 1971:195). Except for the Black Panthers, it had the youngest and most radical adherents of all major black liberation organizations. SNCC's work at first was primarily among rural blacks in the South, although it later expanded its activities into Northern urban areas. SNCC reached national prominence during the summer of 1964 when the provocative statements of Rap Brown and Stokely Carmichael became familiar TV and newspaper fare for millions of Americans. SNCC became one of the most militant black protest organizations, advocating a philosophy of Black Power and Black Nationalism that pointed to a new direction for the Black Liberation Movement, but as an organization, SNCC did not survive the 1960's.

THE BLACK PANTHER PARTY The Panthers started out as the Black Panther Party for Self-Defense in Oakland, California, in the fall of 1966. Its co-founders were Huey Newton and Bobby Seale. Designating themselves as Minister of Defense

---

*As used here, and in most political literature of the 1960's, "Black Power" refers to an attitude and a policy on the parts of many American blacks that they should seek *collectively* to make themselves felt, as blacks, in various institutions and arenas of American life, such as in public demonstrations, in collective black voting for black candidates, in black boycotts, or in selective purchasing from black merchants, and the like. The term did not necessarily imply violent behavior, although it was sometimes so construed by fearful whites. "Black Nationalism," which overlapped somewhat in meaning with Black Power, referred more specifically to *separatism,* i.e. that blacks should have their own institutions, separate from those of whites. In its extreme form, the Black Nationalist outlook called also for a separate territory in the United States for blacks only. Perhaps the distinction between these two terms could be clarified by reference to the educational institutions: "Black Power" would signify the assertion of such political and economic leverage as would gain for blacks the same advantages and opportunities as whites enjoyed in the public schools, whereas "Black Nationalism" would call for *separate* schools as well. (See also Chapter 14.)

and as Chairman, respectively, of their new organization, their primary objective was to organize their fellow blacks locally into a defense league against white harassment. In their early days, the main activity of the Panthers was "patrolling the pigs." In 1967, Eldridge Cleaver became the Panther's "Minister of Education," as well as their most articulate and thoughtful spokesman. A number of Black Panther chapters established programs in the late 1960's to provide free breakfasts for ghetto children, some have made efforts to improve community health service, and in several communities there are Black Panther schools devoted to indoctrinating the young with an awareness of their identity and rights. In Panther chapters, membership records are carefully guarded to prevent them from falling into the hands of the police. As a result, it is virtually impossible to estimate, with any certainty, the size of the movement. The popular press suggested, as of about 1970, that there were about forty-five chapters with a total of fewer than two thousand members, but as many as perhaps sixty thousand "sympathizers" (Mead, 1971:195). Police pressure has led to the arrest, killing, or exile of most of the Panthers' national leadership and many of their local leaders.

Other political publics and interest groups include the Black Muslims, the National Urban League, the Revolutionary Action Movement (RAM), and the Mississippi Freedom Democratic Party (MFDP).

The Countermovement Interest Groups

The countermovement which grew concurrently with the radical one has its base in a large "middle-America" public that is suspicious of the motives and methods of the radicals. The countermovement has been spearheaded by several right-wing organizations that mix moral and political interests. All have claimed that their primary interest is to defend "American" values presumably threatened by protesting blacks and students. More specifically, these groups can be said to represent a frame of mind that sees "law and order" in American society threatened by radical protest. Some of these moral and political interest groups have been prepared to utilize coordinated violent action in order to restore or defend what they perceive as "law and order," and thus represent a modern vigilante phenomenon. Examples would be such organizations as Newark's North Ward Citizen's Committee; "Break Through" in Detroit, led by Donald Lobsinger; "Fight Back" in Warren, Michigan, led by Ronald Portnoy; the Home Defense Association of Oakland, California, led by Herbert Clark; and the Minutemen, with heaviest concentration in the West and Midwest, led by Robert DePugh.

The John Birch Society is one of the few right-wing organizations in the United States that has succeeded in building a broadly based and highly active membership. The organization that Robert Welch created in 1958 consists of two separate entities, the John Birch Society itself and an affiliated publishing arm, Robert

Welch, Inc. The Society's official organ is the *Bulletin,* written entirely (some 15,000 words) by Welch himself. In the mid-sixties, the JBS claimed a membership of about 60,000, distributed among some 4,000 chapters throughout the fifty states. The ideology of the John Birch Society contends that an international Communist conspiracy now largely controls not only most of the other nations of the world but also the major social, economic, and political institutions in the United States. The conflict with Communism is perceived as the central issue of our time, dominating and overshadowing all others. Those in the Society view the black and student protest of the sixties in the light of this subversive conspiracy.

One of the more recent of the activist countergroups is the North Ward Citizen's Committee of Newark, New Jersey, whose leader, Anthony Imperiale, was elected to the Newark City Council. In 1969, this organization claimed a dues-paying membership of two hundred, and thousands of enthusiastic followers. Members operate radio-equipped car patrols in their neighborhoods (North Ward) and train members in karate. Their militant quest for "law and order" is rooted in the anxieties aroused by the Newark disorders of the sixties. Accompanying the fear of black protest is a strong sense of concern for the "lack of discipline on our college campuses."

Occupational Interest Groups

A third type of interest group we might include here would be the occupational interest groups, such as the police, who, in the line of duty, come into contact with student, black, and anti-war protestors. In some ways, the police can be seen as part of the conservative countermovement, but they have other special interests, so we are not considering them here as a part of either movement. Radical protest poses an unusual problem for the policeman. In protest situations, the police are in the public eye, and frequently they find themselves in violent confrontation with students and blacks. Faced with mounting pressures to quell the protest, the police have naturally sought to understand the origins and nature of radical protest. With a few exceptions, they have adopted an explanation of radical protest that is based on the "rotten apple" theory of human nature; that is, radical protest is attributed mainly to the efforts of evil individuals. This theory tends to view radical protest as the conspiratorial product of authoritarian agitators—usually Communists—who mislead otherwise contented people (Skolnick, 1969:260). Such an approach has serious implications. The police are led to view protest as "illegitimate misbehavior," rather than as legitimate dissent against policies and practices that might be wrong. The police are bound to be hostile to "illegitimate behavior," and the reduction of protest tends to be their principal goal. Such an attitude automatically produces great hostility between police and protestors.

A similar outlook, sometimes evidenced by the FBI and other governmental agencies, is the "riffraff" theory of radical protest. This theory attempts to explain "riots" in terms of three major assumptions: that a small minority of the black population engages in riot activity, that this minority is composed of the unattached, uprooted, and unskilled, and that the overwhelming majority of the black population deplores riots (Tomlinson and Sears, 1967). This theory helps to dramatize the "criminal" aspect of riots, to undermine their political aspect, and to uphold the argument that social change is possible only through lawful and peaceful means. If such riots can be explained as the work of a few "agitators" or "hoodlums," radical protest can be more widely discredited. Implicit in the "riffraff" theory is the idea that riots are unilaterally violent, that public officials and agencies merely respond in defense against the violence of "irresponsible advocates," and that such disturbances have little wider meaning in the black community.

Scientific Interest Groups

Social scientists have developed a variety of explanations for the nature and causes of radical protest, which derive in many respects from the theories reviewed in Chapter 1.

They usually place radical protest under the heading of "collective behavior." The crucial element of collective behavior is that it is qualitatively different from the "normal" group processes of society. Radical protest is thus conceived as nonconforming or even "deviant" mass behavior. Under this conception, the routine processes of any given society are seen as stable, orderly, and predictable, operating under the normative constraints and cumulative rationality of tradition. The instability, disorder, and irrationality of radical protest therefore are attributed to those groups that are experiencing "social strain" or "tension" (Smelser, 1962:1), leading to frustration and hostility on the part of marginal or dissatisfied groups.

Contemporary social theorists also attempt to explain radical protest in terms of "a breakdown of normal social controls," in the sense of both widespread social disorganization and the inability of local authorities to maintain order in the face of emergent disorder. This perspective is affirmed in a recent work directed specifically at the causes and control of ghetto disorders, where it is argued that while "social tensions" clearly underlie riots, they amount to only a partial explanation;

"a key element in the outbreak of riots is a weakness in the system of social control" (Janowitz, 1968:7).

Kenneth E. Boulding, in developing a theory of protest, says that a protest movement is likely to succeed only if it expresses a view that is widespread but not yet publicly proclaimed. However, if the society is sharply divided, protest movements might raise even stronger counterprotests. Boulding goes on to say that, even if its time is ripe, a protest movement may provoke repression if it takes an inappropriate form or if the object of protest is not clear (Boulding, 1969).

Another sociological theory, put forth by Jerome H. Skolnick, is that radical protest must be analyzed in relation to crises in American institutions generally. He suggests that a serious analysis cannot focus solely on the character or culture of the protestors, but that protest must be viewed as an outgrowth of genuinely "oppressive" social, economic, and political conditions within basic institutions (Skolnick, 1969).

Another theory, which is socio-psychological in nature, tends to find the roots of protest in permissive child-rearing practices. Some analysts contend that changes in the child-rearing pattern are the underlying causes of student protest. The basic tenet of this theory is that parental authority and control are lacking in the home; consequently, by the time they enter college, students are "spoiled" and have no respect for authority (Stewart, 1972:101).

A much more sophisticated resort to parent-child explanations of protest is that of Lewis S. Feuer. In his book *The Conflict of Generations,* Feuer explains the student movement as a breakdown in the "generational equilibrium" of the society:

> We may define a student movement as a combination of students inspired by aims which they try to explicate in a political ideology, and moved by an emotional rebellion in which there is always present a disillusionment with and rejection of the values of the older generation; moreover, the members of a student movement have the conviction that their generation has a special historical mission to fulfill where the older generation, other elites, and other classes have failed. (Feuer, 1969:11)

The generational conflict approach sees the activism of the American student movement as resulting from basic differences in the perception of society between students and the older generation. This difference is responsible for a cultural and political discontinuity between age groups, which leads to the student's rejection of the values and institutions of society.

Obviously, there are many different theories of radical protest, depending on whether the interests of the theorist are occupational, scientific, moral, or political. We will now turn to a more thorough analysis of radical protest as a social problem by looking at the careers of the protest and counterprotest movements.

RADICAL PROTEST AND COUNTERPROTEST AS SOCIAL MOVEMENTS

Student Protest

Recruits and Leaders

An interesting and important conclusion to be drawn from a large number of studies, particularly those of Kenneth Keniston and Richard Flacks, is that recruits into the student movement have been largely children of leftist or liberal parents (Flacks, 1967; and Keniston, 1969:29) and have come, for the most part, from affluent, upper-middle-class, professional homes, with high educational standards and attainment. Their families, by and large, have been close-knit and psychologically supportive (Flacks, 1967; and Keniston, 1969:29). The parents of these students are themselves deviant from conventional middle-class values and attitudes and represent, in their convictions and behavior, a value orientation that is idealistic, liberal, and humanitarian. Styles of family life place a strong emphasis on independence, personal fulfillment, and democratic, equalitarian interpersonal relations. Flacks notes a special concern for "values other than achievement." Keniston, whose observation of the New Left in *Young Radicals* is limited (unlike Flacks' study) to a small elite group, insists that parental emphasis upon academic achievement was considerable and effective with the young leaders studied. At any rate, there seems to have been in the homes of these young activists "stress on the intrinsic worth of living up to intellectual, aesthetic, political or religious ideals" (Flacks and Keniston, 1969:13). According to both investigators, there is an impressive degree of continuity between the attitudes and values of the youth and those of their parents. Moreover, they point out, the social base of the general student recruit did not differ markedly from that of the leaders. Indeed, the small elite sample that Keniston investigated was primarily composed of "young leaders."

Strategies and Tactics

During their earlier years, SDS and other student activist groups preferred to work in local urban situations, in grass-roots community organization among the poor. The involvement of students in this kind of action rose steadily for a number of years, but as the war in Viet-Nam became increasingly important, SDS abandoned its practice of concentrating on domestic issues and began to become involved in foreign policy issues.

During this period of new involvement, "resistance" and "confrontation" came to occupy an increasingly prominent position in the strategy and tactics of the student movement. "Resistance" and "confrontation" refer to such forms of direct action as deliberate disruption of, or interference with, normal, routine operations of persons; deliberate violation of authoritative orders to disperse; forceful retaliation against police use of clubs, chemicals, or other weapons; the use of barricades or "mobile tactics" to prevent or delay police efforts to disperse a crowd; the use of ridicule, rudeness, obscenity, and other "uncivil" forms of speech and behavior to shock, embarrass, or defy authorities; and refusal to comply with orders or to accept authoritative commands or requests as legitimate (Skolnick, 1969:106).

Other tactics utilized by SDS and the student movement groups included "teach-ins"; protest against Dow Chemical Company and other campus recruiters for what Kenneth Boulding calls the "World War III industries"; disruption of recruitment efforts of Marine, Army, and Navy recruiters; and disruption of the military induction process by burning draft cards, defacing and ransacking military files, and the like (Horowitz, 1969:11).

The general strategy of SDS and the student movement as a whole has been a "strategy of confrontation" to promote reform. This strategy has been outlined in Skolnick's *The Politics of Protest* (Skolnick, 1969: 107-08):

1. *Confrontation and Militancy as Methods of Arousing Moderates to Action.* The creation of turmoil and disorder can stimulate otherwise quiescent groups to take more forceful action in their own ways.

2. *Confrontation and Militancy Can Educate the Public.* Direct action is not intended to win particular reforms or to influence decision-makers, but rather to bring out a repressive response from authorities—a response rarely seen by most white Americans. When confrontation brings violent official response, uncommitted elements of the public can see for themselves the true nature of the "system." Confrontation, therefore, is a means of political education.

3. *Confrontation, Militancy and Resistance Are Ways to Prepare Young Radicals for the Possibility of Greater Repression.* If the movement really seriously threatens the power of political authorities, efforts to repress it through "police state measures" are inevitable. The development of resistant attitudes and action toward the police at the present time is a necessary preparation for more serious resistance in the future.

4. *Combative Behavior with Respect to the Police and Other Authorities, Although Possibly Alienating "Respectable" Adults, Has the Opposite Effect on the Movement's Relationships with Nonstudent Youth.* Educated, middle-class, nonviolent styles of protest are poorly understood by working-class youth, black youth, and other "dropouts." Contact with these other sectors of the youth population is essential and depends upon the adoption of a tough and aggressive stance to win respect from such youth.

5. *The Experience of Resistance and Combat May Have a Liberating Effect on Young Middle-Class Radicals.* Most middle-class students are shocked by aggressive or violent behavior. Militant confrontation gives resisters the experience of physically opposing institutional power, and it may force students to choose between "respectable" intellectual radicalism and serious commitment to revolution, violent or otherwise.

Through such strategy and tactics, SDS hoped to invigorate and democratize American politics.

The Natural History of the Student Protest Movement

The SDS and other elements of the recent student protest movement offer particularly good illustrations of the "natural history" model introduced in Chapter 2.

The *incipiency* stage of the student movement extended from the late 1950's to about 1962. During this period, it was a fluid and open movement that emphasized persuasion, urged broad popular participation in all important decisions, and concentrated its energies in organizing the poor, both black and white; it was especially active in Newark, Cleveland, and Chicago. Also during this stage, student campaigns employed such normal channels as student government and such conventional protest techniques as petitions, picketing, and public meetings.

The intensification of the Viet-Nam war by the United States in late 1964 stirred up activist concern among many students previously relatively passive. SDS was one of the few leftist organizations—on many campuses the only one—with chapters or organizers on the campuses, and it was natural that the newly aroused students should find in SDS an opportunity for expression and group identification (Kazin, 1969:647). While the movement took in new individual members, it also became something of a coalition of leftist groups that found the open structure of SDS and its well attended conventions a convenient framework within which to operate. The Progressive Labor Party, pro-Chinese and Marxist-Leninist in its orientation, was the best organized of the groups to find a home in SDS (Mead, 1971:197).

The *coalescence* stage of the SDS was marked by its official organization in 1962 and continued for about three years, during which time the Viet-Nam war was greatly escalated and the Berkeley campus was rocked by a series of massive protest demonstrations, a sit-in at the administration building, mass arrests, and a strike. It seems fair to say that the Free Speech Movement at Berkeley at the end of 1964 marked the formation of a cohesive "public" in the American student movement as a whole. The Free Speech Movement began, conventionally enough, over suddenly imposed restrictions on students who used the campus "to support or advocate off-campus political or social action" (Towle, 1964). The FSM grew from a protest against particular violations of students' rights to a vehicle for expression of an underlying conflict between students as a "class" and the administration of the "multi-versity," a struggle between two fundamentally opposed interests in, and orientations toward, higher education. The FSM demonstrated further the feasibility of involving large numbers of students in direct action techniques on campus, and suggested that such techniques might be necessary to effect campus reforms (Skolnick, 1969:93).

The *institutionalization* stage of SDS and the rest of the movement occurred during 1965-1969. This was a period of organization and routinization for SDS. The movement began to develop its mechanisms of coping with the establishment and absorbing a new influx of members.

In April, 1965, a national student march in Washington, D.C., against the war achieved wide recognition as a nationally organized expression of the student movement. After the march, hundreds of campuses witnessed "teach-ins" and other organized activities concerning Viet-Nam. The Indo-China war soon became the central, overriding preoccupation of SDS. The anti-Viet-Nam war activity that followed was characterized by marches, some draft card burning, and the use of civil disobedience to dramatize the movement's cause.

By the end of 1965, increasing disillusionment with the efficacy of such protest began to develop. Each major march had more participants but was shortly followed by some new escalation of the war. Many disillusioned students argued that the main function served by peace marches was to maintain America's image as a democratic society permitting dissent, so that the war effort could continue without significant internal or external opposition (*New Left Notes,* 1965-1967). The establishment was coping with the movement all too well.

During the ensuing three or four years, SDS and the student movement engaged in a struggle, over a number of issues, with an establishment showing increasing skills in repression and co-optation. The interaction over each issue left SDS a little less unified and focused. In 1966, there was the issue of student draft deferments and the propriety of using college class standings as a basis for granting the deferments. In the controversy, student sit-ins and seizures of college and university administration buildings occurred across the country (Visick, 1967). Some limited success for the students was achieved in the form of a few refusals by college administrations to submit class rankings to the Selective Service Director, and such non-cooperation came into use in other ways as a tactic for resisting the draft (Visick, 1967). However, the results overall were discouraging, for the movement had little net impact on the government or on public opinion. For a time, this discouragement was reflected in a changing leadership in SDS and a turn toward a philosophy of "student syndicalism" or "student power," which focused less on national politics and more on campus issues *per se*—the abolition of grades, the revision of the curriculum, and student participation in university government (Skolnick, 1969:97). However, the continued escalation of the war and other grievances felt by college youth soon led to a return to a more national focus (Teodori, 1969:228). This focus centered on a cause especially well suited to student radicals, combining their campus and national interests, namely, the various ties between universities and the military—not only ROTC, but war-related research and military recruiting. This issue strengthened the mobilizing efforts of SDS and produced a great many campus confrontations and disorders, during this heyday of the institutionalized student movement.

During the late sixties, the responses of the government, the police, campus administrations, and other agencies of the establishment showed the usual combination of co-optation and repression: government commissions were appointed to study the problem; students were admitted to policy committees on many campuses; a third "radical" political party (the Peace and Freedom Party), advocating many of the students' demands, eventually made a strong showing (in the 1968 election); and the Republicans in the same year elected a candidate committed to ending the Viet-Nam war. These developments symptomized both the institutionalization of the movement and its increasing co-optation. On the repression side of the process, meanwhile, student agitation that continued in spite of these co-optive efforts was opposed with increasing harshness: many students in the movement were suspended or expelled from their campuses; national guard and police contingents began quelling campus uprisings with force that was very heavy and of doubtful legitimacy, even according to a government commission (Cox Commission, 1968). The behavior of the Chicago police toward student demonstrations before and during the 1968 Democratic National Convention was especially controversial (Sparling, 1968). The 1968-1969 school year saw the peak of SDS strength, with a dues-paying membership of 8,000 in 300 campus chapters and a record number of campus disruptions (Mead, 1971:197).

Disagreement over how to respond to this co-optation and repression ushered in the *fragmentation* stage of the movement, beginning in 1969 or 1970. At the national convention of SDS in Chicago in June, 1969, it became clear that a spirit of solidarity had ceased to characterize the SDS coalition. At this convention, the SDS split into an extremely violent faction, Revolutionary Youth Movement I (sometimes called "Weathermen") and the more moderate RYM II, which regarded most violence as futile. Each faction "excommunicated" the other. RYM II, the larger faction, was charged with opposing most of the demands and programs of the Black Liberation Movement and with being disaffected over what it had labeled the "student elitism" of SDS. The Weathermen, far less disciplined and more militant, were a smaller group advocating immediate destruction of the social structure through sabotage and guerrilla warfare.

SDS as an organization emerged from the convention in complete shambles (Mead, 1971:197). For the next year, it was the Weathermen who captured the headlines. By their provocation of street violence in the fall of 1969 and their bombings throughout the following months, this self-styled revolutionary vanguard dismayed and disgusted virtually all segments of the moderate and radical left.

The *demise* of SDS was apparent from the limited amount of protest created by the renewed bombings in Indo-China from 1970 to 1973. The last showings of student radicalism were in the Kent State and Jackson State protests of early 1970, both of which were severely and successfully repressed. SDS is no longer an umbrella-type organization able to mobilize and coordinate large numbers of protestors in activities across the nation.

The ironies of the establishment's co-optation of the student movement have sometimes been acute, especially at the level of rhetoric. As early as 1970, former President Nixon, without a murmur from the students, described his legislative program to Congress as "a new American revolution." More recently, Army recruiting billboards have featured an appeal which the SDS alumni must find galling: just as they used to admonish the military to "make love, not war," the Army, as though in belated reply, now offers the poignantly ironic appeal, "A country needs love, too." (See Mauss, 1971 [b], for more on this movement's "career.")

Terrorist and extremist remnants of the protest movement of the sixties have continued into the seventies. Though apparently very few in number, and racially mixed, the terrorists have formed themselves into a series of small and ephemeral bands which have generated shock waves and publicity far out of proportion to their numbers. One of the most notorious of these bands has been the Symbionese Liberation Army (SLA), which first appeared on the scene by claiming "credit" for the 1973 assassination of Marcus Foster, a tremendously able and respected Superintendent of Schools in Oakland, California. Even though he was black, Foster was accused by the SLA of aiding and abetting the establishment's oppression of the common people. More spectacular yet was the SLA's kidnapping of newspaper heiress Patricia Hearst in early 1974, and holding her for a ransom that eventually took the form of the distribution by her wealthy father of two million dollars' worth of food to variously defined "needy people" in California. Rather than returning Miss Hearst, however, the SLA kept her on, perhaps as a new recruit and willing participant, in a series of subsequent bank holdups, shootouts, and other serious incidents. In May, 1974, most of the SLA was apparently destroyed by the police in a shootout and fire at their Los Angeles hideout, but a few of the members, accompanied by Miss Hearst in one way or another, remained at large. While continuing to use the rhetoric of political protest which many of them learned as participants in the Berkeley student agitations of the late 1960's, the SLA has perpetrated violent acts in the 1970's which are generally regarded as crimes against life and property.

Black Protest

Recruits and Leaders

Objective studies on the social characteristics of members of black protest organizations are limited. With the exception of SNCC (students only), generalizations about the social status of membership in these protest organizations are risky. Blacks of all social classes are potential recruits of protest organizations in nearly equal proportions. However, "grass roots" blacks, often expressing more intense overt anti-white attitudes than middle- and upper-class blacks, provide a social base from which the Black Liberation Movement has drawn increasingly in recent years. Black ministers, who once had a virtual monopoly on leadership in the black liberation movements, have begun to be displaced by militant young student activists (Thompson, 1963:34).

Black sociologist Harry Edwards has suggested that there are five types of black students participating in the Liberation Movement: "the radical activist, the militant, the revolutionary, the anomic activist, and the conforming Negro" (Edwards, 1970). SNCC recruits have been drawn mainly from the first three of Edwards' classifications.

The "radical activists" typically have relatively long histories of activism in the movement, usually dating back to participation in SNCC before its Black Power days. Thus, they are usually sophisticated in organizing and mobilizing people and have a substantial amount of firsthand experience in confronting entrenched, legally established institutions and authorities. The radical activist is usually older than the normal SNCC recruit. He may be a senior or graduate student in his middle or late twenties, usually coming from a middle-class black family.

The "militant" is by far the most numerous of the black student activists. He is usually an undergraduate in his late teens or early twenties. He typically possesses neither practical experience in dealing with political issues nor any cohesive philosophy, for the militant is the "nouveau noir" of the Black Liberation Movement. Hence, the campus militant is usually the follower in SNCC and other organizations. He does no organizing, but rather is organized and politicized by the radical activist and others. The militant also comes from a middle-class black family, and he has typically been protected from the harsh experience of the black community by his parents, who have maintained tight control over him.

The "revolutionary" repudiates almost all means except premeditated and calculated violence as a legitimate tactic in the black liberation struggle. It is the revolutionary who has popularized, and who staunchly believes in, the statement that "more political solutions have come from the barrels of guns than from the halls of the United States Congress." In black student organizations such as SNCC, the revolutionary seldom becomes active until a crisis arises. He is not usually elected to positions of authority, and, when he is, his tenure in office is usually shortlived. He tends to push the militant membership too fast and in too radical a direction to suit them. The revolutionary's socio-economic class origin and his age do not show any distinguishable pattern.

The strategies and tactics of SNCC are based upon concepts of Black Power. In the spring of 1966, with the election of Stokely Carmichael as president, SNCC put forth a position paper stating that "our organization (SNCC) should be black-staffed, black-controlled, and black-financed" (Teodori, 1969:273). SNCC took the attitude that blacks should organize blacks to help bring about an increase in respect for "blackness" and that whites should lend their organizing efforts to the white community, to build a base for a future coalition between poor whites and poor blacks (Buckman, 1970:131).

Strategies and Tactics

Formed to facilitate communication among sit-inners in 1960, SNCC's major tactic was that of mass nonviolent direct action, so characteristic of the early civil rights movement. Voter registration and education in rural black belts also characterized SNCC in the early sixties. Beginning in 1967, SNCC participated in the anti-war movement, at least at the leadership level (Horowitz, 1969:26). During this same period, SNCC moved to direct confrontation, under the leadership of Stokely Carmichael and H. Rap Brown. Their strategy of confrontation was similar to the SDS strategy described earlier.

The Natural History of the Black Protest Movement

In its *incipiency* stage (before 1963), black protestors challenged the very legitimacy of government in the South, first in an effort to organize within the established structure of party politics and, when that failed, outside that structure. SNCC began to take form in the early 1960's, and, in 1963 and 1964, it helped to organize the now famous Mississippi Freedom Democratic Party (MFDP) with a slate of black and white candidates. Both SNCC and MFDP began as black and white coalitions, and the MFDP goal was to gain seats in the national convention of the Democratic Party to be held in August, 1964 (Chambers, 1968:265). The resulting convention struggle gave national prominence both to the MFDP and to its support base, SNCC.

The convention struggle marked SNCC's *coalescence* from a small band of student sit-ins to a formidable organization involved in "protest politics," largely in response to harassment from local law enforcers and racist citizens across the South. Coalescence was somewhat retarded by the growing preoccupation of the whites in SNCC with other issues and the partial eclipsing of SNCC by the emerging student movement.

Between 1966 and 1968, SNCC began to organize around the concept of Black Power and to exclude its white members. In the summer of 1969, H. Rap Brown, then chairman of SNCC, explained that the organization had changed the second word of its name from "nonviolent" to "national" because it wished to make clear its readiness to retaliate with violence when met with violence (Mead, 1971:196).

As SNCC moved away from a commitment to nonviolence and began to focus on black issues exclusively, it quickly moved into its *institutionalization* stage, becoming an important part of the emerging black united front. The eventual merger between SNCC and the Black Panther Party meant the end of the former as a separate entity. Eldridge Cleaver, then Minister of Information of the California Black Panther Party, explained:

We feel that we add to each other—this was the whole motivation behind the merger. The Black Panther Party manages to reach people in the Black community that no other organization in history has reached. . . . SNCC has great success in getting, say, college students together. Add the college students that SNCC is able to get to the hard brothers on the block that the Black Panther is able to get and you have a mighty force that could do a helluva job here in Babylon [America]. (Teodori, 1969:286)

By the time of its merger with the Black Panthers, signs were already starting to appear of the *fragmentation and demise* of SNCC. Its association in public opinion with the urban disorders of the 1960's was only confirmed by the merger, and it became with the Panthers a target for the heaviest repressive measures by the government and the police of various cities. Its two main charismatic leaders, Stokely Carmichael (1966-1967) and H. Rap Brown (1967-1969), were only the most highly publicized of the many SNCC leaders and members who faced arrest and exile toward the end of the decade. Concurrently, governments at the federal, state, and local levels passed a series of civil rights and anti-discriminatory laws which had the effect of co-opting and dissipating much of the thrust of the civil rights movement in general, and particularly of the more militant and radical organizations like SNCC. The co-optation was perhaps also symbolized and personified by the career of Carmichael, who began to find himself in demand as a highly paid speaker at rallies and campuses and then went on to marry a celebrated black singer and virtually to withdraw from public life.* (See Chapter 14 for more on the Black Protest Movement.)

---

* Since the end of the 1960's, H. Rap Brown has been serving a long prison term on conviction for charges stemming from his SNCC days. Stokely Carmichael has spoken on a number of campuses in recent years but is currently living in Africa. For a recent history of the rise and decline of SNCC, see Cleve Sellers, *River of No Return* (1972).

Counterprotest

Probably a large majority of Americans have always seen radical protest by blacks and youth as a serious threat to "law and order," even though many have agreed with the general goals of the protestors, such as peace and equality. A Harris poll in September, 1969, of a cross section of 1,895 households showed that 59 percent of those polled felt that anti-war and black protestors were harmful to America. Student demonstrators were regarded as harmful by 72 percent. Out of this large public, there had been emerging for a decade an inner core of such militant counterprotest organizations as Newark's North Ward Citizen's Committee (NNWCC), the Minutemen, the John Birch Society, Detroit's Break Through (DBT), and the Oakland Home Defense Association (OHDA).

The most widely publicized and influential of these counterprotest organizations has been the John Birch Society. The programs of the JBS are aimed to eradicate what it sees as Communism and to return the American people to the "pure" and "fundamental" economic, political, and religious beliefs, values, and institutional forms of an idealized past. The chief remedy for the social ills of our time, as proposed by the JBS, is to extirpate all "thought and leadership to the left of Adam Smith in economics, Barry Goldwater in politics, Carl McIntire in religion and the three R's in education" (Broyles, 1964:6). In their reactionary definitions of reality, and occasionally in their disruptive tactics as well, the *counterprotestors* have been as "radical" as the protestors themselves, but public and official opinion has reserved that label for the latter.

Recruits and Leaders

The Birchers seek to accomplish their purposes by enlisting the support of a dedicated, zealous, disciplined, and thoroughly indoctrinated ideological cadre of workers. The members of the JBS are believers in the "conspiracy theory" of history and in "absolute political truth," which they alone claim to possess (Epstein and Forster, 1966:93). Their operating premise is that "over all our lives and over all the events of our time, there rules a powerful and protected establishment, perpetuated by a secret conspiracy of vast dimensions" (Epstein and Forster, 1966:93).

The typical counterprotest movement recruit is characterized by an easy willingness to believe that the state should initiate certain "offensive" actions in order to preclude trouble from radical protestors. "Getting tough" is the phrase often used. It does not mean just getting tough on rioters. It means getting tough on the entire life-style of so-called radical youth: clipping long hair, rousting people from parks for carrying concealed guitars, stopping and questioning anyone who does not look like a member of the Jaycees, drafting all the anti-war protestors to "straighten them up," ridding our theaters and bookstores of "filth," and, always above all, putting "those" people in their places (Hess, 1969:102-04 and 178-85).

The supporters of the anti-protest movement are usually middle class and have been described as "nouveau riche," uneasy in a status higher than that of their parents (Riesman and Glazer, 1963:89-90). Property has become an idol for members of these organizations. They are active in and sometimes control many reputable community organizations: parent-teacher associations, veterans' groups, civic clubs, and boards of local churches. High officials, especially certain professional police authorities, appear sometimes to be influenced by the JBS outlook. A former associate director of the FBI, for example, finds a common denominator between civil rights demonstrators, the anti-war movement, student protest, and "racketeers, Communists, narcotic peddlers, filth merchants and others of their ilk who hold themselves above the law" (Stringfellow, 1966:73).

Program and Tactics

The JBS has always relied primarily on typical pressure-group tactics: propaganda, large-scale importunings of school boards and city councils, letter-writing campaigns to legislatures, and the like. During the early sixties, the JBS directed its attention toward generating public pressure to reverse what it perceived as Communist trends within American society. The Society claimed that 60 to 80 percent of the United States was Communist-controlled. In this belief, it selected targets for action. The Society's early scattered shots at enemies was narrowed down into a Standard Agenda that was presented in the September, 1963, publication of the *Bulletin*. It is into this agenda, with only slight variations, that the national program finally crystallized:

1/ Recruiting
2/ The movement to impeach Warren
3/ The United Nations (Get us out)
4/ Civil rights opposition
5/ The Liberty Amendment (Abolish income tax)
6/ Support local police
7/ American Opinion Magazine
8/ American Opinion Libraries
9/ American Opinion Speakers Bureau
10/ Conduct study clubs
11/ The review of the news
12/ Your own readings

The official action taken by the JBS in disseminating propaganda on these projects included books, flyers, tapes, films, rally speeches, petitions, bumper stickers, and the writing of letters (Epstein and Forster, 1966:38-39).

The Natural History of Counterprotest

The *incipiency* stage of the counterprotest movements began in the McCarthy era with the emergence of several radical right publications (e.g., *Liberty Letter* and *Christian Beacon*) during the early and mid-fifties. A propaganda medium of special importance in the incipiency stage was the radio. During the early and mid-fifties, there were several hundred broadcasts each week carrying the message of the radical right to various parts of the country. The battle cry of these propaganda broadcasts was the cry of conspiracy: that a secret, diabolical, Communist clique actually plans and executes the major events affecting our personal and national destinies.

From the right-wing public receptive to such propaganda, Robert Welch, a wealthy Massachusetts candy maker, invited eleven men, most of them older businessmen, to a meeting in Indianapolis in December, 1958, to consider ways of reversing the direction he felt the country was taking. Some of these men had already been introduced to Welch's fairly standard right-wing views through their reading of his magazine *One Man's Opinion* and his controversial "private letter," *The Politician* (Broyles, 1964:7). During the two-day meeting, Welch presented his analysis of the sad state of the union and proposed the formation of the John Birch Society as the remedy. Those assembled accepted Welch as the leader of the new society and named it for an American who had died in a Chinese prison after being captured by Communist forces. The transcript of this two-day organizational meeting was published in 1959 as the *Blue Book,* which is the bible of the JBS. Thus occurred the *coalescence* of the JBS out of the incipiency of a more general anti-radical movement.

During the early 1960's the JBS moved steadily toward *institutionalization* in American political life. By the mid-sixties, it was far and away the most fully organized and effective right-wing pressure group in the country, with a formalized, hierarchical structure under Welch, forty paid full-time field coordinators, and a large central administrative staff. Its active and successful participation in the Republican Party during this period, culminating in the nomination of right-wing candidate Barry Goldwater in 1964, marked the high point of JBS influence and institutionalization, as well as the beginning of its co-optation by regular party politics. Undaunted by the disastrous defeat of Goldwater in the election of that year, JBS in fact used that very development, together with the increasingly frequent urban and student disorders of the mid-sixties, as a basis for a renewed membership campaign, with the slogan, "*Now* will you join the John Birch Society?" The Society enjoyed a large membership increase during this period, largely from the ranks of "middle Americans" forming that large public which polls have shown were so unappreciative of black and student movements then also in full bloom.

In the call for "law and order" in the cities, and for more discipline on the campuses, JBS was second to none (Epstein and Forster, 1966:38-39).

In 1968, the Republicans succeeded in electing their candidate, Richard Nixon, whose public image at that time was far more conservative than it later became. His anti-Communist and his "law and order" commitments seemed unambiguous to the American public, and his promise to end the Viet-Nam war offered the hope of removing from the dissidents their chief issue. The election, therefore, while it may not have reassured the JBS hard core, did co-opt much of its supporting public and greatly reduce the success of its membership drive. From that time, JBS influence has declined. Its *demise* is still far from evident, but the *fragmentation* of its supporting public, if not of its very membership, has taken the form of a turning back to more regular establishment organizations, such as the Republican, Conservative, and American Independent parties. The co-optation which contributed so much to this process was accompanied by a return to apathy in many circles, as the decline in black and student unrest made the JBS once again seem rather extreme and as scandals surrounding Richard Nixon and Spiro Agnew somewhat discredited the cry for "law and order" which they once personified. The fates of the protest and counterprotest movements were tied together in a great many ways. In a very real sense, their relationship was symbiotic; they fed on each other. The government and other established institutions often responded simultaneously to both movements, repression of the one constituting a kind of co-optation of the other, and vice versa. It is understandable, then, that their declines should be roughly simultaneous also.

THE LEGACY OF THE PROTEST AND COUNTERPROTEST MOVEMENTS

The protest and counterprotest movements of the 1960's offer a particularly good illustration of the main thesis of this book, namely, that the social movements which arise to define and carry "social problems" have a kind of natural history or life cycle of their own without any particular or necessary connection to the "real" social conditions which they deplore. As one reviews the grievances which are supposed to have brought these protest and counterprotest movements into being, one is hard put to argue that the obvious and rapid decline of these movements in recent years has been the result of a fundamental redress of such grievances. To be sure, some changes remain as a legacy of these movements, but they do not seem to have been basic or far-reaching.

The black protest movement has left us certain cultural fads and fashions, such as the Afro hair style. One also sees more blacks and other minorities in commercial advertisements, on television shows, and in comic strips like "Peanuts" and

"Doonesbury." Many of our college campuses have black studies and other ethnic studies curricula, though these are declining rapidly in popularity and enrollment. Under pressure from the militant young black protestors of the 1960's, such as the Panthers, the more traditional civil rights organizations of the country, like the NAACP, have taken on a noticeably more militant stance themselves on many issues, and they have made room for younger "firebrand" leaders (Connery, 1968:134). In the realm of law and politics, one surely sees more blacks in government and in civil service than was true in the 1950's, and great strides have been made in the passage of civil rights laws and of "affirmative action" programs. A much larger proportion of the blacks in the South are registered to vote and are holding public office than was true a decade or so ago. Yet, in spite of this legacy of cultural and legal innovations, black spokesmen themselves are quick to point out that this apparent progress boils down to an illusionary tokenism. The gap between average black and white incomes has changed little or none since 1960; *de facto* school segregation remains on a massive scale, but now, ironically, more in the North than in the South. Blacks continue to experience social slights and affronts, though these are perhaps more subtle than in the past. There is still little acceptance of blacks by whites on a social level; indeed, one of the implications of the Black Power perspective, and of the "Black Is Beautiful" slogan, is to maintain, if not to intensify, the very social segregation which presumably generated the black protest movement. In other than symbolic ways, then, it is a moot question just what progress was wrought by this movement. (See Chapter 14 for further information.)

A similar observation is justified with respect to the youth or student protest movement. Here too we see some relatively superficial "fallout" from the movement. Long hair, beards, and sideburns, once the hallmark of "unruly campus dissidents," can now be seen on a good many younger members of the establishment and on some of their fathers as well! The "peace symbol" has become a prosaic design in youthful jewelry. Slogans, like "make love, not war," have inspired a number of variations on the "love" theme in our popular media, including the ironic use of that theme by Army recruiters, mentioned earlier: "A country needs love, too." The "generation gap" (supposedly evidenced by campus disorders but never demonstrated by opinion polls) became a household phrase, an oft-discussed "social problem," and an underlying theme of the family television show "All in the Family." On college campuses, many student representatives were installed on committees and invited to participate in the policy-making process, but with the passage of time fewer and fewer have actually participated. A few more "student-oriented" courses were installed in some college curricula, but many of these have become casualties of more recent fiscal austerity (Rudolph, 1965:1-10; Skolnick, 1969:19). The war in Southeast Asia was greatly reduced in scope and intensity, as students had been demanding, the draft was ended, and the legal age for voting and for many other adult practices was reduced to eighteen from twenty-one. All these and similar changes might appropriately be considered a part of the legacy of the student movement.

At the same time, the war did not really end in response to student pressure. More than four years after Richard Nixon's commitment to end the war, massive bombing was still going on, and even the withdrawal of American troops took years to accomplish. During all this time, the student movement was clearly moribund and ineffective. Student power and "freedom" on the college campuses, which were the issues that generated the student movement, have not been noticeably enhanced. Indeed, the responses of legislatures and other appropriating agencies to the student movement, and the implementation of those responses by campus administrations, have added up to a fiscal and administrative "backlash," leaving students with less financial support and more disciplinary regulations than they had before 1964. Thus, neither the ending of the war nor the acquisition of greater student freedoms can realistically be attributed to the student protest movement.

The counterprotest movement left, perhaps, the scantiest legacy of all. One might, however, fairly credit the Birch Society, and the more general, middle-America public which surrounded it, with limiting the extent of the legacies from the two protest movements. The propaganda and political agitation from the counterprotestors no doubt did much to help create the "law-and-order" mentality so important to the two Nixon campaigns and to the "war against crime" with which these campaigns tried to identify themselves. Police and National Guardsmen have lately gained much more training and skill in riot control than they had a decade ago, and new riot-control laws have been passed by the score, even being included as amendments to civil rights laws themselves (Zinn, 1968:3-8). Police have become more active politically in the face of criticism and pressure about their handling of rioters and other offenders to the peace. Both on and off duty, policemen have actively campaigned, in some of our larger cities, in favor of "law-and-order" candidates, against the establishment of "citizen review commissions," and in favor of anti-riot laws. In a few cities, indeed, it became apparent that police had joined the John Birch Society and other right-wing groups in some considerable numbers (*San Francisco Chronicle,* 1968). In addition to the police, citizens themselves began to purchase private weapons in greater numbers than ever before, to form themselves into vigilante-type organizations for protection against "lawless elements" such as black and youthful protestors, and to practice military drills and maneuvers with paramilitary groups like the Minutemen (Connery, 1968:134). In some respects, it might even be fair to attribute the Watergate scandal of the early 1970's to the influence of extreme counterprotest thinking: after all, the extraordinary, bizarre, and illegal measures uncovered during the Watergate investigations were clearly attributable to the inordinate concern of people in the Nixon administration about "subversive" elements in the country, in the McGovern camp, and even in the federal government itself.

Aside from these developments, which might be considered almost a "negative legacy" of the counterprotest movement, one is hard put to think of any real change in the social and political conditions that were supposed to have produced organizations like the John Birch Society in the first place. The students may be quieter, but campus protest *per se* was not what generated the counterprotest movement; it was, rather, "subversion" of a more general kind issuing from the "worldwide Communist conspiracy." Not only is the American Communist Party in a more secure position legally and politically than at any time since Senator Joseph McCarthy, but Richard Nixon himself has energetically led the country to détent with Russia and China, the two great Communist powers of the world. Welch himself explains such developments by denouncing most of our political leaders as part of the conspiracy, but that is only to admit the extraordinary lack of a positive legacy for the JBS after a decade and a half of work. While the Warren Court, with its "permissive" attitudes toward criminals and subversives, has been replaced by a somewhat "tougher" Nixon-Burger Court, even that Court has rendered many verdicts in favor of "subversives" and "dissidents"; it has thrown out capital punishment (for the time being, at least); it has approved of abortion-on-demand; and it has generally supported enforcement of desegregation and other civil rights measures from the tumultuous sixties. In very few developments of this past decade can the remnant of the counterprotest movement take much satisfaction.

For all three of the movements with which this chapter has been concerned, then, it is fair to say that they have left their legacies, but in few respects, if any, have these legacies included the crucial social and political changes which the movements began by demanding. The movements finally declined for reasons relating to their own life cycles, and to their interaction with the establishment, rather than to social progress itself.

PART THREE

PERSONAL DEVIATION

Chapter 7

Drug Use

The fact is that America is a drug-prone society. Adults have set this standard by their own behavior and, even more, by the advertising they allow on all the mass media. If there's one message that comes through sharp and clear in all American advertising, it's that every time you have a pain, a problem or trouble of any sort, there's a salesman just around the corner who has the snake oil that you need. After all, this is the age of "better living through chemistry." Pop a pep pill to cram for an exam. Pop a barbiturate to get to sleep at night. Pop a tranquilizer or gulp a martini if you're nervous about a social occasion. And, of course, our teenagers have all been preconditioned to marijuana by cigarette commercials, which all play on the theme of escapism and suggest that you can find some magical release from the ills of the flesh by putting a dried plant in paper, lighting it and inhaling the result. It isn't really much of a step from that to marijuana; and pot, of course, seems to have the advantage that it really gives you a boost and tobacco doesn't. (Fort, 1970:56)

THE SOCIAL CONSTRUCTION OF REALITY

Drugs and Relativity

The above quotation hints at the difficulties involved in considering all the issues related to drug use and abuse in a given social context. Most adult members of this society engage in some form of drug taking during their lifetimes. Yet, it is fairly evident that only a small minority of such users are ever presumed or ever consider themselves to be part of a "drug problem." It is thus extremely important for any investigation of drug use to define exactly what is meant by a "drug problem," to what extent it exists, whom it affects, and finally, why it is a problem for society in the first place.

We can start this investigation by asking the question, "What counts as a drug?" As the National Commission on Marijuana and Drug Abuse points out, to answer

TABLE 7-1   SUBSTANCES REGARDED AS DRUGS

	Adults (N=2411)	Youth (N=880)
Heroin	95%	96%
Cocaine	88%	86%
Barbiturates	83%	91%
Marijuana	80%	80%
Amphetamines	79%	86%
Alcohol	39%	34%
Tobacco	27%	16%
No opinion	1%	1%

Source: National Commission on Marijuana and Drug Abuse, Drug Use in America: Problem in Perspective, 1973, p. 9

this question from a scientific orientation means including as a drug "any substance other than food which by its chemical nature affects the structure or function of a living organism" (National Commission, 1973:9). Obviously, such an all-inclusive definition is *not* the one commonly associated with public conceptions of a "drug problem" in America. Rather, from a social point of view, those drugs which are seen to create a "drug problem" belong primarily to a narrow group of psychoactive ("mind-altering") substances such as marijuana, heroin, barbiturates, and the like. As the findings of the National Commission clearly indicate (Table 7-1), the public is most likely to regard as "drugs" those psychoactive substances associated with the public conception of the "drug problem." Alcohol and tobacco are seldom considered drugs by this same public, even though their power to alter body functions and behavior is well-known.

This anomaly is even more curious if we consider what the public means by the term "drug abuse." The National Commission found the following statements describing drug-taking behavior to be mentioned most often in connection with drug abuse: (1) non-medical purposes, (2) prone to excess, (3) habit-forming, (4) damaging to health, and (5) using for pleasure (to feel good, to get high, and so on) (National Commission, 1973:12). Yet, significantly, only 4 percent of the persons surveyed equate the taking of illegal drugs *per se* (e.g., marijuana, heroin) with the term "drug abuse."

It is obvious that each of the statements listed in the National Commission survey apply as well to alcohol and tobacco as they do to the more exotic psychoactive substances. In fact, by a large margin, the most widely used drugs under the circumstances described are alcohol and tobacco. Yet, the public does not consider these latter two substances as part of the "drug problem" or, for that matter, as drugs at all. They are set off as somehow fundamentally different from the other psychoactive drugs, although in both circumstances of use and general effect, they are quite similar.

The above description is not intended to set the stage for a continuation of the rather belabored debate over the relative merits of alcohol versus marijuana, or other such unresolvable issues. Rather, the purpose is to draw attention to a most striking aspect of drug use—its basis in the cultural meanings ascribed to it. Drug-taking behavior runs the gamut of social meanings from exalted to condemned, dependent primarily on time and place. Presumably, the range of pharmacological effects of a given drug is fairly constant both across cultures and throughout history, so that differing evaluations of particular drugs can be validly linked to the prevailing social climate. Further, these evaluations often show little correspondence to the demonstrated properties of the drugs. Instead, as the National Commission concluded, they are usually based on untested assumptions centering on particular qualities of the drug or drug user. The importance of social context in such evaluations is illustrated by Dr. Joel Fort (1969) in describing certain qualities of one drug as:

. . . massively used for decades; its mechanism of action on the brain and other body organs is unknown; it accounts for thousands of deaths and illnesses each year, and it produces not only chromosomal breakage, but actual birth defects in *lower* animals . . . On the basis of the foregoing, an ambitious politician or other demagogue could call for a march on the Capitol to urge a legislature always willing to enact new, albeit harmful and expensive, laws to make criminals out of those who use this chemical. The substance described is aspirin, and of course when one looks at the full picture, it is easily recognized that millions of people regularly and beneficially use tons of this drug without untoward consequences. (Fort, 1969:5)

Fort's hypothetical case has many real-life parallels. In the mid-1960's America's "flower children" were extolling the mind-expanding properties of LSD and similar hallucinogens. At the same time, most of their elders were condemning the same drugs as leading to moral, mental, and physical decay. Typical of the sensationalism which surrounded the use of hallucinogens were the front-page stories describing six Pennsylvania college students who purportedly were blinded after staring at the sun while under the influence of LSD. That this was later shown to be a total fabrication was given but little media coverage (Fort, 1969:139-40). Similarly, other lurid "properties" of LSD were sensationalized (e.g., chromosomal breakdown) without much regard for substantial evidence. Additionally, the drug was linked with a dissenting life style ("Tune in, turn on, drop out") which was said to be an inevitable consequence of its use. Basically ignored were the vast majority of LSD users who went quietly about their business, occasionally "dropping acid." Within such an unfavorable climate, the youth lost the definitional battle, and harsh anti-hallucinogen laws were rapidly passed at both the state and federal levels.

While LSD is certainly a dramatic example, even the more commonplace drugs in American society have undergone differential treatment both over time and in different cultures. Most familiar is the American prohibition of alcohol which thrived and then died a slow death in the early 20th century. (See Chapter 8.) Also, it is fairly well-known that most Moslem countries have forbidden the use of alcohol at various periods in their existence while, at the same time, the use of hashish has been allowed. Less well-known are the 17th-century rules in Eastern Mediterranean regions prohibiting coffee-drinking. The death penalty was provided for anyone frequenting or owning a coffee house. (Caffeine was not the problem. The coffee house served as a meeting place for persons suspected of plotting revolutionary deeds!) (El Mahi, 1962). In a similar vein, use of tobacco in Germany, Persia, Russia, and Turkey at one time was considered morally "dangerous" and brought death—not from heart disease or cancer—but at the hands of the executioner (Kolb, 1962).

A review of cross-cultural and historical instances, such as that sketched briefly above, lends credence to Blum's (1967) statement that drug-taking behavior is "common to mankind." Equally evident is that most societies throughout time have sought to proscribe certain kinds of drugs for reasons unrelated to health practices. Societies can and do offer many socially legitimate avenues for drug use, while circumscribing use of similar drugs as inappropriate (i.e., illegal). Thus, what constitutes a drug problem appears to derive less from the drug-taking behavior *per se,* and more from the socially constructed meanings of what is a legitimate motive, place, and mode for engaging in such behavior.

Parameters of Consensual Reality

If ingestion of drugs with potentially harmful effects constitutes America's drug problem, then the degree of severity of the problem can be measured simply by the prevalence of drug use. In this respect, the most serious problem in terms of frequency of use would be alcohol, followed closely by tobacco (nicotine). Use of sedatives/tranquilizers, stimulants, marijuana, other hallucinogens, and narcotics would follow, in that order. It is obvious that this listing of prevalence of drug use bears little correspondence to what is publicly defined as the "drug problem." Most of the public concern is limited to the last three substances—marijuana, other hallucinogens, and narcotics. Alcohol and tobacco, despite their demonstrated deleterious effects, have gained a measure of respectability, or at least widespread acceptance. Sedatives, tranquilizers, and stimulants occupy a middle ground and are widely (and legitimately) sold.

In 1970, 214 million prescriptions were filled by mood-altering drugs. Figure

Chapter 7 / Drug Use

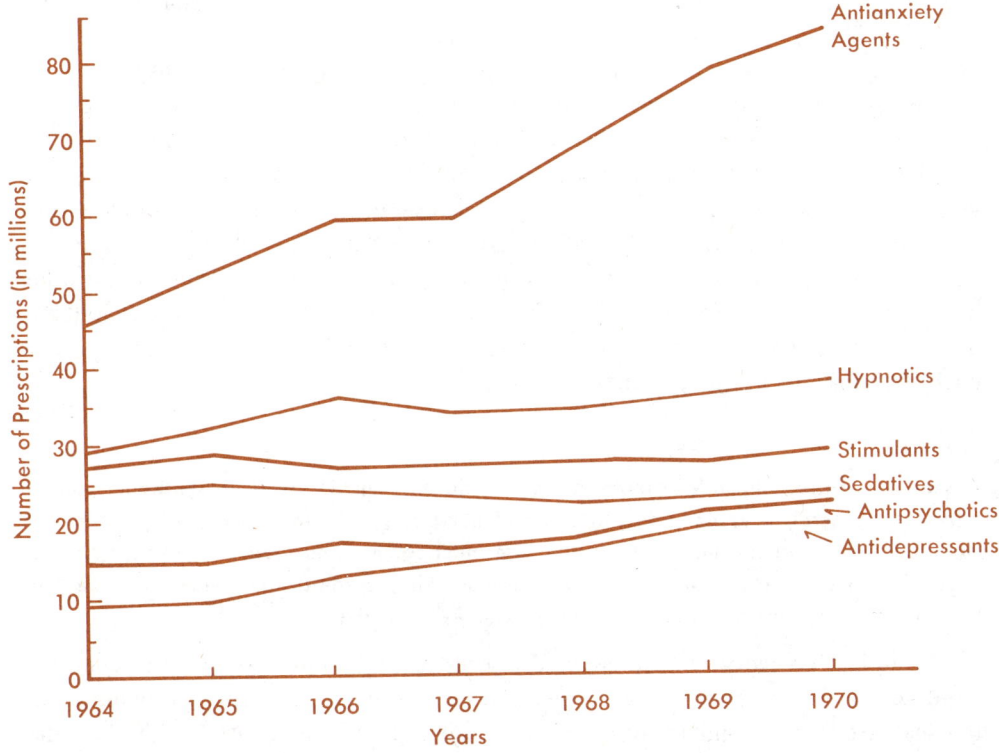

Figure 7-1   Psychotherapeutic Drugs: Prescriptions Filled in U.S. Drug Stores, 1964-1970

SOURCE: M. B. Balter and J. Levine, 1971

7-1 shows that over 80 percent of these were substances which tranquilized or sedated (an effect similar to that produced by the opiates). The magnitude of this legal drug supply might warrant the charge that physicians' prescriptions are the major cause of increased drug use. In fact, as early as 1919, the Treasury Department levelled this charge at the medical profession with respect to the addiction problem. The accuracy of this statement is still open to dispute, but it does draw attention to the continuing position occupied by the medical field in a social consideration of the drug problem in America.

Following the public definition, two drugs, alcohol and tobacco, will be virtually ignored in the remainder of this chapter. Alcohol is discussed in its own right in Chapter 8; tobacco is simply *not* considered a "drug" by the vast majority of Americans. It may be thought of as unhealthy, socially harmful, sinful, and the like, but it is seldom included in the drug problem. That distinction is reserved for more illicit substances. To paraphrase Wittgenstein, a drug problem is what people say a drug problem is. In this respect, tobacco does not qualify.

The drugs which will be discussed here can be placed in five general categories: (1) opiates, (2) stimulants, (3) sedatives/tranquilizers/hypnotics, (4) marijuana, and (5) other hallucinogens. As most researchers have pointed out, we know very little about the extent of use of these drugs in America. The estimates that are offered are generally extrapolations from arrest data in the case of narcotics addicts, or based on survey responses obtained from users of marijuana or other hallucinogens. While, for greater clarity, we will break down our discussion into the five categories mentioned above, we should remember that users of one drug have probably also used one or more of the others.

Opiates

This group of drugs includes opium, morphine, heroin, and Demerol (a synthetic), among others. In general, they act upon the central nervous system to relieve pain, reduce the metabolic rate, and produce drowsiness. The most common method of consumption is by injection into either a muscle or vein, although smoking, sniffing, and swallowing the drug are not unknown. Each of these drugs is physically addictive.

The opiate category in general, and heroin in particular, usually first comes to mind when the drug problem is mentioned. However, in terms of actual non-medical use, heroin and its relatives are used but little compared with the other substances being considered here. Of all the drugs included in the National Commission survey, heroin had the "lowest reported rate of incidence . . . 1.3% of the adults [surveyed] and .6% of the youth reported that they had tried heroin at least once . . ." (National Commission, 1973:69). The Commission does note that this is, in all likelihood, an underestimation since "street users" do not usually show up on household surveys.

In order to take account of these "street users," statements about the prevalence of opiate use are usually based on some general estimate of the number of *addicts* in a given society. Since opiates are addictive, it is assumed that any kind of regular use will eventually show up on addiction records; and since regular addiction is thought to be fairly difficult to conceal in a society with strict prohibitions, the addiction records are considered a relatively reliable indicator. Unfortunately, even with these qualifications, the extent of opiate use remains open to debate. For instance, it was estimated in 1963 that over one billion doses of true narcotics were legally administered or prescribed. At present, there is no way of knowing how such legal use contributes to a drug problem. Thus, we are left only with addict counts as an indicator.

In 1966, the Federal Bureau of Narcotics, based on their arrest records, esti-

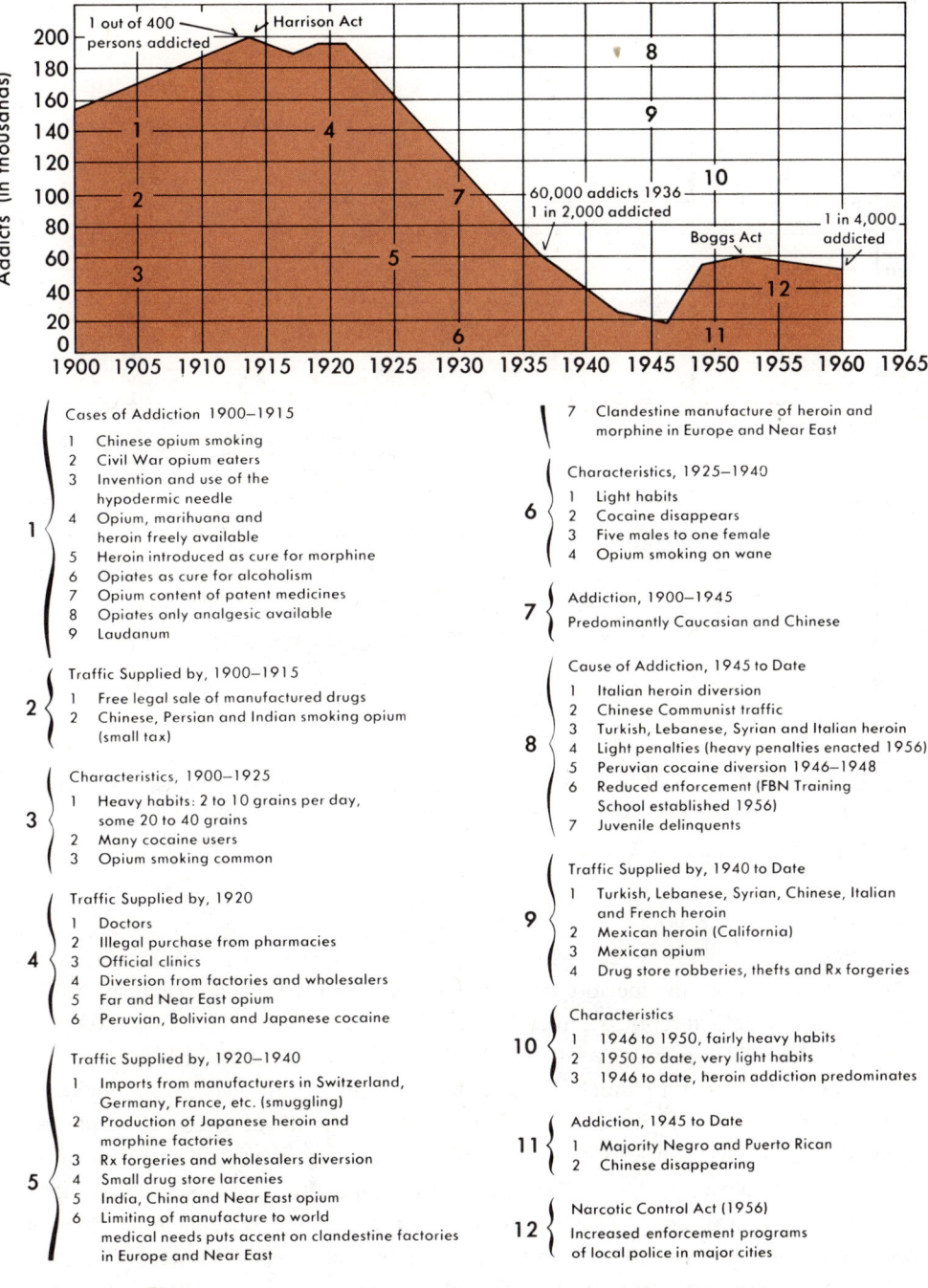

Figure 7-2 History of Narcotic Addiction in the United States
SOURCE: Bureau of Narcotics, U.S. Treasury Department, "Prevention and Control of Narcotic Addiction," Washington, D.C.: Government Printing Office, 1962, p. 5

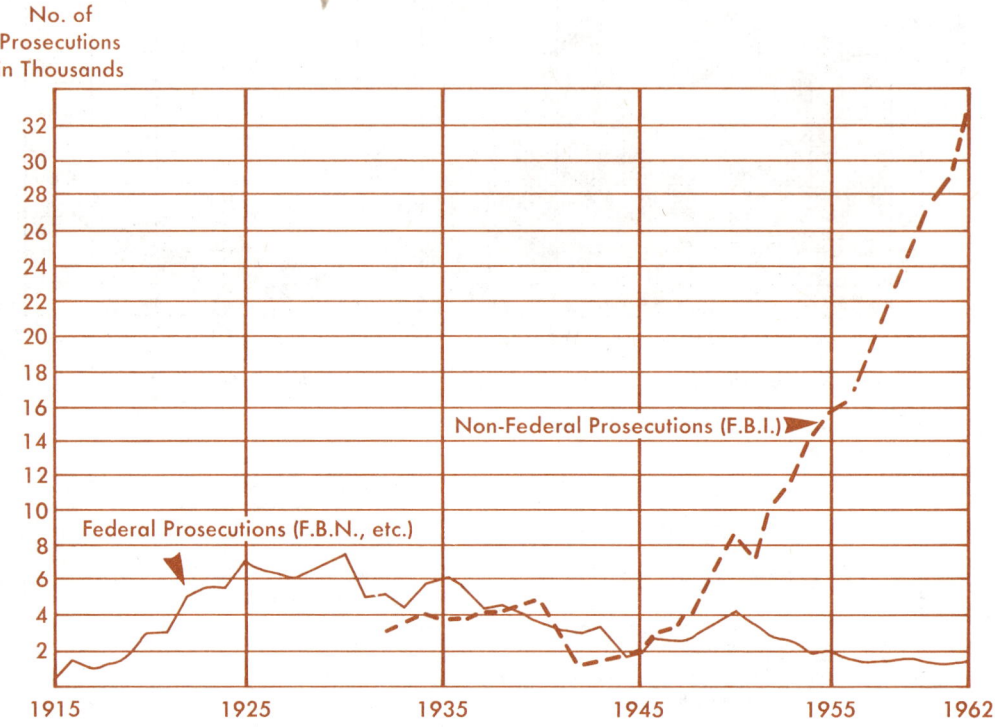

Figure 7-3 Federal and Non-Federal Narcotics Prosecutions in the U.S., 1915-1962 (Gross Annual Totals)

SOURCE: Lindesmith, 1967:108

mated there were 60,000 opiate addicts in the United States. As seen in Figure 7-2, this was publicized as a significant reduction from an estimated 200,000-500,000 addicts in the period immediately prior to 1914, the year of the first major federal anti-narcotic statute.

While these figures argue well for the Bureau's effectiveness in reducing opiate use, they are subject to much debate. Alfred Lindesmith, who has long been a scholarly figure in drug research, questions the estimate of 60,000. Utilizing the same data available to the Bureau, he convincingly argues that the total number of addicts comes closer to the 100,000-200,000 range. It is Lindesmith's contention that the "ski-jump" curve (Figure 7-2) presented by the Bureau more accurately represents *federal* arrest totals while ignoring the activities of state and local law enforcement agencies. An entirely different picture is obtained if non-federal arrest prosecution records are examined. In Figure 7-3, Lindesmith shows how federal arrest statistics, and not actual addict counts, parallel the Bureau of Narcotics' "ski-jump" estimates. If non-federal prosecutions are added to this graph, a distinctly different trend is apparent.

Additional support for a higher estimate of addicts than the Bureau's comes from other social scientists. Ball, Englander, and Chambers (1970) combined three indices of addict population in 1967 to come up with a nationwide estimate of 108,424. Blum and his associates (1969), in probably the most extensive survey of materials in recent years, placed a ceiling of 200,000 on the addict population in their 1969 report on society and drugs.

Recent Bureau estimates show an increase in "active addicts" to more than half a million. While there has probably been a significant rise in heroin use, this drastic change in the Bureau's own figures is primarily a function of a different accounting system. As will be demonstrated later on, the Bureau's estimate must be viewed as an indicator of the agency's particular needs and interests, rather than as a reliable index of addicts. At this point, the actual number of opiate addicts is not known.

In addition to computing the addict population, sociologists have attempted to delimit the characteristics of these users. Although there have been some marked demographic changes over the last 35 years, the addict populations studied have remained remarkably stable with respect to a number of social characteristics, which are enumerated below. The most notable changes have occurred in type of drug used, age, race, and to some extent, sex. Heroin has replaced morphine as the principal addicting opiate. The addict population has become younger. For example, 24 percent were under 30 years of age in Dai's study in the 1930's, whereas Ball found 49 percent under 30 in his 1965 report. Further, Dai's population was primarily white, while 30 years later those of Ball's sample came more often from minority groups. Finally, the sex ratio has increased from Dai's findings of 3:1 (men predominating) to about 5:1.

The stable characteristics of users over time are noteworthy in terms of life-style implications. Generally, the male addict is most often single or, if married, it is a broken marriage with no children. Irregular employment and low-status occupations are typical. Finally, the addicts are strikingly similar in education and intelligence to their respective base populations (DeFleur, 1970). However, there is little evidence that these latter characteristics are causative factors in opiate usage. On the contrary, their stability over time, as compared to other demographic indicators, would suggest that they are products of the life style imposed on addicts. In other words, the punitive stance toward addiction held by the larger society forces unemployment, broken homes, and so on. If this is the correct conclusion, then no matter who comprises the addict population (e.g., young/old, white/minorities) the enforced life style will remain historically constant.

Most recent studies indicate that while the addicts' social traits continue to remain stable, changes in demographic characteristics are taking place. For one, the addict population is still getting younger. In the studies reviewed for the National Commission report, persons under 30 years of age were consistently reported as comprising over 60 percent of the population taking opiates. Sex and racial characteristics also appear to be changing to include more women and Caucasians. Studies are somewhat inconsistent on this last point, but such a trend does seem to be emerging as more middle- and upper-middle-class high school or college age students experiment with opiates (Blum, 1969b). Such factors should be kept in mind when the various theories accounting for drug use are introduced later on.

Stimulants

Although this category of drugs includes such often abused substances as nicotine and caffeine, the major concern has been with amphetamine-type substances. These include Benzedrine ("bennies"), Dexedrine ("dexies"), and Methedrine ("meth," "crystals"). Cocaine, while not an amphetamine, also qualifies as a powerful stimulant. Each of these drugs works on the central nervous system to produce feelings of well-being, prevent fatigue, curb the appetite, and, in general, to radically accelerate all bodily functions. The amphetamines can be injected, but are most commonly taken orally. Cocaine is usually sniffed, but it also can be injected. These drugs are not physically addictive, but cessation of use is usually accompanied by depression and extreme fatigue, thus making it more attractive to remain on the drug than to experience the hard comedown.

The extent of amphetamine use in the United States is difficult to determine, since there is such a large variety of drugs and so many modes of using them. Clouding the picture is the fact that most of the drugs in this category are widely prescribed by physicians in treating depression, weight control, fatigue, and so on. However, from the meager data available, their illicit use seems both prevalent and on the rise.

Indicative of the prevalence of amphetamines in American society is their large-scale production by legitimate pharmaceutical companies. In 1959, 75,000 pounds of amphetamines were produced legitimately in the United States—or 20 tablets for every man, woman, and child. In 1964, this figure had risen to 4.5 billion tablets or 25 tablets per capita (Blum and Funkhouser-Balbaky, 1965). By 1969, total production had reached the 153,000 pound mark with the hypothetical ration per person increased to 45 tablets (Fort, 1970). It is estimated that half of this legitimate production eventually finds its way into illicit distribution systems (Blum, 1969a:111).

Until recently, most illicit amphetamines were used for more practical purposes than just "getting high." Students, truck drivers, and others used various stimulants to improve their performances. However, there was a growing sense of crisis in the late 1960's about the use of such drugs for their mood-changing effects. Smith (1969) noted a pattern of stimulant use in urban areas, where amphetamine use reached large proportions among segments of drug-using subcultures as they experimented with a wide variety of drugs. The source of supply for this group of users was supplemented by the advent of "street" labs to manufacture Methedrine, a drug which peaked in popularity about 1967 (Smith, 1969).

The use of Methedrine differed from most prior illicit amphetamine use. The drug was injected instead of taken orally, producing intense euphoria. The extreme of Methedrine use was typified by the "speed freak," who would inject the drug several times a day and stay awake for several days. When the Methedrine user sought a way of temporarily halting his "run" without going through a gradual tapering-off process, the use of heroin and other depressants became an integral part of the "speed scene." The heroin brought the speed freak down immediately, and sleep ensued. There is some evidence that this use of heroin eventually took precedence over "speed" and, as a city experienced a stabilization of its amphetamine population, it simultaneously faced a drastic increase in heroin addiction (R. Smith, 1969).

The material gathered for the National Commission report (1973) indicates that intravenous use of amphetamines, and particularly Methedrine, has diminished rapidly in recent years. However, the oral use of amphetamine substances for non-medical purposes (e.g., to "get high" or facilitate performance) continues, for 5 percent of the adult population and 6 percent of the youth surveyed by the Commission reported such non-medical use. Additionally, the Commission noted substantial evidence of chronic use of amphetamines among middle-class adults, particularly women. When asked the purpose of such use, 43 percent of these adults responded that these substances "helped them accomplish something."

Barbiturates and Other Hypnotics, and Tranquilizers

Barbiturates, as a class of drugs, are classified as sedatives or depressants. The most common are Amytal ("blue devils"), Nembutal ("yellow jackets"), Seconal ("reds," "red devils"), and Phenobarbital ("pheno"). The drugs depress the central nervous system, slowing down (and possibly stopping) normal bodily functions, thus producing drowsiness, reduced coordination, and similar symptoms commonly associated with drunkenness. Barbiturates are most commonly taken orally, although they are occasionally injected. Very often, this group of drugs is taken in combination with alcohol, increasing the chance of an overdose and possible death. These drugs are addictive and, when used over a long period of time, the withdrawal symptoms are more severe than those associated with heroin. Withdrawal is best accomplished in a hospital or under a doctor's supervision in case seizures occur. (Some of the preparations popularly called "tranquilizers," however, are not usually addictive.)

As with stimulants, the extent of barbiturate and tranquilizer use is practically impossible to assess. In a recent year, ten billion doses of barbiturates, or 50 doses per person, were manufactured legally (Cohen, 1969). The legal production of tranquilizers is even higher. Estimates of the number of persons addicted to these drugs range from 200,000 (Fort, 1970) to over one million (Weinswig and Doerr, 1969).

An overwhelming number of persons addicted to barbiturate-type substances comprise what Moffett and Chambers (1970) have called the "hidden addiction" problem. These addicts usually obtain the drug legally, through medical prescriptions. They may not be aware they are addicted, even though they would undergo potentially severe withdrawal symptoms if they ceased drug-taking. For all intents and purposes, they are the "respectable addicts"—the businessman, housewife, student, and so on—who are dependent on pills to ease anxiety, get to sleep, or generally, to make life a little easier to face. The National Commission concludes that this group of people might constitute "the modern equivalent of the hidden opiate dependence of the late 19th century" (1973:145). In both cases, the drug was legally obtainable and often prescribed for emotional problems. (Nineteenth-century opiate addiction will be discussed in a later section of this chapter.)

Until the mid-1960's, the heavy use of barbiturate-type drugs was primarily limited to adults. However, recent reports indicate they are becoming increasingly popular with junior high, high school, and college age youths. Data on actual use are sketchy, but the National Commission (1973) indicates 3 percent of the youth surveyed report ever having used such substances for non-medical reasons. Unlike the experience of their elders, youthful experience with these drugs has been largely confined to occasional use with little actual dependence or addiction occurring. School-age users appear to seek the "drunk-like" high from these drugs, while the older user is said to be more interested in the relaxation or relief the substances offer. However, with approximately half of the massive legal production of barbiturates entering the illicit marketplace (Cohen, 1969), one can reasonably predict that youthful use of the drug will increase as will, concomitantly, the incidence of addiction.

Marijuana

Marijuana is a mild hallucinogen produced from the hemp plant, *Cannabis sativa*. Its effects range from increased appetite to euphoric relaxation. Alteration of time and space perception and reduced coordination often accompany use of the drug. Hashish, made from the resin of the same plant, is a much more potent drug with increased hallucinogenic effects and seemingly less sedative ones than marijuana. Some forms of psychosis have been associated with chronic hashish use in India, but it is not known if this is a result of the drug use or of the person's meager life style. Neither marijuana nor hashish is addictive in the physical sense.

The National Commission on Marijuana and Drug Abuse (1972) recently released its comprehensive report on marijuana, which estimated that 24 million Americans had tried marijuana at least once. Of these, 8,340,000 were thought to be current (1971) users. In its follow-up survey the next year, 1972, the Commission's conclusion, of course, was that marijuana use was pervasive in American society.

Although most media attention and drug surveys have focused on the use of drugs by the nation's youth, the National Commission (1972) reports that about one-third of those having ever used marijuana were above 25 years old. Table 7-2 shows the age distribution of persons reporting they had ever used marijuana, according to the two National Commission surveys.

TABLE 7-2 INCIDENCE OF MARIJUANA USE BY AGE, 1971 AND 1972

Age	1971	1972
12 - 13	6%	4%
14 - 15	10%	10%
16 - 17	27%	29%
18 - 21	40%	55%
22 - 25	38%	40%
26 - 34	19%	20%
35 - 49	9%	6%
50 and over	5%	2%

Source: National Commission on Marijuana and Drug Abuse, Drug Use in America: Problem in Perspective, 1973, p. 65

It is obvious from these data that marijuana use is not limited to the 18-25 age bracket, although it is certainly pervasive among this group.

TABLE 7-3 EXPERIENCE WITH MARIJUANA

Frequency	Adults (18 and over)	Youth (12 - 17)	Category Designation
Have used marijuana but no longer use	41%	45%	Experimenters
Once a month or less	9%	15%	Experimenters
2 - 3 times per month	8%	10%	Intermittent users
Once per week	4%	9%	Intermittent users
Several times per week	5%	4%	Moderate users
Once daily	1%	1%	Moderate users
More than once daily	2%	4%	Heavy users
No answer	30%*	12%*	

*The Commission ran a detailed analysis comparing this "no answer" group with the other respondents and concluded that the overwhelming majority would fall in the "experimenters" group.

Source: National Commission on Marijuana and Drug Abuse, Marijuana: A Signal of Misunderstanding, 1972, p. 41

Further Commission findings show substantial use across all socioeconomic and ethnic groups, with a slightly higher prevalence among those with above-average incomes and some college education. This is in sharp contrast to similar studies carried out in the 1930's and 1940's, which found marijuana use to be primarily a phenomenon associated with lower income, urban, minority youth.

Table 7-3 shows the distribution of use and the National Commission's categories for all those reporting having used marijuana.

The motivation for the use of marijuana by the largest group, that of "experimenters," has been characterized by the Commission as primarily "curiosity and a desire to share a social experience" (1972:44). With the exception of occasional marijuana use, the "experimenters" are quite similar to non-users in most respects. The next group, the "intermittent" group, shares the "experimenters'" basic motivation but with the increased marijuana use attributed to a greater sense of its value in social relationships. Again, the "intermittent" group is quite similar to non-users in terms of life style and beliefs, although they tend to be somewhat more liberal politically and socially than the "experimenters."

Little is known of the motivations and characteristics of the last two groups in the Commission typology—the "moderate" and "heavy" users. The use of marijuana by the "heavy" user group is probably an organizing feature of their life style (e.g., alleviate boredom, stay "high"), which is at variance with the values of the larger society. "Moderate" users would probably occupy a middle ground between the "intermittent" and "heavy" user groups, sharing some of the characteristics of each.

It should be noted that 41 percent of the adults and 45 percent of the youth who reported ever trying marijuana no longer used this substance. Of this group, the overwhelming majority (61 percent) of the adults specified that among other reasons for quitting marijuana, they had simply lost interest in the drug. From these data (and the data previously presented), the Commission concludes that marijuana use can best be viewed as an age-related phenomenon which may soon be approaching its peak use in the population.

Hallucinogens

The category of hallucinogens derives its name from the primary effect of the drugs it subsumes. Very simply, in one form or another, they cause "hallucinations"—visual imagery that ordinarily would not be perceived. The list of drugs in this group is large, but most common are LSD ("acid"), PCP ("angel dust"), STP, DMT, psilocybin ("magic mushroom"), mescaline/peyote, and MDA. Some, like STP and MDA, have an amphetamine base. PCP is a large-animal tranquilizer with hallucinogenic properties. Others, like peyote and psilocybin, are found naturally in cactus and mushrooms, respectively. These hallucinogens are usually swallowed, although they can be injected or smoked. It is difficult to make sweeping statements about the effects of the various drugs found in this category since their quality and, in fact, the actual substance ingested, is often questionable if purchased on the illicit market. None of these drugs is addictive, but all may cause "bum trips" —an ill-defined, overused term which usually refers to a person's being unable to deal with the hallucinations provoked by the drug.

Historically, the use of hallucinogens has been linked to ritualistic settings in non-literate societies. Highlighting such use was the ascription of a vast array of meanings, imputing magical or religious properties to the drugs involved. With such a background, it is not surprising that with the widening introduction of hallucinogens into American society in the early 1960's, similar claims were advanced in the secular terms appropriate to a "civilized" culture. Promoted as facilitating "a new awareness," "expansion of one's consciousness," and the like, hallucinogens rapidly became the most controversial and emotion-laden category of drugs used in America. Curiously, they were (and still are) one of the least used substances among the drugs being considered in this chapter.

The most publicized and widespread of the hallucinogens is LSD (D-lysergic diethylamide). One knowledgeable source has estimated that ten million doses of this drug are illicitly sold each year (Pawlak, 1973:6). A sizable portion of this annual output appears to be consumed by regular devotees of the drug, rather than being dispersed throughout the drug marketplace. The experimentation with LSD, which once marked one's entry into the "hip culture," diminished in the late 1960's as reports of LSD-related chromosomal damage, "bum trips," and various other maladies were sensationalized in the media. Persons inclined to experiment turned to other drugs with hallucinogenic properties similar to LSD, but without the reported dangers of what was once the "glamor drug" of the youth counter-culture.

Most notable of the "safe" hallucinogens have been psilocybin and mescaline. Both drugs have a long history of use in non-literate societies, since they are available in natural (or "organic," as it was soon to be called) form—psilocybin from a type of mushroom, and mescaline from the buttons of the peyote cactus. Unfortunately, both the cactus buttons and "magic mushrooms" were in somewhat short supply in the 1960's, so synthetic mescaline and psilocybin were produced to meet the growing demand for "safe" hallucinogens.

Although LSD remains the most prevalent hallucinogen (primarily since it is the most available), its surrogates—psilocybin and mescaline—have increased in popularity since they are reportedly relatively free of "bum trips." This shift in first choice among hallucinogens strongly attests to the influence of the power of suggestion over how one will perceive the effects of a given drug. Repeatedly, chemical analysis of the substances being sold on the illicit market, such as mescaline and psilocybin, has shown most of them to be LSD or LSD compounds —the very drug supposedly being avoided because of its undesirable properties! (See Table 7-4.)

TABLE 7-4 STREET DRUG ANALYSIS PROGRAM. RESULTS FOR APRIL 1971 TO JULY 31, 1972

Sold as:	LSD	LSD-PCP	PCP	LSD-Amphetamine	Psilocybin	Mescaline	Marijuana	Hashish	Cocaine	Cocaine-local Anesthetic	Opium	Heroin	Local Anesthetic	Amphetamine	Methamphetamine	MDA	STP	Barbiturate	Heroin-Procaine	DMT	Other	No Drug	No Results	Totals
Mescaline	141	38	12	2		3							2	1			2				10	4	8	223
LSD	92	4											1	1			1				1	1	1	101
Psilocybin	44	8	1	1	1								1								1		5	62
THC	3	24											4								2		3	34
Marijuana							78																	81
Hashish							3	14																17
Amphetamine														21							5	2		28
Methamphetamine														4	2									6
MDA	4		1											1	1	8	1							16
Cocaine			3						21	16		1	8	1			1							51
Barbiturates																		19			4		1	24
Heroin									1			3							2			1		7
Opium							3				4	1									2		1	10
DMT																				1				1
Psilocin	2	1																						3
Other	2	1	3												1		1				5	5		21
Not Identified	16	2	1				4		1	2		2		4			1	7			15	7	1	62
Totals	301	56	46	2	2	4	90	14	22	18	4	7	19	33	2	10	4	27	2	1	45	15	25	747

Actual Breakdown After Analysis:

Source: Vic Pawlak, "Conscientious Guide to Drug Abuse," Phoenix, Ariz.: Do It Now Foundation, 4th Edition (1973):46

Note: For more comprehensive and somewhat later data on the same subject, see the 5th edition (1974) of the same publication, and also, "Street Drug Survival," vol. 4, no. 1 (1974), published by the Do It Now Foundation.

Reliable information on the extent of hallucinogen use, as on the drugs considered previously, is quite scant. Most studies depend on surveys of student populations, since the 18-35-year-old age bracket was the initial source of heaviest use. For instance, a 1971 Gallup poll showed an increase in LSD experiences among American college students from 1 percent in 1967 to 14 percent in 1970 (Gallup, 1971). The most recent data from the National Commission's survey suggest a diffusion of substantial hallucinogen use in high school populations. Among youth (12-17 years), 4.8 percent reported ever using LSD or similar hallucinogens. Of those 18 years of age or older, 4.6 percent indicated they had used these substances at least once. Interestingly, 60 percent of these adults reported their most recent use was over six months ago, while 70 percent of the youth reported hallucinogen experience within the last six months. Finally, the Commission reports that 1.2 percent of the adults and 2.5 percent of the youth stated that they would probably try LSD-type drugs if they were legal and available.

It should be emphasized that each of these statistics indicates the proportion of the respondents who had *ever* used LSD and like substances. As Goode (1972:119) notes, LSD "is the experimental drug *par excellence*." These substances are typically *not* taken on a regular basis. Rather, the pattern of use shows a sharp drop-off after initial experimentation, and often a total cessation.

The description of drug use here has necessarily been brief. However, even this limited presentation reveals substantial evidence of a pervasiveness of drugs in American society. The question becomes, "What of the future?" Figure 7-4, depicting the trend of use among college students over the last five years, lends itself to some interesting speculations.

The data here show marked increases in the number of persons trying the various types of drugs at least once. The major exceptions to this trend are the slight decreases in number of persons with alcohol experience and the fluctuating figures shown for the use of tobacco. Perhaps this change indicates the future will witness a redefinition of which substances constitute the drug problem.

Public Opinion

Public tolerance or intolerance of certain behaviors has been linked by some investigators to the level of accuracy of general knowledge about these behaviors, and, concomitantly, to the perceived danger to the individual and society engendered by them (Rooney and Gibbons, 1966). Thus, the public's definition of "what counts" as a problem for the "man on the street" could be derived from the amount and accuracy of information about drug-use behavior available to the public.

With the possible exception of marijuana, drug use as a problem is an abstract question for the vast majority of Americans. The public must rely almost exclu-

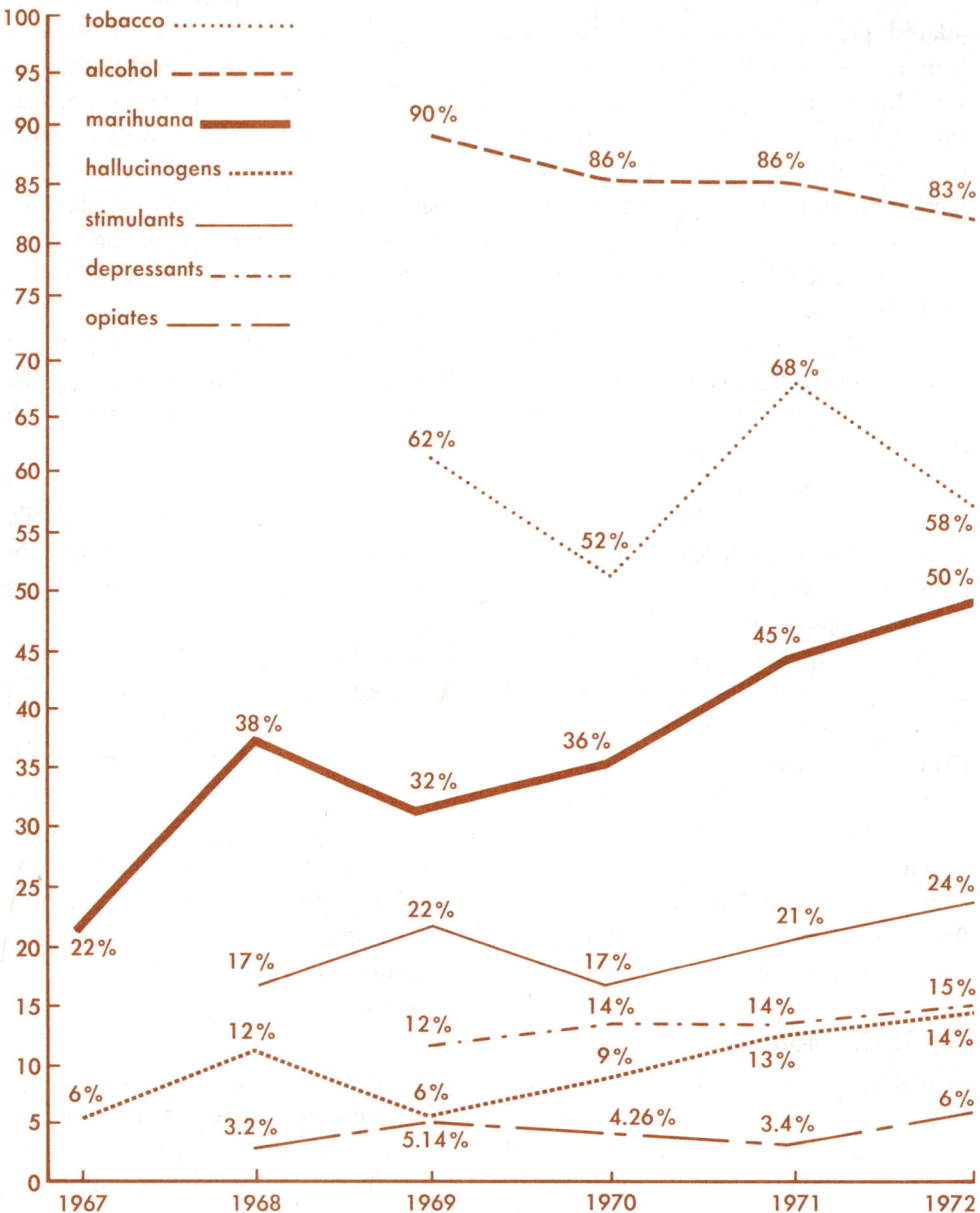

Figure 7-4 Mean Percentage of College Students Who Have Used Drugs (Ever Used) by Type and Year of Survey

SOURCE: National Commission on Marijuana and Drug Abuse, 1973, p. 83

TABLE 7-5 INCIDENCE OF HEROIN AND MARIJUANA USE, 1971

	Adults (N=2411)	Youth (N=880)
Heroin	9%	10%
Marijuana	26%	31%

Source: National Commission on Marijuana and Drug Abuse, Drug Use in America: Problem in Perspective, 1973, p. 129

sively on newspapers, television, magazines, movies, and so on, for its understanding of the many facets that make up the drug problem. Through such vicarious experiences, opinions, often erroneous or inaccurate, are formed and solidified. Two cases are instructive in this regard—the "dope fiend" mythology and the marijuana issue.

The Dope Fiend Mythology

Alfred Lindesmith (1940) has termed the media-disseminated view of drug users "the dope fiend mythology." By this he means the idea that drug use is associated with crime, violence, low morals, and a contagion effect that spreads the affliction. Whereas little of this mythology is based in fact, it is a common view presented to the public (Reasons, 1971). Not surprisingly, when the same public is questioned about drug use in general, they repeat this same story line, i.e., the various associations linked to drug use in the mythology (Rooney and Gibbons, 1966). Correspondingly, the public exhibits very poor knowledge of the properties of the drugs themselves. For example, as Table 7-5 indicates, in 1972 the National Commission survey found that only a small proportion of the public agreed with the *true* statement that "You can use (heroin or marijuana) occasionally without becoming addicted to it."

The fears promoted by such misinformation find expression in the public support of a punitive approach to drug users and sellers. Public tolerance for drug users is low. The National Commission survey revealed that 53 percent of the adults questioned thought drugs were one of the most serious problems facing the United States and demanding attention (1972:154). In this regard, the majority of the public supports the laws against the various drug offenses and often advocates even more severe penalties (Rooney and Gibbons, 1966; Chambers, 1970; Gallup Opinion Index, 1970; Harris Poll, 1971; Hadden, 1971). The marijuana issue is a specific example of this general trend.

The Marijuana Issue

The most comprehensive nationwide study of attitudes and beliefs about marijuana was undertaken in 1971 under the auspices of the National Commission on Marijuana and Drug Abuse. One of the conclusions reached by the Commission was:

Bombarded in recent years with contradictory "findings" and statistics about the effects of marijuana, and with conflicting arguments about public policy, the public tends to believe everything, whether pro or con. *Particularly important in this regard is the wide-spread acceptance of beliefs which have little basis in fact.*

Approximately half of the adult public believes that "many crimes are committed by persons who are under the influence of marijuana," and that "some people have died from using it." Seven of every 10 adults believe that "marijuana makes people want to try stronger things like heroin." Although the probability that a person believes these statements increases with age, a significant percentage of all groups are represented. (1972:152, italics added)

It should not be surprising to find that in the same survey the statement, "using marijuana is morally offensive," was agreed upon by 64 percent of the adult population sampled. Additionally, while stressing leniency for first-time users (i.e., no jail term), 74 percent of those queried were against removing the criminal sanctions for possession of the drug. In fact, the majority of respondents thought increasing the penalties for possession would be an acceptable "solution" (National Commission, 1972).

A recent empirical test of the general public's attitudes toward marijuana took place in the California election in November, 1972. An initiative was placed on the ballot to "decriminalize" the use of marijuana. This proposition, if passed, would have removed the criminal sanctions against personal use of marijuana and have allowed persons to grow their own supply. The laws prohibiting *sale* of the drug would have been maintained. (This was quite similar to the National Commission's recommendation.) The proposition was defeated by a 2:1 margin, having been approved in only one county (San Francisco). A 1974 election in the state of Washington had a similar outcome.

It seems fairly well established that the public as a whole believes both that drug use is a problem and that the punitive approach is the most effective one in coming to grips with the problem. The next task is to assess how, why, and where such feelings are harbored. To do this, we will first enumerate the various publics and groups having vested interests in the drug issue, delineate their particular concerns, and evaluate their contributions to the present drug situation in American society.

CHAMPIONS AND THEIR INTERESTS

Public and official governmental attitudes toward drug use in this country have undergone a radical change in the past century and a half. In order to understand the more recent concern for the drug problem in this country, and the subsequent social policy intended to deal with it, we must look at the publics and the interest groups that have been active in defining the realities about drugs and drug users.

In this section, we will be concerned with describing these publics and groups. Later we shall assess their influence and their present-day relevance.

Drug-related publics and groups have been mainly of five kinds: (1) moral and religious; (2) users; (3) economic; (4) professional and occupational; and (5) scientific. Of course these are not totally separate groups; there has been a great deal of overlap both in membership and in policy advocacy. Also, the relative importance and influence of each group has varied over time.

Moral and Religious Interests

The initial moral involvement of Americans in a drug problem came about through a curious combination of Christianity, racial problems, and world affairs. Missionaries in the Far East, witnessing opium smoking on a large scale, began agitating for international control of this drug. Their reaction can be understood in terms of the prevailing philosophy of the Christian tradition. Not only did opium smoking produce "unnatural" sensations of bodily pleasure, but perhaps more importantly, it undermined the discipline and responsibility required of every individual by the Christian ethic (Reasons, 1971). It was, thus, within the Christian "humanitarian framework" of saving persons from themselves, that the anti-opium movement gained its initial impetus.

Nineteenth-century America has been called by one author, "a dope fiend's paradise" (Brecher, 1972:3), for opium and opium derivatives were widely and legally available at low cost. Most of these drugs were dispensed and utilized for medical purposes, without much regard for their addictive properties. Prescriptions were not usually required; many of the substances were sold in the patent medicines readily available as "cure-alls." It was during this period that opiate use, although pervasive, was considered as a lesser evil than the use of alcohol or tobacco (Isbell, 1963), and was often even medically prescribed. Accordingly, the user population was largely composed of older women from middle- to upper-class backgrounds (Terry and Pellens, 1970:475-488). Any concern over a "drug problem" was limited mostly to the smoking of opium, and not its ingestion through other means. And even this selective sensitivity seems to have had at least partly a racist rather than a moral basis.

The first anti-opium law was a San Francisco city ordinance passed in 1875 which prohibited the *smoking* of opium. This was passed at a time when smoking the drug was a practice characteristic only of the Chinese and was "insignificant as compared to the number of individuals [primarily whites] using opium in other forms . . ." (Terry and Pellens, 1970:808). It wasn't long until most states and municipalities had enacted similar ordinances prohibiting the smoking of opium, while ignoring other and more pervasive uses of the substance. It does not appear to be merely coincidental that these laws were enacted in a period of concern about the "yellow peril." The first anti-drug prohibitions are thus easily seen as part of a larger concern about the "moral behavior" of the Oriental (Reasons, 1971). Smoking opium had become a symbol of depravity indigenous to the Chinese, and the statutes prohibiting such use became a reaffirmation of white moral superiority over the Oriental (Smith, 1966).

It should be pointed out that the use of these racial motivations has not been confined to any one group or amalgamation of groups or to any point in time. Rather, they constitute a psychological orientation which several interest groups have applied to their own purposes. Some of the more blatant examples can be seen in the emotional appeals issued over the years for statutes restricting various forms of drug use. It appears that, regardless of the drug under attack, reformists have often made racial references in their arguments. For example, Reasons (1971) reports on one 1914 article (prior to the Harrison Act) proclaiming that "most of the attacks upon white women of the South are the direct result of a cocaine-crazed Negro brain." Even 33 years later, Harry J. Anslinger, then director of the Federal Bureau of Narcotics, resorted to a similar appeal in "evidence" given in the House Hearings on Taxation of Marijuana (resulting in the Marijuana Tax Act of 1937). In a letter he submitted in support of the Bureau's position on marijuana, after relating a sex crime which was attributed to a marijuana-smoking Mexican ("a sex-mad degenerate"), he goes on to say, "I wish I could show you what a small marijuana cigarette can do to one of our degenerate Spanish-speaking residents" (House Hearings, 1937, p. 32 as cited by Reasons, 1971).

Even without an explicitly racial rhetoric, however, much of the moralistic fervor in the past has reflected a "white man's burden" line of thinking. Typical of this line was the Right Reverend Charles Brent, Episcopal Bishop of the Philippine Islands at the turn of the century. For Bishop Brent, the opium problem was first and foremost an international moral issue (Taylor, 1969). He saw opium as ruining the lives of whole nations (e.g., China and the Philippines) and pressed for international control. His efforts resulted in the Shanghai Opium Conference of 1908, which eventually gave rise to further international meetings on the subject, leading both to international treaties and to domestic legislation in the United States. (See next section for more on this movement.)

Contemporaneous with Bishop Brent's international activities, concern about drug use was increasing on the domestic front. It was becoming readily apparent that the various opium preparations (both prescriptions and patent medicines) were being used for other than medicinal purposes. The non-medicinal use of such substances, although it continued to be legal, came to be equated, in the moral climate of the Progressive Era, with other "immoral" acts such as gambling, smoking, prostitution, and, of course, consumption of alcohol. Like alcohol, drug use was seen as contributing to loss of self-control, motivation, and responsibility and therefore antithetical to the prevailing moral philosophy of the times (Reasons, 1971). Several *ad hoc* public compaigns were waged to alert the public to the dangers of patent medicines. The most notable of these was led by Dr. Harvey W. Wiley, Chief of the Bureau of Food and Drugs, U.S. Department of Agriculture, and carried out in the popular press. Dr. Wiley's efforts eventually resulted in the Pure Food and Drug Act of 1906.

The role played nowadays by distinct moral and/or religious convictions in present drug policy is much more vague than it was in the days of Bishop Brent, Dr. Wiley, and their colleagues. While drug use is still condemned from most pulpits in America, the explicit role of the clergy in defining and combatting the drug problem has lost much of its importance. However, the values espoused by these earlier efforts still enjoy a certain currency.

User Interests

One group which is very seldom considered in discussing drug-related issues comprises the persons most involved: the drug users themselves. Historically, this amorphous aggregate has been a silent witness to the ongoing debate about its social existence. However, in more recent years, it has become active in two significant areas having public implications: (1) First has been the growing trend on the part of drug users to reject the societal definition of their behavior as destructive, as acts of personal weakness, and so on. Instead, they have promulgated the view that at least certain kinds of drug use are virtuous, enhancing to the individual, or just plain fun. They have denied that societal harm stems from drug-using behavior *itself;* instead, they have redefined the harm to society as a consequence of the *criminal sanctions* against such behavior.

This new interpretation was marked by the proselytizing of Timothy Leary and Richard Alpert in the early 1960's concerning the benefits to be derived from the use of various hallucinogens. At one end of the spectrum, some users were claiming the value of a variety of drugs as a help in the "search for identity"; at the other end was a less dramatic assertion of civil liberties, claiming drug use as an individual prerogative. Numerous *ad hoc* groups of users and sympathizers were established in an attempt at legal validation of the latter point of view. One of the most effective of these has been BLOSSOM, which has been working for the decriminalization of marijuana use. As mentioned earlier, marijuana proponents succeeded in an effort to place an initiative on the 1972 California ballot to decriminalize the personal use of marijuana. Similar efforts were made in the state of Washington during the same year, but failed to receive the requisite number of signatures for placement before the general public until 1974. (Once on the ballot, however, the initiatives were defeated by votes in both states.)

(2) The second area receiving considerable effort, especially from former drug users, is the rehabilitation of those who have been "hooked" on *addictive* drugs. Unlike the users who have been trying to change societal definitions of drug use (except in respect to civil liberties), this group generally concurs in the official definition of addiction as an undesirable human condition, affecting mostly weak individuals. Best typified by Synanon, a private treatment organization founded by ex-addicts, this segment of the user (and ex-user) public promotes a different conception of how best to deal with drug users. Their underlying assumption is that no one knows the problems, the tactics, the "hustles," or the whole life style of an addict better than another addict. The treatment routine at Synanon calls for the voluntary association of such individuals in a drug-free, socially supportive environment. What is offered is a substitute life style, in contrast to the usual societal response of incarceration or punishment, followed by a return to the same (i.e., drug-user) life style.

Economic Interests

The work of the moral reformers mentioned earlier has always created difficulties for the manufacturers of the drugs under attack. Throughout the 19th century, their preparations had been both legal and profitable. With increasing governmental regulation (resulting from the efforts of "moral entrepreneurs"), the task for the 20th century manufacturers has become one of retaining the profits. Even legitimate drug producers (i.e., those in the pharmaceutical industry) have been implicated in our national drug problem (however unintentionally), because of thei large-scale marketing of certain products which have been found to contain "dangerous" drugs. Recall also that a large proportion of the traffic in certain restricted drugs originates from legitimate pharmaceutical sources. To protect its public image and its access to the resource market, the pharmaceutical industry has advertised and lobbied very effectively to promote its viewpoint that only a minimum of government regulation is desirable (more on this later in the chapter).

A second, and perhaps more sinister, economic interest is that of the illicit producers and peddlers of drugs, whether they are small-scale operators or organized criminal syndicates. Such segments of our population actually thrive, in a way that legitimate drug interests cannot, on legislation which restricts public access to "dangerous drugs." They do not, therefore, oppose such legislation but perhaps even promote it. As legislative restrictions and penalties increase, higher prices and higher profits are the result.

Professional and Occupational Interests

Two categories of experts have traditionally been charged by our society with the responsibility for handling the drug problem: (1) the medical profession, and (2) the law-enforcement officers. Each group has its professional or occupational interests involved in the issue of "what to do" about drug use, and the history of the development of drug policy in our society (see next section) is in large part a history of the see-saw struggle between these two interest groups for the official "custody" of the definition and treatment of the drug problem.

The image of the drug addict at the turn of the century was predominantly that of a sick person, needing treatment by the medical profession. As we shall see later, this image underwent some transformation, and by 1922, addiction and addicts were portrayed instead mainly as criminal problems. This basic redefinition of the drug problem led to the conflict of interests between the medical profession and agencies charged with enforcement of the drug laws.

Immediately before and after the Harrison Act of 1914, the medical model of addiction prevailed. In a very real sense, physicians were society's "keepers of the problem" (Reasons, 1971). Addiction was seen as a "disease" for which physicians could diagnose the symptoms and provide treatment. Often this "treatment" consisted merely of supplying the addict with his drug in order to stave off withdrawal symptoms. Thus, addicts could legally maintain their addiction under the auspices of the medical profession.

The Harrison Act, which restricted the importation of opium, specifically excluded the medical profession from its restrictions. Strong medical interests secured appropriate modifications to the original Harrison Act legislation (introduced in 1910) so that upon its actual passage in December of 1914, a clause provided exemption from the Act for "the dispensing or administration of these drugs to a patient by a physician, dentist, or veterinary surgeon in the course of his professional practice and *for legitimate medical purposes*" (Terry and Pellens, 1970:754. Italics added). Thus, even after the passage of the first major drug control bill, physicians retained their right to provide drugs to addicts.

The erosion of this medical privilege came about through a series of progressively limiting interpretations by the Treasury Department's Narcotics Division (backed up by the courts) of the clause "for legitimate medical purposes." Following the court cases, and subsequent vigorous prosecution based upon them, the medical profession in general (with few exceptions) ceased in its efforts to reassert the medical definition of addiction. In thus virtually abdicating their claim as the "keepers of the problem" they left the door open to the view of addiction as a criminal activity (as promoted by the Treasury Department).

However, the American Medical Association continued to maintain its active opposition to other drug-related restrictions. In consort with the pharmaceutical industry, the medical profession has consistently and successfully resisted government intrusion into drug-dispensing activities involving the "non-addict" population. Their success in these matters is such that many physicians freely prescribe "a pill-for-every-problem . . . [redefining] normal problems in living as medical problems" (Rogers, 1971:16).

During most of the present century, the creation and enforcement of drug policy in this country has been left mainly in the province of the Narcotics Division of the Treasury Department and its successors: the Bureau of Narcotics, and later, the Bureau of Narcotics and Dangerous Drugs of the Justice Department.

The federal agencies charged with enforcement of drug legislation have been mentioned several times in previous sections of this chapter and will play a prominent role in the later historical discussion of the rise of the drug problem. The concern in the present section is merely to specify the special areas of interest of these agencies.

The Harrison Act of 1914 was an attempt to place controls on the use of narcotics in the United States. Basically, it required all persons handling opiates to keep accurate records and pay a tax of one cent per ounce on such substances. There is no reference to addicts, addiction, or any restrictions on who could or could not receive the drugs. The duties of the Narcotics Division, established in the Treasury Department, were clearly and simply to supervise the record-keeping and insure the collection of the stipulated tax. As Dickson (1968:149) notes, with the passage of time, "the Narcotics Division was faced with a severely restricted scope of operations." The agency either had to be satisfied with these somewhat marginal duties or else increase the scope of its authority. Again, Dickson (1968) captures the essence of the situation:

> Given the normal, well-documented bureaucratic tendency toward growth and expansion, and given the fact that the Division was a public bureaucracy and needed to justify its operations and usefulness before Congress, it would seem that increased power and jurisdiction in the area of drug control would be a desirable and, in fact, necessary goal. Adaptation to the Harrison Act limitations would preclude attainment of this goal. Operating under a legislative mandate, the logical alternative to adaptation would be to persuade the Congress and public that expansion was necessary and to extend the provisions of the Harrison Act. (149)

The Division chose the latter course, and in 1919 initiated a campaign to marshal public support for a conception of the drug addict as a criminal and to expand the purview of the Harrison Act. Some earlier Supreme Court cases had firmly established control of addicts and addiction as a concern of the Harrison Act and consequently of the Narcotics Division. Simultaneously, public reprehension of opiate use was cultivated through an extensive barrage of Division-sponsored newspaper articles and public reports which depicted opiate use as linked to crime, poverty, corruption of youth, insanity, and the like. With such activities, the Division not only created the social need for its specialized activities but also greatly increased the scope of these operations.

In 1930, after having been a part of the Department of Prohibition for ten years, control and enforcement of drug-use laws was vested in the newly created Bureau of Narcotics. Harry J. Anslinger, then the Assistant Commissioner of the Bureau of Prohibition, was named to head the new agency. Most analyses of Anslinger's 32-year tenure as head of the Bureau of Narcotics have emphasized the moral zeal with which he approached the drug issue. Becker (1963) has, in fact, termed Anslinger a "moral entrepreneur," and credits him with leading the moral crusade which culminated in the Marijuana Tax Act of 1937. While Anslinger and the Bureau were certainly the leading forces in this campaign, it is easy to see that their interests were not exclusively moral (Dickson, 1968).

Scientific Interests

One might expect that in an area of such great concern as the drug problem, scientific involvement would be of paramount importance in the formulation of social policy. This has not been the case. Rather, the historical evidence indicates that either most policy decisions are formulated in opposition to the findings of science, or that such findings are selectively scanned in order to find "evidence" to support a policy already decided. In any event, both the social and the physical sciences have been relatively impotent in affecting rational public attitudes and social policy with respect to the drug issue.

The physical sciences have primarily been concerned with physiological effects of the various drugs. The history of drug policy in America reveals an almost conscientious indifference to such findings. For instance, in the only scientific testimony before Congress pertaining to the Marijuana Tax Act of 1937, Dr. William Woodward, legislative counsel of the American Medical Association, argued against the view of the drug being espoused by the Bureau of Narcotics. Specifically, he stipulated that there was no reliable scientific evidence indicating marijuana to be addictive, leading to sexual excess, insanity, or any of the other nebulous claims being advanced by the Bureau. He was personally assailed for his efforts, and the Act was passed anyway.

Scientific interests have not fared better even in more recent times. In 1970, the Comprehensive Drug Abuse and Control Act was passed by Congress and set forth five categories (schedules) of drugs, presumably based on a combined consideration of each drug's potential for abuse and for medical utility. Schedule I contains the hallucinogens, heroin, cocaine, and marijuana derivatives. These drugs are said by the Act to have a high abuse potential and no medical use, and are thus tightly restricted or even outlawed. Schedule II includes most of the amphetamines plus certain narcotics which also have a high potential for abuse but are medically useful. The Act establishes strict regulations and monitoring systems to control the dispensing of these drugs by physicians. Schedule III drugs are seen as low in abuse potential and as having medical utility. Included here are the barbiturates, some less potent narcotics, and major tranquilizers. Restrictions on these are less severe than with the Schedule II drugs, although prescriptions to purchase them are still required. Minimal controls are applied to the Schedule IV and V drugs, which include minor tranquilizers such as Librium and Valium.

If we recall the information presented in the first part of this chapter, describing the effects and prevalence of the various drugs, it becomes fairly obvious that this classification system bears little resemblance to the real abuse potentials of the various drugs. Goode (1972), in a similar critique of this legislation, reiterates the high addiction potential of barbiturates and tranquilizers (Schedule III and IV drugs, respectively) as opposed to non-addictive marijuana and other hallucinogens (Schedule I). Similarly, he points out that barbiturates are "the number one cause of death from drug-related overdoses" (Goode, 1972:126). Even if prevalence is accepted as a criterion of abuse, the Schedule II-V drugs far outdistance those found in Schedule I. Even if we discount the barbiturates, amphetamines, tranquilizers, and so on, taken legally, the volume of these drugs reaching the illicit market (from legitimate production) is still overwhelming. As such, it appears the 1970 classification scheme is more reflective of previously formulated policy than of any consideration of available scientific evidence.

It is perhaps indicative of the weak role played by the sciences in drug policy formation that even in those instances where attention is paid to scientific information, it is sometimes "quasi-science" or even just plain bad work. The LSD-chromosome scare of 1967 is a case in point. Here a geneticist from New York, after viewing the unkempt hippies of San Francisco, set out to prove LSD to be harmful. Joel Fort (1969) relates this "scientific" endeavor as follows:

> ... using an enormous sample of three people, two "normals" and one paranoid schizophrenic (who had had electroshock and tranquilizer therapy), he took a sample of their white blood cells, and after exposing the cells of the two normals to varying concentrations of LSD in test tubes, he examined all three with an electron microscope and reported finding significant increases in chromosomal breakage *due to* the effects of LSD. This nonarticle was rushed into press by *Science*, the official journal of the American Association for the Advancement of Science, while an article showing the opposite results was delayed for months, and articles about many more important things continued the usual waits for publication. Within 24 hours of the publication in this relatively esoteric journal, there were national headlines to the effect that LSD had been shown to produce *human birth defects*. A new mythology had been created. (1969:141, italics in original)

Fort goes on to say that the chromosome issue is still undecided at this point. While many drugs (such as caffeine and aspirin) are known to affect chromosomes, the meaning of "broken chromosomes" for human reproduction is not known. Finally, he points out that some of the most recent and rigorous scientific work "found no evidence of LSD producing increased chromosomal breaks" (p. 142).

However, by the time of Fort's reasoned critique and rebuttal, science had already fulfilled its role as fodder for moral and legislative canons.

The social sciences have not fared much better in drug-related matters, although millions of dollars are spent each year on research and treatment programs. In the last 15 years, it has increasingly fallen to psychology and sociology to devise treatment remedies for drug users, which would seem to be based upon an implicit theory of drug-using behavior in those fields. A brief review of the major theoretical emphases of both psychology and sociology illustrates the input of these disciplines into the American drug problem.

Psychological explanations of drug use have traditionally accepted the society's view that such behavior is by definition undesirable, so that the task is to explain "why individuals do that sort of thing." In one way or another, psychological theories have stressed the idea that *personality types* exhibited by addicts (and other users) involve strong dependency needs and pronounced feelings of inadequacy. Therapeutic programs based on some variant of this view have dominated society's approach to "curing" its drug users (discounting jail as "therapy"), with very little success. One possible reason for failure may lie in the reliance upon the premise that the drug user has an "abnormal" personality. In so doing, the psychologist is put in the doubtful position of treating as a crucial variable something (a personality trait) which may not be very important to the behavior in question. The result is an explanation of drug behavior which fails to provide a specific, consistent, and universally applicable theory which is able to explain variation in group addiction rates, as well as how psychologically "normal" people become addicted (cf. Lindesmith, 1940b).

For sociologists, attention has been focused largely on the influence of the group in promoting and maintaining drug use. Here again, the societal definition of drug use as "bad" is not usually challenged. Consequently, sociologists also ask, "Why do they do it?" and arrive at answers stressing deprived background or environment, peer-group influence, institutional decay, and the like, all intent on explaining this deviant act. Unfortunately, even if the sweeping institutional changes called for by these analyses were carried out in policy (which they inevitably are not), chances are that drug-using behavior would not be altered significantly. Sociologists, in accepting the premise of drug use as "deviant behavior," typically ignore the fact that illegal drug use is only *one kind* of "drug abuse" (Hadden, 1973), as we pointed out in our earlier discussion on the prevalence of barbiturate use. If we are to have a realistic sociological theory of drug abuse, it should account for the various patterns of such behavior, from the garden-variety street user and occasional marijuana smoker to the physician-addict and the barbiturate-dependent housewife. Two sociological theories about distinct types of drug-using behavior have been more helpful in this regard.

Twenty-five years ago, Alfred Lindesmith formulated his classic proposition about opiate addiction. Disturbed by the circularity of psychological pronouncements on the subject, Lindesmith (1948) sought an internally consistent, universally applicable statement on the causality of addiction. His thesis posited addiction as the direct result of knowledge on the part of users that their withdrawal distress was linked to the use of opiates. In other words, persons using opiates come to recognize that continued use of the drug will enable them to avoid withdrawal symptoms. Desire for such avoidance will then become a motivating factor for continued use (i.e., addiction). In essence, this formulation calls attention to the role of *learning* in the process of becoming addicted. A person can learn to "crave" the drug simply as a means of warding off withdrawal symptoms.

A second formulation, this time dealing with marijuana use, also employs a learning perspective. Becker's (1963) classic treatment on becoming a marijuana user details the process whereby persons learn from others to become habitual marijuana users. This entails gaining knowledge about the effects of the drug, and how to recognize such effects and define them as pleasurable. In addition, his formulation incorporates the process whereby a novice marijuana smoker learns how he can engage in such behavior without being readily detected.

The distinct advantage of both Becker's and Lindesmith's approaches to drug use is that they draw attention to what can be called the "normalcy" of such behavior. In this perspective, use of illicit drugs is but one of many alternative behaviors open to persons in a society, and is explainable by the same principles of social learning which are applied to more conventional behaviors. (See Chapter 1 on "learning theories" of deviance.)

Not all physical and social science contributions to drug use theory and control have been totally ignored. One federal agency, the Food and Drug Administration, is specifically charged with receiving and acting upon such ongoing scientific research. However, on a broad policy level, scientific interests are scarcely heeded, as witnessed by the almost total neglect of the recommendations of the National Commission on Marijuana and Drug Abuse (1972 and 1973)—perhaps the most comprehensive study of the subject ever accomplished.

THE DRUG PROBLEM AS A SOCIAL MOVEMENT

The discussion above indicates clearly that the issue of drugs in American society has not lacked for interested parties. At various points in time, each of the publics and interest groups discussed here has figured prominently in the definition of drug use and abuse. Sometimes their recommendations and influence were counter to prevailing notions of what should be done with drugs and drug users; at other times, they were in the vanguard of significant changes in social definitions and policies.

As we look back over the last century or so, we can see four distinct social movements which have addressed the drug issue. These movements have overlapped somewhat in the manner indicated by Figure 2-4, but they have been different. The four are: (1) the Anti-Opiate Movement; (2) the Early Anti-Marijuana Movement, which was aborted; (3) the Anti-Narcotics Revival; and (4) the Modern Reform Movement. Each movement (except the second) has had a life-cycle approximating the five-stage model that we have been using in the book so far. Let us look briefly at each of these movements in order to understand how they have contributed to the present public and official definitions and policies relating to drug use in our society.

The Anti-Opiate Movement

In the late 19th and early 20th centuries, opium preparations were widely available even without a prescription. The drug problem at this time was narrowly defined as the smoking of opium, which, as we noted earlier, was associated with the Chinese populations in the larger American cities. The first law proscribing that behavior was a San Francisco city ordinance passed in 1875, followed by similar laws in some other cities. After that, the problem was considered largely contained, or else was informally tolerated, as long as it could be kept within the Chinese communities (Reasons, 1971).

Incipiency

The origins of the anti-opiate movement are to be found in the moral interests and early efforts of American missionaries, especially overseas. Basing their concern on a Christian ideology which stressed discipline and responsibility, the missionaries played a leading role in the formation of international anti-opium societies, which lobbied and agitated for control of the "opium menace" in the "uncivilized" (i.e., non-Christian) countries of the world. Anti-opium societies first began to emerge in China and England (e.g., The Society for the Suppression of the Opium Trade), with American missionaries playing the leading roles, and Christian precepts furnishing the ideological base (Reasons, 1971). British policy toward the use of opium was scarcely affected by such efforts, but America was influenced considerably more. Led by such untiring workers as the Right Reverend Charles Brent, the missionary entrepreneurs successfully lobbied for a succession of international conferences to discuss means for establishing international restrictions on world traffic in the drug, starting with the Shanghai Opium Conference of 1908. This pioneering work culminated in The Hague International Opium Conference of 1912, which passed a resolution calling for international controls. (The United States was a signatory to this agreement, and in 1914 passed its own domestic legislation, the Harrison Act, which complied with the Hague guidelines.)

Coalescence

Early in the 20th century, the international movement to control opium converged with a similar campaign in the United States, only in this country the movement was aimed also at exposing the "evils" of the patent medicine business. Led primarily by Dr. Harvey Wiley, Chief of the Bureau of Food and Drugs (USDA), the intent of this campaign was to make the public aware of a new and growing "menace," the "drug fiend." The literature of the campaign portrayed persons as enslaved by the various opium preparations, which robbed them of their wills, as did alcohol and tobacco (the more notorious evils of that time).

However, the major target of Dr. Wiley's campaign was not the addict himself, but the patent medicine trusts which furnished the preparations. The addict was primarily looked upon as one who was "sick" but could be saved by "humanitarian efforts." One such humanitarian effort, and the first major test for the pharmaceutical industry, was the Pure Food and Drug Act of 1906. In the early 1900's the patent medicine industry had reached its peak, and practically all of its remedies for physical ills contained opium or its derivatives (Terry and Pellens, 1970:75). So widespread was the industry, that one wholesale house alone was said to distribute in excess of 600 different preparations containing opiates (Brecher, 1972:3). Dr. Wiley, head of the Bureau of Food and Drugs, launched a campaign with the ultimate goal of driving the patent medicines off the market. The passage of the Pure Food and Drug Act was a direct consequence of Wiley's activities. Under this Act, preparations containing opiates and similar drugs were required to be so labeled. However, to their advantage, the manufacturers did manage to have some of the original portions of the Act dropped: Those parts which would have required the quantity of each drug to be listed on the label, and would have provided for standards of purity. Thus, the first confrontation ended in an Act which reflected, in large part, a co-optation by the pharmaceutical industry.

Institutionalization

The passage of the 1906 Pure Food and Drug Act was the result of a coalescence of national and international segments of the growing anti-opiate movement, and it was also an indication that institutionalization of the movement had begun. The passage of the Harrison Act of 1914 was the next development in this stage. But this Act, referred to earlier in this chapter, was directed more specifically at the supposedly illegal, non-medical users of opium, those who used it as a source of pleasure. The "menace" of opium smoking *per se* was seen as qualitatively different from patent medicine addiction, as it represented a deliberate attempt to induce intoxication. Associated also with various other "vices" (e.g., prostitution), and racially linked to a lower-class ethnic group (the Chinese), free use of opium aroused the public to demand laws to prohibit it, and to prevent this "alien practice" from spreading to other communities.

It was within such a moral climate that Congress passed the Harrison Act of 1914, to "prohibit the importation and use of opium for other than medicinal purposes." The Act specifically prohibited the importation of opium prepared for smoking, while at the same time safeguarding medical and drug industry interests. Other use and addiction, which was enormously more prevalent, was not even mentioned in the Harrison Act. It was still considered a "medical problem," necessitating little social concern. Once again, the medical and pharmaceutical establishments succeeded in co-opting the law: The patent medicine trust managed to obtain exemptions from the restrictions of this bill for "preparations containing not more than two grains of opium, one-fourth grain of morphine, one-eighth grain of heroin, or one grain of codeine, or any preparations of them, in one ounce" (Terry and Pellens, 1970:753). Also exempted from this Act was the importation of decocainized coca leaves, at the request of the coca leaf industry (e.g., Coca-Cola).

Another step in the institutionalization of the anti-opiate movement, the role of the Narcotics Division of the Treasury Department (charged with the enforcement of the Harrison Act) in changing the official definition of narcotic use from a medical to a criminal problem, has been briefly outlined above. Also very important, however, was the Division's success in changing *public* conceptions about such behavior.

Dickson (1968:49) notes that following the passage of the Harrison Act, the attitude of the general public toward narcotics use "could be characterized as only slightly opposed." At this point, the addict was still seen as "sick" and, hence, as a medical concern. Only opium *smoking* raised the public's ire, since it was a deliberate attempt at intoxication, antithetical to the prevailing moral ethic (cf. p. 258). As noted earlier, in order to expand its limited scope of operations and increase its power, it became the Narcotic Division's task to change this mildly negative feeling from "neutrality or slight opposition to strong opposition." The task was made easier by the Division's status as a public bureaucracy, with access to the means of communicating a view which would be given legitimacy by the public (Dickson, 1968). After all, here was one agency which would be in a position to "know" about such matters. Further, the pronouncements about the "evils" of drug use would be made in the name of both strongly held moral values and concern for public safety, so that the agency could avoid counter claims of selfish interests. Thus, within such a social climate, and with such excellent tools at its disposal, the Narcotics Division began to "educate" the public about a new social problem—the drug addict.

The new image of the drug addict was built upon a five-point mythology: (1) The drug addict is a violent criminal. (2) He is a moral degenerate, e.g., liar, thief, and so on. (3) The drug peddler wants to convert others into addicts. (4) The drug addict wants to convert others into addicts. (5) The addict takes drugs because of an abnormal personality, e.g., psychopathic, weak-willed, and so on (Lindesmith, 1940a, and 1940b). The Narcotics Division made extensive use of the media in disseminating publicity about each of the above facets of "addiction." The articles which they disseminated usually contained additional references to the dangers for unsuspecting youth; to the insanity caused by the use of drugs; and to various physical ills, ranging from rotting of the skin to sterility, all attributable to such drug use. Also, since the Division was the agency charged with patrolling the problem, it was also the "authoritative" source on the extent of such behavior. Thus, in 1919, it announced there were over one million addicts in this country.

At the same time, the Division sought to increase its jurisdiction over drugs at the expense of the medical profession. Thus, in a series of court cases brought by the Treasury Department against medical doctors, the ability of a physician to prescribe narcotics to an addict was progressively removed. Within three years (1919-1922), the Treasury Department secured a number of favorable Supreme Court decisions (*Webb* v. *U.S., Jin Fuey Wong* v. *U.S.,* and *Behrman* v. *U.S.*) which culminated in the prohibition of physician-supplied narcotics to addicts, regardless of the "medical purpose." Thus the influence of the strong medical lobby in Congress, which had secured and maintained the original exemption for physicians, was circumvented through the use of the judiciary.

Fragmentation and Demise

In the absence of any significant public opposition to its view, the Division of Narcotics was successful in establishing the addict as "a problem" for America. It succeeded in splitting off and isolating its former ally, the medical profession. The latter, in light of the growing public concern over the "drug fiend," and the judicial rebukes suffered in Division-instigated prosecutions, abandoned its role of treating the addict as "sick," and, by its silence, acquiesced in the Division's new definition of addiction. By 1922, addicts, unorganized and powerless, found that, in addition to their other problems, they were now defined as criminals!

This first era of America's "drug problem" thus ended with the Narcotics Division having successfully created both a public consensus favoring its definition of opiate users, which was soon to encompass all narcotics users, and a new scope of operations for itself. At that point, the Division withdrew from active agitation and enjoyed its new "watchdog" role, except for occasional budgetary struggles with Congress. Its supporters turned to other causes for the time being, and the movement which it had fostered disappeared. It was not until the 1930's that the next major campaign was mounted, this time against marijuana.

The Early Anti-Marijuana Movement

In 1930, the Narcotics Division was reorganized as the Bureau of Narcotics. For the first few years under this new organizational structure, the Bureau was satisfied with the continuation of its "educational function," dealing with the evils of drugs, and with demonstrating its effectiveness in appearances before Congress. As evidence of this effectiveness, the Bureau continued to point to the "rapid decline" in addiction, due to its efforts.

Incipiency

As late as 1932, the Bureau did not consider marijuana use a significant "problem." Moreover, the Bureau suggested that marijuana regulation was more easily and effectively provided under state jurisdiction, and thus was not a concern of the federal government. In 1934, state statutes were still being advocated as a means of controlling marijuana use, even though warnings were beginning to appear in Bureau publications about the increases in youthful marijuana use. By 1936, all 48 states had passed laws regulating the possession and sale of marijuana for other than medical purposes.

In 1937, the Bureau, in a curious reversal, appealed successfully for federal legislation, which resulted in the passage of the Marijuana Tax Act in August of that year. Becker (1963) has argued that the Bureau, out of both moral and occupational interests, mounted a public campaign to generate mass concern and support for the new federal law. As Dickson (1968) points out, however, only four magazine articles concerning the evils of marijuana appeared in the two years previous to the passing of the marijuana statute, and only one such article was printed in the seven months immediately prior to enactment. His conclusion is that, as in the period preceding passage of the Harrison Act, public awareness of, and opposition to, the drug in question was only slight. In other words, as far as the public was concerned, the movement remained only "incipient." However, again paralleling the era of the Harrison Act, the Bureau initiated an intensive "educational" effort concerning the evils of marijuana, *after* the legislation was already passed. Using the same tactics and mythology that had proven effective in earlier years, marijuana was portrayed as an addictive drug, leading to violence, insanity, sexual crimes, and so on. Thus, at a time when *narcotic* addiction was reportedly on the wane (as a result of Bureau efforts), a new threat was defined, and a new federal law was passed. This process, again, is reminiscent of the proposition put forth by Kai Erikson (1966), and reviewed in Chapter 2, to the effect that a control apparatus tends to define the boundaries of deviance in accordance with its own logistical capacities, rather than in accordance with any particular objective reality.

If Harry Anslinger, as head of the Bureau of Narcotics, had indeed been singularly motivated by moral concern about the marijuana evil, then the existing state statutes would have sufficed for him. However, coincidental with the new concern, 1936 was the fourth straight year in which the Bureau's budgetary requests were being given low priority. Except for a $4,500 increase in 1936, the budget had been slashed at the average rate of $110,000 a year since 1932. Indeed, the Bureau was in danger of decline through fiscal neglect—a condition which bureaucracies historically have fought against tenaciously. Viewed from this perspective, this early campaign against marijuana can as much be understood as a struggle for bureaucratic survival as it can a moral campaign (cf. Dickson, 1968).

Unfortunately for the Bureau, however, before the marijuana threat could acquire full public status as a social problem, the movement was temporarily aborted by increasing American involvement in World War II. In spite of its efforts to define marijuana as Japan's secret weapon, the Bureau was unable to generate much further interest, so the movement remained only incipient until the early 1950's, when the drug problem was "rediscovered." Once again we are reminded of the discussion in Chapter 2 about how all-out wars usually preempt a society's logistical capacity to generate and maintain other social problems.

The Anti-Narcotics Revival

Concern for the "drug problem" thus decreased drastically during the 1940's, paralleling a decrease in addiction reported by the Bureau of Narcotics. However, in 1950 the Bureau began calling attention to a "tremendous increase" in teenage addiction. This was, in fact, borne out by the data to some extent, for the "heroin plague," as it was later called, had started in the ghetto areas of the nation's large cities.

Coalescence

Resuming the movement that had lain dormant during the war, the government now began giving a great deal of attention to narcotics, including marijuana. The Kefauver Committee on Crime in 1951 turned to this issue, and, in a massive media campaign, in which most of the material was furnished by the Bureau, the nation was told how drugs were enslaving and corrupting the schoolchildren of America. Drugs were now also linked to Communism, as a means of capturing the minds and spirits of decent people everywhere (Reasons, 1971). The result of all this was a re-emergence and reaffirmation of the punitive approach to drug control. The unwary youth of the nation had to be protected from the unscrupulous pushers, who were lurking around school yards waiting to ensnare the innocent.

The Bureau was asking for new weapons (laws) with which to combat the menace and was rewarded in 1951 with the Boggs Amendment, which contained provisions enabling easier prosecution of users and pushers and stipulating mandatory minimum sentences.

Institutionalization

The year 1951, with the convoking of a congressional committee on drugs, and the passage of the Boggs Amendment, probably marked the beginning of institutionalization for this revived movement. The new "get tough" approach was so successful that only a year later the Bureau could report that the rate of increase in teenage addiction was on the wane.

The Bureau continued to acclaim the effectiveness of the "get tough" approach; and in 1956, the Narcotic Control Act was passed, which extended the maximum punishments of the 1951 legislation, eliminated parole for all but first offenders, and, in general, incorporated a more severe and inflexible approach to the problem (Lindesmith, 1967). Several states followed suit with more restrictive statutes of their own, including laws prohibiting addiction itself. Thus, even if a person was not caught with drugs in his possession, if he was shown to be an addict, he could still be prosecuted!

Fragmentation and Demise

The enforcement of the punitive "cure" for the drug problem continued unabated throughout most of the 1950's, with little opposition. However, toward the end of that decade, voices were beginning to be heard, questioning the value of the Bureau's point of view. Alfred Lindesmith, long a critic of the punitive approach to drug matters, was joined by the American Bar Association and the American Medical Association in reasserting a medical approach to addiction as a viable alternative to the criminal definition taken by the Bureau. This was the first major challenge in 40 years to the Bureau's sole prerogative and authority to define the "realities" of the drug problem, and this challenge ultimately has cracked the solid position which the moral and occupational champions have maintained through the Bureau. Although the Bureau interests clearly seem to be declining in power in the struggle with the new Reform Movement, they are by no means yet in demise.

The Reform Movement

It should not be surprising that much of the preceding discussion of drug-related social movements reads like a history of the Bureau of Narcotics. From 1919 to 1960, the drug problem in the United States was practically the exclusive province of that agency. Led for 32 years by its crusading director, Harry Anslinger, the

Bureau successfully defined who and what constituted the problem, and to what extent it existed. The Bureau influenced policy decisions to such a degree that the punitive approach became the "only" solution. But some winds of change were starting to blow.

Incipiency

In August, 1962, Anslinger retired as Director of the Bureau; and one month later the First White House Conference on Narcotic and Drug Abuse was convened to reassess the drug situation in America. Among the findings released by this Conference of scientific and governmental leaders was a call for modified public and professional attitudes about addiction, and a statement that several misconceptions and stereotypes about drugs and their users had hindered progress in solving the drug problem (Reasons, 1971).

Coalescence

Later in the 1960's, there occurred the first serious confrontation for the Bureau since its victories over the medical profession in the 1920's. The confrontation came from an unintended coalition between two quite disparate groups: the scientific community and the drug users themselves. Both groups had been increasingly angered by the activities of the Bureau and related enforcement agencies, and they began to assail the premises on which the current laws were based. The interests and some of the activities of the users have been noted in an earlier section of this chapter. One additional observation that needs to be made here is that proselytizing by certain drug users was associated with a particular life style which stood in direct opposition to the dominant culture. This was the era of the "hippie," whose general life style was perceived by the public and its officials as conducive to drug use (which it was), and to the "consequences" thereof, such as long hair, free sex, unkempt appearance, and so on. By linking the *effects* of drug use with the hippie life style, as the Bureau and its adherents had attempted to do, the more serious hippie assault on dominant values (e.g., the *right* to take drugs, to reject steady employment, to dress as they pleased, and so on) could be weakened or avoided. However, as it became increasingly apparent that the youthful drug-hippie movement included many young people from "good families" (or even prominent ones), and that this movement would not yield to a strictly punitive approach, the scientific community was called upon to furnish "answers" to what was causing "our youth" to behave in such a way, and what could be done about it. In spite of a tremendous outpouring of research in both the physical and the social sciences, it soon became obvious that both legislators and enforcement personnel were, in effect, partly co-opting the scientists by giving selective credence to that information which best fit in with the assumptions underlying the criminal approach. The combination of the influence of the user and scientific influence, however, eventually did lead to a new trend and a partial reform of the existing approach to "drug abuse."

Institutionalization

While the criminal laws continued to be enforced, new medically based treatment programs were gradually institutionalized. The first major difficulty with those programs was that apparently most addicts did not want to quit, and no matter what type of program was tried, the best prospect for "cure" was the addict who entered treatment voluntarily. Scientists, backed by certain sympathetic people in the federal government, decided that some "painless" and legal way had to be found to induce addicts to give up their drugs.

In the late 1960's, a "new" treatment regimen was introduced—methadone maintenance. The addict was placed on a daily dose of methadone, itself an addictive drug, and maintained on methadone in lieu of heroin. Methadone, in small doses, does not produce the euphoria of heroin and thus has the advantage of allowing individuals to maintain a fairly normal life, although still remaining addicted. The initially high "cure" rates led some persons to hail methadone as a panacea. However, expansion of this program proceeded at a slow pace, for it went against the long-held notion that it was "immoral" to sustain any kind of addiction. When it became obvious that no other program was working as well as methadone, much of the resistance broke down. Unfortunately, the rapid expansion of methadone clinics soon proved that, removed from its carefully selected test population, the cure rate for methadone maintenance declined sharply. At present, it remains a very effective treatment mode for voluntary patients. The involuntary patients, those for whom the program is a condition of probation or parole, fail rather frequently to be "cured."

Another symptom of reform was that several myths about drug users and drugs themselves were coming under attack. The best example is the case of marijuana. With so many otherwise "normal" youth trying this drug in the 1960's, it became very difficult to maintain the fictions of its addictive properties, its causal connection to heroin, and so on. Several government-sponsored research projects were thus established to find out the "truth" about marijuana. In actuality, however, this research seemed designed more to find out what was "bad" about the drug in order to justify the laws prohibiting it. One such project, supported by the National Institute of Mental Health, issued a press release that they had found that massive doses of THC (a psychoactive ingredient of marijuana) caused brain damage in laboratory tests with rats. Fortunately, they also reported that for comparable findings in human beings, persons would have to smoke 40 to 60 high-grade marijuana cigarettes a day for several years before any brain damage would occur (U.P.I., 1971).

Perhaps indicative of the attitude with which most research results contrary to established policy on the drug problem have been received was the almost total neglect of the National Commission's Report on Marijuana (1972). This was perhaps the most extensive study ever conducted on any one drug, and after reviewing the medical and social findings, the Commission recommended the decriminalization of marijuana. This recommendation has yet to be seriously considered in Congress, and was summarily rejected by the Nixon Administration.

In 1968, a new agency, the Bureau of Narcotics and Dangerous Drugs, was created and placed within the Department of Justice. Although this agency has ceased to promote many of the myths associated with marijuana and other drugs (e.g., the "dope-fiend mythology"), the criminal approach to the problem is still dominant. Since the prime task of this agency is still the containment of the drug problem, it is not unreasonable to expect that such a problem will continue, if only to convince the rest of society of the need for the agency.

Thus it appears that both the older punitive approach and the newer medical approach both remain partly institutionalized and still in conflict with each other. While the newer definition has made some inroads, in both the public and the official views, it is yet too early to tell which one will prevail. Both have been backed by important movements carried by strong interest groups, and both continue to have large followings.

THE LEGACY OF THE DRUG MOVEMENTS

The most obvious legacy of America's drug-problem movements is the survival of the punitive approach engendered by the Bureau of Narcotics, which has resulted in the criminalization of a large segment of the population. At present, the dominant mode of dealing with drug-using behavior is to pass laws prohibiting or restricting such use. Such laws and their corresponding penalties vary from state to state. To compound the situation, additional variation is often encountered in the differential application of these laws between locales within most states. The handling of marijuana offenses provides an illustration of the range of this diversity.

In Texas in 1972 and 1973, conviction for possession of small amounts of marijuana warranted prison sentences of up to 99 years. At the same time, a similar offense in Ann Arbor, Michigan, most often entailed receiving a citation similar to a traffic ticket and, if conviction followed, the assessment of a nominal fine ($5 to $25).

The federal guidelines for drug-related laws emanate from the 1970 Comprehensive Drug Abuse and Control Act. As discussed earlier, this Act sets forth five categories (schedules) of drugs, presumably on a basis of potential for abuse as balanced against medical utility of the substances. The rationale for the particular schedules and their restrictions has been called into question, but the fact remains that most law enforcement activity is concerned with those substances falling within Schedule I (hallucinogens, heroin, cocaine, and marijuana derivatives).

The punitive approach to control of these substances has most recently undergone a rhetorical shift consistent with a shift in user populations. As the latter become more representative of the general population (i.e., more middle class and Caucasian), it is becoming increasingly unbelievable to the public to depict the users of such substances as "fiends," "junkies," and other "dangerous" types. Instead, the official law enforcement focus has been publicly shifted to a concentration on the drug distribution system. Consequently, most recent legislation has concentrated on stiffening penalties for those trafficking in drugs. So far there is little evidence that this shift in focus has had a visible effect either on the quantity of illicit drugs available, or on their actual consumption. However, several other more subtle consequences have become apparent.

The history of the punitive approach in America has had extensive consequences for the drug-using population. In one sense, it has perpetuated the problem by making drug users "outsiders" (Becker, 1963) and thus fostering the development of an addict subculture, replete with its own argot, survival techniques, recruitment incentives, and, of course, distribution system for the drugs. A subculture provides the addict with the necessary support to carry on his activities outside the law. In effect, ties to the dominant culture are severed and the addict associates primarily with other addicts, paying allegiance to subcultural values, subscribing to its ideology which views the dominant culture as "square," and generally living in opposition to the society which has cast him out.

The prohibition of drug use also creates a market to supply the demand which can no longer be satisfied legally (if it ever could). True to the theory of supply and demand, prices for limited goods escalate with increased demand. Periodic vigorous enforcement of the prohibition not only drives the prices up, but may cause people to experiment with other drugs. For instance, Operation Intercept in 1969 (an intensive federal effort to cut off importation of marijuana and other drugs, especially at the Mexican border) temporarily reduced the flow of marijuana into the country. Besides causing prices to rise to as much as double their previous mark, the absence of marijuana led several persons into the use of drugs which they normally would not have consumed, e.g., stronger hallucinogens, amphetamines, alcohol (Brecher, 1972).

The high prices of the drug marketplace contribute to the association of addiction and crime. Drugs do not make one impulsively commit crimes. To the contrary, most addicting drugs are depressants and, when under their influence most people prefer to simply relax. However, the high price of supporting an addiction on the black market creates the need for revenue that usually exceeds that available from legitimate sources. Hence, the addict resorts to crime. Ironically, if the same drug were available legally, the average addict could support his habit for a few dollars a day.

Prohibition has other than monetary consequences for the drug user and his source of supply. By making certain drugs illicit, the government foregoes any chance for quality control over the substances being consumed. As Table 7-4 clearly demonstrates, what a user buys is not necessarily a pure version of the drug he wants, or of a passable quality. For those using certain hallucinogens, this means they may be ingesting substances other than the one intended. For those shopping on the heroin market, it may mean death. It is another irony of prohibition that several deaths a year caused by heroin overdoses are attributed to addicts accidentally obtaining *higher* quality drugs than they are used to (e.g., getting hold of substances which are 25 percent to 30 percent heroin when the usual street heroin is only 3 percent to 5 percent pure).

On a broad cultural level, the punitive stratagem and attendant stereotypes have legitimatized one life style over another (Goode, 1969) on at least two levels. First, by identifying certain drugs with particular life styles, the dominant culture has been able to reject out of hand what it views as potential attacks on its moral code. For example, the social impact of legislation prohibiting marijuana and the stronger hallucinogens leads to an implicit view of the user as a person who is not to be trusted (he breaks laws), personally weak (he must resort to drugs in order to cope), and possibly dangerous (from the effect of the drug). Similarly, the whole life style of the user is discredited. The hippie cult, radical politics, and the like are viewed as both cause and effect of illicit drug use.

Perhaps more damaging to the society as a whole is the second consequence of the punitive strategy on the general culture. Such an approach must be unambiguous in order to be enforceable. As such, the lines between what is legally (and morally) acceptable and what is not, are clearly drawn. This leads the general public to believe that they *know* what constitutes a drug problem, and to an erroneous public definition of legal substances, such as alcohol, tobacco, caffeine, prescribed barbiturates, and the like as fundamentally different from the illegal substances. Such beliefs have no correspondence to the actual properties of the substances. All are drugs. All are potentially harmful. All have psychoactive effects. The consideration of alcohol as acceptable and marijuana as not acceptable not only reflects a misguided value commitment, but it also obscures the deleterious effects of the former.

A final consideration of the impact of the punitive approach on the American conception of its drug problem has to do with the social meanings of laws. The passage of laws in areas of social concern promotes the complacent view that something is being done to alleviate a disagreeable situation. We have tried to show in the pages of this chapter that the laws dealing with America's drug situation have had the direct effect of insuring only that some people will be arrested and locked away. The "problem" has not gone away. If anything, the laws have aggravated and worsened the situation by supporting the punitive approach as society's main response to the drug situation. It is within this context that the "drug problem problem," as Nowlis (1969) has termed it, has become real.

An interesting throwback to the Anslinger days, with its total reliance on a non-medical and criminal approach to drug use, appeared in the state of New York in 1973 (Farber, 1973). At the urging of Governor Rockefeller, who was disillusioned by the ineffectiveness of the usual punitive and medical mixture of prevailing drug legislation, the state legislature passed a harsh bill to deal with drug pushers. The new law abandoned the medical definition of addiction entirely, in favor of a strictly criminal one. Among its features were: (1) a mandatory life sentence for selling or possessing "hard" drugs; and (2) a one-to-fifteen-year sentence for the possession of one ounce or more of marijuana, or sale of any amount.

In urging passage of such provisions, the Governor predicted that they would force addicts and pushers off the streets and into treatment. However, after several months of implementation, the new law had not yet, in the opinion of a variety of expert observers, made any change in the incidence of addiction, in the number or activities of pushers, or in the number of clients rushing from the streets to the methadone treatment clinics. In fact, the statistics indicated that the severity of the law had disinclined the police to arrest any but the "big-time" operators, and that juries had shown a reluctance to find defendants guilty as charged under such a harsh law. A special narcotics prosecutor in New York City claimed that the new law had frightened "private adventurers and college kids" away from drugs, but that the street pushers and "big-time" dealers were still as active as ever—only their prices were higher! There is thus no reason to believe that this latest punitive legislation will be more effective than its predecessors.

Equally important as a legacy of drug-related movements in our society has been the survival of the enormous influence of the pharmaceutical industry, and its partial and continuous co-optation of movements aimed at restricting the use of "dangerous" drugs. The fact is that a fair number of drugs with high abuse potential remain legitimate and available. The manipulations by the pharmaceutical industry were noted above in our discussion of the Harrison Act of 1914. Similarly, the paint, hempseed oil, and birdseed industries received exemptions for sterilized marijuana seeds in the enactment of the Marijuana Tax Act of 1937. Thus, even though there have been increasing governmental regulations placed on the type and quality of drug preparations and their raw materials, vested economic interests have managed to maintain some semblance of the *status quo*. In fact, the new regulations have served more to inhibit new competition than to restrict old interests. As long as certain regulations pertaining to taxes, registry, and the like are adhered to, manufacture of the substances can continue unabated. Typically, quantities are limited only by the demands of the marketplace.

A less obvious effect of the pharmaceutical industry on the drug scene in America has been discussed at some length by Erich Goode. It is Goode's argument that the pharmaceutical industry "is to a large degree producing and nurturing the drug problem in the United States" (1972:126). His reasoning is based on the economic premise that it is to the advantage of this industry to create a need or desire for its legitimate products under as many circumstances as possible. He points to the enormous advertising programs of the industry as evidence of these efforts.

A case in point is the industry's campaign in the late 1960's promoting a drug known by the generic name of methaqualone (brand names include Parest, Quaalude, Sopor, Optimil, and Somnafac). This particular drug was promoted as the answer for physicians concerned with prescribing addictive barbiturates for their patients. Methaqualone is a non-barbiturate, sedative/hypnotic which is prescribed as a sleeping pill or tranquilizer. Goode (1972:127) describes one advertisement citing the need for the drug, which appeared in the May 17, 1971 issue of *The Journal of the American Medical Association*. The text, accompanied by photographs of distraught faces, describes a middle-aged housewife unable to sleep the night before her daughter's wedding. The advertisement clearly depicts life circumstances as more manageable with the help of a drug. Goode's (1972) conclusion about this kind of promotion, side by side with an escalating drug problem, is: "The greater the number of circumstances in which prescription drugs are called for, the greater the climate of tolerance of drug use, both legal and illegal."

Even if one rejects Goode's analysis of the pharmaceutical industry's function in increasing overall drug use and concomitant social tolerance for such behavior, a second, perhaps more important, contribution to the drug problem is evidenced by the methaqualone example. In 1965, the first American brand of methaqualone, Quaalude, was marketed with a promotional campaign which highlighted it as a drug producing similar effects to barbiturates, but claimed it was "non-addictive." This claim was advanced, even though there was evidence from Japan, where methaqualone had been used for a number of years that, in fact, the substance was addictive. Even after methaqualone addicts began appearing in America in some numbers (late 1970), the drug companies were still promoting the claim that such dependence was not clearly indicated. The legacy in our society of acceptance for "legitimate" drug use thus still may have an impact on efforts to eliminate "illegitimate" use.

Chapter 8
Alcohol Use

> Civilization may be conceived of as the dignifying of human existence through adornment, and is achieved by the exploitation of surplus to devise need, gratifications not strictly related to survival. . . . Civilization thus conceptualized necessarily imposes a two-sided problem on man. In order to keep these two aspects analytically distinct, they will be referred to as the source and the burden of civilization. (Harold Fallding, 1964:714)

THE SOCIAL CONSTRUCTION OF REALITY
Alcohol and Relativity

Alcohol is one of the products of "surplus" that many have become dependent upon, and the effects of the abuse of alcohol have had far-reaching consequences in our society. The abusive use of alcohol, which generally means a condition of alcoholism, is a complex and confusing phenomenon found among peoples throughout the world. The problems of alcohol use and abuse vary from nation to nation, and even within the same society. Some cultures are basically abstinent by tradition, but this does not mean that they are free of the problems of alcohol use and abuse. The Islamic peoples and the Hindu peoples both have a strong anti-alcohol component in their cultures, and both equate the drinking of alcohol with amoral or anti-religious behavior. Despite the power of religion within their cultures, many who live in those cultures still drink alcoholic beverages (Bales, 1946:87). An interesting point about drinkers in a non-drinking culture is that they have a very high rate of alcoholism, or alcohol-related problems. This is true not only in exotic cultures, but in North America as well. For example, though there is very little drinking among Mormons in the United States (that being a traditionally abstinent religious subculture), among Mormon *drinkers* the rate of alcoholism is very high

(Bacon, 1957:179-181). Western culture in general is rather ambivalent toward the use of alcohol. This ambivalence tends to interfere with the development of concrete and stable attitudes toward drinking, and, in turn, with the development of social controls which the culture can exert upon the drinking behavior of the individual.

In order to study alcohol use and abuse, one must be aware of the cultural context within which each society defines these practices. Differences in definition occur relative not only to the use, non-use, or abuse of alcohol, but even to the very reasons or goals for its use. In nations such as France, Italy, Spain, and Portugal, alcohol, primarily wine, is regarded as a staple food, that is, as a necessary component of the daily diet. These people do not need alcohol in the sense of being addicted to it; rather, it is the common liquid accompaniment to the meal (Sadoun and Lolli, 1963:449-458). Even though the extensive use of alcohol as a beverage is acceptable in all of these societies, only the French appear to demonstrate a high rate of problems related to its use. Other cultures, such as the Jews and the Japanese, use alcohol extensively in a ritualistic and institutional context. While not tolerated within the Jewish culture, alcohol abuse and its accompanying anti-social behavior are excusable in Japan, since, according to the Japanese interpretation, the alcohol is to blame and not the drinker (Pitman, 1967:10-11). Some peoples, such as the Lepchas of the Himalayas and the Cambas from Bolivia, often drink until they are very intoxicated. However, in both of these societies, the drunkenness takes the "form of jollification and loquacity" (Horton, 1959:257-258); aggressive, violent, and obnoxious behavior are noticeably absent during drinking episodes in both of these cultures. In contrast, here in North America, drunkenness is often associated with obnoxious, anti-social, and aggressive behavior.

Definitions and Interpretations

Alcoholism, as distinct from drunkenness, has a wide range of definitions. Just as drinking practices and behavior differ throughout the world, so does the conception of the problems related to the "abuse" of alcohol, or alcoholism. However, at this juncture we will confine ourselves primarily to the definition of alcoholism accepted here in North America. There is no uniformity as to what constitutes alcoholism, even within our own culture. The definition is dependent on many factors, not the least of which is the social characteristics of the person whose behavior is being defined, and the characteristics of those individuals or groups who are doing the defining, that is, the labeling. Definitions of alcoholism are usually associated with a particular theory of etiology, and give more attention to one kind of symptom than others—e.g., physiological factors over psychological or sociological factors. However, when we look at the various definitions of alcoholism, it appears that they generally have two elements in common. One is drinking, and the other is some type of damage to the person caused by the drinking. The damage may be physiological, psychological, or social.

The most prevalent conception of alcoholism, at least among professionals, is that alcoholism is a disease. This suggests, of course, that the definition of alcoholism should be sought for and found in the medical literature. Medicine has referred to alcoholism as a disease or an illness for well over 150 years. However, it was not until the middle 1930's that this definition actually came to be accepted by a majority of the medical profession. The American Medical Association's standard nomenclature of diseases and operations defines alcoholism in the following way: "Alcoholism is a disease in the category of addictions. It is a personality disorder of a sociopathic variety" (Plunkatt and Hayden, 1961:11).

E. M. Jellinek, until his death in the 1960's, was recognized as the world's leading authority on alcoholism. He used a very simple operational definition of alcoholism: "Any use of alcoholic beverages that causes any damage to the individual or society, or both" (Jellinek, 1960:35). This definition is simple and understandable, but not specific enough for scientific purposes.

Another definition was offered by an early research committee of the World Health Organization, which concluded that alcoholism is a chronic disease, and that it is etiologically associated either with personality deviation or with the pharmacological properties of alcohol, or perhaps with both, either simultaneously or successively. This definition allows for either a psychological or a physiological interpretation (World Health Organization, *First Report,* 1954).

One clear psychological definition of alcoholism has been advanced by psychologists with a behavior-modification orientation, who define alcoholism as a psychological ailment, a learned response to stress. In other words, alcoholics learn to use alcohol as a means of avoiding or alleviating psychic pain. Many sociologists, on the other hand, use a "labeling" perspective when defining alcoholism, according to which alcoholism is a "label" externally applied to an individual's drinking pattern by the social-control institutions and their agents, which define his behavior as deviant. While both of these definitions recently have gained considerable support in the academic world, they are regarded with much skepticism by those directly concerned with the treatment of alcoholics.

The one definition probably most acceptable to those professional and lay people who are working in the field of alcoholism was provided by the World Health Organization in its second report on alcoholism in 1955. This definition states that alcoholism is a condition which is said to exist when an individual's drinking has reached such a degree that it is creating increasingly serious problems in one or more areas of his normal life, i.e., domestic, social, or vocational; and defines the chief characteristic of the illness as the inability to control one's drinking

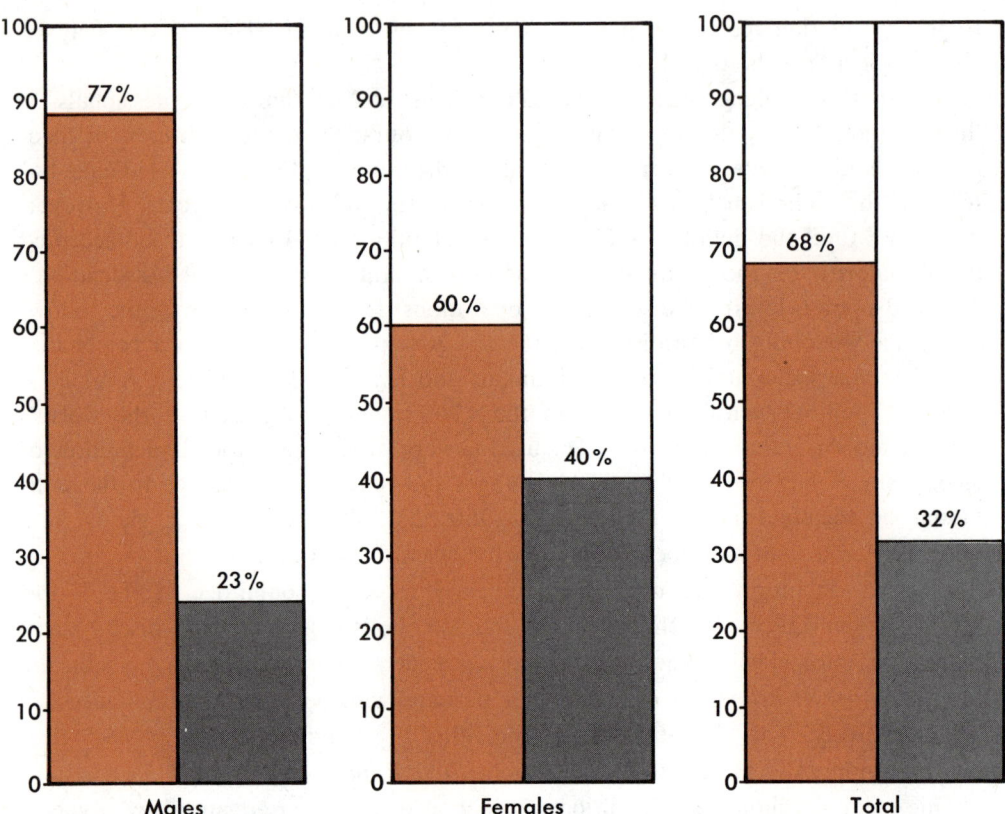

Figure 8-1 Percent of Adult Population Who Are Drinkers, by Sex
SOURCE: U.S. Department of Health, Education, and Welfare, "First Special Report to the U.S. Congress on Alcohol and Health," DHEW publication no. (HSM) 72-9099, Washington, D.C.: Government Printing Office, 1971

once it has started (W.H.O., 1955). Throughout this chapter, we will use this definition of alcoholism, unless otherwise indicated.

Parameters of Consensual Reality

In most areas of the United States, drinking of alcoholic beverages is typical behavior, while both serious alcohol-related behavior problems and total abstinence are atypical behavior. Nevertheless, the problem of alcoholism is generally considered the third most serious public-health problem in the United States today, surpassed in magnitude only by cancer and heart disease. Some even feel that it is our number one health problem (Bell, 1970). Estimates of the number of alcoholics are among the most publicized and most challenged statistics on the problem of alcoholism. Among the most recent statistics presented was an estimate of between nine and ten million alcoholics, regarded as a conservative figure (U.S. Department of Health, Education, and Welfare, 1971). If we couple this estimate with the fact that each alcoholic directly affects four or five other persons (family, close friends, working companions, and so on), then the problem involves at least 40 or 50 million people. The effects of alcoholism are seen not only in the loss of human potential, but also in the loss of economic goods and services. According to Bell (1970), alcoholism is costing American industry over 7.5 billion dollars annually. The unknown and/or unreported effects of the alcoholic employee and

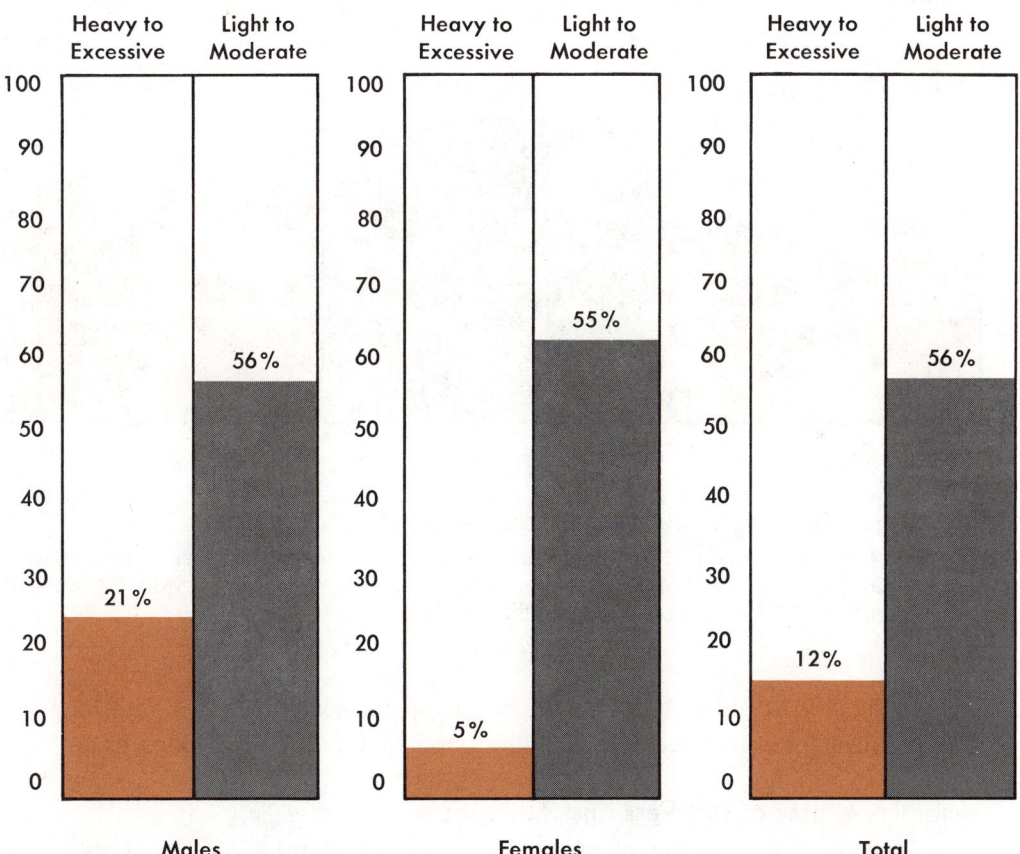

Figure 8-2 Percent of Adult Population Who Are Heavy-Excessive and Light-Moderate Drinkers, by Sex

SOURCE: U.S. Department of Health, Education, and Welfare, "First Special Report to the U.S. Congress on Alcohol and Health," DHEW publication no. (HSM) 72-9099, Washington, D.C.: Government Printing Office, 1971

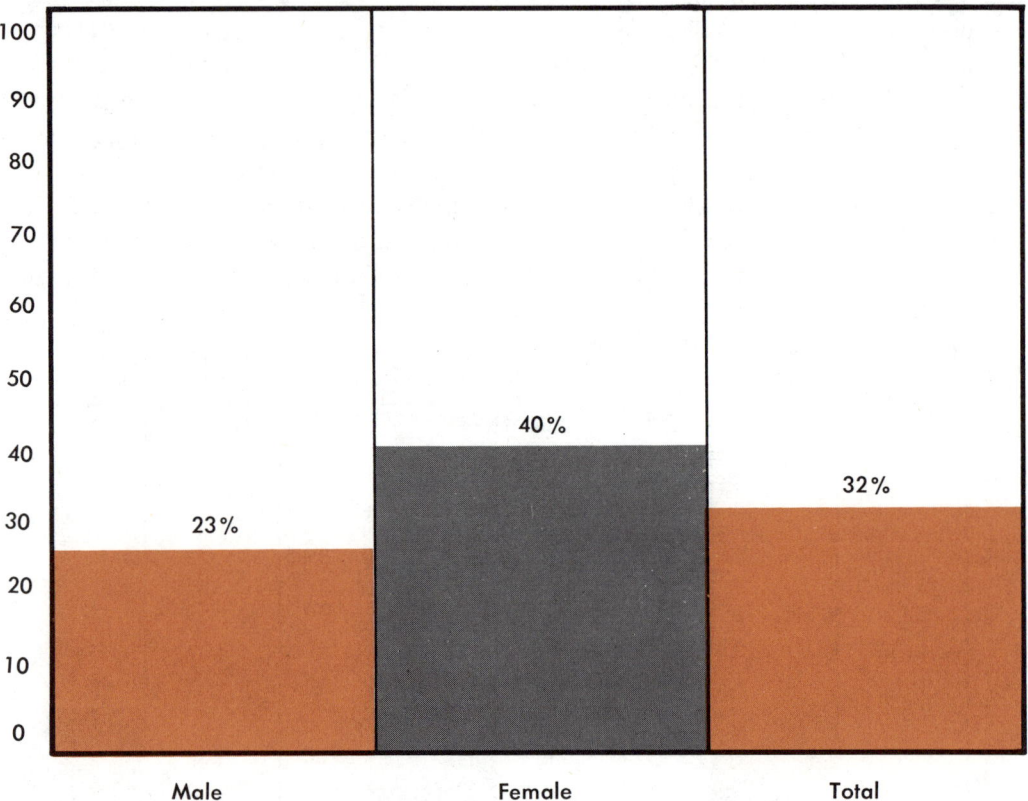

Figure 8-3 Percent of Adult Population Who Do Not Drink, by Sex
SOURCE: U.S. Department of Health, Education, and Welfare, "First Special Report to the U.S. Congress on Alcohol and Health," DHEW publication no. (HSM) 72-9099, Washington, D.C.: Government Printing Office, 1971

employer might match this figure. Before discussing further the question of drinking as a "problem," however, let us look at the extent and nature of drinking itself.

Social Correlates of Drinkers and Abstainers

SEX According to a number of national surveys and reported studies (Cahalan, Cissan, and Crossley, 1969; Cahalan, 1970; Cahalan and Room, 1972; Harris, 1971), about 68 percent of the adult population are defined as drinkers while 32 percent are defined as abstainers (see Figure 8-1). The figure for drinkers can be further broken down by sex differences, in which case approximately 77 percent of the males and 60 percent of the females are drinkers. Among the male drinkers,

Chapter 8 / Alcohol Use

21 percent are heavy-to-excessive drinkers, while 55 percent are light-to-moderate drinkers. When the figures for male and female drinking are combined, 12 percent are found to be heavy-to-excessive drinkers, while 56 percent are light-to-moderate drinkers (Figure 8-2). When the combined group of male and female abstainers of 32 percent is broken down by sex, we can see that this figure is derived from an abstinent male population of 23 percent and an abstinent female one of 40 percent (Figure 8-3). It should be noted that one-third of these abstainers, both male and female, were formerly drinkers who stopped due to alcoholism, physical problems, old age, or other reasons.

AGE The Harris survey of 1971 presented the following breakdown for drinkers

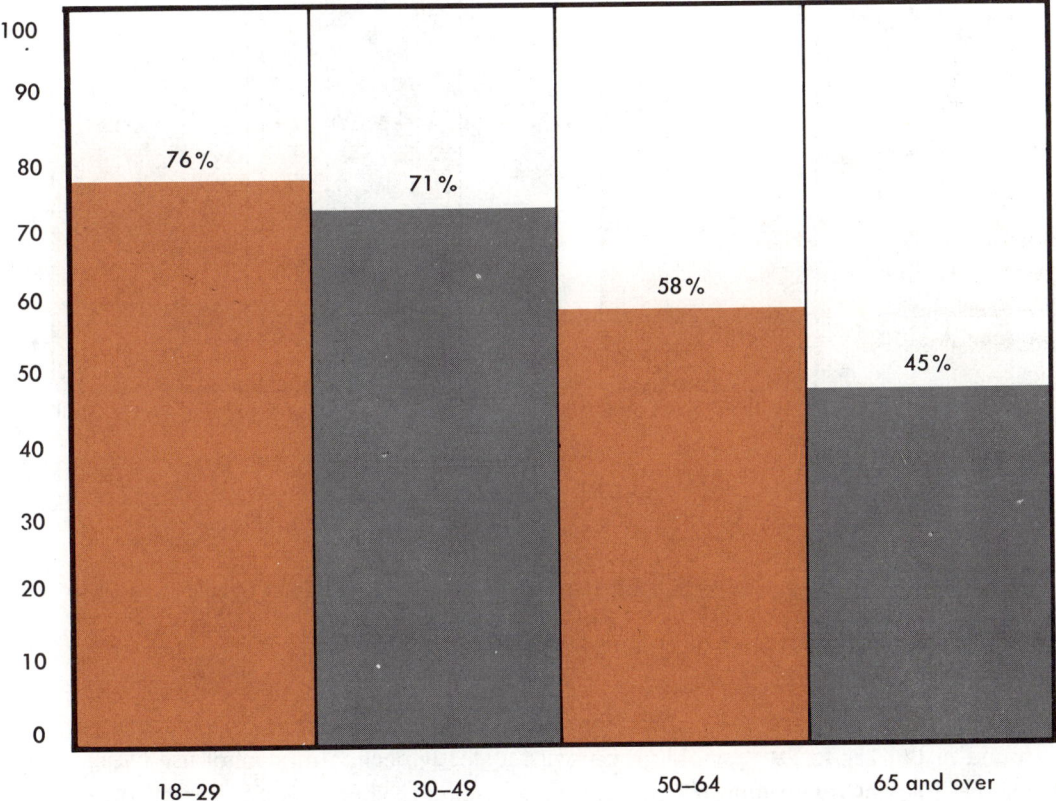

Figure 8-4 Percent of Adult Population Who Are Drinkers, by Age Grouping
SOURCE: U.S. Department of Health, Education, and Welfare, "First Special Report to the U.S. Congress on Alcohol and Health," DHEW publication no. (HSM) 72-9099, Washington, D.C.: Government Printing Office, 1971

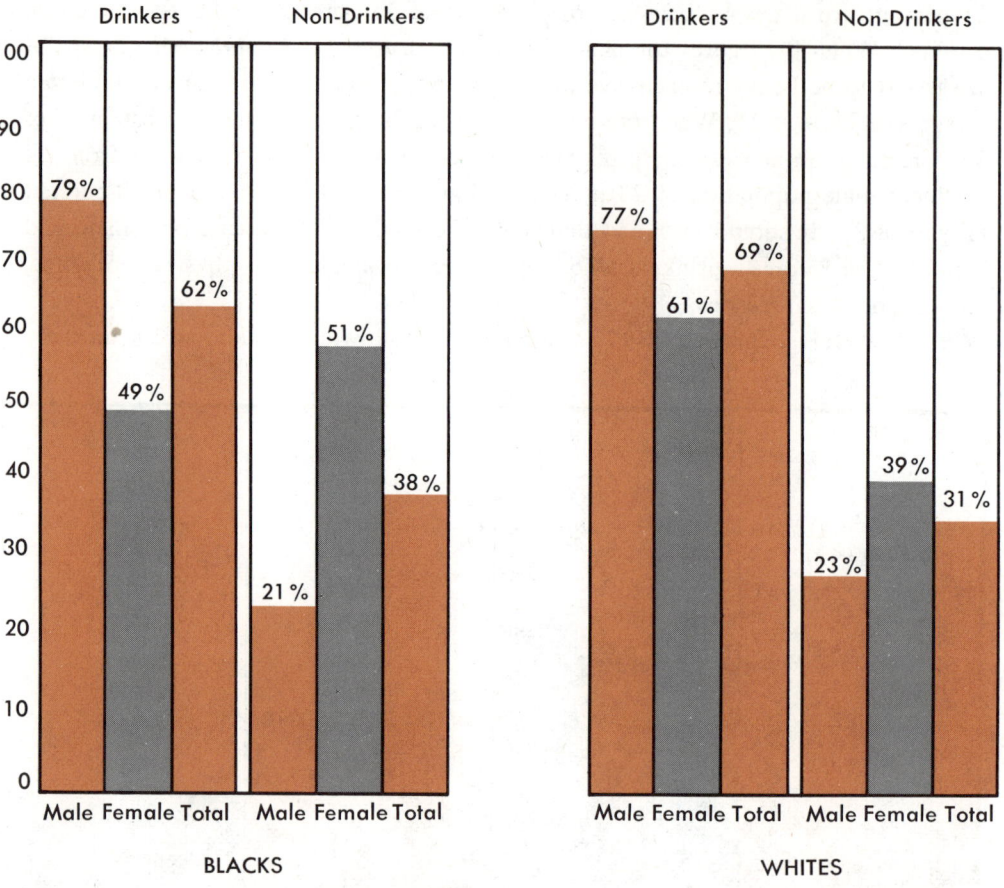

Figure 8-5 Percent of Adult Population Who Are Drinkers and Non-Drinkers, by Race (Black and White) and Sex

SOURCE: U.S. Department of Health, Education, and Welfare, "First Special Report to the U.S. Congress on Alcohol and Health," DHEW publication no. (HSM) 72-9099, Washington, D.C.: Government Printing Office, 1971

by age groups (Figure 8-4). The highest percentage of drinkers, 76 percent, was found in the 18- to 29-year-old group, with a steady decline in alcohol use by age. Of the 30- to 49-year-olds, 71 percent were drinkers, while only 58 percent of the 50- to 64-year-old group drank. The smallest percentage of drinkers was found in the over-65 group, in which only 45 percent were still drinkers. The highest percentage of drinkers, for both males and females, is thus found in the young-adult age groups. Also, the figures show that if a person drinks, the probability that he will continue to drink stays relatively high until he reaches about the middle

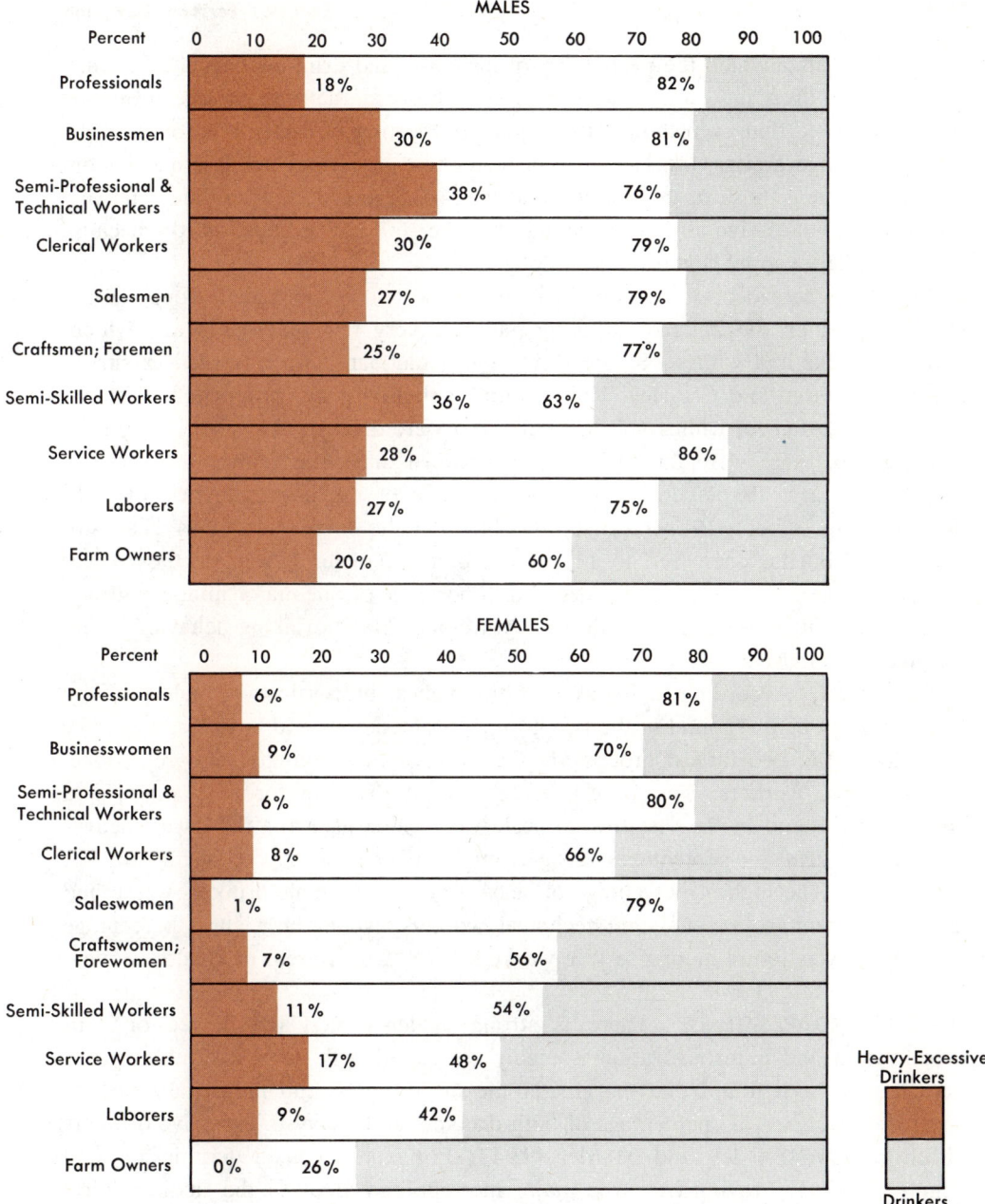

Figure 8-6 Percent of Adult Population Who Are Drinkers and Heavy-Excessive Drinkers, by Occupation and Sex

SOURCE: U.S. Department of Health, Education, and Welfare, "First Special Report to the U.S. Congress on Alcohol and Health," DHEW publication no. (HSM) 72-9099, Washington, D.C.: Government Printing Office, 1971

or late 30's, after which the probability of his continued drinking begins to decline. The steepest drop in drinking occurs among those in the over-65 age group. It should be noted that even though the highest proportion of drinkers is found in the young-adult age groups, the incidence of heavy-to-excessive drinking is much more prevalent among those in the middle- and late-40's age group. There are relatively few heavy-to-excessive drinkers among the over-60 age groups, partly because heavy drinkers simply don't live very long.

RACE   If we consider the differences between the two major racial groups in the United States on the basis of drinking patterns, very few differences are evident between blacks and whites (Figure 8-5). The American drinking-practices survey (Cahalan, Cissan and Crossley, 1969) found a slightly lower proportion of blacks (62 percent) than of whites (69 percent) who were drinkers. However, within the black group, there were large differences between male and female drinkers. Of the black males, 79 percent were drinkers, while of the black females, only 49 percent were. About 19 percent of the black males were classed as heavy-to-excessive drinkers, compared to 11 percent of the females (Cahalan, Cissan and Crossley, 1969). Considering the size and importance of our major minority group, beyond these figures relatively little is known about black drinking behavior, either normative or abusive.

OCCUPATION   According to Figure 8-6, the highest proportions of male drinkers by occupation can be found in the two groups, professionals and businessmen, while for females the two largest groups are the professionals and the semiprofessional and technical workers. The lowest percentage of drinkers for both males and females was found in the farm-owners category, which also had the lowest heavy-to-excessive drinkers percentages, 20 percent for males and 0 percent for females, respectively. The highest percentage of heavy-to-excessive male drinkers was found among the semiprofessional and technical workers, while the highest percentage for females was found among service workers (U.S. Department of Health, Education, and Welfare, 1971:27-28).

REGION AND RESIDENCE   There is strong evidence that the degree of both urbanization and industrialization is highly correlated with general drinking practices. It has been found that the greater the urbanization and industrialization of an area, the higher the percentage of both drinkers and heavy-to-excessive drinkers (Mulford, 1964; Riley and Marden, 1947; Fox and Lyon, 1955; deLint and Schmidt, 1974). Moving from the major metropolitan areas to the smaller cities, to the towns, and finally to the rural areas, there is a steady decline in both normative and abusive drinking. According to Akers (1973:117-120), the rate of drinking in urban areas compared to rural areas is about two-to-one. The highest proportion of both normative drinking and heavy-to-excessive drinking is found in the Middle Atlantic, Northeast, Pacific, and East North Central states. The lowest proportions of both drinking and heavy-to-excessive drinking are found in the "Bible Belt" states, running from Oklahoma to the Carolinas. The western and midwestern states have moderate rates of both normative and abusive drinking (Mulford, 1964:640-641, and Cahalan, 1970).

EDUCATION It appears that the higher the education, the more likely a person is to be a drinker. For both males and females, the lowest proportion of drinkers was found in the category of those with only a grammar-school education. The proportion increases as the education increases, with the group of college-educated males and females having the highest proportions of drinkers. However, the highest proportion of heavy-to-excessive drinkers was found among those who had completed only high school and those who had attended, but not completed, college (U.S. Department of Health, Education, and Welfare, 1971).

Social Correlates of Alcoholism

The social correlates of drinking behavior presented above indicate that drinking is an accepted part of the American way of life. However, while drinking *per se* is accepted, "abusive drinking" (alcoholism) is not accepted by the average citizen. It is one thing to drink; it is another to be a "drunk." So let us turn next to the question of who are the alcoholics in our society. The statistics on alcoholism and the alcoholic are usually not reliable or of scientific quality. Most statistics are gathered from known alcoholic populations, especially from those who have been participants in some type of treatment facility or program. Not included in the statistics are probably many alcoholics whose condition has not yet become public, either because their condition is still barely under control, or because their families and friends are "covering" for them. In spite of these limitations, we do have some descriptive data about the alcoholic population in America today.

First, most alcoholics, about 95 percent, are employable, family-centered individuals, meaning that their families and jobs are still central concerns to them as individuals. Probably less than 5 percent of the alcoholic population are the stereotyped skid row, unemployable social isolates (Wiseman, 1965:65; Bahr, 1973:228). Of those alcoholics who are employed, about 45 percent hold professional and/or managerial positions, 25 percent are white-collar workers, and 30 percent are manual laborers. Only about 13 percent of the alcoholic population have only a grammar-school education or less, while 37 percent have at least some high-school education. Interestingly, about 50 percent of the alcoholics have attended college, with a significant number being college graduates (U.S. Department of Health, Education, and Welfare, 1971). The average age of the alcoholic appears to be somewhere in the late 30's and early 40's (Trice, 1966:39). However, this age group is probably more representative of the alcoholics in treatment than of all alcoholics, because of the fact that most alcoholics do not become readily known or available to be counted until the illness has progressed to a fairly severe stage. Another characteristic of the alcoholic population is that the ratio of male to female alcoholics has been steadily declining for the past few years as the female alcoholic has become a more common phenomenon and/or perhaps more involved in traditional alcoholism treatment programs, thus beginning to appear in the statistics (Mulford, 1964). Recently, a ratio of three male to one female alcoholic was estimated (Kinsey, 1966:4-6), but many researchers in the field of alcoholism feel that the ratio is closer to two-to-one. If we were to draw a "profile" of the typical alcoholic, he would be a 40-year-old white middle-class male with a wife and two children, living in an urban area, and employed. Interestingly, the typical alcoholic profile resembles the profile of the average male American!

Public Opinion

Alcoholism is what we may term an "involuntary problem"; that is, the alcoholic neither tries nor wants to be a problem, but by the nature of the alcoholic process, he cannot help ending up in conflict with the social world. The alcoholic often appears to the general public as an alienated individual. The common conception of the alcoholic as either a skid row bum, homeless and helpless, or as a solitary drinker who is attempting to escape from the reality of his life situation, has influenced the thinking of many about alcoholism and the alcoholic process (Trice, 1966:14; Plaut, 1967:21-22; Cahn, 1970:2; Fort, 1973:10). The definition of the alcoholic as a "drunk who lacks willpower to control his drinking" is not an idea that died with Prohibition (Bell, 1970:53-54); it is still very prevalent and will continue to exist as long as people remain ignorant about the etiology and development of alcoholism. If a random sample of the public was asked to describe the alcoholic, the characterization probably would closely resemble the "skidder"—a late-middle-aged, slovenly dressed, unshaven, staggering, intoxicated "bum." His face would be flushed; perhaps he would have a bulbous nose; and cuts and bruises would be evident. He would live in a hotel or flophouse on skid row, and would be supported by public assistance or a veteran's pension. He would have no assets, and would be considered a complete liability to society. Public reaction to this characterization might range from, "He's a no good, lazy drunk," to "He's a lost soul."

Thus in 1946, in a national survey on public opinion about alcoholism, conducted by J. W. Riley of Rutgers University, over 50 percent felt that alcoholics were nothing more than people who got drunk too often, and that they could stop drinking if they really wanted to (Riley and Marden, 1947:265-273). In 1958, the Roper polling organization also conducted a national survey, in which they found that over 35 percent of those polled still saw the alcoholic as a morally bad person, rather than as someone suffering from an illness (Jellinek, 1960: 182-183).

But within this larger and somewhat homogeneous picture of the alcoholic as a morally reprehensible figure, there is a definite difference of public opinion on alcoholism according to the perceived social class of the individual alcoholic. The middle-class alcoholic is seen as a person with a drinking problem, an illness, and in need of medical help. The lower-class alcoholic is seen as a derelict, a lush, or a bum (Pittman, 1967:8). Another misconception derives from the fact that the middle-class alcoholic is not as visible, and is more likely to be protected by his environment. Thus the average citizen receives his impressions from the alcoholic he may see in bars and public places, and mistakenly characterizes him as a "public drunk." Even two of the very best Hollywood-produced movies in which alcoholism was depicted, "The Lost Weekend" (1940's) and "Days of Wine and Roses" (1960's), gave the impression that the alcoholic was a person with easily identifiable characteristics, chief of which was the ever-present public drunkenness syndrome. This labeling process has extended so far as to influence the goals and perceptions of those in the positions of power who could do something about the problem of alcoholism. This inaccurate identification of the alcoholic, and consequently of the alcoholism problem, has resulted in more time, money, and energy spent in dealing with that 5 percent of the alcoholic population found on skid row, as opposed to the 95 percent of the alcoholic population found in middle-class America (Fort, 1973:15-16). In the end, we find that as a result of the lack of agreement as to who is labeled alcoholic, the resources that have been brought to bear on alcoholism have been dispersed and diffused, and have had little impact on the control and prevention of alcoholism.

Public opinion on alcoholism is obviously negative, whether it derives from moral indignation or from humanitarian concerns. On the other hand, the public attitude toward social drinking is primarily a positive one. We are continually bombarded with the image of drinking as a necessary component of success in our society. In television, the movies, magazines, and books, alcohol, often a particular type and brand, goes hand in hand with happiness, relaxation, success, sex, upward mobility, and the good life. Ads such as the following are typical:

Pleasure without end. . . . Get your party off the ground with Smirnoff. . . . The world's most popular Christmas club—Canadian Club. . . . Give the people *you* like . . . whiskey they like. . . . I never say no to Catto. . . . In beer going first class is Michelob.

Drinking is always portrayed in ads as being enjoyable and desirable, and never is there a hint of the possible negative consequences of alcohol abuse. Thus, we have a conflict in public opinion relative to the use of alcohol. Obviously, to drink is to be part of the American scene and all that it entails; however, to be a "drunk," i.e., an alcoholic, is to be rejected and avoided. We desire the positive identification with alcohol, but not the negative identification, and the interesting thing is that many Americans have achieved the total separation of these two phenomena, i.e., drinking and alcoholism. We may be aware that drinking can lead to alcoholism; however, in most cases, we say, "It couldn't happen to me."

CHAMPIONS AND THEIR INTERESTS

The ambivalence toward alcohol in American public opinion has expressed itself also in a variety of interest groups on both the "wet" and the "dry" sides of the alcohol consumption issue, and in a proliferation of scientific theories of alcoholism. With respect to the *consumption* of alcohol, the interest groups are primarily economic or moral and religious.

Economic Interests

Industry in general has developed a strong interest in the "problem of alcoholism" because of the effects of that problem upon industrial output. It is estimated that, through lost time and productivity, medical expenses, and accidents, American industry loses about six-billion dollars annually (Fort, 1973:117), as a direct result of worker alcoholism. It is this economic loss, coupled with the belief that alcoholism is a treatable illness, that has triggered the concern over alcoholism and the subsequent development by a number of major corporations and labor unions of industrial alcoholism rehabilitation programs. The following is only a partial list of more than 350 companies and organizations that have initiated alcoholism programs:

Alcoa
Allis-Chalmers Manufacturing
American Can
American Cyanamide
American Telephone & Telegraph
Bell Telephone of Canada
Bethlehem Steel
Burlington Northern
Caterpillar Tractor
Commonwealth Edison
Consolidated Edison (NY)
Corning Glass Works
Carpenter Technology Corporation
Detroit Edison
Employers Insurance of Wasau

Eastman Kodak
E. I. duPont de Nemours
Kennecott Copper (Utah Division)
Lever Brothers
Lockheed
Merrill, Lynch, Pierce,
   Fenner & Smith
Metropolitan Life
New England Telephone & Telegraph
New England Electric System
New York Telephone Company
New York Times
New York Transit Authority
North American Aviation
John Hancock

Endicott Johnson Corporation
Equitable Life Assurance Society
Fireman's Fund American
General Dynamics, Electric
   Boat Division
General Electric
General Motors
Hughes Aircraft
Humble Oil & Refining
Imperial Oil Company, Ltd.
Ingersoll-Rand
Inland Steel
IBM
Kemper Insurance Group
The Norton Company
Olin Corporation
Owens-Illinois Glass
Peoples Gas, Light, and Coke
Prudential Insurance
Standard Oil of New Jersey
The Texas Company
Tulsa Bar Association
Union Carbide
U.S. Civil Service Commission
U.S. Postal Service
Western Electric

Most industrial programs attempt to identify the alcoholic employee on the basis of his job performance. Supervisors and foremen are trained to look for the symptoms of decreased job performance, rather than to diagnose alcoholism *per se*. Diagnosis is usually handled by the medical staff, consultants, or, in some cases, the company alcoholism personnel. The alcoholic employee, once diagnosed, is referred to a treatment center with the company stipulation that if recovery progresses, employment will be maintained. Often, even if the treatment requires hospitalization or in-patient residency at an alcoholism center, the company and/or union will maintain the employee on salary or will grant him sick leave.

The success rates claimed by industrial programs range from 65-80 percent, which are probably the highest rates of any treatment program. One of the obstacles to the spread of such industrial programs, however, is the hesitancy of many companies and unions to admit that "such a thing could be present in our organization."

While industry in general may have an interest in reducing the consumption of alcohol among its employees, there are other economic interests which stand to benefit from increased alcohol consumption among the public at large. Though the United States does not have the highest per capita alcohol consumption (this dubious honor goes to France), its consumption rate is easily among the ten highest in the world. Such high consumption represents billions of dollars annually in both business profits and tax revenues. However, since the sheer amount of alcohol consumed is not necessarily related to alcoholism, the liquor industry and the government have been able to justify their roles in the production, distribution, and taxation of alcohol. Judging from the scope and intensity of the advertising of a multitude of alcoholic beverages, the alcohol industry constitutes one of America's largest economic interests.

The liquor industry has traditionally avoided the question of excessive alcohol abuse, relying on the argument that "if the public didn't want it, they wouldn't buy it." On the other hand, many governments, including the federal government, have found themselves in the ironic position of funding alcoholism treatment and rehabilitation programs through the direct allocation of liquor tax revenues. In many state and local jurisdictions, the more the public drinks, the greater the amount of money flowing into government bureaucracies which can be used for the control of liquor consumption and the treatment of alcoholics.

The states of Washington, Georgia and Iowa, to name only a few, have contributed considerable sums of money to establish, develop and maintain state alcoholism prevention and treatment programs. More recently, due primarily to the efforts of Senator Harold Hughes of Iowa, the federal government has enacted legislation, the Comprehensive Alcohol Abuse and Alcoholism Act of 1970, and appropriated about 300 million dollars for treatment and prevention programs and research over a three-year period.

Moral and Religious Interests

Where alcohol behavior is concerned, no interests have been more intense, or more vigorously pursued, than moral and religious ones. Sometimes the churches themselves, and individual clergymen, have been in the forefront of the struggle against what has been called "demon rum," particularly those churches most closely associated with the conservative Protestant tradition. More often, however, the organizations seeking to restrict or prevent drinking have been moralistic social and political ones, often backed by religious groups, but distinct from them. They offer classical examples of Becker's "moral entrepreneurs," and will be described in the next section on social movements, since they are primarily responsible for the creation of alcohol drinking as a "social problem." Historically, these interest groups made no distinction between alcohol use and alcohol "abuse"; they considered both part of the same problem. If drinking were not allowed, they reasoned, there would be no drunkenness or alcoholism. Their efforts, therefore, were concentrated on eliminating drinking altogether, and their point of view eventually came to be embodied in the 18th Amendment to the Constitution, which prohibited the sale or manufacture of alcoholic liquors. After the debacle and repeal of that amendment, however, prohibition organizations lost most of their power and prominence, and, for the past few decades, the focus of alcohol "moral entrepreneurs" has been more upon alcohol abuse or alcoholism than upon drinking.

Anti-Alcohol Organizations

Temperance, which originally was used to mean moderation in drinking, came to be defined as total abstinence by the "temperance movement" (Mann, 1973:6). As early as 1812, temperance societies began to spring up in the United States.

One of the better-known of these was the Washington Temperance Society (later known as the "Washingtonians"), started in Baltimore in April, 1840, by six drinking companions (Bell, 1970:56). Their original aim, like that of most early temperance organizations, was mainly to help alcoholics and those who were "excessive" drinkers, but they were eventually absorbed into the broader prohibition movement. While the organization welcomed non-drinkers to their cause, they wanted mainly to offer their knowing and sympathetic help as "reformed drinkers" to those who were suffering from alcohol problems. After a few decades of effort by the temperance societies, the anti-alcohol movement acquired a more specifically political expression in the form of the Prohibition Party, started in 1853 by some of the more militant temperance people, and still with us as the oldest third-party movement in our country. While its principal goal was to eliminate all liquor commerce and industry, it was in many respects part of the larger populist movement of that period, which had a rural base and a general hostility toward big business and urban industrial life.

During the 1850's and 1860's, the prohibition issue was eclipsed temporarily by the abolition controversy and the ensuing Civil War, but afterward, with the arrival of the "Gilded Age" in the "sinful seventies," the Prohibition Party was rejuvenated and joined by still another powerful organization of moral entrepreneurs who were able to tie religious organizations even more tightly to pressure politics: the Anti-Saloon League. Growing out of an alliance of temperance societies in the 1870's, the Anti-Saloon League was officially organized in 1895 under the leadership of Reverend R. Russell. The League was dedicated both to the elimination of alcoholic beverages and to the destruction of the saloon as an evil institution in American life. Its propaganda attempted to create a public abhorrence of the saloon, and to tie alcohol to subversive and unAmerican influences. A great deal of attention was given, for example, to the fact that the major beer brewers all had German names, such as Pabst, Schlitz, Blatz, or Miller, a theme that became increasingly prominent with the onset of World War I. Racist and ethnocentric propaganda was very common in the League's official publication, *The American Issue,* such as, for example, this passage in the April, 1912, issue (page 1): "The Anglo-Saxon stock is the best improved, heartiest and fittest. . . . If we are to preserve this nation in the Anglo-Saxon type, we must abolish saloons."

Of all the anti-alcohol organizations in our history, perhaps the best-known is the WCTU, or Women's Christian Temperance Union, organized in 1874 as "an organization of Christian women banded together for the protection of the home, the abolition of liquor traffic, and the triumph of Christ's Golden Rule in custom and in law" (Gordon, 1924:4). One early commentator suggested that the WCTU was one of the most powerful moral reform movements in the history of the world (Cherrington, 1920), second only to organized religion. From the beginning, the WCTU stood for conservative Protestant middle-class respectability, and its reformist efforts tended to be directed mainly at the looser, if more downtrodden, lower classes. The WCTU offered the first (or surely one of the first) opportunities in American history for the large-scale political participation of women, and a good many women who received their "training" in WCTU went on to involvement in other political causes, such as female suffrage. Indeed, with Frances Willard as its president in the 1880's, the WCTU branched out and took an interest in a number of the other social issues taken up by the rising Progressive movement, such as feminism, penal reform, child labor, and prostitution.

Alcoholism Organizations

The best-known and most effective interest group in the fight against alcoholism is undoubtedly Alcoholics Anonymous (AA), founded in 1935, in Akron, Ohio, by a surgeon and a broker, both alcoholics. This organization drew partly upon the Washingtonian tradition, mentioned earlier, and partly upon the Oxford movement, a more generalized moral reform or "rearmament" group founded in the early 1920's by Dr. Frank N. Buchman, a Lutheran minister. From the Oxford movement, AA took the ideas of confession, openness, testimonials, small discussion groups, and prayer, while from the Washingtonians they took the ideas of fellowship and mutual dependence in the struggle with alcoholism, weekly meetings, and total abstinence from alcohol (Gellman, 1964:22, and Bell, 1970:55-59). Besides promoting some of the ideals of the Oxford and Washingtonian movements, the two AA founders adopted and nurtured the idea of alcoholism as a disease, which could not be cured but could be indefinitely arrested through abstinence. Also instead of the more aggressive recruiting techniques of the Oxford and Washingtonian groups, AA emphasized the "fellowship of attraction." Other principles that have characterized AA from the beginning have been anonymity, and the avoidance of alliances with other groups, however well-intentioned. This latter rule was so that their energies would not be siphoned off into other causes, as had happened to so many of the earlier organizations we have mentioned.

In 1935, shortly after the founding of AA, the Yale Group came into existence at Yale University's Laboratory of Applied Physiology, under the leadership of Dr. Howard W. Haggard. This group is somewhat remarkable for its combining of academic and scientific interests in alcoholism with those of rehabilitation of the alcoholic. Dr. Haggard had become interested in alcoholism after observing that only a few drinkers developed serious problems related to alcohol use, while most drinkers did not (Mann, 1973:7). This phenomenon called for extensive research. The well-known alcoholism expert Dr. E. M. Jellinek joined the Yale Group, and he and Dr. Haggard developed an extensive program of research and education on alcoholism. They founded the Yale Center of Alcohol Studies (1940) and the *Quarterly Journal of Studies on Alcohol* (1940), the most important professional journal in the field. Other important activities of the Yale Group have been the Yale Summer School of Alcohol Studies (beginning 1943), and the Yale Plan Clinic (mid-1940's), the first out-patient diagnostic and treatment clinics for alcoholics in the United States (Jellinek, 1960:9). In more recent years, the Yale Group has moved to Rutgers University.

Scientific Interests and Theories

Within the academic and scientific communities we can find a number of groups devoted to the study of alcoholism with varying theories and interests. Scientists have focused primarily upon the question of the etiology and development of alcoholism. Scientific concern, furthermore, has been with the discovery and development of causal explanations, rather than with preventive measures, new treatment methods, and so on. Let us briefly review the various theories or constructions of reality about alcoholism that have been promulgated by scientific disciplines and theorists.

Alcoholism is a complex and complicated problem, the etiology of which is still far from understood. Theories about its causation are almost as numerous and varied as the number of scientific and professional disciplines that are concerned with the problem. As of yet, no single theory has proved adequate to explain all of the aspects of the multifaceted problem termed "alcoholism," "alcohol dependence," or "alcohol addiction" (U.S. Department of Health, Education, and Welfare, 1971). It is most likely that the condition of alcoholism reflects an interactive combination of sociological, psychological, and physiological factors in an individual, and between an individual and his social environment (Chafetz and Demone, 1962). However, the most common theories have been advanced exclusively under the banner of one or another of the major academic disciplines, i.e., the physiological, psychological, or sociological perspectives.

Physiological Theories of Alcoholism

Under the rubric of physiological theories, we can find a number of competing conceptions of the etiology of alcoholism, all attempting to explain various aspects of the phenomenon by examining biochemical mechanisms or physiological functions and processes. The methods used have included both the observation of naturally occurring phenomena, and experimental studies. The major divisions of the physiological perspective comprise the genetic, endocrine, genetotrophic, and disease theories.

GENETIC THEORIES Genetic theories basically expound the idea that alcoholism is an inherited problem. Since alcoholism is more prevalent in the families of alcoholics than it is in the general population, it is possible that one can either inherit alcoholism directly, i.e., like one inherits color-blindness or blood type (Cruz-Coke,

1965:1131; Cruz-Coke and Varela, 1966:1282), or that one may inherit a susceptibility to the problem which is triggered by the introduction of alcohol into the system (McClearn and Rodgers, 1961:116-119; Jellinek, 1945:105). While genetic theories cannot be ruled out, the evidence for them is far from conclusive (U.S. Department of Health, Education, and Welfare, 1971:63; Edwards, 1970: 140-163).

ENDOCRINE THEORIES Alcoholism seems to lend itself readily to an explanation of endocrine malfunction, judging from the many studies to that effect (Gross, 1945:25-35; Lovell and Tintera, 1951:96-107; Richter, 1956:472-478; Tintera, 1949:274-278; Zarrow, Addus and Denison, 1960:400-413). Again, however, though there is some interesting evidence, it is not clear so far whether it shows alcoholism to be the effect or the cause of endocrine and glandular problems (U.S. Department of Health, Education, and Welfare, 1971:64).

GENETOTROPHIC THEORIES The basic idea of the genetotrophic theory is that each person has unique nutritional requirements, and that in some cases, due to an inherited defect, some individuals may require unusual amounts of some of the essential vitamins found in particular foods, i.e., they have a genetically caused nutritional deficiency. Given contact with alcohol, such individuals somehow develop a craving for and consequent addiction to it. Again, the evidence surrounding this view is mixed, with substantial studies both for (R. J. Williams, 1959: 452-463; Beerstecher et al., 1951; von Wartburg, 1970) and against (Lester and Greenberg, 1952:553; Mardones, 1960:41-76; Segovia-Riquelme et al., 1970) the theory.

DISEASE THEORIES The "disease" approach to the study of alcoholism might also be called a psychobiological one. This approach sees the development of alcoholism as a disease which progresses through a series of stages, culminating in a biological dependency on alcohol. The early psychobiological discussions were more concerned with biological causative factors than with the disease concept (Richmond, 1971:425-433). However, after the presentation of E. M. Jellinek's disease concept of alcoholism in 1946, psychobiological theory rapidly assumed a primary position in the study of the etiology of alcoholism (Jellinek, 1946:1-88).

Jellinek's theory holds that alcoholism is a disease which begins with a psychological dependency on alcohol, usually psychodynamic in origin, and in time develops into a biological dependency on alcohol. This process will, if the drinking continues, proceed through three stages: the prodromal, the crucial, and the critical. The key factor in the movement from a psychological to a physiological dependence is the loss of ability to control one's drinking.

The disease concept or theory of alcoholism has been adopted by more people working in the field of alcoholism than any other single theory. However, the theory has at least two very serious problems: (1) there is little or no empirical evidence for biological dependency on alcohol; and (2) there is no question that the disease concept as a model is an oversimplification of a complex phenomenon (Cahn, 1970:11).

Psychological Theories of Alcoholism

Increasingly, over the last few decades, science has been moving away from the purely physiological theories of etiology and turning more to psychological conceptions of alcoholism. The three major types of psychological theories are psychoanalytic, reinforcement-learning, and personality-trait theories.

PSYCHOANALYTIC THEORIES Clinical psychology and psychoanalysis have tended to view alcoholism as a manifestation of severe underlying neuroses. Many of the widely accepted psychoanalytic theories have emanated from classical Freudian thought, or are related to it in some way. Freud regarded alcoholism as an expression of self-destructive urges: the alcoholic is plagued with strong death wishes and wants to destroy himself (Norman, 1972:5). Karl Menninger suggests the Freudian variation that alcoholism is a form of self-destruction, addiction being the result of aversion toward even greater self-destruction (McCord and McCord, 1960: 28-29).

Freud also argued that the alcoholic is fixated at the oral stage of psychosexual development, that is, he still derives an abnormal pleasure from the insertion of objects into his mouth. A similar idea has been presented by Fenichel in his theory of neurosis; he feels that passive, narcissistic, dependent urges underlie alcoholism, and that the alcoholic wishes to use his mouth as the primary means to achieve gratification. He also notes that the cyclical nature of the "bender alcoholic" is very similar to the pattern of the manic-depressive psychotic, thus clearly tying the phenomenon of alcoholism to abnormal psychic states (Fenichel, 1945:378-379).

Perhaps the best-known psychoanalytic theory is that of alcoholism as a form of latent homosexuality. Freud discussed this theme, but it was Ferenczi and Abraham who popularized it. Ferenczi, using actual case studies, postulated that, because of a failure in the mother-child relationship, the child becomes fixated at the oral stage and develops an overidentification with the father (McCord and McCord, 1960:31). According to Abraham also, the alcoholic experiences severe frustration during the oral stage of development, and turns to the father to find solace from the frustrating mother. Overidentification with the father results in latent proclivities toward homosexuality, which are displaced by alcoholism (Fenichel, 1945:366-386).

Psychoanalyst Alfred Adler has argued that alcoholism is motivated by a need to strive for power, and a positive reaction to a pervasive feeling of power while drinking. Alcohol, through its anesthetizing qualities, temporarily decreases feelings of inferiority and leaves the person with a better self-concept (U.S. Department of

Health, Education, and Welfare, 1971:64). In a similar social vein, Robert White considers alcoholism to be "a result of suppressed conflicts between dependent drives and aggressive urges" (White, 1948:417).

Empirical evidence in support of the psychoanalytic theories has been inconclusive, primarily because these theories do not lend themselves readily to experimental investigation. McCord and McCord, in a 1956 follow-up study of participants in a 1945 study of delinquent youths, concluded that, generally speaking, the psychoanalytic theories had little utility in predicting alcoholism. Even though they found some support for the notion of oral dependency, their findings were far from significant. Like Landis (1945), furthermore, they found no support for a latent homosexuality theory (McCord and McCord, 1960:35), even though some earlier support for psychoanalytic theory as an explanation of alcoholism had been reported by Knight, as a result of his use of psychoanalysis in therapy (Knight, 1938:1443-1446).

REINFORCEMENT-LEARNING THEORIES An approach to the study of alcoholism which has gained wide acceptance in the therapeutic field is the reinforcement-learning theory, which sees alcoholism as the result of a drinker's learned responses to painful stimuli. In an attempt to avoid unpleasantness, he drinks and thereby achieves a feeling of well-being, blotting out a painful or tension-producing state.

> From observation, we know that many people who have once made the response of drinking alcohol continue to do so, and that some of them do so to excess. Through experience, the drinking response becomes learned. . . . it is learned because it is rewarding. (Conger, 1956:201-304)

This approach, although it has gained considerable support from a segment of the scientific community, also has some serious deficiencies as a general theory of alcoholism. There has been very little empirical evidence, outside of animal studies, that would support the contention that alcoholics experience any more fear, anxiety, or other learned tension-induced states than do non-alcoholics or even non-drinkers (Cahn, 1970:15). One could take the learning theory one step further and argue that, if the theory holds, then the very advanced alcoholic should stop drinking when his drinking behavior is no longer rewarded but rather is constantly punished. However, the application of learning theory to treatment has shown some success (Lemere and Voegtlin, 1955; Abrams, 1964:1160-1165; Kepner, 1964: 279-291; Keehn, Bloomfield, and Hug, 1970:602-615; Akers, 1973).

PERSONALITY TRAIT THEORIES A number of writers in the field of psychology have advanced the view of a distinct "alcoholic personality" type. In order to support this theory, both Blane and Lisansky have presented sets of personality characteristics which they felt are common to all alcoholics. These include high dependency needs, low frustration tolerance, inferiority complex, unresolved love-hate ambivalences, and low sociability (Blane, 1970:16-28). These and similar studies have failed, however, to identify a common personality structure which would be predictive of the onset of alcoholism (U.S. Department of Health, Education, and Welfare, 1971:66; Sutherland et al., 1950:547-561).

In general, psychological theories have stimulated considerable research and have broadened the scope of thinking on the subject of the etiology of alcoholism. While they have led to some successful applications in treatment, these theories have been generally unsuccessful in predicting or preventing alcoholism.

Sociological Theories of Alcoholism

Sociologists, like physiologists and psychologists, have comprised a scientific interest group in support of certain explanations of alcoholism. Generally, they have drawn upon all of the theories or deviance which we introduced in Chapter 1, particularly those of cultural transmission and differential association, symbolic interaction, and anomie.

CULTURAL TRANSMISSION THEORIES Probably the most comprehensive study of the relationship between alcoholism and sociocultural factors was conducted by Bales. He suggested three ways in which the culture and social organization of a society can influence the rates of alcoholism:

First is the degree to which culture operates to bring about acute needs for adjustment, or inner tensions, in its members. [Second is] . . . the sort of attitudes toward drinking which the culture produces in its members. . . . The crucial factor seems to be whether a given attitude toward drinking positively suggests drinking to the individual as a means of relieving his inner tensions, or whether such a thought arouses strong counter-anxiety. [Third is] . . . the degree to which the culture provides suitable substitute means of satisfaction. (Bales, 1959:263)

To substantiate the first point, Bales cites a previous study of Horton on the function of alcohol in primitive societies (Horton, 1959:251-262). In support of his second point, Bales used the results of his own study of the drinking practices of the Jews and the Irish (Bales, 1946:482-493). He distinguished four different sets of attitudes among people which he felt affected the alcoholism rates: (1) complete abstinence, found in some religious groups who totally forbid the use of alcohol; (2) ritualistic drinking, found in the ceremonial use of alcohol by orthodox Jews; (3) convivial drinking, a social ritual which may symbolize group unity or solidarity (this type of drinking was very evident among the Irish, who tended to drink on any and all occasions); and (4) utilitarian drinking, seen only in terms of the self-interest and personal satisfaction of the individual. Bales felt that the greatest number of alcoholics began as the fourth type of drinker (Bales, 1959: 267-277).

Bales discovered that the orthodox Jews had a very low alcoholism rate, which he concluded was related to their attitude limiting drinking to ritualistic purposes. On the other hand, the Irish exhibited a substantially higher alcoholism rate, which he attributed to their use of alcohol to escape from the problems they faced. A convivial attitude toward drinking also seemed to lend itself to the development of alcohol problems (Bales, 1946:490-493). Support for Bales' results relative to Jewish drinking behavior was supplied by Snyder in his study of the drinking practices of Jewish students and adults (Snyder, 1958). Other studies have also demonstrated the relationship between cultural and ethnic group values and alcoholism (Lolli, 1952; Williams and Strauss, 1952, 1953; Skolnick, 1954; Ullman, 1958).

A variation of the idea of cultural learning is that of differential association, first applied by Sutherland to the study of crime. The basic premises of this theory are that (1) all behavior, normative or deviant, is learned; (2) learning takes place in a cultural context; and (3) the individuals involved in this learning process are integrated into a social collectivity. The application of this perspective to alcoholism has been expressed as follows:

> . . . a subculture may condition its members to perform behaviors classified by another subculture as deviant. The significant other or other reference group in a person's life encourages such deviant behavior because of its own need to be permissive or to otherwise reward the behavior. (U.S. Department of Health, Education, and Welfare, 1971:67)

An individual may become an excessive drinker due to the interactive process in his group or subculture. This behavior, which is regarded as deviant by society in general, is accepted and rewarded within the group, thereby justifying the behavior to the individual. (For a detailed critique of Sutherland's theory of differential association, see Cressey, 1970:47-58; Gibbons, 1968:200-208; and Akers, 1973.)

SYMBOLIC INTERACTION THEORIES In the symbolic interactionist perspective, the alcoholic is seen as a person who, through a variety of circumstances, has become publicly labeled as a deviant and is forced by societal reaction to play a deviant role (Becker, 1963; Lemert, 1967, 1969; Rubington and Weinburg, 1971). Lemert has distinguished between primary and secondary deviance. Primary deviance is that behavior which causes a person to be labeled initially. This labeling can then lead to secondary deviance, which results from the societal reaction to the labeling, and culminates in the acceptance by the person of a deviant identity (Lemert, 1967:40-64).

One of the few writers to have actually utilized an interactionist approach in the study of alcoholism is Cahn. He outlined the process in this way:

... Alcoholism is a label attached to a drinking pattern defined as deviant by the social control institutions. There are at least eight variables involved in this labeling process. The way these variables interlock in time and social context determines whether someone is called an alcoholic. These variables are: (1) The quantity of alcohol consumed (It is obvious that there can be no alcoholism without alcohol, but quantity alone is insufficient for attaching an alcoholism label). . . . (2) The rate of consumption. . . . (3) Frequency of drinking episodes (A person who gets drunk three or four times a year is less likely to be labeled an alcoholic than someone who gets drunk every week). . . . (4) The effect of drunkenness upon self and others (A man who commits deviant sex acts or beats his wife while drunk is more likely to be labeled an alcoholic than a man who quietly gets drunk and leaves others alone). . . . (5) Visibility to society's significant labeling agents (The police, the judiciary, school personnel, welfare personnel, employers, and in some situations, social peers and helping agents, e.g., psychiatrists, physicians, psychotherapists, lawyers, are the key instruments of alcoholic labeling). . . . (6) The total social matrix of the person (There are different norms for different classes and status groups in the social system). . . . (7) The total problem syndrome of the drinking behavior (Problem drinking occurs in a problem behavior syndrome). . . . (8) The effectiveness of the formal and informal social controls (The social mores and legal controls are effective determinants of drinking patterns. Social mores that strongly regulate drinking behavior tend to keep drinking within socially acceptable limits). (Cahn, 1970:36-37)

While in a strict sense this approach does not specifically deal with the etiology of alcoholism, it does have possibilities for broadening the study of alcoholism.

ANOMIE THEORIES Probably the one theoretical outlook on the etiology of alcoholism that has been prevalent in the sociological literature has been anomie theory. Recall that we discussed the concept of anomie in Chapter 1 as part of the strain and control theoretical perspective on deviance. Principally, we find at least two conflicting versions regarding the relationship between the development of anomie and the development of alcoholism: (1) that anomie precedes alcoholism and is therefore a causal factor in its development or etiology; and (2) that anomie does not precede alcoholism but rather is a concomitant problem that develops after the onset of the alcoholic process.

Relative to the first, the most generally accepted version, the general scientific opinion has been summed up by Snyder in his statement that at both the inception and terminal stages of alcoholism, the alcoholic is an anomic person (Snyder, 1964:204). Evidence in support of this statement was found also in Park's study, in which he concluded that the personality dispositions of incipient alcoholics show a marked inability to act out social roles in accordance with the requirements of society (Park, 1962:431-456). Other work in support of this position includes that of Connor (1962:458-468); McCord and McCord (1962:413-430); Roman and Trice (1970:424-435); and Keith (1964).

The second version of the anomie/alcoholism theory is that the two problems develop together. Kinsey (1966) held that the concomitant development of anomie and alcoholism had much to do with the alcoholic's loss of control. Other important studies on this version of the anomie theory are by Kinsey and Phillips (1968), and by Phillips (1967 and 1973). In these studies, the general conclusion was that anomie was not found to be significantly present among early-stage alcoholics, and therefore should not be regarded as a causal factor in etiology of alcoholism, but that there was concomitant development of anomie after the onset of the illness.

The basis for all current theories about alcoholism and anomie, and one that favors the first relationship expressed above, was laid by Merton (1957:151-160), who distinguished several different types of anomie. One of these was retreatism, e.g., a retreat to alcohol by the individual who felt unable to gain access to legitimate means for achieving socially prescribed goals. The reaction of the retreatist is in the form of withdrawal from society or, as explained by Merton, the retreatist is "... strictly speaking *in* society but not *of* it ... not sharing the common frame of values (Merton, 1957:153). Merton definitely conceives of anomie as a predisposing factor in the advent of alcoholism. In his discussion of the feedback relationship between anomie and deviant behavior, he claims that anomie leads to deviance, which then leads to an increase in anomie (Merton, 1957:179-180). Cloward amplified Merton's theory by adding the idea of differential access of the deviant, not only to legitimate means but also to illegitimate means to socially prescribed goals (Cloward, 1949:164-176). And then Cloward and Ohlin went on to describe the alcoholic (especially the skidrower) as a "double failure," i.e., as one who has failed to utilize either the legitimate or the illegitimate means to achieve success (Cloward and Ohlin, 1960).

There is some support for all the different theories of alcoholism we have discussed, but particularly for the sociological ones. The interests of the various scientists and disciplines in advancing their respective theories are not only scientific and academic, but frequently occupational as well. Professional reputations are sometimes built and maintained upon a theory that gains and holds currency. For those professionals who are involved in alcoholic treatment programs, their success in gaining a clientele and in acquiring financial support often depends upon their ability to convince the interested parties of the validity of the particular "explanation" that they advocate for the cause and cure of alcoholism.

THE ALCOHOL PROBLEM AS A SOCIAL MOVEMENT

In order to understand the "problem" of alcohol use and abuse, it is imperative that we understand the developmental process of the social movements around this problem during the past 150 years. Alcoholism and its effect on the population have become serious problems in our society only recently, within the last forty years; they were not initially the major concern of those persons and social movements that have had the greatest impact upon alcohol behavior in our society. Most of the time and effort devoted to the question of alcohol problems have been directed toward the pros and cons of drinking itself, and not toward the effects of alcoholism. If we take an historical perspective, it is not difficult to see that, at the zenith of its development, the prohibition movement actually created the social problem of alcohol use. Previously such a problem was not defined as present. This is not to say that people were not becoming alcoholics, or that the abuse of alcohol was not causing great harm and hardship to many. The point is simply that prior to the passage of the Volstead Act in 1919, which contained provisions for the enforcement of the 18th Amendment, the use of alcoholic beverages was not legally defined as deviant behavior; with the passage of that law, a whole new class of crimes and criminals was created, and a consequent social problem. As we will see later on, it was not until the anti-alcohol movement began to wane that a new movement directed at the alcoholic really began to appear on the American scene, though some of the roots of that newer movement can be found in the early anti-alcohol movement.

The Early Temperance (Anti-Alcohol) Movement

The American anti-alcohol movement was actually part of the broader populist and progressive reformist streams that flowed out of the 19th century and remained strong until after World War I. This larger movement was a combination of humanitarian, religious and social concerns for the "social ills" which America was believed to be suffering during this historical period (Hofstadter, 1955). These were concerns not only about alcohol, but also about slavery, female suffrage, poverty, and many other things. The reformism that characterized these groups of moral entrepreneurs was definitely elitist, in that it expressed itself as an attempt by those who were "more fortunate" to help those who were "less fortunate." The reformists were not out to change themselves or "the system," but rather to change others who did not conform to their standards. Their paternalistic stance, couched in their moralistic rhetoric, was a clear expression of the American Protestant ethic. Let us now review the activities and development of a component of this movement, the anti-alcohol organizations.

The anti-alcohol movement of the 19th and early 20th centuries had three main channels of expressions, as we have indicated earlier: temperance societies, the Anti-Saloon League, and the Prohibition Party. The first of these, the temperance groups, were primarily propaganda and education organizations. The second, the Anti-Saloon League, was more of a pressure group in the activist sense of engaging directly in the political process. The third, of course, was an out-and-out political party in its own right, becoming an important "third force" in American political life as few other third parties have succeeded in doing. While these were formally separate organizations, they overlapped a great deal in their membership, and they all had in common a base of support in conservative American Protestantism. In these respects, it is proper to consider them as part of the same movement.

Membership and Leadership

We have already given some emphasis to the importance of the support given to the anti-alcohol movement by the Protestant churches. Churches provided much of the leadership of the movement from clergymen and interested laymen, and its financial backbone was made up mainly of grassroot pledges from church members (Cherrington, 1913). Even before the organization of strong political arms such as the Prohibition Party, temperance societies in the country had grown rapidly during the 1830's and 1840's, and by midcentury, they had reached a total membership of nearly 200,000 in 2,200 local chapters (Gusfield, 1963). The Prohibition Party itself, once it got going, commanded more than 200,000 votes in every election from the turn of the present century until the passage of the prohibition amendment in 1920. Part of the success of the temperance movement, particularly of the WCTU, was a result of its decision late in the 19th century to broaden its focus to include a variety of issues important to the progressive movement more generally, and particularly the feminist issue. The constituency of the temperance movement thus came to overlap significantly with that of other reform movements of the period, almost all of which had an upper-class or upper-middle-class base—the "good genteel people." The loss of that social-class base—indeed, its rejection of that base—by the temperance forces after 1920 was a consequence of changing drinking norms in the upper social strata, from abstinence to "fashionable moderation." Since then, the social-class base of the anti-alcohol movement in our society has steadily "eroded" downward to embrace a primarily lower-middle-class and working-class constituency with more conservative, fundamentalist Protestant preferences than the earlier elite membership (Gusfield, 1963:129-31).

Strategies, Tactics, and Activities

The WCTU, the Anti-Saloon League, and the Prohibition Party, while united in the common anti-alcohol cause, all had somewhat different strategies and used somewhat different tactics. The Prohibition Party was a straight political party in the usual sense. Its strength, however, never became national in the sense of a random distribution of adherents across the states and counties of the country, and it was by no means solely responsible for the passage of the anti-liquor legislation and amendment. Its base was situated at state and local levels, and it was much more popular and strong in some localities than others (e.g., the "Bible

Belt"). Its origins go back to 1853, when a number of the more militant representatives of the temperance societies throughout the country got together and decided that the time had come to use more political muscle to attain their goals. In an effort to make their presence known to the two major political parties, these militants declared that:

> While we do not desire to disturb political parties, we do intend to have and enforce a law prohibiting liquor manufacture and traffic as a beverage, whatever may be the consequence to political parties, and we will vote accordingly. (Sait, 1927:110)

Neither main party, however, was ready to take up this cause at that time, so pressure mounted among the prohibitionists to form a separate party, which they did in Chicago in 1869, with delegates from 20 states. From the very beginning, the Prohibition Party attempted to cast as wide a net as possible to attract supporters, and during the next 20 years it added to its anti-liquor platform planks calling for many other reforms: federal income tax, female suffrage, teaching of the Bible in public schools, an anti-polygamy amendment, direct election of senators, abolition of stock exchanges, and government control of railroads. In taking these positions, the Prohibition Party was clearly appealing to the wider interests of the rural Protestant American, much the same constituency as that of the Populist Party (Cherrington, 1920). Much later, after prohibition and its repeal, the Prohibition Party continued (in vain) to try to build and maintain a wider appeal. The result has been that it has drifted further and further to the political right wing of the current spectrum, exhibiting intense nationalism and economic conservatism. In addition to liquor-related matters, the Party's official publication, *The National Prohibitionist,* deals with anti-communism, water fluoridation, education, and many other issues (Gusfield, 1963).

The WCTU, by contrast, never allowed itself to be distracted from its anti-liquor preoccupation (even down to the present time), and it made no special attempt at political compromise in order to build a political organization or party as such, though it was willing to let other issues (such as female suffrage) ride with it in the "same wagon." Its chief activities were those of persuasion and propaganda, and its political efforts were directed largely at the passage of laws to facilitate anti-liquor indoctrination. Thus, from 1882 to 1902, laws were passed in every state requiring school instruction in the effects of alcohol and the benefits of total abstinence (Gusfield, 1955:221-232). The WCTU tended to define abstinence in the terms and context of general middle-class values and virtues, such as thrift and industry. They took it upon themselves to display and exemplify such virtues in their own conduct, and they promulgated their point of view with a strong, evangelical zeal, which doubtless added much to the public momentum behind the passage of both the 18th and 19th Amendments to the Constitution. The present situation of the WCTU, however, is a much less healthy one. As Gusfield points out (1963:129-131), the term "moralizers in retreat" (Reisman, 1950:195) would now be an appropriate term to describe the condition of the organization. After the debacle of prohibition and its repeal, the abstinence norm was discredited by a large portion of the middle class, especially that portion made up of the newer, upwardly mobile ethnic groups and others. The Protestant and middle-class "mainstream" became increasingly hostile toward WCTU stands and favorable toward the "moderate social drinker" norm. The WCTU has reacted with withdrawal and hostility of its own, cutting itself off from this mainstream and allying with a more sympathetic, less affluent, and more fundamentalist social base, as indicated above. In thus choosing a strategy of "holding fast" in the face of changing drinking norms, the WCTU, and any other surviving temperance organization, has probably sealed its own doom.

The Anti-Saloon League, in many respects, functioned as a kind of bridge between the propaganda/education temperance groups like WCTU and the Prohibition Party itself. The ASL was neither strictly a propaganda organization nor a regular political party. Indeed, it deliberately chose the tactic of trying to infiltrate and pressure the other parties, rather than separating itself from them as a new party in its own right. Thus one of its main strategies was to try to coordinate the anti-liquor activities of all the other organizations in the movement, to serve as a kind of "umbrella" organization for all the rest, and in this effort the ASL had considerable success. Other features of the ASL approach to the issue were the building of a strong organizational discipline under a centralized authority, and the political mobilization of Protestant churches (Odegard, 1966). It began to operate on a national level from about 1895 on, and focused much of its attention on towns, counties, and other localities in an effort to get "local option" exercised in favor of "dry" ordinances. It succeeded in bringing about one local "dry law" after another around the country through its skillful anti-saloon propaganda, its intensive lobbying with all parties and legislative bodies, and its occasional "infiltration" of these groups. By 1910 its efforts had resulted in widespread dry laws in many states, and, after a brief temporary setback in the dry movement for a year or so, the influence of the ASL and its allies was strongly felt in the federal Congress. In 1913, responding to the pressures of these groups, Congress passed the Webb-Kenyon Bill, outlawing the interstate shipment of liquor through, or into, locally "dry" territories, making possible more effective local enforcement. Shortly thereafter, an early version of the 18th Amendment was introduced into Congress (Odegard, 1966). In its efforts to secure passage of the amendment, the ASL bent all its efforts toward the election of "dry" congressmen and senators in the 1916 election. After that election, two-thirds of the Congress was "dry," and it set about immediately to pass a number of anti-liquor and anti-beer measures ostensibly as part of the war effort, making much (as we observed earlier) of the subversive influence which "German" breweries had on American war productivity and morale. In 1918, Congress passed a war prohibition act (the Hobson Joint Resolution), which forbade the manufacture or sale of intoxicating beverages, to go into effect by June 30, 1919. This had the effect of actually instituting prohibition six months before the 18th Amendment itself was ratified in January, 1920. The Volstead Act, passed to facilitate enforcement of that amendment, was itself little more than a codification, on the federal level, of ASL-sponsored ordinances that had earlier been passed at state and local levels. Thus, as the country turned away from the war which was fought to "make the world safe for democracy," it entered the era of Prohibition.

The Natural History of the Anti-Liquor Movement

There is a record of temperance activities, and of an occasional temperance society organization, as early as 1812, so the incipiency of the anti-liquor movement may well go back to colonial times (Gusfield, 1963:32-33). During the first half of the 19th century, temperance societies grew rapidly in both numbers and membership, as we reported above. Also, just before midcentury, the Washingtonian Movement (mentioned earlier) was started, and though its focus was originally on anti-drunkenness or anti-alcoholism, rather than anti-liquor as such, it was soon absorbed by the larger anti-liquor movement. These developments would suggest that, according to our natural history model, the coalescence of this movement was complete by around 1850. Its growth was apparently arrested temporarily by the climax of the abolition movement and the concomitant Civil War, illustrating once again, incidentally, the point made in Chapter 2 about the "quota" of social problems and reforms that a society is logistically capable of handling at the same time. Within a decade or so after the Civil War, however, we can see the institutionalization of the anti-liquor movement in the nationwide organization of the WCTU and the establishment of the Prohibition Party (the Anti-Saloon League came along a little later). This institutionalization can be seen both in the widespread legitimization of the movement through its alliance with mainstream Protestantism, and in the influence of the movement in legislative halls from the local to (eventually) the federal levels. As usual, however, the very legislative success of the movement, climaxing in the 18th Amendment, also constituted a co-optation of the movement (see our definition in Chapter 2) and the beginning of its decline, all very well-documented in the work of Gusfield (1955 and 1963). The institutionalization of a movement's program typically results in the de-institutionalization of the movement itself, and this is precisely what occurred with the anti-liquor movement. The Prohibition Era, bringing, as it did, a discrediting of a law-enforcement approach to the liquor problem, resulted in a gradual shift in the sentiments of former prohibition supporters, and by the time of repeal an actual hostility to the temperance forces had become evident. From there on, abstinence and its advocacy became objects of general opprobrium or even persecution, as the mood in most of the society's institutions turned from one of co-optation to one of repression of the movement. The fragmentation of the anti-liquor movement occurred in two senses: (1) the movement was "cut adrift from a specific institutional mooring" (Gusfield, 1963:165), that is, from the Protestant church, middle- and upper-middle-class base it had enjoyed earlier; and (2) the movement began to diffuse its efforts into a number of other causes, thereby losing its strength of focus on liquor, and alienating some of its supporters on the liquor issue by its stands on other issues (Gusfield, 1955; 1963:126-133). The demise of the movement is clearly underway at present. Votes for the Prohibition Party, once as high as 200,000, fell to 103,000 in the 1948 election and have been fewer than 55,000 ever since (Gusfield, 1963:163). WCTU membership has fallen drastically, particularly among young people, and the legitimacy of temperance as an ideal has almost been destroyed in our society (Gusfield, 1963:8-10, 160-165).

The Anti-Alcoholism Movement

While the anti-liquor movement has been declining during the past generation, a new movement has been rising with a related but different thrust, overlapping somewhat with the old movement in the manner suggested by Figure 2-4 of Chapter 2. While the newer movement is very much concerned with the abuse of alcohol (defined in various ways), it does not address the issue of "moderate" drinking. The new movement is different also in that much (if not most) of its strength comes from "insiders," people who have been afflicted by alcoholism, rather than from outside "reformers" bent on getting everyone else to conform to their moral ideals. Thus, while both movements have been carried mainly by moral entrepreneurs or interest groups, the nature of their moral interests has been quite different. It could be argued that the more recent movement represents a kind of "rear-guard" action, or of making the best out of a losing situation; i.e., if complete prohibition is not possible, then let us at least get rid of drunks. On the other hand, there is the argument that the real issue has always been alcohol "abuse," and the country could not turn to that issue until it had resolved its "hangups" about drinking in general. In any case, the current concern about alcoholism is a product of the generation following repeal.

Membership and Leadership

Starting with the abortive Washingtonian Movement of the 1840's, the membership of anti-alcoholism groups has been largely made up of problem drinkers themselves (Bell, 1970:56). Although, as we have observed, the Washingtonians were quickly absorbed by the anti-liquor forces, the extremely widespread support they received from drinkers across all social classes was a significant harbinger of more recent developments (Maxwell, 1950:410-451). Alcoholics Anonymous, the most important interest group in the current movement, also has attracted a large, cross-sectional membership. After its founding in 1935, described earlier, AA grew slowly at first, reaching a membership of only 40 by 1937. However, under the vigorous leadership of founders "Dr. Bob" and "Bill W.," and with the help of a small grant from J. D. Rockefeller, the message of AA was circulated more effectively by a series of publications and educational meetings (Clinebell, 1965:126). By 1949, there were more than 80,000 members in 3,000 chapters throughout 30 countries of the world; and by 1968, membership in the United States alone had grown to 150,000, and, in the world, to 425,000 (Bell, 1970:59). Members are not always required to be total abstainers, but they must commit themselves to work toward resolution of their drinking problems in a serious and committed way. Drawing its members from all walks of life, AA has benefited by the leadership of many talented and eminent men, who must, however, remain anonymous under the rules of the organization. The Yale Group, as we indicated earlier, and its derivative allied organization, The National Council on Alcoholism, are also products primarily of the 1930's and 1940's, with a membership that is (in NCA, at least) largely made up of recovered or recovering alcoholics. These latter two groups are allied with scientists and researchers in a cooperative program of research and education. In a less dramatic way, the Yale Group and NCA have been as important as AA itself in promoting the current anti-alcoholism movement (Mann, 1973; Cahn, 1970).

Strategies, Tactics, and Activities

Education is a major activity of both the AA and the NCA/Yale Group. The major publications of AA have been the book, *Alcoholics Anonymous* (1939 and 1955), published by its two founders; Bill W.'s *The Twelve Steps and the Twelve Traditions* (1953); the monthly journal, *The Grapevine* (started in 1944), and a variety of small pamphlets. Taken together, these publications set forth the definitions and constructions of reality which AA holds about the nature of the alcoholism problem. The Yale Group publishes the important professional journal, *Quarterly Journal of Studies on Alcohol,* runs the Yale (now Rutgers) summer schools on alcoholic studies, and engages in many other educational endeavors.

Besides education for the public and for practitioners in alcoholism therapy, the Yale people have maintained an extensive program of scientific research, and their out-patient treatment clinics have offered a prototype of treatment practice to the nation (Jellinek, 1960; Cahn, 1970). Both the research and the treatment methods of the Yale Group have been multi-disciplinary, drawing upon the social sciences, as well as upon medicine and social work. One important result of their scientific and educational work has been the general acceptance by the society of a "disease" definition of alcoholism—i.e., that alcoholism is a treatable disease, the causes and cure for which can be discovered through scientific research, as with any other disease.

Alcoholics Anonymous has also contributed to the currency of the definition of alcoholism as a "disease," though that term is not necessarily used in AA circles. However, AA does see alcoholism as a condition that is beyond the ability of the individual to "cure" permanently, and which stays with him the rest of his life. He can "arrest" the condition, or keep it in abeyance as long as he admits that he *has* it, but he cannot actually get rid of the condition through any amount of moral rejuvenation. At the same time, however, AA defines the role of the individual in his own "treatment" as a critical one. It is he who must realize that he needs help, and that he cannot "go it alone." A frequently heard AA saying is that: "You've got to hit bottom before you can go back up" (Tiebout, 1961). In that sense, AA discriminates among prospective members; it won't accept anyone who does not feel an almost desperate need for their help, and this kind of "selectivity" might help to explain the relatively high rate of success that AA has, compared to other treatment programs, in keeping alcoholics "dry" (Blum and Blum, 1967: 164-166).

A number of other features of the AA program might help to account for its success: (1) its use of primary group affiliation, a sense of group solidarity or "we-ness"; (2) the social control which results from the AA friendship network and face-to-face interaction; (3) its use of religious supports, based on the idea that there is a Power greater than oneself to whom one can turn; and (4) its casting of the ex-alcoholic in the role of a helper and rescuer, which gives him a sense of meaning and importance in a life that otherwise may be quite empty, and helps him to work off his own feelings of guilt and impotence (Edwards, et al., 1967; Maxwell, 1962; Trice, 1957 and 1959).

The Natural History of the Anti-Alcoholism Movement

As we pointed out, the incipiency of this more recent movement extends back to the early Washingtonians, in the 19th century. However, as long as the thinking of prohibition held sway, it was not really possible for coalescence to take place among the anti-alcoholism reformist tendencies. After the prohibition movement was discredited, such a coalescence did take place, starting with the organized efforts of AA and the Yale Group, beginning in the 1930's. The strength and influence of these organizations have grown steadily, and have had a great impact upon public opinion, and upon the thinking of both scientists and legislators. In more recent years, particularly during the 1960's and 1970's, there has been evidence of the institutionalization of this movement, and its partial co-optation, in the form of a general acceptance of the disease-and-treatment approach to alcoholism, large-scale government appropriations for research and treatment on the basis of this newer concept, and changes in many state and local ordinances relating to public drunkenness, to make them less punitive. The main ideas of AA and of the Yale Group, and their definitions and constructions of reality about alcohol and alcoholism, are clearly the emerging and dominant ones. The decline of the present movement into fragmentation and demise is not predictable from our current historical vantage point.

THE LEGACY OF THE ALCOHOL PROBLEM MOVEMENTS

America has always had ambivalent feelings about alcohol in its culture, going back to its earliest Protestant beginnings. The division in Protestantism over alcohol, between its fundamentalist and liberal branches, has only deepened that ambivalence, which has been further complicated by the input from Roman Catholicism, which has never had an anti-alcohol tradition (Gusfield, 1963:9-10). Catholicism in America (unlike that in Canada) has never approved of total abstinence, though it has been as opposed as any other group to alcoholism, drunkenness, and so on (Bell, 1970:48-49). The legacy from the earlier prohibition movement and the thrust of the current anti-alcoholism movement have also contributed to our cultural ambivalence. The fact is that we are not sure, as a people, whether drinking is all right or not. Many of our cultural practices reflect this contradictory attitude. Most current laws do not permit "hard liquor" to be advertised on television, but beer and wine may be advertised as long as the ads do not show them actually being consumed! The legal age for the consumption of alcoholic beverages is between 18 and 21, and varies from one state to another, even though 18 is, for all practical purposes, now the legal age for assuming the responsibilities of citizenship. One positive cultural consequence of the recent movement seems to be a gradually spreading change in the definition of the alcoholic from a "sinner," or "deviant," to a "sick person."

These two movements, then, the anti-alcohol and the anti-alcoholism movements, have had an extensive and long-lasting effect upon American society on at least three levels: a general cultural level, a normative level, and a legal level. First, culturally, the anti-alcohol movement has probably affected us in more ways than we realize, while the anti-alcoholism movement is really just beginning to make itself felt on the American scene. The anti-alcohol movement provided us with one of the most colorful and exciting eras in American history—Prohibition. From this era came a new argot: words like "Demon Rum," "bathtub gin," "King Alcohol," "the speakeasy," "bootlegger," and "Wets and Drys," have become common to our vocabulary. Slogans such as the WCTU's "Lips that have touched liquor shall never touch mine," were not a humorous retort to drinking companions but rather a serious declaration of belief in the crusade against alcohol. Probably the most impressive cultural effect that the anti-alcohol movement had upon society was that it changed our manner and mode of drinking. The intended goal of the movement was to eliminate drinking; however, its actual effect was that it changed the type and place of drinking. During Prohibition there was an increase in the number of females who would now drink in "public." Also, the liquor industry, previously an open, capitalistic endeavor, became an underground, clandestine operation which promoted the illegal manufacture, distribution, and sale of alcohol. A number of America's present prominent philanthropists became wealthy running whiskey from Canada to the United States during this period of time. The anti-alcoholism movement has really not, as of yet, contributed substantially to the general cultural context of American society.

On the normative level, too, the anti-alcohol movement has had a considerable impact. Through the temperance movement, new values, attitudes, and behavior patterns emerged and became ingrained in the American way of life. Temperance—and then abstinence—replaced drinking as the accepted social norm. Feminism and the power of moral indignation marched hand-in-hand on the alcohol issue and produced the first major breakthrough for womankind as a political and social force. On the other side of the fence, the fact that prohibition laws were actually unenforceable and unacceptable to many produced a new attitude toward the power structure, an attitude of ambivalence. Laws were good to have, but bad laws were a nuisance, and, therefore, to be ignored. The law said drinking was wrong, but most did not seem to care; the people just bypassed it. The expectation of the laws of a sober America was never achieved, because it was out of touch with the actual behavior of the people.

The anti-alcoholism movement has also affected the normative structure of American society. The recovering alcoholic is now showing society that he can change and can lead a full and productive life without alcohol. We are now beginning to realize that the alcoholic is different from other people, not in a moral sense, but in a medical sense. The role of the recovering alcoholic has become for many a role of helper, therapist or rescuer of others caught up in the problem of alcoholism. Prior to the rebirth of this movement, this role was reserved for the clergy and the medical doctor. The anti-alcoholism movement has also promoted the study of alcoholism as a legitimate field, and through the work of people such as those at Yale, and later Rutgers, it has promoted the involvement of scientists and academics in the pursuit of answers to many of the questions in the alcoholism field.

On the legal level, both movements have had an impact on society. Through the various organizations and groups which promoted its goals, the anti-alcohol movement was very successful in establishing legal principles which brought about sweeping changes relative to the use of alcohol. The most notable, of course, was the 18th Amendment and its accompanying enforcement law, the Volstead Act. With the passage of these acts, a previously normative behavior pattern, the drinking of alcoholic beverages, became a deviant social act; and those who continued to engage in such behavior were not only socially wrong but also legally wrong, i.e., they were lawbreakers. The number of local, state and federal laws enacted relative to drinking and drunkenness are too numerous to mention. However, the effects of these archaic laws are still being felt in many parts of the country today. The anti-alcohol movement also changed the police role relative to drinking, from one of a peace-keeper to one of a gate-keeper during the period of Prohibition.

In the area of the law, the anti-alcoholism movement has made some of its greatest strides. One of the major breakthroughs in the legal pattern which had been developed for dealing with the alcoholic actually began with a court decision on a narcotics addiction case. In the case of *Robinson* v. *California,* decided in 1962, the California Supreme Court ruled that to penalize a drug addict for being an addict was in violation of the provision of the 8th Amendment against cruel and unusual punishment, because conviction of Robinson was based on nothing more than the fact that he was ill. For many decades those engaged in alcoholism treatment and research had been attempting to convince the legal system of this nation that the incarceration of the alcoholic without treatment and/or rehabilitation was a cruel and useless act, since the alcoholic was really not a criminal, but rather a sick individual. The Robinson decision followed this same logic, i.e., that an individual should not be punished for a "crime of status," that is for being an addict or alcoholic (Grad, Goldberg, and Shapiro, 1971:19). In 1966, two more decisions were handed down which have further changed and defined the role and function of the legal system toward the alcoholic, primarily toward the public inebriate. In *Driver* v. *Hinnant,* the U.S. Court of Appeals for the Fourth Circuit ruled that Driver was a chronic alcoholic and that to convict him of public drunkenness was "cruel and unusual punishment" according to the 8th Amendment, since he was suffering from the disease of alcoholism, and his acts were symptomatic of that disease. Shortly after the Driver decision, in *Easter* v. *the District of Columbia,* a similar situation presented itself, and the court, relying on the Driver decision, ruled that proof of chronic alcoholism was a valid defense against a public drunkenness conviction, since the chronic alcoholic is not able to control his drinking (Plaut, 1967:110). It appeared that the anti-alcoholism movement had finally brought about significant reversal in the prevailing attitudes and legal treatment of the alcoholic. However, in 1968, the U.S. Supreme Court in *Powell* v. *Texas* failed to support the rulings of the lower courts on the subject of alcoholism as a defense against public drunkenness (U.S. Department of Health, Education, and Welfare, 1971:86-87). The court majority argued that the defense testimony was "utterly inadequate" (Bahr, 1973:237). Since there was (is) no truly effective treatment for alcoholism known, a short jail sentence for the defendant was, after all, more just and advisable than an indefinite commitment to an alcoholism treatment facility (Driver, 1969). But by this time many states had already proceeded to pass laws favoring the treatment rather than punishment of the alcoholic, based on the decisions of the Driver and Easter cases. States such as Hawaii, North Dakota, Maryland, Washington, and the District of Columbia have passed new public drunkenness laws, while a number of other states are in the process of doing the same. These include Minnesota, Pennsylvania, Kentucky and Massachusetts, among others (Grad, Goldberg and Shapiro, 1971). It is now an established fact that the anti-alcoholism movement has had a definite effect upon the legal system. This movement has also been the motivating force behind changes and new developments on the federal level related to the problem of alcoholism in the United States. It was not until 1966, when President Lyndon Johnson established the National Center for the Prevention and Treatment of Alcoholism, and the National Advisory Committee on Alcoholism, that the federal government really became involved with alcoholism, as distinct from just alcohol use. In 1970, primarily due to the efforts of Senator Harold Hughes, a recovering alcoholic, the Comprehensive Alcohol Abuse and Alcoholism Act of 1970 was passed. This Act included the establishment of a federal alcoholism program, the formation of the National Institute of Alcohol Abuse and Alcoholism, and the appropriation of about $300,000,000 to be used over a three-year period for the development and continuation of alcoholism treatment and prevention programs (Mann, 1973:7). The NIAAA has already begun to effect a significant change on public attitudes toward alcoholism and the alcoholic, and this legitimation of the anti-alcoholism movement will undoubtedly allow for a more enlightened approach to alcoholism on a national level.

It is now apparent that the anti-alcohol movement has for the most part become a dead movement, and will probably not enjoy a rebirth. Drinking *per se* has become a social fact in the American way of life, and the experience of prohibition has convinced us that America wants to drink. On the other hand, the anti-alcoholism movement, while being less spectacular than its predecessor, has slowly grown and will probably continue to do so. Alcoholism as a disease, uncurable but treatable, is now the accepted ideology. However, this does not mean that this ideology will not be challenged or that it will not change. Perhaps now, with the help of the cultural, normative and legal systems which support them, the academic-scientific groups and the recovering alcoholic groups will begin a unified attack on the enormous problems that alcoholism produces for the individual, his family, and society.

Chapter 9
Mental Illness

> The most important assumption about mental illness in Western Society is that it *is an illness,* and should be considered and treated as an illness.
>
> —Thomas Scheff

THE SOCIAL CONSTRUCTION OF REALITY

As the United States moves toward the last decades of the 20 century, a widespread notion exists that a rather large number of people in this country, and elsewhere, suffer from a particular malady known as "mental illness." One professional observer sums up this idea as follows:

> It is widely believed today that just as some people suffer from diseases of the liver or kidney, others suffer from diseases of the mind or personality; that persons afflicted with such "mental illnesses" are psychologically and socially inferior to those not so afflicted; and that "mental patients," because of their supposed incapacity to "know what is in their best interests," must be cared for by their families or the state, even if that care requires interventions imposed on them against their will or incarceration in a mental hospital. (Szasz, 1970:xv)

A psychiatrist named Karl Menninger, an influential perpetrator of this belief, even maintained that "all people have mental illness of different degrees at different times" (Menninger, 1963:32).

Historical Relativity

Yet such a view has hardly been predominant throughout history—even American history. Throughout time, societies have had to cope with those members whose behavior seemed to deviate from what was judged to be "normal." While some forms of deviance were regarded to be the purposeful acts of responsible human beings, other instances of deviance led observers to call into question the mental state of the deviant individual.

The early Israelites, looking at what they called "madness," sometimes saw this condition as one produced by a just and sovereign God, and reversible only by His action:

If [you] will not obey the voice of the Lord your God or be careful to do all His commandments and His statutes . . . the Lord will smite you with madness and blindness and confusion of mind. (Deuteronomy, 28.15, 28)

In ancient Greece such deviants were considered to be possessed by a divine power or being, and consequently were viewed with a sense of awe and mystery. Socrates, for example, once wrote:

The greatest blessings come by way of madness, indeed of madness that is heaven sent. It was when they were mad that the prophetess at Delphi and the priestess at Dodona achieved so much for which both states and individuals in Greece are thankful: when sane they did little or nothing. (cited in Rosen, 1968:84)

Other Greek and Roman observers of mental deviance perceived such "differences" as evidence of physical and/or psychological pathology. For example, near the end of the Greek civilization, Hippocrates (ca. 460-377 B.C.), regarded by many as the "father of medicine," wrote that epilepsy

. . . appears to me to be nowise more divine nor more sacred than other disease, but has a natural cause from which it originates like other affections. (cited in Bromberg, 1963:737)

As the Judaeo-Christian tradition developed, it acquired the idea that such "mental deviants" were possessed not by God, but by demons representing the forces of evil. Such an interpretation had a widespread following within Christendom up until at least the 17th century, and beyond. An early example, a classic biblical story of healing, describes how Jesus dealt with a man having "an unclean spirit who lived among the tombs," a man who "no man could bind . . . with chains." He was "always, night and day . . . in the mountains and in the tombs, crying and cutting himself with stones." The narrative states:

And all the devils besought him saying, "Send us into the swine, that we may enter into them." And forthwith Jesus gave them leave. And the unclean spirits went out, and entered into the swine: and the herd ran violently down a steep place into the sea . . . and were choked in the sea. (Mark, 5)

During the medieval period, various religious and magical techniques were used to remove demons and restore normality to a person regarded as possessed. Shrines were dedicated to various saints and were credited with miraculous cures (Council of State Governments, 1950:17), and witchcraft was used to deal directly "with the powers of darkness." The varied and composite nature of such attempts at remedy is illustrated by this Anglo-Saxon prescription:

When a devil possessed the man or controls him from within the disease: a spew drink or emetic, lupin, bishopwort, henbane, corpleek: pound these together, add ale for a liquid, let it stand for a night, add fifty bibcorns of cathartic grains and holy water—to be drunk out of a church bell. (cited in Bromberg, 1963:739)

Beliefs other than demon possession were given credence in the Middle Ages, and later on. One of these was the idea, not uncommon, that mental aberrations were related to lunar or astrological factors; hence came the word "lunatic." Other people saw the mental deviants as suffering from the loss of rational truth. Therefore, their "error" could be rectified through disciplinary measures. In late medieval Europe, for example, such people were commonly imprisoned and beaten. Some observers, however, saw such a fall from rationality as irreversible, and punishable by death. One man in Konigsberg, Germany, in 1636 made the mistake of claiming he was God. The local folk responded by cutting out his tongue, cutting off his head, and burning his body to ashes. A somewhat related response to mental problems was also made in Germany, some 300 years later, this time by Hitler. Asserting in September of 1939 that "incurably sick persons should be granted mercy death," the Nazi leader proceeded to build gas chambers in mental hospitals, and within two years he had rid Germany of some 50,000 (non-Jewish) Germans (Szasz, 1970:314).

Yet for some, including many medieval writers and artists, the madman was regarded as the only one in touch with ultimate reality (Clausen, 1971:64). In many works of this period, and of the Renaissance, including the works of William Shakespeare, the mentally deviant

... is no longer simply a ridiculous and familiar silhouette in the wings: he stands center stage as the guardian of truth. ... If folly leads each man into a blindness where he is lost, the madman, on the contrary, reminds each man of his truth. ... He speaks love to lovers, the truth of life to the young, the middling reality of things to the proud, to the insolent, and to liars. (Foucault, 1965:14)

However, in more recent times, and in our own times, such deviants have been perceived as rather ordinary people—not possessed, irreversibly irrational, or sick—who are simply experiencing problems in living. That is, they have difficulty interacting with other people, coping, for example, with conflicting needs, aspirations, and values. Thus their mental problems represent their inability to manage life—their unsuccessful struggle with the problem of living with others. According to this position, explanations along demonological or medical lines are myths. In the words of a major proponent of this position, the concept of mental illness, for example,

is a true heir to religious myths in general, and to the belief in witchcraft in particular; the role of all these belief-systems was to act as *social tranquilizers,* thus encouraging the

TABLE 9-1 ESTIMATED PATIENT CARE EPISODES IN MENTAL HOSPITALS (SELECTED)

Year	All Facilities	Inpatient Services All	State and County	Private	General	VA	Outpatient Psychiatric Services	Community Health Centers
1971	4,038,143	1,721,389	745,259	126,600	542,642	176,800	1,693,848	622,906
1969	3,572,822	1,678,371	767,115	123,850	535,493	186,913	1,603,303	291,148
1967	3,139,742	1,659,391	801,354	124,258	578,513	128,196	1,383,000	97,351
1965	2,636,525	1,565,525	804,926	125,428	519,328	115,843	1,071,000	N.A.
1955	1,675,352	1,296,352	818,832	123,231	265,934	88,355	379,000	N.A.

Source: The 1974 World Almanac and Book of Facts, New York: Newspaper Enterprise Association, Inc., 1973

TABLE 9-2 STATISTICS ON STATE AND COUNTY MENTAL HOSPITALS (SELECTED)

Year	Total Admitted	Net Releases	Deaths in Hospital	Residents End of Year	Expense Per Patient
1972	390,000	401,567	23,282	275,995	$7,576.24
1971	414,926	418,750	26,835	308,024	$6,420.79
1970	393,174	394,627	30,804	338,592	$5,435.38
1969	379,838	373,287	35,962	373,984	$4,593.61
1960	234,791	191,386	49,748	535,540	$1,702.41
1955	178,003	126,498	44,384	558,922	$1,116.59

Source: The 1974 World Almanac and Book of Facts, New York: Newspaper Enterprise Association, Inc., 1973

hope that mastery of certain specific problems may be achieved by means of substitutive (symbolic-magical) operations. (Szasz, 1960:118)

Szasz argues that "good mental health" is not a quality which can be possessed, like its physiological analogue, enabling people to make the "right" choices in life. Rather such a label refers to a condition which results from making the choices that seem "right" under the circumstances, and thus harmonious and satisfying social relationships will occur as people become better able to relate successfully to each other, and not by casting out demons or "healing sick people."

Very closely tied to this interpretation is the idea that defining behavior as normal or deviant, healthy or sick, is an extremely risky undertaking, based not on some set of absolute criteria, but rather on those relative to a given group and even a given individual. Shakespeare puts it well:

HAMLET: Ay, marry, why was he sent into England?
FIRST CLOWN: Why, because a' was mad; a' shall recover his wits there; or, if a' do not, 'tis no great matter there.
HAMLET: Why?
FIRST CLOWN: *'Till not be seen in him there;* there the men are as mad as he.
(Rosen, 1968:90; italics added)

In Greco-Roman culture there seem to have existed two main explanations for mental problems, one attributing such phenomena to supernatural forces, the other to natural causes. Significantly, these two interpretations have persisted side by side throughout history until recent times, when the latter gained ascendancy. However, these approaches have not always been mutually exclusive. For example, having medically treated a 14-year-old girl unsuccessfully, three 16th-century doctors concluded that "som cause beyond naturall was in it" (cited in Rosen, 1968:147). A 17th-century cleric turned psychiatrist, Robert Burton, summed up the combined supernatural-medical approach well:

Tis a common practice of some men to go first to a witch, then to a physician; if one cannot, the other shall; if they cannot bend Heaven they will try Hell. (cited in Bromberg, 1963:740)

With the 19th and 20th centuries, the medical interpretation of mental illness gained prominence in much of the world. This interpretation has placed an increasing emphasis upon mental as well as organic factors. Psychiatry, as a specialized field of medicine, has come to play the major role in the diagnosis and treatment of mental illness. Therapies tend to be mental, organic, and social, including, for example, various forms of psychotherapy, drugs, and even surgery, as well as group and milieu forms of therapy. Increasingly, the psychiatrist has been giving his attention not so much to an institutional clientele as to the non-hospitalized population, often dealing with what might be regarded as the "less severe" types of mental illness.

Unlike the ancient Hebrew, who saw "a difference" in the mental deviant and attributed it to God, or the early medieval peasant who attributed it to demons, or the late medieval jailer who attributed it to a fall from rationality, or even the modern social scientist who attributes it to problems in social relationships, the 20th-century psychiatrist is inclined to see mental deviance as an illness in need of a cure.

Parameters of Consensual Reality

It has been estimated by the Committee Against Mental Illness (1966:1) that approximately 10 percent of all Americans are suffering from mental illnesses of one kind or another. About 37 percent of hospital beds in the United States are occupied by mental patients, which is, however, actually a considerable reduction over a decade ago (Horton and Leslie, 1974:528). Obviously, the exact amount of illness is difficult to determine, since not all the people who are afflicted seek out medical help.

Nevertheless, we do know that the number of people receiving psychiatric treatment at some time during 1969 numbered close to 3.5 million (see Table 9-1), exclusive of private psychiatric treatments which involved an additional 750,000 people annually (Clausen, 1971:77). Table 9-1 also indicates that Americans are increasingly using outpatient facilities rather than being hospitalized for their disorders. The trend toward short treatment periods and the use of outpatient services is further reflected in the fact that while total admissions in state and mental hospitals continued to increase in 1970, the resident populations continued to decrease (see Table 9-2).

The exact meaning of the term mental illness is not clear, nor are the origins of the symptoms to which the term supposedly refers. While an international classification system for these symptoms and their labels has been in existence for most of the present century, each country has tended to use its own system, and the United States itself did not conform to the international system until 1968. Even in the mid-1970's there continue to be major differences among countries and schools of psychiatric thought in the criteria for diagnosis of various kinds of mental illness (Clausen, 1971:34). The two major categories generally used are *neuroses* and *psychoses,* which differ mainly in the degree to which the afflicted person has lost touch with "reality." A neurosis is believed to arise from severe feelings of anxiety, guilt, depression, or the like, which, for some reason, certain people are not able to handle very well. As a result, they display certain eccentricities or hang-ups, but they do not lose their grasp of reality enough that their social functioning is severely hampered. So defined, a "neurotic condition" has probably

TABLE 9-3 NUMBER OF ADMISSIONS TO PSYCHIATRIC FACILITIES BY DIAGNOSIS, 1969

Diagnosis	State and County	Out-Patient Services	Private	Total
Schizophrenia	100,398	148,031	17,471	265,900
Neuroses	31,264	164,860	6,626	202,750
Alcohol disorders	94,589	43,250	9,873	147,712
Transient situational disorders	—	133,369	—	133,369
Personality disorders	27,315	94,447	4,530	126,292
Organic brain syndromes	39,831	25,117	4,010	68,958
Child and adolescent disorders	—	43,923	698	44,621
Conditions with no manifest disorders	—	42,749	122	42,871
Mental retardation	9,897	28,243	256	38,396
Affective disorders	13,553	22,675	—	36,228
Other psychoses	12,048	13,145	1,685	26,878
Drug disorders	10,531	12,867	2,356	25,754
Social maladjustment	—	—	291	291
Other disorders	28,537	24,682	3,416	56,635
Undiagnosed	—	83,415	6,833	90,248
Total	367,963	880,763	92,057	1,340,783

Source: National Institute of Mental Health, HSM 72-9045, 1971; HSM 72-9048, 1971; HSM 72-9089, 1972

been experienced by a great many people at one time or another (Clausen, 1971: 41-42).

More serious are the psychotic disorders, the main categories of which are manic-depressive reactions and schizophrenia. The first is characterized by alternating periods of euphoria and despair ("highs and lows"), and recovery is fairly common. Schizophrenia (sometimes called dementia praecox) combines psychological withdrawal from others with delusions, bizarre flights of ideas, and other severe distortions. Classified into various subtypes, schizoprenia in some form is diagnosed relatively frequently, but such diagnoses have proved very unreliable in general (Clausen, 1971:39). Paranoia, characterized by delusions of grandeur and persecution, was once considered only a subtype of schizophrenia, but more recently it has come to be regarded as a symptom of a number of different disorders.

The origins, causes, and etiology of the various neuroses and psychoses are very much open to debate. There is strong evidence for a genetic or other physiological basis for at least some kinds of schizophrenia (Clausen, 1971:58), but these account for a very small proportion of all diagnosed cases (Horton and Leslie, 1974:533). Mental difficulties and deficiencies associated with old age (senility) or with retardation, of course, are primarily physiological in their origins, but these are in a class apart and are not included among the usual "functional" categories of mental illness. Thus, for the overwhelming majority of mental illness cases, no physiological origin is known, or even suspected. Furthermore, mental illnesses of various kinds have been disproportionately associated with certain social factors, including age, sex, urban living, and social class (Clausen, 1971:49-62; Horton and Leslie, 1974:534-538). Accordingly, some important scholars in the study of mental illness insist that it cannot be considered an illness or disease in the usual sense, that it is, in fact, simply an especially dangerous label that is applied to certain socially obnoxious people as a pretext for incarcerating them (Horton and Leslie, 1974:529-533). (See below discussions of scientific interest groups and of legacy.) Nevertheless, the tables we have presented here suggest that in a given year in the United States of the 1970's, at least five million people, or roughly one in forty, will seek psychiatric help for some kind of "mental illness." Many others will fail or neglect to seek such help, even though they too have some kind of mental disorder.

Public Opinion and Mental Illness

Today, as in the past, the American "man-on-the-street" has been reluctant to accept the "illness-cure" model of the psychiatrist. In a study of popular conceptions toward mental illness conducted in the 1950's, Nunnally (1961:51) found that

Old people and young people, highly educated people and people with little formal schooling—all tend to regard the mentally ill as relatively dangerous, dirty, unpredictable, and worthless.

He also noted that while general medical practitioners held reasonably "correct" information about mental disorders, their attitudes toward the mentally ill were as negative as those expressed by the general public. Nunnally further concluded, on the basis of an extensive content analysis of television, radio, newspapers, and magazines, that the ideas about mental health portrayed in the mass media are actually less accurate, according to expert opinion, than are the beliefs of the public-at-large.

Since extensive non-institutional mental health services are being used by the public more and more, we might think that acceptance of the "normalcy" of mental problems and their treatment would be more and more widespread. Yet Derek Phillips' study of a New England town in the early 1960's found that people who seek help are increasingly rejected as they move from (1) seeking no help, to (2) seeing a clergyman, to (3) seeing a physician, to (4) being admitted to a mental hospital. While seeing a psychiatrist was not specifically considered by this study, according to the scale of public evaluation it used, such action would seemingly result in a rejection rating somewhere between seeing a physician and being in a mental hospital (Phillips, 1963).

Another study, that of Simmons in the late 1960's, revealed that former mental patients as a general category ranked 12th with respect to the aversion adults felt toward various categories of people. To give some indication of the low status of the mental patient, the list showed that ranking ahead of patients in public acceptance were homosexuals, prostitutes, alcoholics, gamblers, ex-convicts, and atheists (Simmons, 1969).

But perhaps the clearest indication of contemporary national opinion concerning the mentally ill was provided by the famous "Eagleton incident," in the summer of 1972. Because of the profound insights the affair provides into public attitudes toward the mentally disordered—far more than a myriad of small-sample statistical studies—it is worth examining in some detail.

The story is well-known.* At the Democratic Convention in Miami Beach in July, 1972, Senator Thomas F. Eagleton of Missouri was selected as the running-mate for presidential candidate George McGovern. However, within days Eagleton—aware that the story was going to break—was forced to reveal that on three occasions, in 1960, 1964, and 1966, he had been hospitalized for "nervous exhaustion." Twice he had received shock treatments. In unveiling this facet of his medical history, the Senator said that he was "an intense and hard-fighting person" who sometimes pushed himself "too far." He pointed out that he had been hospitalized of his own volition. "Now," he said, "I have confidence that I've learned how to pace myself and know the limits of my own endurance." At the same press conference, McGovern added:

I think Tom Eagleton is fully qualified in mind, body and spirit to be the Vice President of the United States and, if necessary, to take on the presidency at a moment's notice.

Psychiatric experts, including representatives from the American Psychiatric Association, were quick to point out that Eagleton's illness was a common form of depression which is a treatable, curable condition. Thus Senator Eagleton provided an interesting prototype of a most capable American who followed doctors'

---

*Much of the material in this section, notably quotations at news conferences, etc., is drawn from *The New York Times, Newsweek,* and *Time,* August, 1972, editions and issues.

advice in seeking medical attention when he felt he needed it, was treated, and returned to normal life healthier, he claimed, for the experience.

Yet the press asserted that the Eagleton revelations threatened to wreck the McGovern candidacy. Campaign manager Gary Hart was quick to "take the blame" for the inadequate research which had resulted in "the error." There was a national outcry, and Democrats across the country protested the Eagleton nomination. Newspapers called for Eagleton to quit the ticket, among them *The New York Times, The Washington Post, The Baltimore Sun,* and *The Los Angeles Times.* Party leaders, labor leaders, and campaign contributors all passed the word publicly or privately that Eagleton had to go or the McGovern ticket would be doomed. A woman in California wired McGovern: "Since you have conceded election to Nixon by selection of psychotic, I would like refund of money contributed when you were a viable candidate" (cited in *Newsweek,* August 7, 1972:14).

A special Gallup poll sought American responses to the statement,

As you may know, Sen. Thomas Eagleton, the Democratic candidate for Vice President, has reported that he has been hospitalized three times for nervous exhaustion and has twice had electric-shock treatment. Do you feel that this makes it likely that he is unfit to be Vice President or not?

Some 28 percent answered "yes," 59 percent said "no," while 13 percent were undecided.

Ironically, a *Time* magazine survey of depression patients who had been "cured," or were well on the way to recovery, revealed that most respondents were leery of Eagleton's candidacy for the vice-presidency. A California woman of 49, who had gone some 15 years without further treatment for her depression and was enjoying a successful career as an office manager, had this to say:

I'm sorry for Tom Eagleton, but from my own experience I say he's not qualified to run for the vice-presidency. I don't think anyone ever knows whether he or she is cured. *He did not have a broken leg. It's more like a bad heart attack*—even after an excellent recovery you still can't be sure that it won't occur unexpectedly again at an awkward time. (cited in *Time,* August 14, 1972:41; emphasis added)

A skeptic wrote to the editor of *Newsweek* (August 21, 1972:4): "To have equated these serious things with a misfortune no more significant than a broken arm is an appalling revelation in itself!"

Called variously "lacking candor," "dishonest," and "unwise" for failing to tell McGovern about "skeletons in his closet," Eagleton retorted:

I never have viewed the hospitalization in terms of being skeletons. I view skeletons as something you've done that is sinister, corrupt, evil, filthy—something in that sense. . . . I'm not ashamed. There is nothing dirty or corrupt or evil about the fact that I had voluntarily gone into a hospital. (personal interview, *Time,* August 7, 1972:14)

Chapter 9 / Mental Illness

The widespread concern about Eagleton's competence in the light of his medical history was expressed succinctly in a widely circulated comment by one Democrat:

I know Senator Eagleton was not really mentally disturbed, just fatigued . . . but the public can't make that distinction. They're just going to say, "I can't vote for a guy who might go nuts if the Russians or whatever put the pressure on him." (*Newsweek*, August 7, 1972:13)

Thus it was that Thomas Eagleton was "dumped" by politicians and a public who believed a candidate with a history of mental illness would frighten off many voters.

The incident vividly draws attention to the fact that in the eyes of at least a very large segment of the population, mental disorders are *not* analogous to physical disorders: they are not permanently curable. The "once ill always ill" belief is far from dead. To seek out treatment for a mental disorder is to risk receiving a possibly permanent, stigmatizing label.

The Eagleton incident had a sobering effect upon the National Association of Mental Health, which subsequently launched a new "National Commitment for Mental Health Emphasis." The fall, 1972 issue of *MH,* the body's official magazine, stated:

. . . the disqualification of Senator Eagleton from running for the position of the Vice President of the United States because of fear of the possible implications of earlier psychiatric attention makes it apparent that the job is far from done and that to press on we need this new commitment. (MH, Fall, 1972:18)

Perhaps the editors of *Time* have best summed up the present public perception of the "mentally ill." On the cover of their August 7, 1972 issue was the face of a dismayed Eagleton—with a Cain-like mark on his forehead.

CHAMPIONS AND THEIR INTERESTS

In setting the stage for an analysis of the social sources of the dominant, although not undisputed, "illness" interpretation of mental disorders in the United States and elsewhere, we will now briefly discuss those publics and interest groups that have a vested interest in the issue.

Moral Publics and Interest Groups

Among the "moral entrepreneurs" on the mental illness issue have been at least three identifiable publics, which have occasionally spawned fairly well-organized interest and pressure groups. These three are the civic and humanitarian public, the patients and former patients, and the family and friends of the latter.

The Civic and Humanitarian Public

Roger Williams is cited by Deutsch (1949:47) as "the earliest known colonial champion of the right of the mentally ill to humane treatment." Similarly, as one looks at the "moral-treatment" hospitals which the Quakers erected or campaigned for in England, Frankfort (Pennsylvania), and New York, one cannot but appreciate the humanitarian qualities of men like Tuke, Scattergood, and Eddy. Likewise, one has to be impressed with the efforts and motives of a woman like Dorothea Dix, who seemingly almost single-handedly moved legislatures to action. Indeed, more so than with most of the social-problem movements discussed in this book, the mental-illness issue involved a number of truly outstanding and effective individual champions.

One of the earliest and most influential of these was Dorothea Dix. At a time when the belief in the curability of mental illness was at its peak, this diminutive retired school teacher went to the East Cambridge jail in Boston to teach a woman's Sunday school class on a wintery Sunday morning in 1841. Appalled at the cold and filth, and the incarceration of the mentally disordered with the criminal, she began a long crusade to improve the conditions of those with mental problems.

While it seemed as though legislators and the public were receptive to the building of institutions dedicated to the cure of the insane, as late as the 1840's, no provisions for mental hospitals had yet been made in many parts of the country. In 1843 there were only about 24 hospitals, public and private, with a total bed capacity of only 2,561 devoted specifically to the care of the mentally disturbed (Rosen, 1968:277). One commentator suggests that the leaders among the proponents of the modern concept of mental illness were too "dignified" and "scientific" in their demeanor to arouse the common man; indeed, there is little evidence that the public was much aroused at all about the illness-cure idea prior to 1940, at the earliest (Shryock, 1944:19).

Thirty-nine-year-old Dorothea Dix came to play a vitally important role in the perpetuation of the illness interpretation of mental disorders, calling upon legislatures across the country to establish mental hospitals, and propagating the "cult of curability" through an emphasis upon the economic advantages of building state hospitals:

> No fact is better established in all hospital annals than this: that it is cheaper to take charge of the insane in a curative institution than to support them elsewhere for life. (cited in Deutsch, 1949:172)

Born in Maine and raised in Massachusetts, Miss Dix had had a severe physical breakdown at age 34, which had cut short her career as a teacher. After her recovery, it appeared that she would live out the remainder of her life at a sharply reduced level of activity. A bequest from her grandmother, together with personal savings, gave her the assurance of a comfortable income for life. Having helped to remedy some of the physical problems of the mentally disordered in the East Cambridge jail, she became interested in their plight and spent two years surveying jails and almshouses in Massachusetts. Concluding that the situation at East Cambridge had not been an exceptional case, she came before the state legislature and presented her findings. The solution which she proposed was the construction of state hospitals. Miss Dix gathered around her influential supporters, who included Samuel G. Howe, R. C. Waterston, Luther V. Bell, and Horace Mann. The eventual result was the Worcester State Hospital.

Because of the fact that mental-health problems have potentially disruptive effects upon a society as a whole, such deviance generally draws the concern of certain civic groups. When productive members of society are either partially incapacitated or removed completely from active involvement in social life, there is a general societal loss. Furthermore, the inability of most families adequately to care for and treat such mental deviants usually leads to calls for state intervention; and insofar as the mentally disordered become involved in violations of the law, the state can be expected to take some action.

In the United States, local, state, and federal governments have only recently attempted to treat the mentally disturbed in any specific manner. During the colonial period, governments generally left the problem of handling the mentally troubled up to their families and relatives, grudgingly providing aid when there were no alternatives. Before the advent of almshouses in the 18th and 19th centuries, the unmanageable mentally deviant were commonly placed in jails, and even in the "almshouse era," such people were institutionalized not as mentally ill, but as paupers. Not until the founding of the Pennsylvania Hospital in Philadelphia (1752)—the first institution in the English colonies to care exclusively for the mentally sick—did a state government actively move in the direction of such care. The first *state* hospital—the Lunatic Hospital at Williamsburg, Virginia—was opened in 1769, but no widespread construction of state hospitals took place until well into the 19th century.

Former Patients

Patients and former patients have an obvious stake in the mental-health issue. They are the people who receive the label from society, experience the available forms of treatment, live in or utilize the physical facilities, and to varying degrees face the problem of regaining or maintaining the definition of "normal." Their personal involvement can lead them to a unique comprehension of what it is to be mentally ill in American society, and sometimes to a demand for changes.

Thus it was that a former patient, Clifford Beers, on the basis of his own experiences in three mental institutions at the turn of the century, saw the need for reform in both institutional practices and public attitudes. Beers' influence on the mental health movement in this country will be more fully assessed further on in the chapter. Largely as a result of his autobiography, *A Mind That Found Itself* (1908), and his zeal in campaigning for better treatment of mental patients, "mental-hygiene organizations," preventive and educative groups, came into being in the United States and abroad. In more recent times, although not by an individual's crusade, Senator Eagleton's incident has stimulated new activity on the part of the National Association for Mental Health, and drawn nationwide publicity to the problems of the stigma facing the person with mental disorders.

It is perhaps ironic that it took a war—World War II—to stir the government and the public to action in the area of mental health. Only when it was discovered that the incidence of "mental illness" among draftees and soldiers was unusually high, did the federal government, with some public pressure, pass the National Mental Health Act in 1946, which opened a new era for psychiatrists in the United States. This Act will be examined in detail later on. Also growing out of the war were the efforts of certain conscientious objectors who, after serving on the staffs of mental hospitals during World War II, felt so concerned about conditions that they formed the National Mental Health Foundation (1947) to promote improvement of conditions in mental hospitals.

Family and Friends

One of the most obvious publics with an interest in mental-health issues is the patient's relatives and friends. Their personal involvement with and investment in the patient would seem to make them acutely sensitive to the problems of the mentally ill. A particularly noteworthy example of such a public is Dr. Philippe Pinel, the famous French physician who 200 years ago made history by removing the chains from patients in Paris' Bicêtre hospital. He appears to have been drawn to a concern with mental disorders through the tragic death of a mentally disordered friend. Similarly, the establishment of "The Retreat," by the Quakers in England in 1796 was stimulated to a great extent by the death of a Quaker lady at the nearby York Asylum. Concerned Quakers, including William Tuke, vowed to establish a different kind of asylum. The result was The Retreat, with its emphasis on a calm, nonstressful, positive environment, known as moral treatment. Clifford Beers writes that when he was still a patient, he received much support from his brother, and his Connecticut Society for Mental Hygiene (1908) significantly included among its 14 pioneers both his father and his brother. The late President John F. Kennedy, a strong champion of "mental health," had an older sister who was retarded.

Professional and Occupational Interest Groups

A more organized and focused kind of group with mental-health interests would be those professionals who work with the mentally ill. It is to be expected that their definitions of mental illness, and the kinds of therapy they would advocate, would be in accord with their interests in the status of their own profession, as well as with their altruistic goals.

Up until our own century, the so-called experts in the field of mental disorders were often magicians, shamans, medicine men, priests, and ministers. (In some of the less-developed countries in the world, this is still the case.) In the Middle Ages, it was commonly held that doctors had no business studying and treating mental disorders, a position which the clergy, in all likelihood, had some role in establishing. Yet as far back as Hippocrates, there have been those who have argued for the medical interpretation of mental problems. Opposing the supernatural tradition and its legacy have been such prominent people and groups as the 16th-century Belgian physician Johann Weyer, Dr. Benjamin Rush, the American Psychiatric Association, and the National Committee for Mental Hygiene. Of these proponents, one of the earliest, and certainly the most influential, was Dr. Benjamin Rush (1745-1813), often hailed as the father of American psychiatry, who joined the staff of the Pennsylvania Hospital at Philadelphia in 1783. Even when the hospital was newly opened in 1752, it included among its patients people with mental disorders. When the Pennsylvania Assembly offered financial aid to the hospital, one requirement which they stipulated was that such individuals should receive medical attention. However, the insane were hardly treated as "ill." Rather, they were initially relegated to the basement, and in a subsequent permanent building they were quartered in cells underneath the hospital. For years chains were used on the patients, as were severe and barbarous forms of punishment. With time the "insane department" of the Pennsylvania Hospital became a well-known Philadelphia "exhibit" which could be observed by sightseers for a fee. Attendants were known as "cell-keepers," and their duties more closely resembled those of prison guards than of servers of the sick. This kind of treatment was roundly criticized by Dr. Benjamin Rush. Regarded as the most famous doctor in Philadelphia at the time, Rush so successfully propagated the disease approach to mental disorders that historian Albert Deutsch (1949:87) asserts: "None of his contemporaries exercised a greater influence than he did on American medicine in general and psychiatry in particular."

Born in Philadelphia of Quaker parents, Rush graduated from what is now Princeton University at age 15, and then went on to study medicine at the University of Edinburgh. Soon after graduation, he returned to Philadelphia where he developed a successful private practice. Rush was a member of the Continental

Congress at age 30, as well as a signer of the Declaration of Independence. His accomplishments were significant in a wide variety of fields. His involvement in reform extended to prisons and punishment, education, prohibition, poverty, and abolition.

In the same year that he established his own practice (1769), Rush began teaching at Philadelphia College as the first American teacher to offer a comprehensive course in "mental disease." He is said to have attracted a larger number of students than any other medical teacher during the last quarter of that century. His teachings were subsequently carried to every part of the country by his students (Deutsch, 1949:73). In 1812, Rush published the first general treatise on psychiatry in America, *Medical Inquiries and Observations Upon the Diseases of the Mind.* For 71 years this work remained the only one of its kind in this country, serving as a primary textbook for American students of mental disease. It was not until 1883 that new works appeared, those of William A. Hammond and Edward C. Spitza. Consequently, the influence of Rush on the conception and treatment of mental illness in this country was extensive.

His belief that mental problems are analogous to physical problems is made explicit in a letter to his friend John Adams:

The subjects of mental diseases have hitherto been enveloped in mystery. I have endeavored to bring them down to the level of all other diseases of the human body, and to show that the mind and the body are moved by the same causes and subject to the same laws. (cited in Szasz, 1970:139)

Rush theorized that mental disorders are to be understood as arterial diseases which have their primary location in the blood vessels of the brain. When these blood vessels become overcharged with blood, mental disorganization takes place. He therefore maintained that the brain must be relieved of such pressure by venesection, or blood-letting. Indeed, Rush was regarded as the foremost proponent of venesection in the country. On one occasion he claims to have extracted 200 ounces of blood from one patient within a few months, and from another 470 ounces in 47 bleedings (Deutsch, 1949:77). It is interesting to note that Rush was the inventor of two mechanical devices related to the treatment he advocated: the gyrator and the tranquilizer. The former was a rotating board to which patients were strapped, with their heads furthest from the center. It could be rotated at great speeds, causing the blood to rush to the head, thus supposedly increasing bodily activity. The tranquilizer was a chair to which patients were strapped with their heads in a fixed position, in order to reduce muscular action.

While Rush, in the Hippocratic tradition, held to a physiological interpretation of mental disorders, he nevertheless believed that bodily punishment (e.g., whippings) was sometimes of value. However, it was his position that punishment should be limited only to therapeutic activity, and that hospital staff interaction with patients should generally be characterized by kindness and respect. Largely through his efforts, the mental patients at the Pennsylvania Hospital were given their own hospital wing and eventually their own hospital. By defining mental deviance as a medical phenomenon (a disease or illness), Rush made it possible for people to replace fatalism with hope in an eventual cure. The 19th century thus witnessed the rise of what has been called the "cult of curability," and increasingly up until about 1875, physicians and psychiatrists proclaimed the good news that mental disorders could be cured. Later in the century, when the newly formed professional groups of neurologists and psychiatrically oriented social workers began to compete with the state hospitals for clients, it is interesting to note that their primary tactic was to criticize the performance of the mental hospital superintendents. Although improvements in the state hospitals probably were needed, these critics were mainly trying to call attention to their own competencies. They even went so far as to form a short-lived, National Association for the Protection of the Insane and the Prevention of Insanity (1880).

The 20th century has not in general been dominated by crusading individuals like Rush and Dix in the earlier centuries. The rapid growth of the psychiatric and social work professions in the present century has provided the base instead for important professional interest groups. Chief among these has been the National Committee for Mental Hygiene (which later became the National Association for Mental Health). Though founded originally (1909) largely through the efforts of Clifford Beers, a former mental patient, this organization was rapidly taken over by mental health professionals, especially after World War I, and became closely tied to the American Psychiatric Association. (See discussion below under The Mental Health Movement). Through the publication of its magazine *Mental Hygiene* (recently renamed *MH*), and through various other means, the National Association has strongly advocated and promoted its definition of mental disorders as *illnesses* to be treated according to a general medical model.

The extension of the illness concept to cover crime, juvenile delinquency, and many other forms of anti-social or "deviant" behavior, has been a chief interest of the American Orthopsychiatric Association, founded in 1924 with the support of both the National Committee for Mental Hygiene and the American Psychiatric Association. To define deviance more generally as a problem of mental hygiene not only represents an aggrandizement of the professional territory of the constituent interest groups, but it has also made for a certain amount of rivalry between the proponents of the orthopsychiatric point of view and those social workers and criminologists who see deviant behavior as the result of more "normal" social factors like poverty, differential association, and labelling.

Scientific Interest Groups

Aside from the professional practitioners concerned with the treatment and "cure" of mental disorders, various kinds of behavioral scientists have done research from a variety of theoretical perspectives in an effort to understand the nature and origin of mental illness. Most have focused in one way or another upon family and/or other social environmental factors. In particular, sociologists have historically stressed the social factors associated with mental disorders. The classic studies of Faris-Dunham (1939), Hollingshead-Redlich (1958), Srole (1962), and the Leightons (1959, 1963) have found a greater propensity for mental illness to exist among the members of the lower social classes. Urban sociologists have suggested the relationship between the rising incidence of mental illness and the rise of industrialization. Some forms of mental illness among the elderly have been attributed to their withdrawal from meaningful activities and relationships.

Psychologists and psychoanalysts also have been inclined to emphasize the influence of environmental factors upon the individual, commonly "explaining" a good deal of mental illness in terms of personality disorders resulting from defective socialization experiences. By way of example, psychoanalytic research has pointed to the importance of childhood experiences in shaping adult attitudes and behavior. The extensive research work of Bateson, Lidz, and Wynne-Singer (see Mishler and Waxler, 1965) has sought to explore the relationship between family interaction and schizophrenia. Following a somewhat different direction, a neo-Freudian, Karen Horney (1937), has asserted that neurosis results primarily from fears and mental conflicts experienced by individuals living in the highly individualist, competitive Western society.

More recently, writers such as Scheff (1967) and Szasz (1970) have questioned the validity of the disease model of mental illness, stressing instead the *social processes* which are involved in the recognition, commitment, and treatment of the mentally deviant. Such, in fact, is the point of view of this chapter, generally speaking.

THE MENTAL ILLNESS MOVEMENTS

The fact that the illness interpretation of mental disorders predominates in America today is in large part the result of the work of individuals and groups who diligently disseminated it. We will now review the historical processes through which our current interpretations and definitions have evolved.

Historical Review

At the time of the settling of America, the view that the mentally disordered were actually ill was held by very few. Such people were primarily seen as incurable deviants, who at best should be only physically maintained. Consequently they were confined in homes, often chained in attics, cellars, and sheds, where they would pose a minimum threat to safety and respectability. In other instances, they were placed in jails or in the cells and dungeons of almshouses. Some who were not regarded as dangerous were allowed to wander about the country. When expert judgment was needed concerning the diagnosis of insanity, such responsibility rested not with medical men, but rather with civil officers. In fact, few colonial doctors were acquainted with the nature of or means of treating mental problems.

While the 18th century brought with it asylums in Europe and almshouses in America, these developments only seemed to represent moves to get the mentally disordered "off of the streets," rather than reflecting significant changes in the attitude toward this form of deviance. These new institutions largely served a custodial function, and were characterized by extremely heterogeneous populations of unfortunates.

In 1785, Jean Colombier, Inspector-General of French hospitals and prisons, summed up the situation of the mental deviants as follows:

The half-mad are mingled with those who are totally deranged, those who rage with those who are quiet; some are in chains, while others are free in their prison . . . unless nature comes to their aid . . . the duration of their misery is life-long . . . (Rosen, 1968:151)

One commentator understates the case when he notes that the European asylum movement of this period "was not accompanied by increased knowledge and understanding of mental disease" (Council of State Governments, 1950:17). American almshouses likewise knew no more than a containment approach to the insane.

At approximately the turn of the 19th century, American attitudes toward the insane began to feel the effects of a new mood which was sweeping the Western world. That new trend of thought was the Enlightenment, which had begun in 18th-century Europe. It was an age of rationalism in which

. . . many believed that human reason could free men from the errors and misfortunes of the past and lead them to perpetual peace, utopian government, and a perfect society. *Reason* would discover the *natural laws* regulating existence, thereby insuring the *progress* of the human race. (Brinton, et al., 1957:274)

Human misery was seen to be the result of ignorance; therefore, given the illumination of reason, misery would eventually disappear. In this period in history, a number of reform movements began to emerge in Europe and America, pertaining to the care of children, prisons, working conditions, and public health (Rosen, 1968:275).

This was a time of extreme optimism. Medicine, in particular, was making great promises. Having largely defeated plague, leprosy, and smallpox, it was preparing to move on to bigger and better things, including the successful treatment of mental problems (Shryock, 1944:9, 18). This was the exhilarating environment in which Dr. Benjamin Rush and other medical pioneers advanced various medical therapies for the cure of mental illness. Most of these were very crude by modern standards.

Meanwhile, throughout much of the 19th century, physicians became leaders in the attempts to establish mental hospitals and more often than not ended up in charge of them. (At the same time, English institutions were still being managed by wardens in the prison-system tradition.) From their newly found vantage point, these American physicians-turned-"medical superintendents" proclaimed astonishing cure rates. The Hartford Retreat in Frankfort, Pennsylvania, for example, claimed that 90 percent of the patients admitted during one year had been cured, a figure which was cited in an English novelist's book and subsequently widely quoted in newspapers and periodicals. As a result Hartford gained a reputation as the most successfully operated institution for the mentally ill in the entire world. Not to be outdone, other mental hospitals entered into a numbers competition, manipulating figures to create a largely fictitious picture of cures.

Observers of the era argue that, to some extent at least, such fictitious figures were aimed at legislators who would recognize not only the humanitarian but the economic advantages of cure over custody, and grant funds for new hospitals. If that was the intention, it sometimes worked well. In 1832, a Massachusetts legislative commission presented a report, drawn up by Horace Mann, which read in part:

Until a period comparatively recent, insanity has been deemed as an incurable disease. . . . It is now abundantly demonstrated that with appropriate medical and moral treatment insanity yields with more readiness than ordinary diseases. (cited in Deutsch, 1949:137-8)

By 1844, the medical superintendents of the state and private hospitals had become sufficiently organized to form The Association of Medical Superintendents of American Institutions for the Insane. Concerned primarily with institutional problems, this exclusive association later evolved into the American Psychiatric Association. The legacy of Benjamin Rush is perhaps illustrated in the following statement by one of the most prominent early figures in the Association, Dr. Thomas Kirkbride (1809-1883):

Insanity should be classed with other diseases. . . . It should never be forgotten that every individual who has a brain is liable to insanity, precisely as every one who has lungs is liable to pneumonia . . . (cited in Deutsch, 1949:207)

In the latter part of the 19th century, the work of Dorothea Dix and her allies, described above, was as influential as the earlier pioneering efforts of Benjamin Rush had been. Within five years or so, she carried her cause personally to every state east of the Rockies. Her method usually consisted of three steps: (1) surveying conditions, (2) rallying public opinion, through the press and personal appearances, and (3) presentations in the state legislature. In nearly every instance her presentation eventually resulted in the erection of a state hospital, or in the enlargement and improvement of an existing one. Her role was not so much one of creator as of catalyst, stimulating action that had been desired before her arrival but which, without her presence, might have been delayed for years (Deutsch, 1949:172). It is estimated that Miss Dix was directly responsible for the founding or enlarging of over 30 state hospitals.

Deutsch (1949:183-4) has noted that throughout her career, Miss Dix "played the role of the lone eagle." He suggests that this may have been partly because of the nature of humanitarian reform in her time, which was geared to the individual crusader, and secondly, partly due to her own peculiar temperament. So while she did mobilize others at times (e.g., the influentials who aided her in Massachusetts), her work did not usher in a sustained, cohesive, social movement. Her effectiveness seems largely due to the fact that although the "cult of curability" had put her audiences in a mood receptive to her reforms, the physicians and psychiatrists of the day, because of their self-styled non-activist roles, scarcely "poked their heads around the curtain," whereas she had the audacity to walk out on the stage and come to grips with the issues. As Deutsch (1949:185) puts it, "She had effected a revolution in the care of the mentally ill . . . where . . . reformers had almost despaired of progressive reform."

The aftermath of Dorothea Dix's crusade for the erection of state mental hospitals is an intriguing one with respect to a central thesis of this book, that social problems are products of collective definitions and behavior, existing independently of reality. The medical people had asserted that mental disorders were forms of illness. Miss Dix, a convert to their position, had gone around the country expounding the need for hospitals for mental "patients." Yet, once the hospitals were built, nothing changed! In her inspection tours made late in her career, Miss Dix not only found that the sick were not being cured, but she discovered that in state after state, the very conditions she had fought to eliminate were still present.

It seems that the "cult of curability" had produced the idea that the asylums or hospitals were somehow magical; that once the medical profession had the mentally disordered under the right kind of roof, they would all be made well. The illness/cure interpretation had been oversold. People awoke to find boarding houses rather than hospitals, isolated "monasteries for the mad" rather than therapeutic homes for the disturbed. It became apparent that physicians playing leadership roles in such institutions often had only a superficial understanding of mental problems and that even the supposedly expert psychiatrist was actually working without any clear picture as to the nature, to say nothing of the causes, of the conditions confronting him (Shryock, 1944:11). With the bursting of the "curability" bubble, disillusionment revived the familiar adage: once insane, always insane. In some ways, the reformers' efforts in the 19th century added up to an abortive social movement, which remained in the doldrums until rejuvenated in somewhat different form in the current mental health movement.

The Mental Health Movement

A number of events close to the turn of the 20th century contributed to important changes in the social climate of the Western world. Following the optimism regarding social progress which had characterized the late 18th and early 19th centuries, a mood of caution had set in as a result of a number of disappointments, for example, the failure to successfully combat cholera epidemics and childhood diseases. But by the opening of the 20th century, the effects of the discoveries of bacteriologists like Pasteur, Koch, and the American, Walter Reed, were being realized in the prevention of a variety of historically fatal diseases. New impetus was thus given to the optimistic humanism which had been so rampant a century before. Given the hope of new scientific possibilities on the one hand, and widespread social changes and dislocations in the United States on the other, reform movements again began to spring up during America's Progressive Era.

Stimulated by the Muckrakers, a group of "energetic journalists who made it their chief concern to discover and exploit in popular articles the seamy side of business and political behavior" (Hicks, et al., 1963:326), reformers gave their attention to changes in the political structure at the federal, state and municipal levels. They also focused on reform in such areas as labor, child employment, prohibition, woman suffrage, juvenile delinquency, housing, and public health generally.

In retrospect, in such a climate it seems clear that the time was ripe for the issue of mental disorders to be reopened. The impressive advances of medicine in other areas offered renewed hope for the semi-defunct, "illness-cure" definition of mental disorders.

Incipiency of the Movement

A case could certainly be made for tracing the incipiency of the modern mental health movement back to the early (if abortive) efforts of pioneers like Rush and Dix. But the revival was stimulated by an autobiography that appeared in 1908 entitled, *A Mind That Found Itself,* written by a former mental patient, Clifford Beers (1876-1943). The book told how Beers had experienced a severe mental breakdown shortly after graduating from Yale in 1897, and barely escaped death in a suicidal attempt. He spent three years in three different Connecticut mental hospitals, both state and private. During the course of his hospitalization, Beers was appalled by the common incidence of indifferent, cruel and brutal handling of patients by physicians and attendants. He purposely had himself assigned to the most violent wards in order that he might observe and experience first-hand the treatment of patients at all levels of hospital life, and he kept extensive notes. During his hospitalization Beers fought tenaciously for self-respect not only for himself but also for his fellow-patients. His protestations took both spoken and written form, directed at personnel attendants, on up through institutional superintendents, and finally to the Governor of Connecticut. Beers believed that people with mental disorders suffered from mental diseases or illnesses. Hence, his outrage was the result of seeing the mistreatment not merely of *deviants* but of *sick people*.

While still in the hospital, Beers began to think of how he might work to improve the conditions of mental patients. Upon his release, he devoted himself to the organization of a permanent campaign for improvement in the care and treatment of the mentally troubled, as well as for the prevention, whenever possible, of mental illness itself. Beers dreamed of the day ("within a few generations, I believe") when his future employer, reflecting a whole new attitude toward mental illness, might say:

When an employee is ill, he's ill, and it makes no difference to me whether he goes to a general hospital or a hospital for the insane. Should you ever find yourself in need of treatment or rest, I want you to feel that you can take it when and where you please, and work for us again when you are able. (Beers, 1945:210)

Impressed with the influence which the book *Uncle Tom's Cabin* had had in stimulating support for the anti-slavery movement, Beers abandoned his business career and devoted himself to the writing of *A Mind That Found Itself*. Lest he be accused of writing either an irresponsible or sensational type of book, Beers showed the manuscript first to William James, and then to other psychologists, psychiatrists, and leaders in related fields for criticism and comment. Introduced by an excerpt of a letter from William James, the book was published in 1908, "intended to serve as the opening gun" of his campaign (Beers, 1945:255). In the book, he called for the formation of an agency whose primary task would be to wage an educative war against ignorance about insanity:

This, to cure the disease by preventing it, is the only effective cure known. The watchword of such an organization might well be the significant phrase: Mental Hygiene. Its purpose: the spreading of a common-sense gospel of right thinking in order to bring about right living . . . (from Beers, 1945:393)

He urged that a "National Committee for Mental Hygiene" be created without delay, whose foci would be reform, education, research, treatment, and prevention.

Coalescence

In 1908, Beers and 14 others founded the Connecticut Society for Mental Hygiene, the first state association of its kind. One year later, with 12 others, he founded the National Committee for Mental Hygiene. It is of critical importance to recognize that in starting the movement, Beers intended to enlist the top leadership of the day, both lay and professional, especially professional. He succeeded. Beers was not trying to gather up an assorted array of volunteers for his National Committee in order to "see what could be done"; rather, he was carefully selecting the renowned specialists of the day and enlisting their help to carry out a clearly defined plan. In keeping with his own perception of mental disorders as "illnesses," he drew heavily from the ranks of psychiatrists. Representing that profession in the early planning stages of the movement were three key figures, Drs. Adolph Meyer, William Russell, and Frankwood Williams, while a fourth leader, Dr. William Welch, was a pathologist. And as for those laymen who were part of the movement, Kingsley Davis wrote in the 1930's:

> They are mostly upper-middle-class professionals, predominantly of British ancestry, identified with the Protestant church and frequently reared and educated in New England. Many of them apparently had well-to-do parents who themselves had risen in life through effort and initiative. (1938:58)

Quite clearly, prior to about 1950, the National Committee did little to try to arouse or engage the general public. One searches in vain for historical accounts which describe attempts to win converts among the general public. One historian, for example, writes that with respect to educational materials, the National Committee over time

> ... had utilized what distribution channels seemed appropriate (such as meetings and professional journals) but ... had never set out aggressively to capture the large mass audience—that elusive "man-in-the-street" who had never heard of "mental hygiene." (Ridenour, 1961:118)

Indeed, the chief sources of information on mental hygiene for almost half a century were pamphlets which had to be paid for. Ridenour (1961:119) puts the case mildly when she notes that prior to the late 1940's "The National Committee for Mental Hygiene . . . had never developed public relations and fund-raising campaigns after the manner of some of the other national health organizations."

Rather, from its inception, the National Committee was primarily run by medical professionals and was very closely tied to the American Psychiatric Association. Men active in one organization were commonly also active in the other. Indeed, more than 20 former APA presidents have been actively involved in the National

Committee or its successor, the National Association for Mental Health. Such an interconnection can be clearly seen in the following statement of Dr. Douglas Thom in the October 1922 issue of the National Association's journal:

> Nothing that has happened in modern medicine during the past decade has been a greater boon to mankind than the development of an interest in psychiatry, both medical and social. . . .

Thus, the 20th century mental health movement, led by the National Committee for Mental Hygiene, represents an attempt of the psychiatric profession to re-establish the credibility of an illness interpretation of mental disorders. The method was not so much to secure the interest and aid of the public as to reach out for recognition and support by the federal government, in order to advance the profession and its illness frame of reference.

For the first three years, the National Committee existed primarily on paper, receiving little financial support beyond personal loans obtained by Beers. However, a $50,000 gift from railroad magnate Henry Phipps in 1912 placed the work on an active basis. Dr. Thomas Salmon was lured away from the U.S. Public Health Service to become director of special studies in that same year, and was redesignated medical director in 1915. Prior to the outbreak of World War I the National Committee gave its attention to basic stock-taking: preparing lists of psychiatrists and mental institutes, compiling bibliographies on mental and nervous diseases, and gathering information on laws concerning mental disorders. Surveys of facilities for the mentally disordered were conducted throughout the country, gradually financed by the Rockefeller Foundation. Resultant materials were made available to legislative bodies, professionals in the field, civic groups, and the public generally. In 1917 the Committee began to publish a quarterly, *Mental Hygiene,* which until the 1970's was primarily a scholarly journal with a small and select readership. Anticipating imminent U.S. involvement in World War I, Salmon and two associates succeeded in convincing the Surgeon General that mental disorders had been a common problem among U.S. soldiers on the Mexican border, and that it was imperative for plans to be made for handling mental problems among soldiers about to become involved in the World War. As a result, the Surgeon General put the National Committee in charge of organizing psychiatric units, and Salmon was named the Director of Psychiatry for the American Expeditionary Force. Deutsch comments (1949:317):

> It is one of the grotesque ironies of history that wars, with their frightful carnage in lives lost and wrecked, do tend to give impetus to various health movements. Governments which, in times of peace, gave little or no thought to the problems of protecting and preserving the health of their citizens, turned their attention increasingly to the problems of physical and mental health of the million forces during the World War. Not to make

robust citizens, to be sure, but to make more efficient fighting machines of their soldiers. . . .

Salmon's plan for early examinations, prompt treatment, and post-release care meant that soldiers having mental breakdowns in France stood a good chance of getting better psychiatric care there than they would have received as civilians at home (Ridenour, 1961:53)!

Yet while the National Committee was pushing for the appointment of competent medical personnel to deal with mental problems in the armed services, it was not uncommon for army officials to regard mental breakdowns as a form of cowardice requiring punishment. The stigma which occurs when mental disorder is regarded as a type of deviance, rather than an "illness," is illustrated in the following extract:

One shipload of 250 returning "shell-shock cases," most of whom were suffering from neuroses and required no supervision at all, were kept below decks on the whole trip across, without fresh air or exercise. (Ridenour, 1961:54)

While the rejection of large numbers of men on the grounds of mental defects and the large number of cases of mental problems among the troops attracted wide attention, there were still no significant reforms (Connery, 1968:4). Nevertheless, the war did put the issue of mental disorders on center stage, and furthered the efforts of psychiatrists in their propagation of the mental-"illness" thesis.

Around the time of World War I, psychiatry's willingness to recognize the role of environmental factors in the causes, treatment, and ultimate "cure" of mental disease led that discipline to closer ties with social workers, who, conveniently, were placing increasing stress on personality factors in such areas as delinquency and family disorganization. The war also revealed the need for clinical psychologists in testing subjects; they had administered mental tests to some 1.75 million potential soldiers.

This alliance of fields became particularly strong with the rise of a new institution in the 1920's. With resources provided by the Commonwealth Fund to invest in the health of America's social life, the National Committee established a new Division on the Prevention of Delinquency. Following the precedent of Dr. William Healy in Chicago and then Boston, in 1922 the Committee began to send out psychiatric field-service teams to organize clinics in various cities. Thus the "child guidance clinic" was born.

Such clinics housed psychiatrists, psychiatric social workers, and clinical psychologists, working together. The psychiatrist was usually in charge of administration, physical and psychiatric examinations, and psychotherapy; the psychologist, the assessment of the child's mental abilities; and the social worker, the social history and ties with family and community. Initially aimed primarily at delinquent children, the services of the clinics were gradually broadened to include all types of children, later reflected in the Committee's change of the division name to Division on Community Clinics (1927).

Paralleling the extension of the illness concept into the child guidance field was the establishment of an organization of professionals and citizens committed to the extension of that concept into all sorts of social problem areas; namely, the American Orthopsychiatric Association, organized in 1924 through the efforts of such well known psychiatrists as Karl Menninger, and with William Healy as its first president (Ridenour, 1961:69). Through a variety of promotional efforts, the AOA sought for several decades to influence the public and the National Committee to apply the medical or neuropsychiatric illness model in explaining and treating crime, juvenile delinquency, and many other forms of deviant behavior then considered as "social problems" (Deutsch, 1949). The influence of that point of view was considerable for awhile, and it still remains to the extent that people (and textbooks) are inclined to refer to any form of deviance as a pathology.

Another important post-war development was the effort to train people in the psychiatric traditions and methods of treatment. In 1923, the Committee was placed in charge of administering fellowship grants for psychiatric training, which were provided by the Commonwealth Fund and the Rockefeller Foundation. With the blessing of the Committee, training in psychiatric social work was instigated in Boston and New York. By 1931, the National Committee was collaborating with the American Psychiatric Association in studying medical-school curricula and promoting the improvement of training.

Yet, despite this new emphasis on guidance clinics and the efforts to train competent personnel, one observer of the period notes, "With respect to mental-health education, the most significant characteristic of the early period was the lack of public interest" (Ridenour, 1961:94). When the First International Congress on Mental Hygiene was held in Washington, D.C. in 1930 with over 3,000 people from 50 countries attending, perhaps it is significant that while many were applauding the occasion as the realization of Clifford Beers' greatest dreams, one avid supporter of the movement, Dr. William Welch, had this to say:

[The Congress] was rather terrible and an example of arousing the public before the foundation of sound knowledge and doctrine has been laid. (cited in Ridenour, 1961:67)

Up through the 1930's and early 1940's, the psychiatric profession was influenced largely by the ideas of Freud and strongly committed to the idea, implicit in the illness definition, that mental disorders could be "cured." While the large, remotely located, and deplorably overcrowded mental hospital continued to be the chief resort of psychiatrists and courts in the treatment of mental patients, the 1930's saw the introduction of a variety of new cures which were hailed by psychiatrists as the eventual solution to the problem of mental illness. These therapeutic innovations included psychosurgery (such as lobotomy), insulin shock treatment, electric convulsive shock therapy, and a few other strictly physical methods, along with the usual Freudian-based psychotherapy. These new "cures" fell far short of the psychiatrists' optimistic projections, and they often constituted travesties on professional ethics and on the civil liberties of patients (Deutsch, 1948). Thus, not only did the National Committee for Mental Hygiene during this period make but few gains in convincing the public of the illness and cure definition of mental disorders, but psychiatry generally failed to produce the therapeutic results that would have supported such a definition.

A good example of the failure of people outside of psychiatric circles to take seriously a medical approach to mental problems was the fact that, despite Salmon's energetic mental-health program during World War I, in World War II the Surgeon General hadn't seen fit to even read the summary volume of this activity, let alone initiate a similar program. It was only through the efforts of the National Committee that such a plan was introduced two years after the war started. At that point, Dr. William C. Menninger became head of the Psychiatric Division of the Surgeon General's office, and psychiatrists were hurriedly recruited. By the end of the war the number of psychiatrists in the military had increased from 35 in late 1941 to 2,400 in 1945. It was this development, more than any other, which indicated that the mental health movement had passed from the stage of coalescence to that of institutionalization.

Institutionalization

This wartime alliance between psychiatry and the federal government, although relatively brief, was to have a profound influence upon the definition of mental illness in this country. Between January, 1942 and June, 1945, an estimated 1,875,000 men among the 15 million examined were rejected for service because of alleged psychiatric disabilities (Mechanic, 1969:55). Further, it is estimated that as many as 750,000 men were eventually discharged because of mental and emotional problems (Ridenour, 1961:60). Such figures naturally came as something of a "shock" to Americans, creating concern, which in turn stimulated moves toward finding a remedy to the problem.

Psychiatrists now were not only in a position to state the nature of the mental-health problem (illness or "defects"), but also to determine its incidence. As Deutsch points out:

It had been recommended that one psychiatrist be assigned to draft examining boards for every 50 registrants, and that a minimum of 15 minutes be devoted to every psychiatric examination. When the many millions began to pour through selective service centers, however, these proposals became scraps of paper on the wind. Instead of 15 minutes, an average of barely two minutes was devoted to the psychiatric examination of Army recruits. It was not unusual for a single psychiatrist to examine 200 men daily. (cited in Mechanic, 1969:55)

David Mechanic (1969:56) puts it succinctly: "Most of the incentive for psychiatric screening came from groups within the psychiatric profession, so psychiatrists were in no sense innocent maidens in this affair." One interesting result was that more veterans were receiving compensation and "treatment" for mental illness than ever before in history (Szasz, 1970:38).

Nonetheless, the country finally was alerted to "mental-health needs." The wartime rejections, apart from the mental "casualties," suggested that an extremely high level of mental disorders existed among the U.S. population. Media coverage of the mental-health question began to expand, stimulated by the efforts of a group of men who, as conscientious objectors, had been assigned to work in U.S. mental hospitals as attendants during the war. This group, which was later to form the National Mental Health Foundation (1947), was committed to improving mental hospital conditions and care by means of a constructive arousal of public opinion. They therefore released materials which they had accumulated on the hospitals to *Life* magazine in the spring of 1946, which were published as a feature story, "Bedlam, USA" (May, 1946). This article was reprinted shortly after in *Reader's Digest* as "The Shame of Our Mental Hospitals" (July, 1946). Appearing in two of the magazines with the widest circulation in the U.S., these articles triggered a barrage of exposés and features in other magazines and papers which continued for several years. One of the most widely printed in the series was Albert Deutsch's *The Shame of the States* (1948), a comprehensive survey of mental hospitals which first appeared in 1945 in the New York papers. The radio carried documentaries; the movie industry offered "The Snake Pit" (1946).

Meanwhile, the National Committee for Mental Hygiene had been working on a legislative bill since 1940, which it brought to Congress in 1945. In the face of the strong post-war sentiment favoring action on mental-health problems, the bill received wide support, and in 1946 the National Mental Health Act was passed. The Act established the National Institute of Mental Health as one of the Institutes of Health of the Public Health Service (it is now under the Deparment of Health, Education, and Welfare). Its primary points of focus were to be research, professional training, and the development of community mental-health programs. A House subcommittee report summed up the deficiencies of psychiatric "knowledge" of "mental illness":

... research on the causes, prevention, diagnosis, and treatment of psychiatric disorders has not kept pace with research in the other branches of the medical sciences, nor has the training of specialists in this field kept pace with the growing demands for psychiatrists. ... Finally, services for prevention and early diagnosis of psychiatric disorders, such as those which have been developed and made available in other fields of medicine during the past decade, have not been available to the public to a sufficient extent. (cited in Connery, 1968:18)

Organizationally, with the passage of the National Mental Health Act, the National Committee for Mental Hygiene had run its course. In the 1930's and '40's many state societies had discarded the hygiene tag and become Mental Health Associations. In 1948, the Third International Congress on Mental Health, meeting in London, gave the functions of The International Committee for Mental Hygiene over to the United Nation's World Federation for Mental Health. And in 1950, the U.S. National Committee merged with the National Mental Health Foundation and the Psychiatric Foundation to form the new National Association for Mental Health. This new "citizen group" has continued to stress the goals of the National Committee, namely:

1/ to bring about excellent facilities for diagnosis, treatment, and rehabilitation of persons suffering from mental disorders, at the earliest stage of their illness
2/ to achieve more positive attitudes on the part of the public toward the mentally ill
3/ to promote, reinforce, and help maintain mental health. (Linzer, 1963:1286)

As for the mental health movement, we have argued that its life history has followed the pattern of the other social movements analyzed in this book: The stage of incipiency at the time of Beers, a long period of coalescence, and a third stage of institutionalization, stimulated primarily by the developments of World War II. This most recent stage has involved government absorption of the movement's main point of emphasis, namely, concern for mental health. The result, however, has not yet been the *demise* of the mental health movement. Rather, with government co-optation, psychiatrists and others have been given access to new means of propagating their orientation as the "official" one. Whereas in past times an organization such as the National Committee represented an important channel for advocating the psychiatric interpretation of mental problems, now an organization such as the government-funded but psychiatrist-laden National Institute of Mental Health plays a decisive role in the promotion of mental health. The National Committee lives on as the National Association for Mental Health, playing a largely complementary role to that of the government in the field of mental health. Its growing obsolescence, though, is likely to bring about its demise.

THE LEGACY OF THE MENTAL HEALTH MOVEMENT

We began this chapter by pointing out that it is commonly believed in the United States that a phenomenon known as mental illness exists. Behavior so called, however, has been defined in various ways at different points in history. Thus the question we have attempted to answer is, how did Americans come to possess their particular view? After considering the types of people who might have an interest in defining such behavior, we proceeded to show how the influence of Benjamin Rush in shaping American psychiatric thought, the achievements of Dorothea Dix in crusading for hospitals for the "sick," and the efforts of the National Committee for Mental Hygiene to promote and educate the government and the nation in its orientation, have all played major roles in creating the present concept of mental illness as a curable disease.

The Definition and Treatment of Mental Illness

This illness and curability perspective on mental disorders is perhaps the single most important element in the legacy of the movements of the past, and particularly of the mental health movement of the current century. Not only has this perspective inspired and influenced the public allocation of resources and the policies of government (see below), but it has determined the nature of treatment and therapy. As we have seen, history has brought a number of changes in the latter to correspond with the changing professional (and sometimes public) definitions of mental health and illness. Though certain therapeutic holdovers from earlier periods remain (e.g., large "custodial" hospitals, drug therapy, and occasional shock therapy), the contemporary and emerging trends are away from hospitals and toward community maintenance or community therapy programs. These usually involve keeping a patient in the home of his (her) family, relatives, or friends, with professional supervision and treatment being provided on an outpatient basis at various clinics. More emphasis is placed also on prevention of at least the more severe symptoms through early diagnosis by clinics or private practitioners, and through educational programs intended to make the public more aware, alert, and sympathetic toward mental illness symptoms. While tranquilizing drugs continue to be used, especially for the more "dangerous" cases, the more modern use of drugs has tended to emphasize instead the correction of imbalances in glandular secretions, which are sometimes implicated in mental disorders; at least a few cases of mental illness seem thereby to be preventable if diagnosis and treatment occur early enough. In general, though, modern therapy seems to be relying less on treatment in the isolation of a hospital, and more upon group-based or community-based social therapies (Clausen, 1971:75-84).

The gradual abandonment of hospitals, and of much of the treatment traditionally administered within them, can be attributed partly to their extraordinary lack of demonstrable therapeutic results, in spite of an extraordinary expenditure of public and private funds (see below); it can be attributed also to the rising crescendo of criticism from within the professional and scientific communities. Goffman (1961) and Scheff (1967) have led the way from a sociological perspective, while from within psychiatry itself have come the trenchant and persuasive criticisms of Thomas Szasz (1960 and 1970). The legal point of view has also been represented among the critics (Dershowitz, 1969). In general, the critics have focused on two main charges: (1) Commitment to mental hospitals has not only subjected hundreds of thousands of citizens to outrageous and abusive treatment of dubious therapeutic value, but it has done so in gross violation of the usual due process and of their civil liberties; and (2) Mental illness is mostly a contemporary social construction or definition of reality, more akin to the earlier notion of devil-possession than to an objective medical pathology like appendicitis; except in a relatively small number of cases having a demonstrable medical or physiological origin, "mentally ill" is a label, bestowed by the psychiatric profession upon an individual whose behavior is especially obnoxious, as a pretext for removing him from public participation, whether his behavior is actually dangerous to others or not. The process is, in other words, very much like that which takes place when a person is labelled criminal or delinquent, except that the mental case does not get the benefit of a trial!

While this interpretation of mental illness is very controversial and raises a number of difficult questions, it has been supported by a certain amount of research, as well as by the varied range of diagnoses and recommendations which psychiatrists have made of cases having essentially the same symptoms. One wonders whether even the professionals can tell the difference between the mentally ill and the mentally well, especially once the labels have been attached. Such skepticism is especially well borne out by research of the kind conducted by Dr. David Rosenhan, a professor of law and psychology at Stanford University. In 1973, Dr. Rosenhan selected 30 persons, including himself, other professors, doctors, psychologists, and a housewife, from among volunteers who agreed to pose as mental patients. They all concocted the same symptom of mental illness, "empty, depressed feelings," and were admitted to mental hospitals, usually with the diagnosis of paranoid schizophrenia. Immediately upon admission, the patients dropped the symptom and proceeded to act in every way as they normally did. Their change in behavior made no difference to the hospital staff, however, for, as Dr. Rosenhan put it, "We were diagnosed as schizophrenic, (so) all of our behavior had to be (considered) schizophrenic." Some of the volunteer patients even took notes on their experiences in the hospitals, and when asked by the staff what they were doing, they told the truth. Nevertheless, the staff took every kind of behavior to be a further symptom of paranoid schizophrenia, with one psychiatric nurse making the note that "patient exhibits writing behavior." Interestingly enough, however, the other *inmates* caught on immediately and recognized the volunteer patients as "phonies." A rather humorous sequel to this investigation occurred when Dr. Rosenhan, having publicized his exposé, warned the director of another mental hospital that he planned to slip in a pseudo-patient there also sometime between January and March of the next year. Of the 193 patients admitted to that hospital during that 3-month period, 43 were culled out by the hospital staff as pseudo-patients. Even the psychiatrists rated 23 of them as pseudo-patients. However, as Dr. Rosenhan explained, "none were pseudo-patients. Our pseudo-patients got the flu and never could go through with (that part of) the experiment." (The preceding paragraph was based upon "Hospitals can't handle sanity," an article in the *San Francisco Examiner* [Associated Press release], March 30, 1974, page 6.)

Such imprecision in the diagnosis of mental illness makes estimates of cure or recovery rates as difficult (or even meaningless) as the estimates of actual incidence, leading an official government report on mental illness to conclude:

The present state of scientific development in the mental health professions does not permit as yet the formulation of exact tests of "cure." (Joint Commission, 1961:54)

Little has happened since that observation to increase our confidence in the definition or diagnosis of mental illness, but the legacy of the influence of the mental health movement has continued to be felt nevertheless.

Allocation of Resources

In the last 20 years the federal government, urged by both the National Association for Mental Health and the National Institute of Mental Health, has continued to generate legislation aimed at combatting mental illness and ensuring improved mental health in this country. Among the more important laws, the Mental Health Study Act was passed in 1955, providing funds for a Joint Commission on Mental Health and Illness "to survey the resources and to make recommendations for combatting mental illness in the United States" (*Joint Commission,* 1961:v). In its report, the Commission called for the establishment of prevention-oriented community mental-health clinics to serve both children and adults:

. . . a national mental health program should set as an objective one fully staffed, full-time mental health clinic available to each 50,000 of population. (Joint Commission, 1961:xiv)

In response to these recommendations, the Community Mental Health Centers Act was passed in 1963, authorizing federal funding for the construction of such clinics, with a 1965 Amendment to the Act providing funds for their staffs.

Congressional appropriations to the National Institute of Mental Health have increased tremendously over the years. The NIMH budget was increased from $9,000,000 in 1950, to $68,000,000 in 1960, to $338,000,000 in 1967. The Nixon administration, however, in attempting to tighten the nation's economy, proposed drastic cuts—including a phaseout of the community-health clinics created in President Kennedy's era. Recently, the proposed move was sharply criticized by the president of the National Association for Mental Health. Their positions are in total conflict, since while the federal government is proposing a phaseout, the NIMH is striving to increase the present 325 centers to 1,500 by 1980 (*MH*, Winter, 1973:34).

However, despite occasional disputes, the federal government is very much in support of the psychiatric interpretation of mental disorders. The mental health movement has succeeded in making a "believer" out of Washington. Enormous sums of money are being invested in present mental-health programs in the belief that the illness model corresponds to reality. Mechanic (1969:vii) writes:

> Mental health is a major American industry. In one way or another, mental health programs are being developed by a wide range of government agencies, private voluntary groups, schools and universities, commercial and industrial enterprises, and even religious organizations.

Three billion dollars are spent annually for maintaining mental-health facilities other than those provided within general hospitals (Clausen, 1971:71). As previously noted, the NIMH annual budget has been approaching 400 million dollars. Indeed, a large segment of the psychiatric profession owes its very existence to the faith the federal government has placed in the illness model. In his 1967 Presidential Address, Harvey J. Tompkins, president of the American Psychiatric Association, commented:

> We are approaching a psychiatrist population of nearly 20,000, about four times as many as two decades ago. This gratifying growth could not have occurred without the government subsidies which have been channeled into professional education . . . (Tompkins, 1967:3)

In addition to our 20,000 psychiatrists, we have some 325 state and county hospitals and 2,500 outpatient clinics. Psychiatric facilities are found in many of the country's general hospitals. Larger and larger numbers of people are receiving varied forms of psychiatric care. One might even argue that among the upper-middle class, there is a certain amount of social prestige attached to seeing a private psychiatrist. In addition to these treatment sources, untold thousands of Americans make use of a plethora of counselling services which allegedly serve a positive, preventive function.

Legislation

In the past few decades, laws have increasingly come into being which are intended to safeguard the rights of those people diagnosed as mentally ill. An important reference point for state legislation on commitment of the mentally disordered to an institution or hospital is the Federal Draft Act (1952). Defining the mentally ill person as "having a psychiatric or other disease which substantially impairs his mental health," the Draft Act permits involuntary hospitalization of the individual only if a judicial hearing deems him: (1) mentally ill, (2) likely therefore to injure himself or others if allowed to remain at liberty, and (3) in need of custody, care, or treatment but unable because of his illness to make a responsible decision regarding hospitalization.

Although the Draft Act offers guidelines for state legislation, in actual fact the states vary greatly in their laws on commitment procedures. While almost all the states provide for (and encourage) voluntary hospitalization, in the majority, temporary and emergency commitment of individuals to hospitals is permitted by law. In about one-third of the states, a board of doctors and attorneys may decide to admit a patient involuntarily. In another one-third of the states, a medical certificate, usually signed by two doctors, may be used for the same purpose. In about one-fourth of the states nonprotested admission is allowed; this procedure is used for patients who, because of their mental condition, do not (or cannot) oppose the admission, yet will not go for treatment on their own initiative. (Martindale and Martindale, 1971:67). Responsibility for the commitment in such cases lies with the next of kin, with psychiatrists, with the courts, or with all three, depending upon which state.

Writers like Scheff (1967) and Szasz (1970) remind us however, that the idea of "mental illness as just like any other illness" simply is not reflected in the laws of the land, which often discriminate against those who suffer from mental problems. This point appears to be well-taken. Although the laws governing the rights of the mentally ill differ from state to state, the following generalizations can be made. Under common law, a person officially judged as "lacking in mental capacity" is prohibited from marrying; many states include the insane in this group. In addition, as of 1971, approximately one-half of the states permitted divorce on the grounds of mental illness of one partner. At that time, while some 21 states did not allow mental illness to be used specifically as grounds for divorce, they did permit divorce on the grounds of reasons such as cruel and inhuman treatment, which could have resulted from the "mental problems" of one of the marriage partners. As Scheff (1967:15) perceptively points out:

The marriage vows explicitly state that the marriage contract is to be honored in "sickness and in health." Physical sickness, no matter how chronic or incurable, is not grounds for divorce, but mental illness is. The discrepancy between the institution of mental illness, and physical illness, and the legal institution of divorce is apparent in this case.

A final note with regard to laws on mental illness and marriage and the family: in some 38 states the consent of the mentally disabled parent or parents is not required in order for their children to be adopted, the assumption being that in cases of parental incapacitation—in some cases for only one year—adoption is best for the children (Martindale and Martindale, 1971:52-53).

Mental incapacity in some states leads to a declaration of incompetence, which in turn results in the appointment of a guardian over a person and his estate. In some states, previous hospitalization for mental illness is sufficient evidence for one to be declared incompetent. Moreover, the person who is mentally ill is prevented from making contracts in some 21 states (Martindale and Martindale, 1971: 53-54). By way of example:

Jane Brown was committed to the state mental hospital when she became extremely withdrawn, refused to leave her house, and suffered from delusions. After a course of treatment lasting about five months, she was provisionally discharged. Shortly after returning to the community she purchased a set of encyclopedias from a salesman who came to her home. When she failed to pay the $175.00 after receiving the books, the company threatened to take her to court. But when the company learned of her commitment on the grounds of mental illness, the contract was deemed to be void. Jane returned the books to the company and the court charges were dropped. (Martindale and Martindale, 1971:55)

Still further, a will executed under the "influence of insanity" is invalid legally. Approximately 40 states (80 percent) do not allow the mentally ill to vote, and approximately 50 percent do not allow them to hold office—a rather ironic inconsistency. In most states, an official diagnosis of mental illness leads to the revocation of the person's driver's license.

It is also widely known that mental illness sometimes excuses people from criminal responsibility. States have, to varying degrees, exhibited such leniency in laws influenced by the M'Naghten Rule of 1843 (inadequate awareness of actions), the 1954 Durham Rule (product of disease or defect), and the 1961 Currens Rule (jury convinced of defendant's incapacity).

Finally, many observers would concur with Kutner (1962) in his assertion that procedures of commitment of the mentally ill are hardly analogous to admittance to a hospital for physical treatment. Noting the conflict between the law profession, with its insistence on the protection of individual rights, and the medical profession, with its preference for medical judgments over legal formalities, Kutner (1962:387) writes:

The law is not yet convinced that, even under modern practices, commitment to a mental institution is more analogous to hospitalization than it is to criminal imprisonment.

We can recall also that "the law has historically dealt with the insane as a species of quasi-criminal, often incarcerating them in so-called hospitals where conditions were far worse than those in prisons for criminals" (Pearlstein, 1967:67).

Thus the laws pertaining to the mentally ill in the United States rather forcefully announce that mental illness is *not* "just like any other illness."

However, the recent Eagleton affair has demonstrated rather forcefully the fact that while Americans may accept the basic idea of mental illness, a certain amount of stigma is definitely attached to those who have undergone certain forms of psychiatric treatment. Moreover, the incident raised important questions concerning public faith in the actual "curability" of mental disorders. Many people in this country have adopted the basic idea that mental deviance represents illness, but they regard the mentally deviant person as having departed from normality to such an extent that he will never be quite the same again. Such a conception is thus analogous to the attitude toward the person who has suffered a bad heart attack: he needs to take life much easier than before, for at any time he may have a relapse. He continues to live and have a measure of sympathy and acceptance, but there are definite limits as to what he can do.

This leads us to ask the obvious question: Given the "big business" of modern-day mental-health programs, when the therapies have been rendered, the lights turned out, and the checks cashed, are people really "healthier" for the experience? In the case of disorders having a definite organic basis, such as general paresis, it would seem that the answer is yes. However, with respect to the non-organic or functional illnesses—the neuroses and psychoses—the jury seems to be out for a long debate. The hospitals are built, the clinics well-furnished, and the private offices lushly carpeted. Well-trained, professional staff members communicate an air of confidence and ability to their patients. Dr. William Menninger used to point to the danger of hospitals having "bricks without brains." In the contemporary situation, we may well have "luxury without light."

The fact of the matter is that the interpretation of mental disorders as "illnesses" was never based on the "discovery" of specific diseases. Rather, a host of behavior patterns formerly known by names such as heresy, sin, and possession were simply renamed and classified as illnesses (Szasz, 1970:137). And now, in the decade of the '70's, our actual knowledge of the causes and treatments of such illnesses is still embarrassingly limited. Psychiatry has alternated between emphases upon physiology and psychogenesis without significantly advancing its understanding of these diseases. It has heralded as cures the new shock treatments of the 1930's and the tranquilizing drugs of the 1950's, only to have to attach asterisks to their findings later on indicating limitations or failures, necessitating a resumption of the search. The words of President John F. Kennedy in his 1963 "Message to Congress Relative to Mental Illness and Mental Retardation" sound strangely reminiscent of the words of the Horace Mann Massachusetts legislative committee in 1832:

I propose a national mental health program to assist in the inauguration of a wholly new emphasis and approach to care for the mentally ill. This approach relies primarily upon

the new knowledge and new drugs acquired and developed in recent years which make it possible for most of the mentally ill to be successfully and quickly treated. (cited in Szasz, 1970:319)

With respect to an old problem, the Joint Commission on Mental Health and Illness noted in its 1961 report:

... the information we have leads us to believe that more than half of the patients in most State hospitals receive no active treatment of any kind designed to improve their mental condition. (Joint Commission, 1961:22-23)

Thomas Scheff wrote in 1967:

The cycle of exposé, reform, and apathy which has characterized the treatment of the mentally ill in the United States for over a hundred years, finds us still with hospitals that are more like prisons than hospitals. (Scheff, 1967:15)

Perhaps the problem being voiced with respect to mental hospitals—and undoubtedly applicable to other treatment facilities—is simply a reflection of a more serious problem: "luxury without light." Having "sold out the house," the psychiatric profession finds itself without sufficient knowledge to put on its advertised performance.

Evidence of the way in which psychiatry has become a part of American life is found in the psychiatric argot which is common to everyday vocabulary. Words like neurotic, schizophrenic, psychotic, and pathological are in regular—if somewhat questionable—use among the general public. The psychiatrist and his couch have become favorite targets of cartoons and jokes. The media have come to be largely supportive of the "mental-illness" emphasis in their news stories and program content involving such subjects. The public is willing to make an exception for the mentally ill lawbreaker, and be patient with the senile. Thus the concept of mental illness seems to be institutionally and culturally well-grounded in the United States.

As David Mechanic (1969:19-20) points out, there is nothing intrinsically wrong with adopting a disease orientation. But in doing so, one must consider both the gains and the disadvantages. Among the latter is the possibility of creating extensive personal stigmatization, and, most important, limiting knowledge of the problem by insisting on using an inadequate model. In view of the limited understanding the "illness" frame of reference has provided in dealing with the phenomena it labels, perhaps the time has come to consider experimenting with an alternative type of interpretation.

Chapter 10

Sexual Behavior: Prostitution, Pornography, and Homosexuality

THE SOCIAL CONSTRUCTION OF REALITY

We can imagine a social system in which the motive for prostitution would be completely absent, but we cannot imagine that the system could ever come to pass. It would be a regime of absolute sexual freedom.... [F]ree intercourse for pleasure and friendship, rather than for profit, is the greatest enemy of prostitution ... [and] prostitution is not so great a danger to the family as [is] complete liberty. Where the family is strong, there tends to be a well-defined system of prostitution ... the two opposite types of institutions ... function side by side without confusion. This is why a decline of the family and a decline of prostitution are both associated with a rise of sex freedom. (Davis, 1937:754-755)

Sexual Behavior and Relativity

It is a matter of theoretical conjecture whether, as Davis implies above, prostitution is a functional and necessary concomitant of strong family life, providing a somewhat controlled "safety-valve" or an outlet for monogamous boredom. This view provides one "construction of reality" from an expert social scientist, who was, in part, attempting to explain why prostitution has existed virtually everywhere, and at every time, from the beginning of recorded history. Elsewhere (1971), Davis illustrates the variety of forms which prostitution has taken in different societies, including the miserable brothels of ancient Greece and modern America, to the honored *hetaerae,* the cultured courtesans of ancient Greece; the highly trained *geishas* of traditional Japan, who were occasional and selective with their sexual favors; and the *deva-dasis,* types of religious prostitutes in the early temples of India. In the United States, during most of the 19th century, prostitution was generally tolerated as a "necessary evil," particularly in frontier communities having a shortage of women, and such laws against it as were enforced were aimed more at a kind of rational control of prostitution than at outright prohibition (Lemert, 1951; Bullough, 1964).

Pornography is scarcely less universal than prostitution in the history and cultures of mankind, and the degrees of tolerance for it are no less varied. There is an enormous collection of pornographic literature and pictures, amounting to some 25,000 volumes and 100,000 prints, stored in the Vatican Library at Rome, its contents spanning many centuries and cultures (Ginzburg, 1958:103). It takes the form of verse, prose, novels, songs, and drawings, some of them originally found on the walls of temples. Controversy about pornography is as ubiquitous as pornography itself: as early as 378 B.C., Plato advocated the censorship of portions of Homer's *Odyssey* for the protection of the youth of Athens, although he apparently approved of male homosexuality. Since the mid-1960's, both Denmark and West Germany increasingly have been liberalizing their laws relating to pornography, in the belief that the easy availability of pornographic materials is accompanied by a declining public interest in it, and perhaps also by a declining rate of sex crimes. This belief is compatible with the findings of the research done in this country in 1970 by the National Commission on Obscenity and Pornography (*U.S. News & World Report,* October 18, 1971).

In English-speaking countries, the concern over pornography seems to have begun in early 18th-century England, with an attempt on the part of the Crown to ban a spicy little book entitled *Fifteen Plagues of a Maidenhead,* and, a generation later, to ban an "exposé" called *The Nun in her Smock.* The Crown lost its case in the courts over the first book, but obtained a conviction in the second case, the prosecution having established that publishing "obscenities" was an offense against the common law (Ginzburg, 1958:43; Craig, 1942:32-34). A little later in the same century, an impoverished former British diplomat, John Cleland, secured his own release from debtor's prison by writing *Memoirs of the Life of Fanny Hill, a Woman of Pleasure,* first published in 1749. The British government (this time the Privy Council), apparently moved as well as appalled by the extreme measure to which his circumstances had taken him, issued Cleland a stern censure and a lifetime pension that would insure him against further poverty (Ginzburg, 1958: 64-66).

In the United States, it was this same book, *Fanny Hill,* that was the cause of the first prosecution for distributing "obscene" literature in 1821, when two Massachusetts men were jailed for six months for peddling copies of the book. Until the middle of the 19th century, the pornography available in America was imported, mainly from France and England, but after that a domestic pornography industry developed to which contributions were made even by some esteemed authors;

Mark Twain's *1601*, for example, by now has had more than 40 printings (Ginzburg, 1958:73-77). D. H. Lawrence and F. Scott Fitzgerald are among the many well-known authors in the English language whose works have, at various times and places in the United States, officially been declared obscene.*

The legislative and judicial history of the laws against obscenity in the United States is filled with complications, ambiguities, and inconsistencies, a point which will be amply illustrated in the rest of this chapter. The first federal law on the subject, in 1865, sought to outlaw a growing mail-order business in "obscene" materials. Of even wider scope was the notorious 1873 Comstock Act, named for Anthony Comstock, whose outstanding moral entrepreneurship extended over a period of 41 years (more on Comstock further on). Under its provisions, the Postal Inspection Service was given principal enforcement responsibility, and the numerous arrests and convictions made covered such offenses as mailing information on birth control, and sending postcards that used the word "radical" (cf. the Tennessee case of U.S. vs. Davis, 1889) (Kilpatrick, 1960:43). Around the turn of the century, a Mrs. Mary Dennett was arrested and fined $300.00 for mailing a copy of her pamphlet, "The Sex Side of Life," to a postal inspector who had requested it under an assumed name, even though the pamphlet was highly regarded and in general educational use by the YMCA, the YWCA, the Union Theological Seminary, and hundreds of religious, welfare, and state public health agencies. Although Mrs. Dennett's conviction was later reversed, her case illustrates the awesome jeopardy in which the Comstock Act placed a variety of literature. The maximum penalty was as much as five years in prison, and there was a $5000 fine for the first offense! The Dennett case also illustrates the difficulties in obtaining a general consensus, even within the Establishment, on what constitutes "obscenity" (Kilpatrick, 1960:157).

Homosexuality is also a form of sexual expression that was recorded in antiquity, and that has been met with a great variety of cultural responses over time. There are clear homosexual allusions, and sometimes even urgings, in the philosophical writings of Socrates and Plato, and in the love poems of Catullus, Virgil, and Horace, as well as (more recently) in the literature of André Gide and Oscar Wilde. Pomeroy (1969) has observed that homosexuality is "natural" in the sense that it occurs widely in nature, and in his review of anthropological data on 193 cultures, he found that in 86 percent male homosexuality is at least partially acceptable (including 28 percent in which it is fully acceptable). Among the same cultures,

---

* As any standard dictionary indicates, "pornography" refers to the *content* of written or other sex-related materials, while "obscenity" indicates a *definition* (usually legal) of that content as beyond the range of public tolerance. The word "pornography," as derived from the Greek, means simply "writing about prostitutes" (or, by extension, about sexual indulgence). When something has been declared "obscene," however, it is by definition illegitimate or unacceptable to the community making the judgment.

10 percent accept female homosexuality totally, 79 percent accept it to some extent, and only 11 percent outlaw it (Pomeroy, 1969:4). Compared to most other societies, the United States and the Soviet Union are especially repressive toward homosexuality, particularly of the male variety. In American culture there are no types of sexual activity as frequently condemned as mouth-genital contacts and homosexual activities. There are practically no other societies which have become as disturbed over male homosexuality as we have here in the United States (Gebhard, 1972).

Parameters of Consensual Reality

Prostitution

Having seen some of the variations in the way in which prostitution and certain other controversial forms of sex behavior are defined, let us look now at some of the generally accepted evidence about the incidence of such behavior, particularly in our own society. It is easily understandable why reliable data should be hard to obtain on sexual behavior, such as prostitution and homosexuality, that is illegal in most parts of the nation. It is probably impossible ever to get beyond informed estimates. One journalist who has specialized in prostitution research has estimated that there are about one-quarter of a million prostitutes in the United States, who engage in ten million different acts of prostitution every week, an "average caseload" per girl of about 40 per week (Sheehy, 1972a). As an example, in New York City ordinary streetwalkers (the hardest worked and most poorly paid of all classes of prostitutes) were earning between $200 and $500 per week, even at the peak of a police crackdown on prostitution during 1972 (Sheehy, 1972a). Prostitutes are especially likely to be in demand in places and circumstances in which large numbers of men are deprived of the company of women for long periods of time, such as in early frontier towns and, more recently, in Alaska along the course of the oil pipeline now under construction (*The New York Times*, May 6, 1974). While unmarried men of all ages are more likely than married men to seek the services of prostitutes, according to Kinsey (1948:288), the great majority of prostitutes' customers are married, since the total number of unmarried men is relatively small. For certain of the less conspicuous and "higher-class" varieties of prostitution, such as the professional call girls and the massage parlor girls, the customers are not only nearly all married men, but are also substantial middle-class men (Sheehy, 1972b).

From the point of view of the police, the incidence of prostitution is only occasionally an enforcement problem in its own right. While technically it is the object of "vice-squad" surveillance in most of our cities, it receives serious enforcement efforts only when citizen pressure groups succeed in getting city governments and police departments to launch special campaigns or "crackdowns" (Sheehy, 1972a and 1972b). The rest of the time, prostitution is likely to be tolerated by the police unless it becomes too blatant, or unless it is tied up with other more serious problems, such as venereal disease epidemics or criminal activities. It has been estimated, for example, that although prostitution itself accounts for only 5 percent of the police activity in downtown New York City, more than one-half of all the robberies there (and many assaults and murders as well) are related to prostitution, i.e., prostitutes are either the offenders or the victims in these crimes (Sheehy, 1972a). As far as venereal disease is concerned, the part played by prostitutes is probably highly overrated these days: in San Francisco, the incidence of venereal disease among accused prostitutes was 12 percent in 1974, which was exactly the same as that for the general population there between the ages of 15 and 30 (H. Berman, 1974). Nevertheless, enforcement efforts against prostitutes are costly: in 1971, San Francisco spent $375,000 on prostitution arrests and trials, while Seattle spent $1 million in the same year (Will, 1974). Such figures are indicative not only of the general cost to the public of laws against prostitution, but also of the differential importance attached to the "prostitution problem" from one city to another. The San Francisco metropolitan area not only has a much larger population than Seattle's, but also a much larger tourist and convention business; yet it devotes only 37.5 percent of the amount of public money spent by Seattle to fighting prostitution.

Pornography

There is somewhat more systematic data available on the consumption of pornography in our society, partly because much of it is more publicly observable, but mostly because an extensive investigation into the "smut industry" was conducted between 1968 and 1970 by the National Commission on Obscenity and Pornography (see *The New York Times* report, 1970). In 1969, the annual retail value of various kinds of "sexually-oriented" materials for "adults only" was estimated in the Commission report as follows: books, $45-$55 million; periodicals, $25-$35 million; motion picture box-office receipts (including R-rated, X-rated, and "underground"), $450-$460 million; mail-order materials, $12-$14 million; and various surreptitiously distributed, or "under the counter" materials, $5-$10 million, for a total well in excess of half-a-billion dollars. In 1969, there were more than 2,000 retail outlets for pornographic books and periodicals across the country, found mainly in urban areas of at least half-a-million in population. Judging from Internal Revenue Service records, the 20 largest publishers of pornography averaged $450,000 in profits during 1968 (*The New York Times* report, 1970).

It was the printed pornography and pornographic advertisements sent through the mails that became enforcement problems, rather than the literature sold in local "adult" bookstores. This is because of the prohibitive provisions of the long-standing Comstock Act, plus the effects of the more recent Pandering Advertisement Act of 1968, according to which a recipient of unsolicited pornographic ads or materials through the mails can obtain an order from the Postal Inspector prohibiting a distributor from sending him any more. Although sexually oriented ads constitute only one-quarter of 1 percent of the huge volume of mailed advertising handled by the U.S. Postal Service, there were 234,072 pornographic items and complaints registered with the Postal Service in 1969, a 58 percent increase over the previous year. As a result, 9,731 investigations produced 369 mail pandering convictions, and the discovery that only 15 distributors were responsible for 95 percent of the complaints. In 1970, these statistics increased somewhat, resulting in convictions for 14 of the big distributors and indictments for 58 others. (These figures came from the 1969 Annual Report of the Postmaster General and were reported in *The New York Times* report, 1970.)

The film industry also makes its contribution to the production of pornography, according to *U.S. Industrial Outlook* (as cited in *The New York Times,* 1970:13). In that year an estimated 200 theaters across the country were showing pornographic films exclusively, with their fare accounting for about 20 percent of the total movie receipts in the country, or a retail sales volume of about $200 million, and this mostly from films that were very inexpensive to make. This includes the X-rated and unrated sex films, but not the R-rated. Since 1970, the cinematic quality of many of these films, while seldom very good, has noticeably improved, giving rise to the term "porno-chic," which refers to 35-millimeter color productions with some semblance of a plot, and with a hi-fidelity sound track. An especially well-known example of this genre is *Deep Throat,* which cost only $25,000 to produce and grossed more than $3 million during its first year.

Since the beginning of the present decade, however, the greater availability of pornography has been followed by a drastic decline in demand, just as was the case in Denmark. The largest decrease has come in the mail-order part of the industry, though many bookstores are also closing. As the mid-seventies approached, theatres also began to switch away from X-rated films and back to the more conventional kinds (*U.S. News & World Report,* 1970 and 1972).

Homosexual Behavior

Assessing the amount of homosexual behavior in our society is no less complicated than measuring other kinds of sexual behavior that are widely disapproved of; if anything, it is more complicated, and not merely for the obvious reason that so much of it is hidden. In part, it is a matter of what questions we are asking. If we are asking how much "homosexuality" there is in general, then we are asking not about actual behavior or the number of practicing homosexuals, but about erotic inclinations or "orientations" toward a person of the same sex. This is neither illegal nor unusual, for many people occasionally are attracted, to a greater or lesser degree, to people of their own sex, especially in adolescence, but never act upon that attraction; indeed, they may not fully be aware of it (Pomeroy, 1969). In other cases, people may engage in homosexual relations on an "experimental" basis (as frequently occurs in adolescence), or because no other kind of sexual relations is available (as in prisons), but for them it is only a temporary phenomenon, and does not represent their true sexual preference. The "true homosexual" is one who exclusively prefers a sexual partner of his or her sex, and acts upon that preference. Many homosexuals, perhaps most, keep their sex lives secret and are sometimes called "closet queens." Others have "come out of the closet" and have publicly declared themselves as homosexuals, even though homosexual behavior is illegal in most parts of the country.

The early and classic studies of sexual behavior by Kinsey (1948 and 1953) included an investigation into the extent of admitted homosexual involvements in a sample of "normal" people. Among his findings were: 37 percent of the males in his sample reported having had at least one overt homosexual experience after puberty, and an additional 13 percent had had erotic reactions to other males but had not had sexual experiences. Of the females in the Kinsey sample, 21 percent had had one or more overt homosexual experiences since puberty, and an additional 8 percent had experienced homosexual feelings or reactions without acting upon them. About 4 percent of the men, and a slightly smaller proportion of the women, were exclusively homosexual in their preferences; and an additional 25 percent of the men, and 10 percent of the women, were "mixed" cases, having some measurable degree of homosexual inclination (Kinsey, 1948 and 1953). More recently, Gebhard (1972) reviewed a number of other surveys and concluded that from one-fourth to one-third of college-educated adult males have had some overt homosexual experiences since puberty, mostly during adolescence. Gebhard's conclusions for female homosexual behavior were similar to Kinsey's, and, in addition, he found a number of similarities in homosexual patterns between the United States and certain European countries (Gebhard, 1972).

Most surveys of this nature have tended to oversample the college-educated and white-collar occupational groups, leaving us with relatively less knowledge about the other strata. Homosexual behavior is especially censured, and carries an exceptionally high risk of career damage in many of the high-status occupations, particularly in civil service. Thus it is more likely to be hidden where it exists in such occupational groups, and probably to be underreported in surveys. In lower-ranking occupations, or those which are peripheral to the industrial establishment, such as those of artist, interior decorator, or hairdresser, male homosexual preferences and activities tend to be somewhat more open (Leznoff and Westley, 1967; *Civil Service Journal,* 1972). There is some evidence, in fact, that because of stigmatization and discrimination in many of the more desirable occupations, homosexual men are somewhat "over-recruited" to the lower-status jobs such as hospital orderly, restaurant worker, technician, and salesman (Humphreys, 1972).

For male homosexuals who have "come out," the so-called "gay bar" is an important part of their social lives. It is a "social institution, where friends meet, the news of the homosexual world is to be heard, gossip exchanged, invitations to parties issued, and warnings given about current danger spots and attitudes of the police" (Hooker, 1967:30). In 1965, there were more than 60 gay bars in Los Angeles and 40 in San Francisco; in 1969, the number in the latter city had risen to 70 (Hooker, 1967; *Time,* 1969). In many cities, gay bars are generally tolerated by the police if they are operated discreetly and the patrons create no disturbances; they thus constitute a kind of "sanctuary" for homosexuals. The same safe conditions do not exist in certain other public places where male homosexuals sometimes make their contacts, such as public baths and restrooms, beaches, parks, restaurants, and gymnasiums. Most arrests occur in public restrooms, or "tearooms," as they were called by Laud Humphreys in his book on the subject (1972). In one such Ohio "tearoom," 65 men were arrested over a two-week period for homosexual activities.

We know much less about patterns of meeting and socializing for female homosexuals, or lesbians. There are lesbian gay bars, but they are much less common than male ones (e.g., 1 out of 17 in Seattle). For lesbians, sex is apparently less impersonal; it is also less likely to be publicly noticed than is the case with men. Lesbianism also appears to produce less of a special way of life or pattern of behavior than male homosexuality; as Simon and Gagnon have observed (1967: 215), the lesbian closely resembles her heterosexual sister, and differs radically from both homosexual and heterosexual males in patterns of sexual activity.

A considerable amount of expense and energy go into the enforcement of our laws against homosexual behavior. While we have no nationwide figures at hand, a study conducted in Los Angeles disclosed that between 1962 and 1964, there were 493 men charged in Superior Court as felons for committing deviant sex acts with other consenting adult men. Between May, 1964, and April, 1965, 2,994 men were charged with misdemeanors in the Los Angeles Municipal Court for intent to commit, or for actually committing, homosexual acts with consenting adults (Gallo, 1966). This indicates that where the police or the vice squads choose to carry out a rigorous enforcement of the laws against homosexual behavior, they can generate quite an enforcement burden.

Public Opinion and Deviant Sexual Behavior

The collective definitions of deviant sexual behavior of the kinds we have been discussing are especially important because of their presumed support for the laws attempting to regulate such behavior. Actual public opinion data, however, are rather rare, and when such data are collected they do not by any means necessarily support the laws and enforcement efforts against deviant sexual behavior, though they may not approve of such behavior itself. For example, Davis has reported on a large-scale survey conducted by *McCalls* magazine in February, 1965, in which only 7 percent of the respondents said that they would clear the streets of prostitutes if they had the power; 67 percent said that they would not, and the rest were undecided. This survey was conducted in New York City and in Newark, New Jersey, but it is unlikely that the results would be very different in other big cities (Davis, 1971:342). This does not necessarily mean that the public sampled approved of prostitution, but merely that most people in the survey did not seem to feel that very much police effort should go into enforcement against it.

In the case of pornography, the importance of public opinion is a direct and formal part of the law, since the prevailing judicial decisions make local "community standards" the basis for deciding whether or not certain materials should be declared obscene and therefore illegal (see the last section of this chapter for more on the law). As part of the study conducted by the National Commission on Obscenity and Pornography, in 1968, a careful national sample of about 3,200 persons (including about 800 youths between 15 and 20 years of age) was asked to indicate what they thought were the "two or three most serious problems in the country today." Only 2 percent of the total sample mentioned a concern about erotic materials, compared to 54 percent for the Vietnam War, 36 percent for racial conflict, 32 percent for the problems of the economy, and so on down the list of public issues. The 2 percent concerned about erotic materials was even a smaller number than the 9 percent who indicated a concern about the "moral breakdown in society," and so it would appear that, compared to other current moral issues, pornography didn't rank very high in the public consciousness (Abelson, et al., 1970).

During May of 1969, the Gallup organization included in its standard survey a number of questions related to pornography and obscenity. When asked specifically about this subject, rather than simply being allowed to bring it up themselves, as in the above poll, people showed somewhat higher levels of awareness and concern about it. Twelve percent of the Gallup sample had received "sex literature" in the mail which they regarded as offensive; 38 percent had been exposed to something "dealing with sex" on television which they had found "objectionable"; 23 percent had reacted to something "objectionable" in the movies; and 25 percent had reacted to something "objectionable" in print (i.e., magazines, newspapers, etc.) (Gallup,

1969:16-17). In this poll, those segments of the population most likely to have been offended by media exposure to sex were the rural or small town people, those in the South, those over 30 years of age, and those relatively high in education and occupation. In general, however, the differences among the various categories of the public were quite small, especially between men and women, who had almost identical levels of reaction to offensive material.

As for what should be done about dissemination of erotic materials to the public, the same 1969 poll revealed that 85 percent of the population wanted to see stricter laws regulating the use of the mails for such materials; 75 percent preferred stricter laws on what materials could be sold at newsstands; and 50 percent indicated a willingness to join a neighborhood protest group to work for such laws. Less than one-tenth, however, had ever actually taken any action in the past to restrict the sale of objectionable literature. The differences among the various segments of the population were again rather small, but there was a clear tendency for people from the younger age groups, the urban areas, and the western states to be somewhat more permissive (i.e., less willing to impose restrictions) than others (Gallup, 1969:18-21). It is both interesting and noteworthy that there was so little variation in attitudes among different segments of the populace, both in levels of offense taken to sex-related materials, and in willingness to take restrictive action; this is indicative of considerable consensus regarding public experience and outlook. For many people, the issue is more one of how *harmful* pornographic materials are, rather than one of maintaining civil liberties. Abelson, et al. (1970: 92-93), in one of the staff reports for the National Commission, determined that whereas about 80 percent of the population would oppose the widespread availability of erotic material if they were convinced of its harmfulness, half of our society would be inclined to approve of its availability if convinced that it produced no harmful effects. At the same time, for one-third of the public, harmfulness was not the issue: they would oppose the availability of sexual materials in the media *even if shown that there were no harmful effects.*

We can see, in the above review of public opinion on the various facets of the pornography issue, that there are some areas in which the consensus is fairly strong, and others in which there is considerably less agreement. Somehow, out of all of these nuances of public opinion, our courts must assess, in a given case, what constitutes the prevailing views of a "community" on the subject, for the Supreme Court (U.S. v. Roth, 1957) has made that assessment the criterion for the application of restrictive anti-obscenity statutes to specific pornographic materials, i.e., "whether to the average person, applying contemporary community standards, the dominant theme of the material, taken as a whole, appeals to the prurient interest." One could scarcely ask for a better illustration of relativity in collective definitions of a "social problem."

Whatever levels of tolerance of pornography that may exist in our media, there seems to be little acceptance of homosexuals in our midst, and the disapproval of them reaches emotional peaks at times. In Nashville, Tennessee, in 1973, two national charitable organizations refused to accept a large cash donation that had been raised through a benefit pageant held there by homosexuals (the Miss Gay Pageant), for fear that doing so would cost them the support of other potential donors (*The Advocate,* June 20, 1973:17). Eventually, the charity-minded group found willing recipients for their money, but the incident does illustrate the observation by Pomeroy (1969:4) that the "Judeo-Christian heritage of our society is one of the severest in its condemnation of homosexuality."

A 1969 Harris poll asked a large representative sample of Americans whether they felt certain categories of people on a given list were "more helpful or more harmful to American life or don't help or harm much one way or the other." Sixty-three percent of the sample chose homosexuals as a category that was "more harmful than helpful" (Geis, 1972:38). A CBS-TV survey the same year concluded that "two out of every three Americans look on homosexuals with disgust, discomfort, or fear, and one out of ten regards them with downright hatred" (*Time,* October 24, 1969:82). More recently, a 1973 survey by Indiana University's Institute for Sex Research, again based upon a large representative American sample, found similar results: two-thirds regarded homosexuality as "very obscene and vulgar," and almost one-half feared homosexuality as "a corruption that can cause the downfall of a civilization" (*Human Behavior,* October, 1973:44). More than one-half of the respondents in this same survey approved of denying gays the same treatment accorded other groups, including job discrimination. One-third of the sample wanted homosexuals to be jailed or placed on probation, while the remaining two-thirds would prefer to have them labelled as "sick" rather than considered criminals.

Having obtained some idea of similarities and varieties in public opinion concerning prostitution, pornography, and homosexuality, and therefore the basis of collective definitions for the formation of certain interest groups on these issues, let us turn now to an examination of the interest groups themselves.

CHAMPIONS AND THEIR INTERESTS
Prostitution Interests and Publics

As with the other issues discussed in this book, there are competing viewpoints and interests on questions of sexual deviance, including prostitution, though few of the public issues in our history have generated as much emotion as have sex-related ones. In the case of prostitution, it is not a simple matter of "pro vs. con."

Some people may advocate the commercial sale of sexual favors, commonly called "prostitution"; presumably many prostitutes do. The principal controversy, however, is not so much over whether prostitution is itself good or bad, as whether prostitution should be *legal,* or *legalized* where it is not now legal. Thus, the interest groups that are pro on this issue are not necessarily in favor of prostitution as an occupation, or as a way of life, but they are pro-legalization. Let us look at some of these groups and their interests.

Pro-Legalization Interest Groups

The interest group most directly involved in the prostitution issue is, of course, that of the prostitutes themselves. Their interest is largely economic, but it quickly becomes political as well whenever their occupation is threatened by the passage or enforcement of anti-prostitution statutes. In general, prostitutes have not been an organized interest group in the usual sense of that term, although every large city has had a kind of subculture or "grapevine" to which many of the practicing prostitutes have belonged (Sheehy, 1972a). In quite recent years, however, there are signs of growing coalescence and militancy among prostitutes on a nationwide basis: on June 27, 1974, an organization named Call Off Your Old Tired Ethics (COYOTE) held what was apparently its first national convention in San Francisco at the Glide Memorial Methodist Church. Described by its "founding mother," retired prostitute Margo St. James, as "a loose woman's organization," COYOTE works for the legalization of prostitution and for the protection of prostitutes' civil liberties. Until prostitution is legalized in a given area, however, COYOTE advocates the arrest of customers, as well as prostitutes, not only in the interest of equal justice, but also because, as Ms. St. James has put it: "Men won't change the laws unless they get their nuts caught in the cracker too." COYOTE also is working to enhance the public image of prostitutes and to destroy certain myths or misconceptions about them, such as that they are the main spreaders of venereal disease (H. Berman, 1974).

Besides the prostitutes themselves, other economic interest groups in favor of more permissive laws are the so-called "pimps" and procurers, operators of the "houses of ill fame" and of the particular "shady" hotels or motels which prostitutes (or their customers) rent to conduct their business. These auxiliary economic interest groups frequently include some prominent and highly respected "absentee owners" of hotel or motel properties, and some executive officers in large corporations which employ the services of "high-class" call girls as part of their "customer relations" programs. Needless to say, all such prominent citizens take great pains to be sure that their interests in the matter are not made public, so it is difficult to uncover them (Sheehy, 1972b).

Other interests in favor of legalization, or at least of more permissive laws, are usually of a moral or political kind. Feminist groups, such as NOW (see chapter on the feminist movement), regard the present anti-prostitution laws and ordinances in most places as highly discriminatory against women (i.e., the prostitutes), and while they would prefer the abolition of such laws, on the grounds that a person's sexual behavior is properly her (his) own private affair, they insist that as long as there are laws, these should be made to apply to the male customers as well as to the female prostitutes. The same position seems to emerge, in general, from the literature of the American Civil Liberties Union (ACLU), which has been prominent in efforts to abolish all kinds of discriminatory laws and enforcement practices, especially those that are moralistically inspired (H. Berman, 1974; Roby, 1969). Perhaps surprising to some, another political interest group on the side of legalization has been the conservative intellectuals, or at least those of a libertarian bent. As part of their general opposition to government intervention into the economic and moral realms of social life, conservative writers of the kind appearing in William F. Buckley's *National Review* are usually critical of various kinds of "morality legislation." An editor of that magazine, Washington columnist George F. Will, for example, recently presented "The Conservative Case for Legal Prostitution" (1974). Police groups sometimes also favor legalization, since many of them find enforcement of vice laws a futile and distasteful job.

Anti-Legalization and Anti-Prostitution Interest Groups

While, as we observed earlier, those who favor legalization of prostitution do not approve of it as an occupation necessarily, when we come to the opposition groups, such a distinction is rarely, if ever, made. Those who oppose legalization do so almost surely because they oppose prostitution itself, or, at least, this is true for the moral and political interest groups, which are the most public and prominent ones found in the opposition movement. It may well be true, as many have charged (e.g., Sheehy, 1972a and 1972b), that legalization is also opposed by certain illegitimate economic interests which stand to gain by a continuation of the current restrictions against prostitution in many places. We refer here to policemen and vice squad officers who may be getting "pay-offs" from prostitutes and procurers to "take it easy" in their enforcement activities, and to organized crime, which is often involved in the sponsorship, control, and profits of prostitution. However, these interests are difficult to identify specifically.

Much more easily identifiable are the moral interest groups, which have frequently resorted to political action (Roby, 1969). Little in the way of organized opposition to prostitution appeared in this country until the early 20th century, as part of the vast moral and political wave of the progressive movement. The so-called "muckraking literature" of that time included the "epidemic" of prostitution in its indictment of the many aspects of city life in America at that time. The rapid industrialization, urbanization, and immigration and its attendant evils were alarming to populists and progressives, most of whom had small-town origins. A barrage of magazine articles appeared early in the century in *Harper's, Collier's, McClure's,* and *The Arena,* outlining the horrors of prostitution (Filler, 1950: 285-295). The specter of "white slavery" was a major theme in this literature: prostitution was depicted as perpetrated by a class of "merchants in flesh" who rounded up innocent, unsophisticated young girls of foreign extraction, often minors, through the use of falsehood, drugs, and coercion. The immigrant was portrayed as both the main cause and the main victim of prostitution (Feldman, 1967). Probably the most conspicuous and the most prominent organization in the anti-prostitution crusade of this period was the American Social Hygiene Association, founded in 1913 as a merger of the American Vigilance Association and the American Federation for Sex Hygiene. Its earliest and most prominent founders and leaders were Charles W. Elliot, president emeritus of Harvard University; David Starr Jordan, president of Stanford University; the Right Reverend Walter Sumner and James Cardinal Gibbons, both former vice-presidents of the American Vigilance Association and very prominent churchmen; and Miss Jane Addams, the well-known philanthropist and social worker. Miss Addams' 1912 book, *A New Conscience and An Ancient Evil,* served as the major reference work for the new organization (Elliot, 1914:1-5; Snow, 1946:242). Largely through the influence of this pressure group, vice commissions were organized in all major urban areas to draft, promote, and oversee the enforcement of strong anti-prostitution laws (Filler, 1950:285-295).

The arrival of World War I added an important stimulus to the efforts of the "social hygienists" because of the "camp followers" near military installations, and the anti-prostitution movement waxed strong through the 1920's. By the depression years, however, the movement had subsided somewhat, with very few organized groups left besides the American Social Hygiene Association (Waterman, 1932). The years of World War II once again renewed somewhat the interests of the anti-prostitution forces in the "camp follower" issue, but this renewal scarcely survived the war years. Within a decade or less after World War II, for all practical purposes, the American Social Hygiene Association was dead (see further on under "natural history"), and there has been very little anti-prostitution interest-group activity since that time. Such efforts as there have been have come largely from some of the other interest groups opposed to "sexual permissiveness," as a part of their campaigns against pornography and homosexuality. Therefore we will turn next to a consideration of some of the interest groups related to those issues.

Pornography Interests and Publics

As with the interest groups that are pro-prostitution, we must distinguish here between those favoring the production and distribution of pornographic materials as a worthy occupation, and those favoring the *freedom to do so legally* (i.e., freedom from censorship). It may be that ultimately this distinction is lost in the actual proposals and demands of these two kinds of interests; however, although they both call for an end to censorship and to legal restraint of any kind for adult markets, their motives are different. We will consider all such interests as pro-legalization ones (i.e., anti-censorship), and review their positions on the pornography issue, before examining those interests which are opposed to the production or consumption of pornographic materials, either legally or illegally.

Pro-Legalization Interest Groups

Perhaps the largest category of persons favoring the legal availability of pornographic materials would be the consumers themselves, who, while not organized or cohesive enough to be considered an "interest group" as such, certainly constitute an important *public*. Far from being the sleazy, perverted, "low-life" bums portrayed in some of the stereotypes in the media, pornography consumers are almost entirely middle or upper-middle class, male, Caucasian, married, well-educated, and well-dressed, according to research done for the National Commission on Obscenity and Pornography (Abelson, et al., 1970). Their values seem to be very similar to those of non-consumers of pornography, and they may even feel somewhat guilty about their visits to pornographic bookstores or theaters, judging from the furtiveness of their behavior as reported by observers and interviewers for the Commission. Cleanup or censorship laws and campaigns harm these consumers by increasing the stigma which they feel if apprehended, and by driving up the prices they have to pay. They are, however, too substantial and respectable as citizens ever to be likely to organize in any way in order to protect their interests as pornography consumers.

Economic interests favoring the availability of pornography include the producers of it, the distributors, and, to some extent, the owners of the locations where pornographic materials are sold. There is some reason to believe that organized crime may be involved in the pornography market at least occasionally (Sheehy, 1972b), but the evidence produced by the investigation of the Commission indicated little such "big-time" criminal involvement, mainly because pornography was not profitable enough (Sampson, 1970). The money behind the pornography industry seems as likely to come from prominent "straights." A New York City investigation, for example, linked the pornography business there with several prominent businessmen, a well-known surgeon, and some government officials (Sheehy, 1972b). For the most part, the pornographer (whether producer or distributor), while he may be a serious nuisance to some, is neither a dangerous criminal, a subversive agent, nor a noticeably evil character. More likely, he is "a grubby businessman producing a minor commodity for which there is a limited market and a marginal profit, and which requires that he live in a marginal world" (Gagnon and Simon, 1970). The Commission concluded that while a few operators may make a living from "hard-core" pornography,* they generally "only supplement their regular income from other gainful employment through such sales" (Sampson, 1970).

Less often thought of as profiting from pornography are certain respectable occupational categories: some large Manhattan landlords (including some well-known business firms) turned out to be owners of some of the most lucrative pornographic stores and theaters there, and of some of the "massage parlors" as well (Sheehy, 1972b). Obscenity trials have provided lawyers on both sides (especially the defense lawyers) with some very large fees. The so-called "expert witness" at such trials, frequently an academic specialist, also has reaped some indirect profits from the pornography enterprise: Professor Albert Goldman, for example, in his article, "Witnessing Obscenity for Fun and Profit" (1972), claims that it took him years to realize that everyone in the courtroom was making money on obscenity trials except himself, and he thereafter began charging $500 per day (two-day minimum) for "rehearsals" and court appearances as an expert witness (1972:50). Publishers and film producers, including some large and prominent ones which rarely, if ever, produce pornography themselves, also are frequently found on the side of legalization for pornography, partly out of interest in potential profits, but more often out of a general interest in keeping any kind of government censorship at bay.

Quite apart from any indication of the profit motive is the political and civic interest which many people have in promoting the broadest possible interpretation of 1st Amendment guarantees of freedom of expression. This would include a public made up mainly of the younger, better-educated, and more urban segments of the population (though not even a majority of these). The 1969 Gallup polls referred to earlier in this chapter showed that in these segments of society, there was twice as much disapproval of censorship laws as in the other segments (though still a minority of only around 15 percent). These are the people from among whom come recruits to organizations such as the American Civil Liberties Union (ACLU), which often is involved in the fight against censorship, even in obscenity cases, as

---

* The distinction sometimes made between "hard-core" and "soft-core" pornography may be difficult to make in a given case, but in general the first refers to highly explicit and closeup scenes of copulative organs "at work" in various ways, while the latter refers more to simulated copulation scenes, with the sex organs themselves scarcely, if at all, visible. The film *Last Tango in Paris* would probably qualify as "soft-core," and *Deep Throat* as "hard-core" pornography.

will be clear from a perusal of any recent year's file of their national monthly publication, *Civil Liberties*. Much of the basis of the ACLU's opposition to censorship in these cases rests upon their oft-repeated charge that the law is hopelessly vague on the definition of "obscenity," and that therefore the tremendous variation and relativity in both legislative policy and judicial decisions make attempts at censorship unconstitutional almost by definition.

Anti-Pornography Interest Groups

Let us recall from our discussion of public opinion earlier in this chapter that many citizens claimed to have taken some degree of offense at sex-related materials that had come to their attention in the media, and that as many as one-half of those polled by Gallup (1969) indicated a willingness to join in some kind of organized effort to restrict dissemination of such materials. This anti-pornography public, however, itself would include quite a variety of opinions; it ranges from those who would be interested only in keeping children from being exposed to pornography, to those who would like to restrict it to certain parts of town, all the way to the extreme anti-pornography exponent, who regards the production and consumption of pornographic (or any sex-related) materials as evil, degrading, and corrupting *in and of itself,* and for any person, without regard to whether or not there are any social or psychological consequences.

Through the research efforts of the staff of the National Commission on Obscenity and Pornography, we have some data on the nature and composition of this strong anti-pornography psychological interest group (or public). Compared to the average citizen, they are much more likely to be politically and religiously conservative, and to be dogmatic, authoritarian, and intolerant in their approach to various social issues (Birkelbach and Zurcher, 1970:19). They tend to regard the dissemination of pornography as a fundamental threat to their entire value system, and their response is a defense of their claim of the universality and power of their value system (Zurcher and Cushing, 1970:211). They regard pornography as a more serious social problem than war, racial conflict, air pollution, or poverty; and they believe pornography is an important cause of prostitution, venereal disease, divorce, and even of some nonsex-related social problems such as crime, violence, and race riots (Zurcher and Cushing, 1970:211). Perhaps an ideal personification of such hot-eyed moral fervor can be provided from an earlier age in the figure of Anthony Comstock, who was the leader of a far-reaching moral crusade a century ago. This crusade produced a series of state and federal laws, beginning with an 1873 federal statute bearing his name, which was aimed primarily at preventing the use of the mails for the distribution of sex-related materials. As mentioned earlier, the provisions of this law made the dissemination of even birth-control information by mail illegal, though, with the passage of the intervening decades, these provisions gradually were eroded by court interpretations, and eventually, in 1965, they were declared unconstitutional by the Supreme Court (see Chapter 16). Comstock was so dedicated to the eradication of "smut" that he worked for years without pay as a postal inspector in search of it. His critics have described him as a cruel, vindictive, and perverted genius, who reportedly boasted of having caused 16 suicides, casualties of his war against smut (Craig, 1942:123; Ernst and Lindey, 1940:60). Understandably, people who actively pursue the anti-pornography cause have come to be called "comstocks" and their enterprises "comstockery." In large part, they provide the recruits for the organized moral and religious interest groups, although it must be pointed out in fairness that such organizations include a great many more temperate people as well.

The most prominent organized interest group of moral entrepreneurs in the pornography field is the Citizens for Decent Literature (CDL), which has been in existence for several decades, and has been joined in more recent years by a sister organization, Morality in Media. CDL is a large national organization with many local chapters. One of its basic premises is that the "public morality is being undermined and that in order to restrain this trend, ordinary citizens must be galvanized into effective action for the enforcement of law and order" (Nawy, 1970:189).

Many important religious organizations have made special efforts to mobilize their members in opposition to the spread of "smut." The National Office for Decent Literature (NODL) was founded in 1938 by the Catholic Bishops of the United States, "to devise a plan for organizing a systematic campaign in all dioceses of the United States against the publication and sale of lewd magazines and . . . literature"; to promote strict legislation against pornography, and rigorous enforcement of laws against it; and to make a monthly list of objectionable publications and try to persuade dealers not to handle any items on the list (Kilpatrick, 1960: 244). In Protestant circles, there is the Churchmen's Commission for Decent Publications, embracing representatives of thirty-two different denominations, and the Board for Christian Social Action of the American Lutheran Church, two religious organizations that give special attention to the pornography "problem." Especially important among religious groups taking a strong stand against the dissemination of pornography in the western part of the United States is the Church of Jesus Christ of Latter-Day Saints (or Mormon Church), a highly placed spokesman for which was quoted in recent years as saying: "If there is pornography or obscenity in bookstores, on television or radio, or in places of entertainment . . . it is our duty and responsibility as individuals to speak out, to organize and to protect ourselves and our community against such encroachments" (*Idahonian*, April 7, 1973).

The political interests on the side of censorship are generally those of the right-wing persuasion. In recent years the Ku Klux Klan has included "smut peddlers" among its enemies, along with ethnic minorities and subversives. The American Opinion Library of the John Birch Society has defined sex-oriented materials as "political subterfuge by left-wing organizations" and, in general, as part of the Communist plot to weaken the moral fiber of the nation (Nawy, 1970:187). Often, however, concern over the spread of pornography is expressed by politicians of much less extreme temperament. Indeed, the establishment of the National Commission on this subject was itself the result of a widespread belief in Congress, in 1967, that the traffic in pornography was "a matter of national concern." There were enough congressmen holding such a belief to legislate the establishment of such a commission, to which Congress gave the charge, "after a thorough study which shall include a study of the causal relationship of such materials to antisocial behavior, to recommend advisable, appropriate, effective, and constitutional means to deal effectively with such traffic in obscenity and pornography" (*The New York Times* report, 1970:1). When the Commission eventually turned in its recommendation, which played down the harmful social effects of pornography, and recommended no measures of censorship for adults, many in the Congress felt betrayed.

Other interests on this side of the issue are involved only occasionally and sporadically. Sometimes certain economic interests are threatened by the spread of pornographic materials, or by the prospect of legalization. Again, as with prostitution, such interests may include organized crime or policemen "on the take" in some areas, whose profits stand to be cut off if buying and selling pornography can be done in the open by anyone. More often, however, the economic interests threatened are those of various neighborhood merchants, who fear that their customers will be driven away by the "deterioration" that will inevitably follow the arrival of "smut shops" in the area. In New York City, particularly, the "legitimate" merchants have always supported laws restricting the trade in various kinds of "vice" (Roby, 1969), and more recently were mainly responsible for the creation of the Times Square Development Council, which launched a huge (but apparently futile) campaign against the prostitutes and pornographic shops that had moved into Times Square (Sheehy, 1972b). They succeeded in forcing the city government into a "cleanup" effort that was neutralized in large part by the counter-efforts of other interest groups that were benefiting from the existence of the "vice." The police, as an occupational interest group, aside from those "on the take," seem to have mixed feelings about the availability of pornography. On the one hand, those who are characterized by the "comstock mentality" are strongly against it; others, however, regard the enforcement of censorship laws as an onerous and frustrating duty.

Homosexuality Interest Groups

Much more so than is the case with prostitution or pornography, the interests of homosexuals are promoted mostly by homosexuals themselves, and a multiplicity of homosexual organizations can be found in the forefront of the effort to legalize homosexual behavior between consenting adults. Homosexuals have very few allies in religious and civil libertarian groups. Let us first consider the homosexual organizations and their allies, and then we will review the interest groups opposed to "liberation" for homosexuals.

Pro-Liberation Interest Groups

It may seem strange to some for us to consider here as "moral interest groups" organizations which are made up mostly of homosexuals to promote their own sexual interests. However "selfish" might be the interests of the members of such organizations, though, their interests surely are moral in the sense that they are aimed at making changes in the moral and legal norms of society. They take the moral position, in the interest of themselves as well as others, that a person's sexual preferences and activities, as long as they are not imposed upon others, should be of no interest whatever to the state, and should not be matters regulated by laws. Such groups also promote the idea that homosexuals in general are entitled to be treated with the same dignity and respect accorded all other citizens, since their sexual preferences have no bearing on their inherent worth as human beings. Discriminatory practices in business, industry, education, or other institutions are thus as much a target of their efforts as are restrictive laws.

The oldest organization in this category is the Mattachine Foundation, established in Los Angeles in 1950 as a secret society primarily to promote the interests of male homosexuals. It grew fast, and by 1952 there were 18 chapters in the Los Angeles area. Later on, the organization dropped its secrecy and moved to San Francisco. Its original tactics were of a "consciousness-raising" kind, rather than political, and it has apparently lost strength and membership in recent years to some of the more politically active groups (Gunnison, 1969). A related organization, and a kind of offshoot of Mattachine, is ONE, Inc., founded and directed by Dorr Legg in 1952 to promote research and counseling on homosexuality. From 1953 to 1969, it published a magazine, *One,* but in more recent years it seems to have become less active (Humphreys, 1972:54-57).

The earliest organization for female homosexuals (lesbians) was the Daughters of Bilitis (DOB), originally founded mainly for consciousness-raising purposes by Del Martin and Phyllis Lyon in San Francisco in 1955. For some years this was the only lesbian organization, and in 1956 it began publishing *The Ladder,* which continued until 1972. There are about 16 chapters of DOB around the country as of the mid-seventies (Tobin and Wicker, 1972). An allied group which developed in a more political direction is San Francisco's Society for Individual Rights (SIR), which began in 1964 and has gained some prominence in California (Gunnison, 1969:124). Other lesbian organizations have been formed to meet certain special needs, such as the Lesbian Mothers' Union, started in the early 1970's, which deals with such problems as custody litigation, child care, and related issues. Still other lesbian organizations have maintained ties with the larger women's liberation movement, such as the Lesbian Feminists and the Radicalesbians (products of the early 1970's), both of which regard male dominance and oppression as a major problem for lesbians in particular, as well as for women in general. The larger women's movement, however, has been rather ambivalent about its position concerning lesbians (see Chapter 11). (See Martin and Lyon, 1972.)

Though there is a large variety of both male and female homosexual organizations, spanning a wide range of ideological positions, some efforts have been made at national unification of all of both kinds of organizations. The earliest of these seems to have been the North American Conference of Homophile Organizations (NACHO), formed in 1966 but defunct by 1970 because of internal dissension. Since 1972, the National Coalition of Gay Organizations has been trying to pull together the various homosexual groups, with only limited success. Probably the earliest homosexual organization of a militant political kind to come along and to embrace some of these varying positions was the Gay Liberation Front, organized in New York City in 1969. Internal ideological differences put an end to the New York organization, but the Front is still alive in certain other cities. In 1972, at least 20 percent of the homophile organizations in existence (both male and female) used the name Gay Liberation Front (Humphreys, 1972). An important, if unintended, function of the GLF was that it sowed the seeds for the rise of the Gay Activists' Alliance (GAA) in New York City, in December, 1969. Whereas GLF had involved itself in a variety of "liberation" causes, including black liberation, the GAA resolved to avoid the entanglements and dissension resulting from such a variety of interests, and has concentrated entirely on the one issue of gay liberation (Humphreys, 1972:124). By April, 1971, membership in GAA had grown to 300 (from an original 19). The preamble to the GAA constitution contains, in part, a demand for "the immediate end to all oppression of homosexuals and the immediate unconditional recognition of . . . the right to our own feelings, the right to love, the right to our own bodies, and the right to be persons." More specific GAA goals include fair housing and fair employment legislation for gays, repeal of New York State laws against sodomy and solicitation (i.e., homosexual unions and "courting"), legislation prohibiting police enticement and entrapment, and an end to police harassment of gay bars (Bell, 1971:21-22; Tobin and Wicker, 1972:36). To promote the interests of homosexuals within specific occupational groups, certain newer organizations such as the Gay Nurses' Alliance and the Association of Gay Psychologists have come into existence in the early 1970's.

While religion traditionally has been harshly repressive of homosexual behavior, more recently some religious groups have joined with homosexual organizations to promote their freedom from legal and social harassment, while not necessarily approving of homosexuality itself. The Council on Religion and the Homosexual, originally founded as an interdenominational organization in San Francisco in 1964, has since spread to several other cities. It has received both moral and financial support from some of the larger denominations, beginning with the United Church of Christ (Gittings, 1969:164). The Unitarian-Universalists, several Episcopalian churches, the Quakers, and the Lutheran hierarchy are all among those who have at least expressed some recognition and sympathy for the plight of homosexuals. In order to escape the stigmatization they often find in churches, however, many homosexuals have formed their own churches, the best known of which is probably the Metropolitan Community Church, with more than 40 local congregations across the country (Humphreys, 1972:143-145).

Economic interests of homosexuals mainly take the form of fighting for job security and protection against various kinds of discrimination in their employment and careers. Most state and federal agencies still have laws that discriminate against homosexuals. Those whose economic interests are threatened would include the owners and operators of "gay bars," which often are subject to harassment in the form of intensive police surveillance and the withdrawals of their liquor licenses. In fighting against all such discriminatory treatment, homosexual organizations are often joined by the ACLU, which is about the only politically oriented interest group, outside of gay organizations themselves, working for legalization and liberation of male and female homosexuals.

Anti-Homosexual Interest Groups

Those opposed to legalization and liberation for homosexuals and lesbians tend to be very much the same people as those who oppose legalization for the other forms of deviant sexual behavior discussed so far: they are the older, less educated, small-town, southern or midwestern citizens, especially those with fundamentalist Protestant backgrounds (*Human Behavior,* October, 1973:44-45). In the words of one observer, "some of the most forceful opposition to changes in homosexual status arises from religious sources and is buttressed by theological doctrine" (Geis, 1972:51). Aside from some of the "social hygiene" or "decency" organizations mentioned earlier, which occasionally "branch out" from their specific concerns with prostitution or "smut" to condemn homosexuals, there seem to be no organizations directed specifically against male or female homosexuals. What happens, rather, is that many people hold such hostile feelings toward gays as have been indicated above, or they partake somewhat of the "comstock" outlook on the subject, and such people are spread throughout the various institutions and agencies of society, where they lend support to various kinds of restrictive and discriminatory laws against male and female homosexuals. Even such an "enlightened" group as the American Psychiatric Association (APA) defined homosexuality as a mental "disorder" until the designation was dropped at the 1974 national convention.*

Scientific Interest Groups

In addition to the various interest groups that have a position, pro or con, on prostitution, pornography, or homosexuality, social and behavioral scientists over the years have had their own definitions of these forms of sexual "deviance." It is probably accurate to state that scientific theories, research, and explanations on these three issues are among the most poorly developed and least agreed upon of any that we have discussed in the book so far. Plainly, scientists really don't know why some women become prostitutes, why some men purchase their favors, why some people like pornography, or why some men and women are homosexuals. In general, if any consensus among scientists about these forms of behavior can be said to exist, it would boil down to the following simple postulates: (1) Prostitution, pornography, and homosexuality have existed all over the world since the beginning of recorded history. (2) They probably serve some kind of widespread need or function in the societies where they are found. (3) There is little or no evidence that they, in and of themselves, are causes of crime, social disorganization, the decline of civilization, or of anti-social behavior of any particular kind. (4) The laws which currently attempt to outlaw or restrict these kinds of behavior have generally not succeeded in their purpose, but have been extremely costly in terms of money and civil liberties. (5) They have themselves created a whole class of "crimes without victims," as these have been called by Schur (1965).

There have been specific theories advanced to explain some aspects of these forms of behavior. Kingsley Davis (1937), for example, used a typical "functionalist" explanation for prostitution, arguing that it thrived in monogamous societies precisely because it had a reciprocal or symbiotic relationship with sexually restrictive forms of marriage; that is, marriage survives because prostitution provides (for some men, at least) an outlet or "safety valve" without which marriage would be intolerably restrictive, and prostitution survives because marriage provides

---

* After some debate on a proposal drafted by its governing board, the membership of the APA at large finally adopted the proposal on April 8, 1974, and voted to drop homosexuality from its list of "mental disorders" requiring treatment. In so doing, it reversed a position which it had held for a century. The new official position of the APA is that homosexuality requires treatment only if a patient requests treatment (*New York Times*, April 9, 1974, 12:4).

it with a steady stream of husbands seeking such an outlet. Marriage and prostitution need each other, and they both are being eroded by the spread of a more general sexual freedom (see the quotation at the beginning of this chapter). Others who have studied prostitution have tended to regard it as a special "deviant subculture" which must be understood on its own terms (Greenwald, 1958). Even those who, like Greenwald, have tried to find some deep-rooted "causes" for prostitution in the background experiences of prostitutes have not succeeded in explaining how girls who become prostitutes are systematically different from girls who do not.

On pornography, the best scientific work that we have (and virtually the only such) is that which was done by the National Commission on Obscenity and Pornography in 1968 and 1969 (see *The New York Times* report, 1970). Among the most important conclusions of the research done under the Commission's auspices are that: (1) exposure to pornography has no effect on attitudes or values about either sex or sexual morality; (2) pornographic materials produce sexual excitement in a large number of people, but repeated exposure to such materials results in satiation of both arousal and interest; (3) it is highly doubtful that pornography affects the extent or nature of a person's habitual sexual behavior; and (4) there is no evidence that exposure to explicit sexual materials plays any significant role in causing delinquent or criminal behavior among either youth or adults (pp. 169, 174, 198, and 232-233).*

Sigmund Freud had an explanation for homosexual behavior, as he did for most other kinds of deviant behavior: he regarded a homosexual person as one whose psychosexual development had been "arrested" at a pre-adolescent stage; by psychoanalysis, such a person might be brought through the normal stages to the final, mature heterosexual one. More recently, the American sex researcher Kinsey hypothesized that exclusively heterosexual and exclusively homosexual persons were both rare; most people are on a continuum somewhere in between those two extremes. They are almost always *predominantly* homosexual or heterosexual, but most people also have some homosexual tendencies, which can be "brought out" by certain experiences (Pomeroy, 1969:7).

It is apparent that science has very few specifics to offer by way of explanations for these kinds of sexual deviance, although we have presented only a sampling of the better-known scientific opinions. With some dissent, to be sure, most social and behavioral scientists would probably agree, however, with the five postulates given at the beginning of this section.

---

* See also Goldstein and Kant, 1974, which supports most of the same four conclusions. This work came to our attention only after the chapter was largely completed, but it is a valuable and thorough empirical study.

SEX-PROBLEM SOCIAL MOVEMENTS

Space will not permit as thorough a treatment of the three "sex problems" as social movements as we have devoted to some of the other social problems in this book. However, we will review briefly each of the three in turn, and demonstrate the usefulness of our "natural history" model as it is applied to sex-related social problems.

Prostitution

There seems to have been little general concern about prostitution in our society until the progressive era, around the turn of the present century. To be sure, individual clergymen, feminists, and others had cried out against such vice and evil in earlier times, but there was seldom, if ever, any sustained drive against prostitution in the 18th and 19th centuries, and it was widely tolerated (and even encouraged) in many of the frontier towns, where "respectable" women were in short supply. As the progressives increasingly decried the various kinds of "social evils" associated with the rapidly growing urban areas, they began to include prostitution among their targets and to call for the eradication of the rather conspicuous "red-light districts" to be found in the "seamier" sections of cities (Lemert, 1951:260). The belief that the social environment of mankind could be improved greatly, or even perfected, by enlightened and sustained social and political action, a belief so strongly characteristic of the progressive movement in general, was acted upon nowhere more ardently than in the case of prostitution (Feldman, 1967). This is demonstrated clearly in the pronouncements of Charles W. Elliot (1914) himself, first president of the American Social Hygiene Association (ASHA).

The founding of the ASHA in 1913 represented the *coalescence,* in its own right, of an anti-prostitution movement that earlier had been only an *incipient* trend in the larger progressive movement. The buildup toward coalescence can be traced in the popular and scientific literature of the period. *The Reader's Guide to Periodical Literature,* a standard index of popular magazine articles, lists a total of 157 articles on prostitution during the years 1909 through 1914, compared to only 18 such articles from 1890 through 1908, and comprising nearly one-half of all of the prostitution articles listed between 1890 and 1968. A similar pattern appears, though with some time lag, in the *International Index to the Social Sciences and Humanities,* an index of articles in professional and literary journals, which lists 78 articles on prostitution, from the "experts'" point of view, published between 1911 and 1920, compared to virtually none before that time, and accounting for one-third of all such articles listed for the entire 20th century (up through

1968). Clearly, then, the years just prior to World War I brought the coalescence of the anti-prostitution movement.*

The *institutionalization* of the movement seems to have occurred later during this same general period, i.e., with the U.S. entry into the war in 1917 and 1918. The chief symptoms of this development were the increased "social muscle" enjoyed by the American Social Hygiene Association, including its establishment in 1914 of a respected "professional" journal, *The Journal of Social Hygiene,* and the growing official recognition of the ASHA by government agencies. With the help of considerable ASHA influence, 19 state legislatures enacted "vice" legislation that included the punishment of both prostitutes and their customers; a section also was included by Congress in the Selective Service (Draft) Act of 1917, which prohibited prostitution near military or naval bases and camps; and nearly 200 red-light districts were effectively closed down in our large cities during 1917 and 1918, so that scarcely half-a-dozen remained by the end of the war. During the war, the ASHA was "co-opted" by the government for the war effort. All of the staff and officers of the Association were assigned to active duty with either the War Department, the Navy Department, or the Commission on Training Camps. Fighting prostitution and its concomitant diseases came to be identified with patriotism itself, as well as with righteousness and enlightenment (Snow, 1946). *The Journal of Social Hygiene,* thriving under such quasi-official sponsorship, published feverishly during this period, with its articles accounting for most of those listed in the *International Index* from 1914 on, particularly up to 1920. (The fact that the *Journal* should even have been indexed in the *International Index* was itself a sign of the movement's institutionalization.)

After 1920, public and official interest in the "prostitution problem" dropped off sharply: from about half-a-dozen articles a year on prostitution during 1915-1919, the *Readers' Guide* was down to no listings for 1920 or 1921; the *International Index* listings for prostitution dropped from 19 in 1919, to 9 in 1920, and to only one in 1921; and even the *Journal* listings on prostitution dropped from 17 in 1919 to 5 in 1920, to none in 1921. In accordance with what our "natural history" model would predict, the "social problem" of prostitution was clearly in decline, whether or not there still were prostitutes to be found in the cities. While the more flagrant red-light districts may have been wiped out, prostitution continued apace, becoming more decentralized and more surreptitious, as Walter Reckless, among others, pointed out in his book, *Vice in Chicago* (1933). Waterman (1932:50) makes essentially the same point after reviewing 30 years of efforts to suppress prostitution in New York City: ". . . changes in the law have been followed in all

---

* For the data in these paragraphs, and for much of the material on prostitution in this chapter, we are indebted to Professor Charles E. Reasons, of the University of Calgary, whose work and permission to draw upon it we here gratefully acknowledge.

instances by the necessary adjustments on the part of the (vice operators) to meet the new conditions" (see also Sheehy, 1972a and 1972b). The ASHA, of course, continued to sound the alarm in various ways, though on a somewhat reduced scale, but the "problem," for all practical purposes, became the ASHA's alone. Those agencies and organizations that had been its allies during the war became halfhearted or turned to other issues of the 1920's, such as prohibition and organized crime, indicating some *fragmentation* of what once had been a mighty movement.

From 1920 to 1940, the movement was dormant. Only in a few of the intervening years did the number of listings of prostitution-related articles in any index reach 10 or more, and for many of those years there was only one or none. The approach of World War II, however, gave the ASHA a renewed opportunity to tie its campaign to the war effort, and there was some resurgence of the official concern and attempt at suppression that had occurred during World War I, though on a much reduced scale. The indexes that we have cited reflected this development in a renewed flurry of popular and professional articles on prostitution during the war years, particularly from 1941 to 1943. The ASHA was brought in once again as an ally of the government to combat prostitution, and during 1940 and 1941, the ASHA conducted a number of important studies on prostitution near military bases. In the same period, it produced a "training film," *In Defense of the Nation,* in which prostitution was portrayed as an important hindrance to national defense, and the Association also helped to draft a variety of new legislation to control prostitution in urban areas. Once again, many red-light districts were eliminated, but there was little change in the actual incidence of prostitution, as far as we can tell.

The period of World War II saw the last great national effort to "clean up" prostitution. From that point on, the movement reverted to a fragmented condition, and seems to have continued in this way until its *demise* by about 1960. The decline in official and public concern can be seen once again in the low frequency with which articles on prostitution appeared. The listings in the indexes we have cited began to drop off after the war, with a slight "flare-up" of concern, perhaps, during the Korean War years of the early fifties, but on a much reduced scale, until 1960 to 1962, when there were altogether two articles listed in the *Reader's Guide,* and one in the *International Index.* The ASHA *Journal,* after several months of ever-thinner issues, finally stopped publication in 1954. Since 1960, articles on prostitution have appeared very rarely in *Reader's Guide* and have virtually disappeared from the *International Index,* except for historical treatments. Enforcement of anti-prostitution statutes is much slacker around the nation than it was in the 1940's and earlier, except for spasmodic and occasional "busts" or "crackdowns" that take place in scattered local settings. This process of decline was already painfully evident to the ASHA at an early point. A 1946 article in the *Journal* asked in alarm, "Is Commercialized Prostitution Returning?" In a 1949 "progress report" to the readers of the *Journal,* the editor, while still apparently optimistic that concerted action could keep prostitution under control, had to admit that the "line against prostitution continues to sag in some places [and] more breakthroughs are evident than two years ago . . ." (Snow, 1949:160). As the *Journal,* and the movement which it represented, moved inexorably toward their demise, there is evidence that movement spokesmen were starting to redefine the goals of the movement in somewhat more modest terms, leading to the point where the "problem" might be defined credibly as "solved." By 1953 one important spokesman admitted that "about as much as can be done" against prostitution is to make things so difficult for the average customer that he "must spend considerable effort, time, and money to locate [a prostitute], and risk danger of arrest" (Kinsie, 1953:248). This seems to have set the stage for an article in the final volume of the *Journal* by ASHA President Mather, in which he asks if the mission of his Association has not been accomplished, so that the organization can disband. "We shall not," he points out, "perpetuate our services beyond the time when they are needed" (*Social Hygiene,* 1954:163).

Thus ended a 45 year campaign against prostitution in the United States. It had its ups and downs, and it left behind a large body of legislation at different levels of government. Once again, though, it is a moot question whether the movement has had any effect on the actual incidence of prostitution, or if it ever did. There is no reason to believe that the amount of prostitution has changed at all, and still less reason to believe that it has declined. The occasional "cleanup" campaigns in our large cities offer recurring evidence that prostitution is still very much in evidence. Further, it is interesting to note that the same "natural history" or "life-cycle" pattern that we have seen on a nationwide basis is characteristic of these occasional local anti-prostitution movements. Roby (1969), for example, studied in great detail the process by which a new prostitution statute in New York in the mid-1960's was buffeted about by a variety of interest groups in its formulation and modification, ending up finally as a product of many compromises among the competing interests. Familiarly, it also turned out to produce much collective agitation and temporary enforcement activity, but very little change in the incidence of prostitution.

Pornography and Obscenity

There are, and historically have been, interest groups opposed to censorship of pornographic or other materials which they insist are protected by the 1st Amendment. In the previous section of this chapter, we reviewed some of these anti-censorship (or pro-legalization) interest groups, not only on the pornography issue,

Chapter 10 / Sexual Behavior: Prostitution, Pornography, and Homosexuality 385

but on the other two sex-related issues as well. Rarely, however, have these pro-legalization interest groups ever been welded together into sustained and cohesive social movements on any of these issues. They usually have responded on an *ad hoc* basis to perceived threats against libertarian values which have come from those interest groups and movements attempting to censor and restrict "unpopular" forms of sexual behavior. Thus, as we saw earlier with the issue of prostitution, the social movements that have resulted have been those made up of interest groups trying to *eliminate* prostitution, or to get it publicly *defined as "a problem."* With the possible exception of a very recent, fledgling, and localized organization of "loose ladies" (i.e., COYOTE), whose prospects are not yet clear, there have not been any pro-prostitution movements—only occasional intervention in the legislative or enforcement process on the part of some group or organization like the ACLU to assist or protect the rights of prostitutes. The same is true of the pornography issue: censorship efforts have frequently been sustained and well-organized, and have taken on the proportions of a social movement more than once, whereas pro-legalization interests have seldom, if ever, been on this scale. Accordingly, in our discussion of pornography, as we did with prostitution, we will limit our study to the history and activities of the anti-sex or pro-censorship movement, which is, of course, the social phenomenon responsible for defining the behavior as a problem in the first place.

Anti-pornography agitation has been with us for a long time, certainly at least since Comstock days one hundred years ago, and, in some places, much earlier. California in the 19th century, for example, saw the rise of the so-called League of Deliverance in the 1860's, an offshoot of the "Vigilante" movement there, which devoted itself to the suppression of all kinds of "vice" attributed to the Gold Rush nomads and to the Chinese immigrants. Pornography was only one of their concerns (Nawy, 1970). Thoroughly supported, as they were, by both public and official opinion, campaigns like the League's on the West Coast, and Comstock's at about the same time on the East Coast (and the Midwest), very effectively kept pornography and other "vices" under cover well into the 20th century. The contemporary censorship movement perhaps could be traced in some ways to those early Comstock days, but its real *incipiency* is to be found in the 1950's, when our society was experiencing a strong and repressive general movement against Communists and other "subversive" elements, with which pornography and other "vices" frequently were identified.

Examples of the movement's incipiency on a local level would include an event in Youngstown, Ohio, where, in 1953, the police chief, in cooperation with the local federation of women's clubs, compiled a list of 335 books that the police defined as "obscene." In attempting to compel local book dealers to remove the listed books from their stock, the chief ran into gradually stiffening *ad hoc* opposition, until finally he was restrained by court action initiated by the New American Library of World Literature, eleven of whose titles were on the list, and seven of which were in the Youngstown Public Library (Kilpatrick, 1960:252). In Detroit, at about the same time, some policemen were engaging willingly in censorship and obscenity investigations during their off-duty hours, and at one point they, too, compiled a list of more than 300 books to be banned from local libraries and retail outlets. Included on their list were *The Psychology of Sex* (Havelock Ellis), *1919* (John Dos Passos), and Hans Christian Andersen's *Fairy Tales* (Kyle-Keith, 1961:114-115).

Whenever local censorship efforts of these kinds were tested in the courts, more often than not the decisions went against the censors during the late 1950's and the 1960's. A particularly disappointing case for the pro-censorship forces was the 1957 *Roth v. U.S.* case, in which the Supreme Court laid down, as the three criteria for legally defining material as "obscene," that (1) its "dominant theme," when taken "as a whole," must appeal to a "prurient interest" (not otherwise defined); that (2) the materials must be offensive according to "contemporary community standards" (also not otherwise defined); and that (3) the materials must be lacking in any "redeeming social significance." The practical effect of this decision was to make obscenity convictions very difficult to obtain, considering the vagueness and many obvious "loopholes" in the decision. Accordingly, during the next several years, movies became much "bolder," and printed material with sexual themes came out increasingly from "under the counter" (Wilson, 1972: 115). To the censorship forces, all of this added up to simply one more assault by the "liberal Warren court" upon the basic and traditional values of "Americanism," and their response took the form of increasing coalescence into several new nationwide organizations which began to emerge during this period. They regarded the courts as having betrayed them, and the local law enforcement agencies as ineffectual; they were prepared to take matters into their own hands (Zurcher and Monts, 1972).

Foremost among the anti-pornography organizations to arise during this period is the Citizens for Decent Literature, Inc. (CDL), founded by Charles H. Keating, Jr., in Cincinnati, Ohio (but since moved to Los Angeles). As we indicated earlier, CDL membership tends to be relatively older, less educated, more conservative in religion and politics, and more rural than average Americans (Birkelbach and Zurcher, 1970). CDL has a tax-exempt status as a non-profit organization, and an annual budget of about $100,000, and devotes its energies in large part to court assistance for groups and individuals attempting to promote censorship (McCormick, 1972).

Another prominent organization to come forth as part of the coalescence of this movement is Morality in Media (MM), led by Reverend Morton A. Hill, S.J., whose members more often tend to be Catholics than is the case with CDL, but who otherwise resemble CDL membership. They have a much larger budget than CDL's, which goes for both research and "endowments." A chief target of this organization is eliminating the "socially redeeming value" criterion from state obscenity laws. It is estimated that for every 6 cents in profits taken by pornography producers, CDL and MM spend 14 cents in promoting censorship, most of which goes into legal battles (McCormick, 1972).

One of the more recent organizations in the *coalescence* phase of the censorship movement is the Leadership Foundation, organized late in 1972, with headquarters in Washington, D.C. Probably the main focus of the Foundation's attention is television, which it has undertaken to clean up by means of complaints and pressures directed at the Federal Communications Commission (FCC), by organizing boycotts against sponsors of "objectionable" programs, and by a series of public meetings and rallies which emphasize the need for more patriotism, morality, and spirituality. In the words of one of the founders, the organization represents a great "crusade against moral pollution" and an effort to "get our great nation back on the right track, morally, socially, and spiritually" (*Spokesman-Review,* December 8, 1972, p. 9).

In addition to the establishment of such nationwide organizations as CDL, MM, and the Leadership Foundation, the coalescence of the "anti-smut" movement also was evident in the increasing crescendo of local censorship efforts around the country during the 1960's, in an effort to get at least the local courts to interpret the "community standards" clause of the 1957 *Roth v. U.S.* decision in favor of local censorship. This multifaceted (if not fully coordinated) campaign included moves against not only "hard-core" materials, but also against some "soft-core" books and films that were widely consumed by the general public, including some D. H. Lawrence novels, and movies like *The Killing of Sister George,* with the frequent result of more avid consumption of the condemned work. There were also occasional statewide efforts, such as that led by "Clean, Incorporated," a California citizen's group, aimed at getting more stringent obscenity laws passed by statewide referendum or initiative (Friedman, 1970). Sporadic efforts of the same general kind on a local basis have continued around the country even into the 1970's, for example in the New York City 1972 campaign against smut and prostitution, and the 1971 incident in Laguna Beach, California, where the District Attorney, acting on citizen complaints, closed down a bookstore which specialized in texts on religion, art, parapsychology, astrology, organic foods, and certain "underground" comic books (Nordheimer, 1974; Sheehy, 1972a and 1972b). Convictions in such cases have been hard to obtain, because of the vagueness of the 1957 Supreme Court criteria (e.g., what constitutes community standards), and because of growing public apathy. The main result of all these miscellaneous local cases around the nation, and the enormous variety and unpredictability in their outcomes, has been general confusion about what the standards are for defining anything as "obscene." Nevertheless, in an earlier period (the 1960's) there were several convictions under the 1957 criteria, the best-known probably being that of Ralph Ginzburg for distributing *Eros*.

Such confusion led to increasing efforts by state governments, and eventually by the Congress itself, to come to grips with the social importance of pornography and the definition of obscenity. For a few years during the mid-1960's, Senator Karl Mundt tried to get Congress to pass legislation against "noxious" literature, but with only partial success. In 1967, the House Select Subcommittee on Education addressed the issue with a substitute proposal to create a National Commission on Obscenity and Pornography, whose research would be carried out for two years, from 1968 to 1970. The unanimous adoption of this bill by both houses of Congress was the most important and conspicuous indication that the "anti-smut" movement had reached the stage of *institutionalization*: the highest echelons of the establishment had decided to take on the pornography issue.

After extensive investigation of the effects of pornography, including its psychological and sociological impact, the research staff of the Commission found, in essence, that there was no basis for a belief that pornographic consumption was implicated in any kind of anti-social behavior, or that it had any lasting impact on individual consumers. Accordingly, 12 of the 18 members of the Commission joined in a majority report, which recommended that federal, state, and local legislation prohibiting the sale, exhibition, or distribution of sexual material to consenting adults should be repealed (*The New York Times* report, 1970:62). What followed that recommendation was something of a fiasco: the dissenting members of the Commission, led by Charles H. Keating, Chairman of CDL, first attempted to delay publication of the Commission Report and then to modify it; failing to do that, they issued dissenting statements based more upon the emotional appeal of what "everybody knows," and upon the value premises of CDL, than upon any of the evidence produced by the Commission's research (*Economist*, October 3, 1970). Keating's statement first attacked the empirical evidence and findings of the Commission's staff:

Credit the American public with enough common sense to know that one who wallows in filth is going to get dirty. This is intuitive knowledge. Those who will spend millions of dollars to tell us otherwise must be malicious or misguided, or both. The report of the majority of the Commission does not reflect the will of Congress, the opinion of law enforcement officials throughout our country, and, worst of all, flaunts the underlying opinions and desires of the great mass of American people. (*The New York Times* report, 1970:622)

Nor was Keating, it appears, primarily concerned with the question of social consequences of pornography: "The government interest in regulating pornography has always related primarily to the prevention of moral corruption and *not* (merely) to prevention of overt criminal acts and conduct, or the protection of persons from being shocked and/or offended" (*The New York Times,* 1970:457; italics in original).

The views of Keating and the other dissenting Commission members are important not merely because of the contrast they provide to those of the majority, but also because they turned out to be the prevailing views of both Congress and the President. By a vote of 60 to 5, the Senate repudiated the Commission's (majority) findings and recommendations (Wilson, 1972:119), and, in the same vein, then President Nixon labelled the report "morally bankrupt" and called upon all the states to enact anti-obscenity legislation (*Los Angeles Times,* as quoted in Funston, 1971). Contrary to the intentions of the majority of the Commission, its report thus produced a stimulus for CDL and other pro-censorship organizations, which, after having been frustrated by court decisions, were now, in effect, legitimated by Congress and the President. The Leadership Foundation increased their pressure on the FCC, some of whose leaders expressed sympathy for the Foundation's goals. The FCC is hopeful also that the court cases brought by the Leadership Foundation, CDL, and their allies will help to resolve the difficult dilemma in which FCC finds itself as a result of being required by law *both* to refrain from censorship (following the 1st Amendment) *and* to penalize TV stations which broadcast obscene materials (*Idahonian,* April 14, 1973). Increasingly, the Justice Department began to put its pressure on the trafficking in pornography, including not just "back alley theatres in run-down neighborhoods, but also the established movie houses who are being 'porno-chic'" (*Idahonian,* February 27, 1973). Eventually, a number of cases began to come up before the Supreme Court, and the censorship forces were hopeful that with the four new Nixon appointees there might be a reversal of the 1957 "permissive" decision. These hopes were borne out in part by the 1973 *California v. Miller* decision, out of Orange County, California, in which, by a 5 to 4 vote, the high court ruled that individual states should be the principal authorities for the determination of what is "patently obscene" by "prevailing community standards" (Nordheimer, 1974). While far from what the censorship people had hoped, this decision was hailed as "reversing a decade-long trend toward permissiveness," by giving the individual states "much greater authority to move against obscenity" (*Idahonian,* June 21, 1973:1). While *California v. Miller* was thus a key element in an encouraging trend for the censorship movement after their bitter disappointment over the National Commission's report, neither that decision nor any other court action to date has provided an impartial, equitable, universal, or satisfactory standard by which to judge what is "obscene." The issue, or "problem," remains in highly institutionalized form, and the censorship movement is still very much alive. There are some indications, however, that the movement is headed for *fragmentation* and *decline,* not only because of continuing difficulties in getting court support for its position, but also because of a growing public apathy (or perhaps tolerance) over the issue (Nordheimer, 1974).

While it may be too early to speak of the final stages of the anti-obscenity movement on a nationwide basis, we can find reason to predict that our natural history model eventually will be followed to its conclusion, not only because of our general theoretical perspective, but also because of the experiences of certain local expressions of the movement. One of these was the outcome of a movement in the 1960's in a town with the pseudonym, "Midville," led by the local Interfaith Citizens' Council for Decency (ICCD), an affiliate of the CDL (Zurcher, et al., 1971). This movement was fed by the usual moral entrepreneurship that has characterized the national movement; it also followed the usual "rise and fall" pattern we have plotted, eventually fragmenting as a result of the variety of interests that had made up the movement from the beginning. These included not only the "anti-smut" interests, but also the hyperpatriotic and anti-Communist elements, and the opponents of "student rebels." Also in line with the expected outcome, the "obscene" bookstores in town (one, in particular), which had been closed temporarily through the local movement's efforts, continued to thrive long after the movement died down. As is characteristic of a movement in demise, the ICCD also redefined and scaled down its goals to meet the new reality: ". . . maybe that bookstore will stay open, but the decent people in this town have gone on record about how they feel, and what they can do if they want to, and everybody knows it" (Zurcher, et al., 1971:231).

A journalistic judgment, originating with the New York Times News Service late in 1974, suggests that the predicted outcome of fragmentation and demise for the anti-obscenity movement has begun on a nationwide basis as well (Sterba, 1974). Under the heading "Fight Against Pornography Fizzles Out," this article reviews the opinions of state and local prosecutors and vice officers in Denver, Los Angeles, Chicago, Seattle and even a rural county in Iowa, and finds that there is little public outrage left and little official interest in suppression, where pornographic materials are concerned. All those interviewed seemed to blame the hopeless "quagmire" of judicial decisions and interpretations from the federal Supreme Court on down, in which it is impossible to get any judicial consensus about what constitutes *obscenity*. Thus, the establishment seems to have co-opted the anti-obscenity movement without actually solving the problem toward which the movement was directed. We are reminded again also of the "logistical quota" idea of Erikson (1966), which we discussed in Chapter 1, when we see a Chicago prosecutor's observation that the decline of public and official interest in pornography has occurred because "there are enough other problems in America today that pornography is not an issue that outrages a large number of people" (Sterba, 1974).

Homosexuality

The movement around homosexuality presents the reverse situation to the movements that have grown up around prostitution and pornography: whereas the movements focusing on those issues were *opposition* movements, the one related to homosexuality is a *pro-legalization* one, promoting the interests of male and female homosexuals as citizens and as a minority group that frequently experiences discrimination. To be sure, there is frequent opposition to homosexuals, but that opposition so far seems to have taken the form mainly of local *ad hoc,* uncoordinated "busts" and harassment. As the homosexual (or homophile) movement picks up momentum, we may see the rise of an organized national opposition campaign, but for the time being, homosexual behavior (compared to prostitution and pornography) is generally considered so bizarre and incomprehensible as not, apparently, to constitute any fundamental threat to "straight" values and institutions.

As we indicated toward the beginning of this chapter, there have been homosexuals of both sexes since recorded history began, but it is only in very recent years, and in modern industrial societies like our own, that we can see the rise of organizations and movements for homosexuals. The current movement in America seems to have had its *incipiency* during the early 1950's. Kinsey's work on male sex behavior (actually published in the late 1940's) had gained some currency, and had indicated that (1) homosexual episodes had been admitted by a great many of his respondents; and (2) most people had at least some homosexual tendencies (i.e., could be ranked on a scale somewhere between the extremes of "pure" homosexual and "pure" heterosexual), although very few were exclusively homosexual. Such conclusions suggested that maybe homosexuals were not as totally unique and bizarre as most people had thought, an idea that was reassuring both to homosexuals and to the rest of the population. In 1951, Donald Cory published his book, *The Homosexual in America,* a thoughtful and sympathetic treatment of the subject, which, among other things, encouraged homosexuals to join the "group life of the gay world" and to start engaging in collective action in their own interests (Cory, 1951:264-66).

A few small and struggling organizations were formed during the early 1950's, including the Mattachine Society, mentioned earlier in this chapter, and One, Inc. As the decade progressed, the incipient "homophile movement," as it was called, was broadened by the addition of female (lesbian) organizations, most notably the Daughters of Bilitis in the mid-fifties. The male monthly magazine, *One* (from

1953), and the lesbians' newsletter, *The Ladder* (1956), gave homophiles at least limited media for communication and for the building of a sense of community, though these publications survived for only a few years.

Legal developments during this incipient period were both encouraging and discouraging for the homophile organizations. In 1955, the American Law Institute drafted a Model Penal Code intended as a pattern after which states might begin modernizing their respective constitutions and laws. This model code recommended dropping entirely from the criminal statutes any laws concerning sexual relations (homosexual or otherwise) between consenting adults in private. In 1957, the well-known and highly respected Wolfenden Report to the British Parliament made the same recommendation. These recommendations were adopted in England, but not in the United States. In 1958, *One,* Inc., was victorious in a Supreme Court case which secured the rights of homophiles and their organizations to send their publications through the U.S. mails (Tobin and Wicker, 1972:8).

Rather discouraging to homophiles, however, was the 1957 case of Frank Kameny, a scientist who was fired from federal government service on a charge of homosexual behavior. Kameny contested his firing all the way to the U.S. Supreme Court, which upheld the government's action in a 1961 decision. Kameny's response was to form the Mattachine Society of Washington, D.C. (MSW) that same year, in the belief that homophiles would have to get organized and become much more active in their own cause, both politically and legally, if they were to enjoy their civil liberties. MSW was thus a far more militant homophile expression than its earlier West Coast counterpart. While neither the Kameny case nor the MSW was widely known in the society at large, they provided for the homophiles of the nation both a unifying *cause célèbre* and a model for a new militancy that was to emerge during the coalescence period of the 1960's (Tobin and Wicker, 1972).

Except for the rather singular initiative and organization of Kameny and the MSW, however, the early 1960's ushered in only an incipient and not very robust homophile movement. There were only half-a-dozen homophile organizations in the country (encompassing a number of local chapters as well), and they were "on the run" in some respects as a result of the "anti-subversive" sentiments of both the public and the government during much of the previous decade (the 1950's). It was still very unsafe for a homosexual or lesbian to disclose publicly his or her sexual preferences, or to support homophile causes (Gunnison, 1969). The efforts of the incipient movement during this period were primarily introspective, rather than activist, seeking to "raise public consciousness" and to provide mutual support and exchange of information, rather than engage in struggle with society. As Gunnison expressed it (1969:118):

Little was done to come to grips with the firing personnel manager, the evicting landlord, the reservation-cancelling restaurant, the insurance-cancelling underwriter, the entrapping policeman, the blackmailing extortionist, the license-revoking alcoholic beverage commission—to say nothing of municipal regulations, state laws, and federal, state, and local official policies and practices. . . .

During the early years of the 1960's, the incipiency of the homophile movement gradually gave way to a period of *coalescence,* which began in the middle years of that decade and lasted until the beginning of the current decade. The work of Kameny and the MSW made an important contribution to this coalescence process during the early sixties. In contrast to the style of secrecy and timidity which most homophiles felt compelled to adopt, Kameny was open and outspoken. He and his MSW colleagues openly confronted the establishment by appearing at legislative hearings, organizing picket lines, and joining other homophiles in legal battles. MSW published literature both for the education of the general public on the subject and for the guidance of fellow homophiles. An example of the latter was the 1963 pamphlet, "How to Handle a Federal Interrogation." By 1964, Kameny had recognized, and was urging upon his colleagues, an awareness of the parallels between their goals and those of the civil rights movement more generally:

Blacks tried the education/information approach for fifty years and got almost nowhere. [They] are beginning to get what they wanted through a vigorous social-protest, social-action, civil-liberties type of program. Let not this lesson be wasted on us. (Tobin and Wicker, 1972:97)

In large part through the inspiration provided by Kameny and MSW, other Mattachine and homophile organizations began to revitalize or to appear for the first time. This development occurred mainly at certain centers along the East Coast (especially New York City and Washington, D.C.) and along the West Coast (Los Angeles and San Francisco), with much less development in between. In 1964, SIR (Society for Individual Rights) appeared in San Francisco and purchased a downtown building for a homophile community center. It was especially effective during that period in promoting "outreach" activities and forming alliances not only with other homophile groups, but also with various sympathetic "straights" and straight organizations. An example of the latter kind of alliance was the Council on Religion and the Homosexual (CRH), which involved a number of even the more "respectable" religious denominations in San Francisco; the Tavern Guild, a protective association for gay bars and restaurants; and the National Legal Defense Fund for homophile test cases (Gunnison, 1969). The CRH was joined in 1964 by two founders of the Daughters of Bilitis, Phyllis Lyon and Del Martin, who decided to try to interest church people in the gay cause (Tobin and Wicker, 1972:53). Ms. Lyon became a vice-president of the CRH, whose activities have included not only the sponsorship of "mixed" social functions for gays and straights, but also "initiation and support of court actions testing civil liberties issues, to pressure for fair employment, . . . confrontations with police and other public officials in regard to harassment and other abuses . . ." (Gittings, 1969:153).

Relatively late in the coalescence process of the movement, some churches began to emerge whose ministries were interested primarily in homophiles. One of the most prominent of these was the Metropolitan Community Church, which held its first service in the Los Angeles living room of the Reverend Troy Perry in late 1968, with an attendance of 12. The message of the Reverend Perry was not welcome in the pentecostal tradition from which he had come, but it attracted many homophiles. By early 1971, more than 1,000 were in attendance at the dedication of a newly acquired MCC church building in Los Angeles, and since then the work of the organization has spread to many other cities. Even before 1970, though, MCC had set up a 24-hour "hotline" or crisis call center for homophiles, a class in sign language for deaf homophiles, a youth organization for gay teenagers, a medical and legal referral service, and free food (for three days) and clothing to the needy among them. As MCC spokesmen have defined the function of their organization, it has been presented as a reaction to Christians who have "forced blacks, Chinese, homosexuals, and others out of their congregations. If the churches would open their doors to homosexuals, we would close our doors tomorrow" (Tobin and Wicker, 1972:13-27).

By the mid-sixties, the number of national homophile organizations had reached 17 (a tripling in only five or six years) and was still growing. The first actual organizational expression of the movement's coalescence was the 1966 North American Conference of Homophile Organizations (NACHO), held in San Francisco, the first of a series of annual conferences to help unify the movement and promote its basic goals of political, economic, and sexual freedom for homophiles. Projects and task forces were organized to deal with the various aspects of the homophile interests (Gunnison, 1969:119-126). Another important expression of coalescence during this period was the 1967 establishment of the *Los Angeles Advocate* (later simply *The Advocate*), a national newspaper for homophiles, with a large circulation, compared to earlier homophile attempts at publication, and an emphasis upon keeping the homophile "community" abreast of the most important current national news relating to their interests.

By 1969, as the decade was coming to a close, there were countless homophile organizations across the country, and a fairly high degree of coalescence had been achieved under the NACHO "umbrella" and by means of a national newspaper. In June of 1969, a precipitating incident occurred in New York City, which seems to have capped the coalescence of the movement (at least symbolically) and to have launched the *institutionalization* phase, which began to gain momentum as the movement entered the new decade. On June 27, 1969, the New York City police raided the Stonewall Inn, an after-hours gay bar. Instead of the usual response of passively pouring out into the streets under police prodding, the bar patrons became actively hostile and forced the police inside the bar, throwing bottles and stones at them, and generally roughing them up. When police reinforcements arrived, some of the patrons defiantly broke into a rousing gay chorus line (Tobin and Wicker, 1972:173). The following night, homophiles and their sympathizers gathered in strategic places in the city to protest the police actions, using a protest style and technique very much like those which had been institutionalized by the black and student protest movements of the same era, except, of course, that the slogan now being shouted was "gay power!"

This incident was only the beginning of the development of a new style of militancy and protest very much in the established tradition of civil rights agitation. The establishment would now have to begin to take account of the movement in a serious way, and to try to develop coping mechanisms for handling it (one of the signs of a movement's institutionalization). New, more militant coalitions were organized in the movement during 1969 and 1970, such as the Gay Liberation Front (GLF) and the Gay Activist Alliance (GAA). GLF had a distinctly left-wing political stance and collaborated with a variety of other "liberation" movements then current in the society, whereas GAA tried to avoid such entanglements and to concentrate solely on the interests of homophiles. One of the tactics popularized by GAA has been the so-called "zap," which is a kind of very annoying harassment of key public officials and others on certain strategic occasions when media coverage is especially likely to be present. On one such occasion in 1970, 40 GAA members obtained tickets to a special New York City program on ecology, featuring Arthur Godfrey and (then) Mayor John Lindsay, and, as the program began, various GAA members began shouting from the audience and asking the mayor what his administration was doing to end job discrimination against gays. They were removed from the audience, but their interruptions had to be deleted from the TV tape, and, as a compromising measure, they were promised a conference with the deputy mayor (Bell, 1971:56-57). That the "zaps" also served to boost morale within the movement is apparent from the following comment made by a GAA member on another occasion:

That evening we watched ourselves on ABC-TV news, gloating at the sight of our own happy faces, proud that our march on City Hall was successful, and ready and eager for another full-scale attack on the forces that oppressed us. (Bell, 1971:39)

The 1969 to 1970 period marked not only the beginning of institutionalization of relations between the movement and society, as a result of the new gay militancy, but also there emerged a new consciousness and a new rhetoric among the gays themselves. Terms like "activist" and "liberation" began to appear in the names of organizations and publications. The term "gays" itself, once a label of ridicule, rapidly was adopted during this period by the gays themselves in place of the older term "homophile," and the term "gay revolutionary" ("gayrev") was used to denote a much more militant, and generally much younger, person than the homophile of the 1950's. The new gay was also more eager to "come out of the closet" and publicly declare himself or herself and his or her sexual preferences, while demanding a right to enjoy these preferences along with his or her civil liberties. Unlike the term "homophile," "gay" is taken by its adherents to refer not merely to a unique sexual proclivity, but also to a commitment to an entire life style or subculture (Humphreys, 1972:103).

Institutionalization of the movement has occurred more rapidly and more completely in some parts of the country than in others, particularly in New York City and in the two largest California cities. Former New York mayor Lindsay quietly abolished job discrimination against gays in his city, and apparently the New York City police have really tried to improve their relations with the gay community. In 1973, two gay men were permitted to join the Brooklyn Heights auxiliary police, with a reasonably good reception from the other police (*The Advocate,* May 9, 1973:22). In other cities, where gay power is not as strong or as widely tolerated by the public, the police have been much less cooperative (see the *Seattle Gay Liberation Front Newsletter,* May, 1973:3).

One of the most important and pervasive recent expressions of the gay movement's institutionalization has occurred on college campuses, where younger gays have been especially active. On a number of campuses, gay students have been given official recognition among student clubs, financial backing, and even the support of campus health officials. These developments did not occur without considerable effort on the part of the gay activists, however. Early in the 1970's, homosexual students launched a number of court suits around the country to gain this recognition, which were usually resolved in their favor. The National Gay Student Center is a branch of the National Student Association, and, as of the mid-1970's, there were between 200 and 250 gay student groups around the nation, most of them officially recognized along with the Young Republican Club! At Cornell, during the mid-seventies a group called the Ithaca Gay Liberation received about $2,000 a year from the university's student finance commission, mostly for rent on its two-room Gay People's Center, where (among other things) it publishes its own newspaper, *Lavender Opinion.* Perhaps the most striking example of on-campus institutionalization was the grant of $30,000 a year (probably for three years) which the California State Department of Health gave in 1974 to Stanford

University's Gay People's Union to help meet the mental health needs of campus homosexuals!*

While the mid-seventies finds the homosexual movement strongly institutionalized, there are signs of *fragmentation*. The 1970 conference of NACHO, for example, was disrupted by confrontations between the more and the less militant factions. The result was a debacle which ended the life of NACHO as an organization and sent the various factions off in different directions. The GLF (which took over NACHO in 1970) has pretty much died out, along with the other left-wing radical movements of the 1960's (cf. Chapter 6), but the GAA retains some viability (Humphreys, 1972:108). During 1970, various women's organizations broke off from the larger homophile or gay movement to form separate lesbian organizations of varying degrees of militancy. The West Coast Lesbian Conference, held during April, 1973 in Los Angeles, was an attempt to restore some unity to the lesbian branch of the "gay" movement, with only partial success. Since homosexual preferences cut across various political, social, and occupational lines, mere commonality of sexual orientation often becomes a rather thin unifying thread. In general, however, the greatest casualties have been suffered by the more politically radical and militant groups, but the movement as a whole may have peaked during the 1972 to 1974 period. Only time will tell how long the *demise* of the movement will take (*Off Our Backs,* 1973).

THE LEGACIES OF THE SEX-PROBLEM MOVEMENTS
General Cultural Developments

Apart from developments in the field of law and law enforcement, which we shall consider shortly, all three of the movements which we have reviewed here have had a broad impact upon our culture and society. Where prostitution is concerned, an important development has been a general increase in public tolerance as long as the prostitution is not too blatant. We might refer again here to the 1965 public opinion data which we reported early in this chapter, in which only seven percent of the representative sample showed any interest in clearing the streets of prostitutes. Even the social problems textbooks now being used in our colleges rarely include a chapter on prostitution (which was not the case up to about 1960), and where the subject is treated at all, it usually is included as a part of a larger chapter (as is the case with the present book). Recent books and films have even presented the prostitute sympathetically, as a kind of heroine with perhaps loose morals but with a heart of gold (e.g., *Suzie Wong, Klute,* and others).

Just why a greater public tolerance for prostitution has developed is not clear;

---
* Most of the above paragraph is based on Peterson, 1974.

possibly, moral entrepreneurs have found other issues more pressing. It may also be true that the actual incidence of prostitution has decreased, concurrently with an increase in sexual permissiveness among the young women of our society, as predicted by Davis (1937), Hall (1936), and Scott (1936), but there are no reliable data on which to base a statement to that effect. Further, a couple of myths that used to make prostitution appear especially repugnant to the public have been pretty thoroughly discredited. These are: (1) the so-called "white-slave" myth that most prostitutes are naive and helpless girls who have been pressed into service against their wills or under the influence of drugs; and (2) the claim that prostitutes are the chief spreaders of venereal disease, which recent data make clear is a false claim (Lemert, 1951:262; H. Berman, 1974).

The impact on our culture of the pornography censorship movement and its opponents has been a very mixed one. On the one hand, it seems clear that the normative boundaries defining the limits of public tolerance have been expanded greatly by comparison with the 1950's: most of our larger cities, at least, have theaters and bookstores where the most "hard-core" kind of pornography is legally available to interested customers. This new permissiveness also has made inroads into the more standard public fare in literature and films. The works of the late Jacqueline Susann, for example, make the best-seller lists, and big-name actors like Marlon Brando can be seen in Hollywood "soft-core" productions like *Last Tango in Paris*. These developments would have been inconceivable in the early 1950's, and they probably represent as much a "co-optation" of popular trends by the "straight" film and literary worlds as they do an incursion by "smut" merchants. At the same time, the level of public demand for pornography lately seems to have fallen off drastically (*U.S. News & World Report,* July 10, 1972).

The film industry has attempted to forestall more vigorous censorship efforts by conservative interest groups through a kind of "self-policing." This mainly takes the form of the rating system, in which "G" indicates "general" audience appeal, or films that are appropriate for "family" consumption, since they are totally free (presumably) of sex or violence overtones; "PG" means "parental guidance" recommended, placing the responsibility on parents to determine what they will permit their own minor children to view; "R" indicates "restricted," which means that minors have to be accompanied by parents (or other responsible adults) in order to be admitted to see a film; and "X"-rated films are films that legally are unavailable to minors under any circumstances. Though this rating system has been rather loosely enforced in many places, it is an attempt of the movie industry to respond to (and, if possible, co-opt) the pressures from the censorship movement.

The research that has been done on pornography and its social impact is directly attributable to the struggle between the censorship movement and its opposition forces during the 1960's and early 1970's. Never has so much scholarly and scientific investigation been done on this subject as during this period, and much of it officially sponsored (e.g., the work by the staff of the National Commission on Obscenity and Pornography). This research, however, has been no more effective in resolving the general societal ambivalence about censorship than have the legislative and judicial actions of the same period (see further below). The fact is that the issues of pornography and its censorship cannot be resolved on a "rational" empirical basis; they can be resolved only according to one set of value-commitments or another. Those who favor censorship cannot be dissuaded by evidence that pornography has no social consequences; they are convinced intuitively that it does have evil consequences, both for the society and for the individual consumer being "corrupted" by it. To them, pornography is repugnant *per se* to their values and feelings. Those who oppose censorship simply are demanding the broadest feasible interpretation of the 1st Amendment as a higher value than protecting the moral sensitivities of even large segments of the population. As a result, we have coexisting in the same society the "wide-open" pornographic market of San Francisco, and the bitter and violent school textbook struggle that took place in West Virginia during the fall and winter of 1974, in which censorship-minded citizens even tried to have the story "Jack and the Beanstalk" banned from use in the public schools (*Harper's Magazine,* 1974).

In the case of homosexuality, while there is no reason to believe that the general public finds it any less repugnant than it did a generation or so ago, there does seem to be a greater willingness to accord homosexuals their constitutional rights and to assume a "live-and-let-live" stance toward their life style. Both private organizations, like churches, and public organizations, like colleges, have recognized the needs which homosexuals have for acceptance, counseling, and social support. A number of state agencies concerned with public health and social services also have accorded both recognition and financial support to those needs. Partly as a cause of and partly as a result of these gradual improvements in the social environment, homosexuals have increasingly "come out" and publicly declared their commitments to a "gay" life style and sexual orientation. This itself is a startling change to anyone who recalls the public and official attitudes toward homosexuality from about 1960 on back. This "coming out," furthermore, has taken place not only on an individual basis, but also on a collective basis, with a variety of special organizations and institutions for gays: gay bars, gay films, gay religious groups (e.g., the Metropolitan Community Church), and "gay" centers for counseling and socializing, such as the GAA "Firehouse" and the DOB Lesbian Center in San Francisco. The vocabulary of the homosexual subcultures has also gained some general currency in our society, with the term "gay" gradually replacing the more derogatory terms which had been used earlier in reference to homosexuals. The phrase "coming out," once a reference only to an attitudinal change by homosexuals, also has started to be applied to a similar public acceptance of one's "unique situation" by other deviant groups and individuals, such as alcoholics. A related development also has been the "coming out" of *bisexuals,* those claiming a more or less equal attraction to *both* sexes. Winick (1968) has claimed that the number of people exclusively homosexual has been declining, while the number of bisexuals has been increasing. If this is true, it may be a reflection of a growing recognition both by "gays" and by "straights" that, as Kinsey suggested a generation ago, the heterosexual/homosexual distinction is in reality not so much a dichotomy of mutually exclusive categories as it is a *continuum* of mixed preferences. The popular 1972 film, *Sunday, Bloody Sunday,* which dealt with bisexuality and showed both homosexual (male) and heterosexual embraces, was itself a clear sign of growing popular tolerance.*

Legal Developments

Unlike some of the other social problems we have considered in this book, there is a fairly close correspondence, for the three kinds of sexual behavior here, between the general societal and cultural outlooks, on the one hand, and the actual law enforcement practices, on the other. This means that for pornography and obscenity, laws and their enforcement are in a hopeless state of confusion and inconsistency as one goes from place to place in society, while for prostitution and homosexuality, some extraordinarily strict and repressive laws remain "on the books," but their actual enforcement has become increasingly spasmodic and lighthanded.

Where pornography is concerned, the legal situation is a reflection of a see-saw battle, on both the local and the national levels, between the anti-pornography (pro-censorship) and the anti-censorship forces, with the producers and distributors of pornography often caught in the middle (and occasionally the ordinary citizen as well). On the one hand, the research staff and the great majority of an official National Commission on Obscenity and Pornography recommended the abolition of legal restrictions and penalties for the production or consumption of pornographic materials by adults, but, on the other hand, these recommendations were rejected and denounced by the (then) president of the United States and many members of Congress. The Supreme Court has only added to the confusion (Sterba, 1974). In its 1957 *Roth* decision, the Court seemed to bring erotic and pornographic materials under the protection of a very broad interpretation of the 1st Amendment, requiring, as a constitutional test, little more than that the materials in question have some "redeeming social significance" and that they be tolerable by "prevailing

---

* In general, the portrayal of male homosexuality has been harder for the public to tolerate than that of lesbianism. A popular film of the late 1960's, *The Fox,* already had dealt at some length with female homosexuality and bisexuality.

community standards" *somewhere* in the country. On the other hand, in its 1973 *Miller* decision, the Court ruled that states and local areas could apply their own respective "community standards" (rather than the varied national ones) in ruling materials obscene, nor did they any longer need to find a film or book "utterly without redeeming social significance" in order to outlaw it (*Idahonian,* June 21, 1973). Thus, while the hard-core film *Deep Throat* can be shown in nearly all major cities of the country, the works of Anton Chekhov and Hans Christian Andersen can be banned in the schools of Charlestown, West Virginia (*Harper's Magazine,* 1974), or the work of Kurt Vonnegut, Jr., in the schools of Drake, North Dakota (*Idahonian,* November 24, 1973). Even the relatively "liberal" locales will sometimes show a confusing (and humorous) inconsistency: Los Angeles, one of the national centers of pornographic production and consumption, passed a city ordinance in May, 1974, banning from the city's newsstands any publications with nude pictures, in its haste forgetting, as a subsequent ACLU suit pointed out, that such a ban would outlaw many works of art ("Nude Pictures OK in L.A.," p. 7). A recent nationwide review of such local differences turned up numerous examples of films or books that would be perfectly acceptable in some places, while bringing their purveyors heavy fines or jail sentences in others that were sometimes only a few miles away (Nordheimer, 1974).

In the cases of prostitution and homosexual behavior, there is also considerable local variation in laws and law enforcement, but in general there is much less disposition on the parts of the authorities to enforce "vice" statutes, than there was a generation ago, unless the sexual behavior in question is blatantly public or becomes the focus of a crusade by a powerful interest group. In other words, enforcement (and, to some extent, even legislation itself) is a function of the "tolerance quotient" which the authorities perceive to exist in their local communities. Prostitution is actually legal in some places (e.g., Nevada, outside the urban areas), and in most other places it is subjected to only occasional "busts" (e.g., New York City; Sheehy, 1972a and 1972b). Even then it is only the "street girls" who get rounded up, while the high-priced call girls serving business and political elites are almost never bothered.

Homosexuals still receive considerably more pressure from the law and law enforcement than do prostitutes, though things are easier for them than before. As of the mid-seventies, eight states had followed the recommendations of the American Law Institute's Model Penal Code and had abolished laws against any kind of sexual behavior (homosexual or otherwise) between consenting adults in private. In Los Angeles, the City Attorney won his election to office in 1973 largely on a promise to be guided by this same philosophy in his enforcement practices, and it is probable that in many other cities a similar official attitude prevails, even if not publicly stated (Sterba, 1974). At the same time, however, most states still prohibit homosexual acts under any circumstances, or even overtures to such acts in the form of "soliciting," "lewd conduct," or "loitering" in certain places. Where there is not sufficient evidence to arrest a person for an actual homosexual act (usually called "sodomy," "buggery," or "unnatural acts," in the law), the police sometimes will use a soliciting or loitering charge to "run in" a known or suspected homosexual. The penalties for sodomy vary greatly among the states, with prison sentences running anywhere from one year to life, and fines from $100 to $5,000 (Cantor, 1969).* Obviously, such unevenness around the nation raises serious constitutional questions of equal treatment under the law. Further, the constitutionality of arrests for loitering and lewd conduct has come under increasing criticism from interest groups such as the ACLU and various gay organizations, with convictions becoming much harder to obtain than before the gay movement began. Accordingly, in some places the police have been resorting instead to charges of drunk in public to "run in" suspected gays, but that tactic also is being resisted with some success (*The Advocate,* April 25, 1973).

All in all, while there are still many local examples and periodic incidents of public and official repression against prostitution, pornography, and homosexual behavior, it is probably fair by way of generalizing to say that since about 1955, those interest groups and movements that have promoted censorship and restriction of civil liberties have lost ground both in public opinion and in law enforcement, while those interest groups and movements that have favored broader legalization and less censorship have made significant gains.

---

* It is very difficult to determine how many people are currently serving what kinds of sentences for homosexual offenses, since the FBI Uniform Crime Reports do not keep track of arrests in that category separately. Furthermore, once arrested and sentenced, a person is as likely as not to be put on probation or to serve time in local jails, rather than in federal or state penitentiaries. Comprehensive records covering all these different situations are simply not available. However, the 1972 UCR shows 62,900 *arrests* around the nation for sex offenses *other than* rape and prostitution, including such charges as statutory rape (i.e., intercourse with a girl below the age of consent); "morals" (where most of the homosexual cases would probably be recorded), and so on. There is no separate category for "sodomy" or homosexual behavior itself.

PART FOUR

THE CHANGING STATUS OF WOMEN

Chapter 11

Feminist Movements as Social Problems

Dat man ober dar say dat womin needs to be helped into carriages, and lifted ober ditches, and to hab de best place everywhar. Nobody eber helps me into carriages, or ober mudpuddles, or gibs me any best place! . . . And a'n't I a woman? Look at me! Look at my arm! . . . I have ploughed, and planted, and gathered into barns, and no man could head me! And a'n't I a woman? I could work as much and eat as much—when I could get it—and bear de lash as well! And a'n't I a woman? I have borne thirteen chilern, and seen 'em 'mos all sold off to slavery, and when I cried out with my mother's grief, none but Jesus heard me! And a'n't I a woman?

. . . Den dat little man in black dar, he say women can't have as much rights as men, 'cause Christ wasn't a woman! Whar did your Christ come from? . . . From God and a woman! Man had nothin' to do wid Him. (Sojourner Truth, as quoted in Adams and Briscoe, 1971:445)

THE SOCIAL CONSTRUCTION OF REALITY
Female Roles and Relativity

Thus Sojourner Truth, a former slave, throughout her impromptu speech at a woman's suffrage assembly in 1851, noted the inconsistency with which sex roles have been defined in our culture. In responding to objections raised by some about women's right to vote, she pointed out the discrepancy between the Victorian image of middle- and upper-class white women as fragile, pure, and innocent, and the totally different picture of lower-class black women as slaves or former slaves, and as laborers possessed of great physical strength.

Sojourner Truth's perceptions help to emphasize a concept we discussed earlier in Chapter 2: the cultural and temporal relativity that is built into any normative system. Just as norms and values change according to different situations, times, and places, so do role definitions, or systems of normative expectations. An excellent example of how the factors of time and situation can act to change women's roles can be seen in the history behind the protective legislation for women. During the period of early industrialization in this country, it appeared to some that women and children were working under "dangerous" conditions and for too long hours. Later we will see under what circumstances such conditions came to be defined as dangerous, but for now, let us look at these conditions and at the rationale behind some of the legislation that emerged during this early period.

Progressive supporters of protective legislation for women called for the banning of all night work for women on the grounds that it was physically harmful, due to a resulting lack of sleep, and that it was morally dangerous for women to be on the streets late at night and to associate ". . . with all kinds of men employers at late night hours . . ." (Goldmark, 1906:262). The number of hours of labor had to be limited because it was believed that "(n)o woman of any age can toil for a 12- or 15-hour day in a laundry, for instance, involving the heaviest physical exertion, without physical injury" (Goldmark, 1906:270). The progressives also demanded seats at the place of work so that women could rest periodically during the day, and separate toilet facilities. Further, female employees should no longer be required or allowed to take work home with them from the factory to finish, thus further lengthening the work day. Generally, then, the progressives felt that:

Only the state, through laws, can protect its weaker laborers, and hitherto such protection has been almost wholly lacking. To enforce the few beneficent statutes prohibiting night work and fixing hours of labor for women in states where no such laws exist, and to obtain and enforce similar laws in other states—is a task imperiously demanded by the ever-widening employment of women and the influence of their unregulated employment upon the nation's life. (Goldmark, 1906:275-6)

The progressives' image of women that spawned such demands for protection was one that is very different from that held by today's liberals. Then, a woman was regarded as fragile, sensitive, easily harmed, innocent, and in need of guidance and protection from others that she could not give herself. Because of her timid "nature," this protection was seen as her right. Time has brought us a slightly different definition of women, and circumstances no longer seem to require legislation to prohibit such abuses as those mentioned above on the part of employers. Today's woman is not now usually regarded as quite so fragile, or easily harmed, or so "innocent," but she is still regarded by some as "sensitive," and in need of some kinds of protection; and therein lies the basis for conflict.

As Ms. Truth's statement testifies, role definitions are affected not only by time. Great variation may also exist concomitantly among subcultures and cultures throughout the world. Although in Europe and the United States, the middle and upper classes restrict the performance of heavy manual labor mainly to the male sex, this is not the case in those same countries among the lower classes, or in any peasant or subsistence economy in other countries. In these latter populations, the heavy manual labor is most often shared by both sexes, or sometimes allocated to the women alone. Although a variety of "explanations" can be found for such divisions of labor, one of the most intriguing comes from one so-called primitive society in Central Africa:

Everybody knows that men are not suited by nature for heavy work, that women are stronger and better workers. Men drink too much and do not eat enough to keep up their strength; they are more tense and travel about too much to develop the habits or the muscles needed for sustained work on the farms. (Albert, 1963:110)

Sexual aggressiveness, traditionally thought to be inherent in the male personality by western standards, is defined as a female trait in many African and American Indian societies. The characteristics of sensitivity, inability to control one's emotions, and the "gift" of intuition have all been defined by western society as female properties. In Iran, however, this is not the case:

In Iran . . . men are expected to show their emotions . . . If they don't, Iranians suspect they are lacking a vital human trait and are not dependable. Iranian men read poetry; they are sensitive and have well-developed intuition and in many cases are not expected to be too logical. They are often seen embracing and holding hands. Women, on the other hand, are considered to be coldly practical. They exhibit many of the characteristics we associate with men in the United States. (Hall, 1963:10)

Many more examples can be cited to show that what we in the United States define as appropriate sex-role behavior today may not be appropriate in a different culture, subculture, time, or circumstance. Sometimes the differences may seem interesting or amusing to us. At other times, however, the changes in attitudes about sex-role definitions in certain segments of the population may lead to demands for social reform, as in our own society during the past century.

Parameters of Reality

Probably no aspect of social reality has been more criticized by women recently than the economic one. If society is divided between the haves and the have-nots, then women may be the haves only to the extent that they have employment or income independent of their fathers, husbands, or other males. In 1970, 42 percent of all American women 16 years or older were either working or looking for work, and half of those age 18 to 64 were actually in the labor force. Two-fifths of all the American workers in 1970 were women. Who are these women and why are they working? The largest female group in the labor force is from 20 to 24 years,

TABLE 11-1 LABOR FORCE PARTICIPATION RATE FOR MARRIED WOMEN (MARCH, 1969)

	Percentage in Labor Force
Women with no children under 18	41
Women with children age 6-17 only	49
Women with children under age 6	29

Source: E. Waldman, *Changes in the Labor Force Activity of Women,* 1970, p. 32

TABLE 11-2 LABOR FORCE PARTICIPATION RATE FOR ALL WOMEN BY EDUCATIONAL LEVEL (MARCH, 1969)

	Percentage in Labor Force
Grade school only	30
High school graduate	30
College graduate	54
More than 4 years of college	69

Source: E. Waldman, *Changes in the Labor Force Activity of Women,* 1970, p. 32

and the second largest is from 45 to 54 years. More than half of both these categories were employed in 1970. From these figures we can surmise that the two heaviest contributors to the female work force seem to be those starting their working careers, and those re-entering the work world after having raised families and having filled the more "traditional" female roles. Although the presence of children seems to influence the decision to work, as can be seen in Table 11-1, we still find nearly 30 percent of those women with children under age six participating in the labor force. Black women tend to be working in larger proportions than white women, regardless of their own age, the ages of their children, or the income of their husbands. Generally, we also find (as we would expect) that the more education a woman has had, the more likely she is to be working (see Table 11-2 and U.S. Department of Labor, *Expanding Opportunities for Girls: Their Special Counseling Need,* 1971; Waldman, 1970; and Oppenheimer, 1973). According to surveys and to Department of Labor statistics, the reasons women give for working relate less to career aspirations than to economic necessity. More than half of all the women working are either single, widowed, divorced, or separated (and thus self-supporting), or are married to husbands earning less than $5,000 a year (and are thus supplementing a low family income) (*U.S. News & World Report,* April 13, 1970:35-37; U.S. Department of Labor, *Why Women Work,* 1968).

Three-fourths of the women holding jobs in this country are working full-time, a proportion that hasn't changed a great deal over the years. The majority are still in traditionally female occupations such as teaching, domestic work, and clerical work. Two-thirds of those in the professions are either nurses or teachers (Waldman, 1970). It has long been noted that no matter what occupation a woman holds, she will earn less than a man in that same occupation. For example, a male school teacher earns on the average of $10,000 per year; a female schoolteacher earns about $7,200. A male salesperson earns $7,400 and a female, $3,600. Male operatives earn $7,000, and female operatives, $4,000. Statistics for women also tend to cluster around their average salary more than is true for men; that is, men's incomes show more variation, more extremes in both directions. "The absence of marked variation means that most women were receiving 'just average' wages, regardless of training, job status, or experience" (Suter and Miller, 1973: 211). Some of the reasons for the "earnings gap" between the sexes can be found in the protective legislation mentioned earlier. In many areas, the kinds of work women are allowed to do are limited; often women are not allowed to work overtime, etc. Thus the originally well-intentioned protective legislation has contributed to the income differential between the sexes (Suter and Miller, 1973; *U.S. News & World Report,* April 13, 1970).

At retirement, this income discrepancy combines with an early mandatory retirement age for women to further extend the difference into social security benefits. In many states, the mandatory retirement age for women is 62. This, in effect, prevents them and their employers from contributing to social security for the three more years that are allowed to men, which, in turn, reduces the dollar amount of women's benefits. Since Medicare is not available until age 65, women also must pay for private medical insurance for those three years (Collins, 1971). Throughout women's period of employment and retirement, then, the income differential between the sexes continues.

More recent legislation, however, which we will discuss in more detail later on, has contributed to eradicating such discrepancies. Title VII of the Civil Rights Act of 1964 prohibits discrimination on the basis of sex. Presidential Executive Order 11246 of 1968 prohibits discrimination in federal jobs. Whether or not these acts are enforced and obeyed is an issue which has been raised by many women. However, they do provide a legal basis on which women can seek parity in both positions and salaries (Kanowitz, 1969).

Practices relating to aspects of a woman's life other than her occupation are also regulated by legislation. Young women retain their "innocence" in sexual matters under the law. In fact, the law states that a woman under a certain legal age (usually 16 or 18, depending on the state) cannot legally consent to sexual intercourse with a man who is not her husband. (It is interesting to note that there is no such parallel law for young men.) The legal age at which women may marry, however, is consistently lower than that for males. Thus it is very often the case that a young woman may consent to marry a man (and thus engage legally in sexual intercourse), but she may not consent to intercourse with a man who is not her husband. In other words, she may not consent to a transitory relationship, but she may consent to a relatively long-term or permanent and legally complex one (Kanowitz, 1969).

Marriage, for the woman, involves legal ties with her husband that stem from the belief that:

By marriage, the husband and wife are one person in the law; that is, the very being or legal existence of the woman is suspended during the marriage, or at least is incorporated and consolidated. (Blackstone Commentaries 433 as quoted in Kanowitz, 1969)

As part of this new legal status at the time of marriage, it is mandatory in most states that a woman adopt her husband's surname. If she does not wish to do this, she must go through a legal process to change her name back to her maiden name (or any other name she should choose). If her husband objects, she is prohibited from making this change. Upon marriage, she is also legally bound to her husband's domicile (home) in many states. Because it is the man who becomes legally responsible for support of the wife and family at marriage, the woman, in most states, encounters a great deal of difficulty in establishing credit on her own if the marriage terminates. It seems, then, that the woman may receive a great deal of legal economic security through marriage, but that she must lose "her very being or legal existence" in exchange (Kanowitz, 1969).

If a woman becomes a kind of "legal non-entity" in the marital realm, what of her political self? She has the right to vote and to perform such civic duties as jury duty. (However, as late as 1962, three states completely excluded women from jury duty.) She has the legal right to run for political office, and to take part in the governing of the country. Relatively few women, though, have chosen to participate in the governing process. Fewer still have been elected to do so. At the federal level, a total of 65 women have ever served in the House of Representatives. Seventeen states (34 percent) have never had a female representative in Congress; another 17 have had only one throughout their entire histories. Thus 68 percent of the states (34 states) have had no more than one female representative ever sent to Congress. Only ten women have served in the U.S. Senate, five of whom were elected (others were appointed to fill seats vacated by death, etc.), and seven of whom served less than one year. Three women have made serious attempts at running for the presidency: Belva Lockwood ran in 1884, and received the entire electoral vote of the state of Indiana; in 1964, Margaret Chase Smith actively but unsuccessfully campaigned for her party's nomination for president; and in 1972, Shirley Chisholm ran as a third-party candidate. None of these women

Chapter 11 / Feminist Movements as Social Problems

TABLE 11-3 ATTITUDES TOWARD WOMEN WORKING (1938)

Do you approve of a married woman earning money in business or industry if she has a husband capable of supporting her?

	Approve	Disapprove
Total	22%	78%
Men	19%	81%
Women	25%	75%

Source: G. Gallup, The Gallup Poll: Public Opinion 1935-1971, 1972, p. 131

TABLE 11-4 ATTITUDES TOWARD WOMEN WORKING (1972)

Do you approve or disapprove of a married woman earning money in business or industry if she has a husband capable of supporting her?

Approve	64%
Disapprove	34%
Don't Know	2%

Source: National Opinion Research Center, University of Chicago, 1972, p. 27

received an appreciable number of votes. The record of women participants in the executive and judicial branches of government is even more sparse. It appears, then, that women have held about 2 percent of the legislative posts and even fewer executive or judicial positions (Gruberg, 1968).

Public Opinion

It is interesting to compare the actual involvement of women in various aspects of civic and social life with the opinions of Americans about such involvement. Later, we will discuss the effect public opinion can have on legislation and on political participation. For the moment, however, let us just define what the opinion of the public has been toward women's involvement in social and economic life and how it has changed in recent years.

In 1938, according to a Gallup poll, when the public was asked, "Do you approve of a married woman earning money in business or industry if she has a husband capable of supporting her?" 78 percent disapproved. In 1972, when asked exactly the same question in a NORC-Roper poll, only 34 percent disapproved. Thus even though social disapproval has declined, it is still far from absent (see Tables 11-3 and 11-4).

In response to the question, "Would you vote for a woman for president if she were qualified in every other respect?" 66 percent of the 1937 public said "no";

TABLE 11-5 WOMAN FOR PRESIDENT (1937)

Would you vote for a woman for President if she were qualified in every other respect?

	Total	Male	Female
Yes	34%	27%	41%
No	66%	73%	59%

Source: G. Gallup, The Gallup Poll: Public Opinion 1935-1971, 1972, p. 67

TABLE 11-6 WOMAN FOR PRESIDENT (1971)

If your party nominated a woman for President, would you vote for her if she were qualified for the job?

	Total	Male	Female
Yes	66%	65%	67%
No	29%	35%	33%
No opinion	5%		

Source: G. Gallup, The Gallup Poll: Public Opinion 1935-1971, 1972, p. 2139

TABLE 11-7 WOMAN FOR CONGRESS (1970)

If your party nominated a woman to run for Congress from your district, would you vote for her if she were qualified for the job?

	Total	Male	Female
Yes	84%	83%	84%
No	13%	13%	13%
No opinion	3%	4%	3%

Source: G. Gallup, The Gallup Poll: Public Opinion 1935-1971, 1972, p. 2261

but in 1971, in response to a similar question, "If your party nominated a woman for president, would you vote for her if she were qualified for the job?" only 29 percent voted "no." Note that this question concerned only the highest office, for the public apparently does not feel as negative about women holding lesser offices: in 1970, only 13 percent responded "no" to the question, "If your party nominated a woman to run for Congress from your district, would you vote for her if she were qualified for the job?" The public, for the most part, seems to be more willing to be represented by a woman at the lower (and less powerful) levels of government (see Tables 11-5 through 11-7).

TABLE 11-8 WOMEN GETTING AS GOOD A BREAK AS MEN

Women were asked: In your opinion, do women in the United States get as good a break as men?

	Yes	No
All women	65%	35%
Women with children under 21	66%	34%
Women/attended college	53%	47%
Women/high school	68%	32%
Women/grade school	69%	31%

Source: G. Gallup, The Gallup Poll: Public Opinion 1935-1971, 1972, p. 2260

TABLE 11-9 WOMEN'S CHANCES AT EXECUTIVE POSITIONS

Women were asked: If a woman has the same ability as a man, does she have as good a change to become the executive of a company or not?

	As Good	Not as Good	No Opinion
All women	39%	54%	7%
Women/children under 21	33%	60%	7%
Women/attended college	22%	75%	3%
Women/high school	39%	54%	7%
Women/grade school	54%	36%	10%

Source: G. Gallup, The Gallup Poll: Public Opinion 1935-1971, 1972, p. 2260

TABLE 11-10 EASY LIFE

Women were asked: Which do you think has the easier life in the United States today—men or women?

	Men	Women	No Opinion
All women	30%	46%	24%
Women/children under 21	31%	49%	20%
Women/attended college	28%	44%	28%
Women/high school	30%	50%	20%
Women/grade school	34%	39%	27%

Source: G. Gallup, The Gallup Poll: Public Opinion 1935-1971, 1972, p. 2261

The final question that we will address here is perhaps the most important one. How do women perceive their own situation in this society? In 1970, women had an opportunity to respond to a series of questions in a Gallup poll regarding sexual equality. The results are shown in Tables 11-8 through 11-10. We see that when asked whether or not women get "as good a break as men," 35 percent of the women believed that they did not. When asked about the chances for a qualified woman to become an executive of a company, 54 percent felt that a woman would not have as good a chance as a man to get such a position. Furthermore, 40 percent of the women surveyed did not believe a woman could run a business as well as a man. It is interesting to note, however, that 46 percent of the women did feel that women have an easier life than men in the United States.

What do all these statistics mean, and why have we brought them up? When we assess these data, we can see a considerable disparity between the actual situation for women in our society and the level of their satisfaction with it. One-third to one-half of the women sampled do not feel that they have achieved equal status with the males in our society, feel that they are not getting as good a break in society as the men, and feel that their chances of succeeding in professional careers are limited by their sex. Perhaps to compensate for these feelings, some of the women (only about half) feel that their lives are easier than men's lives. These perceptions provide the soil for the germination and growth of a women's movement. Throughout the rest of the chapter, we will examine the development of that movement, as it is affected by, and affects, both the social realities and the collective opinions about those realities.

FEMINIST MOVEMENTS AND THEIR CHAMPIONS
The Early Feminist Movement

Although the women's liberation advocates claim that theirs is the cause of all women, it is apparent that some women stand to gain more than others from the changes brought about by the movement. This fact is even more apparent when one examines the various interests that gained—and lost—from the early feminist movement, culminating in the passage of the 19th Amendment. The first feminist movement concerned itself mainly with obtaining protective legislation for women and with agitating for woman suffrage. To a lesser extent, early reformist women also favored prohibition, easier divorce laws, and equal rights for women generally. Agreement on these issues was far from complete, however, and various organizations arose to represent various interests.

Moral Interest Groups

The Progressive era spawned many moral interest groups whose efforts were directed toward reform of social conditions. Many women had the time and affluence to devote to the various social causes that arose during these years. Children's rights, as discussed earlier (see Chapter 4), was one area in which women's influence was encouraged. Other causes were less popular but equally powerful in their eventual impact. Probably the best-known was the temperance issue. The largest organization formed to promote this cause was the Women's

Christian Temperance Union (WCTU), formed in 1874 under the direction of Frances Willard. Its primary goal was abstinence from alcohol on a national scale, but it later became an instrument for "consciousness-raising," and by 1876 it was openly supporting woman suffrage. Other organizations that concerned themselves with the "moral uplift" of women took the form of consciousness-raising or self-improvement groups such as the Working Girls Club, which discussed issues like "How to Get a Husband" and "Money—How to Get It and Keep It" (Flexner, 1973:206).

Economic Interest Groups

Of more direct significance to the working women of this period, however, were the interest groups that concerned themselves with labor reform. As Flexner (1973:247) has noted:

> It cannot be repeated too often that for women working a ten- or twelve-hour day, whose earnings were almost half of those of men, whose lives were often bounded by the sweatshop, and whose relation to their employer lacked any safeguards to personal dignity or job tenure, "equal rights" was a question of more than education or getting the vote. For them, equality also meant better pay for their labor, security from fire and machine hazards or the unwanted attentions of a foreman and a chance to get home to their domestic tasks before complete exhaustion had overtaken them. Until more of them could work for these goals through a trade union, other issues were remote and unreal, a fact partially attested to by the relatively small degree of participation by such women in the suffrage movement.

Perhaps the first attempt to organize women laborers to work for reform was Sarah Bagley's effort in 1845 to form the Female Labor Reform Association, whose aims included shorter working hours for women. It is in some ways telling that the organization fell apart relatively soon due to a lack of money, and the fact that members were unable to contribute sufficient time to furthering its goals (pay was low and hours long). This attempt was followed in 1881 by the opening of the Knights of Labor to all laborers (and to some non-workers who were interested in labor reforms). It soon became apparent, though, that any effective efforts on behalf of women were going to have to come from working women themselves. Although the Knights elected a woman as Master Workman (or head of the Knights) in 1886, and formed a Department of Women's Work to investigate matters of pay, hours, child labor, etc., they were unsuccessful in their efforts at labor reform. Other than the Knights, organizations such as the National Consumers League, founded in part by Mrs. Josephine Shaw Lowell, lobbied for such reforms as shorter hours, better wages, seats, and toilet facilities for women. This organization was responsible for initiating many of the court cases favoring protective legislation. Perhaps the most lasting of the labor organizations to develop was the National Women's Trade Union League. Organized in 1903 by Mary E. Kenney, it represented an alternative to the American Federation of Labor, which was disinclined to become involved with the labor problems of unskilled and poorly paid men or women. This organization worked strongly until 1950 for protective legislation for women, and against the early versions of the Equal Rights Amendment (ERA). (See Flexner, 1973; Gruberg, 1968; and O'Neill, 1969 for entire paragraph.)

Political Interest Groups

While the organizations just discussed represent the economic interests of those in the early feminist movement, probably the most widely known goal of this movement was woman suffrage. The organizations that formed around the struggle for the vote began with the formation of the American Equal Rights Association, founded shortly after the Civil War to further both the black and the female causes. In May, 1869, however, a group of women headed by Elizabeth Cady Stanton and Susan B. Anthony broke away from the Association to form the National Woman's Suffrage Association (NWSA). Membership was open to all women, and the goals of the organization extended far beyond suffrage to include easier divorce laws, greater political and economic participation, and more social freedom (including free sex, according to Virginia Woodhull, an early member). Just six months later, the American Woman Suffrage Association (AWSA) was formed, with a membership composed only of carefully selected delegates of various women's groups. The AWSA worked solely for suffrage, thus purposely avoiding other controversial issues that might alienate powerful segments of the population. By 1890, however, the NWSA and AWSA had merged to form the National American Woman Suffrage Association, under the leadership of Elizabeth Cady Stanton, its president. The National Council of Women of the U.S. also was formed in 1888 to improve the status of women by acting as a clearinghouse for information; it also drew up a list of women qualified to fill government positions. Finally, in 1913, Dr. Alice Paul founded the Congressional Union for Woman Suffrage, later renamed the National Women's Party, whose purpose was to work for women's rights through a women's political party. Perhaps the distinctive characteristic of this organization was its unwillingness to work within the existing male-dominated system. Mrs. Oliver P. Belmont, the Party's first president, was quoted as follows: "I do not want to see any woman elected to a man's party. I do not want to see any woman in the Senate as a Republican or a Democrat" (Gruberg, 1968:100). It is interesting to note, however, that this position was dead by 1928, when the National Women's Party supported Herbert Hoover for president of the United States. (See Flexner, 1973; Gruberg, 1968; O'Neill, 1969.)

Racial Interest Groups

Special note needs to be taken of the black women's organizations that developed during this period for the purpose of furthering the rights of black women. Although most white organizations claimed to represent black women as well, they neither spoke for the unique needs of black women nor allowed black women to speak for themselves within the organizations. Black women were concerned about issues that scarcely affected white women: their physical safety, health care, education, and freedom from assault or lynchings. In 1895, in response to these problems, the National Federation of Afro-American Women was established, with Mrs. Booker T. Washington as its first president. The following year it merged with the Colored Women's League of Washington to form the National Association of Colored Women, under the leadership of Mrs. Mary Church Terrell, who was a well-educated and experienced advocate of women's rights. It cannot be said that black women worked exclusively through black organizations, but the establishment of such bodies points out the need many black women felt to have certain issues addressed, and their exclusion from, or disillusionment with, many white organizations (Flexner, 1973; Gruberg, 1968; O'Neill, 1969).

Before discussing the interests and publics that are represented in the present feminist movement, we shall briefly look at those segments of society that opposed the early movement. Later, we will see how these two "sides" interacted throughout this period.

Opposition Interest Groups

There is a clear division pertaining to specific issues among the factions opposing the feminists during the reform era. The drive for protective legislation evoked the least opposition. Only factory owners and business interests protested this legislation openly, for their economic interests stood to suffer from an increase in wages, a decrease in working hours, and the installation of certain safeguards and facilities for women. Legislators reacted to women's needs rather slowly, due primarily to their concern over the opinions of some of their wealthier constituents. When the feminists expanded their goals to include woman's suffrage, an array of opposition interests emerged. Then, as now, one of the strongest cries of opposition came from women themselves. The women of Boston, for example, formed the Boston Committee of Remonstrants. (In accordance with their principles, they hired men to represent them before legislatures, courts, etc.) In 1890, they started a publication, *The Remonstrance,* to voice their position. By 1911, Mrs. Arthur Dodge had founded the National Association Opposed to Woman Suffrage. The main arguments used by these interests were that voting was unfeminine, that women simply could not take time out from their home duties to concern themselves with politics, and that the men represented them adequately (Flexner, 1973:298). Opposition to giving women political power came also from religious leaders like Cardinal Gibbons, who opposed woman suffrage on the grounds that it threatened traditional family patterns and roles. The position of the early feminist movement was further weakened in the eyes of the Church when a few of its more liberal members began advocating dissemination of birth control information. Further opposition was found among the political machines and certain economic interests, which stood to lose if women obtained the franchise; they feared that since women favored reform and "clean" politics, their votes could be neither controlled nor predicted on issues such as protective legislation, income tax, or prohibition. The "solid South" saw in woman suffrage the danger that women might press for black enfranchisement and challenge their position on states' rights. Generally, then, opposition came from many segments of society that saw feminist goals as a threat to the established social patterns of interaction.

The Modern Liberation Movement

Even the most cursory look at the groups that claim to represent the interests and goals of the present women's movement reveals a very different kind of composition from that of the first feminist movement or, for that matter, of the other social reform movements of the 1960's and 70's. While the earlier feminist movement was characterized by many distinct organizations, the present one is characterized by few. While the modern movement has a number of leaders, such as Kate Millet, Germaine Greer, and Gloria Steinem, few of these women have aligned themselves exclusively with one particular organization.

Moral Interest Groups

To some extent, in the women's liberation movement traditional organizational structure has been deliberately avoided in favor of neighborhood or local "consciousness-raising" groups that remain formally leaderless. Howard (1974) defines these groups as "expressively oriented" or, in Smelser's (1962) terms, "value-oriented." They are not linked to any kind of organization and eschew leaders, in the belief that women have been followers for too long. In order to free themselves from the dependence they have been socialized to accept in the traditional hierarchical structure, formal leadership must be removed. In this setting where each woman is an individual, women may air their grievances and gain strength from each other. These groups are less interested in changing economic conditions of society, or in actively lobbying for passage of the ERA, than they are in "raising" the consciousness of themselves, other women, and ultimately of society concerning the injustices which they have experienced as women, and more basically, concerning the discrepancies in values based on sex that exist in our society.

A secondary function of these groups is to create a new respect for and awareness of women and sisterhood among women themselves. Thus the term "consciousness-raising group" has been adopted to describe these informal gatherings.

Political and Economic Interest Groups

PRO-FEMINIST Another type of women's organization can be termed "instrumental" (Howard, 1974) or "norm-oriented" (Smelser, 1962) groups. These groups tend to be political in nature and devoted to promoting social change. They include professional groups and caucuses, e.g., Sociologists for Women in Society (SWS). Howard feels that these ". . . caucuses provide a mechanism whereby women [can] develop both analytical and political skills for confronting sexism at the institutional level . . ." (Howard, 1974:154). Perhaps the best known of these political organizations is the National Organization for Women (NOW), formed in 1966 by Betty Friedan " 'to bring women into full participation in the mainstream of American society *now*' " (Gruberg, 1968:105). There is probably no better statement as to the organization's purpose than NOW's Bill of Rights, as summarized by Morgan (1970:512):

I/ Equal Rights Constitutional Amendment
II/ Enforce Law Banning Sex Discrimination in Employment
III/ Maternity Leave Rights in Employment and in Social Security Benefits
IV/ Tax Deduction for Home and Child Care Expense for Working Parents
V/ Child Day Care Centers
VI/ Equal and Unsegregated Education
VII/ Equal Job Training Opportunities and Allowances for Women in Poverty
VIII/ The Right of Women to Control Their Reproductive Lives

More recently, one prominent spokesperson of the movement, Gloria Steinem, founded *Ms.* magazine, which represents moral and political interests at the same time—moral because it addresses value discrepancies in sex role traditions and political because of its impact on female opinion.

The efforts of NOW have been aided by professional and occupational groups such as the American Association of University Women, which, with a membership of some 155,000, promotes women's participation in community affairs in government, business, and education, and supports the ERA. Another group, the National Federation of Business and Professional Women's Clubs, founded during World War I, is a non-partisan group that supports female political candidates, ERA, equal pay, and uniform retirement age under Social Security. This organization, incidentally, was largely responsible for initiating the drive to establish the President's Commission on the Status of Women. Through their actions, these groups hope to get certain political measures passed, and to legalize equality of opportunity for women in the labor market without regard to sex or motherhood status (Hernandez, 1971; Howard, 1974; and Morgan, 1970).

An organization that works primarily for the political progress of today's women's movement is the Women's Joint Congressional Committee (WJCC), which was originally created during the first feminist movement as a national coordinating body for various women's groups. Although in its earlier stages it pressed for opposition to the ERA, that stand has changed over the years. The organization operates informally now to disseminate information to reform-minded women (Gruberg, 1968). In 1961, the President's Commission on the Status of Women was established; it set out to document the discrimination and inequality women feel they face in our society (Gruberg, 1968).

ANTI-FEMINIST While "male chauvinism" has often been blamed by today's feminists as largely responsible for women's subordination, the most vocal opposition to emerge in response to the feminist movement has come from women. The "Stop ERA" movement has been led by Mrs. Phyllis Schlafly. She claims that the passage of ERA will destroy women's privileged position in this society, and will threaten the traditional family system by taking away a woman's right to be a full-time wife and mother. Her position has been supported by many women who have been successful in the domestic sphere and see the movement as threatening the meaning of that success. Organizations that have formed around this theme include MOM (Men Our Masters), HOW (Happiness of Womanhood), Fascinating Womanhood, and the Pussycats, whose motto is "The lamb chop is mightier than the karate chop" (Brothers, 1972:56 for quote; Staines, *et al.*, 1974; and Wohl, 1974).

"Traditional" women are not the only source of female opposition to the movement, however. Staines, *et al.* (1974) have noted what they term the "Queen Bee Syndrome": the highly successful woman in a professional (and male) world who is against feminism. The so-called Queen Bee is against feminist goals, claim Staines, *et al.*, because she has been co-opted by the system by being rewarded for not "rocking the boat," and because she fears competition from newly emancipated women.

While the movement has heard opposition from various conservative groups, it seems that women have raised the loudest collective anti-feminist voice during the current movement.

Scientific Interest Groups

Various scientific interests have addressed the subject of women over the years. For the most part, in this area scientists have tended to reflect the intellectual fashions of their times. Early theorists thus took for granted the theory of inherent biological and psychological differences between men and women, and sought to identify their consequences. More recently, however, scientists have reflected the mood of equality of the 1960's and 70's in calling into question traditional assumptions about certain inherent differences between the sexes.

Biological differences have long been thought to set the "limits" of sex-role behavior. During the early feminist movement, a great many physiological differences were believed to distinguish men from women, including different ways of breathing. While men breathed abdominally, women were thought to breathe costally, or from the chest (Klein, 1971). While women's apparent inability to breathe deeply was actually due to their clothing (and especially to very restrictive corsets), this biological "fact" affected attitudes toward protective legislation for women. In much the same way, accepted "facts" about women's hormonal peculiarities have helped to form popular definitions about women's roles in the present as well. A prominent gynecologist of the 1960's, for example (Overstreet, 1964), asserted that hormonal changes related to the menstrual cycle had profound effects on the activities and behavior of women. Immediately prior to menstruation, he tells us,

there is a tendency to depression, irritability, emotional instability, hair-trigger emotional responses, decreased concentration ability, increased frequency of headaches, and other personality changes. (Overstreet, 1964:18)

Throughout menopause, according to Dr. Overstreet, conditions become even more unstable in the female, with such symptoms as

hot flashes and night sweats—which are so thoroughly documented over women's bridge tables that it is almost unfashionable not to have them. Along with these come variable degrees of emotional instability, irritability, depression, lack of concentration, weepiness, headaches, and the like.

And, finally, after menopause a woman's estrogen deficiency accelerates the onset of senility (Overstreet, 1963:22).

Dr. Overstreet's response to research which contradicts his findings by showing the cultural relativity of "inherently female" traits (e.g., Mead, 1935) is simply to ignore it:

From puberty onward, the woman's general body-muscle strength is never again equal to that of a man's. . . . Naturally, this strength difference has manifold implications for the tasks and activities to which the woman will turn—*despite certain of the primitive societies where what we think of as the male and female roles are reversed.* (Overstreet, 1963:19; italics added)

Recent research has called into question scientific "facts" about menstruation such as those which Overstreet advances by suggesting that the mood changes and cramps sometimes associated with the menstrual cycle are all learned in a given social setting (Paige, 1973). According to this research, the effects of the "bridge table" discussions of women are more significant than Dr. Overstreet suspects, for they may teach women what to expect and how to behave around the time of their menstrual periods. Furthermore, anthropological studies continue to document the cultural basis for differences in sex roles. Consensus on these more recent theories is far from complete, but they do seem to be emerging as the more acceptable ones for the coming generation.

The same congruence of scientific theories with popular beliefs can be seen in the history of some of the psychological and psychoanalytic theories that seek to explain sex-role differentiation. Until the time of Freud, for example, hysteria was thought to be a malady that could affect only women. The very name of this condition, which comes from the Greek word *hyster,* meaning womb, disqualifies men as victims, since they do not have wombs. Freud questioned this assumption, and eventually destroyed it. At the same time, however, he set forth his own theories on sexual and psychological development which attributed basic personality differences between the sexes to their genital differences. He postulated that female envy of the male penis caused women to be jealous, vain, and morally "weaker" than men. Furthermore, penis-envy was the basis for the two kinds of female orgasms: clitoral (or immature, emulating the male) and vaginal (mature and "healthy") (Freud, 1930 and 1933).

Female psychoanalyst Karen Horney (1924) turned the tables, so to speak, by proposing that motherhood gives women superiority over men. This advantage elicits an envy from men, for, as Horney asks,

. . . is not the tremendous strength in men of the impulse to creative work in every field precisely due to the feelings of playing a relatively small part in the creation of living beings, which constantly impels them to an overcompensation in achievement? (Horney, in Klein, 1971:79)

The psychology of Horney is not in keeping with that of the women's movement, however, for throughout her analysis, she implicitly accepts the popular belief that a woman's "worth," her greatest achievement, lies in motherhood.

In many ways, the theories of Freud and Horney are still with us today in the work of modern psychoanalysts like Erikson (1950). More recently, however, those theories, or scientific constructions of reality, are being called into question by the work of sexologists, psychiatrists, and medical practitioners such as Masters and Johnson (1966), Lenton (1970), and by many others, who have challenged traditional beliefs about the inherent social implications of human sex differences.

While most psychologists and psychoanalysts have remained basically within the Freudian and other traditional perspectives, some alteration of that stance has begun in recent times. Erikson (1964), for example, has modified the emphasis placed on the penis-envy theory and acknowledges that cultural differences do affect definitions of sex roles. Kohlberg (1966) has emphasized that "cognitive judgments" made in early childhood are probably more important than either biological or cultural factors in the development of sex-role definitions, and that these judgments are built upon a process of learning through rewards and penalties. Marmor (1968) has pointed out how modern psychoanalysis must and can accommodate a feminist interpretation of the modern woman's resistance to tradition by regarding it as "healthy" rebellion against male "infantilization" of her, and as "a laudable effort at self-realization." Other psychologists and psychoanalysts such as Bardwick (1971) have warned against either the extreme advocacy of genital determinism on the one hand, or the total denial of sex differences on the other:

In truth, one ought not to insist that boys and girls develop in an identical or even parallel fashion, and one should not permit the importance of genitals to be uniquely exaggerated in a theory of normal development. The ego is a body ego, but the genitals are not the only area of the body. We ought to explore the effect on the ego of the difference in body erogeneity. (Bardwick, 1971:11)

Traditionally, sociologists and anthropologists also have tended to go along with the popular notions that "a woman's place is in the home," and that differences in family roles can be attributed to inherent physiological and psychological differences between men and women. This point of view has been especially characteristic of family sociologists, e.g., Landis (1954) and Blood (1962) (see Chapter 13). Blood (1962), for example, in discussing the sexual behavior of married couples, explains in some depth that most women are by nature simply not very interested in sex for a variety of reasons:

One of the myths of modern man, a myth assiduously cultivated by Dr. Kinsey, is that males and females do not differ in sex drive. . . . [On the contrary, however] . . . males are driven by hormonal chemistry, by seminal pressures, by genital awareness, and by the more predictable and rewarding nature of their sexual climax far more than females. Such biological differences contribute heavily to the higher salience of sex in the consciousness and value system of the average male. (Blood, 1962:358)

Thus, according to Blood, the differences between men and women are primarily physiological, and are reflected in the lesser capacity of women for orgasm. Women cannot, Blood tells us, achieve orgasm as quickly or as frequently as men. While there has recently been an increase in the proportion of women experiencing orgasm, Blood cautions us against jumping to hasty conclusions:

While this trend reminds us that orgasmic response is not a purely biological phenomenon, it should not delude us into believing that the further emancipation of women will make them the equal of men in orgasm capacity. Though such notions are advocated by feminist females and sex hungry males, scientific caution suggests that they exceed the facts. (Blood, 1962:356)

When Blood's assessment is viewed in relation to the growing body of anthropological and sociological research running counter to his statements (e.g., Mead, 1935; Masters and Johnson, 1966; Reuben, 1972) it appears that he is exercising more than "caution." For, all along, there have been a few sociologists and anthropologists who have questioned the notion of inherent sex differences. As early as 1907, W. I. Thomas noted that personality results from an interaction between one's "original nature" (whatever that may be) and social factors. In other words, the social definition of sex roles is learned from significant others and contributes greatly to one's construction of reality.

Much better known is the work of Margaret Mead, who, in her classic study, *Sex and Temperament in Three Primitive Societies* (1935), demonstrated that the relation between sex and "temperament" (psychological traits) is strictly culturally determined.

In the last decade, inspired by the consciousness-raising spirit of the times, contemporary social scientists more generally have emphasized the cultural determination of sex roles and of the relations between the sexes (e.g., Rossi, 1970; Epstein, 1970). In the discipline of sociology itself, as in other disciplines, a pressure group, Sociologists for Women in Society (SWS), representing a combination of scientific and political interests, has been active since 1969, printing newsletters and promoting the professional status of women in the discipline of sociology. In the professional journals, much attention has been given to the status of women in sociology (e.g., Wolfe, *et al.,* 1973; La Sorte, 1971; Patterson, 1971). Moreover, the women's caucus has not always been hospitable to the publication of research results that run contrary to the ideology of the current feminist movement (American Sociological Association Committee on the Status of Women in Sociology, 1973).

While there have always been a few people like Margaret Mead, who were ahead of their time, the scientific disciplines have generally not been far out of step with the prevailing intellectual currents of their time, as is succinctly pointed out by Giele (1971:xliii):

Thus in a generation the sociology of sex roles has changed its stance from accepting and explaining inevitable role conflict to one that labels needless suffering that can be avoided by changed institutional arrangements and redefinitions of male and female roles.

FEMINIST SOCIAL MOVEMENTS
The Early Feminist Movement

Smelser (1962) has suggested three conditions that must be present in a society in order for a new movement to get started. The first is "structural conduciveness," which, for the early feminist movement (and many others in the 19th century), was represented by industrialization and the so-called domestic revolution. With industrialization had come the need for many more workers in the factories. Women and children were able to do the work and could be paid less than men. The same technology that brought long hours and low pay in the factories for working-class women, however, gave more leisure time to others by providing domestic aids such as the washing machine, electricity, running water, etc. In this additional free time, women had the opportunity to reflect upon certain apparent social inequities.

A second way in which 19th-century society contributed to the feminist movement's development was by providing Smelser's second condition, which he has called "structural strain." One source of strain developing among working-class women at this time was their failure, as they perceived it, to get the help of trade unions in their efforts to improve their working conditions and circumstances. Still another kind of strain existed between the "male establishment" and many nonworking, well-educated, wealthy women. These women had little opportunity to use the skills and education they had acquired (in 1900, 20 percent of the college graduates were women), and they began to resent a political process which denied them the vote, while giving it to illiterate immigrant and black males.

Smelser's third precondition for a social movement is the "growth of a generalized belief," or definition of the situation as problematic and requiring change. The circumstances described above were not seen by the public as inherently problematic until a re-definition of the situation took place, prompted by the actions of both working-class women in the factories and upper-class educated women, and other allied groups and sympathizers, toward the end of the 19th century. In time, two general issues became defined as problematic: (1) protection for female industrial workers, and (2) woman's suffrage.

During the Civil War, many women began to work in the factories. At the close of the war, these women began to press for higher wages and for better and safer working conditions, or for protective legislation. Many of those who were not working in the factories had been actively involved in the slavery abolition movement. At the close of the war, some of these women, feeling that ". . . the Negro's hour must be theirs also, assumed in the flush of Union victory that they would soon win the vote" (O'Neill, 1969:16). However, a lengthy struggle awaited them, for the idea of woman's suffrage or female activism challenged the very foundations of 19th-century society:

> It [feminism] was disquieting because its very existence was a contradiction in terms for the Victorians, who believed that they had accorded women a higher and more honorable estate than had any previous generation. That so many women failed to agree with them called into question the whole system of values which revolved around the home and the chaste Mother-Priestess who made it possible. In this very special sense, feminism was a radical movement. On the face of it, equal rights for women was not a demand likely to compromise the essential Victorian institutions. In fact, it threatened to do so because the Victorians had given the nuclear family a transcendent significance all out of proportion to its functional value. In this process they created a social problem which threatened to undo a patiently constructed domestic system and, what was worse, by its very existence, undermine the animating principles of the Victorian ethos. (O'Neill, 1969:6-7)

By the late 19th century, then, there were two dissatisfied segments of the female population advocating change: (1) the social feminists who worked for protective legislation, and (2) the political feminists, or suffragists, who pressed for the right to vote.

Leadership and Recruitment

While these two segments merged in the later days of the movement, it is important to remember that in the early stages, they drew their support, membership, and leadership from different populations.

Some early social feminists were upper-middle-class women who had the time and resources to devote to working for protective legislation. Some formed clubs or organizations to work for young women's moral and cultural improvement. Other social feminists were working-class women like Mrs. George Rodgers. A housewife and mother of 12, she was elected Master Workman for the Knights of Labor in 1886. When the Knights later formed a Department of Women's Work to investigate pay, hours, and child labor, it was headed by Leonora Barry, an uneducated stocking-machine worker. She faced many difficulties which characterized most working-class attempts at reform: she had little education, and even less time to devote to her investigation of women's working conditions because of her own long working hours. She also found herself barred from many factories, and the working women she approached were often unwilling to discuss factory conditions with her, for fear of reprisals from their employers.

Suffragists, by contrast, tended to be disproportionately well-educated middle- and upper-class women who had married later in life and had had fewer children than average (Rossi, 1972; Flexner, 1973; Howard, 1974; O'Neill, 1969). The leadership, or "hardcore of activists . . . were women without marital and family ties, ex-wives, non-wives, childless wives, whose need to support themselves triggered concern for equal rights to vote, to work, and to advance in their work" (Rossi,

1972:349). Elizabeth Cady Stanton, one of the Seneca Falls Convention leaders, was a daughter of a judge and well-educated in the legal subordination of women. Bored with her life as a wife in Seneca Falls, she shared her frustrations with Lucretia Mott, a Quaker teacher, who also felt deprived of social participation and its rewards. Together, they helped call the Seneca Falls Convention of 1848, the first woman's rights convention in the United States. Other leaders in the movement, like Lucy Stone, who led the American Women Suffrage Association, which worked through state legislatures, had received a formal education but found no outlet for their skills except in working for social reforms.

By 1890, the early feminists had gained both legitimacy and relative affluence from their many speaking engagements. They were joined by a new generation of leaders, such as Rachel Foster and Carrie Chapman Catt, who resented the influx of immigrants, because the political machines were using the male-immigrant vote to deny suffrage to "educated and responsible women." Other leaders founded organizations like the National College Women's Equal Suffrage League, an early consciousness-raising group founded by M. Carey Thomas, the president of Bryn Mawr College. By 1910, the influence of a third generation was felt through women like Harriet Stanton Blatch (Elizabeth Cady Stanton's daughter), who were introducing "radical" tactics such as marches and hunger strikes (imported from England) into the movement.

By 1917, a professional leadership had developed in the suffrage movement that enabled the NAWSA to form a board comprised of women of independent means who could devote full time to working for suffrage. Through the work of this professional board and Carrie Chapman Catt, its president, the NAWSA was able to embrace all but the most radical suffrage groups (Flexner, 1973; O'Neill, 1969).

The Natural History of the Early Feminist Movement

Prior to the Civil War, during the *incipiency* phase of the movement, few women's organizations appeared, since there was no generalized belief in the need for reform. Isolated efforts like Sarah Hale's *Godey's Lady's Book,* which campaigned for education, professional opportunities, and physical education for women, had little practical effect, since even those women who had the resources and education to become involved in women's self-help programs, like Mrs. Stanton, complained only individually of their frustrations. Attempts to organize for labor reform also failed due to lack of money, time, and sponsorship.

By 1848, a small group of reformers, led by Mrs. Stanton and Mrs. Mott, met at Seneca Falls, New York, to share their discontents and aspirations, and to organize for reform. The women attending the Seneca Falls Convention declared their "independence" as follows:

> We hold these truths to be self-evident: that all men and women are created equal. . . .
>
> This history of mankind is a history of repeated injuries and usurpation on the part of man toward woman, having in direct object the establishment of tyranny over her. . . .
>
> In entering upon the great work before us, we anticipate no small amount of misconception, misrepresentation, and ridicule; but we shall use every instrumentality within our power to effect our object. We shall employ agents, circulate tracts, petition the State and national legislatures, and endeavor to enlist the pulpits and the press on our behalf. (quoted in Flexner, 1973:75)

Their efforts at independence at this time were short-lived, however, for the abolition movement and the oncoming Civil War consumed all the time and energy of reformers.

While the end of the war did not bring the hoped-for woman's suffrage, it did enable women finally to turn their energies solely to suffrage and/or to labor reforms. Women like Mrs. Stanton began exhausting speaking tours, and at a few factories, women's organizations were formed to change working conditions.

By 1869, the stage of *coalescence* was clearly starting. In that year Elizabeth Cady Stanton and Susan B. Anthony founded the NWSA, which pressed for labor reforms, suffrage, educational opportunities, and other progressive measures for women. In response to this rather radical organization, the more conservative members of the feminist movement, such as Henry Blackwell, Lucy Stone, and Julia Ward Howe, formed the AWSA. Realizing that women possessed no real power with which to bargain, the AWSA tried to maintain ties with the more conservative (and powerful) elements of society by focusing on the suffrage issue alone, and avoiding the more radical causes of the NWSA.

"Social feminists," meanwhile, were trying to work through existing labor organizations such as the Knights of Labor and the AFL. Because these labor organizations seemed unwilling to offer much to young, unskilled, and predominantly temporary workers, the National Women's Trade Union League and the National Consumer's League were founded respectively in 1903 and 1890 as ". . . one more expression of the fusion of two streams—the educated, middle-class women, sometimes, but not always, professionals, and working women—for the common effort on the latter's behalf" (Flexner, 1973:212).

During this period, racial conflict seemed to threaten this fusion. Since the passage of the 15th Amendment (1870) giving the franchise to the newly freed blacks, there had been resentment among the feminists and other women about black males voting and therefore governing white females. Now, this antagonism spread to include immigrant European males, who were also allowed to vote. Anglo-Saxon American women saw both of these groups as inferior to themselves, and even leaders like President William Howard Taft openly questioned a policy that allowed black and immigrant males to vote, while denying white females that right. Many of the female factory workers, however, were also immigrants from Europe, and they became alienated from the larger group of feminists as racial arguments continued to be used by suffragists (Flexner, 1973; O'Neill, 1969).

By 1910 or 1912, these differences began to fade in importance as the social feminists realized that they had but little power unless they aligned themselves with the suffragists. The suffragists also began to see suffrage as a means to further reform, rather than as an end in itself. Adopting the protective-legislation issue as an argument for suffrage also proved useful:

We have women working in the foundries, stripped to the waist, if you please, because of the heat. Yet the Senator says nothing about these women losing their charm. They have got to retain their charm and delicacy, and work in the foundries. Of course you know the reason they are employed in the foundries is that they are cheaper and work longer hours than men. Women in the laundries, for instance, stand for thirteen or fourteen hours in the terrible steam and heat with their hands in hot starch. Surely these women won't lose any more of their beauty and charm by putting a ballot in a ballot box once a year than they are likely to lose standing in foundries or laundries all year round. There is no harder contest than the contest for bread, let me tell you that. (as quoted in Flexner, 1973:258-9)

Throughout the last half of the 19th century, the progress that was made toward suffrage was accomplished largely through the efforts of the AWSA. In the early years of the NWSA, Virginia Woodhull, a journalist and writer member, effectively discredited that organization in the eyes of the public by advocating free love and licensed prostitution. Coming in the wake of the Comstock legislation (see Chapter 10), this stand so thoroughly destroyed the legitimacy of the NWSA that it was forced to merge with the AWSA in 1890, to form the National American Women's Suffrage Association (NAWSA), headed by Carrie Chapman Catt. This merger climaxed the coalescence of the movement.

The suffrage "problem" was sufficiently *institutionalized* by 1912 to be included in the Progressive Party platform of that year, but war again threatened to dissipate its thrust. While most active women became involved in the peace movement, a few like Mrs. Catt realized the political necessity of supporting the war effort and of submitting to a degree of co-optation. Personally, she

... took an entirely cold-blooded view of the situation. She had her doubts that the war would make the world a better place to live in, but she never for a moment thought the suffragists had any choice but to endorse the President's policy. They were too near their goal to risk challenging an inflamed public temper. (O'Neill, 1969:184-5)

Her reasoning proved sound. After much political maneuvering, by August of 1920, the 19th Amendment to the Constitution was ratified by the required number of states, and women were given the right to vote in federal elections. Shortly thereafter, most states passed individual laws enabling women to vote in all elections.

In many ways, the war marked the end of the progressive era and of the reform movements that it had engendered, and the beginning of the *fragmentation* and *demise* of the early women's movement. Following the war, the prohibition or 18th Amendment was passed, which some women in the feminist movement (though certainly not all) had supported. Laws regulating the influx of unskilled and uneducated immigrants also had been passed, woman's suffrage had been achieved, and much new protective legislation was in force (see the section on the legacy of the feminist movements). The war had ended, and the country wanted a "return to normalcy": Americans were tired of trying to reform the world. In this setting, few of the groups that had supported the feminist movement had any interest in its continuance. The National League of Women Voters (NLWV), for example, turned its attention to other social issues, such as pure food and drug legislation, and support of the Tennessee Valley Authority. A very few groups, most notably the National Women's Party, which had originally been organized to achieve woman's suffrage, became more radical after the passage of the 19th Amendment, and began campaigning for the Equal Rights Amendment and against the protective legislation that was being passed. Other groups, like the National Consumer's League, the Women's Trade Union League, and the YWCA, worked to broaden protective legislation to include men as well as women (Lemons, 1973). These efforts largely failed because the intellectual and emotional energies of the nation were being consumed by the new and more pressing problems of (1) organized crime that had emerged in the prohibition era, and (2) the "Red scare" sparked by the Bolshevik Revolution and the radical labor and political activities of many recent immigrants to America. In the face of these new problems, then, the early women's movement gradually went into demise.

The Modern Feminist Movement: Women's Liberation

The three preconditions of a social movement mentioned earlier can also be seen in the setting from which the modern feminist movement has emerged. Structural conduciveness, the first of these, could be found in the "New Frontier" spirit which characterized the Kennedy years, the New Left and civil rights movements which came into their own in the 1950's and 1960's, and in the ready availability of government funds for reform projects in the 1960's (Mitchell, 1971).

Of special importance were the successes of the civil rights movement. As Yinger has explained,

If those who lack income, power, and prestige have caught a dream of something different because some of their fellows have demonstrated the possibility of change, their status becomes uncrystallized in their imaginations, if not in fact.

. . . A fully crystallized stratification system must distribute dreams as unequally as it distributes other values if it is to remain unchanged. (1965:12)

For many women in the 1960's, dreams were distributed more freely than were the opportunities to fulfill them. While the sex discrimination article of the Civil Rights Act of 1964 was being virtually ignored, women watched the courts take up the cause of implementing racial equality. Black victories there contributed much to the dreams of women.

The second precondition, structural strain, appeared in three forms. The first was a kind of "status inconsistency" which develops when one's social position or role is not consistent with one's self-concept and aspirations. While women were receiving about 50 percent of the bachelor's degrees in college during the 1960's, few were getting permanent, full-time jobs or entering professional careers. Those who did tended to receive less prestigious and responsible positions and were paid less than their male counterparts (Howard, 1974). A different kind of strain was felt by women who had devoted much of their lives to their homes and families, but found themselves with little identity or status of their own after their children were grown. A third kind of strain was experienced by women who had both job and family responsibilities. These women questioned the dual roles they had been forced to accept, while men had only to deal with their occupational responsibilities. In these three ways, then, structural strains emerged that contributed to the rise of the modern feminist or women's liberation movement.

The emergence of such strains, ironically, was due in large part to the legacy of the earlier feminist movement (discussed further at the end of this chapter). The large body of protective legislation for women in industry, passed early in the century, had now become one of the main obstacles to full social and economic equality for modern women, for it blocked their access to certain kinds of jobs, to overtime pay, and to other occupational advantages.

A few dedicated feminists in and out of Congress had been working to strike down this protective legislation, beginning with the introduction of the Equal Rights Amendment into Congress in 1923 (and every year thereafter). Also, the early feminist movement left in its wake a few political organizations, such as the League of Women Voters, that have given a few women training in the political arena that they have been able to draw upon in launching the modern liberation movement (Gruberg, 1968).

None of these structural factors, however, would have been sufficient to produce the women's liberation movement, and the concomitant social problem it represents, without the third factor: namely, the growth of the generalized belief, or "collective definition," that the situations of most modern women are grossly unfair and in need of radical change. The dissemination and popularization of this definition are attributable largely to the successful efforts of Betty Friedan, Simone de Beauvoir, and other early harbingers of women's liberation, about whom we shall have more to say later.

Leadership and Recruitment

We mentioned earlier that the modern movement has had two rather different segments: instrumental and expressively oriented groups. The instrumental groups draw most of their membership and leadership from middle- and upper-middle-class women of post-college age, who are highly educated and often career-oriented. Able not only to articulate their grievances, but also to use social institutions such as the media to their advantage, these women have provided the impetus for goal-oriented organizations like NOW. Well-educated white middle- and upper-class women also provide most of the membership of the expressively oriented, or consciousness-raising groups. However, the latter tend to be younger than the goal-oriented members, and rather than being experienced in "establishment" and professional matters, they have been involved in more grassroots social reform movements like civil rights and the New Left. While the younger women organize at the community level, the professional women are working through more established social and political institutions. Freeman has noted the complementary relationship between the two segments: "It [the "younger branch"] often seems mired in introspection, but it is in fact creating a vast reservoir of conscious feminist sentiment which only awaits an appropriate opportunity for action" (Freeman, 1973:47). Conspicuously absent from both segments, however, are working-class or blue-collar women. We will see later how the goals of the present movement do not encompass the needs of these women (Freeman, 1973; John Howard, 1974; Lear, 1968).

The Natural History of Women's Liberation

The incipiency of the current movement was characterized by more or less isolated expressions of disillusionment and frustration among individual women in the 1950's. Prior to their involvement in feminism, the younger members of the movement were involved in working for the civil rights of others. They had yet to recognize their roles in these efforts or in society as subordinate. Professional women, however, were beginning to define the strains they experienced. The sociologist Helen Hacker (1951), for example, noted early the similarities between the status of blacks and of women in the United States, since both lacked the political, legal and social rights and opportunities held by white males. Few took note of her ideas, however. Simone de Beauvoir (1953) wrote about women's secondary position in society, but few were aware of her writings in *The Second Sex* at that time. Isolated cries were rising, but the collective voice was not yet strong enough to be heard.

Coalescence, or the formation of that collective voice, began in 1961 with the establishment of the President's Commission on the Status of Women. While there was not yet sufficient pressure to act on the findings that the Commission clearly documented about discrimination against women, the effect of the Commission was still important:

> (1) it brought together many knowledgable, politically active women who otherwise would not have worked together around matters of direct concern to women; (2) the investigations unearthed ample evidence of women's unequal status, especially their legal and economic difficulties, in the process convincing many previously uninterested women that something should be done; (3) the reports created a climate of expectations that something would be done. (Freeman, 1973:36)

Little was actually done at this time, however. In fact, at a meeting of the Third National Conference of Commissions on the Status of Women, the delegates (mostly men) refused to let the question of implementation of the recommendations of the Commission come to the floor (Freeman, 1973). Even Title VII of the Civil Rights Act of 1964 remained unenforced because most agencies were preoccupied with racial violations. What did occur during this period was a continuing rise in the expectations and dissatisfaction of professional women, leading to what Freeman (1973:40) has called the "essential elements contributing to the emergence of the women's movement:"

> (1) the growth of a pre-existing communications network which was (2) co-optable to the ideas of the new movement; (3) a series of crises that galvanized into action people involved in this network, and/or (4) subsequent organizing efforts to weld the spontaneous groups together into a movement. (Freeman, 1973:40)

It was not until 1966 that the movement actually began to take shape. In response to Betty Friedan's *The Feminine Mystique,* which documented, in especially compelling terms, the "second-class citizenship" accorded women, a group of professionals created the National Organization for Women (NOW). Charter members included Dr. Kathryn Clarenbach, an educator; Dr. Alice Rossi, a sociologist; Aileen Hernandez, a lawyer; Caroline Davis, a United Auto Workers executive; and Ms. Friedan (Lear, 1968). NOW was the first (and principal) national organization to promote women's rights. It represented the climax of the coalescence phase of the movement, and the beginning of its institutionalization.

NOW's membership grew quickly, and provided an effective communications network for the movement. In response largely to the pressure from the growing movement, in 1968 President Johnson issued Executive Order 11246, which banned all sexual as well as racial discrimination in federal jobs (Kanowitz, 1969). In an effort to redress somewhat the losses that had already been suffered through discrimination, in 1969 President Nixon issued Executive Order 11375, which established "Affirmative Action" committees in public institutions. The function of these committees is to see that women and minority groups are given priority in recruitment to positions in public and government life.

Meanwhile, the younger women who were involved in the reform movements of the 1960's were becoming increasingly disillusioned:

All of the radical movements of the 1960's called for a redefinition of social roles: blacks would no longer shuffle; students would no longer grovel; the male would no longer have to define his manhood as a readiness to kill for his country. None of the radical movements went so far, though, as to pose a new and different role for women. Indeed, some of the most radical voices spoke in reactionary terms when conversation turned to women. (Howard, 1974:145)

Leaders in those movements were uncomplimentary and even hostile in their references to the women's movement. Eldridge Cleaver, for example, once suggested that women exercise "Pussy Power." Abbie Hoffman claimed that, "The only alliance I would make with the Women's Liberation Movement is in bed." Stokely Carmichael stated that "The only position for women in SNCC is prone" (Morgan, 1970:35-6). Women's disillusionment was deepened by the expulsion of whites from the more militant black organizations, and by the eventual co-optation and demise of the New Left in the early 1970's. Thus, with some bitterness, much disillusionment, and many organizational skills, these women comprised the wellsprings of the rising women's liberation movement.

While the goals of the instrumentally oriented NOW and *Ms.* magazine are issue-specific, those of the expressively oriented groups remain purposely more diffused: to become aware of woman's position in society, to share mutual concerns, and to communicate with other feminists in an open and non-competitive environment (Howard, 1974; Epstein and Goode, 1971). As the movement expands to include a broader spectrum of the female population, however, the concerns of these expressive groups may become antithetical to those of the original founders of the movement. A good example of this tendency can be seen in one of the concerns of the working-class women, who are poorly represented in the movement at the present time:

A common complaint among working-class women who have formed their own consciousness-raising groups is that, after they become "fat and forty," their husbands lose sexual interest in them. In a sense, they seek to extend the period during which they are viewed as sex objects by their husbands. (Howard, 1974:158)

In general, the values of working-class women, in terms of how they wish to be viewed and treated by men, differ from those of the middle- and upper-class women who have formed the core of the movement up until now. With the growing numbers of working-class women becoming interested in the movement, some modification of the original aims will probably occur.

The prospects for the movement's fragmentation and demise thus can be viewed from many perspectives. The movement has not had, and probably will not have, much support or membership from lower-class or minority women, for, as Shirley Chisholm has noted,

The use of the word "Ms." is not a burning issue to them [black and Mexican-American women].... They are more concerned about the extension of the minimum wage ... about welfare reform. (San Francisco Sunday Examiner & Chronicle, February 18, 1973:9)

The current movement rarely addresses these issues.

There seems to be an ideological split developing among some of the original founders of the movement as well. Betty Friedan, for example, has criticized some of the more radical members in the movement (e.g., Gloria Steinem) for being "female chauvinists" who have gone "too far" in defining marriage as legalized prostitution. "Such sexual definition," says Friedan, "whether it seems to put us down or glorify us, denies us human identity, personal definition—the right to spell our own names as people by our own actions in society—which is what this movement is all about" (Friedan, 1972:83). Moreover, it is probable that the passage of the ERA will satisfy many feminists and cool their enthusiasm for the movement (Rossi, 1964). Howard (1974) also suggests that as more women enter the professions and are given the opportunity to compete for top positions, they will have less time to devote to the movement, less stake in the more radical demands, and much invested in the establishment. Probably, then, the prospects for fragmentation and demise will grow as gains are made, tensions within the movement develop, and more pressing social issues are discovered.

THE LEGACY OF THE FEMINIST PROBLEM-MOVEMENTS
The Early Feminist Movement
The feminist movement of the progressive era ended, for all practical purposes, with the passage of the 19th Amendment. The net result of that movement fulfilled neither the dreams of the most ardent feminists, nor the nightmares of the movement's critics. Indeed, there was little progressive effect at all from either of the two main thrusts of the movement.

The first thrust, which was political, culminated, of course, in the 19th Amendment extending suffrage to women in 1920. This new constitutional development, however, has made little difference in the outcomes of elections, or in other aspects of the political process. Many moral entrepreneurs had hoped (and machine politicians had feared) that the women's vote would bring about a "cleansing" of politics, since women somehow had a moral sensitivity, and commitment to moral issues was felt to be lacking in most men. As it has turned out, however, there has never been a women's bloc or a women's vote; with very few historical exceptions, women have distributed their votes in about the same way as have men on almost all candidates and issues. Nor have women generally organized themselves politically into special pressure groups, lobbies, or caucuses to try to influence the political process from a particular "women's point of view." Organizations growing out of early feminist times, such as the League of Women Voters, have encompassed neither large numbers nor any representative cross-section of American women, and they have tended to avoid partisan politics. If political institutions were not much affected by female suffrage, neither were other institutions. Dire predictions by anti-suffragists about the neglect of motherhood and the consequent destruction of the American family were certainly not fulfilled by the extension of the franchise to women. If anything, perhaps the political socialization of their children was enhanced.

The second main thrust of the early feminist movement, however, did leave an impact, but, in retrospect, it certainly does not seem to have been a progressive one. We refer here to the web of protective social and economic legislation that was generated by the earlier movement. At least implicitly, and often explicitly, this legislation both expressed and reinforced the 19th-century stereotypes of women as essentially innocent, helpless, fragile, and domestic. Society in general, and the legislatures in particular, still regarded extra-domestic jobs or careers for women as irregular, generally undesirable, and in need of careful surveillance. Occupations regarded as "dangerous" for women, either physically or morally, were closed to them by both law and custom, and differential pay scales were recognized (and sometimes required) by law in the belief that women had "special" physical, emotional, or social constraints making them in general less productive than men in the same jobs. Nor were women usually permitted to gain extra compensation from overtime work, since unduly long work days and work weeks were considered harmful for them. Even in matters such as property ownership, they were sometimes placed by the law under the protection of their fathers until marriage, and then under that of their husbands, with but few legal prerogatives of their own until relatively recent times. All of this protection, let us keep in mind, was offered in a "progressive" spirit as a solution to some of the pressing social problems around the turn of the century. It is ironic that this legacy of an earlier feminist movement should now become part of "the problem" being attacked by the contemporary movement. (For an extensive review of this early legislation, with citations of specific laws, see Kanowitz, 1969.)

The Modern Feminist Movement

Though it has been in progress for a relatively short time, the modern feminist movement (often popularly called women's lib) has already had a widespread impact on our general cultural context, our behavioral norms, and our laws.

General Cultural Impact

While changes in women's clothing fads and fashions have occurred with increasing rapidity over the past several generations, recent changes have begun to reflect the influence of the liberation theme in current feminism. Differences between male and female clothing have diminished with the unisex trend, and the pants-suits that once would have been unacceptably immodest for women are increasingly in vogue. Women have gained greater freedom of physical movement (as men have had for some time) with their new clothing fashions, and they have discarded the earlier confining "foundation garments," and even their brassieres in many cases.

Innovations in language have accompanied this new movement as they usually have other movements. The phrases women's lib and women's libber are much bandied about, and cannote a jocular, if somewhat condescending, popular designation for the movement and its adherents. The term of address, Ms., has become common (and sometimes mandatory) parlance, replacing both Miss and Mrs., and thus according women privacy regarding their marital status. Widespread as such usages might be, however, their currency ought not to be overestimated: A Gallup poll taken in March, 1973, indicated that one-third of the women polled, and almost one-half of the men, had never heard of the title Ms. (pronounced Miz), and that most of those who had heard of it disapproved of its use. Of the married women, 89 percent preferred to be called "Mrs.," and 67 percent of the single women preferred "Miss."

Perhaps nowhere has the general cultural influence of the new movement been as noticeable as in the mass media. A number of new (or remodeled) popular magazines have carried a great deal of feminist material and sentiment. *Ms.* is probably the best-known of these, for the explicitly liberationist themes and articles which it features. It is published by Gloria Steinem, a well-known leader in the women's movement. *Cosmopolitan,* while strongly criticized by many in the women's movement for continuing to present women as "sex objects," nevertheless seems somewhat influenced by that movement. It caters to the single career woman, and plays up her sexual freedom. While many of the articles have a "how-to-please-your-man" sort of theme, they nevertheless deal with it in a general context of female freedom and independence. More recently, as though reflecting one of the motifs of the movement even further, *Cosmo* has been carrying articles with a "how-to-be-happy-even-though-you-don't-have-a-man" theme. *Playgirl* and *Viva* have a more explicitly sexual orientation, complete with nude pictures of men and women in sexual embraces. They represent what might be called the "centerfold segment" of the liberationist movement, seemingly declaring their equality with men by showing that if male magazines can feature nude women, then female magazines can feature nude men. These magazines have been criticized by the more serious segments of the women's movement for their preoccupation with sex, and their alleged function as new means for capitalist male exploitation of women. It is probable, however, that such publications would not have been possible or have been able to acquire "respectable" audiences without the generally liberating impact of the women's movement.

The popular daily and Sunday comics in our newspapers have also picked up the problematic aspects of the new women's movement as good topical plot material. In 1973, "Apartment 3-G" featured such a plot, as did "Steve Roper" in 1974, as well as many others in the early and middle 1970's. In these comic strips, however, tradition often wins out, as the women libber heroine either succumbs to the pressures of convention or else gets herself into some serious predicament from which she has to be saved by a man. "Peanuts" occasionally features the competent young girl camp counselor who is irritated all summer by the little tot who calls her "sir" because she is functioning as an authority figure, thus making for a kind of spoof on women's lib. More sophisticated and probably more supportive of the movement's outlook is "Doonesbury," where all the absurdities and ironies of male chauvinism are presented to the reader. Many other examples of the influence of the women's movement on the comics could be cited.

Television has been another medium showing strong influence from the themes of the women's movement, not so much in the daytime soap operas as in the evening programs, which are more likely to be viewed by non-traditional women. The good-natured traditional submission to abuse by Archie Bunker's wife, Edith, in "All in the Family" is presented sympathetically, and Archie as a tyrannical husband is the butt of satire in this and other areas. "Maude," on the other hand, asserts herself, with much audience approval, as the embattled middle-aged housewife with a considerably "raised consciousness." "Mary Tyler Moore" is in some ways a "model" single career girl with whom modern young women can identify, but she remains subordinate to a male boss. Even the TV commercials show the influence of the women's movement, as they do of the civil rights movement. Most of us have probably seen that female Ph.D. biophysicist (or other professional) who makes sure that her children get a certain orange drink each morning. In this commercial, the feminists get their professional career woman, but domestic traditionalists (i.e., most consumers) still win out in the end, for the "heroine" is still a mother and still has the responsibility of getting breakfast for her family!

Normative Influences

In both societal attitudes and behavior, we can see changes that have recently been wrought by the women's movement. We have already alluded to the greater sexual freedom which women seem to have, and which is urged upon them in certain magazines. Beyond the rather narrow issue of sexual behavior, however, the larger arena of sex-role definitions in general shows much influence from the movement. The traditional normative requirements of marriage and motherhood for women have been severely weakened. Career girl or career woman is no longer a pejorative term, and some of the traditionally unflattering labels like spinster and old maid are falling into disuse, indicating a higher status for the unmarried woman. The fact that a married couple does not have children is not nearly as likely as it once was to bring stares of disapproval or gushes of sympathy for the infertility of the wife or husband. The childless and/or unmarried and/or divorced woman, while still clearly limited in circles of friendship, is no longer the oddity that she was even a decade ago.

That is not to say, however, that women have lost all interest in romance and marriage, or that they have altogether thrown over their traditional "feminine" behavior and preferences. Actually, the present is a very ambiguous, transitional time for standards of behavior in male-female relationships. Men and women both are sometimes at a loss to know how to act with each other. Do women still like to have their beauty or sex appeal noticed by men, or will they respond with anger or indignation at being "treated as sex objects?" It clearly depends upon the woman. Psychologist Joyce Brothers (1972:56) reported on a national poll in 1971 which showed that a majority of women under 25 years of age objected to being "treated as sex objects," but that an even larger majority "enjoyed being whistled at!" We have already seen above that the title Ms. is not widely accepted by women. Questions of traditional male chivalry are also closely related to sex-role norms. Are women still "on the pedestal," or aren't they? Again, it depends upon the woman. A 1972 national poll showed that only 12 percent of the women and 15 percent of the men felt that men should no longer be expected to open doors for women (Etzioni, 1972). In this respect, at least, more than 80 percent of both sexes still believe in good old-fashioned male chivalry, and one wonders what the future will bring in such attitudes. Meanwhile, the hapless male who opens a door for one of the female 12 percent may be rewarded with a snide remark!

An unexpected normative "fall-out" from the women's movement has been the genesis of a small but growing men's liberation movement (Farrell, 1971, and

Spokesman Review, 1974). This is not a countermovement to the women, but one which seeks to extend to men the same liberation from traditional role expectations and demands. Why, this movement asks, should men be stereotyped by women, or by other men, in the traditional masculine image? Why must men be "studs" in the *Playboy* and *Playgirl* fashion? Why can they not cultivate sensitivity, cry when moved or hurt, touch each other without embarrassment, or give way to any other so-called "feminine" modes of behavior that may appeal to them as individuals?

Legal and Institutional Developments

The new feminist movement has already succeeded, as part of its own process of institutionalization, in bringing about many new developments in society in legal and other institutional respects. There have been great increases in the past decade or so in the number of women who are participating in our political life, beyond merely voting. Even in the early 1960's, there were two female senators and 18 female representatives in the U.S. Congress (Etzioni, 1972). While these numbers have not increased lately (in fact, they have decreased), there has been a dramatic increase in the number of women running for public office: In 1974, more than 3,000 women filed for election to city, state, or national offices, compared with 1,072 in 1972. Sixty-three percent of the voters, furthermore, have indicated in national polls that they would be willing to vote for women for these various political offices (Harvey, 1974). While such developments would not have been possible without the old 19th Amendment, they are neither natural nor direct consequences of that amendment, for they have occurred only since the beginning of the recent women's liberation movement.

In an effort to implement the demands of modern feminists and liberals for equal access on the part of women to all political and economic opportunities, Congress has passed civil rights legislation covering women as well as ethnic minorities, and at least two executive orders (#11246 and #11375) have been issued intended to prevent discrimination on the basis of sex in government or industry. An Affirmative Action bureaucracy (which functions with varying degrees of efficiency) has been set up at federal, state, and local levels to see to the enforcement of these laws. The Equal Rights Amendment (ERA), which has been up for passage for half a century, interestingly enough, has only since the late 1960's shown any real prospect of being ratified by the requisite number of states. When it is finally ratified, which seems rather likely, the Constitution will then require considerable revision to eliminate all sex distinctions under the law, and this will present some very interesting and complex problems of enforcement.

Meanwhile, even without ERA, we have been seeing some very important developments by and for women in industry. Openings for women in many traditionally male careers and positions are appearing in rather large numbers. In 1973 (*Daily Idahonian*, February 7, 1973), a large commercial airline appointed its first female officer. In the same year, the first Women's Bank and Trust Company was opened in New York to handle the financial needs of women who still felt they were experiencing discrimination in other banks (*Parade Magazine*, June 24, 1973). Since the early 1970's, women have been enrolling in college ROTC programs in all three branches of the military service (Malcolm, 1972).

One of the more curious, and perhaps undesirable, symptoms of the increasing equality of the sexes is in the "institution" of crime, where, for the first time in our history, the rates for women are beginning to approach those for men. According to the *Uniform Crime Reports* for August of 1972, the arrest rates for males under the age of 18 rose 32 percent between 1966 and 1971, compared to a 79 percent rise for women. During the entire decade of the 1960's, arrest rates for male minors rose 73 percent and for female minors 202 percent. The same general trends have occurred in adult crime (Moblit and Burcart, 1973). The crime rates for women also show a growing shift from the "traditional female" kinds of crime (e.g., prostitution and drugs) to property crimes and violence of the kind once considered exclusively male (Moblit and Burcart, 1973). These trends might mirror the new definitions of sex roles found in legitimate social life, or they might represent a greater inclination on the part of the police to press charges against women for certain kinds of offenses. In either case, or for whatever reason, the trend toward parity between the sexes continues. For the women not criminally inclined, however, the modern feminist response to the growing crime rate has been an increased female enrollment in classes on judo, karate, and other arts of self-defense.

Sobran (1974) has suggested that, as we look toward the future, we can expect the increasing participation of women in business, industry, and politics to be accompanied by their increased susceptibility to the traditional male maladies such as heart disease, ulcers, high blood pressure, and a variety of psychological tensions. The questions posed by Etzioni (1972:35) on this issue might well cause the more faint-hearted feminists to reconsider their aspirations:

Will they all end up dashing to work in a competitive world, seeking some elusive status and measuring their success against their take-home pay, to finally collapse at the end of the day in a neurotic exhaustion, using liquor and the television set as psychiatric first-aid for winding down?

To which some of the more committed feminists may respond, "It sounds almost as bad as motherhood!"

Chapter 12

Abortion

No Papuan woman deems a large brood a desirable goal of her marriage. Naturally it would be different if no pains were involved, if a nursemaid took care of the children, and a governess took care of raising them! But all such wishes must remain unfulfilled. As a result, the Papuan woman seeks help elsewhere and believes that she will find this succor. In their belief, a formula uttered into the palm of the hand, with which she then smites her abdomen, has the desired effect. All kinds of tree and herb roots which must be ingested perform the same service, by expelling the fetus. An interesting abortifacient is a fruit kernel, taken from the excrement of the cassowary bird. This kernel is cooked together with some legumes, which the woman must then eat. The kernel itself is left uneaten, since all they seek to accomplish is that the soul-substance, which resides in the kernel expelled from the abdomen of the cassowary, should communicate itself to the herbs. This soul-substance then initiates in the body of the woman the expulsion of the fetus. If all "natural" animistic medicine fails, one has to take recourse to ghosts. Two ghost women, Godewa and Laulabu, are thought to have at their disposal abortifacient powers; therefore, one solicits their help by means of a magic formula, although, as the women themselves now concede, this is done in vain. . . . Abortion is not deemed here a wrongful act, because nobody is harmed thereby, and the woman is permitted to do with her own body as she pleases. (Keysser in Devereux, 1955: 251-252)

ABORTION AND THE SOCIAL CONSTRUCTION OF REALITY
Cultural Relativity

Abortion is an ancient and universal practice. According to Himes (1936), abortion was the primary method of birth control in many primitive societies. In a classic analysis of anthropological material on the institution of abortion, Devereux (1955:161) concluded that "there is every indication that abortion is an absolutely universal phenomenon. . . ." In his history of European morals (1900), the 19th-century historian, William E. H. Lecky, drew the same conclusion. Devereux further noted that in primitive societies, abortion was practiced for a wide variety of reasons. Among the Mataco, it was assumed that subsequent births would be facilitated by aborting the first fetus; in times of famine, Ngali and Yumu women aborted their fetuses and fed them to their starving children; and in Fiji, for reasons lost in tradition, it was customary for women to abort intermittently. Other motivations for abortion included disposing of the fruits of incest or adultery; but "in many cases we do not know whether we are confronted simply with inadequate data or with some definite kind of motivation which was forgotten after the practice became customary or fashionable" (Devereux, 1955:10).

Attitudes toward and penalties for abortion also varied widely among primitive societies. According to Devereux (1955), although the practice of abortion was virtually universal, few groups gave it their unqualified approval. Lecky, however, stated that "the practice of abortion was one to which few persons in antiquity attached any deep feelings of condemnation" (1900:20). Depending upon the strength of the proscription against abortion under given circumstances, penalties might be administered by supernatural powers (e.g., plagues or injuries); by natural powers (e.g., sterility being caused by abortion); or by public or private powers (e.g., beating, killing, or divorcing the "guilty" party) (Devereux, 1955).

References to the practice of abortion are found in the writings of the ancient Hebrews, Egyptians, Greeks, Romans, and Orientals. According to Himes (1936), the earliest abortifacient recipe, contained in the royal archives of China, is almost 5,000 years old. Although both the Babylonian Code of Hammurabi and the Jewish Old Testament at the time of the Egyptian exodus (e.g., Exo. 21:22) set penalties for abortion, according to Lader (1966:75), "these were strictly limited to the payment of compensation when an assault on a pregnant wife resulted in miscarriage."

In early Rome, due to the institution of *pater familias,* abortion was the concern only of the family, and not of the state. Under this system, the husband/father held the power of life and death over other members of the family. Although he might order his wife to procure an abortion, he also had the power to punish, divorce, or even kill her if she had an abortion performed without his knowledge and consent. However, by 700 B.C., Roman women were "demanding emancipation and using abortion, not only for family limitation, but also for personal vanity and social ambition" (Lader, 1966:76-77). Thus, several direct and indirect efforts were made by the state in an attempt to reduce the frequency of abortion, but they were largely unsuccessful due to the strength of pro-abortion traditions over seven centuries old.

Christian dogma, however, came into conflict with Roman custom; "it was

Christianity which revolutionized moral ideas in this matter by endowing the embryo with a soul" (de Beauvoir, 1952:110). Lader (1966) stated that Christian philosophy is the primary source of prohibition against abortion. The condemnation of abortion in the earliest Christian writings in the *Didache* (ca. A.D. 80) was followed by numerous denunciations of abortion by men of the Church throughout the centuries. However, it should be noted that the New Testament does not include any clear prohibition of abortion (Granfield, 1969). Taylor (1954) maintained that the pronouncement of Tertullian, an early Christian theologian, that abortion constituted "murder by advance" derived from his inaccurate translation of Exodus 21:22, which, in turn, led to the idea that the Old Testament defined abortion as a crime. Although this mistranslation, perpetuated by Jerome, has been exposed (Taylor, 1954), the Roman Catholic Church's position on the issue has remained essentially unchanged.

Cultural variations in the practice of and attitudes toward abortion have persisted in modern times. In some of the Eastern European countries, there has even been a certain amount of vacillation on the abortion issue; that is, liberal abortion laws have been passed and then later repealed in favor of more restrictive ones. Contrary to popular stereotypes, the Scandinavian countries may be termed moderate or middle-ground in regard to their current abortion legislation, although some (notably Denmark and Sweden) are moving toward a more permissive position. "It appears to be the case that most Scandinavians do not believe that abortion is equivalent to the taking of a human life" (Callahan, 1970:199). Western European countries are characterized by restrictive abortion laws, but in France, Italy, West Germany, and Belgium, the number of illegal abortions is purported to equal the number of live births, despite the strong anti-abortion influence of the Catholic Church. Clearly, Japan's laws with regard to abortion are the most permissive in the world at this time, virtually allowing abortion on demand; this policy apparently stems from the necessity of controlling a national population problem.*

Definitions and Interpretations

For several centuries in Christian countries, abortion was generally punished by the Church as murder only if the fetal soul was rational or animated (defined as 40 and 80 days after conception for male and female children, respectively). A very brief and unsuccessful attempt was made in the 16th century by Pope Sixtus V to enforce stringent sanctions for abortion at any time after conception. Then, in 1869 Pope Pius IX declared that all abortion would be considered murder, thus eliminating the earlier distinction between the animated and non-

---

* However permissive Japan may be considered on abortion, though, contraceptive pills are not legally available there, except for research purposes!

animated fetus. (More recent developments in the official position of the Roman Catholic Church will be discussed at a later point.)

In our time, and among secular bodies, according to Pressat (1971:120), "The very definite distinction which has become established in the West between contraception (prevention of conception) and abortion (destruction of the fetus and therefore of a living being) does not exist in Japan, where the dividing line is established at birth." Stockwell (1970:89), however, includes abortion and infanticide together in one category, and equates these with contraception, distinguishing between two broad classes of population control: "(a) those used after the fact of conception or birth (such as abortion or infanticide), and (b) those used before, during, or immediately after intercourse to prevent conception from taking place."

Further problems of definition of abortion versus contraception are illustrated in the use of the IUD (popularly known as the loop or coil) and the morning-after pill, both generally considered as means of contraception. While there is disagreement among medical authorities as to exactly how an IUD works, there is one school of thought which views it as speeding the passage of an egg (possibly fertilized) through the uterus so that implantation is prevented. Similarly, the morning-after pill acts as "an instant abortifacient" (Westoff and Westoff, 1971: 77). In addition to these two methods, although the procedure involved is not new, menstrual extractions are increasingly being used in cases of suspected pregnancies even before conception is or can be definitely confirmed (before the fifth week). By means of this technique, the contents of the uterus are removed, including a fertilized egg, if present. While the term interceptive has been coined to cover techniques like the IUD, and the morning-after pill, the removal of a fertilized egg by any such artificial means (including menstrual extraction) is considered by some as tantamount to actual abortion (*Time,* September 11, 1972:47; *Newsweek,* July 24, 1972:69).

A number of labels have been applied to the term abortion, depending upon the perspective of the defining individual or group. While on the one hand, abortion has been termed feticide, "war on the unborn," and "slaughter of the innocent" by its opponents, it has also been described as merciful, humanitarian, a back-up method of birth control, and a necessary means of limiting population growth by its defenders:

Free associations to the word "abortion" would probably yield a fantastic array of emotional responses: pain, relief, murder, crime, fear, freedom, genocide, guilt, sin. Which of these associations people have no doubt reflects their age, marital status, religion or nationality. To a forty-four-year-old Japanese or Hungarian woman, the primary response might be "freedom" and "relief"; to an unmarried American college

girl "fear" and "pain"; to a Catholic priest, "murder" and "sin"; to some black militants, "genocide." (Rossi, 1969:338)

The emotional nature of the definitions attached to the term have been clearly recognized by the medical profession. In his abortion clinic ethnography, Ball (1967) discussed abandoning the use of the term abortion in the presence of the patron in favor of medical terminology, in order to emphasize the clinic's professionalism and thus to contradict the stereotyped image of deviance and disgrace. Also along these lines Chisholm (1971) suggested that the negative connotations surrounding the abortion procedure might be eliminated by following the British precedent of referring to "pregnancy termination." In its pamphlet, *Portrait of the Opposition,* the National Association for Repeal of Abortion Laws emphasized the use of emotionally loaded terms by Right to Life and similar anti-abortion groups as a major weapon in their "threat" to the repeal movement.

In medical terms, abortion refers to "the induced termination of pregnancy before the normal fetus has attained viability, or the capacity for life outside the womb" (Lader, 1966:18). This definition applies only to induced, intentional abortion as distinguished from spontaneous abortion or miscarriage. Therapeutic abortion involves "the intentional termination of pregnancy for reasons of medical necessity" (Schur, 1965:13). As will become clear in the course of this chapter, variations in the latitude allowed physicians in determining what constitutes "medical necessity" have been more or less severely restricted by the statutory definitions of any given state as well as the interpretations allowed by the courts. Lader (1966:3) argued that the term "therapeutic" is misapplied in this context, and that "hospital" abortion would be a more accurate term "since many abortions performed outside the law are equally therapeutic." This leads us to the lexical distinctions between legal and illegal abortion.

Like the divorce laws, legislation concerning abortion has varied widely from state to state, but in January, 1973, the United States Supreme Court struck down the criminal abortion statutes of at least 46 states. Prior to the Supreme Court decision, only four states and the District of Columbia allowed, in effect, "abortion on request," so that the decision could be made by a woman and her physician. Even in these states, the permissive legislation was scarcely five years old. In New York, abortions were legal up to and including the 24th week of pregnancy, with no residency requirement. The laws in Alaska and Hawaii were very similar, but there was a 30-day-residency requirement in the former state and a 90-day requirement in the latter. In the state of Washington, there was a 90-day-residency requirement, and abortions were legal up to and including the 16th week of pregnancy (Trotter, 1972).* The statutes in the remaining states ranged widely

---

* Laws of this kind rarely specify whether the number of permissible elapsed weeks is to be reckoned from the last menstrual period, from the first period missed, or from the estimated date of conception. Doctors are thus given a discretionary time span of about two weeks.

along the permissive-restrictive continuum, those states with the most restrictive statutes allowing abortion only if necessary to save the life of the mother, and those with less restrictive laws allowing a rather wide interpretation of provisions regarding the preservation of the mental health of the mother as grounds for abortion.

Parameters of Consensual Reality

Because of the legal sanctions and the social stigma associated with obtaining an abortion until quite recently, reliable statistics on the phenomenon are very limited. Estimates of the incidence of abortion in the United States have varied "wildly" (Callahan, 1970:132). Taussig (1936) estimated that 681,600 abortions were performed annually during the early 1930's and that approximately 60 to 65 percent of these were illegal. In several other studies, varying ratios of the incidence of abortion to the incidence of live births were found among samples whose representativeness has been criticized on several grounds. These figures, as well as those from later studies, are summarized in Callahan (1970), but Taussig's estimate has been perhaps the most influential of the early calculations, and he has been described as "author of the first authoritative study of abortion" (Lader, 1966:7). In the Kinsey sample of 1966, of the white, non-prison, never-married women studied, 22 percent had had at least one abortion by the age of 45 (Kinsey, 1966). While this sample has been criticized as nonrepresentative, the data nevertheless provide one of the few cases for comparison with Taussig in that an extrapolation from these figures yields a total of approximately 600,000 illegal abortions per year (Callahan, 1970). Other studies have also been deemed inadequate on the basis of their sample design (Calderone, 1958). Perhaps the most influential figures have been those reported by the statistics committee of the 1955 Planned Parenthood Conference on abortion:

> Taking into account the probable trend of the abortion ratio since the interwar period, a plausible estimate of the frequency of induced abortion in the United States could be as low as 200,000 and as high as 1,200,000 per year, depending upon the assumptions made as to the incidence of abortion in the total population as compared with the restricted groups for which statistical data are available, and upon the assessment of the direction and magnitude of bias inherent in each series of data. There is no objective basis for the selection of a particular figure between these two estimates as an approximation of the actual frequency. (Calderone, 1958:180)

As Callahan (1970) pointed out, in spite of Calderone's and the statistics committee's caveats regarding the unavailability of a reliable, exact figure on abortions for the total population, advocates of legal reform have tended to select the upper limits of these estimates as representing the incidence of abortion in the United States. One million is an often-quoted figure, however, even in the national news media (*Newsweek, Time,* etc.), which also usually put the number of deaths resulting from illegal abortions at about 10,000 annually. However, Tietze (1963), a physician and a leading authority on abortion, estimated that approximately 500 deaths occur per year from both legal and illegal abortions. Even earlier, in 1948, Tietze stated that the death rate from abortion had declined by approximately 80 percent from 1927 to 1945. Registered deaths from abortion numbered 247 in 1964 and 235 in 1965 (Cooke, 1968).

Tietze (1970) has estimated a ratio of about two therapeutic abortions per 1,000 deliveries, so that the estimated total number of legal abortions in the United States per year in 1970 was about 8,000. There has been considerable agreement on this figure (Callahan, 1970). Westoff and Westoff (1971), however, indicated that the figure of 8,000 is applicable for the mid-1960's, and that approximately 20,000 legal abortions were performed in 1969, and 200,000 in 1970. The number of legal abortions, then, has been greatly affected by the passage of more permissive legislation in recent years.

During the first year in which New York's liberal law allowing "abortion on demand" was in effect (beginning in July, 1970), approximately 165,000 abortions were performed in New York City alone, and more than 50 percent on women who were not residents of New York state. Both maternal-mortality rates, infant-mortality rates, and illegitimate-birth rates for this same time period are reported to have dropped. Furthermore, although it was widely recognized that the earlier restrictive abortion laws discriminated against poor and non-white women, during the first year in which the new law was in effect over 50 percent of the abortions involving New York state residents in New York City were performed on black and Puerto Rican women (*Newsweek,* July 19, 1971:50-52). However, the majority of those who obtained legal abortions in the United States in the late '60's and early '70's were white, single, and between the ages of 20 and 30 (*Time,* September 27, 1971:67-70). During the same period of time, approximately 50 percent of the legal abortions performed in New York involved married women; this is in sharp contrast to the estimates, commonly made prior to the general availability of "abortion on demand," that 85 to 90 percent of all illegal abortions involved married women (for example, see Rossi, 1966), but of course it must be recognized that New York may be atypical in this regard.

Completely accurate and reliable statistics on the incidence of and reasons for abortion are yet to come. The Joint Program for the Study of Abortion (JPSA) has been established by the Population Council in order to fill such gaps. In the first of a series of studies, Tietze and Lewit (1971) reported on records submitted by 56 institutions participating in JPSA. Of 22,593 reported women who had aborted, 23 percent were under the age of 20; 55 percent were single; and 30 percent were currently married. Although the ethnic affiliation was unknown for

TABLE 12-1 ATTITUDES TOWARD ABORTION

Would you favor or oppose a law which would permit a woman to go to a doctor to end a pregnancy at any time during the first three months?

	Percent Favor	Percent Oppose	Percent No Opinion
NATIONAL	40	50	10
SEX			
Men	40	46	14
Women	40	53	7
RACE			
White	40	50	10
Non-white	45	50	5
EDUCATION			
College	58	34	8
High School	37	53	10
Grade School	31	57	12

Source: Gallup Opinion Index, Report no. 54, December, 1969

over seven percent, approximately 63 percent were white, and approximately 25 percent were black; the remaining four to five percent belonged to other ethnic groups.

Public Opinion

Having reviewed the statistical facts on the actual incidence of abortion, let us see what the public has been thinking about the abortion issue. According to Tietze and Lewit (1971:137), "the past few years have witnessed growing acceptance and increasing utilization of induced abortion as a legitimate medical procedure in the United States." Although abortion remains a highly controversial topic in our society, there is growing evidence that public opinion on the subject is changing. Table 12-1 presents the results of the 1969 Gallup poll, in which 40 percent of the sample of about 1,500 indicated that they would favor a law which would permit abortion during the first three months of pregnancy. More recently, however (June, 1972), the Gallup organization reported that "64 percent of American voters favor abortion reform [i.e., making it more permissive], an astonishing reversal of sentiment. In 1968, voters were [had been] 85 percent against abortion reform" (Hacker, 1972:4). Similarly, in 1970 Ehrlich and Ehrlich presented statistics demonstrating that approval of abortion in six out of seven circumstances rose an average of 15 percentage points within two years, from 1965 to 1967 (see Table 12-2).

TABLE 12-2   INCREASE IN APPROVAL OF ABORTION

Reasons	Percentage Approval 1965	Percentage Approval 1967
Woman's health endangered	87	86
Victim of rape	52	72
Pregnancy due to incest*	—	69
Possibility of deformed child	50	62
Woman unmarried	13	28
Can't afford child	11	25
Child unwanted	8	21

* Not surveyed in 1965.
Source: Ehrlich and Ehrlich, 1970:225
Original source cited by Ehrlich and Ehrlich: Data from Studies in Family Planning, no. 30 (Supplement), The Population Council, 1968

Rossi (1967) thoroughly analyzed the data gathered by the National Opinion Research Center in December, 1965, when a representative sample of 1,484 adult Americans was surveyed in regard to their attitudes toward abortion under specified conditions. A more recent survey by NORC (Spring, 1972), in which the same questions were asked of 1,613 adults, provides valuable comparative data. Table 12-3 shows the change in attitudes toward abortion from 1965 to 1972. One of the most striking findings consists of the fact that more than twice the proportion of the 1972 sample, as compared with the 1965 sample, indicated approval of legally accessible abortion under what are considered the three most controversial conditions on the list: if a low-income family cannot afford more children, if the woman is not married, and if a married woman does not want any more children.

Table 12-4 shows the differences in attitudes toward abortion between males and females at various education levels. While men are, on the whole, more liberally disposed toward abortion than are women, in 1972 there is very little difference between them if they have had at least "some high school." In the area of religion, the gap between Protestants and Catholics in their attitudes toward abortion, termed a "relatively slight difference" by Rossi in 1967 (p. 39), appears to have narrowed even more in 1972 (see Table 12-5). It would appear, moreover, that the views of Protestant and Catholic women are more closely aligned than those of the men in these two religious groups.

In looking at the next three tables (all based on data from the National Opinion Research Center), however, we notice (Table 12-6) that there is some decline in the percentages approving abortion under the various specified conditions with advancing age, for both sexes. In Table 12-7 we see that the percentages of approval under each condition are higher among the never-married than among the married, both male and female. Also, although women generally indicate less

TABLE 12-3 ATTITUDES TOWARD LEGAL ABORTIONS UNDER SPECIFIED CONDITIONS

Please tell me whether or not you think it should be possible for a pregnant woman to obtain a *legal* abortion....

	1965[b] (N = 1,482)			1972[c] (N = 1,613)			1965-1972
	Yes	No	Don't Know	Yes	No	Don't Know/ No Answer	Percent Increase in Approval
If the woman's own health is seriously endangered by the pregnancy	71	26	3	83.0	12.5	4.6	12.0[a]
If she became pregnant as a result of rape	56	38	6	74.1	19.6	6.3	18.1[a]
If there is a strong chance of serious defect in the baby	55	41	4	74.3	20.3	5.4	19.3[a]
If the family has a very low income and cannot afford any more children	21	77	2	45.6	47.9	6.6	24.6[a]
If she is not married and does not want to marry the man	18	80	2	40.5	52.6	6.9	22.5[a]
If she is married and does not want any more children	15	83	2	37.6	57.1	5.3	22.6[a]

[a] "Percent increase in approval" figures may be slightly misleading. They are approximations, as the 1965 figures were rounded to the nearest whole percent, while the 1972 figures were rounded to the nearest tenth of a percent.
[b] Source: Rossi, 1967:36 (1965 NORC data)
[c] Source: National Opinion Research Center, Survey 4139, Spring, 1972

TABLE 12-4 ATTITUDES TOWARD ABORTION UNDER SPECIFIED CONDITIONS BY SEX AND EDUCATION

(Percent who believe abortion should be legally accessible under specified conditions)

	Males (N = 803)[a]					Females (N = 805)[b]			
	Elementary School or Less	Some High School	High School Graduate	Some College or More		Elementary School or Less	Some High School	High School Graduate	Some College or More
Maternal health	59.7	81.4	89.4	89.4		48.3	78.7	86.9	89.2
Rape	41.6	66.1	76.8	87.2		38.3	67.9	80.1	87.6
Defect	46.8	70.3	77.3	88.0		41.7	69.0	77.0	82.8
Poor (income)	20.8	32.6	50.0	65.0		20.0	31.3	48.8	62.9
Unmarried	16.9	30.1	45.4	59.5		20.0	25.7	42.6	55.9
Child unwanted	9.1	30.1	42.6	56.2		13.3	25.0	37.1	53.2
N	77	236	216	274		60	268	291	186
X̄ percentage	32.5	51.8	63.6	74.2		30.3	49.6	62.1	71.9

[a] Four (4) males were classified as having no formal education (total N = 807).
[b] One (1) female was classified as having no formal education (total N = 806).

Source: National Opinion Research Center, Survey 4139, Spring, 1972

TABLE 12-5 ATTITUDES TOWARD ABORTION UNDER SPECIFIED CONDITIONS BY SEX AND RELIGION

(Percent who believe abortion should be legally accessible under specified conditions)

	Males (N = 807)					Females (N = 806)			
	Protestant	Catholic	Jewish	None, Other, No Answer		Protestant	Catholic	Jewish	None, Other, No Answer
Maternal health	84.0	79.0	96.2	95.6		81.8	79.9	96.4	82.6
Rape	73.0	69.4	100.0	82.6		74.7	69.6	92.8	82.6
Defect	76.3	67.6	96.2	89.8		74.7	66.0	85.7	73.9
Poor (income)	46.0	36.5	76.9	76.8		43.3	34.5	75.0	73.9
Unmarried	40.8	33.3	80.8	72.5		37.7	28.9	78.6	60.9
Child unwanted	39.1	29.2	65.4	73.9		33.3	27.8	75.0	60.9
N	493	219	26	69		538	194	28	46
X̄ percentage	59.9	52.5	85.9	81.9		57.6	51.1	83.9	72.5

Source: National Opinion Research Center, Survey 4139, Spring, 1972

TABLE 12-6 ATTITUDES TOWARD ABORTION UNDER SPECIFIED CONDITIONS BY SEX AND AGE

(Percent who believe abortion should be legally accessible under specified conditions)

	Males (N = 807)						Females (N = 806)					
	18-25	26-35	36-45	46-55	56-65	66-75	76 & over	18-25	26-35	36-45	46-55	56-65	66-75	76 & over
Maternal health	91.3	87.1	87.8	82.4	81.7	67.2	72.4	87.2	89.8	78.5	84.4	77.4	71.2	72.3
Rape	74.6	76.0	74.8	77.1	72.2	58.2	75.9	79.4	78.4	74.6	75.5	74.2	62.5	68.1
Defect	76.8	82.4	79.7	79.1	68.2	58.2	69.0	84.3	82.4	72.3	72.8	64.5	60.0	59.6
Poor (income)	55.8	47.4	46.3	54.2	38.9	29.8	44.8	51.0	50.0	47.7	41.5	41.1	32.5	31.9
Unmarried	50.0	42.7	43.9	47.7	35.7	29.8	37.9	46.1	41.5	40.0	40.8	35.5	25.0	27.6
Child unwanted	52.2	40.4	39.8	44.4	33.3	22.4	34.5	43.1	38.6	36.2	36.7	30.6	25.0	23.4
N	138	171	123	153	126	67	29	102	176	130	147	124	80	47
$\bar{X}$ percentage	66.8	62.7	62.0	64.2	55.0	44.3	55.8	65.2	63.4	58.2	58.6	53.9	46.0	47.2

Source: National Opinion Research Center, Survey 4139, Spring, 1972

TABLE 12-7 ATTITUDES TOWARD ABORTION UNDER SPECIFIED CONDITIONS BY SEX AND MARITAL STATUS

(Percent who believe abortion should be legally accessible under specified conditions)

	Males (N = 807)					Females (N = 806)				
	Married	Widowed	Divorced	Separated	Never Married	Married	Widowed	Divorced	Separated	Never Married
Maternal health	84.4	75.0	78.3	45.4	88.0	82.3	72.2	92.8	78.6	88.2
Rape	75.0	58.3	60.9	45.4	75.2	73.9	67.8	88.1	60.7	85.9
Defect	76.3	70.8	73.9	45.4	76.8	74.4	58.3	85.7	64.3	80.0
Poor (income)	45.4	50.0	39.1	36.4	57.6	45.5	30.4	57.1	28.6	51.8
Unmarried	40.2	37.5	56.5	45.4	53.6	36.6	28.7	57.1	35.7	54.1
Child unwanted	36.8	37.5	43.5	27.3	58.4	34.3	26.1	54.8	25.0	44.7
N	624	24	23	11	125	536	115	42	28	85
$\bar{X}$ percentage	59.7	54.8	58.7	40.9	68.3	57.8	47.2	72.6	48.8	67.4

Source: National Opinion Research Center, Survey 4139, Spring, 1972

TABLE 12-8 ATTITUDES TOWARD ABORTION UNDER SPECIFIED CONDITIONS BY SEX AND RACE

(Percent who believe abortion should be legally accessible under specified conditions)

	Males (N = 807)			Females (N = 806)		
	White	Black	Other	White	Black	Other
Maternal health	86.9	68.7	*	84.4	68.5	*
Rape	78.0	52.7	*	77.8	58.5	*
Defect	79.6	55.0	*	76.1	56.2	*
Poor (income)	48.6	39.7	*	46.5	31.5	*
Unmarried	44.7	33.6	*	40.3	28.5	*
Child unwanted	42.0	32.1	*	36.4	27.7	*
N	673	131	3	675	130	1
$\bar{X}$ percentage	63.3	47.0	—	60.2	45.2	—

* Too few cases to calculate percentages.
Source: National Opinion Research Center, Survey 4139, Spring, 1972

approval of abortion than do men, according to the NORC data, divorced women indicate greater approval under every condition specified than do divorced men. Finally, we can see in Table 12-8 that while whites generally show a much more liberal attitude toward abortion than do blacks, the gap between the races narrows significantly under the specified conditions of poor, unmarried, and child unwanted. For more detailed discussion and analysis of public opinion on the abortion issue, see Blake, 1971; Rossi, 1967; Ryder and Westoff, 1971; and Westoff, et al., 1969.

CHAMPIONS AND THEIR INTERESTS

Though the practice of abortion is, as we have seen, gaining wider acceptance, it is still regarded by many as a social problem because of the variety of interests which it involves, and the many ways in which it is defined. As Callahan has said, in introducing the subject,

Abortion is at once a moral, medical, legal, sociological, philosophical, demographic and psychological problem. . . . It is a moral problem because it raises the question of the nature and control of incipient human life. It is a medical problem because the doctor is the person normally called upon to perform an abortion; both his conscience and his medical skills come into play. More broadly, the question is raised of the use of technological developments for the purported improvement of human life. It is a legal problem because it raises the question of the extent to which society should concern itself with unborn life, with motherhood, with family life, with public control of the medical profession. It is a sociological problem because, as Edwin M. Schur (1955) has pointed out, it touches on "woman's role in our social system, family organization and disorganization, national demographic policy, and the role of informal and formal sanctions." It is a demographic problem because, at one level, it raises the question of whether abortion provides a useful, desirable and legitimate method of population limitation where such limitation is needed. At another level, there is the fact that, for good or ill, it is already being so used in many parts of the world. It is a psychological problem because in one way or the other, the attitude of human beings toward conception, pregnancy, birth, and child-rearing touches deep-rooted drives, instincts, emotions and taboos. (Callahan, 1970:1-2)

For each of the many interests mentioned by Callahan, there exist publics and interest groups with varying constructions of reality on the issue. Arguments against abortion are, in the final analysis, generally of a religious or moral nature. These take the form of an argument that at conception (when the egg and sperm unite), there is not only human life, but a human being, and that the destruction of this being at any stage of its development (zygote, blastocyst, embryo, or fetus) is tantamount to murder. This is the position, in particular, of the Roman Catholic Church, which holds that the body and the soul are united at the time of conception. Less theologically oriented arguments refer to the "humanness" of the embryo, rather than its ensoulment. Other opponents of abortion contend that its practice, or even its availability, will lead to infanticide, euthanasia, sexual promiscuity, and the weakening of family ties.

On the other side of the question, those who advocate greater liberalization, reform, or repeal of existing abortion laws generally believe that there is room for legitimate debate on the question of when a fetus becomes a human being, and that no one moral position on the subject should be enforced by the law and imposed upon a woman. Even in religious organizations, there are clergymen and laymen who favor the liberalization of abortion laws because of their belief that compulsory pregnancy is inhumane, and that many social problems result from denying a woman the right to make her own decision in this matter. Most advocates of repeal of restrictive abortion laws hold that the health and the rights of the pregnant woman transcend those of the fetus; and, furthermore, that a child deserves to be born under conditions where it is wanted and healthy. In this view, also, moral concerns based on traditional theology are regarded as too narrow; its proponents hold that greater moral concern should be given, instead, to the idea of forcing a woman to bear an unwanted child, and to public-health problems connected with illegal abortions under the more restrictive laws.

Interests and Publics

The Psychological Public

Having outlined the *general* interests and arguments found on both sides of the abortion issue, let us look more closely at some of the publics and interested parties found in the "outer ring" of the abortion movements. There is some reason to believe that a kind of psychological public may exist with respect to the abortion issue. In an attitudinal study with a limited population of clergymen, Bonham and Santee (1971) found significant correlations between negative attitudes toward induced abortion and conservative or negative attitudes toward women, sex, and politics; this would also be in line with certain traits of the authoritarian personality which we mentioned in Chapter 1 (cf. pp. 16-17). Further substantiation for this proposition has come from the findings, in several studies, of a relationship between religiosity and prejudice, with prejudice here being generalized to refer to negative attitudes toward women (Bonham and Santee, 1971). In further defining this psychological public, Bell (1971:129) has observed that according to some traditional authorities, a woman should not be allowed to make her own decision regarding her right to abortion, the assumption being that "they know what is better for a woman than she knows for herself" [sic]. Still other observers have detected what they call a "Comstock mentality" on the part of abortion opponents: "Deeply buried beneath the discussion of abortion are unresolved attitudes toward sex . . ." (Rossi, 1967:33); that is, punitiveness toward female sexuality, which is manifested in pregnancy, is expressed through denial to the woman of the option of abortion (Rossi, 1967, and Bell, 1971). The "hidden issue" behind abortion, then, as Hoffman (1972) also points out, is an ambivalence toward sex which demands punishment for sensuality. Intriguing as these studies on the "anti-abortion" personality may be, they are based on limited data and measures, and they do not purport to provide a sufficient explanation for all of the opposition to abortion. There do not yet appear to be any studies on a "pro-abortion personality."

Professional Publics and Interest Groups

Physicians and lawyers have certain professional interests at stake in the abortion issue. Physicians are divided. Some of them favor abortion under varying circumstances and are opposed to the imposition of legal strictures upon their medical judgment in the use of abortion as a proper medical procedure; yet other physicians feel that performing abortions is contradictory to their training as guardians of life, and are therefore not in favor of abortion. Psychiatrists sometimes disagree about the psychological implications for the parent(s) involved: while some believe that irreparable guilt feelings on the part of the parent-to-be or the unmarried parent may result from abortions, others believe that the forced birth of an unwanted child may have even graver consequences for all concerned—mother, child, family, and society.

Legal interests in the abortion issue center primarily on the issue of constitutionality. Among the contentions of those who have favored reform or repeal of restrictive abortion laws are that such laws enforce "cruel and unusual punishment" upon women, deny the right of marital privacy, do not afford the poor equal treatment, and violate the principle of separation of Church and State. On the other hand, some lawyers argue that there is ample precedent for considering the fetus to be human, and thus entitled to full protection under the law.

Economic Interests

As is the case with almost all social problems, economic interests are also involved. If, as it has been suggested by Bell (1971), a large percentage of the estimated $350,000,000 spent annually for illegal abortions in the United States is funneled into crime syndicates, and if, as indicated by Schur (1965), illegal abortions account for the third largest criminal racket in the United States, then we can expect that those who profit from them are interested in maintaining restrictive abortion laws. On the other hand, certain other economic interests would undoubtedly favor liberalization and repeal of stringent laws: Edmiston (1971) has reported that several hospitals and clinics in New York which cater almost exclusively to abortion patients are realizing a handsome profit. In addition, more than a dozen commercial abortion referral agencies* have sprung up, some of which receive substantial kickbacks from abortionists or clinics to which patients are referred, and some of which charge exorbitant sums for their services. (It is important to note here that such services can be obtained free of charge or for a nominal fee from legitimate, nonprofit agencies—many of them backed by feminist organizations—which have greatly increased in number since the Supreme Court decision.)

Interests and their Pressure Groups

Growing out of the above-mentioned publics and their interests, various organizations have emerged to carry on the battle in the central circles of the movements for and against abortion. The members of these interest groups are often recruited from a mixture of these publics. Some groups are concerned exclusively with the abortion issue, while others derive their concern about abortion from related interests. Let us now consider the principal organized groups.

---

* In New York, a lawsuit has been brought against at least one of these agencies (Abortion Information Agency, Inc.) by the state Attorney General's office; others are under investigation (Edmiston, 1971).

Two organizations, with the same broad goals of making abortion available on request as a medical service, are the Association for the Study of Abortion (ASA) and the National Association for Repeal of Abortion Laws (NARAL), both with headquarters in New York. While both groups have lobbied for less restrictive abortion laws, NARAL has been more active in organizing and promoting repeal of existing laws, while the ASA has been more concerned with distribution of information about the availability of abortions. Yet another national group which has been devoted to repeal is the Women's National Abortion Action Coalition. All three of these interest groups have generated affiliates at state and local levels, and have aided them in various ways, including providing them with finances, suggestions as to tactical maneuvers, and so forth.

At the other end of the spectrum are groups strongly opposed to abortion. Foremost among these are the National Right to Life Committee, headquartered in Washington, D.C., and the Toronto-originated Birthright, both of which have also spawned groups of a similar nature at state and local levels. While Right to Life coordinates related groups which share its philosophy, Birthright groups, which have formed in many population centers, function primarily to persuade unwillingly pregnant women to consider alternatives other than abortion.

A rather neutral counseling organization operating at the national level is the National Clergy Consultation Service on Abortion, which comprises a kind of federation of consultation services run by members of the clergy, most of whom are willing to recommend abortion in some circumstances, unless it appears that termination of the pregnancy would lead to severe psychological problems for the woman (Mace, 1972; Remsberg and Remsberg, 1972). In addition to such services as these, counseling can also be obtained from a number of local agencies not specifically formed around the abortion issue, such as Planned Parenthood clinics and Zero Population Growth referral services.

Interest groups on both sides of the fence have increasingly come to recognize the political nature of the abortion issue and, accordingly, to act upon the basis of this realization:

> With forces on the one hand arrayed in favor of liberalization of existing laws (or for no laws at all), and forces on the other intent on maintaining present laws (or tightening them), the issue has taken the form of various pressure groups struggling against each other for the legislative ear. . . . Abortion seems particularly apt to bring out the mentality of the crusader, whether of liberal, radical, or conservative stripe. (Callahan, 1970:3)

At the present time, as a result of the landmark Supreme Court ruling of 1973—that restrictive abortion laws are unconstitutional—it appears that the pro-abortion faction* has the upper hand. In this struggle, the broad theme of women's emancipation and women's rights, more popularly known as "women's lib," has been one of the major elements of the social milieu which has facilitated the movement toward liberalization of both attitudes toward, and laws regulating, abortion. The culmination of the repeal/reform movement in the Supreme Court decision of 1973 was greeted by both sides with surprise—happy amazement on the part of proponents, and dismayed shock by opponents. When the decision and its extensive legal ramifications are considered in a historical context, the rapidity with which the ruling was made is indeed amazing in view of the relative recency of the repeal/reform movement on the public scene. Before the high Court's decision, Lader (1971:52) remarked that "the soaring trend toward legalization . . . has been called the fastest social revolution in recent history." This is not to imply, however, that the movement's goals have been realized without difficulty, or, more importantly, that the opposition has given any indication of retreating or admitting total defeat.

We will turn shortly to a review of the movements which these pressure groups have led, but first let us look briefly at how some social scientists define the abortion controversy. We have "heard from" most of the other interest groups, and let us recall from Chapter 1 that social scientists also have their own constructions of reality regarding social problems.

Scientific Interests: Sociological Theories on the Abortion Problem

Becker's Moral Entrepreneurship

While not addressing the abortion problem in particular, in his theory of moral entrepreneurship Howard S. Becker (1963) has identified a quasi-religious feature of many social movements in which moral considerations are as prominent as they are in the case of the abortion movement. He discusses the roles of two kinds of moral entrepreneurs in generating "social-problem" definitions of practices such as abortion, and in the formation of pressure groups on either side of an issue. In the issue being disputed, in this case abortion, the content of the present rules is always profoundly disturbing to the crusading reformer no matter which side he is on: for the opponent of abortion, this means that "evil" reform laws must be repealed; for the proponent, "immoral" restrictive laws must be repealed or reformed.

According to this social-scientific explanation, crusading reformers "typically believe that their mission is a holy one" (Becker, 1963:148). "Both sides [in the

---

* Strictly speaking, of course, this faction is not really "pro-abortion" so much as it is "pro-free choice" on abortion.

political struggle over abortion] claim the angels (whether 'traditional Christian' or 'progressive humanist') as their allies" (*America,* September 11, 1971:135). Likewise, Hoffman (1972:712) has remarked that the abortion debate involves "two sharply conflicting views of moral excellence and human welfare." Again, in Becker's terms, humanitarian motives are displayed by each group. The crusader "believes that if [people do what he—the reformer—thinks is right] . . . it will be good for them" (Becker, 1963:148). Those who oppose abortion, then, believe it is best for society, the child, the woman—for all involved—if abortion is legally prohibited. The crusader may also feel, according to Becker (1963:148), "that his reform will prevent certain kinds of exploitation of one person by another." Proponents of repeal or reform of restrictive abortion laws, although they recognize that the majority of women, and especially those of lower socio-economic status, do not approve of abortion on demand, nevertheless feel that these groups are being exploited by more powerful groups who deny them their right to abortion, and that it should be made available to them. In the other direction, anti-abortion forces have petitioned in a few states for appointment of a "guardian of unborn fetuses" for the purpose of establishing that the fetus is a "person" entitled to equal protection under the law; in this way they feel that the fetus may be protected from "exploitation" by abortion.

Becker notes further that "moral crusaders typically want to help those beneath them to achieve a better status. . . . moral crusades are typically dominated by those in upper levels of the social structure" (Becker, 1963:149). This is clearly evident in the following statement made by an advocate of the legislation of elective abortion: ". . . it is to the educated and influential that we must look for effecting rapid legislative change, in spite of conservative opinion among important subgroups . . ." (Blake, 1971:548). Aid to those who are less favorably situated in the social scale and who have less power to control their destinies is also intended by the proponents of the restrictive legal position; a fairly clear implication of this stance, by whichever side, is the view that the "morally inferior" are in need of "guidance."

Because the moral crusader "is more concerned with ends than means, he frequently relies on the advice of experts [in drafting legislative proposals]" (Becker, 1963:150). Thus, crusaders on both sides of the abortion issue have marshalled the theories and findings of experts in various fields in support of their respective arguments and the legislation which they propose.

"Crimes without Victims" and the Latent Functions of Law

Another sociologist, Edwin Schur, has commented that ". . . abortion relates significantly to many questions of policy, pattern and process which should be of interest to the sociologist. . . . It seems surprising that a topic which so clearly invites sociological analysis has received relatively little attention in sociological journals" (1955:94). Over a decade later, Finner and Gamache (1969:1) noted that "induced abortion, as a sociological phenomenon, has received relatively little attention." Indeed, it appears that by far the majority of the popular and academic literature on the topic is polemical; and within the social sciences, only a handful of investigators have devoted extensive study to the subject.

Schur has characterized abortion as one of several "victimless crimes," in that it essentially involves "the willing exchange, among adults, of strongly demanded but legally proscribed goods and services" (Schur, 1965:169). As a result of this strain between norms and laws, enforcement of restrictive laws has been sporadic, and corruption is facilitated. In addition, the self-image of the deviant (the pregnant woman seeking an abortion) may be adversely affected to a significant degree by the criminalization of her behavior by the law, and secondary crime may result from her desperate need to finance the operation.

Some of the concepts discussed in his earlier book, *Crimes Without Victims* (1965) are further developed in Schur's later analysis (1968) of the social dysfunctions of restrictive abortion laws. These include: the dangers of illegal abortions; the problems caused by socio-economic differentials among the "deviants" (access to abortion is directly related to a woman's socio-economic status); and the socio-psychological impact which may result from the fact that criminal law has been applied in an area of private morality. Ball (1967), in his ethnographic study of an [illegal] abortion clinic, noted the deliberate emphasis on medical procedure or the rhetoric of "legitimization" (which may be compared with the rhetoric of "criminalization" resulting from restrictive laws) in the treatment of the patients, an attempt to minimize the patient's anxiety and allay any feelings of regret or guilt.

While abortion *per se* may be considered a victimless crime, according to Rossi (1966), restrictive abortion laws do have victims to whom too little attention has been paid. Rossi has suggested that most Americans are unwilling to face the reason for which the majority of women seek abortions: because a child is not wanted. Confronting this fact "goes counter to the expectation that women are nurturant, loving creatures who welcome every new possibility of adding a member to the human race" (Rossi, 1966:7). In a similar vein, a Houston psychiatrist has wondered whether women themselves are not the victims of the stringent abortion laws, if it is possible "that the pregnant woman symbolizes the proof of male potency and that if we loosen our rule over women and grant them the right to dispose of that proof when *they* want to, we men feel terribly threatened lest women can at will rob us of the proof of our potency and masculinity?" (White, quoted in Worden, 1972:13-14). An earlier statement provides a partial response to this question: "Legal prohibitions can have the effect of forcing women to bear unwanted children and, in this sense, be means to further women's subservient social status in an age when emancipation of women is a major cultural theme" (Johnson, 1969:336-337).

THE ABORTION PROBLEM AS A SOCIAL MOVEMENT

Although we will not attempt a comprehensive historical treatment of the abortion movement in the United States, it is important to trace briefly its legal and social backgrounds. Abortion was not considered a punishable offense in English common law until "quickening" of the fetus had occurred; and even after quickening, it was at first regarded only as a misdemeanor (Tietze and Lewit, 1969). In the United States, the replacement of this common law by specific legislative prohibitions was gradual and "fragmentary until well after the Civil War" (Lader, 1966: 85 ff.). This change was the legal expression of two ideological streams: (1) mid-19th-century humanitarianism: "governments were playing an increasing role in the protection of the health and safety of their citizens"; and (2) the mid- and late-century Victorian puritanical influence seen, for example, in the passage of the Comstock Act in 1873, which included prohibitions against mailing or advertising through the mails abortifacient or contraceptive drugs or devices, and against their manufacture or sale in the District of Columbia and federal territories. In the years following, state laws modeled on this federal statute were passed in rapid succession. According to Lader (1966), the inheritance of the Victorian era was a "tangle of laws" on abortion, with the now-outmoded objectives of expanding population, banishing sin and sexual immorality, and "protecting" women from charlatans who passed themselves off as competent physicians capable of performing safe abortions.

Before discussing in more detail the major organizations and processes contributing to the institutionalization of the movement, let us consider briefly some susceptibility factors within the social milieu which have been conducive to the growth and development of the movement. Although it has been proposed that the Finkbine case (see below) was a precipitating factor, a combination of societal elements has contributed to the movement's growth and development.

Already mentioned as one such factor is the growing women's movement—especially in regard to its emphasis upon a woman's right to control her own body and reproductive processes. "Indeed, freedom of abortion—and hence control over maternity—has, at times, been considered to be the touchstone of a complete emancipation of women . . ." (Schur, 1968:145). Lader (1971:51) concurred: "The nationwide campaign to give every woman the right of choice in childbearing through legalized abortion [is] possibly the crucial feminine issue of this decade."

The increasing prominence of the issue of abortion also has been a result of the growing openness in sexual discussion throughout American society (Rossi, 1969). Further, Schur (1968:145) noted "broad and complex patterns of social change" behind "the development of an increasingly liberal outlook on abortion in our society." Among these patterns are new norms governing fertility and the social roles of women, and also a growing disapproval of applying criminal law to matters of private morality. This, in turn, is related to the growing tendency for other, more serious crimes to consume the quota of deviance issues to which we can give our attention at a given time. For Schur, the hallmark of all of these changes is increased free choice for the individual. Bell (1971) and Callahan (1970) have also seen here a reflection of a normative shift from institutional to individual responsibility.

A final factor which has facilitated the reform/repeal movement deserves mention. Growing collective concern about overpopulation and the depletion of our natural resources has led to increasing approval of the option of abortion in the absence of any foolproof method of birth control (short of sterilization). Abortion, in fact, figured significantly among the major issues considered by the Presidential Commission on Population Growth and the American Future (1972).

The Reform Movement

Incipiency

Significantly, abortion did not loom as a widely discussed problem until what [demographer] Judith Blake describes as the "reproductive renaissance" of the 1946-1960 era came to an end. By the 1960s fourth or fifth pregnancies that had been welcomed by so many American couples in the preceding two decades, were no longer desired. (Rossi, 1969:342)

While it is impossible to trace the origins of the movement to ease the restrictions on abortion laws in any definitive sense, it appears that its first stirrings were perhaps signaled by the Planned Parenthood Federation's conference on abortion in 1955, a condensed report of which has been edited by Calderone (1958). While there had been even earlier discussions of the problem (in a book on abortion by Taussig in 1936 and at a 1942 conference held under the auspices of the National Committee on Maternal Health), the intervention of World War II postponed the possibility of taking any positive action. Planned Parenthood's call for a model abortion law was eventually answered by the 1962 American Law Institute (ALI) Model Penal Code, the provisions of which include the following:

Justifiable Abortion. A licensed physician is justified in terminating a pregnancy if he believes there is substantial risk that continuance of the pregnancy would gravely impair the physical or mental health of the mother or that the child would be born with grave physical or mental defect, or that the pregnancy resulted from rape, incest, or other felonious intercourse. All illicit intercourse with a girl below the age of 16 shall be deemed felonious for purposes of this Subsection. Justifiable abortions shall be performed only in a licensed hospital except in case of emergency when hospital facilities are unavailable. . . . (American Law Institute, 1962)

Coalescence

These events comprise the inception of the movement to reform abortion laws, but the precipitating incident, which appears to have led to the movement's coalescence, was the tragic experience of a Phoenix family.

In July, 1962, Mrs. Sherri Finkbine had been scheduled to have an abortion approved by a medical board, after discovering that she had inadvertently taken the drug thalidomide (which had caused the deformity of thousands of infants throughout Europe and Great Britain when taken by the mother in the early stages of pregnancy). Before the operation, Mrs. Finkbine impulsively reported the story to an Arizona newspaper, motivated by a desire to warn other women of the potential danger of thalidomide. The newspaper account triggered a barrage of adverse national publicity, which resulted not only in "hate-mail" directed at the Finkbine family, but also in the cancellation of the scheduled abortion. The Finkbines finally resorted to obtaining the desired abortion in Sweden, although not without some delay. Collective concerns of various kinds were mobilized across the nation. While Schur (1965) noted that the experience of the Finkbines produced tremendous concern throughout the United States over the inadequate testing of drugs, he concluded that it led to "surprisingly little pressure for the reform of American abortion laws. Apparently there was but slight dismay that a respectable mother of four should be required to go to another country to obtain socially and legally sanctioned medical help" (Schur, 1965:12). In retrospect, however, it appears that the projection of one family's ordeal into national prominence did, in fact, have a significant impact on the coalescence of the abortion-reform movement, even if it did not bring legitimacy to abortion-reform advocates.

From the early 1960's on, pressure mounted for reform of restrictive abortion laws, as called for by the ALI Model Code. During the mid-1960's, the issue became, in Ross and Staines' (1972) terms, "salient" (though not yet legitimate) as a result of increasing attention drawn to the subject in the mass media (publication of books, magazine and newspaper articles, editorials, and even television documentaries). The Finkbine case was referred to by several authors writing on the topic of the abortion problem during this period (e.g., Schur, 1965; Lader, 1966; Rossi, 1967), and interviews with the Finkbines were featured widely in the media.

Institutionalization

The erosion of restrictive abortion statutes began in 1967, with the passage of Colorado's reform law (based on the ALI Model Code), sometimes characterized as an "abortion on demand" law. This probably marked the start of the stage of institutionalization of the reform movement. Shortly thereafter, in 1969, NARAL was organized (see page 458), as pressure for repeal of restrictive laws gained legitimacy (Callahan, 1970). Seemingly in response to a spreading reform movement, two anti-abortion groups, the National Right to Life Committee, and Birthright, were both organized in 1968, although a number of these organizations had already been in operation for a few years at the state level. The New York State Right to Life Committee, for example, founded in late 1965, claimed over 500,000 members as of 1972 (Shapiro, 1972). Such forces fighting the liberal trend—in the form of the "right-to-life" countermovement—became increasingly determined to halt the pro-abortion advance as other organizations joined NARAL in the push for repeal. The ensuing struggle marked the entry into the stage of institutionalization for both movements, which adopted strategies and counterstrategies involving political lobbying, rallying for public support, etc. The abortion issue had attained legitimacy at this point (Ross and Staines, 1972) in that a large number of people agreed that a genuine social problem existed, although there were, as we have seen, significant differences between their conceptions of the problem and their proposals for its solution.

Let us turn now to the factors contributing to institutionalization from within the reform movement itself. Lader (1966) cites the San Francisco-based Society for Humane Abortion, founded in the early 1960's, as the first organization to be formed specifically around the abortion issue. The Association for the Study of Abortion (ASA) is, however, a more broadly based, nationwide, non-profit educational organization, founded in 1965 "in recognition of the . . . urgent abortion problem (in the United States)." The goals pursued by this Association are:

- to ascertain and evaluate the attitudes of lay and professional groups toward existing abortion practices;
- to assess the effect of present abortion practices upon the physical, mental, and social well-being of the individual and society as a whole;
- to inform the lay and professional public of the results of these findings;
- to improve understanding of the abortion problem through public meetings and the use of the mass media;
- to cooperate with other individuals, organizations, and agencies in furthering the purposes of the Association.

Both the ASA and NARAL list among their officials an impressive array of professionals in the fields of law, medicine, theology, sociology, social work, and so forth, so that at the national level, most of the leaders of these organizations comprise a kind of professional elite. Leaders of both their state and local affiliates also tend to be professionals, but membership is open to any individual who wishes to support the organization's goals.

While NARAL is also oriented toward distribution of information and serves as a clearinghouse for local groups,* its action-orientation, as contrasted with the more educational ASA, is stated in Article II of the organization's by-laws:

> NARAL, recognizing the basic human right of a woman to limit her own reproduction, is dedicated to the elimination of all laws and practices that would compel any woman to bear a child against her will. To that end, it proposes to initiate and coordinate political, social, and legal action of individuals and groups concerned with providing safe abortions by qualified physicians for all women seeking them regardless of economic status.

NARAL's suggested formula for success is: "Repeal = Public support × Organization + Legislative pressure." To this end, state and local repeal groups are provided by the national organization with a systematic and detailed outline of tactics for winning legal repeal battles, including fact sheets on how to organize, build a support base, and push a bill into law, together with a "Portrait of the Opposition." Even a cursory review of the literature distributed by NARAL shows that the importance of political strategy is well-recognized by this organization.

Armed with the slogan, "Abortion: a woman's right to choose," the Women's National Abortion Action Coalition (WONAAC) began coordinating a national campaign in July, 1971, for "the repeal of all anti-abortion laws and the corollary demands of no forced sterilization and the repeal of all restrictive contraception laws." With affiliates throughout the United States, WONAAC has organized a number of rallies, including the first national abortion rights demonstrations held concurrently in Washington, D.C. and San Francisco in November, 1971. Other women's groups such as NOW (National Organization for Women), WLM (Women's Liberation Movement) and WITCH (Women's International Terrorist Conspiracy from Hell) have employed similar strategies (including lobbying, pickets, petitions, and sit-ins) to express the belief that restrictive abortion laws are unconstitutional. Both WONAAC's membership and the tenor of its campaign and literature are different from those of the more restrained ASA and NARAL. The image projected by WONAAC is that of angry (mostly young), active feminists for whom the abortion rights issue constitutes only one aspect of their struggle to control their own lives. The professionals (physicians, attorneys, etc.) involved in the organization have usually become leaders and spokeswomen. The tone of the *WONAAC Newsletter* issued after the Supreme Court decision was

---

* Both the ASA and NARAL provide reprints of relevant journal and magazine articles, speeches, etc., on request.

still far from subdued. The organization claimed credit for being in the vanguard of the fight which resulted in the Court's decision, but it was noted that "although our victory is sweeping and decisive, the job of winning total control over our reproductive lives is not yet completed" (Mutnick and LaMont, 1973:7). For this reason, as well as the threat of foes of abortion to overturn the Court's decision, WONAAC members and sympathizers were warned of the vital necessity of continuing support for the abortion-rights movement both in the United States and internationally.

In addition to these national organizations which are specifically concerned with the abortion issue, a growing number of other groups began to align themselves with the reform/repeal movement. In *Who Shall Live?* put out by the American Friends Service Committee, position statements issued by a variety of religious groups, professional associations and voluntary organizations are given (1970). In 1967, the House of Delegates of the American Medical Association endorsed reform measures congruent with the ALI Model Code. Other proponents of repeal indicated their feeling that the ALI reform code was inadequate and too restrictive, and it would affect only "the periphery of the social problem" (Hardin, 1968: 246). Thus increasing support was marshalled in favor of repeal of restrictive abortion laws, and as of September, 1972, according to NARAL, no less than 64 national organizations were on record as recommending repeal; among these, to name only a few, were the American Baptist Convention, the American Civil Liberties Union, the American Friends Service Committee, the American Psychiatric Association, the American Public Health Association, the Presidential Citizens Advisory Council on the Status of Women, Planned Parenthood-World Population, and Zero Population Growth (ZPG).* While the National Crime Commission had earlier made recommendations along the lines of liberalization of existing abortion laws in 1966 (Callahan, 1970), further impetus to the gathering momentum of the reform/repeal movement was provided by the majority report of the United States Commission on Population Growth and the American Future (issued in March, 1972), which included the following recommendations:

Therefore, with the admonition that abortion not be considered a primary means of fertility control, the Commission recommends that present state laws restricting abortion be liberalized along the lines of the New York State statute, such abortions to be performed on request by duly licensed physicians under conditions of medical safety.

In carrying out this policy, the Commission recommends:

---

* ZPG, in fact, has a nationwide, computerized data information bank which provides women requesting abortion information with a list of eight to ten doctors and/or clinics in their area, fee information, and other pertinent facts. (There is no charge for this service, although a $5.00 donation is accepted from women who can afford it.) (*Time,* March 15, 1971:64)

That federal, state, and local governments make funds available to support abortion services in states with liberalized statutes.

That abortion be specifically included in comprehensive health insurance benefits, both public and private. (U.S. Commission on Population Growth, 1972:178)

Parallel developments in the legislative sphere included the adoption of laws generally based on the ALI Model Code in 12 states during the period from 1967 to 1972 (U.S. Commission on Population Growth, 1972).

However, the trend was not entirely in the liberal direction: "while in 1970 New York passed a liberal abortion law, the governor of Maryland vetoed one" (Bell, 1971:126); other such examples are given in a *New York Times* article, "Anti-abortion Forces Demonstrate a Growing Influence in State Legislatures across the Country" (June 28, 1972:21). Perhaps the first widely recognized empirical indicator of the strength of the gathering force of the anti-abortion faction was the backlash which occurred in New York state. In May of 1972, two years after its passage, the liberal New York abortion law was repealed by the state assembly, but rescued by the veto against repeal by Governor Nelson Rockefeller. The political potential of the still-controversial issue had been seized by opponents of abortion, including "right-to-life" groups, the Roman Catholic Church, and leaders of the orthodox Jewish groups, who together had mobilized further opposition to the liberal statute. As Shapiro (1972:10-11) put it, Right to Life had a message for New York legislators: "repeal the abortion-reform law or face political extinction."

Of course, the institutionalization of the abortion-reform movement, including its great success in winning support from government sources and in the legal and medical professions, will create a definite possibility of complete co-optation of this movement by the establishment in the next few years, and its subsequent decline. The "stay-on-your-guard" tone of WONAAC, mentioned just above, is a sign of some awareness of this danger, at least among the more militant "central-core" members of the movement. Further, the strength of the counter-movement in the immediate future will depend upon the future of the reform movement itself. The two movements are clearly in a symbiotic relationship, so that the decline and demise of one will most likely bring about a similar outcome for the other. Let us therefore briefly consider the history and development of the counter-movement.

Rise of the Anti-Abortion Counter-Movement

The rise of the abortion counter-movement is an expression of the repressive side of traditional society. It has been a concomitant of the reform movement from the latter's beginnings, and its passage through the stages of incipiency and coalescence are hard to pinpoint. However, an incipiency can be seen in the outraged reaction of many abortion opponents in the Finkbine case as early as 1962, and in some widespread criticism of the ALI proposals at about the same time. Coalescence progressed rapidly in response to the new, more permissive laws in a few of the states in the mid- and late 1960's. In any case, the movement's institutionalization, which seemed to be approaching just prior to the Supreme Court decision of 1973, was set back only temporarily, if at all, by that decision. After its show of strength in New York (which led to the necessity of using a governor's veto to save a liberal abortion law), and prior to a referendum on Michigan's restrictive abortion law, it was reported that:

> The Michigan Catholic Conference and the Right to Life Movement, allied with the Voice of the Unborn, are preparing a last-minute blitz by handbill, radio and TV. Reform spokesmen say the opposition will spend $400,000 to prepare and mail 1,500,000 four-color leaflets to voters. The leaflets show barrels full of fetuses. (Hacker, 1972:4)

Foremost among the organizations opposing abortion is the National Right to Life Committee, founded in 1968 to provide national coordination of allied groups from its headquarters in Washington, D.C. It also distributes various materials advocating the anti-abortion viewpoint. Among Right to Life's literature are color pamphlets picturing fetuses aborted at various stages of gestation. The organization's strategies range from mass mailings of such materials to demonstrations and political pressure in the form of lobbying (as in the instance of the New York State campaign). Rallies stress such themes as The Celebration of Life and The Rights of the Unborn. Although the tactics of the anti-abortion groups are generally similar to those used by pro-abortion groups (letter-writing campaigns, propaganda literature, buttonholing legislators, and so forth), at least one of their techniques has been dramatically different—a resort to grossness and threats. In New York, one assemblyman displayed an aborted fetus in a bottle while making his impassioned plea for repeal of the liberal New York law. The threatening phone calls received by another New York assemblyman who favored the liberal law seem to represent "a common theme" expressed by many legislators in other states who "would like to vote for easier abortions [but who] 'have been terrorized' out of doing so" (*The New York Times,* June 28, 1972:21).

While there are several doctors and attorneys among the officers and on the board of directors of the National Right to Life Committee, "most anti-abortion groups are 'grass-roots' organizations . . . formed in reaction to the move toward more liberal policies on abortion" (*The New York Times,* June 28, 1972:21). Shapiro (1972:10) describes those attending the annual caucus of New York State's Right to Life group as "average middle-class ladies and gentlemen, none of whose names or faces would register at first with the average newspaper reader or television watcher." For example, the founder of the New York State Right to

Life group, Edward Golden, began the movement from his kitchen table "just after the first liberalized abortion proposal drafted by a committee of the American Law Institute was submitted to the [New York] Legislature" (Shapiro, 1972:10). The continuing impetus for such groups has been provided by the increasing pressure for repeal of abortion laws. Golden has denied both Roman Catholic participation in the New York group's formation and Catholic control of the organization, but he has estimated that 85 percent of the members are Catholics, and that "basically [the group's] opposition to abortion comes from the teachings of the Church" (Shapiro, 1972:41). In fact, among the pamphlets distributed by the National Committee are copies of Statements and Declarations on Abortion issued by the National Conference of Bishops, and reprints from such publications as *The Catholic Lawyer*. While members of anti-abortion groups are predominantly Catholic, a small proportion of conservative Protestants and Jews are also to be found among the constituents (*The New York Times,* June 28, 1972:21).

Birthright, another significant organization among those opposed to abortion, was begun in 1968 by a Toronto housewife and mother of seven, Louise Summerhill (Keene, 1970). Birthright offices, which are staffed by trained volunteer counselors, have sprung up in a number of cities in both Canada and the United States since the founding of this group. Dedicated to the slogan "It is the right of every pregnant woman to give birth and the right of every child to be born," the counselors do not provide abortion referral services. Instead, alternatives to abortion are suggested, and the distressed pregnant woman is offered whatever help necessary to carry her pregnancy to term (Burns, 1972). Such services may include anything from counseling, to providing maternity clothes and baby layettes, to placing girls in maternity homes where they may continue their schooling. Like Right to Life, Birthright distributes pamphlets and reprints publicizing its viewpoints. It also advertises widely on billboards and in newspapers, presenting simple messages such as, "Pregnant and Distressed? Call Birthright" (the telephone number of the local center is listed).

Although Birthright also has no formal association with the Catholic Church, its founder, Mrs. Summerhill, is a Roman Catholic, as are many of the Toronto center's volunteers (Keene, 1970). In New York, the Catholic Archdiocese helped implement the Birthright program in that city. Also in New York, Birthright telephones are manned primarily by Right to Lifers, although the two organizations are formally separate (Shapiro, 1972). One significant difference claimed by Birthright is that it "is not a lobby as such" (Kucharsky, 1971:36), so that the group's action is not directed toward legislators but toward reorienting pregnant women considering abortions to consider other alternatives. Birthright's first national conference, held in June, 1972, featured Eunice Kennedy Shriver as the keynote speaker.

Institutionalization of the Counter-Movement

The evidence of nationwide coordination, together with a series of strong statewide campaigns, suggests that the counter-movement had achieved institutionalization by the late 1960's or very early 1970's. Perhaps one of the best indicators of the arrival of both movements at the stage of institutionalization has been the rising volume of their coverage in the mass media, as evidenced, for example, by a count of articles listed in the *Reader's Guide to Periodical Literature*. Going back to the 1950's, only about six articles per year were listed beneath the topic of "abortion," and many of these actually dealt with miscarriage, rather than abortion. By contrast, the articles listed in the same category during the 1960's ranged upward from a dozen annually. By the early 1970's, this number had shot up to more than 50 per year. We should keep in mind, however, that such an assessment provides only a rough approximation because of changes in time periods covered by volumes of the *Reader's Guide* during the dates under consideration, and because of a few duplications in listings as the topic became subheaded in the later years mentioned.

The Decline of the Counter-movement

While both the pro-abortion and the "right-to-life" forces have enjoyed some important successes, we predict that the 1973 Supreme Court decision has sounded the death-knell of the reform movement by adopting its position. Concomitantly, the membership of the counter-movement will gradually experience a feeling of futility and begin turning to other causes, resulting in their fragmentation and eventual demise as a specific movement. For the time being, however, they have reacted strongly to the Supreme Court decision, promising to draft a constitutional amendment in order to "go over the gray heads of these seven old men" (cf. *Newsweek,* February 5, 1973:27). Another tactic being developed by the anti-abortionists is to persuade the courts to define the embryo as viable by definition, and therefore legally a "person," with constitutional rights, from the moment of conception. Pro-abortionists, who have been just as swift in responding to that decision, and aware of the determination of their opposition, have vowed steadfast support for the ruling. The prognosis is not good for the amendment campaign, in view of the massive nationwide support and large congressional majorities that would be necessary for its ratification.

Opponents of abortion, meanwhile, whose "lawmaking efforts appear dead now," even at the state level (Malloy, 1973:3), have expressed a belief that some day the Court's opinion will be reversed by means of a change in the composition of its judges. Pending that day, however, they are devoting themselves to a series of "rear-guard" actions, such as counseling centers and the distribution of educational materials. Following the classical pattern for declining movements, the "pro-life" forces may displace their goals altogether and focus mainly on counseling centers as the most effective form of opposition to abortion for the future. Some of the counter-movement members and leaders have also been advocating a campaign for use of better methods of birth control and more education about contraception as a means of reducing the recourse to abortion. Others in the movement, especially the Roman Catholics, strongly oppose such an effort. Thus some fragmentation has already begun (*The New York Times,* June 28, 1972).

Similar efforts at adaptation, incidentally, are being made by the survivors of the more successful reform movement, the most significant being the opening of abortion clinics. The Planned Parenthood organization, for example, is working toward the establishment of such facilities throughout the United States (*Time,* February 5, 1973:50-51). NARAL's executive director has emphasized his organization's interest in the same project, which would include non-profit referral services, and require high medical standards and the distribution of contraceptive information (Malloy, 1973). Others from the reform/repeal movement will doubtless find new causes altogether. Thus, both movements, to some extent, are already starting to experience the process of decline in the form of displacement and redefinition of goals. (The reader interested in following the on-going struggle between the two movements on a monthly basis will find the *ASA Newsletter* extremely valuable.)

THE LEGACY OF THE ABORTION MOVEMENTS

We began this chapter by considering how abortion has been regarded throughout history, as well as in various contemporary societies. Focusing upon the United States, we have briefly traced the history of "the abortion problem," and we have noted the development of interest groups as a result of opposing definitions of both the problem and the ways in which it might be ameliorated. The reform/repeal movement has been considered the primary movement in our framework (with the ASA, NARAL, and WONAAC as representative organizations); and "right to life" or "pro-life" forces have constituted a counter-movement (with Right to Life exemplifying politically oriented groups and Birthright counseling and education-oriented groups). Until only recently, it might have been predicted—and perhaps quite accurately—that these movements would remain at the stage of institutionalization for some time. With the Supreme Court decision, however, the picture has been radically altered, leading us to predict the imminent decline of both movements.

Just what was the nature of so momentous a decision? The seven-judge majority grounded their opinion in the right of personal privacy guaranteed by the 9th and 14th Amendments, and thereby judged restrictive abortion laws to be unconstitutional. According to the guidelines set by the Court, an abortion decision during the first trimester (12 weeks) of pregnancy is left to a woman and her physician, free of any regulation by government. During the last six months of pregnancy, states are permitted to pass laws related to the health of the pregnant woman, but not to prevent abortion altogether. Only in the last ten weeks of pregnancy, when the fetus is judged to be viable, may states proscribe abortion (except where it may be necessary to preserve the life or health of the mother). However, the right to abortion granted through the Court's decision is not unqualified; the ruling was not tantamount to legalizing abortion "on demand." Private doctors can still refuse to abort private patients without referral. Clinics and hospitals can also refuse unless there are no others within a "reasonable" distance (Weaver, 1973; *Newsweek,* February 5, 1973:27; *Time,* February 5, 1973:50-51).

At the present time, many practical questions are still unanswered, and it is uncertain exactly what implications the Supreme Court decision entails for the laws of individual states. Certainly, those states whose laws permitted abortion only to save the mother's life were, in effect, left without an abortion law when the ruling was handed down. Even the four states which had relatively liberal laws prior to the ruling may have to revise their laws to eliminate any provisions which are inconsistent with the decision.

The Supreme Court decision of 1973 is, clearly, the most important legacy of the two movements we have been considering. At this time it is virtually impossible to foresee all the implications which the Court's majority opinion will have for American society. Even those social commentators who are usually outspoken have remained rather reticent on the subject. Some predictions, however, may be made. Tietze, who has studied the effects of the New York law on abortion patterns and practices, has suggested a number of possible outcomes if "aspects of the New York experience are repeated nationally" (quoted in Malloy, 1973:3). Included among such effects are: an increase in the number of abortions performed; a decline in birth rates and rates of illegitimate births; a decrease in the number of women with dependent children on welfare; lower maternal-mortality and infant-mortality rates; and a stabilized population size in the early part of the 21st century. As abortion becomes more widely available, it is also likely that there will be a significant decrease in the cost of an abortion (this has been found to be the case in New York state; Malloy, 1973). There is also evidence, however, that more frequent abortions may result in more problems of infertility and of premature deliveries (from cervical incompetence) for women who have had abortions.

Beyond the Supreme Court ruling, the reform/repeal movement has had considerable normative impact. Discussion of abortion is no longer regarded as taboo, but instead is considered an acceptable, albeit controversial topic of conversation. Before "abortion on demand" was available in a few states, it became rather fashionable to arrange for an abortion overseas; some agencies, in fact, offered a "travel package" which included a tour of the country (or continent) after a woman had obtained her abortion. Now that abortion will be widely obtainable throughout the United States, the search for the safe abortion will be ended. In addition, the ability of women to exercise greater control over their reproductive lives will have a tremendous significance for the changing role of women in our society.

Chapter 13

Emerging Modes of Marriage

THE SOCIAL CONSTRUCTION OF REALITY

The bride wore nothing. Neither did the groom or, for that matter, the officiating cleric, a minister of the religious-diploma mill known as the Universal Life Church, Inc. The ceremony was as stark as the apparel. Dropping a stick before the couple, the pastor pronounced the legal essentials in mod vernacular: "You're married, so long as you dig it." (*Time*, July 4, 1969:57)

Social Relativity and the Search for Definition

What does that little tableau mean to you? Many of us probably have mixed feelings about it. However, if it makes you feel rather uncomfortable, and produces in you at least a mild revulsion, or fear for the future of the family, then chances are that you are part of that large American public that we shall call "defenders of the traditional family." On the other hand, if you are somewhat delighted by the event (which, of course, actually happened), and feel that it points in the direction of a new, more "enlightened," freer family style, in which each couple can "do its own thing," then we would probably classify you as a part of that other emergent public, the "challengers of the traditional family." This distinction between these two publics is an important one to understand at the outset of our discussion, for the definition of the "problem" in modern family life is dependent upon which of these two publics one listens to.

All of us are at least vaguely aware that there is no one style of family life that is universal and common to all peoples around the world, and we know from talking to our parents and grandparents that what was "proper" in family relationships in the past is no longer considered so. Thus, we find much variation and relativity in modes of family life, both across time and across cultures, and more recently, even across subcultures in our own society, as the above quotation suggests. In parts of the Middle East, a girl is often married by the age of 13, while in Ireland she may be close to 30. In both places, the families of the spouses will have a lot to say about who their children marry, and where, how, and under what conditions. Some Moslem countries permit polygyny, but so did the Mormons in 19th-century America. Divorces were illegal in Italy until only recently, and are still difficult to obtain, while in parts of the United States, new "no-fault" divorce laws state that a marriage can be "dissolved" if only one of the spouses thinks the couple's differences are "irreconcilable." And so it goes: marriage laws and traditions are tremendously varied around the world with respect to number of spouses, age at marriage, kind of marriage rites, means of obtaining divorce or dissolution of marriage (if any), number of children encouraged, whether sexual relations are permitted before (and outside of) marriage, and every other aspect of family life.

One way in which family life in America is especially distinctive is in its relatively large amount of freedom: freedom of choice in marriage partners; predominance of personal factors over economic ones in the selection of spouses; freedom of the nuclear family from obligations to relatives and grandparents; and considerable privacy in living quarters and day-to-day life. Each family member is regarded as an individual who is expected to develop his (her) own preferences and live his (her) own life, rather than to subordinate his (her) life to the welfare of the family as a whole, which is the expectation, for instance, in traditional Japanese families. The weakening of economic interdependence in American family life has led to a special emphasis on affectional ties as the primary bonds holding a family and a marriage together. For this reason, hostility and aggression on the part of family members are probably more disruptive in American families than in families in societies where economic ties are still important in holding the family unit together (Nimkoff, 1965:330–39). In fact, economic arrangements are among the most important determinants of the nature of family bonds around the world. Only those societies that have undergone considerable industrialization and economic development have experienced changes in family life in the same general direction as our own society, toward greater freedom.

This point is emphasized by Winch and Blumberg (1953), although they note that the nuclear family is typical of hunting and gathering societies, as well as of modern industrial societies. It is only at the intermediate level of subsistence—herding and sedentary agriculture—that the extended family system, with many relatives grouped together into one large family unit, is dominant. In a study conducted in the United States, they also found that the degree of isolation of the nuclear family was greater for those families that were geographically mobile, lived in urban places, were Protestant, and had high socioeconomic status. Economic bonds are obviously not the most vital factor holding these families together.

This does not mean, however, that the industrial revolution is the only force responsible for producing this more independent kind of family arrangement. After surveying 60 cultures drawn at random from Murdock's extensive ethnographic atlas, Yehudi A. Cohen (1969) concluded that the political organization of the state was an important factor in determining the way in which sex relations and family relations were controlled. He found that states in which the central ruling bodies have not yet gained complete dominance over local elites tend to have stronger controls over sex relations than do states in which the dominance of the central ruling bodies is more secure. The theory behind these findings is that isolated nuclear families are more easily controlled by the ruling power than are larger kin groups, which usually form the basis of local elite structures. Less centralized states thus maintain and support the nuclear family by having strong laws against adultery, incest, and other kinds of sexual behavior outside of the marital pair.

We see, then, that the definition of the type of family life, or even of the meaning of the term "family" itself, differs from culture to culture, and may be influenced by such divergent factors as economic, political, or social differences. Is it possible, therefore, to come up with a universally valid general definition? According to *Webster's Third New International Dictionary,* marriage is "the institution whereby men and women are joined in a special kind of social and legal dependence for the purpose of founding and maintaining a family" (p. 1384). This kind of definition would satisfy those who hold a traditional view of the family, but it does not include some of the more "far-out" forms of marriage practiced by some of the contemporary "challengers" (e.g., homosexual marriages). Webster's definition also appears to discriminate against childless marriages, though that is not made explicit.

In *The Encyclopedia of Sexual Behavior,* Joseph K. Folson defines the family as "an enduring social group of individuals whose interrelationships are defined primarily by the process of biological reproduction" (1961). Further on in the same publication, M. F. Nimkoff defines marriage as "a social status defining the rights and duties of persons of opposite sex living in a more or less durable union" (1961). Folson's definition would include group marriages, but excludes homosexual and childless marriages. Nimkoff's is a bit more general, including childless and group marriages, but still excluding homosexual marriages (as does the law in the United States so far). Some authors, such as Freeman and Jones (1970), manage to discuss marriage and the family in their texts without ever really pinning down these terms with a formal definition.

As a working definition for this chapter, our definition of the family will include an element of relative permanence, and other essential points such as its existence as a social group, the sharing of everyday life tasks, and the mutuality of psychological support. (In order to be truly inclusive, a definition of the family can no longer include a reference to reproduction.) Following Nimkoff, our definition of marriage is a social status defining the rights and duties of persons living together as spouses.

Definitions of the Problem

Finding agreement on the definition of "family" or "marriage" is perhaps not as difficult as getting people to agree on the definition of what is "wrong" with family life in America, or, in other words, what the "problem" is. The "defenders" of traditional family life tend to see the problem as one of the "decline and fall" of a wholesome family life of the kind enjoyed by our parents and grandparents. (Seldom does anyone question whether our conceptions of earlier family life are realistic, or whether they are somewhat idealized and romanticized.) The "symptoms" of the modern "decline" of the family are seen by its "defenders" as: (1) a constantly increasing divorce rate; (2) an increasing illegitimacy rate; (3) increasing sexual promiscuity before and during marriage; (4) a ready resort to abortion; (5) a shrinking family size (or even childlessness); and (6) an increase in the number of working mothers. The latter two points are taken by the "defenders" to indicate a decline in "motherhood" or in general family-centered values.

For the "challengers" to traditional family life, on the other hand, the "symptoms" of the "oppressiveness" of family norms and expectations in our society are: (1) the difficulties and bitterness that usually characterize divorce proceedings in most states; (2) the stigma which society places on "illegitimate" children, who should not even be treated as a separate category on our records; (3) the laws and social restrictions that make it difficult for consenting adults to do as they please in sexual matters; (4) the traditional laws against abortion, which ought to be a matter solely for a woman and her doctor to decide (or, since the Supreme Court decision legitimizing abortion, the complaint of the "challengers" has been against those citizens and legislators who want to restore the earlier laws); and (5) the expectations on the part of society that a "woman's place is in the home," that "working mothers" are not good mothers, and that the only "normal" or "decent" family is one with children, preferably more than one.

Parameters of Consensual Reality

To what extent do our "statistics" or other official measurements of reality bear out the fears and allegations of the "defenders" or the "challengers?" In some ways, of course, both sides can support their claims statistically, since the question is not only one of what the statistics "say," but also what they "mean," and the meaning is likely to be imposed by the point of view that each side brings with it. Furthermore, statistics can be gathered with only a specific group(s) in mind, or they may take on a whole new meaning when compared with statistics from an earlier period. Take divorce, for example (or "dissolution," as it is now called in some of the more "liberal" states): There are various ways to present the "statistics" on divorce, some of which are based on the calculation of the number of divorces per 1,000 women, or per 1,000 people, etc. In the early 1970's, for example, there were 4.1 divorces per 1,000 people in the United States (*Monthly Vital Statistics Report,* 1973), a figure that was considerably higher than it had been in the 1950's, but no higher than in the 1940's. A more meaningful figure, perhaps, is the ratio of divorces to marriages, which has risen in recent years to about one in three (Goode, 1971:482), though there is considerable variation in that figure from one place to another, and from one group to another. Again, the ratio is scarcely higher, if at all, than it was in the late 1940's. Actually, overall for the past generation, the divorce rate, however it is figured, has fluctuated very little. It was relatively high in the '40's and early '70's, relatively low in the '50's and early '60's, but even those peaks and valleys have not been very severe. Before judging, however, whether any divorce rate is "high" or "low," "bad" or "good," we must keep in mind a number of relevant facts and considerations: (1) The divorce rate has been rising steadily in virtually all industrialized or "western" countries in recent years, so it is questionable whether the rate in the United States is unusually high (Goode, 1963). (2) The great majority of people who get divorced do not stay divorced; they remarry (Udry, 1971). In fact, in the early 1970's, only 3 percent of the adult population in the United States was currently divorced (i.e., not remarried) (*Monthly Vital Statistics Report,* 1973). (3) Finally, a divorce rate, whatever it is, does not tell us much about the *quality* of marriage relationships; couples who do not get divorced are not necessarily staying together out of happiness or satisfaction. A great many homes or marriages may be "broken" in actual fact, but remain legally intact for the benefit of "appearances," or "for the children," or for any number of reasons. This was even more likely to have been the case in earlier generations, when divorces were harder to get and more frowned upon by public opinion. So we cannot conclude, just because earlier generations may have had lower divorce rates, that their marriages were any happier (Gurin, Veroff, and Feld, 1960; Cuber and Harroff, 1965).

With respect to "fatherless" homes and illegitimacy, which are often issues related to the divorce rate, official statistics show that both parents are present in 87 percent of American families (*Statistical Abstract of the United States,* 1970: 38); and that about one in 15 births is illegitimate (Ventura, 1969). There are some differences in the figures, however, both for fatherlessness and illegitimacy according to race. About 8 percent of Caucasian families have been fatherless for the last 20 or 30 years, with little fluctuation in the rate during that period, while in black families there has been no father living at home in around 20 percent of the cases, and this rate has been steadily increasing over this same time period. Similarly, illegitimacy may run as high as one birth in three in the ghetto areas of the country, with many cases of "repeaters"—i.e., mothers who repeatedly produce illegitimate children (Ventura, 1969; *U.S. News & World Report,* 1966 and 1967). Such differences in rates of fatherlessness and illegitimacy, however, are probably really social-class differences rather than racial ones, since black Americans are disproportionately found in the lower classes, where historically most illegitimacy has occurred.

The issue of sexual relations outside of marriage (both premarital and extramarital) has provoked much public interest and discussion in recent years, but, because this tends to be a very personal matter, there is very little extant reliable data on what proportions of men and women actually engage in sex outside of marriage. Research done by Kinsey in the late 1940's and early 1950's found that a majority of males at that time, and a rather large minority of females as well, admitted in their interviews that they had had premarital sexual intercourse, though for many of these, especially the women, the intercourse had occurred only with partners who later became their spouses (Kinsey, 1953). One wonders whether, in the generations since the one studied by Kinsey, the incidence of premarital sex is any higher, or whether there is just more openness in discussing sexual matters, especially among youth; this latter explanation has been suggested by Reiss (1967). In a July, 1972, Gallup poll, 63 percent of American college students admitted to having had premarital sex.

A practice that may be more common among youth now than in the past is nonmarital "cohabitation" or "shacking up." We call it "nonmarital," rather than premarital, because it does not necessarily involve any assumptions about eventual marriage, either to each other or to anyone else. Figures on this practice are also difficult to find, but estimates from census data indicate that more than 143,000 unmarried people (of all ages) were cohabitating without marriage in 1970 (only about 0.072 percent), almost 10 times the 1960 census estimate (Safire, 1973). The percentage might be a lot higher for certain populations (e.g., college students), especially when compared to the previous decade, but on a subject which most people consider somewhat delicate and private, it is difficult to be very sure of any figures.

Extramarital sex, like premarital sex, has been with us a long time. Kinsey's estimates indicate that around 1950 half of the married men in America, and about a quarter of the married women, admitted to at least one extramarital affair (Goode, 1963:367; and Kinsey, 1965:426-437). One fairly recent study (Cuber and Harroff, 1965) suggests that extramarital affairs are both more common and more tolerated among what they call "significant Americans" (i.e., the upper-middle class) than among most others. Neubeck (1969) indicates, however, that extramarital affairs tend to be rather short-lived, about half of them lasting less than a year and two-thirds less than three years. If "shacking up" is a relatively new development in premarital (or nonmarital) sex, then the newest form of extramarital sex may be the practice known as "swinging," sometimes called "mate-swapping," which may involve two couples or more. Some estimates of the incidence of "swinging" (impossible to verify) go as high as 8-million people (Bartell, 1971; Gilmartin and Kusisto, 1973; Varni, 1972; and Denfield and Gordon, 1970). The chief distinction between this behavior and the more traditional kind of extramarital sex is that in "swinging" both spouses participate with the knowledge and approval of each other, so that no deception is involved; thus it is sometimes called "comarital" intercourse, indicating that it exists alongside of marriage and without any threat to it. However, it is very debatable whether "swinging" is in fact any more "healthy and open," or any less a threat to marriage, than the traditional kind of extramarital sex. "Swingers" have reported that jealousy remains a big problem for them, and it is not uncommon for the practice to precipitate (though not necessarily to *cause*) divorces between "swinging" couples (Gilmartin and Kusisto, 1973).

The "decline and fall of motherhood," a process which some have claimed is taking place in our society, is another of those unsettled questions about modern family life. Motherhood has both a biological and a social aspect. Biologically, there is the question of childbearing itself: Are mothers indeed having fewer children now than formerly? If so, is that a fact to be deplored or applauded? And however many children mothers are having (or not having), what are the "acceptable" means of regulating the frequency of childbirth, or of preventing it altogether? Contraception? Abortion? The social aspect of motherhood has to do with the way in which a mother acts out this social role. Does she create a more "healthy" family life by having one or two children, or by having many? If she has a greater or smaller number, what are the implications of her decision for society at large? Is a continuing "baby boom" a good thing for the economy, or a threat to the survival of the whole species? If a mother has children, should she renounce any career of her own outside the home, in order to be with her children "full-time," or can she reconcile a career with being a mother, just as her husband does with being a father? It is apparent from these questions that important matters of a moral nature are as much at issue as the "facts" themselves.

Some of the questions raised above are important only for certain segments or subcultures of our society; contraception of one kind or another, for example, though practiced by nearly all American couples, whatever their religious commitments, is an important issue only for Roman Catholics and for certain small conservative Protestant bodies. Some of the other questions, such as the "liberation" of women's roles inside and outside of the home, or the issue of abortion, are explored at considerable length in other chapters, so we will not dwell on them here. We might report, however, that many wives and mothers do have jobs outside the home, and have had for a long time. Statistics from the Bureau of Labor show that women have comprised about one-third of the entire labor force of the nation since at least World War II. Looked at another way, we can say that the proportion of married women employed outside the home has gradually increased from about 25 percent in 1950, to 30 percent in 1960, to 40 percent in 1970 (*Statistical Abstract of the United States,* 1970). Even among mothers with children under six years old, 28 percent are employed. The "working mother" is clearly a fact of modern life. Whether that makes her less adequate or successful as a mother is open to debate. One pair of family experts has argued, with evidence, that it does not (Nye and Hoffman, 1963). In any case, to portray the family of "the good old days" as one in which mother stayed home with the children and father went out into the world is an inaccurate and romanticized picture. The distinction between "men's work" and "women's work" may actually have been less clear in the past than it is in the present. Men and women in past centuries usually worked together, often side-by-side in the fields, to make their farms produce, and as industrialization developed in early America, women provided much of the labor in the factories (and, for that matter, so did children). In short, the "working mother" is not a new phenomenon, and an interesting question for the sociologist is why that reality should have come to be regarded by some as "a problem" just now.

Whatever may be new, however, about styles of marriage and family life, or about sexual customs, there is certainly no reason to believe that the good old standard marriage is on the way out. Three-fourths of all Americans over the age of 13 are currently married, and many of the remainder either have been married (and widowed or divorced) or probably will be married. Furthermore, young people are still in a considerable hurry to get married, for the median ages of marriage in the United States are only 21 for the bride and 23 for the groom. Since men are the more frail sex, however, and are dying at a faster rate than women in all age groups, the women are more likely to be left spouseless as time goes on. By age 75, three-fourths of American women have been widowed, as compared to only one-third of the men (*Monthly Vital Statistics,* 1973; and *Statistical Abstract of the United States,* 1970).

While Americans are thus still very much "the marrying kind," they have not been producing as many children per family lately as they did in the 1940's and 1950's, and so there has been a "decline in family life," at least from the point of view of numbers. Our birth rate is now below 15 children per 1,000 people annually, the lowest it has been in about 40 years. At the beginning of the 1970's,

34 percent of all American families had only two members (i.e., either a parent and a child, or just the two parents), 21 percent had only three members, and the remainder of the families (45 percent) had four or more members. Clearly, more than half of families do not have more than two children (*Monthly Vital Statistics,* 1973; and *Statistical Abstract of the United States,* 1970). More information on birth rates and number of children will be given later in the chapter on population.

Public Opinion

Although official and scientific data such as those cited above can give us an approximate picture of what is actually happening in the world of marriage, sex, and the family, there is still the separate but important question of what people think about what is happening. It is out of such public and collective beliefs that social problems and other social movements are born. One very clear indication of such beliefs (besides poll data, which we shall examine presently) can be found in the popular magazines, and perhaps there is no magazine more typical of the tastes of "middle America," or what has been called "the average American," than the *Reader's Digest*. The May, 1970, issue, for example, carried an article about marriage which pointed up the importance of mutual sensitivity in verbal exchanges between spouses. The following month the same magazine had an article about the functions of jealousy in marriage, and how it should be handled. The important assumption underlying all these articles is the necessity of the survival of traditional marriage and family life, an assumption no doubt taken for granted by virtually all of its readers.

Another popular magazine with a "middle-America" readership, *Better Homes and Gardens,* in 1972 attempted to report what its readers believed about marriage and the family. As a basis for this report, the magazine solicited and received the opinions of an unsystematic but rather large sample of 350,000 Americans. Most of the respondents said that they believed that the traditional family was in great difficulty, due to such powerful threats as materialism, permissive parenthood, drugs, and loose attitudes about sex and divorce (Lindberg, 1972). About three-fourths of all respondents to this magazine survey felt that the traditional roles of wife and mother were "fulfilling," that a working wife was not good for family life, and that most of the couples they knew were happy in their marriages. Even larger majorities favored family planning, and thought that better birth-control methods contributed to marital adjustment. These opinions are not too different from what more systematic poll data tend to show, but on the other hand, 40 percent of these respondents were in favor of legalizing abortion, 26 percent were in favor of unmarried cohabitation, and a mere 2 percent believed that extra-marital sex could contribute to happiness in a marriage. In giving their opinions on why marriages failed, 65 percent of the magazine readers mentioned immaturity,

48 percent pointed to selfishness, 39 percent to financial problems, and 37 percent to a lack of mutual interests or goals.

We may have greater confidence in these findings than we have in other non-random or unsystematic surveys, because of the large number of respondents. There is really no substitute, however, for the surveys and polls that are carried out by professionals using careful and scientific sampling techniques, such as those used by Roper, Gallup, and others. These surveys are frequently reported in the popular media, although they are not conducted by the media. A few years ago, the Roper Public Opinion Corporation published the results of a survey in the *Saturday Evening Post* that was partly comparable to one they had done some 30 years earlier (Brown, 1966). They found that Americans in general were still strongly behind the traditional concept of the family. Three-quarters of the respondents thought that it was realistic for a husband and a wife to love each other throughout their lives, and a similar proportion disapproved of adultery no matter what the circumstances. Five out of every six bachelors and two out of every three single women planned to marry some day. A slight majority felt that both husbands and wives should be virgins before marriage. These proportions were very similar to those reported in a 1973 Roper poll. The only significant change was a greater leniency expressed about divorce in the more recent poll.

Probably the most prominent of the polling organizations is the Gallup Public Opinion Research Corporation, which publishes *The Gallup Opinion Index* monthly. There have been a number of Gallup polls since the mid-1960's that have included questions on the family, or on sexual behavior. A 1969 poll found that a slight majority of Americans had seen or read anything that they thought was objectionable dealing with sex on television, in the movies, or in print. There was little difference between men and women on this question, but there was a considerable difference by region. People from the West were much less likely to find something objectionable than were people from the East or the Midwest, while people from the South were the most likely to find something offensive (Gallup, 1969, #49).

In 1970, Gallup did an extensive comparison of the opinions of men and women on a variety of family-related issues. Only a few questions yielded large differences between the sexes. About two-thirds of both women and men felt that there was no significant discrimination against women in the United States. A majority of both men and women were in favor of making divorce more difficult to obtain than it currently was, of setting up government-funded day-care centers for children, of passing stricter laws against sending pornography through the mails, of abstaining from premarital sexual intercourse, of permitting legal abortions where the mother's health or a deformed child were involved, and of allowing sterilization operations under a variety of conditions (Gallup, 1970, #63).

Two Gallup polls carried out in 1972 showed a similar picture. Offense at pornography was still strong among the respondents, as was disapproval of premarital sex. Considerable support was found for sex education in the public schools, and for the liberalization of abortion laws. There were noticeable differences of opinion on these issues by age, however, with people age 30 and over being much more conservative in their views than those under 30. Particularly striking were the responses of college students: 72 percent of male and 55 percent of female college students held that premarital coitus was not wrong, and about three-quarters of both male and female respondents did not think it important that they marry virgins. Nearly half of the females and three-quarters of the males indicated that they had already had sexual intercourse, with the percentage rising steadily from the freshman to the senior category (Gallup, 1972, #85 and #87).

These latter figures are supported, in more detail, by the 1971 surveys of Daniel Yankelovich reported in his book, *The Changing Values on Campus*. He found that only 25 percent of his sample of college students viewed casual premarital sexual relations as morally wrong. Having an abortion was seen as wrong by 26 percent, extramarital sexual relations by 57 percent, "swinging" by 59 percent, and having children without a formal marriage arrangement by only 42 percent. Approximately one-third of the students considered marriage obsolete, a significant rise over 1969 (about one-fifth), and a similar percentage expressed a willingness to try living in a commune. Nevertheless, a strong majority was looking forward to being married, was interested in having children, and believed that the traditional family structure still worked (Yankelovich, 1972).

An even more recent poll released by Gallup showed that the proportion of Americans favoring large families was at the lowest point in the organization's 37 years of polling history. Only one adult in five said that the ideal number of children in a family was four or more, compared with twice that number of large-family supporters just six years ago. The decline in preference for large families was greatest among women and among Roman Catholics, though both of these groups still favored large families slightly more than did the general population (Gallup, 1973, #92).

What do all of these figures mean? It is clear that the vast majority of Americans are still very much in favor of the continuation of the traditional American family. The "liberalization" of attitudes regarding marital and sexual behavior that has occurred across all segments of the population has seldom represented a threat to the fundamentals of our family system. The only serious challenges to traditional family outlooks have come from college students, who may change some of their views when they are older.

CHAMPIONS AND THEIR INTERESTS

As we indicated at the beginning of this chapter, those having an interest in "family problems" in our society can be divided into two main publics: the "defenders" of traditional family life, and the "challengers" of traditional family life. Both publics would feel both comfort and alarm on reading the various statistics we have just reviewed on the social "realities" of family life. Both are fairly large and amorphous publics made up of a variety of organized and semi-organized groups focusing on special interests. Let us first examine the main elements of the "defenders" public, and then we will look at the "challengers" in a similar fashion.

The Defenders of Traditional Family Life

Psychological Publics

Whenever a traditional institution seems to be undergoing change, or is being somehow called into question, as traditional family life is today, there are likely to be certain segments of the population who feel personally threatened by the ferment. Generally, these are people who have invested a great deal of time, effort, and personal commitment in helping to maintain the status quo. To attack (or even seriously question) the status quo is to attack those things for which they personally have stood, perhaps for many years. Nowhere is there a better example of this psychological phenomenon than in those who have given years of their lives in conscientiously acting out the roles of the "good father," or the "good mother," the "good wife," or the "good husband," as these roles were traditionally defined. Since commitments of these kinds are likely to have been more total and higher in priority for women than for men, the public we are talking about here is perhaps most likely (but by no means exclusively) to be found among middle-aged and older women. These women see themselves as having devoted the greater part of their lives to their husbands and their children, and they are now being told, in effect, by the challengers of such traditions, that they have done the wrong thing all these years: that they allowed themselves to be confined too much to the home; that they should have had careers of their own; that they should not have had so many children; and perhaps also that their marital fidelity was neither necessary nor especially virtuous. From their social context, we can understand why these "solid mothers and fathers of middle America" resist the new sex-role definitions, and the new styles of family life being advocated by the "challengers." Their resistance is far more profound than obstinate adherence to tradition for tradition's sake; it is a defense, sometimes a desperate one, of their own self-concepts, and of the source of their feelings of self-worth. Small wonder that a conscientious and self-sacrificing middle-aged mother, for example, would argue against the notion that motherhood is no longer very important for society; or that, in her own family life, she might develop what Pauline Bart (1970:70) has called "the Jewish mother syndrome" (whether she is Jewish or not), characterized by ". . . rigidity, a need to be useful in order to feel worthwhile, obsessive-compulsive supermother, superhousewife behavior, and generally conventional attitudes." Certainly some of the widespread defense of conventional forms of marriage and family life in our society today springs from such deep psychological and emotional interests.

Moral and Religious Publics and Interest Groups

Many of the interest groups among the "defenders" are religiously and/or morally motivated. Chief among the "defenders," in fact, are the conservative churches, not only Protestant, but also Roman Catholic and Latter-Day Saints (Mormon). Some denominations (including the Catholics and the Mormons) have launched special programs aimed at strengthening and promoting traditional family life among their members, and in society as a whole. In recent years many issues of the conservative Protestant magazine, *Christianity Today,* have carried articles defending traditional teachings about marriage and the family, using both theological and social arguments. Even at the height of the "Age of Aquarius," *Christianity Today* carried an article on adultery that left its readers no doubt about the position of conservative Christianity:

Sex, like life itself, is a gift of God. Like life, however, it is to be conducted within certain limits. Failure to observe these limits entails consequences. To exceed life's boundary brings death . . . the death or at least the degeneration of the marriage is brought on . . . by adultery. (1969:35-36)

Similar sentiments are frequently heard in the sermons of well-known evangelists, such as Billy Graham.

Such moral entrepreneurship and guardianship over the values of traditional family life are not only found among religious spokesmen. The views of the traditionalists also find wide expression in the mass media, particularly in the so-called "women's magazines" such as *Ladies Home Journal, Good Housekeeping, McCall's Magazine,* and in the various "family magazines" such as *Reader's Digest.* Syndicated newspaper columns, like those of Ann Landers, "Dear Abby," and Dr. Joyce Brothers, also regularly advocate moral positions that clearly constitute defenses of the ideals of the "good old-fashioned American family." Even high school and college textbooks have not been free of traditional moral biases in treating the subjects of marriage and the family, as we shall see later on. It would be fair to say, in fact, that advocates of the traditional family have had a virtual monopoly on what the media (including television) have to say on marriage- and family-related topics, since they have the power to determine what is "good taste." Unconventional notions are likely to appear only in such "far-out" publications as *Playboy* or *Cosmopolitan*.

Economic and Political Interest Groups and Publics

Interest groups and publics which defend traditional family life in order to protect strictly economic and political vested interests are rather hard to identify, largely because both the political and economic establishments in our society are already so oriented toward traditional definitions of marriage and the family that private or separate groups are hardly necessary. Politicians all pay their respects to the "family as the basic unit of society," or they fail to do so at their political peril. Until recently, a divorce in a politician's past was considered a political handicap, and a divorce while in office an even more serious public-relations problem. "Families of America," "the home," motherhood, and children have always been highly valued institutions in our political rhetoric. The official political bias in favor of large families is nowhere more tellingly expressed than in the income-tax exemption or allowance which for generations Congress has granted to the taxpayer for each dependent or increase in family size. Under this provision of the tax law, a "breadwinner" can deduct from his or her taxable income several hundred dollars for each parent and each child, a provision which, in effect, rewards large families at the expense of smaller ones. The tax savings for married couples who file a "joint return" is another provision in the law which favors the traditional institution of marriage. With biases of these kinds already "built into" the political thinking of legislators and public officials, there is hardly any need for special "pressure groups" to promote family interests.

Our economic institutions, too, depend upon the persistence of the conventional American family, although there are no actual pressure groups in the business world which specifically devote themselves to furthering this institution. Life-insurance companies, toy manufacturers, home builders, and a variety of other industries have a considerable stake in the perpetuation of traditional family life, and advertisers have recently been criticized for underhandedness in "getting at" mothers through the commercials directed at children during television cartoon shows. Actually, the appeal of a great deal of the advertising in television, radio, magazines, and so forth, is based on family values, family togetherness, and family stability. It is not necessary to postulate a conspiracy theory about American business to be aware of the kind of support which it subtly (and not so subtly) gives to the institutions of traditional marriage and the family in the normal course of "doing business." It is also well known that American industry favors a very traditional kind of wife and home life for its male executives, and that more than one man has failed to advance in his career despite his abilities because he did not have the "right kind" of wife, or because she did not behave in the manner expected of company wives. A generation ago, William H. Whyte, Jr., laid out the "rules" for "Mrs. Executive" to follow for her husband's good in a series of *Life* and *Fortune* articles in 1955, some of which were later included in his well-known book, *The Organization Man* (1956). To be sure, the women's movement and other forces for social change have made some modifications in the picture Whyte presented, but much of it still survives.

Occupational Interest Groups

Certain occupations or professions are, in effect, devoted to maintaining and improving traditional forms of marriage and the family, and therefore they automatically receive both practical and ideological support from the efforts of their professional organizations or associations. We are referring here to family-life educators and marriage (or family) counselors. The former group is found on the faculties of high schools and colleges, and these educators write textbooks on family living. They are frequently the same people who in part make up the scientific interest groups discussed below, and it is apparent from the content of their books and courses that most of them have a strong (and doubtless sincere) bias in favor of traditional family life. Their growing importance as an influence in society and as an interest group is indicated by the enormous increase during the past generation of marriage- and family-life course enrollments and textbook sales (Horton and Leslie, 1965:220-222).

While family-life educators work mainly in educational institutions, many family counselors are found either in social-work agencies or in private practice (or both), and others can also be found in the counseling centers on college campuses. There is little data or objective evidence available that would enable us to evaluate whether such counselors provide any help in solving family problems (Horton and Leslie, 1965:222-223), but the mere fact that the profession of family counselor has grown so prominent, and that they are included on the staffs of public agencies and institutions, indicates the existence of a publicly and officially defined "need" for them and for the traditional interests which they represent.

Scientific Interest Groups

In recent years, medical and social scientists have appeared in increasing numbers in the camp of the "challengers," but for the most part such scientists have given their weight instead to the support of the "defenders" of traditional family life. Both in their textbooks and in their scientific articles, they have tended to equate "normal" family life with "traditional" family life, and to consider variations as somewhat pathological (or at least deviant), and in need of explanation. Their standard of normal and desirable is the "stability" of a family, that is, its maintenance during at least the child-rearing period. They do not seem to consider seriously the possibility that some marriage relationships might better be terminated, regardless of the stage they are in. The "normalcy" of the marriage relationship as a way of life has also generally been taken for granted by this group, without giving due consideration to why some people do not wish to marry (Kephart, 1966; Blood, 1969).

The promulgation of traditional ideas about marriage and the family in the name of science can be seen as early as the work of Sigmund Freud (1930), who (ironically) was considered rather radical for his time. Although he recognized that the requirement by "civilization" of repression of the individual's sexual desires might produce a variety of psychological problems, Freud accepted as "normal" the monogamous style of family life common to his time and culture. In sexual matters particularly, Freud had very conservative and fixed ideas about what was "natural," particularly for women, and he tended to attribute sexual habits and practices that were out of the ordinary to the pathological or "arrested" psychological development of individuals.

In our own time, most psychological and psychiatric counseling or therapy has tended to focus on helping the individual "adjust" to traditional family roles and rules. As Whitehurst has put it,

The (traditional) psychological explanation views adultery as immature behavior, infantile regressiveness, hostility toward the spouse, deep self-uncertainty, or as a symptom of marital maladjustment at other levels. (1969:132)

Marital and family experts in sociology also have tended to defend the more traditional views of marriage and the family in our society in the name of science. Consider the following excerpts from standard family textbooks of a generation ago:

Marriage makes possible such a conditioning of the sexual relationship as to give it the greatest significance of which it is capable. In marriage, sex . . . acquires a depth and a breadth of meaning which it otherwise lacks. Thus marriage regulates sex to make it more meaningful. (Nimkoff, 1934:55-56)

Men always boast about their abilities, but few if any of us can possibly achieve this ideal development with more than one woman! Those who find themselves unable to achieve monogamy are either poor judges of their prospective mates for one reason or another, or else they are incapable of mating in the fullest sense. . . . As a form of sexual behavior [sic], monogamy comes closest to our ideal. (Landis, 1952:415-416)

It may seem somewhat incongruous that at about the same time that the latter author, J. T. Landis, was writing the above words, his brother, P. H. Landis, also a family sociologist, wrote an article for *Reader's Digest,* entitled, "Don't Expect

Too Much of Sex in Marriage" (Landis, 1954). In this article even monogamous sex was de-emphasized, especially for women, and it was claimed that sexual fulfillment was unimportant for women, and was secondary to the joys they derived during sexual intercourse from contemplating their child-bearing potential. One can almost hear the shrieks of outrage from the modern women's movement at the following selection:

With many wives, also, the thought of possible motherhood is more important than anything else—the ultimate joy they feel in sexual intercourse stems from the realization that they may bear children. The emotion experienced may be tender and completely gratifying, without any need for physical climax. (Landis, 1954:27)

More recent sociological and psychological treatments of sex in marriage have tended to place far more importance on it, and to regard sexual "adjustment" or "success" as an important ingredient in a happy marriage. This has led to a rash of "how to" manuals in the last couple of decades, but these have almost all made clear that they were dealing with marital sex (Lewis and Brissett, 1967).

The point of all of these examples of traditional thinking about marriage and the family by psychologists and sociologists is not to belittle their ideas, or to present them as "wrong"; it is to show that their "scientific" outlooks and interests have not been totally free of the collective definitions of the traditionalists and "defenders" of conventional family life. At the appropriate place in the next section, it will become apparent that there are also social scientists who espouse a "challengers'" point of view, and whose "science" is therefore no freer of bias.

The Challengers of Traditional Family Life

Psychological Publics

As we have seen, people who have committed themselves for many years to a conventional kind of family-role behavior and outlook may develop a strong ego-involvement in and commitment to traditional definitions of such roles. Similarly, people who have been living in an unconventional manner can be expected to share collectively a variety of ideas which challenge the traditional definitions of right and wrong in matters of sex, marriage, and the family. Included in this group are homosexuals of both sexes; thousands of heterosexual couples who have been cohabiting without a formal marriage (and without necessarily any deep philosophical basis for their arrangements); many others who are formally married, but who have what Cuber and Harroff (1965) call a "utilitarian marriage" in which "discreet" extramarital sex is tacitly accepted (but never openly acknowledged) by both parties; and even some couples who, in the face of the strong child-oriented biases of our society, have elected to remain childless for the benefit of the wife's career, or for any number of reasons. All of these categories of people, and others whose family arrangements deviate noticeably from traditional patterns, have an obvious psychological "stake" or interest in promoting legal and social acceptance for deviant family styles, regardless of whether they have anything else in common, or ever organize or communicate with each other.

Moral and Religious Publics and Interest Groups

Drawn in part from such a psychological public, and overlapping somewhat with it, are other publics and organized groups who openly challenge family traditions and promote new ones, because they think it is morally right to do so. The moral ideals on which they base their advocacy of such new practices are, of course, different from those of the "defenders." Instead of ideals such as chastity, self-restraint, selfless devotion to children and family, and life-long companionship with one spouse, the "challengers" are likely to hold up the ideals of individual choice and liberation; tolerance of variety among consenting adults in all matters of sex, cohabitation, contraception, abortion, and the duration of relationships; and charity, or suspended judgment, toward all other individuals, regardless of how strange or weird their life-styles may appear. Interestingly enough, certain of the more liberal denominations and individual churches are found in the camp of the "challengers," as the quotation at the beginning of this chapter suggests. It is not only in churches of doubtful legitimacy like the Universal Life Church that we find support for some of the moral ideals of the "challengers." Among the more established religious groups, the Glide Memorial Methodist Church in San Francisco is a well-known advocate of such ideals, and a haven for those who hold them. *Honest Sex,* by Rustum and Della Roy (1969), a publication under Christian auspices, uses a general framework of "situational ethics" to promote varieties in marital and sexual styles. Even such a "mainline" denomination in the Christian establishment as the United Presbyterian Church (USA), in its 1970 General Assembly, discussed a committee report containing a number of statements of the "new morality":

Increasingly, the expectation of premarital virginity is not being met either by men or women. This change is not necessarily to be regarded as a sign of the lowering of the moral standards of young people. . . . [and later in the report] . . . [Our concern] for the Church is that it might see the question of marital fidelity in broad enough terms to understand that faithfulness in marriage and coital exclusivity are not synonymous. . . .

Although some religious spokesmen are thus found on the "challengers" side, we cannot say that they are in the vanguard, and probably, on balance, we would have to conclude that religion in America stands mostly on the side of the "defenders."

The chief source of moral entrepreneurship for the "challengers" comes from a variety of secular organizations, most of which have fairly specific moral interests and which focus on particular issues such as abortion, family planning, and women's liberation. Since we have devoted other chapters to abortion and to the women's movement, we will not discuss them further here, except to emphasize that these issues, and their respective interest groups, are very much a part of the social problem of the family as well. Other moral interest groups on the side of the "challengers" would include homosexual organizations such as the Mattachine Society and the Daughters of Bilitis (also discussed in another chapter), "swingers' clubs" (Denfield and Gordon, 1970; Varni, 1972; Bartell, 1971), and "group-marriage" communes (Bell, 1971; Rogers, 1972). Though many such groups operate "underground," in the sense that their members do not publicly identify themselves, they may number in the thousands, and their memberships in the millions, if we can rely on the estimates of some of the researchers cited above. An outspoken "challenger" organization that is not underground in any sense is the Sexual Freedom League, whose position has been stated as follows by one of its leading members:

Sexual expression, in whatever form agreed upon between consenting adults of either sex, should be considered an inalienable right. . . . Sex without guilt and restriction is good, pleasurable, relaxing, and promotes a spirit of human closeness, compassion, and good will. We believe that sexual activity . . . has a wealth of potential for making life livable and enjoyable. (quoted in Bell and Gordon, 1972:96-97)

In addition to such organized groups among the "challengers," there are quite a number of philosophers, novelists, and publicists whose published work has had quite an impact on and gained some following from among the moral interest groups we are discussing. Among individual works we include here Rimmer's *The Harrad Experiment* (1966), *Open Marriage* by O'Neill and O'Neill (1972), and *Becoming Partners* by Rogers (1972). The O'Neills and Rogers have had scientific training and sometimes speak as scientists, but in these works they are clearly taking a moral position in favor of the "challengers." They do not necessarily advocate extramarital (or nonmarital) sex (the O'Neills are particularly non-committal on this point), but by developing the concept of "open marriage" they are promoting new rules and styles of married life that are free of the customs of mutual "possession," total exclusivity in relationships with members of the opposite sex other than one's spouse, and rigid sex-role definitions. We could also perhaps include here, as moral entrepreneurs for the "challengers," the publishers of magazines for the "modern" young man and woman, such as *Playboy*'s Hugh Hefner and *Cosmopolitan*'s Helen Gurley Brown. The moral values and standards advocated in these publications are clearly those of "challengers" of family traditions, but since commercial interests are mixed with moral ones in these publishing enterprises, they might also be included under the next heading.

Economic and Political Interest Groups and Publics

In addition to a great variety of "avant-garde" popular magazines like *Playboy* and *Cosmopolitan* (which might be considered the "challengers'" legitimate counterparts to some of the "defenders'" magazines mentioned earlier), there is a large and thriving "pornography" industry (both "hard-core" and "soft-core"). A more thorough treatment of pornography as a "social problem" in its own right appears in another chapter, but let us point out here that it is clearly in the economic interests of the producers and distributors of pornographic books, magazines, films, and "implements" to promote the views of the "challengers" in general, and the "new" sexual attitudes in particular. The same is true of the business of organized prostitution, of the "massage-parlor" enterprises in some of our large cities which serve as "fronts" for various kinds of prostitution (by no means true of all or even most massage parlors), and of any other enterprise which offers its customers sexual indulgences and gratifications outside the traditional marriage bond. Because so many of these enterprises are still illegal in so many places, their economic interests are frequently intertwined with political ones, for they constantly need to find legal and political support in their confrontations with the police and in their fight against city ordinances that seek to prevent them from operating. It was probably due in large part to political pressure from such interest groups that the city of Boston, Massachusetts, in mid-1974, set aside a certain section of the city as a "haven" or special district in which the operation of all such sex-related enterprises would be legal.

In addition to the political activities of the economic interest groups that are directly involved in the outcome of political and legal decision-making, there are a few strictly political interest groups among the "challengers" who are concerned with political principles, and who operate mainly out of civil libertarian motives and interests. Chief among these is the American Civil Liberties Union (ACLU), whose lobbying, court defenses, and publicity are frequently found on the side of one or another sort of challenger of traditional family life. Perusal of, say, the last three years of its publication, *Civil Liberties,* indicates that the ACLU has advocated abolition of all obscenity rules as unworkable and contrary to 1st Amendment guarantees, legality of abortion at the discretion of a woman and her doctor, the repeal of any laws or policies which discriminate against women and keep them locked into traditional family roles, and the abolition of laws against any kind of sexual relations between consenting adults. Some of the more political organizations associated with the women's movement (discussed in another chapter) have also functioned at times as political pressure groups on the side of the "challengers," since their interests converge with those who challenge the traditional wife-and-mother images of women.

Scientific Interest Groups

The "challengers" of traditional marriage and family life, like the "defenders," can draw support from segments of the scientific community, especially psychologists and sociologists, whose research often convinces them that changes should be made in some of the values and norms surrounding the institutions of marriage and the family. Like the social scientists on the side of the "defenders," those on the side of the "challengers" have also allowed their own biases to influence their science, but their views do lean upon systematic research. Of course, scientists and philosophers have been among those advocating new forms of marriage and the family for some time. Among the philosophers, in ancient times Plato is known to have advocated a radically new system of "mating," at least for the ruling class, in his ideal society. Karl Marx, in *Das Kapital* (1906), and his colleague Friedrich Engels, in an essay on the origin of the family (1846, quoted in Skolnick and Skolnick, 1971, chapter 5), both attributed the negative aspects of the traditional family forms of their time to the demands of a private property system and of the inheritance laws. Further, Engels saw the "oppression" of women by men as the original form of class oppression. Psychologists Albert Ellis (1954) and Wilhelm Reich (1969 and 1971) have both been critics of monogamy and other western family traditions for a long time. Reich, drawing in part upon his discipleship of Freud, but rejecting the conservatism of the Freudian analysis, observed that:

The difficulties described in the case of the permanent sexual relationship are accentuated by the economic bonds and in reality made insuperable. The permanent sexual relationship, with its biological and psychological foundation, thus turns into compulsive marriage. This institution is ideologically characterized by the ecclesiastical demands that it must be (a) lifelong, and (b) strictly monogamous. (1969:129)

Carl Rogers, sometimes called a "humanistic psychologist," has not gone so far as to rule out monogamy as a viable form of marriage, but, as a result of his counseling work and research with many couples, he does approve of a variety of "experimental" innovations in marriage, including extramarital or "comarital" sex. He has compared those couples who elect to venture out into such "experimentation" to Daniel Boone and the great pioneering explorers. His picture of the emerging type of marriage is a far cry from tradition:

They are just as truly pioneers, exploring the far reaches of the relationship between a man and a woman. . . . They have broken many of the conventional rules of "what marriage should be" and are striving, with real dedication to each other, to build a new model for a permanent . . . relationship. It is built on . . . a commitment which is real but fluctuating, on a changing, flowing union which carries no guarantee except that of further change. (1972:66)

For radical advocacy in the name of sociology, it would be hard to find a more able or representative collection of essays than that presented in Libby and Whitehurst (1973), in which a number of scholars from sociology and other disciplines examine the institution of monogamous marriage and its alternatives. While some of the essays are relatively detached, trying simply to "tell it like it is," the general intent of the book is to find monogamy seriously defective as a modern family style, and to advocate variety in marriage and family life.

Although they fall short of actual advocacy, a number of social and other scientists, in the name of research on human behavior, have published a number of works which have had the effect of supporting the position of the "challengers." Such works have a supportive effect because: (1) the "challengers" quote liberally from the findings of these researchers, which often point up a wide discrepancy between cultural norms and actual behavior; and (2) the reading public, on either a first-hand or a second-hand basis, becomes acquainted with the findings of these scientists, and often gains the impression that "everybody's doing it," the "it" being premarital or extramarital sex, divorce, abortion, "swinging," or whatever the scientists have discovered. Perhaps the first example of such science pressed into the service of the challengers was the well-known work by the late Alfred C. Kinsey (1948 and 1953) on the sexual behavior of American men and women. This research, which showed, among other things, that surprisingly large percentages of both men and women had participated in premarital and extramarital sexual experiences, has been widely quoted by various "challengers" of the traditional-family pattern to show that the traditional rules don't really "work." More recently, the findings of Masters and Johnson (1966 and 1970) also have been used by various moral entrepreneurs among the "challengers" as evidence for their views.

Other scientific efforts to describe and analyze the realities behind the institutions of marriage and the family, which have been used by the "challengers" to bolster their position, would include a classical essay by Kingsley Davis (1937), which argues, in effect, that monogamous marriage and prostitution are symbiotic institutions, or that one keeps the other going; the comprehensive and revealing work of Ira Reiss (1967) on premarital sex; and the study by Cuber and Harroff on sex among the "significant Americans" (1965), which can easily be interpreted as an "everybody's-doing-it" look at sex and marriage in the upper-middle class. Morton Hunt (1971), too, concludes his study of extramarital sex with the statement that the extramarital affair is an "institutionalized" part of American family life. And so it goes. It is rather rare, in recent years, for any scientist to conclude from his or her research that traditional forms of marriage or the family are "working," or are commanding the exclusive commitment of the overwhelming majority of Americans; and even when such findings are reported, they are scarcely regarded as newsworthy by the media.

An interesting collection of articles by two social scientists (Skolnick and Skolnick, 1971) which contains a variety of scientific findings and conclusions about the "transitional" state of contemporary family life, provides a good sampling of the various "explanations" which social and other scientists have been offering about what has "happened" to the "good old American family." In one way or another, most scientific explanations draw upon what we called "strain theories" in Chapter 1. That is, they focus on the disorganizing or disorienting social impact on traditional family life of such important changes as industrialization and urbanization, population trends, and new methods of contraception. They consider that these changes have made the family unit "obsolete," or, from a slightly different theoretical perspective, "dysfunctional" (see also Goode, 1963). For the "challengers," the obvious implication of these findings is that the family and the marital institution must be changed in various ways in order to meet the demands of the modern world; whereas the "defenders" are likely to urge upon us the opposite conclusion that all this social change has created "threats" to the family institution, which necessitate our moral "retrenchment" and our most earnest efforts to strengthen family life. Thus the meaning of the same "scientific findings" may be different, depending upon whether one is a "defender" or a "challenger" of the traditional views. On the whole, however, the "challengers" seem to have been the more effective of the two groups in their use of science to back up their preferences.

Having reviewed the various kinds of "champions" found on either side of the social problem of the family, let us look briefly at the social movement(s) they have generated.

THE FAMILY PROBLEM AS A SOCIAL MOVEMENT

There can be little doubt that the nature of marriage and family life in our society has been changing, no matter what statistics or other "objective indicators" we look at. Virtually all scientific and other official observers of family life agree that, compared to earlier generations, family life now is characterized by a somewhat higher divorce rate and a higher number of illegitimate children, lower cultural expectations of premarital chastity and even of marital fidelity, a smaller average family size, greater resort to contraceptives and tolerance for abortion, more working mothers, less parental authority over children and authority of husband over wife, and a number of other indicators which show that Ameircan family life has become more equalitarian and oriented toward the individual, rather than patriarchal and family-group oriented as it was earlier. (In addition to the material presented earlier in this chapter, see F. J. Davis, 1970, chap. 6, for a comprehensive review of these developments.) Most "experts" on the subject attribute these changes in one way or another to the industrial revolution, and to the concomitant shift of American population from rural to urban living areas.

Whether these changes add up to a "problem," however, is another question in itself. There is no inherent reason why we cannot collectively define the changes which have occurred in marriage and the family as simply "normal" and "natural" adaptations to the historical changes taking place in the other institutions of society, particularly in the economy. It is doubtful whether changes in family life have been any more profound or extensive than changes in, say, religion or education, but public opinion in general (always with some dissent, to be sure) seems more inclined to regard the changes in those institutions as "progress" rather than as "problems." Even among those numerous publics in our society who agree that the changes which have taken place in the family constitute problems, we see a basic division over the next question, which is one of defining just what the problem is (or problems are) in all these changes. As we have seen, this latter question has produced two main "camps" or schools of thought, the "defenders" of traditional family life and the "challengers," each of whom reads a different meaning into the same "facts." For the "defenders," the meaning of all those changes in family life is one of deterioration, indicating the imminent "decline and fall" of the American family, and perhaps of American society as a whole, since the family is the "basic unit" of society. For the "challengers," on the other hand, the changes in family life point to obsolescence, and the problem is one of "liberating" the individual and the family as an institution from the "crippling vestiges" of an earlier cultural tradition which no longer "works." The different interpretations attached by these two camps to the same facts and figures have, of course, produced different courses of action by their respective publics and interest groups.

The Defenders

While our focus so far has been on the more contemporary "defenders," we would not want to leave the impression that the controversies about marriage and the family in our society are of only recent origin. An early standard (and quaintly traditionalist) work on the history of the family (Calhoun, 1960—originally published 1919) makes it unmistakably clear that many of the issues that we associate with modern family controversies are generations old, including the issues of patriarchal authority and the "woman's place," working wives and mothers, illegitimacy, "free love," prostitution, divorce, the "erosion" of the importance of the family in favor of the school and other institutions, parent-child relations, and a number of other matters which we would recognize today as very "modern" issues. As Calhoun (1960, vol. III) points out, these issues began to gain a special urgency in public and official opinion right after the Civil War, and continued to preoccupy the public mind for a good 50 years thereafter. This was already a period of "the precarious home" (chap. 9), and of "the passing of patriarchism and familism" (chap. 8). This was also the period of great reformist zeal known in American history as the Progressive Era, which (as we have observed elsewhere in this book) spawned a large number of the "social problems" and movements that are still with us.

The "defenders" of traditional family life, then, first made their appearance as a social movement during the decades on either side of the turn of the present century. In a very real sense, they were a part of the larger Progressive Movement which itself was generated by the response of middle- and upper-middle-class Americans to the changes brought about by the greatly increased industrialization, urbanization, and immigration in the years following the Civil War (Hofstadter, 1960). In keeping with the stages of our natural history model of social movements, the incipiency of the "defenders'" movement can be found even before that war in the series of unfriendly exchanges between northern and southern journalists and ministers about the state of the family and sexual morality in the two parts of the country (Calhoun, 1960, vol. II). While the northerners pointed to rampant "miscegenation" and "sexual debauchery" between southern slave owners and their female slaves as "proof" of the evil impact of slavery on family life, the southerners criticized the North in terms that sound surprisingly "modern" for 1857:

In eighty years, the social system of the North has developed to a point in morals only reached by that of Rome in six centuries. . . . Already married women, moving in the fashionable circles of the North, forego the duties of domestic life, . . . and refuse to no inconsiderable extent to undergo the pains of child-bearing. . . . Already the priceless gem of chastity in women has been despoiled of its talismanic charm with men. [The rule seems to be], so long as exposure is avoided, no wrong is done. (quoted in Calhoun, 1960, vol. II:157)

This general consciousness of the "deterioration" of family life in mid-19th century, shared by both North and South (though by different interests and using different definitions), was doubtless a reflection of social changes of a very "modern" kind which had already begun in America. The consciousness had to remain incipient, however, for the onset of the Civil War and the task of Reconstruction, which became the great "social problem" of the time, pre-empted all other problems for a couple of decades. Up to about 1880, the family as an essential and traditional institution had been largely taken for granted. When divorce was discussed in the public arenas, it was mostly with respect to its legal or ecclesiastical aspects, rather than in connection with the family. The great public speakers and universities of the time gave almost no attention to the family as a "problem," and there were no books devoted to the family (Calhoun, 1960: vol. III, 8-10).

During the late 1880's and early 1890's, however, the stage of incipiency gave way to coalescence, as a number of local and national organizations began to spring up to work for improvement in family life. Chief among these was the National League for the Protection of the Family, founded in New England as a "divorce-reform" organization. In a slightly earlier period the Children's Protective Society had been organized (1875), interestingly enough as an offshoot of the Society for the Prevention of Cruelty to Animals. The child-centered aspects of the "defenders'" movement are discussed further in the chapter on juvenile delinquency. Here, let us note only that organizations and societies devoted to "reforming" family life in a variety of ways, many of them coordinated under the auspices of the League for the Protection of the Family, became active in publication, lobbying, and educational activities. Largely as a result of such efforts, periodical literature and books on family life began appearing in large numbers around the turn of the century, many of them purporting to take a newer, more "scientific" approach to the subject. At the same time courses in marriage and family life gradually began to work their way into the curricula of high schools and colleges, particularly women's colleges.

The entry of this movement into the stage of institutionalization seems to have occurred roughly around 1910, or near the end of that first decade. One indication of such institutionalization was the official recognition accorded to the "family problem" by the American Sociological Society (as the American Sociological Association was originally called), which, in its 1908 annual convention, devoted all of its sessions to that subject. At about the same time, or slightly later, official governmental recognition and response (the surest sign of a movement's institutionalization) came rapidly in a series of developments such as new divorce laws, the establishment of courts of "domestic relations" to specialize in family problems, and the creation in the federal executive branch of the U.S. Children's Bureau to gather data on children's "problems." Academic institutionalization followed as more family-related courses were established and eventually grouped together into departments (and even colleges) of "domestic economy" (Calhoun, 1960: vol. III, 8-10, and 172-178).

Since this early institutionalization of the movement, the "defenders" have clearly dominated the establishment in matters relating to family life. Though it has waxed and waned somewhat, particularly during periods of societal involvement in other, more pressing problems such as the world wars and the Great Depression, the "defenders'" movement has succeeded, during the past half-century, in getting passed an enormous body of state and federal legislation intended to "protect" the family in a variety of ways. This legislation includes divorce laws which have given greater protection to the rights of women and children, perhaps, than they had in the 19th century, but which have made divorces rather difficult to get without severe legal battles; laws making contraceptives and abortions very difficult to get until quite recent years; laws favoring families with children, especially many children; and so on. One of the most interesting and (in retrospect) ironic bodies of legislation to come out of the Progressive Era was that dealing with the "protection" of women, the overall effect of which has been to keep women out of certain lines of work, to prevent them from working for higher overtime wages, and in general to make them less desirable as employees because of all the special "privileges" they have had to be given due to their supposedly more "delicate natures." It is precisely such protective legislation that has recently been under attack by the current women's movement (which we considered in an earlier chapter), and, of course, also by today's "challengers" of traditional family life. In other words, much of the legislation generated by the institutionalized defenders' movement, under the guise of protecting families and mothers, has had the effect of making it difficult (and somewhat stigmatizing) for a woman to be anything but a housewife and mother.

After a period of dormancy in its promotional activities during the 1930's and early 1940's, the well-institutionalized family-"defenders'" movement has been aroused to renewed efforts by a number of new "threats" to family life since World War II. The well-publicized jump in the divorce rate during the mid- and late 1940's, combined with the "scandalous" revelations of the Kinsey reports about what people were *really* doing in their sex lives, helped to reawaken the complacent "defenders." The rise of a new "challengers'" movement has also greatly contributed to the revival of the "defenders." The "defenders" have responded by (1) flooding the media with articles, books, and programs promoting their position; (2) lobbying for more family-oriented legislation; (3) trying to keep sex education out of the schools and in the home, "where it belongs"; (4) promoting the establishment and growth of more family-life education courses in colleges; (5) promoting more family-guidance and counseling programs, both in social-welfare agencies and in private practice, which are intended to help "strengthen" traditional family life; and (6) establishing *ad hoc* and continuing organizations to oppose the changes sought by the "challengers" in matters of divorce, abortion, women's rights, and so on. Interestingly enough, however, the social composition of the "defenders" now has changed somewhat compared to the period before 1945. Whereas earlier in the century, the "defenders" were largely Protestant, middle and upper-middle class, well-educated, and of Anglo-Saxon stock, the modern "defenders" (while still espousing largely the same values and ideology) are mostly working class, lower-middle and middle class, much more likely to be Roman Catholic or Mormon in religion (though the more conservative and fundamentalist Protestant groups are also active), and as likely as not to be of Irish, German, Italian, or other non-Anglo origins. These social elements, ironically, are precisely the ones considered to have been partly the "cause" of our "family problems" by "defenders" during the Progressive Era!

The "defenders," though newly aroused, still remain in the stage of the institutionalization of their social movement. They are now engaged in a crucial battle with the "challengers" for control over the definitions of "normal" and "problem" or deviant family-life patterns during the coming generations. They may well carry the day, given the current support they enjoy both in public opinion and in establishment policy. There are signs, however, that they are losing ground to the "challengers," and that some fragmentation is occurring among their traditional supporters. Most surveys show that preferred family size is much smaller than it used to be, and that contraception is practiced almost universally in our society, even among Roman Catholics. Further, the "defenders" seem to have lost the battle on abortion with the 1973 Supreme Court decision on that matter, and it seems most unlikely at this time that efforts to overturn the Court's decision with a constitutional amendment will succeed. Official government policy discriminating against the single, the divorced, the female, the illegitimate child, and the informal cohabitation of the sexes is rapidly receding and promises to disappear totally within the present generation. Furthermore, the "challengers" seem to be thriving.

The Challengers

Just as the "defenders" of traditional marriage and the family have a longer history than most people think, so the "challengers" go back a long way, too; indeed, if the record were complete, we might find that there have been "challengers" as long as there have been "defenders," for one supposes that the "defenders" were, after all, responding to someone's challenges! What is unique about the current age, however, is that the challengers have acquired an audience and taken on a status of a legitimacy that they have probably never before enjoyed in our society. The few scattered advocates of "free love" in the 19th century were considered a disgrace by the public-at-large. Utopian communities attempting variations on the monogamous tradition were severely persecuted and repressed (e.g., the Oneida Community under John Noyes). The Mormon experiment with polygyny, though carried on hundreds of miles away from non-Mormon settlements, was the target of the Republican Party Platform of 1856 (pledged to stamp out "those twin relics of barbarism, slavery and polygamy"), of federal legislation (the Edmunds-Tucker Act of the 1860's), and, eventually, of a Supreme Court decision in 1887. (Ever since losing that battle, the Mormons have been very much on the side of the "defenders"!)

However many instances there may have been in our history of departures from traditional forms of the family, when their actions were not totally acceptable, those involved have generally had the good sense to keep quiet and maintain at least a front of respectability. Kinsey (1953) found a surprising number of respondents, who were willing, under the cloak of anonymity, to admit to "mate-swapping"; and a more recent study of "significant Americans" (i.e., generally upper-middle class) mentioned above indicates that "discreet adultery" has been more common for some time than was generally known or expected (Cuber and Harroff, 1965). Quietly admitting to doing it, however, is a far cry from advocating it, and it is the latter action which constitutes the greatest weapon of the "challengers," not just with regard to sexual deviance, but also with regard to abortion, divorce, female sex-roles, and many other things. Nor have the "defenders" been able to silence them with the legal repressions and censorship that have worked well in the past. One after another, restrictive laws or city ordinances have gone down before an increasingly broad application by the courts of constitutional guarantees. In this respect, the challengers' movement has been the beneficiary of the litigational efforts of the civil rights movement of the 1950's and 1960's, of the "counterculture" and New Left efforts in the 1960's, and of the more recent legal pressures brought to bear by movements more specifically related to the "challengers," e.g., the women's movement.

Such studies as we have of the social composition of the "challengers" indicates that they are far from being "low-life debauchers," as they are sometimes characterized by the "defenders." Indeed, relatively high levels of education, occupational prestige, and political participation are associated with those who have given support to the issues of abortion reform, "no-fault" divorce laws (i.e., "dissolution"), contraception, smaller family sizes, women's rights, and many other causes closely identified with the "challengers." To take an extreme example, there are even some studies of "swingers" which have found them to be generally above average in education and occupation, generally happily married and sexually satisfied before beginning their "swinging," and generally committed to the maintenance of the traditional nuclear family in all respects except sexually (Bartell, 1971; Gilmartin and Kusisto, 1973; and Varni, 1972).

While the incipiency of the "challengers'" movement may go back some distance, it is very clearly indicated at latest by the rise of such magazines as *Playboy* in the mid-1950's, which has become not only a widely read journalistic endeavor but also a chain of men's clubs and a foundation dedicated to the promotion of the "playboy ideals." Just as a magazine, though, *Playboy* marks a significant departure from the past. It is not merely that the magazine advocates a variety of values which are at odds with traditional marriage and family values, but rather that it does so "over-the-counter" in a format and layout of high quality and some intellectual appeal. It is neither a standard men's pulp magazine nor an embarrassing underground "smut" piece. It clearly appeals to the "establishment man," and its phenomenal growth in the last two decades is clear evidence of at least an incipient constituency for the "challengers" during that entire period, evidence which is strengthened by the rise of a number of imitators such as *Penthouse.* Nor has the incipiency of the "challengers' " movement been limited to popular literature for men. Shortly following the appearance of *Playboy,* the women's magazine, *Cosmopolitan,* was taken over and transformed by Helen Gurley Brown, whose "daring" book, *Sex and the Single Girl,* is yet another evidence of the movement's incipiency. The new *Cosmopolitan,* while not taking a position quite as extreme as *Playboy* in some ways, and certainly not taking a "women's-lib" line, has nevertheless condoned, and even glamorized, a sexual code for women that the "defenders" would surely find "loose," and a "career-girl" style of life that makes the lot of the "everyday housewife" seem very dull by comparison! Early in the 1970's, some considerably more risqué (but equally "high-class") magazines for women appeared, most notably *Playgirl* and *Viva,* both featuring male nudity. One can find other signs of incipiency of the "challengers' " movement in the media of the 1950's and 1960's, particularly in popular films. In a number of Hollywood productions, e.g., *Love Is a Many-Splendored Thing, Diary of a Mad Housewife,* we were told that adultery is permissible under some circumstances, and in a lighter picture, *Suzie Wong,* we were introduced to a number of examples of the lovable prostitute with the heart of gold.

It is questionable whether these developments in the media, which we are presenting as indicators of the incipiency of the "challengers' " movement, were only symptoms, or were themselves important influences in promoting the rise of this movement. For the purposes of our argument, it doesn't really matter; the very fact that there is such an obvious and eager market for such media products makes it clear that many people were open to most of the ideas which the "challengers" represented. For incipiency to become coalescence, however, it was necessary for those ideas to be advocated by some organizations, and these began to appear (at least to public view) mainly in the mid-1960's. We are thinking here of women's liberation organizations such as the National Organization for Women (NOW), discussed earlier; Zero Population Growth (ZPG); homosexual or "gay liberation" organizations; abortion reform organizations; certain "counterculture" phenomena like the "communal families"; "swinger" and "mate-swapping" clubs; and many other such examples of collective efforts to experience and advocate alternatives to the traditional American family. In order to promote specific legal issues or causes that appeared from time to time, coalitions would take place between two or more of these special-interest groups. For instance, lesbian organizations joined with NOW on some issues, and NOW helped ZPG at other times. Virtually all of these organizations could be expected to combine in a given urban area in order to resist passage or enforcement of laws restricting sexual activities between consenting adults.

The mid-1970's has witnessed the beginning of the institutionalization of the "challengers'" movement, but only the beginning. The extent to which the "defenders" are taking the "challengers" seriously, and organizing to resist or repeal their accomplishments, is one indication of institutionalization, as in the case of the abortion and women's-rights issues. The Equal Rights Amendment campaign, carried on mainly in the halls of state legislatures, the Supreme Court's "liberal" decision on abortion in 1973, and the gradual trend in some states toward the new "no-fault" dissolution laws to take the place of divorce are clear indications also that the "challengers'" movement is being institutionalized at the governmental level. In all such cases, the government has had to respond to the pressure and enterprise of the "challengers" in concrete, and partially co-opting, ways. The survival of the multi-faceted "challengers'" movement as a coalition depends upon the future responses of both the "defenders" and the government, and upon the extent to which it can be successful in acquiring continued legitimacy for increasingly novel, or even radical, definitions of what is "desirable" in marriage and family life.

THE LEGACY OF THE FAMILY MOVEMENTS

The competing movements around the issue of the family in our society have succeeded, over the years, in obtaining varying degrees of public and official acceptance for their respective definitions of "the problem." As a result, the current body of custom and law on the family in our culture is a curious mixture of Old Testament, Puritan, Anglo-Saxon, Latin, libertarian, patriarchal, equalitarian, and many other strains. This mixture is not only a general characteristic; it is manifest in the enormous variety of state and regional laws and customs, depending upon the relative power of "challengers" and "defenders" in the different parts of the country. In other words, what the "problem" is in American family life depends in large part upon where one lives in the country, as well as upon what one's religion is and who one's peers are. What Bell (1971) has said about sex in America could be said as well about most aspects of family life, namely, that it has a "schizoid" quality!

Let us consider the state of marriage and family law around the country (as reviewed, for example, in Folkman and Clatworthy, 1970: chap. 14). In almost all states, the husband is still legally defined as the provider, even if the wife is employed. The wife, on the other hand, is still legally responsible for the household chores, even if she is employed outside the home; she can be required by her husband to work without wages in his business; she must live where he chooses to live; and she must provide him with "reasonable" and "normal" sexual gratification. The laws vary considerably with regard to requirements for marriage, including minimum age, age with parental consent, blood tests required, waiting period after tests, and so on, but despite these requirements, it is much easier to get married under the law than it is to get a divorce. A few states (notably Washington and California) have abandoned the traditional divorce laws, with their court proceedings which make husband and wife into adversaries, in favor of the new concept of "dissolution," which is relatively easy to obtain; but most states by far still have the old divorce battles. Where children are concerned, parents are still held responsible for their physical, educational, and emotional well-being, and gross parental failure in any of these respects can result in a loss of custody of the child to the state. Children, for their part, are legally obliged to obey their parents and, if their parents require it, to turn over to parents all their earnings outside the home.

Sex relations are still regulated by law in most states, even for married persons. Fornication, adultery, and cohabitation ("shacking up") are illegal in nearly every state, with jail terms up to five years and fines from $20.00 to $2,000.00 for violators, depending upon the state and upon the "seriousness" of the violation. Interracial sex used to be especially seriously regarded by the law, and, in fact, interracial marriage was illegal in 40 states before the 1960's! (All interracial or "miscegenation" laws were finally struck down by a Supreme Court decision in 1967.) Various sexual "perversions," including mouth-genital contact of any kind, are still illegal in most states, even for married persons, with some very serious penalties usually involved, even though surveys as far back as Kinsey's indicate that such "perversions" are extremely widespread among married couples. Kinsey (1953) reports on a 1943 decision in the Minnesota Supreme Court in which a wife was granted a divorce on the grounds that her husband's expectation of intercourse three or four times a week constituted an "uncontrollable craving," even though (as Kinsey's study showed) that weekly rate of intercourse was close to the national average for married couples of that age. Thus our laws have not kept up with social change in the area of the family, and many can be considered archaic. The product of an "illicit" sexual union, namely, an illegitimate child, is still stigmatized by the law in most states, and may lose his or her rights to inheritance and other legal rights. Legal children, however, are still very much favored by the law, for parents are still being given income-tax breaks, which have, in fact, been getting more generous in recent years to keep up with inflation.

Tradition has held up fairly well in matters of custom, as well as in law. A woman is still expected to take her husband's surname at marriage (partly as a matter of law, and partly as a well-established custom), and even if she opts to keep her "maiden name," it is her father's! Men and women who live together as couples are still expected to marry, eventually if not in the beginning, and they still meet with most people's disapproval if they do not. Indeed, even the practice of informal cohabitation that has grown in recent years among the younger people is, on second look, a very traditional kind of behavior; it is essentially monogamous, after all, and it may result in break-up no more often than legal marriages. A "couple" of some duration also continues to be the "basic unit" of our society for most social and recreational occasions, as many widowed, divorced, and single adults will dolefully attest. Our media, such as television, also take for granted and reinforce in many ways the traditional familial values of our society; one thinks here of the afternoon "soap operas," as well as of extremely popular evening programs like "All in the Family" and "Maude." To be sure, there are also opposing values alluded to in these and other programs, but, on balance, our TV fare is very marriage- and family-oriented.

However, the "challengers," for their part, have made strong inroads into law and custom. Although many of the existing laws regulating marriage, the family, and sex, which we have mentioned above, are still "on the books," they are no longer enforced, or they have yet to face a court test, or both. There is simply no longer the will, on the parts of either the police or the courts, to enforce laws that have lost their underlying legitimacy in the norms and values of the society. Where enforcement or penalty does occur, it is likely that the offense has either been extremely flagrant, or has simply been used by the authorities as a pretext for holding a person who is suspected of other (unproved) violations. Aside from sexual matters, the views of the "challengers" have prevailed increasingly in the public and official definitions about divorce or dissolution, abortion, the woman's role in society, contraception, and preferred family size. For example the recent rapid growth in the number of nurseries and children's day-care centers, many of them government-subsidized, is in part a response to the pressure of the "challengers," but it is also partly a co-optation effort which has had the effect of muting some of the "challengers'" more radical attacks on the traditional family.

On a less formal level, the "challengers" have also had an extensive influence upon our culture, and will doubtless continue to do so. It is certain that sex as a topic is much more discussed (and discussable) publicly than ever before, and in "respectable" places. As Salzman and Bernard (1969) have suggested, there is probably also a lot less guilt than formerly on the part of those who deviate from traditional sex standards, whether we are talking about unmarried college-student couples who move in together, or about their parents who may be experimenting with one or another kind of extramarital relationship. Divorce (increasingly called "dissolution") is also rapidly losing the stigma it once had, both for men and for women. New kinds of relations between the sexes, married or not, and sexual or not, seem in general to be more open and publicly acceptable. The old code of "chivalry," with its patronizing and condescending attitudes toward women, is rapidly breaking down, as women are increasingly expecting to open their own doors, pay their own checks, and do many other things for themselves that were once considered "unladylike." Partly as a result of official "affirmative action" policies, and partly as a cause of them, women are increasingly expecting to combine careers with motherhood, just as men have always combined careers with fatherhood. Perhaps the most fundamental, and yet the most subtle, development in American married life, however, has been the gradual change in the very "cement" of marriage and family life: i.e., where families were once held together by economic necessity and social or legal pressure, they will henceforth be held together only by the mutual interests and emotional bonds of the family members themselves.

As various "experts" look ahead to the future of family life in America, when some of the "problems" in contemporary family life will presumably have been "solved," they give us somewhat different projections. Since the same "data" and information on "trends" are available to all of the "experts," we can attribute some of the differences in their projections to the different meanings which they see in the same data; these, in turn, are doubtless also affected by their varying scientific and/or ideological interests. Pope and Knudsen (1965), for example, look a couple of generations into the future, where they see general social acceptance for "permissiveness with contraception," once contraceptive techniques have become foolproof. Davids (1972) goes so far as to predict that citizens of the future will have to be licensed to have children, and that good grades on standardized examinations will be a prerequisite for such licensing. He estimates that only 25 percent to 30 percent of the population will be willing to undergo the rigorous training and evaluation required for their parenthood licenses. He expects a complete equalization of husband and wife to occur under the law, legal acceptance not only of abortion but of various kinds of marriage styles, and popular acceptance of short-term affairs and limited-term marriages.

Winch (1970) has predicted a number of fairly profound consequences of the development of a safe contraceptive, including the disappearance of moral and legal sanctions against nonmarital sex, a decline in the rates of both marriages and births, fewer unwanted and rejected children, and the rise of more "positive" kinds of marriages. The several intervening years since these predictions were first offered have brought scant fulfillment of them.

It might be interesting and appropriate to close with some observations by one of America's most distinguished family sociologists, Reuben Hill, whose optimistic outlook for the future is somewhat more reassuring for the "defenders" of traditional family life. In a 1964 article on the future of the American family, Hill reviewed four different ways in which social scientists have tried to predict future family trends, and he concluded that all their predictions were in a positive direction:

None of the products of these methods justifies the lugubrious picture of a disintegrating family without future functions; in fact, the findings suggest accelerating upgrading in the amenities, increasingly flexible family organization, and improved competence in planning and decision-making. (1964:27)

PART FIVE
GENERAL SOCIETAL ISSUES

Chapter 14

Race and Ethnic Relations

THE SOCIAL CONSTRUCTION OF REALITY

> An image of a Caucasian with white skin, deep-set eyes, wavy hair of a color other than black, a tall, stout, hairy body, and large hands and feet, seems to evoke in many Japanese an association with "vitality," "superior energy," "strong sexuality" or "animality," and the feeling that Caucasians are basically discontinuous with Asians. (Wagatsuma, 1967:422)

This Japanese image of Caucasians is particularly interesting, since it contains some of the same value judgments and stereotypes that white Americans have typically held about black Americans.

Race and Social Relativity

There is an immense range in the social definitions of racial and ethnic groups around the world. From paintings in the royal tombs of Biban al-Muluk, it is clear that the early Egyptians recognized four racial groups—red, black, yellow, and white—and rated them in that order. The Eskimo has recognized only two races, his own and that of the white man, whom he has considered to be an inferior being. The Iroquois perceived three racial groups, rating red men above blacks and both of them above whites (Conrad, 1964). In human affairs, one's own group is always considered to be superior, with other groups usually ranked in terms of their similarity to oneself. This negative bias in evaluating other groups is called *ethnocentrism*.

In order to illustrate the variety of racial and ethnic opinions, we will briefly characterize intergroup relations in eight areas of the globe: northern Brazil, Mexico, Southeast Asia, Japan, Central Africa, South Africa, the Caribbean, and Switzerland. The people of northern Brazil exhibit a decided preference for Caucasian physical features, but factors such as wealth, occupation and education are more important in determining social position than are racial factors. Upward mobility is possible for members of all racial groups, though a remnant of the old white aristocratic class, which denies membership to blacks, still persists. In most areas, the status of the Indian is between that of the white and the black. However, in the Amazon lowlands the Indian's status is the lowest of any group, perhaps because of the history of slavery involving Indians in the Amazon basin (Wagley, 1969).

In Mexico, 85 percent of the people belong to the broad racial category of *mestizo* (mixed), which means that they speak the Mexican dialect of Spanish, and that they are not of recent European origin (van den Berghe, 1967). There is a correlation between social class and color, but there are many dark-skinned and Indian-looking people in all classes. This situation has developed partially because the Spanish rulers of early Mexico derived their pride from their culture rather than from their racial characteristics (van den Berghe, 1967). As mixed racial groups acquired the cultural characteristics of the Spanish conquerors, they found the door open to a reasonable degree of upward mobility.

Chinese migrants in Southeast Asia occupy a position similar to that of the Jews in medieval Europe. They are a middle-class minority, owning a disproportionately large number of businesses. They are tolerated by other groups when times are good, but persecuted when times are bad. The Chinese migrants have matched the poor images their hosts hold of them with stereotypes of their own. Shibutani and Kwan report that in Thailand, the Chinese see the Thais as indolent, morally loose, and corrupt. In Indonesia, they find the natives to be "inferior in ability, intelligence and energy. [Even] the Peranakan, offspring of Chinese fathers and Indonesian mothers, were assumed (by the Chinese) to be less capable because of their 'blood'" (Shibutani and Kwan, 1965).

As the quotation opening this chapter shows, the Japanese have ambivalent feelings about Caucasians. They consider themselves to be white rather than yellow, and they valued white skin over dark skin long before they had contact with western civilization. Skin color in Japan has always been associated with a complex of physical characteristics that were considered to be indicators of degrees of spiritual refinement or crudeness (Wagatsuma, 1967).

There were three main racial groups in Central Africa during the last years of colonial domination by European nations—African, European and Asian. Additional racial groups (often mutually hostile) existed among the Africans, but these were ignored under colonial rule. In this setting, the European saw the Asian as hard-working, clever, crafty, and materialistic. The African was seen as ignorant, immature, untrusting, and uncooperative. Asians shared the European view of the African, but they also rejected the European because they considered him to be hypocritical. From his position at the bottom of the status ladder, the African resented the Asian, perceiving him as basically dishonest and unscrupulous. The

European was worse: powerful and clever but haughty and manipulative, always seeking his own advantage at the expense of others (Banton, 1967).

In South Africa, segregation practices have not been declared unconstitutional as they have in the United States. Instead, the Reservation of Separate Amenities Act provides for separate and unequal facilities under the law (van den Berghe, 1970). Pierre van den Berghe has defined three levels of segregation in South Africa. *Microsegregation* insures that public and private facilities have separate provisions for whites and blacks, following a pattern much like the one in the southern United States in the 1940's. *Mesosegregation* produces racially homogeneous ghettos, called Group Areas, in multiracial urban areas, in order to assure that blacks and whites do not live together in the same neighborhood. *Macrosegregation* goes beyond white American practices toward blacks in the recent past, establishing "native reserves," where natives both live and work in an almost completely segregated fashion, except when they are needed for labor in the white South African industrial complex (van den Berghe, 1970). This combination of a reservation system and the exploitation of labor is, however, different from the American system of reservations for Indian tribes, where jobs are rarely available at all.

The Caribbean is at the other end of the racial continuum from South Africa. Because there were never many whites in the Caribbean, there was little opposition to the creation of a middle class of mixed racial origins (mulattos) that could become an ally to the upper-class whites in the event that a revolution ever occurred among the lower-class blacks. Though slavery in the 17th century was initially devastating to the imported Africans, a racial balance has now been achieved in the Caribbean. Men of color are considered "white" if they are successful in the society. Whites still control the business world, but politics has become the province mainly of blacks and mulattos (Mason, 1970).

Nearly three-fourths of the citizens of Switzerland are of German origin (as determined from the language they speak), one-fourth are French, and small minorities are Italian and Romansch. Despite their numerical majority, the German-speaking Swiss do not dominate the other groups. Two or three of the seats on the seven-seat Federal Council are reserved for French or Italian-speaking politicians. Government documents are published in German, French, and often Italian, as well. There is no evidence that the French, Italian or Romansch groups in Switzerland are discriminated against in any way (Mayer, 1951).

In the United States today, the major racial and ethnic minorities are considered to be blacks, who comprise almost one-eighth of the population; Spanish-speaking Americans (mostly Chicanos of Mexican origin), about 2½ percent of the population; and "Native Americans" (i.e., American Indians), less than one percent. Other minorities are more assimilated into the dominant white Anglo-Saxon groups although Oriental-Americans, Jews, and European immigrant groups (e.g., Italians and Polish) still experience some degree of discrimination. The official ideology of the United States, of course, is one of equality for all, but in the next few pages we will show that basic inequalities and disadvantages still affect minorities in America, though perhaps not as much as in the past or in certain other contemporary societies.

Parameters of Consensual Reality

Various agencies of the federal government, such as the Bureau of the Census and Bureau of Labor Statistics, keep detailed records of statistical differences in the areas of population, family composition, education, and income between whites and non-whites in the United States. In addition, many specialized studies have been carried out by academic researchers, pollsters, and private industry. Unfortunately, most sources of official information are limited to the categories of white or non-white, without breakdowns into specific minority groups such as Spanish-surnamed Americans or native Americans.

The best estimates available indicate that in 1970, there were somewhat under 25 million blacks in the United States, plus five million Mexican-Americans, less than a million native Americans, and much smaller numbers of members of other minority groups. Approximately two out of every three Americans were living in Standard Metropolitan Statistical Areas (SMSA's). The proportions of whites and non-whites living in SMSA's were similar, but the populations of central city areas within the SMSA's show a very different picture. More than half of all American non-whites live in central cities, compared to only one-quarter of American whites (U.S. Bureau of Census, 1970). Many of these central-city areas are ghettos in which large numbers of minority people face housing discrimination, high population density, high crime rates, and many other conditions usually considered deplorable in contemporary America. Blacks move nearly as often as whites, but they are more likely to move to a residence in the same county.

The median age of blacks is considerably below that of whites: in 1969, 21.2 as compared with 29.3 (U.S. Bureau of Census, 1970). This is due to a number of factors, among which are higher birth rates and a shorter life expectancy among blacks.

In 1970, nine out of every ten white families included both a husband and a wife, while only seven out of ten non-white families were "complete" (U.S. Dept. of Labor, 1971). The proportion of broken homes rises as income level decreases, so that in black families with incomes below $3,000 per year, only one-quarter of the children are living with both parents (U.S. Dept. of Labor, 1971). More than half of the illegitimate children born in the United States are non-white.

Health and health care are significantly poorer for non-whites than for whites.

A good index of the quality of health care is the death rate for infants under one year old. The 1971 estimate was 16.8 infant deaths per thousand live births for whites, as compared to 30.2 for non-whites (National Center for Health Statistics, 1972). Evidence presented by Moore and Cuellar (1970) and Wax (1971) indicates that Mexican-American and Native American babies are more than three times as likely as white babies to die before their first birthday.

A higher proportion of whites than non-whites are enrolled in school at each age level, and the difference is greatest for college students. The average white student spends two and one-half more years in the classroom than does the average black student. A national program of academic achievement testing showed that even in the first grade, white students are better prepared than Native Americans or Mexican-Americans, who are, in turn, better prepared than blacks. By the twelfth grade, the rank-order of the groups has not changed, but all three minority groups have lost ground relative to whites (U.S. Bureau of Census, 1970). Despite the desegregation program of the federal government, most black students in 13 southern states go to schools that are 95 percent or more black, and the situation is not very different in many northern states, such as Illinois (U.S. Bureau of Census, 1970). Plans for busing students to schools outside their neighborhoods have been put into effect in many states, in an effort to counteract the effects of the residential segregation which characterizes most American cities. The U.S. Commission on Civil Rights (*Mexican American Education Study,* 1970) reported that the situation in the schools among Mexican-American children in the Southwest was considerably less segregated, with only one-tenth of them attending schools that were 95 percent or more Mexican-American. However, fully 45 percent of these children do attend schools that are at least half Mexican-American.

Unemployment is somewhat higher for non-whites than for whites everywhere, but in certain ghettos and on the Indian reservations, it soars to ten times the national average. This high rate of unemployment is often associated with a high crime rate, particularly among adolescents and young adults (Pettigrew, 1964). In an attempt to combat these problems, the U.S. Department of Labor has developed a number of job-oriented training programs which in 1969 contained from 32 percent to 87 percent minority enrollees (U.S. Bureau of Census, 1970). Nearly one in every seven employees of the federal government is black, Native American, Oriental or Spanish-surnamed, but these workers are concentrated at the lower pay levels (U.S. Bureau of Census, 1970).

Even when they are able to secure employment, minority persons have usually been paid less than the going wage rate for whites. As a result of these and other factors, one-third of all non-whites in the United States live on incomes below the official poverty level. The proportion of non-whites earning more than $15,000 per year is less than half that for whites (U.S. Bureau of Census, 1970). Further, few non-whites are able to start and sustain their own business enterprises. Most whites live in homes that they own themselves, but most non-whites live in rented dwellings which are owned by whites.

Race and Public Opinion

In the previous section, we examined the "reality" of the race problem as defined in official reports, statistics, and other empirical data from scientific studies of race relations in the United States. However, as we have seen with other social problems, the public's definition of the situation is not always the same as that indicated by such empirical facts. Here we shall outline the views on race relations held by blacks and whites in America, as they have been expressed in a number of national surveys, as well as in material gathered from specific locations. These studies, although they do not always reflect a knowledge of the situation as it really exists, reveal a decrease in prejudice toward blacks on the part of whites, fundamental misperceptions of the attitudes of blacks by whites, and a preponderance of blacks who favor integration with whites.

In 1971, the Gallup poll reported that more than two-thirds of the American people claimed that they would have voted for a black man for president if he were the best-qualified candidate, while only one-third of the population expressed this opinion in 1958. Fourteen percent of the sample indicated that they would be more likely to vote for a presidential candidate if he had a black vice-president on the ticket, but 23 percent said they would be less likely to vote for an integrated ticket (Gallup, 1971b). A 1970 survey showed that the Ku Klux Klan (who are militantly anti-black) and the Black Panthers (who are militantly pro-black) were equally rejected by Americans, while the National Association for the Advancement of Colored People (moderately pro-black) received more favorable than unfavorable ratings (Gallup, 1970b). Whites were strongly opposed to busing students in order to create integrated schools (Gallup, 1971a), but there was general agreement that white people do not have the right to keep blacks out of their neighborhoods (Campbell, 1971). Few whites objected to sending their children to a school in which there were a few black students, but most whites did object if the school were more than half black (Gallup, 1969b).

In a pioneering study of American race relations done in the late 1940's, Robin Williams pointed out that whites often assume that minority group members are happy with their place in life. However, survey data from Elmira, New York, Steubenville, Ohio, Savannah, Georgia, and Bakersville, California, indicated that only from 12 percent to 41 percent of the blacks found living in these cities to be satisfactory, as compared with 51 percent to 72 percent of the whites (Williams, 1964). More recent research documents the same basic dissatisfaction with American life on the part of minority groups. Many blacks are bothered by the sight of

European immigrants having more success than native-born Americans like themselves (Marx, 1969). With respect to changing their social situations, most blacks think that the civil-rights "revolution" is moving too slowly (Campbell, 1971). Very few believe that most whites want to give blacks a better break (Campbell, 1971), and only one-quarter believe that lately the federal government has been helpful in the struggle for black rights (Goldman, 1970).

Using national samples taken from 1949 to 1969, the Gallup poll has demonstrated that whites have been consistently more satisfied with their jobs, income, housing and children's education than have non-whites (Gallup, 1969a). Most whites are aware that at least some blacks suffer from discrimination in housing or at work, but less than one in five believe that black inequalities in these areas are mainly due to discrimination (Brink and Harris, 1967; Campbell, 1971). Whites typically feel that racial integration is proceeding too quickly (Gallup, 1970a), and that relatively few blacks are in favor of desegregation, while, in fact, over two-thirds of American blacks strongly support desegregation (Campbell, 1971). Whites commonly believe that most black civil-rights actions have been violent and have not helped the cause, but blacks have just the opposite opinion (Campbell, 1971). These differences in the perceptions of blacks and whites about race relations testify to the pervasiveness of the mutual misunderstanding between these groups in America.

Lionel Lokos (1971) has argued that the small minority of militant blacks who receive a large amount of publicity and attention cause whites to perceive blacks as much more militant than they actually are. In fact, few blacks want to use force to win their rights (Goldman, 1970), or would prefer a separate black nation (Goldman, 1970), or are suspicious of whites who try to help them (Marx, 1969). More blacks are in favor of busing than of "black power," and an overwhelming proportion of them are in favor of integration at work, in school, and in housing (Goldman, 1970). Four out of every five black people believe in America strongly enough to be willing to fight for it (Goldman, 1970).

All of these research findings show that black people still want very much to get into the mainstream of American life, just as other minority groups have done before them. White people have some awareness of the situation of blacks in the United States, but the beliefs and opinions of the two groups sharply differ on a number of basic issues.

CHAMPIONS AND THEIR INTERESTS

It may seem incredible to anyone growing up in an era of civil rights movements that there ever was a time when there was no "race problem" in the United States. However, one of the most penetrating and popular histories of reform movements in America, covering the period between the Civil War and World War II, fails even to mention a "race problem" or a "civil rights movement" of any kind during this period (Hofstadter, 1960). That is not to say that no prejudice, discrimination, or racial tension existed in those times, but only that such conditions were not generally defined as a "social problem." The classical "race problem" in the United States, namely, slavery, was generally considered to have been "solved" by the Civil War and the Reconstruction of the South. The new kinds of political and economic constraints against blacks, such as the "Jim Crow" laws* in the South and certain counterparts in the North, which arose in the generation after the Civil War, have been explained by one historian in terms of the political compromises within the white establishment of that time (Woodward, 1955).

At the beginning of the 20th century few, if any, whites, in either South or North, had any interest in promoting the civil rights of blacks. Indeed, most people were not prepared to grant such rights even to white European immigrants, who were streaming into this country by the millions during this period. The occasional race riot in the North, and the more frequent lynchings of blacks in the South, were simply looked at as unpleasant episodes which most Americans were as likely as not to blame on the black victims. There was simply no room for a "Negro problem" in a period when the "quota" of "social problems" was already filled by large-scale immigration, several simultaneous reform movements already generated by the progressive era, World War I, waves of organized crime and "subversives" in the 1920's, the Great Depression, and then finally World War II. After all, a nation which still denied naturalized citizenship to immigrants from the Orient; which summarily, even under the leadership of liberals like Franklin Roosevelt and Earl Warren, moved native-born citizens of Japanese ancestry into concentration camps; and which was still sending its black and white soldiers to war in segregated military units, was not likely to be terribly concerned about a "race problem."

Black Self-Help Programs of the Early 20th Century

Accordingly, such a social movement as there was in the first half of the present century took the form of black "self-help" efforts primarily, with only occasional white help. The NAACP (see below) was organized early in the century, with a largely white membership, but it had very little impact on society until more

---

* The origin of the term "Jim Crow" is not known. It may have been an early term of derision applied to American blacks because of their color, presumably resembling that of crows. In any case, "Jim Crow laws" comprised an enormous body of local, state, and federal legislation which mandated racial segregation in various aspects of social life, including some of the most minute. Segregated military units would be an example on the federal level; laws against mixed marriage on the state level; and ordinances providing for separate public restrooms, drinking fountains, swimming pools, schools, and bus sections on the local level (although some of the latter were also sometimes embodied in state law). Applied more broadly, the term "Jim Crow" also referred to a variety of laws which restricted or denied political power to blacks, such as poll tests and taxes, gerrymandering of electoral districts, racial discrimination in jury selection, and so on.

recent times. In the beginning, black interests had to be promoted mainly by black people. Whatever moral or religious interests and leadership that existed came almost entirely from black churches; but by far the main interests expressed by reform groups of this period, since they were those of blacks themselves, were political and economic interests. Let us review some of the black interest groups which promoted the cause of "the Negro" during this period.

Booker T. Washington and the Tuskegee Institute

In 1895, Booker T. Washington gave an address at the Atlanta Cotton States and International Exposition, at which he (in effect) urged blacks to be happy with their place in life and to try to improve themselves in their present situation. He made it clear that he felt agitation by blacks would be unwise and unproductive (Quarles, 1964). This position was repeated in other public presentations by Washington, and was very well-received by whites since it posed no threat to them. His philosophy and approach to black self-help were institutionalized in a vocational school for blacks, the Tuskegee Institute, founded in 1881, which became the model for other black schools in the South.

Because his definition of the situation was so acceptable to whites, Booker T. Washington moved into the position of the national representative of black people to white society. He had considerable control over money being donated for black educational institutions, and his influence with three successive Republican presidents was so great that most black government appointees during these administrations were hand-picked by him (Quarles, 1964; Logan, 1970). His interest in black economic development led to his founding of the National Negro Business League around the turn of the century, of which he was president (Meier, 1968a). While the number of individuals who could be counted as members of specific organizations headed by Washington was never very large, his influence on race relations in the United States was immense.

W. E. B. Du Bois and the Niagara Movement

In 1895, W. E. B. Du Bois became the first American black to receive a Ph.D. degree. Du Bois was more interested in the "talented tenth" of educated blacks than in the masses who were addressed in the programs of Booker T. Washington. He first criticized Washington in his book, *The Souls of Black Folk* (1903), charging that his approach was a tacit acceptance of the alleged inferiority of the Negro, and that it tended to place the blame for the status of Negroes on themselves, instead of on whites (Davie, 1949; Quarles, 1964; and Myrdal, 1944).

In 1905, a group called the Niagara Movement was formed at a meeting of Du Bois and 28 members of the "talented tenth," held on the Canadian side of Niagara Falls, because accommodations for blacks were unavailable on the American side (Logan, 1970). They declared a battle against all caste distinctions based simply on race and color (Aptheker, 1964). Some 30 branches of the Niagara Movement were formed nationwide, with Du Bois as its executive officer, but membership numbers were always small and mostly limited to blacks who were from a class background above that of the masses (Quarles, 1964). The elitist attitude of Du Bois excluded the average black man, and his aggressive anti-white definition of the situation eliminated any possibility of receiving financial support from the white establishment.

Marcus Garvey and the Universal Negro Improvement Association

When Marcus Garvey organized the Universal Negro Improvement Association (UNIA) in Jamaica in 1914, his model was at first the vocational-occupational one of Booker T. Washington. In 1916 he came to Harlem, a black ghetto in New York City, and soon changed his definition of the race relations situation to a more radical one. In 1918, he began the publication of the *Negro World,* which soon built up a circulation of some 200,000 readers. By the mid-1920's, when he was at the height of his influence, he could count more than one-million followers (Quarles, 1964). His message was that black was beautiful, and that blacks should develop their own institutions in the ghetto. An outgrowth of his ideological orientation was a movement to bring blacks back to Africa, which was supported, for obviously different reasons, by such diverse groups as poor blacks and the Ku Klux Klan (Cronin, 1968; Logan and Winston, 1971).

Garvey organized a number of black businesses, including the Universal Black Cross Nurses, the Black Eagle Flying Corps, and the Black Star Steamship Line. Like both Booker T. Washington and the modern black militants, he preached complete economic self-sufficiency, arguing that blacks should have their own stores and factories (Quarles, 1964). Unfortunately, his business ventures were more flamboyant than financially solid, and so their economic effect on Harlem and other ghettos was more psychological than economic.

Modern Civil Rights Organizations

The civil rights movement is often said to have begun with the Montgomery, Alabama, bus boycott in 1955, although the National Association for the Advancement of Colored People (NAACP) was founded as early as 1909. This organization, though neither very militant nor very strong, was still the major force for civil rights through decades of struggle, until a change in the social climate encouraged the rise of more militant sister organizations at mid-century. Of these, two especially important and durable ones have been the Congress of Racial Equality (CORE) and the Southern Christian Leadership Conference (SCLC).

The National Association for the Advancement of Colored People

As the Niagara Movement weakened, it gave birth to the NAACP, and at this time, both organizations shared the goals and talents of W. E. B. Du Bois. At first, Du Bois was the only non-white among the national officers of the organization, but black control has increased through the years. By the early 1960's, there were over 1,600 local units of the NAACP, with a total membership of more than 400,000 (Meier, 1970). The organization has always been integrated, but the bulk of the rank and file members has become increasingly black. The national budget has exceeded one-million dollars annually since 1963, with an additional million dollars being spent annually by the affiliated National Legal Defense Fund. Presently, the professional staff under the direction of Roy Wilkins includes more than one-hundred employees (Simpson and Yinger, 1965).

Compared to Booker T. Washington or the National Urban League, the NAACP has been a fairly aggressive organization, but in the light of more recent black power movements, it seems quite conservative. Local branches participate in a wide variety of activities, depending on their interests, but the national organization has concentrated its energies on furthering the civil rights of blacks by engaging in court cases of strategic importance in the civil rights field, particularly those which have had a good chance of success. These cases have included such issues as the admission of blacks to schools supported by public funds, ending the white residential segregation permitted by municipal ordinance, and ending private residential restrictive covenants (Simpson and Yinger, 1965). The NAACP has not ignored the needs of ghetto blacks, but its definition of their needs has not always been the same as their own definitions (Broom and Glenn, 1965).

The Southern Christian Leadership Conference and Martin Luther King

On December 1, 1955, Rosa Parks sat down in the white section of a Montgomery, Alabama, bus and refused to move when a white man entered the section. She was arrested, and blacks decided to boycott the bus company at a meeting the same night. Dr. Martin Luther King, Jr., the pastor of the Dexter Avenue Baptist Church, was elected president of the group, which named itself the Montgomery Improvement Association. Within four days, the bus company had lost three-fourths of its passengers.

The Southern Christian Leadership Conference grew out of this incident. It was founded in 1957 by one-hundred black clergymen, mostly Baptist ministers, who defined the civil rights struggle in moral terms, and urged the use of non-violent direct-action techniques to resist segregation and other forms of discrimination in the South (Quarles, 1964; Simpson and Yinger, 1965). The organization grew only a little from 1957 to 1960, when it had a staff of six and a budget of less than 100,000 dollars, but it expanded rapidly between 1960 and 1963, by which time it had a staff of more than 30 workers and a budget of nearly one-million dollars (Cameron, 1966).

Under the leadership of Martin Luther King, the SCLC functioned as a channel of communication between blacks and the larger society, as well as between radical and conservative factions within the civil rights movement. The SCLC is actually composed of other organizations, rather than having a membership of individuals. Most of the demonstrations it has sponsored have had only a small number of active participants, though sensationalistic press coverage and white anxiety have tended to inflate the popular perception of the size of the demonstrations and thus to increase their impact on the social system (von Eschen, 1970).

The Congress of Racial Equality (CORE)

CORE was founded in 1942, but it lacked a paid staff until the mid-1950's (Meier, 1970). Originally operating as a primarily white liberal organization based in the North and upper South, it gradually took on an increasingly black membership and became more militant, in contrast to the NAACP and SCLC. CORE pioneered in the use of the sit-in and other non-violent tactics developed so effectively by other groups in the 1960's. (See Chapter 6.)

Black Nationalist Organizations

Black nationalism has been present in the doctrines of black social movements since the days of Marcus Garvey at least, and has included such ideals as economic self-sufficiency, separatism, and "black power." In a more general sense, the so-called black nationalist organizations can be considered a part of the civil rights movement itself, since they exerted a strong influence upon that movement and frequently joined forces with it. However, they are different enough in their basic ideological stance to warrant brief separate treatment here. Perhaps the three best contemporary examples of black nationalism are the Black Muslims, the Black Panthers, and the Student Non-Violent Coordinating Committee (SNCC).

The Black Muslims

In 1930, the prophet W. D. Fard began preaching among blacks in the Detroit ghetto, where eventually he founded the Black Muslims. As the shock of the Depression reached the ghetto, many blacks began to view whites as "devils," or as basically evil. In 1934, Fard vanished, and he was succeeded by Elijah Muhammed, who led this new movement dedicated to a rejection of white American society and culture, including American citizenship, Christianity, and even the goal of racial integration (Lincoln, 1972a). A few years later, membership began to decline from its peak of about 10,000. Many Muslims were imprisoned for refusing to serve in the Armed Forces during World War II. Muhammed himself spent three years in prison for draft evasion, and for influencing other blacks to refuse the draft. Malcolm Little, a younger leader who joined later on, changed his surname to "X" (as did many other Muslims) to signify his freedom from white-given names of the slavery period. Malcolm X had been a criminal in his youth, and was converted to the movement while in prison for armed robbery. He was a charismatic leader, and he quickly rose to prominence within the Muslim organization. In the early sixties, he had a falling out with Elijah Muhammed, at which time he rejected the separatist doctrines of the Muslims, and founded his own group, the Muslim Mosque, Inc. (Logan and Winston, 1971). In October, 1965, he was assassinated, but his place as one of the "saints" of the black militancy movement is assured by the popularity of his many writings and recordings (Malcolm X, 1964; and Breitman, 1965 and 1968).

The Student Non-Violent Coordinating Committee (SNCC)

At the request of SCLC, a large group of student activists, representing various organizations in the South, met in Raleigh, North Carolina, in April, 1960 (Simpson and Yinger, 1965). They decided to coordinate their activities, hired a secretary, and, in another meeting later that year, formed the SNCC (Matusow, 1970). In line with its direct-action philosophy to end segregation and discrimination in public and private places, its sit-in campaign was so well-coordinated and so successful that by 1961, more than one-hundred cities in the South had ended racial segregation in their restaurants (Waskow, 1966). When CORE was forced to call off its own "freedom rides" because of mob violence, many of the SNCC student volunteers rushed to Alabama to continue them (Matusow, 1970).

The Black Panthers

The term "Black Panther" was first used in 1965 during a voter registration drive in Lowndes County, Alabama. Huey P. Newton and Bobby Seale organized the Black Panther Party in California, shortly after the Watts riot, with the main purpose of helping ghetto residents resist false accusations by the police. As the movement developed, it added the goals of full employment, adequate housing, resistance to police brutality and to consumer exploitation, and the teaching of black culture and history, to its roster. However, these goals were usually overlooked by the press, which reported the Panthers' militant and threatening language in detail, and always gave top coverage to its conflicts and confrontations with the police (Logan and Winston, 1971).

When Black Panther Huey Newton was convicted of voluntary manslaughter in the killing of a white police officer in 1968, the group received a large amount of national publicity. Newton claimed that the shooting was in self-defense, and blacks all around the country rallied to his cause (Logan and Winston, 1971). Eldridge Cleaver, Huey Newton, and Bobby Seale were the major personalities in the transformation of a local California organization to a national movement overnight (Marine, 1969). Cleaver's charisma made his books, *Post-Prison Writings and Speeches* and *Soul on Ice* best-sellers (Cleaver, 1967 and 1970), and his speeches were in demand by liberal whites as well as by blacks. By 1970, there were chapters and branches of the Black Panthers in 28 American cities, but the number of individual members was a closely guarded secret (Pfaff, 1970).

Mexican-American (Chicano) Organizations

Mexican-Americans, like blacks, have joined a bewildering assortment of organizations in an attempt to achieve fuller participation in American society. Most of these organizations are based in the West, mainly in the far West. They include the Alianza Hispano Americana, the League of United Latin-American Citizens, various United Leagues, the Community Service Organization, the American G.I. Forum of the United States, the Council of Mexican-American Affairs, the Association of Mexican-American Educators, the Mexican-American Political Association, the Political Association for Spanish-Speaking Organization, the Alianza Federal de Mercedes, the National Task Force de la Raza, the National Farm Workers' Association (later renamed the United Farm Workers' Organizing Committee), and a great many others (Briegal, 1970).

The oldest organizations are probably the mutual benefit societies, which began in the early 1800's. Neither these original groups nor the more recent organizations have been successful in dealing with discrimination by Anglos (a Mexican-American term for most whites) in a variety of crucial areas such as education, housing and jobs. These failures, combined with the comparative successes of the black civil rights movement, encouraged Chicanos (a term preferred by many Mexican-Americans for themselves) to form more militant organizations. Perhaps the two most outstanding examples of militant Chicano groups are the Alianza Federal de Mercedes and the United Farm Workers' Organizing Committee, which we shall discuss below (Briegal, 1970). Most Chicano organizations, however, are not very militant, but instead prefer a combination of self-help activities and legitimate political pressure to improve the position of Chicanos in the areas of education, career advancement, and income. To this end, many Chicano organizations participate in local election campaigns and maintain a vigilant pressure on government and industry to see that guidelines of "affirmative action" are implemented. These tactics, of course, do not gain the publicity given to the more militant organizations such as Alianza and UFWOC.

The Alianza Federal de Mercedes

When the United States acquired what is now New Mexico, there were more than 50,000 Mexican settlers living there, with a well-developed class structure. There was little violence associated with the takeover, and the entire Mexican society was absorbed into the United States (Moore, 1970). However, as Anglo settlers arrived in increasing numbers, they were able to manipulate land taxes, mortgages, and litigations over disputed land titles in their favor, and to gain control over most of the existing privately held lands. When, in addition, the state and federal governments appropriated much of the common land that had belonged to the incorporated towns and villages, the land loss to Spanish-speaking citizens totaled nearly four-million acres (Love, 1970).

The Alianza Federal de Mercedes was founded in 1963 by Reies Lopez Tijerina in New Mexico, with the goal of regaining the land lost by Mexican-Americans to Anglos since the conquest of Mexico by the United States (Briegal, 1970). Alianza was to hold in trust any lands it regained, and its tribunals were to decide which Spanish-speaking people should be given lifetime land allotments. The organization was also working for the use of Spanish as a second language in grade schools, and the requirement that all elementary schoolteachers in New Mexico should be fluent in Spanish (Gonzalez, 1970).

At first, Alianza tried legal means to achieve its goals, but in 1966, with no success in sight, it turned to militant tactics. It proclaimed the Republic of San Joaquin del Rio de Chama (in Rio Arriba County, New Mexico), and tried to take over part of the Kit Carson National Forest (Love, 1970). At that time, it claimed as many as 20,000 members, drawn largely from lower-class Spanish-speaking residents of New Mexico and the adjacent states (Gonzalez, 1970). As a result of continuing militant activity, some of it illegal, Tijerina and some of his followers were jailed in 1967, and the organization has been dormant since then (Gonzalez, 1970).

The United Farm Workers

In California, the rapid influx of Anglo settlers, beginning in the mid-19th century, further separated the sparsely distributed Mexicans and left them disorganized. This political disorganization has continued into modern times, as large numbers of Mexican workers have been shuffled back and forth across the border according to the labor needs of the farm economy in California and the Southwest. The more settled Mexican immigrants in the urban areas have been "ghettoized" in *barrios* and discriminated against in much the same way as blacks have been. Joan Moore (1970) has applied the label "economic colonialism" to this situation.

Beginning in the mid-1960's, a farm workers' organization began to take shape under the leadership of Cesar Chavez; it eventually developed into the United

Farm Workers' Organizing Committee (UFWOC), and then became a full-fledged farm workers' union with AFL-CIO affiliation. While open to all farm workers, its membership is overwhelmingly Chicano, and it mainly promotes the basic "bread-and-butter" interests of the Mexican-American *braceros,* or farm workers. Since its inception, UFWOC has been embroiled in controversy over its legitimacy as a truly democratic representative of all farm workers, and it has been strongly challenged by a rival membership in the Teamsters' Union.

Native American (Indian) Organizations

The destruction of Native American or Indian tribal cultures that resulted from contact with European pioneers when this country was first settled led to the rise of many messianic social movements, among them the Peyote Cult, the Earth Lodge Cult, the Dream Dance of the Menomini, the Ghost Dance, and groups led by Handsome Lake, Smohalla, Kolaskin and Isatai (Lanternari, 1963). Only in recent years have Native Americans moved from retreatist religious and mystical movements to the political offensive. In this section, we will examine the Ghost Dance of 1890 as an example of messianic movements, and then two contemporary elements of the "red power" movement: the National Indian Youth Council (NIYC), and the American Indian Movement (AIM).

The Great Ghost Dance of 1890

In 1889, a Paiute shaman called Wovoka rose in a trance to see God. God taught him how to dance a ceremony that would hasten reunion with the dead, and gave him charge over the West. The movement spread rapidly among various tribes of Plains Indians, with each tribe having its own version of how whites would lose their control over the Indians. At this time, the Sioux were the largest and strongest tribe on the Great Plains, with 26,000 members. The years from 1868 to 1890 had brought a long series of tragedies—land losses to whites, loss of the buffalo, disease epidemics and loss of crops due to poor weather conditions. Under the leadership of Sitting Bull, the Sioux tribes became particularly excited by the idea that the time of punishment for red men had come to an end, and the movement gained momentum (LaBarre, 1970).

The Sioux believed that if they wore ghost shirts painted with the sun, moon and stars, and if they danced the ghost dance, they would never again become sick, and the bullets of the white men could no longer hurt them. The dancing alarmed the Indian agents, who sent for federal troops. Short Bull and Kicking Bear escaped from the reservation into the Badlands with a large party of tribal members. Sitting Bull stayed in camp and was killed when the troops came. Later that year (1890), Yellow Bird led a short revolt which resulted in the massacre of many Sioux men, women and children at the Battle of Wounded Knee (South Dakota).

This ended the Ghost Dance as a militant movement, as well as the military threat of the Native Americans to the whites (Mooney, 1896; and LaBarre, 1970).

The term "red power" was first used in public at the 1966 Convention of the National Congress of American Indians (NCAI), which, together with the National Indian Youth Council (NIYC), leads the red power movement (Day, 1972). Vine Deloria, Executive Director of the NCAI, defines red power as: "We simply want the power, the political and economic power, to run our own lives in our own way" (Day, 1972). The general goals of the red power movement for the native Americans include increased education, improved health, retention of reservations as a land base, economic development, political sovereignty at the tribal level, and the development of Indian culture (Witt, 1970).

The pan-Indianism that was inherent in the Ghost Dance of 1890, and in contemporary movements such as the Peyote religion, has continued to develop. This trend has been accentuated among tribes on the Great Plains, who have been forced to live together on multi-tribal reservations, treated by whites as "Indians" instead of as members of distinct individual tribes, and pressured to assimilate into white culture (Thomas, 1970). One reaction to these pressures has been a broadly based movement aimed at preserving both Indian and tribal identity (Howard, 1970a).

Two important organizations in the red power movement are the National Indian Youth Council (NIYC), and the American Indian Movement (AIM). The first of these, NIYC, was organized in the early 1960's by ten young Native Americans (Day, 1972). Originally, it was intended to be mainly a forum for working out ideas and developing leadership techniques for the improvement of Indian conditions (Witt, 1970). Since 1964, however, beginning with the leadership of Mel Thom, NIYC has grown increasingly militant, and has been an active participant in the "fish-ins" of western Washington, which will be discussed further on. Even more militant, however, is the American Indian Movement (AIM), which came into being in 1972 and gained national attention a year later with its military occupation of Wounded Knee, South Dakota. Led mainly by young but mature, educated activists of urban origin, AIM has posed a strong challenge to the more moderate Indian leaders of the country, particularly those among the Oglala Sioux of South Dakota. Its appeal to a long downtrodden people can perhaps best be illustrated by the comment of a Sioux woman who excitedly watched an AIM contingent return to Pine Ridge, South Dakota, from a successful confrontation with white leaders of a nearby Nebraska town in 1972:

[H]ere came carload after carload (of) these virile-looking men with their long braids. We hadn't seen long braids in so long. (Aarons, 1973:18)

The chief federal agency that has been assigned responsibility for relations with American Indians is the Bureau of Indian Affairs (BIA), which has received much criticism lately for its record of Indian treatment. While it is probably no more or less humane than other federal bureaucracies, and no more or less well-intentioned, many modern Indians, especially the more militant, characterize the BIA as paternalistic, insensitive, and even oppressive in its relations with Indians. Many social critics, white as well as Indian, have called for changes in the mission and goals of the BIA, and for many more Indian staff members in the agency, in order to make it more responsive to the needs of the Native Americans. It remains, however, the focus of much of the hostility of AIM and other newer Indian organizations.

Opposition Publics and Interest Groups

So far we have been largely concerned with various representative interest groups (mainly of a political and economic nature) which have promoted the interests of racial minorities in our recent history. We say that these are "representative," rather than exhaustive, groups, not only because they by no means constitute a full list of the groups supporting black, Chicano, and Native American interests, but also because they do not include the innumerable groups that have arisen during the past century or so to represent the interests of the host of immigrant ethnic groups to our shores from Europe, Asia, and elsewhere. Time and space here do not permit a review of the experiences of all these other ethnic groups, although their history provides many parallels and precedents to the more recent efforts of the black, Chicano, and Indian minorities to gain entrance to the larger American society particularly in its urban areas (Handlin, 1951). One of the many similarities between the experiences of all of these groups has been the continuing opposition of established interests in the larger society. It seems that newcomers to "the system" have always had to fight their way in by one means or another. The opposition interests seem to have been mainly economic and political, although we can see evidence also of what might be called psychological opposition interests. Let us look briefly at these latter interests first.

Psychological Opposition

By "psychological opposition" in this instance we mean opposition that has its origins in the socialization of a person (including his "upbringing"), rather than in his economic or political interests. One form of this opposition may derive from the cultural norms of the society or region in which the person grows up (Rose, 1964). A person who is reared to believe that blacks should be subordinate to whites, or that they are somehow inferior to whites, is likely to resist any changes in such definitions as "unnatural" or even "immoral." While we generally associate such an attitude toward blacks with the traditional South, it has been widespread throughout all sections of the nation, though perhaps less overt in some places than in others. Invidious definitions have been applied as well to other ethnic groups in our history, not only the Indians, the Chicanos, the Orientals, and other more "visible" groups, but also to the Italians, the Irish, and the Scandinavians. It is largely this cultural heritage of welcoming "outsiders," on the one hand, while trying to keep them in their (subordinate) "place," on the other hand, that has led some social critics to refer to ours as a "racist society".

Another kind of psychological opposition to the efforts of ethnic groups or movements to improve their circumstances takes the form of a certain personality syndrome that has been called variously the "authoritarian personality," the "closed mind," "prejudice," or "bigotry" (Allport, Adorno, et al., Rokeach, and others). To some extent, such a personality type may result from the kind of cultural norms discussed above, but social scientists usually consider it instead as a product of certain kinds of parent-child relations, and/or of various kinds of "status-anxiety" in adult life. In other words, regardless of whether the surrounding culture defines an "outgroup" as inferior, dangerous, etc., an individual may have learned from the way his parents treated him and others that the world is divided into "high" and "low" types, and that "they" (blacks, Jews, Irish, or whomever) are among the "low." Or, his own insecurities about himself, his job, or his social standing may cause him to look for scapegoats to blame for his difficulties, or lower-status people in comparison to whom he feels superior. Psychological interests which oppose ethnic movements are seldom, if ever, expressed in separate organizations based only on such interests; however, they are often important in motivating people to join political or economic opposition groups.

Economic Opposition

The range of economic segments which benefit (or think they benefit) from the continued subordination of certain ethnic groups is large and varied. One of the oldest and most militant economic interests which is aligned against ethnic minorities is the working-class public, whose opposition has often been crystallized and institutionalized through labor unions. Under pressure from recent legislation and from the federal government, unions in more recent years have softened their opposition and have even (in some cases) worked actively to integrate and promote the interests of blacks and Chicanos. Historically, however, and even now to some extent, the "aroused" minorities of each generation have been considered a threat to the jobs and the status of the working class, particularly if such minorities have been willing (as they often have been) to work for lower wages and under poorer conditions than those generally prevalent. The opposition of the established working class, while understandable in a way, is all the more ironic because that class itself has so often been made up of older minorities or immigrants.

A great many other economic interests, both national and local, have felt themselves threatened in one way or another by the newest minorities on the scene (nowadays, mainly blacks, Chicanos, and Indians). For example, many localities have formed homeowners' associations which have attempted to keep minorities from moving into their neighborhoods. These associations have had euphemistic names such as community associations or neighborhood improvement associations, but their purpose has been mainly to prevent neighborhood integration, and thereby to "protect" property values in the area. They have been aided and abetted at times by realtors and real-estate organizations using a variety of ruses to turn away minority customers, or entering into restrictive covenants with housing developers. Hotel and restaurant operators have also feared that service to minority customers would drive away their "established clientele," and it was common for blacks and other minority groups to be refused service in hotels, restaurants, barber shops, and other places until the various civil rights acts were passed in the 1960's. When the NAACP, through legislative lobbying and court actions, strove to make all such restrictions against minority groups illegal, many of the business interests involved organized an opposition movement and worked vigorously to keep "free enterprise free." There is an irony inherent in this situation as well, for one of the basic principles of the classical theory of capitalism is the "color-blindness" of the marketplace; if two people can trade to their mutual advantage, it is not supposed to make any difference in capitalist theory what their race, color, or creed might be.

Political Interests and Minorities

Minority groups in our history have often been treated as "political commodities," and the position that various political parties and interest groups has taken toward them has varied according to the political advantage they have perceived. If the parties could gain political advantage by opposing one or more minority groups, then such action was taken; if, on the other hand, they could amass votes and receive other political benefits by championing the cause of the oppressed minorities, then these minorities sometimes found powerful allies in the political establishment. C. Vann Woodward (1955) has written an historical account of the process by which blacks, especially in the South, were subordinated by whites, and it is clearly a process which was suited to the political needs of the various white parties. Indians, and even Spanish-speaking Americans, have not been very popular causes for any politician to sponsor, largely because they are relatively small in numbers and have been geographically concentrated in only a few states. By contrast, more recently blacks have come to be considered political assets by both major political parties, since they have migrated from the South to become more of a nationwide political force, and have grown in numbers to more than 10 percent of the population. Blacks have been more successfully recruited to the Democratic than to the Republican Party, as have many immigrant groups, but until the 1960's the powerful southern bloc of the Democratic Party held it back from really promoting minority interests. Aside from political parties themselves, there have been a number of special political pressure groups that have generally opposed the growth of power of blacks and other minorities. Perhaps the best-known of these is the Ku Klux Klan, which has operated both inside and outside the law to preserve the legacy of white Protestant domination, and to intimidate any who have tried to challenge that domination. The KKK has had its own ups and downs. Its periods of strength have occurred just after the Civil War, again in the 1920's and 1930's, and then in the 1950's and 1960's. Since the mid-sixties, it has declined in influence considerably. Although it is primarily based in the South, its fiery crosses and ghost-like white-hooded garb have been seen in many other places, too. Another group which has opposed minority-group rights, but which is much less disposed to illegitimate means of terrorist tactics, is the John Birch Society. The Society has operated throughout the nation since the 1950's to stem the "communist menace," but in general it works against any change in the traditional power relations between dominant and minority cultures (Forster and Epstein, 1964; and Broyles, 1966). In fact, most organizations generally identified as "far right" on the political spectrum have stood in opposition to legislation or other action that would promote the interests of the minorities at the expense of the dominant white middle class.

Scientific Interest Groups and Race Relations

Scientists have left us a very mixed heritage of information and "truth" on the subject of racial differences and race relations. Over the past century or so, scientific literature has, at one extreme, advocated the importance of racial differences, and the superiority of some races over others, and then, at the other extreme, has taken the position that the genetic differences between races are unimportant as determinants of behavior. Furthermore, it has taken most of the positions between these two extremes as well (Snyder, 1962). Actually, it appears from an historical perspective that biological and social scientists have generally held scientific positions that were in accord with the prevalent intellectual fashions of their times. In the late 19th and early 20th centuries, when most people in Europe and America believed that certain behavior patterns around the world were innate or "inbred" in the various races, and that the "white race," on balance, was superior, most scientists said about the same thing. More recently, the great majority of scientists in all fields have held to the more liberal ideology, now especially fashionable in academic circles, that there are no innate differences in behavior or ability among the races; that no race is inherently superior to any other; and that there is no scientific or any other justification for racial segregation and discrimination. The ideas of scientists such as William Shockley and Arthur Jensen, who have suggested in recent years that some cognitive and intellectual traits may systematically differ among the races, have not been well-received by the modern scientific establishment. The question of the relative importance of heredity versus environment in racial differences is unanswered in scientific research, although the great majority of scientists today favor a primarily environmentalist explanation.

Aside from the issue of the nature and causes of racial differences, social scientists have been interested mainly in two other issues: (1) how and why societies make the kinds of racial or ethnic distinctions that they do, and subordinate certain ethnic groups, or, what are the "structural-functional" determinants of interethnic relations; and (2) how and why some individuals, or categories of individuals, come to hold negative or hostile attitudes against other racial or ethnic groups. The second issue, that of prejudice, has probably been dealt with most in social-science research and literature. Some of the theories and research focusing on the structural-functional explanation of interethnic relations have held that ethnic distinctions are made in every multi- (or bi-) racial society, and that these processes of stratification simply represent different ways of organizing societies to accomplish the tasks and goals which are collectively believed in by most members of the society (Merton, 1949; Parsons, 1951; and Davis and Moore, 1945). From this point of view, racial conflicts are seen as limited and temporary in nature, and as often leading to the assimilation of the ethnic minority groups. Other social scientists emphasize instead the importance of the conflict between the dominant and the minority ethnic groups. They see this conflict as an ongoing struggle over power and economic assets, which is potentially destructive of the society and which can be kept within bounds only by some kind of mutual dependence or interests between the conflicting groups, or by out and out coercion on the part of the dominant group (e.g., Dahrendorf, 1958; and van den Berghe, 1967).

An enormous body of social science literature has been produced on the subject of racial or ethnic prejudice, especially since World War II, beginning with the pioneering work of psychologists such as Allport (1954), Adorno, et al. (1950), and Rokeach (1960), and continuing up to the present time with the more sociological approaches of Myrdal (1944), Williams (1964), A. Rose (1965), P. Rose (1964), Yinger (1965), Glock and Stark (1966), and many others. In virtually all of the scientific writing on prejudice, it has been considered, implicitly or explicitly, as "pathological"; that is, prejudice has been considered as an unfortunate and undesirable personality trait. Much has been written about its causes, its consequences, and how it might be eliminated. In the scientific literature it has generally been attributed either to unenlightened socializing influences in the home or community, especially in the South, or to abnormal or neurotic personality patterns such as "authoritarianism," both of which were discussed earlier in the section on psychological opposition. The development of such personality patterns has usually been blamed either upon misguided parental behavior, or else upon the difficulties which the prejudiced person has had in coping with his own frustrations while striving for status, recognition, or economic security. Some of the more recent literature, in order to counterbalance the preoccupation of scientific research with the subject of prejudice, has attempted to develop theories about other aspects of interethnic relations, and to synthesize the various theoretical notions that have been put forth earlier (see especially Blalock, 1967, and Schermerhorn, 1970).

RACE RELATIONS AND SOCIAL MOVEMENTS

Having provided brief descriptions of the various interest groups and organizations that have been involved in defining the "race problem" of our society, we will next review some of the structural conditions which helped to generate the movements for racial reform, some of their more important strategies and tactics, and their respective "natural histories."

The Early Black Self-Help Movement

Booker T. Washington was at the height of his power during the worst years of oppression of blacks between the Civil War and the present. The Niagara Movement also began during these years, but it quickly faded without having had much impact. Marcus Garvey began his career at a time when things were just "bottoming out" for blacks, and the early 1920's, when the UNIA flourished, witnessed the first real advances for black citizens since the Reconstruction period.

Perhaps the best way to illustrate the tenor of these times is to list some of the significant events which promoted black interests of the years from 1905 to 1925. In 1905, the Niagara Movement was organized, and R. S. Abbott began publishing the radical newspaper, the *Chicago Defender,* which urged blacks to move from the South to the urban North. In 1909, the NAACP was founded, followed one year later by the National Urban League. The UNIA was organized in Jamaica in 1914, and moved to the United States two years later. In 1919, W. E. B. Du Bois organized the first Pan-African Congress, which met in Paris. In 1920, the UNIA convention in Harlem captured the imagination of ghetto blacks, and Marcus Garvey filled Madison Square Garden with a primarily black audience for a speech. As the final event in this 20-year span, A. Philip Randolph organized the Brotherhood of Sleeping Car Porters in 1925.

At the beginning of this period, conditions for American blacks were deteriorating. Near the end of the period, conditions were just beginning to improve. After World War I, when black soldiers returned home to face a changing environment, blacks began to question their place in American society. The sudden postwar increase in violent racial conflict (83 confirmed lynchings, over 200 public Ku Klux Klan meetings, and 25 major race riots in 1919 alone) suggests that whites may have been aware of and reacted to the threat to the social structure posed by black social movements which were attempting to redefine the black condition as an American social problem.

The view held by Booker T. Washington was that the only way for blacks to reach the goals of full citizenship and integration was to hide them beneath a passive mask that did not threaten the status of whites (Meier, 1968a). His approach was heavily criticized by W. E. B. Du Bois and Marcus Garvey, but unlike Washington, neither of these latter two leaders made any significant inroads into the white power structure, nor did they penetrate the black masses in the deep South. Washington honestly believed that the strategy of increasing black economic strength would lead to racial advancement on all fronts (Quarles, 1964). However, he also covertly contributed to court cases against discrimination in a number of ways, and attacked discrimination publicly in many speeches made after 1904 (Logan, 1970).

In contrast to Washington, who had a broader appeal, W. E. B. Du Bois used the strategy of intellectual expression through books and articles. This approach never won him the admiration of the black masses, but it later resulted in important documents for black equality such as the NAACP-sponsored *An Appeal to the World,* which unsuccessfully petitioned the United Nations for redress against the denial of black civil rights in the United States (Davie, 1949).

Booker T. Washington appealed to rural blacks in the South, W. E. B. Du Bois had his success largely with intellectuals in the international community, but Marcus Garvey captivated urban blacks in the North. His main tactic was the "big sell." He was a showman who never missed a chance to put on the biggest possible extravaganza for any occasion. Some of his financial schemes, however, were disastrous, and, since he had raised some of his money through the mails, he was prosecuted by the federal government for using the mails to defraud. In 1923, he was convicted and sent to prison, which effectively ended his movement (Drimmer, 1968), though it survived another decade in attenuated form.

The Modern Civil Rights Movement

The participation of black troops in two world wars had a significant effect on American race relations. The period of World War I was a low point in the black struggle for freedom, but the agitation which followed it began the long struggle toward black power. During World War II, large numbers of black soldiers had the experience of being treated as equals in many foreign countries, and they were not willing to accept the "black Sambo" role when they returned to the United States. By the early 1950's, many small improvements in the blacks' situation had led to expectations for still further advances, which most whites were unwilling to deliver. In addition, the frustration that most blacks felt in the face of the rather slow progress they made through court actions made them ready to accept more militant modes to obtain racial equality.

The NAACP was in existence long before the civil rights explosion of the 1950's, of course, but its strategy up until that time had been largely the legal recourse. At first, it pressed cases under the "separate-but-equal" theory of the Plessy v. Ferguson decision of 1896, believing that the South would abandon its segregated black facilities if it were required to bring them up to the white standard. But as the South demonstrated its willingness to improve black education somewhat, rather than permit integration in the schools, it became clear that tactical victories in the "separate-but-equal" cases were strategic failures. As a result, in 1954 the NAACP decided to make a more direct attack on segregation (Quarles, 1964).

In May, 1950, the NAACP filed a suit in South Carolina to force the schools of Clarendon County to admit students without regard to race. When this and related cases reached the Supreme Court four years later as Brown v. Board of Education of Topeka, Kansas, the Court, in a historic reversal of precedent, promulgated the principle that separate educational facilities were inherently unequal and therefore unconstitutional (Quarles, 1964). This meant that the NAACP would now have the backing of the federal government in getting school districts in the South (and eventually in the North, too) reorganized to eliminate segregated schools. In the late 1950's, more militant organizations mounted a challenge to the NAACP's dominance of the civil rights field. To meet this challenge, the NAACP took on a more militant style, giving greater support to "direct action," while at the same time continuing its support of legal cases (Broom and Glenn, 1965). For example, in 1962, the NAACP took on more than 90 percent of the costs of legal fees for civil rights cases (Quarles, 1964).

Unlike the NAACP, Martin Luther King, Jr., and the SCLC have had little time to argue the fine points of the law. King's success rested on the fact that he clearly articulated the needs and goals of blacks, both to themselves and to their white fellow-citizens. His rhetorical strategy was to call forth feelings of guilt in whites, and then to relieve these feelings, leaving his audiences anxious to support such a reasonable and moderate man (Meier, 1968b). CORE pioneered in such non-violent direct-action tactics as sit-ins, boycotts, picketing, and marching, but King elaborated upon them, extended them further into the deep South, and tied them to the prestigious non-violent philosophy of Gandhi. White reaction to the early boycotts was bitter, but black participation was so nearly complete that it was impossible for the white establishment to bring enough pressure to bear on the boycotts to break them. Subsequent court decisions against Montgomery's bus segregation ordinance vindicated the boycott (Broom and Glenn, 1965). Through the techniques of non-violence, black protestors gained a moral edge on whites, which made serious resistance to blacks impossible in the long run, and made it seem incongruous to portray blacks as morally inferior to whites (Bell, 1970; and Smith, 1970). Since the assassination of Martin Luther King in 1968, SCLC has not been nearly as effective and influential as it was in its early days.

CORE began as a small, predominantly white-liberal middle-class movement, which concentrated its work in the North and upper South. Members were among the best-educated in their communities. White intellectuals joined forces with blacks who were in the process of moving up from the working class into the middle class (Bell, 1970). In 1956, CORE began work in the deep South, and in 1961, it selected James Farmer as its director, thus changing its image to a more militant and separatist one, and increasing its support among younger black people (Meier, 1970).

The sit-in and other non-violent techniques had been pioneered by CORE, but the college students who began the sit-in movement in Greensboro, North Carolina, on February 1, 1960, had never heard of these early protests. The rapid spread of the sit-ins across the South was generated in part by the failure of the states to carry out the 1954 Supreme Court public-school desegregation decision, and by the success of Martin Luther King's Montgomery bus boycott in 1958.

CORE was temporarily forgotten in this surge of protest. It regained the focus of public attention with its freedom rides through the South in 1961, in which many protestors were beaten by mobs of angry whites (Waskow, 1966; Meier and Rudwick, 1969). By 1963, CORE had grown to as many as 10,000 active and 60,000 associate members, with an annual budget of $715,000, a paid staff of 35, and a number of unpaid "subsistence workers" (Simpson and Yinger, 1965). It has, however, declined somewhat in numbers and influence since then.

Black Nationalist Movements

The civil rights movement in the South was based on the existence of an indigenous black subculture, which gave its members a sense of identity and integrity. Northern blacks were marginal to this movement, since they were several generations removed from their Southern origins and subject to a white culture that was very different from the one in the South, which was the target of most of the civil rights actions. The black power movement fulfilled the cultural needs of ghetto blacks in the North in much the same way as the civil rights movement had done for rural blacks in the South (Laue, 1972). Expressing the sentiments of many ghetto blacks, Stokely Carmichael said:

We must face the fact that, in the past, what we have called the movement has not really questioned the middle-class values and institutions of this country. If anything, it has accepted those values and institutions without fully realizing their racist nature. (Carmichael and Hamilton, 1967:21)

The black power movement rejects white culture as a source of black identity, and expresses distrust of whites and middle-class blacks who try to accommodate to the standards and values of white society (Lincoln, 1972b).

The Student Non-violent Coordinating Committee has always followed the strategy of direct action against discrimination, but their tactics became increasingly militant during the 1960's. Believing that the federal government under President John F. Kennedy had guaranteed them the protection of the law, they moved into a massive voter registration campaign in the deep South. By 1963, SNCC had a staff of 70 headed by John Lewis and an annual budget of $160,000 (Simpson and Yinger, 1965). In 1964, its staff numbered 150, four-fifths of them black. The failure of the government to protect SNCC workers in the South, conflicts between blacks and whites within the movement during the "freedom summers" of 1964 and 1965, and the failure of the Democratic Convention in 1964 to seat the black delegates from the Freedom Democratic Party in Mississippi, all pushed SNCC toward a more radical "solution" to the American race relations "problem" (Matusow, 1970).

In 1966, the SNCC national conference rejected the non-violent doctrines of John Lewis, and elected Stokely Carmichael their new chairman (Matusow, 1970). He had originated the "black power" slogan in 1965, which he subsequently defined as control of political power by blacks where they were in the majority, and proper representation and sharing of control where they were in the minority. Black power also meant liberating internal and external "colonies" of blacks from white economic exploitation (Logan and Winston, 1971). Carmichael rejected the goal of assimilation of blacks into middle-class America, which he viewed as inherently racist. From this viewpoint, black group solidarity was necessary before a minority group could bargain effectively with the white liberal establishment (Cleaver, 1967).

In 1969, SNCC changed the word "Non-violent" in its name to "National," thus removing the last vestige of the organization's formal commitment to non-violence. By this time, the success of the Black Panthers had already led to a proliferation of black groups who approved of the use of violence as a legitimate means to achieve their ends, such as the Black Liberators, the Republic of New Africa, the

Mau Mau, the Revolutionary Action Movement, and the Black Liberation Army (Logan and Winston, 1971).

The trend toward a rhetoric of violence, and away from the pacifistic Gandhian strategy of Martin Luther King, was based on a number of factors.

1/ The unintended violence caused by non-violent protests came to be defined by blacks as necessary to the success of the movement.
2/ The success of the Civil Rights Movement caused it to recruit greatly increased numbers of protestors, thus weakening discipline and training within the movement.
3/ The composition of the protestors shifted from heavily middle class to predominantly working class.
4/ Having achieved many of the initial and most easily reached goals of blacks, the movement had to select other goals such as welfare rights and white acceptance of the legitimacy of black culture which whites could resist with much less guilt.
5/ Whites developed new elites to resist the black demands, and techniques for coping with non-violent protests which rendered them rather useless as tactics. (von Eschen, 1970)

When Elijah Muhammad, of the Black Muslims, was released from prison in 1946, he began organizing Islamic temples in the major American ghettos. Each temple organized a unit of the "Fruit of Islam," a paramilitary defense corps designed to keep and protect Muslims from attack (Logan and Winston, 1971). By the early 1960's, the successful recruitment of ghetto blacks had produced more than 50 temples and missions, with a total membership in the movement of perhaps 100,000. The Black Muslims was at first composed mainly of poorly educated blacks recently immigrated from the rural South, but as the organization grew, it recruited more people with urban backgrounds. Members now are generally young, and men greatly outnumber women. Many are former addicts and prostitutes, or other deviants, who appear to have been successfully rehabilitated by the movement (Quarles, 1964; Broom and Glenn, 1965; and Lincoln, 1972b).

As other groups became more militant, the Black Muslims have become less so. Their tactics have all been directed at blacks, ignoring whites rather than challenging them in the manner of the Black Panthers. Religious conversions of black members have led to personal reform, dignity, and self-reliance. In addition to religious services, the Muslims conduct black history and culture classes and urge the total support of black businesses, particularly those run by Muslims themselves (Lincoln, 1972b). They have benefited from the increasing separatist sympathies of young ghetto blacks (Prager, 1971). Upon seeing the strength of white hostility and resistance to the Black Panthers (Schanche, 1970), the Muslims have changed their position to one of non-violence. Elijah Muhammad, who still leads the movement after almost 40 years, has said, "If a Muslim is caught using arms, I punish him for it because this is not the way to win freedom, justice and equality" (*U.S. News & World Report,* September 21, 1970:84).

However, there remain factions within the Black Muslim movement which advocate violence under certain circumstances. This is especially true of the "Sunni" sect of the Muslims, which was implicated in the siege of a Brooklyn, New York, sporting-goods store in early 1973, and of certain "free-lance" Muslim factions. Elijah Muhammad's leadership has been challenged both by these groups and by more "orthodox" Muslims, who do not recognize the legitimacy of the black variant of Islam (Briggs, 1973).

Mexican-American (Chicano) Movements

The Delano, California, grape strike of 1965, led by Cesar Chavez, combined ideas from his previous work under the Community Service Organization with traditional labor union tactics (Briegal, 1970). Resistance to the strike by farm owners has been intense, but national publicity, plus solid support from many Chicanos, has helped to turn *La Huelga* (the strike) into *La Causa,* a crusade to assert the dignity of all Chicanos (Howard, 1970b). After a victory in the grape boycott, Chavez moved on to the lettuce fields, where migrant farm workers (*braceros*) were still receiving relatively low wages (*IFCO News,* May/June, 1972). It appears that "brown power" arose to challenge Anglo dominance in Chicano areas in much the same way that black power arose in the black ghettos (Torgerson, 1968; Ericksen, 1970).

John R. Howard (1970b) has identified three factors which were responsible for the rise of the United Farm Workers' Organizing Committee and Cesar Chavez. An important structural factor was the termination by the federal government of the *bracero* program in 1964. The *bracero* program had provided the growers with a continuing, mobile supply of cheap Mexican labor. Once this program was cut off, the agricultural labor force stabilized and increased its bargaining power vis-à-vis the growers.

A second factor was the earlier success of the black protests. These protests not only gave the Chicanos hope that the tactics of the blacks could be successfully applied to Chicano problems, but they also trained a corps of young Anglo activists, many of whom made themselves available for the UFWOC strike activity. The final factor was that the leadership of the new movement was Chicano. In previous efforts to organize Chicano workers, the leadership had been composed of Anglos who "spoke for" Chicano communities without being a part of them, and who thus did not legitimately represent their interests (Howard, 1970b). These three factors combined to produce a situation that was conducive to the development of a potent Chicano protest movement.

The Alianza Federal de Mercedes began several years before the UFWOC grape strike, and under very different conditions. The general situation in New Mexico had been one of rapid economic change since World War II with some accompanying dislocations and racial tensions; but the movement would probably not have developed without the dynamic leadership of Reies Tijerina (Love, 1970). His charisma held the movement together, though his recent removal from the group does not seem to have led to its total demise. The UFWOC is a modern movement—a product of urban society despite its rural nature. In contrast, Alianza is a classic "primitive revolt," more characteristic of developing nations than of modern industrial societies. It has more in common with the millenarian Sioux Ghost Dance Cult than with the UFWOC. Like other millenarian groups, Alianza believes that divine justice is at hand, and that God will see to it that the movement is victorious (Love, 1970). The strategic decisions of the leadership are supported by supernatural elements such as dream interpretation and revelation, which endow the movement with a quasi-religious nature (Gonzalez, 1970).

Tactics used by the various Chicano groups range from strikes, sit-ins, marches, and outright violence to conventions and publicity stunts. Basically, Chicano movements have used tactics that are common to other protest groups in American society, rather than developing unique tactics of their own (Gonzalez, 1970). Reies Tijerina has had some success at preaching violence in private and permitting these threats to be reported in the press, while consistently retracting or denying these statements in front of Anglos (Gonzalez, 1970).

In 1966, Chicano students staged a strike at a largely Chicano high school in Los Angeles. When 12 students and a teacher were arrested and charged with conspiracy to interrupt the educational process, and the teacher suspended, a sit-in was staged at the offices of the Los Angeles Board of Education. This resulted in the reinstatement of the teacher, and influenced Chicano groups in Denver and other Southwestern cities to use the same strategy in their protests (Briegal, 1970). Today, there is continued activism directed toward educational reform, which has spread to a number of college campuses, where "brown-power" advocates have been successful in establishing Chicano studies programs (Howard, 1970b).

Native American Movements

The succession of tragedies that preceded and prompted the Great Ghost Dance of 1890 was not repeated in the social setting in which the "fish-ins" and other elements of the red power movement developed in the 1960's. Instead, the essential dynamic behind the development of "red power" as a national force has been the progressive growth of a pan-Indian definition of the problem, which has replaced the former individual tribal definitions. Formerly, tribe was sometimes pitted against tribe, and their separate tribal identities kept them from concerted action in their own interest against the larger white-controlled society. Paradoxically, the white man's definition of every Native American as an "Indian," rather than as a member of a specific tribe, has contributed much to the development of this common consciousness.

The tactics of the Ghost Dance Movement relied upon appeal to other-worldly elements, and were not really directed against the white man. In contrast, modern Native American social movements, like contemporary Chicano ones, have adopted a wide range of direct-action techniques aimed at the white power structure, and already tested by the civil rights movement. The "fish-in" is a particularly good example of a tactic derived from the latter movement, but given a peculiarly Indian adaptation.

Long-standing federal treaties with the Indians have guaranteed them certain ancestral fishing rights on and near their reservations, but certain state governments (e.g., Washington) have recently sought to place some restrictions on these rights. In 1964 and 1965, there were Native American confrontations with authorities on the Nisqually River in the State of Washington, and demonstrations in Olympia, Washington (American Friends Service Committee, 1970). In 1966, the United States Department of Justice defended Indian fishermen in court cases, and in 1968, the U.S. Supreme Court confirmed the right of Native Americans to fish off the reservation, subject only to the appropriate general regulations of the States (American Friends Service Committee, 1970). Though the catch of Native Americans accounted for only 6.5 percent of Washington State salmon landings from 1958 to 1967, opposition by the State of Washington has continued (American Friends Service Committee, 1970). Accordingly, Native American spokesmen in Olympia have threatened to bring 700 Indians from South Dakota to join with members of Washington tribes still fighting to maintain their right to unrestricted fishing on the Nisqually River (*Walla Walla Union Bulletin,* 1973).

In 1964, under the leadership of Mel Thom, the National Indian Youth Council (NIYC) came to the aid of the Makah and other tribes in western Washington who were fighting to maintain their right to fish in the waters of the Quillayutte, Puyallup, Hoh, Yakima, Nisqually, and Columbia Rivers. The movement was carried on largely by militant youth, but it also had the support of many tribal elders (Day, 1972). Steiner has described the first "fish-in" from an Indian perspective:

And some of the Indians took out their cameras and began taking pictures of the game wardens. Most times you see white people taking pictures of Indians, but this time it was the Indians taking pictures of mad white people. That made them madder. It was our turn.

You could feel there was a squaring off . . . (it was) the first time in recent history that we were publicly demonstrating what we privately felt. (1968:23)

In the Indian view, ancestral fishing rights cannot possibly be bought or sold. They tie the people to the world in which they live. To detach Native Americans from their world in this way would sever their continuity with the past and cut them off from an important and meaningful source of existence (American Friends Service Committee, 1970).

Since 1970, the red power movement has been in full swing, and the newspapers have frequently carried stories of confrontations involving sit-ins, the closing of Indian lands to whites, Indian take-overs of government lands (such as at Alcatraz Island), the blocking of construction on projects deemed harmful to Indian interests, and the occupation of government offices (Day, 1972; *Akwesasne Notes*). One of the most serious of these incidents was the 1973 confrontation at historic Wounded Knee, South Dakota, which began at the end of February and lasted 70 days. Early one winter evening, under the leadership of the militant American Indian Movement (AIM), about two hundred well-armed Indians suddenly invaded and occupied the small village of Wounded Knee, located on the remote Pine Ridge Sioux reservation; they looted the trading post, destroyed a nearby museum, and took a few elderly hostages (Dollar, 1973). Surrounded by a number of federal authorities and marshals, the invaders refused to leave until the government agreed to meet certain demands, including implementation of an 1868 treaty providing (e.g.) for most of South Dakota to be made an Indian reservation (a treaty the government considered obsolete), a congressional investigation of the BIA, and ousting the entire elected council of the Oglala Sioux on charges of corruption. From time to time during the occupation, other demands were added and some withdrawn.

The AIM action was a challenge not only to the federal government, but also to the established leadership of the Sioux, which condemned the occupation as a criminal act and prepared to make its own counterinvasion. The intervention of many government leaders, civil rights leaders, church people, and others, succeeded in keeping the two Indian sides apart, and in preventing the incident from erupting into bloody violence. At length, the AIM invaders surrendered, after their leaders had, one by one, done so with great fanfare. Once arrested, the perpetrators of the incident were released on bail, and they proceeded to tour the country to raise money for their defense, and to capitalize on the Wounded Knee publicity in order to focus public attention on their goals. The village was left in shambles, but very little bloodshed actually occurred (including one or two deaths). The expenses connected with the incident for the government, however, reached five-million dollars (Dollar, 1973), and in September, 1974, the courts dismissed all charges against the AIM defendants, because of the prosecution's mishandling of their case! The major significance of the episode was that it catapulted AIM into national prominence.

Race Relations Movements and the Natural History Model

The rise and fall of movements related to ethnic minorities in our country's past offer particularly good examples of the "life-cycle" or natural history process in the development of social problems. It is truly difficult to see any relation in American history between the "objective realities" of the conditions surrounding our ethnic minorities, on the one hand, and the occasional collective definitions of them as "problems," on the other hand. Our "original minority," the American Indians, constituted a problem from the beginning, but not a "social problem" in the usual sense of that term. Rather, the Indians were a problem in the same sense as the wild frontier—they were something to be removed ("The only good Indian is a dead Indian"), or, at the very most, "converted" as the missionaries preferred. The same has been true, for most of our history, of the Mexicans (forefathers of today's Chicanos), who stood in the way of the "manifest destiny" of our nation to stretch from sea to shining sea.

Even more of an anomaly in terms of objective reality versus the public definition of the situation was black slavery, which flourished in the land of the free for two centuries before it was defined as a "social problem" by the abolitionists of the 19th century. Slaves graced the estate of many a signer of the Declaration of Independence, despite its affirmations of universal equality. The point of all of this, of course, is not that our ancestors were hypocrites, or at least not uniquely so; rather, the point is that no matter how cruel, inhuman, or intolerable a certain social condition or institution may seem to some, and especially to those of a later generation, that condition or institution does not become a social problem until a society so defines it. Thus, the abolition movement featured all kinds of moral entrepreneurs (including some outrageous fanatics) and some powerful political and economic interest groups on both sides, most of whom were willing to push all the way to a devastating civil war in order to resolve the issue. Once the war was over, the "social problem" of slavery was collectively defined as "solved," even though the general lot of the blacks was not appreciably improved, and, indeed, may even have been worsened, especially after the white political compromise of 1876, which gave rise to the "Jim Crow" laws of the South (Woodward, 1955).

It was, in fact, the total dissipation of the emancipation spirit after the Civil War, and the general desertion of the black causes by whites, that led to the black self-help movement, which we have discussed above. Featuring outstanding early black leaders of varying persuasions such as Booker T. Washington, W. E. B. Du Bois, and (a little later) Marcus Garvey, this movement began late in the 19th century and extended into the 1920's. In many ways, it was an abortive movement. For a time, it gave some hope, encouragement, and material support to young blacks trying to rise above their heritage of slavery and "make it" in the white man's system, especially in the South. The various organizations which comprised the movement, however, such as the Tuskegee Institute of Booker T. Washington, the Niagara Movement, and the UNIA, never pulled together very often. Each had a somewhat different regional focus and social base. Yet in a very loose way, they did constitute a fledgling movement, which became *institutionalized* enough to be courted quietly by Theodore Roosevelt in the White House, to found a viable and enduring educational program at Tuskegee, and to arouse the wrath of the Ku Klux Klan. Eventually, however, the movement was doomed by the relatively low level of interest on the part of whites, its limited regional base (almost entirely in the South), and its limited appeal outside the South to a black bourgeois constituency. The nation's preoccupation with World War I, followed by the "red scare" of the 1920's, brought an end to this movement, which had begun to peter out even before the war. Washington died (partially disgraced by scandal) in 1915, having lost his tie to the White House with the election of Wilson in 1912 (Logan, 1970). The Niagara Movement was virtually dead by 1910, and deserted by Du Bois (Quarles, 1964). The UNIA of Garvey lasted a little longer, sustained by the support of many poor northern blacks, until it began to experience rifts and dissension, which culminated in a big split in 1929 over whether the organization should move from New York back to Jamaica. Garvey eventually moved to London in the 1930's. The black self-help movement thus had reached some degree of institutionalization by the eve of World War I, but it *fragmented* and declined after that, without having had any large-scale impact on the black minority, or any impact at all on the whites. For all practical purposes, and except for an occasional riot or lynching, the "race problem" in America was forgotten until the 1950's.

The civil rights movement, more recent and vivid in our memories, also has followed a general natural history of the kind we are postulating. The *incipiency* of the movement can be seen in the 1950's, probably the early part of that decade, in the accelerating activity of the NAACP and other organizations against school segregation. Since schools had been segregated for nearly a century, it is open to question why the issue became a "social problem" only then; it may have been that the NAACP leaders (both black and white) sensed that the new "Warren Court" would be more amenable to considering a reversal of the historic "separate-but-equal" doctrine than previous Supreme Courts had been. In any case, the 1954 Brown v. Board of Education decision by the Court not only fulfilled that hope, but it also raised many other aspirations long dormant among black leaders, and helped greatly to push the civil rights movement along toward coalescence. The success of the Montgomery, Alabama, bus boycott a little later in the decade was another important contribution to the growing unity of the movement, and, in fact, gave rise to the Southern Christian Leadership Conference (SCLC) and the joining to the civil rights cause of the charismatic leadership of Martin Luther King, Jr.

By the early 1960's, the movement was showing clear signs of *coalescence*. The various separate organizations such as NAACP, SCLC, SNCC, and CORE were cooperating and coordinating their efforts (though not without some strains and rivalries, to be sure) to produce further boycotts, many successful sit-ins, voter registration drives, and important court cases. The support and leadership of white liberals (adults and students), which had contributed much to the rise and coalescence of the movement up to that time, began to give way to the ascendancy of new black spokesmen and leaders, some of them very militant and even violent in their preferred tactics. This coalescence of the more militant new "black power" organizations and leaders with the older civil rights "establishment" was important for both elements: it gave the newer groups a legitimacy they would otherwise not have had (especially with white liberals), and it pushed the entire civil rights movement in the direction of greater militancy and solidarity. At the same time, however, this development led to the increasing separation of whites from the movement and their involvement in other causes (e.g., the Viet-Nam War), so that the coalescence that was occurring in the civil rights movement was increasingly one of black people with rapidly rising aspirations and consciousness.

The middle- and late-1960's was the period of greatest *institutionalization* for the civil rights movement, not only in the sense that it became a "going concern" and developed a series of successful strategies and tactics of its own, but also in the sense that the rest of the society (especially the government) responded with a variety of coping routines to deal with the movement. While continuing repressive efforts against the more militant leaders (e.g., H. Rap Brown) and organizations (e.g., Black Panthers), the government also passed and implemented a series of very important new laws and policies to meet the grievances of the more moderate core of the movement, which had the usual effect of co-opting and softening the movement's main thrust. This was the period (from about 1964 to 1968 or 1969) of greatest proliferation of civil rights acts, desegregation efforts, anti-poverty programs, affirmative action policies, and so on. A kind of high point was reached in 1969, when the NAACP took some 500 cases to court.

An important expression of the movement's institutionalization on the campuses was the establishment of "ethnic-studies" programs across the nation, especially black studies, Chicano studies, and Native American studies. The academic status and integrity of these programs has been rather controversial, but for a time many universities and colleges poured considerable resources into them. While these programs were without precedent in the college curriculum, they were simply the modern counterparts of the private "ethnic-studies" programs instituted earlier in the century by the several immigrant groups, who ran their own schools, in their own languages, after normal public school hours (Handlin, 1951). Some of these schools (e.g., for the Chinese) still survive. They represent an important means for ethnic minorities to cope with outside prejudice and pressures, and to maintain self-esteem and pride in their heritage.

The origins and development of the Chicano and Native American elements of the civil rights movement are somewhat more obscure, partly because they did not receive the media coverage that the blacks did, and partly because they have never been very numerous in proportion to our total population. It may be that the "heydey" of the Chicano and Indian movements is yet to come, but for the time being they seem to have benefited greatly by the efforts and experiences of the blacks. They have received the protection and support of the new laws and "affirmative action" policies brought in by the civil rights movement, and they have also gained increased ethnic consciousness and aspirations. In a real sense, the legitimacy and institutionalization which the nation has come to bestow on the black mainstream of the movement have extended to the other minorities as well. In their own right, however, both Chicanos and Indians have gained a considerable degree of institutionalization for their own segments of the movement. The federal and state governments and the BIA are increasingly coming to terms with Indian claims by means of court cases and meaningful negotiations with Indian leaders. The UFWOC has become an AFL-CIO union, and many of the labor laws originally written for the protection of factory workers have been extended to cover the migrant farm workers (mostly Chicano). The successful boycotts of the UFWOC are also a sign of the institutionalization of the Chicano part of the civil rights movement.

While the civil rights movement has continued to be institutionalized, and the "race problem" associated with it has continued to be collectively defined as one of our modern "social problems," there are signs that this extremely important and historic movement is losing steam, and that the "race problem" is beginning to lose the high degree of popular and official interest that it once evoked. The conditions of blacks, once considered so problematic, were already, in the early 1970's, beginning to be redefined as less problematic, or even as "solved." Signs of *fragmentation* began to appear in the late 1960's, even as the movement was reaching its zenith, partly because of disagreements over new strategic directions in the face of establishment co-optation, and partly because of the death, arrest, or dropping out of some important leaders. The SCLC, which was making some real headway under Dr. King, never recovered from his assassination in 1968. Rap Brown and some of the other more militant leaders were in and out of jail, and others, like Carmichael, just gradually dropped out in favor of a more comfortable and less hazardous life. SNCC died out, and some of its members joined with the Black Panthers, who began to have a series of bloody encounters with the police.

In 1971, the Panthers split into two factions, with one, led by Cleaver in Algeria, calling for more violence, and the other, led by Newton in Oakland, focusing increasingly on community organization, "ghetto breakfast" programs, and so on. A strong showing by Panther candidate Seale in a 1972 election for Mayor of Oakland (California) increased the co-optation of Panther forces into regular politics, and since then their numbers and influence have steadily declined (*Newsweek,* January 25, 1971).

Fragmentation has beset the Black Muslims, too, sometimes in the form of some rather bloody vendettas between factions, particularly during 1971 through 1973. Not all Black Muslims have remained loyal to Elijah Muhammed, with his emphasis on middle-class values, clean living, and business enterprises. Some, notably the so-called "Sunni" sect, take their inspiration from a more "orthodox" variant of Islam, including the notion of *jihad* or "holy war," and are more oriented toward ideology and various "third-world" causes. This split was involved to some extent in the 1963 schism led by Malcolm X, but his leadership was ended by his assassination in 1965 (Briggs, 1973).

With fragmentation having set in the more militant wing of the civil rights movement (e.g., the Panthers and the Muslims), as well as in the more "moderate" wing (e.g., SCLC, SNCC, etc.), the NAACP remains the single most important and effective representative of black civil rights interests. This is a great shrinkage in numbers since the proliferation of black organizations in the 1960's. The rise of AIM signifies a trend toward fragmentation in the Indian branch of the movement also, and even Chavez and the UFWOC have begun to be criticized by those Chicanos who apparently prefer the Teamster affiliation to that of the AFL-CIO. Nor are the boycotts working as well as they once did. It would be rash to predict the total demise of the civil rights movement for the time being, but it has been largely "tamed," blunted, and co-opted. Even such symbolic protest efforts as the "black boycott" in the House of Representatives of President Nixon's 1971 State of the Union Address have had little or no impact. On the campuses, meanwhile, ethnic-studies programs are dying out, since student interest and enrollment have dropped drastically and budgets have consequently been cut.

Probably the most crucial sign of the impending *demise* of the movement, and therefore of the "social problem," has been the loss of white interest in it, and the flagging of governmental zeal for "solving" the race problem. Nowhere is this more apparent than in the issue of school desegregation. Northern and western white interest groups were strongly in favor of civil rights and integration as long as these were southern problems, but attitudes have changed now that laws and policies, originally directed against "southern racism and bigotry," have now been turned against northern cities as well. The "social problem" of racial segregation in the schools is now a northern problem: 45 percent of black children in the

South attend majority white schools, compared to 30 percent in most northern cities, and the figure is rising in the South while dropping in the North. By fleeing to the suburbs and making our cities increasingly black, whites in the North have achieved with their moving vans what whites in the South had been doing with "Jim Crow" laws. As they have deserted the cities, they have also redefined the "race problem." A dissipation of enthusiasm for desegregation in both Congress and the Supreme Court has been the inevitable consequence (Taylor, 1974).

THE LEGACY OF RACE RELATIONS MOVEMENTS
General Cultural Legacy

One of the popular conceptions about minority groups in American society is that of the "melting pot," in which minority groups are seen as eventually merging with the majority, each contributing its own unique traits (Gordon, 1964). While the melting pot notion has had its critics, it is nevertheless true that at least certain subcultural traits of minority groups have been absorbed into our general cultural heritage. We have also acquired certain traits of language and style from the protest movements of minority groups.

Black culture in the United States started almost from the zero point because of (1) the care taken by plantation owners to separate each slave from all others of his tribe in order to minimize the possibility of revolts, and (2) the high level of repression in the slave system (Rex, 1970). Black culture has developed through the simultaneous processes of the survival of certain elements of African tribal cultures, and ethnogenesis, or the creation of a culture out of nothing in the "pressure cooker" of the native black American experience.

Among the cultural contributions of blacks to the larger society are clothing styles, music, art, argot and the "hip" social role. Black clothing includes both loose-fitting colorful African styles and ghetto styles of relaxed and "flashy" clothing. Black "soul food" has not had much of an impact on the general public, but black music has made a significant contribution to American culture. African music appeals to a rather specialized audience, but jazz, which is truly a black art form, and is perhaps the most significant American musical development in this century, has a tremendously broad appeal. In the art world, there is some trade in African art objects, but not as much as in Native American crafts and jewelry.

A considerable amount of the slang developed in the ghetto has come to be used commonly by at least some elements of the white social structure. Terms and phrases such as "cool" and "right on" are heard as much from whites as from blacks these days. This argot is part of the general "hip" social role in which people act "cool." This social role greatly influenced the development of the hippie subculture, and other predominantly white "deviant" groups in American society.

Mexican and Chicano influences on American art and music have been rather modest, except in the Southwest. The same can be said of clothing styles. Mexican "ponchos," for example, are well-known in Anglo culture, but not widely used. Architecture in the Southwest has been significantly influenced by adobe construction techniques and Mexican spatial designs, e.g., as can be seen in the placement of walled gardens in the front yard of many houses. The acceptance of Mexican food has been more national in scope. It is difficult to find a city in any part of the United States without "Mexican" restaurants and taco stands.

Leather clothing and other goods modeled after "Indian" styles are standard craft items in white society, and native American tribal music is becoming fashionable outside of anthropological circles. Indian art—pottery, rugs, paintings, and jewelry—is becoming extremely popular, and has had some effect on white art styles. At the present time, Indian food, unlike Chicano food, is not well-known to the general public.

All three groups have had a significant effect on the values and beliefs of white Americans as a result of their protests of the last 20 years. Their repeated demonstrations against the lack of justice and equal opportunity in all dimensions of the lives of blacks. Chicanos and Native Americans have reduced the smugness of many white Americans about equalitarian democracy and the Horatio Alger myth, which maintain that all Americans can reach any level of success they desire by dint of hard work and perseverance (Remmling, 1967; Rieff, 1966).

Normative Changes

There have been a number of normative changes in American society occasioned by the social movements discussed in this chapter. These normative changes are perhaps more far-reaching in their effects than the factors cited above, but as yet they have not been formalized into laws or resulted in any changes in the legal system.

One example of this class of effects is ethnic jokes. As a result of the civil rights movement, for the first time ethnic jokes about blacks became socially inappropriate, in the media and in the theater, and in many parts of white society. We no longer find "minstrel shows," Amos 'n' Andy programs, or other forms of "entertainment" which present blacks as ignorant buffoons. However, jokes about Chicanos and native Americans have continued somewhat longer. As late as 1967, Louis Filler commented that while it was now the fashion to be sympathetic toward blacks, the Indian was "still the subject of derogatory jokes, blank ignorance, and indifference" (Filler, 1967).

By 1973, continued Native American and Chicano agitation had resulted in such changes as the dropping of the nickname "Indians" by the Stanford University athletic teams, and the banning of the Frito Bandito ad from television and radio commercials. A black comedian may still joke about blacks, but it is rare to see a white comedian making similar jokes. It is, however, quite acceptable for black comedians such as Flip Wilson to make fun of white ethnic habits.

The early black social movements probably had little normative effect on the larger society. Perhaps the greatest accomplishment of the Niagara Movement was that it eventually led to the formation of the NAACP. Booker T. Washington secured jobs and training for many blacks, but in the process he reinforced white stereotypes of black docility and black affinity for manual labor. Marcus Garvey may not have had much of a normative effect on whites, but he had a lasting effect on American blacks. The beginnings of black racial pride can be found in Garvey's program of the Universal Negro Improvement Association. The first large-scale production of black dolls dates from this time, as black parents developed sufficient racial pride to believe that their children should play with black rather than white dolls (Cronin, 1968).

The NAACP's Legal Defense Fund has influenced the race relations scene beyond just the legal changes forced through its cases. In 1968, it set up an extensive scholarship fund for black college students, and influenced the White House to make it possible for public school children to have better school lunches than ever before. During 1969, it was responsible for 280 complaints against discrimination in employment filed with the Equal Employment Opportunities Commission, which resulted in 2,300 new jobs or promotions for blacks, and it won many test cases to end discrimination against the poor in law enforcement, public housing, and the schools. The next year, it initiated a program to double the number of black lawyers practicing in the United States within a period of seven years (Haines, 1971).

The sit-ins and freedom rides did not change the basic educational and economic problems that beset American blacks, but they did show whites that blacks could fight back, and they helped black morale considerably. In the past, most blacks had passively watched NAACP lawyers force whites back inch by inch, but with the civil rights movement, they could feel a part of the national struggle for equality (Broom and Glenn, 1965). Though blacks gained pride and enhanced self-esteem from the civil rights movement, poor blacks gained less than blacks in the middle class, and blacks in the ghettos of the North gained less than blacks in the South. Poor blacks could not afford to use many of the public facilities that were integrated, and were not qualified for most of the jobs to which black applicants could now be admitted (Broom and Glenn, 1965).

The overall effect on whites of the Black Panthers and other militant groups in the black power movement has probably been counterproductive. White definitions of the situation have conveniently ignored the positive aspects of these groups, and selectively emphasized their threatening and destructive tendencies. Turning away from a militant approach, the Black Muslims have put their money (estimated at 20 million dollars) into black businesses, including restaurants, supermarkets, and a slaughterhouse. They have bought over 18,000 acres of farmland in Alabama and Georgia, plus additional land in other states. Their massive food-production industry cost between five- and eight-million dollars to set up, but it includes every aspect of the process, from growth to consumption. Their membership is stabilized at about 100,000, but their newspaper, *Muhammad Speaks,* has a circulation in excess of 500,000 (*U.S. News & World Report,* September 21, 1970:84). White opposition to Muslim doctrines is still strong, but the Muslims' quiet determination has won a new respect for black nationalism among many whites.

Thomas Sowell (1973) in an article entitled "Radical Chic Is Vicious," suggests that one cultural effect of the black power movement has been to create a new set of stereotypes about blacks. This is partially due to differential press coverage in which small militant black groups, such as the Black Panthers, receive much more extensive coverage than large moderate groups such as the NAACP. This coverage is generally biased and ignores the following basic points:

1/ Most Negroes are not on welfare, and most people on welfare are not Negroes.
2/ Most black families have both parents present, and have incomes above the official poverty level.
3/ Organizations such as the NAACP and leaders such as the late Martin Luther King, Jr., have had many times more supporters than various extremist groups or their highly publicized spokesmen. (Sowell, 1973)

Selective media coverage also produces an artificial stereotype of the "authentic" ghetto black, who is portrayed as terribly disadvantaged and hostile, but proud of his race and committed to helping his black brothers out of poverty (Sowell, 1973). This image is often complemented by a snide characterization of working- and middle-class blacks who favor integration as "Uncle Toms."

The Alianza de Federal de Mercedes has been somewhat successful in the area of attracting the attention of the state and federal governments to the discrimination suffered by lower-class Chicanos (Gonzalez, 1970). However, the effects of Cesar Chavez and the United Farm Workers' Organizing Committee have been broader. Their victory over the grape growers in the summer of 1970 forced the growers to recognize the UFWOC as the bargaining agent for migrant laborers and other field workers (*Newsweek,* January 25, 1971). However, the effect on the *barrio* may have been even greater, for the East Los Angeles *barrio* erupted with three major protests within one year after the grape victory (Dunne, 1971).

Native American protest movements have generally been unsuccessful in bringing about changes in the legal system, but they have been able to preserve their capital in land and resources sufficiently to maintain their own communities. An emerging cultural practice of some significance is the development of successful models of rural cooperatives, seen in tribes such as the Navajo, which Chicano and black minority groups have begun to emulate (Deloria, 1969). Other kinds of cultural changes which they have been able to effect have been relatively minor, such as the removal of signs reading "No Dogs or Indians Allowed" from bars in white cities near Indian reservations.

Changes in the Law and Justice System

The changes perpetrated by the law and justice systems in response to racial social movements have been fairly important, though there has been some strong resistance to the new laws by individuals who work within the system as a strong in-group, which enables them to oppose attempts to change their definitions of the situation. Changes in the law due to the actions of Native American and Chicano social movements have been comparatively minor, but a few major changes have resulted from black actions. The Southeastern states, with their long "Jim Crow" tradition, have constituted the main "battleground" for the civil rights movement in the 1950's and 1960's, but events of the early 1970's indicate that the battle is shifting northward.

In Gwin and Beal v. United States (1915), the Supreme Court for the first time struck down the "grandfather clause," which had enabled southern states to keep blacks from voting. In Norris v. Alabama (1935), the Court ruled that the systematic exclusion of blacks from juries was *prima facie* evidence of denial of the right of equal protection under the law, as guaranteed by the 14th Amendment. Three years later, in Missouri ex rel. Gaines v. Canada, the Court ruled that the state of Missouri had to admit blacks to its state law school, since its practice of providing a scholarship to attend a school in another state did not meet the requirement for equal facilities. In a decision based on the 15th Amendment, the Court, in Smith v. Allright (1944), forced the Democratic Party in Texas to permit blacks to vote in its primary elections. Further, in a series of decisions from 1941 to 1950, the Court ruled against segregation of blacks on trains engaged in interstate commerce (Broom and Glenn, 1965).

After 1950, the number of cases and laws related to the civil rights of blacks increased greatly, but we will discuss only six of the major documents in this period. These are: the case of Brown v. Board of Education of Topeka, Kansas in the Supreme Court in 1954, the Civil Rights Acts of 1957, 1960, 1964 and 1968, the Voting Rights Act of 1965, and President Nixon's Executive Order 11478 issued in 1969. In the 1954 decision, the Supreme Court reversed the Plessy v. Ferguson decision of 1896 which had allowed separate but equal educational facilities for blacks and whites to be imposed by the states, saying that "segregation, with the sanction of the law, therefore has a tendency to retard the educational and mental development of Negro children and to deprive them of some of the benefits they would receive in a racially integrated school system . . ." (Marden and Meyer, 1968). This decision was rendered in such a way as to imply that all public segregation in the United States was unconstitutional and would be found so if tested in the courts (Marden and Meyer, 1968).

The Civil Rights Act of 1957 followed on the heels of the early victories of the civil rights movement, and constituted a counter measure to the strong opposition of the South to the Brown v. Board of Education decision of the Supreme Court. It was the first civil rights legislation to be enacted since 1875. Its accomplishments were to establish a Civil Rights Commission to gather data on voting violations, to empower the Justice Department to initiate action where voting violations occurred in federal elections, and to require nondiscriminatory qualifications for the selection of juries in federal courts. This relatively innocuous legislation was topped by the Civil Rights Act of 1960, which "was designed to impede interracial violence without eroding the power and authority of state officials" (Blaustein and Zangrando, 1968).

In 1964 and 1968, Congress enacted civil rights acts that were far more extensive than any such preceding laws in American history. They included detailed provisions to insure equality in the areas of voting, public accommodations and facilities, education, and employment. Desegregation problems of school districts were to be aided by funds and training handled by the Department of Health, Education, and Welfare. The Civil Rights Commission was given greater powers, and was joined by two new civil rights agencies—the Equal Employment Opportunities Commission and the Community Relations Service (Blaustein and Zangrando, 1968).

The 1965 march from Selma to Montgomery, Alabama led to another piece of legislation—the Voting Rights Act of 1965. This assigned federal examiners to register voters and observe elections in states or counties where voting discrimination existed. Literacy tests and other discriminatory means of limiting voter participation were outlawed. The act was constructed so as to help the poor, uneducated and other minority groups as well as blacks. States that were included under the guidelines for discrimination in the act were Alabama, Alaska, Georgia, Louisiana, Mississippi, South Carolina, North Carolina and Virginia (Blaustein and Zangrando, 1968).

In Executive Order 11478, Richard M. Nixon went beyond former more or less passive federal support of equality of opportunity in employment and ordered that federal agencies develop affirmative programs in which minority applicants would be actively sought out and specially trained to perform at their highest potential. The Civil Service Commission was given the power to enforce the Executive Order, and in particular to consider all complaints of discrimination in federal employment based on race, color, religion, sex or national origin (*Equal Employment Opportunity in the Federal Government,* 1969). Affirmative action programs, however, have also left their legacy of complications, with critics complaining that such policies simply constitute "reverse discrimination." A number of lawsuits have been initiated by white males, who feel that the affirmative action policies of employers or universities have caused their applications to be rejected in favor of those of less qualified minority people and/or females. Perhaps the best-known of these cases is that of Marco DeFunis, who was turned down for admission to the Law School at the University of Washington, even though his credentials were apparently stronger than those of some minority applicants who were admitted. DeFunis sued, and his case went all the way to the Supreme Court, which, in 1974, declined to act on the case, on the grounds that by then it was no longer relevant; for DeFunis had subsequently gained admission to the Law School, and was nearly finished with his studies there.

In addition to the advantages offered under affirmative action programs, minority groups have made some real gains as a result of the civil rights movement. The gains of blacks are documented in a special study published by the U.S. Department of Commerce (*The Social and Economic Status of Negroes in the United States,* 1971). This study shows that the enormous gaps that have always existed between blacks and whites in income, employment, education, housing, health, voting behavior, and so on, were significantly reduced during the 1960's. Most of those gaps, however, remain fairly large. This is especially the case in the area of educational opportunity. A 1973 report of the Senate Select Committee on Equal Educational Opportunity (cited in Taylor, 1974) indicates that most cities, especially in the North, have barely begun the task of eliminating school segregation, although more than 20 years have passed since the decision of Brown v. Board of Education of Topeka. The Committee found evidence of severe segregation, teacher labeling and classifying of students by background instead of by potential, and unequal disbursement of funds so that poor children attend poor schools and wealthy children attend well-funded schools (*San Francisco Examiner & Chronicle,* January 21, 1973).

In a sense, then, the society has come full circle in dealing with the "social problem" of racial segregation in the schools. Since the 1954 Brown decision, the South has reluctantly but effectively achieved a large measure of integration in its schools. The legacy of the integration "problem" for the North, however, has "come home to roost," as it were, in the form of bitter debates and confrontations over busing black and white children into each others' neighborhoods to achieve integration (e.g., Boston in late 1974). The opposition is probably strong enough, in Congress and in the courts, to prevent any further integration of schools in the North, especially by means of busing. Already, however, the "integration legacy" has left the North with a new "problem." In order to avoid the consequences of an integration policy which they forced with so much moral zeal upon the South, northern whites have made a mass exodus to the suburbs, creating a problem of residential, and consequently further educational, segregation. The schools in Washington, D.C., are now 96 percent black or Puerto Rican, those of Chicago, 70 percent, and those of Philadelphia, Detroit, and New York, 65 percent. The problem is no longer viewed as one of "segregation"; it has now become a problem of "preserving neighborhood schools" (Taylor, 1974). And redefinition, let us remember, is one of the ways in which social problems are "solved."

Chapter 15

The Environment as a Social Problem

THE SOCIAL CONSTRUCTION OF REALITY*

If (a) country was ever uncertain of the ends it should pursue, that day has passed. There may be doubts among philosophers and heart-searchings among poets, but to the multitude the kingdom of God is to be realized here, and now, on this earth; and it is to be realized via technological innovation, and at an exponential rate. Its universal appeal exceeds that of the brotherhood of man, indeed comprehends it. For as we become richer, surely we shall remedy all social evils; heal the sick, comfort the aged and exhilarate the young. (Mishan, 1970:4)

(The) striking dualism in contemporary science and technology—monumental achievements beside astonishing omissions and misdirections—deserves the most careful scrutiny. If the present destructive course is to be altered, we must understand not only the operational details of past and present errors, but also the way in which society's institutions, goals, and prejudices have interacted with science and technology to produce such imperfect results. (Ehrlich, Holdren, and Holm, 1971:2)

Relativity and the Environment

Cultural definitions of man's relationship with his environment have varied from society to society and within societies at various historical periods. These cultural definitions are critical determinants of the effect man will have on his environment. This is especially true today for, as McHarg (1969:26) argues: "In times long past, when man represented no significant power to change nature, it mattered little to the world what views he held. Today when he has emerged as potentially

---

* All of the issues discussed in this chapter are closely related to that of population size. However, since another chapter is devoted to that topic, little will be said about it here.

the most destructive force in nature and its greatest exploiter, it matters very much indeed."*

Attitudes toward nature and the environment of primitive societies, as well as of contemporary eastern societies, can be contrasted with those of dominant western themes. Many of the pantheistic religions of primitive groups emphasized harmonic relationships between man and nature. Man was only the custodian of the land, and therefore many of the acts of man in relationship to the natural environment took on a sacramental nature—that is, of clearly defined religious significance (see Durkheim, 1954). Similarly, the traditional Oriental view has been one of man submerged in nature, rather than opposed to it.

On the other hand, many of the values of western man have stressed conquest of nature rather than unity with it. This tradition goes back at least to the biblical injunction that man should have dominion over the world. McHarg (1969:26) argues that "If the highest values in a culture insist that man must subdue the earth and that this is his moral duty, it is certain that he will in time acquire the powers to accomplish that injunction."

Just as cultural definitions about man's relationship with his environment have varied, so also have the effects of man on his environment. Early man utilized the wild plants and animals found in abundance in his natural environment as a source of food and fuel. The food-gathering and hunting peoples of the Old Stone Age, as noted by Bates (1969:21) "were closely interacting parts of the biological communities in which they lived. Tools and language made them unusually efficient hunters but not really different in their impact on the community from other kinds of social carnivores or omnivores."

This situation soon changed, however. Perhaps such changes in early man's relationship with nature began with his ability to make fire. With this ability, along with an increased capacity to make and utilize tools, man became a modifier of his environment. Ehrlich, et al. (1971:6) suggest that:

The long history of this phenomenon makes instructive reading at a time when many people believe that man's environmental impact began with the industrial revolution. Some commentators have erroneously implied that our environmental problems can be traced primarily to misuses of technology since World War II. . . . Such views seriously underestimate the degree to which Homo sapiens had altered the face of the planet before he had harnessed steam and other surrogates for muscle power.

---

* Numerous books and articles have been written on the attitudes of Americans toward their environment. For example, Allen and Wilkinson (1966) analyze the attitude of people who founded the American democracy, and how that attitude has persisted and influenced the use of natural resources to the present time. McConnell (1954) traces the history of the conservation movement and the force of ideas of men such as Marsh, Muir, and Leopold. For an annotated bibliography of sources dealing with this topic and related issues, see Suljak (1971).

These authors go on to document some of these effects of early man on the environment. They argue, for example, that over-grazing and lumbering were at least partly responsible for the "desertification" of much of northern Africa, and for the expansion of the Thar desert of India, that logging and clearing of land for agricultural uses stripped many of China's watersheds, leading to destructive flooding of her rivers, and that over-grazing by the shepherds of the early Navajo tribes turned first-rate grazing lands into desolate expanses of sandy desert.

In those days, our early ancestors possessed enormous ability to change their environment. That ability, however, has become even greater as man has progressed through what Bates calls four basic "revolutions" (1969:22). The first of these, the *agricultural revolution,* led to man's cultivation of plants and his domestication of animals. This had important effects both on man's relationship with his fellows and with his natural environment. In the first instance, the growing and harvesting of crops led to more stable and permanent villages, with concomitant effects on human social relationships and patterns. In the second case, man came to have a greater impact on his environment by his removal of natural vegetation, and his replacement of it with crops grown for foodstuffs and other purposes. The second or the *urban revolution* was, in many ways, a natural outgrowth of the early establishment of villages, with their permanence and growing division of labor. However, it was also based upon man's ability to transport and store food, which then made possible the formation of larger cities and the increased specialization of labor and knowledge. The third revolution, the *industrial revolution,* led to the harnessing of power beyond the muscles of man and his domesticated beasts. This, in turn, resulted in dramatic increases in man's ability to influence his natural environment, and it continues to affect life-styles and consumption patterns both in industrialized societies and in societies just entering the stage of industrialization. Finally, in the very recent past, man reached the stage of the *scientific revolution.* This revolution, in reality a continuation or extension of the industrial revolution, has given rise to the dramatic and drastic increase in power available to 20th-century man, including the development of nuclear power and electronic devices almost beyond imagination. The important point is that each of these revolutions has allowed man to have an ever-increasing impact on his natural environment. He has become, in this process, not only a part of his ecosystem, but the most powerful influence on it. As the National Academy of Sciences Committee on Resources and Man has put it, man is simultaneously the potentially most precious resource of the ecosystem and its most serious threat (Committee on Resources and Man, 1969:3).

Definitions and Interpretations

Perhaps now, more than ever before in history, many of the scientists who have participated in advancing man's knowledge of science and technology are questioning the outcome of his utilization of that knowledge. As Kenneth Boulding (1966:14) has stated: "In the West, our desire to conquer nature often means simply that we diminish the probability of small inconveniences at the cost of increasing the probability of very large disasters." An increased desire for ever-expanding per capita consumption (perhaps more and more often of a "conspicuous" nature) has led, Boulding and others feel, to a situation where the limits of the earth's finite resources will be reached fairly soon. Thus, if in the past natural resources have been viewed by western man as something to be exploited to increase his wealth and pleasure, at least a portion of western men now view them as something to be carefully preserved or consumed with minimal waste, and in a more measured and equitable manner. Pollution, environmental degradation, and resource depletion have become full-scale social issues, embellished with "crisis rhetoric," serving as rallying points for powerful social movements, and certified as worthy foci of study by the student of human society.

Each of these concerns has aspects which are of interest to the social scientist. For example, the decisions as to how the available resources are to be used are reflections of societal attitudes and value systems. The quality of life in any given society is dependent upon the quantity and quality of resources available, as well as upon the technological skills that have evolved for their utilization. Resource utilization and pollution issues provide numerous areas for open societal conflict. There is, for example, the very important question of who will receive the ill-effects of the pollution. Minority groups living in the less desirable areas of the central city argue that when the city decides to put in a new sewer plant, that plant is more likely to be located in their area of town. On the other hand, the new swimming pool or high school often goes into a more affluent neighborhood. A related concern revolves around the current issue of separating the power source—and the pollution involved in the manufacture of power—from the user. Should the huge industrial and population centers of southern California, for example, have been allowed to build gigantic fossil fuel-burning power plants in the Four Corners Area of the Southwest, taking the clean electrical power to California and leaving the pollution behind?

Part of the social end of the problem, too, is related to the fact that mankind is in the midst of a "revolution of rising expectations" (Chapman, 1969:32). This involves a somewhat universal commitment to the concept of growth as an irreversible "need." This growth-ethic is not just an affliction of the U.S., because as Mishan (1970:3) notes: "Like a national flag and a national airplane, a national plan for economic growth is deemed an essential item in the paraphernalia of every new nation state."

Parameters of Consensual Reality

Numerous indicators which suggest the scope and nature of environmentally related problems can be cited. These deal with such things as the "energy crisis" (and the related depletion of natural resources), pollution, and congestion in the cities, crowding of national parks and recreation areas, and so on. Table 15-1 presents a list of some of the major issues that constitute the focus of current environmentalist concern, a matter which we shall discuss more fully in the next section.

As is obvious from this list, the range of issues is indeed diverse, and it seems that we hardly have time to become concerned about one issue before another bursts upon our consciousness. One of the most recent problems to attract attention, for example, is that of noise pollution. According to Ehrlich and Ehrlich (1972: 176), this problem "has recently been thrown into sharp focus by the discovery that some teen-agers were suffering permanent hearing loss following long exposures to amplified rock music, and by public concern about the effects of sonic booms that would be caused by supersonic transports (SST), if they were put into commercial service." Although the facts surrounding this issue, and many other environmental concerns, are extremely interesting, space here will permit us to discuss in any detail only three of the problems listed in Table 15-1: resource depletion, air pollution, and water pollution.

Resource Depletion and the Energy Crisis

One of the clearest indicators of the existence of an "energy crisis" is the multitude of scientific reports and documents published each year which spell out the nature of this problem. Starr (1971:3) points out in one of these studies that in the next 30 years the United States will consume more energy than it has in its entire

TABLE 15-1 SOME OF THE ISSUES THAT CONSTITUTE THE FOCUS OF ENVIRONMENTAL CONCERN

Air Pollution
Water Pollution
Noise Pollution
Resource Depletion—Including Minerals, Water, Forests, Land, Fossil Fuels, etc.
Post-War "Development" Blight of the Cities
Erosion of the Countryside
Highway and Other Littering
Overcrowding and Destruction of National Parks and Related Areas
Coal Strip-Mining
Solid Waste Disposal
Pesticides
Oil and Sewage on the Beaches
The Supersonic Transport (SST)
Changeover from Animal Farming to Animal Factories

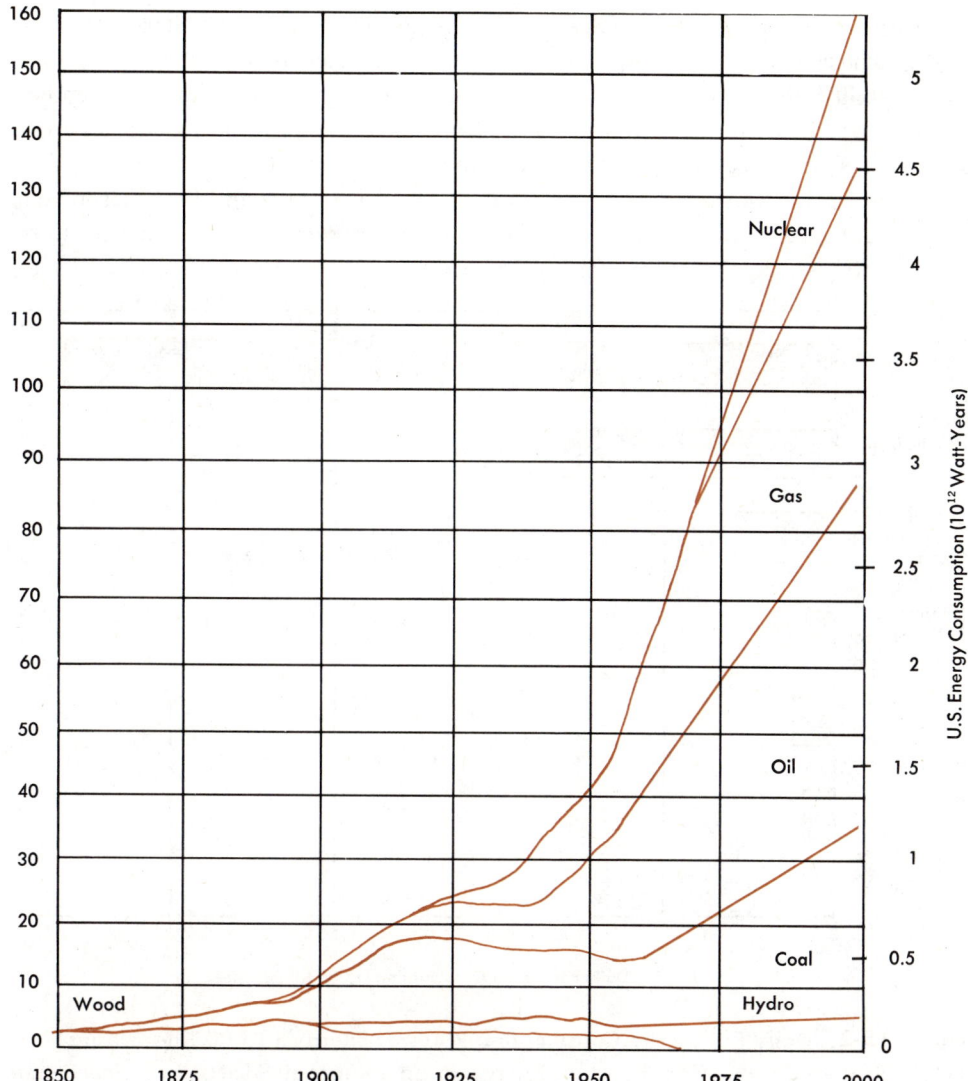

Figure 15-1   U.S. Energy Consumption
SOURCE: Chauncey Starr, "Energy and Power," in *Energy and Power, a Scientific American Book,* San Francisco: W. H. Freeman and Company, 1971, pp. 3-15

history to this point. By 2001, the annual U.S. demand for energy in all forms is expected to double, while the annual worldwide demand will probably triple. The more rapid increase in the world demand results from continued industrialization of underdeveloped areas, and a move on the part of many countries toward energy consumption patterns more similar to those in the U.S. today. As Starr (1971:3) further suggests, there is no question that such projected increases will sorely tax man's ability to discover, extract, and refine energy fuels in the tremendous volumes which will be required, to transport them safely, to find locations for the hundreds of new electrical power stations in the U.S. (thousands worldwide), and to dispose of the waste products with minimal harm to man and his environment.

As is depicted in Figure 15-1, U.S. energy consumption has multiplied 30 times since 1850. At the same time, oil and natural gas have replaced wood and later

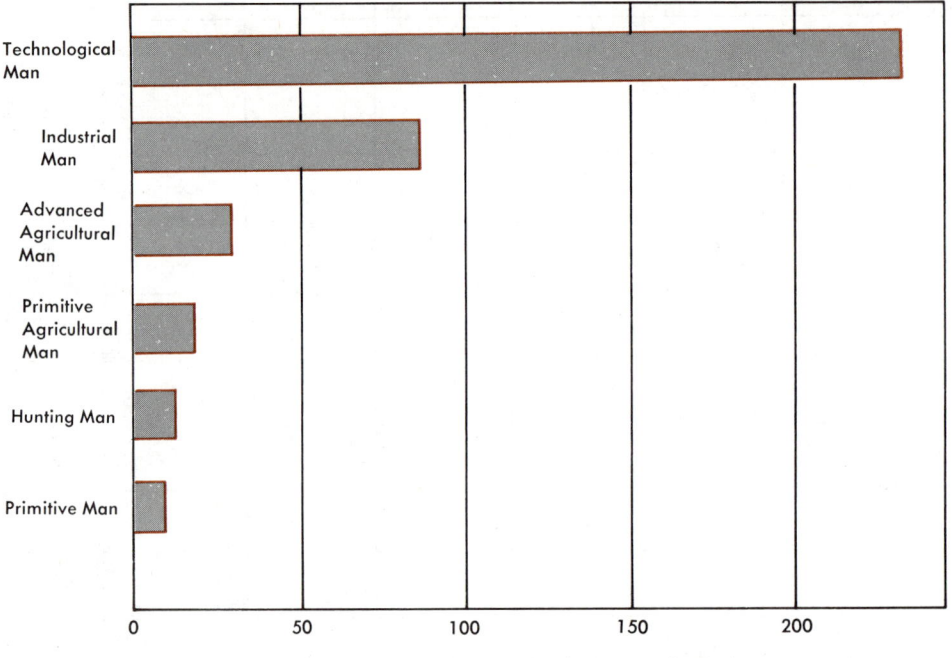

Figure 15-2 Daily Per Capita Consumption Rates of Energy (1,000 Kilocalories)

SOURCE: Earl Cook, "The Flow of Energy in an Industrial Society," in *Energy and Power, A Scientific American Book*, San Francisco: W. H. Freeman and Company, 1971, pp. 83-91

Daily consumption of energy per capita was calculated by Mr. Cook for six stages in human development (and with an accuracy that decreases with antiquity). Primitive man (East Africa about 1,000,000 years ago), without the use of fire, had only the energy of the food he ate. Hunting man (Europe about 100,000 years ago) had more food and also burned wood for heat and cooking. Primitive agricultural man (Fertile Crescent in 5,000 B.C.) was growing crops and had gained animal energy. Advanced agricultural man (northwestern Europe in A.D. 1400) had some coal for heating, some water power and wind power and animal transport. Industrial man (in England in 1875) had the steam engine. In 1970 technological man (in the U.S.) consumed 230,000 kilocalories per day, much of it in the form of electricity.

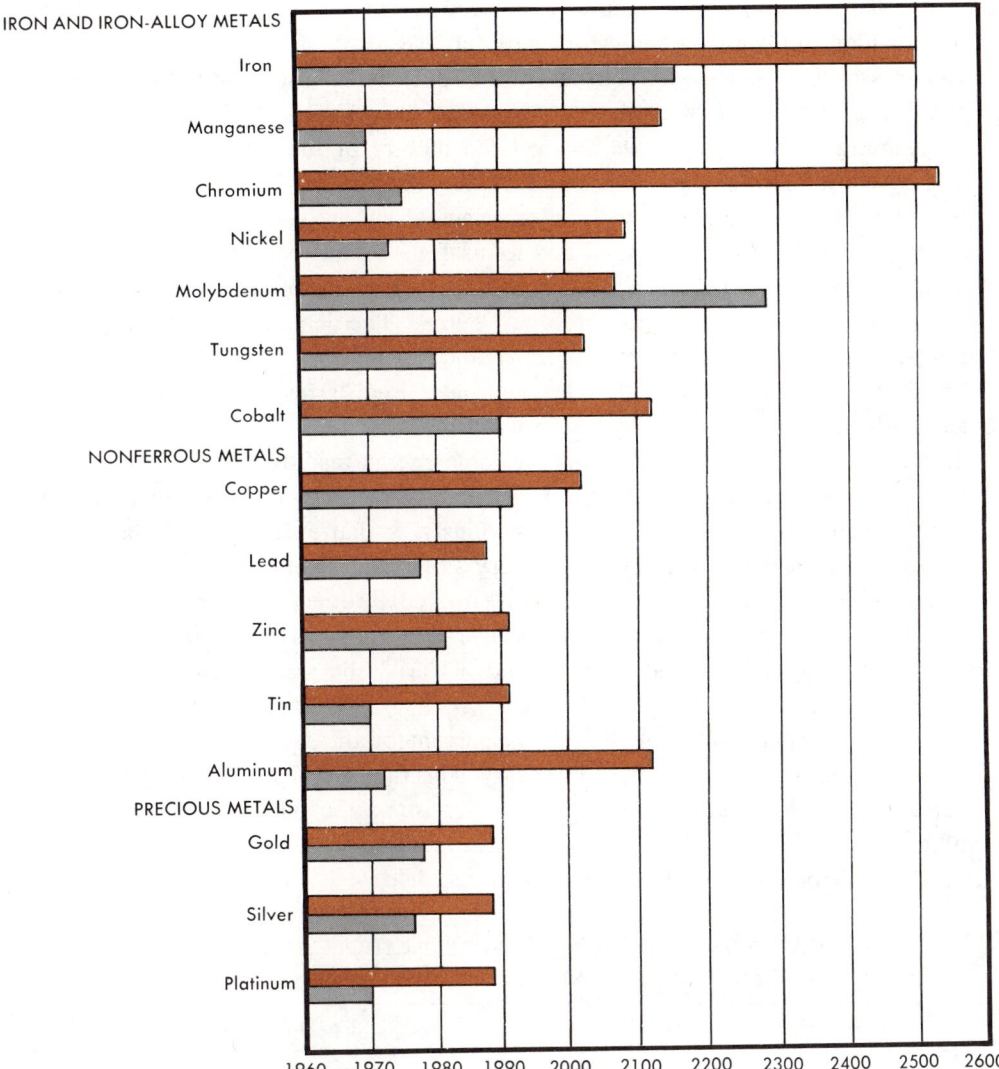

Figure 15-3   Lifetimes of Metal Reserves

SOURCE: Harrison Brown, "Human Materials Production as a Process in the Biosphere," in Paul R. Ehrlich, John P. Holdren, and Richard W. Holm, *Man and the Ecosphere*, San Francisco: W. H. Freeman and Company, 1971, pp. 107-114

Lifetimes of metal reserves are indicated for the world (dark) and the U.S. (light). These rough estimates are based on the assumption that the utilization of metals will continue to increase with population growth and rising per capita demand. They take into account, however, that new reserves will be discovered by exploration or created by innovation. It is estimated that U.S. demands will increase four and a half times by the year 2000.

coal as the principal energy sources. Projections to the year 2000 indicate an ever-expanding utilization of nuclear energy as a source of power.

Changes in daily per capita consumption of energy are also indicative of what is happening in the energy field. Such changes are illustrated in Figure 15-2. Simply by examining the bar graph, we can get the picture of the tremendous increases in energy consumption in a technological society such as the U.S.

The move toward nuclear power as a principal energy source may, in part, be necessitated by the depletion of oil and natural gas as inexpensive sources of fuel. In fact, the virtual depletion of all types of fossil fuels with the exception of coal is projected for the next century (Hubbert, 1969). The depletion of major types of metal reserves appears to be even more imminent. Figure 15-3 shows that by the year 2000, it is estimated that the U.S. will have used its reserves of all the metals listed, with the exception of iron and molybdenum.

In addition to the depletion of nonrenewable energy resources, there is mounting concern that we are also using up our renewable resources much faster than they are being replaced. The problem here, obviously, is that even many of the renewable resources are renewable only at a very slow rate. Many of the forests of the world, for example, have been virtually destroyed through such processes as soil erosion, and through heavy use to satisfy ever-growing needs for fuel, construction materials, and residential and grazing land. Clearly, the restoration of a forest is not a short-term undertaking.

Today the United States, with just six percent of the world's population, consumes about 35 percent of the world's energy. This fact, coupled with projections that other areas of the world are moving toward consumption patterns more and more similar to those in the United States, leads to many of the gloomy prognostications that are forthcoming from the energy resource field.

TABLE 15-2 MAJOR U.S. SOURCES OF AIR POLLUTION AND YEARLY AMOUNTS EMITTED INTO THE ATMOSPHERE

Sources of Pollutants	Millions of Tons of Pollutants Emitted				
	Carbon Monoxides	Sulfur Oxides	Nitrogen Oxides	Hydrocarbons	Particulate Matter
Motor Vehicles	66	1	6	12	1
Principal Industrial Sources, (pulp and paper mills, petroleum refineries, smelters and chemical plants)	2	9	3	1	3
Fuel Burned for Houses and Offices	2	3	0	1	1
Trash Burning	1	0.1	1	1	1

Source: Paul R. Ehrlich and Anne H. Ehrlich, Population, Resources, Environment, p. 147

Air Pollution

One of the results of the rapid increase in per capita consumption can be seen in the man-made hazes that have been hanging over an ever-increasing number of the world's major population centers, caused by industrial and private fuel wastes. While some progress has been made in legislating more restrictive automobile and industrial emission standards, which will be detailed further on (cf. page 603), the condition persists. The seriousness of the air pollution problem is evident from data presented in Table 15-2 on the tonnage of major air pollutants emitted each year into the atmosphere of the United States.

A total of more than 140 million tons of these air pollutants is added to the atmosphere each year. This amounts to almost three-quarters of a ton for every man, woman, and child in the United States. For some years now, this emission of such a high tonnage of pollutants has increasingly taxed the capacity of the atmosphere to absorb and carry it away, particularly from areas of high population density (Ehrlich and Ehrlich, 1972:147).

Fortunately, air pollution has reached the serious "killer" stage only a few times in history—the Meuse Valley in Belgium in 1930, Donora, Pennsylvania, in 1948, and London, England, in 1952. While public-health officials are still not completely sure of all of the effects of exposure to less than lethal doses over a fairly long period of time, Ehrlich and Ehrlich (1972:147), indicate what some of these long-term effects might be:

Cigarette smokers from smoggy St. Louis, Missouri, have roughly four times the incidence of emphysema as smokers from relatively smog-free Winnipeg, Canada. At certain times, air pollution increases the frequency of head colds. Ten years after the Donora smog disaster of 1948, those residents who had reported severe effects during the smog showed the highest subsequent death rates. (This, of course, does not prove that the smog hurried them toward their graves; perhaps only previously weakened people suffered severe effects.) Pneumonia deaths are more frequent in areas of high pollution. Chronic bronchitis is more serious among British postmen who work in areas of high air pollution than in those who serve in relatively smog-free areas. Emphysema death rates have skyrocketed as air pollution has increased. England has higher overall rates of air pollution than the United States, and death from lung cancer is more than twice as common among British men as it is among American men. The lung cancer death rates in England are correlated with the density of atmospheric smoke. The lung cancer rate for men over 45 in the smoggiest part of Staten Island, New York is 55 per 100,000. In a less smoggy area just a few miles away, the rate is 40 per 100,000.

As the Ehrlichs note, though air pollution probably kills, it usually does so in a slow, unobtrusive manner. Therefore, the deaths it causes are not called to the attention of the public in any dramatic fashion, and relatively little public concern was expressed until the recent steep rise in environmental-"crisis" rhetoric.

Water Pollution

Water, like forests, is a renewable natural resource. However, the available supply of fresh water is being severely taxed in many parts of the globe. Though successful efforts have been developed over the years to treat water chemically so that it can be used again and again, most of us are not too excited by the possibility that the drinking water that flows from our taps may have already been used by seven or eight other persons. Ehrlich and Ehrlich (1972), not completely with tongue in cheek, cite the graffiti on the walls of public restrooms in numerous towns along the Mississippi River which reads: "Flush the toilet, they need the water in St. Louis." Of course, the concern is for the effects of water pollution not only upon the waterways themselves, but also upon some of the wildlife dependent upon these waterways for survival.

As in so many other things concerning the earth, mankind, in its use of water resources, has failed to realize all of the probable consequences of its various actions. For example, the damming of the major rivers and waterways of the Pacific Northwest is now threatening the extinction of important types of fish life. Another example has recently come to the attention of residents of the state of Texas. The U.S. Army Corps of Engineers, as well as various state and private organizations, have for years followed a policy of damming the Texas rivers that flow southeastward to the Gulf of Mexico. While some of the dams have been built to meet municipal and agricultural needs, many have been for the explicit purpose of flood control. However, recently officials have discovered that one of the beneficial results of intermittent flooding is the cleansing and flushing out of the bays and estuaries. Without this occasional cleansing, many of these smaller bodies of water are dying and taking with them fish and other water life. The seriousness of this matter is evident from a recent proposal to pipe water from the Mississippi down the coast of Texas to be used to flush out the bays.

Perhaps the best way to summarize the water-resources situation is to quote from a recent speech made by Thomas L. Kimball, executive vice president of the National Wildlife Federation (1972:1-2):

The present situation for water use is . . . poor with the future outlook uncertain. More than one-third of all fresh water is in Canada and the Soviet Union with relatively thin human population densities. Worldwide demands for this vital liquid are skyrocketing. Industry now uses approximately 6,000 liters (about 1,585 gallons) of water a day to produce the goods and services for only one person living in an industrialized society. To keep up with the accelerating demand, we are increasingly draining our fresh water capital—groundwater. In one recent year, India drove more than 78,000 new wells and, while this helps India feed hungry millions, it poses some acute long-term problems for future generations. Lakes and rivers are polluted faster than natural processes can cleanse them. Persistent, toxic, and, in some cases cumulative chemical poisons and fertilizers are causing increasing concern in all nations. Also, in terms of human health, waterborne viruses adversely affect nearly one out of seven persons, primarily in developing nations. Only one in eight of the urban families in these nations is served by a sanitary sewer system.

In addition to resource depletion, and air and water pollution, numerous other areas have attracted the serious attention of scientists and policy makers on both the national and the international scene. Some of the items from the list in Table 15-1 that have been receiving special attenion are synthetic pesticides, nuclear radioactive exposure, oil spills in the oceans and on the beaches, and the pervasive concern with what to do with all of our garbage. Concerning the latter, the United States now produces a ton of garbage per person per year. The U.S. Public Health Service estimates that it takes $3 billion annually to get rid of it, including about $150 million in New York City alone (Einstein, 1970).

In concluding this section, it should be noted that not all experts who study resource availability or some of the related issues discussed are in agreement as to the exact parameters of the situation. Highly respected individuals often argue on very different sides of the issue. While this is perhaps to be expected, the variety of positions taken by the "experts" is terribly confusing to the interested layman. More will be said about this later in the chapter.

Public Opinion

While the "expert" concerns himself with resource depletion estimates and increases in per capita consumption rates, the general public responds to the issue of environmental control only as it feels it is affected personally by environmental problems. Recent indications are that more people are feeling personal effects—from pollution in the air, from urban "brown-outs," and from crowding and congestion both in the urban centers and in the national parks, where ever-increasing numbers flee to escape the urban centers.

Numerous efforts by government as well as by private organizations and individuals have been expended to stimulate public interest in environmental issues. In summarizing such efforts, Murch (1971:101) states:

The spring of 1970 was a milestone in the effort to increase public awareness of environmental problems. During this period, the nation's attention was increasingly drawn to pollution and other threats to the environment. A dozen special television broadcasts examined the issue, while numerous magazines picked up the theme, and environmental groups were formed in an attempt to coordinate local conservation efforts, and extend their concern to the entire community. A climax was reached on April 22, when communities across the nation were urged to observe Earth Day.

TABLE 15-3 CONCERN OVER POLLUTION

Year	Percent Who Feel Pollution Is Very or Somewhat Serious	
	Air	Water
Total Sample		
1965	28	35
1966	48	49
1967	53	52
1968	55	58
1970	69	74
Big City Residents Only		
1965	52	45
1966	70	59
1967	76	62
1968	84	73
1970	93	89

Source: ORC data reported in Erskine (1972a)

In summarizing the data from the major polls that have asked environment-related questions (California, Gallup, Harris, Minnesota, Opinion Research Corporation, and Roper), Erskine (1972:120), suggests that concern with ecological issues has burst upon the American consciousness with unprecedented speed and urgency. There is ample evidence that public alarm about the environment sprang from almost nowhere to major proportions in only a few years. When the first polls appeared about 1965, relatively few people indicated much concern about environmental issues. In fact, activities that occurred in the early 1960's which were directed at influencing public opinion on environmental matters had had little noticeable impact. For example, in 1960 the Izaak Walton League sponsored a national "Clean Air Week" to try to acquaint the public with the existence of a national crisis. Little popular interest and support was generated by this campaign (Trop and Roos, 1971). This indifference and lack of serious interest has changed to the point where today, some of the polls show the environment to be *the* major concern of the American public, even surpassing the perennial worries about war, the economy, and law-and-order issues. Further, an ever-increasing number of individuals are concerned to the extent that they are willing to pay some of the cost to help solve the problem, as we will see in the analyses of the various polls.

We will be able to present public-opinion data only on the *pollution* issue, since little or no survey data can be found on the other issues in Table 15-1. The data summarized from some of the national polls in Tables 15-3 through 15-6 depict the recent increased levels of public concern about pollution. Table 15-3 shows the significant changes that have taken place in attitudes since 1965. While in 1965, 28 percent and 35 percent of the respondents in NORC's national sample perceived air and water pollution, respectively, to be serious problems in their area, these figures had doubled by 1970. Big city residents, though starting with a higher level of concern about pollution, have now reached the point where 9 out of 10 feel that air and water pollution are serious problems where they live.

Essentially the same conclusion is evident from Tables 15-4 and 15-5, the latter

TABLE 15-4 CHANGING PERCEPTIONS ON SERIOUSNESS OF POLLUTION

Compared with a few years ago, do you feel that air (and water—1970) pollution has become worse around here, that the situation has improved, or that it has remained the same?

	Worse	Improved	Same	Not Sure
1967	38%	5%	52%	5%
1970	53	3	39	5

From what you have heard, do you think there is a lot of air pollution around here, some but not a lot, only a little, or hardly any?

	A Lot, Some	Little, Hardly Any	Not Sure
1967	56%	40%	4%
1970	70	28	2

Source: Harris data reported in Erskine (1972b)

TABLE 15-5 PERCEPTIONS OF MAJOR PROBLEMS

What are the two or three top problems facing people such as yourself that you would like to see the new Congress do something about? (1971)

State of the economy	63%
Control of air and water pollution	41
War in Vietnam	31
Taxes and spending	31
Crime	28
Drugs	18
Student unrest	15
Education	11
Increase social security	9
Racial problems	8
National health insurance	7
Housing	6
Farm problems	5
Labor problems	4
Cut foreign aid	4
Abolish the draft	4

Source: Harris data reported in Erskine (1972a)

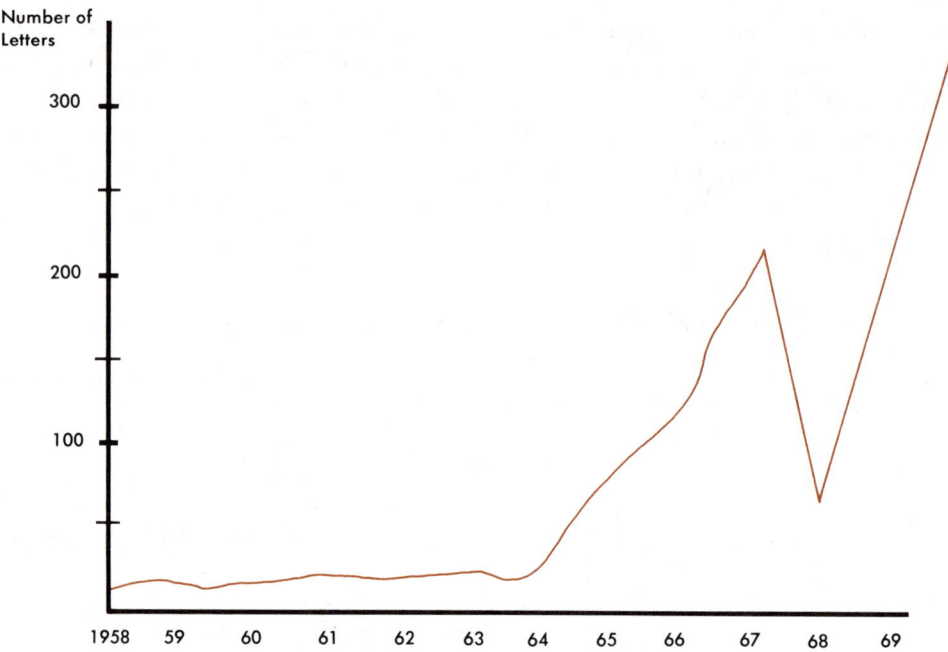

Figure 15-4 Number of Letters-to-the-Editor of *The New York Times* on Environmental Problems, 1958-1969

SOURCE: Donald Munton and Linda Brady, "American Public Opinion and Environmental Pollution," *The Behavioral Science Laboratory Research Report,* Ohio State University, November 1970, graph 2, p. 5

showing that by 1971 only the state of the economy worried people more than did the pollution problem.

Figure 15-4 presents another type of data (other than survey data) compiled by Munton and Brady (1970), which demonstrates increased public interest in and concern about environmental issues. The graph depicts the number of letters on environmental issues received (as opposed to those only printed) by *The New York Times*. The data show that only a negligible number of letters on such issues was received prior to 1964, followed by a sharp increase for every subsequent year except 1968. (Munton and Brady suggest that perhaps for this year public attention was focused on presidential and congressional elections, during which time pollution and environmental deterioration were seldom mentioned as political issues.) While *The New York Times* does not constitute a representative sample of American newspapers, the data do provide some indication that substantially more Americans have become concerned about environmental problems than was true a few years ago.

Perhaps a more convincing indicator of increasing public concern is willingness to pay some of the costs of pollution control or clean-up programs. The national polls have consistently shown that the financial sacrifices persons are willing to make are not very large. However, findings from the Harris poll show that the percentage willing to pay 15 dollars a year more in taxes to finance federal air-pollution control programs has increased steadily since 1967, when the question was first asked (see Table 15-6).

Data from regional studies have generally been quite consistent with the national opinion data. In a statewide sample of respondents living in the state of Washington, Dillman (1971) found that a greater percentage of his respondents felt that more money should be spent for pollution control (69 percent) than for any other area except for crime prevention and control. Another environment-related problem, protection of forests and other natural areas for human enjoyment, ranked fourth in Dillman's list of 15 expenditure areas. Fifty-one percent of his respondents favored more money being spent in this area.

An interesting finding, perhaps not yet sufficiently documented, is that the *actual* pollution level at a particular time or in a particular place is not strongly related to public perceptions of the seriousness of the problem. For example, Murch (1971), found that respondents in his Durham, North Carolina, study admitted that the U.S. had a serious pollution problem, but felt that the situation in the community of Durham was not nearly as bad as the national situation—this, despite the fact that measures of air quality show that air pollution in Durham exceeds the national average! Similarly, Albrecht (1972) found that his respondents in the Four Corners Area of the Southwest felt that they did not have a serious pollution problem compared with the situation in the U.S. as a whole, nor would they have one even if six major coal-burning power plants were built in their area. They expressed this opinion despite the fact that the six plants, if built, would emit daily more than 200 tons of fly ash, 1,365 tons of sulfur oxides, and 1,000 tons of nitrogen oxides.

TABLE 15-6 WILLINGNESS TO PAY FOR PROGRAM TO CURB POLLUTION

Would you be willing to pay $15 a year more in taxes to finance a federal program to control air pollution?

	Willing	Unwilling	Not Sure
1967	44%	46%	10%
1970	54	34	12
1971	59	34	7

Source: Harris data reported in Erskine (1972a)

TABLE 15-7 MEAN MONTHLY COLUMN-INCHES OF SPACE THE NEW YORK TIMES INDEX DEVOTED TO ENVIRONMENTAL ISSUES

Heading	1950	51	52	53	54	55	56	57	58	59	60	61	62	63	64	65	66	67	68	69	70
Environment[a]	—	—	—	—	—	—	—	—	—	—	—	—	—	—	—	.1	.2	.2	.5	1.5	5.7
Pollution[b]	—	—	—	—	—	—	—	—	—	—	—	—	—	—	—	—	.3	.1	2.1	.7	—
Air Pollution	1.3	2.7	2.3	1.3	1.7	2.3	1.2	1.5	1.3	1.7	1.6	1.8	1.3	1.3	1.5	3.6	7.9	11.2	4.1	8.3	25.4
Water Pollution	.8	.6	.7	.5	.8	.6	.6	.5	1.0	1.1	1.3	2.3	1.8	2.0	1.4	4.8	4.4	3.7	5.2	15.4	17.0

[a] Not listed, 1950-1964.
[b] Used as heading only, 1950-1965. Reference was "See kinds, e.g., Air, Water." Used as heading only in 1970. Reference was to "Environment." "Ecology," when included, was used only as a heading. In the earlier years, the references were mainly to single entries under "Biology." In the later years, the references were to "Environment." One additional category not included in this table was that of "U.S.—Pollution." The pattern of increasing space here paralleled that for the general categories.
The 1970 figures cover January-July only.

Source: Taken from table 7, p. 19 in Donald Munton and Linda Brady, American Public Opinion and Environmental Pollution

TABLE 15-8 EMPHASIS ON POLLUTION COVERAGE, JANUARY 1970

	Average Number of Stories Run		
	Large Papers	Small Papers	Combined Average
Page-one local stories	6.6	2.8	4.6
Page-one wire stories	3.6	4.0	3.8
Editorials	5.8	3.2	4.5

Source: John C. Maloney and Lynn Slovonsky, "The Pollution Issue: A Survey of Editorial Judgments," The Politics of Ecosuicide, 1971

Another interesting observation from the survey data which requires further explanation is that *concern* for such things as air pollution has *risen* steadily at the same time that *levels* of a number of common air pollutants have *declined* in a broad sample of urban areas (Ludwig, Morgan, and McMullen, 1970). This finding can be explained, at least in part, by the attention created by mass media coverage and emphasis on pollution, as shown by Munton and Brady (1970:19a). For example, Table 15-7 shows the mean monthly column-inches of space devoted by *The New York Times Index* to environmental issues from 1958 to 1970. The nationwide high point reached in newspaper coverage on pollution by 1970 can be seen also in Table 15-8, a vastly different picture from that just a short time earlier, according to Maloney and Slovonsky (1971).

These surveys lend credence to the argument that public concern comes in part from the emphasis the mass media have placed on environmental problems. As Munton and Brady (1970:23) put it: "Article after article, book after book, and commentator after commentator have informed the public about environmental pollution and told them they should be worried." The result as evidenced in the public opinion data has been, simply, that they have become worried—perhaps frequently without really understanding why or exactly what it is that they are supposed to be worried about.

CHAMPIONS AND THEIR INTERESTS

The data presented above clearly suggest that the interest and concern of the general public relating to environmental issues has been increasing rapidly since at least 1965. However, a closer examination of the polling data reveals that such interest and concern are not equally distributed across all segments of the population. There are several "special publics" for whom the environment has become a much more salient issue. Further, within these publics one does not find anything approaching a consensus of attitudes toward environmental issues, or even agree-

TABLE 15-9 PERCEPTION OF EFFECTS OF AIR AND WATER POLLUTION

	Yes	No	Not Sure	Total
Total	29%	68%	3%	100%
Sex				
Men	33	64	3	100
Women	26	71	3	100
Race				
White	30	68	2	100
Black	21	69	10	100
Age				
16–20 years	31	64	5	100
21–29	41	58	1	100
30–34	25	72	3	100
35–49	36	60	4	100
50 plus	21	76	3	100
Education				
8th grade	15	81	4	100
High School	30	67	3	100
College	42	55	3	100
Income				
Under $5,000	15	82	3	100
$5,000–$9,999	29	67	4	100
$10,000 plus	43	56	1	100
Community Type				
Cities	31	64	5	100
Suburbs	43	55	2	100
Towns	25	73	2	100
Rural	18	79	3	100
Region				
East	31	66	3	100
Midwest	33	65	2	100
South	17	79	4	100
West	39	58	3	100

Source: Taken from table 4, p. 11 in Donald Munton and Linda Brady, American Public Opinion and Environmental Pollution. The Munton-Brady table utilizes data from a July 1969 Gallup poll done for the National Wildlife Federation.

ment that the environment deserves the amount of attention it is receiving. In fact, some would argue that the heavy emphasis on environmental problems diverts attention away from more crucial issues such as war, racism, and poverty. These special publics have provided the impetus and manpower behind both the environmentalist social movement and an opposition or counter-social movement. This section will single out some of the major interest groups involved in order to demonstrate both the distribution of environmental concern across the population, and the conflicting orientations toward the environment. (The range of interests of these groups is indicated in Table 15-1.) The next section will then discuss the major social movements which have been generated by the special publics and interest groups.

Demographic and Structural Distribution of Environmental Interests

The *distribution* of concern about the environment across the social structure constitutes a rather interesting paradox. The polls and surveys show that it is generally those persons who have access to the better, rather than the poorer, environments, who are most concerned about environmental deterioration. Further, persons of lower socio-economic class, who both exhibit less concern and who frequently must survive in the poorer environments of crowded, dirty urban centers, are likely to define an "improvement" in their environment in the very terms that environmentalists are increasingly calling into question—higher levels of consumption and material convenience (see Morrison, Hornback, and Warner, 1972).

A closer examination of public opinion data on what is happening to the environment reveals more about the above paradox: both perceptions of being personally affected by a deteriorating environment, and level of concern about environmental issues are closely related to the socio-economic characteristics of the respondents. Table 15-9 shows responses to the question, "Have air and water pollution affected your personal enjoyment of your surroundings and your life in any way?" Major differences in response to this question are evident according to race, education, income, community type, and region of the country. Whites are more likely to feel that their personal enjoyment of the environment has been affected by pollution than are blacks. Those who were most likely to respond affirmatively to this question were persons with a college education, with incomes of $10,000 or over, or who lived in the suburbs. Table 15-10 indicates that concern for environmental problems is also related to most of the same demographic and socio-economic characteristics. Whites are more deeply concerned than are blacks, and degree of concern rises rather significantly with increases in level of education, income, or occupation.

Economic and Occupational Interests

It seems particularly paradoxical that the poor and the minority groups are least concerned about environmental pollution since, as suggested above, it is probably accurate to suggest that in many instances, they are the ones likely to suffer most from the effects of pollution. Schnaiberg (1971:25-26), has argued:

If we turn to costs of environmental degradation, the following appears to be an accurate statement: regardless of the particular cost dimension examined, environmental costs to

TABLE 15-10 RESPONDENT'S CONCERN ABOUT ENVIRONMENTAL PROBLEMS RELATED TO DEMOGRAPHIC AND SOCIO-ECONOMIC CHARACTERISTICS

	Deeply Concerned	Somewhat Concerned	Not Very Concerned	Don't Know, No Answer	Total	N
Total	51%	35%	12%	3%	100%	3192
Sex						
Men	56	32	10	3	100	1488
Women	46	38	14	2	100	1712
Race						
White	52	35	11	2	100	2922
Black	34	32	25	9	100	253
Age						
21–34	51	41	7	1	100	886
35–49	50	38	10	2	100	1032
50+	52	28	16	4	100	1249
Education						
Grade School	39	34	20	7	100	856
High School	52	37	10	1	100	1615
College	62	32	6	—	100	721
Income						
$4,000	37	35	23	6	100	787
$4,000–$6,999	55	34	8	3	100	774
$7,000–$9,999	53	38	8	1	100	720
$10,000+	58	34	7	—	100	877
Occupation						
Farm	43	37	17	3	100	169
Blue Collar	48	39	12	2	100	1310
Clerical, Sales	52	37	9	2	100	366
Professional, Busn.	57	33	9	1	100	733
Community Size						
2,500	46	37	14	3	100	954
2,500–49,000	52	31	16	1	100	479
50,000–249,000	55	35	16	1	100	505
250,000–999,000	52	35	11	2	100	642
1,000,000+	51	36	8	5	100	620
Region						
East	47	38	11	4	100	944
Midwest	57	34	9	1	100	859
South	45	36	16	4	100	873
West	59	32	10	—	100	524

Source: Taken from table 6, p. 17 in Donald Munton and Linda Brady, *American Public Opinion and Environmental Pollution.* The Munton-Brady table utilizes data from a January 1969 Gallup poll.

the individual are consistently higher for the poor than for the more affluent. Whether in terms of air pollution (higher in central city areas, where high concentrations of poor reside), water pollution (more severe in high-density areas, again where the poor reside), or land pollution (impact of DDT spraying is most severe for migrant laborers, for example), the poor are in a position of entrapment. . . . And, if we project current environmental decay to the apocalypse that many forecast, one would have to be incredibly naive to believe that such a catastrophe would strike uniformly across social lines. If air deteriorates, oxygen is available to the more affluent; if water deteriorates, water purifiers or bottled water will go to the highest bidders; and the choicest land already belongs to the corporate elite!

However, the polling and attitude results are perhaps not too surprising when we consider Whitney Young's observation that,

People live in blighted housing, can't find decent jobs, send their kids to second-rate schools, die too soon because they can't afford doctors, and the cities they live in are sinking under the weight of countless unresolved problems of poverty and discrimination. That's where our national attention should be focused. The war on pollution is one that should be waged after the war on poverty is won. . . . (quoted in Munton and Brady, 1970:18)

Dolbeare and Dolbeare (1971:9), using a somewhat Marxist orientation, have argued that the more closely we analyze the beliefs and values of any group of individuals, the more likely we are to find a coherent relationship between their perception of the world and their priorities and aspirations. Similarly, according to Gusfield (1970:11), "What may be greeted with warmth and acceptance by one group is responded to with hostility and repulsion by those whose life conditions differ." These ideas suggest, and the data seem to bear out, that one's perceptions of, and orientations toward, the environment are likely to vary greatly according to life conditions and chances. A higher level of education, for example, may lead to a greater ability to comprehend the problem of environmental degradation, and more leisure time to theorize about the issue. The suburban dweller with a high income and level of education is not likely to feel economically dependent upon the forest and the river for his livelihood. To him, they can be a source of beauty and aesthetic appreciation rather than a source of income. On the other hand, to the person needing a job, the haze of smoke over a valley can be something he values and sees a kind of beauty in, since it means employment and support for his family. Utilitarian values rather than preservationist values are likely to characterize such a person's orientation toward the environment.

This point has been made very clearly by Harry, Gale, and Hendee (1969: 248-249), particularly as related to place of residence:

> . . . since rural occupations are mainly based upon the exploitation of nature, we suggest that, for ruralites, nature is primarily significant as a utilitarian object. Because the relevant occupations are lumbering, mining, fishing, and agriculture, the most organized opposition to the conservation movement is found in these rural-based industries which are able to exert political influence through their occupational and industrial associations.

There are some interesting parallels between the notion that attitudes toward the environment are closely related to life circumstances and chances, and Maslow's (1943) theory of a hierarchy of needs. According to Maslow, only when certain lower-level needs (physical, safety, etc.) are satisfied can one develop an enduring concern for higher-level needs (self-esteem, self-actualization, etc.). It may be that only when economic needs are met can one develop an enduring concern for the quality of the environment. Until one has reached a certain level of economic security, aesthetic values may be much less important. Data which will be presented at a later point in this chapter on the makeup of the environmentalist movement (cf. pages 592-593) would seem to support this hypothesis.

An alternative hypothesis, which would also explain the above findings about differing values placed upon the environment, has been suggested by Munton and Brady (1970:18). Each of the variables associated with high concern about environmental degradation is highly related to educational level, and Munton and Brady note that the higher one's educational attainment, the more information he is likely to have about public issues. They argue further, that the fact

> that the better-educated person is more likely to receive and is more capable of ingesting information, and therefore tends to be more aware of public issues may seem merely obvious. The connection, though, is crucial to an understanding of present opinion about environmental problems. Since no one favors pollution, we assume that, in general, greater information and thus greater awareness, leads to greater concern. In short, we are arguing that information . . . is the main underlying basis for concern.

These authors note that a similar argument has been advanced by Davies: "People have to be taught that air pollution is bad for their health. One may even have to be taught to consider air pollution aesthetically unattractive. Thus, unlike problems such as unemployment or crime or poor housing, perception of air pollution as a problem is heavily dependent upon exposure to channels of information" (quoted in Munton and Brady, 1970:18). More data are required before a decision can be made on the explanatory power of these alternative hypotheses.

Social-class and economic differences in response to environmental issues, whatever their motivational basis may be, have recently evolved into a more general conflict between industry (including labor here) and the environmentalists. This basically boils down to a conflict between making jobs and markets, on the one hand, and the philosophy of "no growth" expounded by many of those concerned with environmental deterioration, on the other. While economic growth and expansion means more jobs, it also frequently means more pollution and a more rapid depletion of the earth's resources. Harold Gilliam, in a recent article in the *San Francisco Sunday Examiner and Chronicle* (1972:41), cites some important quotes which indicate a growing feeling on the part of many labor leaders and entrepreneurs toward the environmentalists:

> Too many environmentalists regard nature as higher than people; they have contempt for human beings. . . . We don't want combat with environmentalists, but we won't surrender.
> —John F. Henning, *California Labor Federation*

> The no-growth philosophy is an upper-middle-class-elitist view, an attempt to convince the poor that they should stay on the bottom rung of the ladder.
> Michael R. Peevey, *California AFL-CIO*

> People are more important than pollywogs.
> —William Leonard, *East Bay Associated Home Builders*

These economic concerns were translated, in the 1972 elections, into bitter opposition on the part of some labor unions to several environmental measures. If forced to choose between a payroll with pollution and a clean environment with no payroll, many individuals and communities are going to respond, "to hell with the environment."*

Special economic or class-structured publics are thus emerging with definite opinions in response to the environmental clamor. As we examine these publics, it seems rather clear that their orientation toward environmental issues is closely related to their personal life circumstances and interests. Noteworthy, too, is the fact that many of the same issues that are influenced by social-class differences *within* countries are also influenced by a social or economic hierarchy *between* countries; that is, orientation toward the environment is, at least in part, dependent upon whether one is a "have" or a "have not" country. The proposals presented by industrialized countries in the United Nations, for a worldwide environmentalist policy, are a case in point:

> It is one thing for the affluent nations of the world to propose a freeze on consumption rates as a means of saving the environment, but it is quite a different matter to suppose that underdeveloped nations would receive such a proposal with any degree of enthusiasm. The realities of such a proposal are that it would virtually condemn citizens in the underdeveloped world to live forever as second-class passengers in "spaceship earth." (see Castro, 1972)

---

* The opposition of industrialists (as compared to organized labor) is usually exerted less publicly through political alliances and pressures, which are discussed somewhat below under "political interests."

Whether or not underdeveloped countries can ever hope to achieve the level of consumption of developed countries is an interesting question. For example, if a country like India were to use fertilizers at the per capita level of the Netherlands, it would consume one-half of the world's total output of fertilizers (Castro, 1972:241). However, does this give the developed countries the right to propose that the underdeveloped countries should sacrifice their desires for economic and consumptive growth as their part in saving the world's environment?

For many of the countries of the world as well as for the poor and the minorities within developed countries like the United States, perhaps the "pollution of poverty" is a far more real and salient issue than is the pollution of the environment.

Political Publics and Interests

Both major political parties in the United States have claimed a high degree of interest in environmental protection, though perhaps official Republican Party interest has been somewhat slower in developing. The 1964 platform of the Democratic Party made brief mention of environmental issues, while no mention at all was made by the Republicans. By the 1968 conventions, the Democrats devoted a complete section of their platform to environmental conservation and natural resources, while the Republicans acknowledged the existence of air and water pollution, and the need for their correction (Trop and Roos, 1971).

In 1965, at about the same time that public interest in environmental matters was increasing, President Lyndon Johnson proclaimed the beautification of our natural environment as a national goal. Support from both political parties helped Congress to pass several important environmental bills between 1965 and 1970, including the Highway Beautification Act, the Water Quality Act, the Water Resources Act, and the Rural Water Sewage Act (Trop and Roos, 1971).

The political rhetoric about the environment, aside from some important exceptions which we will examine shortly, has continued to be non-partisan. For example, by 1970 President Richard Nixon in his State of the Union Message asserted: ". . . the great question of the seventies is, shall we surrender to our surroundings, or shall we make peace with nature, and begin to make reparations for the damage we have done to our air, our land and our water?" He abandoned his earlier statements, which were more favorable to industrial needs and interests, and, to the surprise of almost everyone, even the tone of the public pronouncements by his Secretary of Interior, Walter Hickle, changed. While the President's indecisive response to the Santa Barbara oil spill in 1969 angered the environmentalists, as well as Santa Barbara citizens, he was no longer making remarks as he had done while still a nominee to the effect that the United States should not establish very strong water-pollution standards, so as not to hinder industrial development.

Despite these observations, there is still some evidence that concern with the environment is not strictly non-partisan in nature. Recent data supporting this contention have been collected by Dunlap and Gale (1974). They begin by noting important characteristics of environmentalist politics that could possibly contribute to partisan interests: first, pro-environmental legislation is frequently opposed by business and industry because these are the groups most likely to feel that their economic interests are threatened by stringent anti-pollution laws; second, environmental legislation frequently entails an extension of governmental regulatory powers; third, in order to be effective, it is almost an absolute necessity that environmental legislation be innovative. Given these characteristics of environmental legislation, Dunlap and Gale argue that it is only natural that partisan differences will emerge for the following reasons: (1) the Republican Party has traditionally been the party of big business, and as such is likely to be more concerned with the interests and desires of the business community on environmental issues; (2) a central tenet of the Republican Party has been that the least government is the best government; (3) the Republican Party has traditionally been less innovative in using government to solve social problems. Based on this logic, Dunlap and Gale hypothesized that Republicans would be significantly less likely to support pro-environmental legislation than would Democrats. Using data from a western state legislature, the hypothesis was supported, even when controlling for other variables that the researchers felt had some importance.

TABLE 15-11 POLITICAL OUTLOOK (in percentages)

Of the following terms, which one best describes your political outlook at the present time?

	Random Sample	Eco-Activists	SDS Activists
Radical left	5	18	91
Very liberal	24	47	9
Moderately liberal	35	18	—
Slightly liberal	14	8	—
Slightly conservative	14	6	—
Moderately conservative	8	2	—
Very conservative	—[a]	—[a]	—
Radical right	—[a]	2	—
Total	100	101[b]	100
(N)	(229)	(51)	(22)

[a] Less than one percent.
[b] Rounding error.

Source: Taken from table 1, p. 384 in Riley E. Dunlap and Richard P. Gale, "Politics and Ecology: A Profile of Student Eco-Activists," Youth and Society, 3 (1972):379-397

These same authors (Dunlap and Gale, 1972) have also examined political orientations of students who have had some involvement in various types of environmental organizations. Student eco-activists were compared with a random sample of other students, as well as with a small sample of members of the Students for a Democratic Society (SDS). Table 15-11 shows how each of the groups classified themselves in terms of political outlook. It is rather clear that politically the eco-activists fall somewhere between the random sample and the SDS members, though they are generally much closer to the former. They are clearly more "liberal" than the random sample, but far less likely to view themselves as "radical left" than were members of SDS.

In terms of political party orientation, the eco-activists were found to be just as likely to indicate a traditional political-party preference as were those from the random sample. The percentage of both groups identifying themselves as Democrats was almost identical, with the eco-activists slightly less willing to indicate a Republican preference. Dunlap and Gale conclude:

The composite view of Oregon eco-activists which emerges from these data definitely does not support the popular view of the "eco-freak" as "turned on" to the environment but not to politics. Yet, our data also fail to support the right-wing view of eco-activists as "radicals with a new cause." Although the eco-activists are quite politically active, and have often taken part in demonstrations, their willingness to identify with a traditional political party, and their self-descriptions as "liberals," clearly differentiates them from SDS-type activists. All things considered, the view of eco-activists as "good liberals," put forth by the Left, seems to receive the most support from our data. (1972:386)

In terms of future partisan involvement in environmental issues, however, some important changes may become evident. For example, as indicated earlier, labor is becoming more strongly involved in opposition to pro-environmental legislation because of the fear that such legislation will cost jobs for workers. The Democratic Party has traditionally been the party of labor. How, then, will this party deal with the environment issue in the future? Clearly the issue is a complex one. In addition to these more general and partisan political interests, furthermore, there are the specialized environmentalist organizations, such as the Sierra Club and the Audubon Society, both of whom attempt to influence the political process in favor of environmental preservation. Their efforts will be taken up in the next section of this chapter.

Orientations toward the environment will continue to vary greatly, depending upon the interests involved. The crisis rhetoric of the environmentalists is loudly scoffed at by other publics. As we have noted, some right-wing groups have defined the environmentalist movement as a communist-inspired conspiracy designed to deny the United States access to minerals and resources vital to her survival (see

Albrecht, 1972). Some left-wing groups have seen the movement as an attempt by the power structure to draw attention away from more important social issues, such as war and poverty. Many black leaders in the country have tended to agree with this prognosis. To quote Richard Hatcher, mayor of Gary, Indiana: "The nation's concern with environment has done what George Wallace was unable to do: distract the nation from the human problems of black and brown Americans" (*Time,* August 3, 1970:42). A number of citizens, who belong to neither the right nor the left, have probably wondered whether or not mankind will suffer "a whole hell of a lot if the whooping crane doesn't quite make it" (quoted in *Time,* August 3, 1970:42).

Scientific Publics and Interests

In the United States interest in environmental problems has, in the past, been limited largely to the academic community and to those public agencies, such as the Park Service, which have been given special charge and responsibility in areas of natural-resource protection and preservation. Certainly, there have been other individuals and small groups who have taken a special interest in the environment, but, until recently, widespread concern has been minor outside the academic world and the world of public agencies.

The academic and scientific communities have played a significant role in the recent popularization of the environment as a major social problem. Much of the larger public has been sensitized to environmental issues through the rhetoric and actions of individuals with university and similar educational affiliations. Center stage has been held in recent years by such eminent figures as Paul Ehrlich (*The Population Bomb* and *Population, Resources, Environment*), Barry Commoner (*Science and Survival, The Closing Circle*), Rachel Carson (*Silent Spring*), and Dennis Meadows, et al. (*The Limits of Growth*). These "doomsday prophets" have made both the public-at-large and governmental decision-makers aware of the magnitude of the environmental deterioration that has been occurring. Probably few books have been more widely read and quoted in recent years than have those listed above. All of these important works forecast worldwide environmental catastrophe unless important, large-scale, immediate and successful efforts are made to control population, pollution, and resource depletion.

More recently, important parallels have become evident in the divisions among the economic publics and the divisions among the scientific ones. The "doomsday prophets" are now being challenged by a growing number of their scientific peers. The following quote from a column in *The New York Times,* written by Jeffrey St. John, discusses one group that has recently challenged the ideas of Dennis Meadows and his colleagues at the Massachusetts Institute of Technology:

A trio of researchers at Amsterdam's Konninklijke Shell-Laboratorium this past summer did a deft demolition on Meadows and his team of "doomsday futurists" at M.I.T. Among the many points the Amsterdam group made was that "The Limits of Growth" lacked "theory, evidence or experience" and that it was based largely on unproven assumptions—a corrosive and chronic intellectual affliction of many futurists. The singular false assumption of so many doomsday determinists is that the problems which they project into the future will not be modified or changed by what the Amsterdam group called "social feedback," a process by which men of the mind intervene in positive terms to solve such problems without recourse to coercion. Nor do the futurists care to comprehend the process by which freely inquiring minds produce new systems of thought which could change the character of current problems. (December 5, 1972)

Probably the most important critique of the environmental prophets of doom is John Maddox's recent book, *The Doomsday Syndrome* (1972). Maddox enters the debate with rather impressive credentials. He is editor of *Nature* magazine, a theoretical physicist, and widely recognized as one of England's leading scientists. In his book, Maddox unhesitatingly takes on Ehrlich, Commoner, Carson, Hardin, Dubos and others who have helped popularize the current "environmental crisis." Maddox is convinced that the predictions of these writers are wrong. The facts, he argues, do not support their case. The threat of famine is not getting closer but is receding; the growth of the world's population is leveling off, and will do so more rapidly as developing countries industrialize; minerals are still plentiful for man's needs, and, as current sources run out, new ones will be found.

One of the major mistakes made by the doomsayers, Maddox feels, is that they fail to take into account man's adaptability and his problem-solving abilities. As evidence of this, he notes that pollution in many American and British cities is decreasing, and the quality of the water in many areas is better now than a few years ago. All of this has happened because of the "deliberate exercise of human ingenuity." In other words, technology and prosperity do not inherently lead to environmental destruction but, instead, contain within themselves the very means by which a better environment may be created. Maddox's critique will, no doubt, evoke a strong response. Though his aim is not to argue for "do-nothingism," it has already been suggested by some critics that his whole book simply presents "the case for complacency."

Whatever the outcome of this growing debate, the long and illustrious history of "fads and foibles" in scientific research suggests that the scientist is not immune to bandwagon effects, and that many of us quickly devote our attention to fashionable problems. (The production of this chapter is, in part, confirmation of this observation.)

THE ECOLOGY PROBLEM AS A SOCIAL MOVEMENT

The environmentalist movement is not a product only of the 1960's and 1970's. Its historical roots can be traced back before the turn of the present century. In understanding the current movement, therefore, it is of some importance to take a brief look at some of its antecedents and their probable impact on current environmental interests and action.

The Early Conservation Movement

In referring to interest in the environment in this country, it is quite impossible to point to some particular date, event, or individual and say, "this is where it all began." It would probably not be inaccurate to suggest that from the time of the very founding of this country, there were some individuals who were vitally concerned with preserving and protecting its pristine character from the ravages of their fellowmen.

To a large majority of the early settlers of America, however, the country appeared so vast that there was probably little widespread concern about protecting it or maintaining its unspoiled nature. Rather, the challenge was more one of conquering the vast wilderness, taming the mighty rivers, clearing the forests for villages and crop lands, and gaining access to the seemingly unlimited supply of natural resources in order to increase wealth and power. Gale (1972) has noted, however, that two early interests emerged some time around the turn of the present century which were to play important roles in the formation of early environment-related movements, and, indirectly, in environmentalist movements as well. These two themes were resource conservation and outdoor recreation. The first of these included two subthemes—one emphasizing "conservation-wise use," and the other "preservation."

The issue of resource conservation was a major political issue during the decade from 1900 to 1910. There is some evidence that the conservationist movement had more fire during this period than at any other time, until the recent rebirth of major interest in environmental issues. This early movement had its major roots in the progressive movement, a multifaceted reform movement of that period. In the resource area, conservation meant not preserving the bounties of the land, but conserving them or using them wisely for the good of the people. McConnell (1954) has argued that without a more cohesive set of ideas than the vision of "the use of the earth for the permanent good of man," this early progressive orientation was destined to have little real impact. However, early concern for resource conservation on the part of such well-known public figures as Teddy Roosevelt and Gifford Pinchot did draw conservation issues to the attention of a much broader public. These individuals, and others, became increasingly alarmed at the destruction and deterioration of forests, wildlife, and soil, and so pushed for "strong governmental support of a 'conservation-wise use' policy" (Gale, 1972:283).

This "conservation-wise use policy," emphasizing efficient development and use of natural resources, soon found itself in conflict with another perspective that was gaining wide support—what Gale refers to as a "conservationist-preservationist" orientation. This latter orientation was frequently expressed by private citizens who were concerned about the destruction of the natural environment, the misuse of natural resources contained in that environment, and the disregard of the wildlife that inhabited it. This concern led to the formation of such interest groups as the Sierra Club in the San Francisco area in 1892, and the first national Audubon Society in 1905 (Gale, 1972:283). Gale notes that while both those who held the "conservation-wise use" perspective and the "conservation-preservation" perspective considered themselves conservationists, the management and development orientation of the former frequently conflicted with the preservation and protection orientation of the latter.

McConnell (1954) has suggested that the conservationist-preservationist orientation became almost a religious set of ideals for those who adopted it. This fervor is projected in the writings of such figures as George Perkins Marsh, John Muir, and Aldo Leopold. As such, this orientation attracted a strongly dedicated core of true believers, who were able to maintain a commitment to the philosophy of preservation that has carried even into the present environmentalist movement.

Concerning the second of the early environmental interests, outdoor recreation, Gale (1972:285) has observed:

Outdoor recreation as an important leisure activity was a second major factor in the development of the environmental movement. Especially in those regions which offered high-quality outdoor recreation, persons joined together to enjoy outdoor sports in a group setting and to train others in outdoor skills. On occasion, these groups actively defended a favorite recreational area or other natural resource which was crucial to the continued enjoyment of the recreational activity. Some of the organizations were national —like the Izaak Walton League and Ducks Unlimited—while others were regional or local—like the Seattle Mountaineers, Appalachian Mountain Club, or Association of Northwest Steelheaders.

One of the major controversies of this period that did so much to arouse public concern over environmental issues, and a controversy in which John Muir and other early conservationists played important roles, was the move by the city of San Francisco to build a reservoir for water-supply purposes in the Hetch Hetchy Valley, which had been included as a part of Yosemite Park. This case is particularly interesting, because in it we can see the same issues being fought out that are present in most, if not all, of today's major environmental controversies (such as the SST or the Alaskan pipeline issues). The leaders of San Francisco argued that without the increased source of water that would be supplied by the new dam, the city could not continue to grow. Thus, the issue then, as so frequently now, was one of continued growth versus environmental protection and preservation. According to Nash (1965:xi),

The struggle over Hetch Hetchy seemed to many at the time to be symbolic of a larger conflict between beauty and materialism, sentiment and the utilitarian viewpoint, morality and irreligion. At stake, it appeared, was not just a wild valley but whether Americans would ever be able to place the finer things of life above the pursuit of the main chance.

The composition of the early environmentalist movement was basically upper-middle class. As such, it neither attempted to define goals in a way to make them more palatable to a wider, more heterogeneous public, nor made efforts to mobilize mass support for their achievement (Gale, 1972). Therefore, in terms of membership, it never did attain any significant size, and its impact was neither major nor sustained, except for the first decade of the present century when the "conservation-wise use" philosophy was closely tied to the political program and ideals of progressivism. Otherwise, during this early period, the efforts made by the early environmentalists were confined by the limited range of issues that attracted their interest—preserving a back-country area, or blocking the construction of another dam.

The life-cycle of the early conservation movement was pretty well linked with that of the larger progressive movement as a whole, which is to say that it declined sharply after World War I. By that time, much of its program had been co-opted by the government. The preservationist interest, for example, was taken over, for the most part, by the establishment of the National Park Service. Similarly, the "conservation wise-use" interest has been adopted by the U.S. Forest Service.

The Contemporary Environmentalist Movement

Spurred by the belief that the world faces an ultimate "eco-catastrophe" unless immediate and successful efforts are made to halt the deterioration of the environment, thousands and even hundreds of thousands of persons have joined together to make up what is now being referred to as the "environmentalist movement." This current environmentalist movement has clearly become one of the major politico-economic developments of 20th-century America (Hendee, Gale, and Harry, 1969), and, both in terms of size and ultimate impact on life styles, legal systems, and so on, it threatens to surpass such influential predecessors as the civil rights movement and the anti-Viet-Nam war movement. In fact, Schnaiberg (1971:1) argues that if we define success in the American context of size and rate of growth, the environmentalist movement is already far more successful than these predecessors.

Since the pollution of the environment has been going on for centuries, why only recently has there been such an upsurge of popular interest? We cannot rely entirely on the answer that this new perception of the environment as a serious social problem is a wholly rational response to objective conditions—that is, that finally things have gotten so bad that it's impossible to ignore them any longer. This argument has been advanced by numerous writers, who suggest that the concern of the 1960's evolved from the fact that the devastation of the environment and the threat of overpopulation had reached ultimate crisis proportions. However, the identical argument was used to account for the birth of the early preservationist movement in 1890 in this country. Certainly things did not get better during the period of about 1910 to 1960, but the rhetoric of this interim period seems to have only rarely reached "crisis" proportions, and only in the writings of rather small circles of scientists and nature lovers.

Possibly more important was the publicity given to environmental issues by the media during the late 1960's. We have noted earlier that the growth of public concern about the environment, as reflected in attitude and opinion surveys, follows rather closely the increased attention and coverage given these issues by the media. As has been noted by Marx (1970:946): "Once again, as in the coverage of the Viet-Nam War, the close-up power of the medium was demonstrated. The sight of lovely beaches covered with crude oil, hundreds of dead and dying birds trapped in the viscous stuff, had an incalculable effect upon a mass audience."

The following observation by Chapman (1969:32) is reminiscent of one of our arguments in Chapter 2.

. . . that as a society reaches some threshhold of economic development, with its attendant scientific and technological capabilities, it can afford to concern itself less with materials and quantity and more with quality of life. Whether this implication is true or not, and however we define our terms, attaching utility to the quality of environment has the effect of perceiving as resources some aspects of the environment not previously considered to be resources—animal life, plant associations, and the like. A range of new problems thus emerges.

The reader may again note the similarity between these ideas and Maslow's theory of a hierarchy of needs (cf. p. 578). Aesthetics, quality of the landscape, wild rivers, and wilderness may be important social values only in those societies or in those strata of any given society that have reached a certain level of economic security and well-being.

Incipiency and Coalescence

The environmentalist movement of today is in many ways a revival of the earlier one; in other words, it follows the pattern represented by Figure 2-3 in Chapter 2. The incipiency of this new movement occurred during the decades of quiescence of the last one, for that one never fully died. The Sierra Club and Audubon Society, for example, are holdovers from those early days, and have slowly been joined by other such organizations (see Table 15-12). These groups have never let society really forget about the environment as a social problem. The coalescence and rise of the current movement, as a movement in its own right, however, is a phenomenon of the 1960's. Gale (1972) suggests for us the signal event which indicated that coalescence had taken place: "Though there had been some prior interest in environmental issues which were outside the traditional preservationist concerns . . . the environmentalist movement was launched in the fall of 1969 with the nationwide coordination of activity culminating in the first Earth Day on April 22, 1970." Schnaiberg (1971) generally agrees by noting that before the late 1960's though there were numerous organizations concerned with the environment, few of these were actively interested in the total environment, and fewer still were acting to prevent what many were coming to believe would be an apocalyptic environmental collapse. He (1971:7) further argues that previously "none of these movements ever captured the attention of large numbers of people, nor did they mount the political campaigns to convince the political and economic elites of the seriousness of the situation . . . the present movement is unique in its scope and intensity."

While it would perhaps be impossible to delineate all of the important reasons why a major environmentalist movement coalesced in the late 1960's, several factors seem to stand out. We would agree with Schnaiberg's argument that it was neither a sudden crisis nor an abundance of new information describing environmental deterioration that led to the environmentalist movement. As discussed earlier in this chapter, degradation of the environment has been occurring for centuries, and scientific data evaluating the seriousness of this degradation were available long before the 1960's. Schnaiberg feels that the two precipitating factors that provided the impetus for the movement were: (1) the precedent set by the civil rights and the anti-Viet-Nam war movements in the late 1950's and the 1960's, and (2) the emergence of a popularized perspective on environmental problems epitomized by Rachel Carson's *Silent Spring* (1962).

There is little question, however, that the special conditions which Cameron (1966:10) argues must be present for the formation of a social movement were present in the case of the environmentalist movement. Significant numbers of individuals have consciously recognized that they have shared or common moral and aesthetic interests at stake in the continuing deterioration of their natural environment; they have come to believe in their own ability to change the situation (it must be changed, they feel, in order to avert an "eco-catastrophe"); and they have lived under conditions in which they have seen that joining together to bring about desired changes is both possible and plausibly effective (both the civil rights and the anti-war movements increased such expectations). The social climate, in other words, has been conducive to the development of a major environmentalist social movement.

Institutionalization

The environmentalist movement is currently in the third stage of its development, the stage of institutionalization, at the peak of its success, enjoying strong public support and public involvement. Environmentalist organizations such as the Sierra Club continue to grow in numbers, in organizational structure, and in impact on the larger social order. In the decade of the 1960's, the nationwide enrollment of the Sierra Club increased from 15,000 to approximately 85,000, while in the East, its membership expanded from 750 to 19,000 (Trop and Roos, 1971:62). The success of the movement has contributed, in part, to the more recent growth of an organized counter-movement (see Albrecht, 1972) and has, in turn, been stimulated by it. Unlike the usual response to many social movements, the counter-movement is not a broad-scale societal reaction to the environmentalists, but rather is a reaction from those interest groups discussed earlier who feel seriously threatened by this group.

While the current movement involves many of the traditional concerns of the early conservationists and preservationists, its interests and ideology go further in several important ways. Four of these have been identified and discussed by Morrison, Hornback, and Warner (1972:261). According to these authors, the current movement, in the first place, "involves a much broader conception of the features of the environment that are of concern." While the early conservationists concentrated on what were characterized as non-renewable or slowly renewable natural resources such as forests and wildlife, the current environmentalist movement involves concern with virtually all aspects of the natural as well as the man-made environment. Evidence to support this contention can be found in recent research on changes in ideological orientations and activities of groups such as the Sierra Club. Faich and Gale (1971:282) have noted that priorities of Sierra Club members have "shifted in recent years from outdoor recreation, mixed with an occasional concern for protecting certain wilderness areas, to an almost exclusive emphasis today on general environmental quality issues, ranging from wilderness protection and outdoor recreation, to urban pollution and population control. The members, in short, are no longer the outdoor recreationists of yesterday, but rather today's environmental politicos, in the vanguard of society's newest social movement."

The second way in which the present movement goes beyond its predecessors ideologically is closely related to the first. Not only does the contemporary movement have a broader range of interests in the environment, but Morrison and his colleagues believe that it also takes a broader view of man and how his "values, institutions, technology, social organization, and, in particular, population, influence the long- and short-term quality and quantity of all resources available." In the third place, the current movement is seen to involve a more sophisticated understanding of the relationship between man and his environment. Living organisms, including man, are viewed as existing in a complex interrelationship, the ecological balance of which may be upset by population, consumption, and technological growth. Finally, the current movement is characterized more by a feeling or sense of urgent crisis than was true of the earlier conservationist movement. Only by taking immediate and even drastic action, many adherents believe, can eco-catastrophe be avoided.

Up to this point, we have been talking about "the" environmental movement as though there existed a single, monolithic body of individuals compacted into one single-purpose organization. Such, obviously, is not the case. There are many hundreds and even thousands of organizations in the U.S. that comprise the public behind the "environmentalist movement." Some of these are national in scope, and

TABLE 15-12 ENVIRONMENTAL ORGANIZATIONS

National	Regional and Issue-Specific[a]
Sierra Club (over 100,000 members) (1892)	Black Mesa Defense (Four Corners Area)
Friends of the Earth (1970)	Escalante Wilderness Club (Utah)
National Audubon Society (1905)	New Mexico Citizens for Clean Air and Water (New Mexico)
National Wildlife Federation (1936)	"Save French Pete" (Oregon)
Environmental Defense Fund (1968)	Native American Rights Fund
Conservation Foundation (1948)	Trout Unlimited
Zero Population Growth (1969)	Save-the-Redwoods League (California)
Izaak Walton League of America (1922)	Defenders of Wildlife
National Recreation and Parks Association (1966)	Desert Protective Council
National Parks Association (1919)	Ducks, Unlimited
Wilderness Society (1936)	Citizens League against the Sonic Boom
	Citizens for Clean Air
	International Shade Tree Conference
	Appalachian Trail Conference

[a] Some of these organizations, e.g., Trout, Unlimited and Ducks, Unlimited, have been in existence for many years. Most, however, are products of the 1960's and 1970's.

extremely broad in terms of their outlook and approach to environmental problems. Others are highly localized and very issue-specific. Table 15-12 lists what are generally recognized as the major national environmental organizations, along with the year of their inception. The table also includes some examples of more localized, issue-specific environmental organizations. To understand the diversity of the movement, one must have some conception of the range of issues around which environmental-concern organizations have developed. Table 15-13 presents a very brief and limited list of "targets." Though the list is short, practically every group could be placed under one or another of the headings.

Recruits to the contemporary environmental movement, like those to the earlier one, have come mainly from the upper levels of education, income, and occupational status (cf. pp. 575-579, 587). Much of the research that has been done on environmental activists has been limited to a very few organizations (the Sierra Club has received the most attention), and to student participants in environmental-related activities. In general, this research has concluded that the environmental movement is basically an upper-middle class social movement. Faich and Gale (1971:276), in a mailed questionnaire to Sierra Club members in the Puget Sound area, reported that, "Professional positions are held by fully 73.8 percent of our respondents, an additional 9.8 percent are administrators and 9.2 percent students; only 2.8 percent are clerical workers and another 2.8 percent are unemployed. A mere 3 percent of the members have never attended college, while 25 percent have doctorates, 45.5 percent have master's degrees, and 17.4 percent the baccalaureate."

Similarly, Devall (1970b:123), from a mailed questionnaire to a random sample of the Sierra Club, found that "seventy-four percent of the respondents had at least a four-year college degree. Thirty-nine percent had an advanced degree. . . . Forty-nine percent of the male respondents were 'higher professionals,' i.e., physicians, lawyers, college professors, engineers, and 21 percent were 'lower

TABLE 15-13   PRINCIPAL TARGETS OF THE MOVEMENT

Freeway Engineers
Dam Builders (with special emphasis on the U.S. Army Corps of Engineers)
Subdividers
Industrial Polluters (whose chemical waste affects both the air and waterways)
High Rise Builders
Forest Clear-Cutters
Agricultural Chemical and Pesticide Users
Litter-Bugs
Drivers of automobiles, snowmobiles and motorbikes (noise)
(Us All?)

professionals,' i.e., school teachers, free-lance writers, artists. Only 5 percent of the males were in clerical or sales occupations, owners of small businesses or unskilled workers.... Forty-eight percent of the respondents said their family income was over $12,000 a year, and 30 percent said their income was over $18,000 a year."

These findings do not paint a picture of Sierra Club members as typical Americans. However, the above characteristics are typical of people who have more time, more resources and more energy to address and pursue social problems, as we discussed in Chapter 2. Generally, persons who have developed intense aesthetic appreciation of their environment are most frequently persons who do not have to battle that environment for livelihood and survival, i.e., through dependence upon such occupations as mining, lumbering, farming, and so on. They have the leisure time and the education to cultivate aesthetic tastes and to rationalize these with appropriate constructions of reality. While the Sierra Club membership may be typical of many other major environmental organizations, however, it is not typical of them all. For example, the Black Mesa Defense includes many Native Americans who have joined together in an attempt to block powerplant construction and strip-mining on the Black Mesa, an area of religious significance to the Hopi Indians.

Whatever the socio-economic makeup of the membership of any particular component of the environmentalist movement, the ideological range of orientations toward environmental issues held by movement participants is exceedingly broad and diverse. Schnaiberg (1971) has developed a most interesting typology of the major "participants" that bears this out. The types he discusses are: (1) cosmetologists, (2) meliorists, (3) reformists, and (4) radicals. Each of these four types is discussed in terms of its respective definition of "the environmental problem," and its proposed means and goals for amelioration.

(1) COSMETOLOGISTS According to Schnaiberg, the cosmetologists deal only with the byproducts of consumption. Their orientation toward environmental deterioration, in other words, is extremely limited and superficial. They are the most "naive" of the environmentalists. Cosmetologists engage in anti-litter campaigns, and a successful environmental action, from their point of view, would be "collection of paper and other wastes from public places." Representative groups would be the Boy Scouts, Garden Clubs, and Parent-Teacher Association groups. Such groups are likely to view environmental problems as separate from other issues, and are most likely to be supported (and co-opted) by the creators of environmental problems, since the actions of the cosmetologists are not generally effective.

(2) MELIORISTS Schnaiberg's meliorists are, again, rather ingenuous and simple in their approach to environmental problems. Like the cosmetologists, they focus primarily on consumption-related activities. A principal aim of their environmental-related activity is to transform "waste" into "usable material." Thus, the meliorist is likely to be the person who is responsible for the community "recycling center." However, like the cosmetologist, the meliorist does "not attempt to locate the source of the waste in areas of production, or at a later stage, in the realm of consumer preferences (and lack of consumer sovereignty)." Also, like the cosmetologist, the meliorist believes that environmental problems are solvable at relatively minor cost and with minor inconvenience.

(3) REFORMISTS   The reformists constitute ". . . the first group which begins to consider both the consumption and production aspects of environmental decay. In addition, they are generally more knowledgeable about the physical-biological aspects of environmental processes. . . ." In addition, the reformist groups are more involved in trying to influence public decision-making relating to environmental issues. Thus, they are likely to be participants at public hearings, to mount campaigns against producers of products that degrade the environment, and to engage in broad consumer-education programs. Instead of focusing only on littering and recycling, reformists are likely to oppose auto-pollution, highway and dam construction, nuclear power facilities, and so on. Further, as individuals, they model their personal behavior after their ideals, and try to convince their friends to do likewise.

(4) RADICALS   Radicals go beyond the meliorative stance of the reformists, and "aim at total restructuring of the social and especially the economic system. This varies from a direct attack on capitalist economic systems *per se* to a rather more wide-reaching critique of industrial society in general (although with heavy emphasis on the U.S.)." Many of the radical environmentalists are former supporters of the anti-Viet-Nam War movement, exemplifying the contentions of Eric Hoffer and others about the "true believer" and the substitutability of his causes (cf. Chap. 1, p. 17). For them, the destruction of the environment is largely a result of the operation of the same forces that seek to destroy third-world revolutionary movements. The radical perspective is basically one of "no-growth," since an expansive industrial society is seen as incompatible with the preservation of environmental quality. "For the radicals, there is little meaning in separating environmental problems from the 'corporate' or 'industrial state,' and the inequalities therein." Environmental activity on the part of the radicals has tended to reinforce the view they already hold concerning the basic materialistic and undemocratic nature of American society.

As we consider the four categories of followers which Schnaiberg sees in this movement, we are reminded of the three-ringed model of social-movement membership put forth in Chapter 2 (see pp. 47-48). The "cosmetologists" and the "meliorists" would fit the description of members in the third or outermost "ring" of a movement; the "reformists" would fit into the middle ring; and the "radicals," perhaps along with some of the more militant "reformists," would comprise the innermost central ring. The radicals would also be among those "die-hard" members who, in Smelser's terminology, would react to failure or frustration by trying constantly to convert a "norm-oriented" movement into a "value-oriented" one (Smelser, 1962).

This range of orientations on the part of the environmentalists suggests that the tactics they are likely to employ would also vary greatly. While this may be the case to some extent, Gale (1972) argues that most action taken by environmentalist groups to this point has been well within the confines of middle-class politics. Major emphasis has been placed on such strategies as lobbying, petition signing, and court suits aimed at blockage of programs which the environmentalists have viewed as potentially harmful to the environment.

This has generally been true of student environmental activists as well. For example, while Dunlap, Gale and Rutherford (1973) found that about 50 percent of their sample of University of Oregon students had participated in some action on an environmental issue, these actions could not be viewed as being of a particularly radical nature. The environmental involvement of most of their students related to two issues: (1) a U.S. Forest Service plan to allow the cutting of timber in a virgin area near the university community, and (2) the highly publicized plan advanced by the U.S. Army to store nerve gas in Oregon. The most common actions taken by the students on these issues were attendance at a rally or demonstration (27 percent), and signing a letter or petition (25 percent). However, Dunlap and his colleagues also found that a significant portion of their respondents expressed a willingness to engage in certain other types of political activity that could be classified as falling outside of middle-class political traditions, such as illegal sit-ins.

There are reasons for expecting a continuation of "middle-class politics" as the tactical preference in the environmental movement, in view of recently developed legal processes for handling environmental issues. For example, under new legislation, most projects which would have any effect on the environment now require public participation and open hearings before approval of the project is granted by the appropriate governmental agencies. Also, an extensive legal framework for the protection of the environment has been evolving. Each new congress has added to the federal legislation designed to safeguard the environment. Among the most significant pieces of such legislation passed to date are the Wilderness Act, the National Environmental Policy Act, and numerous federal air- and water-pollution statutes, the contents of which will be described further on. At the state level, too, the movement has been active in developing an effective conventional strategy. For example, the Sierra Club Handbook for environmental activists contains a chapter which argues that time and money spent on state and local efforts may have a greater pay-off in effecting change than work at the federal level (Mitchell, 1970).

Since, however, the implementation of state and federal legislation often falls short of environmentalists' expectations, some of them may turn to other tactics. Morrison, Hornback, and Warner (1972:264) argue that "the environmentalists are increasingly turning to *power* strategies (i.e., attempting to achieve sufficient group influence to coerce changes) and away from *participation* strategies (i.e., educating and urging people voluntarily to make changes)." Examples of such "power" strategies are attempts to prevent land developers from desecrating wildlife refuges by litigation procedures, restraining orders, sit-ins, boycotts, law-enforcement campaigns, pressures on state and local governments to outlaw sale of nonreturnable bottles, polluting detergents, etc. Furthermore, as Gale (1972: 302) suggests, even more radical tactics could emerge: "Green Panthers, 'eco-tactics,' hike-ins, and a growing radical ecology are, together with an occasional advocacy of violence, indications of disillusionment with the older middle-class politics. Citizens who are compelled to take political action because of an environmental crisis, as occurred in Santa Barbara during the oil spill in 1969, may find that traditional tactics accomplish little." Molotch (1971) has also observed that during the Santa Barbara incident, the tactics of frustrated local residents gradually changed from conventional politics to increasingly ideological and even radical approaches. Even talk of blowing up the oil platforms in the channel was widely heard.

Signs of Fragmentation in the Environmentalist Movement

There has been some fragmentation within some of the major organizations that constitute the movement. For example, a former president of the Sierra Club left that organization in a disagreement over the main focus of the club's effort, and he helped to found another environmentalist group, Friends of the Earth. Both organizations are thriving so far, however. On a somewhat broader basis, recreationists in the movement have recently come into direct conflict with the environmentalists in several areas. A case in point is the "battle over Mineral King" (Hano, 1971), which has been waged between recreational developers—Walt Disney Enterprises, in this case—and the protectionists. Recreationists see Mineral King as an ideal location for the development of a major recreation complex within easy reach of hundreds of thousands of outdoor recreation-starved Californians. Protectionists, on the other hand, fear the rape and destruction of an area they would prefer to see preserved in its natural state. Of course, there are numerous other instances in which the interests of recreationists and preservationists still overlap to a considerable degree.

Prospects for the Environmentalist Movement

Some of the problematic issues that have contributed to the growth of the environmental movement are being solved. Pollution-abatement technology is advancing at a rapid rate, new sources of energy are being studied and developed, and many industrialized nations are reaching zero population growth. The provisions of the National Environmental Policy Act of 1969, including the formation of the Environmental Protection Agency of the federal government, offer some threat of co-optation of the movement by the government and its subsequent "taming," as occurred at the end of the earlier conservation movement. The frustrations faced by the rapidly rising expectations of many environmentalists, together with co-optation of much of their program by the government, has caused the less committed members to start dropping out. Perhaps it is significant that, as Gale (1972:296) notes: ". . . in spite of . . . feeling of frustration on the part of many environmentalists, no environmental equivalents of Stokely Carmichael or Martin Luther King have stepped forward, no militant environmental organization has successfully challenged the leading role played by established organizations such as the Sierra Club and the Wilderness Society, and no environmental campaign has brought about a nationwide mass mobilization. Further, the environmental movement has remained nonviolent, using public pressure as a means of forcing negotiation on specific environmental issues." Judging from our expectations about the "life-cycle" of such movements, and from the history of the earlier conservation movement, we might expect a demise of the current environmentalist movement within the decade. However, the legacy it has already produced is enormous.

THE LEGACY OF ENVIRONMENTAL MOVEMENTS
The Early Conservation Movement, 1890-1910
Cultural and Normative Changes

With the passing of the frontier era late in the 19th century, there developed a growing realization in some circles that natural resources were, indeed, exhaustible (Moncrief, 1970). The conservation movement helped to popularize this idea. Traditional emphasis had been on civilizing wilderness "in the name of prosperity and progress" rather than on preserving it. One of the products of the early movement, then, was a change in attitude toward preservation of certain of nature's wonders for the benefit and enjoyment of posterity. As noted by Nash (1965:x), "In the closing decades of the nineteenth century the appreciation of wilderness, which previously had been confined to a small group of intellectuals, broadened to include increasing numbers of the American people." John Muir, who eventually founded the Sierra Club, played a major role in the popularization of the wilderness concept through his publications and tireless efforts to share his concerns with his fellow-countrymen.

Legal Changes

One of the outcomes of the controversies of this era, and certainly a part of the legacy of this early movement, was the widespread acceptance of the doctrine that in some instances the laissez-faire methods of obtaining and utilizing natural resources would have to be modified to permit government interference in such forms as the "withdrawal of public lands from private exploitation and the wise management of these lands for the optimum economic and social benefit of the people as a whole" (Jones 1965:4). Probably nowhere did this developing doctrine create more controversy than in the state of Colorado. Here, the conservation movement ignited one of the bitterest political disputes between state and federal governments since the Civil War. As McCarthy (1973:27) has noted:

> The conservation crusade, initiated by American preservationists in the late 1870's and finally joined by the federal government in the early 1890's for the purpose of saving . . . the vanishing natural resources of the western public domain, gave rise to the critical question of precisely where the rights of the states left off and the power of the federal government began.

Colorado, like most of the other western states, was more concerned with attracting new settlers, exploiting mineral and forest resources within her borders, and clearing land for the growth of new towns and cities than with preservation. It should be recognized, of course, that the idea of exhausting the supply of land, forests, and other natural resources appeared almost incredible to many people, particularly in the western United States. Thus, angry westerners charged federal violation of "both the principal of state sovereignty and the 'rights' of American citizens to settle and establish 'civilization' where they pleased" (McCarthy 1973:27).

Conservationists soon became aware that eastern legislators were much more willing to support the passage of bills setting aside vast tracts of western land for preservation than were westerners. Therefore, much of their effort was concentrated on Congress rather than on the states. Congress responded by passing several major preservation measures, among the most important of which was the Forest Reserve Act of 1891, which gave the President of the United States the right to set aside public lands as forest reserves. McCarthy (1973:27) notes that it became the reasoning of the federal government "that if the forests and waters and mineral wealth of the West were to be saved for the use of 'future generations,' it would have to be done through federal regulation. The fact that western states like

Colorado never agreed formed the crux of the conservation furor for the next two decades."

Numerous bills important to the conservationists were passed during this period, and their passage, at least in part, must be viewed as a part of the legacy of the early conservationists. The Yosemite National Park was set apart as a "forest reservation" in 1891. This was followed by several other national parks and wildlife refuges, the first of which was established on Pelican Island, Florida, in 1903. In 1907, the "forest reserves" became "national forests" with the name change indicating, more than anything else, that these large tracts of land were now viewed as the continuing heritage of all of the American people.

The passage of many of these laws was aided by the fact that during part of this period, the White House was occupied by a President who was among the most sympathetic of all American presidents to the cause of conservation—Theodore Roosevelt. In one of the most important steps in the history of conservation, President Roosevelt, in May, 1908, called a Conference of Governors of all the states to introduce a policy of "protection, preservation, and wise use" of natural resources. This conference was later followed by the appointment of Conservation Commissioners in a majority of states and the appointment of a National Conservation Commission. Though the role of the state commissioners was later greatly curtailed and sometimes abolished in states such as Colorado, the precedent had been set. And, though later presidents and congresses were less concerned with the cause of conservation, the groundwork was certainly laid upon which later efforts would build. This must be viewed as part of the legacy of the early environmental movement.

The Contemporary Environmentalist Movement

The large numbers of changes in environmentally related attitudes and behavior evident in the United States during the past few years border on the amazing. While perhaps not all of these changes can be attributed to the current environmental movement, there are many cultural, normative, and legal changes which can be.

Broad Cultural Changes

Perhaps the major change that can be observed at the cultural level is the fashionable widespread interest that has been generated in environmentally related issues. Data presented earlier in this chapter from the polls clearly show the suddenness with which Americans have become interested in and concerned about their environment. This issue came from almost nowhere to the point of being rated in some polls as a more serious concern than Viet-Nam, crime, or any of the other problems that worried Americans in the late 1960's and early 1970's. As we have noted, certainly the environmentalist movement played a crucial role in defining the environment as a significant problem for much of the American public. All across the country, schoolchildren, social clubs, and "little old ladies in tennis shoes" are now engaged in clean-up programs, and in efforts to educate the public on matters concerning pollution, resource conservation, and related issues. Hendee, Gale, and Harry (1969:214) argue that "now, more than ever before, nature appears to have acquired expressive meaning for the American people rather than being, as before, merely an object for consumptive use and conquest." They feel, in other words, that more people have been developing a greater appreciation for their natural environment. The public opinion data presented earlier suggest that while this may be the case, it is not true for all major segments of the American public. Further, these data provide support for the argument that the greater appreciation of the environment that has occurred may be as much of an effect as a cause of the environmentalist movement.

Another of the basic societal changes that has been a result of the movement is the demand that we now consider more than just the economic effects of continued growth. This is clearly reflected in the defeat of plans to build supersonic airlines (supersonic transport or SST) in the U.S. The question "what does it cost?" has come to be significant in other than financial terms. Strip-mining, which constitutes by far the most efficient means of extracting coal and minerals from the earth, is now being outlawed in many states. The environmental scars that strip-mining leaves behind are now being considered as costs that must be calculated in the cost-benefit equation. If nothing else, this realization on the part of the public has forced large industries and utility companies to spend millions in public-relations campaigns to convince the American public that they are concerned about the environment. Oil companies show pictures of fishermen making trophy catches just below an active oil well to demonstrate that the wells do not have negative effects on the eco-system. The largest automobile company in the United States takes out full-page advertisements in *The New York Times* which contain only two well-aimed sentences:

> DOES G.M. CARE ABOUT CLEAN AIR?
> YOU BET WE DO!!

This is a far cry from the days when industry felt it could pollute with impunity. While some of the changes probably go no deeper than the Madison Avenue public-relations work, cases in which industries are being forced to clean up have become increasingly common occurrences.

One also finds recent additions to the vocabularies of many Americans that seem to have found their way into everyday argot through their repeated use by spokesmen of the environmentalist movement. Thousands of people from all walks of life now use the word "ecology," though few of them may be able to define it.

"Energy crisis," "pollution," "eco-system," and similar words are bandied about by newscasters, politicians, and the man on the street. A new national symbol, Woodsey the Owl, has recently been created, and one even hears Archie Bunker quoting the environmentalist slogan, "Give a hoot, don't pollute."

Normative Changes

Important consequences of the environmentalist movement can also be seen in changes in the life-styles and norms of many individual Americans. One sees this in the automobile driver who asks for non-leaded gasoline, the homemaker who

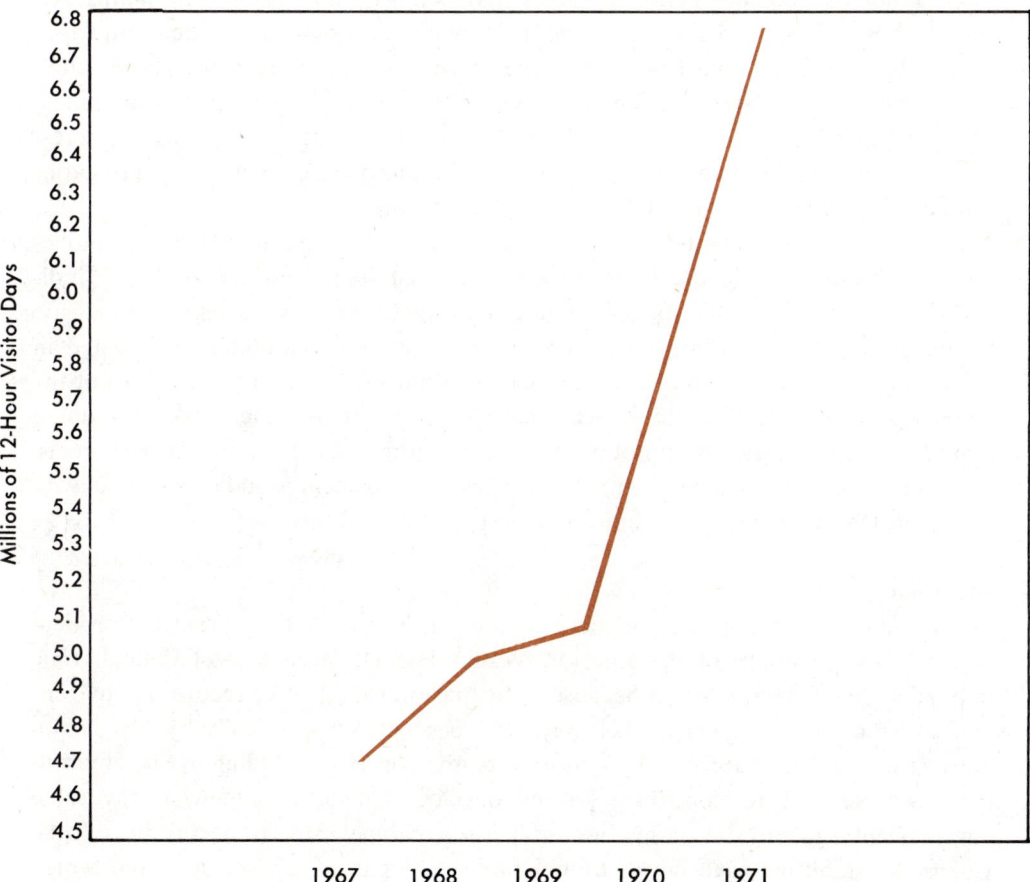

Figure 15-5 Use of National Forest Wilderness and Primitive Areas, 1967-1971 (in 12-Hour Visitor Days)

SOURCE: John Baden, "Neospartan Hedonist Adult Toy Aficionados, and the Development of Bureaucratic Purgatory: A Casual Model," paper presented at the Meetings of the Pacific Sociological Association, Scottsdale, Arizona, May 1973. Baden's data are taken from a U.S. Forest Service report.

purchases low-phosphate detergents, and the teenager who walks or rides a ten-speed bicycle instead of taking the family car. Everywhere, one sees individuals involved in personal efforts to "get back to nature." Certainly, those actively involved do not make up a majority of the population. However, it is no longer difficult to find persons who prefer "cross-country skiing or snow shoeing over snowmobiling (or even riding lift chairs), boots over trail bikes, and canoes over motor boats" (Baden, 1973:2). More and more people seem to prefer retaining certain areas of the country as wilderness preserves or wild rivers rather than covering them over with four-lane highways and full-facility campgrounds. Baden (1973) has assembled a series of tables that demonstrate some of the points discussed above. Figure 15-5 is taken from his work. It shows the sudden and rapid rise in the use of national forest primitive and wilderness areas since about 1969. The number of visitor-days spent in these areas increased by over two million in the four years from 1967 to 1971. These data make evident the growing interest of natives in contact with the out-of-doors. They also make obvious future problems the forest service will face in managing such areas.

It would probably not be too far-fetched to relate the recent communal movement in this country to the larger environmentalist social movement. Many individual participants in this movement are seeking to establish a less materialistic relationship with the natural environment. Many of the communes are located in more isolated wilderness areas, where their inhabitants, far from the symbols of the larger consumer society, can reject them. Many commune members view these items of conspicuous consumption as contributors to the environmental crisis. Here one can live without synthetic fabrics and artificial foods, and live with nature instead of having to subdue (or destroy) it.

Legal Changes

Other important changes are evident in the legal and political arenas. President Nixon's first Secretary of the Interior, Walter Hickel, faced a most difficult time in gaining Senate confirmation because of his past nonsupportive record on environmental issues. And though Hickel may have been chosen originally by Mr. Nixon because he was recommended by oil interests, the constant prodding by the environmentalists seemed to contribute to his development of a somewhat favorable environmental record during his brief stay in the cabinet. Due in part to his efforts, Congress established five new national parks and passed a wilderness bill which added 23 areas to the National Wilderness Preservation System.*

During the 1972 national elections, environmentalists joined together to defeat

---

* The new wilderness areas were designated by Public Laws 91-58, 91-60, 91-82, 91-504, 91-505 and located in the states of Alaska, California, Colorado, Washington, Oregon, New Mexico, Florida, Oklahoma, Michigan, Wisconsin, Maine, Massachusetts, and Arizona. Areas classified

a number of Congressmen who had compiled the poorest environmental track records. Among these was the powerful chairman of the House Interior and Insular Affairs Committee, Wayne Aspinal of Colorado. Aspinal was labeled by the environmentalists as the most notorious of the "dirty dozen," and this label plagued him continually in his unsuccessful run for re-election.

It seems quite clear that in the political arena, the environmentalists have become a powerful interest group that cannot be ignored. As it has been rhetorically asked: "Is there now a politician anywhere who is in favor of smog, sewage-laden rivers, or the uncontrolled automobile exhaust?"

As the result, largely, of such political developments, numerous new laws have been passed, agencies created, and significant court decisions rendered. While it would require far too much space here to document all of these events, several of the most outstanding will be discussed briefly.

AIR POLLUTION   Almost every year now brings several new bills dealing with the problem of air pollution. The Air Pollution Control Act of 1967 began an important trend of putting teeth into efforts to greatly reduce levels of air pollution in the United States. The Clean Air Act of 1970 provided the means to establish nation-wide air-quality standards which are to be implemented in all of the states by May 31, 1975. In effect, states have been required to file plans indicating how they will meet the air-quality levels that have been specified. For many urban areas, this has meant the development of transportation and exhaust emission controls to reduce smog levels, and in numerous areas, city planning and other government agencies are now working on mass transportation plans to help implement this law. Two-year delays approved earlier for some areas have recently been rescinded by a federal appeals court, thus requiring national compliance with the mid-1975 deadline.*

WATER POLLUTION   As with the area of air pollution, the number of measures dealing with water pollution has increased rapidly in the past few years. Certainly the most far-reaching of these has been the Clean Water Act of 1972. This act

---

* As is so often the case in the legacies of social-problem movements, however, the laws that have been passed during the recent environmental movement have not always worked out as expected, as indicated by the following news report:

"The Environmental Protection Agency disclosed that its studies had confirmed that the catalytic converters which will be standard equipment on 70 percent of all 1975 model automobiles, in order to meet federal air pollution standards, do indeed change carbon monoxide and other hydrocarbons to water and harmless gases—but they also cause sulfur and water in gasoline to combine with oxygen and produce sulfuric acid" (*San Francisco Sunday Examiner and Chronicle,* September 8, 1974, "This World," page 10).

---

as part of the wilderness preservation system are protected from most encroachments by man except in the forms of hiking and backpacking. The five new national parks included Florissant Fossil Beds in Colorado, Apostle Islands National Lakeshore, Gulf Islands National Seashore in Florida and Mississippi, Sleeping Bear Dunes National Lakeshore in Michigan, and Voyageurs National Park in Mnnesota.

seeks to end all water pollution by 1985, and calls for spending $24.6 billion for this purpose in its first three years. Despite claims that he advocated environmental clean-up and protection, the Clean Water Act was vetoed by former President Nixon. However, the veto was quickly overridden by wide margins in both houses of Congress.

OTHER MEASURES Numerous other bills dealing with the environment have been passed or are under consideration. New standards are being set for noise pollution relating to such things as motor vehicles and construction equipment. Studies are underway to recommend air-craft and airport noise limits. Scenic highway bills have been passed directed at "visual pollution," and designed to bring about the removal of unsightly billboards along certain highways and streets. Laws now require that environmental, aesthetic, and social impacts be considered, along with the traditional economic impacts, by almost any type of development that is contemplated. To protect the interest of the general populace, public hearings are now required by law on most types of development before they are given approval.

THE COURTS One of the most significant occurrences in recent years has been the growing number of court suits directed at blocking developments that may have possible negative environmental impacts. Citizens in many states can now go to court and challenge governmental policies which they view as having possible harmful consequences for the environment. Recent court decisions have given citizens this right even in cases where they cannot demonstrate personal financial loss or injury. Aesthetic values now constitute legitimate bases for argument in court cases.

With support from powerful elements of the environmentalist movement such as the Sierra Club and other organizations (e.g., some of those in Table 15-12) more and more citizens have been willing to take such action. As an example, members of the Navajo and Hopi Indian Tribes in the Southwest have joined with environmentalists in filing suit against the U.S. Government to block the development of a series of proposed coal-burning electrical power plants in their area. The Navajo and Hopi not only fear the effects of the power plants on vegetation, farming, and water supplies, but are also concerned with possible effects on religion, culture, and traditional life-styles.

Certainly, not all such efforts by the environmentalists to block new and potentially harmful developments have been successful. For example, in an important recent case, the Sierra Club has been unsuccessful in its attempts to keep the U.S. Forest Service from allowing Walt Disney Productions to build a ski resort in Mineral King Valley in the Sierra Nevada. Nevertheless, the batting average of the environmentalists is probably much higher than it would have been without the interest and concern the movement has generated.

NEW FEDERAL AGENCIES Several new federal agencies have been established in recent years, both to monitor compliance with the numerous existing pollution and environmental protection laws, and to help establish new policies. Probably the most important of these are the President's Environmental Quality Council and the Environmental Protection Agency. The Environmental Quality Council was established by the National Environmental Policy Act of 1969. The stated purposes of this Act were:

To declare a national policy which will encourage productive and enjoyable harmony between man and his environment; to promote efforts which will prevent or eliminate damage to the environment and biosphere and stimuate the health and welfare of man; to enrich the understanding of the ecological systems and natural resources important to the Nation; and to establish a Council on Environmental Quality.

Under the chairmanship of Russell Train, the Council has played an important role in defining environmental issues and in prodding bureaucratic agencies to action.

Clearly the most active and powerful of the new agencies is the Environmental Protection Agency. The EPA was created in 1969 to pull together a broad scattering of agencies in the anti-pollution field. Since its creation, the EPA has shown little reluctance to take on even some of the country's most powerful firms over pollution issues. The roles of the EPA are many and varied. Environmental impact studies must be filed with and approved by the EPA before most developments such as new highways, dams, and power plants can be built. The agency sponsors a good deal of much needed research on environmental questions, and also plays an important regulatory role in checking to see that industries, cities, etc., are complying with environmental quality standards.

One of the most controversial of recent EPA proposals would cut gasoline consumption in the Los Angeles Basin by 86 percent. While many argue that such a move would totally paralyze the city, some EPA officials note that this drastic cut in consumption is necessary to meet the standards established by the 1970 Clean Air Act. Air-pollution levels defined as acceptable by this act were exceeded in Los Angeles on more than 220 days in 1971.

Whatever its future history, the legacy of the environmental movement is an important one. To many, the accomplishment that stands out most is that for perhaps the first time in our history, we are carefully considering other than economic costs of continued growth. While in the past, pollution and resource depletion may have been considered side effects of increased production at the lowest possible expense, they are now being considered important social and environmental costs that deserve as much or more attention as does growth and profit. The environmentalist social movement has played an important role in changing attitudes to create such an outlook.

Chapter 16

Population

THE SOCIAL CONSTRUCTION OF REALITY

The explosive growth of the human population is the most significant terrestrial event of the past million millenia. Three and one-half billion people now inhabit the Earth, and every year this number increases by 70 million. Armed with weapons as diverse as thermo-nuclear bombs and DDT, this mass of humanity now threatens to destroy most of the life on the planet. Mankind itself may stand on the brink of extinction; in its death throes it could take with it most of the other passengers of Spaceship Earth. No geological event in a billion years—not the emergence of mighty mountain ranges, nor the submergence of entire subcontinents, nor the occurrence of periodic glacial ages—has posed a threat to terrestrial life comparable to that of human overpopulation. (Ehrlich and Ehrlich, 1972)

Crowded, crowded, crowded, we are told. Slums are crowded, suburbs are crowded, megalopolis is crowded, and more and more and more people are eating up, burning up, and using up the beauty and wealth of America—turning the land into a polluted, depleted sprawl of scummy water and flickering neon, an ecological catastrophe stretching from the Everglades to the Pacific Northwest. . . . That so very much of this is preposterous . . . should come as no real surprise to those who follow the fads of crisis in America. There are no plain and simple problems any more. From poverty to race to crime to Vietnam all we face are crises which threaten to bring down the world upon our heads. And now it is ecology-environment—which is a perfectly good problem to be sure—but with its advent comes dragged in by the heels our old friend the super crisis of the population explosion, which is not nearly as real or immediate a problem in America, and ends up serving unfortunately as a political smokescreen that can obscure a host of legitimate concerns. (Wattenberg, 1972:19)

Population and Relativity

Of the host of "social problems" that confront mankind today, none has received a fraction of the combined attention that scientists, laymen, and governments throughout the world are giving to the "population crisis." To many, the ever-expanding world population has become a short-fused bomb, the explosion of which threatens the very destruction of human life on our planet. On the other hand, there are others who argue that again, as so frequently has occurred in the past, we have been caught up in the crisis rhetoric of an issue and, in so doing, have lost our ability to evaluate objectively the facts relating to that issue. This chapter is designed to confront some of those facts and to examine their meanings from various points of view. We will begin by looking briefly at how population growth has been defined by various societies during different historical periods. The bulk of the chapter will then deal with defining population growth as a major social problem, and with the evolution of a powerful social movement along with this definition.

In the cultural tradition of every society, living is more valued than dying. It is this emphasis on the prolongation and sanctity of life that has been the major causative factor in the recent burgeoning of the world's population. Technological and medical advancements that have the capability to prolong life and reduce infant mortality have been adopted in most societies, while cultural norms relating to the regulation of fertility have lagged behind. Therefore, the world is now experiencing tremendous population growth due to low mortality rates, coupled with consistently high fertility rates.

In contemporary societies, the problem is usually seen as one of fertility control and reduction. Yet, until World War II, nearly every government had policies that encouraged population increase by promoting greater fertility and in-migration. The prospect of a stable or declining population was viewed in a negative light, and many nations enacted legislation favoring population increases, in addition to the pro-growth customs and traditions which they already had.

The first recorded effort to increase population through legislation was the Babylonian Code of Hammurabi, enacted during the 20th century B.C. (Glass, 1940). Later on, in the early Roman Empire, Caesar Augustus promulgated certain laws directly related to increasing population, including some which removed obstacles to marriage, increased the difficulty of unmarried persons to inherit estates, gave preferential consideration to fathers with large families in granting public offices, and conferred honors on mothers with large families (Glass, 1940: 86-87). While originally the purpose of such laws was mostly to increase the numbers of the aristocratic segment of Roman society, later laws enacted by Trajan and Nerva were aimed at increasing the total population through family allowances based on the number of children in a family. According to Glass, however, these legislative efforts eventually proved ineffectual.

During the 17th century, both France and Spain passed legislation designed to encourage fertility and immigration, and to reduce emigration. Examples of these enactments include: (1) tax exemptions to men who married early in life, (2) tax exemptions to immigrants, (3) exemption from all taxes for fathers of ten living legitimate children, and (4) punishment by death for anyone attempting to emigrate or helping others in their emigration (Glass, 1940:91-95). Also, during this same period, Prussia and Russia adopted policies designed to make immigration to these countries attractive to potential settlers.

In France and Spain, policies aimed at effecting population growth were very explicit. In England, on the other hand, practices were more subtle, but directed at similar outcomes. In Elizabethan England, certain public offices were reserved for married men, and special trades could be filled only by married persons (Glass, 1940). Even in 19th-century Japan, the 1873 Code outlawed the prevalent practices of abortion and infanticide, and provided for a family-allowance fund for subsidizing children. It was only a little more than 70 years later that Japan reversed its official position completely and instituted an effective anti-natalist policy.

Before and during World War II, several nations established demographic policies aimed at increasing their growth rates. France, in the depression years of the thirties, faced an impending population decline and strove to combat this "catastrophe" by establishing a widespread family-allowance system. Subsidies were based on the number of children in each family, and were intended to offset the economic liabilities of rearing a large family unit. Germany, under Adolf Hitler, embarked on a grandiose program of pro-natalism. Restriction of birth control information and devices, the availability of marriage loans, family allowances, tax exemptions, and the removal of the stigma on illegitimacy were practices directed at reducing the economic hardships of bearing children and creating pronatalist values (Thomlinson, 1965:404-405). Italy and the Soviet Union also followed policies of granting family allowances and glorifying the fertile mother.

While nearly all early population legislation was directed at increasing population size, there was a decree passed in Wurttemburg as early as 1712 prohibiting marriage unless the prospective groom could prove that he was able to support a family. The effect of this type of policy is a reduction in the marriage rate, which directly affects the fertility rate.

Such growth-limiting policies have become much more common in recent years. Following World War II, many nations adopted policies designed to replace population losses incurred through the war. However, it was only a few years before national goals shifted. Japan, for example, was one of the first nations to enact laws that were specifically designed to reduce the birth rate, in 1948. The effectiveness of the new policies can be documented by noting the gross reproduction rate* in that country before and after such legislation. While the gross repro-

---

* Average number of daughters a woman would have if she were to bear children at the prevailing age-specific fertility rates and to live through the entire reproduction span from age 15 to age 50.

duction rate was 2.2 in Japan in 1947, this rate had dropped below 1.0 by 1957 (Heer, 1968:105).

India, since about the mid-1950's, has placed heavy emphasis on family planning practices. However, despite efforts by the government for the past 20 years to promote birth control practices among the population, around one-million new children are born to Indian mothers each month. Indian newspapers are filled with information on contraceptive methods, most of which are government-subsidized to bring them within the financial reach of even the most impoverished villagers. Billboards are displayed throughout the country depicting happy, smiling, two-child families. But with a birth rate of almost 40 births per 1,000 population, it is obvious that for many the message simply has not gotten through. Many Indian villagers continue to define the "problem" as one of *food shortages,* rather than one of population surplus! Such experience in India casts a shadow over the successful establishment of similar governmental programs in other developing nations. Since 1964, Pakistan, Tunisia, Turkey, Ceylon, Korea, Thailand, Egypt, and other countries have attempted to implement various family planning approaches, with the results in most instances yet to be determined.

The two great communist powers, the Soviet Union and Communist China, have had widely fluctuating population policies in the post-war era. According to Marxist thought, the concept of overpopulation is solely a product of the capitalistic system, and could not exist in a smoothly running socialistic state. Even so, the leaders of both these nations have taken problems of population into account in establishing national priorities and policies.

The Soviet Union suffered heavy losses during World War II, and in 1944, adopted a family-allowance program for parents with three or more children to attempt to offset staggering war casualities. Since its enactment, the financial benefits accruing from the program have been gradually reduced, so that by 1964 the monthly payment to parents after their fifth child (with their fourth child still eligible for payments) was only 12 percent of their average wage, compared to 51% in 1944 (Heer and Bryden, 1966:144-156). This reduced economic advantage indicates that Soviet pro-natalism has become a token policy in some of its aspects. In line with symbolic gestures toward approval of large-family size, women with ten living children, or those who would have had ten children if not for war casualties, are given the Order of Mother Heroine, enhancing their prestige in the community. Yet, alongside these pro-natalist policies, the Soviet Union has promoted certain population-control programs: it relegalized abortion in 1955, and offers birth control information and devices at government clinics. There is no one consistent program being followed. Probably the best indication of the original Soviet policy can be garnered from an official statement by Premier Khrushchev in 1955, though it is perhaps now obsolete:

Bourgeois ideology invented many cannibalistic theories, among them the theory of overpopulation. Their concern is to cut down the birth rate, reduce the rate of population increase. It is quite different with us, comrades. If about 100 million people were added to our 200 million, even that would not be enough. (*Pravda*, January 8, 1955)

Communist China is the world's greatest demographic enigma. The seemingly impenetrable "bamboo curtain" also prevents the world's demographers from analyzing the conditions and policies of its most populous nation. With the recent entry of China into the United Nations, it is hoped that the mysteries surrounding the Chinese population will be opened up for study. Yet, there are several facts that are known about the Chinese situation. Following the 1953 census, which showed a much larger population than was anticipated, Chinese officials sanctioned the use of contraceptive techniques and legalized abortion. Since then, their policy has vacillated between pro- and anti-natalism and is probably dependent on yearly agricultural success or failures (Aird, 1962). As of 1967, China was discouraging early marriage, providing contraceptives, utilizing abortion, and denying additional food rations to large families (Heer, 1968:105-106). Also, external and internal migration are strictly controlled. The government is currently attempting to relocate much of the population from the densely settled coastal areas to the sparsely populated western provinces.

Like Russia and China, the United States is another country which has had no systematic population policy. The nation was founded on a growth ethic that included population growth, but this value-orientation is increasingly coming under attack from demographers, ecologists, economists, and others. Early population policies of the U.S. were designed to restrict the utilization and sale of contraceptives, and to encourage high fertility and immigration; but at present, a reversal of these priorities is occurring. Below is a partial list of some U.S. laws and practices which have demographic consequences:

Laws and Practices	Major Process Affected
1. Child labor laws (since turn of century)	mortality
2. Marriage and divorce laws (19th century)	fertility
3. Public sanitation laws (20th century)	mortality
4. Social Security Act of 1935	mortality
5. Free public education (20th century)	fertility
6. Food and drug laws (since 1914)	mortality
7. Unemployment insurance (since 1930's)	fertility
8. Medicare and Medicaid (1965)	mortality
9. Federal income tax laws (1913 on)	fertility
10. Selective service laws (20th century)	fertility
11. Immigration Act of 1965	migration
12. Supreme Court Abortion Decision of 1973	fertility
13. Reversal of "Comstock laws" restricting contraceptive information (1966)	fertility

Most of these laws and practices were not designed deliberately to affect population phenomena, but their impact has often been greater than that of consciously planned programs. Still, it is evident that, at least in the past, the United States has not followed a consistent program of either pro- or anti-natalism, but rather, has shifted about as economic and other factors have changed.

The major part of this section has been concerned with state intervention in population processes, but the critical impact of any legislation is the effect it exerts on the normative structure of the society. Just as certain legislation which is not specifically designed to affect population size, composition, or distribution may have more important though unintended demographic consequences than official population policy, so many social customs not related to population phenomena also exert influences on population processes. Practices associated with religion, magic, politics, and economics often have latent consequences in the demographic sphere. This relationship is normally reciprocal in nature; thus population phenomena in a society comprise a type of servo-system that is constantly engaged in a feedback process among the other elements.

Anthropological studies have picked out social practices in primitive groups that appear to have an integral relationship with the ecological and demographic characteristics of those societies. Practices such as infanticide have been noted in nearly all areas of the world. As Thompson (1953:10-11) has stated:

Infanticide was an almost universal custom from very early times and is still quite common in many parts of the world. Almost all the so-called primitive peoples regularly practice infanticide and have done so for ages.

Thomlinson (1965:196) indicates that many societies practicing this custom do not consciously use it as a population-control device, but rather, employ it to satisfy magical and religious prescriptions. Douglas (1972:54), who has studied population control in primitive groups, believes that population stability does occur among these primitive tribes, but that it is related to systems of social prestige rather than to conscious regulation of the resources necessary for survival. That is, those groups lowest in status are the most likely to be "thinned out" by one means or another. She looked at four groups who attempted to control their fertility through various means.

Group	Practices
1. Pelly Bay Eskimos	Female infantcide
2. Rendille camel herders	Emigration, non-division of inherited herd, late age of marriage for women, killing of boys born on Wednesdays or after the circumcision of the eldest brother
3. Tikopia Islanders	Contraception, abortion, infanticide, pushing undesirables out to sea
4. Nambudiri Brahmins	Allowing only the eldest son and daughter to marry, seclusion of all other daughters

The outcome of these practices in each case was a reduction in fertility that was in harmony with the exigencies of the related physical and social environments.

The effectiveness of population policies is not very clear in many cases. The most popular argument against the practicality of dictated policies is that population size, rate of growth, composition, and distribution are affected more by technological and organizational developments than by official proclamations and practices. Goldschmidt (1959) has divided the evolution and growth of human society into five stages, based on the complexity of technology and the elaboration of the division of labor in each stage. What is critical in this model is that each stage of development is accompanied by increased population density, regardless of place and time (Heer, 1968). The relationship which Heer postulates between development and population provides support for those who argue that programs such as family planning are useless, unless the country has reached a commensurate level of technological and organizational development. These people hold that the conditions of industrialization, urbanization, and bureaucratization must be somewhat advanced in order for planned parenthood programs to succeed.

This section has attempted to illustrate various roads leading to population control taken by a variety of peoples over a great period of time. What comes through in a historical and cross-cultural survey such as this is that the problems of population are hardly ever defined similarly by any two societies, or in the same society over time. Many different policies have been implemented to increase, decrease, stabilize, or shift populations, but as yet, no definite plan of action appears to have completely solved population issues for any country or group. Before we can find an answer to the "population problem," we must first define what the question actually is. For the student, as well as the initiator of population control, five questions must be posed (Thomlinson, 1965:393):

1/ Control of what?
2/ To what ends?
3/ By what means?
4/ In what direction?
5/ With what result?

Today's confusion over the population issue revolves around the fact that different nations and interest groups have different answers to these five questions.

Parameters of Consensual Reality

Demographic analysis focuses its research activities on three basic human events: (1) the size of the population, (2) the composition of the population, and (3) the spatial distribution of the population (Bogue, 1969). The critical thrust of the research process, though, is the determination of change in these events over time, since the dynamic aspect of population phenomena occupies the researchers'

Chapter 16 / Population

central area of concern. These three areas of analysis also form the parameters of the present population debate. While the study and discussion of population size and rate of growth tends to attract major attention, the other two parameters, composition and distribution, are also of crucial importance in comprehending the totality of the "population problem."

Size and Growth of Population

As of 1970, the world's population was estimated to be approximately 3.632 billion, with an annual rate of growth of two percent (*Statistical Abstract of the United States,* 1972:803, Table 1318). These figures do not reveal much by themselves, until they are contrasted with other historical data. At the time of the birth of Christ, there were around 200 million people covering the face of the earth. The rate of growth was fairly static, hovering at about .000005 percent per year (Thomlinson, 1965). It took around 1,300 years for the entire population of the world to double. Yet, at the present rate of world growth, it will take only 35 years for the 3.6 billion inhabitants of 1970 to double themselves. This dramatic decrease in the time it takes for the earth's populace to double its numbers has given rise to the term "population explosion." See Table 16-1.

TABLE 16-1 GROWTH OF WORLD POPULATION*

Year	Population	Percent Increase Per Year Since The Previous Date	Years To Double Since The Previous Date
10,000 B.C.	100,000–10,000,000	—a	—b
5,000 B.C.	5,000,000–20,000,000	—a	—b
0	200,000,000	—a	—b
1300 A.D.	400,000,000	—a	—b
1650	.5 billion	.1	1000
1700	.6 billion	.2	300
1750	.7 billion	.3	230
1800	.9 billion	.4	180
1850	1.2 billion	.5	140
1900	1.6 billion	.6	120
1950	2.4 billion	.8	90
1960	2.8 billion	1.7	40

a *Smaller than .05 percent.*
b *A very large number of years.*

All figures are rounded to avoid a false impression of accuracy. Even today world population totals are not highly accurate; early figures are best described as informed guesses. However, the overall import of the table is factually substantiated.

* United Nations, Demographic Yearbook: 1949-50, New York, p. 10; United Nations, press releases, 1959-62; A. M. Carr-Saunders, World Population, The Clarendon Press, Oxford, 1936, p. 42; and Kingsley Davis, "Future Population Trends and Their Significance," Transactions of the Eighteenth North American Wildlife Conference, Wildlife Management Institute, 1953, pp. 8-21.

Source: Ralph Thomlinson, 1965:13, Table 2

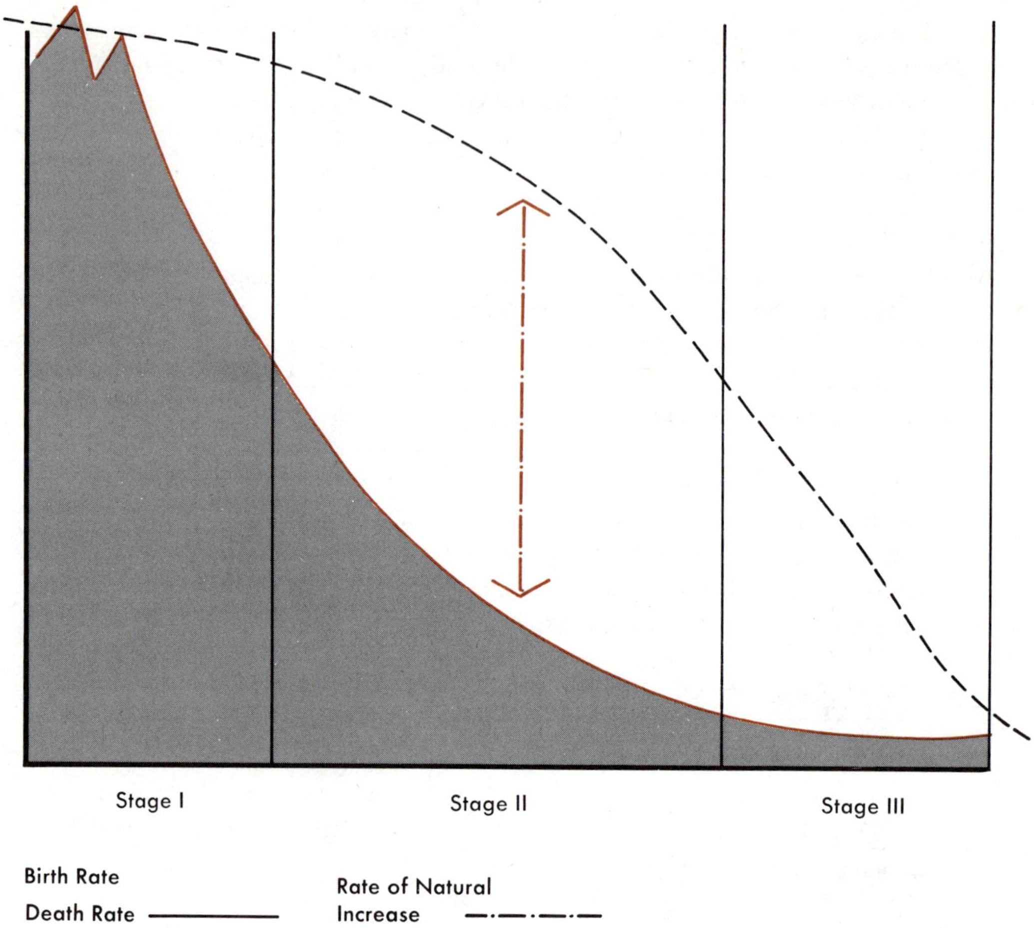

Figure 16-1 Demographic Transition Theory

The "demographic transition theory" is often employed to explain the recent burgeoning of the world's population. Originally, it was formulated to describe the transition of the western nations from high birth and death rates to low birth and death rates (Thompson, 1928). According to the demographic transition theory, eventually the fertility rates of the developing areas will decrease to a level comparable to the mortality rates, but this is only a prediction, with no concrete assurances. See Figure 16-1.

A comparison of current regional growth rates around the world reveals the existence of great differentials between western and developing nations. It can be readily seen that the three extremely high rates of growth are in Asia, Africa, and

South America, while the lowest rate occurs in Europe. This reveals the fact that the largest rates of growth are operating on the largest base populations: 2.6 billion for the developing areas, versus one billion for the rest of the world. Viewing population increase from this perspective, it can be seen that the effect of the U.S. rate of growth on the world population is almost inconsequential, since its base population is only a small fraction of that of all the developing countries. See Table 16-2.

The present U.N. projections for the world's population in the year 2000 range from 5.5 to 7 billion people (*U.N. Population Studies,* 1966, no. 41). If the current rate of growth of two percent per annum continues, the size of the earth's population will be approximately 10 billion by the year 2020. Of course, the problem with this particular type of projection is that it is based solely on current trends, and is therefore subject to great error. The figure 10 billion simply tells us what will be "if" present trends continue into the future.

The principal population question is one of *world* population, but where does the United States fit in? As was previously mentioned, the population of the U.S. is only a small portion of the world's total, numbering approximately 209 million in 1972 (*Current Population Reports,* 1972, no. 493:1). The annual rate of growth in this country has been 1.1 percent per year, thus creating a doubling time of 63 years if the current rate continues. But the U.S. has experienced a complex demographic history that does not lend itself to simplistic doubling projections.

The first census in 1790 counted roughly four-million people within the continental United States. During the 19th century, the population increased rapidly through expansion of boundaries, immigration, and natural growth. At the close of the century, the population had risen to 76 million persons. The 20th century saw a curtailment of immigration and a reduction of boundary expansion, thus reducing the importance of these sources of growth. During the depression of the thirties, the total fertility rate* bottomed out at approximately 2.1, with a crude birth rate† of 18.7 in 1935. These low fertility rates appeared at the end of a constantly declining curve since 1800, and thus were consistent with the demographic transition theory. But following World War II, the U.S. experienced a "baby boom," with a total fertility rate approaching 3.6-3.7 at its peak, and a crude birth rate of 24.9 in 1955 (Thomlinson, 1965:167). The reasons for this resurgence of high fertility are attributed to postponement of child-bearing by families during the depression, reuniting of service families after the war, and a favorable post-war economy. This boom era greatly affects the U.S. population at the present time and

---
* Total fertility rate—average number of birth to women living through childbearing ages under constant age-specific birth rates.
† Crude birth rate—total births per year per 1,000 population.

TABLE 16-2 POPULATION, RATES OF GROWTH, AND AREA, BY REGION

Country	Latest Population Census		Midyear Population Estimates			Population per Square Mile, 1970	Area in Square Miles
	Year	Number (1,000)	1963, Number (1,000)	1970, Number (1,000)	Annual Rate of Change, 1963-70 (percent)		
World total	(x)	(x)	3,162,000	3,632,000	2.0	69	52,425,382
North America	(x)	(x)	283,708	321,000	1.8	34	9,361,730
South America	(x)	(x)	157,057	190,000	2.8	28	6,885,449
Europe	(x)	(x)	437,000	462,000	0.8	242	1,905,893
U.S.S.R.	(x)	(x)	225,000	243,000	1.1	28	8,649,485
Asia	(x)	(x)	1,754,000	2,056,000	2.3	193	10,630,156
Africa	(x)	(x)	289,000	344,000	2.5	29	11,706,594
Oceania	(x)	(x)	16,800	19,400	2.1	6	3,286,076
United States	1970	203,235	189,197	204,800	1.1	57	3,615,191

[Population data generally are present-in-area estimates for the present territory. For some countries however, estimates include national armed forces and diplomats stationed outside the country and exclude alien armed forces, foreign diplomats, and enemy prisoners of war stationed within the country. Except as noted, area data include inland waters. See source, pp. 800, et passim, for general comments concerning the data, and for details of methodology, coverage, and reliability.]

Source: Statistical Abstract of the United States, 1972, p. 803, Table 1318

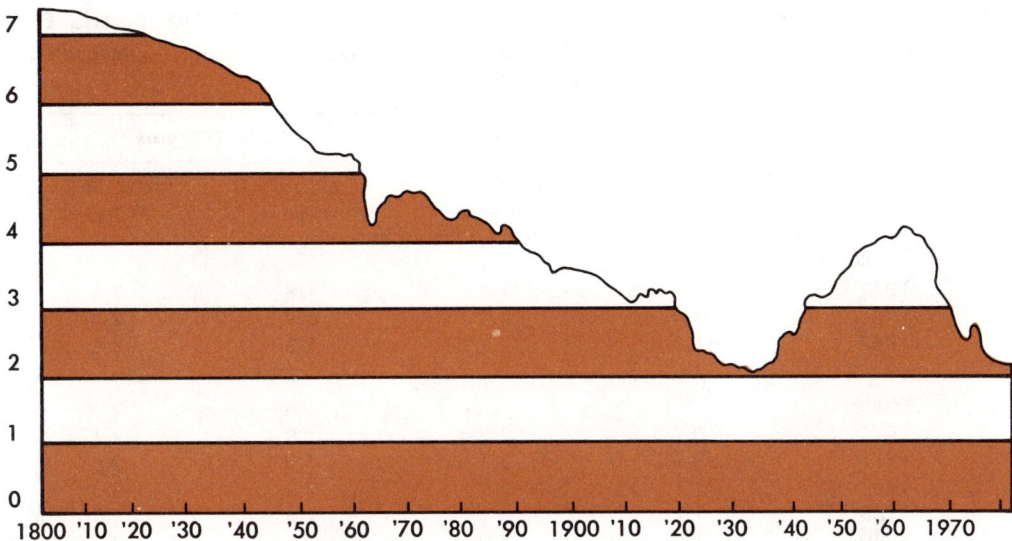

Prior to 1917, data available only for white population; after 1917, total population.

Annual births, expressed in terms of implied completed family size, declined until the 1930's, rose, and fell again.

Figure 16-2 Total Fertility Rate, 1800-1971

SOURCE: *Population and the American Future,* p. 13. Sources: Prior to 1917: Ansley J. Coale and Melvin Zelnik, *New Estimates of Fertility and Population in the United States,* Princeton: Princeton University Press, 1963; 1917 to 1968: U.S. National Center for Health Statistics, *Natality Statistics Analysis,* Series 21, no. 19, 1970; 1969 to 1971: U.S. Bureau of the Census, Current Population Reports, Series P-23, no. 36, "Fertility Indicators: 1970," 1971; the figure for 1971 is based on an unpublished census staff estimate

will continue to do so in the future. The babies born during that period are now entering the job market, the universities, and parenthood. It is this large base of prospective parents that ensures substantial future growth for the United States, even if replacement-level fertility rates* were achieved immediately (*Current Population Reports,* 1972, no. 480). See also Figure 16-2.

The crude death rate† of the U.S. has dropped from 17 in 1900 to approximately 9 in 1970, with the average life expectancy estimated to be around 70 years (*Population and the American Future,* 1972:11). This reduction in mortality has

---

* Replacement-level fertility—the fertility level required for the population eventually to reach zero growth under projected mortality rates and in the absence of immigration (2.11 births per woman currently).

† Crude death rate—total deaths occurring per year per 1,000 population.

TABLE 16-3 AVERAGE NUMBER OF BIRTHS TO DATE AND TOTAL BIRTHS EXPECTED FOR WIVES 18 TO 29 YEARS OLD REPORTING ON EXPECTATIONS, BY AGE: 1955 TO 1972

Year and Race	18 to 24 Years		25 to 29 Years	
	Births to Date	Total Births Expected	Births to Date	Total Births Expected
All Races				
1972	0.9	2.3	1.8	2.5
1971	1.0	2.4	1.9	2.6
1967	1.2	2.9	2.3	3.0
White				
1972	0.9	2.2	1.8	2.4
1971	0.8	2.4	1.9	2.6
1967	1.1	2.9	2.3	3.0
1965	1.2	3.1	2.4	3.3
1960	1.3	3.0	2.3	3.3
1955	1.1	3.2	1.9	3.1

Source: Current Population Reports, Series P-25, No. 240, p. 1, Table A

greatly reduced the infant and youthful mortality rates,* so that any future declines in the death rate will have to take place among the older sector of the populace, and it is not expected that the mortality rate will drop considerably in the near future. Therefore, fertility and immigration are now viewed as the two main determinants of population growth in the United States.

It was expected that when the boom-era babies reached the age of parenthood, they would start another boom ripple in the age structure with their own children. The fertility rate had continuously dropped since its high peak in the fifties, until a small rise was observed between 1968-1970. But after this upward fluctuation, the fertility rate for 1971 and 1972 began again to fall, a trend not expected by demographers as a whole (*Population and the American Future,* 1972:14). (See Table 16-3.) In 1972, the crude birth rate was 15.6, and the general fertility rate† was 73.4, the lowest annual rates ever recorded in U.S. history (*Monthly Vital Statistics Report,* 1973, 21, 12). Although the fertility rate of the U.S. is now near the replacement level, the future expansion of the population is already ensured by the age-structure of the populace. The number of prospective parents is so large, that even if replacement-level fertility were to be reached immediately,

---

* Mortality rate—synonymous with crude death rate (interchangeable).
† General fertility rate—number of births per year per 1,000 women of childbearing ages (15-49).

and even with no more immigration, the population of the U.S. would gain 44 million people from this population base by the year 2000 (*Current Population Reports,* 1972, no. 480:3). With immigration, the population would gain almost 60 million additional persons by the close of the century.

The recent series projections of the population of the U.S. from 1972-2020 by the Census Bureau* has dropped a B series (3.1 births per woman upon completion of childbearing) and added an F series (1.8 births per woman upon completion of childbearing). This alteration was made as a result of a change in two factors: (1) a sharp drop in fertility since 1970, and (2) a drop in the birth expectations of young wives (*Current Population Reports,* 1972, no. 493). It has already been mentioned that the general fertility rate for 1972 was 73.4, the lowest in U.S. history. The other factor, birth expectations, is a more elusive concept, since it is based on attitudinal measures. In 1967, the average number of births expected by wives 18-24 years of age was 2.9. In 1972, this expectation had dropped to 2.3 (*Current Population Reports,* 1972, no. 240:4).

The four fertility assumptions made by the Census Bureau between 1960 and 1972 produced projections of 2.78, 2.45, 2.11, and 1.8 births per woman upon completion of childbearing (see Table 16-4). Depending upon which assumption

TABLE 16-4 SUMMARY OF PROJECTIONS OF TOTAL POPULATION: 1960 TO 2020

Year (July 1)	Series C (2.78 births)	Series D (2.45 births)	Series E (2.11 births)	Series F (1.8 births)
Estimates				
1960			180,671	
1965			194,303	
1970			204,879	
1972			208,837	
Projections				
1975	215,872	215,324	213,925	213,378
1980	230,955	228,676	224,132	221,848
1985	248,711	243,935	235,701	230,913
1990	266,238	258,692	246,639	239,084
1995	282,766	272,211	256,015	245,591
2000	300,406	285,969	264,430	250,686
2005	321,025	301,397	273,053	255,209
2010	344,094	318,156	281,968	259,332
2015	367,977	335,028	290,432	262,631
2020	392,030	351,368	397,746	264,564

(Population in thousands. Total population including Armed Forces abroad.)
Source: Current Population Reports, Series P-25, No. 493, p. 1, Table A

* Series Projections of the U.S. Bureau of the Census—projections of future size and composition of the U.S. population employing various fertility, mortality, immigration, and timing birth-pattern assumptions. Published under the P-25 series of the *Current Population Reports,* 1972.

is utilized, a very different picture of the future U.S. population is obtained. Not only is the total size of the population affected, but the age structure also will vary depending on the particular fertility assumption. Looking at the age structure simplisticly, we see a median age of the population of the U.S. in the year 2000 as either 29.1, 31.1, 34.0, or 35.8 for the various assumptions (*Current Population Reports,* 1972, no. 493:3). Thus the fertility rate has a critical impact on whether the population will be younger (low median age) or older (high median age).

Replacement-level fertility figures are based on a no-migration assumption, but immigration has a very real effect on population growth. At the present time, approximately 400,000 legal immigrants are admitted to the United States annually. Between 1970 and 2000, assuming all families had an average of two children and immigration continued at its present level, these immigrants plus their children would account for nearly one-quarter of the total population growth for that 30-year period, or 15 million persons (*Population and the American Future,* 1972:201). Yet, even this projection does not reveal the total picture, since a great deal of immigration is illegal and escapes federal control. In 1971, over 420,000 deportable aliens were found within U.S. borders, more than the legal immigrant quota (*Population and the American Future,* 1972:202). This amount of population inflow to the U.S. can have significant consequences for future national growth.

The United States is assured of future growth, but the extent of the increase is mainly dependent on future fertility patterns. The most recent data on population growth in the United States indicate that for the first time in history, the rate at which American women are having children has declined to a level just below the 2.1 necessary to achieve zero population growth (the figures for 1972 are 2.08 children per family). If this rate of child-bearing were to continue, it would eventually lead to an actual decrease in the country's population. However, as noted above, even at this rate the population will not level off until around 2035, at which time the country would have a population of approximately 280 million people. The 60-65 years required for a general population leveling-off results from the fact that there are now so many young potential child-producing families in the United States, a product of the post-World War II baby boom.

The 1972 figures are interesting not just because of the rapid drop in birth rate, but also because the estimated number of births in 1972 was the lowest total since 1945. These figures, combined with the lowest net civilian immigration since 1964, contributed to the lowest level of population growth in the United States in 35 years—7.8 persons per 1,000 population.

The declining rate is significant, but its causes are difficult to pinpoint. Certainly, the increased availability of contraceptives and abortion are important, as are increased concern on the part of the American population about environmental issues, increasing economic pressures resulting from spiraling inflation, increased

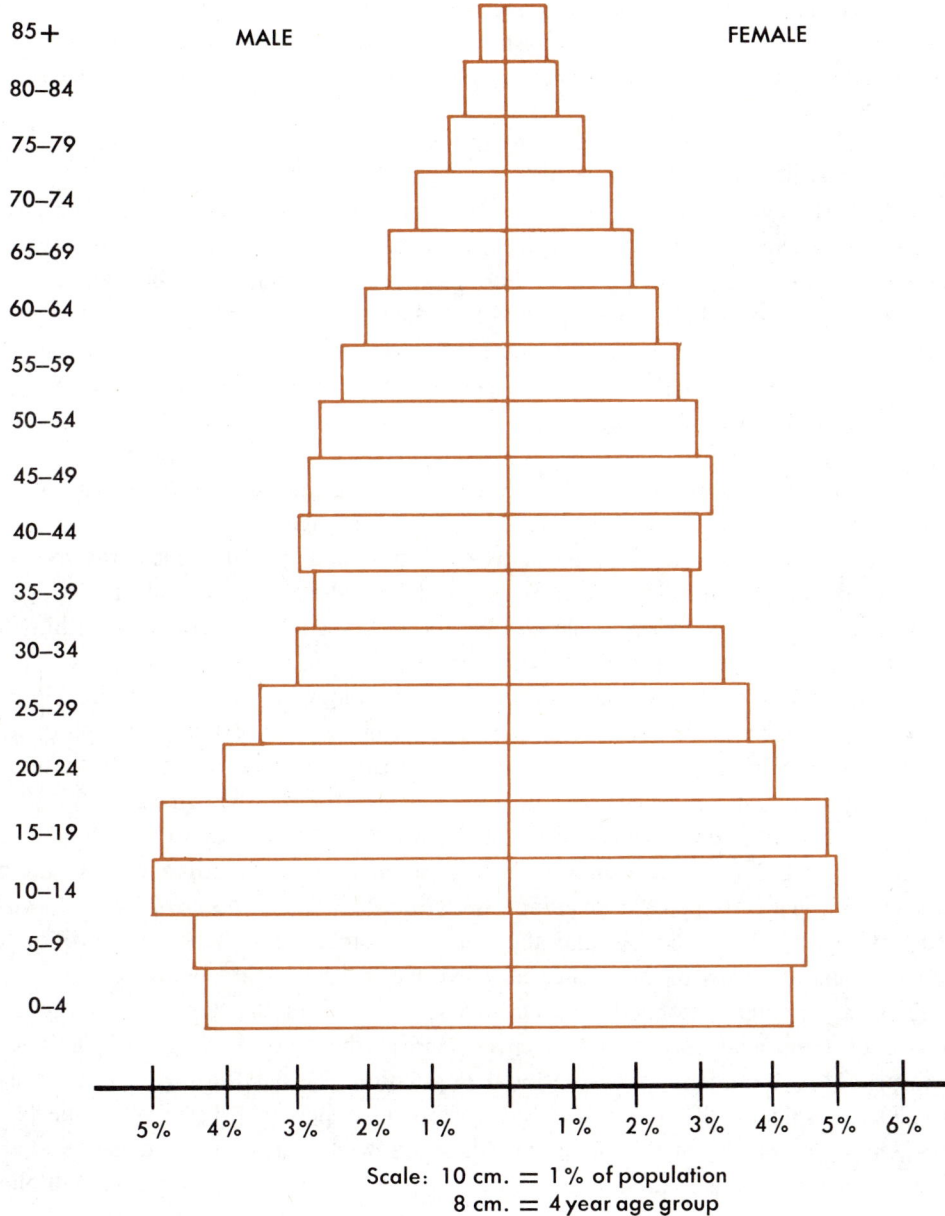

Figure 16-3 Age-Sex Pyramid for the Population of the United States as of July 1, 1972

costs of education, the new independence of women, and population movement from rural to urban areas (where, traditionally, birth rates have been a good deal lower). All of these factors probably have contributed to the changes we see occurring in the country, but which ones are the most important will have to be determined by additional research.

The Composition of Population

Size is probably the critical factor in the population debate, but it is often overshadowed by considerations of population composition. The "quantity versus quality" mode of thought applies to population phenomena, since the size and rate of growth of a population are inexorably linked to its present and eventual composition. In this section, we will present an outline of two basic components of the U.S. population: age and race. In the case of the United States, where the rate of growth is on the decline, the quality of the population takes on increased importance in study and planning.

The age-sex pyramid of the U.S. (Figure 16-3) graphically displays the "baby-boom" bulge in the 5-9, 10-14, 15-19, and 20-24 age categories. This "ripple" presents the U.S. with an assured source of continued growth, unless the average number of offspring of all families is dropped immediately to around one, which is highly unlikely. This pyramid shows the reduced fertility experienced within the last ten years within the United States in the 0-4 and 5-9 age categories. This decreasing fertility, if continued, will result in an older national population. Populations grow younger or older depending upon whether they experience high or low fertility, respectively (Coale, 1964). By contrasting low and high fertility assumptions, Figure 16-4 shows two of the possible age distributions in the year 2000. Thus, the future course of fertility will determine the age makeup of the population. Also, if the U.S. ever attains a stabilized population, its median age would be around 37, with 16 percent over age 65 (*Population and the American Future*, 1972:94-96). This indicates that the nearer a nation approaches a condition of zero population growth, the higher its aged-dependency ratio* becomes.

The racial composition of the country has received much attention recently as a result of the racial turmoil experienced during the sixties. As of 1970, blacks comprised 11.1 percent of the national population. This is the highest percentage for blacks since 1900, when they comprised 11.6 percent of the populace. The percentage of blacks in the population has followed a curious trend, since at the time of the first census in 1790, almost one in five persons were black. Although their absolute numbers increased, due to the heavy influx of immigrants from European nations, their relative percentage in the population decreased.

---

* Aged-dependency ratio—the proportion of those members of the populace aged 65+ divided by the populace in the working ages (15-64).

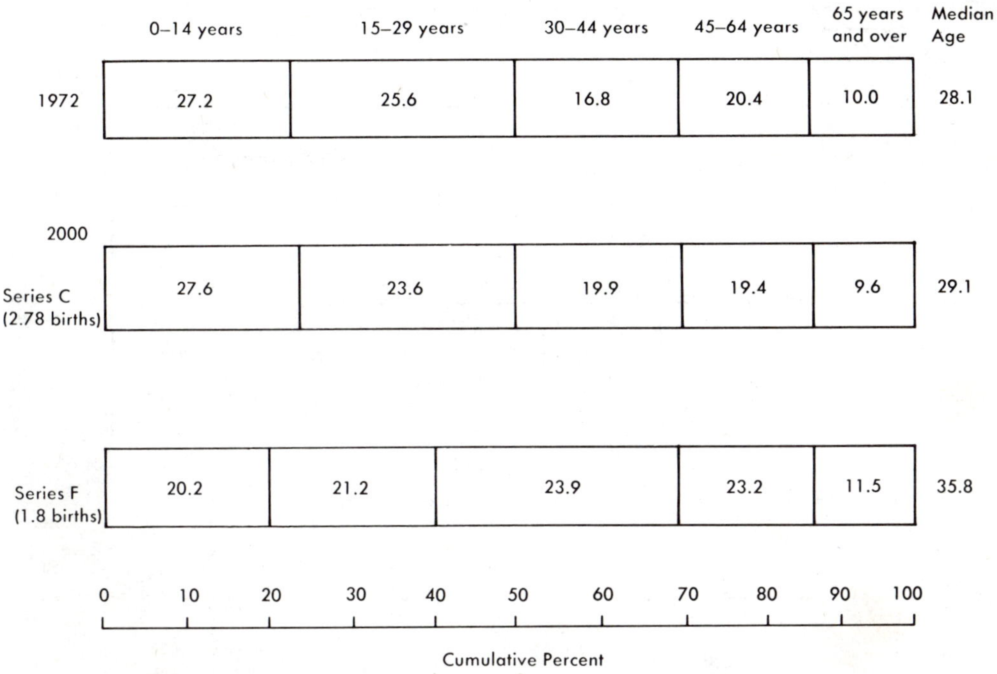

Chapter 16 / Population

	0–14 years	15–29 years	30–44 years	45–64 years	65 years and over	Median Age
1972	27.2	25.6	16.8	20.4	10.0	28.1
2000 Series C (2.78 births)	27.6	23.6	19.9	19.4	9.6	29.1
Series F (1.8 births)	20.2	21.2	23.9	23.2	11.5	35.8

Cumulative Percent

Figure 16-4   Percent Distribution of Population by Age: 1972 and 2000 (Series C and F)

SOURCE: *Current Population Reports,* Series P-25, no. 493, p. 3, fig. 3

The birth rate for blacks and other non-whites was 25.2 in 1970, while it was only 15.6 for whites. This differential of approximately 10 in the crude birth rate between the two groups has existed for many years. Another reason for the upswing in the number of blacks is the higher expectation of number of births by black women. In 1971, the number of births expected per 1,000 white women aged 18-24 was 2,363, while the comparable figure for black women was 2,634 (*Statistical Abstract of the United States,* 1972:54, Table 71). Along with high birth rates and expectations of births is the increasing expectation of life for blacks. From 1920-1970 white males increased their life expectancy 13.7 years to 68.1 years of life, while black males increased their life expectancy 15 years to 60.5 years of life. The increase for black women was even more substantial, raising their life expectancy by 23.7 years to 68.9 years of life, while white women raised theirs 19.8 years to 75.4 years of life (*Statistical Abstract of the United States,* 1972:55, Table 74).

Racial minorities are not randomly distributed throughout the nation, but are

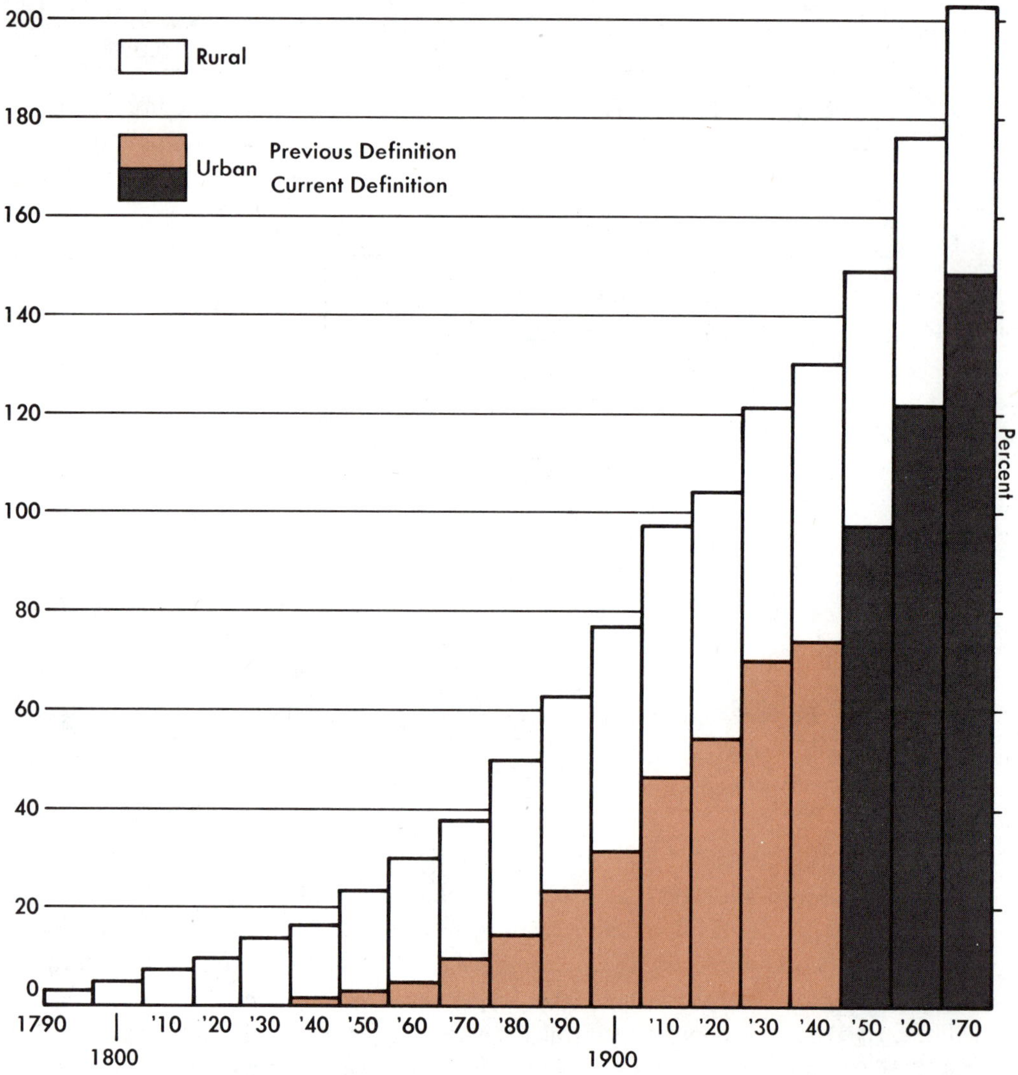

Figure 16-5 Urban and Rural Population, 1790–1970
SOURCE: "Census of the Population, 1970," Vol. 1, *Characteristics of the Population,* Series PC (1)-A, "Number of Inhabitants," p. 1, fig. 34.

concentrated in urban areas, especially in city centers. In 1970, 80.7 percent of all blacks and non-whites were classified as urban compared to 72.4 percent of all whites. Fifty-eight percent of all blacks lived in central areas of cities, while only 27.8 percent of whites did (*Statistical Abstract of the United States,* 1972:16, Table 15). The percentage has been increasing for blacks, while it has been decreasing for whites. It is this concentration of blacks in large, deteriorating city centers that prompted Silberman (1962:89) to state, "The city can be saved only if it faces up to the fact that 'the urban problem' is in large measure a Negro problem."

Projections of future trends to 1985 envision a growth of 918 million non-whites in the central city areas, with a corresponding drop of 2.4 million whites. Thus, increasing racial segregation is predicted for the future of this country.

Spatial Distribution of Population

As we indicated in the first section of the chapter, some people consider the population problem to be one of distribution, rather than one of growth. As one Hollywood star put it on a late-night talk show, "There's a lot of empty land in Arizona." This is an oversimplified view of the distribution problem, but no serious student of demography can deny that it is an important issue that must be faced. In this section, the processes of metropolitan growth and migration will be presented in order better to analyze the present and future spatial distribution of the U.S. population.

At the time of the first U.S. census in 1790, only 5.1 percent of the populace was classified as urban. This country had its origins in the land, and the rural ethic has been a predominant mode of thought up to the present day. Yet, in the 1970 census, 73.5 percent of the American people were classified as urban dwellers. It is this astounding shift from a rural to an urban nation that has brought the attention of researchers to the study of the spatial distribution of the population. See Figure 16-5.

As the report of the Commission on Population Growth and the American Future (1972:25) stated, "Population growth is metropolitan growth in the contemporary United States . . ." During the period from 1960-70, the total U.S. population grew by 13 percent, while the metropolitan population increased by 23 percent. Not all metropolitan areas grew at the same rate, as Table 16-5 indicates. Areas of two million or more actually grew at slower rates than did the population as a whole, but areas between one and two million increased at a rate of 27 percent. Also, during this same time period, the number of Standard Metropolitan Statistical Areas (SMSA's)* increased from 212 to 243.

The sources of metropolitan growth are basically: (1) natural increase, (2) migration, (3) political annexation, (4) reclassification, and (5) change in the

---

* Standard Metropolitan Statistical Area (SMSA)—a county or group of contiguous counties which contains at least one city of 50,000 inhabitants or more, or "twin cities" with a combined population of at least 50,000. In addition to the county, or counties, containing such a city, or cities, contiguous counties are included in an SMSA if, according to certain criteria, they are essentially metropolitan in character and are socially and economically integrated with the central city. (See U.S. Bureau of the Census, U.S. Census of Population: 1960, Number of Inhabitants, United States Summary, PC (1)-IA, p. xxiv.)

TABLE 16-5   GROWTH OF METROPOLITAN AREAS: 1960-1970

Metropolitan Area Population, 1970	Number of Areas, 1970	Population in 1970 Boundaries (millions)	Population Increase 1960 to 1970 (in 1970 boundaries)	
			Number (millions)	Percent (increase)
All Areas	243	139	20	14
2,000,000 or more	12	52	6	12
1,000,000 to 2,000,000	21	28	6	27
500,000 to 1,000,000	32	22	3	18
250,000 to 500,000	60	20	3	16
Under 250,000	118	17	2	14

Source: U.S. Bureau of the Census, Census of Population and Housing: 1970, General Demographic Trends for Metropolitan Areas, 1960 to 1970, Final Report PHC (2), 1971. The figures shown in this table differ somewhat from those cited elsewhere in the text due to differences in areal definitions. If one compares the population of metropolitan areas as defined in 1960 to the corresponding population within areas as defined in 1970, there is an increase of 26 million people. But, if we look at growth occurring within fixed metropolitan boundaries as defined in 1970, as in this table, there is an increase of 20 million. The latter figure does not allow for territorial extension of existing areas or the growth of additional areas to metropolitan status between 1960 and 1970.

definition of "metropolitan" by the Census Bureau (Thompson, 1965:148). One-third of all metropolitan growth between 1960-70 took place through extension of territorial limits and redesignation of new metropolitan areas due to their expansion to requisite size qualifications. The other two-thirds of the growth occurred as a result of natural increase (74 percent) and migration (26 percent) within 1960 boundaries (*Population and the American Future,* 1972:27). Although, in the past in-migration to metropolitan areas was a major source of growth, this source of increase has nearly been eliminated at the present time, since only 31.4 percent of all Americans live outside SMSA's, and the great bulk of internal migration now occurs *between* metropolitan areas (*Statistical Abstract of the United States,* 1972: 16, Table 15).

Even the lines separating urban from rural are beginning to blur, as the influence of the dominant metropolitan regions touches nearly all parts of the nation. Although rural people constitute 26.5 percent of the population, rural farmers make up only around five percent of the total. Rural non-farm people are often as oriented to a cosmopolitan way of life as are the inner-city dwellers, who themselves often have a rural background. This extension of the influence of the city into the rural hinterlands prompted the Census Bureau to develop the concept of the SMSA. This takes into account the fact that counties containing the large central cities and certain contiguous counties are completely intertwined with the city as a functioning or "ecological," if not political, unit.

Although metropolitan areas as a whole are growing rapidly, some central cities are actually losing population. Fifteen central cities with populations of over one-half million lost population between 1960-70. Those who flee the city relocate themselves in the suburban areas surrounding the core city, thus creating a dualistic system within a metropolitan area. Those who remain behind in the inner city are predominantly poor and/or black. The percentage of whites in central cities decreased between 1960 and 1970, while the percentage of blacks increased. This results in further segregation of the races within the metropolitan area, with the central city losing its economic base to the suburban regions. Although SMSA's or metropolitan areas are considered as units by the Census Bureau, the different areas that comprise them operate as independent political structures, creating an uncoordinated system of politically autonomous and economically unequal districts.

Presently, the United States is moving beyond the metropolitan concept to a "megalopolis" or "urban region" mode of organization. Urban regions are now defined as "areas of one-million people or more comprised of a continuous zone of metropolitan areas and intervening counties within which one is never far from a city" (*Population and the American Future,* 1972:40). Such an area exists along the Atlantic coastline, and extends over to the Chicago area. It is a constellation of large and small cities with their hinterlands; a maze of varying geographical types combining to produce a new demographic phenomenon that appears to be the direction of the future. It is predicted that by the year 2000, one-sixth of the continental U.S. land space will be classified as falling within an urban region, while five-sixths of the American population will be living within this area (*Population and the American Future,* 1972:41-42). Thus, the concentration of the populace in urban agglomerations seems to be a continuing process, one that has been underway since the origins of the country.

Migration within the United States is not a regulated movement, but one that is basically determined by the exigencies of the market economy. It is often viewed as an adaptive phenomenon, in that its purpose is the relocation of population from regions of economic depression to areas of economic prosperity. Rural to urban migration has been the predominant mode of movement in this country, but this type of migration is becoming less important as the rural-farm population continues to decrease. The Report of the Commission on Population Growth and the American Future (1972:28) indicated three basic migratory phenomena existing today: (1) moves from economically depressed regions to areas of gainful employment, (2) moves from the central cities to the outlying suburbs, and (3) moves among metropolitan areas due to the existence of a nationwide job market. All of these forms of migration have a significant impact on the social, economic, and political structures of the affected areas.

The U.S. is a nation of movers. Vance Packard, in *A Nation of Strangers,* attempted to document the deterioration of neighborhood ties and lasting relationships due to the ever-increasing mobility of the American populace. According to estimates made by the Census Bureau for the period March, 1970-March, 1971, approximately "17.9 percent of the 201,506,000 persons of 1-year old and over living in the U.S. in March 1971 had moved within the country during the preceding twelve months. This 17.9 percent represents about 36,161,000 persons, with 23,018,000 moving within counties and 13,143,000 moving between counties" (*Current Population Reports,* 1972, no. 235:1). On the average, in roughly six years, there are as many moves made as there are people in the country. It is no wonder that Petersen (1958) has referred to the United States as a "nation of nomads."

We now have an abbreviated picture of the demographic circumstances and prospects for the world and for the United States. The factors of size and growth, composition, and spatial distribution have been described in order to present the empirical realities of the population issue. The implications of these figures in terms of policies and planning will be discussed later, for the curious fact about the population debate is that sets of figures can be, and usually are, interpreted in many ways depending upon the value orientation of the interpreter. Simply put, one man's "birth dearth" is another man's population "explosion."

Public Opinion

After having reviewed some of the facts and figures relating to population growth, we now turn to a brief discussion of public reaction to this phenomenon. Specifically, we will look at three areas: (1) public perceptions of population growth or change as being problematic; (2) public attitudes relating to ideal and desired family size; and (3) attitudes relating to birth control and abortion.

Population as a Public Issue

Along with the broader issue of "environmental deterioration," problems relating to population growth have received an increasing amount of attention in the media in recent years. If nothing else, this focus on population by the media has increased public awareness of the issues involved. By 1965, Erskine (1967), in summarizing a nationwide poll of 1,620 adults and 551 teen-agers, reported that 82 percent of those surveyed had read or heard about predictions of great increases in population size. However, in this poll, undertaken for *Look* magazine by the Gallup organization, less than one-third (29 percent) of the respondents indicated that they were worried about the projected increase. In other words, though a majority of those surveyed were becoming aware of projections of the population explosion, few of them felt a particularly high level of concern about it at that time. Those who did indicate such concern were either college-educated or had incomes of $10,000 a year, or more, and were thus the least likely segment of the population to have large families themselves anyway.

The level of expressed public concern about the population issue has apparently increased significantly since the 1965 survey. Kantner (1968), again using national survey data, reports that a study conducted in the fall of 1967 found that 54 percent of the respondents felt that the rate of growth of the United States' population constituted a "serious problem." An even higher percentage of those questioned may have felt a serious concern about the rate of growth of the world population, though data on this question were not available.

In a survey of the residents of the state of Illinois, Simon (1971) found that a significant majority of her respondents were concerned about population growth in the United States. In response to the question, "Do you think population in the United States is growing too fast, not fast enough, or just about right?", 66 percent felt that the population is growing too fast. Most of the respondents felt that general ignorance or ignorance about birth control methods were primarily responsible for what they perceived as a too rapid rate of growth.

The general conclusion that emerges from an examination of polling data is that from at least the time of the middle 1960's up until the present, more and more Americans have indicated concern about the rate of population increase. Two general observations about this which will be discussed in more detail later are in order. First, this increase in concern about population growth has closely paralleled the increase in concern about environmental deterioration in this country. Clearly the two problems are closely related in the views of the American public. Second, the growth in concern about population growth comes at about the same time as, or even later than, *actual significant decreases in the rate of population growth*. While concern (as reflected in attitudes) may be related to behavior (as reflected in lower fertility behavior), it seems clear that much of the decrease in fertility in the United States is traceable to other factors. Some leading possibilities are the economic uncertainty that has been characteristic of recent years, which has prevented families from becoming too large; and the growing popularity of smaller families, quite apart from any real concern for population growth.

Ideal and Desired Family Size

Research relating to ideal and desired family-size preferences has been going on now for a number of years in the United States, as well as in other countries. Historically, family-size preference data have shown that individuals in the lower socio-economic levels have been more likely to desire larger families than those in the middle- and higher-income levels. This finding is supported by recent data which show that, generally, people in the poorer, less-developed areas of the world desire larger families than do those in the more industrialized (and wealthy) nations. Suggested reasons for such findings are numerous and include such explana-

TABLE 16-6 IDEAL NUMBER OF CHILDREN

	1973
One, Two	46%
Three	23
Four	14
Five, Six, or more	3
None	1
No Opinion	9

Source: George Gallup, "Few Favor Large Families," reported in the Salt Lake Tribune, February 5, 1973

TABLE 16-7 PERCENT SAYING 4 OR MORE IS IDEAL NUMBER OF CHILDREN

	1967	1973	Point Change
National	40%	20%	—20
Men	34	18	—16
Women	45	21	—24
Under 30 years	34	12	—22
30 to 49 years	40	22	—18
50 and over	42	24	—18
Protestants	37	20	—17
Roman Catholics	50	23	—27
College	34	12	—22
High School	40	19	—21
Grade School	44	31	—13

Source: George Gallup, "Few Favor Large Families," reported in the Salt Lake Tribune, February 5, 1973

tions as: (1) a large family has been valuable as a labor pool in agrarian areas, (2) traditional cultural norms stressing pro-natalism have died out more slowly among the poor and in more backward areas, and (3) religious prohibitions against birth-control practices have been more influential in such areas and have changed less rapidly.

Whatever the reasons, such findings create a series of dilemmas for demographers. For example, it is in the countries that face the most serious population problems that family-size preferences frequently remain the highest. In addition, it has been found that largest families are desired by the lower socio-economic classes in industrialized societies, who are the least able to support their offspring, and by the poorer populations of the countries where they can least be afforded. While such data suggest that increased affluence, with its attendant benefits of education and a better living environment, is one of the most likely means of decreasing the desired family size, the difficulty of increasing the level of affluence in developing countries is compounded by the tremendous rate of population growth that such countries currently face.

In the United States, changes in family-size preferences have coincided rather closely with the increased awareness of the population controversy. The most recent data on family-size preferences of Americans (Gallup, 1973) show that the proportion who favor large families is at its lowest point in the nearly 40 years that regular surveys on the subject have been conducted. At this point, only one adult in five states that the ideal number of children in a family is four or more. This figure constitutes a dramatic drop in only six years. For instance, in 1967, 40 percent of those surveyed selected four or more as the ideal number of children. In the 1973 data, almost half (46 percent) say that one or two children would constitute the ideal number.

The data also give further evidence of a convergence of Catholic and non-Catholic attitudes toward ideal family size. Twenty percent of the Protestants and 23 percent of the Catholics surveyed favored four or more children. Six years earlier, Gallup data had shown 37 percent of the Protestants selecting this category, in contrast to fully 50 percent of the Catholics.

Table 16-6 summarizes the most recent polling data on attitudes relating to the ideal number of children for a family to have, and Table 16-7 shows the change in views that has occurred since 1967 for various groups.

As can be seen from the data, the most significant attitude changes have occurred among Roman Catholics and women, though important shifts are evident for all population groups. As suggested earlier, this attitude change has already been reflected in the recent figures on the fertility levels of the American family.

Attitudes Relating to Birth Control and Abortion

Just as Americans have become more concerned about population growth, so also have they become more likely to approve and to practice various methods of family-size limitation. And, despite the strong teachings of the Catholic Church to the contrary (see the next section), this has been just as true for Roman Catholics in the United States as for non-Catholics.

Erskine's (1967) report of the 1965 Gallup poll shows that when respondents were asked what should be done to control the increase in population, a majority of the adult sample favored increased use of birth control methods, or increased education about such methods combined with increased use. Significantly, almost one-fourth of the sample felt that nothing should be done. However, at the same time, a large majority of both the adult and the teen-age samples felt that birth control information should be available to anyone who wants it (see Table 16-8).

A majority of the adult sample (55 percent) felt that the policy of the Catholic Church on birth control would be changed in the near future. This held true for Roman Catholics as well as for other religious groups. A strong majority of all respondents, except the Roman Catholics, indicated disapproval of the policy of the

TABLE 16-8 ATTITUDES TOWARD AVAILABILITY OF BIRTH CONTROL INFORMATION

Do you think birth control information should be available to anyone who wants it, or not?

	Adults	Teens
Should be available	80%	75%
Should not be available	13	16
Don't know	7	9

Source: Hazel Erskine, "The Polls: More on the Population Explosion and Birth Control," *Public Opinion Quarterly*, 31 (Summer, 1967), p. 306

Catholic Church in trying to prevent the distribution of birth control information. Seventy-eight percent of the adult sample and 75 percent of the teen-age sample were in favor of the United Nations supplying birth control information to different nations of the world.

In a later study using a sample of Rhode Island housewives, Bouvier (1972) sought to determine the extent to which Catholic women, regardless of the official teaching of their Church, were becoming more like non-Catholic women in their family-planning attitudes and practices. In reviewing past research, Bouvier notes that national family planning surveys have shown that as early as 1955, 58 percent of all couples with Catholic wives had used contraceptives. By 1960, this figure had climbed to 70 percent and by 1965, to 78 percent. Comparable figures for Protestant women for these periods are 75 percent for 1955, 84 percent for 1960, and 87 percent for 1965. These figures clearly reflect a narrowing of the gap in birth-control behavior between Catholic and non-Catholic women.

Of perhaps further significance is the fact that the data show that one year after the issuance of Pope Paul's *Humanae Vitae,* which opposed birth control (to be discussed in the next section on special interest groups), the proportion of Catholics using non-approved birth control practices had continued to increase.

In his Rhode Island study, Bouvier (1972) reports that by 1969, 80 percent of Catholic women were using birth control methods as compared to 87 percent of the non-Catholic women surveyed. When comparing wives under 30 years of age, the difference is only 1.7 percent (83.8 percent of the Catholic wives and 85.5 percent of the non-Catholic wives practice birth control). Despite these similarities, Bouvier notes significant differences when it comes to method of birth control selected. Catholic women were more likely to select the less effective methods such as rhythm and withdrawal, which are not opposed by the Church, while non-Catholic women were much more likely to use the pill and the diaphragm—generally safer methods. Bouvier concludes that, at least in Rhode Island, Church teaching may not be stopping Catholic women from practicing birth control, but it is affecting the method they are likely to select.

Since its introduction, the pill has gained wide approval as a method of birth limitation in the United States as well as in many other countries. It now clearly constitutes the most popular and widely used contraceptive method in the United States. However, attitudes toward other, perhaps more harsh or permanent methods of population control, which were unpopular not too long ago, are also now acceptable to large majorities of Americans, at least under certain circumstances. For example, some questions were included in a September 1966 Gallup poll on the issue of sterilization as a means of birth control (Erskine, 1967). Subjects in the United States and Canada were presented with several case situations, and asked if they would approve sterilization in these situations. Results are presented in Table 16-9.

As can be seen, a large majority of the subjects would approve sterilization in each of the situations presented even in 1966. While the results for both the United States and Canada were similar, Canadians appeared to be somewhat more favorably disposed in each situation than the Americans. Perhaps the most definitive expression of opinion on this matter is the actual demand for sterilization operations. According to a 1970 survey, of all married couples who were practicing any kind of contraception, one-sixth had resorted to sterilization, "the ultimate contraceptive." Indeed, among couples with wives between 30 and 44 years of age, sterilization was the single most popular form of contraception,

TABLE 16-9 ATTITUDE TOWARD STERILIZATION

Do you approve or disapprove of sterilization operations in the following situations?	Approve	Disapprove	No Opinion
Women who have more children than they can provide for and ask to be sterilized.			
U.S.	64%	24%	12%
Canada	68%	22%	10%
Persons who have mental or physical afflictions and ask to be sterilized.			
U.S.	76%	15%	9%
Canada	83%	9%	8%
Sterilization in cases where the health of the mother would be endangered by having additional children.			
U.S.	78%	13%	9%
Canada	81%	9%	10%

Source: Hazel Erskine, "The Polls: More on the Population Explosion and Birth Control," Public Opinion Quarterly, 31 (Summer, 1967), p. 312

accounting for a quarter of the cases. Since 1970, sterilizations have been performed (on either men or women) at the rate of about one million cases a year, so that by 1975 at least six million adult Americans had been sterilized, and the rate seems to be growing, especially among women (Westoff, 1974).

In 1971, about 80 percent of the sterilizations were performed on men, probably because the male vasectomy is a relatively short and simple operation. By 1973, however, the male/female ratio in sterilizations had approached half and half, perhaps reflecting the development of "laparoscopy," a new sterilization operation for females which is much simpler and faster than the conventional tubal ligation. Unlike the case in India and in some of the other "underdeveloped" countries, where sterilizations (especially for men) have been urged upon the people as a matter of official policy, Americans desirous of sterilizations have had to cope with a variety of state laws and hospital regulations restricting their efforts. Those who have succeeded in getting sterilizations have therefore had to be highly motivated. Their motivations, according to one survey, have included both altruistic and more self-centered elements; that is, some of them have cited concerns over population growth, while others have cited the desire to avoid being tied down by children. Since the operations range in cost from $50 to $200 for men, and up to $500 for women, it is not surprising that the sterilizations have been obtained almost entirely by people of above average income (Westoff, 1974).

Attitudes toward the other controversial method of birth limitation, abortion (prior to the 1973 Supreme Court ruling), have followed a somewhat paradoxical pattern in the United States. For a complete treatment of the history of abortion in this country, see Chapter 12.) It has frequently been argued that certain groups —specifically, women and the less advantaged—should support legalized abortion on a priori ideological grounds (Blake, 1971:548). However, this has not been the case. In fact, these two groups have consistently been among those ranking highest in their opposition to legalized abortion. On the other hand, abortion has been most strongly supported by non-Catholic, well-educated, "Establishment-type" males (Blake, 1971).

In analyzing changes in public opinion relating to abortion for the decade from 1960 to 1970, Blake notes that opposition declined in some cases, though not to any considerable degree. In national opinion surveys conducted between 1962 and 1969, the percentage disapproving of abortion in various situations has, in fact, been fairly stable. Throughout the decade, about 10 percent disapproved of abortion in cases where the mother's health is endangered, and approximately one-fifth disapproved in cases where the child might be deformed. However, opposition in situations where the reasons for an abortion are economic is much higher. In 1962, 71 percent of those surveyed disapproved of abortion where the family could not afford another child. This figure declined to 65 percent by 1969.

Similarly, in 1962, 90 percent disapproved in cases where the family simply didn't want another child, while the figure was 78 percent in 1969.

Our examination of public opinion and behavior on population-related matters can be briefly summarized as follows: Since at least the middle-1960's, Americans have become progressively more concerned about population-growth problems. This concern is reflected, in part, in their changing family-size preferences. More Americans now desire smaller families than ever before. Changing family-size preferences are, in turn, reflected in more wide-scale approval and use of contraceptive methods. We now turn to an examination of positions of more specific publics in the population debate.

CHAMPIONS AND THEIR INTERESTS

As indicated above, more Americans than ever before now view population growth as a problem that requires action, both at the individual and at the governmental levels. Clearly, the discussion of population phenomena has drawn a greater audience within the last several years. In addition to the growing broad-scale public concern with population matters, there are numerous, clearly defined special-interest groups in the debate that merit special attention. Pseudo-demographers, lay prophets, and religious authorities have all joined professionals in the field of population study to create a vast, uncoordinated compilation of facts, speculations, and plain mumbo jumbo. The incredible number of conflicting interpretations and projections may make the average citizen wonder how any rational person could consider demography or population study a science.

What are the most important special interests and publics in the population debate, and what are their positions? While no effort will be made to discuss them all, we will look at several groups that have received and are receiving the most attention.

Religious and Moral Interests

The Pro-Natalist Churches*

There certainly is no *one* religious point of view on population growth in the United States. The official attitude expressed depends upon the particular church being examined. Several churches have taken strong stands in support of population-control efforts, both in the United States and abroad. Some of these stands are backed by religiously-supported action and information programs which disseminate birth control information, family planning literature, and so on. However, most

---

* Churches that oppose artificial or planned interference with conception and birth processes.

attention has been focused on the churches that have taken a pro-natalist position, and, more specifically, on the Roman Catholic Church.

The official teaching of the Roman Catholic Church is to have large families. The following quotation from Pope Pius XII presents the core of the Church's basic doctrine on family size:

> Large families are most blest by God and specially loved and prized by the Church as its most precious treasures. For these families offer particularly clear testimony to three things that serve to assure the world of the truth of the Church's doctrine and the soundness of its practice, and that redound, through good example, to the great benefit of all other families and of civil society itself. Where you find families in great numbers, they point to: the physical and moral health of a Christian people; a living faith in God and trust in His Providence; the fruitful and joyful holiness of Catholic marriage. (quoted in Blake, 1966:31)

Blake (1966:31) notes that this position is further supported in the following quotation from the Director of the Family Life Bureau, National Catholic Welfare Conference, Monsignor John C. Knott:

> The mind of the Church has been and is in favour of life. She is not frightened by the statistical data presented by demographers and described in nightmare terms by propagandists. Whatever solution she may approve for the population problem will be informed by the life-loving, and optimistic spirit of the late and beloved Pope John XXIII, who said:
> "Do not be afraid of the numbers of your sons and daughters. On the contrary, ask Divine Providence for them."

The Church further states that even restrictions of size through the use of the rhythm method (the only method of family planning that receives official approval) should not be done for selfish reasons. For example, Catholics are taught that material aspirations for the family or for the children do not constitute sufficient reason to use even rhythm to limit the number of offspring (Blake, 1966). "For the Christian couple, the decision to limit births will not be a happy way to get out from under responsibility, but a necessary step taken with the knowledge that it is depriving them of a great opportunity to serve in partnership with God in one of the most important works possible" (quoted in Blake, 1966:29).

Despite these official statements (and perhaps, in part, because of them), the period of the 1960's became a period of conflict among Catholics regarding birth control and family-planning practices. The birth-control pill was introduced in the early 1960's and became widely available, and it was soon evident that many Catholic women were using the pill, though without the official approval of the Church (Bouvier, 1972:514). A nationwide poll conducted in the mid-1960's (Erskine, 1967) had found that a majority of respondents, including the Roman

Catholic respondents, felt that the policy of the Roman Catholic Church regarding birth control would soon be liberalized. It was widely assumed that when the Second Vatican Council acknowledged that many Catholics were not following the proscriptive doctrine of the Church, a new theological position would be approved. However, as noted by Bouvier (1972:514) and others, "Despite the advice of a substantial majority of his Commission to study population and family problems, on July 25, 1968, Pope Paul VI issued *Humanae Vitae*," reinforcing the position of the Church in opposition to birth control.

Controversy has raged both among Catholics and non-Catholics since the Pope's ruling. Many individuals in positions of leadership in the Church have chosen to ignore the ruling. As one Catholic priest has put it concerning his reaction to *Humanae Vitae,* "Since there is no scripture and no history, there can be no theological ground either" (quoted in Baker, 1970:149). Other Roman Catholics have been even more explicitly negative in their response. For example, a Roman Catholic biologist, has stated:

> My first duty as a Catholic is to do what I believe is morally correct. There is no doubt in my mind that the position of the Church with respect to birth control is morally wrong. The price of doctrinaire insistence on unworkable methods of birth control is high. It contributes to misery and starvation for millions and perhaps the end of civilization as we know it. As a scientist I know that Catholic Doctrine in this area is without biological foundation. It is therefore my duty, both to myself and to my Church, not just to ignore this doctrine, but to do everything within my power to change it. After all, without drastic world-wide measures for population control in the near future, there will be no Church anyway. If the Church, or, for that matter, any organized religion is to survive, it must become much more humanitarian in focus. If it does, the theology will take care of itself. (quoted in Baker, 1970:150)

These quotes are indicative of the response of a good many members of the Catholic Church in the United States, and in many other industrialized countries. The attitudinal and behavioral data presented earlier make it very clear that a significant percentage of Catholic women in this country are ignoring the Pope, are practicing birth control and are using methods other than rhythm. Furthermore, a large majority of Catholics now view smaller families as ideal. As Blake (1966) has put it in response to the question of how closely the ideals of American Catholics accord with the Church's strong preference for large families, lay Catholics "are generally farther from sharing their Church's view concerning family size than they are from sharing those of non-Catholics." In other words, American Catholics are "more 'American' than Catholic."

Critics of the position of the Catholic Church, however, are quick to point out that the effect of the Pope's ruling will be most strongly felt in the more underdeveloped nations of the world, rather than in industrialized nations. And, they emphasize, it is in the underdeveloped nations that the problem of population control is most critical. Moreover, even if most Catholics in the United States do choose to ignore the ruling of the Pope, that ruling will remain a point of conflict and controversy among those who take different sides in the population debate.

It should be noted that the Catholic Church is certainly not alone among established religions in taking a strong pro-natalist position. The Church of Jesus Christ of Latter-Day Saints (Mormon) also stresses the importance of reproduction among its members. Largely due to their belief in the pre-existence of spirits, Mormons are enjoined to bear as many children as possible in order to offer the spirits mortal bodies in which to dwell. Certain spokesmen of the Church are therefore adamantly opposed to the use of contraceptive practices, except where the health of the mother may be endangered. The following passage from former Secretary of Agriculture Ezra Taft Benson, who is also president of the Quorum of the Twelve Apostles of the Mormon Church, is indicative of the Mormon position on birth control:

> The world teaches birth control. Tragically, many of our sisters subscribe to its pills and practices when they could easily provide earthly tabernacles for more of our Father's children. We know that every spirit assigned to this earth will come, whether through us or someone else. There are couples in the Church who think they are getting along just fine with their limited families but who will someday suffer the pains of remorse when they meet the spirits that might have been part of their posterity. (1969:12)

The importance of this religious philosophy as it affects the reproductive patterns of members of the Mormon Church is clearly reflected in their birth rate. The crude birth rate for members of the Mormon Church was 28.41 in 1970, while it was only 18.2 for the United States as a whole (Spicer, 1973, Table 2).

Planned Parenthood Federation

Until the relatively recent establishment of Zero Population Growth (cf. below), probably the best-known and most influential group in the population control movement was the Planned Parenthood Federation. Planned Parenthood is an organization devoted to counseling, training, and educating families in birth control and family planning procedures. It frequently enjoys the cooperation and support of Protestant denominations affiliated with the National Council of Churches, which tend not to share the pro-natalist position of Catholicism and of the more conservative Protestant churches.

Staffed largely by volunteer middle- and upper-middle-class persons, Planned Parenthood has devoted thousands of hours to helping people prevent unplanned and unwanted pregnancies. With the help of this group, many young mothers in the United States and abroad have learned to limit the number of their offspring, in accordance with their family-size preferences.

Academic and Scientific Interests and Publics

Among the principal actors in the population controversy, members of the scientific community occupy a prominent position. It is probably quite safe to argue that the majority of that part of the scientific community which deals extensively with population matters has a neo-Malthusian orientation. McCracken (1972), for example, has noted the importance of the neo-Malthusian outlook in the writings of many of the population-growth critics, who generally accept the proposition that one of the critical reasons for the population problem is that population increases at a more rapid rate than does the supply of food and other crucial materials. Thus, the earth's resources are simply not capable of keeping up with a constantly expanding population, and ultimate crisis in the form of starvation faces much of the earth's population. Many of the neo-Malthusians note an additional contemporary problem related to trying to keep the food supply equal to the population growth—that of pollution of the earth's food resources and crops from ever-expanding industry and manufacturing, and from increased use of chemical fertilizers and sprays.

In the words of H. M. Raulet, a public health anthropologist, the common neo-Malthusian summary of the population problem in the underdeveloped countries of the world would be as follows: "The less developed countries . . . are caught in a kind of low-level equilibrium trap in which high rates of population growth impede economic development, and economic backwardness and traditionalism hold back the completion of the 'demographic transition'" (1970:211-234). Pradervand (1972:81) has also suggested that "neo-Malthusian interpretations now tend to dominate the whole development scene. For the Agency for International Development (AID) of the United States State Department, the idea that rapid population growth is the main obstacle to development in many countries has become the cornerstone of official wisdom. This is not only stated in official publications, but it also influences budgetary considerations. This position—that one dollar invested in family planning is worth 100 dollars invested in more traditional fields—is still used as a justification for western concentration on population control.

Acceptance of the neo-Malthusian thesis contributes, no doubt, to much of the rhetoric of the emotionalism and crisis so evident in the writings of many of those in the population field. The dramatic quote from the writings of the Ehrlichs at the beginning of this chapter is the type of expression very frequently found in the work of the population-growth critics. Paul Ehrlich, who is both influential and widely respected, is one of those most convinced that doomsday is just around the corner unless drastic (and successful) steps are taken to halt the mushrooming population. The following quote from Anne and Paul Ehrlich quite adequately sums up this position:

> Spaceship earth is now filled to capacity or beyond and is in danger of running out of food. And yet the people traveling first class are, without thinking, demolishing the ship's already over-strained life-support systems. The food-producing mechanism is being sabotaged. The devices that maintain the atmosphere are being turned off. The temperature-control system is being altered at random. . . . In the past few years some people have begun to face the immensity of the spaceship's peril and have begun to grope for ways of avoiding catastrophe. But, unaware that there is no one at the controls of their ship, most of the passengers ignore the chaos or view it with cheerful optimism, convinced that everything will turn out all right. (Ehrlich and Ehrlich, 1972:3-4)

The Ehrlichs have accepted the challenge of combating the "cheerful optimism" of the ship's passengers in the hope that, if enough people are aroused and frightened, the necessary effort to salvage spaceship earth may be put forth.

Another widely respected scientist who has taken a strong position in favor of immediate efforts to halt population growth is Kingsley Davis. Davis is well-known for his emphasis on the need to change popular attitudes on desired family size. In this regard, he feels strongly that the many family planning organizations, which provide individuals with the knowledge and skills to have only a given number of children, are a highly ineffective method of population control. Noting that surveys confirm a popular desire for family limitation, Davis points out that if people continue to desire the number of children they currently desire, this will still result in rapid population growth. Davis feels that by sanctifying the doctrine that each woman should have the number of children she wants, and by assuming that if she has only that number, this will automatically curb population growth to the necessary degree, the leaders of current policies neglect the real issue of finding out why women desire as many children as they do, and how this desire can be modified. Further, many experts overlook the fact that a desire for and use of contraceptives is often compatible with high fertility, where desired family size remains high. According to this position, the problem of population limitation is basically a problem of attitude change, rather than a problem of technology, particularly in the developed countries. We know how to use the control techniques, and we desire to use them, but we don't use them to the degree necessary to stop population growth, according to Davis. Numerous other scientists and academicians are basically in agreement with the positions taken by Ehrlich and Davis. Some are willing to go even further.

Many of the individuals most concerned with the problem of continued population growth have played important roles in organizing or supporting groups such as Zero Population Growth (ZPG), International Planned Parenthood Federation, Congress on Optimum Population and Environment, Planned Parenthood-World Population, and related groups. Each of these organizations has developed ideologies around the necessity of population stabilization. The organizational and ideological characteristics of some of these groups will be covered in greater detail in the section on the population control movement.

Though their numbers may not be nearly as large, one also finds in the scientific community those who are unwilling to accept the assumptions upon which many of the doomsday predictions are made. One of the most eloquent spokesmen of this latter group is Samuel McCracken, Professor of Literature and Humanities at Reed College in Oregon. According to McCracken (1972:45), "Even though everyone knows that extravagance and intellectual fad are inextricably linked, the absurdities governing the thinking of many in the current population-control movement are likely to prove far more important to the course of society than almost any amount of countercultural nonsense."

According to McCracken, two problems seem to underlie the fear of those who say that disaster is imminent unless we attain zero population growth immediately. The first of these is the widespread espousal of the philosophy of neo-Malthusianism. The second concern, and one that has become very popular in the recent literature, is the problem of simple population density. It is the belief of many contemporary writers dealing with population growth that ". . . when people live together in numbers too great for a given area, the overcrowding thus induced causes that very fabric of society to be rent. It is in the teeming cities and gargantuan campuses that violence breaks out, for it is there that humans huddle together, compacted quite beyond their natural tolerance for each other" (McCracken, 1972:45).

Whether or not one concurs philosophically with such a view on the evils of population density, it must be recognized that there is simply not much reliable empirical data available about its effects. The data on certain animal populations show that overcrowding under experimental conditions leads to fighting, infanticide, and reduced population density. Whether the same would occur with a culture-producing animal such as man remains highly debatable. Most generalizations relating to the effects of density on human populations are based on limited observations and laboratory-type empirical data.

While McCracken certainly does not argue in favor of infinite population growth, he does urge a less biased and emotional look at the situation. As he notes (1972:46), "when someone asserts that the United States is overpopulated, I find myself wondering which United States he means. For the truth is that most Americans live at densities well below, sometimes startlingly so, the inhabitants of such well-conducted realms as Denmark and the Netherlands (which has a population density fifteen times greater than our own)."

What McCracken and many like him most fear about the population-control writers is the lengths to which some of them would go to achieve their ends. Most would start with the removal of any and all pro-natalist governmental policies and cultural practices, such as the income-tax deduction for children, and the glorification of motherhood and child-rearing in this country. It is only a short step to utilizing disincentives to reproduction such as breeding taxes, and then to more coercive restrictive practices such as fines and compulsory sterilization and abortion. Such proposals raise some very important questions if we think of them within the context of a free society. Should the right of dissent be denied to those who, because of their religious, philosophical, or other views, do not accept the premises upon which such policies are based? As McCracken (1972:50) puts it: "The extreme callousness of the movement's chief advocates when it comes to the rights of others is nowhere more apparent than in their treatment of the religious issues involved in such questions as abortion and contraception. Ehrlich divides the religious world as it relates to population control thus: there are two sorts of Catholics (or insert the religion of your choice). Enlightened Catholics agree with Ehrlich. Unenlightened Catholics, like Dwight Eisenhower's 'undiscerning Democrats,' exist only by implication, and while they must be pretty numerous, their views, being unenlightened, are worth neither credence nor constitutional protection."

Thus, while generally agreeing that unlimited growth is neither possible nor desirable, many cannot go along with those who would greatly limit the freedoms of today's society in order to attain the population policy they want. At the same time, many of the true believers in the population movement are convinced that any policy which strictly conforms to the notion of a free society, and holds back from using coercive measures, can only lead to the ultimate destruction of life on this planet.

McCracken has received support from other well-known figures in the scientific community. For example, Ben Wattenberg (1970:18-23), an anti-zero population growth advocate, argues that there simply is no need to implement radical programs to achieve population control, since the United States is already experiencing reduced growth through the operation of existing social, economic, and political factors. In his words: "The critical facts are that America is not by any standard a crowded country and that the American birth rate has recently been at an all-time low." According to Wattenberg, the problem is not one of population explosion, but rather one of population distribution. Here, of course, he is referring to the continued concentration of Americans in metropolitan areas. Wattenberg also feels that the hyper-emotional language used to describe the population crisis acts as a smokescreen to obscure many other legitimate related problems in the United States. This position has recently been echoed by a number of sociologists, including Bahr, Chadwick, and Thomas (1972:16), who argue that:

Identification of population growth as the critical problem of our time is a misplaced alarm that threatens us in at least two ways. First, it diverts attention and resources from other problems . . . second, there are the drastic costs to human freedom and dignity if many of the proposals for widespread population control are taken seriously and adopted.

McCracken, Wattenberg, and those who agree with them constitute a minority, perhaps a small minority, of the academic community. Nevertheless, their position is important if for no other reason than that it calls into question some of the excesses of the rhetoric of the doomsday prophets.

Political Publics and Interests

The religious, moral, and scientific interests discussed above have attracted much of the attention in the population debate. Other interests, however, are also noteworthy because of the particular position they express in relationship to the growth-no growth controversy.

Shifting Official Policies

Population control has now received the official support (at least verbally) of the United States government. On July 18, 1969, President Nixon made the following statement:

One of the most serious challenges to human destiny in the last third of this century will be the growth of the population. Whether man's response to that challenge will be a cause for pride or for despair in the year 2000 will depend very much on what we do today. If we now begin our work in an appropriate manner, and if we continue to devote a considerable amount of attention and energy to this problem, then mankind will be able to surmount this challenge as it has surmounted so many during the long march of civilization. (Commission on Population Growth and the American Future, 1972)

This statement indicates a basic shift in the traditional American mode of thought concerning population. America has been a growth-oriented nation, linking an expanding economy with an ever-increasing population. Also, the agrarian roots of American thought have infused the general culture with pro-natalism and an orientation against the restriction of family size. That is why President Nixon's speech takes on such importance; it is an official recommendation to view growth and population planning in a new light.

Zero Population Growth

The most widely known formal organization spearheading the anti-population growth movement today is Zero Population Growth, Inc. (ZPG). This organization, first incorporated in Connecticut in 1968, has been called "the only organization focusing on population control in the United States which is openly involved in political action" (Barnett 1971:759). Paul Ehrlich was elected as its first president in the spring of 1969. ZPG was formed as a nationwide nonprofit organization with the very explicit purpose of stabilizing population in the United States. From its onset, the organization has stated a willingness to utilize political, educational, and legal action to achieve its goals.

A number of other interest groups and organizations not dedicated primarily to containing population growth are nevertheless sympathetic to that objective and often lend cooperation and support to the no-growth movement. We have already discussed most of these in the chapters on the women's movement, abortion, family, and environment.

Anti-Population-Control Interests

We have noted above that some groups and individuals have taken an opposing position, for religious or scientific reasons, to the no-growth movement. More recently, representatives of several minority groups and of third-world governments have been making themselves known who oppose population control for essentially political reasons; i.e., because they fear it as an attempt by the dominant groups in the industrialized nations to maintain their own favored positions of power and control.

Dr. Charles V. Willie (1972:51-53), for example, has expounded on American minority group fears that family planning is simply a ruse for a plan of extermination initiated by whites. He states:

The genocidal charge is neither "absurd" nor "hollow" as some whites have contended. Neither is it limited to residents of the ghetto, whether they be low-income black militants or middle-aged black moderates. Indeed, my studies of black students at white colleges indicate that young educated blacks fear genocide. . . .

This fear has recently been echoed in a Progressive Labor Party Position Paper (1971), which argues that the essence of the zero population growth movement is nothing more than racist hysteria. The principal argument centers around the fact that political power comes from numbers, and that zero population growth is a program designed to stabilize or reduce minority numbers. Recent revelations that government funds and programs have been used to sterilize young black girls from poor families in the South, without their knowing what was really happening, have fed fuel to the fire.

However, it should not be assumed that the position of the PLP and of Willie is accepted by all blacks. The following quote clearly illustrates this:

Finally, one tall, lean dude went into deep knee-bends as he castigated the sisters to throw away the pill and hop to the mattresses and breed revolutionaries and mess up the (white) man's genocidal program. A slightly drunk lady from the back row kept interrupting with, for the most part, incoherent and undecipherable remarks. But she was encouraged finally just to step into the aisle and speak her speech, which she did, shouting the brother down in gusts and sweeps of historical, hysterical documentation of mistrust and mess-up, waxing lyric over the hardships, the oatmeal, the food stamps, the diapers, the suffering, and bloody abortions, the bungled births. She was mad as hell and getting more and more sober. She was righteous and beautiful and accusatory, and when she pointed a stiff finger at the brother and shouted "And when's the last time you fed one of them brats you've been breeding all over the city, you jive-ass so-and-so?" she tore the place up. (Cade, 1970:162-169)

Fears similar to those expressed by Willie have also been heard from several third-world nations in recent years. In some of these countries, nationalism, aspirations to great-power status, and racial pride combine to make successful family planning programs a near impossibility (Rowan, 1972). In interviews with government officials in several Latin American countries, Rowan (1972) reports that the majority express the belief that they need more, rather than fewer, people. For example, in Brazil the government emphatically disavows any policy of birth limitation. With an economic growth rate of 11 percent a year, Brazilian officials are convinced that they can afford a 3 percent population increase per year. Government leaders acknowledge that while in the past opposition to birth control programs may have been based on religious dogma, now such policies are based on the desire for Brazil to become a major world power.

A leader in Argentina also has frankly expressed the belief that the industrialized nations' preoccupation with birth control in underdeveloped countries is nothing more than racist escapism. Other third-world leaders are quick to point out that many leaders in the industrialized nations define the population problem as basically only a problem of the underdeveloped countries. They also note that consumption and use of natural resources per capita is much greater in the rich countries, and that, therefore, population increases in these countries means a much greater drain on the global supply of resources. Because of this, attempts by the United States and by the United Nations to commit some countries to a program of population control have become a touchy issue. Some countries simply do not care to have others telling them what to do. Each country is likely to consider its own national interests as more important than global problems.

Recognizing the delicacy of this issue, the United Nations, in the Tehran Conference on Human Rights in 1968, stated a policy supporting the right of every family to determine its own size. At the same time, the actions of the United Nations have been directed toward a policy of guaranteeing every individual the right to obtain necessary information so that he will be able to make a free and responsible choice on this important matter.

The differing interests of the industrial and the emerging nations came to the fore more sharply than ever at the UN-sponsored World Population Conference attended by 135 nations in Bucharest during August, 1974. The industrial nations had hoped to get widespread consensus for a global program of population control, but their proposals were so coolly received by the "third world" nations, and so watered down through compromises with them, that the 10,000-word "plan" finally adopted by the conference placed primary emphasis upon "economic and social development" (rather than upon population control itself) "in the solutions of population problems." In the process of its deliberations, the conference was presented with the anomaly of seeing the Vatican and Communist China on the same side as leaders of the so-called "anti-Malthusian bloc," opposing a strong position in favor of birth control. While many delegates and observers felt that the mere occurrence of such a conference at all was a hopeful sign, French agricultural expert Rene Dumont commented as the conference closed: "It will be said that the conference was convened on the eve of the greatest famine and that the conference failed to recognize it" (*San Francisco Sunday Examiner & Chronicle,* September 8, 1974:14).

National sovereignty and individual rights become critical concerns when national and international bodies become more involved in population policy and decision-making. It is clear, however, that so long as many of the beliefs expressed above are held by leaders and representatives of minority groups and of third-world countries, efforts to curb the world's population growth are likely to fail.

THE POPULATION-CONTROL MOVEMENT

While the call of God, according to Genesis 1:28, has been to "be fruitful and multiply," the call that goes out across the land today is likely to stress "making love, not babies," or "stopping at two, or one, or none." The focus of this book has been directed toward stressing the relation between social problems and their concomitant social movements. Certainly, we see that linkage in our problem for this chapter. Out of the growing population controversy there has been evolving a major population-control social movement which, in turn, has helped to define further the parameters of the problem and to increase the level of public concern about its nature.

Overview of the Population Control Movement

The movement to halt population growth in the United States has been largely a spontaneous public movement, but it is more and more frequently attracting support from influential groups as well as from governmental agencies. We have seen that, at least until quite recently, almost all action on the part of governmental bodies has been directed at increasing rather than decreasing population growth. Some recent changes that constitute an important component of the population control movement are now very evident.

As early as 1946, the United Nations had established a Population Commission concerned with population issues. Numerous foundations were also already at work in the United States and elsewhere promoting population study and analysis. Among the most important of these were the Rockefeller and Ford Foundations, the Population Council, and Pathfinder Fund. The International Planned Parenthood Federation* was helping to establish private family planning associations both here and abroad (Claxton, 1971).

However, the most important efforts to halt population growth were to come later. In 1959, President Eisenhower rejected, as inappropriate U.S. government interference, a recommendation that the United States assist countries asking for help to deal with their rapidly growing populations. President Kennedy, only two years later, recognized a need for action where population growth was outpacing economic growth, and took some of the first steps to help alleviate the situation (Claxton, 1971). In 1962, the United States joined with 68 other countries to adopt a United Nations resolution recognizing that economic and social development are closely interrelated with population policy, and authorizing studies to determine what type of birth-control assistance was needed, particularly in underdeveloped countries.

By 1965, President Johnson had brought the United States to full support of world population-control efforts. The United States Agency for International Development was authorized to set up missions in developing countries to assist with their family planning programs. From that point to the present, population-control efforts of the U.S. government have continued to expand, and now include involvement by the State Department, the U.S. Information Agency, the Peace Corps (volunteers in some countries devote most of their time to family-planning efforts), and numerous other agencies. The government has also supported and encouraged such efforts by private organizations, both national and international.

Official developments in the past decade, then, have changed remarkably and now constitute an important part of the population-control effort. Of perhaps even greater interest, however, is the development of citizen-based interest groups working to halt population growth. The earliest of these was Planned Parenthood (cf. above), which, at least until recently, has been more concerned with child-spacing and with preventing unwanted pregnancies than with population control

---

* The International Planned Parenthood Federation (IPPF) was founded in 1952, in large part through the influence of Margaret Sanger, as a federation of already existing national planned parenthood organizations. By 1960, IPPF included organizations from 54 countries, which were supported in part by funds from their own governments, from other international organizations, and from grants (Ehrlich and Ehrlich, 1972:310-311).

as such. The most important organization dedicated to curtailing population growth *in general* is Zero Population Growth (ZPG), whose activities are carried on at many levels.

Politically, ZPG actively lobbies both at the national level and in several key states. The organization currently maintains three full-time lobbyists in Washington, D.C., working to influence the passage of legislation favorable to efforts to curb population growth. Many of the local chapters are actively involved in political campaigns to support candidates who favor ZPG ideology. Unlike many similar organizations, ZPG has never sought tax-exempt status because of its desire to be free to lobby actively and to support political candidates favoring population stabilization policies.

Educationally, ZPG maintains a very active media campaign to familiarize the populace with its position, and with the dangers it sees in continued population growth. In support of this effort, ZPG has distributed over 500 "spot" television announcements to stations across the country. Filmstrips and other educational packets have been prepared by local chapters for distribution to and utilization in schools, churches, and other organizations.

On the legal level, ZPG has been involved in lawsuits in several states, opposing anti-abortion laws and fighting for the legalization of the dissemination of birth control information and materials. ZPG has also joined with several environmental concern organizations in bringing suit against companies with policies which they define as having detrimental environmental consequences.

The growth rate of ZPG has been nothing short of phenomenal. Beginning with approximately 100 members in 1968, the size of the organization had grown to roughly 3,500 by January, 1970, to 29,000 by January, 1971, and to 36,000 by May, 1971, with almost 400 local chapters (Barnett, 1971).

Barnett (1971, 1974) has conducted two mailed-questionnaire studies of the membership of ZPG. The first, conducted in the fall of 1970, when the membership was approximately 17,500, included a sample of 165 ZPG members drawn randomly from the organization's membership list. The second study, conducted in the spring of 1971, when the membership had almost doubled, produced 359 completed questionnaires. The following discussion of the movement's participants is taken largely from these two Barnett studies.

In the first place, Barnett notes that ZPG has been loosely structured from its very inception. Local chapters, as opposed to a clearly defined national hierarchy, have constituted the principal bases of the organization. Both at the national and the local levels, ZPG has had to rely heavily on volunteer workers to carry on much of the effort. However, there apparently has been no shortage of persons dedicated to population control who have been willing to work.

As for the background characteristics of the members of ZPG, Barnett's first study indicated the following: (1) members were highly homogeneous in race (only one of the 165 respondents was a non-Caucasian); (2) males outnumbered females almost two to one; (3) over one-third of the respondents were students; (4) slightly over half (56 percent) of the subjects were married; (5) 60 percent classified their political outlook as liberal, with 30 percent defining themselves as middle-of-the-road and only 10 percent as conservative; (6) in terms of religious preference, 65 percent were Protestant, 15 percent Catholic, 8 percent Jewish, 5 percent other, and 7 percent selecting no religion.

ZPG members were generally young (probably because many of the ZPG chapters are located on college and university campuses) and highly educated (57 percent had a bachelors degree or a graduate degree—again reflecting the university setting of many of the organization's chapters). The demographic characteristics of the respondents included in the second sample were not very different. A higher proportion of fulltime students and a lower proportion of Protestants were the only significant differences that appeared between the samples in the two studies.

Several questions in the studies dealt with attitudinal and behavioral patterns of the ZPG membership. As might be expected, since the ZPG upsurge coincided closely with the growth of environmental concern in this country, there was a significant overlap of membership in the two types of organizations. Forty-three percent of the ZPG members indicated membership in an environmental or conservationist organization such as the Sierra Club, or Friends of the Earth. Frequently, the goals as well as the concerns of the environmentalists and the population control groups are identical, and so one would expect their organizations to draw from the same general population.

The majority of ZPG members studied were childless at the time of the research, though this finding, again, must be viewed in light of the large number of student members. In terms of family-size intentions, most respondents were committed to having a maximum of two children (the mean number of intended children in the second study was about 1.5).

Respondents in both samples were asked to indicate what they felt would be the ideal population size for the United States. The results showed a mean ideal size for the first sample of 163 million, and for the second, 151 million. Most ZPG members, then, felt that the population of the United States has already become a good deal larger than they desired it to be.

Most of the members studied were in favor of government policies that would facilitate the limitation of population growth, though usually not for mandatory restrictions. Table 16-10 shows the attitudes of the two samples toward four general types of possible population control policies.

The approach most favored in both surveys was to place a tax on families that

TABLE 16-10 ZPG MEMBERSHIP ATTITUDES TOWARD CERTAIN POPULATION CONTROL POLICIES

	First Survey		Second Survey	
	Approve	Disapprove	Approve	Disapprove
Abolish all income tax deductions for children born in the future.	64%	32%	57%	34%
Give payment each year to those adults who have had no more than the number of children necessary to halt our population growth.	60%	29%	57%	32%
Place a tax on those adults who, in the future, have more children than necessary to halt our population growth.	78%	13%	77%	14%
Have the government limit, by law, the number of children a person can have to what is necessary to halt our population growth.	33%	51%	30%	52%

Source: Larry D. Barnett, "Zero Population Growth, Inc.," BioScience, 21 (July 5, 1971), 759-765; and Larry D. Barnett, "Zero Population Growth, Inc.: A Second Study," Journal of Biosocial Science 6 (January 1974):1-22

had more than the number of children necessary to halt population growth. Only about one-third of both samples approved of going so far as to have the government limit by law the number of children a family could have. It therefore appears evident that the more coercive policies advocated by some of the most vocal spokespersons of the population control movement in this country do not receive wide support from the general membership of groups interested in population limitation, even from those with the high level of commitment generally characteristic of joiners of ZPG. The more radical proposals, such as those calling for mandatory sterilization or abortion after a given number of children, would presumably receive even less support.

In terms of what are considered acceptable efforts to control population growth, Greene (1972:42-43) has noted that the movement as a whole can be divided into roughly three camps. First, there are the family-planning advocates who believe that through public information programs and through making available easy and safe means to prevent conception, individual families will reproduce, on their own throughout society, at a rate to attain ZPG. Second, there are those who feel that some sort of compulsion or coercion is necessary, and that a voluntary system will fail. According to this latter group, parenthood is not a right, and so methods of compelling adherence to a norm of small-family size should be adopted. Between these two groups fall what may be a majority (according to Barnett's data presented above) of members of the anti-population growth movement. Such persons stress economic incentives (eliminating tax advantages for larger families, rewarding couples with small families, etc.), but reject more coercive efforts.

The Natural History of the Population-Control Movement

An important part of the analysis of social movements throughout this book has been the use of a "natural history" model. Movements have been viewed as having their incipiency in shared frustration, need deprivation, or concern about the present course of events. Through the stage we have called coalescence, the movement then evolves into a more structured and cohesive organization of groups and individuals seeking to promote and influence change. Social problems, in this analysis, are seen largely as products of the efforts of movement participants and adherents. Continued coordination of the groups and individuals that have come to accept the movement's definition of social reality leads to more specific role definitions, divisions of labor, ideological developments, and so on. At this, the institutionalized stage of the movement's life-cycle, its influence on the host society is likely to be at its highest peak. Programs and philosophies are then frequently co-opted by the host society and, rather than continuing as blueprints for change, become a part of the status quo in rather attenuated form. At the same time, the host society suppresses the more extreme elements of the movement and destroys their influence. The history of the movement from this point on is usually one of fragmentation and demise.

The question of chief concern here is the extent to which this model can usefully be applied to the population movement. Clearly, this is one movement that has not yet worked itself through all the stages of its life-cycle. Nevertheless, the pattern that has developed is the familiar one. During the *incipient* years, organizations such as Planned Parenthood were little more than voices crying in the wilderness and were not primarily concerned with overall population trends. However, in the 1960's, a *coalescing* of other interests around some of the implicit elements of the Planned Parenthood ideology began to be evident. New and more radical voices were later added, leading to the formation of organizations such as ZPG, which espoused a more restrictive and interventionist philosophy on population issues. With growing public interest in environmental problems generally, the time was ripe for the rapid dissemination of the belief that the most serious environmental problem, and one out of which most of the others grew, was continued population growth. However, in accordance with what we have so often noted about the common discrepancy between "actual" reality and collectively defined reality, it is important to notice here that the founding of ZPG in 1968, amidst an atmosphere and rhetoric of crisis, took place a whole decade *after* the population growth rate in the United States had *already* begun a clear trajectory toward zero. Nevertheless, concurrent with the rapid growth in membership in the movement, was the growing acceptance of its beliefs by the general public and by official agencies. The previous section has shown the major changes in public attitudes and behavior patterns related to population growth which have taken place since the mid- to late-1960's.

The population-control movement is probably now in the stage of *institutionalization,* as indicated by the fact that many of the ideas espoused by the movement have evoked official responses from U.S. government agencies, from the United Nations, and from many other official bodies. Many of the policies supported by the movement have been reflected in changes in laws (for example, the 1973 Supreme Court ruling on abortion; cf. Chapter 12 on abortion), as well as in the attitudes and behavior patterns of the general public (cf. the concluding section of this chapter). As illustrated by the earlier discussion on publics involved in the population debate, the position taken by ZPG and related organizations has not been totally adopted, but it has been accorded widespread legitimacy, and finds ready advocates in government, in the media, and in numerous other arenas.

Will the future of the movement lead to *fragmentation* and *demise,* as our model predicts, or is the "problem" of population growth so well established that the movement will continue to grow and expand, both in size and in its impact on policy, on law, and on public preferences and lifestyles? Greene (1972) has noted what he feels is a mellowing of ZPG and other population control groups, as they increase in size, age, and public respectability—a pattern that appears again and again in our study of social movements. Thus, at this stage, it appears rather safe to predict a life-cycle for the population control movement that is consistent with the pattern of other groups examined in this book. Whatever the ultimate outcome of the movement, its legacy is already an important one. It is to this legacy that we now turn.

THE LEGACY OF THE POPULATION PROBLEM-MOVEMENT

In previous sections of this chapter it has been demonstrated that there is no one population problem and no one answer to the dilemmas posed by the various demographic processes occurring in this country and throughout the world. It is almost axiomatic that any "social problem" generates divergent groups and solutions. The actors in the American and world population debates usually have access to, and knowledge of, the same empirical data, but the varied, and often contradictory, interpretations of these data underscore the difficulty of attempting to analyze any social phenomenon from only one perspective. The introduction of ethics, ideology, perceived group needs, etc., adds extra ingredients to the debate, thus ensuring an almost incomprehensible tangling of the basic threads of the social problem with strands of different arguments. But it is these additional themes that sometimes become critical elements in viewing the full scope of the present population problem. This is particularly true of any attempt to assess the impact or legacy of the current population-control social movement.

Killian (1964) has noted that the significance of any social movement must be found in the consequences that movement has had for the larger society or social order from which it emerged. That is, has the movement led to any significant social or cultural change? Unless the answer to this question is in the affirmative, Killian feels, the movement is little more than a passing curiosity or a sidelight of history.

The Question of Cause and Effect

To evaluate the impact of the population-control movement is difficult for several reasons. In the first place, the movement is very much a contemporary one. ZPG is only a few years old and is still growing rapidly. Therefore, any comprehensive assessment of the legacy or impact of this group, and the various related population-control organizations, can probably not be made for several years. In terms of the natural history model that has been employed throughout this book, the population-control movement is scarcely in the middle of its "career." More problematic than this, however, in terms of the impact of the population-control movement, is the fact that many of the effects one would normally attribute to the movement have occurred concurrently or even prior to its recent rapid growth. For example, earlier we noted the significant changes that have occurred in attitudes and behavior related to population growth in the United States. More Americans than ever before view population increase as problematic, are more favorably disposed to using various birth control methods and practices, and desire smaller families. Fertility rates have been declining rapidly. However, most of these patterns had already become well-established before the rapid growth of the population control movement (cf. Figures 16-2 and 16-3). Consequently, it would be rather doubtful to attribute these changes to the movement itself. In fact, the causal arrow may very well run the other way: individuals who have already changed their attitudes and behavior patterns may be joining the movement as a more public expression of their commitment.

The central thrust of our argument here is that the relation of special interest groups to population changes is not at all clear. Although it appears that the philosophies and actions of these groups are greatly dependent upon the future course of demographic developments, it is not so apparent that the reverse proposition is true. If it is in fact correct to view population changes as resulting ultimately from such phenomena as industrialization, bureaucratization, and urbanization, then the impact of the population-control social movement itself may be seen as negligible.

However, we cannot be sure that the population-control movement has not had *any* effect in changing attitudes and fertility patterns. ZPG was founded in 1968 for the explicit purpose of publicizing the necessity of stopping population growth in the United States, and since that time, the following rather dramatic changes have taken place in population-related attitudes and behavior: the percentage of Americans who believe that population growth is a serious national problem has climbed by 65 percent, the birth rate has declined by 12 percent, the fertility rate has declined by 17 percent, and the expected family size has declined by 21 percent. These changes may or may not have occurred without the influence of ZPG and related interest groups.

Perhaps the most significant change is the major decline in desired family size. Kingsley Davis has convincingly argued that there is no reason to expect that decisions about ideal family size made by married couples will result in population control, unless they desire *small* families. It will result in more *planned* families, but could still lead to a rapidly expanding population. The problem, in Davis' view, is basically a motivational one—only when couples are strongly motivated to have small families will significant changes occur in population-growth patterns. As we have noted above, American couples now desire smaller families than at any other point in our history. Whatever their causal connection with the movement, these are important changes.

Also pointed out earlier is the fact that groups such as ZPG seem to be having their major impact on college campuses. Their information campaigns may be having important effects in influencing the newly married and the yet unmarried to have smaller families. It is also no doubt true that the population debate, spurred in significant part by the efforts of the population control groups, has played an important role in bringing the population issue to the attention of much of the broader public. The results of this are likely to include effects on fertility patterns such as those noted above.

Worldwide Changes in Official Policies

Attitude changes have not occurred among U.S. citizens only. To quote from Philip Hauser (1972:4):

Never before in the history of the world has there been so much attention devoted to the so-called "population problem." Individuals, public and private organizations, governments and international agencies are focusing on various aspects of population and are setting policies and devising programs on an unprecedented scale. To those who have been concerned with population problems over the course of the last generation . . . it is probably amazing to contemplate the developments in the last several years. It was unthinkable for most of the past generation that events that are now before us—the actions of the United Nations, of the World Health Organization, of the United States

Government, and of various religious bodies—could have occurred within the span of time over which we have been doing our work. . . .

That several of the specific changes implied in the Hauser quote can be seen, at least in part, as the legacy of the environmental movement, can be documented. Concerning U.S. population policy, when President Dwight D. Eisenhower indicated in 1959 that he felt the problem of population control was outside the realm of governmental concern, he probably rather accurately reflected the feelings of most Americans. In the decade and a half since then, official governmental statements have reflected the same types of changes as those which have occurred in public attitudes. The first official changes in the policies of the U.S. government were directed toward population growth in underdeveloped countries of the world. President Johnson's 1968 State of the Union Message pledged the support of the United States to help governments in developing countries to control their populations. At that point, official concern with U.S. population growth was not so clearly registered. However, only a year later, President Nixon was making it amply clear that the official position of his administration was one of concern with controlling population growth in the United States and elsewhere.

Since the late 1960's, agencies of the government such as the Department of Health, Education, and Welfare have become more and more actively involved in population control programs. In 1967 HEW appointed a Deputy Assistant Secretary for Population and Family Planning. And, though numerous statutes still on the books at that time prohibited the new secretary from actively disseminating birth control information, the new course had been established.* At present HEW is actively involved in providing assistance to various state and local family planning efforts all across the nation.

---

* Public advocacy of birth control through contraception actually began quite early, during the Industrial Revolution in England. Handbills and books on the subject began to appear as early as the 1820's and continued to circulate until the 1870's, when laws began to be passed to suppress them, both in England and in the United States. In the latter country, the most important legislation at the federal level was included in the so-called Comstock Act (see Chapter 10), which forbade the dissemination of birth control information and, of course, other sex-related literature, through the mails. Many states followed suit with what came to be called "little Comstock laws." In 1890, the importation of such literature, including birth control information, into the United States was forbidden. Family planning pioneers like Margaret Sanger, however, continued to circulate birth control information at considerable personal risk, and in 1916 she was jailed after opening the first birth control clinic in Brooklyn, New York. However, largely as a result of her efforts, the courts began to take an increasingly permissive posture toward birth control legislation and its enforcement, first allowing physicians to prescribe contraceptives for medical reasons, and gradually permitting wider dissemination of birth control information. Finally, in 1965, the Supreme Court ruled unconstitutional a Connecticut statute forbidding the use of contraceptives, and from that time on most states have struck down their own "Comstock laws." The old federal Comstock Law of 1873 still remains on the books, but it has of late received scant enforcement by the courts because of the many difficulties in interpreting it (Ehrlich and Ehrlich, 1972:305-306).

Both as a result of the efforts of HEW and of various voluntary units, most communities of significant size now operate birth control clinics. Only a decade ago, few cities had such units. Their effectiveness is greatest among minorities and lower-income persons. The middle class have always had their own private physicians available for counseling, and to provide them with the necessary technology and advice. To a greater extent now than ever before in history, birth control devices are generally available to all segments of the population.

Perhaps the most significant legal event that has occurred in this country, and given the population control movement a tremendous boost, was the 1973 Supreme Court decision approving abortion (cf. Chapter 12). This decision by the Supreme Court was no doubt influenced by the efforts of the participants in the population control movement. And, once the decision was made, several of these organizations moved quickly to help facilitate its implementation. *Newsweek* magazine (February 5, 1973) reported that almost immediately staffers at Planned Parenthood-World Population began making plans to help establish non-profit abortion clinics in 40 states, all of which would be linked by a toll-free nationwide telephone referral system. It is too early yet to assess the impact which the new abortion law has had, or is likely to have, upon our population figures. However, judging from the experience of Japan, which has permitted easy abortions for some years, we ought not to overestimate the difference that abortions are likely to make here upon our birthrates. A Japanese scholar has shown, through very thorough and careful research, that even in an age of "easy abortion," couples in Japan have continued to rely primarily upon contraceptive techniques, rather than upon abortion, for controlling family size. In fact, it appears from his research that abortion made only a negligible contribution to the relative stabilization of population in Japan during the 1950's and 1960's (Aso, 1971 and 1975). It is probably reasonable to infer from such research that while ready and legitimate access to abortion will be very important to individual women and their families, it will not make much of an impact upon population trends in general, beyond what is already made by sterilization and contraception.

ZPG and other groups in the movement have also had a good deal of success in challenging various state and local laws and statutes having implications for population control. Birth control information and devices have now been made available in many areas where they were outlawed only a few years ago.

Significant changes in attitudes toward population control are also readily evident on an international scale. The United Nations and its various agencies, such as the Pan American Health Organization, United Nations Children's Fund (UNICEF), the Food and Agricultural Organization (FAO), and the Economic Commission for Asia and the Far East (ECAFE), are all actively involved in supporting the efforts of individual countries directed toward population limitation. As mentioned above, the U.N.-sponsored World Population Conference in Bucharest in August, 1974, brought together most nations of the world for joint planning and policy-making to deal with problems of world population growth. This was the first world conference in which the problem of population control had comprised the principal business.

Also on an international scale, voluntary and private organizations such as International Planned Parenthood Federation, Planned Parenthood-World Population, Population Council, Population Crisis Committee, the Ford Foundation, and the Rockefeller Foundation are all now providing active leadership and assistance to many nations of the world. Further, as of the mid- or late 1960's, the U.S. Agency for International Development has become more active in furnishing technical and advisory help for population projects and programs in underdeveloped countries.

As for future projections, the opinions and actions of the interest groups discussed earlier in this chapter will continue to influence, as well as to depend upon, what happens in the United States and in the world, with respect to population growth, composition, and distribution. The further establishment of relationships between these phenomena and environmental deterioration, economic development, social disorganization, and individual rights will also play an important role in the future of these organizations. Those groups arguing more from an ethical than a utilitarian standpoint, such as the Catholic Church, will probably not alter their position greatly with respect to fertility control and the emphasis on large families; yet, even this may change if the problems of growth are greatly compounded in the future. It has already been shown that American Catholic families are more "American" than "Catholic," and the influence of this laity, combined with outside social pressure, could conceivably dictate a basic shift in papal philosophy.

Groups such as ZPG owe their existence to the perceptions and reactions of certain "moral entrepreneurs" concerning population trends and changes. Thus, their survival in their present form is directly linked with future demographic developments. Even ZPG has begun to shift its basic emphasis from national to global priorities. As the rate of growth of the United States' population slows down, more attention is being focused on the more serious issue of world overpopulation. Of course, the present trends in the United States are still unstable and in doubt, and the organization plans to continue its fight to reduce growth on the home front by attempting to inculcate its basic values in the American populace as a whole (Greene, 1972). But, if the trend toward replacement-level fertility continues indefinitely, the organization will, no doubt, need to shift its focus of interest, as has been done by numerous other social movements discussed in other chapters.

The future is not easily predictable in the sphere of population. The world's prospects appear to be more growth and increased spatial concentration in large metropolitan and supra-metropolitan areas. Combined with these processes, the United States can reasonably expect more racial segregation and increasing suburbanization. The basic question regarding the relationship between the groups that are involved in the population debate and these prospects is likely to remain one of to what extent their pronouncements, arguments, and rationales actually affect demographic processes. Again, this question awaits further analysis at a later stage of the life-cycle of the population control movement.

About the Contributors

This book is the joint endeavor of a number of sociologists, who have carefully integrated their efforts into a single work with a common theoretical perspective. The principal author of the book, Armand L. Mauss, is the sole author of Chapters 1 and 2, as well as coauthor of all the other chapters. The principal authors of Chapters 3-16 are identified below in alphabetical order, with their respective chapters indicated in parentheses.

Stan L. Albrecht (Chapters 15 and 16) is Associate Professor of Sociology at Brigham Young University (MA and PhD, 1970, Washington State University).

Richard R. Bennett (Chapter 3) (MA, 1970, Florida State University), is an NIMH Fellow and 1975 PhD candidate at Washington State University.

Reginald W. Bibby (Chapter 9) is Assistant Professor of Sociology at York University, Ontario (MA, University of Calgary, and PhD, 1974, Washington State University).

Lee H. Bowker (Chapters 13 and 14) is Associate Professor and Chairman of the Department of Sociology, Whitman College, Walla Walla, Washington (MA, University of Pennsylvania, and PhD, 1973, Washington State University).

Robert Davis (Chapter 6) (MA, 1969, Atlanta University), is an NIMH Fellow and 1975 PhD candidate at Washington State University.

Stuart C Hadden (Chapter 7) is Assistant Professor of Sociology at Indiana University (MA and PhD, 1973, Washington State University).

Clay W. Hardin (Chapter 16) (MA, 1973, Utah State University), is a 1975 PhD candidate and teaching assistant at Utah State University.

Jill Gilbert McKelvy (Chapter 10) (MSW, 1965, University of Washington) is a teaching assistant and 1976 PhD candidate at Washington State University.

Armand L. Mauss (principal author) is Associate Professor of Sociology at Washington State University (MA and PhD, 1970, University of California, Berkeley).

Michael J. Ohr (Chapter 4) (MA, 1972, Texas Christian University) is a teaching assistant and 1976 PhD candidate at Washington State University.

Lorne A. Phillips (Chapter 8), is Assistant Professor of Sociology and Associate Director of the Alcohol Studies Program at Washington State University (MS, Oklahoma State University, and PhD, 1973, Washington State University).

Vicki L. Rose (Chapter 12) (MA, 1972, University of Tulsa), is an NIMH Fellow and 1976 PhD candidate at Washington State University.

John M. Taves (Chapter 5), is Assistant Professor of Sociology at the University of Texas, Arlington (MA, University of Missouri, Kansas City, and PhD, 1975, Washington State University).

Julie Camille Wolfe (Chapter 11) (MA, 1973, Washington State University), is a teaching assistant and 1975 PhD candidate, Washington State University.

Bibliography

PROLOGUE, CHAPTERS 1 AND 2

Adorno, T. W., Else Frenkel-Brunswik, Daniel J. Levinson, and R. Nevitt Sanford
1950 The Authoritarian Personality. New York: Harper & Row.

Akers, Ronald
1973 Deviant Behavior: A Social Learning Approach. Belmont, Calif.: Wadsworth Publishing Co.

Banfield, Edward
1970 The Unheavenly City. Boston: Little, Brown & Co.

Becker, Howard S.
1963 Outsiders: Studies in the Sociology of Deviance. New York: The Free Press.
1966 Social Problems: A Modern Approach. New York: John Wiley & Sons.
1967 "Whose side are we on?" Social Problems 14 (Winter):239-247.
1971 "Reply to Riley's 'Partisanship and objectivity'." The American Sociologist 6 (February):13.

Berger, Peter L., and Thomas Luckmann
1967 The Social Construction of Reality. New York: Doubleday Anchor Books.

Birenbaum, Arnold, and Edward Sagarin
1972 Social Problems: Private Troubles and Public Issues. New York: Charles Scribner's Sons.

Blumer, Herbert
1951 "Collective behavior." *In* Alfred M. Lee (ed.), New Outline of the Principles of Sociology, 2nd ed., rev. New York: Barnes & Noble.
1971 "Social problems as collective behavior." Social Problems 18 (Winter):298-306.

Bredemeier, Harry C., and Jackson Toby (eds.)
1960 Social Problems in America. New York: John Wiley & Sons.

Breton, Albert, and Raymond Breton
1969 "An economic theory of social movements." American Economic Review 59 (May):198-205.

Brinton, Crane
1952 The Anatomy of Revolution, rev. ed. New York: Vintage Books.

Bryant, Clifton D. (ed.)
1970 Social Problems Today: Dilemmas and Dissensus. Philadelphia: J. B. Lippincott Co.

Cameron, William Bruce
1966 Modern Social Movements. New York: Random House.

Cantril, Hadley
1941 The Psychology of Social Movements. New York: John Wiley & Sons.

Carnoy, Judith, and Marc Weiss (eds.)
1973 A House Divided: Radical Perspectives on Social Problems. Boston: Little, Brown & Co.

Case, Clarence M.
1924 "What is a social problem?" Journal of Applied Sociology 3:268-273.

Chambliss, William J. (ed.)
1973 Problems of Industrial Society. Reading, Mass.: Addison-Wesley Publishing Co.

Chasteen, E.
1969 "Public accommodations: Social movements in conflict." Phylon 30 (Fall): 234-250.

Clinard, Marshall B.
1974 The Sociology of Deviant Behavior, 4th ed. New York: Holt, Rinehart & Winston.

Cloward, Richard, and Lloyd Ohlin
1960 Delinquency and Opportunity. New York: The Free Press.

Cohen, Albert K.
1955 Delinquent Boys. Glencoe, Ill.: The Free Press.
1959 "The study of social disorganization and deviant behavior." *In* R. K. Merton, et al. (eds.), Sociology Today. New York: Basic Books.

Cole, William E., and Charles H. Miller
1965 Social Problems: A Sociological Interpretation. New York: David McKay.

Cuber, John F., Robert A. Harper, and William F. Kenkel
1956 Problems of American Society: Values in Conflict, 3rd ed. New York: Henry Holt.

Davis, F. James
1970 Social Problems. New York: The Free Press.
Davis, Kingsley
1937 "The sociology of prostitution." American Sociological Review 2 (October): 746-755.
Denisoff, R. Serge
1968 "Protest movements: Class consciousness and the propaganda song." Sociological Quarterly 9 (Spring):228-247.
Dentler, Norman A. (ed.)
1972 Major Social Problems, 2nd ed. Chicago: Rand McNally.
Denzin, Norman K.
1970 "Who leads: Sociology or society?" The American Sociologist 5 (May):2.
Durkheim, Emile
1933 The Division of Labor in Society. New York: The Macmillan Co.
1951 Suicide. Glencoe, Ill.: The Free Press.
1961 The Elementary Forms of Religious Life. New York: Collier Books.
1964 The Rules of the Sociological Method. New York: The Free Press.
Duster, Troy S.
1970 The Legislation of Morality: Law, Drugs, and Moral Judgment. New York: The Free Press.
Dynes, Russell R., et al.
1964 Social Problems: Dissensus and Deviation in Industrial Society. New York: Oxford University Press.
Erikson, Kai T.
1966 Wayward Puritans. New York: John Wiley & Sons.
Frank, L. K.
1925 "Social problems." American Journal of Sociology 30:462-473.
Fuller, Richard C.
1937 "Sociological theory and social problems." Social Forces 4:496-502.
Fuller, Richard, and Richard Myers
1941a "Some aspects of a theory of social problems." American Sociological Review 6:24-32.
1941b "The natural history of a social problem." American Sociological Review 6: 320-328.
Gerson, Walter M. (ed.)
1969 Social Problems in a Changing World. New York: Thomas Y. Crowell.
Gliner, Robert
1973 American Society as a Social Problem. New York: The Free Press.
Glock, Charles Y. (ed.)
1973 Religion in Sociological Perspective (Chapter 16). Belmont, Calif.: Wadsworth Publishing Co.

Goffman, Erving
1961 Asylums. Garden City, New York: Doubleday & Co.
1963 Stigma: Notes on the Management of a Spoiled Identity. Englewood Cliffs, N.J.: Prentice-Hall.
Gouldner, Alvin W.
1968 "The sociologist as partisan: Sociology and the welfare state." The American Sociologist 3 (May):103.
Gusfield, Joseph R.
1955 "Social structure and moral reform: A study of the Women's Christian Temperance Union." American Journal of Sociology 61:221-232.
1967 "Moral passage: The symbolic process in public designations of deviance." Social Problems 15 (Fall):175-188.
1968 "The study of social movements." In International Encyclopedia of the Social Sciences. New York: Crowell, Collier, and Macmillan.
1970 (Ed.) Protest, Reform, and Revolt: A Reader in Social Movements. New York: John Wiley & Sons.
Heberle, Rudolf
1951 Social Movements. New York: Appleton-Century Crofts.
Heidt, Sarajane, and Amitai Etzioni (eds.)
1969 Societal Guidance: A New Approach to Social Problems. New York: Thomas Y. Crowell Co.
Hirschi, Travis
1969 Causes of Delinquency. Berkeley: University of California Press.
Hoffer, Eric
1951 The True Believer. New York: Harper & Row.
Hopper, Rex D.
1950 "The revolutionary process: A frame of reference for the study of revolutionary movements." Social Forces 28:270-279.
Horton, John
1966 "Order and conflict theories of social problems." American Journal of Sociology 71 (May):701-713.
Horton, Paul B., and Gerald R. Leslie
1970 The Sociology of Social Problems, 4th ed. Englewood Cliffs, N.J.: Prentice-Hall.
1974 The Sociology of Social Problems, 5th ed. Englewood Cliffs, N.J.: Prentice-Hall.
Hubbard, Jeffrey C.
1973 Mass Communication and Social Problems. Unpublished Ph.D. dissertation, Washington State University.
Huff, Darrell
1954 How to Lie with Statistics. New York: W. W. Norton & Co.

Johnson, Donald M.
1945 "The phantom anesthetist of Mattoon: A field study of mass hysteria." Journal of Abnormal and Social Psychology (April):145-186.

Johnson, Elmer H.
1973 Social Problems of Urban Man. Homewood, Ill.: Dorsey Press.

Julian, Joseph
1973 Social Problems. New York: Appleton-Century Crofts.

Kallen, David J., Dorothy Miller, and Arlene Daniels
1968 "Sociology, social work, and social problems." The American Sociologist 3 (August):3.

Kane, John J.
1962 Social Problems: A Situational-Value Approach. Englewood Cliffs, N.J.: Prentice-Hall.

Kavolis, Vytautas (ed.)
1969 Comparative Perspectives on Social Problems. Boston: Little, Brown and Co.

Killian, Lewis
1964 Social movements. In R. E. L. Faris (ed.), Handbook of Modern Sociology. Chicago: Rand McNally.

King, C. W.
1956 Social Movements in the United States. New York: Random House.

Kitsuse, John I., and Malcolm Spector
1973 "Toward a sociology of social problems: Social conditions, value-judgments, and social problems." Social Problems 20 (Spring):407-419.

LaBarre, Weston
1970 The Ghost Dance: Origins of Religion. Garden City, N.Y.: Doubleday & Co.

Landis, Judson R. (ed.)
1973 Current Perspectives on Social Problems, 3rd ed. Belmont, Calif.: Wadsworth Publishing Co.

Lang, Kurt, and Gladys Lang
1961 Collective Dynamics. New York: Thomas Y. Crowell.

Lemert, Edwin
1951 "Is there a natural history of social problems?" American Sociological Review 16:217-233.
1972 Human Deviance, Social Problems, and Social Control, 2nd ed. Englewood Cliffs, N.J.: Prentice-Hall.

Lindenfeld, Frank (ed.)
1973 Radical Perspectives on Social Problems, 2nd ed. New York: The Macmillan Co.

Lofland, John, and Rodney Stark
1965 "Becoming a world-saver: A theory of conversion to a deviant perspective."

Lofland and Stark, *cont.*
American Sociological Review 30 (December):6.

Lowry, Ritchie P.
1974 Social Problems: A Critical Analysis of Theories and Public Policy. Lexington, Mass.: D. C. Heath & Co.

McDonagh, Edward C., and Jon E. Simpson (eds.)
1969 Social Problems: Persistent Challenges. New York: Holt, Rinehart and Winston.

McLaughlin, Barry (ed.)
1969 Studies in Social Movements: A Social Psychological Perspective. New York: The Free Press.

Malcolm, Andrew H.
1974 "The great toilet tissue scare." San Francisco Sunday Examiner & Chronicle, February 17: "This World" section, p. 17.

Mauss, Armand L. (ed.)
1971a "The New Left and the Old." Journal of Social Issues 27 (July): entire issue.

Mauss, Armand L.
1971b "The lost promise of reconciliation: New Left vs. Old Left." Journal of Social Issues 27 (July):1-20.
1971c "On being strangled by the stars and stripes: The New Left, the Old Left, and the natural history of American radical movements." Journal of Social Issues 27 (July):185-202.

Medalia, Nahum Z., and Otto N. Larsen
1958 "Diffusion and belief in a collective delusion: The Seattle windshield-pitting epidemic." American Sociological Review 23 (April):180-186.

Merton, Robert K.
1957 Social Theory and Social Structure. Glencoe, Ill.: The Free Press.

Merton, Robert K., and Robert A. Nisbet
1971 Contemporary Social Problems, 3rd ed. New York: Harcourt, Brace, Jovanovich.

Messinger, Sheldon L.
1955 "Organizational transformation: A case study of a declining social movement." American Sociological Review 20 (February):3-10.

Miller, Walter B.
1958 "Lower-class culture as a generating milieu of gang delinquency." Journal of Social Issues 14:5-19.

Mills, C. Wright
1943 "The professional ideology of social pathologists." American Journal of Sociology 49 (September):165-180.
1959 The Sociological Imagination. New York: Oxford University Press.

Molotch, Harvey, and Marilyn Lester
1974 "News as purposive behavior: On the strategic use of routine events, accidents, and scandals." American Sociological Review 39 (February):101-112.

Moore, Wilbert
1963 Social Change. Englewood Cliffs, N.J.: Prentice-Hall.

Oberschall, Anthony
1973 Social Conflict and Social Movements. Englewood Cliffs, N.J.: Prentice-Hall.

Perrucci, Robert, and Marc Pilisuk (eds.)
1968 The Triple Revolution: Social Problems in Depth. Boston: Little, Brown & Co.

Petersen, William, and David Matza (eds.)
1963 Social Controversy. Belmont, Calif.: Wadsworth Publishing Co.

Quinney, Richard
1970a The Problem of Crime. New York: Dodd, Mead, & Co.
1970b The Social Reality of Crime. Boston: Little, Brown and Co.

Raab, Earl, and Gertrude J. Selznick
1964 Major Social Problems, 2nd ed. New York: Harper & Row.

Reissman, Leonard
1972 "The solution cycle of social problems." The American Sociologist 7 (February): 7-9.

Rose, Arnold M.
1968 "Law and the causation of social problems." Social Problems 16 (Summer): 33-43.

Ross, Robert, and Graham L. Staines
1972 "The politics of analyzing social problems." Social Problems 19 (Fall):2.

Rubington, Earl, and Martin S. Weinberg
1971 The Study of Social Problems: Five Perspectives. New York: Oxford University Press.
1973 (Eds.) Deviance: The Interactionist Perspective, 2nd ed. New York: The Macmillan Co.

Scanzoni, John (ed.)
1967 Readings in Social Problems. Boston: Allyn & Bacon.

Schaffer, Albert, et al.
1970 Understanding Social Problems. Columbus, Ohio: Charles E. Merrill Co.

Schur, Edwin M.
1965 Crimes Without Victims. Englewood Cliffs, N.J.: Prentice-Hall.
1971 Labeling Deviant Behavior. New York: Harper & Row.

Skolnick, Jerome H., and Elliott Currie (eds.)
1970 Crisis in American Institutions. Boston: Little, Brown & Co.

Skolnick and Currie (eds.), cont.
1973 Crisis in American Institutions, 2nd ed. Boston: Little, Brown & Co.

Smelser, Neil J.
1962 A Theory of Collective Behavior. New York: The Free Press.

Spector, Malcolm, and John I. Kitsuse
1973 "Social problems: A reformulation." Social Problems 21 (Fall):2.

Stewart, Elbert W. (ed.)
1972 The Troubled Land: Social Problems in Modern America. New York: McGraw-Hill Book Co.

Sumner, William Graham
1960 Folkways. New York: New American Library (Mentor).

Toch, Hans
1965 The Social Psychology of Social Movements. Indianapolis: The Bobbs-Merrill Co.

Troeltsch, Ernst
1931 The Social Teaching of the Christian Churches, 2 vols. New York: The Macmillan Co.

Tumin, Melvin M.
1968 "Some social consequences of research on racial relations." The American Sociologist 3 (May):117-123.

Turner, Jonathan H.
1972 American Society: Problems of Structure. New York: Harper & Row.

Turner, Ralph H., and Lewis M. Killian
1957 Collective Behavior. Englewood Cliffs, N.J.: Prentice-Hall.

Waller, Willard
1936 "Social problems and the mores." American Sociological Review 1 (December): 922-933.

Weber, Max
1957 The Theory of Social and Economic Organization. Glencoe, Ill.: The Free Press.
1964 The Sociology of Religion, esp. chapter 4. Boston: Beacon Press. (first published 1922)

Weinberg, S. Kirson
1970 Social Problems in Modern Urban Society, 2nd ed. Englewood Cliffs, N.J.: Prentice-Hall.

CHAPTER 3

Abrahamsen, David
1960 The Psychology of Crime. New York: John Wiley & Sons.

Alpren, David M.
1972 "Living with crime: U.S.A." Newsweek 80 (December 18):31-36.

Bibliography

Baker, Robert K., and Sandra J. Ball
1969 "Mass media and violence." Vol. 9 of The President's Commission on Causes and Prevention of Violence. Washington, D.C.: Government Printing Office.

Banton, Michael
1964 The Policeman in the Community. New York: Basic Books.

Bayley, David H., and Harold Mendelsohn
1969 Minorities and the Police: Confrontation in America. New York: The Free Press.

Becker, Howard S.
1963 Outsiders: Studies in the Sociology of Deviance. New York: The Free Press.

Bellush, Jewel, and Stephen M. David (eds.)
1971 Race and Politics in New York City. New York: Praeger Publishers.

Bennett, Richard R.
1971 "Towards a concept of police militancy." Paper delivered at the 16th Annual Conference on Corrections, Tallahassee, Florida.

Black, Donald J.
1970 "Production of crime rates." American Sociological Review 35 (August):733-748.

Black, Donald J., and Albert J. Reiss, Jr.
1967 "Patterns of behavior in police and citizen transactions." Studies in Crime and Law Enforcement in Major Metropolitan Areas, Volume II, Section I. Report of a Research Study Submitted to the President's Commission on Law Enforcement and the Administration of Justice. Washington, D.C.: Government Printing Office.

Block, Herbert A., and Gilbert Geis
1970 Man, Crime and Society. New York: Random House.

Block, Richard L.
1971 "Fear of crime and fear of the police." Social Problems 19 (Summer):91-101.

Blumberg, Abraham S.
1970 Criminal Justice. Chicago: Quadrangle Books.

Blumer, Herbert
1971 "Social problems as collective behavior." Social Problems 18 (Winter):298-306.

Bulletin, The
1974 "Citizens give reasons for unreported crime." Philadelphia, April 16.

Cameron, Mary Owen
1964 The Booster and the Snitch. New York: The Free Press.

Chevigny, Paul
1969 Police Power: Police Abuses in New York City. New York: Vintage Books.

Cipes, Robert M.
1968 The Crime War. New York: The New American Library.

Clark, Ramsey
1971 Crime in America. New York: Pocket Books.

Cloward, Richard A., and Lloyd Ohlin
1960 Delinquency and Opportunity: A Theory of Delinquent Gangs. New York: The Free Press.

Cohen, Albert K.
1955 Delinquent Boys: The Culture of the Gang. Glencoe, Ill.: The Free Press.

Conklin, John E.
1971 "Dimensions of community response to the crime problem." Social Problems 18 (Winter):373-385.

Conner, Walter D.
1972 "The manufacture of deviance: The case of the Soviet purge, 1936-1938." American Sociological Review 37 (August):403-413.

Cray, Ed
1972 The Enemy in the Streets. New York: Doubleday Anchor Books.

Cressey, Donald R.
1969 Theft of the Nation. New York: Harper & Row.

Daily Idahonian
1973 "Death penalty needed sometimes, says Nixon." (March 10). (Moscow, Idaho)

Dinitz, Simon, Russell R. Dynes, and Alfred C. Clarke
1969 Deviance: Studies in the Process of Stigmatization and Societal Reaction. New York: Oxford University Press.

Durkheim, Emile
1964a The Division of Labor in Society. New York: The Free Press.
1964b The Rules of Sociological Method. New York: The Free Press.

Eastman, George D., and Esther M. Eastman (eds.)
1969 Municipal Policies Administration. Washington, D.C.: International City Management Association.

Erikson, Kai T.
1966 Wayward Puritans. New York: John Wiley & Sons.

Federal Bureau of Investigation
1970 Uniform Crime Reports. Washington, D.C.: Government Printing Office.

Furstenberg, Frank F.
1971 "Public reaction to crime in the streets." The American Scholar 40 (Autumn):601-610.

Gallup, George
1967 Gallup Opinion Index: Report no. 27. Princeton, N.J.: American Institute of Public Opinion. (September):20.
1968 Gallup Opinion Index: Report no. 33. Princeton, N.J.: American Institute of Public Opinion. (March):14-17.
1972 Gallup Opinion Index: Report no. 82. Princeton, N.J.: American Institute of Public Opinion. (April):13.

Garmire, Bernard L.
1970 "The ghetto effect." Unpublished Police Research Project, Miami Police Department, Miami, Florida.

Glasser, William
1965 Reality Therapy. New York: Harper & Row.

Goffman, Erving
1959 The Presentation of Self in Everyday Life. Garden City, N.Y.: Doubleday Anchor Books.

Gourley, Douglas G.
1970 Effective Municipal Police Organization. Beverly Hills, Calif.: Glencoe Press.

Halleck, Seymour L.
1967 Psychiatry and the Dilemmas of Crime. New York: Harper & Row.

Haskell, Martin R., and Lewis Yablonsky
1970 Crime and Delinquency. Chicago: Rand McNally & Co.

Hissong, Jerry B.
1968 "The role of the church in preventing crime and delinquency." Federal Probation 32 (December): 50-54.

Hudson, James R.
1970 "Police-citizen encounters that lead to citizen complaints." Social Problems 18 (Fall):179-193.

Jones, Robert
1969 "Black vs. white in the station house." The Nation (October 13):368-370.

Kamisar, Yale
1969 When wasn't there a "crime crisis?" In Simon Dinitz, et al. (eds.), Deviance: Studies in the Process of Stigmatization and Societal Reaction. New York: Oxford University Press, pp. 30-40.

Knudten, Richard D.
1970 Crime in a Complex Society: An Introduction to Criminology. Homewood, Ill.: The Dorsey Press.

Kuykendall, Jack L.
1970 "Police and minority groups: Toward a theory of negative contacts." Police 15 (September-October): 47-54.

LaFave, Wayne R.
1965 Arrest: The Decision to Take a Suspect into Custody. New York: Little, Brown & Co.

Leary, Mike
1973 "Drinkers, not addicts, to blame for muggings, panel says." The Miami Herald (March 23):31A.

Leonard, V. A., and Harry W. More
1967 The General Administration of Criminal Justice. Brooklyn, N.Y.: The Foundation Press.

Levine, James P.
1970 "Methodological concerns in studying Supreme Court efficiency." Law and Society Review 4 (Summer):583-611.

McNamara, John H.
1967 "Uncertainties in police work: The relevance of police recruits' backgrounds and training." In David Bordua (ed.), The Police: Six Sociological Essays. New York: John Wiley & Sons.

Mannheim, Hermann
1967 Comparative Criminology. Boston: Houghton Mifflin Co.

Manning, Peter K.
1972 Observing the police: Deviants, respectables, and the law. In Jack D. Douglas (ed.) Research on Deviance. New York: Random House.

Marx, Gary T., and Dane Archer
1973 "The urban vigilante." Psychology Today 6 (January): 45-50.

Mass, Peter
1969 The Valachi Papers. New York: Bantam Books.

Miller, Walter B.
1958 "Lower-class culture as a generating milieu of gang delinquency." Journal of Social Issues 14:5-19.

More, Harry W.
1967 "A law enforcement association as a pressure group." Police 11 (May-June): 26-34.

Nation's Business
1967 "Businessmen-Partners in crime-busting." 58 (January):58-62, 89-90.

Nieburg, H. L.
1969 Political Violence: The Behavioral Process. New York: St. Martin's Press.

Niederhoffer, Arthur
1967 Behind the Shield. Garden City, N.Y.: Doubleday Anchor Books.

Nixon, Richard M.
1967 "What has happened to America?" Reader's Digest 46 (October):49-54.

Quinney, Richard
1970 The Social Reality of Crime. Boston: Little, Brown & Co.

Packer, Herbert L.
1972 "Two models of the criminal process." In George F. Cole (ed.), Criminal Justice: Law and Politics. Belmont, Calif.: Duxbury Press, pp. 35-52.

President's Commission on the Causes and Prevention of Violence.
1969 Law and Order Reconsidered. Washington, D.C.: Government Printing Office.

President's Commission on Law Enforcement and the Administration of Justice
1967a The Challenge of Crime in a Free Society. Washington, D.C.: Government Printing Office.
1967b Task Force Report: Crime and Its Impact—An Assessment. Washington, D.C.: Government Printing Office.
1967c Task Force Report: Organized Crime. Washington, D.C.: Government Printing Office.

Remsberg, Charles, and Bonnie Remsberg
1968 "The amazing anti-crime crusade of Indianapolis women." Good Housekeeping (February):86-87.

Sheehy, Gail
1972a "Cleaning up hell's bedroom." New York Magazine 5 (November 13):50-66.
1972b "The landlords of hell's bedroom." New York Magazine 5 (November 20): 67-80.

Skolnick, Jerome H.
1967 Justice Without Trial: Law Enforcement in Democratic Society. New York: John Wiley & Sons.
1969 The Politics of Protest: Violent Aspects of Protest and Confrontation. A Staff Report to the National Commission on the Causes and Prevention of Violence. Washington, D.C.: Government Printing Office.

Stark, Rodney
1972 Police Riots. Belmont, Calif.: Wadsworth Publishing Co.

Sutherland, Edwin
1947 Principles of Criminology. Philadelphia: J. B. Lippincott Co.
1969 The diffusion of sexual psychopath laws. In William J. Chambliss (ed.), Crime and the Legal Process. New York: McGraw-Hill Book Co.

Taylor, Ian, et al.
1973 The New Criminology: For a Social Theory of Deviance. New York: Harper Torchbooks.

Turner, William W.
1970 Hoover's F.B.I. New York: Dell Publishing Co.

Tyler, Gus
1971 Organized Crime in the United States. Ann Arbor: The University of Michigan Press.

United States Civil Rights Commission
1965 Law Enforcement: A Report on Equal Protection in the South. Washington, D.C.: Government Printing Office.

U.S. News & World Report
1967 "Johnson's War on Crime." 62 (February 20): 48.
1970 "Citizens War on Crime: Spreading across the United States." 68 (March): 55-58.

Wilson, James Q.
1968 Varieties of Police Behavior. Cambridge, Mass.: Harvard University Press.

Wilson, Orlando W., and Roy C. McLaren
1972 Police Administration. New York: McGraw-Hill Book Co.

Wolfgang, Marvin E., and Franco Ferracuti
1967 The Subculture of Violence. London: Tavistock.

CHAPTER 4

Addams, Jane (ed.)
1925 The Child, the Clinic and the Court. New York: New Republic.

Baker, Gordon H., and W. Thomas Adams
1963 "Glue sniffers." Sociology and Social Research 47:298-310.

Blackman, A.
1971 "Street gangs go conservative." Spokane Daily Chronicle (November 22):35.

Bowlby, John
1952 Maternal Care and Mental Health. Geneva: World Health Organization.

Brace, Charles Loring
1876 The Dangerous Classes of New York and Twenty Years' Work Among Them. New York: Wynkoop and Hallenbeck.

Brockway, Zebulon R.
1878 "Prison discipline in general." Proceedings of the Annual Conference of Charities. Cincinnati:106-111.
1912 Fifty Years of Prison Service. New York: Charities Publication Committee.

Caldwell, Peter
1886 "The reform school problem." Proceedings of National Conference of Charities and Corrections. St. Paul:71-76.

Carver, Lyell, and Paul A. While
1968 "Constitutional safeguards for the juvenile offender." Crime and Delinquency 14 (January):63-72.

Cavan, Ruth S., and Jordan T. Cavan
1968 Delinquency and Crime: Cross-Cultural Perspectives. New York: J. B. Lippincott Co.

Cloward, Richard A., and Lloyd E. Ohlin
1960 Delinquency and Opportunity. New York: The Free Press.

Cohen, Albert K.
1955 Delinquent Boys. New York: The Free Press.

Cohen, Albert K., and James P. Short, Jr.
1971 "Juvenile delinquency." *In* Robert K. Merton and Robert A. Nisbet (eds.), Contemporary Social Problems, revised ed. New York: Harcourt-Brace & World.

Deutscher, Irwin
1960 "Some relevant directions for research in juvenile delinquency." *In* Arnold M. Rose (ed.), Human Behavior and Social Processes. Boston: Houghton Mifflin Co., 1962, pp. 468-480.

Durkheim, Emile
1938 Rules of Sociological Method. New York: The Free Press.
1951 Suicide: A Study in Sociology. New York: The Free Press.

Empey, LaMar
1967 "Delinquency theory and recent research." Journal of Research in Crime and Delinquency 4 (January):28-42.

Folks, Homer
1891 "The Care of Delinquent Children." *In* Proceedings of National Conference of Charities and Corrections. Indianapolis: 136-150.

Gallup Opinion Index
1972a Report No. 82 (April).
    Princeton, N.J.: American Institute of Public Opinion.
1972b Report No. 87 (Sept.).
    Princeton, N.J.: American Institute of Public Opinion.

Glueck, Sheldon, and Eleanor T. Glueck
1934 One Thousand Juvenile Delinquents. Cambridge, Mass.: Harvard University Press.
1963 "Toward further improving the identification of delinquents." Journal of Criminal Law, Criminology and Police Science 54:178-180.

Gould, L.
1969 "Who defines delinquency." Social Problems 16 (Winter):325-336.

Henderson, Charles R.
1905 "Juvenile courts: Problems of administration." Charities 13 (January):340-343.

H. E. W.
1969 Juvenile Court Statistics, Stat. Ser. 2, Children's Bureau, U.S. Dept. of Health, Education, and Welfare. Washington, D.C.: Government Printing Office.

Humphrey, Mary E. (ed.)
1939 Speeches, Addresses, and Letters of Louise de Koven Bowen, 2 vols. Ann Arbor, Mich.: Edward Brothers.

Kittrie, Nicholas N.
1971 The Right to Be Different. Baltimore: The Johns Hopkins University Press.

Lefstein, Norman, Vaughan Stapleton, and Lee Teitelbaum
1969 "In search of juvenile justice—Gault and its implementation." Law and Society Review 13 (May):491-537.

Lees, J. P., and L. J. Newsome
1954 "Family or sibship position and some aspects of juvenile delinquency." British Journal of Juvenile Delinquency 5 (July):46-65.

Lemert, Edwin M.
1970 Social Action and Legal Change: Revolution Within the Juvenile Court. Chicago: Aldine Publishing Co. (esp. p. 4)

Loble, Lester H., and Max Wylie
1967 Delinquency Can Be Stopped. New York: McGraw-Hill Book Co.

McKay, Henry D., and Solomon Kobrin
1966 Nationality and Delinquency. Chicago: Institute of Juvenile Research, Department of Mental Health, State of Illinois.

Mead, George
1934 Mind, Self and Society. Chicago: University of Chicago Press.

Merton, Robert K.
1957 Social Theory and Social Structure. Glencoe, Ill.: The Free Press.

National Council on Crime and Delinquency
1972 Children's Rights. Crime and Delinquency Literature 4 (3):449-477.

Ohr, Michael J.
1972 "Some Factors in Juvenile Delinquency: An Interactionist Study." Unpublished M.A. thesis, Texas Christian University.

Platt, Anthony M.
1969 The Child Savers. Chicago: The University of Chicago Press.

Pound, Roscoe
1944 "The juvenile court and the law." National Probation and Parole Association Yearbook. New York: 1945.

Powell, J. C.
1891 The American Siberia. New York: H. J. Smith.

Bibliography

President's Commission on Law Enforcement and Administration of Justice
1967 "Facts about delinquency." *In* Rose Giallombardo (ed.), Juvenile Delinquency: A Book of Readings, 2nd ed. New York: John Wiley & Sons, pp. 37-42.

Reckless, Walter C., Simon Dinitz, and Ellen Murray
1956 "Self-concept as an insulator against delinquency." American Sociological Review 21 (December):744-746.

Richardson, Anne B.
1892 "The cooperation of woman in philantrophy." *In* Proceedings of National Conference of Charities and Corrections. Denver:216-222.

Schwartz, Michael, and Sheldon Stryker
1970 Deviance, Selves and Others. The Arnold and Caroline Rose Monograph Series in Sociology. Washington, D.C.: American Sociological Association.

Shaw, Clifford R., and Henry D. McKay
1942 Juvenile Delinquency and Urban Areas. Chicago: University of Chicago Press.

Short, James F., Jr.
1973 "Gangs, Politics, and Social Order." Unpublished paper for the National Institute of Mental Health, Research Grant MH 2072.

Short, James F., Jr., and I. Nye
1957 "Reported behavior as a criterion of deviant behavior." Social Problems 5 (Winter):207.

Slocum, W. L., and Carol L. Stone
1961 "Delinquent-type behavior of farm and non-farm teenagers." Unpublished paper read at Conference on Current Research in Delinquency of the Washington State Department of Institutions, University of Puget Sound, Tacoma, Wash.

Spielberger, Adele, and Roland Chilton
1971 "Is delinquency increasing?" Social Forces 49 (March):487-493.

Sutherland, Edwin H., and Donald Cressey
1966 Principles of Criminology, 7th ed. New York: J. B. Lippincott Co.

Tangri, Sandra S., and Michael Schwartz
1967 "Delinquency research and the self-concept variables." Journal of Criminal Law, Criminology and Police Science 58 (June):182-190.

Teeters, Negley K., and John Otto Reinemann
1950 The Challenge of Delinquency. Englewood Cliffs, N.J.: Prentice-Hall.

Thomas, Shailer, Wilber B. Brookover, Jean LePere, Don Hamachek, and Edsel Erickson
1964 "The Effects of Three Treatment Conditions on Changing Self-Concept and Achievement." Unpublished.

Wines, Enoch C.
1880 The State of Prisons and of Child-saving Institutions in the Civilized World. Cambridge, Mass.: Harvard University Press.

Winslow, Robert W.
1969 Juvenile Delinquency in a Free Society. Belmont, Calif.: Dickenson Publishing Co.

Yablonsky, Lewis
1970 The Violent Gang. Baltimore: Penguin Books (rev. ed.).

CHAPTER 5

"A 'bill of rights for prisoners' is backed by 450 civic leaders."
1972 The New York Times 23 (February 16):4.

"Abolishing the death penalty."
1925 Literary Digest 86 (August):29.

Alexander, Myrl E.
1954 "Do our prisons cost too much?" Annals of the American Academy of Political and Social Science 293 (May):35-41.

Alper, Benedict S., and Jerry F. Boren
1972 Crime: International Agenda. Lexington, Mass.: D. C. Heath & Co.

"Attica's legacy."
1971 Newsweek 78 (October 4):23.

Auditor General and the Legislative Analyst, State of California
1971 "A review of the economic efficiency of California correctional industries." Sacramento.

Augustus, John
1939 John Augustus: First Probation Officer. New York: National Probation Association.

Barnes, Harry E., and Negley K. Teeters
1959 New Horizons in Criminology, 3rd ed. Englewood Cliffs, N.J.: Prentice-Hall.

Bates, Sanford
1954 "The prison: asset or liability?" Annals of the American Academy of Political and Social Science 293 (May):1-9.

Bedau, Hugo A.
1967a The Death Penalty in America. Garden City, N.Y.: Doubleday Anchor Books.
1967b "The issue of capital punishment." Current History 53 (August):82-87 ff.

Bennett, James V.
1964 "Evaluating a prison." Annals of the American Academy of Political and Social Science 293 (May):10-16.

Berck, Martin G.
1973 "The death penalty: A lot of Americans don't want to let it go." Lewiston (Ida.) Morning Tribune (July 19):5.

Brockway, Zebulon R.
1912 Fifty Years of Prison Service. New York: Charities Publication Committee.

Burns, Robert E.
1932 I Am a Fugitive from a Georgia Chain Gang. New York: Grosset & Dunlap.

Calvert, Roy
1971 Capital Punishment in the Twentieth Century. Port Washington, N.Y.: Kennikat Press.

Christian Century
1961 "Episcopalians oppose the death penalty." 78 (March 29):382.

Chute, Charles L., and Marjorie Bell
1956 Crime, Courts and Probation. New York: The Macmillan Co.

Clemmer, Donald
1968 The Prison Community. New York: Holt, Rinehart & Winston.

"Closing death row."
1972 Time 100 (July 10):37.

Cohen, Morris R.
1971 "Moral aspects of punishment." *In* Leon Radzinowicz and Marvin E. Wolfgang (eds.), Crime and Justice 2. New York: Basic Books, pp. 27-42.

Commission on Vocational Education in Correctional Institutions
1971 "Interim report." Legislative Research Checklist 14 (November):210.

Conrad, John P.
1967 "Prisons and prison reform." Current History 58 (August): 88-93.
1971 "The need for prison reform." Current History 61 (August):87-91.

"Counsel for the doomed."
1963 Newsweek 61 (March 25):36-37.

"The Court on the death penalty."
1972 Newsweek 80 (July 10):20.

Crawford, William
1969 Penitentiaries of the United States. Montclair, N.J.: Patterson Smith.

Daniels, Stephanie
1974 "Looking at prison reform." San Francisco Sunday Examiner & Chronicle (March 3):California Living magazine section.

Darrow, Clarence
1922 Crime: Its Cause and Treatment. New York: Thomas Y. Crowell.

"Death for the death penalty."
1965 Time 85 (April 2):62-63.

"The death penalty."
1920 The Survey 43 (February 21):619-620.

"The death penalty as a preventive of crime."
1901 Annals of the American Academy of Political and Social Science 17 (March): 366-369.

England, Ralph W.
1961 "New departures in prison labor." The Prison Journal 41 (Spring):21-36.

Erikson, Kai T.
1966 Wayward Puritans: A Study in the Sociology of Deviance. New York: John Wiley & Sons.

Federal Bureau of Investigation
1960-72 Uniform Crime Reports. Washington, D.C.: Government Printing Office.

Federal Prison Industries
1966 Annual Report. Washington, D.C.: Government Printing Office.
1967 Annual Report. Washington, D.C.: Government Printing Office.
1971 Annual Report. Washington, D.C.: Government Printing Office.
1972 Annual Report. Washington, D.C.: Government Printing Office.

Felkenes, George T.
1968 "Sterilization and the law." *In* Harold K. Becker, et al. (eds.), New Dimensions in Criminal Justice. Metuchen, N.J.: Scarecrow Press.

Georgia Legislature Penal Affairs Study Committee
1971 Report (February).

Gibbons, Don C.
1974 "Punishment, treatment, and rehabilitation." New York: MSS Modular Publications, no. 67.

Glaser, Daniel
1970 "Prison work and subsequent employment." *In* Norman Johnston, Leonard Savitz, and Marvin Wolfgang (eds.), The Sociology of Punishment and Correction. New York: John Wiley & Sons, pp. 509-516.

Grünhut, Max
1948 Penal Reform. Oxford, Eng.: The Clarendon Press.

"History of the movement to establish a house of detention for untried adults in Philadelphia."
1961 The Prison Journal 41 (Autumn Supplement):1-8.

Hopper, Columbus B.
1970 "The conjugal visit." *In* Norman Johnston, Leonard Savitz, and Marvin Wolfgang (eds.), The Sociology of Punishment and Correction. New York: John Wiley & Sons, pp. 455-459.

Irwin, John
1970 The Felon. Englewood Cliffs, N.J.: Prentice-Hall.

Kirchway, George W.
1927 "The question of capital punishment." Congressional Digest 6 (August-September):219-244.

Koeniger, Rupert C.
1951 "What about self-mutilation?" The Prison World (March-April):3-6, 30.

Koestler, Arthur
1957 Reflections on Hanging. New York: The Macmillan Co.

Lawes, Lewis E.
1924 Man's Judgment of Death. New York: G. P. Putnam's Sons.

Leary, Mary E.
1972 "California views the death penalty." America 127 (August 5):55-59.

Life
1960 "Big debate on capital punishment." 48 (May 9):45.
1971 "Opening the gates to new prison reform." 71 (August 13):24-29.

McAnany, Patrick D.
1971 "Punishment as reflected in prevailing ideologies." *In* Leon Radzinowicz and Marvin E. Wolfgang (eds.), Crime and Justice 2. New York: Basic Books, pp. 113-144.

McClellan, Grant S.
1961 Capital Punishment. New York: The H. W. Wilson Co.

McCorkle, Lloyd W.
1970 "Group therapy with offenders." *In* Norman Johnston, Leonard Savitz, and Marvin Wolfgang (eds.), The Sociology of Punishment and Correction. New York: John Wiley & Sons, pp. 517-524.

MacCormick, Austin H.
1954 "Behind the prison riots." Annals of the American Academy of Political and Social Science 293 (May):17-27.

Marshall, Jack
1974 "Death penalty bid rejected." Lewiston (Ida.) Morning Tribune (June 27):5.

Martinson, Robert
1974 "What works? Questions and answers about the rehabilitation of prisoners." Public Interest (Spring).

Mather, Boyd P.
1971 "Iowa: death penalty abolished." Christian Century 82 (March 24):382.

Menninger, Karl
1968 The Crime of Punishment. New York: The Viking Press.

Merrill, Lois T.
1945 "The puritan policeman." American Sociological Review 10 (December):766-776.

Mitford, Jessica
1971 "Kind and usual punishment in California." Atlantic Monthly (March).
1973 Kind and Usual Punishment: The Prison Business. New York: Alfred A. Knopf.

Morris, Albert
1934 Criminology. New York: Longmans, Green & Co.

Morris, Norval
1965 "Prison in evolution." *In* Tadeusz Grygier, Howard Jones, and John C. Spencer (eds.), Criminology in Transition. London: Tavistock Publications Ltd., pp. 267-292.
1971 "Reform: It must come." Life 71 (September 24):36.

Nation
1971 "The churches and the noose." 213 (September 20):228.

National Opinion Research Center
1972 Spring Social Survey Codebook. Chicago: National Opinion Research Corp., University of Chicago.

New York Prison Association
1910 Annual Report. Albany, N.Y.: J. B. Lyon.

New York State Special Commission on Attica
1972 Attica: The Official Report of the New York State Special Commission on Attica. New York: Praeger Publishers.

New York Times
1972 "Attica prisoners have gained most points made in rebellion." (September 12):1.

"No. 77."
1967 Time 89 (June 9):33.

Ohlin, Lloyd E.
1971 "The effect of social change on crime and law enforcement." *In* Leonard J. Levy (ed.), The Challenge of Crime in a Free Society. New York: Da Capo Press, pp. 24-36.

"Outside on the job."
1962 Time 80 (September 14):33.

Petersen, Larry R.
1974 "Religion and the right to life: Religious and social determinants of attitudes toward abortion and capital punishment." Unpublished M.A. thesis, Washington State University.

Playfair, Giles
1957 "Is the death penalty necessary?" Atlantic Monthly 200 (September):31-35.

Powers, Edwin
1966 Crime and Punishment in Early Massachusetts: 1620-1692. Boston: Beacon Press.

Powers, Sanger B.
1958 "Day-parole of misdemeanants." Federal Probation 22 (December):42-46.

"The question of capital punishment."
1927 The Congressional Digest 6 (August-September):219-244.

Robinson, Louis N.
1931 Should Prisoners Work? Philadelphia: John C. Winston.

Rose, Gordon
1961 The Struggle for Penal Reform. Chicago: Quadrangle Books.

Schardt, Arlie
1973 "Washington report: Death penalty." Civil Liberties 297 (July). New York: ACLU.

Silver, Isidore
1972 "Death and the judges." Commonweal 96 (April 4):136-138.

Steiner, Jesse F., and Roy M. Brown
1927 The North Carolina Chain Gang. Chapel Hill, N.C.: University of North Carolina Press.

Stewart, Tom
1974 "The death rows are filling up." San Francisco Sunday Examiner & Chronicle (April 14):This World section, p. 20.

Sutherland, E. H., and D. R. Cressey
1966 Principles of Criminology, 7th ed. Philadelphia: J. B. Lippincott Co.
1970 Principles of Criminology, 8th ed. Philadelphia: J. B. Lippincott Co.

Taft, Donald R., and Ralph W. England, Jr.
1971 Criminology, 7th printing. New York: The Macmillan Co.

Tannenbaum, Frank
1933 Osborne of Sing Sing. Chapel Hill, N.C.: University of North Carolina Press.

Teeters, Negley K.
1937 They Were in Prison. Philadelphia: John C. Winston.
1952 "A limited survey of some prison practices and policies." The Prison World 14 (May-June):5-8, 29.
1955 The Cradle of the Penitentiary: The Walnut Street Jail, 1773-1835. Philadelphia: University of Pennsylvania Press.
1967 Hang by the Neck. Springfield, Ill.: Charles C Thomas.

Teeters, Negley K., and John D. Shearer
1957 The Prison at Philadelphia: Cherry Hill. New York: Columbia University Press.

Time
1967 "Stirrings on death row." 89 (April 21):25.
"Toward a more humane society."
1965 Christian Century 82 (March 3):261.
"The ultimate question."
1971 Nation 212 (May 17):610-611.

United States Bureau of Prisons
1930 Annual Report. Washington, D.C.: Government Printing Office.
1952 National Prisoner Statistics, Bulletin no. 5. Washington, D.C.: Government Printing Office.
1963 National Prisoner Statistics, Bulletin no. 42. Washington, D.C.: Government Printing Office.
1969 National Prisoner Statistics, Bulletin no. 45. Washington, D.C.: Government Printing Office.
1971a National Prisoner Statistics, Bulletin no. 46. Washington, D.C.: Government Printing Office.
1971b Statistical Report: Fiscal Years 1969 and 1970. Washington, D.C.: Government Printing Office.
1973 Statistical Report: Fiscal Years 1971 and 1972. Washington, D.C.: Government Printing Office.

U.S. News & World Report
1971 "Signs of an end to death row." 70 (May 31):37-38.

Warren, Marguerite Q.
1970 "The community treatment project." In Norman Johnston, Leonard Savitz, and Marvin Wolfgang (eds.), The Sociology of Punishment and Correction. New York: John Wiley & Sons, pp. 671-683.

Wilkins, Leslie T.
1969 Evaluations of Penal Measures. New York: Random House.

Wilson, James Q.
1974 "Crime and the criminologists." Commentary 58 (July):47-53.

Wisconsin Council on Criminal Justice
1972 Final Report of the Citizens Study Committee on Offender Rehabilitation. Madison, Wis.

"Women poisoners: Death meted out in U.S. and England, despite opposition."
1936 Literary Digest 122 (July 25):30.

Zalba, Serapio R.
1970 "Work-release." In Norman Johnston, Leonard Savitz, and Marvin Wolfgang (eds.), The Sociology of Punishment and Correction. New York: John Wiley & Sons, pp. 693-698.

CHAPTER 6

American Council on Education
1971 Campus Unrest, 1969-70. Washington, D.C.

Aries, Philippe
1965 Centuries of Childhood. New York: Vintage Books.

Altbach, Philip G., and Patti Peterson
1971 "Before Berkeley: Historical perspectives on American student activism." The Annals of the American Academy of Political and Social Science 395 (May):12.

Bayer, A. E., and A. W. Austin
1969 "Violence and disruption on U.S. campuses." Educational Record (Fall): table 6.

Bayley, David H.
1962 "The pedagogy of democracy: Coercive public protest in India." American Political Science Review 56 (September):663-672.

Boskin, Joseph, and Robert A. Rosenstone
1969 "Protest in the sixties." The Annals of the American Academy of Political and Social Science 382 (March):1.

Boulding, Kenneth E.
1969 "Toward a theory of protest." *In* Walt Anderson (ed.), The Age of Protest. Pacific Palisades, Calif.: Goodyear Publishing Co.

Broyles, Allen J.
1964 The John Birch Society. Boston: Beacon Press.

Buckman, Peter
1970 The Limits of Protest. New York: Bobbs-Merrill Co.

Chambers, Bradford (ed.)
1968 Chronicles of Negro Protest. New York: Parents Magazine Press.

Connery, Robert H. (ed.)
1968 Urban Riots: Violence and Social Change. New York: Columbia University Press.

Cox Commission
1968 Crisis at Columbia. New York: Vintage Books.

Edwards, Harry
1970 Black Students. New York: The Macmillan Co.

Ehrlich, Howard J.
1971 "Social conflict in America: The 1960's." The Sociological Quarterly 12 (Summer):297.

Epstein, Benjamin, and Arnold Foster
1966 The Radical Right. New York: Random House.

Etzioni, Amitai
1970 Demonstration Democracy. New York: Gordon & Breach.

Feuer, Lewis S.
1969 The Conflict of Generations. New York: Basic Books.

Flacks, Richard
1967 "The liberated generation: An explanation of the roots of student protest." Journal of Social Issues 23 (July):66-68.

Flacks, Richard, and Kenneth Keniston
1969 "Notes on young radicals." Change 1 (November-December).

Graham, Hugh Davis and Ted Robert Gurr
1969 Violence in America: Historical and Comparative Perspectives. A Staff Report to The National Commission on the Causes and Prevention of Violence, vol. 2. Washington, D.C.: Government Printing Office.

Grubery, Martin
1968 Women in American Politics. Oshkosh, Wisc.: Academia Press.

Hess, Karl
1969 "The death of politics." Playboy 16 (March):102-104, 178-185.

Horowitz, Irving L.
1970 The Struggle Is the Message: The Organization and Ideology of the Anti-War Movement. Berkeley: The Glendessary Press.

Janowitz, Morris
1968 Social Control of Escalated Riots. Chicago: University of Chicago Center for Policy Study.

Kazin, Michael
1969 "Some notes on S.D.S." American Scholar 38 (Fall):647.

Keniston, Kenneth
1968 Young Radicals. New York: Harcourt, Brace & World.

Keniston, Kenneth, and Michael Lerner
1971 "Campus characteristics and campus unrest." The Annals of the American Academy of Political and Social Science 395 (May):44.

Kerner Commission
1968 Report of the National Advisory Commission on Civil Disorders. Washington, D.C.: Government Printing Office.

Lemberg Center for the Study of Violence
1968 Riot Data Review, No. 2. Waltham, Mass.: Brandeis University.

Life
1968 "The defiant voices of SDS." (October 18):81.

Lipset, Seymour M.
1971 Rebellion in the University. Boston: Little, Brown & Co.

Luce, Phillip
1965 "Why I quit the extreme left." Saturday Evening Post 238 (May 8):33.

McReynolds, David
1966 "Chinese Communism, USA." Commonwealth 83 (February 4).

Marx, Gary T. (ed.)
1971 Radical Conflict. Boston: Little, Brown & Co.

Mauss, Armand L.
1971a "The lost promise of reconciliation." Journal of Social Issues 27 (July):1-20.
1971b "On being strangled by the stars and stripes: The New Left, the Old Left, and the natural history of American radical movements." *Ibid.*, pp. 183-202.

Mead, Walter B.
1971 Extremism and Cognition. Iowa: Kendall-Hunt Publishing Co.

Meier, August, and Elliot Rudwick
1970 Black Protest in the Sixties. Chicago: Quadrangle Books.

Miller, Collin
1965 The press and the student revolt. *In* Michael V. Miller and Susan Gilmore (eds.), Revolution at Berkeley. New York: Dial Press.

Mouat, Lucia
1966 "Dubois Club pick targets." Christian Science Monitor (July 19):3.

National Advisory Commission on Civil Disorders
1968 The Report of the National Advisory Commission on Civil Disorders. Washington, D.C.: Government Printing Office.

National Commission on the Causes and Prevention of Violence
1969 The Report to the National Commission on the Causes and Prevention of Violence. Washington, D.C.: Government Printing Office.

New York Times
1968a "Cleaverism" (Letter to the Editor) New York Times Magazine, September 28, p. 22.
1968b James Reston column, October 23.

Peterson, Richard E.
1968 The Scope of Organized Student Protest in 1967-68. Princeton: Educational Testing Service.
1970 Cambodia, Kent, Jackson, and the Campus Aftermath. Report prepared for the Carnegie Commission on Higher Education. New York: McGraw-Hill Book Co.

Riesman, David, and Nathan Glazer
1963 "The intellectuals and the discontented classes (1955)." *In* Daniel Bell (ed.), The Radical Right. New York: Doubleday & Co.

Rudolph, Fredrick
1965 "Changing patterns of authority and influence." *In* Owen Knorr and John Minter (eds.), Order and Freedom on the Campus. Boulder, Col.: Western Interstate Commission for Higher Education.

San Francisco Chronicle
1968 "Political tack by police." December 16, p. 12.

Scranton Commission
1971 Presidential Commission on Campus Unrest, Report. Washington, D.C.: Government Printing Office.

Skolnick, Jerome H.
1969 The Politics of Protest. New York: Simon & Schuster.

Smelser, Neil J.
1962 Theory of Collective Behavior. New York: The Free Press.

Solomon, Fredrick, and Jacob R. Fishman
1963 "Youth and peace: A psychological study of student peace demonstrations in Washington, D.C." Journal of Social Issues 20 (July):54.

Sparling, Edward J. (Chairman)
1968 Dissent and Disorder: A Report of the Citizens of Chicago on the April 27 Peace Parade. Chicago: Office of the Mayor.

Stewart, Elbert W.
1972 The Troubled Land. New York: McGraw-Hill Book Co.

Stringfellow, William
1966 Dissenter in a Great Society. New York: Holt, Rinehart & Winston.

Teodori, Massino (ed.)
1969 The New Left: A Documentary History. New York: The Bobbs-Merrill Co.

Thompson, Daniel C.
1963 The Negro Leadership Class. Englewood Cliffs, N.J.: Prentice-Hall.

Time
1967 "The fire this time." 90:5 (August 4), pp. 13-18.

Tomlinson, T. M., and David O. Sears
1967 Los Angeles Riot Study: Negro Attitudes Toward the Riots. Los Angeles: Institute of Government and Public Affairs, University of California.

Towle, Katherine
1964 Letter to the Students. Daily Californian (September 14). Berkeley, Calif.: Associated Students, University of California.

Turner, Ralph
1969 "The Perception of Protest." American Sociological Review 34 (December).

U.S. News & World Report
1968 "Violence hits schools, colleges: What's causing it?" May 20:36-38.

Visick, Vern
1967 The Rank Protest of 1966-67. Chicago: University of Chicago Divinity School.
Zinn, Howard
1968 Disobedience and Democracy. New York: Random House.

CHAPTER 7

Ball, John C.
1965 "Two patterns of narcotic drug addiction in the United States." Journal of Criminal Law, Criminology, and Police Science 56:2.
Ball, John C., David M. Englander, and Carl D. Chambers
1970 "The incidence and prevalence of opiate addiction in the United States." *In* J. C. Ball and C. D. Chambers (eds.), The Epidemiology of Opiate Addiction in the United States. Springfield, Ill.: Charles C Thomas.
Balter, Mitchell B., and Jerome Levine
1971 "Character and extent of psychotherapeutic drug use in the United States." Presented at the Fifth World Conference on Psychiatry, Mexico City (November). (Cited in Brecher, 1972.)
Becker, Howard S.
1963 Outsiders: Studies in the Sociology of Deviance. New York: The Free Press.
Berstein, A., and H. Lennard
1973 "Drugs, doctors, and junkies." Society 10 (May-June):14-25.
Blum, R. H.
1967 "Dangerous drugs." *In* Task Force Report: Narcotics and Drug Abuse. Report to the President's Commission on Law Enforcement and the Administration of Justice. Washington, D.C.: Government Printing Office, pp. 21-39.
Blum, R. H., and associates
1969a Society and Drugs. San Francisco: Jossey-Bass.
1969b Students and Drugs. San Francisco: Jossey-Bass.
Blum, R. H., and M. L. Funkhouser-Balbaky
1965 "Legislators on social scientists and a social issue: A report and commentary on some discussion with law makers about drug abuse." Journal of Applied Behavioral Science 1:84-112.
Brecher, Edward M., and the editors of Consumer Reports
1972 Licit and Illicit Drugs. Mount Vernon, N.Y.: Consumers' Union.

Cohen, Sidney
1969 In Hearings Before the Subcommittee to Investigate Juvenile Delinquency of the Committee on the Judiciary. Washington, D.C.: Government Printing Office.
Dai, Bingham
1970 Opium Addiction in Chicago. Montclair, N.J.: Patterson-Smith Publishing Co.
DeFleur, Lois B.
1970 "Chicago addiction in contemporary perspective." *In* Introduction to Bingham Dai. *Ibid*. (1970), pp. v-xx.
Dickson, Donald
1968 "Bureaucracy and morality: An organizational perspective on a moral crusade." Social Problems 16 (Fall):143-156.
Eli Mahi, T.
1962 A Preliminary Study of Khat Together with the International History of Coffee in Relation to Khat. World Health Organization, Regional Office for the Eastern Mediterranean (March). (Cited in Blum, 1969a.)
Erikson, Kai T.
1966 Wayward Puritans. New York: John Wiley & Sons.
Farber, M. A.
1973 "Users, pushers, haven't noticed it so far." The New York Times (December 2).
Fort, Joel
1969 The Pleasure Seekers. Indianapolis: The Bobbs-Merrill Co.
1970 "The drug revolution." Playboy (February).
Gallup, George
1970 Gallup Opinion Index. (May):11-13. Princeton, N.J.: American Institute of Public Opinion.
1971 "Accelerating drug use." The Washington Post (January 17).
Goode, Erich
1972 Drugs in American Society. New York: Alfred A. Knopf.
Goode, Erich (ed.)
1969 Marijuana. Chicago: Aldine-Atherton Co.
Hadden, Stuart C.
1971 A Survey of Public Opinion Towards Local Drug Problems. Pullman, Wash.: Social Research Center, Washington State University.
1973 The Social Creation of a Social Problem. Unpublished Ph.D. dissertation, Washington State University, Pullman, Washington. (unpublished paper)

House Committee on Ways and Means, 75th Congress
1937 Hearings on the Taxation of Marijuana, H.R. 6385. Washington, D.C.: Government Printing Office.

Isbell, H.
1963 "Historical development of attitudes toward opiate addiction in the United States." *In* Seymour Farber and R. H. L. Wilson (eds.), Man and Civilization: Conflict and Creativity. New York: McGraw-Hill Book Co.

Kolb, L.
1962 Drug Addiction: A Medical Problem. Springfield, Ill.: Charles C Thomas.

Lindesmith, Alfred R.
1940a "Dope fiend mythology." Journal of Criminal Law, Criminology, and Police Science 31:199-208.
1940b "The drug addict as a psychopath." American Sociological Review 5 (December):914-920.
1948 Opiate Addiction. Bloomington, Ind.: Principia Press.
1967 The Addict and the Law. New York: Random House.

Moffett, Arthur, and Carl Chambers
1970 "The hidden addiction." Social Work 15: 54-59.

National Commission on Marijuana and Drug Abuse
1972 Marijuana: A Signal of Misunderstanding. New York: The New American Library.
1973 Drug Use in America: Problem in Perspective. Washington, D.C.: Government Printing Office.

Nowlis, Helen
1969 Drugs on the College Campus. Garden City, N.Y.: Doubleday.

Pawlak, Vic
1973 A Conscientious Guide to Drug Abuse, 4th ed. Phoenix, Ariz.: Do It Now Foundation.

Reasons, Charles
1971 An Inquiry in the Sociology of Social Problems: The Drug Problem in Twentieth Century America. Unpublished Ph.D. dissertation, Washington State University, Pullman, Washington.

Rogers, J. M.
1971 "Drug abuse: Just what the doctor ordered." Psychology Today 5 (September):16.

Rooney, Elizabeth A., and Don C. Gibbons
1966 "Social reactions to 'Crime Without Victims'." Social Problems 13 (Spring): 400-410.

Smith, Roger
1966 "Status politics and the image of the addict." Issues in Criminology 2:157-175.
1969a The Marketplace of Speed: Violence and Compulsive Methamphetamine Abuse. Unpublished. (Cited in Brecher, 1972.)
1969b "The world of the Haight-Ashbury speed freak." Journal of Psychedelic Drugs 2 (2):172-188.

Taylor, Arnold H.
1969 American Diplomacy and the Narcotics Traffic, 1900-1939: A Study in Humanitarian Reform. Durham, N.C.: Duke University.

Terry, Charles E., and Mildred Pellens
1970 The Opium Problem. Montclair, N.J.: Patterson-Smith Publishing.

UPI
1971 "Pot-using rats become 'bizarre'." San Francisco Chronicle (September 16):3.

Weinswig, Melvin H., and Dale W. Doerr (eds.)
1969 Drug Abuse: A Course for Educators. Indianapolis: Butler University College of Pharmacy.

CHAPTER 8

Abrams, S.
1964 "An evaluation of hypnosis in the treatment of alcoholics." American Journal of Psychiatry 120 (June):1160-1165.

Akers, Ronald L.
1973 Deviant Behavior: A Social Learning Approach. Belmont, Calif.: Wadsworth Publishing Co.

Alcoholics Anonymous
1939 The Story of How More than 100 Men Have Recovered from Alcoholism. New York: Works Publishing Co.
1955 The Story of How Many Thousands of Men and Women Have Recovered from Alcoholism, new and rev. eds. New York: Alcoholics Anonymous Publishing.
1953 Twelve Steps and Twelve Traditions. New York: Harper & Brothers.

Bacon, Selden D.
1957 "Social settings conducive to alcoholism: A sociological approach to a medical problem." Journal of the American Medical Association 164 (May):177-181.

Bahr, Howard M.
1973 Skid Row: An Introduction to Disaffiliation. New York: Oxford U. Press.

Bales, R. F.
1946 "Cultural differences in rates of alcoholism." Quarterly Journal of Studies on Alcohol 6 (March):482-493.

Bales, *cont.*
1959 "Cultural differences in rates of alcoholism." *In* R. G. McCarthy (ed.), Drinking and Intoxication. New York: Free Press, pp. 263-277.

Becker, H. S.
1963 Outsiders: Studies in the Sociology of Deviance. New York: The Free Press.

Beerstecher, E. J., J. G. Reed, W. D. Brown, and L. J. Berry
1951 "The effect of single vitamin deficiencies on the consumption of alcohol by white rats." Individual Metabolic Patterns and Human Disease. University of Texas Publication No. 5109, Austin: University of Texas.

Bell, R. Gordon
1970 Escape from Addiction. New York: McGraw-Hill Book Co.

Blane, H. T.
1970 "The personality of the alcoholic." *In* M. E. Chafetz, H. T. Blane, and M. J. Hill (eds.), Frontiers of Alcoholism. New York: Science House, pp. 16-28.

Blum, Eva Marie, and Richard H. Blum
1967 Alcoholism. San Francisco: Jossey-Bass.

Cahalan, D.
1970 Problem Drinkers. San Francisco: Jossey-Bass.

Cahalan, D., I. H. Cisin, and H. M. Crossley
1969 American Drinking Practices: A National Survey of Drinking Behavior and Attitudes. New Brunswick, N.J.: Rutgers Center of Alcohol Studies.

Cahalan, D., and R. Room
1972 Problem Drinking Among American Men. Monographs of the Rutgers Center of Alcohol Studies, No. 7. New Brunswick, N.J.: Rutgers Center of Alcohol Studies.

Cahn, S.
1970 The Treatment of Alcoholism. New York: Oxford University Press.

Chafetz, Morris E., and Harold W. Demone, Jr.
1962 Alcoholism and Society. New York: Oxford U. Press.

Cherrington, Ernest H.
1913 History of the Anti-Saloon League. Westerville, Ohio: The American Issue Publishing Co.
1920 The Evolution of Prohibition in the United States. Westerville, Ohio: The American Issue Publishing Co.

Clinebell, H. J., Jr.
1965 "Who is qualified to treat the alcoholic? Comment on the Krystal-Moore discussion." Quarterly Journal of Studies on Alcohol 26 (March):124-127.

Cloward, Richard A.
1959 "Illegitimate means, anomie and deviant behavior." American Sociological Review 24 (April):164-176.

Cloward, Richard A., and Lloyd E. Ohlin
1960 Delinquency and Opportunity. New York: The Free Press.

Conger, John S.
1956 "Reinforcement theory and the dynamics of alcoholism." Quarterly Journal of Studies on Alcohol 17 (June):296, 301-304.

Connor, Ralph G.
1962 "The self-concepts of alcoholics." *In* David J. Pittman and Charles R. Snyder (eds.), Society, Culture and Drinking Patterns. New York: John Wiley & Sons, pp. 455-467.

Cressey, Donald R.
1970 "Epidemiology and individual contact: A case from criminology." Pacific Sociological Review 11 (Fall):48-58.

Cruz-Coke, R.
1965 "Colour-blindness and cirrhosis of the liver." Lancet 1 (May 29):1131.

Cruz-Coke, R., and A. Varela
1966 "Inheritance of alcoholism." Lancet 2 (December 10):1282.

deLint, J., and W. Schmidt
1974 "Alcoholism and mortality." *In* B. Kissin and H. Begleiter (eds.), Biology of Alcoholism 4. New York: Plenum Publishing Corp.

Driver, Richard J.
1969 "The United States Supreme Court and the chronic drunkenness offender." Quarterly Journal of Studies on Alcohol 30 (March).

Edwards, G.
1970 "The status of alcoholism as a disease." *In* R. V. Phillipson (ed.), Modern Trends in Drug Dependence and Alcoholism. New York: Appleton-Century Crofts, pp. 140-163.

Edwards, G., C. Hensman, A. Hawker, and V. Williamson
1967 "Alcoholics Anonymous: The anatomy of a self-help group." Social Psychiatry 1:195-204.

Employee Alcoholism Control Program
Pamphlet produced and distributed by Schick's Shadel Hospital (Labor Management Division). Seattle, Washington.

Fallding, Harold
1964 "The source and burden of civilization illustrated in the use of alcohol." Reprint from Quarterly Journal of Studies on Alcohol 25 (December):714.

Fenichel, O.
1945 The Psychoanalytic Theory of Neurosis. New York: W. W. Norton Co.

Fort, Joel
1973 Alcohol: Our Biggest Drug Problem. New York: McGraw-Hill Book Co.

Fox, Ruth, and Peter Lyon
1955 Alcoholism: Its Scope, Cause, and Treatment. New York: Random House.

Gellman, I. P.
1964 The Sober Alcoholic: An Organizational Analysis of Alcoholics Anonymous. New Haven: College and University Press.

Gibbons, Don C.
1968 Society, Crime and Criminal Careers. Englewood Cliffs, N.J.: Prentice-Hall.

Gordon, Elizabeth P.
1924 Women Torch-Bearers. Evanston, Ill.: National Woman's Christian Temperance Union Publishing House.

Grad, F. P., A. L. Goldberg, and B. A. Shapiro
1971 Alcoholism and the Law. Dobbs Ferry, N.Y.: Oceana Publications.

Gross, M.
1945 "The relation of the pituitary gland to some symptoms of alcoholic intoxication and chronic alcoholism." Quarterly Journal of Studies on Alcohol 6 (June):25-35.

Gusfield, J. R.
1955 "Social structure and moral reform: A study of the Woman's Christian Temperance Union." American Journal of Sociology 61 (November):221-232.
1963 Symbolic Crusade. Urbana: University of Illinois Press.

Harris, L., and associates
1971 American Attitudes Toward Alcohol and Alcoholics, Study No. 2138. Report prepared for the National Institute on Alcohol Abuse and Alcoholism, Rockville, Md.

Hofstadter, Richard
1955 The Age of Reform. New York: Alfred A. Knopf.

Horton, Donald
1959 "Primitive societies." In R. G. McCarthy (ed.), Drinking and Intoxication. New York: The Free Press, pp. 251-262.

Jellinek, E. M.
1945 "Heredity of the alcoholic." Quarterly Journal of Studies on Alcohol 6 (June): 105.
1946 "Phases in the drinking history of alcoholics." Quarterly Journal of Studies on Alcohol 7 (June):1-88.
1960 The Disease Concept of Alcoholism. New Brunswick, N.J.: Hillhouse Press.

Jessor, R., T. D. Graves, R. C. Hanson, and S. L. Jessor
1968 Society, Personality and Deviant Behavior. New York: Holt, Rinehart and Winston.

Keehn, J. D., F. F. Bloomfield, and M. A. Hug
1970 "Use of reinforcement survey schedule with alcoholics." Quarterly Journal of Studies on Alcohol 31 (September):602-615.

Keith, Harold L.
1964 Alcoholism, Tuberculosis, and Occupational Factors: An Exploratory Study of Anomie. Unpublished doctoral dissertation. Washington State University, Pullman, Washington.

Kepner, E.
1964 "Application of learning theory to the etiology and treatment of alcoholism." Quarterly Journal of Studies on Alcohol 25 (June):279-291.

Kinsey, Barry A.
1966 The Female Alcoholic: A Social Psychological Study. Springfield, Ill.: Charles C Thomas.

Kinsey, Barry A., and Lorne Phillips
1968 "Evaluation of anomie as a predisposing or developmental factor in alcohol addiction." Quarterly Journal of Studies on Alcohol 29 (December):892-898.

Knight, R.
1938 "The psychoanalytic treatment in a sanitarium of chronic addiction to alcohol." Journal of the American Medical Association 111 (October 15):1443-1446.

Landis, C.
1945 "Theories of the alcoholic personality." In C. Landis (ed.), Alcohol, Science and Society. New Haven: Quarterly Journal of Studies on Alcohol, pp. 129-142.

Lemere, F., and W. L. Voegtlin
1955 "An evaluation of the aversion treatment of alcoholism." In E. Podolsky (ed.), Management of Addictions. New York: Philosophical Library, pp. 173-180.

Lemert, E. M.
1967 Deviance, Social Problems and Social Control. Englewood Cliffs, N.J.: Prentice-Hall.
1969 "Sociocultural research on drinking." In M. Keller and T. G. Coffey (eds.), 28th International Congress on Alcohol and Alcoholism, Vol. 2. Highland Park, N.J.: Hillhouse Press, pp. 56-64.

Lester, D., and L. Greenberg
1952 "Nutrition and the etiology of alcoholism. The effect of sucrose, saccharin and fat on the self-selection of ethyl alcohol

Lester and Greenberg, *cont.*
by rats." Quarterly Journal of Studies on Alcohol 13 (December):553-560.

Lindesmith, Alfred R.
1948 Opiate Addiction. Bloomington, Ind.: Principia Press.

Lisansky, E. S.
1960 "The etiology of alcoholism: The role of psychological predisposition." Quarterly Journal of Studies on Alcohol 21 (June): 314-343.

Lolli, Giorgio
1952 "The use of wine and other beverages by a group of Italians and Americans of Italian extraction." Quarterly Journal of Studies on Alcohol 13 (March):27-48.

Lovell, L. H., and J. W. Tintera
1951 "Hypoadrenalism in alcoholism and drug addiction." Geriatrics 6 (January-February):1-11.

McClearn, G. E., and D. A. Rodgers
1961 "Genetic factors in alcohol preference of laboratory mice." Journal of Comparative and Physiological Psychology 54 (March-April):116-119.

McCord, William, and Joan McCord
1960 Origins of Alcoholism. Stanford, Calif.: Stanford University Press.
1962 "A longitudinal study of the personality of alcoholics." In David J. Pittman and Charles R. Snyder (eds.), Society, Culture and Drinking Patterns. New York: John Wiley & Sons, pp. 413-430.

Mann, Marty
1973 "America's 150-year war: Alcohol vs. alcoholism." Alcohol Health and Research World 1 (Spring):5-7.

Mardones, J.
1960 Experimentally induced changes in the free selection of ethanol. *In* C. C. Pfeiffer and J. R. Smythies (eds.), International Review of Neurobiology, Vol. 2, pp. 41-76.

Maxwell, Milton A.
1950 "The Washingtonian movement." Quarterly Journal of Studies on Alcohol 11 (September):410-451.
1962 Alcoholics Anonymous: An interpretation. *In* D. J. Pittman and C. R. Snyder (eds.), Society, Culture and Drinking Patterns. New York: John Wiley & Sons.

Merton, Robert K.
1957 Social Theory and Social Structure. Glencoe, Ill.: The Free Press.

Mulford, Harold A.
1964 "Drinking and deviant drinking, U.S.A., 1963." Quarterly Journal of Studies on Alcohol 25 (September).

Norman, J. H.
1972 An Overview of Alcoholism: Theories and Problems. Unpublished manuscript, Washington State University, Pullman, Washington.

Odegard, Peter H.
1966 Pressure Politics. New York: Octagon Books.

Odegard, Peter H., and E. Allen Helms
1928 American Politics. New York: Harper & Brothers.

Park, Peter
1962 Problem drinking and role deviation: A study of incipient alcoholism. *In* David J. Pittman and Charles R. Snyder (eds.), Society, Culture and Drinking Patterns. New York: John Wiley & Sons, pp. 431-454.

Phillips, Lorne A.
1973 Anomy and Alcoholism: A Causal and/or Concomitant Relationship. Unpublished doctoral dissertation, Washington State University, Pullman.
1967 A Study of the Relationship between Anomie and Alcoholism. Unpublished master's thesis, Oklahoma State University, Stillwater.

Pittman, David J. (ed.)
1967 Alcoholism. New York: Harper & Row.

Plaut, Thomas F. A.
1967 Alcohol Problems: A Report to the Nation. New York: Oxford University Press.

Plunkett, R. J., and A. C. Hayden (eds.)
1961 Standard Nomenclature of Diseases and Operations (published for the AMA), 5th ed. New York: McGraw-Hill Book Co.

Riesman, David
1950 The Lonely Crowd. New Haven: Yale University Press.

Richmond, Mary Ellen
1971 Social Diagnosis. New York: Russell Sage Foundation.

Richter, C. P.
1956 "Loss of appetite for alcohol and alcoholic beverages produced in rats by treatment with thyroid preparations." Endocrinology 59 (October):472-478.

Riley, J. W., and C. F. Marden
1947 "The social pattern of alcoholic drinking." Quarterly Journal of Studies on Alcohol 8:265-273.

Roman, P. M., and H. M. Trice
1970 "The development of deviant drinking behavior; occupational risk factors." Archives of Environmental Health 20 (March):424-435.

Rubington, Earl, and Martin S. Weinberg
1971 The Study of Social Problems. New York: Oxford University Press.

Sadoun, Roland, and Giorgio Lolli
1962 "Choice of alcoholic beverage among 120 alcoholics in France." Quarterly Journal of Studies on Alcohol 23 (September): 449-458.

Sait, Edward McChesney
1927 American Parties and Elections. New York: The Century.

Segovia-Riquelme, N., A. Dederra, M. Anex, O. Barnier, I. Figuerola-Camps, I. Campos-Hoppe, N. Jara, and J. Mardones
1970 "Nutritional and genetic factors in the appetite for alcohol." In R. E. Popham (ed.), Alcohol and Alcoholism. Toronto: University of Toronto Press, pp. 86-96.

Skolnick, Jerome H.
1954 "A study of the relation of ethnic background to arrests for inebriety." Quarterly Journal of Studies on Alcohol 4 (December):622-630.

Snyder, Charles R.
1958 Alcohol and the Jews. New York: The Free Press.
1964 "Inebriety, alcoholism and anomie." In Marshall B. Clinard (ed.), Anomie and Deviant Behavior. New York: The Free Press, pp. 189-212.

Sutherland, Edwin H.
1961 White Collar Crime. New York: Holt, Rinehart & Winston.

Sutherland, Edwin H., H. G. Schroeder, and C. L. Tordella
1950 "Personality traits and the alcoholic." Quarterly Journal of Studies on Alcohol 11 (December):547-561.

Tiebout, H. M.
1961 "Alcoholics Anonymous—An experiment of nature." Quarterly Journal of Studies on Alcohol 22:52-68.

Tintera, J. W., and L. H. Lovell
1949 "Endocrine treatment of alcoholism." Geriatrics 4 (September-October):274-278.

Trice, H. M.
1957 "A study of the process of affiliation with Alcoholics Anonymous." Quarterly Journal of Studies on Alcohol 18 (March):39-54.
1959 "The affiliation motive and readiness to join Alcoholics Anonymous." Quarterly Journal of Studies on Alcohol 20 (September):313-320.
1966 Alcoholism in America. New York: McGraw-Hill Book Co.

Ullman, Albert D.
1958 "Sociocultural backgrounds of alcoholism." The Annals of the American Academy of Political and Social Science 315 (January):50.

U.S. Department of Health, Education, and Welfare
1971 First Special Report to the U.S. Congress on Alcohol and Health, Shirley Sirota Rosenberg, ed. DHEW Publication No. (HSM) 72-9099. Washington, D.C.: Government Printing Office.

von Wartburg, J. P.
1970 "Alcohol dehydrogenase distribution in tissues of different species." In R. E. Popham (ed.), Alcohol and Alcoholism. Toronto: University of Toronto Press, pp. 13-21.

White, Robert
1948 The Abnormal Personality. New York: The Ronald Press Co.

Williams, Phyllis H., and Robert Straus
1950a "Drinking patterns of Italians in New Haven: Utilization of the personal diary as a research technique." Quarterly Journal of Studies on Alcohol 11 (March): 51-91.
1950b "Drinking patterns of Italians in New Haven: Utilization of the personal diary as a research technique." Quarterly Journal of Studies on Alcohol 11 (September):452-483.
1950c "Drinking patterns of Italians in New Haven: Utilization of the personal diary as a research technique." Quarterly Journal of Studies on Alcohol 11 (December):586-629.

Williams, R. J.
1946 "The etiology of alcoholism: A working hypothesis involving the interplay of hereditary and environmental factors." Quarterly Journal of Studies on Alcohol 7 (March):567-585.
1959 "Biochemical individuality and cellular nutrition: Prime factors in alcoholism." Quarterly Journal of Studies on Alcohol 20 (September):452-463.

Wiseman, Jacqueline P.
1970 Stations of the Lost: The Treatment of Skid Row Alcoholics. Englewood Cliffs, N.J.: Prentice-Hall.

World Health Organization
1954 Expert Committee on Alcohol: First Report. W.H.O. Technical Report Series, No. 84. Geneva.
1955 Alcohol and Alcoholism. Report of an Expert Committee. W.H.O. Technical Report Series, No. 94. Geneva.

Zarrow, M. X., H. Addus, and M. Denison
1960 "Failure of the endocrine system to influence the alcoholic drive in rats." Quarterly Journal of Studies on Alcohol 21 (September):400-413.

CHAPTER 9

Associated Press
1974 "Hospitals can't handle sanity." San Francisco Examiner (March 30):6.

Becker, Howard S.
1963 Outsiders. New York: The Free Press.

Beers, Clifford W.
1945 A Mind that Found Itself. New York: Doubleday, Doran, & Co. (first published 1908)

Brinton, Crane, John Christopher, and Robert Wolff
1957 Modern Civilization. Englewood Cliffs, N.J.: Prentice-Hall.

Bromberg, Walter
1963 History of the treatment of mental disorders. In Albert Deutsch (ed.), The Encyclopedia of Mental Health. New York: Franklin Watts, Inc.

Committee Against Mental Illness
1966 What Are the Facts About Mental Illness? Washington, D.C.

Clausen, John
1971 "Mental disorders." In R. K. Merton and Robert Nisbet (eds.), Contemporary Social Problems. New York: Harcourt, Brace, Jovanovich.

Connery, Robert H.
1968 The Politics of Mental Health. New York: Columbia University Press.

Council of State Governments
1950 The Mental Health Programs of the Forty-Eight States. Chicago: Council of State Governments.

Davis, Kingsley
1938 "Mental hygiene and the class structure." Psychiatry 1 (February):55.

Dershowitz, Alan M.
1969 "The psychiatrist's power in civil commitment: A knife that cuts both ways." Psychology Today 2 (February): 42-47.

Deutsch, Albert
1948 The Shame of the States. New York: Harcourt Brace.
1949 The Mentally Ill in America. New York: Doubleday, Doran, & Co.

Faris, Robert E. L., and H. Warren Dunham
1939 Mental Disorders in Urban Areas. Chicago: University of Chicago Press.

Felix, Robert H.
1963 "The National Institute of Mental Health." In Albert Deutsch (ed.), The Encyclopedia of Mental Health. New York: Franklin Watts.

Foucault, Michel
1965 Madness and Civilization. New York: Pantheon Books.

Goffman, Erving
1961 Asylums. Garden City, N.Y.: Doubleday Publishing Co.

Hicks, John D., George E. Mowry, and Robert E. Burke
1963 The American Nation, 4th ed., 2 vols. Boston: Houghton Mifflin Co.

Hollingshead, A. B., and F. Redlich
1958 Social Class and Mental Illness. New York: John Wiley & Sons.

Horney, Karen
1937 The Neurotic Personality of Our Time. New York: W. W. Norton & Co.

Horton, Paul B., and Gerald R. Leslie
1974 The Sociology of Social Problems, 5th ed. Englewood Cliffs, N.J.: Prentice-Hall.

Joint Commission on Mental Illness and Health
1961 Action for Mental Health. New York: John Wiley & Sons.

Kutner, Luis
1962 "The illusion of due process in commitment proceedings." Northwestern University Review 57 (September):38.

Leighton, Alexander
1959 My Name is Legion. New York: Basic Books.

Leighton, Dorothea C., et al.
1963 The Character of Danger. New York: Basic Books.

Linzer, Edward
1963 "National Association for Mental Health." In Albert Deutsch (ed.), The Encyclopedia of Mental Health. New York: Franklin Watts.

Martindale, Don, and Edith Martindale
1971 The Social Dimensions of Mental Illness, Alcoholism, and Drug Dependence. Westport, Conn.: Greenwood Press.

Mechanic, David
1962 "Some factors in identifying and defining mental illness." Mental Hygiene 46 (January):66-74.
1969 Mental Health and Social Policy. Englewood Cliffs, N.J.: Prentice-Hall.

Menninger, Karl
1963 The Vital Balance: The Life Process in Mental Health and Illness. New York: Viking Press.

MH (Journal for the National Association of Mental Health)
1972 Fall.
1973 Winter.

Mishler, Elliot G., and Nancy E. Waxler
1965 "Family interaction processes and schizophrenia: A review of current theory." Merrill-Palmer Quarterly of Behavior and Development 11 (October):269-315.

Nunnally, Jim C., Jr.
1961 Popular Conceptions of Mental Health. New York: Holt, Rinehart & Winston.

Perlstein, Stanley
1967 Psychiatry, the Law, and Mental Health. New York: Oceana Publications.

Phillips, Derek L.
1963 "Rejection: A possible consequence of seeking help for mental disorders." American Sociological Review 28 (December):963-972.

Ridenour, Nina
1961 Mental Health in the United States: A Fifty-Year History. Cambridge: Harvard University Press.
1963 "The mental health movement." *In* Albert Deutsch (ed.), The Encyclopedia of Mental Health. New York: Franklin Watts.

Rosen, George
1968 Madness in Society. Chicago: University of Chicago Press.

San Francisco Examiner
1974 "Hospitals can't handle sanity." March 30, p. 6.

Scheff, Thomas J. (ed.)
1967 Mental Illness and Social Process. New York: Harper & Row, Publishers.

Shore, Maurice J.
1950 Twentieth Century Mental Hygiene. New York: Social Sciences Publishers.

Shryock, Richard H.
1944 "The beginnings." *In* American Psychiatric Assn., One Hundred Years of American Psychiatry. New York: Columbia University Press.

Simmons, D. L., and Hazel Chambers
1965 "Public stereotypes of deviants." Social Problems 13 (2):223-232.

Srole, Leo
1962 Mental Health in the Metropolis. New York: McGraw-Hill Book Co.

Szasz, Thomas
1960 "The myth of mental illness." The American Psychologist 15 (February):113-118.
1970 The Manufacture of Madness. New York: Dell Publishing Co.

Tompkins, H. J.
1967 "The presidential address: The physician in contemporary society." American Journal of Psychiatry 124 (July):1-6.

Waller, Willard
1936 "Social problems and the mores." American Sociological Review 1 (December):922-933.

CHAPTER 10

Abelson, H., R. Cohen, E. Heaton, and C. Suder
1970 National Survey of Public Attitudes Toward and Experience with Erotic Materials. Technical Reports of the Commission on Obscenity and Pornography, Vol. 6. Washington, D.C.: Government Printing Office.

The Advocate: Newspaper of America's Homophile Community
1973 April 25, May 9, May 23, and June 20.

Bell, Arthur
1971 Dancing in Gay Lib Blues. New York: Simon & Schuster.

Berman, Harriet Katz
1974 "Quarantine: Policing prostitution." Civil Liberties 301 (March):1.

Birkelbach, R. D., and L. A. Zurcher
1970 "Some socio-political characteristics of anti-pornography campaigners: A research note." Sociological Symposium 4 (Spring):13-21.

Bullough, Vern L.
1964 The History of Prostitution. New Hyde Park, N.Y.: University Books.

Cantor, Gilbert M.
1969 "The need for homosexual law reform." *In* Ralph W. Weltge (ed.), The Same Sex. Philadelphia: Pilgrim Press.

Civil Service Journal
1972 U.S. Civil Service Commission 13 (October-December).

Cory, Donald Webster
1951 The Homosexual in America: A Subjective Approach. New York: Greenberg Publishers.

Craig, Alex
1942 Above All Liberties. Freeport, N.Y.: Books for Libraries.

Daily Idahonian
1973 Various issues. (Moscow, Idaho).

Davis, K.
1937 "The sociology of prostitution." American Sociological Review 2 (October):744-755.

Davis, *cont.*
1971 "Sexual behavior." *In* Robert K. Merton and Robert A. Nisbet (eds.), Contemporary Social Problems, 3rd ed. New York: Harcourt, Brace & World.

Economist
1970 "Who's for porn?" 237 (October 3):51.

Elliott, C. W.
1914 "The American Social Hygiene Association." Journal of Social Hygiene 1 (December):1-5.

Erikson, Kai T.
1966 Wayward Puritans. New York: John Wiley & Sons.

Ernst, Morris, and Alexander Lindey
1940 The Censor Marches On. New York: Doubleday, Doran & Co.

Feldman, E.
1967 "Prostitution, the alien woman, and the progressive imagination, 1910-1915." American Quarterly 19 (Summer):192-206.

Filler, Louis
1950 Crusaders for American Liberalism. Yellow Springs, Ohio: The Antioch Press.

Friedman, Jane
1970 Regulation of Obscenity by Federal Agencies. Technical Reports of the Commission on Obscenity and Pornography, Vol. 5. Washington, D.C.: Government Printing Office.

Funston, Richard
1971 "Pornography and politics: The court, the Constitution, and the commission." Western Political Quarterly 24 (December).

Gagnon, John H., and William Simon
1970 "Pornography: Raging menace or paper tiger?" *In* W. Simon and J. H. Gagnon (eds.), The Sexual Scene. Chicago: Aldine Publishing Co.

Gallo, Jon J., et al.
1966 "The consenting adult homosexual and the law: An empirical study of enforcement and administration in Los Angeles County." UCLA Law Review 13 (March).

Gallup, George
1969 Gallup Opinion Index. Report no. 49 (July):16-24. Princeton, N.J.: American Institute of Public Opinion.

Gebhard, Paul H.
1972 Incidence of Overt Homosexuality in the United States and Western Europe. National Institute of Mental Health Task Force on Homosexuality: Final Report

Gebhard, *cont.*
and Background Paper. Washington, D.C.: Government Printing Office.

Geis, Gilbert
1972 Not the Law's Business? An Examination of Homosexuality, Abortion, Prostitution, Narcotics and Gambling in the United States. Rockville, Md.: National Institutes of Mental Health.

Ginzburg, Ralph
1958 An Unhurried View of Erotica. New York: The Helmsman Press.

Gittings, Barbara B.
1969 "The homosexual and the church." *In* R. W. Weltge (ed.), The Same Sex. Philadelphia: Pilgrim Press.

Goldman, Albert
1972 "Witnessing obscenity for fun and profit." New York Magazine 5 (April):47-53.

Goldstein, Michael J., and Harold S. Kant
1974 Pornography and Sexual Deviance. Berkeley, Calif.: University of California Press.

Greenwald, Harold
1958 The Call Girl: A Social and Psychoanalytic Study. New York: Ballantyne Books.

Gunnison, Foster, Jr.
1969 "The homophile movement in America." *In* Ralph W. Weltge (ed.), The Same Sex. Philadelphia: Pilgrim Press.

Gusfield, J. R.
1963 Symbolic Crusade: Status Politics and the American Temperance Movement. Urbana, Ill.: University of Illinois Press.

Hall, Gladys Mary
1936 Prostitution in the Modern World: A Survey and a Challenge. New York: Emerson Books.

Harper, James
1974 "The text war freezes minds, hardens hearts." San Francisco Sunday Examiner & Chronicle (November 17), A:4.

Hooker, Evelyn
1967 "The homosexual community." *In* John Gagnon and William Simon (eds.), Sexual Deviance. New York: Harper & Row.

Human Behavior
1973 "Homosexphobia." A report on the paper presented at the 50th Annual Meeting of the American Orthopsychiatric Association, May 1973, by Eugene E. Levitt and Albert D. Klassen, Jr., on "Public Attitudes Toward Sexual Behavior: The Latest Investigation of the Institute for Sex Research."

Humphreys, Laud
1972 Out of the Closets. Englewood Cliffs, N.J.: Prentice-Hall.
Kilpatrick, James J.
1960 The Smut Peddlers, Garden City, N.Y.: Doubleday & Co.
Kinsey, Alfred C., W. B. Pomeroy, and C. E. Martin
1948 Sexual Behavior in the Human Male. Philadelphia: W. B. Saunders Co.
1953 Sexual Behavior in the Human Female. Philadelphia: W. B. Saunders Co.
Kinsie, P. M.
1953 "Prostitution—Then and Now." Journal of Social Hygiene 39 (June):241-248.
Kyle-Keith, Richard
1961 The High Price of Pornography. Washington, D.C.: Public Affairs Press.
Lemert, Edwin M.
1951 Social Pathology. New York: McGraw-Hill Book Co.
Leznoff, Maurice, and William A. Westley
1967 "The homosexual community." In John Gagnon and William Simon (eds.), Sexual Deviance. New York: Harper & Row.
McCormick, Kenneth D.
1972 "The guardians of virtue mount a new offensive." Saturday Review 55 (July):24-25.
Martin, Del, and Phyllis Lyon
1972 Lesbian/Woman. New York: Bantam Books.
Mather, J.
1954 Various editorials, status reports, etc., in his capacity as last president of American Social Hygiene Association. Journal of Social Hygiene 41 (esp. last issue).
National Institute of Mental Health
1972 Task Force on Homosexuality: Final Report and Background Papers. Washington, D.C.: Government Printing Office.
Nawy, Harold
1970 The San Francisco Erotic Marketplace. Technical Reports of the Commission on Obscenity and Pornography, Vol. 4. Washington, D.C.: Government Printing Office.
New York Times
1970 The Report of the Commission on Obscenity and Pornography. New York: Bantam Books.
1974 "Prostitutes attracted to Alaska by oil pipeline." (May 6).
Nordheimer, Jon
1974 "A nationwide boom in smut." San Francisco Sunday Examiner & Chronicle (May 26):18.
Off Our Backs: A Women's News Journal
1973 Washington, D.C. 8 (May):3.
Peterson, Iver
1974 "Campus gays have come a long way." San Francisco Sunday Examiner & Chronicle (June 30):19.
Pomeroy, Wardell B.
1969 Task Force on Homosexuality: Background Papers. Washington, D.C.: Government Printing Office.
Reckless, Walter C.
1933 Vice in Chicago. Chicago: University of Chicago Press.
Riegel, R. E.
1968 "Changing American attitudes toward prostitution, 1800-1920." Journal of the History of Ideas 29 (July):437-452.
Roby, Pamela
1969 "Politics and criminal law: Revision of the New York State penal law on prostitution." Social Problems 17 (Summer):83-109.
Sampson, John J.
1970 Commercial Traffic in Sexually Oriented Materials in the United States (1969-1970). Technical Reports of the Commission on Obscenity and Pornography, Vol. 3. Washington, D.C.: Government Printing Office.
Schur, Edwin M.
1965 Crimes Without Victims. Englewood Cliffs, N.J.: Prentice-Hall.
Scott, George Ryley
1936 A History of Prostitution from Antiquity to the Present Day. London: T. Werner Laurie Ltd.
Seattle Gay Liberation Front Newsletter
1973 May issue.
Sheehy, Gail
1972a "Progress report on the clean-up of Hell's Bedroom." New York Magazine 5 (November 13):50.
1972b "The landlords of Hell's Bedroom." New York Magazine 5 (November 20):67.
Simon, William, and John H. Gagnon
1967 "Femininity in the lesbian community." Social Problems 15 (Fall):212-221.
Snow, William
1946 "The American Social Hygiene Association: Some notes on the historical background, development, and future opportunities of the National Voluntary Organization for Social Hygiene in the United States." Journal of Social Hygiene 32 (June):241-250.

"The state of the Union regarding commercialized prostitution—A 1949 summary."
1949 Journal of Social Hygiene 35 (April): 146-161.
Sterba, James P.
1974 "Fight against pornography fizzles out." Daily Idahonian (originating from The New York Times) (December 3):4.
Time
1969a "Coming to terms." October 24, p. 52.
1969b "The homosexual: Newly visible, newly understood." (October 31):56-66.
Tobin, Kay, and Randy Wicker
1972 The Gay Crusaders. New York: Paperback Library.
U.S. News & World Report
1970 "When pornography curbs are lifted." 69 (October 19):68.
1971 "The Smut Era—On the decline." 71 (October 18):43-45.
1972 "Smut: A boom that is faltering." 73 (July 10):66-67.
Waterman, Willoughby C.
1932 Prostitution and Its Repression in New York City. New York: Columbia University Press.
Will, George F.
1974 "The conservative case for legal prostitution." San Francisco Sunday Examiner & Chronicle. September 1 (Sunday Punch section):3.
Wilson, W. Cody
1972 "The American experience with pornography." In National Institute of Mental Health, Social Change and Human Behavior: Mental Health Challenges of the Seventies. Washington, D.C.: Government Printing Office.
Winick, Charles
1968 The New People. New York: Pegasus.
Zurcher, L. A., and Robert G. Cushing
1970 Participants in Ad Hoc Anti-pornography Organizations: Some Individual Characteristics. Technical Reports of the Commission on Obscenity and Pornography, Vol. 5. Washington, D.C., Government Printing Office.
Zurcher, L. A., and R. George Kirkpatrick
1970 Collective Dynamics of Ad Hoc Anti-pornography Organizations. Technical Reports of the Commission on Obscenity and Pornography, Vol. 5. Washington, D.C.: Government Printing Office.
Zurcher, L. A., and R. G. Kirkpatrick
1971 The Natural Histories and Member Characteristics of Anti-Pornography Organizations (under auspices of the Commission on Obscenity and Pornography).

Zurcher and Kirkpatrick, cont.
Washington, D.C.: Government Printing Office.
Zurcher, L. A., R. George Kirkpatrick, Robert G. Cushing, and Charles K. Bowman
1971 "The anti-pornography campaign: A symbolic crusade." Social Problems 19 (Fall):217-238.
Zurcher, L. A., and J. Kenneth Monts
1972 "Political efficacy, political trust, and anti-pornography crusading: A research note." Sociology and Social Research 56 (January):211-220.

CHAPTER 11

Adams, Elsie, and Mary Louise Briscoe
1971 Up Against the Wall, Mother. Beverly Hills, Calif.: Glencoe Press.
Albert, Ethel M.
1963 "The roles of women: Question of values." In Seymour M. Farber and Roger H. L. Wilson (eds.), Man and Civilization: The Potential of Woman. New York: McGraw-Hill Book Co.
American Sociological Association Committee on the Status of Women in Sociology
1973 "Comment on Wolfe, et al., Sex discrimination in the hiring practices of graduate sociology departments: Myths and realities." American Sociologist 8 (November):165-167.
Artandi, Susan
1972 "Misrepresented by women's lib." Science 178 (November 10):565.
Babchuk, Nicholas, Ruth Marsey, and C. Wayne Gordon
1960 "Men and women in community agencies: A note of power and prestige." American Sociological Review 25 (June): 399-403.
Bardwick, Judith M.
1971 Psychology of Women: A Study of Bio-Cultural Conflicts. New York: Harper & Row, Publishers.
Benedict, Ruth
1934 Patterns of Culture. New York: Houghton Mifflin Co.
Blood, Robert O., Jr.
1962 Marriage. New York: The Free Press.
Brothers, Joyce
1972 "Women's lib backlash." Good Housekeeping 175 (September):54.
Collins, Thomas
1971 "The golden years: Working women and retirement." The Spokesman Review Sunday Magazine (March 28):11.

Daily Idahonian
1973 "A first: Woman flight officer is airborne." (February 7).

de Beauvoir, Simone
1953 The Second Sex, tr. by H. M. Parshley. New York: Alfred A. Knopf.

Dector, M.
1972 "Toward a new chastity." Atlantic Monthly 230 (August):42-46.

"Discrimination: Women charge universities, colleges with bias."
1970 Science 168 (May 1):559-561.

Epstein, Cynthia
1970 "Encountering the male establishment: Sex-status limits on women's careers in the professions." American Journal of Sociology 75 (May):965-982.

Epstein, Cynthia, and William J. Goode (eds.)
1971 The Other Half: Roads to Women's Equality. Englewood Cliffs, N.J.: Prentice-Hall.

Erikson, Erik H.
1950 Childhood and Society. New York: W. W. Norton & Co.
1964 "Inner and outer space: Reflections on womanhood." Daedalus 93 (2):582-606.
1968 Identity: Youth and Crisis. New York: W. W. Norton & Co.

Etzioni, A.
1972 "Women's movement. Tokens vs. objectives." Saturday Review 55 (May 20):31-35.

Farber, Seymour, and Roger H. L. Wilson (eds.)
1963 Man and Civilization: The Potential of Woman. New York: McGraw-Hill Book Co.

Farrell, Barry
1971 "You've come a long way, buddy." Life 71 (August 27):52-59.

Federal Bureau of Investigation
1972 Uniform Crime Reports. (August).

Flexner, Eleanor
1973 Century of Struggle: The Woman's Rights Movement in the United States. New York: Atheneum Publishers.

Freeman, Jo
1973 "The origins of the women's liberation movement." In Joan Huber (ed.), Changing Women in a Changing Society. Chicago: University of Chicago Press.

Freud, Sigmund
1930 Three Contributions to the Theory of Sex, 4th ed., tr. by A. A. Brill. New York: Nervous and Mental Disease Publishing Co.

Freud, cont.
1933 "The psychology of women." In New Introductory Lectures. London: Hogarth Press.

Friedan, Betty
1963 The Feminine Mystique. New York: W. W. Norton & Co.
1972 "Beyond women's liberation." McCalls 99 (August):82-83.

Fuchs, Victor R.
1971 "Differences in hourly earnings between men and women." Monthly Labor Review 94. Washington, D.C.: U.S. Department of Labor, Bureau of Labor Statistics, pp. 9-15.

Gallup, George
1972 The Gallup Poll: Public Opinion 1935-1971. New York: Random House.
1973 Gallup Opinion Index Report no. 93. (March). Princeton, N.J.: American Institute of Public Opinion.

Gardner, Burleigh
1974 "The awakening of the blue collar woman." Intellectual Digest 4 (March):17-19.

Giele, Janet Zallinger
1971 New developments in research on women. In Viola Klein, The Feminine Character. Chicago: University of Chicago Press.

Gilman, Richard
1971 "Where did it all go wrong?" Life 71 (August 13):48-55.

Goldmark, Josephine C.
1906 "Working women and the laws: A record of neglect." Annals of the American Academy of Political and Social Science 28 (July-December):261-276.

Green, Arnold, and Eleanor Melnick
1950 "What has happened to the feminist movement?" In Alvin W. Gouldner (ed.), Studies in Leadership: Leadership and Democratic Action. New York: Harper & Brothers.

Gruberg, Martin
1968 Women in American Politics: An Assessment and Sourcebook. Oshkosh, Wisc.: Academia Press.

Hacker, Helen
1951 "Women as a minority group." Social Forces 30 (October):60-69.

Hall, Edward L.
1963 The Silent Language. Greenwich, Conn.: Premier Books.

Harvey, Paul
1974 Radio commentary, June 8. (nationally broadcast)

Hernandez, Aileen
1971 Editorial from NOW's president, July, 1970 newsletter. *In* June Sochen (ed.), The New Feminism in Twentieth-Century America. Lexington, Mass.: D. C. Heath & Co.

Horney, Karen
1924 "On the genesis of the castration complex in women." International Journal of Psychoanalysis 5 (January).
1926 "The flight from womanhood: The masculinity complex in women as viewed by men and by women." International Journal of Psychoanalysis 7.

Howard, Jane
1971 "Is women's lib a dirty word in Milwaukee?" Life (August 27):46-51.

Howard, John R.
1974 The Cutting Edge: Social Movements and Social Change in America. Philadelphia: J. B. Lippincott Company.

Howell, Mary
1974 Conference on "Women and the Law." Civil Liberties 6 (May-June):4.

Kanowitz, Leo
1969 Women and the Law: The Unfinished Revolution. Albuquerque: University of New Mexico Press.

Klein, Viola
1971 The Feminine Character: History of an Ideology. Urbana, Ill.: University of Illinois Press.

Kohlberg, Lawrence
1966 "A cognitive-developmental analysis of children's sex-role concepts and attitudes." *In* Eleanor M. Maccoby (ed.), The Development of Sex Differences. Stanford: Stanford University Press.

Landis, P. H.
1954 "Don't expect too much of sex in marriage." Reader's Digest 65 (December): 25-28.

La Sorte, Michael A.
1971 "Sex differences in salary among academic sociology teachers." American Sociologist 6 (November):304-307.

Lear, Martha Weiman
1968 "The second feminist wave." *In* The New York Times Magazine (March 10):24-25, 50-60.

Lemons, J. Stanley
1973 "Social feminism in the 1920's: Progressive women and industrial legislation." Labor History 14 (Winter):83-91.

Lenton, Sally
1970 "Primate studies and sex differences." Women: A Journal of Liberation (Summer):43-44.

Lydon, Susan
1968 "Understanding orgasm." Ramparts (December):14-28.

McCabe, Charles
1971 "The lib industry." San Francisco Examiner (November 17):63.

Maccoby, Eleanor E.
1963 "Woman's intellect." *In* S. M. Farber and R. H. L. Wilson (eds.), The Potential of Woman. New York: McGraw-Hill Book Co.

McDowell, Margaret B.
1970 "The new rhetoric of woman power." The Midwest Quarterly 12 (Autumn): 187-198.

Malbin, Nona Glazer, and Helen Youngelson Walhrer
1972 Women in a Man-Made World: A Socioeconomic Handbook. Chicago: Rand McNally & Co.

Malcolm, Andrew H.
1972 "Navy needs female officers." San Francisco Examiner & Chronicle (December 17):This World section, p. 26.

Marmor, Judd
1968 "Changing patterns of femininity: Psychoanalytic interpretations." *In* S. Rosenbaum and S. Alger (eds.), The Marriage Relationship: Psychoanalytic Perspectives. New York: Basic Books.

Masters, W. H., and V. E. Johnson
1966 Human Sexual Response. Boston: Little, Brown & Co.

Mauss, Armand L.
1971 "On being strangled by the stars and stripes: The New Left, the Old Left, and the natural history of American radical movements." Journal of Social Issues 27 (July):183-202.

Mead, Margaret
1935 Sex and Temperament in Three Primitive Societies. New York: William Morrow & Co.

Mitchell, Juliet
1971 Woman's Estate. New York: Vintage Books.

Moblit, George, and Janie M. Burcart
1973 "Crime and women in America: Some preliminary trends of a decade (1960-1970). Paper presented at the Pacific Sociological Association Meetings, Scottsdale, Arizona. May.

Montagu, Ashley
1968 The Natural Superiority of Women. New York: The Macmillan Co.

Morgan, Robin (ed.)
1970 Sisterhood Is Powerful: An Anthology

Morgan (ed.), *cont.*
of Writings from the Women's Liberation Movement. New York: Random House.

National Opinion Research Center
1972 Codebook for Spring Social Survey. Chicago: NORC, University of Chicago.

Nye, F. Ivan, and Lois Wladis Hoffman
1963 The Employed Mother in America. Chicago: Rand McNally & Co.

Oakley, Ann
1972 Sex, Gender and Society. New York: Harper Colophon Books.

Office of Public Information
1970 The United Nations and the Status of Women: A Survey of United Nations Work in This Field. New York: United Nations.

O'Neill, William L.
1969 Everyone Was Brave: A History of Feminism in America. Chicago: Quadrangle Books.

Oppenheimer, Valerie Kincade
1973 "Demographic influence on female employment and the status of women." *In* Joan Huber (ed.), Changing Women in a Changing Society. Chicago: University of Chicago Press.

Overstreet, Edmund W.
1964 "The biological make-up of woman." *In* Seymour M. Farber and Roger H. L. Wilson (eds.), The Potential of Woman. New York: McGraw-Hill Book Co.

Paige, Karen E.
1973 "Women learn to sing the menstrual blues." Psychology Today 7 (September):41-46.

Patterson, Michelle
1971 "Alice in Wonderland: A study of women faculty in graduate departments of sociology." American Sociologist 6 (August):226-234.

"Rebelling women—The reason."
1970 U.S. News & World Report (April 13): 35-37.

Reeves, Nancy
1971 Womankind: Beyond the Stereotypes. Chicago: Aldine-Atherton.

Reuben, David
1972 Any Woman Can! New York: David McKay Co.

Roiphe, Anne
1972 "What women psychoanalysts say about women's liberation: An interview with H. Deutsch." The New York Times Magazine (February 13):12-13.

Rossi, Alice
1964 "Equality between the sexes: An immodest proposal." Daedalus 93 (Spring).

Rossi, *cont.*
1970 "Status of women in graduate departments of sociology, 1968-1969" American Sociologist 5 (February):1-12.
1972 Sex equality: The beginnings of ideology. *In* Constantina Safilios-Rothschild (ed.), Toward a Sociology of Women. Lexington, Mass.: Xerox College Publishing.

San Francisco Sunday Examiner & Chronicle
1973 "Social issues win out." (February 18): This World section, p. 9.

Seward, Georgene H., and Robert C. Williamson
1970 Sex Roles in Changing Society. New York: Random House.

Smelser, Neil
1962 A Theory of Collective Behavior. New York: The Free Press.

Sobran, M. J., Jr.
1974 "Of Ms. and men." National Review (May 24):579-581.

Spokesman-Review (Spokane, Wash.)
1973 "Women's Lib Bank." Parade magazine (June 24):13.
1974 "Men's liberation movement seen gaining strength across United States." (July 14):5.

Staines, Graham, Carol Tavris, and Toby Epstein Jayaratne
1974 "The queen bee syndrome." Psychology Today 7 (January):55-60.

Steinmetz, Urban G.
1970 The Male Mystique. Notre Dame, Ind.: Ave Maria Press.

Suter, Larry E., and Herman P. Miller
1973 "Income differences between men and career women." *In* Joan Huber (ed.), Changing Women in a Changing Society. Chicago: University of Chicago Press.

Tanner, Leslie B.
1970 Voices of Women's Liberation, Sojourner Truth Reminiscences by Frances D. Gage. New York: The New American Library.

Thomas, W. I.
1907 Sex and Society, Studies in the Social Psychology of Sex. Chicago: University of Chicago Press.
1918 "The persistence of primary group norms in present day society and their influence in our educational system." *In* Suggestions of Modern Science Concerning Education. New York: The Macmillan Co.

U.S. Department of Labor
1968 Why Women Work. Wage and Labor Standards Administration, Women's Bu-

Bibliography

U.S. Department of Labor, *cont.*
    reau. Washington, D.C.: Government Printing Office.
1970 American Women at the Crossroads: Directions for the Future. Report of the Fiftieth Anniversary Conference of the Women's Bureau of the Department of Labor. Washington, D.C.: Government Printing Office.
1971 Equal pay. Publication no. 1320. Washington, D.C.: Government Printing Office.
1971 Expanding Opportunities for Girls: Their Special Counseling Need. Employment Standards Administration. Washington, D.C.: Government Printing Office.
1971 The Myth and the Reality. Employment Standards Administration. Washington, D.C.: Government Printing Office.
1971 Report of the Office of Equal Employment Opportunity, November 1, 1967 to December 31, 1970. Washington, D.C.: Government Printing Office.

U.S. News & World Report
1970 "Rebelling women—The reason." April 13, pp. 35-37.

Viorst, Judith
1974 "What worries me most about women's lib." Redbook 143 (May):51-52.

Waldman, Elizabeth
1970 "Changes in the labor force activity of women." Monthly Labor Review. Washington, D.C.: U.S. Department of Labor, Bureau of Labor Statistics (June):10-18.

Wohl, L. C.
1974 "Phyllis Schlafly: The sweetheart of the silent majority: Chairman of an organization to stop the ERA." Ms. 2 (March):54-76 *et passim*.

Wolfe, Julie C., Melvin L. DeFleur, and Walter L. Slocum
1973 "Sex discrimination in the hiring practices of graduate sociology departments: Myths and realities." American Sociologist 8 (November):159-165.

"Women's rights: Some like it not."
1973 Newsweek (January 15):17-18.

Yinger, J. Milton
1965 A Minority Group in American Society. New York: McGraw-Hill Book Co.

Zelditch, Morris
1955 "Role differentiation in the nuclear family: A comparative study." *In* Talcott Parsons and R. I. Bales (eds.), Family, Socialization, and Interaction Process. Glencoe, Ill: The Free Press.

CHAPTER 12

Alexander, Shana
1972 "The politics of abortion." Newsweek 80 (October 2):29.

America
1971 "Roundup on Abortion Reform." 125 (September 11):134-135.

American Friends Service Committee
1970 Who Shall Live? New York: Hill & Wang.

American Law Institute
1962 Model Penal Code. Philadelphia: American Law Institute.

Association for the Study of Abortion
1973 ASA Newsletter. (New York: Various years.)

Ball, Donald W.
1967 "An abortion clinic ethnography." Social Problems 14 (Winter):293-301.

Bates, Jerome E., and Edward S. Zawadzki
1964 Criminal Abortion. Springfield, Ill.: Charles C Thomas.

Becker, Howard S.
1963 Outsiders: Studies in the Sociology of Deviance. New York: The Free Press.

Bell, Robert R.
1971 Social Deviance. Homewood, Ill.: The Dorsey Press.

Blake, Judith
1971 "Abortion and public opinion: The 1960-1970 decade." Science 71 (February):540-549.

Bonham, Sharon Price, and Barbara D. Santee
1971 "Ministers' attitudes toward abortion." Unpublished paper presented at the 1971 Meetings of the Southwestern Social Science Association.

Burns, Ruth Ann
1972 "Abortion opponents active." The New York Times 121 (June 11):104.

Calderone, Mary Steichen (ed.)
1958 Abortion in the United States. New York: Hoeber and Harper.

Callahan, Daniel
1970 Abortion: Law, Choice and Morality. London: The Macmillan Co.

Chisholm, Shirley
1971 "Foreword." *In* Diane Schulder and Florynce Kennedy (eds.), Abortion Rap. New York: McGraw-Hill Book Co., pp. vii-xi.

Cooke, Robert E., et al. (eds.)
1968 The Terrible Choice: The Abortion Dilemma. New York: Bantam Books.

Day, Lincoln H., and Alice Taylor Day
1965 Too Many Americans. New York: Dell Publishing Co.

de Beauvoir, Simone
1952 The Second Sex. New York: Alfred A. Knopf.
"Desperate Dilemma of Abortion."
1967 Time 90 (October 13):52.
Devereux, George
1955 A Study of Abortion in Primitive Societies. New York: Julian Press.
Edelstein, Ludwig
1967 Ancient Medicine. Baltimore: The Johns Hopkins University Press.
Edmiston, Susan
1971 "A report on the abortion capital of the country." The New York Times Magazine (April 11):10-11ff.
Ehrlich, Paul R., and Anne H. Ehrlich
1970 Population, Resources, Environment. San Francisco: W. H. Freeman & Co.
Finch, B. E., and Hugh Green
1963 Contraception through the Ages. Springfield, Ill.: Charles C Thomas.
Finner, Stephen L., and Jerome D. Gamache
1969 "The relation between religious commitment and attitudes toward induced abortion." Sociological Analysis 30 (Spring): 1-12.
Gallup, George
1969 Gallup Opinion Index Report Number 54 (December). Princeton, N.J.: American Institute of Public Opinion.
Gastonguay, Paul R.
1971 "The fourteenth amendment and human life." America 126 (April 15):400-401.
Granfield, David
1969 The Abortion Decision. Garden City, N.Y.: Doubleday & Co.
Group for the Advancement of Psychiatry
1970 The Right to Abortion: A Psychiatric View. New York: Charles Scribner's Sons.
Guttmacher, Alan F. (ed.)
1967 The Case for Legalized Abortion Now. Berkeley, Calif.: Diablo Press.
Hacker, David W.
1972 "Polls show abortion reform winning big. . . ." National Observer (October 21):4.
Hall, Robert E.
1970 Abortion in a Changing World, Vols. 1 and 2. New York: Columbia University Press.
Hardin, Garrett
1967 "Semantic aspects of abortion." ETC: A Review of General Semantics 24 (September):263.
1968 "Abortion—Or compulsory pregnancy?" Journal of Marriage and the Family 30 (May):246-251.

Himes, Norman E.
1936 Medical History of Contraception. New York: Gamut.
Hoffman, Paul
1972 "Nixon vs. Rockefeller: The politics of abortion." Nation 214 (June 5):712-713.
"In center of latest dispute on abortion: Nixon, Rockefeller."
1972 U.S. News & World Report 72 (May 22):50.
Johnson, Elmer H.
1969 "Abortion: A sociological critique." In Jeffrey K. Hadden and Marie L. Borgatta (eds.), Marriage and the Family. Itasca, Ill.: F. E. Peacock Publishers, pp. 332-337.
Kanowitz, Leo
1969 Women and the Law. Albuquerque: University of New Mexico Press.
Keene, Roger
1970 "The woman who tells girls in trouble: 'Have your baby'." MacLeans (May).
Kinsey, Alfred C.
1966 "Illegal abortion in the United States." In Robert W. Roberts (ed.), The Unwed Mother. New York: Harper & Row, pp. 191-200.
Kucharsky, David
1971 "Rebirth of opposition? The abortion issue." Christianity Today 15 (April 23): 36.
Lader, Lawrence
1966 Abortion. Boston: Beacon Press.
1971 "A guide to abortion laws in the United States." Redbook 137 (June):51-58.
Lecky, William E. H.
1900 History of European Morals from Augustus to Charlemagne, Vol. 1, 3rd ed., rev. New York: D. Appleton & Co.
Mace, David R.
1972 Abortion: The Agonizing Decision. Nashville, Tenn.: Abingdon Press.
Malloy, Michael T.
1973 "Despite court's ruling, abortion fight goes on." National Observer (February 3):3.
Mutnick, Barbara, and Susan LaMont
1973 "The meaning of the Supreme Court decision." Women's National Abortion Action Coalition Newsletter (February-March):3, 7.
National Opinion Research Center (NORC)
1972 Codebook for Spring, 1972, General Social Survey. Chicago: NORC, University of Chicago.
Newsweek
1971 "Abortion: How it's working." 78 (July 19):50-52.

Newsweek, *cont.*
1972 "Pre-emptive abortion." 80 (July 24): 69.
1973 "The abortion revolution." 81 (February 5):27-28.

New York Times
1972 "Antiabortion forces demonstrate a growing influence in state legislatures across the country." 121 (June 28):21.

Noonan, John T., Jr.
1970 The Morality of Abortion. Cambridge, Mass.: Harvard University Press.

Osofsky, H. J., and J. D. Osofsky
1973 The Abortion Experience. New York: Harper & Row.

Pilpel, Harriet
1969 "The right of abortion." Atlantic Monthly 223 (June):69-71.

Pressat, Roland
1971 Population. Baltimore, Md.: Penguin Books.

Reeves, Nancy
1971 Womankind. Chicago: Aldine-Atherton.

Remsberg, Charles, and Bonnie Remsberg
1972 "Abortion." Seventeen 31 (September): 140-141.

Ross, Robert, and Graham L. Staines
1972 "The politics of analyzing social problems." Social Problems 20 (Summer): 18-40.

Rossi, Alice S.
1966 "Abortion laws and their victims." Transaction 3 (September-October):7-12.
1967 "Public views on abortion." *In* Alan F. Guttmacher (ed.), The Case for Legalized Abortion Now. Berkeley, Calif.: Diablo Press, pp. 26-53.
1969 "Abortion and social change." Dissent 16 (July-August):338-346.

Ryder, Norman B., and Charles F. Westoff
1971 Reproduction in the United States, 1965. Princeton, N.J.: Princeton University Press.

Schulder, Diane, and Florynce Kennedy
1971 Abortion Rap. New York: McGraw-Hill Book Co.

Schur, Edwin M.
1955 "Abortion and the social system." Social Problems 3 (October):94-99.
1965 Crimes Without Victims. Englewood Cliffs, N.J.: Prentice-Hall.
1968 "Abortion." Annals of the American Academy of Political and Social Science 376 (March):136-147.

Shapiro, Fred C.
1972 " 'Right to Life' has a message for New York State legislators." The New York Times Magazine (August 20):10-11ff.

Stern, Loren G.
1968 "Abortion reform and the law." Journal of Criminal Law, Criminology and Police Science 59 (March):84-95.

Stockwell, Edward G.
1970 Population and People. Chicago: Quadrangle Books.

Taussig, F.
1936 Abortion, Spontaneous and Induced: Medical and Social Aspects. St. Louis, Mo.: C. V. Mosby Co.

Taylor, Gordon R.
1954 Sex in History. New York: The Vanguard Press.

Tietze, Christopher
1948 "Abortion as a cause of death." American Journal of Public Health 38 (October):1434-1441.
1963 "Some facts about legal abortion." *In* Roy O. Greep (ed.), Human Fertility and Population Problems. Cambridge, Mass.: Schenkman Publishing Co., pp. 222-236.
1970 "Induced abortion as a method of fertility control." *In* S. J. Behrman, et al. (eds.), Fertility and Family Planning. Ann Arbor: The University of Michigan Press, pp. 311-337.

Tietze, Christopher, and Sarah Lewit
1969 "Abortion." Scientific American 220 (January):21-27.
1971 "Early complications of abortions under medical auspices: A preliminary report." Studies in Family Planning 2 (July): 137-143.

Time
1971 "Dial for abortion." 97 (March 15):64.
1971 "Legal abortion: Who, why and where." 98 (September 27):67-70.
1972 "Unofficial abortion." 100 (September 11):47.
1973 "A stunning approval for abortion." 101 (February 5):50-51.

Trotter, Robert J.
1972 "Abortion laws still in ferment." Science News Letter 101 (January 29):75.

U.S. Commission on Population Growth and the American Future
1972 The Report of the Commission on Population Growth and the American Future. New York: Signet.

Weaver, Warren, Jr.
1973 "High court rules abortions legal the first three months: National guidelines set by 7-2 vote." The New York Times 122 (January 23):1ff.

Westoff, Charles F., Emily C. Moore, and Norman B. Ryder
1969 "The structure of attitudes toward abortion." Milbank Memorial Fund Quarterly 47 (January):11-38.

Westoff, Leslie Aldridge, and Charles F. Westoff
1971 From Now to Zero: Fertility, Contraception and Abortion in America. Boston: Little, Brown & Co.

Worden, Portia
1972 "Current opinion on abortion." PTA Magazine 66 (May):12-14.

Ziff, Harvey L.
1969 "Recent abortion law reforms (or much ado about nothing)." Journal of Criminal Law, Criminology and Police Science 60 (March):3-23.

CHAPTER 13

Bart, P.
1970 "Mother Portnoy's complaints." Transaction 8 (November-December).

Bartell, G. D.
1971 Group Sex. New York: Peter H. Wyden.

Bell, R.
1971 Marriage and Family Interaction. Homewood, Ill.: Dorsey Press.

Bell, Robert R., and Michael Gordon (eds.)
1972 The Social Dimension of Human Sexuality. Boston: Little, Brown & Co.

Blood, R.
1969 Marriage. New York: The Free Press.

Brown, Sandford
1966 "May I ask you a few questions about love?" Saturday Evening Post 239 (December 31):24-27.

Calhoun, A. W.
1960 A Social History of the American Family. New York: Barnes & Noble.

Christianity Today
1969 "Incidence of adultery." 13 (September):35-36.

Cohen, Y.
1969 "Ends and means in political control: State organization and the punishment of adultery, incest, and violation of celibacy." American Anthropologist 71 (Fall):658-687.

Cuber, J. F., and P. B. Harroff
1965 Sex and the Significant Americans. Baltimore: Penguin Books.

Davids, L.
1972 "Tomorrow's marriage styles." Current 136 (January):33-35.

Davis, J. F.
1970 Social Problems: Enduring Major Issues and Social Change. New York: The Free Press.

Davis, K.
1937 "The sociology of prostitution." American Sociological Review 2 (October):746-755.

Denfield, D., and M. Gordon
1970 "The sociology of mate swapping: The family that swings together clings together." Journal of Sex Research 7 (May):85-99.

Ellis, Albert
1954 The American Sexual Tragedy. New York: Twayne Publishers.

Folkman, J. D., and N. M. Clatworthy
1970 Marriage Has Many Faces. Columbus: Charles E. Merrill Publishing Co.

Folson, J. K.
1961 "Family, sexual and affectional functions of the." *In* A. Ellis and A. Abarbanel, The Encyclopedia of Sexual Behavior. New York: Hawthorn Books.

Freeman, H. E., and W. C. Jones
1970 Social Problems: Causes and Controls. Chicago: Rand McNally.

Freud, S.
1930 Sexuality and the Psychology of Love. (republished 1963 by Collier Books, New York.)

Gallup, G.
1969 The Gallup Opinion Index no. 49 (July). Princeton, N.J.: American Institute of Public Opinion.

1970 The Gallup Opinion Index no. 63 (September). Princeton, N.J.: American Institute of Public Opinion.

1972 The Gallup Opinion Index no. 85 (July). Princeton, N.J.: American Institute of Public Opinion.

1972 The Gallup Opinion Index no. 87 (September). Princeton, N.J.: American Institute of Public Opinion.

1973 The Gallup Opinion Index no. 92 (February). Princeton, N.J.: American Institute of Public Opinion.

Gilmartin, B. G., and D. V. Kusisto
1973 "Some personal and social characteristics of mate-sharing swingers." *In* Roger W. Libby and R. N. Whitehurst, Renovating Marriage. Danville, Calif.: Consensus Publishers.

Goode, W. J.
1963 World Revolution and Family Patterns. New York: The Free Press.

Goode, *cont.*
1971 "Family disorganization." *In* R. K. Merton and R. Nisbet, Contemporary Social Problems. New York: Harcourt, Brace, Jovanovich, pp. 467-544.

Gurin, G., J. Veroff, and S. Feld
1960 Americans View Their Mental Health: A Nationwide Interview Survey. New York: Basic Books.

Hill, Reuben
1964 "The American family in the future." Journal of Marriage and the Family 26 (February):20-28.

Hofstadter, R.
1960 The Age of Reform: From Bryan to F.D.R. New York: Vintage Books.

Horton, P. B., and G. R. Leslie
1965 The Sociology of Social Problems. New York: Appleton-Century Crofts.

Hunt, M.
1971 The Affair. New York: New American Library.

Kephart, W. H.
1966 The Family, Society and the Individual. Boston: Houghton Mifflin Co.

Kinsey, A. C., W. B. Pomeroy, C. E. Martin, and P. H. Gebhard
1948 Sexual Behavior in the Human Male. Philadelphia: W. B. Saunders Co.
1953 Sexual Behavior in the Human Female. Philadelphia: W. B. Saunders Co.

Landis, J. T., and M. G. Landis (eds.)
1952 Readings in Marriage and the Family. New York: Prentice-Hall.

Landis, P. H.
1954 "Don't expect too much of sex in marriage." Reader's Digest 65 (December): 25-28.

Lewis, L. S., and D. Brissett
1967 "Sex as work: A study of avocational counseling." Social Problems 15 (1967): 8-17.

Libby, R. W., and R. N. Whitehurst
1973 Renovating Marriage: Toward New Sexual Life-Styles. Danville, Calif.: Consensus Publishers.

Lindberg, P.
1972 "What's happening to the American family?" Better Homes and Gardens 50 (October):52-53; 128-129.

Masters, W. H., and V. E. Johnson
1966 Human Sexual Response. Boston: Little, Brown & Co.
1970 Human Sexual Inadequacy. Boston: Little, Brown & Co.

Marx, K.
1906 Das Kapital. New York: Modern Library.

Monthly Vital Statistics Report
1973 Vol. 22. (May 22).

Neubeck, G.
1969 Extra-Marital Relations. Englewood Cliffs, N.J.: Prentice-Hall.

Nimkoff, M. F.
1934 The Family. Chicago: Houghton-Mifflin Co.
1961 "Marriage." *In* A. Ellis and A. Abarbanel, The Encyclopedia of Sexual Behavior. New York: Hawthorn Books.
1965 Comparative Family Systems. Boston: Houghton Mifflin Co.

Nye, I. F., and L. Hoffman
1963 The Employed Mother in America. Chicago: Rand McNally & Co.

O'Neill, N., and G. O'Neill
1972 "Open marriage: a synergic model." The Family Coordinator 21 (October).
1973 Open Marriage: A New Life-Style for Couples. Philadelphia: M. Evans & Co.

Park, R. J., and P. C. Glick
1967 "Prospective changes in marriage and the family." Journal of Marriage and the Family 29 (May).

Pope, H., and D. D. Knudsen
1965 "Premarital sexual norms, the family, and social change." Journal of Marriage and the Family 27 (August).

Reich, W.
1969 The Sexual Revolution. New York: Farrar, Straus & Giroux.
1971 The Invasion of Compulsory Sex Morality. New York: Farrar, Straus & Giroux.

Reiss, I. L.
1967 The Social Context of Premarital Sexual Permissiveness. New York: Holt, Rinehart & Winston.

Rimmer, R. H.
1966 The Harrad Experiment. New York: Bantam Books.

Rogers, C.
1972 Becoming Partners: Marriage and Its Alternatives. New York: The Delacorte Press.

Roy, R., and D. Roy
1969 Honest Sex. London: George Allen & Unwin, Ltd.

Safire, W.
1973 "On cohabitation." The New York Times (September 24).

Salzman, L.; J. Bernard, and others
1969 "Changing standards: Discussing adultery." Time (May).

Skolnick, A. S., and J. H. Skolnick
1971 Family in Transition: Rethinking Marriage, Sexuality, Child Rearing, and

Skolnick and Skolnick, *cont.*
Family Organization. Boston: Little, Brown & Co.

Statistical Abstract of the United States
1970 Washington, D.C.: Government Printing Office.

Time
1969a "Changing standards: Discussing adultery at the annual meeting of the American Psychiatric Association." 93 (May 16):52.
1969b "Rites." 94 (July 4):57.

Udry, J. R.
1971 The Social Context of Marriage. Philadelphia: J. B. Lippincott Co.

U.S. News & World Report
1966 "Illegitimacy in the U.S.—It's on the rise." 61 (July 18):87.
1967 "Startling story of illegitimate children in U.S." 63 (October 2):84-85.

Varni, C.
1972 "An exploratory study of spouse-swapping." Pacific Sociological Review 15:4 (October), pp. 507-522.

Ventura, S. J.
1969 "Recent trends and differentials in illegitimacy." Journal of Marriage and the Family 31 (August).

Whitehurst, R.
1969 "Extramarital sex: Alienation or extension of normal behavior." *In* G. Neubeck (ed.), Extramarital Relations. Englewood Cliffs, N.J.: Prentice-Hall.

Whyte, W.
1956 The Organization Man. New York: Simon & Schuster.

Winch, R.
1970 "Permanence and change in the history of the American family and some speculation as to its future." Journal of Marriage and the Family 32 (February): 12-13.

Winch, R. F., and R. L. Blumberg
1953 "Societal complexity and familial organization." *In* Selected Studies in Marriage and the Family. New York: Holt, Rinehart & Winston, pp. 70-92.

Yankelovich, D.
1972 The Changing Values on Campus. New York: Pocket Books.

CHAPTER 14

Aarons, Leroy F.
1973 "For Indians it's a life with built-in failure." San Francisco Sunday Examiner & Chronicle (March 18): This World section, p. 18.

Adorno, T. W., et al.
1950 The Authoritarian Personality. New York: John Wiley & Sons.

"Akwesasne Notes."
1969 Published by the Indian Studies Program at Wesleyan University for the Mohawk Nation.

Allport, Gordon W.
1954 The Nature of Prejudice. Garden City, N.Y.: Doubleday Anchor Books.

American Friends Service Committee
1970 Uncommon Controversy. Seattle, Wash.: University of Washington Press.

Aptheker, Herbert
1964 A Documentary History of the Negro People in the United States. New York: Citadel Press.

Banton, Michael
1967 Race Relations. New York: Basic Books.

Bell, Inge Powell
1970 "CORE and the strategy of nonviolence." *In* Minako Kurokawa (ed.), Minority Responses: Comparative Views of Reactions to Subordination. New York: Random House.

Blalock, Hubert M.
1967 Toward a Theory of Minority Group Relations. New York: John Wiley & Sons.

Blaustein, Albert P., and Robert L. Zangrando
1968 Civil Rights and the Black American: A Documentary History. New York: Simon & Schuster.

Breitman, George (ed.)
1965 Malcolm X Speaks. New York: Grove Press.
1968 The Last Year of Malcolm X. New York: Schocken Books.

Briegal, Kaye
1970 "The development of Mexican-American organizations." *In* Manuel P. Servin, The Mexican-Americans: An Awakening Minority. Beverly Hills, Calif.: Glencoe Press.

Briggs, Ken
1973 "Signs of unrest among the U.S.'s Black Muslims." San Francisco Sunday Examiner & Chronicle (February 18):This World section, p. 28.

Brink, William, and Louis Harris
1967 Black and White: A Study of U.S. Racial Attitudes Today. New York: Simon & Schuster.

Broom, Leonard, and Norval D. Glenn
1965 Transformation of the Negro American. New York: Harper & Row.

Broyles, J. Allen
1966 John Birch Society: Anatomy of a Protest. Boston: Beacon Press.

Cameron, William Bruce
1966 Modern Social Movements: A Sociological Outline. New York: Random House.

Campbell, Angus
1971 White Attitudes Toward Black People. Ann Arbor, Mich.: Institute for Social Research.

Carmichael, Stokely, and Charles V. Hamilton
1967 Black Power: The Politics of Liberation in America. New York: Random House.

Chasteen, Edgar
1969 "Public accommodations: Social movements in conflict." Phylon 30 (Fall): 234-250.

Cleaver, Eldridge
1967 Post-Prison Writings and Speeches. New York: Random House.
1970 Soul On Ice. New York: Dell Publishing Co.

Conrad, Jack
1964 The Many Worlds of Man. New York: Thomas Y. Crowell Co.

Cover, R.
1970 "Year of harassment." The Nation 210 (February 2):110-113.

Cronin, E. David
1968 "Marcus Garvey: One aim! One God! One destiny!" In Melvin Drimmer (ed.), Black History: A Reappraisal. Garden City, N.Y.: Doubleday & Co.

Dahrendorf, Ralf
1958 "Out of Utopia: Toward a reorientation of sociological analysis." American Journal of Sociology 64 (September):115-127.

Davie, Maurice R.
1949 Negroes in American Society. New York: McGraw-Hill Book Co.

Davis, Kingsley, and Wilbert E. Moore
1945 "Some principles of stratification." American Sociological Review 10 (April): 242-249.

Day, Robert C.
1972 "The emergence of activism as a social movement." In Howard Bahr, et al., Native Americans Today: Sociological Perspectives. New York: Harper & Row.

Deloria, Vine, Jr.
1969 "The war between the redskins and the Feds." The New York Times Magazine (December 7).
1971 "Divided panthers." Time 97 (February 22):23.

Dollar, Clyde D.
1973 The second tragedy at Wounded Knee. The American West 10 (September).

Drimmer, Melvin (ed.)
1968 Black History: A Reappraisal. Garden City, N.Y.: Doubleday & Co.

Dunne, J. G.
1971 "To die standing: Cesar Chavez and the Chicanos." Atlantic Monthly 227 (June).

Ericksen, Charles A.
1970 "Uprising in the barrios." In John H. Burma (ed.), Mexican-Americans in the United States. Cambridge, Mass.: Schenkman Publishing Co.

Filler, Louis
1967 "Dynamics of reform: The antislavery crusade and others with something about the Negro." Antioch Review 27 (Fall).

Forster, Arnold, and Benjamin Epstein
1964 Danger on the Right. New York: Random House.

Gallup, George
1969a The Gallup Opinion Index, Issue no. 47 (May). Princeton, N.J.: American Institute of Public Opinion.
1969b The Gallup Opinion Index, Issue no. 51 (September). Princeton, N.J.: American Institute of Public Opinion.
1970a The Gallup Opinion Index, Issue no. 58 (April). Princeton, N.J.: American Institute of Public Opinion.
1970b The Gallup Opinion Index, Issue no. 62 (August). Princeton, N.J.: American Institute of Public Opinion.
1971a The Gallup Opinion Index, Issue no. 75 (September). Princeton, N.J.: American Institute of Public Opinion.
1971b The Gallup Opinion Index, Issue no. 77 (November). Princeton, N.J.: American Institute of Public Opinion.

Glock, Charles Y., and Rodney Stark
1966 Christian Beliefs and Anti-Semitism. New York: Harper & Row.

Goldman, Peter
1970 Report from Black America. New York: Simon & Schuster.

Gonzalez, Nancie L.
1970 "Alianza federal de mercedes." In Manuel P. Servin, The Mexican Americans: An Awakening Minority. Beverly Hills, Calif.: Glencoe Press.

Gordon, Milton M.
1964 Assimilation in American Life. New York: Oxford University Press.

Haines, Aubrey B.
1971 "Legal defense fund after 30 years." Christian Century 88 (April 21).

Handlin, Oscar
1951 The Uprooted. New York: Grosset & Dunlap.

Hofstadter, Richard
1960 The Age of Reform: From Bryan to F.D.R. New York: Vintage Books.

Howard, John R.
1970a "American Indians: Goodby to Tonto." *In* John R. Howard, Awakening Minorities. Chicago: Aldine Publishing Co.
1970b "Mexican Americans: The road to Huelga." *In* John R. Howard, Awakening Minorities, Chicago: Aldine Publishing Co.
1974 The Cutting Edge: Social Movements and Social Change in America. Philadelphia: J. B. Lippincott Co.

IFCO News
1972 "United Farm Workers union victory undermined." 3 (May-June):1.

Jensen, Arthur R.
1969 "How much can we boost IQ and scholastic achievement?" Harvard Educational Review 39 (Winter):1-123 and 39 (Summer):449-483.

"Jesse Jackson quits the SCLC after being suspended."
1971 Christian Century 88 (December 22).

LaBarre, Weston
1970 The Ghost Dance: Origins of Religion. Garden City, N.Y.: Doubleday & Co.

Lanternari, Vittorio
1963 The Religions of the Oppressed. New York: New American Library.

Laue, James S.
1972 "The changing character of the Negro protest." *In* Minako Kurokawa (ed.), Minority Responses: Comparative Views of Reactions to Subordination. New York: Random House.

Lincoln, C. Eric
1972a "The Black Muslims." *In* Arnold M. Rose and Caroline B. Rose, Minority Problems. New York: Harper & Row.
1972b "The Black Muslims in America." *In* Minako Kurokawa (ed.), Minority Responses: Comparative Views of Reactions to Subordination. New York: Random House.

Logan, Rayford W.
1970 The Negro in the United States, Vol. 1. New York: Van Nostrand Reinhold Co.

Logan, Rayford W., and Michael R. Winston
1971 The Negro in the United States, Vol. 2. New York: Van Nostrand Reinhold Co.

Lokos, Lionel
1971 The New Racism: Reverse Discrimination in America. New Rochelle, N.Y.: Arlington House.

Love, Joseph L.
1970 "La ràza: Mexican-Americans in rebellion." *In* John R. Howard, Awakening Minorities. Chicago: Aldine Publishing Co.

Malcolm X
1964 The Autobiography of Malcolm X. New York: Grove Press.

Marden, Charles F., and Gladys Meyer
1968 Minorities in American Society. New York: American Book Co.

Marine, Gene
1969 The Black Panthers. New York: New American Library.

Marx, Gary T.
1969 Protest and Prejudice: A Study of Belief in the Black Community. New York: Harper & Row.

Mason, Phillip
1970 Race Relations. New York: Oxford University Press.

Matusow, Allen J.
1970 "From civil rights to black power: The case of SNCC, 1960-1966." *In* Bracey Meier Rudwick (ed.), Conflict and Competition Studies in the Recent Black Protest Movement. Belmont, Calif.: Wadsworth Publishing Co.

Mauss, Armand L.
1971 "On being strangled by the stars and stripes: The New Left, the Old Left, and the natural history of American radical movements." Journal of Social Issues 27 (January):183-202.

Mayer, Kurt
1951 "Cultural pluralism and linguistic equilibrium." American Sociological Review 16 (April):157-163.

Meier, August
1968a "Booker T. Washington: An interpretation." *In* Melvin Drimmer (ed.), Black History: A Reappraisal. Garden City, N.Y.: Doubleday & Co.
1968b "On the role of Martin Luther King." *In* Melvin Drimmer, Black History: A Reappraisal. Garden City, N.Y.: Doubleday & Co.
1970 "Negro protest movements and organizations." *In* Bracey Meier Rudwick (ed.), Conflict and Competition: Studies in the Recent Black Protest Movement. Belmont, Calif.: Wadsworth Publishing Co.

Meier, August, and Elliott Rudwick
1969 "The first freedom ride." Phylon 30 (Fall):213-222.

Merton, Robert
1957 Social Theory and Social Structure. Glencoe, Ill.: The Free Press.

Mooney, James
1896 The Ghost Dance Religion and the Sioux Outbreak of 1890. Chicago, Ill.: University of Chicago Press.

Moore, Joan W.
1970 Colonialism: The case of the Mexican-Americans. Social Problems 17 (Spring).

Moore, Joan, with Alfredo Cuellar
1970 Mexican Americans. Englewood Cliffs, N.J.: Prentice-Hall.

Myrdal, Gunnar
1944 An American Dilemma. New York: McGraw-Hill Book Co.

Nabokov, P.
1970 "La ràza, the land, and the hippies." The Nation 210 (April 20):466-467.

National Center for Health Statistics
1972 Monthly Vital Statistics Report no. 20 (August 30). Washington, D.C.: Government Printing Office.

"New meaning for the N in SNCC."
1969 U.S. News & World Report (August 4):8.

Newsweek
1971 "Chavez Strikes Again." 77 (January 25).

Nixon, Richard M.
1969 Executive Order 11478: Equal Employment Opportunity in the Federal Government. Washington, D.C. (August 8, 1969).

Parsons, Talcott
1951 The Social System. Glencoe, Ill.: The Free Press.

Pettigrew, Thomas F.
1964 A Profile of the Negro American. Princeton, N.J.: Van Nostrand Co.

Pfaff, Alma D.
1970 The Black Panther Party: Its Origin and Development as Reflected in Its Official Weekly Newspaper, the Black Panther Community News Service. Washington, D.C.: Government Printing Office.

Prager, K.
1971 "Right on toward a new black pluralism." Time 97 (February 22):14.

Quarles, Benjamin
1964 The Negro in the Making of America. New York: The Macmillan Co.

Remmling, Gunther W.
1967 Road to Suspicion. New York: Appleton-Century Crofts.

Rex, John
1970 Race Relations in Sociological Theory. New York: Schocken Books.

Rieff, Philip
1966 The Triumph of the Therapeutic. New York: Harper & Row.

Rogers, Cornish
1970 "SCLC: Rhetoric or strategy?" Christian Century 87 (September 2).

Rokeach, Milton
1960 The Open and Closed Mind. New York: Basic Books.

Rose, Arnold, and Caroline Rose
1965 Minority Problems. New York: Harper & Row.

Rose, Peter I.
1964 They and We. New York: Random House.

San Francisco Sunday Examiner & Chronicle
1973 "A grim segregation report." (January 21).

Schanche, D. A.
1970 "Panthers against the wall." Atlantic Monthly 225 (May):55-61.

Schermerhorn, R. A.
1970 Comparative Ethnic Relations: A Framework for Theory and Research. New York: Random House.

Shibutani, Tamotsu, and Kian M. Kwan
1965 Ethnic Stratification: A Comparative Approach. New York: The Macmillan Co.

Simpson, George E., and J. Milton Yinger
1965 Racial and Cultural Minorities. New York: Harper & Row.

Smith, Donald H.
1970 "An exegesis of Martin Luther King Jr.'s social philosophy." Phylon 31 (Spring).

Snyder, Louis
1962 The Idea of Racialism. Princeton, N.J.: Van Nostrand Co.

Sowell, Thomas
1973 "Radical chic is vicious." Psychology Today 6 (February).

Steiner, Stan
1968 The New Indians. New York: Dell Publishing Co.

Taylor, Paul
1974 "America cools off on integration of schools." San Francisco Sunday Examiner & Chronicle (January 20).

Thomas, Robert K.
1970a "Pan-Indianism." *In* Stuart Levine and Nancy O. Lurie (eds.), The American Indian Today. Baltimore, Md.: Penguin Books.
1970b "Tijerina sentenced in New Mexico." Christian Century 87 (January 28).

Toch, Hans
1965 The Social Psychology of Social Movements. Indianapolis, Ind.: Bobbs-Merrill Co.

Torgerson, Dial
1968 "Brown power unity seen behind school disorders." Los Angeles Times (March 17):1.

U.S. Bureau of the Census
1970 Statistical Abstract of the United States: 1970. Washington, D.C.: Government Printing Office.

U.S. Commission on Civil Rights
1970 Mexican American Education Study. Washington, D.C.: Government Printing Office.

U.S. Department of Commerce
1971 The Social and Economic Status of Negroes in the United States, 1970. Washington, D.C.: Government Printing Office.

U.S. Department of Labor
1971 Black Americans: A Chartbook. Washington, D.C.: Government Printing Office.

U.S. News & World Report
1970 "Whatever happened to the Black Muslims? Negroes building a farming empire." 69 (September 21):84.

van den Berghe, Pierre L.
1963 "Dialectic and functionalism: Toward a theoretical synthesis." American Sociological Review 28 (October):695-705.
1967 Race and Racism: A Comparative Perspective. New York: John Wiley & Sons.
1970 "Racial segregation in South Africa: Degrees and kinds." In Pierre L. van den Berghe, Race and Ethnicity. New York: Basic Books.

von Eschen, Donald, et al.
1970 "The disintegration of the Negro nonviolent movement." In J. Bracy, A. Meier, and E. Rudwick (eds.), Conflict and Competition: Studies in the Recent Black Protest Movement. Belmont, Calif.: Wadsworth Publishing Co.

Wagatsuma, Hiroshi
1967 "The social perception of skin color in Japan." Daedalus 96 (Spring).

Wagley, Charles
1969 "From caste to class in North Brazil." In Melvin M. Tumin (ed.), Comparative Perspectives on Race Relations. Boston: Little, Brown & Co.

Walla Walla Union Bulletin
1973 "Indian fishing dispute turning more violent." (February 16).

Waskow, Arthur I.
1966 From Race Riots to Sit-In. New York: Doubleday & Co.

Wax, Murray L.
1971 Indian Americans, Unity and Diversity. Englewood Cliffs, N.J.: Prentice-Hall.

Williams, Robin M., Jr.
1964 Strangers Next Door. Englewood Cliffs, N.J.: Prentice-Hall.

Witt, Shirley
1970 "Nationalistic trends among American Indians." In Stuart Levine and Nancy O. Lurie, The American Indian Today. Baltimore, Md.: Penguin Books.

Woodward, C. Vann
1955 The Strange Career of Jim Crow. New York: Oxford University Press.

Yinger, J. Milton
1965 A Minority Group in American Society. New York: McGraw-Hill Book Co.

Zinn, Howard
1967 SNCC: The New Abolitionists. Boston: Beacon Press.

CHAPTER 15

Albrecht, Stan L.
1972 "Environmental social movements and counter-movements: An overview and an illustration." Journal of Voluntary Action Research 1 (October):2-11.

Allen, Shirley Walter, and Leonard Justin Wilkinson
1966 Conserving Natural Resources: Principles and Practices in a Democracy. New York: McGraw-Hill Book Co.

Baden, John
1973 "Neospartan hedonism, adult toy aficionados, and the development of bureaucratic purgatory: A causal model." Paper presented at the Meetings of the Pacific Sociological Association, Scottsdale, Arizona, May 1973.

Bagge, Carl E.
1971 "Radicalism perils supply of minerals." From a speech quoted in The Salt Lake Tribune (June 29):17.

Bates, Marston
1969 The human ecosystem. In Resources and Man, A Study and Recommendations of the National Academy of Sciences. San Francisco: W. H. Freeman & Co., pp. 21-30.

Boulding, Kenneth
1966 Human Values on the Spaceship Earth. New York: National Council of Churches of Christ in the U.S.A.

Cameron, William Bruce
1966 Modern Social Movements: A Sociological Outline. New York: Random House.

Bibliography

Carson, Rachel
1962 Silent Spring. Boston: Houghton Mifflin.
Castro, Joao Augusto de Araujo
1972 "Environment and development: The Case of developing countries." *In* David A. Kay and Eugene B. Skolnikoff, World Eco-Crisis: International Organizations in Response. Madison: University of Wisconsin Press, pp. 237-252.
Chapman, John D.
1969 "Interactions between man and his resources." *In* Resources and Man, A Study and Recommendations of the National Academy of Sciences. San Francisco: W. H. Freeman & Co., pp. 31-42.
Committee on Resources and Man
1969 Conserving Natural Resources: Principles and Practices in a Democracy. New York: McGraw-Hill Book Co.
Commoner, Barry
1971 The Closing Circle: Nature, Man and Technology. New York: Alfred A. Knopf.
Cook, Earl
1971 "The flow of energy in an industrial society." *In* Energy and Power, A Scientific American Book. San Francisco: W. H. Freeman & Co., pp. 83-91.
Coser, Lewis A.
1957 "Social conflict and the theory of social change." The British Journal of Sociology 8 (September):197-207.
Creer, Ralph, Robert Gray, and Michael Treshow
1970 "Differential responses to air pollution as an environmental health problem." Journal of the Air Pollution Control Association 20 (December):814-818.
Davies, Clarence J., III
1970 The Politics of Pollution. New York: Pegasus.
Devall, W. B.
1970a The Governing of a Voluntary Organization: Oligarchy and Democracy in the Sierra Club. Ph.D. dissertation, University of Oregon.
1970b "Conservation: An upper-middle class social movement: A replication." Journal of Leisure Research 2 (Spring):123-126.
Dillman, Don A.
1971 "Public values and concerns of Washington residents." Agricultural Experiment Station Bulletin No. 748, Washington State University, Pullman, December 1971.

Dolbeare, Kenneth M., and Patricia Dolbeare
1971 American Ideologies: The Competing Political Beliefs of the 1970's. Chicago: Markham Publishing Co.
Dunlap, Riley E., and Richard P. Gale
1971 "Student recruitment into the environmental movement: A test of a reformulation of 'mass society' theory." Paper read at the annual meeting of the Rural Sociological Society, Denver, Colorado.
1972 "Politics and ecology: A political profile of student eco-activists." Youth and Society 3 (June):379-397.
1974 "Party membership and environmental politics: A legislative roll-call analysis." Social Science Quarterly 55:4 (December).
Dunlap, Riley E., Richard P. Gale, and Brent M. Rutherford
1973 "Concern for environmental rights among college students." The American Journal of Economics and Sociology 32 (January):45-60.
Durkheim, Emile
1954 The Elementary Forms of Religious Life. Tr. by Joseph Ward Swain. Glencoe, Ill.: The Free Press.
Ehrlich, Paul R., and Anne H. Ehrlich
1972 Population, Resources, Environment. San Francisco: W. H. Freeman & Co.
Ehrlich, Paul R., John P. Holdren, and Richard W. Holm
1971 Man and the Ecosphere. San Francisco: W. H. Freeman & Co.
Einstein, Charles
1970 "Who's going to take out the garbage?" *In* Walt Anderson (ed.), Politics and Environment. Pacific Palisades, Calif.: Goodyear Publishing Co., pp. 100-106.
Erskine, Hazel
1972a "Polls: Pollution and its costs." Public Opinion Quarterly 36 (Spring):120-135.
1972b "Polls: Pollution and industry." Public Opinion Quarterly 36 (Summer):263-280.
Faich, Ronald G., and Richard P. Gale
1971 "The environmental movement: From recreation to politics." Pacific Sociological Review 14 (July):270-287.
Fischer, John
1971 "How I got radicalized." In E. A. Schuler, T. F. Hoult, D. L. Gibson, and W. B. Brookover, Readings in Sociology. New York: Thomas Y. Crowell.
Gale, Richard P.
1972 "From sit-in to hike-in: A comparison of the civil rights and environmental movements." *In* W. Burch, N. Cheek, and L.

Gale, *cont.*
Taylor (eds.), Social Behavior, Natural Resources and the Environment. New York: Harper & Row, pp. 280-305.

Gilliam, Harold
1972 "Jobs vs. the environment." San Francisco Examiner & Chronicle (December 10):This World section, p. 41.

Gusfield, Joseph R. (ed.)
1970 Protest, Reform, and Revolt: A Reader in Social Movements. New York: John Wiley & Sons.

Hano, Arnold
1971 "Protectionists vs. recreationists—The battle of Mineral King." *In* Roy L. Meek and John A. Straayer, The Politics of Neglect: The Environmental Crisis. Boston: Houghton Mifflin Co.

Harry, Joseph, Richard P. Gale, and John C. Hendee
1969 "Conservation: An upper-middle class social movement." Journal of Leisure Research 1 (Summer):246-254.

Hendee, John C., William R. Catton, Larry D. Marlow, and C. Frank Brockman
1968 Wilderness Users in the Pacific Northwest—Their Characteristics, Values, and Management Preferences. USDA Forest Service Research Paper PNW-61. Portland, Ore.: Forest and Range Experiment Station.

Hendee, John C., Richard P. Gale, and Joseph Harry
1969 "Conservation, politics and democracy." Journal of Soil and Water Conservation 24 (November-December):212-215.

Hubbert, M. King
1969 "Energy resources." *In* Committee on Resources and Man. San Francisco: W. H. Freeman & Co., pp. 157-242.

Jones, Holway R.
1965 John Muir and the Sierra Club. San Francisco: Sierra Club Publication.

Killian, Lewis M.
1964 "Social movements." *In* Robert E. L. Faris (ed.), Handbook of Modern Sociology. Chicago: Rand McNally, pp. 426-455.

Kimball, Thomas L.
1972 "Status of our environment and our efforts to improve it." A talk presented before the Joint International Conference developed by the Atomic Industrial Forum and the American Nuclear Society, November 13, 1972. Copies available from the National Wildlife Federation, Washington, D.C.

Krizek, John
1970 "How to build a pyramid: A kit of PR tools helps win San Francisco's approval for a new high-rise office building." Public Relations Journal 26 (December):17-21.

Ludwig, John H., George B. Morgan, and Thomas B. McMullen
1970 "Trends in urban air quality." Transactions, American Geophysical Union 51 (May):468-475.

McCarthy, G. Michael
1973 "Retreat from responsibility: The Colorado legislature in the conservation era, 1876-1908." Rocky Mountain Social Science Journal 10 (April):27-36, 1972.

McConnell, Grant
1954 "The conservation movement—past and present." The Western Political Quarterly 7 (September):463-478.

McHarg, Ian L.
1969 Design With Nature. Garden City, N.Y.: The Natural History Press.

Maddox, John
1972 The Doomsday Syndrome. New York: McGraw-Hill Book Co.

Maloney, John C., and Lynn Slovonsky
1971 "The pollution issue: A survey of editorial judgments." *In* Leslie L. Roos, Jr. (ed.), The Politics of Ecosuicide. New York: Holt, Rinehart & Winston, pp. 64-78.

Marx, Leo
1970 "American institutions and ecological ideals." Science 170 (November 27):945-952.

Maslow, A. H.
1943 "A theory of human motivation." Psychological Review 50 (July):370-396.

Mauss, Armand L.
1971 "On being strangled by the stars and stripes." The Journal of Social Issues 27 (1):183-202.

Meadows, Donella H., et al.
1972 The Limits to Growth: A report for the Club of Rome's Project on the Predicament of Mankind. New York: Universe Books.

Mishan, E. J.
1970 Technology and Growth: The Price We Pay. New York: Praeger Publishers.

Mitchell, John G. (ed.)
1970 Ecotactics: The Sierra Club Handbook for Environmental Activists. New York: Simon & Schuster.

Bibliography

Molotch, Harvey
1970 "Oil in Santa Barbara and power in America." Sociological Inquiry 40 (Winter):131-144.
1971 "Santa Barbara: Oil in the velvet playground." *In* Roy L. Meek and John A. Straayer (eds.), The Politics of Neglect: The Environmental Crisis. Boston: Houghton Mifflin Co.

Moncrief, Lewis
1970 "The cultural basis for our environmental crisis." Science 170 (October 30):508-512.

Morrison, Denton E., Kenneth E. Hornback, and W. Keith Warner
1972 "The environmental movement: Some preliminary observations." *In* W. Burch, N. Cheek, and L. Taylor (eds.), Social Behavior, Natural Resources and the Environment. New York: Harper & Row, pp. 259-279.

Morrison, Denton E., and Allan D. Steeves
1967 "Deprivation, discontent, and social movement participation evidence on a contemporary farmer's movement, the NFO." Rural Sociology 32 (December):414-434.

Munton, Donald, and Linda Brady
1970 American Public Opinion and Environmental Pollution. The Behavioral Science Laboratory Research Report, Ohio State University.

Murch, Arvin W.
1971 "Public concern for environmental pollution." Public Opinion Quarterly 35 (Spring):100-106.

Nash, Roderick
1965 "Introduction." *In* Holway R. Jones, John Muir and the Sierra Club. San Francisco: Sierra Club Publication, 1965.

Petric, Nick
1971 Letter to the editor of The Salt Lake Tribune (July 14).

Public Law Establishing the Council on Environmental Quality
1970 Public Law 91-190, 91st Congress, 1970.

Rappaport, Roy A.
1971 "The flow of energy in an agricultural society." *In* Energy and Power, A Scientific American Book. San Francisco: W. H. Freeman & Co., pp. 69-80.

Reissman, Leonard
1972 "The Solution Cycle of Social Problems." The American Sociologist 7 (February):7-9.

Schiff, Ashley L.
1971 "Innovation and administrative decision making: The conservation of land resources." *In* Leslie L. Roos, Jr. (ed.), The Politics of Ecosuicide. New York: Holt, Rinehart & Winston, pp. 273-298.

Schnaiberg, Allan
1971 "Politics, participation and pollution: The 'environmental movement'." Mimeographed, Northwestern University.

Smelser, Neil J.
1962 A Theory of Collective Behavior. New York: The Free Press.

Starr, Chauncey
1971 "Energy and power." *In* Energy and Power, A Scientific American Book. San Francisco: W. H. Freeman & Co., pp. 3-15.

St. John, Jeffrey
1972 "Fear and fantasy in future folly." The New York Times, December 5, 1972.

Suljak, Nedjelko D.
1971 Public Policymaking and Environmental Quality: An Annotated Interdisciplinary Bibliography. Institute of Government Affairs, University of California, Davis.

Time
1970 (August 3):42.

Toch, Hans
1965 The Social Psychology of Social Movements. New York: The Bobbs-Merrill Co.

Trop, Cecile, and Leslie L. Roos, Jr.
1971 "Public opinion and the environment." In Leslie L. Roos, Jr. (ed.), The Politics of Ecosuicide. New York: Holt, Rinehart, & Winston.

Wagar, J. Alan
1970 "Growth vs. the quality of life." Science 168 (June 5):1179-1184.

White, Lynn
1967 "The historical roots of our ecological crisis." Science 155 (March 10):1203-1207.

Zald, Mayer N., and Roberta Ash
1966 "Social movement organizations: Growth, decay and change." Social Forces 44 (March):327-341.

CHAPTER 16

Aird, John S.
1962 "Population policy in mainland China." Population Studies 16 (July):38-57.

Aso, Takenori
1971 "The factors affecting fertility in Japan since 1955." Unpublished master's thesis, University of North Dakota, 1971.

Aso, *cont.*
1975 "The year of the fiery horse and fertility control in Japan." Unpublished Ph.D. dissertation, Washington State University, 1975.

Bahr, Howard, Bruce Chadwick, and Darwin Thomas (eds.)
1972 Population, Resources, and the Future: Non-Malthusian Perspectives. Provo, Utah: Brigham Young University Press.

Baker, Jeffrey J. W.
1970 "Science, birth control, and the Roman Catholic church." Bioscience 20 (February):143-150.

Barnett, Larry D.
1971 "Zero Population Growth, Inc." BioScience, 21 (July 15):759-765.
1974 "Zero Population Growth, Inc.: A Second Study." Journal of Biosocial Science 6 (January):1-22.

Benson, Ezra Taft
1969 Official Report of the One Hundred Thirty-ninth Annual Conference of the Church of Jesus Christ of Latter-Day Saints. Salt Lake City, Utah: Church of Jesus Christ of Latter-Day Saints (April):12.

Blake, Judith
1966 "The Americanization of Catholic reproductive ideals." Population Studies 20 (July):27-43.
1971 "Abortion and public opinion: The 1960-1970 decade." Science 171 (February 12):540-549.

Bogue, Donald J.
1969 Principles of Demography. New York: John Wiley & Sons.

Bouvier, Leon F.
1972 "Catholics and contraception." Journal of Marriage and the Family 34 (August):514-522.

Cade, Toni
1970 "The pill: Genocide or liberation?" The Black Woman: An Anthology. New York: Signet Classics, pp. 162-169.

Claxton, Philander P., Jr.
1971 "The development of institutions to meet the world population crisis." Department of State Bulletin 65 (August 16):165-172.

Coale, Ansley J.
1964 "How a population ages or grows younger." *In* Ronald Freedman (ed.), Population: The Vital Revolution. Garden City, N.Y.: Doubleday & Co.

Commission on Population Growth and the American Future
1972 Population and the American Future. New York: New American Library.

Douglas, Mary
1972 "Population control in primitive groups." *In* Sue T. Reid and David L. Lyon (eds.), Population Crisis: An Interdisciplinary Perspective. Glenview, Ill.: Scott, Foresman & Co.

Ehrlich, Paul R., and Anne H. Ehrlich
1972 Population, Resources, Environment. San Francisco: W. H. Freeman & Co.

Erskine, Hazel
1967 "The polls: More on the population explosion and birth control." Public Opinion Quarterly 31 (Summer):303-313.

Gallup, George
1973 "Few favor large families." Salt Lake Tribune (February 5).

Glass, David V.
1940 Population Policies and Movements in Europe. Oxford: Clarendon Press.

Goldschmidt, Walter
1959 Man's Way. A Holt-Dryden Book: Henry Holt & Co.

Greene, W.
1972 "Militant Malthusians: Zero Population Growth movement." Saturday Review 55 (March 11):40-44.

Hauser, Philip
1972 "The emergence of the population problem." *In* Sue Titus Reid and David L. Lyon (eds.), Population Crisis: An Interdisciplinary Perspective. Glenview, Ill.: Scott, Foresman & Co.

Heer, David M.
1968 Society and Population. Englewood Cliffs, N.J.: Prentice-Hall.

Heer, David M., and Judith G. Bryden
1966 "Family allowances and fertility in the Soviet Union." Soviet Studies 18 (October):153-163.

Kantner, John F.
1968 "American attitudes on population policy: Recent trends." Studies in Family Planning 30 (May):1-7.

Killian, Lewis M.
1964 "Social movements." *In* Robert E. L. Faris (ed.), Handbook of Modern Sociology. Chicago: Rand McNally, pp. 426-455.

McCracken, Samuel
1972 "The population controllers." Commentary 56 (May): 45-52.

Packard, Vance
1972 A Nation of Strangers. New York: David McKay Co.

Peterson, William
1958 "Internal migration and economic development in Northern America." Annals of the American Academy of Political and Social Science 316 (March):52-59.

Pollara, Frank
1971 "Trends in U.S. population." *In* Daniel Callahan (ed.), The American Population Debate. Garden City, N.Y.: Doubleday & Co., pp. 55-67.

Progressive Labor Party Position Paper
1971 "ZPG: A Fascist movement." *In* Daniel Callahan (ed.), The American Population Debate. Garden City, N.Y.: Doubleday & Co., pp. 68-76.

Rowan, Carl T.
1972 "Efforts to curb world's population growth will fail." Salt Lake Tribune (December 19).

San Francisco Sunday Examiner & Chronicle
1974 "Two meetings, two failures?" (September 8):This World section, p. 14.

Silberman, Charles E.
1962 "The city and the Negro." Fortune 65 (March):88-154.

Simon, Rita James
1971 "Public attitudes toward population and pollution." Public Opinion Quarterly 35 (Spring):93-99.

Spicer, Judith C.
1973 "Mormon fertility through half a century: Another test of the Americanization hypothesis." Paper presented at the Pacific Sociological Association Meetings, Scottsdale, Arizona, May 1973.

Thomlinson, Ralph
1965 Population Dynamics. New York: Random House.
1967 Demographic Problems. Belmont, Calif.: Dickenson Publishing Co.

Thompson, Warren S.
1928 "Population." American Journal of Sociology 34 (July):959-975.
1953 Population Problems. New York: McGraw-Hill Book Co.

Thompson, Warren S., and David T. Lewis
1965 Population Problems. New York: McGraw-Hill Book Co.

United Nations
1966 "World population prospects as assessed in 1963." U.N. Population Studies, No. 41.

U.S. Bureau of the Census
1972a Statistical Abstract of the United States, 93rd edition. Washington, D.C.: Government Printing Office.
1972b "Birth expectations and fertility: June 1972." Current Population Reports, Series P-20, No. 240. Washington, D.C.: Government Printing Office.
1972c "Mobility of the population of the United States: March 1970 to March 1971." Current Population Reports, Series P-20, No. 235. Washington, D.C.: Government Printing Office.
1972d "Illustrative population projections for the United States: The demographic effects of alternate paths to zero growth. Current Population Reports, Series P-25, No. 480. Washington, D.C.: Government Printing Office.
1972e "Projections of the population of the United States, age and sex: 1972 to 2020." Current Population Reports, Series P-25, No. 493. Washington, D.C.: Government Printing Office.

U.S. Department of Health, Education, and Welfare
1973 "Births, marriages, divorces, and deaths for 1972." Monthly Vital Statistics 21 (March).

Wattenberg, Ben
1970 "The nonsense explosion." The New Republic (April 4-11):12-23.
1972 "Overpopulation as a crisis issue." *In* Howard Bahr, Bruce Chadwick, and Darwin Thomas (eds.), Population, Resources, and the Future: Non-Malthusian Perspectives. Provo, Utah: Brigham Young University Press.

Westoff, Leslie Aldridge
1974 "People who gave up more children." San Francisco Sunday Examiner & Chronicle, Sunday Punch section (October 6):2.

Willie, Charles V.
1972 "The genocide issue—Two views." *In* the Population Reference Bureau, Inc., The World Population Dilemma. Washington, D.C.: Columbia Books, pp. 51-53.

Index

NAMES AND CITATIONS

Aarons, Leroy F., 527
Abbott, R. S., 533
Abelson, H., 365, 366, 371
Abernathy, Rev. Ralph David, 214
Abraham, R. B., 301
Abrahamsen, David, 98
Abrams, S., 302
Abzug, Bella, 53
Adams, Elsie, 405
Adams, W. Thomas, 119
Addams, Jane, 18, 131, 132, 134, 138, 370
Addus, H., 300
Adler, Alfred, 301
Adorno, Theodore, 16-17, 49, 529, 532
Advocate, The, 367, 396, 402
Agnew, Spiro T., 231
Aird, John S., 610
Akers, Ronald L., 30, 126, 290, 302, 304
Akwesasne Notes, 542
Albert, Ethel M., 407
Albrecht, Stan L., 571, 582-583, 590
Allen, Shirley W., 557*n*
Allport, Gordon W., 529, 532
Alper, Benedict S., 178
Alpert, Richard, 259
Alpren, David M., 95, 105
Altbach, Phillip G., 212
American Council on Education, 204
American Friends Service Committee, 542
American Law Institute, 464
Andersen, Hans Christian, 386, 401
Anslinger, H. J., 106, 258, 263, 272, 273-274
Anthony, Susan B., 416, 428
Aptheker, Herbert, 520
Archer, Dane, 94, 103
Aries, Philippe, 201
Aso, Takenori, 656
Aspinal, Wayne, 603
Augustus, Caesar, 607
Augustus, John, 122-123, 162
Austin, A. W., 204

Bacon, Sheldon D., 282
Baden, John, 601-602
Bagley, Sarah, 415

Bahr, Howard M., 291, 318, 642-643
Baker, Bobbie, 88
Baker, Gordon H., 119
Baker, Harvey, 123
Bales, R. F., 281, 303-304
Ball, John C., 245, 461
Balter, Mitchell B., 241
Banfield, Edward, 66-67
Banton, Michael, 107, 513
Bardwick, Judith M., 423
Barnes, Harry E., 151, 153
Barnett, Larry D., 643, 648-650
Barry, Leonora, 426
Bart, Pauline, 487
Bartell, G. D., 481, 493, 503
Bates, A. B., 557, 558
Bayer, A. E., 204
Bayley, David H., 106, 202
Becker, Harold K., 151
Becker, Howard S., 16, 31-32, 35, 58, 70, 99, 100, 106, 263, 266, 271, 277, 296, 304, 459-460
Bedau, H. A., 149, 150, 152, 153, 188, 189
Beecher, Rev. Thomas K., 178, 182
Beers, Clifford, 331-332, 340-342, 343, 345
Beerstecher, E. J., 300
Bell, D., 98, 162, 284, 285, 292, 297, 298, 312, 313, 315, 377, 395, 456, 457, 463, 468, 493, 505, 536
Bell, Luther V., 331
Bellush, Jewel, 107
Belmont, Mrs. Oliver P., 416
Bennett, James V., 97, 162
Bensen, Ezra Taft, 638
Berck, Martin G., 164, 171, 192
Berger, Peter L., 3, 4-5, 7-8, 18-19, 20, 44, 53
Berghe, Pierre van den, 512, 513, 532
Berman, Harriet, 361, 368, 369, 398
Bernard, J., 507
Birkelbach, R. D., 373, 386
Black, Donald J., 106, 107, 108
Blackman, A., 145-146
Blackwell, Henry, 428
Blake, Judith, 454, 460, 634, 636
Blalock, Hubert M., 533
Blane, H. T., 302, 303
Blatch, Harriet Stanton, 427
Blaustein, Albert P., 553

Block, Richard L., 92, 101
Blood, Robert O., Jr., 423-424, 490
Bloomfield, F. F., 302
Blum, Eva Marie, 240, 314
Blum, Richard H., 240, 245, 246, 314
Blumberg, R. L., 94, 476-477
Blumer, Herbert, 44-45, 57, 58, 61, 66, 70, 109, 110
Bogue, Donald J., 612
Bonham, Sharon P., 456
Boren, Jerry F., 178
Boskin, Joseph, 202-203, 207
Boulding, Kenneth E., 218, 220, 559
Bouvier, Leon F., 632, 636-637
Bowen, Louise De Koven, 130, 131, 132, 138
Bowlby, John, 119
Brace, Charles Loring, 122, 135
Brady, Linda, 570, 572, 573, 574, 576, 577, 578
Branch, Elmer, 191*n*
Brecher, Edward M., 257, 268, 277
Breitman, George, 523
Brennan, Justice William J., 191*n*
Brent, Rt. Rev. Charles, 258, 267
Briegal, Kaye, 524, 525, 539
Briggs, Ken, 539, 547
Brink, William, 517
Brinton, Crane, 49, 57, 60, 337
Briscoe, Mary Louise, 405
Brissett, D., 491
Brockway, Zebulon, 135, 169, 177, 178-179, 182
Bromberg, Walter, 321, 323
Broom, Leonard, 521, 535, 536, 538, 550, 552
Brothers, Joyce, 420, 439, 487
Brown, Harrison, 563
Brown, Helen Gurley, 493, 504
Brown, H. Rap, 214, 226, 227, 227*n*, 545, 546
Brown, Roy M., 151, 154
Broyles, Allen J., 228, 531
Bryden, Judith G., 609
Buchman, Dr. Frank N., 298
Buckley, William F., 369
Buckman, Peter, 226
Bulletin (Philadelphia), 83, 85
Bullough, Vern L., 358
Burcart, Janie M., 441
Burger, Justice Warren, 234
Burke, Stephen W., 208

706

Index

Burnham, David, 86
Burns, Robert, 151
Burns, Ruth A., 470
Burton, Robert, 323

Cade, Toni, 644-645
Cahalan, D., 286, 290, 291
Cahn, S., 292, 301, 302, 304-305, 313
Calderone, Mary S., 447, 463
Caldwell, Peter, 133
Calhoun, A. W., 498-500
California Auditor General, 155
Callahan, Daniel, 444, 447, 448, 454-455, 458, 463, 465
Cameron, Mary O., 93, 589
Campbell, Angus, 516, 517
Cantor, Gilbert M., 402
Cantril, Hadley, 49
Carkett, Ross, 142
Carmichael, Stokely, 214, 226, 227, 227n, 434, 537, 546
Carnoy, Judith, 33
Carr-Saunders, A. M., 613
Carson, Rachel, 583, 584, 589
Carver, Lyell, 147
Catt, Carrie Chapman, 427, 429
Catullus, 359
Cavan, Jordon T., 115, 116
Cavan, Ruth S., 115, 116
Census, U.S. Bureau of the, 514, 515, 616-620, 623, 624, 625, 626, 627, 628
Chadwick, Bruce, 642
Chambers, Bradford, 226, 245, 248, 255
Chambliss, William J., 33, 34
Chapman, John D., 559, 588
Chavez, Cesar, 525-526, 539, 547, 551
Chekhov, Anton, 401
Cherrington, Ernest H., 297, 308, 309
Chessman, Carryl, 170, 189
Chevigny, Paul, 92, 108
Chisholm, Shirley, 410, 435
Christian Century, 167
Christianity Today, 487
Chute, Charles L., 162
Cipes, Robert M., 94, 95, 100, 101, 102, 103, 105, 106
Cisian, I. H., 286, 290
Civil Service Journal, 364
Clarenbach, Dr. Kathryn, 433
Clark, Herbert, 215
Clark, Ramsey, 87, 90, 96, 96n
Clatworthy, N. M., 505
Clausen, John A., 321, 324-326, 349, 352
Claxton, Philander P., Jr., 647
Cleaver, Eldridge, 215, 227, 434, 524, 537, 547
Cleland, John, 358
Clinard, Marshall B., 20, 29, 32
Clinebell, H. J., Jr., 313
Cloward, Richard A., 29, 98, 126, 306
Coale, Ansley J., 617, 622
Cohen, Albert, 30, 99, 117, 126, 127, 248
Cohen, Yehudi A., 477
Collins, Thomas, 409
Colombier, Jean, 337

Commission on Population Growth and the American Future, 467-468, 617-618, 620, 622, 626, 627
Commoner, Barry, 583, 584
Comstock, Anthony, 18, 359, 373-374, 385
Conger, John S., 302
Conner, Walter D., 97, 106
Connery, Robert H., 232, 233, 344, 347-348
Connor, Ralph G., 305
Conrad, Jack, 511
Conrad, John P., 169, 173, 193-194
Cook, Earl, 562
Cooke, Robert E., 448
Coolidge, Pres. Calvin, 162
Cory, Donald, 391
Council of State Governments, 337
Cox Commission, 206, 207, 223
Craig, Alec, 358, 374
Cray, Ed, 92
Cressey, Donald R., 30, 87, 177, 179n, 304
Cronin, E. David, 520, 550
Crossley, H. M., 286, 290
Cruz-Coke, R., 299-300
Cuber, John F., 479, 480, 491, 496, 503
Cuellar, Alfredo, 515
Currie, Elliott, 33, 34
Cushing, Robert G., 373

Dahrendorf, Ralph, 532
Dai, Bingham, 245
Daily Idahonian, 374, 389, 401
Daniels, Stephanie, 168, 169, 171, 186, 200
David, Stephen M., 107
Davids, L., 508
Davie, Maurice R., 519, 534
Davies, Clarence J., III, 578
Davis, Caroline, 433
Davis, F. James, 35, 498
Davis, Kingsley, 27, 342, 357, 365, 379, 398, 496, 532, 613, 640, 654
Day, Robert C., 527, 541-542
de Beauvoir, Simone, 432-433, 444
DeFleur, Lois B., 245
DeFunis, Marco, 554
Deloria, Vine, Jr., 552
Denfield, D., 481, 493
Denison, M., 300
Dennett, Mrs. Mary, 359
DePugh, Robert, 215
Dershowitz, Alan M., 350
Deutsch, Albert, 330, 333-334, 338, 339, 343-344, 345, 346-347
Deutscher, Irwin, 127-128
Devereux, George, 442-443
Dickson, Donald, 262, 263, 269, 271, 272
Dillman, Don A., 571
Dix, Dorothea, 330-331, 335, 338-339, 340, 349
Dodge, Mrs. Arthur, 417
Doerr, Dale W., 248
Dolbeare, Kenneth, 577
Dolbeare, Patricia, 577

Dollar, Clyde D., 542
Dos Passos, John, 386
Douglas, Just. William O., 191n
Douglass, Mary, 611
Downes, Byran T., 208
Drimmer, Melvin, 534
Driver, Richard J., 318
Du Bois, W. E. B., 519-521, 533, 534, 543-544
Dumont, René, 584
Dunham, H. Warren, 336
Dunlap, Riley E., 581-582, 595
Dunne, J. G., 551
Durkheim, Emile, 3, 23, 26-28, 29, 42-43, 71, 98, 125, 134, 557
Dwight, Theodore W., 178
Dynes, Russell R., 27, 32

Eagleton, Sen. Thomas F., 327-329, 332, 355
Economist, 388
Edmiston, Susan, 457, 457n
Edwards, Harry, 225, 300, 314
Ehrlich, Anne H., 560, 564, 565-566, 606, 639-640, 647, 655n
Ehrlich, Paul R., 207, 449, 450, 556, 557-558, 560, 565-566, 583, 584, 606, 634-640, 642, 643-644, 647, 655n
Einstein, Charles, 567
Eisenhower, Dwight D., 647, 655
Elliot, Charles W., 370, 381
Ellis, Albert, 495
Ellis, Havelock, 386
El Mahi, T., 240
Empey, LaMar, 126
Engels, Friedrich, 495
England, Ralph W., 148, 150, 153, 154, 160-161, 168, 179, 180, 181, 196
Englander, David M., 245
Epstein, Benjamin, 228, 229, 231, 424, 434, 531
Ericksen, Charles A., 539
Erikson, Erik H., 422-423
Erikson, Kai, 9, 16, 27, 31, 41-43, 71, 98, 125, 148, 166, 175, 271-272, 390
Ernst, Morris, 374
Erskine, Hazel, 568, 569, 571, 628, 631, 632, 633, 636-637
Etzioni, Amitai, 202, 205, 439, 440, 441

Faich, Ronald G., 590, 592
Fallding, Harold, 281
Farber, M. A., 279
Fard, W. D., 522
Faris, Robert, 336
Farmer, James, 213, 536
Farrell, Barry, 439
Federal Prison Industries, Inc., 155, 161, 181, 181n
Feld, S., 479
Feldman, E., 370, 381
Felkenes, George T., 151
Fenichel, O., 301
Ferracuti, F., 99
Feuer, Lewis S., 218
Filler, Louis, 370, 549

Findlay, Gov. William, 177
Finkbine, Mrs. Sherri, 12, 462, 464, 469
Finner, Stephen L., 461
Fishman, Jacob R., 205, 206
Fitzgerald, F. Scott, 359
Flacks, Richard, 219
Flexner, A., 415-418, 426-429
Flynn, Frank T., 180n
Folkman, J. D., 505
Folks, Homer, 122, 135
Folson, Joseph K., 477
Foucault, Michel, 321
Ford, Pres. Gerald, 102
Forster, Arnold, 228, 229, 231, 531
Fort, Dr. Joel, 239, 248, 264-265, 293, 294
Foster, Marcus, 224
Foster, Raches, 427
Fox, Ruth, 290
Franklin, B. A., 184
Franklin, Benjamin, 176
Freeman, J., 432, 433, 477
Freud, Sigmund, 11, 130, 301, 336, 345, 380, 422, 490
Friedan, Betty, 419, 432, 433, 435
Friedman, Jane, 387
Fuller, Richard C., 35, 58
Funkhouser-Balbaky, M. L., 246
Funston, Richard, 389
Furman, William Henry, 191n
Furstenberg, Frank F., 89, 90, 101

Gagnon, John H., 364, 372
Gale, Richard P., 577-578, 581-582, 585-587, 589, 590, 592, 595, 596, 597, 600
Galileo, 4
Gallo, Jon J., 364
Gallup, George, 88-89, 121, 164, 254, 255, 328, 365-366, 372, 373, 411-413, 437, 449, 480, 484-485, 516, 517, 568, 628, 630-633
Gamache, Jerome D., 461
Garmine, Bernard L., 108
Garvey, Marcus, 520, 533, 534, 543, 544, 550
Gebhard, Paul H., 360, 363
Geis, Gilbert, 367, 378
Gellman, I. P., 298
Genovese, Kitty, 9
Georgia Report (Penal Affair Study), 161
Gibbons, Don C., 194, 199, 200, 254, 255, 304
Gibbons, James Cardinal, 370, 418
Gide, André, 359
Giele, Janet Z., 424
Gilliam, Harold, 579
Gilmartin, B. G., 481, 503
Ginzburg, Ralph, 358, 359, 388
Gittings, Barbara B., 378, 394
Glaser, D., 99
Glass, David V., 607-608
Glasser, William, 97
Glazer, N., 229
Glenn, Norval D., 521, 535, 536, 538, 550, 552
Glock, Charles Y., 17, 49, 532

Glueck, Eleanor T., 119
Glueck, Sheldon, 119
Goffman, Erving, 31, 108, 349-350
Goldberg, A. L., 317, 318
Golden, Edward, 470
Goldman, Albert, 372
Goldman, Peter, 517
Goldmark, Josephine C., 406
Goldschmidt, Walter, 612
Goldwater, Barry, 228, 230
Gonzalez, Nancie L., 525, 540, 551
Goode, Erich, 254, 264, 278, 280, 434, 479, 480, 497
Gordon, Elizabeth P., 297
Gordon, Milton M., 481, 493, 548
Gould, L., 118, 121
Gourley, Douglas G., 108
Grad, F. P., 317, 318
Graham, Billy, 487
Graham, Hugh Davis, 208
Granfield, David, 444
Greenberg, L., 300
Greenwald, Harold, 380
Greer, Germaine, 418
Gross, M., 300
Gruberg, Martin, 411, 416, 417, 419, 420, 431
Grünhut, Max, 178, 182
Gunnison, Foster, Jr., 377, 392-393, 394
Gurin, G., 479
Gurr, Ted Robert, 208
Gusfield, J. R., 48, 308-312, 315, 577

Hacker, Helen, 432, 449, 469
Hadden, Stuart C., 265
Haggard, Dr. Howard W., 298
Haines, Aubrey B., 550
Hale, Sarah, 427
Hall, Gladys M., 398
Halleck, Seymour L., 98
Hamilton, Charles V., 537
Hammond, William A., 334
Handlin, Oscar, 528, 546
Hano, Arnold, 596
Hardin, Garrett, 467, 568
Haroff, P. B., 479, 480, 491, 496, 503
Harper's magazine, 399, 401
Harris, L., 210, 228, 255, 286, 287-288, 517, 568, 569, 571
Harry, Joseph, 577-578, 587, 600
Hart, Gary, 328
Harvey, Paul, 440
Hatcher, Richard, 583
Hauser, Philip, 654-655
Hayden, Thomas, 53, 213
Health, Education, and Welfare, U.S. Dept. of, 284-290, 291, 300, 301-302, 303, 304
Healy, Dr. William, 344-345
Hearst, Patricia, 224
Heberle, Rudolph, 49, 54, 58
Heer, David M., 608-609, 610, 612
Hefner, Hugh, 493
Hendee, John C., 577-578, 587, 600
Henderson, Charles R., 137
Henning, John F., 579
Henrotin, Helen, 131
Hernandez, Aileen, 420, 433
Hess, Karl, 229

Hickle, Walter, 580, 602
Hicks, John D., 340
Hill, Rev. Morton A., 386-387
Hill, Reuben, 508
Himes, Norman E., 443
Hippocrates, 320, 334
Hirschi, Travis, 29, 126
Hissong, Jerry B., 94, 104
Hitler, Adolf, 53, 321
Hobbes, Thomas, 11
Hoffer, Eric, 17, 18, 49, 54, 58, 594
Hoffman, Abbie, 53, 434
Hoffman, Paul, 456, 460, 482
Hofstadter, Richard, 307, 499, 518
Holdren, John P., 556, 557-558
Hollingshead, A. B., 336
Holm, Richard W., 556, 557-558
Homer, 358
Hooker, Evelyn, 364
Hoover, George, 131
Hoover, Pres. Herbert, 100-101, 416
Hoover, J. Edgar, 90, 96
Hopper, Rex D., 49, 58, 195
Horace, 359
Hornbach, Kenneth E., 575, 596
Horney, Karen, 336, 422
Horowitz, Irving Louis, 205, 206, 208, 220, 226
Horton, John, 282, 303, 324, 326, 489
Horton, Paul B., 10, 28, 32
Howard, John R., 418, 419, 420, 426, 431, 432, 434, 435, 527, 539, 540
Howe, G. E., 131
Howe, Julia Ward, 428
Howe, Samuel G., 331
Hubbard, Jeffrey C., 10
Hubbert, M. King, 564
Hudson, James R., 92, 107, 108, 109
Huff, Darrell, 9
Hug, M. A., 302
Hughes, Sen. Harold, 296, 318
Human Behavior, 367, 378
Humphrey, Mary E., 130-131
Humphreys, Laud, 364, 377, 378, 396, 397
Hunt, Morton, 496
Hurley, Timothy, 123

Idahonian, 374, 389, 401
IFCO News, 539
Imperiale, Anthony, 216
Innis, Roy, 214
Irwin, John, 199
Isbell, H., 257

Jackson, Lucius, Jr., 191n
James, Jesse, 112
James, William, 341
Janowitz, Morris, 218
Jellinek, E. M., 283, 293, 298-299, 300, 313
Jenkins, E. Fellow, 135
Jensen, Arthur, 532
John XXIII, Pope, 636
Johnson, Donald M., 7
Johnson, Elmer H., 462
Johnson, Pres. Lyndon, 41, 88, 102, 145, 165, 198n, 205, 318, 433-434, 580, 647, 655

Johnson, V. E., 422, 424, 496
Joint Commission on Mental Health, 351, 356
Jon, Gee, 152-153
Jones, Holway R., 598
Jones, Robert, 97
Jones, W. C., 477
Jordan, David Starr, 370

Kameny, Frank, 392-393
Kamisar, Yale, 106
Kanowitz, Leo, 409-410, 434, 437
Kantner, John F., 629
Kazin, Michael, 221
Keating, Charles H., 386, 388-389
Keehn, J. D., 302
Keene, Roger, 470
Kefauver, Sen. Estes, 272
Keith, Harold L., 305, 386
Kemmler, William, 152
Keniston, Kenneth, 205
Kennedy, Pres. John F., 41, 145, 165, 332, 355-356, 537, 647
Kenney, Mary E., 416
Kephart, W. H., 490
Kepner, E., 302
Kerner Commission, 209
Khrushchev, Nikita, 609-610
Killian, Lewis, 41, 58, 59, 62-63, 653
Kilpatrick, James J., 354, 374, 386
Kimball, Thomas L., 566-567
King, C. W., 58
King, Rev. Martin Luther, 53, 207, 214, 521-522, 535-536, 538, 545, 546, 551
Kinsey, Alfred C., 292, 306, 360, 363, 380, 391, 400, 423, 447, 480, 496, 501, 503, 506
Kinsie, P. M., 384
Kirchway, George W., 152
Kirkbride, Dr. Thomas, 338
Kitsuse, John I., 59, 63n
Kittrie, Nicholas N., 117, 140
Klein, Viola, 421, 422
Knight, R., 302
Knott, John C., 636
Knudsen, D. D., 508
Knudten, Richard D., 76, 84, 94
Kobrin, Solomon, 119
Kohlberg, Lawrence, 423
Kolb, L., 240
Kusisto, D. V., 481, 503
Kutner, Luis, 354
Kuykendall, Jack L., 108
Kwan, Kian M., 512
Kyle-Keith, Richard, 386

LaBarre, Weston, 68, 526, 527
Labor, U.S. Dept. of, 408, 514
Lader, Lawrence, 443-444, 446, 447, 459, 462, 464, 465
LaFave, Wayne R., 108
LaMont, Susan, 467
Landers, Ann, 487
Landis, J. T., 302, 423, 490
Landis, P. H., 490-491
Lang, Gladys, 49, 58
Lang, Kurt, 49, 58
Lanternari, Vittorio, 526
Larsen, Otto N., 7

La Sorte, Michael A., 424
Lathorp, Julia, 131
Laue, James S., 537
Law Enforcement Assistance Admin., 85, 198n
Lawes, Lewis E., 188
Lawrence, D. H., 359, 387
Lear, Martha W., 432, 433
Leary, Mary, 166-167
Leary, Mike, 102
Leary, Timothy, 259
Lecky, William E. H., 443
Lefstein, Norman, 146-147
Legg, Dorr, 376
Leighton, Alexander, 336
Leighton, Dorothea, 336
Lemberg Center, 207
Lemere, F., 302
Lemert, Edwin, 31, 58, 99, 123, 137, 139, 141, 142-143, 304, 358, 381, 398
Lemons, J. Stanley, 430
Leonard, William, 101, 579
Leopold, Aldo, 557n, 586
Lerner, Michael, 205
Leslie, Gerald R., 10, 28, 32, 324, 326, 489
Lester, Marilyn, 10, 300
Levine, James P., 106, 241
Lewis, L. S., 491
Lewit, Sarah, 448-449, 462
Leznoff, Maurice, 364
Libby, R. W., 496
Life magazine, 170, 195, 213, 347
Lincoln, C. Eric, 522, 537, 538
Lindberg, P., 483
Lindenfeld, Frank, 33
Lindesmith, Alfred, 244, 255, 265, 266, 270, 273
Lindey, Alexander, 374
Lindsay, Mayor John, 102, 395-396
Linzer, Edward, 348
Lipset, Seymour M., 204
Lisansky, E. S., 302-303
Loble, Judge Lester, 124, 143-144
Lobsinger, Donald, 215
Lockwood, Belva, 410
Lofland, John, 50
Logan, Rayford W., 519, 520, 523, 524, 534, 537, 538, 544
Lokos, Lionel, 517
Lolli, Giorgio, 282, 304
Los Angeles Times, 389
Love, Joseph L., 525, 540
Lovell, L. H., 300
Lowell, Mrs. Josephine, 415
Lowry, Ritchie P., 36n
Luce, Phillip, 213
Luckmann, Thomas, 3, 5, 8, 18-19, 20, 44, 53
Ludwig, John H., 573
Lyon, Phyllis, 376, 377, 393-394

McAnany, Patrick D., 172
McCall's magazine, 365
McCarthy, G. Michael, 598
McCarthy, Sen. Joseph, 53, 230, 234
McClearn, G. E., 300
McClellan, G. S., 164
McConnell, Grant, 557n, 585, 586

McCord, Joan, 301, 302, 305
McCord, William, 301, 302, 305
MacCormick, Austin H., 151, 161
McCormick, Kenneth D., 386, 387
McCracken, Samuel, 639, 641-642, 643
Mace, David R., 458
McGovern, Sen. George, 234, 327-328
McHarg, Ian L., 556, 557
McIntire, Carl, 228
Mack, Julian, 123
McKay, Henry D., 98, 119, 126
McMullen, Thomas B., 573
McNamara, John H., 97
Maddox, John, 584
Malcolm, Andrew H., 441
Malcolm X, 523, 547
Malloy, Michael T., 471-473
Maloney, John C., 573
Mann, Horace, 331, 338
Mann, Marty, 296, 298, 313, 318
Mannheim, Hermann, 99
Manning, Peter K., 99
Marden, Charles F., 553
Mardones, J., 300
Marine, Gene, 524
Marmor, Judd, 423
Marsh, George Perkins, 557n, 586
Marshall, Just. Thurgood, 191n, 192
Martin, Del, 376, 377, 393
Martindale, Don, 353, 354
Martindale, Edith, 353, 354
Martinson, Robert, 174
Marx, Gary T., 94, 103, 517, 588
Marx, Karl, 11, 17, 28, 33, 495
Maslow, A. H., 578, 588
Mason, Philip, 513
Mass, Peter, 96, 96n
Masters, W. H., 422, 424, 496
Matusow, Allen J., 523, 537
Mauss, Armand L., 60, 61, 65, 68, 211, 224
Maxwell, M., 313, 314
Mayer, Kurt, 513
Mead, G. H., 31, 128, 213, 215, 221, 223, 227, 421, 424
Mead, Margaret, 424
Meadows, Dennis, 583
Mechanic, David, 346, 347, 352
Medalia, Nahum Z., 7
Meier, August, 213, 519, 521, 522, 535, 536
Mendelsohn, Harold, 106
Menninger, Karl, 199, 301, 319, 345
Menninger, Dr. William C., 346, 355
Merrill, Lois T., 150-151
Merton, Robert, 27, 29, 34, 98, 125, 306, 532
Messinger, Sheldon L., 48, 68
Meyer, Gladys, 553
Meyr, Dr. Adolf, 342
MH (Nat'l. Assn. of Mental Health), 329, 352
Miller, Collin, 210
Miller, Herman P., 409
Miller, Walter, 30, 99
Millet, Kate, 418
Mills, C. Wright, 35
Mishan, E. J., 556, 559
Mishler, Elliot G., 336

Index

Mitchell, Aaron, 189
Mitchell, Juliet, 430, 595-596
Mitford, Jessica, 171, 199, 200
Moblit, George, 441
Moffett, Arthur, 248
Molotch, Harvey, 10, 596
Moncrief, Lewis, 597
Monge, Jose, 189
Montgomery, Paul L., 185
Monthly Vital Statistics Report, 479, 482, 483, 618
Monts, J. Kenneth, 386
Mooney, James, 527
Moore, Joan W., 515, 525
Moore, Wilbert E., 40-41, 532
More, Harry W., 101, 107
Morgan, George B., 419, 420, 434, 573
Morris, Albert, 151, 154-155, 162, 169, 173, 178, 182, 186, 194, 195
Morrison, Denton E., 575, 590, 596
Mott, Lucretia, 427-428
Mouat, Lucia, 213
Mowrers, Robert, 142
Muhammad, Elijah, 522-523, 538-539, 547
Muir, John, 557n, 586, 597-598
Mundt, Sen. Karl, 388
Munton, Donald, 570, 572, 573, 574, 576, 577, 578
Murch, Arvin W., 567, 571
Mutnick, Barbara, 467
Myers, Richard, 35, 58
Myrdal, Gunnar, 519, 532

Nader, Ralph, 18, 53
Narcotics, Bureau of, 243-245
Nash, Roderick, 587, 597
National Academy of Sciences Committee on Resources and Man, 558
National Center for Health Statistics, 515, 617
National Commission on Marijuana and Drug Abuse, 238, 242, 247-250, 253, 255-256, 266, 276
National Institute of Mental Health, 325
National Opinion Research Center (Roper Poll), 164, 292, 411, 450-454, 484, 568, 569
National Violence Commission, 201, 203-204
Nation's Business, 105
Nawy, Harold, 374, 375, 385
Nerva, Emperor, 607
Neubeck, G., 481
Newsweek, 114, 327n, 328-329, 445, 448, 471, 473, 551, 656
Newton, Huey, 214-215, 523-524, 547
New York Prison Assn., 168, 179, 182
New York Times, 86, 152, 158, 160-163, 167, 168, 183-186, 188-191, 194, 196-198, 208, 210, 327n, 360-362, 375, 380, 388, 389, 469-470, 472, 570, 573

Nimkoff, M. F., 476, 477-478, 490
Nixon, Pres. Richard, 87, 100, 102, 113, 224, 231, 233, 234, 276, 328, 389, 434, 547, 552, 553-554, 580, 602, 604, 643, 655
Nordheimer, Jon, 387, 389-390, 401
Norman, J. H., 301
Nowlis, Helen, 279
Noyes, John, 502
Nunnally, Jim C., Jr., 326
Nye, I., 118, 121, 482

Oberschall, Anthony, 50-53, 55, 64
Odegard, Peter H., 310
Ohlin, Lloyd E., 29, 98, 126, 172, 306
Ohr, Michael J., 118
O'Neill, G., 493
O'Neill, N., 493
O'Neill, William L., 416, 417, 426-427, 429
Oppenheimer, Valerie K., 408
Osborne, Thomas Mott, 151, 169, 182
Overstreet, Edmund W., 421-422

Packard, Vance, 627
Paige, Karen E., 422
Park, Peter, 305
Parks, Rosa, 521
Parsons, Talcott, 532
Patterson, Michelle, 424
Paul, Dr. Alice, 416
Paul VI, Pope, 632, 637
Pawlak, Vic, 251, 252
Pearlstein, Stanley, 354
Peevey, Michael R., 579
Pellens, Mildred, 257, 268, 269
Penn, William, 150
Perry, Rev. Troy, 394
Petersen, Larry R., 164
Peterson, Richard E., 204, 212, 397
Pettigrew, Thomas F., 515
Pettis, John A., 141
Pfaff, Alma D., 524
Phillips, Derek, 306, 327
Phipps, Henry, 343
Pierce, Vivian, 188
Pinchot, Gifford, 585
Pinel, Dr. Philippe, 332
Pittman, David J., 282, 293
Pius IX, Pope, 444-445
Pius XII, Pope, 636
Plato, 358, 359-360
Platt, Anthony, 122, 129, 130, 131, 133-135, 137, 139, 140, 143
Plaut, Thomas F. A., 292, 317
Playfair, 188
Pomeroy, Wardell B., 359, 363, 367, 380
Pope, H., 508
Portnoy, Ronald, 215
Pound, Roscoe, 137
Powers, Dorothy, 131
Prager, K., 538
President's Commission on Law Enforcement, 83, 86-88, 89, 101-102, 116
Pressat, Roland, 445
Prisons, Bureau of, 150, 153, 155-160, 163

Quarles, Benjamin, 519, 520, 521, 534, 535, 538, 544
Quinney, Richard, 14, 25-26, 28, 106

Ralmer, Mrs. Potter, 131
Randall, C. D., 131
Randolph, A. Philip, 533
Raulet, H. M., 639
Reagan, Gov. Ronald, 93, 189
Reasons, Charles, 255, 257, 258, 261, 267, 272, 274
Reckless, Walter, 120-121, 128, 382
Redlich, F., 336
Reich, Wilhelm, 495
Reinemann, John O., 122, 133
Reisman, David, 310
Reissman, Leonard, 58-59, 70
Remmling, Gunther W., 549
Remsberg, Bonnie, 103, 104, 458
Remsberg, Charles, 103, 104, 458
Reston, James, 210
Reuben, David, 424
Rex, John, 548
Richardson, Anne B., 131-132
Richmond, Mary Ellen, 300
Richter, C. P., 300
Ridenour, Nina, 342, 344, 345, 346
Rieff, Philip, 549
Riesman, David, 229
Riess, Ira, 107, 108, 480, 496
Riley, J. W., 290, 292
Rimmer, R. H., 493
Robinson, L. N., 180, 181
Roby, Pamela, 369, 375
Rockefeller, J. D., 313
Rockefeller, Nelson A., 102, 279, 468
Rockefeller, Gov. Winthrop, 190
Rodgers, D. A., 300
Rodgers, Mrs. George, 426
Rogers, Carl, 493, 495-496
Rogers, J. M., 261
Rokeach, Milton, 529, 532
Roman, P. M., 305
Room, R., 286
Rooney, Elizabeth A., 254, 255
Roos, Leslie L., Jr., 568, 580, 590
Roosevelt, Franklin D., 518
Roosevelt, Theodore, 544, 585, 599
Roper Poll (*see* National Opinion Research Center)
Rose, Arnold, 70, 528, 532
Rose, P., 532
Rosen, George, 320, 323, 330, 337
Rosenhan, Dr. David, 350-351
Rosenstone, Robert A., 202-203, 207
Ross, Robert, 70, 464, 465
Rossi, Alice, 424, 426-427, 433, 435, 445-446, 448, 450, 451, 454, 456, 461, 463
Rowan, Carl T., 645
Roy, Della, 492
Roy, Rustum, 492
Rubin, Jerry, 213
Rubington, Earl, 31, 304
Rudolph, Fredrick, 232
Rudwick, Elliot, 213, 536
Rush, Dr. Benjamin, 176, 333-335, 338, 340, 349
Russell, Rev. R., 297
Russell, Dr. William, 342

Rutherford, Brent M., 595
Ryder, Norman B., 454

Sadoun, Roland, 282
Safire, W., 480
St. James, Margo, 368
St. John, Jeffrey, 583-584
Sait, Edward M., 309
Salmon, Dr. Thomas, 343-344
Sampson, John J., 371, 372
Sanborn, Franklin, 169, 182
San Francisco Examiner and Chronicle, 86, 88-89, 233, 351, 554, 579, 603n, 646
Sanger, Margaret, 647n, 655n
Santee, Barbara D., 456
Schanche, D. A., 538
Schardt, Arlie, 171, 192
Scheff, Thomas, 319, 336, 349-350, 353, 356
Schermerhorn, R. A., 533
Schlafly, Mrs. Phyllis, 420
Schnaiberg, Allan, 575, 577, 587-588, 589, 593, 594
Schur, Edwin M., 16, 31, 99, 446, 457, 461, 462-463, 464
Schwartz, Michael, 120, 128
Scott, George R., 398
Scranton Commission, 204
Seale, Bobby, 214-215, 523, 547
Sears, David O., 217
Segovia-Riquelme, N., 300
Sellers, Cleve, 227n
Shakespeare, 321, 323
Shapiro, B. A., 317, 318, 465, 468, 469, 470
Shaw, Clifford R., 98, 126
Sheehy, Gail, 95, 100, 102, 103, 360-361, 368, 369, 371, 372, 375, 387, 401
Shibutani, Tamotsu, 512
Shockley, William, 532
Short, James F., 117, 126, 145-146
Shriver, Eunice Kennedy, 470
Shryock, Richard H., 330, 338, 339-340
Silberman, Charles E., 625
Silver, Isidore, 158
Simmons, D. L., 327
Simon, William, 364, 372
Simpson, George E., 521, 523, 536, 537
Sitting Bull, Chief, 526
Sixtus V, Pope, 444
Skinner, B. F., 30
Skolnick, Jerome H., 33, 34, 107, 109, 202, 203, 213, 216, 218, 220, 221, 222, 232, 304, 497
Slovonsky, Lynn, 573
Smelser, Neil, 39-40, 43, 46, 54, 56-57, 61, 64-65, 67, 217, 418, 419, 425, 595
Smith, Adam, 11, 228
Smith, Donald H., 536
Smith, Margaret Chase, 410
Smith, Mrs. Perry, 131
Smith, R., 247, 258
Snow, William, 370, 384
Snyder, Charles R., 304, 305, 531
Social Hygiene, 384

Sociological Quarterly, 204
Socrates, 359
Solomon, Frederick, 205, 206
Sowell, Thomas, 551
Sparling, Edward J., 223
Spector, Malcolm, 59, 63n
Spicer, Judith C., 638
Spitza, Edward, 334
Spock, Dr. Benjamin, 130, 145, 212
Spokane Daily Chronicle, 184
Spokesman Review, 387
Srole, Leo, 336
Staines, Graham, 70, 420, 464, 465
Stallings, Harold, 142-143
Stanton, Elizabeth Cady, 416, 427-428
Stapleton, Vaughan, 146-147
Stark, Rodney, 50, 532
Starr, Chauncey, 560-562
Statistical Abstract of the U.S., 479, 482, 483, 613, 614, 623-624, 626
Steinem, Gloria, 53, 418, 419, 435, 437
Steiner, Jesse F., 151, 154
Steiner, Stan, 541
Sterba, James P., 390, 391, 400, 401
Stewart, Elbert W., 218
Stewart, Justice Potter, 191n, 192
Stinney, George Jr., 158
Stockwell, Edward G., 445
Stone, Lucy, 427, 428
Stowe, Harriet Beecher, 34
Strauss, Robert, 304
Stringfellow, William, 229
Stryker, Sheldon, 120, 128
Suljak, Nedjelko D., 557n
Summer, Rt. Rev. Walter, 370
Summer, William G., 23
Summerhill, Louise, 470
Susann, Jacqueline, 398
Suter, Larry E., 409
Sutherland, Edwin, 30, 93, 99, 102, 104, 109, 126, 177, 179n, 303, 304
Szasz, Thomas, 319, 321, 323, 334, 336, 347, 350, 353, 355-356

Taft, Donald R., 148, 150, 153, 154, 160-161, 168, 179, 180, 181, 196
Taft, Pres. William Howard, 428-429
Tangri, Sandra S., 128
Tarrant County (Texas), Juvenile Probation Dept., 119-120, 136, 144
Taussig, F. W., 447, 463
Taylor, Gordon R., 444
Taylor, Jan, 99, 258
Taylor, Paul, 548, 554-555
Teeters, Negley K., 122, 133, 151, 152, 153, 168, 177
Teitelbaum, Lee, 146-147
Teodori, Massino, 222, 226, 227
Terrell, Mrs. Mary Church, 417
Terry, Charles E., 257, 268, 269
Tertullian, 444
Thom, Dr. Douglas, 343
Thom, Mel, 541
Thomas, Darwin, 642-643
Thomas, M. Carey, 427

Thomas, Robert K., 527
Thomas, W. I., 6, 128, 424
Thomlinson, Ralph, 608, 611, 612, 613, 616
Thompson, Daniel C., 225
Thompson, Warren S., 611, 615
Thornton, Justice, 139, 144
Tiebout, H. M., 314
Tietze, Christopher, 448-449, 462, 473
Tijerina, Reies Lopez, 525, 540
Time magazine, 167-168, 189, 207, 327n, 328-329, 364, 445, 448, 467n, 472, 473, 475, 583
Tintera, J. W., 300
Tobin, Kay, 376, 377, 392-395
Toch, Hans, 49
Tomlinson, T. M., 217
Tompkins, Harvey J., 352
Torgerson, Dial, 539
Train, Russell, 605
Trajan, Emperor, 607
Trice, H. M., 291, 292, 305, 314
Troeltsch, Ernst, 57
Trop, Cecile, 568, 580, 590
Trotter, Robert J., 446
Truth, Sojourner, 405, 406
Tuke, William, 330, 332
Turner, Jonathan H., 62, 90, 96, 96n
Turner, Ralph H., 201-202, 203
Twain, Mark, 359
Tyler, Gus, 96

Ullman, Albert D., 304
Uniform Crime Reports, 6, 10, 78-87, 90-91, 118-119, 174, 402, 441
U.N. Demographic Yearbook, 613
U.N. Population Studies, 616
U.S. Industrial Outlook, 362
U.S. News & World Report, 102, 104, 158, 191, 210, 358, 362, 398, 408, 409, 480, 539, 551

Valachi, Joseph, 96
Varela, A., 300
Varni, C., 481, 493, 503
Ventura, S. J., 479-480
Veroff, J., 479
Virgil, 359
Visick, Vern, 222
Voegtlin, W. L., 302
von Eschen, Donald, 522, 538
Vonnegut, Kurt, Jr., 401
von Wartburg, J. P., 300

Wagatsuma, Hiroshi, 511, 512
Wagley, Charles, 512
Wainwright, Louis, 160
Waldman, E., 408, 409
Wallace, Gov. George, 102, 583
Walla Walla Union Bulletin, 541
Warner, W. Keith, 575, 590, 596
Warren, Justice Earl, 113, 234, 518, 544
Washington, Booker T., 519, 521, 533, 534, 543-544, 550
Washington, Mrs. Booker T., 417
Waskow, Arthur I., 523, 536
Waterman, Willoughby C., 370, 382-383
Waterston, R. C., 331

Index

Wattenberg, Ben, 606, 642, 643
Wax, Murray L., 515
Waxler, Nancy E., 336
Weaver, Warren, Jr., 473
Weber, Max, 18, 53, 57
Weinberg, Martin S., 31, 32, 304
Weinswig, Melvin H., 248
Weiss, Marc, 33
Welch, Robert, 215-216, 230, 234
Welch, Dr. William, 342, 345
Westley, William A., 364
Westoff, Charles F., 445, 448, 454
Westoff, Leslie A., 445, 448, 454, 634
Weyer, Johann, 333
While, Paul A., 147
White, Just. Byron, 191
White, Robert, 302
Whitehurst, R., 490, 496
Whyte, William H., Jr., 489
Wicker, Randy, 376, 377, 392-395
Wickersham Commission, 101
Wilde, Oscar, 359
Wiley, Dr. Harvey W., 259, 268
Wilkins, Leslie T., 174, 199
Wilkins, Roy, 18, 521
Wilkinson, Leonard J., 557n
Will, George F., 361, 369
Willard, Frances, 298, 415
Williams, Dr. Frankwood, 342
Williams, Phyllis H., 300, 304
Williams, Robin M., Jr., 516, 532
Williams, Roger, 330
Willie, Charles V., 644, 645
Wilson, J., 106, 107, 108
Wilson, James Q., 174, 199, 386, 389
Wilson, Pres. Woodrow, 544
Winch, R. F., 476-477, 508
Wines, Enoch C., 130, 178, 182
Winick, Charles, 400
Winslow, Robert W., 117, 119
Winston, Michael R., 520, 523, 524, 537, 538
Witt, Shirley, 527
Wohl, L. C., 420
Wolfe, Julie C., 424
Wolfgang, M., 99
Wood, Jerry M., 144
Woodhull, Virginia, 429
Woodward, C. Vann, 518, 530, 543
Woodward, Dr. William, 263
Worden, Portia, 461
World Health Organization, 283, 289
Wovoka, 526
Wylie, Max, 124, 143

Yablonsky, Lewis, 115, 126
Yankelovich, Daniel, 485
Yinger, J. Milton, 430-431, 521, 523, 532, 536, 537
Young, Whitney, 577

Zalba, Serapio R., 198
Zangrando, Robert L., 553
Zarrow, M. X., 300
Zelnik, Melvin, 617
Zinn, Howard, 233
Zurcher, L. A., 373, 386, 390

SUBJECTS

Abolition movement, 45, 543
Abortion, 442-474, 483-485
   Christian dogma, 443-485
   cultural relativity, 442-444
   definitions and interpretations, 444-447
   incidence, 447-449
   interest groups, 12, 454-462
   laws, 12-13, 446-447, 465, 469, 473
   moral entrepreneurs, 459-460
   opposition arguments, 455
   and population control, 445, 463, 473, 634-635, 656
   as problem-movement, 48-49, 51, 52, 462-474
     anti-abortion countermovement, 468-472
     and feminist movement, 459, 462
     legacy, 472-474
     natural history, 463-468, 504
     and sexual freedom, 462-463
   public opinion, 449-454, 634-635
   sociological theories, 459-462
   as victimless crime, 460-462
Affirmative action programs, 434, 440, 507, 553-554
Africa, 407, 512-513, 558, 614, 615
Agency for International Development, 639, 647, 657
Air pollution, 565, 568, 569, 571, 572, 577, 603, 603n
Alabama:
   bus boycotts, 520, 521, 536, 544
   prisons, punishment, 151, 160
Alaska pipeline, 63, 360, 587
Alcoholics Anonymous, 298, 313-315
Alcoholism, 294-306
   interest groups, 294-306
   physiological theories, 299-301
     disease, 69, 283, 300-301, 314, 317, 318
   programs, 294-296
   psychological theories, 301-303
   public opinion, 292-294, 327
   social correlates, 291-292
   sociological theories, 303-306
   (see also Alcohol use)
Alcohol problem-movements, 306-318
   anti-alcohol, 16, 68, 296-298, 307-312
     early temperance movement, 307-312
     natural history, 311-312
     strategies, tactics, 308-311
   anti-alcoholism, 312-315
     natural history, 314-315
   legacy, 315-318
Alcohol use, 281-294
   advertising, 293, 295
   definitions, interpretations, 282-284
   as drug, 238-239, 253, 254, 278
   economic costs, 285-286, 294-295
   incidence, 284-286, 295
   and liquor industry, 295-296
   relativism, 5, 281-282
   social correlates, 286-291

Alianza Federal de Mercedes, 524, 525, 540, 551
American Civil Liberties Union, 13, 15, 48, 95, 113, 369, 494
   abortion policies, 13, 15, 467, 494
   capital punishment, 190-191
   homosexual rights, 378, 402
   obscenity, censorship, 372-373, 401, 494
   prison reform, 170, 171, 183-184, 186, 187
   prostitution, 385
American Correctional Assn., 173, 178, 182
American Federation of Labor (AFL), 170, 180, 416, 526, 546, 547
American Friends Service Committee, 13, 48, 185, 467 (see also Quakers)
American Indian Movement, 526, 527, 542, 547
American Indians (see Native Americans)
American Law Institute, 194, 392, 401, 463-464, 465, 467-469
American League to Abolish Capital Punishment, 170, 188-189
American Medical Assn., 15, 261, 273, 283, 467
American Orthopsychiatric Assn., 335,
American Psychiatric Assn., 327, 333, 335, 338, 342, 345, 467
American Social Hygiene Assn., 370, 381-384
American Society for the Abolition of Capital Punishment, 188, 190
American Woman Suffrage Assn., 416, 427, 428, 429
Anomie theory, 27-28, 29, 134
   alcoholism, 305-306
   crime, 98-99
   juvenile delinquency, 125
Anti-Saloon League, 297, 307, 310
Association for the Study of Abortion, 48, 458, 465-466, 472
Attica prison riots, 184-185, 186, 194
Auburn Prison (N.Y.), 153, 154, 169, 177
Auburn system (see Puritans)
Audubon Society, 582, 586, 589, 591

Berkeley, Calif., 94-95
   student protest, 204, 205, 210, 221, 224
Birth control, 631-634, 636-637, 655n
   (see also Abortion; Population control movements)
   contraception, 445, 481, 502, 508, 633-634, 655n
Birthright (Toronto), 458, 465, 470
Black Liberation Movement, 214, 223, 225-226, 537, 538
Black Mesa Defense, 591, 593
Black Muslims, 215, 522-523, 538-539, 547, 551
   prisoners' rights, 185, 187
   Sunni sect, 539, 547

Index

Black Nationalism, 214, 214n, 522-524, 534-539, 545
Black Panthers, 94, 113, 214-215, 227, 232, 516, 522, 523-524, 537, 538, 546-547, 550, 551
Black Power, 214, 214n, 226, 227, 232
Black protest movement, 202, 203, 207, 208, 210, 213, 214, 225-228, 231-232
  co-optation of, 227
  legacy, 231-232
  natural history, 226-227
  recruits, leaders, 225-226
Blacks:
  abortion issue, 446
  alcohol use, 290
  birth rate, 622-625
  businesses, 520, 551
  and capital punishment, 158, 164
  cultural contributions, 548
  crime rate, 82-84
  drug use, 258
  families, 514
  genocide theory, 644-645
  illegitimacy rate, 479-480, 514
  juvenile delinquency, 119-121
  militants, 517
  myths, stereotypes, 9
  and police, 92, 97
  and politics, 213-215, 530-531
  pollution concern, 574, 575
  and prison system, 170, 186-187
  protest, 202, 203, 207, 208, 210, 213, 214, 225-228, 231-232
  school segregation, 5
  slavery, 518, 543, 548
  women's organizations, 417
  (*see also* Race and ethnic relations)
Blue laws, 25, 75-76
Boggs Amendment (1951), 76, 273
Boy Scouts of America, 87, 132, 145, 593

California:
  divorce law, 506
  juvenile court system, 137, 139, 141
  marijuana initiative, 256, 259
  prisons, 159, 161, 171, 194, 195-196, 199-200
  recreation developers, 596, 604
  Robinson v. *California*, 317
  vice-suppression, 385
California Adult Authority, 171, 199-200
Capitalism, and social problems, 33, 34, 46
Capital punishment (*see* Corrections and punishment)
Chicago, 86, 105, 119, 207, 555
Chicanos (*see* Mexican-Americans)
Children's Aid Society (N.Y.C.), 122-123, 135
Children's rights movement, 138-144
  due-process constitutionalists, 140-143, 146-147
  legal moralists, 140, 143-144

Child-savers movement, 69, 122, 128-138, 144-146
  and feminist movement, 129-132, 414
  institutional transformation, 135-136
  natural history, 137-138
Child Welfare League of America, 123, 135
China, 4, 558, 610, 646
Citizens for Decent Literature, 374, 386, 389, 390
Civil Rights Acts:
  1957, 552, 553
  1960, 552, 553
  1964, 409, 431, 433, 552, 553
  1968, 552, 553
Civil Rights Commission, 515, 553-554
Civil rights movement, 51, 53, 56, 60, 211, 503, 520-522, 534-536
  and environmental movement, 589-590
  laws, legislation, 552-555
  legacy, 69
  and modern feminist movement, 430-431
  and NAACP, 535, 544
  natural history, 544-548
Civil War, 202, 204, 425, 499
Clean Air and Water Acts (1970, 1972), 603-604, 605
Coalescence stage, of social movements, 61, 62-63
Common Cause, 53-54
Commonwealth Fund, 344, 345
Communism, 46, 234, 272
Community Mental Health Centers Act (1963), 351-352
Comprehensive Alcohol Abuse . . . Act (1970), 296, 318
Comprehensive Drug Abuse . . . Act (1970), 263-264, 276-277
Comstock Act (1873), 359, 362, 373-374, 385, 462, 610, 655n
Congress, U.S., women in, 410-411, 440
Congress of Racial Equality (CORE), 213-214, 520, 522, 523, 535-536, 545
Consensual reality, 6-11, 35
  common sense, 7-8
  formal, 8-9, 11
  imaginary evidence, 7
  informal, 9-11
  media effects, 10
  parameters, 8-11, 36
  public opinion, 9-10
  as social product, 3, 11
Conservation movement (1900-1910), 585-587, 597-599
Conservative movements, 211, 215-216, 228-231
Control theory, 29-30
Co-optation, 60-65, 222-224, 227, 230-231
Corrections and punishment, 148-200 (*see also* Crime; Juvenile delinquency)

Corrections and punishment, *cont.*
  capital punishment, 149-150, 152-153, 155-158, 187-193
    abolition movement, 167-168, 187-193
    decline of, 155-157
    moral interest groups, 169-170
    public opinion, 164-165
    restoration movement, 191-192
  corporal punishment, 150-153
  historical relativity, 148-155
  indeterminate sentence, 171, 177, 177n, 179, 199-200
  interest groups, 165-174, 189-190
  prisons, imprisonment, 150, 153-155, 158-163, 193-194
  probation, parole, 150, 162-163, 169, 173-174, 179, 179n, 180
  public opinion, 163-165
  recidivism, 155, 173-174, 199
  social movements, 175-199
Cosmopolitan magazine, 437-438, 488, 493-494, 504
Courts (*see* Supreme Court)
COYOTE, 368, 385
Crime, 75-100 (*see also* Corrections and punishment; Drug use; Juvenile delinquency; Sexual behavior)
  class definitions, 14, 25-26
  drug addiction, 277-278
  felonies, misdemeanors, 22, 77
  folk crimes, 77, 112
  index (street) crimes, 78-83
    age, 82
    clearance rates, 85, 90
    persons, 78-79
    property, 79-80
    race, 82-83
    region, 80
    sex, 81-82
    urban vs. rural, 80-81
  interest groups, 91-100
  organized, 86-87, 96, 112
  predatory vs. political, 75, 76
  protective organizations, 95, 104-105
  psychological theories, 98, 172-173
  public opinion, 88-91
  rates, 42, 441
  relativity, 6, 10, 75-77
  reporting, 83-86
  secondary, 25, 70
  sociological theories, 30, 98-99, 172-174
  statistics, manipulation of, 15, 90-97, 106
  victimless, 16, 76, 87, 114, 379, 460-462
  victims, 83-86
  white-collar, 86, 87-88, 104, 112
Crime movements, 100-114
  and civil liberties, 113-114
  historic, 100-101
  legacy, 112-114
  loser vs. gainer interests, 104-105
  natural history, 109-112
  police in, 106-109, 113
  and "silent majority," 112-114
  vigilante groups, 103

Index

Daughters of Bilitis, 376, 391, 393-394, 399, 493
Deep Throat, 362, 372n, 401
Demise stage, of social movements, 58-59, 61, 65-66, 67-68
Deviant behavior theories, 26-32, 35-36
  control theory, 29-30
  functionalism, 26-27
  interactionism, 31-32
  social learning, 30-31
  strain, 27-29
Differential association theory, 304, 335
Doomsday theories, 584, 639-641
Driver v. Hinnant, 317-318
Drug movements, 16, 266-280
  anti-marijuana, 271-272
  anti-narcotic revival, 272-273
  anti-opiate, 267-271
  international treaties, 258, 267-268
  legacy of, 276-280
  legislation, 258, 278-279
  modern reform, 273-276
  racism, 257-258
Drug use, 106, 110-111, 114, 237-280
  addiction, 261, 275
    as crime, 261-263, 273, 277-279
    laws, effects of, 278-279
    medical model, 261, 269, 273
  barbituates, tranquilizers, sedatives, 240-241, 247-248, 264, 280
    mental illness, 349
  civil liberties, 259
  cocaine, 238, 246, 263, 269
  coffee, caffeine, 240
  criminal sanctions, 76, 114
  dope-fiend mythology, 255, 268
  hallucinogens, 239-240, 250-254, 263, 264
    proselytizing, 259, 274
  interest groups, 256-266, 277
  marijuana, hashish, 238, 248-250, 255-256 (*see also* Marijuana)
  opiates, 241, 242-246
  pharmaceutical industry, 246, 260, 268, 279-280
  psychological theories, 265
  public opinion, 254-256
  quality control, 252, 278
  relativity, 237-240
  sociological theories, 29, 265-266
  stimulants, 240-241, 246-247, 263
  subcultures, 274, 277-278
  tobacco, 238-239, 240, 241-242, 253, 254, 278

Easter v. Dist. of Columbia, 317, 318
Eastern State Penitentiary (Pa.), 153, 177
Eighteenth Amendment, 57, 70, 77, 307, 309-311, 430
Eighth Amendment, 152, 184, 317
Elmira Reformatory, 162, 177n, 178-179, 182
Environmental movement, 52, 57, 63, 64, 68, 585-605
  and anti-Viet-Nam War movement, 587-590, 594
  and civil rights movement, 589-590

Environmental movement, *cont.*
  conservation movement, 585-587, 597-599
  contemporary movement, 587-597, 599-605
    and communal movement, 602
    cosmetologists, 593, 594
    cultural changes, 599-601
    legal changes, 602-604
    meliorists, 593-594
    natural history, 589-596
    normative changes, 601-602
    organizations, 592-593
    power strategies, 596
    radicals, 581, 582, 594-595
    reformists, 594-595
    targets of, 592
  industry, business, 578-579, 580, 600
  legacy, 597-605
  population control, 649-650, 651
Environmental Policy Act (1969), 595, 597, 605
Environmental problems, 556-605
  air pollution, 565, 571, 572, 577, 603, 603n
    perception of effects, 568, 569, 574
  cultural definition, 556-559
  doomsday prophets, 582-583
  energy consumption, 560-564
  forests, 564
  growth-ethic, 559, 578-579, 594
  interest groups, 575-584
  metal reserves, 563, 564
  need hierarchy, 578, 588, 593
  noise pollution, 560, 604
  nuclear energy, 564
  oil spills, 580, 596, 600
  public opinion, 567-573
  resource allocation, 559
  revolutions, 558-559, 562
  statistics, 560-567
  strip-mining, 600
  student activists, 581, 582, 593-594, 595
  supersonic transports, 560, 587, 600
  water pollution, 566-567, 603-604
    perception of effects, 568-569, 574
  wilderness areas, 601, 602, 602n, 603n
Environmental Protection Agency, 597, 603n, 605
Equal Employment Opportunities Commission, 550, 553
Equal Rights Amendment, 416, 418, 419, 420, 430, 431, 435, 440-441, 505
Euthanasia, 16, 62

Family (*see* Marriage and family)
Federal Bureau of Investigation, 78, 90, 96, 96n
Federal Communications Commission, 387, 389

Feminist movements, 405-441
  abortion issue, 459, 462
  and anti-alcohol movement, 298, 308, 316
  and child-savers movement, 129-132, 414
  early movement, 414-418, 425-430
    interest groups, 414-417
    leadership, recruitment, 426-427
    legacy, 435-437
    natural history, 427-430
    opposition to, 417-418
    protective legislation, 406, 417, 421, 425, 426, 429-430, 431, 436-437, 501
    woman suffrage, 414, 416, 425, 426-430
  employment, 407-409, 411, 441, 482
  labor reforms, 415-416
  legal status, 409-410, 436
  lesbian organizations, 377
  modern liberation movement, 418-424, 430-435
    civil rights movement, legislation, 430-431, 433-434, 440
    collective definition, 431-442
    consciousness-raising, 418-419
    cultural impact, 437-439
    instrumental vs. expressive groups, 432
    interest groups, 418-424
    leadership, recruitment, 432
    legal, institutional developments, 440-441
    mass media, 437-438
    natural history, 432-435
    normative influences, 439-440
    radical protest groups, 433-434
    structural strain theories, 430-431
    working-class women, 434-435
  political offices, 410-411, 440
  prostitution laws, 369
  public opinion, 411-414
  revival pattern, 68
  sex roles, relativity of, 405-407
    biological differences, 421-422
    crime rates, 441
    cultural differences, 406-407, 421, 423, 424
    psychoanalytic theories, 422-423
    sociological theories, 423-424
    sexual freedom, 439-440
Folk beliefs, 9
Folk crimes, 77, 112
Folkways, 22-23
Ford Foundation, 647, 657
Forest Service, 587, 595
Fragmentation stage, of social movements, 61, 64-65
France:
  alcohol use, 282, 295
  mental illness, 332, 337, 344
  population policies, 607-608
Friends of the Earth, 591, 596, 650

Gay Activists' Alliance, 377, 395, 397, 399
Gay Liberation Front, 377, 395, 397

Georgia, prison system, 151, 158, 160, 161
Germany, 321, 358, 608
Ghost Dance of 1890, 526-527, 540-541
Great Britain:
  abortion laws, 462
  air pollution, 565
  birth control, 655n
  common law, 115, 117
  death penalty, 149
  homosexuality, 76
  population policies, 608
  pornography, 358
Greece, 320, 323, 357, 358

Harrison Act (1914), 258, 261, 262, 267, 269, 279
Hawes-Cooper Act (1934), 160, 180
Health, Education, and Welfare, U.S. Dept. of, 655-656
  Children's Bureau, 78, 124, 500
Homosexuality, 76, 112, 114, 358, 359-360, 362-364, 376-379, 391-397, 491
  alcoholism, 301-302
  "coming out," 399-400
  historical background, 358, 359-360
  incidence, 362-364
  interest groups, 376-379, 391-397, 493, 504
    anti-homosexual, 378-379
    pro-liberation, 376-378, 391-397
  job discrimination, 363-364, 367, 378, 392, 395
  labelling theory, 31-32
  laws, 364, 392, 401-402
  lesbianism, 363, 364, 397, 400n, 504
  marriages, 477
  as "mental disorder," 379, 379n
  militant organizations, 395-396
  police harassment, 364, 395, 396, 402
  public opinion, 327, 367
  in prisons, 195
  as problem-movement, 391-397
  religious organizations, 378, 393
  scientific findings, 380, 400
  university organizations, 396-397
Hull House Group, 123, 132

Incipiency stage, of social movements, 61-62
India, 3, 558, 566, 580
  population, birth control, 609, 634
  prostitution, 357
Indian Affairs, Bureau of, 528, 546
Indians, American (*see* Native Americans)
Industrial revolution, 558-562
Institutionalization stage, of social movements, 61, 63-64
Interest groups, 11-20, 36
  economic, 14, 32-33
  individuals' role, 18
  moral, 15-16
  objectivist theories, 33-34
  occupational, 15
  political, 14-15

Interest groups, *cont.*
  vs. pressure groups, 12, 13-14, 36
  psychological, 16-17
  publics, 11, 12, 36
  religious, 12-13
  risks vs. rewards, 50-51
  scientific, 17, 19-20, 36
  ulterior motives, 18-19
International Assn. of Police Chiefs, 97, 100, 124
International Congresses on Mental Hygiene, 345, 348
International Index to the Social Sciences, 381-382, 383
International Planned Parenthood Federation, 640, 647, 647n, 657
International Prison Congress, 178, 179
Izaak Walton League, 568, 591

Jackson State killings, 204, 224
Japan:
  abortion policies, 444, 444n, 445, 656
  alcohol use, 282
  Caucasians, perception of, 511, 512
  families, 476
  population policies, 608, 608n, 609, 656
  prostitution, 357
Jews, 282, 303-304, 320
Jim Crow laws, 518, 518n, 543, 552
John Birch Society, 215-216, 228-231, 233-234, 375, 531
Journal of Social Hygiene, 382, 383-384
Juvenile delinquency, 115-128
  categories, 117-118
  incidence, 118-121, 114
  interest groups, 121-128, 141-143
  psychological theories, 125, 144
  public opinion, 121
  relativity, 5-6, 9
  self-concept, 127
  social class, 118, 119, 127-128
  sociological theories, 125-128
    labelling theory, 31-32
    social learning, 30
Juvenile delinquency movements, 128-147
  child-savers, 16, 69, 122, 128-138, 144-146
  children's rights, 128-129, 138-147
  cottage plan, 134-136, 138
  and courts, 124, 128-129, 138-144
  legacy, 144-147
  reformatory system, 133-136, 138

Kent State killings, 204, 224
Knights of Labor, 415, 428
Ku Klux Klan, 375, 516, 520, 531, 534, 544

Labelling theory, 31-32, 43, 282
  alcoholism, 283, 292-293, 304-305
  crime, 99
  juvenile delinquency, 126-128
  mental illness, 326, 335

Labor unions, racial prejudice in, 529-530
Ladder, The, 376, 392
Last Tango in Paris, 372n, 398
Law and order movement, 52, 57, 60, 64, 86, 88, 90-95, 100-102, 105, 112-114, 163-165, 211, 215-216, 228-231 (*see also* Radical protest)
Law Enforcement Assistance Act (1965), 198, 198n
Law Enforcement Assistance Admin., 85, 105, 113
Laws:
  blue laws, 25, 75-76
  class-based, 14, 25-26, 28
  manifest, latent functions, 27
  as normative systems, 22
  psychopath, 93, 109
  relativity of, 25, 32
  as residues of social movements, 70
Leadership Foundation (Wash., D.C.), 387, 389
Lesbianism, 363, 364, 376-377, 397, 400n
Los Angeles:
  air pollution, 605
  Chicano strike, 540
  crime rate, 86
  homosexuals, 376, 393-394
  pornography laws, 401
LSD, 239-240, 250, 252, 264-265

Marijuana, 25, 100, 106, 110-111, 238, 248-250, 255-256
  addiction myths, 275-276
  anti-marijuana movements, 271-273
  decriminalization attempts, 256, 259, 276
  public opinion, 255-256
  scientific findings, 263, 264, 275-276
Marijuana Tax Act (1937), 258, 263, 271, 279
Marriage and family, 475-510
  business and industry support, 488-489
  challengers of tradition, 478, 491-497
    court tests, 507
    natural history, 504-505
    social movement, 502
  childless couples, 491-492
  counselors, 489, 501
  cultural relativity, 475-478
  decline of, 478
  defenders of tradition, 478, 486-491
    laws, 505-507
    natural history, 499-502
    social movements, 498-502
  definitions, 477-478
  divorce, 5, 478, 479, 488, 499-501
    and mental illness, 353-354
    no-fault, 476, 505, 506, 507
  economic bonds, 476-477
  extramarital sex, 480-481, 483, 495-496
  family life, freedom of, 476-477

Marriage and family, *cont.*
family size, 629-631, 636, 640, 654
future of, 508
"group-marriage" communes, 493-502
illegitimacy, 479-480, 506
in mass media, 487
motherhood, 481-482
nonmarital cohabitation, 480, 483, 485, 491, 495-496, 506-507
norms, oppressiveness of, 478
open marriage concept, 493
premarital sex, 480, 484, 485, 491, 495-496
protective legislation, 500-501
public opinion, 483-485
as social movement, 497-508
legacy, 505-508
statistics, 478-483
swingers' clubs, 493, 503, 504
woman's legal status, 410
Massachusetts:
crime rates (16th cent.), 41-42
prisons, punishment, 153, 159, 167, 176
reform, 194, 196-197
Mass media, creative effects, 7, 9, 10
Mattachine Foundation, 376, 391, 393, 493
Men's liberation movement, 439-440
Mental Hygiene (MH), 335, 343
Mental illness, 319-336
in armed forces, 332, 343-344, 346-347
environmental factors, 336, 344
historical relativity, 319-324
hospitals, 330-331, 338-339
illness, curability model, 33-35, 338-346, 349-351, 355-356
interest groups, 329-336
media coverage, 347
neuroses, 324-325, 336
paranoia, 325-326
psychiatrists and psychiatry, 323-324, 327, 336, 342, 346, 352, 355-356
guidance clinics, 344-345
psychoses, 324, 325-326
psychotherapy, 323, 326
public opinion, 326-329
schizophrenia, 325, 326, 336, 350-351
social processes, 336
statistics, 322, 324-325
strain theory, 29
witchcraft, 320-321
Mental illness movements, 53, 336-356
historical review, 336-340
legacy, 348-356
community programs, 349, 351-352
legislation, 352-356
patients' rights, 351-355
resource allocation, 351-352
mental health movement, 340-348
and federal government, 346-348, 351-352
incipiency, 340-341
institutionalization, 346-348

Mexican-Americans, 513-514, 515
cultural influence, 549
juvenile delinquency, 119-120
organizations, 524-526, 539-540
bracero program, 539
natural history, 546
Minutemen, 215, 228, 233
Montgomery, Ala., bus boycotts, 520, 521, 536, 544
Moral entrepreneurs, 16, 130, 263, 459-460
Morality in Media, 374, 386-387
Mormons:
alcohol use, 281
birth control, 638
marriage, defense of, 487, 501
polygamy, 476, 502
pornography, 374
Supreme Court decisions, 502
Motion pictures:
alcoholism, 293
criminal figures in, 112
marriage, challenges to, 504
mental illness, 347
pornographic, 362, 372n, 398, 401
Ms., 419, 434, 437

Narcotics, Bureau of, 100, 106, 262, 271-275
Narcotics and Dangerous Drugs, Bureau of, 262, 276
National American Woman Suffrage Assn., 416, 427, 428
National Assn. for the Advancement of Colored People, 213, 232, 516, 518-519, 520, 521, 530, 533, 534, 535, 544, 550, 551
capital punishment, 190-191
prisoners' rights, 170, 171, 183-184, 187
National Assn. for Repeal of Abortion Laws, 48, 446, 458, 465-467, 472
National Assn. of Mental Health, 329, 332, 335, 343, 348, 351, 352
National Commission on Obscenity and Pornography, 358, 361, 365-366, 371-372, 373, 375, 388-390, 399, 400
National Committee for Mental Hygiene, 333, 335, 341-348, 349
National Consumers League, 415, 428
National Council of Churches, 168, 184
National Council on Crime and Delinquency, 15, 124, 138, 141, 173, 184, 187
National Indian Youth Council, 526, 527, 541
National Institute of Mental Health, 347, 348, 351-352
National League of Women Voters, 430, 431, 436
National Mental Health Act (1946), 332, 335, 347-348
National Mental Health Foundation, 332, 347

National Organization for Women, 13, 48, 369, 419, 432, 433-434, 466, 504
National Prison Congress, 178, 182
National Prisoners Reform Assn., 186, 187
National Right to Life Committee, 13, 458, 465, 468, 469-470, 472
National Urban League, 184, 215, 521
National Welfare Rights Organization, 14, 145
National Wilderness Preservation System, 602, 602n, 603n
National Women's Party, 416, 430
National Women's Suffrage Assn., 416, 428
National Women's Trade Union League, 416, 428, 430
Native Americans, 9, 35, 513, 515, 543, 551-552
cultural contributions, 549
environmental movement, 593, 604
fish-ins, 541-542
organizations, 526-528, 540-542, 546
racial perceptions, 511
religious movements, 67-68, 540-541
New Left movement (1960's), 65, 68, 430, 432, 434, 503 (*see also* Radical protest)
New York City:
Civilian Review Boards, 98, 106-107
crime rate, 86, 89
homosexual movement, 394-395, 396
juvenile delinquency, 122-123
Neighborhood Guild, 132
pornography, 371, 372, 375, 387
prostitution, 95, 360, 361, 365, 384
protest movements, 202, 205, 207
school racial balance, 555
New York Prison Assn., 168, 179
New York State:
abortion law, 446, 448, 467, 469-470, 473
capital punishment, 188
drug laws, 279
homosexuality, laws on, 377
prisons, punishment, 151, 153, 161, 168-169, 178-180, 196
Niagara Movement (1905), 519-520, 521, 533, 544, 550
Nineteenth Amendment, 68, 309, 311, 414, 429-430, 435-436
Normative theories, 20-26, 37
folkways, 22-23
laws, 22
mores, 22-23
norms, 21-22
power groups, 28
relativity, 24-26
sanctions, 24
values, 21, 23-24
North American Conference of Homophile Organizations, 377, 394, 397

North Carolina, prisons and punishment, 151, 154, 160, 195, 198

Objectivist theories, 32-34
Obscenity (*see* Pornography)
Old age movements, 51, 62
ONE, Inc., 376, 391, 392
Opiates, 241, 242-246
 anti-opium movement, 257-259
  natural history, 267-271
 Chinese use, 257-258, 267, 268
 heroin, 242, 245, 247, 263, 269, 272, 275, 278
 legislation against, 261-262
 and medical profession, 261
 19th-century addiction, 248, 257, 268
 patent medicines, 257, 258-259, 267, 268-269
 withdrawal, avoidance theory, 266

Parens patriae doctrine, 129-130, 137-140
 prisons, correction, 148, 150, 153, 154, 176-177
 rape laws, 76-77
Pennsylvania Hospital, 331, 333, 335
Pennsylvania Prison Society, 168, 176
Peyote, 250, 251, 526, 527
Philadelphia correction system, 148, 165-166, 175-176, 177, 193, 200
Philadelphia Society for Prisons, 122, 133, 137, 168, 176
Planned Parenthood Federation, 638, 647-648, 651
 and abortion, 13, 447, 458, 463, 467, 472
Planned Parenthood-World Population, 640, 656
Playboy magazine, 440, 488, 493-494, 503-504
Police, 96-98, 106-109
 class attitudes toward, 92-93
 crime waves, 106
 enforcement styles, 107-109
 equipment, 95
 and juvenile courts, 139, 142-143
 media portrayals, 112
 political activism, 233
 and pornography laws, 375
 professional associations, 97-98, 124
 and radical protest movement, 216-217
 strikes, 108
Pollution (*see* Environmental problems)
Population, 606-646
 academic and scientific interests, 639-643
 doomsday prophets, 639-641
 neo-Malthusians, 639, 641
 anti-control advocates, 642-643, 644-646
 coercive restrictive practices, 642, 650
 demographic transition theory, 615-616
 density, 641

Population, *cont.*
 growth, in Europe, 614, 616
 migration, internal, 627-628
 political publics, 643-646
 primitive groups, 611
 public opinion, 628-635
  birth control, 631-634, 636-637
  family size preferences, 629-631, 636, 640, 654
  population as problem, 628-629
  relative definitions, 606-612
  religious and moral interests, 635-638
 statistics, 612-628
  age-sex structure, 618, 620-623
  birth rate, 482-483, 616, 616*n*, 618-620, 642
  census figures, 614, 616, 619
  composition of population, 612, 622-625
  death rate, 617, 617*n*, 618
  fertility rate, 616, 616*n*, 617, 617*n*, 618-620, 624
  future growth, 619-620
  immigration, 616, 620
  race, 622-625
  size and growth, 612, 613-622
  spatial distribution, 612, 625-628, 642, 658
  urban and rural, 624-627, 658
  zero growth, 620, 629, 642
 technological, medical advances, 607, 612
 third-world nations, 609, 645-646
 U.S. laws and practices, 610-611
Population control movement, 43, 46, 52, 53, 64, 646-658
 and environmentalists, 649-650, 651
 government agencies, 647, 655-656
 legacy, 69, 652-658
 natural history, 651-652
 zero growth, 648-654
Population Council, 647, 657
Pornography and obscenity, 16, 358-359, 361-362, 371-375, 384-391, 484, 485
 censorship laws, 372-375, 385-386, 398, 400-401
 consumption, 361-362
 films, 362, 372*n*, 398, 401
 hard core vs. soft-core, 372*n*, 398
 historical background, 358-359
 interest groups, 63-64, 371-375, 384-391
 vs. obscenity, 359*n*
 and organized crime, 371
 and Postal Service, 359, 362
 as problem movement, 384-391
 public opinion, 365-366
 scientific findings, 380, 388-389, 398-399
 social impact, 398-399
Poverty, war on, 53, 56, 65, 70, 577
Presidential Executive Orders:
 11246, 409, 433-434, 440
 11375, 434, 440
 11478, 552, 553-554
President's Commission on the Status of Women, 419, 420, 433, 467
Prisoners' Union, 171, 186

Prison Law Collective, 171, 186
Prison Penitentiary Movement, 175, 176-178
Prisons, 150, 153-155 (*see also* Corrections and punishment)
 chain gangs, 154, 160
 employment, 154-155, 160-161, 169, 170, 181*n*
 vs. labor unions, 170, 180-181, 182
 living conditions, 158-160
 prisoners' rights movement, 170-171, 176, 183-187
  natural history, 186-187
 racial segregation, 184
 reform movement:
  accommodations, 196-197
  education, 195
  furloughs and visits, 195-196
  halfway houses, "open institutions," 198-199
  imprisonment, de-emphasis, 193-194
  social science, 173
  work-release programs, 161, 197-198
 riots, 184-185, 187, 194
 staff personnel, 161-162
 wages, 181
Progressive Labor Party, 213, 221, 644
Progressive Movement, 41, 44, 52, 258, 298, 307-308, 340, 381, 518 (*see also* Feminist movements)
 conservation, 585-586
 drug campaigns, 258-259
 family life defenders, 499-501, 502
 and feminist movement, 414-416
 and incidence of social problems, 41, 44
 protective legislation for women, 406
Prohibition Movement, 25, 52, 57, 68, 183, 189, 240, 296, 307, 310-312, 315-316
Prohibition Party, 297, 307-312, 315-316
Prostitution, 9, 14, 27, 95, 100, 357-358, 360-361, 367-370, 381-384
 historical forms, 357-358
 incidence, 360-361
 interest groups, 102-103, 367-370, 381-384, 494
 laws and enforcement, 360-361, 365, 369, 382, 383, 400
 and marriage, 496
 as problem-movement, 381-384
 public opinion, 327, 365
 relativity, 76, 77, 357-358
 tolerance for, 397-398
 venereal disease, 361
Protestant churches, 57, 167, 168, 492
 alcohol campaigns, 296, 308, 310, 311-312, 315
 birth control, 638
 pornography, 374
Protest movements (*see* Radical protest)
Psilocybin, 250, 251, 252

Index

Psychiatry (*see* Mental illness)
Pure Food and Drug Act (1906), 259, 267, 268
Puritans, 16, 35, 134
   Auburn system, 148-149, 165-166, 175, 177, 188, 193, 200
   punishment policies, 150-151, 152

Quakers, 378
   capital punishment, 187-188, 190
   mental asylums, 330, 332
   prison system, 148, 165-166, 175-176, 177, 193, 200

Race and ethnic relations, 511-555
   cultural relativity, 511-514
   ethnic studies programs, 545-546, 547
   European immigrants, 514, 528, 529
   interest groups, 517-533
      black self-help programs, 518-519, 533-534, 543-544
      civil rights organizations, 520-522, 534-536, 544-548
      opposition groups, 528-531
   and labor unions, 529-530
   prejudice, bigotry, 528-529, 532-533
   public opinion, 516-517
   social movements, 533-555
      cultural legacy, 548-549
      laws and justice system, 552-555
      natural history, 543-548
      normative changes, 549-552
   statistics, 514-516
      health care, 514-515
      income, 515-516, 554
      school enrollment, integration, 515-516, 535, 544-545, 547-548, 552-553
      unemployment, 515
Radical protest, 201-234
   anti-war protest, 202, 203, 205-206, 210, 220-224
   black protest, 202, 203, 207, 208, 210
   conservative countermovement, 211, 215-216, 228-231
      legacy of, 233-234
      natural history, 230-231
      program and tactics, 229
      recruitment, leadership, 228-229
   feminist groups, 433-434
   historical relativity, 202-203
   interest groups, 210-218
   public opinion, 210
   riffraff theory, 217
   riots, 217
   as social movement, 219-234
      fragmentation, 65
      leadership, 54
      legacy, 231-234
   sociological theories, 217-218
   statistics, 203-204, 208, 209
   student protest, 202, 203, 204-205, 220-224
   and environmental problems, 581, 582, 594-595
Reader's Digest, 483, 487, 490-491

Reader's Guide to Periodical Literature, 100-101, 381-382, 383, 471
Reformatory movement, 168, 175, 178-183 (*see also* Corrections and punishment; Juvenile delinquency)
Religious interest groups, 12-13, 56
   crime campaigns, 103-104
   drug campaigns, 110, 258-259, 267
   homosexual, 378, 393
   pornography campaigns, 374, 387
   pro-natalist policies, 635-638
   situational ethnics, 25, 492
Repression, of social movements, 60-65
Revolutionary Action Movement, 215, 538
Revolutionary Youth Movement, 223-224
Right-wing movements, 211, 215-216, 228-231 (*see also* Radical protest)
Rockefeller Foundation, 343, 345, 647, 657
Roman Catholic Church:
   abortion, 12, 444-445, 446, 450, 452, 455, 468, 470, 472, 631
   alcoholism policies, 315
   birth control, 202, 481, 631-633, 642, 657
   family size, 485, 631, 636-637
   marriage, defense of, 487, 501, 502
   pornography, 374, 387
   prison reform, 168
Roman Empire, 320, 443, 607

Salem Fraternity (1887), 123, 132
San Francisco:
   anti-opium law, 257, 267
   conservation movement, 586-587
   homosexuality, 374, 376, 393
   pornography market, 399
   prison reform, 168, 169
   prostitution, 361
Scientific revolution, 558-559, 562
Seneca Falls Convention (1848), 427-428
Sex problem movements, 381-402 (*see also* Prostitution; Pornography; Homosexuality)
   cultural developments, 397-400
   legal developments, 400-402
Sexual behavior, 357-402 (*see also* Marriage and family)
   bisexuality, 400
   cultural relativity, 357-360
   extramarital sex, 480-481, 483, 495-496
   homosexuality, 76, 112, 114, 358, 359-360, 362-364, 376-379, 391-397
   interest groups, 367-380
   nonmarital cohabitation, 480, 483, 485, 491, 495-496, 506-507
   premarital sex, 480, 484, 485, 491, 495-496
   pornography, obscenity, 358-359, 361-362, 371-375, 384-391

Sexual behavior, *cont.*
   prostitution, 357-358, 360-361, 367-370, 381-384
   public opinion, 365-367, 397, 399, 400
   sex roles, 405-407
   sociological theories, 379-380
   swingers, 493, 503, 504
Shanghai Opium Conference (1908), 258, 267
Sierra Club, 16, 582, 586, 589, 590, 591, 592-593, 595, 597, 604, 650
Sing Sing Prison 151, 154, 182, 183
Social disorganization theory, 27, 28, 125-126
Social hygiene movement, 370, 382
Social interactionist theories (*see* Labelling theory)
Social learning theory, 30-31
   alcoholism, 302
   crime, 99
   drug use, 266
   juvenile delinquency, 126
Social problem-movements, 38-71
   conduciveness and strain, 39-41
   co-optation, 60-65
   deprivation, role of, 17, 49
   expressive, 45-46
   general vs. specific, 44-45
   host society, 59-61
   ideology, 55-56
   legacy, decline, 66-70
   nationalistic, revival, 45, 46
   natural history, 57-66
   norm- and value-oriented, 40, 43, 46
   organization, 46-57
      formal, informal, 55, 62
      leadership, 51-55
      members, recruitment and retention of, 49-51
      mobilization, 55-57
      strategies, tactics, 56-57
      three-ring structure, 47-49
   precipitating incidents, 56-57, 60
   problems as movement, 58
   psychic and emotional needs, 49-50
   repression, 60-65
   risks vs. rewards, 50-52
   social class, 51-53
   stability and change, 41-44
   time factor, 45
Social problems, 3-37
   interest groups, 11-20
   manifest and latent, 34
   social construction of reality, 3-11
   sociological theories, 20-37
Society for Individual Rights, 377, 393
Society for . . . Roman Catholic Children, 123, 135
Sociological theories, 20-37
   deviant behavior, 26-32, 35-36
   general, 32-36
   normative systems, 20-26, 37
   objectivist, 32-34
   subjectivist, 33, 35-36

Sociologists for Women in Society, 419, 424
Southern Christian Leadership Conference (SCLC), 214, 520, 521-522, 535, 544-545, 546
Standard Metropolitan Statistical Areas, 514, 626, 626n, 627
Statistics, 8-9, 11
  manipulation of, 90-91, 96-97, 106
Sterilization, 151, 633-634
Strain theory, 27-29, 33, 39-40
  alcoholism, 305-306
  crime, 98
  family life, 497
  feminist movements, 425, 430-431
  radical protest, 217
Structural-functional theories, 26-28
  boundary testing, 43, 125
  crime, 98
  dysfunctional behavior, 26, 27, 28
  feminist movement, 425-426, 430-431
  manifest and latent, 27
  race relations, 532
Student Non-Violent Coordinating Committee, 214, 225-227, 434, 522, 523, 537, 545, 546
Student protest, 202, 203, 204-205, 220-224
  child-rearing theories, 218
  co-optation of, 222-224
  generational conflict, 218
  legacy, 232-233
  natural history, 221-224
  parental influences, 219
  political groups, 212-215
  strategies, tactics, 219-221
  terrorists, extremists, 224
Students for a Democratic Society (SDS), 212-213, 581, 582
  confrontation strategy, 219-221
  natural history, 220-224
Subjectivist theories, 33, 35-36
Supreme Court:
  abortion rulings, 12, 446, 458-459, 466-467, 469, 471, 472-473, 478, 502, 505, 656
  capital punishment, 153, 164, 189, 191-192, 193
  drugs, 262, 270
  homosexuality, 392
  juvenile rights, 144, 146-147
  miscegenation laws, 506
  Norman decision, 502
  Native American rights, 541
  obscenity, 366, 386-387, 389-390, 400-401
  police arrest procedures, 113-114
  Rulings:
    Brown v. *Board of Education*, 535, 544, 553, 554

Supreme Court: Rulings: *cont.*
    California v. *Miller*, 389-390, 401
    Defunis v. *Odegaard*, 554
    Gault, 144, 146
    Gwin and Beal v. *U.S.*, 552
    Jin Fuey Wong v. *U.S.*, 270
    Kent, 144, 146
    McKiver v. *Pennsylvania*, 146
    Miranda, 113-114
    Missouri ex rel Gaines v. *Canada*, 552
    Norris v. *Alabama*, 552
    Plessy v. *Ferguson*, 535, 552-553
    Powell v. *Texas*, 317-318
    Smith v. *Allright*, 552
    U.S. v. *Roth*, 366, 386, 387, 400-401
    Webb v. *U.S.*, 270
    Winship, 146
  school desegregation, 535-536, 544, 554-555
  Warren Court, 234, 386

Teamsters' Union, 526, 547
Tobacco, as a drug, 238-239, 240, 241-242, 253, 254, 278
Treasury Dept., Narcotics Div., 261-263, 269-271
Tuskegee Institute, 519, 544

United Auto Workers, 186
United Farm Workers, 186, 524, 525-526, 539-540, 546-547, 551
United Nations, 348, 645, 647, 654, 656-657
United Prisoners' Union, 171, 186, 187
Universal Life Church, 475, 492
Universal Negro Improvement Assn., 520, 533, 544, 550
Urban revolution, 558, 562
U.S.S.R.:
  crime, 76
  homosexuality, 360
  police, 97
  population policies, 608, 609-610, 614

Values, 21, 23-24, 30
  conflict theory, 27, 28
  sacred vs. profane, 23
Victimless crimes, 16, 76, 87, 114, 379, 460-462
Viet-Nam War, 88, 365, 545
  anti-war protest, 202, 203, 205-206, 210, 220-224, 587, 594
  legacy, 232-233

Viet-Nam War, *cont.*
  draft-resisting, 222
  moral interest groups, 212
Virginia:
  Landman v. *Royster* decision, 184
  prisons, 152, 153, 176
Viva magazine, 438, 504
Volstead Act (1919), 307, 311, 317
Voting Rights Act (1965), 552, 553

Walnut Street Penitentiary (Phila.), 150, 153, 168, 176
Walt Disney Enterprises, 596, 604
Washington, D.C., 105
  protests, demonstrations, 202, 205, 207, 222
  school racial balance, 555
Washington State:
  abortion laws, 446
  divorce laws, 506
  marijuana initiative, 256, 259
  Native American fishing rights, 527, 541-542
  pollution control, 571
  prisons, 154, 184, 194, 195-195, 198
Washington Temperance Society, 297, 311, 312-313, 314
Watergate scandals, 6, 87, 88, 93, 104, 231, 233
Water pollution, 556-557, 568, 569, 572, 577, 603-604
Weathermen, 65, 223-224
Wilderness Society, 591, 597
Women's Christian Temperance Union, 16, 297-298, 309-310, 311, 414-415
Women's liberation movement, 13, 23, 43, 51, 56, 64, 68, 466 (*see also* Feminist movements)
Women's National Abortion Action Coalition, 48, 458, 466-467, 468, 472
World Population Conference, 645-646, 657
Wounded Knee, S.D., 526-527, 542

Yale Group, 298-299, 313-315, 316
Yosemite Park, 586, 599
Youngstown, Ohio, 385-386

Zero Population Growth, 13, 458, 467, 467n, 504, 591, 638, 640, 643-644, 648-654
  activities, 648
  impact, 654
  membership, attitudes, 648-650